MAJORITY

1931–1952

MAJORITY

1931-1952

AN ANTHOLOGY OF

21

YEARS OF PUBLISHING

HAMISH HAMILTON

LONDON

First published in July 1952
by Hamish Hamilton Ltd
90 Great Russell Street, London W C 1

PRINTED IN GREAT BRITAIN BY
EBENEZER BAYLIS AND SON, LTD., THE
TRINITY PRESS, WORCESTER, AND LONDON

TO CASS

NOTE

IN *Publishing and Bookselling* (beautifully produced, like all his publications, by my early mentor, Jonathan Cape), Mr. Frank Mumby wrote: 'Hamish Hamilton started publishing under his own imprint in 1931. Half American by birth and with many Transatlantic ties of affection and friendship, his ambition had long been to contribute something to the cause of Anglo-American understanding in the face of the growing menace of German aggression. This he succeeded in doing with books by such illuminating American correspondents as John Gunther, Walter Duranty, Virginia Cowles and Vincent Sheean, which brought him one resounding success after another, and, with novels by Angela Thirkell and other best-sellers, placed the firm securely on its feet. It commemorated its first ten years' harvest in its anthology *Decade* (1931–41).'

I am grateful to Mr. Mumby for his perspicacity, for publishers' imprints are seldom noticed and their policies even more rarely appreciated. In the past eleven years, which bring us to our *Majority*, the same ideal has been before us, save that the aggression is no longer German. My one regret in this new commemorative anthology is that there is no contribution from Italy, for though our list contains Italian authors, nothing of suitable length could be found, so that I can only express my affection and admiration for my wife's country in this note. The literature of France, on the other hand, is well represented.

I wish to thank the authors here represented for their contributions and regret that it was not possible to find suitable self-contained passages from the work of such distinguished writers as Sir Norman Angell, S. N. Behrman, Hilton Brown, Richard Crossman, John Fischer, John Hersey, Walter Lippmann, Rose Macaulay, Malcolm Muggeridge, Mollie Panter-Downes, Hesketh Pearson, Vasco Pratolini, Enid Starkie, Bruno Walter, Chaim Weizmann, Sumner Welles, and Franz Werfel, or to reproduce illustrations by the *New Yorker* artists who have done so much to cheer the Western World in the past twenty-five years.

Finally, I salute my colleagues under the green bay tree of our imprint and hope they may continue to enjoy our adventure.

1952   HAMISH HAMILTON

CONTENTS

GENERAL

GLIMPSES OF CONVENT LIFE   page 1
BY MONICA BALDWIN

ENGLISH RELIGION   19
BY D. W. BROGAN

THE SHORN LAMBS   55
BY JOHN MASON BROWN

THE MOOD OF SQUARES   75
BY R. J. CRUIKSHANK

NEW YORK: SKETCH OF MEGALOPOLIS   87
BY JOHN GUNTHER

GUY DE MAUPASSANT: *A WOMAN'S LIFE*
   AND *BEL-AMI*   123
BY ALAN HODGE

HOME LIFE IN WALES   131
BY JACK JONES

CONFESSIONS OF A TIGHT-ROPE WALKER   151
BY ARTHUR KOESTLER

THE GHOST IN THE VILLA   195
BY ALAN MOOREHEAD

1848: SEED-PLOT OF HISTORY   231
BY L. B. NAMIER

BENJAMIN CONSTANT AND *ADOLPHE*   243
BY HAROLD NICOLSON

THE UNQUIET GRAVE   261
BY 'PALINURUS'
WITH AN INTRODUCTION BY CYRIL CONNOLLY

	page
STANDARD ENGLISH	351
WAR ADOPTIONS	361
BY ERIC PARTRIDGE	
OF ELLEN TERRY: OUR LADY OF THE LYCEUM	367
BY W. GRAHAM ROBERTSON	
CHARLES DICKENS AND *GREAT EXPECTATIONS*	385
BY BERNARD SHAW	
BERLIN AND BLOOMSBURY IN THE THIRTIES	399
BY STEPHEN SPENDER	
CARMICHAELS	465
ARNOLD BENNETT	473
BY FRANK SWINNERTON	
THE RULER IN BERLIN	479
THE SUPERMEN	487
BY A. J. P. TAYLOR	
MRS. GASKELL AND *CRANFORD*	491
BY ANGELA THIRKELL	
MARCEL PROUST	511
BY MARTIN TURNELL	

PLAYS AND POETRY

THE BROWNING VERSION	573
BY TERENCE RATTIGAN	
IN CAMERA (*HUIS CLOS*)	609
BY JEAN-PAUL SARTRE	
SIX POEMS	645
BY PAUL DEHN	
EIGHT POEMS	653
BY KATHLEEN RAINE	

Contents

FICTION

	page
THE PURSUIT OF LOVE BY NANCY MITFORD	663
THE OUTSIDER BY ALBERT CAMUS	807
THE ANIMAL WAITER	881
ART AT THE HOTEL SPLENDIDE BY LUDWIG BEMELMANS	888
THE GENTLEMAN FROM PARIS BY JOHN DICKSON CARR	895
PEARLS ARE A NUISANCE BY RAYMOND CHANDLER	919
DE MORTUIS . . . BY JOHN COLLIER	957
FOR ESMÉ—WITH LOVE AND SQUALOR BY J. D. SALINGER	965
THE SECRET LIFE OF WALTER MITTY	983
THE CATBIRD SEAT	990
THE LILIES AND BLUEBIRD DELUSION	997
A CALL ON MRS. FORRESTER	1006
THE LADY ON THE BOOKCASE BY JAMES THURBER	1011
WHEN I WAS THIRTEEN BY DENTON WELCH	1021

Contents

FICTION

page

THE PURSUIT OF LOVE 603
BY NANCY MITFORD

THE OUTSIDER 807
BY ALBERT CAMUS

THE ANIMAL WAITER 881

ART AT THE HOTEL SPLENDIDE 888
BY LUDWIG BEMELMANS

THE GENTLEMAN FROM PARIS 895
BY JOHN DICKSON CARR

PEARLS ARE A NUISANCE 919
BY RAYMOND CHANDLER

DE MORTUIS 957
BY JOHN COLLIER

FOR ESME — WITH LOVE AND SQUALOR 965
BY J. D. SALINGER

THE SECRET LIFE OF WALTER MITTY 983

THE CATBIRD SEAT 990

THE LILIES AND BLUEBIRD DELUSION 997

A CALL ON MRS. FORRESTER 1006

THE LADY ON THE BOOKCASE 1011
BY JAMES THURBER

WHEN I WAS THIRTEEN 1021
BY DENTON WELCH

GLIMPSES OF
CONVENT LIFE

BY MONICA BALDWIN

from *I Leap Over the Wall* (1949)

GLIMPSES OF CONVENT LIFE

Never had I dreamed of anything like these great Ministries—the power-houses, I supposed, of our Government—into which I had just been permitted a glimpse. Several of them were not even in existence in 1914 when I retired from the world. And even those that were must have been far less vast and complicated than they are to-day.

I was particularly impressed by the gloom of Africa House in Kingsway and the sheer immensity of the Ministry of Information. There was something faintly terrifying in the thought of those gigantic buildings, honey-combed with endless passages, along which men and women scuttled like ants; and the tiny cell-like offices where millions spent their lives clicking away on typewriters or dealing with official forms. But the power and intricacies of our titanic government machine left me without enthusiasm. Some instinct within me even rebelled at the thought of a civilization that had such a system at its nerve-centres. And I began to ask myself frightening and paralysing questions—questions that had no answers, or, if they had, I certainly hadn't a notion what they were.

How different was the government of empires from that of convents!

About the more modern congregations I am confessedly ignorant; but the old mediæval monastic houses were ruled on highly efficient lines.

The communities—which might number anything from a dozen to close on a hundred members—were divided into Choir Nuns and Lay Sisters.

The Choir Nuns—each of whom had brought a dowry—spent their time chiefly in prayer, manual work and the recitation of the Divine Office in choir. The Lay Sisters, who were drawn originally from the peasant class, gave—instead of dowries—their services for the heavier work of the house.

The Superior—known as the Reverend Mother Prioress—was elected triennially by the votes of the Choir Nuns. (Lay Sisters were not allowed a vote.) Her position was less that of mistress than of mother to the Community. The extreme respect shown to her was based upon the idea that in the monastery she held the place of Christ. The nuns, until they had been for a certain number of years in the Community, always knelt when she spoke to them. When she passed, they had to rise and bow to her as she went by. For

3

anything that was in any way an exception to the Rule, her leave had to be asked. Her will was supreme.

She herself was expected to be in all things a model of perfection—a point which, surprisingly, seemed in no way to daunt those members of the community (and they exist in every convent) who felt themselves to be peculiarly fitted by Providence for the office of Prioress.

From among themselves the Choir Nuns also elected perhaps sixteen or seventeen who represented them, much as an M.P. represents his constituency. These Sisters were consulted when important decisions had to be taken by the Prioress; they would be asked to vote, for instance, when there was a question of a novice being allowed to take her Vows.

To these few fell also the choosing of a much smaller and even more carefully selected body. This was the Council: a kind of Privy Cabinet who assisted the Prioress in the administration of the monastery.

The actual work of the house was divided up among the heads of the various departments. These were known as the 'Officers'. The more important were elected triennially; the rest were nominated—usually once a year—by the Prioress.

Each nun had her business laid down for her, even to the minutest details. Thus and thus was each thing to be done, and no otherwise. Short work was made of enterprising novices who came forward with bright ideas for new and better ways of doing things. Moreover, every least object employed by a nun in her 'Office' was entered in an inventory and an exact account had to be rendered when another Sister succeeded her.

First in rank among the Officers was the *Subprioress*, whose chief business was to safeguard the observance and internal discipline of the monastery. She also replaced the Prioress when the latter was unable to preside and, like her, was treated with the greatest reverence by the community. As she was liable to severe criticism if ever she failed to be kind, humble, wise, patient and a living example of religious observance at all times, her Office was hardly one to be coveted.

The *Procuratrix* ordered and gave out the provisions, had charge of the Lay Sisters, and looked after the general upkeep of the house. A Martha-job, if ever there was one, and fatiguing—but apparently a swift highroad to holiness.

The *Cellaress* did a certain amount to help the Procuratrix and had besides quite a number of odd little jobs of her own. One of these was to wash the eggs served to the community; another, to read aloud the life of some saint to the Lay Sisters as they sat over their sewing in the afternoon. She also presided at the hatch between the refectory and kitchen-quarters at meal-times, and gave out any special dish that had to be served to anyone who was ill.

The *Refectorian's* work was to keep the refectory in order, lay the tables, and, with the assistance of the weekly server, to wait upon the community at dinner and supper every day. She had to keep the great oak tables clean and polished, set the salt, lay a plate and porringer at each one's place, and wash the water-jugs in the lavatory outside.

And on Maundy Thursday, when the Prioress served in the refectory and washed the feet of the twelve eldest nuns (in memory of Christ, who on the eve of his Passion washed the feet of his disciples), the whole room had to be scoured, polished and adorned with flowers and draperies.

An *Under-Refectorian* helped the Refectorian to set the mugs and porringers. It was also her task to remove with a moist and malodorous dish-rag all stains from the Refectory floor.

The Office of Refectorian was not particularly sought after. The daily serving could be intensely tiring and it was not easy to keep oneself free from a faint aroma of grease. There was, too, a most unattractive duty attached to it—that of mending the vast sheet-like table-napkins which custom ordained that, when the Prioress gave the signal, each nun should affix to her bosom with a pin. These had to be darned *before* the Lay Sisters washed them. And it was an occupation which—to put it mildly—could be very unpleasant indeed.

The *Sacristan* had one of the most important and arduous Offices in the monastery. Two other nuns—usually chosen from among the strongest in the community—were allowed her as helps. One of them was always responsible for the bell-ringing in choir and cloister which called the nuns to various duties during the day. She had also to start the 'peal' rung in the choir for five minutes or so before each part of the Divine Office. On high festivals, the Under-Sacristan's life was a perfect nightmare of bell-ringing; for, besides the peals for Mass, Office, Strict Silence and Spiritual Reading which enlivened the morning, she had also to ring in the cloister at 2 p.m. for the Lesser Silence; at 3 o'clock in choir and cloister for Strict Silence; again there at 3.15 'because such was the custom'; at 3.25 in the cloister, summoning the nuns to Vespers, and again in the choir at 3.30 to 'start the peal'. And with Compline, a whole programme of evening ringing began. As it was a considerable distance from choir to cloister, the Under-Sacristan seldom put on weight for lack of exercise. Should she be late to ring, or forget altogether, the earth shook and trembled, for the entire community would be seriously inconvenienced.

Between them, the Sacristans were responsible for keeping the church, choir and sacristy in a state of spotless perfection. The High Altar and the Altar of Our Lady had always to be immaculate; there were the huge brass and silver candlesticks to be polished, flowers cut and continually rearranged. Twice daily the massive sanctuary lamp needed replenishing; new candles had to be unpacked and set up in place of others that were scraped and laid away in the long shelves behind a curtain in the outer Sacristy. Vestments were prepared for the two daily Masses and for Benediction; while bells,

censers, crucifixes, incense-boats, lanterns, cruets and holy water-stoups were
constantly in need of a refill or a rub.

The Head Sacristan had the key of the safe in which the sacred vessels were
kept. Amongst them was an exquisite jewelled ciborium of pure gold and a
beaten silver chalice that might have belonged to the shrine of some mediæval
saint. I remember, too, a great gem-encrusted monstrance—magnificent but
hideous—which literally blazed with brilliants when the Host was lifted up
at Benediction on the greater feasts.

The Church linen and vestments were kept in a small, ancient room called
the Custry. Here were long chests with deep drawers full of cottas and albs,
each one folded according to custom, in the tiniest possible accordion pleats
and then bound tightly—like a della Robbia bambino—with strappings of
linen or tape. The snowy gossamer lawn out of which most of them were
fashioned was lace-edged—priceless, historic lace, inducing sharp intakes of
breath and wide eye-openings when shown to connoisseurs. And what
masses of it. Cream, foam-colour, ivory, linen-white, ghost-grey or palest
oyster—all the faint, indescribable quarter-tones between white and white
that exist only in lace. Each piece had its pedigree. Most of it was well over a
yard in depth.

On wide, sliding shelves, inside deep cupboards, vestments were laid full-
length between dust-sheets and damp-proof paper to prevent the gold and
silver embroidery from tarnishing. To describe such a magnificent collection
in these pages is impossible, but I cannot resist the temptation to mention two
or three which, if I ever attempt to burgle the convent, I shall certainly carry
away with me in my bag.

There was a set—complete with cope, chasuble and dalmatics—of stiff,
sprigged Jacobean silk. It dated from the time of James II, and was as much a
masterpiece as any of the ancient Church-pictures in the refectory. Despite
the passage of centuries, neither the lovely old-fashioned gold 'galloon', nor
the enchanting colours in which the silk was woven, were tarnished or faded.
Old rose, pale green and pinkish lilac made a delicate background to embroidery worked in heavy ropes of twisted gold. The linings were mulberry-
colour, shot with a curious green, like shadowed cypress. When you lifted the
chasuble, the faintest possible fragrance—suggesting lavender, pot-pourri and
ancient incense—exhaled from its folds. To me it was a living link with a
historic past. It evoked awareness of all kinds of long-forgotten happenings,
about which nobody would otherwise have known.

There was another complete set of cloth-of-gold, enormously heavy, and
only used once a year at Midnight Mass—perhaps because the embossed
angels on the magnificent material suggested a vision of the first *Gloria in
excelsis Deo* seen through Melozzo da Forli's eyes. It was lined with stiff,
poppy-coloured satin and produced the effect of a fanfare of golden trumpets under a sunset sky.

Another set, presented to the convent when Queen Anne was reigning, was of many-coloured tapestry, thick as a carpet, an unusual medley of curious reds, dull greens, deep purples and mysterious blues. There was white in it, too, and a brownish gold that somehow suggested Byzantine mosaic. This, too, was used only once a year, for the Ceremonies of Holy Saturday. To me, it always seemed like a harmony of the colour and magic of spring.

The more modern vestments, especially the new Gothic chasubles used for the greater festivals of Our Lady, were perhaps faintly reminiscent of evening gowns. But, after all, why not? I remember especially one of silver *peau d'ange* with a lining of palest hyacinth. Its chief glory was a medallion of Fra Angelico's *Coronation of the Virgin*, perhaps unequalled as an example of the technical skill to which the embroiderer's needle can attain. I have never seen anything lovelier of its kind than the way in which the delicate rainbow-hued draperies were treated. They might have been dipped in the heart of an opal. The whole thing was like a key-hole glimpse of heaven's glory, seen through a veil of iridescent mist.

Finally, there were the splendid copes worn for Vespers at Easter and Pentecost. Cloth-of-silver with a stupendous hood and jewelled orphreys; and one of embossed brocade whose magnificent lining suggested firelight glowing dimly behind claret-coloured glass.

Even to handle such vestments gave one emotions that were at once sensuous and æsthetic. The rich hues, exquisite textures, faint, subtle perfumes, were somehow a little intoxicating after so much that was bleak and austere.

The *Vestiarians*, charged with the making, mending and distribution of the habit, were usually about six in number—two head officers and four underlings. Their lives could hardly have been a greater contrast to those of the sacristans. For about five hours daily they sat and sewed in silence in a hot stuffy room whose windows were nearly always tightly shut.

And when, on a green and golden April morning, the blackbirds fluted among the lilac bushes and called them out into the sun-drenched garden to smell the fragrance of spring, the vestiarians had to remember that the Rule—which was the Will of God for them—forbade the lifting of their noses from their work, unless it should be absolutely necessary. The fact that the outer garments worn by the religious had, like the table-napkins, to be mended before being sent to the laundry, certainly did not make the temptation to join the blackbirds easier to resist.

When, every six weeks or so, there was a great 'wash' of some part of the habit, the vestiarians had to ensure that each garment was properly dealt with before being put carefully away. This was a tremendous business. At about eight o'clock in the morning, every member of the community who was able to stand on two legs was expected to scurry along to the long low-raftered garrets under the monastery roof.

Here the Lay Sisters had prepared great baskets of wet linen or woollen garments which the nuns had to shake, lay out on the long wooden tables, slap and flatten by way of ironing, fold across, and finally hang up to dry on the long wire lines that stretched across the garret from end to end.

This business usually took from one to three hours, according to the quantity of the garments and the numbers of those who had come to help. With the exception of the vestiarians, it was not obligatory to show up for 'Garrets'; not to do so, however, was looked upon as shirking and, sooner or later, one would be sure to hear about it from the Superior.

Talking was generally allowed till the bell in the cloister rang for work; after that, silence reigned. In summer, 'Garrets' was a pleasantly cool occupation, but in winter—when the snow was sometimes lying on the roof a few feet above one's head—the cold was frightful. Quite often, the wet linen was frozen stiff in the baskets and one's hands became so numbed that they refused to work. Later on in the morning, when the circulation was restored to them, the pain in one's blue and chilblained fingers was quite agonizing.

The *Infirmarian*, with a Lay Sister as her handmaid, ruled over the Infirmary, which had a special wing to itself. Here the *grandes malades*, with the very old nuns, and anyone who might be recovering from an operation, were looked after with extraordinary kindness and care.

Any infirmarian who carried out all the detailed instructions laid down for her in the Rule and Constitutions could hardly fail to make of the infirmary a place of happiness and peace. The idea, of course, behind all this charity was the one set forth in St. Matthew, xxv. 40, '*Mihi fecistis* . . . I was sick, and you visited Me . . . What you did unto *them*, you did to *Me*.'

In the convent infirmary, the sick were looked upon quite simply as being Christ. The rest followed automatically.

The minor ailments of the community were, as has been said before, attended to by the *Apothecary*. Should you need her services, you knocked at the door of the dark little stone-floored chamber where she plied her trade. Within, the white washed walls were hung with rows of pots, pans and tiny long-handled pipkins of polished copper and brass. An immense, sinister-looking cupboard contained remedies for every emergency: bottles of elder-syrup for coughs in the winter; orange-flower water for insomnia; large, round, gelatinous pills containing black, fishy-smelling liquid to be taken as a 'help' to fasting during the forty days of Lent; bark—another unpopular but efficacious remedy for weakness; 'tilly-tea'—brewed from the flowers of the *tilleul* or lime-tree—sovereign cure for colds . . . and more modern remedies, tubes, boxes, bottles, packets of them; and a small, ancient bookshelf containing endless little old wives' recipes and instructions for the care and healing of the sick.

Here was to be found the short, simple, but absolutely infallible *Remedy for Rheumatism*, which produced its astounding results in under fifteen days.

Here was *Dr. Ralalife's Recipe for a Consumption*, consisting of crabs' claws finely powdered, asses' milk, and crabs' eyes. And here—in *Mr. Jenison's Receipts, Both Galenicall and Chimicall Who First Teach Us to Make Our Drugs in the Year* 1702—is the account of the virtue contained in *Lady Carrington's Cerecloth*, which 'cured ye King's evil or any other sore by washing your sore with milk or butter and beere' and 'applying this cerecloth till it's cured'.

When I myself was given the office of Apothecary, I wrote to one of my aunts, lamenting my ignorance of even the most elementary medical knowledge. She immediately sent me a large and excellent *Encyclopædia of Nursing*. This—though I should have found it quite invaluable—was immediately taken away from me. The reason given was that it contained a great deal which it was quite unnecessary for me to know.

The most responsible office was undoubtedly that of *Mistress of Novices*. To train young and chosen souls in the way of perfection was undoubtedly an exacting occupation; and in some ways the Novice Mistress ruled over her small domain rather like a queen. Canon Law obliged the novices to be separated as much as possible from the community during the earlier stages of their religious life. Until they had made their Vows, the young nuns had their own table in the Refectory, their own living-room (known as the 'Noviceship'), their dormitory, their garden, and a special cloister where they walked up and down for spiritual reading on rainy days. Conversation with the community nuns was prohibited, and—except upon special occasions— they seldom saw the Superior. As a result, the Novice Mistress soon became everything to them—guide, philosopher and friend, as well as mother and confidante.

The position was one of great trust and great importance. It was accompanied by privileges, not the least of which was much intimate converse with the Prioress, to whom everything concerning the novices had to be made known. Small wonder that she who held this office had sometimes to pay a price for it at the hands of certain members of the community.

The *Organist, Choir Mistress, Chantress* and *Succentress* were responsible for the music.

The *Librarian* kept the books in order and watched, argus-eyed, lest any Sister should so far forget herself as to take out a volume without marking it down on the shelf-catalogue.

The *Portress* and her relief opened the *guichet* to visitors, dispensed bread, soup and alms to the poor, and flew backwards and forwards between the Great Door and the Prioress's chamber for 'leaves' and directions whenever the door-bell rang.

One more office—that of the *Prioress' Chaplain*—must be mentioned. The title is misleading, since it suggests that nuns sometimes encroach upon the territory of the priesthood. Actually, the office was simply that of a kind of lady-in-waiting to the Superior. Chaucer's Prioress, it may be remembered, was attended by one:

> 'Another Nonne also with her hadde she
> That was hire chappeleine, and Preestes thre.'

She prepared and marked the places in the Prioress's Plain-chant books and breviary; arranged hours for her interviews with members of the community; accompanied her at the annual visitation of the cells and on Maundy Thursday, when she served in the refectory and washed the feet of the community.

Three times a day she gave round letters to the nuns, after they had been previously examined by the Prioress. This obliged her to be constantly in and out of the Superior's room, so that she had many opportunities of slipping in a suggestion or tactfully sowing the seeds of an idea. This could make her a valuable friend—or, possibly, a dangerous enemy.

Perhaps the most tiresome of her jobs was the adornment of a number of the 'little altars'—wooden brackets on which were set a statue or picture of a saint. These lurked in every corner of the monastery. Practically every nun had charge of one. This meant that a vase or two of flowers, with perhaps a few candles or a lamp on 'occasions', had to be crammed on to the bracket, and the whole affair dusted carefully every day. When the saint's festival came round, the nun was expected to do something spectacular in the way of decoration. So, on the eve, she would spend such free moments as she possessed in decking out the altar and its immediate surroundings with ferns, foliage, flowers and a forest of elegant candlesticks mounted on wooden stands.

(The idea was, I believe, that the larger and more elaborate the 'dress', the more fervour it betokened in the dresser. A meagre 'dress', suggesting that only a short time had been spent upon it, was thus a sure sign of tepidity.)

A carpet, with a cushion supporting a book, was then spread before it; so that when the community assembled at the appointed hour, the Prioress could recite the prayer or litany in honour of the saint.

To me, this business of 'dressing' the little altars always seemed rather a waste of time. Time was so scarce, and there were so many things one longed to do in it. . . . .

The actual mode of government was simple.

It was based upon faith—which has been defined as a supernatural faculty of discerning the divine through, and in, the human.

Those who embrace the Religious Life believe that it contains three special channels by which the Will of God comes to them. These are, (1) the Rule, which outlines the spirit and observances of the Order; (2) the Constitutions and Customs, which fill in details; and (3) the commands of the Superior.

By faith, each Religious sees God in the Superior. 'Never,' says St. John of the Cross, 'look upon your Superior, be he who he may, otherwise than if you were looking upon God, for he stands in his place. If you reflect upon the character, ways . . . or habits of your Superior, you will change your obedience from divine into human . . . and obedience influenced by human considerations is almost worthless in the eyes of God.'

As a result, the more complete the submission of one's will to that of the Superior (sin always, of course, excepted), the more perfectly one's will is united to the Will of God.

I once consulted the famous Dominican, Father Bede Jarrett, about this matter of submission.

He was a man of deep humour, profound learning, and wide experience. I told him about an order which had just been given to me by a Superior and which had struck me as being neither wise nor just.

'I can submit my *will* sufficiently to do the thing I've been told to do,' I explained to him, 'but as for forcing my *mind* . . .'

He looked at me with those intent yet curiously brooding eyes that were so unforgettable.

He said: 'I once took that same problem to my Novice Master. He told me to re-read *The Charge of the Light Brigade*. The idea, you see, is, that you do what you're told, no matter how certain you feel that someone has blundered. To ride fearlessly into the jaws of death without reasoning why adds splendour to your obedience.'

'Even,' I persisted, 'if you feel convinced that what you've been told to do is sheerest lunacy?'

He smiled.

'Ah, but don't you see?—that's just where the heroism comes in.'

This point of view impressed me. Of course, it fits in perfectly with another basic principle of the Christian life—that one is not made or unmade by the things that happen to one, but by one's reactions to the circumstances of one's life.

That, as the Dominican assured me, is all that God cares about.

But there was another theory which helped to influence the decisions of those in authority. This I found harder to assimilate. It was the theory of *la grâce d'état*. In practice, it really meant that if a nun were appointed to an office, that nun—provided that she prayed sufficiently for God's grace and did what lay in her to make the thing a success—was certain not to fail. '*I can do all things*,' one was reminded by one's Novice Mistress, '*in him who*

strengtheneth me'—a heartening belief when the day for the annual Change of
Office came round and a kind of General Post took place in the community.

I have seen a young and quite inexperienced little under-vestiarian summoned on such an occasion to the Superior's room. She came forth in a
terrified daze, unable to realize that she had just been appointed Mistress of
Novices. Another, who knew nothing of medicine and had never nursed
anyone, appeared equally stunned when informed that henceforward she
would hold the office of Infirmarian.

I myself felt the need of all the support which *la grâce d'état* could provide
for me at an extremely early stage of my career. After barely six months in
the convent, I was told suddenly that in a fortnight's time I should have to go
down to the school and give classes in English, Geography and History.

I was panic-stricken.

My own school-days had been delightful, but the classes were dull and I
had never bothered about studying. My time had been spent in devouring
Malory's *Morte d'Arthur*, the works of Kipling and the plays of Oscar Wilde,
whose epigrams dazzled my adolescent mind. As a result, the *lacunae* in my
education were such that it would have been hard to find anyone less fitted
for the instruction of youth.

This I tried nervously to explain to the Prioress.

She assured me, however, that, in the spiritual order, one was never
justified in saying that anything at all 'could not be done'.

'If you put everything you've got into it, and trust God,' she insisted,
kindly but firmly, '*He* will do the thing for you. Remember St. Peter walking on the waves.' And an eminent Jesuit, to whom I confided my apprehension next time I went to Confession, advised me to imitate the apostles when
Christ told them to feed five thousand people with five barley loaves and a
few cold fish.

After that, of course, there was nothing more to be said.

BEING war-time, there were no sleeping or restaurant cars on the train in
which I travelled up to Stirling. So, for a matter of six hours or so, I had to sit
bolt upright in my corner.

I felt as excited as a school-child about the adventure that lay before me.
A journey to Samarkand or El Dorado could hardly have held more potential thrills.

As usual, I was passionately interested in my fellow-travellers: three huge

Commandos, a red-haired sailor with a lovely girl-companion, and a husky-voiced young woman with a husband in Air Force blue, whose head, arm and leg were swathed in cotton-wool and bandages. Amongst their heaped hand-luggage they had a tame brown rabbit in a basket. Half-way through the journey they took it out and handed it leaves of limp-looking lettuce to nibble. It was an enchanting rabbit. When it lifted its split top lip to show long supercilious teeth, it looked like a disdainful elderly spinster. The wounded airman held it close in the crook of his unbandaged arm and appeared to derive much solace from its company.

Presently, I fell asleep.

I was awakened by an alarming sensation of nausea.

Obviously, a certain quantity of oxygen must have been shut in with us several hours before, when the guard had gone round at black-out time to see that windows and doors were hermetically sealed.

Since then, however, eight persons and a rabbit had been breathing it more or less energetically in and out of their lungs.

It now appeared to have reached exhaustion point.

Another two minutes—and, unless something drastic could be done about it, I knew that I should faint.

Now, absurd as it will surely sound to persons who from their cradles have been accustomed to deal with the things, I must here confess that one of the minor nightmares of my post-conventual life has been connected with windows and doors. When, for instance, I try to enter a bank or a post office, my unpractised instinct invariably guides me to pull when it ought to be push. Or *vice versa*. And it is the same with windows. Whenever, in car or taxi, I turn a handle to lower the window, the door flies open. As for buses and railway carriages, no matter how perseveringly I turn, twist, pull, push or press the gadget intended to control their windows, I have never yet encountered one upon which my efforts produced the slightest effect. And I find it humiliating.

This occasion was the solitary exception. Perhaps the saints of Paradise, whom I so desperately invoked as I fumbled with the blind, had something to do with it. Anyhow, the window suddenly yielded to treatment and, lowering itself obligingly a couple of inches, admitted a shaft of cold night air which cut into the fetid atmosphere like a blade. I inserted my nose into the space between blind and window, and drew a long, life-giving breath. By the mercy of Heaven, I was saved.

It is a curious thing, but, as I look back on it to-day, I believe that this trivial incident did almost more to impress me with the sense of my new and bewildering freedom than anything else had so far done.

I had actually dared to open a window, in a place containing several other people, and the universe had NOT rocked to its foundations and then come toppling down about my ears.

It seemed almost too wonderful to be believed.

The reason, of course, is that in convents, windows are such a subject of contention that it is practically impossible to touch one without getting your fingers burned.

Two parties exist in every religious community: the Fresh Air Fiends, who want the windows open, and the Fug Fiends, who want them shut. The odd thing is that, though the first are nearly always in the majority, it is the second who get their way.

It puzzled me when I came up from the Noviceship to the community. Why, since the lovers of fresh air were so numerous, didn't one of them just rise up and fling the windows wide?

The answer is that, in convents, things simply don't happen that way.

I remember one of the older nuns explaining this to me after I had suggested that certain measures should be taken in connection with window-opening. They were excellent measures, inspired by the most elementary rules of hygiene. And I was much surprised by the lack of enthusiasm with which they were always met. It was then that a certain nun, wise, elderly, and enormously kind-hearted, threw up her eyes to heaven at the crude inexperience revealed by my remarks, and said to me:

'Ah, mon enfant, croyez-moi: if it were 'umanlee posseeble for those windows to be flung orpen, flung orpen they would be. Mais—ça ne vaut pas la peine.'

I did not believe her. I experimented with the windows. And—I regretted it.

For, unfortunately, even in convents, one sometimes finds people who will stop at nothing—absolutely nothing—to get their own way.

Most people appear to think that by the very fact of entering a convent, one ought at once to be transformed, automatically, into a saint. The idea of a nun committing even the smallest imperfection profoundly shocks them. This is unreasonable. Nuns and monks—although examples of extraordinary holiness are sometimes found among them quite early in their religious life—would be the first to tell you that they are, generally speaking, a considerable distance from sanctity. They have—and carry with them into the convent—human faults and weaknesses, just like the rest of mankind. Many of those can only be corrected after long years of self-discipline and prayer.

Moreover, it sometimes happens that, after the period of trial known as the noviceship is passed, a nun will develop some idée fixe or eccentricity of character. When this happens, the nun in question can become a positive menace to the community.

In such a case, two courses of action are open to the Superior. The first is to enforce conformity to the accepted standard of life by commanding it 'under Holy Obedience', warning the nun that a refusal to obey will result in expulsion from the community. This method, though drastic, has the advantage of ridding the convent of undesirable members. Of its disadvantages nothing need here be said. They are, I think, too obvious to need cataloguing.

The second course of action is entirely 'supernatural'. Should the Superior decide upon it, the community must just resign themselves to shoulder the cross which Divine Providence has laid upon them, and simply envisage the 'difficult member' as a means of acquiring merit.

I once heard a distinguished Jesuit preach a sermon upon how to use disagreeable persons in the community as a means of acquiring an ever-increasing degree of sanctifying grace.

The old nun from whom I have quoted before had—in her long years of community life—made the most of many opportunities. A window-shutting fixation on the part of a certain 'difficult member' had deprived her for years of the fresh air that she not only loved, but which was essential to her health. It also, now and again, made virtue arduous among the weaker members of the community.

One day the old nun said to me:

'Ah, *chère petite*, you do not onnerstan'.' (It was true; I did not. Perhaps I never shall.) 'You t'ink *cette personne-là* is a gret orbstacle to *la perfection de la communauté*. An' eet ees not so. She ees a cross, yes—*mais*, what is a cross? *C'est une petite gâterie de Notre-Seigneur.*'

As for '*cette personne-là*', she insisted that, far from thinking her the curse of the community, she had come to look upon her as its greatest asset. For—*voyez-vous*—did she not provide her religious sisters with almost hourly opportunities of practising virtue, with the excellent result that most of them were rapidly attaining to a standard of holiness which they might never otherwise have reached? *Enfin*, if *le bon Dieu* had not presented such a person to the community, it would be their duty—*mais oui*, absolutely, their duty!—to 'go out into the 'ighwez an' 'edges an' *chercher, chercher, CHERCHER*, onteel won wass found!'

All of which only goes to show that, in convents, your success or failure in the matter of acquiring virtue depends entirely upon your point of view.

I reached Stirling at daybreak.

Having been told to change there, I climbed out, dragged my two suitcases from the van (the solitary porter was too busy to attend to me) and sat down on a bench to wait for the next train.

The bench was hard and the air extremely chilly. I had an hour before me. To pass the time, I began to say by heart the Office of Prime.

Jam lucis orto sidere
Deum precemur supplices . . .

The sun had just risen. The sky, drained hitherto of every vestige of colour, was dappled with little pink and golden clouds. It made one think of the floor of heaven, as painted by Fra Angelico. And, far below, on the shadowy earth, where the world still appeared to be sleeping, the walls and roofs of Stirling clung huddled together against the steep sides of the hill.

Oddly enough, however, it was neither the flaming sky nor the dim grey city that seized upon my imagination, dragging it forcibly away from the words of the morning hymn upon which I'd only just started. It was the abyss that yawned between.

That abyss had already begun to bother me when, as a child at school, I had been given the *Letters of St. Catherine of Siena* to read. She saw it as the abyss of infinity between God and his creation. To her, Christ was always the *Pontifex*—the 'Bridgemaker'—between the Creator and the creature who had become separated from him by sin. Thinking on these things (when I ought, I suppose, to have been studying arithmetic and *grammaire française*), it always seemed to me that there could never be too many of those who made it the business of their lives to bridge that gulf by prayer. That, I believe, was largely why, when I entered a convent, I chose an Order the *raison d'être* of whose members was to 'stand in the breach' and play the part of 'bridge-makers' between God and man.

For this is the work of those whom the Church officially dedicates to the recitation of the Divine Office in choir.

Among the various questions which are so often hurled at me in connection with convents, one of those which most constantly recurs is, 'What really *is* this thing you call the Divine Office?'

Well, this seems as good a place as any other in which to try to answer that question. It is not easy, since it involves the statement of one or two Catholic dogmas. And this bores—or alarms—a certain type of person. To ignore the basic idea, however, is to miss the point.

Catholics believe that God, being what he is—infinite and completely 'other' from all else in existence—created man *principally* in order to be adored by him. The other purposes of man's life are only secondary. The right order is: God first, man next.

Here, a difficulty arises.

The abyss which, since the Fall of man, yawns between creature and Creator, is infinite. How then can man's 'nothingness' formulate an act of worship which is in any sense worthy of God who is All?

The answer, of course, is that it can't.

So—we find ourselves up against an apparently insoluble problem. God, when he created man, knew—obviously—that this 'nothingness' of the creature would make his adoration of the Infinite entirely valueless. Why, then, did God create him?

Catholic theology replies that, when God made the world, he foresaw the Incarnation. He, the Infinite, would join himself to that which he had made, thus endowing it with a value which, like himself, would be divine. In this way—since the value of a divine action is infinite—the worship offered by those who are truly incorporated with God-made-Man would acquire the value of him into whose Mystical Body they would thus be drawn.

Which is exactly what happens in the Holy Sacrifice of the Mass. Christ, in the Mass, as on the Cross, becomes 'That with which we can at last incorporate ourselves and thus regain our true existence—that of Sons of God.'[1]

He lifts up the hearts and souls of those who assist at Mass and holds them within the white-hot circle of his own divine and infinitely holy Heart. Thus the adoration of Christ and his Christians mount up *together* to the Father, and the creature's worship—valueless in itself—is transformed and 'en-Christ-ed' by that ineffable union and embrace.

Now, the Catholic Church—being Christ-on-Earth and, therefore, speaking with divine authority—has drawn up a public, official worship of God, called the Liturgy,[2] which is more important and more powerful than anyone's private prayer. This is because, being the Church's official prayer, it has an absolute value, independent of the person who prays.

A Catholic who uses liturgical prayer—provided always that he is in a state of grace—prays *officially*, as a member of the Mystical Body of Christ. Through this membership, he can offer to God *a worship adequate to the Infinite*. He can adore God *divinely*, through, with, and in, Jesus Christ.

The Divine Office is that part of the Liturgy contained in the Breviary. Originally, it appears to have actually formed a part of the Mass. The early Christians, meeting secretly at nightfall in the shadowy catacombs for the *synaxis* or Breaking of Bread, prefaced the ceremony by psalms, litanies, invocations, canticles, readings, homilies and hymns. Then, gradually, as time went on, these elements evolved slowly into the Night Office of Matins and Lauds. The Little Hours of the day,[3] Prime, Terce, Sext, None, Vespers and Compline, were added later.

The Mass is the heart of the Liturgy. The Office is a radiation from this divine centre, a kind of *cortège* which should never be separated in thought from the Holy Sacrifice, whence it derives all its meaning and value.

---

[1] See *The Faith of the Catholic Church*, pp. 115-16, by C. C. Martindale, S.J.

[2] 'Liturgical Prayer' is that found in the Missal, Breviary, Ritual, Pontifical and Diurnal.

[3] These, besides being in the Breviary, are also found in a smaller book called a Diurnal or *Horae Diurnae*.

I have written rather a lot about this—the theological—aspect of the Divine Office, because, unless one grasps it, it is difficult to understand how monks and nuns can feel justified in looking upon it as the object of their lives. The Church sets so much store upon it that all her priests are bound—under pain of mortal sin—to the daily recitation of the Divine Office. And large numbers of religious orders of both men and women, have—as the official reason for their existence—the solemn recitation in choir of this, the *Opus Dei*.

ENGLISH RELIGION

BY D. W. BROGAN

from *The English People* (1943)

ENGLISH RELIGION

OF all English institutions, none is more English, less to be interpreted in general terms or judged by general standards than the Church of England. Its very status as 'by law established' is almost impossible to describe or to justify. Modern liberals brought up for the most part to regard Church establishment as an anachronism or an outrage, may well wonder at the continued existence of the Establishment. They may plan to disestablish and disendow and, while planning this great revolution, will find that their object is also the cherished dream of eminent Anglican divines who far from thinking that the Establishment is the strength of the Church of England, think it a fundamental weakness.

'The Church of England as by law established', it is a fine and apparently clear statement, but what does it mean? Or rather, what does Establishment mean and what is established? The Establishment and the Church of England thus linked by law are neither of them easily described. To begin with the Establishment. What does the State do for the Church? It does not, as is widely thought, pay the Church money. There has never been a concordat between Church and State such as those made between the Pope and Napoleon, the Pope and Hitler. In such bargains the secular power, in return for some degree of control of the Church, pays out of the national revenue some or most of the expenses of the Church and the clergy are a special type of civil servant. The English State does not pay anything to the English Church nor are the clergy state servants. The income of the Church is a corporate income which the State helps the Church to collect as it helps other corporate institutions, hospitals, colleges, etc. to collect their income. The State does more; it collects some of the income itself, turning over the net proceeds to the Church, but this is a limitation of Church power, not a privilege.

The erroneous view that the Church of England is directly a beneficiary of the State is fostered by the existence of the Ecclesiastical Commission. The Commissioners are appointed by the 'Crown', that is by the Prime Minister, and they control most of the real estate owned by the Church of England. But that real estate is the 'private property' of the Church, and were that property sold and the proceeds invested in securities, the Church of England would be no better or worse off, morally at any rate. Nevertheless, it is probably true that by being a great landowner the Church finds itself in positions that weaken its spiritual authority. Thus if it leases property in London for ninety-nine years, it has no means of preventing the temporary owners of that property turning some houses into brothels or slums.[1] And as a great landowner, the Church through the Ecclesiastical Commission is in the position of having to drive hard bargains. A great corporation cannot make special concessions and many a pious Anglican has been on the edge of unkind thoughts after argument with the Ecclesiastical Commissioners on questions of repairs and the duties of leaseholders. But all the same the Establishment of the present Church of England is not financial; it is moral.[2]

The Church of England is still, for most Englishmen, the national and proper way of rendering to God the things that are God's even if that belief involves another, that Caesar is to determine what things are God's and what his. The State in theory does lay down what the Church of England believes and how it shall conduct its public services and administer the sacraments. The Church is on this theory a branch of the civil service, its articles of faith and its modes of public worship are set out as schedules to Acts of Parliament. Only the most old-fashioned and unrealistic lawyer now believes that this picture has any real relation to the facts. The relation between God and Caesar is more complicated than that. For if there was ever a time when the Church

[1] It is true that a century ago the Church, like other property-owners, was not very tender-minded about slums. But the Church was no worse a landlord than were great noblemen or Oxford colleges. Under the shadow of the Christ Church of Pusey and Lewis Carroll lay some of the worst slums of Oxford; and New College at a not very remote date spent on not very successful ornament funds that might have been used to rebuild local slums. Such conduct to-day would seem unsocial even in the case of a college dedicated to St. Mary Magdalen. 'We are all Marthas now,' as Sir William Harcourt might have said.

[2] These truths are obscured in the public mind by the question of tithes. These are charges on land. They represent the medieval view that a tenth of the fruits of the earth was payable in kind to the Church. At various times in the past and present centuries they have been reduced in severity and commuted to money. Some owners of land at various times redeemed the tithe, i.e., made a capital payment, other owners did not. The difference in status, in pure economic theory, ought to be represented by a difference in the price of the land. To some extent it is. Like all other burdens on land, tithe is bitterly resented when prices fall as they have been doing in recent years; the English farmer feels like the Iowa farmer in such matters and the grievance of the English farmer against the Church is even more lively than that of the Iowa farmer against the Vermont banker. For the banker in fairly recent times did lend money while it is a long time since the Church's services were as valuable to the average farmer as tithe would suggest. The landowner, naturally, would like to see tithe abolished in most cases, but not all. For tithe is not specifically payable to the Church at all. A great deal of it is payable to laymen or to corporations like Oxford and Cambridge colleges. Thus the Russell family, when they got Woburn Abbey as their share of the loot of the monasteries, also got the great tithes which had been payable to the Abbot. This share of Church plunder is payable to the present Duke of Bedford, not to any parson. A great landowner or an Oxford college may receive more as tithe on land they do not own than they pay as tithe on land they do own, and some of the tithe they pay in one capacity, they pay to themselves in another. To abolish tithe may be an excellent thing, but if the abolition does not take the form of confiscating the tithe revenue for the State, it will be simply a way of making a large present to landowners who have been lucky enough not to have redeemed their tithe. The Church of England might be less unpopular with farmers if this were done, but the community at large has rights as well as farmers and parsons.

of England was willing to allow the State to determine its belief and practice, that time is long past. For, as a not totally unkind critic said, the troubles of the Church of England in modern times are due to the fact that in its old age it has got religion.[1] A series of revivals of old and preachings of new doctrines have made it impossible to say what is the central doctrine of the Church or what is its practice in public worship. Theological positions hard to distinguish from those of Rome, Constantinople, Geneva, are all held with impunity. The barest minimum of ritual is soundly Anglican as is a profusion of ornament that drove, so the famous story runs, one lady to regret the simple worship of the Church of Rome.

The official Thirty-nine Articles of Religion of the Anglican Church were designed to be, or have been found to be, patient of explanations. They can be affirmed (in some sense) by almost every type of Christian. To the Anglo-Catholic they may be the 'forty stripes save one'; to the Modernist something to be swallowed rather than accepted. But we have moved a long way from Tract XC, and the grievance of acceptance of the Articles is purely a clerical grievance and not, it seems, a very lively grievance even for the clergy.

The case of the Prayer Book is very different. The Prayer Book is far more a mark of Anglicanism than are the Articles. By insisting on the formal ritual of Archbishop Cranmer, the Anglican Church insisted on a mode of worship that was not only abandoned by the other Reformed Churches[2] but, in practice, on a mode of public worship by the laity that is far more ritualistic than that commonly practised in the modern Catholic Church. A prayer book is not the same as *the* Prayer Book. Had the whole Anglican communion effectively insisted on the uniform use of the Prayer Book, it could have been claimed, with some justice, that Canterbury rather than Rome had effectively secured uniformity, reverence and continuity in the public prayers of the laity. And it could also be claimed that the admirable English of the Prayer Book had quietly influenced the minds of all sorts and conditions of men who were hardly conscious of what it was that had coloured their views of how God should be worshipped. The old Anglican was not perplexed by temporary innovations and the fancies of parsons or the fashions of the time. The *Pilgrim's Progress* was not Holy Writ nor the eloquence of any modern century a substitute for the traditional prayers of the Church. And the idiosyncratic and self-willed English mind needed such a discipline. As long as uniformity was fairly generally observed, it received it. But with modern times, with the revival of factions within the Church of England, the old, dull, disciplined days were over. Sung Mattins (some hold) concealed

---

[1] I am, of course, aware, that it has always had religion and that, as Professor Sikes and Canon Smythe have shown, even in the dullest days of eighteenth-century torpidity there was more evangelical zeal and work than used to be thought.

[2] I am aware that the Methodists and other Reformed Churches have service-books, but they do not play anything like the pre-eminent part assigned by Anglican theory to the Book of Common Prayer.

the beauties of the Prayer Book from the congregation and the obvious obsolescence of some parts of the Prayer Book became apparent to the critical, a powerful if not a large body.[1]

More serious was the adoption of a kind of Congregationalism by the clergy. Evangelicals had long neglected some parts of the Prayer Book, and their subtractions were held to justify additions by others. Short of the use of the Ordinary of the Mass in Latin, there were hardly any extremes in alteration which the very 'High' clergy did not permit themselves. Anglo-Catholic divines like Bishop Gore might insist on the Prayer Book and the Prayer Book only as the worship of Anglicans, but this Chillingworthian doctrine was defied by many of the most zealous clergy.

The laity too were less attracted or repelled by the variations on the Prayer Book than by the splendour or poverty of ritual. Any visitor could see that there were great differences in the conduct of public worship at Holy Trinity, Brompton, and All Saints, Margaret Street. Not so many noticed whether All Saints or St. Alban's, or, for that matter, Holy Trinity, rigidly followed all the prescriptions of the Book of Common Prayer, weekday and Sunday alike. The educational effect of a common liturgy was lost. The Book of Common Prayer ceased to be a norm, and, in ritual as well as in doctrine, the Established Church ceased to stand for anything defined.[2]

The difficulty, indeed the impossibility, of defining the doctrine or practice of the Church of England, irritates the Erastian lawyer, like Sir William Harcourt and the exact theologian whether he be Anglican or non-Anglican. All are appalled by the toleration of incompatibles that is the genius of Anglicanism. To treat Christianity thus is very English; to treat Marxism thus, as Mr. Bertrand Russell had pointed out, is also very English. The legal establishment of the Church of England is a public recognition by the English State of a vague historical respect for Christianity and still more, for a very old, traditional English institution called 'the Church'. Before the Reforma-

---

[1] 'Yet I do not think that a boy, especially if his education is directed towards the study of words, can hear every morning, from his tenth to his eighteenth year, the measured and formal English of the Prayer Book without submitting his mind in some degree to the discipline which this Prayer Book enjoins. The collect for the week; the prayer for all sorts and conditions of men; the State prayers; the general thanksgiving. I took these things for granted, and never thought that they might be moulding my mind. Yet, even then, I assumed that the purpose of "this ancient school" was "that there may never be wanting" persons qualified for "the service of the Church and State." Not a word about "business"; not a word about the life-jobs of those figures, who, term after term, faded out of the lower and middle reaches of the school to serve neither Church nor State, but someone's bank or someone else's warehouse. Here we are, in the centre of London, at the ganglion point of high capitalism, the tallest pyramid in the modern competitive system; we continued, calmly and without self-consciousness, to use the terms describing an English society which was beginning to disappear even before a sixteenth-century merchant had founded our school. I do not think that this point ever occurred to the Merchant Taylors' Company.' (E. L. Woodward, Short Journey, pp. 19, 20.)

[2] The Episcopal Cathedral in Glasgow bears (1942) a notice affirming that 'prayer-book services' are held within. It is no longer a guarantee of anything that a church is in communion with Canterbury.

tion, the central Roman authority might impose order and doctrinal coherence. But once that control was removed, the absence of any English appreciation of the attractions of consistency, of the repellent character of anomalies, made it certain that, whatever form organized religious life took in England, it would not be coherent and consistent as it was in the Europe of Geneva or the Council of Trent. The establishment of a Church which offers not the doctrinal and ceremonial *table d'hôte* of the other communions, but a varied *à la carte* service in both, is hard to justify. But only too intelligent Englishmen, seeing the Church of England from too close at hand, can think that its representative role is over or that it can be either disregarded or swept on one side. 'C. of E.' may be a very meaningless term. The Church of England may only be the Church that the majority of English people stay away from. But they want it to be there to stay away from; it is their spiritual home whenever (which is not very often) they feel they want one. They would not be at home in a more functional institution, in a Church which knew its own mind and followed out to their logical conclusions the generally accepted premises of its doctrines. Such a Church would be, in one sense, a more respectable institution, but it would be very much less an English institution. No doubt, the vagueness of Anglicanism has contributed to the evasiveness of English thought in more than theological matters. No doubt the vagueness of the national mind has affected the Church. But whether the Church of England bred the English mind or vice versa does not matter:

> Before the Roman came to Rye or out to Severn strode,
> The rolling English drunkard made the rolling English road.

Some time later in English history, the same defiance of Euclidean geometry produced the Church of England.

It is possible to hold that all that keeps the Church of England together is the fact of Establishment, which both gives what little coherence there is and which gives in addition prestige that the Church, as a church, would not otherwise command. While the Anglican Church had a legal monopoly of higher education, of political position, when its privileges were enforced by laws which kept Dissenters and Catholics and Jews in their place, this view had some plausibility. But the Church to-day neither has nor wants such privileges.[1] During the past century, the legal privileges of the Anglican Church have been reduced to very little, until to-day a large body of its active members and leaders see Establishment not as an advantage but as a disadvantage. The Church of England has some rights in the school system. And the

---

[1] What bishop to-day would waste his time, as did the learned and saintly Christopher Wordsworth, fighting to keep the title 'Reverend' off the tombstone of a Methodist minister in a churchyard?

King is by custom a member of the Church of England in England and of the quite different Church of Scotland in Scotland and, by law, a 'Protestant' everywhere. The old legal pre-eminence of 'the Church' is reflected in other ways. For example, the college chaplains of Oxford and Cambridge colleges are Anglicans as are the college chapels.[1] The aristocracy in England are almost entirely Anglican or Catholic.[2]

This social pre-eminence of the Anglican Church has extended from its aristocratic laity to the clergy themselves. Their social rank rose all through the nineteenth century, and is only now falling again as the clergy become recruited more and more from the lower-middle and upper-working classes.

That the English parson in the age of Swift or of Fielding was a kind of superior domestic is true; that Mr. Collins was probably representative of a good many parsons of the age of Jane Austen is also true. But the English parson in modern times became a kind of equal of the squire, ranking above the doctor and the attorney. He had in many cases been to the same kind of school. He might, especially if the living he held were a good one, be a member of a great family. A friend of Newman's, the Reverend Samuel Wood, was a great-uncle of the present Lord Halifax. He might also be a sporting parson, orthodox, popular, but profoundly unprofessional by the standards of Rome or Edinburgh, as was another clerical member of the same family.

It was roughly true that the policy of the Church of England in that happy nineteenth-century heyday was to put a 'gentleman in every parish'. This ideal, though more practicable than that of putting a saint in every parish, was beyond the resources of the Church. A poor gentleman can exist, but he cannot remain a gentleman in a representative capacity if his income definitely declasses him. And the resources of the Church were not adequate to giving to all the incumbents of parishes a gentleman's income. Nevertheless, the gentility, real or presumed, of the parson had some social advantages. In an inequalitarian society like that of England, the levelling tendencies of the Christian faith must always cause difficulties. Where the clergy are the uncontested dispensers of means of grace and cannot be replaced, their spiritual authority may cover their social inferiority, although as Innocent III found out, the untamed feudal noble could square a good deal of anti-clericalism with a conscience that had a genuine horror of unprofitable

[1] This need not mean much; least of all uniformity. (See Brittain and Manning, *Babylon Bruis'd and Mount Moriah Mended.*)

[2] There are, of course, great Presbyterian houses in Scotland and a number of Nonconformist peers of recent creation in England. But although there was at least one peer of reasonably ancient creation who was a Moslem and all other religions may well be represented in the peerage for all I know, in the aristocracy the national passion for religious eccentricity fights a losing battle with the national passion for snobbery when it is a question of belonging to an unfashionable form of Christianity. According to Mr. G. M. Young, the return of the Willoughby of Parham family to the Anglican fold in the eighteenth century ended the last of the great Puritan nonconforming houses.

heresy. So a priest in a Catholic country need not be a gentleman in any sense of the word so long as his priestly prerogatives are unquestioned. And in a rigidly organized Presbyterian society, the authority of the Church may cover the weak social or economic position of the clergy.[1] But England was not Scotland or Prussia, and the choice was not between some form of clerical independence (or, if you like, tyranny) and a tamed Erastian church, but between one form of Christianity adapted to a society highly conscious of social distinction and another. Between German Lutheranism and Anglicanism it is not hard to make a choice. The parson was given a more independent position by the abuse of his 'freehold'; by the lack of system in church organization; by the great social position of the bishops which resulted from their large incomes and great houses.[2]

Quite apart from any general levelling tendency (and such exists in England) the special social prestige of the Church of England is not what it was. But for the officially minded who like to know where they are, 'Church' is nice and 'Chapel' doubtful and this social ranking extends to all aspects of English religious life. More people than would admit it or are conscious of it, are of the mind of the sergeant-major, who classified his recruits into 'C. of E.,' 'R.C.' and 'fancy religions'. The only change they would make would be in putting 'R.C.' definitely under 'fancy religions'. But this customary precedence is very little based on law; it is based on the normal English attitude to organized religion in his own country. The Church of England is the *normal* form of religion; even the Dissenter who dissents from its claims, like the earlier Nonconformist who refused to conform to its practices, admits by his protest its predominant place. An Anglican bishop, even in a city like Liverpool where his Roman rival has more adherents, is by national custom the chief representative spokesman of the Christian viewpoint.[3] And without any legal sanction in modern times, the Church of England is thought of as being the Church of the Empire, a cause of disillusionment to pious Anglicans when they go to Canada or Australia and discover the strength of their Roman and Dissenting rivals.

[1] It should be noted that in Scotland most, though by no means all, of the 'good' families have drifted in the last two centuries away from Presbyterianism to Episcopalianism. (This has had good results as well as bad for Scottish Presbyterianism.) Without agreeing with Charles II that Presbytery is no religion for a gentleman, there is a sense in which a kind of Anglicanism may seem to be pre-eminently the religion for a gentleman to whom gentility is of fundamental importance. On the other hand, Christianity in any fundamental form can hardly seem to be a religion for a gentleman in the usual sense of the term.

[2] When the first Archbishop Temple sold the country estate of the Archbishops of Canterbury because he did not think that, in modern times, an Archbishop of Canterbury had any business parading as a great landed magnate, he was anticipating as great a change in the role of the archbishopric as the marriages of Cranmer and Parker portended.

[3] *Who's Who* carries this principle to an extreme. Although Catholic bishops in Ireland are certainly far more important than bishops of the Church of Ireland, and are legally in exactly the same position, they are entered in *Who's Who* under their proper names, not under the names of their sees. That honour is reserved for the bishops of the disestablished Church of Ireland.

This prestige of the Church of England may be a result of past legal privilege and may owe something to the present connection with the State, but it is possible that a disestablished Church of England, provided it stayed united, would keep this kind of hold on the English people as the Church of France did when it was disestablished in 1905. For it should be remembered that in organization, if not in doctrine, the Church of England has been far more changed in the last century than it was at the Reformation. Its finances have been reformed; not enough, perhaps, but reformed all the same. Its bishops are no longer opulent feudal magnates, representing the distribution of wealth and power that suited the England of Henry VIII.[1] The creation of new sees in the nineteenth century, the increase in income tax, the rise in the standard of episcopal duty that has been accepted since Samuel Wilberforce set the example in the diocese of Oxford, these have all made bishops very different men and officials from what they were in the days of Dr. Proudie of Barchester. A century ago, a bishop appointed to a really good see could leave a quite impressive fortune to his children. To-day he less often has children, and certainly cannot leave them a fortune out of savings from his salary. Among the qualifications that make a man episcopal timber to-day is a private income that will enable him to bear the burden of such white elephants as Farnham Castle, or other 'assets' of the old order that have now become liabilities.

Despite his archaic costume, his official precedence and, in the case of the old sees, the tenancy of a 'palace' that recalls the golden days of golden stalls and the state of great landed magnates, the modern bishop is not a rich or an idle functionary. Promotion to a bishopric is often, in fact, what it has always been in theory, a call to greater labour, reluctantly accepted. Probably at few periods in church history have the words 'Nolo episcopari' been uttered so often and so sincerely as in modern England.[2]

Yet it is in the method of nomination to bishoprics that the connection between Church and State survives in its most important aspect. Since the time of Henry VIII, the nomination to this great spiritual office has been in the hands of whoever effectively disposed of the State patronage, in the hands of Charles II, in the hands of Lord Palmerston. The King or the politicians who chose the shepherds of the Anglican flock could be of any religion or

[1] 'Few changes in our modern England have been more remarkable than that in the character of the Bishops of the Anglican Church and the way they are regarded. Forty or fifty years ago they were usually rich, dignified, and rather indolent magnates, aristocratic in their tastes and habits, moderate in their theology, sometimes to the point of indifferentism, quite as much men of the world as pastors of souls. . . . The revival within the Church of England began from below, and reached the bishops last.' (James Bryce to Thomas Hughes, *Life of Bishop Fraser*, pp. 356-8.)

[2] I was once present when the future of an eminent divine was being debated. His learning, his good looks, his admirable manners, his good business habits, the reasonable orthodoxy of his religious views, all were discussed and admitted. But, it was added, he could not be made a bishop. He had 'no pastoral zeal' and that, it was somewhat reluctantly admitted, was now necessary in a bishop.

none. A Lutheran background in the case of Prince Albert, a fondness for Presbyterian ways and men in the case of Queen Victoria, submission to the Evangelical views of Lord Shaftesbury in the case of Palmerston, a very outside point of view in the case of Disraeli, High Anglican principles in the cases of Gladstone and Salisbury: all affected the character of the episcopate in the second half of the last century. Of the nine persons appointed to the office of Prime Minister in this century, three were Presbyterians, one a Baptist, one a Unitarian, and the Anglican orthodoxy of the remaining four was not in every case above reasonable suspicion. Yet there is abundant evidence that, in making these appointments, modern Prime Ministers, whatever their origin, have shown a strong sense of responsibility. None has behaved as Disraeli did in candidly making appointments to help his party at an election.[1]

Yet there is, at first sight, something distasteful in the thought of spiritual office so bestowed. For although Prime Ministers do not make scandalous appointments, they do make appointments that it is unlikely would be made by any 'free' church. Chosen by an indirect democratic plebiscite, for reasons that have nothing to do with Church questions,[2] with no certainty that they will have either knowledge or interest in this field, Prime Ministers may impose chief pastors on very reluctant flocks. The see of Hereford, for instance, has more than once been used by Prime Ministers to show their indifference to mere local clerical and lay opinion. Where appointments have involved apparent approval of certain types of religious views, a Prime Minister has seemed to some to be, in effect, extending the limits of tolerable variation in doctrine. And, when some appointment has annoyed an important section of Church opinion, the resentment of lay nomination has found expression in threats to exercise the rights of the Church, rights preserved by the 'election' of a new bishop by the cathedral chapter. In form, the Prime Minister merely nominates a candidate to the chapter, but in effect the so-called *congé d'élire* is only permission to elect one person who is named.[3]

[1] It should be remembered that patronage, the modified English version of the spoils system, was just being abolished in Disraeli's times. His attitude, though a little scandalous when looked at from the side of the angels, was not particularly novel or scandalous from the side of the practising politician.

[2] This was one of the flaws in the argument whereby John Richard Green tried to justify the system by a parallel with the popular election of St. Ambrose as Archbishop of Milan. Mr. Gladstone might be the people's choice as much as St. Ambrose was, but he was not chosen to find a modern Ambrose for the see of Winchester.

[3] I have simplified the procedure, but I have not, I think, distorted its meaning. The *congé d'élire* is, in effect, like an American primary. The electors of Texas will by the time this book has appeared have elected Mr. O'Daniel to the United States Senate. But they will have had no real option. By winning the Democratic primary, Mr. O'Daniel has been given the equivalent of a *congé d'élire*. For the electors of Texas to vote for the Republican candidate (presumably there is one) would be as revolutionary an act as for a Cathedral chapter not to vote for the candidate named in the letters missive of the Prime Minister. They would not, of course, be subject to the penalties of *præmunire*. It might be pointed out to uncritical admirers of Magna Carta that one of

No effective resistance has ever been made to this system, although the possibility of a clerical revolt has no doubt had a limiting effect on the choices made by Prime Ministers, who in modern times always consult the Archbishop of Canterbury and are thus in a position to know how much the Church of England will stand.

Yet, seen from the outside, the nomination of bishops by a lay authority has its advantages. It does, in fact, result in making bishops of men who would be very unlikely to reach that high office were bishops elected by the laity, or the clergy, or by any combination of the two or any method practised by other branches of the Anglican communion.

It can be argued that the representative character of an Anglican bishop is in part derived from his secular origin. Because he has been chosen by the lay power, he is more likely to think in a non-clerical fashion of the problems where the lay and clerical points of view are in conflict.[1] The qualities that appeal to a lay Prime Minister may be very valuable qualities that do not appeal to the minority of zealous laity. A bishop so appointed may be able to defy the sectarian opinion of the faithful.[2]

An Anglican dignitary, in such cases, is far more free than leaders of the 'Free Churches' who cannot go too far ahead of their flocks. An American Methodist bishop who had expressed doubts about the wisdom of the 'experiment noble in purpose' would have been a hero, and yet if no American Methodist bishop has ever had doubts on the policy of constitutional Prohibition, the political wisdom of that bench of bishops must be very low. A Catholic Bishop in a region like Brooklyn really 'cracking down' on Coughlinism would be a parallel to Charles Gore criticizing the Boer War in

the chief grievances against King John and one the charter was intended to put an end to, was royal nominations to bishoprics. Back to Magna Carta is a possible battle-cry for the enemies of this system to-day.

[1] It is, I hope, unnecessary to say that by 'clerical' I do not mean 'religious'.

[2] Another form of patronage which might be, but is not now used in a simple politica lfashion, is that of nominations to regius professorships. In Oxford and Cambridge and in the Scottish universities, a number of the most important chairs are 'regius', that is, the professors are appointed by 'the Crown' which in England means the Prime Minister, in Scotland, the Secretary of State for Scotland. In the past, politics of a kind played some part. Thus it is believed that had the Liberal government been defeated a little sooner than it was, Lord Acton would not have been made Regius Professor of Modern History at Cambridge by its Conservative successor. But direct political rewards are rare in this field. I know of only one case and that not very recent. It was widely believed that a very active politician was given a regius chair in a Scottish university in recompense for his effective services as an election agent for a cabinet minister. Whether this be so or not, the professor of whom the story was told became, in the not very long run, world-famous in his own field of medicine. And, as in the case of bishoprics, the outsider's view is sometimes more objective than the domestic view. But there are, of course, drawbacks to the system. In 1870, when Glasgow University had some of the greatest names in the British academic world on its roll of professors, the official academic chief of the future Lords Kelvin and Lister and the two Cairds was Principal Barclay. 'He was without any particular literary or scientific distinction and was commonly reported to have received his appointment from the Crown because of the presence of mind he had shown in the management of a boat by which he had saved the precious life of one of its ministers.' (*John Henry Muirhead Reflections*, p. 27.)

Joseph Chamberlain's good city of Birmingham, or Dr. Hensley Henson, not yet a bishop, denouncing the profiteers of the Putumayo atrocities by name in Westminster Abbey. More instances could be given to support the view that if we are to give any meaning to 'fearless', other than noisy statements of views already known to be popular (the meaning the word has acquired in the cheap Press), the high Anglican clergy are to-day at least as fearless as the ecclesiastical leaders of any part of the English-speaking world. And some of these Anglican leaders would not have been chosen by any 'democratic' method of election.

There is another advantage in the nomination of bishops by politicians. The Church of England is rent by internal ecclesiastical politics. The appointment of bishops from the outside can not only be used by a prudent lay politician to keep the balance true within the Church, but to remind the clerical combatants that they are members of a technically united body. Thus the variations in doctrine and ritual that might well be associated with the changing party positions of successive Bishops of Truro are not without their educational value. A nomination of a well-known party leader (in the Church sense of party) is not necessarily a triumph for the local section of his party in his new diocese; that party has not yet carried an election and is not necessarily much benefited by the arrival of a bishop who has been appointed by a Prime Minister who has had other motives than the desire to promote true Catholic doctrine or to score off ritualists.[1] And the Bishop, once enthroned, has *usually* settled down to the job of being a Father in God to all the faithful, no matter what their ecclesiastical colour. In this the Bishop is, of course, profoundly English. He acts in the spirit of Bishop Sanderson's preface to the Prayer Book of 1662 and avoids the 'sundry inconveniences' that arise from the attempt to remedy evils that may have arisen from things 'advisedly established'.[2] This respect for vested interests, emotional as well as material, makes the good bishop, although possibly a bishop who serves the Church as a semi-secular rather than as a purely religious body chiefly concerned to declare the faith once delivered or to be delivered to the saints. A Bishop Gore in one direction, a Bishop Barnes in another, may not accept this limitation of their functions, may take an un-English view of the importance of intellectual clarity and insist on definitions ('no evident necessity so requiring' such action in the eyes of their brethren), but they are not typical of the men whom the Prime Ministers normally call to the episcopal office.

The connection with the State is important in another way. For twenty-

---

[1] It is not a real solution of the problem of keeping party spirit within due limits to accept what is, in effect, a geographical limitation of parties. The Protestant Episcopal Church of the United States lays more stress on the 'Protestant' in Richmond, Virginia, than in Fond du Lac, Wisconsin. But what of the Virginian member who moves to Wisconsin?

[2] I take this citation from Dr. Hensley Henson's admirable *Church of England*.

six bishops are members of the House of Lords.[1] As the House of Lords has over seven hundred members, the twenty-six bishops would be a tiny minority *if* the lay peers took their legislative duties seriously. But they do not, and the bishops may often be a numerically large as well as intrinsically weighty section of the actual working Upper House. It is less and less common for a bishop to take much part in mere or pure politics, but in questions with a moral content, questions of moral legislation (e.g. drink, gambling and the like), or questions affecting the treatment of natives in the Empire[2] they have a concern. In medieval language, the post of 'keeper of the King's conscience' was entrusted to the Lord Chancellor, who in modern times is a great lay official and judge.[3] But in a non-technical sense, the keeper of the national conscience is now more often the bench of bishops in the House of Lords.

But a church is not a mere matter of bishops. What of the lesser shepherds and what of the flock? Here it is important to notice one effect of the theory of establishment. The Church of England claims to be the Church of the whole English people. In modern times it admits that there are large Dissenting bodies—Methodist, Romanist, Jewish and others—but these, even if lumped together, are still a minority of the English people. And, it is held, the Church of England has the cure of souls of the rest. So it is under obligation to provide means of worship all over the country; in regions where there are few Anglicans; in regions where there are few inhabitants. No more than a Post Office can it refuse to provide service in remote or unprofitable regions in order to concentrate on those fields that are white for the harvest. This means a maldistribution of resources that is not necessarily discreditable. There are sixteen thousand clergy (not all of them doing parochial work), so

---

[1] The two Archbishops of Canterbury and York, the Bishops of London, Durham and Winchester are members by right. The remaining bishops become members by seniority of their appointment to their sees. This curious system has a very English origin. When it became evident in the nineteenth century that there were not enough bishoprics and that those that existed were often in the wrong place, Parliament reluctantly agreed to tamper with the work of Theodore of Tarsus, Lanfranc and Henry VIII. So new sees, beginning with Manchester, were created. But the change was not to be used to increase the clerical membership of the House of Lords so, with respect for the rights of the Archbishops and the three historically most important episcopal sees, all claims were lumped. This means that a bishop may have to wait a long time before he enters the House of Lords. The Archbishops always, and the three *ex officio* bishops usually, have been bishops before so that they come to the House of Lords with some episcopal experience. (The present Bishop of Durham went straight to the episcopal bench in the Lords.) The other bishops have years of utterances on public questions bottled up before they get an official platform to express them from. The pedantically minded among historians still lament a system that may leave a Bishop of Lichfield outside the House of Lords and put a Bishop of Bradford into it.

[2] The Church of England is now a great missionary church with more firsthand knowledge of all parts of the British Empire than any secular body. And among its missionaries have been some of the most zealous defenders of the rights of the natives, men like Bishop Weston and Archdeacon Owen. The English bishops, in such cases, may be spokesmen for a great unrepresented body.

[3] At present Lord Simon (Sir John Simon).

that if the man-power of the Church of England were evenly distributed over the whole country, each parson would have to look after three thousand people, which of course reduces the pastoral office to a formality. So the rural parson is underworked and the town parson overworked, and the fiction that the Church of England is a Church serving all the population is not at all plausible in a big industrial city in the Midlands, whatever surface truth it may have in an agricultural area like Lincolnshire or in central Oxford.[1]

The Church of England has never in modern times had as many bishops or as few parish clergy as it has to-day and the bishop has kept his place as a national figure better than the parson has. And the system of choosing men for given parochial or other posts loses its attractive simplicity as soon as we descend from the high plateau where bishops and deans are made and live.[2]

Lesser patronage is no longer a simple matter of nomination by a Prime Minister. The Prime Minister continues to nominate to some ecclesiastical posts but the Lord Chancellor nominates to more. Other officers of the Crown (e.g. the Chancellor of the Duchy of Lancaster) have other jobs to give away and so have the Universities of Oxford and Cambridge and the colleges which are part of those universities. So far, so comparatively good; clerical patronage is administered by public or semi-public bodies with, on the whole, a due regard to decorum and piety.[3]

But most patronage is private; it is in the hands of private landowners. In the Middle Ages pious landowners often gave the right to take the profits of a parish to an abbey whose abbot thus became the rector and who put in a vicar who did the work and received a stipend which was less, possibly much less, than the income of the parish. At the Reformation, other landowners took their lands away from the suppressed abbeys, but forgot to give back the great tithes to the parsons who did the work of the parishes. Thus in England the average parish priest is a vicar and not a rector, and it is usually a safe guess that a vicar or a perpetual curate is less well off than a rector.[4]

[1] It is significant that the illustrations to Dr. Hensley Henson's book are all taken from the countryside or from the old cathedral towns. There is no illustration of church life in the places where the great majority of the English people live, the great new industrial areas.

[2] Deans of the great cathedrals may be much more like characters out of Trollope than any modern bishop can be. Of course, Trollope, for all that he was a Liberal, would have been astonished at the Bolshevik enthusiasm of the present Dean of Canterbury (Dr. Hewlett-Johnson), and, despite his robust view of popular literature, he might have been a little puzzled by the ease with which Dr. Inge, when Dean of St. Paul's, combined the careers of Paul Elmer More and Mr. Westwood Pegler and had enough time over to fulfil the duties of the great office once adorned by John Donne.

[3] It has been my experience in Oxford and Cambridge, that the difficulty to-day is to find candidates who can afford to accept the average living. I have been told that on the list of possible nominees kept for the use of the Lord Chancellor, some names (and the most favoured) gain attention because they are marked off by the letters 'WHM' which being interpreted stand for 'wife has means'.

[4] Sometimes more than the great tithes were acquired by the new class of hard-faced men who did well out of the Reformation. The Russells got all the assets of the Abbey of Woburn

The old untrammelled days of nomination, at what was practically the good pleasure of the patron, are over. So are scandalous nominations and sales of nominations. The great grievance now is the characteristically English one of 'party trusts'. Instead of the great magnate nominating a kinsman whose call was more to the temporalities than to the spiritualities (and thus raising the social standing while lowering the spiritual tone of the clergy), the right to 'present' to vacant livings is vested in trustees. These trustees buy up, with funds they have been given or left, vacant rights of presentation. They are associated with parties within the Church, especially with the extreme 'Protestant' parties. Their object is to make sure that, in as many cures of souls as money can buy, the Gospel truth, as they see it, shall be preached and no Romish doctrines or practices be tolerated.[1] The patronage system is being more and more limited and it is its approaching extinction that accounts for the current zeal of the purchasers of presentation rights. But in the combination of religious ends and very worldly means, the trusts are among the most English of institutions. And yet they are in some ways un-English. The blind respect for vested interests, which the free hand given to these trusts exemplifies, is in a way reminiscent of the immunity given to American educational foundations since the decision in the Dartmouth College case over a century ago. No English or Scottish college or foundation has any such immunity from the amending hand of the law. Oxford and Cambridge have both reformed themselves and been reformed from outside. But there are many parishes in England whose pastors are chosen for them by trustees determined to see that in the age of Karl Adam and Karl Barth, Maritain and Reinhold Niebuhr, Cadoux and Needham, the intellectual standards of the *Speaker's Commentary* and the religious spirit of the Ecclesiastical Titles Bill shall be preserved. The Church of England as a body may amend and explain, but inside it these ecclesiastical strongholds of the past still hold out, buttressed by money against the spirit of the age.[2] And once appointed, the Anglican

and sometimes styled themselves lay abbots of that great foundation. The present head of the family, the pacifist Duke of Bedford, has ceased making any contribution to the support of Woburn parish church. Its incumbent receives none of the spoil of the Abbey, not even the lesser tithes. The Russells have usually been strongly Erastian and anti-clerical in their views, but this cannot be attributed solely to the fact that like so many other great families, 'their hands are dripping with the fat of sacrilege' as (unless my memory fails me) Mr. Lloyd George vividly put it *à propos* of the eminently clerical Cecils.

[1] It is a matter of controversy whether the 'Protestant' trusts are worse in this respect than the 'Catholic'. But they are better provided with funds, and as it is true that the extreme old-fashioned Protestant view is held by the most old-fashioned section of the Anglican clergy, the nominees of the Protestant trusts tend to have less personal prestige. The ecclesiastical position of the great Lord Shaftesbury is probably that which appeals least of all to the religious mind of to-day. (It is a leader of this section, Bishop Chavasse of Rochester, who has rushed to the defence of the bankers.) Here, the dead hand of Victorian wealth and piety is heavy on the living Church.

[2] Another example of the dead hand which is able to affect contemporary practice is the Lord's Day Observance Society. English sabbatarianism is not dead, but it is less living than it would be, had it to depend on current income to pay for its campaigns. The universities may

incumbent is almost as much his own master as is the bishop. He holds the 'parson's freehold' and, short of very scandalous neglect or misbehaviour, he is secure for life. This permits, of course, the ill-fitted parson to keep his job long after his utility is gone. It even permits the scandalous parson too long a run for his money, or his patron's money. It also allows the saint to go his own way without adjusting his view of life to the wishes of an unsaintly congregation. It is unlikely that this legal guarantee of the right of the parson to do what he likes with his own will last much longer. That it has lasted so long is part of the English conservatism which marked the old establishment.[1]

Bishops appointed by politicians, parsons appointed by private individuals who may not be either resident or absentee landowners with some interest in the peace, or even in the religious wellbeing of a parish, but merely legal agents of a long-dead zealot: how can such a Church have a hold on the English people? It is easy to ask the question, but harder to answer it; yet the parson has a hold, or if that is too strong a word, he is at one end of a rope that, however slackly, binds or till recently bound the English people to the English Church.[2]

'I have never seen, heard, nor read, that the clergy were beloved in any nation where Christianity was the religion of the country. Nothing can

be held by some to be in the same class. But neither Oxford nor Cambridge insist, to-day, on the literal teaching of what was orthodoxy, religious or academic, in the past. The Bampton lecturers are allowed to go beyond Mansel. And the Gifford lectures on natural religion in the Scottish universities have been given, in one case at least, by an avowed opponent of 'natural religion' in its ordinary sense (Karl Barth).

[1] 'The position of an incumbent in the Church of England would be, if they knew of its wild licence, the envy of foreign tyrants. In 1914 an incumbent who conformed to a minimum of legal observances, who refrained from murder, notorious evil living and conspicuous drunkenness, could do pretty much what he pleased—that is, in principle. In practice, as had been proved by a long succession of technical law-breakers, he could, if he were enthusiastic, devout, hardworking and beloved, ignore the legal minimum required of him, and turn his parish church into a colourable imitation of a Papist chapel or a dissenting meeting-house.' (R. Ellis Roberts, *H. R. L. Sheppard*, p. 86.)

[2] The national character of the Church of England is illustrated by the fact that it is the parson, not the priest or minister, who is the traditional butt. He appears in ludicrous roles on comic postcards, being scored off by the village drunk. He is a classical figure of the mildly humorous drawing-room ballad ('I was a pale young curate then'), or the other which tells of the clerical philanderer who is now 'a vicar in the North Country at a salary three times greater'. He is the hero of the joke about the curate's egg and the hero of *The Private Secretary*. There can be no doubt what denomination ordained Mr. G. S. Melvin, or unfrocked Mr. George Robey. The Anglican clergyman is also the hero of innumerable ribald, unprinted jokes. A touchy and thoughtless parson once complained of this fact and was admirably answered by Mr. St. John Ervine. Anti-clerical jokes are common in all countries. And they must be directed against the traditional representatives of religion. In France that is the *curé* not the *pasteur*; in England, it is the parson and not the priest. This merely proves that, as André Siegfried said, the *curé* is part of the furniture of French life as is the parson of English life. And, for that reason, there was wisdom as well as humour in the jest of a friend of mine at the time of the famous and scandalous trial of the unfortunate Rector of Stiffkey. 'This trial has done more to endear the Church of England to the English people than anything since the trial of the Seven Bishops.' Scandals in the Church of England are public property, not the private mortifications of private sects.

render them popular but some degree of persecution.' So wrote one of the most eminent if not most representative of Anglican divines, Dean Swift, and the readiness of the English people to laugh or sneer at their established pastors is partly due to the fact that it is quite a long time since the Church of England has been persecuted, or even thought it was. It is nearly a generation since F. E. Smith declared that the Welsh Disestablishment Bill had 'shocked the conscience of every Christian community in Europe'. Even the boldest rhetorician to-day, on his way to high legal preferment, would have to find some other means of proving his stout Church-of-Englandism than oratorical flourishes like this. The Church may be impoverished; what old Scottish divines called the 'crown rights of Christ' may be affronted by an Erastian Parliament, but the parson is not linked to his people by any bond like that which unites the Irish priest or the Nonconformist minister, by a memory of wrongs suffered in common. A few sections of the Church of England have more recent memories of suffering than the Civil War of three hundred years ago provides, but in the main, until very recent times, Church and State in England have lived more like bickering spouses than like passionate lovers or deadly enemies.[1] Indeed, the neutral observer of the relationship between Church and State in England is sometimes reminded of Mr. Dooley's observation that, in the Archey Road, when a man and a woman find that they can't go on living together, they go on living together.

Yet there are moments when the strain seems about to become intolerable. Thus the House of Commons has twice recently refused to sanction changes in the Prayer Book asked for by the constituted authorities of the Church. The majority of English members of Parliament were willing to give the Church what it wanted, but a minority of English members aided by members from Scotland (where a different Church is established) and Wales and Northern Ireland (where no church is established) refused to permit the cloven hoof of Rome to be inserted in the doorway of a Church which the most vociferous orators never entered anyway. The result was a solution of a type not uncommon in ecclesiastical politics. The Church went its own way; the bishops had no effective means of putting down 'Romanism'; but the Protestant feeling of the British, if not of the English people, was satisfied. To a large section of the practising and believing Christians in the Church of England, the rites and doctrines condemned by that unimpressive version of a Church Council, the House of Commons in a religious mood, were essential and sacred. They refused to give them up, no matter how much that might annoy stoutly Erastian divines from Paisley or Portadown. So in effect

---

[1] The Anglo-Catholic party keeps green the memory of its Victorian confessors. And it is possible that if the lively, riotous days of Lowder of London Docks could return, or a few priests like Green of Miles Platting spent a year or two in jail in defence of what they took to be orthodoxy, religious zeal (at least as it is understood in Belfast), would revive and the churches be filled again, with worshippers as well as rioters.

the State washed its hands of the matter, leaving the battle to be fought out inside the Church.

But what constitutes being 'inside the Church'? It is easy to exclude Presbyterians, Catholics, Jews, Christian Scientists, but what is the position of the occasional conformer, of the Englishman who stays away from the parish church and not from another rival place of worship? Apparently this unwillingness to submit himself to the discipline of churchgoing gives this not untypical Englishman a special right to insist on having his way. It is on this view the duty of the Church of England to be ready at any moment to provide for the religious needs (if such they can be called) of persons who are only in any degree either Churchmen or Christians, because *some* relation to the Church and to Christianity is part of the make-up of any decent Englishman.[1]

It is the prevalence of this view, and the unconscious arrogance that often accompanies it, which irritates the minority of the English people to whom the English Church is part of the Christian Church. For a Church that meets the demand of this simple 'Church-of-Englandism', most certainly does not meet the needs of the devout believer.[2] Less than ever, in these days, when the whole Christian conception is threatened and by more than argument, is the conscious Christian minority in the Anglican Church disposed to make concessions to the Laodicean majority to whom the Church of England is, like cricket, part of the English background. Indeed, the acceptance of so vague a religion as this seems fraught with danger to the more concrete religion of

[1] This view was very candidly expressed by 'A Soldier' in a letter in the *Spectator*, 31 July, 1942: 'Like all my relatives that I ever heard of I was baptized and confirmed into the Church of England, and all of us expect, in due time, to be married and buried according to its rites. . . . I often intend to go to church and succeed in getting there a dozen times a year, when I enjoy and believe myself to be edified by the old liturgy, especially the Psalms, Lessons and Collects which high-falutin' parsons gabble and mutilate. I hate parsons' antics, High or Low Church. . . . To be honest I should admit that I am much more an Anglican Churchman than I am an orthodox Christian.' This is surely a very advanced form of what Gladstone called 'the Erastian theory that the business of an Establishment is to teach all sorts of doctrines and to provide Christian ordinances by way of comfort for all sorts of people, to be used at their own option.' (*Life of Bishop Wilberforce*, vol. ii, p. 353.) The new view seems to be that the customer is always right, even if he is hardly a customer at all.

[2] Many persons brought up outside the Church of England have been astonished (and often irritated) by the phenomenon of 'Church-of-Englandism'. It is over fifty years since Augustine Birrell allowed his normal urbanity to be overclouded by his Scottish and Dissenting ancestry and training. 'Church-of-Englandism is far too robust, too secular-minded, to care a rap about the opinion of bishops and divines, who are but necessary evils, only to be defended when attacked by low-minded Radicals and vulgar Dissenters. It is the external church, the bricks and mortar, the ivy-mantled tower, nestling in the valley hard by the "Blue Boar", the chiming of the bells on a Sunday morning as they fall on the ears of men walking in an opposite direction, that appeal to these stalwart sons of the Establishment. . . . To men of this mould, to cease to belong to the Church of England is to be a renegade from the national flag, to go over to the enemy. Church-of-Englandism is the religion of England, and it is the duty of every Englishman to belong to the English religion. What that religion is doesn't matter, and is perhaps uncertain. But, whatever it is, it is a moderate, decent religion which leaves you alone, or which you can leave alone if so minded.'

the zealous minority, which now realizes fully that it is a minority and that in the old sense England is no longer a Christian country.[1]

The Christian cause in England is not represented solely by the Established Church. For all the passion of the English people for social conformity was not strong enough to control the national individualism in religion. And one of the great dividing lines in English life, one whose effects are not yet exhausted, was that between 'Church' and 'Chapel'. That line was theological (for each Nonconformist body broke away on some specific point of doctrine or practice), but it was also, as has been said, social. And it was political. For to the Nonconformists, the Church of England and the Tory or Conservative Party were aspects of the same intolerant, exclusive attitude in religion and politics. Only the Methodists preserved, until well into the nineteenth century, the Tory politics of their founder. All the other dissenting bodies (and ultimately the Methodists) were Liberals or Radicals. The converse was not equally true. There were Anglicans who were Liberals, but it was an anomaly that Mr. Gladstone in his progress from High Toryism to Radicalism never abandoned any of the High Church principles he had learned at Oxford. He led in his old age a party whose clerical leaders had little in common with him except basic Christian faith, then a less effective bond of union than it is now.[2]

It is probable that Nonconformity reached its height of political power, was most representative of the temper of the English people, round the beginning of this century.[3] Its hold on the middle and working classes was still strong. Its political principles seemed relevant to the problems of the time. Its moral and political optimism seemed justified. It was united while Anglicanism was divided. It knew what it knew and what it believed. It was no longer hampered intellectually by the educational disabilities of the days of Anglican privilege, and its own internal divisions into rival sects were no longer so bitter or weakening as they had been. But in the generation that

---

[1] 'While the humanistic religious sentiment which expresses itself by the catch in the throat at the last Evensong in the old School Chapel, the community singing of "Abide with me" at a torchlight tattoo, and the standing to attention during the Two Minutes' Silence, can be utilized by totalitarianism, a religion which speaks of redemption by the incarnate Son of God, which offers mankind the sacramental means of union with the eternal life of the God-Man Jesus Christ, and which makes the perpetual representation of His atoning Sacrifice its essential act of worship must be the declared enemy of all who see in the state the be-all and end-all of man's life.' (Humphrey Beevor, *Peace and Pacifism*, p. 207, cited in T. S. Eliot, *The Idea of a Christian Society*, pp. 84–5.)

[2] High Churchmen tended to become Liberals as a protest against the favour shown by Disraeli to the Low Churchmen and, still more, as a protest against the ritual prosecutions which he, driven to it by Queen Victoria, made possible. G. W. E. Russell, who was both a Radical and a High Churchman, attributed some of the Liberal success in forlorn hopes like Brighton at the election of 1880 to good Churchmen voting against the author of the Public Worship Regulation Bill. Other Anglo-Catholics later went 'Christian Socialist'. Gore's background, of course, like Lord Halifax's, was Whig.

[3] I have heard it stated, on what authority I know not, that the great Liberal Parliament elected in 1906 was the first since the time of Charles II, most of whose members were non-Anglicans.

has passed since the great Liberal landslide of 1906, one of the greatest changes in the English religious and social landscape has been the decline of Nonconformity. Partly that decline has been due to the general weakening of the hold of Christianity on the English people, partly it has been due to the comparative irrelevance of the peculiarly Nonconformist (as apart from Christian) view of the contemporary world and its problems. Be the causes what they may, the decline is a fact and an important fact.

The decline of the power of Nonconformity in England has undoubtedly weakened a link between the English and American peoples for which there has been no substitute. The common tradition of evangelical religion, the common belief in conversion, in the literal inspiration of Holy Writ, the common taboos (even if they were more rigid in America than in England): all provided a common ethos. Moody and Sankey were almost as great figures in England as in the United States; the common stock of hymns and of devotional books was drawn on with hardly any sense of national difference. The Council on Interchange of Preachers and Speakers may have been optimistic, in the present, when it declared that 'English religious books are more widely read in America, and vice versa, than any other literature. The language of religion is almost the only language of both countries which does not require re-interpretation.'[1] But it certainly was true a generation ago. And if it is not true to-day, the chief reason (after the decline in the importance of organized religion in both countries) is that English Nonconformity has changed more than has American Protestantism.

For a generation past, Nonconformity has been losing its influence over the working classes. In this it is repeating the history of the older Dissent, which by the eighteenth century was overwhelmingly middle-class. The Methodists have followed the Independents and Presbyterians. Their flocks to-day are not at all proletarians, nor are the pastors. Just as the Church of England is going back to the condition of the eighteenth century with its parsons drawn from all ranks of society, with the sons of workmen serving side by side with the sons of professional men and even of the aristocracy, so Nonconformity is going back to its eighteenth-century condition. No member of a Nonconformist chapel is likely to have been at Eton and only one Nonconformist minister is the son of a peer.[2] But it is also unlikely that many members of Nonconformist chapels should be on the dole, or that their ministers should be drawn from as poor families as now supply so many parsons to the Church of England. There is no reason to be unduly surprised at the view expressed by the former Bishop of Durham[3] that the average minister is now of a higher social rank than the average parson.

[1] R. H. Heindel, *The American Impact on Great Britain 1898–1914*, p. 40. Professor Heindel is rightly sceptical of the contemporary truth of this judgment.

[2] His father is a millionaire and a new peer. Whether there are any third generation Nonconformist peers would be an interesting subject of inquiry.

[3] Dr. Hensley Henson.

This development has more than social importance. The minister is at least as likely to have had a good formal education as the parson and to have had that education at a recognized public institution of learning.[1]

The consequences to relations between the two countries are serious. There *is* an interchange of ideas and persons between the leaders, Anglican as well as simply 'Protestant', *at the top*. The Archbishop of Canterbury has given the Gifford Lectures at Glasgow University; Dr. Reinhold Niebuhr has given the Gifford Lectures at Edinburgh University. British divines are easily made at home in Union Seminary or the University of Chicago. But there is no lively demand in England for the old-fashioned, hellfire, fundamentalist preacher of the type still popular in such different American cities as Los Angeles, Minneapolis and Fort Worth. Men who are great public figures, cultivated by politicians and lavishly reported by the Press in their home towns are, when they come to England, either ignored or are the guests and the stars of small and decaying sects. They discover to their pained surprise that English Nonconformist leaders are more likely to be on terms of sympathetic understanding with learned Jesuits or Dominicans than with the heirs of Moody and Sankey. Only in Wales, Cornwall and the Highlands, or in the most strait sect of the Low Churchmen of the Anglican Church, is their language still spoken in the theological sense. Indeed, Welsh (and even Gaelic) would be a more useful introduction to the life of the old-time religionists in Britain than is English.

It is true that the moral principles may still seem the same. But they will be less rigorously held in England. It is likely that leading English Protestant divines would be less surprised, both at finding themselves at a Catholic meeting and at being offered cigars, than were the American divines who met this year to discuss rural problems.[2] Although the 'social gospel' has made a great deal of progress in America, to the extent, some would say, of replacing the Gospel, the old view that personal faith and personal morals (the latter mainly in the form of 'thou shalt nots') are the sole business of the Church, is far stronger in America than in England.[3]

The political responsibility of the Churches in England is seen very largely

---

[1] Readers of Mrs. Oliphant's *Salem Chapel* will appreciate the difference between the status of a minister who had had a brilliant career at a denominational college unknown outside his sect and one who has had a brilliant career at a modern university or at Oxford or Cambridge. To-day, one of the regular theological professors at Cambridge is a Nonconformist and the Nonconformist colleges at Oxford provide some of the greatest ornaments of theological learning in the university world. Dr. Micklem is no more a character out of *Salem Chapel* than he is a character out of *Mark Rutherford*.

[2] See *Time*, 19 October 1942.

[3] I deliberately say 'England'. The Celtic fringe is more American, less progressive than England in these matters. According to the new chief of the Baptist Church in Scotland, the Rev. T. A. M'Quiston, the chief problems facing the Church in war-time appear to be the danger of allowing 'secularists to infringe upon the sanctity of the Lord's Day', the permitting of 'privileges for the drink traffic, the gambling fraternity (and) the cinemas'. (*Glasgow Herald*, 20 October 1942.) Mr. M'Quiston would be at home in Knoxville, Tennessee.

in economic and political terms. Views about the 'profit motive', about the future of international relations, the terms of peace, the organization of the world: these are the themes of Church discussion in England. And they are less the themes in America. English heresy trials are in the future as likely to be over the nature of interest as over justification by baptism; the banker may soon be the typical sinner whom a Christian may have to be told that he has to forgive, rather than the brewer or the bookmaker.[1] And in the great current controversy over war and peace, the emphasis in American Protestantism has been on the degree of sin or innocence involved in taking part in war, rather than on the social problem of the community and war. When an English minister says that there 'must be no more war', he is more likely to mean that society must be organized to prevent war, than that he will free himself from all share in the common sin by refusing to aid the war effort. The American pacifist minister is still very often at the stage of saving his own soul. If the world imitates him the problem is solved: if not, so much the worse for the world. He is not his brother's keeper, except in matters like Prohibition and other sumptuary laws. For it is, to an outsider, a surprising fact that men who do not think that justice or humanity are worth fighting for, are (or were) ready to use the secular arm to impose a taboo on alcohol. If the non-pacifist clergy ought to repent the lives lost in this and other political wars, the pacifist and Prohibitionist clergy should repent the gang wars that their zeal bred and fostered. And if they reply that war does not bring justice or humanity, still less does Prohibition bring sobriety.

This war is an experiment as noble in purpose as the Eighteenth Amendment was; and whatever the claims on our respect of the Christian pacifist who does not want the aid of the secular arm for any real or alleged moral purpose, the position of that not uncommon type, the Christian pacifist who wants the power of the State to be used for *his* ends but for none that he does not think worthy, is not so easy to defend. And it finds fewer defenders in English Church circles than in American, not because the English divine is by nature more clear-sighted than his American brother, but because some grim political truths are more clearly seen in a London that has known the Blitz than in a Chicago that has only known the massacre of St. Valentine's Day.

But the movement of American Protestantism is probably towards the English emphasis on collective religious responsibility, away both from the unconscious anarchy of some modern attitudes and from the emphasis on biblical orthodoxy that is still so strong in American evangelical religion. Whether this means that the Protestant Churches will play a bigger or smaller role in the future than in the present is another question.[2] But at the

---

[1] The indignant bankers who write letters to *The Times* complaining of the harsh words of the Archbishop of Canterbury would be better advised to claim, rightly enough, that they are the representatives of the publicans of New Testament times. *Verb. sap.*

[2] We learn that in 'Middletown', growth in church congregations has been roughly in proportion to the growth in population. But the growth has been among the marginal, unintellectual

moment a more important fact is that the role of the Protestant Churches as a common link is less important than it was a generation ago. In both countries the role of organized religion is less important and the differences in the national view as to what organized religion is *about* are probably greater at this moment than they ever have been or are likely to be in the future, when the natural evolution of American Protestantism has brought it nearer to the new English pattern. The American small town, home of the old-time religion, has no real counterpart in England and less of a counterpart on the religious side than on any other.[1]

Shocked by the paganism that is pertty widespread in England, shocked both by English hypocrisy in some spheres and in the absence of it in others,[2] the common Puritan tradition that does still bind Temple (Texas) and Wolverhampton (England) may seem to the American to have lost all its power. He will be wrong; in great crises it still has power, but it is not what it was in the days of Henry Ward Beecher or Spurgeon, or what it still is in Atlanta or Des Moines.

The decline of the power of Nonconformity has had important consequences in the political field, important and on the whole unfortunate. The division of the English bourgeoisie into two groups, 'Church' and 'Chapel', had deplorable cultural results. English Nonconformity in the days of its power was not aesthetically an attractive spectacle, and its emphasis on com-

poor sects and is in part accounted for by immigration from the South. (R. S. Lynd and H. M. Lynd, *Middletown in Transition*, p. 297.) The same phenomenon might occur in a growing London industrial area, drawing a large part of its new population from Wales. It has occurred in Detroit as well as in Muncie.

[1] One thing that they still have to some extent in common does not make for mutual friendliness. One of the toughest survivals of the old English religion is Sabbatarianism. Since in the seventeenth century the Hebrew Sabbath was imposed on the Christian Sunday, negative observance of the Lord's Day has been to a great many English-speaking Protestants what not eating fish on Friday is to a great many Catholics—all the law and the prophets. So the American soldier stranded in an English small town on a Sunday will find no substitute for the ever-open drug store, for the movie house, for the amusement park. The majority of the inhabitants of these towns are giving no other indication of their belief that Sunday is a sacred day than their negative support for the legal closing of all homes of public relaxation (except the places where booze is sold). The effect, on an American soldier, is less likely to be an admiration for the staunchness of English religious principles than profound irritation with a people that has the folly to have such laws and has not the enterprise to break them. It is then that he wishes himself back where

> You can pick the morning gloria
> Right off the side-walks of sweet Peoria.

As for having to spend a wet Sunday in Glasgow or Holyhead, that is enough to make the American wish himself in a reasonably good penitentiary, for in Scotland and Wales he cannot even get a drink, and in Glasgow, a city rather bigger than Cleveland, the stern moralists of the City Council have reluctantly allowed four cinemas to open, three of them in the suburbs. It is, in fact, impossible to explain these things to Americans in the high moral terms that the natives of these islands command so easily.

[2] The recent public candour of Englishwomen in the matter of smoking, make-up, dress, language, etc., shocks a great many Americans whose standards are nearer those of Toronto than those of the north-west district of Washington or the 'roaring forties' of New York.

paratively minor matters of conduct distorted its view of the national life and weakened its hold on the working classes. It was often negative; it was often smug. But at its worst, Nonconformity was a protest against as well as a victim of English snobbery. When the economic and other power that the squire and the parson then had is reflected on, there is something heroic in the ugly, poor and now neglected chapels that can be seen in so many English villages in East Anglia, Somerset and other strongholds of the old Puritanism. The last great peasant revolt of English history was the Monmouth Rebellion against James II.[1] It is as the scene of the martyrdom of these humble and unlucky heroes that Taunton ought to touch the heart of anybody who likes the English people for what they are, instead of for what they might have been, had English history been entirely different. We may assume without much risk of error that the average

> Village Hampden that with dauntless breast
> The little tyrant of his fields withstood,

withstood him for his erroneous views of the next world, as well as for his tyrannical conduct in this. Religious dissent, accompanied by hardships that are serious but not demoralizing, is a good education in real radicalism. People who have had that training are not usually taken in by the easy sophistries that suggest that liberty is easy to get, easy to keep and not worth any great trouble to keep or get. These people have made more serious sacrifices for their political rights than payment of poll-taxes, and are not tempted to believe that their duty (and an onerous duty) has been done when they have made the effort to register and vote.

In a country where the weaknesses of English Nonconformity are present without the background of political and social handicaps, its political role is likely to be almost entirely harmful, so that nothing said in defence of the Nonconformist conscience in England should be taken as applying (without further consideration) to the United States, Scotland or Wales. To be a minority, if not of active and convinced Christians, at least of the run-of-the-mill conforming Christians, to belong to bodies that were in varying degrees unfashionable in a country where snobbery is the rival religion to Christianity, to be forced to accept companions, to go to schools, to conform to social customs below the social level to which your financial status and education made natural to you: this was to receive a character-building education not provided in many public schools.[2] Nonconformity is in this context a more important phenomenon than mere dissent. To mark yourself

---

[1] I commend this thought to the Belloc school of historians. Their hero, James II, was the last King of England that any serious number of poor Englishmen thought was worth fighting *against*.

[2] A young woman, for instance, forced to go to a Sunday School which few or none of her normal schoolfellows attend and to take part in the social life of a chapel which had hardly any links with her normal social life has a bracing training for existence in England.

out as peculiar is to show courage, if bad worldly judgment. And that may be one important reason why the English Nonconformist, sharing almost completely the theological views of the Low Churchmen, has had far more interesting political views and has had a far more respectable intellectual record, than the Anglicans who made the best of both worlds, by being 'Church' and thus escaping social disabilities in this world, and being 'evangelical' and thus escaping damnation in the next.[1] The Nonconformists, whatever their natural temperament may have been, or the temptations of their economic status, were predisposed to sympathy with rebels.[2]

Thus they resisted the temptation to exploit the national anti-Catholic bias of the English people, since that involved in modern times hostility to Irish Nationalism; and the Nonconformists and the Irish had many common enemies—and some common principles.[3] This alliance continued even after Nonconformists' disabilities had become a less and less heavy burden, and after the Catholic attitude on such questions as the drink traffic and religious instruction in schools had provided grounds for a political divorce.

The decline of political Nonconformity was probably inevitable. Not only was religious zeal growing more tepid, but the character of political problems was changing. As Anglican exclusiveness became more and more anachronistic, as the weakening of the Christian position laid stress on what united rather than on what divided, the obvious course of prudence, the mere dissidence of dissent, came to seem a little silly. It was, in part, the pressure of Anglican privilege that had acted as a training ground for Nonconformist discipline. And, as the history of the French Radical party shows, the survival of the verbal habits of a militant and under-privileged minority into easy and prosperous times is a strong test of character. It became more difficult for the Nonconformist who would valiant be, to find what to be valiant about in the religious field, and the temptation to make the attainment of the Kingdom of Heaven in this world, by the aid of the law, the chief object of corporate activity was often succumbed to. Serious wrongs abroad—the cause of the Armenians, of the oppressed Indians of the Putumayo, of the Congo negroes, of the Balkan Christians, and of the numerous more or less oppressed peoples of the British Empire—these attracted the

---

[1] Politically the Low Churchmen were almost always Tories. And it is worth comparing the intellectual weight of their leaders, Sir William Joynson-Hicks or Sir Thomas Inskip, with such Liberal Nonconformist leaders as Sir Henry Fowler (Lord Wolverhampton) and Sir John Simon.

[2] C. H. Spurgeon was once asked, ironically, why he did not mortify the flesh by voting Tory at times. He replied 'I mortify it by voting Liberal. I'm a Tory by temperament.' He ceased to mortify himself in 1886.

[3] In this they set an example which the old English Catholics did not follow. They were too good Tories to be upset by the fact that their most vociferous political allies were as bitterly anti-Catholic as they were 'loyal'. So it was an eminent Catholic preacher whom Arthur Griffith, the founder of Sinn Féin, described as 'an English Catholic in Christian clothing'. And it was the Anglican Archbishop of Canterbury (Dr. Davidson) who made the most effective clerical protest against the Black and Tan atrocities, not Cardinal Bourne.

genuine and admirable zeal of many. So did the deplorable habits of the English working man, his fondness for putting his money that ought to have gone to keep his wife and children on horses, or into the purchase of what was technically called alcohol. So did other moral problems affecting private conduct. And it is easy, too easy, to sneer at the Puritan zeal of the Nonconformist clergy, especially if it absolves you in your role of Catholic intellectual or columnist from commenting on the life of really Puritan Catholic communities like Ireland, Boston, or Quebec.

But the regulation of (or meddling with) the lives of the poor is not a great cause such as the nineteenth-century Radicals had at heart in their wars against slavery or tyranny or illiteracy or religious intolerance. And the new major questions necessarily divided the Nonconformists, for the rich members of the community had or tended to have different views on regulation of wages and hours, or the role of trade unions or the incidence of taxation, from those naturally held by their poorer brethren. The young men of Nonconformist origin and low economic status now tended to move into the nascent Labour party, as did Arthur Henderson. Other reasons brought about schism in the Liberal party, and when for the first time a Nonconformist became leader of one section of that party, the day of its greatness was past. Mr. Lloyd George was not the chosen hero or leader of the old Liberal orthodox; he was Welsh, not English; and the Labour party tried to take over the assets of the party which it had supplanted with such pride—and such unconscious prophetic self-judgment—as the 'Official Opposition'.

Among the assets whose transfer was attempted was political Nonconformity. The attempt was only partially successful, even when the necessary writing down of the assets is allowed for. Once the old denominational link between Methodist millionaires and Methodist miners was broken, it was difficult to find a substitute for the connection. Religion can be the opium of more than the proletariat, and many old Radical families—and fortunes— quietly went Tory. This would not have mattered if the Labour party had ever got beyond the stage of being the Official Opposition, but one result of the decline of political Nonconformity or its alienation from the Labour party was that the Conservative party had its not too difficult job made even easier. The bright young members of party congresses and readers of papers at intellectual week-ends might not care, but political work is done when not very bright and not teribly young people of indeterminate social class are moved. There are fewer people standing at street corners singing hymns than when I was a child; there are also fewer people at street corners singing the 'Red Flag'.[1]

[1] The older members of the Labour Party knew this. One of the most famous leaders of the party told me that he got elected to the local council for the first time in a district of London where he seemed, on paper, to have little chance. The working-class nucleus was too small to overcome the bourgeois impermeability of the middle-class regions. But it was from one of the bourgeois areas that he got the votes that put him in. And, he discovered, those votes came

But it is not only that the Labour party has failed to take over the assets that political Nonconformity provided for the Liberals; no one else has succeeded in doing what Nonconformity did, in giving a prosperous bourgeoisie a sense of duty and a sense of social obligation. For all the cant and hypocrisy of the Nonconformist conscience it was a real conscience, and as I have said elsewhere, if hypocrisy is the homage that vice pays to virtue, it is real homage and better than no homage at all. If English public policy was driven to pay that homage, it was due more to the influence of political Nonconformity than to any other force. The business man, doomed to smugness, to complacency, to the temptations of the market, was forced to pay some kind of lip service to general principles of morality, and what is more, to principles of political morality which otherwise he does not so much defy as ignore altogether. It is not evident that the Birmingham of Mr. Neville Chamberlain and the Federation of British Industries is in this respect an improvement on the Birmingham of Dr. Dale and John Bright. The defence of Munich as a good thing, as justice, as good business, as something worthy of the English people, would have been harder in the days when Liverpool theatre-goers rose to cheer when the line came in *Othello*:

The Turks are drowned,

and men of every type and school in England combined to condemn the Turkish outrages in Bulgaria and the prophetic indifference of Disraeli.

The English middle classes have not yet found a substitute for the Nonconformist conscience. Many individual members have found it in Labour politics, and a high proportion of them are children of Nonconformist families. But inevitable as it may have been, the decline of political Nonconformity is a national loss. It cannot find an equivalent in general Quaker toleration and charity: Philadelphia shows that Quakerism is not enough, perhaps because there can never be enough Quakers. And no other instrument than militant Nonconformity for making the thriving middle class conscious of general ideas and general principles has yet been found in England. It may be said, of course, that this does not matter, but observers of politics who think, after the experience of the last twenty years, that the failure of the Labour party to get a real hold on the majority of this class does not matter are true political fundamentalists. In this class lies the block of voters which alone can give the Labour party a decisive majority; the technicians who can make the transformation run smoothly; the potential Fascists who can turn the revolution into the counter-revolution.

Church and Chapel do not exhaust the varieties of Christianity that deserve notice as part of the English scene. A few years ago it might have been worth while discussing the role of Buchmanism as the only current example of that

from a Dissenting community of fairly prosperous people who had no strong views on Fabian Socialism, but did know a Tory when they saw him—and so voted for the anti-Tory.

American influence on English Protestantism which was so important in the nineteenth century. But since the outbreak of war the Groupers have not had the good, or at least lively, Press they could once have counted on. They have not even continued their tactics of cashing in on one of the two or three most valuable publicity names in England, Oxford.[1] The ambiguous war role of Dr. Buchman may have something to do with this. Many of the best hotels have been taken over by the Government of Britain or house more interesting guests. And it is possible that the discovery that in Moral Rearmament the military metaphor was so often purely metaphorical has further depressed the market in this once promising issue.

The iniquities of the Bishop of Rome have been common form in England for four centuries, and Gladstone was right in his time in stressing the fact that anti-Popery was one of the few basic articles of English faith. The good old violent days are over. Lewes no longer burns His Holiness in effigy with anything like the old zeal; and when an Ulster M.P. reminds the House of Commons that the Pope *still* has a bad name in Portadown the House is more amused than impressed; and when Lady Astor sees fit to attack the Master of the Rolls (Lord Greene) as a Papist, it is taken as one more proof that Virginia will out. The position of the Catholic Church in England (or, if it is preferred, the 'Italian Mission', to quote a former Archbishop of Canterbury) is odd, that is, English. There is still a great deal of suspicion of Jesuit wiles (which may not be at all connected with the actual English province of the Society of Jesus). There is a suspicion that Catholic influence in the Foreign Office affects policy, and there is irritation, not to put it more strongly, at the nostalgia of certain Catholic papers and individuals for the good old days when Mussolini was a combination of Augustus, Constantine and Justinian. A generation ago there was a more serious conflict, since a majority of the Catholic population in England was of Irish origin and deeply interested in the fate of Ireland. To-day, not only is there a generation more between them and Ireland, but Irish grievances are hard to work up passion over in people who have been through the Blitz, and whose local hero is more likely to be Brendan Finucane than Mr. de Valera. And Ireland, it must be remembered, is close to England, so that the Irish-English population, unlike the Irish-American population, knows a great deal about contemporary Ireland; knows, for example, how different it is from modern England or modern America. The Londoner of Irish origin knows that he would not be much at home in an Irish-speaking agricultural, backward-looking Ireland after the model of Mr. de Valera's Eire. The Irish of Boston have no such opportunities for inspecting and disliking the Ireland run by their distinguished but untypical fellow-citizen.

In addition to the Irish, there are Catholics of French, Italian, German and

---

[1] It is a well-known but inexplicable fact that anything that happens at Oxford is news and that nothing that happens at Cambridge is.

Spanish origin, and from some points of view the Catholic Church is a collection of what the French anti-Semites call *métèques*. But in another sense it is deeply English, far more English than the Catholic Church in the United States is American. For the Catholic Church is, to use a phrase dear to Augustine Birrell, the 'old religion'. It is part of the historical background in a way that it is not in most of the United States. Mr. George Santayana in King's College Chapel, listening to the cool Anglican service and thinking that he, rather than the choristers, is really at home in the shrine of Henry VI, is a typical figure. The claim of the Church of England to continuity with the medieval Church helps to keep the Catholic side of English history alive. The Pope is part of English history; he may have been a bad thing, but there he is.[1]

Not only is the Pope part of English history, but so are some of the great families that refused to follow Elizabeth into schism. For some of the *very* best families remained true to Rome and some very good families have since been reconciled to the Holy See. The reception of Roman Catholicism in the nineteenth century was helped by these two historical facts. The fact that some of the greatest families had remained true to Rome was far from being unimportant in a snobbish country like England. It was less important than some ecclesiastics thought, but it was important all the same that most of the blood of most of the Howards was Catholic; and although the exchange of an Earl of Shrewsbury for a Newman was a good bargain, even though the Earl was a Talbot, his secession was still a loss. The old Catholic family was part of the English (and Scottish) background. Thus when Macaulay met Lord Clifford of Chudleigh in Rome, he was prepared not merely to meet a descendant of a member of Charles II's cabal, but a Catholic nobleman, a standard figure of the English landscape. It is true that Macaulay, like so many of his contemporaries, was deeply influenced in his views of British Catholicism by Sir Walter Scott, and was disappointed when Lord Clifford did not turn out to be gloomy and Gothick like Lord Glenallan in *The Antiquary*, but for all that, Lord Clifford was as much a part of Old England as a learned minister was of New England.[2]

And there are parts of rural England which the Reformation has only formally affected. A generation ago an Anglican parson in certain parts of rural Lancashire was not as much an intruder as a parson in Connaught or a

---

[1] An odd example of the value attached to this papistical prestige is furnished by the soundly Presbyterian University of Glasgow. Although a large proportion of its alumni, for four centuries past, have been doubtless brought up to regard the Pope as Antichrist, the University, far from hiding the fact that it was founded by a Pope, flaunts it, possibly as a snub to the pretensions of the more recent municipal foundation at Edinburgh.

[2] Macaulay even found himself at home in that famous headquarters of the Counter-Reformation, the English College in Rome. He seems to have liked it largely because it smelled like Peterhouse. Although an almost excessively loyal Trinity man, Macaulay had enough general Cambridge patriotism to account this to the English College as a virtue. This example of an *odeur d'Angleterre* among the *parfums de Rome* should have interested Louis Veuillot.

minister in some parts of the Outer Hebrides, but he was a bit of an intruder all the same.

In addition to the old Catholics and the immigrant Catholics, there has been since the Oxford Movement the convert. The list of converts to Rome is long and impressive. Newman and Chesterton are weightier names than Orestes Brownson and Heywood Broun. And it is mainly, though not exclusively, to the converts that the intellectual prestige of English Catholicism is due.[1]

Although the English Catholics are only one tenth as numerous as American Catholics, they are more important in English intellectual life than their co-religionists are in American.[2] Catholic ideas have more prestige than they have in America. The Catholic solution to present troubles is more in the mind of non-Catholics as a possibility than it is in America. And more is known of the Catholic attitude.[3]

Like the Church of England, the Church of Rome is part of the furniture of the English household, whether it is in the basement, or in the attic, or in the new functional, up-to-the-minute living-room. Dr. Inge may assert firmly that English Catholics are not English, but the Pope could tell him differently. And the difference between the Catholics in America and in England can be adequately illustrated by a true story. When the Anglicans of Liverpool planned to build a great cathedral, they employed a Catholic architect to adapt a medieval Gothic cathedral to the needs of Anglican worship. When Cardinal Mundelein wanted a really American chapel for his new seminary outside Chicago, his architect was told to adapt a New England meeting-house to the needs of the Roman rite.

One Christian denomination deserves notice, although it is ostentatiously not English. But the Church of Scotland, from which three of the last six heads of the Church of England have come,[4] deserves note if for that reason alone. The Church of Scotland has even more serious claims on our attention than that. For the proximity in a small island of two different established

---

[1] The most eminent of all Catholic apologists, Mr. Belloc, is not a convert but he is not wholly English either.

[2] I have been convinced by correspondence with a distinguished professor at the University of Notre Dame that an earlier expression of this view was too dogmatic. But, with a few minor corrections, I think it is still true.

[3] It is possible that Catholic private life is less well known, as the leading Catholic novelists of the younger school do not give a very representative picture of English Catholic life. Neither Mr. Graham Greene's *Brighton Rock*, nor Mr. Evelyn Waugh's *Vile Bodies* can be regarded as exceptions to this rule.

[4] Of the last six Archbishops of Canterbury, three have been Scottish Presbyterians by origin. Five have been from Oxford as against one from Cambridge. Of the five Oxford men, four have been Balliol men (two were also graduates of Glasgow University). The present Archbishop is the son of a previous Archbishop and another was the son-in-law of a predecessor. Four have been headmasters of public schools. With data like these, it should be possible to predict the succession with some confidence, making allowance for the fact that the three last Archbishops have had no children.

Churches, asserting different and incompatible views of the nature of the Church of Christ, while it has been an offence to theologians and an irritation to Anglican snobbery, has at least illustrated the almost (ancient) Roman tolerance of the British State. The political authority in the island of Britain may be held to affirm in Scotland that the Church should be Presbyterian in government; in England that it should be Episcopal; in Wales that the State should have no views on this matter. And for the religious peace of the Empire it was a good thing that the legally equal position of the Church of Scotland forced some understanding of the need for tolerance on intolerant Anglicans. Had there been more Anglican leaders like Archdeacon Strachan in Canada, or had they been more powerful, they might have driven English-speaking Canada into the arms of the United States and even driven French Canada too.[1]

By being both established and non-Anglican, the Church of Scotland has taught a useful truth to many Englishman of an Erastian type of mind who might otherwise have identified religious orthodoxy with Parliamentary enactment. It is good for this type of Englishman to go to Scotland and find himself a Dissenter. But the Church of Scotland has had other utilities too. Since it has been reunited, it has given the Church of England the example of a united national Church freely determining its own discipline and doctrine. And as one of the traditionally important Churches of Calvinist origin, it has linked British Protestantism with the most militant Protestants of the Continent. For the Calvinists of the world, Edinburgh ranks well—after Geneva, but with Dort and Heidelberg and Sedan and other cities where the true doctrine has been attacked, defended and expounded. In the Empire, Presbyterianism has been as great a force as Anglicanism, and David Livingstone has a place in the hearts of all British Protestants brought up with a sense of their duty to the heathen sitting in outer darkness. And, of course, the old connection between the Presbyterians of Scotland and the United States, between the Scottish universities and Princeton, is still important.[2]

In the national stocktaking that is going on during the war, there has been a revival of discussion of religion, if not a revival of religion. Many optimistic intellectuals have come to a belated recognition of the fact that there are such things as bad, not merely ignorant, ill-advised men.[3] The failure of optimistic humanism to eradicate evil from the hearts of men, the failure of 'education' without any dogmatic moral bias to provide any reason likely to be found

---

[1] Strachan was, it should be remembered, a Scot, too full of the national *praefervidum ingenium* for the peace of Upper Canada.

[2] Woodrow Wilson got his first name (e.g. 'Woodrow', not the suppressed 'Thomas') from a collateral ancestor, the famous librarian of Glasgow University at the end of the seventeenth century. This Woodrow was the historian of the Scottish Covenant, whence, it is possible, President Wilson took the name for the constitution of the League of Nations.

[3] To the abandonment of the old habit of judging men may be attributed some of the early propaganda successes of Hitler outside Germany. Many Englishmen refused to see the evident fact that Hitler, Goebbels, Himmler, etc., were *bad* men.

convincing by the average man why he should follow certain moral codes and not others or none, the resistance of some prominent European Church-men to Hitler, all have combined to bring about a curiosity about the pros-pects of Christianity. And this discussion centres round the alleged duty of the Church to give a lead in social matters and the alleged duty of the State to encourage the growth of a Christian society by educational reforms.

The Church of England, as far as the Archbishops represent it, gives a lead by protesting against the acceptance by the Church of the pursuit of wealth, or at any rate money, as the chief end of man. If it be replied that modern society does not in fact accept the pursuit of money as the chief end of man, the Archbishops will find a great deal of support for their view that little or nothing is done to shake the conviction of the young that the advertising, newspaper-making, business-adoring world in which they live, conceals very effectively any doubts it may have about the superiority of the millionaire over the mystic.[1] And in a world in which simple economic utilitarian calculation has been proved to have far less driving power than its romantic salesmen thought it had, the Churches may be more in touch with the movement of the world than the belated nineteenth-century leaders of the old Capitalist and Socialist parties. To believe that the chief end of man is higher dividends or higher wages does not seem so modern, so realist to-day, as it did around 1900.

How far that lead will be followed in religious terms remains to be seen. From the Christian point of view, the replacement of bankers by People's Commissars of Public Investment is not necessarily a great gain, if the com-missars and the people seek first the kingdom of this world. Christianity may indeed be the most this-worldly of the great religions, but it is still less this-worldly than the world is.

Another view of the function of the Church which is now being pressed is that it is to give meaning to life, to counter the scepticism of the young, their scorn of ideals, their lack of character. This doctrine is preached with a complacency that will annoy the young, if they ever get round to noticing it. One would have thought that only persons whose own austere upholding of the highest standards of political morality, in home and international affairs, was a national asset, would be ready to lecture with such unction the genera-tion that produced the R.A.F. Or rather, one would think this, if one did not know that England, a kindly country, is the game reserve where people of this type are protected by national good manners from the caustic and ribald answers they would get in, say, the United States.

But leaving on one side the mere preachers, the moralists have something to say. It is true that the experiment of an educational system without a strong

---

[1] I mean the poor mystic. Many millionaires and one or two mystics have managed to take a contemptuous view of money. It doesn't matter at all, provided you have enough of it. The Anglo-American invention of the Mammon of Righteousness is still in good working order.

3

dogmatic framework has yet to prove itself. Germany and Russia have shown that the dogma need not be religious in the ordinary sense of the term, but it is dogma all the same that prevents the young Russian or the young German from thinking, or at any rate from saying, that he owes nobody anything and that if there is any question of debt, he is the creditor. But there are two objections to the schemes of more or less compulsory indoctrination of the English young with Christian patriotism. First of all, Christianity is not as good an instrument for creating national dogmatic union, for eradicating individualism, as is Communism or Nazism. However it may be interpreted or adjusted, Christianity does insist on the individualism of duty, on the need of laying up individual treasure in Heaven. It might be necessary, if Christianity really took, for the sponsors of revival to see that it did not take too well. They should all be made to read Dostoievsky's fable of the Grand Inquisitor before they build up a united, duty-loving, nationally-minded England on Christian foundations. For that kind of building, the foundations may be sand. And any political structure into whose foundations Christianity in any real sense is built, must necessarily be a house divided.

There is another objection. It is not at all certain that there is enough living, concrete religious faith to supply the demands made on it. If it is merely a matter of increasing the dose of vague, sentimental, thoughtless religiosity that colours the English mind, that is one thing and a thing not worth much worrying about. This is already provided for by the educational system. It could be increased without any great strain on the consciences of the typical teacher or the typical Army officer.[1]

But what the reformers want is something more definite than that. They want to restore to all parts of the educational system that conviction of the importance of concrete religious belief that was exemplified in the founding of High Church schools like Lancing, Low Church schools like Dean Close; in the Anglican orthodoxy of Oxford and in the reaction of the agnostic intellectuals against that orthodoxy. They want college chapels in Oxford and Cambridge to be centres of definite religious life, which of course involves their being places worth staying away from as well as worth attending. But this programme will break down the moment any attempt is made to apply it on a great scale. For there has not been in England, since the seventeenth century, religious unity; so that the specific religious content of a

---

[1] Thus a vigorous critic of many sides of the existing educational system, is quite ready to accept religious teaching of this kind, even when it is given by teachers who 'not only have . . . ceased to take part in public devotions, but . . . are no longer Christians in the sense that they could, with unqualified belief, recite even the Apostles' Creed. They teach Scripture, and often Christianity, but they are formal and not active Christians. . . . On the balance, the present arrangements tend decisively towards the upbringing of reasonable, fairminded, unselfish, kindly men and women; towards decency in fact. This may not be a specially religious result. It has, perhaps, little relevance to the great question of the relationship of man to God. It does, however, make this country, for all save the poorest class, the nicest country to live in.' (F. H. Spencer, *Education for the People*, pp. 262–3.)

national system would have to be low. Nor is there present at this moment enough religious belief, even of competing kinds, that is lively enough to carry the weight of a new national religion.

To be thus sceptical is not to deny that religion plays a great part in English life. There is a widespread belief that 'righteousness exalteth a nation', and there are great deposits of moral conservatism that can be drawn on by the Churches in crises like the abdication of Edward VIII. Public morality still has a meaning, and the man in the street does not really resent the preaching of the parson, although he may not pay much attention to it.

As guardians of morals, the clergy, it is true, often seem to the laity a little lacking in proportion, and the Anglican clergy suffer from this fault as do their brethren in other churches and other lands. Nor are they always exempt, whether they be great churchmen or eminent, not to say professionally eminent, laymen, from the weakness that leads to the belief that fearless denunciation (with its accompanying publicity) is a good way of serving God and attracting the attention of Mammon. In England, as in the United States,

> Smut if smitten
> Is front-page stuff.

But they do not so often strain the toleration of the laity as the American minister tends to do. They have no such dreadful error in judgment as Prohibition to explain away. It is true that a great many of the clergy of the Nonconformist Churches would have liked to impose Prohibition, but they did not succeed. It may not be their fault that they have no Bishop Cannon to live down, but it is accounted to them for righteousness all the same.

Christian belief of a vague kind still has a powerful hold on the emotions of the English man in the street. He is a theist; he has a vague belief in Heaven, a very much fainter belief in Hell. This is not what was called Christianity in old or New England a century ago. It is much more like the religion of Washington or Lincoln, even of Jefferson or Franklin, than like the religion of Jefferson Davis or William Jennings Bryan or the elder Pierpont Morgan. But it is not a negligible force. Can it keep its strength as the older, orthodox religion declines in general authority? Unless the cruse of oil is replenished, must not the thin film of Christian belief and standards dry and crack? It seems likely. And as far as it is true that the English people have been the people of one book, the Bible, it is true no longer. It is only necessary to appeal to get the Bible read as literature when it has ceased to be generally read as the Word of God. The English are now more a Bible-buying than a Bible-reading people. Fewer people than ever before in modern English history take the advice of the hymn:

> You should read it every day,
> It will help you on your way.

And if the 'Bible and the Bible only is the religion of Protestants', the Protestant religion in England is in a bad way.

It would be rash indeed to expect much accurate knowledge of the Bible from the man or woman in the English street to-day. Biblical phrases live in common speech (along with phrases erroneously believed to be biblical, like the motto of Broadcasting House, 'And nation shall speak peace unto nation'). But the book from which they are drawn is less and less known, even in Presbyterian Scotland.[1] It would be convenient but deceptive to attribute the weakening of biblical knowledge to the negligence of the State schools but it is far more widespread than such an explanation would account for.[2] It seems likely, therefore, that Christianity in England will for a generation or two to come be the active religious belief of a minority, and that minority conscious of its new status, of its duty to bring about not a revival of religion but a reconversion of England. But outside that minority will be a large, emotional, respectable and very English majority who will have a vague reverence for religion, for Christianity, for Christian ethics. This vague reverence will not matter much at most times, but it will matter if rash, brash and ill-informed political leaders decide to get rid of this apparently superfluous lumber. Then sentiment if not faith may revive and clerks be again troublesome.

And in the crises of the last three years, probably more Englishmen than knew it felt their patriotic stubbornness strengthened, as they contemplated the apparently invincible might of Nazi Germany, by the thought that 'except the Lord build the house, their labour is but vain that build it'. And obviously the Lord did not build the Nazi house. In that solitary but not desolate hour they felt as it is put in the Book of Common Prayer: 'There is none other than fighteth for us, but only Thou, O God'. And that being so, they did not ask for peace in our time, which at that moment was Hitler's time.

---

[1] Thus I find in an excellent thriller the phrase 'like Galileo, cared for none of these things'. Even those who do not confuse Gallio with Galileo would, in many cases, be hard put to it to tell us what Gallio cared for, or who or what he was.

[2] For some years in Oxford I made an experiment. I used to tell my pupils (nearly all of them from schools where the Bible was 'taught') the story of the Lord Aberdeen under whose very reluctant leadership England entered on the Crimean War. The Prime Minister's conscience was very much disturbed. Although he was a man of real piety, he refused to rebuild the ruinous church on his estate of Haddo. When he died, he left money in his will to his son to build the church. He explained his conduct by a reference to a famous episode in the Old Testament. Only one pupil ever spontaneously spotted the reference. About half did not follow it when it was pointed out to them. Readers may test their own scriptural knowledge for themselves.

THE SHORN LAMBS

BY JOHN MASON BROWN

from *Seeing More Things* (1951)

THE SHORN LAMBS

I. CHARLES AND MARY

AMONG the tantalizing 'ifs' of literature is what Charles Lamb might have been like as man and writer if, in a fit of madness, his sister Mary had not slain their mother when he was only twenty-one. The 'gentle Elia' the world loves was the product of ungentle and terrible events. He was the step-child of a calamity as bloody as any to be found in the most bloodstained Elizabethan dramas of which Lamb was later to become a champion. To a tragic extent Lamb's life, hence Elia's character, was carved out for him by the case knife which poor, deluded Mary drove straight and deep into their mother's heart.

Surely never in the strange annals of authorship has the world gained so much in pleasure or an innocent man lost more in freedom than in the instance of the catastrophe which resulted in Lamb's becoming the most beloved bachelor of letters literature has produced.

When he quit his desk at the East India House on the afternoon of 22 September 1796, and started to walk home through the London he loved, Lamb was not without his worries. His sister Mary, ten years his senior, had already shown symptoms of insanity. Not for the first time, either. As a person who had himself been confined the previous year for six weeks in a madhouse at Hoxton, these symptoms may have had a special meaning for him. In any case, Mary's condition was sufficiently disturbing to have sent Lamb, on his way to work that very morning, in search of a doctor who was not to be found. Aware though he was of the gathering clouds, Lamb could not have been prepared for the violence of the storm which had broken out in the house where he lived with his old father, his invalid mother, his sister, and his Aunt Hetty.

The sight he beheld when he opened the door was of tabloid gruesomeness. Above the bustle of Little Queen Street he may have heard the cries of his father and the shrieks of Mary and her assistant as he approached his home. If he had not, the landlord's presence was in itself a warning. Certainly his eyes must have disbelieved the nightmare of reality which confronted them. The room, in which the table was laid for dinner, was in a turmoil. Charles's aged aunt was unconscious on the floor, 'to all appearance like one dying'. His senile father was bleeding from a wound in his forehead. His mother was dead in a chair, stabbed to the heart by Mary who was standing over her with the case knife still in her hand. Lamb arrived only in time to snatch the knife from her grasp.

What had provoked this scene no one knows. Perhaps, as a professional seamstress, Mary had been overworking, and the stress of a dependent household had become too great for her. Perhaps the final straw had been the additional cares which had come her way because of the leg injury recently suffered by her brother John, her elder by a year and a half. Perhaps, as moderns have hinted, an ugly, long-suppressed animosity between her and her mother had at last erupted. In any event, Mary had had an altercation with the young woman who, in her mantua-making, was her helper. Mary had reached for the knives and forks on the table, throwing them at this frightened girl in the hope of driving her from the house. It was one of the forks thus thrown which had struck her father. Her mother might have been spared had she not attempted to intercede in the apprentice's behalf.

'I date from the day of horrors,' wrote Lamb to Coleridge soon after the disaster. Although by this he meant merely to place in time events described in his letter, he unwittingly summarized the rest of his adult life. To these sensational occurrences which cost him dearly, we owe, in part at least, the writer we cherish as one of the least sensational of authors. For the next thirty-eight years Lamb lived a gallant and, on the whole, a cheerful prisoner to the happenings of that fatal afternoon. In no sense of the word a tragic hero, he emerged as the hero of a tragedy. We pity him the more because he was without self-pity.

There are people, luckless mortals, who by the injustice of circumstances or because of a certain granite in their characters are doomed to be caryatids for the suffering of others. Charles Lamb was one of these. He could have fallen back on the law and allowed his sister to be committed to a public insane asylum. He could have walked out on Mary. In other words, he could have done what his older brother John did and wanted him to do.

Yet even when John washed his hands of the whole problem, Lamb was able to rise, 'not without tenderness', to his brother's defence. He knew John to be 'little disposed . . . at any time to take care of old age and infirmities'. Charles went so far as to persuade himself that John, 'with his bad leg, had an exemption from such duties'. He was well aware that John would make speeches about the money needed to maintain Mary in a private institution. But Charles and John, though brothers, were made of very different stuff. Young and poor as he was, Charles faced the fact without complaining that 'the whole weight of the family' had been thrown upon him. From the outset he was determined, regardless of the sacrifices, that Mary should not go into a public asylum.

Nor did she. Instead, he assumed full responsibility for her. More than that, he devoted his life to her. Because of this utter devotion his own life was altered inescapably. Had it not been for Mary, age would not have fallen so suddenly and engulfingly upon him. Without her, we might be able to imagine Lamb as a young man rather than always picturing him as a smoky and eccentric oldish fellow, settled in both his habits and his singleness, whose youth had come to an abrupt end with his childhood. Without Mary, Charles's dream children might have been real. The 'fair Alice W——n', she of the light yellow hair and the pale blue eyes for whom he claimed to have pined away seven of his 'goldenest years', might have been the 'passionate . . . love-adventure' he once described her as being instead of a reference, true or fanciful, which biographers have been unable to track down. He might not have waited so many years to propose to Fanny Kelly, the actress with the 'divine plain face', and Fanny might even have accepted him.

Without his 'poor dear dearest' Mary, Charles might have continued longer to try his hand at poetry and not so soon, as he put it (with wonderful inaccuracy, in his case), have 'dwindled into prose and criticism'. His spirit would have been gayer, his laughs less like sighs. He might not have been so 'shy of novelties; new books, new faces, new years'. The present, not the past, might have been his delight. He would not have been driven, as driven he was by the events of that appalling afternoon, to find happiness by thinking back to happier days. Retrospection would not have become his refuge. The 'boy-man' that he felt himself to be would not have clung with such tenacious affection to his own boyhood. The texture, the range, the very tone and temper of his work would have been different.

From the moment of his mother's murder and the time that he stepped forward to become Mary's legal guardian, Lamb knew that he and Mary were 'in a manner *marked*'. This was bound to be a portion of their fate. There was no hushing their story. It not only pursued them; it ran ahead of them. Sometimes it even forced them to change their lodgings. No shelter could be found from the nudgings, the whisperings, the stares, and the embarrassments it provoked. Charles's determination to care for Mary involved more than living with her. It also meant his living with the knowledge that everyone around them knew her case and their history. If this increased his shyness, it also brought him and Mary closer together. It was only one more of the many bonds, tender and tragic, which united them.

Fortunately, theirs was a relationship based upon more than the perilous stuffs of gratitude or an embittering sense of obligation. Positive as each of them was as a personality, they were united not only by misfortune but by shared tastes and minds which, in spite of dissimilarities, were complementary. When dedicating a volume of his verse, Charles called Mary his best friend. From the dedication of his life she knew she had no better friend than he. Their devotion to each other was genuine and abiding. It shines through their letters. It is unmistakable in every reference to Mary as Bridget in

Charles's essays. They were collaborators in life no less than in literature. No brother and sister in history are more inseparably linked. To Lamb their life as old bachelor and maid was 'a sort of double singleness'.

The glimpses we have of them together are at once heart-warming and heartbreaking. 'You would like to see us,' wrote Mary to Sarah Stoddart, 'as we often sit, writing on one table (but not on one cushion sitting), like Hermia and Helena in the *Midsummer Night's Dream*; or, rather, like an old literary Darby and Joan: I taking snuff, and he groaning all the while and saying he can make nothing of it, which he always says till he has finished, and then he finds out he has made something of it.'

That is a picture of them at their happiest. It belongs with those other pictures we conjure when we imagine them together. Playing cards. Seeing a play. Going to exhibitions. Reading books, she doting on narratives—any narratives; he delighting in the reflective passages of the older authors. Visiting friends. Enjoying the adventure of one of their short summer journeys. Presiding over one of their delectable 'evenings' at home (held first on Wednesdays, later on Thursdays), which Hazlitt immortalized with his 'How often did we cut into the haunch of letters, while we discussed the haunch of mutton on the table!' Or discussing, in the financial comfort of their later years, the greater pleasures they had known when, in their youth, they had been forced to skimp, save, and plan in order to make a purchase or crowd their way into the pit.

Against these brighter moments must be set the darker ones. These are black indeed. By common agreement Mary, in her right mind, was one of the most amiable and admirable of women. But Mary was not always in her right mind. She was 'perpetually on the brink of madness'. If this was Mary's tragedy, it was also Lamb's. Their sunniest days together were never cloudless. The threat under which they lived was fearful and incessant. At all times the Furies stalked them. Small wonder this brother and this sister have been likened to a cockney Orestes and Electra.

Mary's was a recurrent illness. There was no telling when it would return. There was only the certainty that return it would, with ever-increasing frequency, with ever-mounting seriousness. Some hints, such as a sudden moroseness or irritability on Mary's part, preceded its coming. For these dreaded signs Charles watched anxiously. Apparently Mary did, too.

'You would laugh, or you would cry, perhaps both,' Mary wrote in another letter to Miss Stoddart, 'to see us sit together, looking at each other with long and rueful faces, and saying, "How do you do?" and "How do *you* do?" and then we fall a-crying and say we will be better on the morrow. Charles says we are like Tooth Ache and his friend Gum Boil, which though a kind of ease is an uneasy kind of ease.'

Their ease at its best was the epitome of uneasiness. Surely few scenes could be more touching than the one several of their friends had witnessed. It was the common sequel to each reappearance of Mary's symptoms. When these had shown themselves, Charles would get ready to take her to the private asylum at Hoxton. She would gather together a few clothes, replace with a bonnet the mobcap she wore indoors, and prepare for the street. He would lead her, unresisting, to the door. Then they would start out hand in hand, two figures as sombrely dressed as Quakers, walking the whole way, weeping as they walked, and carrying Mary's strait jacket with them.

Even so, Mary, between interruptions, brought Charles a happiness almost as complete as was the unhappiness her madness had brought upon them both. The debt we owe her is at once incalculable and unpayable. If, as readers, we delight in Lamb as he is, we do so because his writing is the product of his life as it was. He never objected to his lot. He faced it squarely, gaily, without whining, and with inexhaustible courage.

The world that knows him as the 'gentle Elia' does Lamb an injustice. Gentle he always was with Mary and in most of his writings. It was, however, his strength which enabled him to be gentle and not any softness which forced him into being so. He hated the phrase 'gentle-hearted' when applied to him as much as Sir James Barrie abhorred the word 'whimsical'. 'For God's sake (I never was more serious),' wrote Charles to Coleridge; 'don't make me ridiculous any more by terming me gentle-hearted in print, or do it in better verses. . . . The meaning of gentle is equivocal at best, and almost always means poor-spirited.'

Certainly Lamb was anything but poor-spirited. He had a resilience unknown to noisier men and a toughness unsuspected by those who have read him sparingly, and then only in his fanciful or sentimental moods. Did he look like a clerk? He did not act like one. He was no Timid Soul. He was fiercely independent. His father may have been a servant, but in a snobbish age Lamb was subservient to no one. He was at all times ready to stammer out his opinions without fear. Everyone who described him noted the sadness of his brown eyes, the thoughtfulness of his expansive brow, the sweetness of his expression, and the smallness of his body. Lamb knew that physically he was 'less than the least of the Apostles'. A friend thought he looked so fragile that 'a breath would overthrow him'. But there was iron in his 'immaterial legs'. His slight body contradicted the largeness of his spirit.

Although Charles knew great sorrow, he was not discontented. If he could refer to Mary and himself, playfully though correctly, as 'shorn Lambs', his belief in the tempering wind was nonetheless strong. Living with sorrow was as much a habit with him as climbing up on his high stool each morning to work as a clerk at the East India House. The prospect of any change so staggered him that he convinced himself he would no more reverse the untoward accidents and events of his life than he would alter the incidents of some well-contrived novel. Such was his love of life that he even loved his own. He meant what he said when he confessed, 'I am in love with this green earth; the face of town and country; the unspeakable rural solitudes, and the sweet security of streets'.

II. THE MAN WHO WAS LAMB

THE portion of the earth that Charles Lamb loved best was not green. He preferred cobblestones to grass any day. He was a city man if ever there was one; a cockney in every inch of his small person. The nightingale never released a song so sweet to his ears as the sound of Bow Bells. Had he been compelled to choose between Skiddaw and Soho, Wordsworth's mountain would have had no chance. The pleasure William found in a daffodil, Charles derived from a chimney sweep.

He did not object to nature—for others. But human nature and the hum of city streets were his delight. Although, with Mary, he liked to venture into the countryside, for a while and as a break, even in the country he was a cockney on vacation. He dared to write to Wordsworth, of all people, 'Separate from the pleasure of your company, I don't much care if I never see a mountain in my life'. Nature to him was 'dead'; London, living. The sun and the moon of the Lake District did not shine for him as brightly as the lamps of London. It was not the beauties of the outdoors which he found 'ever fresh and green and warm', but all the inventions and assemblies of men in the congested boroughs by the Thames.

Few writers have described a city more affectionately than Charles his London. Few have outdone him in making strangers, both by the calendar and geography, feel like citizens of vanished times and places. There were scarcely any aspects of the metropolis he did not cherish. He, to whom much of life was denied, often shed tears of joy on his night walks about London at encountering so much life.

He never tired of the lighted shops of the Strand and Fleet Street; of the innumerable trades, tradesmen, customers, coaches, crowds, wagons, and playhouses; of 'all the bustle and wickedness round about Covent Garden, the very women of the Town, the Watchmen, drunken scenes, rattles'; of the city's pungent smells and the very dirt and mud; of the sun shining upon houses and pavements; or of the print shops, the old bookstalls, and the coffeehouses. He rejoiced in the sense they gave him of London being a pantomime and a masquerade where life itself was at last awake. The city for him was at once a stimulant and an escape. Urbanwise, he lived on it no less than in it. He measured his fortune, good or ill, by his distance from the Strand. He was jubilant when, after one of their frequent changes of address, he found that the house in which he and Mary were then stopping was 'forty-two inches nearer town'.

The city he lived in, though a metropolis, was not for him a capital. Its government was an irrelevance; its politics non-existent. An historian, hoping to find in Lamb's essays or letters some reflection of the great events of turbulent years, would be hard put to determine whether history had by-passed Lamb or he history. He lived through England's wars as if Europe were at peace. So far as he was concerned, they were undeclared and unwaged. He came to admire Nelson, admitted Wellington's existence, had no love for the early Hanovers, in a mild way championed Queen Caroline's cause, and was curious about Napoleon's height. But the French Revolution left no visible mark upon him, and, though he must have heard of Trafalgar, Austerlitz, and Waterloo, we never hear of them through him.

Did the younger Pitt die in 1806? For Lamb he never seems to have lived. Did 'Boney' threaten England with invasion? Did the Peterloo Massacre spill blood in Manchester? Were trade unions allowed for the first time? Did the Prince Regent's marriage to Mrs. Fitzherbert rock society? Were both the Roman Catholic Emancipation and the First Reform Bill passed? Contemporaneous as he was with all of these occurrences, Lamb was apparently the contemporary of none of them.

Unlike such of his intimates as Coleridge, Hazlitt, Leigh Hunt, and Wordsworth, he had no interest in public affairs. Society for him was always a circle of friends and never the collective well-being of a community. 'Public affairs—except as they touch upon me, and so turn into private,' Lamb wrote to Thomas Manning, 'I cannot whip up my mind to feel any interest in.' By his own admission, he was deaf to the noises which kept Europe awake, and could not make present times present to him.

He was as insulated against political events as he was susceptible to human, literary, and gastronomic values. In his scheme of things 'important people' were unimportant, and for him the 'Great World' possessed no fascination. The bearers of titles, more than leaving him unimpressed, left him unamused no less surely than official leaders left him unled. A benevolent eccentric himself, he delighted in the benevolent eccentricities of others. The heads he prized were not those highly placed but those 'with some diverting twist in them'; heads lightened by 'out of the way humours and opinions'.

His absorptions were personal, not public, and small-scaled rather than outsized. Covent Garden was his Buckingham Palace; the art galleries were his House of Commons; the bookstall, his House of Lords. Londoner, utter and complete, though he was, Lamb never felt, thought, or wrote as a citizen but always as an individual. He took the same pleasure in the 'delicious juices of meats and fishes, and society, and the cheerful glass, and candle-light and fireside conversations, and innocent vanities and jests, and irony itself' that he did in the passages, sublime or melancholy, of his favourite old authors. If the oddities of authorship were dear to him, so were the oddities of people and places, and it was these which enchanted him in London.

The London through which Lamb trudged was apt to be two cities—the one he saw as a man, and the other he remembered from his youth. Accordingly, even when solitary, he seldom walked the streets alone. For the author whose attachment to the past was so great that he could exclaim, 'Hang the age; I'll write for Antiquity!' London's past was superimposed upon its present. On his strolls he was attended by the shades of the boys and teachers he had known as a student at Christ's Hospital; by the ghosts of departed players or of journalists with whom he had worked; or by the figures of Old Benchers, long since dead, whom he had watched in his boyhood in the Inner Temple. These rose constantly before his eyes. So double was Lamb's sense of time, so eager his search for reminders of his 'joyful' days, that, in spite of his best known poem, the 'old familiar faces' were for him never 'all, all . . . gone'.

London offered Lamb a source of vicarious life. The city which touched and diverted him by doing so provided him with a release from both his 'cold bed of celibacy' and his long years of confinement at the East India House. During most of his writing life, Lamb was a full-time clerk, a part-time author. He contended that his real 'works'—'more MSS. in folio than ever Aquinas left, and full as useful'—were the great ledgers he had filled day after day for the thirty-three years of his clerkdom, and not the printed volumes to be found at booksellers. There was little of the free-lance in his nature. There could not be. His being married, as he put it, to Mary's fortunes meant that he was unable to run risks with his own. Instead of writing to live, he clerked in order to be free to write. Generous as he was in his gifts and loans to others, he could not afford to be without steady employment himself.

He was horrified when Bernard Barton confided he was thinking of giving up his job in a Quaker bank to live by his pen. 'Keep to your Bank,' he urged Barton, 'and the Bank will keep you. . . . What, is there not from six to eleven p.m. 6 days in the week, and is there not all Sunday?' For Lamb this was writing time enough. It spared him the insecurities of being a 'slave to Booksellers' and 'the miseries of subsisting by authorship'. It meant that, when at last he was at liberty to write, his pen felt its 'promotion'. His writing was thus kept an escape from drudgery, and so avoided being drudgery itself.

He was, of course, fond of seeing himself as a prisoner at the India House, of claiming that he sat there like Philomel all day (but not singing) with his 'heart against this thorn of a desk'. But he liked his job better than he guessed, and was lost when he retired from it. The routine of working at India House from ten to four at once supported and soothed him. It comforted him in his loneliness and appealed to what was essentially gregarious in his nature. He missed the friendly eminence of the high stool upon which he had sat for so many years. He missed not hanging his hat each day on the same peg. He missed the amiable ease of an office where, though he laboured faithfully, he could still find time to write some of his best letters. He missed the companionship of his 'old desk fellows'—his 'co-brethren of the quill'. He missed 'the hot huddle of rational creatures'. He missed, too, being able to excuse his habitual tardiness by such an explanation as 'I m-make up for that by g-going away early'.

The truth is he missed his chains. Like many another, he came to realize they had become a necessary part of his apparel. Nothing in his story is more poignant than the sadness which inundated him when, at fifty, his dream of liberty became a reality and he was freed from what he had thought was bondage. During the next nine years, until his death in 1834, he sensed that freedom in itself could be a bondage. He had lived so long 'to other people' that he could not happily fill his own emancipated hours. Time stood still for him and was empty in its idleness. He lost the 'Wednesday feelings' and the 'Saturday night sensations' he had once known. To his despair he discovered he walked about, not to and from. Having all holidays, it was as though he had none. No Babbitt and no Dodsworth could have been more rudderless upon retirement than was this man, part Yorick, part Jaques, when he was at last freed by a generous pension.

His Yorick side is known to every reader whose knowledge of him does not stop with the *Tales from Shakespeare*, 'The Dissertation on Roast Pig', or 'Dream Children'. Lamb turning suddenly to Martin Burney at cards to comment, 'Martin, if dirt were t-trumps, what a hand you would hold!'; Lamb crying out, 'Wordsworth says he could have written *H-Hamlet* if he'd had the m-mind!'; or Lamb answering Coleridge's question as to whether or not Charles had ever heard him preach in the days of his Unitarian ministry with, 'I never heard you do anything else'—all these are instances of his 'punch-light' humour which, though familiar, have not become tired.

As a conversationalist, his stammer was part of his comic equipment. He relied upon it the way acrobats rely upon a net. He was a fellow whose jests were infinite, instantaneous, impudent, and deflating. He had the virtues, and the wisdom, of not being a continuous conversationalist. His stutter, like his discretion, made that impossible. His hatred for the 'long and much talkers' was as lusty as theirs for him. He knew the value of silences, broken suddenly and unexpectedly, and, one gathers, of dead-panning his way to a joke. Pomposity he despised, dullness he abhorred, and seers he loathed when they were 'seering'.

To be at his best he had to be among people he knew and liked. To strangers and incompatibles he was an enigma, if not an irritant. Carlyle, with his genius for fermentation, was never sourer than on the subject of Lamb. 'A more pitiful, rickety, gasping, staggering, stammering Tomfool I do not know,' fumed he. 'He is witty by denying truisms and abjuring good manners.' Yet to Hazlitt, as to many another, this same Lamb was 'the most delightful, the most provoking, the most witty and sensible of men. . . . No one ever stammered out such fine, piquant, deep, eloquent things in half a dozen half-sentences as he does. His jests scald like tears; and he probes a question with a play upon words.'

Among his friends, on the kind of drinking, talking, smoking evening which he cherished, his relaxation was to enliven the passing moment as certainly as, when alone, his consolation was to dream of the moments that had been. He had a reply—and an unanswerable one—for those who complained he was always aiming at wit. He said that to do so was at least as good as aiming at dullness.

Macready was shocked to hear Lamb confess at Talfourd's one night that 'the last breath he drew in he wished might be through a pipe and exhaled in a pun'. Lamb's fondness for puns was notorious. He loved them as much as all people dislike them who cannot make them. There is no such thing as stooping to a pun. There is only the challenge of being able to rise to a good one. Few cadavers could be deader or more emaciated than those occasional puns which, in his letters, Lamb quotes approvingly, pointer in hand, with the subtlety of a window demonstrator. Lamb, however, knew a pun must be heard, not read, and heard at the moment of its birth if it were to live completely or to be fully enjoyed. 'A pun,' wrote he, 'hath a hearty kind of present ear-kissing smack in it; you can no more transmit it in its pristine flavour than you can send a kiss.'

That Lamb laughed and could make others laugh, everyone knows. But the nature of his laughter, the keen and enjoying manner in which he detected frailty, the amused details which underwrite his fantasy and are the basis of his reveries, along with the man who could be as realistic in his observation of men as he was in facing the unpleasant realities of his own life —these are what the sentimentalists forget who have made him as sentimental as themselves.

Many authors suffer at the hands of their detractors; just as many (and no less cruelly) at the hands of their admirers. Lamb belongs to this well-nigh smothered brotherhood. He has almost been killed, not so much by his own kindness, which was true and very human, as by the bogus, treacly kindness which others have palmed off as being his. Thornton Wilder once described a modern playwright, addicted to cute and elfin phrases and marshmallow thoughts, as writing in the manner associated with Lamb by people who have not read him. This false notion of Lamb, with its attendant misunderstandings and proper revulsions, is a ghost which, worse than haunting the real Lamb, has all too often obscured him.

In his eagerness to canonize Lamb's palpable and radiant virtues, Thackeray may have dubbed him 'Saint Charles'. Charles, however, was the more of a saint because he was so much of a man. Although there are those who choose to bury him in lavender, to cushion him on sachets, and to confuse him with old lace, they do Lamb a genuine injustice.

Lamb could be sweet beyond comfortable endurance. He could be whimsical to a disquieting extent. He could dip his pen far too deep in syrup and produce copy, on occasions, which to modern eyes reads like literate valentines from yesteryear. These, however, were the excesses into which his tenderness led him. They were the expressions of his frustration, his regrets, his loneliness, and, in a way, of his period. Though full of sentiment, Lamb was no sentimentalist as a man, and only as an author when he nodded, which he was mortal enough to do at moments. That he was kind and that he was witty, everyone knows. But that he was both kind and witty at one and the same time has so surprised his admirers that some of them have overlooked entirely the sharpness of his mind and tongue.

In his letters, as in his talk, a spade was a spade. It was only in his essays that it became a shovel, a gardener's utensil, or something like Triptolemus's tool. When he informed Manning that Coleridge's wife was expecting a baby, did he do so by referring to 'a little one' or 'an addition to the family'? He did not. As directly as if he were a GI in the Army, he wrote, 'Coleridge is settled with his wife (with a child in her guts)'.

No one has written about childhood more tenderly than he. Even so, his was not the bachelor's idealization of all children. He knew that the young, like their elders, were either amiable or unamiable. He saw no reason 'to love a whole family, perhaps eight, nine, or ten, indiscriminately—to love all the pretty dears because children are so engaging'. His phrase, when a sick child had at last been removed from his home, after robbing Lamb of his rest, was, quite simply, 'The little bastard is gone'.

He pulled no punches with his friends, and was much too good a friend to do so. His candour was as great as his charm. 'Cultivate simplicity, Coleridge,' wrote he, 'or rather, I should say, banish elaborateness. . . . I allow no hotbeds in the gardens of Parnassus.' No one ever derived more amusement from a friend's faults than Lamb did from those of poor, foolish, bumbling George Dyer. His letters about Dyer, like his references to him in his essays, are as full of mocking laughter as they are of love. Few people have played more knowledgeably, or with greater relish, upon human frailty than Lamb did when, by 'beslabbering' a book Joseph Cottle had written, he so appealed to its author's vanity that Cottle forgot all about his dead brother in the next room.

Although by his own confession he could not hate anyone he knew, Lamb was terrifyingly aware of people's defects. Shelley's voice was to him 'the most obnoxious squeak I ever was tormented with, ten thousand times worse than the Laureat's, whose voice is the worst part about him except his Laureatcy'. Lamb's aversion to Byron's character was 'thorough' and his admiration for his genius 'very moderate'. 'He is great in so little a way' was Lamb's summary of his Lordship.

Once at Godwin's, Holcroft and Coleridge were fiercely disputing which was better, *man as he was* or *man as he is to be*. 'Give me,' said Lamb, 'man as he is *not* to be.' If, in general, he was willing to take all people as they were, he was taken in by no one. His eye for human absurdity was as keen as his enjoyment of human oddity. Was it a poor relation remembering a birthday so as to drop in just in time for dinner? Was it a liar spinning fabulous yarns on a boat to Margate, or a fact-loving bore on the top of a stagecoach? Lamb saw their failings plain. His gentleness did not prevent his feelings from being strong. 'Now, of all God's creatures,' he wrote, 'I detest letters-affecting, authors-hunting ladies.' His loathing for booksellers was equally strong. So was his disrelish for the Scots. Lamb was as 'essentially anti-Caledonian' as ever Dr. Johnson was.

The fact—the fine, the beckoning, the all-conquering fact—about Lamb is that he could look 'with no indifferent eye upon things or persons'. 'Whatever is' was to him 'a matter of taste or distaste'. He knew, as some of his admirers have forgotten, that he was 'a bundle of prejudices—made up of likings and dislikings—the veriest thrall to sympathies, apathies, and antipathies'. Without these prejudices Lamb would not be Lamb. Nor would he be Lamb had he not felt and phrased them in a way so unmistakably and beguilingly his own that, though it has won him countless friends, it has removed him from the reach of imitators.

III. ELIA VERSUS LAMB

AN affectionate rather than a passionate man, Charles Lamb's prejudices were his substitutes for passion. It was in them that he lived, and because of them, in part, that he lives for us. They were the proofs of his awareness, his sensibility, his discernment, his humanity. Characteristically enough, he chose to refer to these prejudices as 'imperfect sympathies' no less than as prejudices.

One of the major paradoxes of his paradoxical mind was that, as a rule, he could be sympathetic even when he was being witty. His wit was the expression of his love, not his contempt, for men. People who would have irritated others amused him. His knowledge of life was too complete for him to be surprised by human frailty. If he never failed to observe it, he seldom failed to enjoy it. Since he expected it, he was tolerant of it.

His was the laughter of acceptance not protest, of recognition instead of revulsion. His gaiety was as divorced from scorn or cynicism as it was wedded to melancholy. It smiles without being insulting. Unchilled by the arrogance which is the curse of professional wits, it is as warm and human as the 'rather smoky, and sometimes rather drinky' little man from whom it emanated. It sprang from a superior mind, unconscious of its superiority; a mind which is the more endearing because its modesty remains unlost in the midst of its most dazzling exhibitions of prowess.

Lamb's mind was the antithesis of neat and officelike. It resembled an antique shop or an old bookstore where, in spite of the clutter, the dust, and the overlay of accumulation, the proprietor can at a moment's notice bring to light whatever treasure is desired. It never judged 'systemwise' but always by 'fastening on particulars'. It was proudly unmethodized, desultory, tangential. If it worked obliquely in ways beyond prediction, it was because it fed upon the tantalizing obliquities of life no less than of literature. Its knowledge was a matter of informed tastes rather than of pursued facts.

Lamb had no desire to keep up with the Joneses. He had a hard enough time keeping up with the whims of his own interest. The topical left him uncoerced; the popular unpersuaded. When a new book came out, he read an old one. He would have been both amused and amazed by the manuals, digests, and sugar-coated textbooks in which those who mistake facts for learning nowadays stalk culture as if it were a butterfly to be pinioned in a net. Although the most bookish of bookish men, he was no chaser after information for information's sake. Instead, he was a savourer, content to taste and retaste what was best or most flavoursome in the volumes he cherished. If his devotion to what was special, limited, and wayward in his preoccupation was one of his limitations, this did not bother him. Lamb was comfortable in his ignorance of what he did not choose to know.

On all matters relating to science, Elia could boast he was 'a whole Encyclopædia behind the rest of the world'. He was equally, and just as proudly, unknowledgable about geography, modern languages, the shapes and textures of the commonest trees, herbs, or flowers, and tools, engines, or mechanical processes. In spite of his attachment to the past, history as a mere sequence of events had so little interest for him that he could brag he had never deliberately sat down to read a chronicle even of his own country. As for astronomy, it did not exist in the orbit of his shining concerns. 'If the sun,' wrote he, 'on some portentous morn were to make his first appearance in the west, I verily believe that, while all the world were gasping in apprehension about me, I alone should stand unterrified, from sheer incuriosity and want of observation.'

One of the reasons for Elia's dislike of the Scots was that no excursions could be taken with them, since they always insisted upon keeping to the path. Lamb's thinking, though it could lead to the summits, was nothing if not excursive. The straight highroads dear to historians were not the routes he either elected or was equipped to travel. When he did not spurn the obvious views and inevitable sights, he preferred to reach them by a back door or secret passage. He gave both his mind and heart (the combination, in his case, meaning his attention) to the ignored vistas and overlooked curiosities. Even these he approached by those unblazed trails which, to the personal essayist, are the royal road.

If these footpaths were roads which led to himself, the reason was his modesty, not his egotism. Lamb was one of the most autobiographical of authors. To read him on virtually any subject is to read about him. It is to know him with a sense of daily intimacy with which few writers are known. In his copy Lamb could no more escape from himself than in his living he could leave Mary. Yet self-centred in the ordinary sense, he was not. The world, for the conceited man, starts and ends with himself. For Elia, Charles Lamb was merely the point of departure to the world around him. Although with him the first person singular was a favourite pronoun, as he used it, it somehow managed to seem printed with a small 'i'.

Lamb was too unpretentious to pretend to be omniscient. He was poignantly aware that few people are able to speak for themselves, much less for others. Speaking of and through himself was his way of speaking for all. He knew his own voice contained the echoes of other voices. In this way he chose to write, intertwining with his identity griefs and affections which were not his own, 'making himself many, or reducing many unto himself'.

Since truth to Lamb was as personal as everything else, facts enjoyed no immunity from his prankishness. It diverted him to distort them when, as Elia, he wrote of his friends, his family, or himself. His love of mystification was one of the abidingly boyish aspects of his character. It pleased him in his essays to mislead his readers by false scents; to write Oxford when he meant Cambridge; to make Bridget his cousin, not his sister; to merge Coleridge's boyhood with his own; or to paint himself as a hopeless drunkard when, as a matter of fact, he was a man who, though he loved to down a drink, was seldom downed by drinking. By deliberate, sometimes mischievous, design his familiar essays were but the 'shadows of fact'. They were 'verisimilitudes, not verities'. Yet Lamb was present, quintessentially if not factually, in their every phrase and sentence. At least an important part of him was present though not by any means the whole man.

Closely related as Elia is to Charles Lamb, they were not—they are not—in any sense of the word identical. When it came to authorship, there were two Charles Lambs. If not that, there was, at any rate, one Lamb who wrote in two styles so different that he could be suspected of employing his left hand for the one, his right hand for the other. As in the case of countless others, ink-stained or ink-free, Lamb had a public and a private manner. He did not write to his friends as he wrote for the magazines. Although in either case a natural-born essayist, and a matchless critic of books and men, his style, which was always intimate, altered according to whether his pen or a printer was to be the transmitter of his words.

Hazlitt's portrait of him as a nobleman of another day caught the spirit, not of Lamb the private letter writer, but of Lamb the public essayist. Certainly, the Lamb who contributed to periodicals was not the Renaissance figure Hazlitt envisaged. Yet Hazlitt was right beyond dispute in dressing this Lamb in the clothes of an age other than his own. When he wrote for publication, Lamb did go into costume as surely as, when he dashed off notes to his friends, he donned a dress so modern that after the passage of more than a century it seems as contemporary to us as it did to them.

The highly, at moments even dangerously, self-conscious artist we cherish as Elia emerged late in Lamb's life as the flowering of his varied career as a professional writer. By that time Lamb had long since mislaid, except for album purposes, the poet of slight endowment he had started out by being. Years before, too, he had discarded the novelist whose all but non-existent talent for narrative stamped *Rosamund Gray* and his contributions to *Mrs. Leicester's School* as no more than apprentice work. He had also buried the dramatist with 'no head for playwriting' whose blank verse tragedy *John Woodvil* was but the feeblest of Elizabethan echoes, and whose little farce *Mr. H* . . . was so disastrous a failure that its author had joined in the hissing.

In the same way Lamb had outgrown those un-Lamblike *Tales from Shakespeare* upon which he had collaborated with Mary. Although he had predicted such a potboiler would be popular 'among the little people', he had never guessed how enduring its popularity would prove among those grownups of little courage who, apparently, are grateful for anything which spares them Shakespeare in the original.

The first volume of the *Elia* essays was published when Lamb was forty-eight; the second, and last, ten years later. In print, and in such memorable papers as his 'On the Genius and Character of Hogarth' and 'On the Tragedies of Shakespeare,' Lamb had already established not only his brilliance as a critic but his unique public manner as an essayist. Yet during all these formative years, in fact from his first preserved letters to Coleridge before and after Mary's murder of her mother, right down to the last note scribbled off to Mrs. Dyer (about a book, appropriately enough) five days before his death thirty-eight years later, Lamb was the possessor of an epistolary style quite at odds with the style we know as Elia's.

More than being the best introduction to Lamb, Lamb's are among the world's best letters. In them we almost hear him talk. To be sure, his stutter is gone, and an incredible fluency has replaced it. But, as in all good letters, the illusion of direct communication is maintained. Both the moment and the mood are captured in all the heat of their passing sorrow or amusement. The small details, the great agonies, the first impressions, the play of mind and the play on words, the reflections by means of which a particular instance is lifted into a generality, the tastes of food, the smells of London, the look of friends, the résumé of last night's party, the book just read, the anecdote just heard, this day's sadness, the next day's gaiety—they are all there, caught hot, caught frankly, and transferred without effort by a pen scratching swiftly against stolen time at the office.

Perhaps the speed of their composition was the guarantee of their simplicity. In any case, again and again Charles's letters deny their datelines by remaining undated. They are not so much the products of an age as they are models for all time. Whether they are 'thank-you' notes for a visit paid or a roast pig sent; apologies for having to be carried home from an overconvivial evening; his proposal of marriage to Fanny Kelly; the gossip of London dispatched across the oceans to Manning in China; religious musings; discussions of death; the account to Coleridge, magnificent in its dignity, of his mother's murder; appraisals of Defoe, Cervantes, Godwin's *Chaucer*, or the second edition of the *Lyrical Ballads*, they are perfect of their kind.

They show the warmth, the originality, the humour, or the grandeur of the astonishing little man who wrote them. They are the spontaneous distillations of a writer, instinctive and superior. They make us companions not only in Lamb's daily living but in his adult life. Their every episodic entry fits into a sequence. Without meaning to do so, they form an autobiography from which Lamb's biographers must quote and to which everyone who would know him must turn. They give us Lamb unadorned; Lamb, the writer, without self-consciousness, hence often at his finest; Lamb, so to speak, at his slippered ease, relaxed, using short sentences, hitting directly; Lamb employing the most vivid and abrupt of colloquialisms, thus avoiding the calculated, beautiful, and antique cadences so dear to Elia.

The difference between the letter writer who signed himself C.L. and the essayist known as Elia is the difference between a candid camera close-up and a full-length portrait in oil, apparelled for effect and so posed that its very casualness is studied. It is the difference between jewels unset and a necklace painstakingly matched. It is, in short, the everlasting difference between the impromptu and the planned.

When Thackeray's 'Saint Charles' wrote for the public prints, he heard voices, Joan-wise. The sonorities of such favourite prose writers as Sir Thomas Browne, Burton, Marvell, and Fuller haunted his ears. 'I gather myself up into the old things,' wrote Lamb. More accurately, he gathered the old authors up into himself. Their outmoded language was an expression of what was backward-glancing in his spirit. It pleased him by being out of date. It orchestrated his melancholy. Not only that. When appropriated for his casual personal essays, its very gravity served as a foil to his humour.

Lamb loved the stately rhythms and obsolete words of these older writers. While playing chameleon to their style, he could achieve a style of his own. He imitated in order to create what is inimitable. The borrowed pencil Hazlitt accused him of employing as an essayist was put by Lamb to his own uses. He was aware that, as Elia, his writings were 'villainously pranked in an affected arrangement of antique modes and phrases'. But he knew these writings would not have been his, had this not been so. 'Better it is,' said he, 'that a writer should be natural in a self-pleasing quaintness, than to affect a naturalness (so called) that should be strange to him.'

Quaint Elia was, and is, and in a manner pleasing not only to himself but to readers everywhere once they have become Elians. This is no hard thing to do, if only in a more hurried age, when prose is thinner and the language employed more often than it is enjoyed, readers are willing to give Elia and themselves a chance. His essays never were *in date*, except for what is dateless in their insight. Stylistically, they were intentional anachronisms when they were published. Their antique flavour was, and remains, a source of their charm.

To modern eyes, accustomed as they are to sentences being the shortest distance between a subject and a predicate (if, indeed, they extend that far), the long, leisurely, and intricate constructions of Lamb the essayist may at first glance appear forbidding. Yet forbidding is the very last word anyone in his right senses, and with the slightest acquaintance with Lamb, would dream of using for those gloriously warm and intimate essays which Lamb wrote as a critic of life, or of art, the theatre, and books. If, at the outset, their subtle and sustained sentences seem difficult, with their 'methink's', their 'thee's' and 'thou's', their 'art's', 'wert's', 'reader's', and other pressed flowers from another day, or their addiction to such words as 'agnise', 'additaments', and 'dulcifying', these difficulties soon turn into delights. However truffled, archaic, or self-conscious was Lamb's formal style, it is rich in its rewards. Costume prose it may be, but costume jewellery it never was because its gems are genuine.

More than taking knowing, Elia survives it. His better essays belong in that class of literature he described as being 'perpetually self-reproductive'. They bear reading and re-reading, and then can be read and re-read again. They are habit-forming rather than time-passing. If the style in their case is not the whole man, it is at any rate the essayist. Elia cannot be separated from it. Nor would anyone who has once cultivated a taste for that style be denied its enjoyment. Although, as a word man, Lamb was deaf to music and could complain about its 'measured malice', Elia was able with words to release an incomparable music of his own.

He was the opposite of those writers he dismissed as being 'economists only in delight'. His prodigality with the pleasures he provides is limitless. The joy he creates from small things is large. The conceits in his phrasing are redeemed by the sincerity of his feeling. If he seldom wrote a bromide, it was because he seldom thought one. The commonest reaction became uncommon in his statement of it. His vocabulary was as much his own as his mind, and both were unpredictable.

As is true of all good essayists, not too much of Elia is to be read at one sitting. He fatigues, not by the ardour of his emotions, but by the incessant probing of his perceptions, by the sudden quiet dartings of his mind and the abundance of his allusions. To be enjoyed fully, he must be lingered over, read with the same disregard for the present that he showed, savoured, as he savoured the subjects of his choice. He is a writer who does not raise his voice.

He avoids emphasis. His finest phrases spill from his pen without warning. They are tucked away, not paraded. They come jostling, one so close upon the other that they are apt to be overlooked. To miss them is to miss the true satisfactions of Elia, because in his phrases he gives the pleasures other authors give in their paragraphs.

His mood is ruminative, his mind associational. For all the amusement to be had from the felicities of his observations, his was an essentially tragic nature. He was a tragedian who smiled instead of crying. This not only deepens his humour. It insures its humanity.

On the subject of his family, his youth, his London, the places he had visited, or the 'characters' he had known, his vision was as detailed and unblinking as it was in his criticism. Yet, uncanny as was his accuracy as a reporter, Lamb was never a journalist. What he wrote as journalism somehow managed to be literature. 'In eternity,' pointed out Sir Thomas Browne, 'there is no distinction of Tenses.' This line in the *Religio Medici* was one which, as both a familiar essayist and a magazine critic, Lamb must have hugged to his heart. For him datelines did not exist. He had no interest in news and less sense of it. News, as he saw it, was whatever happened to interest him, however personal or remote. The measure of his ability is that he made it interesting to his contemporaries, and even now makes us feel contemporaneous with it.

As a critic no less than as a man, Lamb lived in a world where watches had stopped. Yet he creates the illusion that they are still ticking. What he was fond of reviewing was not last night's or last week's play but his memories of twenty or thirty years ago. Although this was all a part of his being unable to make present times present to him, it has never prevented him from making times past present to us.

The same Lamb who had abandoned poetry early in his career wrote as a poet when he was at his best as a critic or a correspondent. The stuttering, jesting, smoking, drinking little fellow, valiantly linked to Mary, was little in an abidingly big way. He was big of heart, large of mind, and unique in his endowments. Victim of life though he was, he was never victimized by it. He lived an interior life externally. It was his mind and the abilities out of which he fashioned his style which made his living, on the whole uneventful, eventful for the world no less than for him. Perhaps Pater, another stylist, wrote the best summary of Lamb in these words, 'Unoccupied, as he might seem, with great matters, he is in immediate contact with what is real, especially in its caressing littleness, that littleness in which there is much of the whole woeful heart of things, and meets it more than half-way with a perfect understanding of it.'

THE MOOD OF SQUARES

BY R. J. CRUIKSHANK

from *The Moods of London* (1951)

THE MOOD OF SQUARES

Had I but plenty of money, money enough and to spare,
The house for me, no doubt, were a house in a city square;
Ah, such a life, such a life, as one leads at the window there?

—BROWNING

ON seeing London from the air, it is the green look of the place that astonishes one. In early summer, the impression one receives is not so much of a city encircled by a sea of greenness, out of which it towers grey and impregnable, as of a city whose dykes, levées and sea-walls are all being broken down. The citizens have cried to the sea as to a liberator, 'Come in—come in'. The green pours in. It broadens out into wide lakes. There are dark, flooding rivers of it, and a hundred thousand little pools. Sometimes the waves leap so high they drown solid piles of masonry, and the sight sets one dreaming of some spring to come when, like an old city of legend, London will be buried deep beneath this green sea, and the ghostly chimes of St. Paul's will be audible at night on the Surrey hills.

At any time of the year, the urban and rural aspects of London flow easily, almost imperceptibly, into one another. That is more true, of course, of the south and western parts of London than of the north and east, the parts that seem to sit too high to be inundated by the green flood. Too much of the north and east remains a waste of bricks, the creation of the speculative builder of Victorian times. But seen in the wide sweep that a plane affords, London looks like a city whose inhabitants have tried very hard to bring the country into the town, and so redress the ugliness of a commercial civilization. To that degree, the character of the Londoner is shown in the face of London. At the heart of the city are the royal parks. Then the eye is taken by a myriad verdant touches that keep the city fresh even in dusty winter. There are such lawns as those of Lincoln's Inn Fields and the Temple, and the tiny pin-points of emerald where gardens have been made out of the disused burial grounds of the old City.

It has become a city of green sanctuaries. The way some of them are hidden is part of the fine fraudulence of London. Riding a bus along Grosvenor Place, one can see that the King and Queen possess a garden behind the smoky back wall of Buckingham Palace. It is plainly a large garden. But how large is not at all apparent except from the other side of the wall. There the garden

77

stretches out in wide vistas. There are sweeps of lawn framed by a forest; an expanse of water that looks almost like the Serpentine; flower gardens, and shrubberies rambling enough for a child to get lost in. At a royal garden party five or six thousand guests make no intolerable crush. A meditative soul can disengage himself from the throng, stroll off to watch the swans and, out of earshot of the Guards' band, reflect upon the awful necessity of kingship to be gracious to a mob.

Above all, one who looks on London from the clouds is attracted by the profusion of the squares and the height of their trees. Those squares of London would alone be worth coming to see if there were nothing else to attract a visitor. Other cities at home and abroad possess their squares, but it is the number, variety and beauty of London's that distinguish our city and give it a quality of its own. Venice is made known by its canals, and Rome by its fountains and gardens. London, I would think, deserves to win some similar fame through its squares. They are among the best and most original ideas that London has to offer. They form one of the best reasons for loving London. They save us from a nightmare of steel and concrete. A stranger could spend many hours, touched by their changing pleasures, in strolling through them. The squares, unlike the streets, encourage leisurely wanderings. Their houses do not, on the whole, resent being looked at. Those squares that remain residential present a happy mode of life, a compromise between the centuries. The severity of doors and windows is tempered by the charm of flowers and grass. The perpendicularness of houses melts into the roundness of trees. The gardens of the squares provide escape from the blankness of streets. Amid the Puritan restraints of London's domestic architecture, this combination of houses and trees affects one like the confession of an income-tax inspector that he writes poetry.

There are more than four hundred squares of one kind or another in London. The pilgrim who would look at all of them must travel far into the depths of East London as well as West. It is a mistake to think that the fine specimens are to be found alone in Mayfair and Bloomsbury. There are some squares in Southwark, decrepit and shabby but undeniably handsome, that are like old patricians who have seen better days. Some turn in fashion in twenty years' time may bring them into their own again. A square may be as large and public as Eaton Square, which is almost like an allée in a provincial French town, laid out for a review and march past of troops, or it may be as sequestered a promenade as Torrington Square, in Bloomsbury, hidden away under rolling clouds of trees. A London square may be a circle, or a lozenge, or a crescent. It may be any shape at all. Nobody can complain of the sameness of the squares. The diversity of their forms and sizes, as they open up out of their connecting streets, robs a stroll through them of any monotony. An appearance is contrived of spontaneous growth; there is an enhancement of the country's invasion of the town. One comes to believe that on some magical summer morning long ago the great trees marched in and took possession.

Inigo Jones planned the square of Covent Garden, and St. James's Square was built, long before the Duke of Bedford laid out his London estate, but the inspiration of what most of us regard as the squares of London was given by the Bloomsbury developments of 1780. The house of Russell bears a name for singular originality, but no unconventional notion of any Russell in politics or religion has been happier in the outcome than the making of Russell Square.

It is odd to think what has happened to Russell Square since. The Russell liking for the unusual has been travestied by other hands. On one side of the square rises the grey Biblical cliff of the University of London building. It looks very like the Tower of Babel. And it has the curse of Babel on it. It aspired too high, and the penalty for breaching the L.C.C. limit is that the three topmost storeys of the tower may not be inhabited. On the other side of the square is one of the most romantic pieces of architecture in London, the Hotel Russell, an example, I am told, of a style rarely seen in these parts, German Renaissance, a flamboyant, heraldic style of which, I feel, we should have more for the sake of keeping things lively. Its interior makes one think of the sets used in a toy theatre—Act IV, scene 1, a hall in the Duke of Mantua's palace; flourish—procession—hautboys—enter the Duke and court. It is the great advantage of not having any taste that one can genuinely enjoy bad architecture. Round the corner from the hotel is the Russell Square Underground station. Its lift is a splendid example of the macabre style of the late Victorians. It looks like the Pit and the Pendulum.

The Duke of Bedford's model square was widely copied in the first part of the nineteenth century, and London was then provided with the ample squares of Belgravia and Tyburnia, where rich merchants, lawyers and doctors, as well as the aristocrats, came to live. The city had become the capital of the Industrial Revolution. It was a London intoxicated by commercial success. It had the thrust, drive, vulgarity and eagerness for display that mark a newly rich class. The squares grew more pompous, there was a falling away from the good manners of the eighteenth century, but the idea of bringing the country into the dusty town was honoured still.

One could wish that Thomas Cubitt, a speculator of unusual taste, as well as energy, might have gone on building new squares for the new plutocracy. But by the middle of the century mock-Gothic mansions at Penge and baronial halls at Clapham Common became the fancy of prosperous business men. It was a case of spiritual pride. The eighteenth-century aristocrats had at least lived in communities—in the squares, in fact. They were exclusive without being remote. The new barons shut themselves up in castellated strongholds in Upper Norwood, and the serfs of the Industrial Revolution could only guess what crimes were done in the dungeons. The walls were high. They were crowned by rusty spikes and broken glass. The worst could be feared.

The best-known squares of London vary considerably in their appeal. It is understood that in this meaning of the word Trafalgar Square is no square at all. It is completely the public place where greedy, stupid pigeons hold their non-stop mass meetings and coo down the Government. Lincoln's Inn Fields, the largest of the real squares, provides one of the most attractive surprises London offers to a visitor. He passes out of bustling Chancery Lane, crushed by a sense of too many buildings and people huddled into too narrow a space, and finds himself in one of the most spacious enclaves of half-rural London. Its trees are noble. In the spring the thrushes and blackbirds flute in its dells, and rarer birds are seen. Butterflies wreathe a dance over the head of some venerable K.C. The children swarm at the foot of Margaret MacDonald's memorial. In Lincoln's Inn, the Law is in Arcady. No place better illustrates the depth of the penetration of Nature's vanguards into the stone and brick wastes of London.

St. James's, one of the oldest squares, is a place apart. The houses of the Whig dukes have long since changed hands, but St. James's remains patrician. It is a fine square, but it has a formal, magisterial look, as though it had to set an example to such rakish squares as Soho Square and Golden Square. St. James's is the erudite square of Chatham House and the London Library. It has a strong flavour of Macaulay about it. Its most celebrated tradition is a literary one, of Samuel Johnson and Richard Savage walking all round it one night for want of a lodging. They paced the square for several hours, inveighed against the Government, and 'resolved they would stand by their country'. Our Whig hero, William of Orange, booted and spurred, primed for action, and looking as if about to plunge down on his horse from his pedestal and charge into the Royal Institute of International Affairs should Professor Arnold Toynbee show a deviation towards Jacobitism, commands the stately scene. The great joy of St. James's Square is not King William but the view it affords of the front of the Haymarket Theatre, as elegant a piece of stage spectacle as anything presented inside it. When the lamps under the colonnade are lighted, and the regal gold and red is sparkling, one half expects Millamant to appear, disorganizing the Haymarket traffic—'here she comes, i' faith, full sail, with her fan spread and her streamers out, and a shoal of fools for tenders'.

The hand of commerce rests heavily upon the handsomest of the Mayfair squares, Berkeley, and no nightingale could be heard above the boom of the traffic. But it is not so spoiled that we cannot guess how well it looked a few years ago when Lansdowne House ran along one side of it. It is still a graceful and elegant, if battered, duchess among squares; a duchess who is hard up, and has gone into business with a 'nice American'. Its plane trees, the oldest in London, soar and spread prodigiously. No matter how often one has passed through it, there is always an element of happy surprise in coming upon those swaying towers of greenery in the centre of the West End. A Gainsborough pageant might still be presented under its trees, with Her Grace of Devonshire in her spreading hat and blue ribands, and young gentlemen following her in classical armour and ostrich plumes.

Grosvenor Square, in which Lady Bracknell feared acts of violence would take place if education were ever taken seriously in England—luckily, it never has been—is now as American as Fifth Avenue. Turning the gardens into a memorial to President Roosevelt has given us a new kind of London sanctuary. Many of our squares have lost their residential character, and there is no turning back. But one fancies most Londoners would prefer that an old square should be adapted to some such ceremonial use rather than be filled by hat shops and motor salesrooms. Grosvenor Square has been made into a contemporary shrine, and the change has given a new vitality to the tradition. Few of the statues in our squares are of any great worth, but Londoners have always had an amused tolerance for the Hanoverian princes and Whig states-men in togas who peep out of the shrubbery—characters like that Duke of Gloucester who was universally known as Silly Billy. The Roosevelt memorial shows us to what finer commemorative ends a square may be put. Around his statue collect the shadows and gleams of the days through which this generation of Londoners have lived together. In these gardens many Londoners recall his voice as they heard it broadcast during the days of the German bombings. The immediate past, that most elusive of all orders of time, gathers around us.

Most of us have our favourites among the squares. Some are impressed by the grand manner of Belgrave Square, which has made few concessions to the spirit of the age and maintains a proud, censorious look. It is possible to admire its spaciousness. It is possible to acknowledge that hearts just as pure and fair may beat in Belgrave Square, etc. But for me this square retains the terror of the annihilating dowagers of Victorian fiction who lived there—it is haunted by their freezing stares and cutting voices—the petrifying rustle of Lady Bracknell is still audible.

LADY BRACKNELL. What number in Belgrave Square?

JACK. 149.

LADY BRACKNELL (*shaking her head*). The unfashionable side. I thought there was something. However, that could easily be altered.

JACK. Do you mean the fashion, or the side?

LADY BRACKNELL (*sternly*). Both if necessary, I presume. What are your politics?

That formidable spectre has outlived the blitz. Walking through Belgrave Square, I suspect the flash of a lorgnette at the window, and, as I hurry away, am pursued by a dowager's unstrung voice asking, 'Who *was* that person?'

It is a relief to reach shadowy and pensive Chester Square where the only ghost to fear is that of Matthew Arnold.

Some amateurs of squares take pleasure in the Bayswater ones with their air of fantasy, soaring Corinthian pillars, and their huge rambling mansions, large enough to billet a regiment—squares that are bathed in the after-glow of Victorian wealth. There are other connoisseurs who ask for nothing better than the Kensington squares, particularly lovely Kensington Square itself, that is like a chapter from *Henry Esmond*, a muted survival of the eighteenth century: 'As Esmond and the dean walked away from Kensington, discoursing of this tragedy, and how fatal it was to the cause which they both had at heart, the street criers were already out with their broadsides, shouting through the town the full, true, and horrible account of the death of Lord Mohun and Duke Hamilton in a duel. A fellow had got to Kensington and was crying it in the square there at very early morning, when Mr. Esmond happened to pass by. He drove the man from under Beatrix's very window, whereof the casement had been set open.' Others again have a liking for Chelsea's retreats, which now and again sprout out in doors and shutters of joyous blue or canary yellow, as though the natives were under the pleasant hallucination that Chelsea is a small town in the South of France, lost among the vines and olives. On the other hand, men of mark in insurance and chartered accountancy approve the solid worth of the squares that lie behind cheerful, rattling, busy Sloane Square, whose trees, and shops, and general arrangement, give it a happy French look, especially on a May morning, Many are still content with Bloomsbury's best, in particular Bedford Square, and its unspoiled aspect of classic contentment. The pavement of Bedford Square has a rainwashed spread and spaciousness, it has an affinity with South Parade at Bath, it is designed for the clatter of social and intellectual shoes, for the meeting of well-known ghosts and living celebrities.

A quiet domesticated taste in man or woman inclines to such squares as Gordon, Brunswick or Mecklenburgh—discreet, homely in the best sense, full of self-effacing felicities of style. Many a Londoner dashes through them without in the least appreciating how admirable are their subdued qualities. They are too well-mannered to seek to detain him by anything showy. They are examples of that reticence in home architecture in which London excels, but are touched by a warmth and dignity that is not to be found in the streets of modern villas. They are like acquaintances who grow on us by an undemonstrative civility, never exhibiting their affections, but always remaining loyal. Perhaps it is on evenings in late spring that one can best savour the charm of domestic ease that these smaller squares provide. The year should be far enough advanced for the trees to be in full dress, but not so late as to rob us of the pleasure of lighted windows early in the evening. That lighting makes the sympathetic difference—it expresses the interior warmth of domesticity, it heightens the 'lived-in' feeling that is the attraction of such corners of London. The typical London square was not made to present a dramatic effect, it was built that families might enjoy easy, half-rural, well-found private lives, with gates to protect them from a noisy world. The ease has gone, and much of the privacy, the gates have been taken for scrap, but these favourite squares still keep something of the old comforting flavours. The grille by the side of the pavement presents a tantalizing series of flashes of basement kitchens—though not such succulent 'still life' as were exhibited fifteen years ago—and there is the glow of a fire in a first-floor room. Sometimes even a pretty housemaid in a cap and frivolous apron—a vision as rare as a unicorn nowadays—may be glimpsed. Certainly we must insist on warm pools of light in chilly spring-time to assure the right effect. From the point, too, of evoking the authentic atmosphere, one regrets the loss of the barrel-organ, of which there can be no more than a dozen now extant in London; even though its music used to be a great nuisance to irritable writers, lawyers, and other natural sufferers from nerves. On a May evening the barrel-organ, presided over by a sad-eyed little monkey, would give tongue to the emotions of the Bloomsbury square by playing some such tinkling Victorian ditty as 'Scenes that are brightest', or 'When other lips and other hearts their tales of love shall tell'. One misses, too, the touches of local colour that used to be supplied by the muffin-man—more especially when his mournful hootings were heard a street away. In the days of one's boyhood the feeling conveyed by these squares was of a wild romanticism smouldering underneath London's sobriety, a feeling well expressed by Gilbert Chesterton in *The Club of Queer Trades*. In such a setting one still hopes on a hazy spring afternoon to look over a wall and find that the flower-beds on the lawn spell out *DEATH TO MAJOR BROWN*; or see a giant head thrust out of the coal-hole in the pavement bawling blood-freezing maledictions.

Nowadays a large number of the houses in these squares have been turned into flats. One is asked to dinner by a friend who lives at the top of the house. His windows frame the crests of big plane trees. The leaves dance an endless ballet. Sometimes the head of a plane tree lurches towards the window in a showering splendour, then its green mane is flung back again. There is the agreeable sense of being in a world of one's own that one gets on a ship; here the waves are all dark green. The upward beams of the street lamps among the leaves make intricate patterns; they are always changing. To watch this play of lights and leaves is cooling on a warm evening; so it is to listen to the sea-murmurs of the tree-tops, a remote Delius kind of music. The ever-moving screen of leaves beyond the window offers a walled privacy wholly assured. We remember once again *The Club of Queer Trades*, and that arboreal house agent who let select residences in the tree-tops to persons of retiring habits. These hidden towers among the plane trees are good places for good talk. They assure a philosophic detachment—problems may be contemplated at one remove—especially when the telephone is three flights down. But women complain of the stairs. Women are seldom philosophers. And convention in London forbids our copying the sensible Continental habit of doing all our business with the outer world by letting down baskets.

It is said that more than half the trees in London are planes. They are the chief tenants of the squares. They are the ones that never move away. I have read somewhere that there is a strange element in their attachment to London, that they invaded the city two hundred and fifty years ago or so, chose it for their own and flourished in discouragement—the prime virtue of a Londoner. No other tree has such an iron constitution. London does its best to kill its best friend. London tries to poison it with soot, smoke, grime, and chemical fumes. London tries to choke it with fog. But the faithful tree lives. It has a tenacity of affection that no ill-usage can kill. The plane tree is the incorrigible Cockney. It prefers the dust and fumes of Leicester Square, the tawdriest square in London, to the valleys of the western shires. Nor is there any look of struggle to exist, of heroic survival about it. London is a bad stepmother, but the plane has nothing of the scrawniness and raggedness of a neglected child. Born and nurtured in London's dust-heaps, it grows into one of the most poetic of trees. In its grace of form, in its crowding luxuriance of leaves, it illustrates that law of life which says that beauty is unpredictable and incalculable, and is often achieved in defiance of the rules of hygiene and eugenics. Out of the grime comes the radiance.

The unconquerable Cockney tree breaks through asphalt and paved yards. It is not only the peculiar glory of the squares and parks, it thrives in dismal alleys where the hardiest old shrub turns its face to the wall and dies, and it throws out an extravagance of leaf in the smoky shafts between warehouses. On sombre days of fog it cheers Londoners by producing a dappling of visionary sunshine on its trunk, due to that shedding of the bark which is the secret of its health in our foul airs. It has a resolve to live and find the sun, such as one has known in children of the London slums. The principle of survival is in its sap. Did you ever see in one of our squares the young shoots sprouting out of the ruined sides of a plane tree that had been splintered in the blitz?

Our squares are better chroniclers of English history than are the streets of London. They bear more eloquently the traces of the changing centuries. At the side of some front doors there remain the sconces for the torches the linkboys carried. This brings back to you our ancestors' London of a perpetual black-out, and the highwayman in Hyde Park who held up Horace Walpole. The houses in an old square record, sometimes through the agency of blue L.C.C. plaques, sometimes by more subtle signs, the struggles for power, the ups and downs of society. Take this particular house—with the rich crumbliness of its brick, its look of distinguished weariness, and its long windows brilliantly streaked by the green reflections of the plane trees. It was built in the last decade of the eighteenth century. It was lived in first by a

Whig aristocrat who despised the King, and thought Tories low, ill-bred fellows. A City of London banker, an Evangelical Tory, had the house in the eighteen-twenties. A pepper merchant, with eleven children, bought it in the 'fifties; later on, a stockbroker; then a fashionable doctor, who believed in shutting windows on consumptives, lived there; next a fashionable doctor who entranced everybody by *opening* windows on consumptives. At the turn of the century it was the home of an actor-manager. In the nineteen-twenties it was a nest of intellectuals, there was discourse of James Joyce and Virginia Woolf and Aldous Huxley, Freud, Pavlov, Maynard Keynes, the Stracheys and 'the psychological implications of the quantum theory'. To-day the ground floor is occupied by a milliner; the officials of a small trade union are on the first; and, higher up, there is to be found the London agent of the Curly Corkscrews Corporation Inc. of Newark, New Jersey, next door to a Big Consultant of Big Business. It is worth turning over the editions for a century back of that fine work of erudition, the London Post Office Directory, to trace the residents of one of the squares. It is a compendium of social history. Everything changes in the squares. The plane trees remain.

NEW YORK:
SKETCH OF MEGALOPOLIS

BY JOHN GUNTHER

from *Inside U.S.A.* (1947)
(revised 1951)

NEW YORK:
SKETCH OF MEGALOPOLIS

Submit to no models but your own O city!
—WALT WHITMAN

New York is all the cities.
—W. L. GEORGE

So now we come to New York City, the incomparable, the brilliant star city of cities, the forty-ninth state, the Cyclopean paradox, the inferno with no out-of-bounds, the supreme expression of both the miseries and the splendours of contemporary civilization, the Macedonia of the United States. It meets the most severe test that may be applied to definition of a metropolis—it stays up all night. But also it becomes a small town when it rains.[1]

New York City is at once the climactic synthesis of America, and yet the negation of America in that it has so many characteristics un-American. One friend of mine, indignant because it seems impossible for any American city to develop on the pattern of Paris or Vienna, says that Manhattan is like Constantinople—not the Istanbul of old Stamboul but of the Pera or Levantine side. He meant not merely the trite fact that New York is polyglot, but that it is full of people, like the Levantines, who are interested basically in only two things, living well and making money.

Also I have heard New York characterized as nothing but 'a cluster of small islets in the North Atlantic'. These at any rate fling their lustre far. The most important single thing to say about Manhattan in relation to the rest of the United States is that it dominates what, for want of a better phrase, may be called American culture. New York is the publishing centre of the nation; it is the art, theatre, musical, ballet, operatic centre; it is the opinion centre; it is the radio and television centre; it is the style centre. Hollywood? But Hollywood often seems to be little more than a suburb of the Bronx. Politically, socially, in the world of ideas and in the whole world of entertainment, which is a great American industry needless to say, New York sets the tone and pace of the entire nation. What books 150 million Americans

[1] Forty-ninth state? In blunt fact the secession of New York City and the formation of a new state based on the municipality has often been discussed. It came forward again in October, 1949, after the Lehman-Dulles senatorial election.

will read is largely determined by New York reviewers. Most of the serious newspaper columns originate in or near New York; so do most of the gossip columns, which condition Americans from Mobile to Puget Sound to the same patterns of social behaviour. In an immense variety of fields, from serious drama to what you will hear on a jukebox, it is what New York says that counts; New York opinion is the hall mark of both intellectual and material success; to be accepted in this nation, New York acceptance must come first. I do not assert that this is necessarily a good thing. I say merely that it is true. One reason for all this is that New York, with its richly cosmopolitan population, provides such an appreciative audience. It admires artistic quality. It has a fine inward grasp of talent. Also New York is a wonderfully opulent centre for bogus culture. One of its chief industries might be said to be the manufacture of reputations, many of them fraudulent.

The field of culture or quasi-culture aside, New York City's tremendous importance has traditionally been based on four factors:

1. It was by far the greatest point of entry for European immigrants. Karl Marx, writing in the New York *Tribune* a good many years ago, predicted not only that these would come, but that the great bulk of them, having arrived, would tend to remain in the New York area.

2. It was by far the greatest American port for exports, primarily of wheat. New York was the city where people came in, and goods went out.

3. It was the financial and credit capital of the United States.

4. It was a wonderful place for residents of other American cities to visit, shop in, and throw money at.

New York has to some extent lost ground in all these categories. First, immigration was largely cut off. Second, wheat and other exports turned to other ports (though New York is still by far the biggest ocean port in the country). Third, Washington more or less replaced it as the financial capital. Fourth (though still the Number One American tourist attraction),[1] New York has lost something of its inevitableness as the place that all Americans want to see before they die.

This situation makes it clear incidentally why New York made such a fight to get the UN, and most New Yorkers applauded heartily the generosity and enterprise of the Rockefellers whereby it was finally enabled to come to Manhattan, safely tucked in between the East River and shabby old Turtle Bay.

'Little Old New York'

More than anywhere else in this book, the author must now steer tightly between Scylla and Charybdis, between saying too much and too little. How can we talk about the Statue of Liberty or Ellis Island without seeming

---

[1] 'New York is a bigger summer resort than Atlantic City and a bigger winter resort than Miami.' (Simeon Strunsky, *No Mean City.*)

ridiculously supererogatory? But how can we omit Brooklyn Bridge and still give an accurate, lively picture? One must either take the space to mention something that everybody knows everything about, or else risk omission of things that everybody will think ought certainly to be included.

Park Avenue in summer near Grand Central, a quivering asphalt shelf, and the asphalt soft, a thin layer of street separating the automobiles above from the trains below; avenues as homespun with small exquisite shops as Madison, and streets as magnificent as 57th; the fat black automobiles double-parked on Fifth Avenue on sleety afternoons; kibitzers watching strenuously to see if the man running will really catch the bus; bridges soaring and slim as needles like the George Washington; the incomparable moment at dusk when the edges of tall buildings melt invisibly into the sky, so that nothing of them can be seen except the lighted windows; the ravishingly pretty girls in their ravishingly pretty dresses under the marquees of the great apartment buildings, waiting for taxis at seven in the evening; how the avenues will be cleared of snow and actually dry a day after a six-inch fall, while the side streets are still banked solid with sticky drifts; how the noon sun makes luminous spots on the rounded tops of automobiles, crowded together on the slope of Park Avenue so that they look like seashells—all this is too familiar to bear mention.

Manhattan was discovered by Henry Hudson in 1609, and bought from the Indians for $25 in 1626. Not so well known are such details as that the city's flag still bears the Dutch royal colours (orange, white, and blue), and that, in 1811, it was decided that only three sides of the City Hall need be finished, since surely there would be no more movement of the city northward. Of course New York has been pushing outwards like a swarm of bees ever since, and not merely to the north. It covers 365.4 square miles to-day; it has upwards of 5,700 miles of streets.

As of 1950 the population of New York City within city limits was 7,835,099. Only two states, Pennsylvania and California (aside from New York state itself), contain more people; of the seventy-five nations in the world, it has a greater population than forty-one; it has more people than the whole of Canada. By 1970, according to census estimates, the population will have risen to 8,500,000; after 1980, along with that of the rest of the country, it is expected to decline. These figures refer to city limits only. In 1950 the New York 'metropolitan district' actually held 12,831,914 people, making the area by all odds the greatest urban concentration the world has ever known. Newark and Jersey City are, to all intents and purposes except politically, subdivisions of Manhattan; I have heard a Pennsylvanian say that even Scranton was 'part of New York'; speaking in the broadest way, 'New York' includes the whole regions from Bridgeport to Trenton and beyond.

The best remark I know in the field of racial fusions is from Bryce, that

New York 'is a European city, but of no particular country'. He might of course have said, 'but of many countries'. Details are well known. For instance *two hundred* newspapers not in English are published in New York; they appear in fifteen foreign languages. More than two million New Yorkers are foreign born; more than two and a half million others are of foreign or mixed parentage. Of the foreign-born the largest group is Italian (more than 400,000), followed closely by Russian (395,000), and with Germans (225,000), Poles (195,000), and Irish (160,000) next. Those of mixed parentage follow the same order. There are 28,593 Greeks, some 25,000 Czechs, and 12,000 Chinese. All told there are representatives of at least seventy nationalities in New York, from Bulgarians to Yemenites. Cutting across national categories are the Jews, of whom the city has about two million; New York is overwhelmingly the first Jewish city in the world.

Hamilton Fish Armstrong, writing in *Foreign Affairs*, once had some illuminating things to say about the New York potpourri. One is that, in spite of all that has been added, the basic Anglo-Dutch stock still gives marked coloration to the city. Another is that New York's conglomerateness dates from the very beginning, and has given it a tolerance unmatched by any other American city except one much smaller, San Francisco. From the early Du Ponts to Otto Habsburg, from Leon Trotsky to Haya de la Torre, Manhattan has been traditionally generous to refugees. It has a cosmopolitanism of the mind as well as pocket. It may be built on islands, but it is not insular.

New York has religions in profusion too. It is a strong Roman Catholic and Episcopalian as well as Jewish city. It is the headquarters of the Collegiate Reformed Protestant Dutch church, and it has a powerful upper sprinkling of Christian Scientists. The best surface indication of the importance of religion in New York is real estate. Stroll down Fifth Avenue. In block after patrician block are churches of various denominations occupying sites of the most prodigious value. Or—as an instance of the influence of religion in another secular field—consider Christmas shopping.

It is a proud boast of New York that, what with its enormous pools of foreign-born, any article or object known in the world may be found there. You can buy anything from Malabar spices to Shakespeare folios. A stall on Seventh Avenue sells about a hundred different varieties of razor blades. Also it is incomparably the greatest manufacturing town on earth; in an average year it produces goods valued at more than four billion dollars. It houses no fewer than 237,000 different business establishments and 36,000 different industrial concerns, representing more than 312 different manufactures—even if you can see deer in Westchester twenty miles away. Also it is by far the first city in the nation in the service industries. Manhattan alone employs more wage earners than Detroit and Cleveland put together; Brooklyn more than Boston and Baltimore put together; Queens more than

Washington and Pittsburgh put together.[1] The three most important New York industries are the garment trade, printing, and foodstuff. To attempt to describe Manhattan without at least one mention of the Garment Centre is impossible. Mammoth trucks choke the streets between 34th and 38th, and men on foot push through the crowds with their movable racks hung with clothes. The Garment Centre means also that New York has two of the most powerful unions in the country, the Amalgamated Clothing Workers which was Sidney Hillman's union, and the International Ladies Garment Workers Union run by as able a man as American labour knows, David Dubinsky. This union has elaborate extracurricular activities, like its famous summer camps. Once it produced a musical comedy, *Pins and Needles*, that became a Broadway hit.

In *Inside Asia* I had a small passage describing the variety of strange occupations in India, like grasshopper selling. I have just thumbed through the classified New York telephone directory, a volume 1,898 pages long. Among occupations in New York are cinders, chenille dotting, bullet-proof protective equipment, breast pumps, bungs, boiler baffles, glue room equipment, abattoirs, flow meters, eschatology, mildew-proofing, pompons, potato chip machinery, rennet, spangles, solenoids, and spats. Also this book contains literally twenty-two columns of associations of one kind or another.

Items in Physiognomy

Well, little old Noisyville-on-the-Subway is good enough for me.
—O. HENRY

New York is divided into five counties called boroughs. The extraordinary tongue of MANHATTAN is only 12½ miles long and 2½ miles wide, but it contained 1,936,540 people in 1950. It has twenty bridges, roughly 100,000 out-of-town visitors a day, more than 1,000 night-clubs, Columbia University, the Polo Grounds, and Central Park, which many people think is the most satisfactory park in the world, with its 840 acres spread out like a carpet for the skyscrapers to tiptoe up to. It has colossal new housing projects like Peter Cooper Village and Stuyvesant Town, and subdivisions as divergent as the Gas House District, Hell's Kitchen and Greenwich Village.

BROOKLYN (population 2,716,347) is a world in itself, with a fierce local nationalism, the Dodgers, the Bush Terminal, and Coney Island. Geographically Brooklyn, which was once spelled Bruekelen, is the huge, bumpy, watery 'head and shoulders' of Long Island. It covers 88.8 square miles; merely to list its street names takes 192 pages in a pocket guide. It delivers the biggest Democratic vote in the nation, speaks a patois all its own, and was

---

[1] New York *Herald Tribune*, 21 June 1945, quoting *A Survey of the New York Market* published by the Consolidated Edison Company.

the original habitat of Murder, Inc. Brooklyn has more people than thirty-one states, and it is the home of the fourth largest savings bank in the country. It has been the home of some remarkable writers, from Walt Whitman to Arthur Miller, and its borough president, John Cashmore, who was once a newsboy and who is one of New York's six 'mayors', is a powerful force in pan-New York political affairs.

The BRONX, which borders on Westchester County and is the only borough on the mainland, covers 54.4 square miles and has 1,444,903 people. It is heavily Jewish like Brooklyn, and likewise a great community for baseball, having the Yankee Stadium; it contains sub-Bronxes like Throg's Neck, Clason's Point, and Mott Haven. It has its own flag, a well-known zoo, the Hall of Fame of New York University, ten farms within the borough limits, and seven hundred miles of streets; for a proud interval it called itself the capital of the world, when the UN sat temporarily at Hunter College.

In the Bronx, one might say in parenthesis, live two notable New York politicians, Edward J. Flynn and Michael J. Quill. Mr. Flynn, its boss for many years, has craggy importance on the national level too; he is a former chairman of the Democratic National Committee, and FDR once named him ambassador to Australia. He was rejected by the Senate, however, because some Belgian paving blocks got found in the wrong place. Of all the American municipal viceroys, Flynn is the most superior, the most civilized and cultivated man. Mr. Quill is on the left-wing side of the political fence. He was born in County Kerry in 1905, and was a soldier in the Irish Republican Army; he came to New York, got a job as a subway worker, and is now head of the powerful Transport Workers Union.

QUEENS, the biggest borough in area (120.6 square miles), has 1,546,294 people; thus it is the fourth subdivision of New York City to be greater in population than any American *city* except Chicago, Los Angeles, Detroit, and Philadelphia. Probably Queens is the most diffuse of the boroughs, the least distinctive. It has Idlewild, La Guardia Field and Forest Hills, the tennis capital of America; it has 196 miles of waterfront and relentlessly unending rows of ugly small houses; in Queens, as well as anywhere in the country, you may see how a great city frays at the periphery; no community has more untidy edges.[1]

Finally, RICHMOND (population 191,015) which is another world in itself, Staten Island. A curious community, half an hour away by boat, Richmond has only one vote out of sixteen in the Board of Estimate (the governing body of New York City); this it resents, and occasionally it threatens to

---

[1] When this book first appeared furious letters descended on me as the result of this paragraph. One mentions the 'silly, useless, cruel slur against a great community, combined with untruth, false implication and plain malice. The outside edges of Queens are not untidy. Hundreds of thousands of families have come to Queens to attain ownership of their homes. It has more detached houses, with more dwelling windows, than all the other boroughs.'

secede. Garibaldi lived on Staten Island once, and the community has an excellent institution of learning in Wagner College.

New York: Neighbourhoods and Spectacle

The city like a ragged purple dream, the wonderful, cruel, enchanting, bewildering, fatal, great city.
                                                                    —O. HENRY

A point to make now is New York's extreme brittleness, its vulnerability. As fascinating as any story in America is how it gets its water; the supply system represents an investment of two billion dollars, and some water comes from points at least a hundred miles away. What might a small bomb or two, at any of several strategic points, do to this enterprise? Also the city's life depends on water in another direction, that is, on the bridges and tunnels by which water is traversed. New York learned grimly about its vulnerability in this respect during a tugboat strike in 1946. A handful of 3,500 workers, manning three hundred tugboats, paralysed the city from stem to stern; the entire Atlantean metropolis was forced to shut down for 16 hours. Most neutral observers thought that the operators had as grave, if not a graver, responsibility for this strike than the AF of L workers who struck; but this is beside the point. What counted (and could count again) is that the city, without these tugboats, cannot live. New York uses about 34,500,000 pounds of food a day, 98,000 tons of coal, and 4,000,000 gallons of oil, which help provide its gas, steam, and electricity. Seventy per cent of all this is moved by tugs and barges. Consider too elevator strikes; a brief one occurred recently. New York City has more than 43,000 elevators (about 20 per cent of all in the entire country), which carry about 17,500,000 passengers daily. Their shafts, put end to end, would stretch 1,600 miles; they go halfway to the moon, 125,000 miles, every day. When the elevators stop, New York stops too.[1]

At the Manhattan skyscrapers, every name in the book has been thrown. They have been called 'the inconceivable spires of Manhattan, repeating the upthrust torch of Liberty', 'gypsum crystals', 'a mass of stalagmites', 'a ship of living stone', 'an irregular tableland intersected by shadowy canyons', 'dividends in the sky', 'a giant cromlech', and, best of all, 'a pincushion'.[2] A more utilitarian-minded description is one by H. G. Wells; the skyscrapers reminded him irresistibly of the commercial nature of our civilization, being like 'piled-up packing cases outside a warehouse'.

[1] These figures are from the New York *Times*, 30 September 1945, and 10 February 1946. A remarkable point is the safety record of the New York elevators. The ratio is one person killed to 196,000,000 carried.

[2] These phrases are from a brilliant essay on New York by Vincent McHugh. It was originally published in New York City volume of the WPA series, and was later reprinted by Clifton Fadiman in his anthology, *Reading I've Liked*.

Perhaps we should have another word on water supply, and, if only space permitted, on the bizarre configuration of underground New York, with its tubes carrying not only water but steam, sewage, electric power, railroad trains, gas, automobiles, mail, and telegrams. 'The most complicated and expensive thing ever built is Manhattan Island,' *Life* wrote recently in a stimulating pictorial essay. 'Under its asphalt skin are 12,100 miles of power cable, more than four million miles of telephone wire, 27 miles of pneumatic tubes to speed mail at thirty miles per hour, 54 miles of steam mains that heat a seventh of the island's 67,601 structures, 1,200 miles of gas mains, 774 miles of cavernous water mains (plus a water tunnel) to supply what the city needs daily, and 560 miles of sewer to carry it off.' Residents of Manhattan will recall the recent scare over water shortage, and the efforts made to ameliorate a situation that could easily have become uncomfortable, if not dangerous. Normally New Yorkers use about 1,200,000,000 gallons of water per day, about half of which goes to domestic consumers, half to industry. Lack of rain dried up the reservoirs. A campaign began to check waste (about one-sixth of the total water supply is wasted every day) and curtail use—public drinking fountains were shut off and restaurants served water only on request—until the rains came again and the crisis wore off.

A related subject, snow, also provides New York with drama on occasion. In Christmas week, 1947, came one of the most ponderous snowfalls in the city's history. The gigantic metropolis was, for a day or two, prostrate, inert, and almost helpless. More than 25 inches of snow fell in a few hours; the cost of removing it came to more than six million dollars, or $225,000 per inch. It took 35,000 men to do the job. Snow of a different sort—ticker tape and torn up telephone books—is a distinguishing mark of New York's municipal parades. For General MacArthur, in April 1951, a record of 2,850 tons of paper fell on the Manhattan streets; this beat anything ever known before. Howard Hughes got only 1,800 tons, Lindbergh, 1,750, Admiral Nimitz 274, and General Eisenhower 77. (But the Eisenhower demonstration took place in June 1945, in the days of acute paper shortage, and the citizenry had been urged not to make a mess.) Winston Churchill, in March 1946, got 50 tons.

Dirt, litter, sewage, street cleaning—all these are major problems in New York as they must be in any sizable metropolis. New York has been called the dirtiest important city in the world, even though it spends something like $50,000,000 per year to keep itself clean. Hardly a day passes without stories in the papers to the effect that some Bronx housewife has been fined $20 for tossing garbage out of a window; recently, in a single building, 216 violations in the health code were discovered. One factor making for untidiness is that there are 188,000 vacant lots, over which the Department of Sanitation has no jurisdiction; another is 'trade waste', or the enormous accumulation of empty crates and cartons that have to be hauled away by private truckers every day. An estimated number of 8,000,000 rats live in New York City, who cause damage that may reach $45,000,000 per year. There were 673 cases of rat bites on human beings in 1950, and a rat control committee under the commissioner of health is functioning.[1]

No city changes so quickly as New York; none has so short a memory or is so heartless to itself; it has an inhuman quality. Few New Yorkers pay the slightest attention to the historical monuments that fill the city, and most know very little about its wonders. How many ever recall that Theodore Roosevelt was born at 26 East 20th Street, or that the oldest building in the city is on Peck Slip, or even that a three-million-dollar treasure ship is supposed to be lying in the East River near 53rd Street? My publisher lives in the east 30's. I had been in his delightful house fifty times before I learned that James Monroe had once lived in it.

Glance at Baedeker's *United States* of 1893. To what sights does this worthy guide give its severely rationed stars? What was the 1893 equivalent of Rockefeller Centre? Let the reader go to the public library and find out. But as to other details the midtown hotels starred are the Everett House, the Westminster, and the Windsor. ('Fees to waiters and bellboys are unfortunately becoming more and more customary in New York hotels.') The first uptown restaurant starred is the Café Brunswick; the chief 'oyster saloon' is Dorlon's; the first theatre mentioned is Daly's ('Shakespearean and modern comedy—Miss Ada Rehan'). As to shops, Baedeker says, 'Many of the New York shops are very large and handsome, easily bearing comparison with those of Europe.' As to baths it mentions that 'hot and cold baths may be obtained at all the hotels (25c–75c) and large barber shops.'[2]

One extraordinary phenomenon all over New York is its unequal rate of growth. On one side of a courtyard in the east 60's is a glittering modern apartment house where, I doubt not, you could find a tolerable small place to live for a rental of $5,000 a year. On the other side, not fifty feet away, is a dirty balcony hung with laundry, part of a frowsy tenement built over squalid shops. Recently I lunched in an exquisitely ornate suite in the Hotel St. Regis. Across the narrow canyon of 55th Street I could watch hurried seamstresses at work for wages that would not have paid the headwaiter's tip.

I live in midtown Manhattan; I have just walked around the block to see concretely what illimitable variety this single neighbourhood affords. Within a hundred yards I can go to church, have my hair cut, buy some flowers, attend an auction, order plumbing material, visit two banks (both

---

[1] Also New York has approximately 10,000 cases of food poisoning per year. See recent stories in the New York *Post* by Charles Abrams, and an article in the New York *Herald Tribune*, by Ben Price, 6 July 1949.

[2] Another item is that the average Englishman will find offensive the American habit of spitting on the floor, but that the Americans are now keenly alive to this 'weak point' and are 'doing their best' to remove it.

low Georgian buildings in red brick), and dine in one of the supreme restaurants of the world or at Hamburg Heaven. Within a slightly greater radius I can buy a Cézanne ($55,000), a chukar partridge ($7.50), a pound of Russian caviar ($28), or a copy of the Civil Service *Leader* (5c). Within two hundred yards are three competing pharmacies comfortably busy, a shop for religious goods and missals, a delicatessen squeezed into a four-foot frontage, a toupee and postiche shop, windows full of the most ornately superior English saddlery, a podiatrist, a good French bookstore, a cheap shoe shine parlour, the most expensive butcher store in the world, a Sport-of-the-Month Club, and, of course, the inevitable small stationery shop with its broad red band across the window advertising a variety of cigar.

New York is so volatile, so diffuse, that it no longer has recognizable social frontiers; it is too big a community to be a community. As *Fortune* once observed, even the greater millionaires no longer live in houses for the most part, but in apartments; the *Social Register* contains upward of 27,000 names. Fifty years ago the '400' constituted a genuine enough inner nucleus. To-day practically anybody who can buy a drink at 'Twenty-One' or be seen in the Club Room of the Stork Club is a member of society, because the criterion is no longer merely wealth or lineage. It is not Mrs. Vanderbilt who draws attention at the opera; it is a visiting movie star. Nor does it matter much nowadays where people live; anybody who has the money can buy a house in the east 70's (if he can find the house). People shoot up; people shoot down. Ask any New Yorker to list the dozen leading citizens of the town. The variety of names you will get is astonishing.

Also New York is the crime capital of the world; its criminal aristocracy may have its ups and downs, and the names of the more celebrated of the élite may change (Louis Lepke has been electrocuted, and Lucky Luciano was packed off to Italy), but the Kefauver investigation and the able recent work of District Attorneys Hogan and McDonald proved once for all, if any proof were needed, how tenaciously crime bites into almost every phase of the city's life. Mr. Costello may have been embarrassed on the witness stand, but he is still a fragrant power. New York spent $102,031,389 on the police department in 1949. In that year there were 296 homicides, 14,229 other felonies, and a total of 963,795 criminal arrests. Some wonderful things happen in the realm of New York crime. In what other city would the mayor himself charge that his own telephone wires were tapped? In what other city would a large sign be posted in a downtown window, '$1,000 Reward for Anyone Killed While Robbing This Office!'

Finally, let us list the chief New York issues to-day, political, semi-political, and otherwise. First, traffic. The violent snarled congestion in bursting streets costs the city at least a million dollars a day. Second, housing. Authorities estimate that it has an 'absolute shortage' of 150,000 apartments, which means that about 500,000 people are living 'under the crudest and most difficult conditions'. Another estimate is that 450,000 families, or roughly one-fifth of the total population, live in 'subhuman' tenements or houses. Third, gambling, political corruption, and police reform.

'Go East, Young Man'

New York City sucks in humanity from all over the world, as it sucks in Louisiana prawns and Idaho potatoes. This city, a parasite, would die without new blood. New Yorkers born in New York City are, as is notorious, rare. Consider some distinguished citizens in various fields and where they came from. John J. McCloy, the high commissioner to Germany, was born in Philadelphia, Judge Sam Rosenman in San Antonio, Herbert Bayard Swope in St. Louis, and Gustav Metzman, president of the New York Central, in Baltimore. Henry R. Luce was born in China, Elsa Maxwell in Iowa, and Judge Learned Hand in Albany. Harold Ross, editor of the *New Yorker*, comes from Aspen, Colorado, and Lewis W. Douglas from Bisbee, Arizona. H. V. Kaltenborn was born in Wisconsin, George Jean Nathan in Indiana, Bruce Bliven of the *New Republic* in Iowa, and Winthrop W. Aldrich, probably the most important banker in the city, in Rhode Island. The Van Doren literary family derives from Illinois, Albert D. Lasker from Texas, and Mrs. Ogden Reid of the *Herald Tribune* from Wisconsin. Walter S. Gifford, ambassador to England, was born in Massachusetts, Sherman Billingsley in Oklahoma, John W. Davis in West Virginia, and Arturo Toscanini in Parma, Italy. There are, of course, a few exceptions. Robert I. Gannon, president of Fordham University, was born on Staten Island, and former comptroller Joseph D. McGoldrick in Brooklyn. Born actually in Manhattan are Gilbert Miller, the theatrical producer, Arthur H. Sulzberger, publisher of the New York *Times*, Hamilton Fish Armstrong, and Charles G. Bolté, the brilliant young chairman of the American Veterans' Committee.

City Hall and Kefauver Committee

Countless times in this book we have mentioned people with a great variety of experience, but I know none who quite matches the former mayor, Bill O'Dwyer (later envoy to Mexico) for abundance in this respect. He was born in 1890 in County Mayo, Ireland, one of eleven children; both his parents were schoolteachers.[1] He ran off to Spain when a boy, and studied for two years with the Jesuits at the University of Salamanca; he planned to be a priest. But he changed his mind, took ship for New York, and arrived

---

[1] Two of his brothers, who also emigrated to America, met violent deaths; one, John, was killed by gunmen in a Brooklyn holdup some years ago; another, James, a New York City fireman, lost his life while answering a false alarm.

here in 1910, twenty years old, with $23.35 in his pocket. In the next few years he held every possible sort of job. First he became a handyman in a Bronx grocery at $9 a week; then he worked as a deckhand on a freighter in the South American trade, as a stoker, and later as a fireman on the river boats between New York and Albany. Meantime, he studied stenography at night school. He had a turn as a hod carrier and plasterer's apprentice, working on a building near Maiden Lane, and he still holds his membership in the Plasterers Helpers Union, AF of L. Also—it pleases him to recall this now—he was a bartender for a brief elegant period in the Hotel Plaza.

Then O'Dwyer decided to become a cop. He had been granted United States citizenship in 1916, and he joined the New York police department a year later. The fact that he was a policeman has considerable importance. At least it should have taught him to know cops. One can talk about issues and involvements like housing, subways, or what you will, but basically the mayor of any great American city stands or falls by his police department. Any time a police department, through corruption or otherwise, chooses to embarrass a mayor by lying down on the job, the mayor is beaten. There are 19,000 policemen in New York City, and it is no easy thing to keep that many men, who may be continuously exposed to temptation, honest all the time, especially if there is no honesty at the top. The average New York cop gets $3,420 a year. The police have nice distinctions in graft. Gambling money, so the legend goes, is 'clean'; vice money is, however, dirty. The terrific difficulty of dealing with gambling may be illustrated by one small point, that at Mr. La Guardia's request the Stock and Curb exchanges for a brief time published no daily sales totals except in round numbers, so that the tens of thousands of people in the 'policy' racket couldn't use the last digits as the basis for their calculations.

O'Dwyer's political career may be outlined briefly. He went to law school at night, and in 1932 was appointed a city magistrate, which meant that he was politically 'right'. Governor Lehman promoted him to the county court in 1938; later he won an election to a fourteen-year term on this bench. This was a well-paid job, and he could have looked forward to security and a pleasant routine existence for years. He dropped it the next year, however, to run for the district attorneyship of Kings County, and won. His record as a prosecutor makes a highly contentious subject still. He broke up Murder, Inc., more or less, and ended the wholesale killings on the Brooklyn waterfront, but much that is unsavoury—like the Reles case—is on the record. In 1941, O'Dwyer ran for mayor; La Guardia beat him. After the war, in 1945, he ran again and won—there were some highly special circumstances connected with this election—with an absolute majority of 285,000 and the biggest plurality in the history of the city. Thus he reached what is generally considered to be the second biggest and most difficult political job in the

United States, and he had the nice numerical luck to be the one hundredth elected mayor in New York City history.

I went down to the City Hall and had an hour with O'Dwyer shortly after he became mayor. He wore a light brown sports jacket; he was as relaxed—working a fourteen-hour day—as a character in the *Crock of Gold*. He was full of Irish wit, modesty, and bounce. Mostly we talked about things personal, But occasionally there were remarks like, 'How the hell *does* democracy work, anyhow?' He is a gregarious man, and loves people; especially he loves those who have fought their way out of a bad environment. What he hates most are stuffy people. ('I am sorry for the selfish ones; they only see one side.') I asked him how he took the load off. 'A thousand ways!' Then suddenly Mr. O'Dwyer was reminiscing about his childhood. 'It was all a series of breaks . . . you know how rebellious Irish kids are . . . and everybody yearning for a piece of poetry.' He wanted to be a doctor. Medicine, the mysterious agencies of disease, the world of pain, fascinated him, and he was bursting with humanity for the sick, although 'healthy as a trout' himself. To contribute to that field, he thought, would be something. 'What is it that makes people happy? To contribute!' He couldn't afford the long years of schooling that medicine entailed; he chose the law as the next best thing. 'When a guy gets along in his twenties he begins to get uneasy; people stare at themselves, and know that they'll be sore as hell at life at sixty if they don't do something to improve themselves.' He asked himself, while he was still a cop on a beat, 'Is life just a process of eating and destroying food?' The urge to get ahead stirred him, as he put it, 'like a bug on an elephant's tail'. And to do something for the little fellow.

A word now on the 1945 mayoralty election that first brought O'Dwyer in. Of all crazy elections in the history of New York City, this was one of the craziest. He was the candidate of both the Democratic and American Labour parties, which was interpreted by anti-O'Dwyer folk as meaning that he was the candidate of (*a*) Tammany and (*b*) the Communists, unnatural as this coalition may seem. Of course O'Dwyer is about as Communistic as Saint Peter. In the old Brooklyn days the Christian Front boys vociferously sided with him for the most part. Nevertheless, he was bracketed with Vito Marcantonio, vehemently left-winger leader of the ALP. O'Dwyer, a good vote-getter with a good record, was obviously going to be a hard man to beat. After ponderous deliberations (in which Governor Dewey shared) the Republicans chose a judge of the general sessions court, Jonah J. Goldstein, to run against him.[1] This was in part a device to catch the Jewish vote which is roughly 30 per cent of the total city vote as a rule. The only trouble with Judge Goldstein was that he was a Democrat! This fact may not be believed but it is true. Judge Goldstein, the Republican candidate to beat O'Dwyer, was a member of the Democratic party until the night before the nomination.

[1] Not to be confused with Attorney General Goldstein.

Meantime, much finagling had been going on in higher reaches of the
Democratic party too—Hannegan and Flynn both played a role. O'Dwyer
would not consent to run until after a stiff fight with Flynn, who wanted to
put people on the slate he would not have. Finally O'Dwyer (Democrat-
ALP) and Goldstein (Republican but a Democrat) squared off against one
another. Also behind Goldstein were the Fusion and the Liberal parties—
which, however, were not parties. All seemed simple. Then entered a new
and disruptive factor—the Little Flower. Previously Mr. LaGuardia had
announced the names of a dozen people who he thought would make good
mayors and whom he would support, among them Adolf A. Berle Jr., Lewis
W. Douglas, Robert Moses, Gordon S. Rentschler, chairman of the board
of the National City Bank, General Brehon Somervell, and Newbold
Morris, then president of the City Council. Now Mr. Morris (an able and
amiable man, about whom the crude witticism was spread that he had been
born with a silver foot in his mouth) decided to enter the race himself. This
made the struggle triangular. LaGuardia vigorously supported Morris, who
ran as a 'No Deal' candidate. He knew of course that this would split the
opposition, and help elect O'Dwyer; the only explanation is that (though in
theory a Republican himself and a mortal foe of Tammany) LaGuardia disliked the Dewey-Goldstein brand of Republicanism so much that he was
willing to see a Tammany Democrat elected. O'Dwyer would have won
anyway. Nevertheless, Morris's candidacy did what Mr. LaGuardia hoped it
would do, and the New York *Herald Tribune* was soon writing that the
fundamental reason why William O'Dwyer became mayor was that Mr.
LaGuardia willed it.[1]

What happened in the elections of 1949 and 1950 we have already discussed. The year 1951 brought new and formidable trials to the bland
O'Dwyer. Millions of citizens rocked, roared, or became stupefied as the
Kefauver hearings, sharpened and magnified by the incredible instrument of
television, put him under scrutiny without mercy.

One highlight was testimony from O'Dwyer about his visit to the illus-
trious Costello, gambling and underworld czar, in 1942. O'Dwyer 'had no
idea' why the leader of Tammany Hall and other eminent personages in
New York City politics happened to be present at the same conference. It
was 'just a coincidence'. Another was the revelation that O'Dwyer appointees
like Frank Quayle, the former fire commissioner, were friends of gritty
hoodlums like Joe Adonis. Above all, there came the conflicting stories of
Mr. O'Dwyer and John P. Crane, president of the Uniformed Firemen's
Association.

[1] A minor but illuminating item is the way the New York newspapers lined up during this
campaign. The *Times* backed Morris; so did the *Post*. *PM* supported O'Dwyer until a day or
two before the election and then switched to Morris. The Brooklyn *Eagle* supported O'Dwyer
and so did the *Daily Worker*. Supporting Goldstein were the *Herald-Tribune*, the *World-Telegram*,
and the *Sun*. What line the *News*, *Mirror*, and *Journal-American* took was difficult to figure out.

O'Dwyer was questioned as follows:

Q. Do you know John P. Crane?
A. I do.
Q. Did you have occasion to be visited by him in connection with business relating to the Firemen's Association?
A. Yes.
Q. Did he in 1949 ever visit you at the Gracie Mansion?
A. It's possible.
Q. Did he ever come alone?
A. I never recall him coming alone; no definite recollection about it, except that they were always planning to get things for their union. They made a lot of trouble.
Q. Do you know whether Crane ever made any campaign contributions?
A. I don't know.
Q. Did he ever make any to or through you?
A. He did not.

Then came Crane, who said promptly, 'I met O'Dwyer on the porch of Gracie Mansion some time around 12 October 1949'.

Q. Were you alone with him?
A. Yes, sir.
Q. Will you tell the committee what transpired?
A. I told the Mayor at that time that I had promised him the support of the firemen and I offered him some evidence of that support on the occasion, in the form of $10,000.
Q. Was that in cash?
A. That was in cash.
Q. Did he say anything?
A. He thanked me. He didn't look in the envelope or anything else.

Crane said the cash was in a red manila envelope. He never received any acknowledgment or receipt.

Somebody, it was obvious, was committing perjury. Why, the innocent may ask, should city firemen want to present gifts, as campaign contributions or otherwise, to the mayor? Because they needed his 'goodwill'. Firemen in New York are at the mercy of City Hall—also Albany—for salary increases and the like. Mr. Crane stated that, in addition to the $10,000 to O'Dwyer, he gave $55,000 to James J. Moran, one of the mayor's closest friends, who had been appointed by him to a life job as commissioner of water supply, just before he (O'Dwyer) stepped out of office. Crane was as a result suspended from his job as international vice president of the International Association of Fire Fighters (AF of L), and Moran was forced to resign his office by the new mayor, Mr. Impellitteri. Mr. O'Dwyer is, however, (as of the moment of writing) still ambassador to Mexico.

Judge Samuel Leibowitz of the Kings County Court, a picturesque figure, stated before the Kefauver committee in Washington that gamblers paid between $20,000,000 and $25,000,000 per year to New York City policemen for protection, and that the graft went 'right to City Hall'. On the same day J. Edgar Hoover, director of the FBI, said that if state and local laws were strictly enforced 'gambling could be wiped out in the United States within forty-eight hours'.

Next to O'Dwyer and the ineffable Virginia Hill, the star Kefauver witness was Costello himself. This prosperous hoodlum is sixty. The pattern is familiar—a desperately petty gangster, by playing politics, got rich; then, towed by greed, he expanded his operations so widely that trouble came. Costello's real name is Francisco Castiglia, and he arrived on American shores at the age of four. He was arrested for assault and robbery at the age of seventeen, and once spent a brief term in jail. He became a gun-toter and bootlegger in the 20's, and then branched into slot machines, horse-racing, real estate, politics, and major gambling. He refused (of course) to tell the Kefauver committee his total wealth. His political interrelations were such that (as in the Aurelio case) he was able to arrange for the appointment of an important judge; he became the king of what was virtually an invisible government, based on crime and and fraud. 'He arranged for the ouster of Hugo Rogers as leader of Tammany Hall, and for the selection of Carmine G. DeSapio as his successor,' the New York *Times* has written frankly. Whether full retribution will ever come to Mr. Costello, is, as these pages go to press, unknown. Senator Kefauver said that he is 'a right cunning fellow'. But he has not found the past few months very comfortable.

As to O'Dwyer the Kefauver report states flatly that he contributed directly and indirectly 'to the growth of organized crime, racketeering, and gangsterism in New York City'. Both as mayor of New York and earlier as district attorney of Brooklyn, 'neither he nor his appointees took effective action against the top echelons of the gambling, narcotics, waterfront, murder, or bookmaking rackets'. Further, as summarized by the New York *Times*, the committee decided:

1. That while Mr. O'Dwyer, as Brooklyn prosecutor, had broken up Murder, Inc., he never touched, by indictment or prosecution, the six men he himself had told a grand jury in 1945 were the big bosses of the crime combination, Adonis, Bugsey Siegel, Lansky, Abner Zwillman, William Moretti, and Charles (Lucky Luciano) Lucania, all of whom were friends of Costello.

2. That Mr. O'Dwyer found various reasons for not prosecuting Albert Anastasia, waterfront racketeer, until after the principal witness against

Anastasia, Abe Reles, was killed by an unexplained fall from a window while in protective custody of the police.

3. That Mr. O'Dwyer, as mayor, made various gestures in the direction of suppressing illegal bookmaking, but . . . that nothing ever came of them.

4. That Mr. O'Dwyer constantly denounced Tammany Hall and Costello, but never told the public he had gone to Costello 'for aid in war contracts frauds', and had met Michael J. Kennedy Jr., then leader of Tammany Hall, at Costello's apartment on that occasion.

Fabulous numbers of television viewers, radio listeners, and newspaper readers were fascinated to satiety by the Kefauver sessions. But not so many demanded answers to the questions that should have been on every lip. What has happened to public morality in this country? Why do people stand for what is going on? What can the ordinary citizen do to break up the alliance between crime and politics? Another question concerned the propriety of television hearings. Mr. Costello won the sympathy of thousands when he refused to allow the cameras to photograph his face. Whether any committee, investigating a witness who may turn out to be perfectly innocent, has the right to force him to sit for hour after hour before a blazing battery of cameras, is a debatable point. Senator Kefauver himself has conceded this, and hopes to bring the whole subject to congressional attention.

Mr. O'Dwyer returned to Mexico when the hearings were concluded; on publication of the committee's report he stated that the charges against him were 'fantastic'.

Tiger and Impellitteri

A reformer is a guy who rides through a sewer in a glass-bottomed boat.
—THE LATE JAMES J. WALKER

Of various puppets and ephemeral riffraff in New York City politics this book tells nothing. Nor have we the space to mention here how New York (just like a village) has red signs near the polls telling people not to loiter, how Fusion is not something that you can call up on the telephone, how the Greater New York City Charter was first set up and how the city has a triple central government the interrelations of which can only be calculated by a slide rule, and how the Liberal party broke off from the American Labour party (the father of which was Mr. LaGuardia) after a vicious left-right split.

But about the institution known as Tammany and its camorra we must, if only for the record, have a brief line. Actually Tammany goes back into American history as far as the federal government itself. One of its founders was Aaron Burr, and it was a quite worthy organization in older days. Bob Wagner and Al Smith both came out of Tammany. It was the first classic example of the American political machine, and its role was indispensable and orthodox—that of being a bridge between the newly arrived immigrant and citizenship. It taught him how to vote and for whom. Also it rendered real service. If Sally Snooks of West 98th Street got measles, the district leader saw to it that she was taken care of. Tammany purveyed help, if not justice. Whether or not the corner cop would let your youngster play under the water hydrant on a hot day depended on Tammany. It could do anything for a man from granting a bus franchise to a suspension of sentence for a serious crime; whether or not you could build a skyscraper—and how cheaply or expensively—or a chicken coop, depended on the Tiger.

Then, after a long period of satiety and deliquescence, came the crushing blows of twenty years ago. Judge Seabury demonstrated that it was extremely unwise for politicians to maintain safety deposit boxes with big amounts of cash in New York City. James J. Walker resigned as mayor rather than be forced out of office by Mr. Roosevelt, and the great days of Tammany were over for the time being.

Aside from scandals and witness leadership two other factors contributed to this loss of prestige and power:

1. The movement of people out of Manhattan itself into Brooklyn and the Bronx. Tammany is the Democratic machine in Manhattan *only*.

2. The New Deal. Tammany favours were small stuff compared to public works through the WPA. These latter, moreover, were administered honestly.

Tammany's leader at the moment, who is also chairman of the New York County Democratic committee, is Carmine G. DeSapio. It was he, along with Ed Flynn, the Bronx suzerain and national committeeman, and Paul E. Fitzpatrick, the state chairman, who created the ill-fated Lynch-Pecora slate in 1950. The defection of Mr. Impellitteri, followed by his victory, caused a profound—but possibly temporary—schism within Democratic ranks. Impellitteri, immediately after his election, appointed Frank J. Sampson, a former head of Tammany, as his administrative assistant in charge of patronage (Sampson had bolted Tammany to back Impellitteri in the campaign) and a pungent struggle began—as has so often happened in New York—for control of the organization. DeSapio meantime sought to close ranks, clean up, and in particular deny that Costello or other racketeers had any controlling influence on the appointment of officials and the like.

Mr. Impellitteri, the new mayor, was born in Sicily in 1900, the son of a village cobbler. He came to this country as an infant, went to parochial school, and joined the Navy in World War I. He went to Fordham law school by day, worked as a bellhop by night, and then became night manager of a west side hotel until he got his degree. He practised law for a time—his wife, incidentally, worked as a secretary in a legal firm for twenty-two years until he was inaugurated as mayor—and in 1929 entered politics; one legend is that Boss Flynn picked him for an early minor office by running through a printed list of names and choosing the one that sounded most Italian. Impellitteri was a member of Tammany, but its sachems never particularly liked him. In 1945 he became president of the city council and a member of the Board of Estimate; he was acting mayor on several occasions when O'Dwyer was absent. Mr. Impellitteri is a hard-working, earnest, warm personality; whether he is strong-shouldered enough to lick the machines, restore the city's prestige, and curtail municipal corruption remains to be seen. Nobody would deny that he has a man's size job.

Mayor Impellitteri once publicly refused to shake hands with Costello—which in those days was something like putting your head in a meat grinder—and has, on the record, always kept clear of the gangsters. His prestige was augmented, when, as acting mayor, he appointed the impressively bulbous, copiously moustached Thomas F. Murphy, the man who prosecuted Alger Hiss, to be commissioner of police.

Wall Street, the Solar Plexus

I must atone for my wealth.
—OTTO KAHN

A bank is the thing that will always lend you money if you can prove you don't need it.
—JOE E. LEWIS

The main thing to say about Wall Street to-day is that it is not what it once was. Much of the brutal golden power is gone. Consider as typical of a whole great evolution what has happened to the 'Corner', i.e., the House of Morgan, J. P. Morgan himself, the Younger, died in 1943, and his will was made public in 1947. After deduction of tax, debts, and expenses, his net estate amounted to the bagatelle of $4,642,791. Nothing could more dramatically illustrate how times have irremediably changed.[1]

Wall Street, the solar plexus of the American capitalist system, is so called because Peter Stuyvesant, in 1653, built a wall roughly where it lies to-day. It is a narrow, noisy, trenchlike little chasm, scarcely six hundred yards long. Here, or in the immediate neighbourhood, are banks like Chase, the National City, and the Guaranty. (Mr. Bell's essay tells much about who owns these banks, for instance of the Giannini holdings in National City, and which are 'Morgan banks' and which are not.) Here are potent underwriting houses like Halsey Stuart and Morgan Stanley; here is the Stock Exchange, on which

[1] The best single thing on Wall Street in short space I have ever read is an essay by Elliott V. Bell in an anthology called *We Saw It Happen*. Mr. Bell was a financial reporter for the New York *Times* when he wrote it. He later became a leading member of Governor Dewey's brain trust and head of the New York state banking department.

are listed 208 billion dollars' worth of securities and which in 1950 transacted
business worth over 1.1 billion dollars in bonds and traded 524 million shares
of stock. But another index of the way things have been going is that in 1929
the price of an Exchange seat was $625,000, and to-day it is $49,500. At the
depth of the depression a seat cost $17,000.

In the vivid, fragrant, days before 1929 Wall Street was, though disliked
and distrusted by many people, an object of profound veneration to the
business world. To become a Morgan partner, or even a Kuhn Loeb partner,
was for most men of the East practically like becoming a cabinet minister.
The path was well beaten for any really bright and ambitious youngster, and
it was often a golden path—St. Paul's or Lawrenceville, Yale or Princeton,
and then the Street. Bankers were really looked up to in those days. Morgan
and Kuhn Loeb had the juiciest parts of the investment business almost without competition, with Morgan concentrating on British and domestic
industrial issues mostly, Kuhn Loeb on German and Scandinavian issues and
some railroads. Another pregnant point is that in this era bankers played a
very definite role in international political affairs. The House of Morgan was
like the Board of Trade in England, to all intents and purposes it was a silently
functioning agency of the American government itself. A Morgan partner
could have much more influence than, say, an assistant secretary of state.
Mr. Bell mentions the way Wall Street kept in close touch with Washington,
and told it, bluntly if necessary, what it was to do. Also the railway empires
of the country were more or less divided between Kuhn Loeb and Morgan,
though other firms in time pushed their way in. The railroads could not
promote their massive issues without money, and it was Wall Street which
gave them money. Finally—and this is still true to-day—the bankers, through
interlocking directorates and otherwise, had germinal influence on the affairs
of almost all the great American manufacturing corporations.

Where do the bright youngsters turn to-day? A good many, if they hope
to become millionaires some day by a conservative route, go into law.
(Many, not exclusively interested in making money, more interested in
making *things* or public policy, go into small businesses or government service, after a period at law.) The great law firms of Wall Street still pick the
best brains in the nation. They have consummate power, ability, and intelligence. Their profits may still be enormous; since the SEC, a great deal more
legal work attends financial issues than heretofore. One point to reflect on is
their inhospitality to Jews. Many leading law firms downtown—and to a
certain extent banks—rigidly exclude Jews; even Jewish underlings and clerks
are uncommon. In no American milieu is this more conspicuous. For a Jew
to get into a really good firm below Chambers Street is almost as difficult as
to get into the Ku-Klux Klan. The upper reaches of the law in Wall Street
are the last frigid citadel of Anglo-Saxon Protestantism.

To proceed. In 1930 James W. Gerard, formerly ambassador to Germany, made a national sensation—it will seem tame now—by listing the sixty-four men who 'ruled the United States'. He included only one politician (Mellon); he did not include the president, Mr. Hoover. These shoguns, he said, were the real powers behind the throne, too busy to run for office themselves but decisive in determining who did run, and in utter control of the nation's politics as well as purse strings. Perhaps the list has relevance to-day, if only because a similar list as of 1950 would be so different.

John D. Rockefeller Jr.
Andrew W. Mellon
J. P. Morgan
George F. Baker, banker
John D. Ryan, copper magnate
Walter C. Teagle, president of Standard Oil of New Jersey
Henry Ford
Frederick E. Weyerhaeuser, lumber
Myron C. Taylor
James A. Farrell, U.S. Steel
Charles M. Schwab, Bethlehem Steel
Eugene G. Grace, Bethlehem Steel
Harry M. Warner, movies
Adolph Zukor, movies
William H. Crocker, San Francisco, banker
O. P. and M. J. Van Sweringen, railway magnates
W. W. Atterbury, president of the Pennsylvania R.R.
Arthur Curtiss James, large holder of railway securities
Charles Hayden, financier
Daniel O. Jackling, president of the Utah Copper Co.
Arthur V. Davis, president of Alcoa
P. M. Gossler, president of the Columbia Gas & Electric Corp.
R. C. Holmes, president of the Texas Corp.

John J. Raskob
Seven members of the Du Pont family
Edward J. Berwind, financier
Daniel Willard, Baltimore & Ohio
Sosthenes Behn, IT&T
Walter S. Gifford, AT&T
Owen D. Young, General Electric
Gerard Swope, General Electric
Thomas W. Lamont
Albert H. Wiggin, banker
Charles E. Mitchell, banker
Samuel Insull
The seven Fisher brothers
Daniel Guggenheim and William Loeb, mining magnates
George Washington Hill, American Tobacco Co.
Adolph S. Ochs
William Randolph Hearst
Robert R. McCormick
Joseph M. Patterson
Julius S. Rosenwald, merchant
Cyrus H. K. Curtis
Roy W. Howard
Sidney Z. Mitchell, chairman of the board, Electric Bond & Share
Walter Edwin Frew, Corn Exchange Bank
A. P. Giannini
William Green and Matthew Woll, labour[1]

What are the main reasons why Wall Street has declined so notably in prestige, authority, and influence? Following are a few. They are not listed chronologically or in order of importance:

(a) First, of course, the crash and the depression, which not only

[1] One singular point in this list is that none of the great insurance companies is represented.

obliterated a great proportion of the national wealth, but drastically lowered confidence in bankers.

(*b*) Scandals. It was a severe blow to Wall Street that men like Richard Whitney, a former president of the Stock Exchange, and in a different category Charles E. Mitchell, the president of the National City Bank, underwent public trial. When Whitney first got into trouble people said, 'Oh, the Morgans will never let him go to jail.' But he went.

(*c*) Income tax. It is, after all, almost insuperably difficult nowadays to accumulate a fortune. It may not be impossible to make big money; to hold on to it is a different matter. What does it profit a man to spend thirty years trying to make money in large amounts, and have his major earnings go to taxes?

(*d*) More pertinent than any of these items so far, the transfer of much of the control of credit from Wall Street to the government. 'Freedom to speculate' became severely limited. Moreover the government extended its direct financial power through such agencies as the RFC (created by Mr. Hoover). Many corporations did not have to go to Wall Street any more. They went to Washington.

(*e*) The growth of corporations themselves. Plenty of companies, especially new companies, do still come to Wall Street for underwriting. But the colossi like AT & T are big enough to be their own bankers for the most part. In the old days a middle western railway could be as dependent on Morgan as a cripple on a crutch. Nowadays even small corporations do their banking locally. Financial power has become much more diffused. For instance Ford (a special case of course) financed himself in an emergency through his own dealers.

(*f*) Various regulatory devices, initiated by the New Deal for the public interest. We accept these to-day, it has been said, almost as automatically as we accept—and welcome—the strictures of the Pure Food and Drug Act. But in 1929 a private bank did not even have to make public its condition. There was no federal regulation whatever of the issue of securities except of certain minor types.

(*g*) Among specific acts, the Banking Act of 1933, which enforced a separation of banks of deposit from investment banking ('and so took all the gravy out of Wall Street') and the Securities Act of 1934 which set up the SEC To-day—something so obviously correct that it seems barbarous that it did not exist fifteen years ago—every underwriter is under strict legal compulsion to declare in the most minute detail every relevant fact about an impending issue. Every material fact bearing on an issue must be made known.

(*h*) One might also mention the Investment Trust Act and similar acts, regulating the operation of investment trusts and councillors, and forbidding the latter to act as brokers, and also in another field, the Johnson Act, which cut off loans to foreign nations in default on obligations to the United States.

(i) Competitive bidding. Except in isolated cases the railroads and utilities are no longer able to negotiate their financing with banking houses of their own choice. Instead they must offer their securities publicly to the highest bidder. This, as much as anything, has served to upset old banking ties, lower the morale of the Street, and cut profits to the bone.

(j) During the hearings of a sub-committee of the United States Senate investigating the banking business and the stock market, a lively press agent managed to put a midget on J. P. Morgan's knee.

Perhaps this last item marked the turning point. With that midget, an impregnability was shattered, a myth was broken, an era ended. The Pecora hearings were the Great Divide, and Wall Street has never been quite the same since.

Some testimony by Mr. Morgan and his associates during this astonishing investigation shows nicely what a Divine-Right-of-Kings world we lived in then:

Q. Should not private banks be examined and forced to publish statements of their condition?
A. Possibly.
Q. What assurance has a depositor of the solvency of Morgan & Company?
A. Faith.
Q. Are not depositors entitled to statements of Morgan & Company's condition?
A. They can have them if they want them; no one has ever asked.
Q. Has any public statement ever been made . . . since the Elder Morgan testified before the Pujo committee twenty years ago?
A. No. That was the only public statement we have ever made about anything.

It was at this hearing, incidentally, that the country learned that neither Morgan nor any of his great partners, men like George Whitney and Thomas W. Lamont, had paid any income tax during the depression years 1931 and 1932, and that in 1930 their payments had totalled only $48,000. This was because the partnership had taken advantage of the capital losses provision in income tax regulations. The late Senator Glass of Virginia snapped in incredulous disgust, 'The fault is with the law'. (It should also be noted that few among those outraged by this non-payment of taxes for two years paid much attention to the fact that from 1917 to 1927 members of the firm had paid taxes of more than 50 million dollars.)

Also in this investigation it became known that the Morgan partners followed the practice of offering certain stocks to a group of selected friends at prices considerably below market, before issuing them. The question was asked, 'Was not the offer of such shares at wholesale prices a kind of bribe?' The answer was, 'No. The shares were only offered to clients and friends who could afford to take a risk . . . regarded as too speculative for the general public.' Among Morgan acquaintances—who got Standard Brands at bargain rates—were Calvin Coolidge (3,000 shares), John J. Raskob (2,000), General Pershing (500), Colonel Lindbergh (500), Bernard M. Baruch (4,000), Norman H. Davis (500), Cornelius S. Kelley of Anaconda (2,000), Charles E. Mitchell (10,000), Alfred P. Sloan (7,500), Clarence H. Mackay (2,000). Similar bargains in Allegheny Corporation went to Charles Francis Adams (1,000), Newton D. Baker (2,000), and Owen D. Young (5,000).

In 1933 the Banking Act was passed. Morgan decided to remain a private commercial bank, and therefore had to drop its security underwriting business, in which it was the leading institution in the country. Morgan's son Henry and two other partners resigned from the parent house to form a new investment firm, totally independent, Morgan Stanley & Company, Inc. Morgan's other son, Junius, stayed on with the parent bank, which was still the largest private bank in the world.

In 1940 came another bruising and revolutionary step—the Morgan bank decided to incorporate itself. This was as if Carry Nation had done a midnight strip tease at Leon & Eddie's. Morgan applied to the authorities for a charter of incorporation and then moved into the sphere of 'government supervision and growing accountability to the public'. The *ancien régime* was no more. This was Louis XVI's head bouncing into the cart. 'It was understood,' wrote the New York *Times*, that 'the firm was incorporated because death and inheritance taxes raised difficulties in keeping the bank's capital intact as partners died or withdrew.' Some time after this—another shock to the old-fashioned—J. P. Morgan & Company, Inc., offered stock to the public for the first time, and in 1942 it was admitted to membership in the Federal Reserve system.

No one should think from the above that Wall Street is powerless these days. It is still incontestably the most important financial centre in the world, and it still has an influence on America pervasive, tenacious, and articulate. All that has happened is that it can no longer play its game exclusively its own way; it must obey house rules.

As to the place in the national economy of some great corporations not so directly in the Wall Street arc, though most are based in or near New York, the most interesting presentation I have seen is that in a pamphlet prepared by Senator O'Mahoney's Temporary National Economic Committee.

There were in 1945 forty-one American corporations with total assets of a billion dollars or more. There are, of course, other and perhaps better ways of measuring the size of a corporation than by its assets. But considered strictly from the point of view of assets, the biggest—and the largest enterprise in the United States—was the Metropolitan Life Insurance Company, with almost six and a half billion dollars in assets; next came Bell Telephone, with more than six billion; next the Prudential Insurance Company with more than five. A fingerful of banks were runners-up, with more than three and a half billion each; then came two more insurance companies, with more than three billion. The first railway on the list was the Pennsylvania, with assets of $2,800,000,000 plus. The first industrial corporation was Standard Oil of New Jersey, with $2,300,000,000 plus. General Motors was thirteenth on the list; U.S. Steel fourteenth; the New York Central fifteenth; the Santa Fe twenty-third; the Union Pacific twenty-fifth; Consolidated Edison twenty-seventh; Du Pont thirty-eighth; and Ford forty-first.

Senate statisticians made much play with this list. They showed, for instance, that only six American states (New York, Pennsylvania, Ohio, California, Michigan, Massachusetts) had a total assessed valuation of property greater than the assets of Metropolitan Life. Both AT & T and the Prudential Insurance Company had greater assets than all but thirteen states. Assets of Chase National ran nip and tuck with those of Kentucky, and Standard Oil (New Jersey) was richer than Virginia. The Northwestern Mutual Life Insurance Company of Milwaukee had assets almost equivalent to those of the state of Georgia; similarly the Chemical Bank & Trust Company of New York ran neck and neck with Florida; the Baltimore & Ohio Railway with Washington; and Commonwealth & Southern with Colorado. Mr. Berle, the former American ambassador to Brazil and now head of the Liberal Party, said once that two hundred companies owned half the wealth of the United States. Probably he was not far wrong.[1]

What happened to Wall Street itself in the past few years may be told briefly. The long bull market collapsed in 1946; after a sharp recession prices began to rise again, and they have been intermittently rising ever since. In February 1951, in fact, the stock market hit a new high for the past twenty years. What will happen next? Will there be another boom like that of 1929, to be followed by another crash? The country has to hand at least some of the techniques that might prevent a new depression. It remains to be seen, however, if it will use them. Plenty of people hate the idea of government

[1] As to concentration of ownership the *New Republic* stated (2 September 1946) that three family groups—Du Ponts, Mellons and Rockefellers—control fifteen of the two hundred biggest non-financial corporations in the country, with assets of eight billion dollars. Nearly a third of the directorships of the two hundred largest non-financial corporations and the fifty largest financial corporations were held by only four hundred men. Morgan partners at one time held 167 directorships in 89 corporations—including 15 banks and trust companies, 10 railroads, 38 industrial companies, 13 public utility companies, and 6 insurance companies.

controls so much that they would rather risk ruining themselves—and everybody else to boot—than attempt to make use of them.

The Harlems

Harlem has a black belt where darkies dwell in a heaven and where
white men seek a little hell.

—ALFRED KREYMBORG

There are several. One is Puerto Rican, one Haitian, and another, verging
into what might be called the Marcantonio territory on the east side, is
Italian. I drove through this area before a recent election; loud speakers
brought campaign speeches—in warm whole-toned Italian—out into the
dreary, chilly streets. Also there are Russians in Harlem, Spaniards, Mexicans,
a considerable salting of Chinese, some Japanese Nisei who do not want to
return to California, and, of all things, the largest Finnish community in the
United States.

Next to the Negroes, the biggest group in Harlem is that from Puerto
Rico, which numbers about 230,000 and presents some shockingly difficult
problems and frustrations. Negroes and Puerto Ricans get on well together
by and large. One Puerto Rican told me that this was natural because his
people want to get Americanized as quickly as possible, and the Negroes
represent Anglo-Saxon culture! Another item in this general field is probably
apocryphal. Harlem had a small angry upsurge in 1943 which, but for
instant sharp work by Mr. LaGuardia and the police, might have become a
serious riot. The Negro community seemed to feel so secure and confident of
adequate protection, however, that a Chinese laundryman is supposed to
have hung a sign on his shop, *Me Coloured Too!* Still another point in Harlem
mixed-upness is the fact that a well-known small community exists of Negro
Jews.

Though not necessarily the biggest, Harlem is by all odds the most
important concentration of Negroes in America. Roughly from 110th
Street to 155th on the east side, and from Madison Avenue to St. Nicholas,
live more than 350,000 Negroes. This is more than the population of whole
cities like Toledo, Omaha, or Miami. Yet Harlem holds only about half the
total number of Negroes in New York City as a whole; there are more than
150,000 in Brooklyn, about 30,000 in the Bronx, and about 30,000 in Queens.
Years ago, New York Negroes lived in a few scattered and isolated enclaves:
Minetta Lane in Greenwich Village, 'San Juan Hill' on West 63rd Street near
the river, and some areas in German Yorkville (especially on East 88th near
Third). Now they have spread all over the city, and Harlem itself is expand-
ing all the time. It has no fixed frontiers.

Since 'Harlem' has become a kind of abstraction (like 'Hollywood'), it is extremely difficult to describe. The easiest thing to say is that it is a profoundly complex cross section of the whole of New York in black miniature. People are tempted to think of Harlem as exclusively a slum; it is also talked about as if it were a cave full of night-clubs. Many Harlemites have of course never seen a night-club. Some parts of it are indeed slums, and one block, near Lenox and 143rd Street, is commonly said to be the most crowded in the world. A recent commissioner of housing and building visited a sixty-four-year-old tenement in the neighbourhood not long ago, and found it 'infested, scaly, shabby', a menace to health, a disgrace otherwise, and a fire-trap. Rats were so much in evidence that the remark was reported, 'They not only come here to eat, but I think they cook their own food, too'.

But Harlem as a whole is by no means a slum. This is not the Bowery. A good many apartment blocks, built before the district became Negro, are still in good shape; the trouble is that they are viciously overcrowded and badly maintained. For instance there will be only one superintendent for six buildings, jammed with sublet flats, and containing literally hundreds of families. Also Harlem has several handsome, modern, and well-maintained apartment buildings. One, at 409 Edgecombe, is in the area known locally as 'Sugar Hill'; here lives, as I heard it put, 'the glamour set of Black America'.[1] But this description makes Sugar Hill sound frivolous, which it is not. A great number of eminent Negroes live there—Walter White, the competent discerning secretary of the National Association for the Advancement of Coloured People, Municipal Judge Charles E. Toney, figures in the arts like Duke Ellington, Canada Lee, and Langston Hughes, Roy Wilkins the editor of *Crisis*, one of the best-known Negro lawyers in the country Thurgood Marshall, William T. Andrews who is one of the senior members of the state assembly, and the most distinguished of them all, Dr. W. E. B. Du Bois.

I went up to Harlem with two Negro friends recently, and tried to learn a little. It is a community constantly in motion. Like New Rochelle, it is a kind of bedroom for the rest of New York; people live here, and work downtown. It has several Negro newspapers, including the conservative *Amsterdam News* and the radical *People's Voice*. There is no Negro department store; most of the shopkeepers on the main street (125th) are Jews. Almost all real estate is white absentee owned, though one Negro businessman, A. A. Austin, is a substantial owner; there is no Negro bank (but local branches of the great white banks employ Negro personnel); about seventy-five saloons and one movie house are Negro owned, but no more; the chief hotel is a remarkable establishment called the Theresa, almost exclusively Negro, but it is white owned, and several whites live in it. The chief Negro business in Harlem on a broad level is insurance (unless you want to count religion as a business), and on a narrower level hairdressing.

The whole community is strongly labour conscious. At least 50,000

[1] For much detail on this and similar matters see Roi Ottley's *New World A-Coming*.

5

Negroes in New York City are members of unions, including laundry workers, garment workers, hod carriers, longshoremen, painters, and members of the United Office and Professional Workers, CIO. Probably some single streets in Harlem have more Negro trade unionists than the entire state of Georgia. In New York as a whole there is probably less discrimination against Negroes, in employment and otherwise, than in any other city in America. In fact many familiar forms of anti-Negro discrimination are illegal in New York. Of course some discriminations, illegal or not, do continue to exist.

Harlem has no single political boss, any more than New York City itself has a single boss. You can find every shade of opinion on any question. Some Harlemites are 'handkerchief-heads'; some frankly call themselves 'anti-white'. Once the community had a picturesque creature, Abdul Hamid Sufi, who was called the Black Hitler, and who, despite this name, operated a 'Temple of Peace and Tranquillity'. There are some extremely conservative Negroes and equally some extreme radicals, as well as many who defy classification. The president of the New York City civil service commission, Ferdinand Q. Morton, is a Negro, and so is a member of the state Committee Against Discrimination set up by the Ives Bill, Elmer Carter. The admirable record and accomplishment of Dr. Ralph Bunche of the UN, who won the Nobel Peace prize in 1950, is well known.

On a street corner near the Theresa we listened to a campaign speech by Congressman Adam Clayton Powell Jr. Many Negroes dislike Powell, and call him a spellbinder. He has a blistering hot voice; he never pauses a second between sentences; he gestures like a piston. This evening, with his words reverberating up and down the street, he denied with ringing animosity that his wife, Hazel Scott, a well-known Negro pianist, was white (as some silly people had alleged); he excused some absences from Congress by saying that, after all, his constituents ought not mind that he had taken a brief honeymoon—how the crowd roared—and, anyway, his mother was very ill. 'Any Negro born of a Negro,' Powell cried out, 'must be a Negro, must be a radical, must be a fighter, all the time!' By profession Powell is a preacher, as was his father before him. His Abyssinian Baptist church has, in fact, what is believed to be the largest Protestant congregation in the world, numbering at least ten thousand. He was the first Negro council-man in New York City, and is one of two Negroes in the Congress.

To sum up: the chief characteristic of Harlem is that, by and large, its Negroes (and others in New York) have greater opportunities in more fields than in any comparable city; they have better chances in education, jobs, social evolution, and civil service; they are the nearest to full citizenship of any Negroes in the nation.

New York Daily News *and Vox Pop*

I have made frequent references to the New York *Daily News*, which has the biggest circulation of any newspaper in America. I wonder how many people read carefully the department which I like to turn to first, the Voice of the People, one of the saltiest things in American journalism. Here are shrieks, moans, and whistles that cover every conceivable variety of topic. These letters prove something well known to most Americans, but occasionally ignored, and also something which many foreign observers do not realize at all, the enormous capacity of American citizens to take sides on public issues with ferocious vigour.

Following are some judgments by *News* readers on international affairs:

AGREES WITH CHURCHILL

Manhattan: Churchill was right. F.D.R. was the best President England ever had.

CHECKING OUT

Newark, N. J.: Strikes, discrimination, prejudice, superiority complexes—that describes the United States. . . . I'm going to England next month to become a British subject. God save the King and long live Great Britain!

RUNNING AWAY FROM WAR

Queens: War with Russia for U.S. and British oil in Iran? Listen; any jackass in Washington, D.C., who thinks I'm sweating out another war is batty. Stand for hours for horse meat, swilly pork, frozen, slimy, stinking chickens? . . . Hell, no.

On things domestic, *News* readers are not less vocal:

RADIO HATE LIST

Hartford, Conn.: The public is taking an awful lot of abuse from the radio. Crooners, preachers, politicians, commentators, swing music and Reds should simply be swept off the ether waves.

REDS VS. UNCLE SAM

Manhattan: Inasmuch as everyone knows the Communists are out to destroy our Government what is the Government waiting for? Why doesn't it execute all Communists guilty of direct or indirect attempts to overthrow it?

WANTS VITO FOR PRESIDENT

Manhattan: Why can't we have Vito Marcantonio running for President? . . . We should have Vito in the White House, and other men like him in Washington, for better conditions.

The *News* supported FDR in 1932, 1936, and 1940, and then turned violently against him. Its readers still find him a favourite object of attack.

WANTS SOULS TO ROT

Bronx: No matter how many crimes the Nazis committed, they never stooped so low as to execute captured generals. That fiendish action remained for the maronic [sic] Roosevelt clique to do. May their souls rot in hell forever.

ROOSEVELT AND DISASTER

Manhattan: What do you mean, News, by that crack in your editorial 'Pearl Harbour Snafu' that Roosevelt was only partly to blame for the disaster? Why, FDR was the greatest warmonger of all time, was itching to get us into the slaughter from 1933 on. Didn't he keep blasting away at Hitler? Didn't he give the order as early as September, 1941, for the Navy to shoot Axis ships on sight? . . . Why, you dumb oxen, have you forgotten so soon? Pearl Harbour was only a smoke-screen for his devilish World War II plans! Wake up, you dopes, to the truth.

Many *News* readers had violent feelings about the UN when it moved into the New York area:

HYDE PARK: DEATH VALLEY

Queens: If the United States MUST be saddled with this white elephant, the UN, then by all means let the world capital be at Hyde Park, N. Y., the graveyard of America's independence. . . . On second thought, how about Death Valley as a world capital site?

Not all *News* letters are on political topics by any means:

EXIT THE LITTLE WOMAN

Bronx: After almost two years overseas, I recently returned home expecting to rush into the arms of my loving wife, only to find that she had cleaned out our bank account and run off with a man who is married and the father of two children. What fools these mortals be! I still love her.

WANTS HIS MUSIC

Milltown, N.J.: There should be more soft, sweet music on the radio after 11 p.m. How can a fellow cuddle up to his girl with some news commentator yapping in the background?

Finally, the *News* takes great delight in printing attacks on itself:

SAYS THEY WERE NO GOOD

Iselin, N. J.: What a lousy sheet The News has turned out to be! . . . and your so-called Voice of the People is a big fraud and frame-up, too. Many people I know have sent you letters praising the Democrats but you did not print any of them. I dare you to print this, you stinkers.

SAYS WE'RE COMMIES

Brooklyn: I think your paper is a dirty, filthy, crummy rag, and it stinks like hell. . . . You are a bunch of Communist rats. I hate everything connected with you, from the editor all the way to the newsboy who sells this stinking paper. I can make my language stronger, but some children might read this.

SAYS WE'RE DECADENT PUNKS

Manhattan: Are the editors of The News a bunch of decadent intellectual punks, or are they fitted to direct the people into a better life? I think they are decadent punks, and if we lived in a virile country where duelling was legal I would enjoy meeting these decadent punks in a duel . . .

SAYS WE'RE OPIUM-COATED

Bronx: The News reminds me of an opium-coated poison pill, with sex and crime stories and comic strips covering up malicious columns that work against the people's interests. Your paper exists as a monument to the stupidity of the human race.

The *News* takes pride in its snappy headlines. When Alger Hiss went to jail the caption was RED HERRING CANNED.

As Others See Us

Recently I have been asking visitors from abroad what impressed them most about the United States, with particular reference to the New York area:

An Austrian diplomat: The copiousness and variety of foreign accents heard in the streets.

A German novelist: Space. *Lebensraum.* The impression that no crisis can be really severe or permanent in this country because people are free to move around so much.

A young English girl: The steam rising from manholes in the streets, and the fact that so many policemen are so fat.

A wealthy central European refugee: 'In the law courts, they have to prove *me* wrong!'

A Norwegian: The lack of capacity of Americans for stable personal relationships.

An English labour leader: Suburban gardens have no hedges, and children are not taught to be responsible.

A radio commentator returning after long absence: That the United States is the only country that raised its living standard during the war.

A Brazilian: Road signs like those warning motorists, DEATH IS SO PERMANENT.

New York Olla Podrida

New York City has more trees (2,400,000) than houses and it makes 14,500,000 telephone calls a day, of which about 125,000 are wrong numbers. Its rate of divorces is the lowest of any big American city, less than one-tenth of that of Baltimore for instance. One of its hotels, built largely over railway tracks, has an assessed valuation of $22,500,000 (there are 124 buildings valued at more than a million dollars in Manhattan alone), and it is probably the only city in the world that has five district attorneys.

New York City has such admirable institutions as the New School for Social Research, the Council on Foreign Relations, Cooper Union, the Museum of Modern Art, and the Century Association. It has 18 billion dollars' worth of real estate, and the Port of New York Authority with a $371,000,000 investment in bridges, tunnels, airports, and the like. It has 492 playgrounds, more than 11,000 restaurants, 3,243 churches, and the largest store in the world, Macy's, which can serve more than 150,000 customers a day. It has the Great White Way, bad manners, 34,777 school-teachers (average pay $3,803), and 500 boy gangs.

Each eye in the Statue of Liberty is two and a half feet wide, and Broadway was originally called Breederweg. The Christmas tree in Rockefeller Centre Plaza has seven miles of wiring and 9,500 lights. The subway system runs 13,179 trains a day, and collects seven million fares. Fourteen thousand babies are still-born every year, and in Manhattan alone 51,373 people received summons in 1949 for making unnecessary noise.

New York employs upwards of 184,000 people, and it has 360 miles of shoreline containing 1,800 docks. It uses six billion pounds of cream and sugar and 70 million pounds of fruit annually for ice cream. Conventions and tourists bring in about $450,000,000 per year, and 400,000 commuters ride in and out every day.

New York makes three-quarters of all the fur coats in the country, and its slang and mode of speech can change hour by hour. It has New York University, a private institution which is the second largest university in the country, with 13,800 Jews in its student body, 12,000 Protestants, and 7,200 Catholics. and a great municipal institution, the City College of the College of the City of New York, one of four free city colleges. In New York people drink 14 million gallons of hard liquor a year, and smoke about 20 billion cigarettes. It has 301,850 dogs, and one of its unsolved murders is the political assassination of Carlo Tresca.

New York has something like 11,000 taxis and 882 parks. Its budget runs to $261,000,000 for education alone, and it drinks 3,500,000 quarts of milk a day. The average New York family (in normal times) moves once every eighteen months, and more than 2,200,000 New Yorkers belong to the Associated Hospital Service. New York has a birth every five minutes, and a marriage every seven. It has more Norwegians than most Norwegian cities and only one railroad, the New York Central, has the perpetual right to enter it by land. It has 22,000 soda fountains, and 171 tons of soot fall per square mile every month, which is why your face is dirty.

GUY DE MAUPASSANT:
A WOMAN'S LIFE AND *BEL-AMI*

BY ALAN HODGE

Introductions from the Novel Library,
of which Mr. Hodge is General Editor

———————

MR. OLIVER SIMON is the Production Editor of the
Novel Library and we should like to thank him here for
contributing so much to its success, both by designing
its attractive and economical format and making available the pattern papers by well-known artists which
have been used on the bindings and have become such
a distinctive feature of the Library.

H. H.

GUY DE MAUPASSANT:
A WOMAN'S LIFE AND BEL-AMI

BY ALAN HODGE

Introductions from the Novel Library,
of which Mr. Hodge is General Editor

Mr. Oliver Simon is the Production Editor of the Novel Library and we should like to thank him here for contributing so much to its success, both by designing its attractive and economical format and making available the pattern-papers by well-known artists which have been used on the bindings and have become such a distinctive feature of the Library.

H. H.

OFTEN there is a fine bloom about a first novel which its writer never quite achieves again, however more expert he becomes in technique, or more nearly universal in his sympathies. Perhaps this is because novelists are apt to write with less calculation in their early books, putting into them more of their first lively and unpremeditated impressions of the world. Readers come away with the feeling that a part of real life has been directly revealed to them, without the complicated shades of forethought and afterthought, the framework of deliberate interpretation, that are to be found in the maturer and more reflective masterpieces of fiction.

At least two English writers have begun their careers as novelists with wonderfully fresh and lively books which have remained their most popular works, though admittedly not their best—Fielding with *Joseph Andrews* and Jane Austen with *Pride and Prejudice*. There are many readers also who prefer the slighter works of Tolstoy as a young man—*Sebastopol*, *Childhood* and *The Cossacks*—to the more ambitious volumes of his middle age. Maupassant in *A Woman's Life* miraculously combines the vivacity of a first novel with the maturity that seems to have been his ever since he first put pen to paper. A part of his achievement must be set down to the fact that in 1882 Maupassant was still in burly good health; and it is, of course, true that this novel is not his first book. Two collections of stories had preceded it, containing such brilliant examples of his art as *Boule de Suif* and *La Maison Tellier*. He was therefore by no means an inexperienced hand when he sat down to write *A Woman's Life*. For all that, a first novel it is, and it ought to rank high on anyone's list of masterly first productions.

The story of Jeanne Lamare is told with a sustained compassion less rare in Maupassant's work than his reputation for cynicism and brutality might suggest. 'Sometimes,' Henry James remarked, in an essay which is admirably just and perceptive for all his shocked yet fascinated squeamishness at Maupassant's grimly frank treatment of sex, 'Sometimes there is a sorrow, a misery, or even a little heroism, that Maupassant handles with a certain tenderness, without insisting on the poor, the ridiculous, or, as he is fond of saying, the bestial side of it. *A Woman's Life* is a capital example of this.' Many of the book's attractive and sympathetic qualities undoubtedly arise from its setting in the country. It is always in his stories of life in Paris, which he despised and detested, that Maupassant is at his most cynical. The more engaging side of his nature seems to have been brought out by the country-side, and particularly by the landscape of the coast of Normandy, where he had lived as a boy and where the happiest days of his later life were spent, boating, swimming and writing at the seaside resort of Etretat.

The country house of *Les Peuples* in which Jeanne passes her life is modelled on Maupassant's own boyhood home. How faithfully he recreates the still charm of Normandy in the summer, and the strange sense of desolation given off by its remote hamlets in winter-time! A remarkably evocative sense of place pervades the whole book. Though the story reaches out over a whole lifetime, it is given a feeling of unity and a sense of completeness by the singular skill with which Maupassant presents the changeless background to the few big events of Jeanne's life. The occasional pleasures in the lives of nineteenth-century gentry, the stretches of contentment and the much longer stretches of boredom, have never been more suggestively portrayed outside the pages of Russian literature. In the midst of this timeless countryside Maupassant has the art to let days of enchantment stand out as well as mourn-ful days of tragedy. What could be more touching than Jeanne's home-coming from her convent, full of girlish dreams of the romantic marriage she will make, and of the happy-ever-after? And there have been few more entrancing scenes in fiction of the dawning of first love than Jeanne's sea-trip with the handsome Vicomte Julien de Lamare and her father, the Baron, on a perfect summer's day.

These touches of innocent bliss form a beautiful contrast to the story of disillusionment that is to follow. For, as in all the relationships of her life, Jeanne is deceived in her husband. The Vicomte turns out to be heartless, snobbish, desperately mean. Delicately Maupassant introduces the first signs of his pettiness during the romantic honeymoon in the wilds of Corsica, when Jeanne is embarrassed and distressed because her husband fusses over bills, takes pride in tipping too little and even deprives her of the pocket money given her by her mother. Seldom has Maupassant's spirit of irony better inspired him than in the scenes where Jeanne begins to recover from her first horror at the realities of making love, and to find pleasure in sex, just when her husband no longer desires her. This is the beginning of many disappointments, dramatically accumulating and leading to the tremendous climax of Julien's death. No one who has read it will easily forget the scene in which the Comte de Fourville discovers his adored young wife in adultery with Julien and furiously heaves the caravan in which they are embraced over the cliff to destruction.

It was Joseph Conrad who wrote of Maupassant that 'such is the greatness of his talent that all his high qualities appear inherent in the very things of which he speaks, as if they had been altogether independent of his presentation'. So it is that the tragedies of Jeanne's life appear to happen in all naturalness; Maupassant's selection of events is so effectively done that they seem never to have been arranged by their author. Jeanne is shown only in the half dozen principal relationships of her life, in nearly all of which her hopes and ideals are betrayed. Yet life is not all disillusion; there are consolations even in the deepest affliction. Though her husband was twice an adulterer, after his dreadful death Jeanne contrives to idolize him in her memory. Though the Baron is feckless and improvident, and marries his daughter to the first eligible young man who presents himself without inquiring into his character, yet he is fond and understanding in his fatherliness. The Baroness is the most slothful of valetudinarians, yet, having in her time betrayed and been betrayed, she is capable of a deeply affectionate insight into her daughter's plight. And who is it who rescues Jeanne when she is finally impoverished and deserted but Rosalie, the maid, who had been her husband's first mistress? Even Jeanne's spoiled and spendthrift son, Paul, renders her one service; he presents her with a grandchild who is the comfort of her old age. A pessimistic philosophy Maupassant's may be, but it is not misanthropic: rewards as well as punishments are meted out in the human relationships of this book.

In a preface to one of his later books Maupassant set out his ideas on how novels should be written. His sense of form, which he owed to the teachings of Flaubert, was outraged by the massive and painstaking detail into which novelists like Zola were drawn, and his sense of drama revolted by involved psychological explanations of the doings of people in fiction. He preferred novels, he wrote, 'which avoid with care all complicated explanations, all dissertations on motives, and confine themselves to making persons and events pass before our eyes'. 'Psychology should be hidden in a book,' he went on, 'as it is hidden in reality under the facts of existence. The novel conceived in this manner gains interest, movement, colour, the bustle of life.' It is with an extraordinary sureness of touch that he put these precepts into practice in *A Woman's Life*. With dramatic economy Maupassant concentrates on the few great turning points in an ordinary existence: birth and death, marriage and adultery, the disaffection and ingratitude of children, the slow ruin of a family fortune. In the simplest and apparently most monotonous of lives the widest horizons are opened. Tremendous experiences befall the most naïve hearts. That is the truth which Maupassant set out to illustrate in this novel, and no one who reads the life story of Jeanne will think it a truism.

MAUPASSANT's life is a tragic story, and one which he might almost have written himself. His parents were Norman gentry—his mother a woman of character whom he adored, and his father a handsome, extravagant man with a capacity for seducing any pretty girl in sight, including his son's nurses. From his schooldays Maupassant had the good fortune to be the literary pupil of Gustave Flaubert who was a close friend of his mother and her family. In his youth he was blessed with a powerful body and strenuous good health—nothing delighted him more than violent physical exercise, particularly swimming, rowing and yachting. He was, in fact a perfect stallion of a man, and that was his undoing. While still in his twenties Flaubert used to reproach him with spending all his energies in boating and whoring; and it was about this time that he contracted venereal disease, for which there was then no cure.

Suddenly at the age of thirty, after eight years spent in the French civil service, Maupassant shot into fame with his story *Boule de Suif*. From 1880 until 1890 he was one of the most prolific and successful writers of the time. But all through these creative years the disease was mounting within him. It reached its tertiary stage in the late 1880's. Maupassant began to have hallucinations; he suffered from insomnia, headaches, failing eyesight, occasional paralysis, and persecution mania. In search of relief he tried out many regimes, but doctors could do nothing for him. Towards the end of 1891 he attempted to commit suicide. During the night after New Year's Day, 1892, he woke up raving and was led away in a strait-jacket. Eighteen months later he died in a private asylum.

Bel-Ami was written midway through Maupassant's years of achievement, and there is no doubt that it is the most striking of his novels. Georges Duroy, nicknamed Bel-Ami, is the supreme cad of fiction. The cads of other novelists usually have some ability to recommend them—or at least a forcefulness of character; but the sole gifts possessed by Maupassant's hero are good looks and a talent for exploiting his fascination for women. At the beginning of the book Georges Duroy is a demobilized non-commissioned officer, earning twenty-five shillings a week as a clerk in a railway office. At the end he is a renowned journalist, feared throughout Paris, who has picked up a fortune on the side, married into wealth and power, and has a glittering future in politics ahead of him. This extraordinary success Bel-Ami owes almost entirely to the brains and influence of the women he captivates—almost entirely, for he has a shrewdness of his own which rapidly teaches him to judge where profit and advantage lie.

In any other hands than Maupassant's such a character would be a monster of immorality. But Bel-Ami is not. At the start he has an eager, diffident, uncouth ingenuousness that is touching. And he is debased not so much by positive faults in his own character as by the corruption of the financial speculators, political climbers and blackmailing journalists into whose company he drifts. At first sight, Maupassant may seem to be an impassive and cynical chronicler of his hero's seamy adulteries. But no one can read *Bel-Ami* without recognizing its author's profound sense of pity. It is impossible simply to despise and condemn Georges Duroy; Maupassant displays his meanness and mediocrity with a compassionate clairvoyance. This sense of pity in Maupassant saves him from indulging in sheer misanthropy. On the other hand, his cynical humour keeps the balance and prevents his pity from spilling over into sentimentality. This balance of qualities is seen at its best in *Bel-Ami* at moments when genuine emotion on Duroy's part is mixed with baser feelings. One of the most moving incidents in the book occurs when Duroy takes his clever and elegant Parisian bride to see his parents, who are rough peasants and café-keepers in Normandy. Embarrassment on all sides soon cuts this honeymoon short. In Duroy's heart the tormenting combination of shame and affection for his parents is described with wonderful penetration. *Bel-Ami* is full of such terrifyingly true readings of the human self. Few incidents better illustrate Maupassant's grim sense of comedy than Duroy's anguished debate with himself as to whether he should accept the money slipped into his pocket by his mistress. It costs him much effort to decide that a needy gentleman may legitimately regard such money as a loan; but shortly afterwards he is spending some of it on an evening with a prostitute. And what more life-like examples of self-deception could there be than the stages by which Duroy works himself into a passion of jealousy for his wife's late husband; then into indignation that she should be left a fortune by an old lover—of which he is nevertheless delighted to accept a half share; and finally into a state of righteous rage over his wife's adultery with the Foreign Minister—as soon as she and the Foreign Minister are no longer useful to him, and he is himself planning a second and more glorious marriage?

There is something essentially logical in every step in Duroy's rise to fame and in every twist of his emotions. Maupassant had learnt well the lessons given him by Flaubert in how to describe coolly, in classical prose and without exaggeration, the meaner convolutions of human desire. In a sense, Flaubert filled the role of a father in Maupassant's life after Mme de Maupassant separated from her husband. He gave advice on Maupassant's schooling, appraised his early poems, and when Maupassant came to Paris to be a junior clerk in the Ministry of Marine at a salary as miserably low as Georges Duroy's, Flaubert became his 'cher maître' and practically his guardian. Through Flaubert, Maupassant met Zola, Turgenev, the Goncourts, and most of the principal writers of the time. He spent many evenings in the country homes of Flaubert and Zola on the outskirts of Paris. But though he wrote a few poems, was driven by lack of money into occasional journalism, and tried his hand at writing plays, no one at first except Flaubert took him seriously as a writer of promise. The truth is that throughout his life Maupassant disliked literary discussions and salon conversations. He kept himself apart from the ideologies of movements and schools. Most people who met him got the impression of a man wholly uninterested in ideas and theories and blankly reticent about his own opinions and feelings. Sport and love affairs were his sole relaxation, and they took him far from the intellectual coteries of Paris.

Maupassant's favourite retreat was his villa at Etretat on the Norman coast. Here *Bel-Ami* was written in the winter of 1884–85—two years after the publication of *A Woman's Life*. His valet François Tassart, who wrote a loyal and affectionate memoir of his master, records that his habit was to write between eight and eleven o'clock in the morning and to spend the rest of the day in exercise and entertainment. One day, François writes, 'At two o'clock I took the daily ration out to the cock and his last companion—all the other hens having gone into the pot. My master was walking around the pond. He followed me to watch the cock eat; he had a spray of fuchsia in his hand, and he said: "I've finished *Bel-Ami*. I hope it will satisfy those who are always asking me for something long. For there are pages and pages of it, and very closely written. There is a special part for the ladies which I hope they will like. As for the journalists they can make what they please of it. I'm ready for them." '

In fact, *Bel-Ami* was widely noticed in the press. It was hailed as 'the young pessimist's masterpiece', and at the same time condemned as 'repulsive' and 'disgusting'. What the reviewers most strongly objected to, however, was Maupassant's picture of the newspaper office of *La Vie Française*. He was obliged to write to *Gil-Blas*, in which *Bel-Ami* first appeared as a serial in April and May, 1885, explaining that he was not satirizing reputable news-papers, only muck-raking and speculative rags. Maupassant took some trouble to promote his own sales, for he had the Norman's traditional care-fulness in money-matters. A month after *Bel-Ami* was published he wrote to his mother, complaining that the funeral celebrations for Victor Hugo had been 'a terrible blow to the book'. Thirteen thousand copies were sold in the first month, a figure which Maupassant professed to find 'respectable, but nothing more'.

In this country Maupassant's reputation has for the most part rested on his short stories. These new translations of *A Woman's Life* and *Bel-Ami* will go some way, we hope, to convince modern readers that his narrative still was equally at home in the broader field of the novel.

HOME LIFE IN WALES

BY JACK JONES

from *Me and Mine* (1946)

WE had celebrated Laura's sixty-second birthday by going to Merthyr on the bus, but we did not go until the afternoon, on the half-past two out of Cardiff. For Bob had been home on leave from Scotland and had returned there only that morning. So I thought it would ease us all off, a ride on the bus to Merthyr, and it would be something for Laura's birthday. So Mary took the afternoon as well as the morning off, and the two boys lost a half-day's schooling. David and Norman were having a spelling competition—no, they were trying to read the letters of the words of the adverts on the bus-windows aloud.

'I can tell you this letter, Nana, it's Ker,' said David. 'No, it's Huh—isn't it, Nana?' said Norman. 'Yes,' said Laura. 'What's this Ker and Huh for K and H?' I wanted to know. 'Oh, that's how they are taught the alphabet,' said Mary. 'H'm, and Norman knows the letters better than you do,' I said to David. 'Things are beginning to come,' said Laura, pointing to stony allotments on the hillside. A number of miners of the night-shift were working on their allotments. 'I wouldn't like to have to dig for victory there,' said Mary. 'Those men have got to dig harder than that for victory about half a mile below where they're digging now,' I told her. And unless something is done soon they'll drop digging and stop the wheels into the bargain.

My sympathies have always been where they will always remain, with the miners, and I knew that trouble was brewing again. So after a cup of tea at my Mother's I left Laura and Mary and the two boys there with my Mother and my sister, Belle, whilst I went to have a talk with some of the miners who were travelling by bus a dozen miles each way night and morning to their work down distant mines. These chaps with whom I spoke told me that they were paying 6s. 6d. a week bus-fare and that that, with other deductions from wages, left many of them with only £3 10s. for a full week's work at the coal-face—and that's not bloody-well good enough, Jack. 'No,' I said, 'but neither is it bad enough to warrant you striking just now. Things are none too good out in the Middle East'—'Ay, ay, that's what they've been ramming down our throats and we've had about enough of it,' said one. 'There's no workers' playtime down there where we work, Jack, but there is where my daughter works and earns more money than I do.'

That was how miners in all parts of the South Wales coalfield were talking, I found while going from one mining valley to the other. A new layer of resentment was forming over the old and deep layers formed by indignities suffered by long years of unemployment between the wars, and this new layer, the creation of a new kind of indignity, that of paying them less than was being paid to many female munition workers, had roused the smouldering fires of ancient grudges and an eruption which might seriously affect the national war effort was imminent. So I wrote another article in support of the miners' wages claim, the claim which looked like causing a crisis. I felt it was a just claim, even a moderate one. All they asked for in May of 1942 was a minimum weekly wage of £4 5s. and a few reasonable increases over and above that for the most skilled miners. I went down a mine with an American journalist—I think it was Humphries of the *Chicago Sun*—to see what the conditions were like before I wrote the article I had in mind. The conditions in the two seams I through went were not too bad but bad enough. The air was thick with dust from the coal-conveyors and it was dark and dangerous down there. There was silicosis in the air and there was roof-pressure and ever so many other dangerous things the people of the world above knew nothing or little about.

I wrote the article and it appeared without alteration in the *Western Mail*. The following day there was an article by one who wrote under the pseudonym of 'Economist'. This chap said that my article of the previous day: '. . . teems with rash and erroneous, if not also at the present time, mischievous statements'. Then he went on to deal with what he called '. . . some of the most misleading of them'. He flayed me with sets of figures and with ratios, and concluded by pointing out that ' . . . out of every £1 received from the sale of coal during the past two and a half years wages and other costs have taken 19s. 5d. and profits only 7d.'. I wrote a letter which appeared in the *Western Mail* on the Friday, and in my letter I asked this 'Economist' or whatever his real name was: 'What, after all, do our wages and profits matter in comparison with what is involved in this titanic struggle of the free peoples against the forces of evil?' I said more than that, of course, but that was the line I took up, and dropped it there. After a lot of haggling the miners were only partly satisfied with the advance of wages they got that time, round about the time of the fall of Tobruk, and it was obvious then to most people that the miners were still dissatisfied and that they would make further demands as time went on.

Anyway, I got stuck into another by-election, the second by-election in which I took part in the first half of 1942. The first was in April, when Sir James Grigg, after he had been made War Minister, came to Cardiff East in the hope of regularizing his position. For he was War Minister and a member of the Cabinet without a seat in Parliament, and I was asked to speak in support of his candidature. Certainly, I said, before I had met the man, and after I had met him I was convinced that he was worthy of all support. For here was a War Minister who was no politician in the usual sense of the word. He struck me as a grand worker, a worker for victory. As a platform speaker he was no great shakes, yet he impressed all who saw and heard him. Not for years and years had I been on a political platform, but now, in support of Sir James Grigg, I addressed more meetings than any other speaker. He was opposed by Fenner Brockway of the I.L.P., whose policy was to make peace with the German people over the head of the German Government. What a hope! I went to one of Brockway's meetings, at which Maxton and others also spoke, and I came away feeling sorry for Maxton, who is a very nice chap. Sir James Grigg was elected and I was glad that he was. For I felt then that in him we had a man who would work hard and intelligently for the cause at the War Office. Time, of course, would prove whether or not my confidence in him was justified.

But this other by-election which took place in June 1942, was different for the reason that I was pressed to stand as an independent win-the-war candidate. The member for the Llandaff and Barry Division, in which I am a resident and voter, died suddenly. His name was Munro and as far as I know he was about the average Conservative member of Parliament. Before he was properly cold people throughout the division were thinking of the names of the possible and probable candidates and my name was mentioned among others. Then certain people came to see me and made certain suggestions.

'Of course, you knew W. J. Brown, M.P.?' said one. 'Yes, I knew him in the trade union movement—and I met him not so long ago in America when we were both speaking out there,' I said. 'Of course—and look how he won Rugby, where he was barely known, as an independent.' 'Now you live in this division and you are very well known and respected, so you ought to walk it,' said the tallest of the two men who had come to see me. 'All the same, walk it or trot it, I'm not going to stand,' I said. 'I shall support the Government candidate whoever he is.' 'Listen,' said the shortest, 'if it's the question of your deposit, then.' 'It's not that at all—thank you all the same,' I said. 'We've got a National Government and I don't feel disposed to do anything that will make things any harder than they are for the Government.' 'Well, think it over,' said the tall chap. 'Yes, sleep on it, Jack,' said the short chap, and off they went. The next thing was that Mary came home to dinner one day and said that a woman living down the road had told her that her husband had told her—the woman down the road—that I was going to stand as an independent candidate—'Nonsense,' I said. 'I'm only telling you what she said,' said Mary. 'If you did stand you'd stand as good a chance as any,' said Laura, after Mary had raised her voice to repeat what she had already told me.

That evening I handed a letter into the office of the Editor of the *Western Mail*, in which my letter appeared next morning. I made it known that I had been invited to stand as an independent candidate in the forthcoming by-election and that I had turned down the invitation, for the reason that I was not prepared to feed my ambition at the expense of my country's cause. I also made it known that I was ready to support, with my voice and my pen, the National Government candidate whoever he or she might be. It turned out to be Cyril Lakin, the Assistant Editor of the *Sunday Times*, and although I had never met him he was good enough for me. An independent candidate whose place of origin was Australia appeared in the field, and he was followed on to the field by the Welsh Nationalist candidate, a Mr. Paton, who had as fine a set of moustache and whiskers as I had seen for a long time. He drew the largest crowds and provided the most entertainment. I went about speaking on behalf of the National Government candidate and also saying what I thought of the so-called independent candidates who were springing up at every by-election. I asked if June 1942, was the time to try and embarrass the Government, to weaken the people's faith in it? I posed many a question which proved rather awkward—anyway, the National Government candidate was returned by a majority of thousands and the genial and most entertaining Welsh Nationalist candidate forfeited his deposit. Still, he could afford it.

We were not hearing from Lawrence, and Laura watched the postman night and morning from the corner of our bedroom window, so the candidates and what they said during the by-election campaign held no interest for her. 'No letter from Lawrie this morning again,' she would sigh, and this morning after morning got on my nerves until I shouted: 'Don't keep on saying that every morning, woman. The boy's all right. No news is good news.' 'I hope so,' she said. 'If it's not one it's the other,' I said. 'Watching the postman all the damned time until you make me feel as anxious as you are. But I've got to go out and face people and talk confidently most nights of the week, remember.' 'I'm not stopping you to talk any way you like,' she said. 'I know you're not, lovely girl—and I'll tell you what's wrong. This full-time job of Mary's is tying you up, keeping you in too much. With her two boys to look to, you can't come about with me same as you did up to the time I went to America. Now I'm getting all the out and you all the in. To-night I'm telling Mary that she must ask Mr. Harris to let her work half-time, mornings only—' 'No, I shall be all right,' said Laura.

Next morning there were letters from three of her boys—and you should have seen Laura when she came dancing into the bathroom as I was shaving myself. 'A letter from Lawrie, look, a letter from——' 'Let me have it quick,' I said, half-shaved. 'Go and get your glasses, woman.' Oh, what a grand letter it was. Again he had been recommended for the Military Cross—'But that's nothing compared to the fact that he's safe and well,' I said. 'Didn't I tell you that he was all right? There you are, see. All that worry and watching the postman wasn't necessary after all.' 'How was I to know?' said Laura.

'Well, you know now, I said, and now you should know better than to do it again.' 'I'll try not to,' she said.

The letter from David said that he and Kathie were both grand, she was working at a nearby war factory. There were rumours that the Squadron was soon to go overseas, but there were rumours to that effect all the time. He hoped to be home for his birthday in August if he wasn't sent overseas before then. If he came it would be only for a couple or three days, for Kathie would not be able to get another holiday—though she could get a doctor's certificate to say she was unwell—'He's fishing for an invitation for her,' I said, 'but I'll tell him when I write. It's true I told them to come again when-ever they could, but once a year is enough for me all the same.' 'Let them come while they can,' said Laura. 'Oh, all right,' I said.

The letter from Clifford said he had played his last part with the Catterick crowd, meaning the amateur players of the Royal Corps of Signals. Soon he would be leaving for London, where, as a first-class wireless operator, he would have more scope and also be able to see more first-class plays. But he hoped to get a spot of leave before leaving for London and—'And he'll be down here again,' I said, interrupting Laura's reading of the letter. 'Where else would he go?' said Laura. 'That's it,' I said, 'where else would any of them damn-well go? That's the beauty of it and you waiting on them hand and foot all the time they're here. This bungalow has been more like a barracks than—' 'You haven't had much to complain about,' said Laura. 'All right, all right, have 'em here one after the other until you've killed yourself waiting on 'em,' I shouted.

That night Glyn came over from Penarth with a bottle of brandy—'Letter from Laurie,' was how Laura greeted him. 'Where is it?' said Glyn, handing me the bottle of brandy. 'That's what you asked me to try and get for granny,' he said. 'How much was it?' I asked him. 'Wait till I read our Law's letter,' he said. 'H'm, again he's been recommended for the Military Cross, Mam.' 'Now,' I said, 'before you start reading those other letters, how much did you pay for this bottle of brandy for your granny?' 'Give me a pound and we'll call it quits,' he said. 'Here's thirty shillings,' I said, 'for you didn't get it for less. This will be a godsend for your granny.' Glyn pocketed the thirty shillings and started reading David's letter. That's how it was and always will be in our house, everybody reading everybody else's letters. 'We'll take this over to my Mother to-morrow, go on the half-past eleven bus, Lol,' I said. 'But how about the children?' she said. 'There you are,' I said. 'All right, we'll have to wait till Mary has her half-day Wednesday and go on the half-past two bus.'

My Mother was pretty bad when we were last up to see her and Belle said it was only the drop of brandy that kept her going and Danny had tried everywhere to get some more—'I'll get her some from somewhere,' I said, and now Glyn had got it from his sergeants' mess for me. But when we took it up to Merthyr on the Wednesday afternoon my Mother was much better and Danny had managed to get a bottle of brandy for her. 'Never mind,' I said, 'now you've got enough to last you till Christmas.' 'That's if I live till then,' said my Mother. 'Stop talking like a funeral,' said my sister Belle. 'I must tell you, John. Mam's a hell of a woman at times.' 'Now, now, Belle,' I said. 'But I tell you she is,' she said. 'Belle's right, John,' said my Mother. 'I'm gone to talk like an old woman and sometimes I give in. Since Jackie's gone to the Navy'—'How is Jackie?' I said. 'Grand—show John his photo, Belle,' said my Mother. Belle handed me the photo of my nephew, Jackie, looking grand in petty-officer's uniform. 'Head-cook he is, you see, John,' said my Mother. 'Our Lawrie's been recommended for the Military Cross,' said Laura. 'And that's the second time,' said Mary.

Little David and Norman missed Jasper, the fine black-and-white grey-hound, and their Auntie Belle was telling them that he was gone far away, but the old dog had died. Frank, our Belle's son, was in the Merchant Navy, and she was worrying because she had not heard from him for ever so long. 'We didn't hear from Lawrie for nearly a month and I was beginning to think—' 'Yes, but you had no need to think that way,' I said, interrupting Laura. All their talk was about 'the boys', how are they?—where are they now?—and so on. 'Where are those children gone to, I wonder?' said Mary presently. 'Don't worry, they're all right out the back,' said Belle. 'That old Rommel is a bit of a flamer, isn't he, John?' said my Mother as Mary went out the back to see what her two boys were up to. 'Yes, but there's too much talk about him, Mam,' I said. 'All our newspapers seem to have Rommel on the brain and now the people are beginning to think he's a war wizard or something of the sort.' 'Like that old De Wet in the last war,' said Mam. 'Not the last war, De Wet was a Boer War general, Mam,' I said. 'Was he?' she said indifferently as she went on knitting, her eyes resting for a few seconds on my brother David's Distinguished Conduct Medal in its frame on the wall. Maybe she was thinking of that day in 1916 when she went with my Dad to Cardiff to receive it on the Barracks' square, where every available man was on parade that day. David her husband at her side and David her son lying quiet over there in Mametz Wood and she parading at Cardiff to receive the Distinguished Conduct Medal he had won—

How old is she now? I wondered, watching her knitting away. I shall be fifty-eight in November, I told myself, so she must be seventy-eight if not seventy-nine—for she had Raddie and had lost the lovely little girl before she had me— 'This war, John,' she said, starting another row with the needle she had knitted off the row before, 'this war will last longer than the one you and your brothers went to.' 'It may, Mam,' I said. 'It will, John,' she said. 'Belle is a good gel, John.' 'Don't I know it, Mam,' I said. 'Yes, a very good gel,' she said. 'Keeps this old house clean as a pin upstairs and down and looks after me, her husband and those three old boys of ours, and her own boy and Jackie when they come on leave. Yes, a good gel, John. All I can do now is sit quiet out of the way and knit a bit.' She raised her voice a little to ask: 'How do you manage for a bit of food down Cardiff, Laura?' 'What?' said Laura. 'I'm gone I can't shout for her to hear. Tell her, John,' said Mam. 'Oh,' said Laura after I had repeated Mam's question. 'We manage very well, but when the boys or Mary's husband write to say they are coming on leave now we ask them to try and remember their ration cards. They didn't use to bother, but now—' 'Yes,' said my Mother, 'when they come one after the other they mustn't forget their ration cards. Our Danny is the one . . . goes round the shops to see what's to be had first thing in the morning.' She looked at Laura and said as loud as she could: 'The wool we're getting now is not so good for knitting as the wool before the war, Laura.' Laura looked at me and I repeated what my Mother had said. 'No, not near as good,' said Laura. 'Her hearing is getting worse, John,' said my Mother. 'No,' I said, 'it's just the habit she's got into of not listening the first time.' Mary brought her two boys in, having washed them ready to leave. 'Ready to go, are you, boys?' said my Mother. 'Yes,' said David. 'I'm in second class now.' 'Well done you,' said my Mother. 'Norman isn't,' said David. 'You're older than he is,' said my Mother. 'Never mind, Norman,' said my sister Belle, kissing him. 'You'll catch up with him, won't you?'

It's no use trying to talk to Laura whilst on a bus, for one would have to shout loud enough for all the other passengers to hear, so I waited until we got home and until Mary and the boys had gone to bed before saying: 'We must go to Merthyr oftener than once a month from now on. My Mother's breaking fast.' After Laura had gone to bed I went to fetch the desk diary to make sure about my engagements, and lucky I did, for if I hadn't I should have forgotten about Quentin Reynolds coming down to me from London next day. So I got an old envelope out of the waste-paper basket and with a fat blue pencil printed 'QUENTIN REYNOLDS ANGEL HOTEL DON'T FORGET' on both sides and put it on the mantelpiece in the living-room to remind me. That's how I keep myself in touch with what has gone into my desk and pocket diaries and I recruit four living reminders when I put hand-printed reminders of each and every engagement on the mantelpiece of the living-room, where Laura and Mary and Mary's two boys can see it. The boys slowly call out the letters I have printed on the reminder before and after their breakfast and I tell them the words the letters make. 'So it's to-day the American is coming, is it?' said Laura. 'This afternoon, round about tea-time,' I told her. 'Did you meet him over in America, Dad?' said Mary, undoing the back of Norman's trousers before he went to the lav'. 'There, you must learn to do the front yourself,' she told him. 'No, I've never met him,' I said. 'Mary, look at that boy sitting all hunched up.' 'I don't think he's up to the mark,' said Mary. 'What's wrong with you?' I asked little David. 'Nothing,' he said. 'He's always the same after a long bus-ride, takes him a day or two to get over it,' said Mary. 'But you are a bit dopey at the best of times, son.' 'No more dopey than the other one—or yourself for that matter,' said Laura, who seems to be able to hear anything said against her favourite, little David, the first time.

Someone in the American Division had written to ask if I would guide Quentin Reynolds through a few of the South Wales mining valleys and I was only too pleased to do anything I could for American visitors. I thought to take Quentin Reynolds on the same run as I had taken Ray Daniell of the *New York Times*, but it was more difficult to accommodate Reynolds. He himself weighed about seventeen stone and he travelled with a secretary and photographer. What he wanted was material for a mining 'story' for *Collier's Weekly* . . . Yes, I said, looking at him as he tossed off his second double-brandy, which appeared to be his favourite drink. No wonder my brother Danny and me had found it difficult to buy a bottle of brandy for our aged Mother in Cardiff and Merthyr. For if there were many more like Quentin around then they were bound to create a brandy shortage. The strange thing to me was that all the brandy he was able to get had no more effect on him than the same amount of water would have had on me. Another thing. When there was no more brandy obtainable Quentin took the next-best in his opinion without a murmur, and he was still cheerful when forced down to a tankard of wartime beer. He had known mighty drinkers in Soviet Russia, and was he not a mighty man himself? Yes, and he and his presented a transportation problem, but Frank Baker, who had a little petrol left over, solved it by giving the biggest of his two cars an outing before putting it away for the duration. Yes, and Frank himself took a couple of days off to drive our near-to-famous American visitor around the coalfield. Frank and his wife also staged at their home a lunch worthy of our American visitor's reputation and size. It was an outsize lunch for an outsize visitor and it had everything down to—well, it was the last of the swell lunches which Britain had in her locker to honour such visitors with. Quentin will remember it gratefully.

We sent Quentin down one of the coal-mines in the Rhondda Valley and we sent his secretary, a most charming young lady, down with him. I stayed at the pit-head with the photographer Quentin had brought along, arranging 'shots' of miners as they were coming towards and walking away from the mine for him. He took scores of shots from all sorts of angles and he must have had enough illustrative material for a big book. Then the secretary took enough notes for a couple of big books, but when Quentin came perspiring up out of the mine he wanted the nearest pint of beer to wash the dust down. No sooner said than done; an admiring steward of a nearby Workmen's Club (licensed premises) invited Quentin and his party to come and have whatever they had a mind to. All he could put was beer and bread and cheese and we were most welcome. We stayed at the club for the best part of an hour before leaving to attend a 'lodge meeting' of one of the Rhondda lodges of the South Wales Miners' Federation, and Quentin, the first visitor to be allowed to remain whilst the miners discussed such questions as then affected them, was invited by the chairman to say a few words— 'That's if you've got a mind to,' he added. Quentin, like myself, never at a loss for something to say, made a neat and effective little speech. And he spoke very much to the point—I wish I could remember all he said. There was a bit from the Russian . . . He quoted a Russian worker who said: 'Our fighting men do not fight by the clock or die by the clock, nor do we, the workers of Russia, work by the clock. We work all we can all the time . . .'

I enjoyed those couple of days with Quentin Reynolds; it was a nice break in between two intensive bouts of talking all over the place. For in July of 1942 words were still weapons of war, and it was felt necessary that I and others like me should go on talking. In addition to meetings at works and factories I was also speaking at camps and gun-sites to men and women of the Forces. As going about the works and factories I met those who in the years leading up to the outbreak of war had been part of what was then called 'the hard core of unemployment'. I also found at work thousands of those classed as unemployable until the demands of the war on labour stopped all that nonsense. Such tags and labels as figure-fuddled so-called experts had made for scores and hundreds of thousands were made to look silly by the progress of the war. They and their surveys and investigations . . . The war, more terrible in many ways than any other war in history, had at least conferred the dignity of work upon those who had been told that they were unemployable and done for, and now they were proving that not by a long shot were they anything near being done for. I don't know into what wartime holes the sometime so-called experts have scuttled for the duration, but wherever they are let them not come out when this war is won and try to tell me that what war can do in the way of providing unemployment peace cannot. The people's reward for winning this people's war must be a people's peace, in which the least that should be made certain is the provision of work and wages and the continuity of self-respect.

Anyway, after another hard week's talking I was too tired to go with Laura, Mary and her two boys, to meet Glyn and Julia and little Lorraine on the pebble beach at Penarth on the Sunday afternoon. Come on, it will do you good, said Laura, but I would not go. It was a long time since I had been left in peace to have a good read, and now that they were leaving just after two and would not be back much before ten I had eight hours' perfect peace to look forward to. First I looked up next week's engagements in my desk diary and printed the next day's engagement, guest-speaker at the weekly lunch of the Cardiff Rotary Club, subject: British-American Comradeship In War And Peace. I printed on an old envelope 'BE AT PARK HOTEL BY ONE AT LATEST FOR ROTARY LUNCH' and put it on the mantelpiece in the living-room. Then, wearing my as good-as-new dressing-gown I went into my own room and started dipping into the books there. I went on dipping until tea-time without the aid of my glasses, but after tea I wore my glasses. Oh, what a grand read I had before they came back home to shatter the peace I had been revelling in. All the same I was glad to see them. 'I don't want any supper,' said Mary, 'just a cup of tea, that's all. I shan't want any rocking to-night.' Her two boys were telling me of the ships they had seen and the big fish a man fishing from the pier had caught and the picnic they had had with the food they and Auntie Julia as well had brought —'Oh, Jack, Julia's feet have gone bad through standing at that lathe she's working at,' said Laura. 'How bad?' I said. 'Well, sore, like the candle of her eye,' she said. 'The doctor told her it's not being used to standing all the time.' 'Oh,' I said. 'If it's only by standing then what about me behind that counter all day?' said Mary. 'Yes, but you do get the chance to move around,' said Laura. 'Julia will have to watch that she don't get varicose veins or something. If she doesn't get better soon Glyn says she will have to give the job up. Now what do you boys want to eat?' 'Not much of anything at this time,' said Mary. 'Oh, let them have food,' said Laura. They had milk to drink and some bread and butter and cake to eat before going to bed. 'Quarter to seven in the morning, Mam,' said Mary. 'Good night, Dad.'

Mary sleeps until half-past eight on Sunday mornings after, as she says, getting up early all the week. This is what she calls early. Quarter-past seven each week-day morning except Mondays; she gets up at a quarter to seven on Monday mornings so as to do the living-room and the bedrooms before going to her work at the shop. Then her Mother can start her washing as soon as she has left for the shop and the boys have left with me to go to school. 'Speaking at the Rotary to-day then, Dad?' she said. 'Yes,' I said, 'in the morning now.' 'Then you won't be home to lunch?' said Laura. 'Woman,' I said, 'that's pretty obvious, isn't it?' 'Good morning, all,' said Mary. 'We'll go with mammy,' said David. 'You'll wait for me,' I said, 'and go when I'm ready.' 'Yes, wait for grampa,' said Mary. David closed his lips and looked resentfully at me. 'Right,' I said presently, and David walked out, followed by Norman, passing their Nana in the scullery without a word. 'Stop!' I shouted. 'What about your Nana, the pair of you?' They turned about and returned to kiss her good morning. 'You two are getting worse,' I said. 'Don't trouble to say good morning to your Nana now.' They didn't say anything then, but when we were going along the road David said: 'We can go to school by ourselves and come home by ourselves.' 'Oh,' I said, 'you can, can you?' 'Yes, can't we, Norm?' he said. 'Never mind asking Norman,' I said. 'Don't try to make him as bad as yourself.' 'Ask him then, you ask him if we can't go to school by ourselves,' said David. 'Walter goes by himself and Christopher Davies——' 'And Gerald and Russell James,' said Norman. 'They don't have their grampas to take them to school,' said David.

'Right,' I said. 'Good enough. Go by yourselves for all I care.' And they went by themselves and David took Norman by the hand to halt him this side of the main road, and after a look left and right they crossed the main road. Not satisfied with that they went on to assert their independence by going off the main road to stand with some other boys who were looking at the books and things in the window of Thomas's shop. 'Go on to school before you have me after you,' I shouted. Hand in hand they went off to school and I knew that they resented my shepherding of them. They were themselves, able to go and come by themselves; at six and a half and five and a half years respectively they claimed their independence. I stood watching them until they were out of sight and I was about to step out to take my morning walk when I saw the postman coming. 'Anything for Sarandai?' I asked. 'Yes, Mr. Jones.' Amongst the letters he handed me was one that made me feel afraid. War Office stamp and a Liverpool postmark. I stuffed the other letters into one of my coat-pockets and opened and read this one. Then I walked slowly back to the house. Some men passed the time of day as on their way to catch buses or trains. My breakfast felt as though it were a stone in my stomach, all over I felt too tight inside the skin of my head and body, and how was I going to tell his Mother?

She had lit the gas under the gas-boiler to boil the clothes and she looked happy and full of work. I stooped and turned off the gas under the boiler and it went out. 'What did you do that for?' she said. 'Come with me, into my room a minute, lovely girl.' 'What's the matter?' she said. 'I'll tell you in a minute. Sit down here with me,' I said. 'It's Lawrie,' she said, and I nodded, and I didn't know what to say or do. He had died of wounds on the 22 July 1942, and there we were, his Mother and me, with only the bit of paper and the few words. 'And me not there to do something for him,' Laura was saying, and she could cry but I couldn't. With the tears streaming down her face she sat there, with the letter in her hand, looking at the two photographs of him, the one a cadet in battle-dress and the other in his officer's uniform. Now the lump in my stomach had gone and my middle part was as weak as though I had been gutted. I looked around at his books, the Navarre Society's edition of Montaigne in five volumes and the volumes of the *Encyclopedia Britannica*, ninth edition, which he had re-bound after I had bought the lot for less than a pound. 'I'll have to go and telephone, Lol,' I said presently. 'Telephone Frank Webber to say I won't be down to speak at the Rotary to-day.' 'No, no, you must try and go,' said Laura, 'and I must—oh, my lovely boy, I must try and finish the bit of washing,' she said, looking at his photographs. 'We'll have a cup of tea first,' I said. 'Come on, lovely.' 'Oh, Jack,' she said. 'Yes, I know, lovely,' I said. 'I'm feeling I don't know how and if I don't have a cup of tea or something——' 'Come on,' she said, 'and I'll make you one.'

She made a cup of tea for me and one for herself and I forget now what we said to comfort each other over the cup of tea. She went and did a bit more washing and I shaved myself and changed into my blue suit and the clock said it was twenty minutes past eleven, I remember. 'Lol,' I said, 'give over now and wash and change and come with me to meet the children out of school at twelve o'clock. For if I'm to go and speak at the Rotary I'm not leaving you here alone or with only the children when they come. We'll meet them and go with them down to the shop to Mary, and she can walk back home with you and I'll go on down town.' And that's how it was, and if ever a man was glad of his daughter's help then it was me that day. As soon as she saw me and Laura and the two little boys walk into the shop she guessed and was round the counter like a shot to stand close to her Mother as I confirmed what she only guessed. 'It's our Law,' I whispered. 'He's . . . he's gone. Tell Mr. and Mrs. Harris and take your Mother home and don't leave her till I get back from the Rotary—now, no snivelling, good girl.' She bit her lip and pressed her Mother's arm and I went outside to catch a breath of air. Mr. Harris followed me out to say how sorry he was and to offer me a cigarette. 'That's how it is,' I said. I waited until Mary and Laura and the two little boys came out of the shop. 'You go, Dad, or you'll be late,' said Mary. 'Don't worry about Mam. She'll be all right,' I pressed Laura's hand and walked away towards town, walked as far as Gabalfa, where I got on a bus. David Prosser, the Editor of the *Western Mail*, was at the Rotary Club lunch that day, and after I had spoken on 'British-American Comradeship In War And Peace' I had a word with him and went across to his office. 'It will save me writing if they see it in your paper,' I said. 'For I would have to write scores of letters to relatives and friend and I don't feel like writing them. Let them hear of it through your paper, and to those I must write I'll send a cutting.' 'Could you let me have a photograph to go with the paragraph?' he asked. 'Yes,' I said. 'I'll let you have it before the day is out.'

When I went back home to Laura, who was feeling better now, thanks to Mary, I asked her what photograph of Lawrence she would like to see next day with the paragraph that was to appear about his passing. 'Oh, the one of him in his officer's uniform,' she said. 'I'll have to take it down after tea,' I said. 'Mamma can go with you for a bit of a walk,' said Mary. 'Will you come, Lol?' I said. 'Yes,' she said. When, after tea, I went into our bedroom to brush my hair a bit, I noticed flowers in a little glass jar in front of the photograph Lawrence and David had had taken together. Then in my room, when we went to get the photograph to take down to the *Western Mail*, there were little glass jars with flowers in them in front of his two photographs in there as well. Laura had started her daily service at the little shrine of Lawrence. It wasn't long before other letters arrived from his brother-officers, and as they give some idea of what sort of a chap our Lawrence was perhaps it would be well if I quoted a passage or two from some of them. His battery commander said:

I feel that 'Jonah', as we always called him, died as he would have wished. His troop was in a sticky spot in the attack of 22 July. The Hun had got a lot too near the guns and was sniping with some sort of a gun from a ridge to the flank. The gun detachments were suffering severely. Jonah was ordered to withdraw his troop half a mile. He got the guns moving in his usual imperturbable style. Then a shell from the sniping gun wounded him in the leg and body. His batman drove him immediately to a dressing-station; where, I have since learned, he died. . . . We, too, will miss Jonah. We officers in the battery have fought together for nearly a year—and Jonah is the first to go. . . . It is too bad that Jonah, who was probably the best of us all, should be the first to go. . . .

There are another half-dozen letters from brother-officers, from the officer commanding the regiment down to the last-joined second lieutenant, but I don't feel like quoting any more. He was four times recommended for the M.C., he knew no fear, and so on, all boiling down to the basic fact that he was a man amongst men and a soldier who did his duty as he saw it to the end. Then he was our boy, Laura's and mine, and he still is and will for ever be our boy. The other boys came to their Mother as soon as they could and when Clifford returned to his duty in London he wrote his Mother, finishing his letter by signing 'Law and Kip'. His brothers agreed that he should continue signing for Lawrence as well as himself from then onwards, but they hadn't reckoned with Lawrence. For it wasn't long before his Mother said to me: 'I don't feel that he's dead any more.' Neither did I, nor did any of the others of the family. For soon he was back home and with all members of the family elsewhere and one night when I fetched a book to have a read after Laura had gone to bed he guided me to Volume The First of the Navarre Society's edition of Montaigne I had bought for him. After I had put my glasses on, the book seemed to open itself and there was Letter V for me to read. I began to read and went on reading until I came to the words which expressed the feelings of me and mine with respect to Lawrence. Then I heard Lawrence reading aloud this bit:

> Insomuch that having loved beyond everything else M. de la Boetie, the greatest man, in my judgment, of our age, I should think myself very negligent of my duty if I failed, to the extent of my power, to prevent so rich a name as his, and a memory so deserving of remembrance, from disappearing and being lost; and if I did not essay by these means to resuscitate it and make it live again. I believe that he something feels this, and that my services effect and rejoice him. In truth, he lodges with me so vividly and so wholly that I am loth to believe him committed to the gross earth, or altogether severed from communication with us. . . .

'Mark that, John,' said Lawrence. 'Too true I will, son,' I said, 'but not with this silk ribbon-marker attached to the book. Here's this letter you left here at home that time, a letter I wrote you when you were at Bulford Camp—' 'Bulford,' he said with a chuckle. 'Let's have a look at it, John.' 'Your

Mamma's letter is in there as well,' I said. 'Of course,' he said, then read the address on the envelope aloud: '931078 Gunner L. Jones, C/7 Troop, Squad 2, 4th Field Training Regiment, R.A., Wing Barracks, Bulford Camp, Wilts.' 'Yes,' he said, chuckling again, 'that was old Jonah in those days. Let's see what Mamma had to say to me then—you mustn't let her worry any more about that bit of a break in the line at El Alamein, John. She's getting over it, sleeping better now too——' 'I expect she's asleep with book in hand and glasses on now,' I said. 'I won't be a sec, son.' 'So she is,' said Lawrence with a chuckle, for he had followed me into the bedroom where we found Laura as we expected. 'Try and take her glasses off without waking her,' said Lawrence. 'That'll take some doing, son, but I'll try,' I said, and for once I did manage to take her glasses off without waking her. Then me and Law went back to the living-room. 'Where's that letter, John?' he said. It was in the left-hand pocket of my dressing-gown and I pulled it out and we read it together. It was dated 16 June 1940, and this is Laura to Lawrence at that time:

Dear Lawrence,

We received your letter and glad to hear that you are well. We are both A1 now, although dadda have had a bad throat these last few days. But it is better now, he have done a lot of speaking lately. He spoke at the Empire, Cardiff, last night on the War Savings campaign. Proud Valley is still drawing crowded houses, dadda and Mrs. Thomas still make personal appearances. I don't think I have ever seen a picture that have drawn the people more than this one. Cliff and Doris and little Pat have gone back, they went back Friday before your letter came. He is going back to hospital on the 21st. He looks very well. Mary is still with Bob at Morcambe and by her letter I think she intends staying as she has rooms at 25/- a week furnished. I suppose she knows best. Had a letter from David, his address is changed and I will put it in, in case you have not got it. Now he is at the School of Photography, Royal Air Force, Farnborough, Hants. He is well, but working very hard. Have not heard from Glyn yet, am writing him the same time as this. Well, Law, how about your washing? The garden is looking lovely. Did I tell you in the last letter that we have had the house painted? We had a little rain last night and it was wanted badly. Now I think I have told you all. So for the present best love and cheerio. Mam. XXXX.

'Now,' I said, 'I'll put that letter to mark old Montaigne where you said, son, and put it back in the bookcase, for I'm getting to feel a bit sleepy. Good night, son.' 'Good night, John,' he said, following me into my room, and I left him there amongst the books. Before very long his name appeared in the *London Gazette* for the Military Cross, and some time later we had the official citation. I read it aloud to Laura, but she would read it herself after-wards.

For conspicuous gallantry and devotion to duty throughout the entire operation

in the Corridor at Tobruk between 21 November and 8 December 1941, also
during the whole period of the withdrawal from Benghazi in February 1942.

  During the whole of these periods, his personal courage was an inspiration to all
with whom he came into contact. It was largely due to the courage, initiative and
resourcefulness displayed by Second-Lieutenant Lawrence Jones which enabled the
rearguard which he commanded during the whole period to extricate itself from
the enemy armed defence guard which he fought off from the 2 to the 9
February. During this period his troop destroyed four enemy armoured fighting
vehicles.

'Well done, our Law,' I said, but Laura began to cry and I had to talk pretty
straight to her once more. 'I'll be all right in a minute,' she said, and in about
a minute she was all right again. On the Wednesday, Mary's half-day off,
we went, the five of us, me and Laura and Mary and her two boys, up to
Merthyr on the bus, to read the official citation to my Mother, who was
surprised to see Laura as good as she was. 'P'raps you'll have to go up to
London to the King for your boy's medal, John,' said my Mother. 'It was to
Cardiff, to the Barracks, remember, me and your Father went for your
brother's medal. How are the other boys?' 'Grand,' I said. 'David will be on
embarkation leave soon and no doubt he and his wife will be down from
Scotland for a few days.' 'Then tell him and his wife to come and see me this
time, for they didn't the last time they were down,' said my Mother. 'I'll see
that they will come on the bus to see you this time,' I assured her. 'Remember
that now,' I said in a loud voice to Laura. 'Remember what?' she said. 'That
David and Kathie must come here to see my Mother when they come down
this time,' I said. 'Of course,' she said. 'They'll be having bed and breakfast
at the Park Hotel this time again,' she went on, 'for we haven't room for
them to sleep—' 'A week's sleep at the Park Hotel and they won't have
much change out of a five-pound note,' said my Mother. 'What's that?' said
Laura. I told her. 'No, you're right,' she said to my Mother.

'Look what Auntie Belle bought us, Nana,' said Norman as running in
followed by David, each with a packet of something sticky. 'Very nice—but
Auntie Belle is your Mammy's auntie and not yours,' I said. 'Can't she be
our auntie as well?' said David. 'Yes, of course she can,' said my Mother.
'How are you managing with the points and things at the shop where you
work, Mary?' 'Oh, she knows all about points and things by now,' I said.
'Brings the week's points home on Saturday to count them on Sunday.'
'It's Jack does the bit of shopping in the mornings,' said Laura. 'Yes, Mam,
I've been in the fish-queue a few times,' I said. 'But no more. Oh, no. The
last time I stood the only man in a queue of women I had enough. Of course
they were only joking, but they had the laugh on me. One woman said to
the others: "We'd better be careful what we say this morning, that's if we
don't want to find ourselves in a book and our talk in it the talk of the place."
The others laughed and looked at me—no, no more queueing-up for me

Mam.' 'Our Danny is the one, he handles our ration-books, points and all,'
said my Mother. 'Mary's two boys are kicking and wearing out my clothing
coupons,' I said. 'Is there a baby on the way with your David's wife, John?'
said my Mother. 'Not that I know of—but Mary would know, for it's to
Mary Kathie writes oftenest,' I said. 'She hasn't said anything in her letters,'
said Mary. 'How long have they been married now?' said Belle. 'About nine
months,' I said. 'Why, Mam, are you in a hurry for another great-grand-
child?' 'No, I was only wondering, that's all, John,' she said, starting to
count stitches on the knitting-needle, and in this way the time went again.
A cup of tea and a little talk about this and that and off to catch the bus
back home again. 'Your Mother was looking fairly well to-day,' said Laura.
'Oh, I don't know,' said Mary.

As soon as the bus for home started off, Norman, who was sharing a seat
with his Mother—David with his Nana as usual—somehow managed to
half-turn and kneel on the seat to get a better view of the street through the
window, and in doing so transferred some of the dirt off his boots on to
Mary's coat. 'My best coat, you little blinder,' she whispered angrily, smacking him on the leg and then twisting him back down on to his behind. He
began to cry. 'Be quiet, boy,' I said. Mary brushed the dirt off her coat with
her hand. She and Laura were wearing the black coats which Mr. Ball, the
tailor, had made ready for them to wear in less than a fortnight after the
news came through about Lawrence. I didn't agree that it was necessary
for them to go into mourning, but they said it was not decent for them to
continue going about in clothes of any other colour. Norman was still
crying—'Let him come here to me,' I said, and he came and sat beside me.
Children are all right on the first half of the journey, I was thinking, but
they're enough to drive a man daft on the return journey. 'Now, sit quiet,
good boy,' I said. After more than three years of total war and its ups and
downs the people in the bus didn't look so bad, neither did we five, Laura
and me and Mary and her two boys. We were fairly well fed and dressed—
the upset about Lawrence hadn't affected Laura's splendid appetite, thank
goodness. It was when left alone she got to feel low, but I was seeing to it
that she was not left alone for long. I had booked seats for three evenings
of Sadler's Wells opera the following week, and already I had told her the
stories of the three operas, *La Traviata*, *The Magic Flute* and *Rigoletto*. Front
row circle and what she would not hear from there in our fairly intimate
theatre she would not miss. The main thing was to keep her feeling that she
was still a part of what bit of life there was going, and I knew the house was
sold out for all performances. A crowded house, in itself, irrespective of
what takes place on the stage, is a bit of a tonic for a woman, and especially
in wartime. It was for Laura, who heard most of what the goodish
orchestra played, anyway. Then on Sunday evenings we went together to
one or other of three chapels, to Tabernacle for the community hymn-

singing, to Beulah Chapel or to Bethlehem in Gwaelodygarth to hear Mr. Berry preach.

So by the time David came down, with his Kathie, to spend a few days of his embarkation leave with us, his Mother was almost her old self again. She was laughing again and she was scolding and sometimes smacking Mary's two boys. David was there on the Sunday when there was an orchestra under Dr. Malcolm Sargent—or was it some other famous conductor?—at the Park Hall in the afternoon. I had booked two seats front row circle and I told Dave to take his Mother, and he did, wearing the suit I had bought in Pittsburgh, U.S.A., which fitted him as well as though he had been measured for it. 'Take Mamma, son,' I said. 'She'll hear the loud parts and look at the audience whilst the soft parts are being played. Anyway, an orchestra playing, even when you can't hear it, is something well worth seeing. Our Law will be there with you and his Mother,' I told Dave, and off he and his Mother went, and a handsome pair they were as they walked along the road to the bus-stop. 'Huh, look at Laura and her baby,' I said to Mary and Kathie. 'The little hound, as our Law used to call him,' said Mary. 'Hound?' said Kathie, her eyes opening wide as her lips closed tight. 'Dad will tell you, I've got to get these two boys of mine ready for Sunday-school,' said Mary. 'Don't look so angry, Kathie,' I said, 'for if ever anyone thought more of David than you do then it was Lawrence. But he used to shout at him and call him a little hound all the same, and especially when he was trying to coach David for the entry exam. to the secondary school, about which David was not very keen. "Now sit down there and work this out with me," Lawrence would say. "No, I'm going out to play," said David. "You are not, you are going to sit here and do this homework," said Law, who in his schooldays was the biggest glutton for homework that his Mother and me had ever known. But as for David—well, he shouted: "I am going out to play, our Law, and you won't stop me. Is our Law my boss, Dad?" "Never mind asking Dad, you little hound—oh, what's the use?" Lawrence would groan as David ran out laughing. Lawrence would continue with his own studies and enjoy himself with his books on one corner of the table. Only in bed did he have a chance to talk seriously to David about his future, and after David had said: "Ay, ay, our Law," a few times he would be asleep and Lawrence would find it was himself he was talking to again. "You little hound," he would say affectionately, then settle down to read until I went in to switch the light off before I went to bed. That was how they were, Kathie, your David and our Lawrence, about ten years ago.' 'I wish I had met Lawrence,' she said. 'He's all over this house and wherever his Mother goes,' I said.

CONFESSIONS OF
A TIGHT-ROPE WALKER

BY ARTHUR KOESTLER

from *The God That Failed* (1950)

CONFESSIONS OF A TIGHT-ROPE
WALKER

I

A FAITH is not acquired by reasoning. One does not fall in love with a woman, or enter the womb of a church, as a result of logical persuasion. Reason may defend an act of faith—but only after the act has been committed, and the man committed to the act. Persuasion may play a part in a man's conversion; but only the part of bringing to its full and conscious climax a process which has been maturing in regions where no persuasion can penetrate. A faith is not acquired; it grows like a tree. Its crown points to the sky; its roots grow downward into the past and are nourished by the dark sap of the ancestral humus.

From the psychologist's point of view, there is little difference between a revolutionary and a traditionalist faith. All true faith is uncompromising, radical, purist; hence the true traditionalist is always a revolutionary zealot in conflict with pharisaean society, with the lukewarm corrupters of the creed. And vice versa: the revolutionary's Utopia, which in appearance represents a complete break with the past, is always modelled on some image of the lost paradise, of a legendary Golden Age. The classless communist society, according to Marx and Engels, was to be a revival, at the end of the dialectical spiral, of the primitive communist society which stood at its beginning. Thus all true faith involves a revolt against the believer's social environment, and the projection into the future of an ideal derived from the remote past. All Utopias are fed from the sources of mythology; the social engineer's blueprints are merely revised editions of the ancient text.

Devotion to pure Utopia, and revolt against a polluted society are thus the two poles which provide the tension of all militant creeds. To ask which of the two makes the current flow—attraction by the ideal or repulsion by the social environment—is to ask the old question about the hen and the egg. To the psychiatrist, both the craving for Utopia and the rebellion against the *status quo* are symptoms of social maladjustment. To the social reformer, both are symptoms of a healthy rational attitude. The psychiatrist is apt to forget that smooth adjustment to a deformed society creates deformed individuals. The reformer is equally apt to forget that hatred, even of the

153

objectively hateful, does not produce that charity and justice on which a utopian society must be based.

Thus each of the two attitudes, the sociologist's and the psychologist's, reflects a half-truth. It is true that the case-history of most revolutionaries and reformers reveals a neurotic conflict with family or society. But this only proves, to paraphrase Marx, that a moribund society creates its own morbid grave-diggers.

It is also true that, in the face of revolting injustice, the only honourable attitude is to revolt, and to leave introspection for better times. But if we survey history and compare the lofty aims in the name of which re-volutions were started, and the sorry end to which they came, we see again and again how a polluted civilization pollutes its own revolutionary offspring.

Fitting the two half-truths—the sociologist's and the psychologist's—together, we conclude that if on the one hand over-sensitivity to social injustice and obsessional craving for Utopia are signs of neurotic maladjust-ment, society, may, on the other hand, reach a state of decay where the neurotic rebel causes more joy in heaven than the sane executive who orders pigs to be drowned under the eyes of starving men. This in fact was the state of our civilization when, in December 1931, at the age of twenty-six, I joined the Communist Party of Germany.

II

I became converted because I was ripe for it and lived in a disintegrating society thirsting for faith. But the day when I was given my party card was merely the climax of a development which had started long before I had read about the drowned pigs or heard the names of Marx and Lenin. Its roots reach back into childhood; and though each of us, comrades of the Pink Decade, had individual roots with different twists in them, we are pro-ducts of—by and large—the same generation and cultural climate. It is this unity underlying diversity which makes me hope that my story is worth telling.

I was born in 1905 in Budapest; we lived there till 1919, when we moved to Vienna. Until the first world war we were comfortably off, a typical Con-tinental middle-middle-class family: my father was the Hungarian represen-tative of some old-established British and German textile manufacturers. In September 1914 this form of existence, like so many others, came to an abrupt end: my father never found his feet again. He embarked on a number of ventures which became the more fantastic the more he lost self-confidence in a changed world. He opened a factory for radio-active soap; he backed several crank inventions (everlasting electric bulbs, self-heating bed-bricks and the like); and finally lost the remains of his capital in the Austrian inflation of the early 'twenties. I left home at twenty-one, and from that day became the only financial support of my parents.

At the age of nine, when our middle-class idyll collapsed, I had suddenly become conscious of the economic Facts of Life. As an only child, I continued to be pampered by my parents; but, well aware of the family crisis, and torn by pity for my father, who was of a generous and somewhat childlike disposition, I suffered a pang of guilt whenever they bought me books or toys. This continued later on, when every suit I bought for myself meant so much less to send home. Simultaneously, I developed a strong dislike of the obviously rich; not because they could afford to buy things (envy plays a much lesser part in social conflict than is generally assumed) but because they were able to do so without a guilty conscience. Thus I projected a personal predicament on to the structure of society at large.

It was certainly a tortuous way of acquiring a social conscience. But precisely because of the intimate nature of the conflict, the faith which grew out of it became an equally intimate part of myself. It did not, for some years, crystallize into a political creed; at first it took the form of a mawkishly sentimental attitude. Every contact with people poorer than myself was unbearable—the boy at school who had no gloves and red chilblains on his fingers, the former travelling salesman of my father's reduced to cadging occasional meals—all of them were additions to the load of guilt on my back. The analyst would have no difficulty in showing that the roots of this guilt-complex go deeper than the crisis in our household budget; but if he were to dig even deeper, piercing through the individual layers of the case, he would strike the archetypal pattern which has produced millions of particular variations on the same theme—'Woe, for they chant to the sound of harps and anoint themselves, but are not grieved for the affliction of the people'.

Thus sensitivized by a personal conflict, I was ripe for the shock of learning that wheat was burnt, fruit artificially spoilt and pigs were drowned in the depression years to keep prices up and enable fat capitalists to chant to the sound of harps; while Europe trembled under the torn boots of hunger-marchers and my father hid his frayed cuffs under the table. The frayed cuffs and drowned pigs blended into one emotional explosion as the fuse of the archetype was touched off. We sang the 'Internationale', but the words might as well have been the older ones: 'Woe to the shepherds who feed themselves, but feed not their flocks'.

In other respects too the story is more typical than it seems. A considerable proportion of the middle classes in central Europe were, like ourselves, ruined by the inflation of the 'twenties. It was the beginning of Europe's decline. This disintegration of the middle strata of society started the fatal process of polarization which continues to this day. The pauperized bourgeois became

rebels of the Right or Left; Schickelgruber and Djugashvili shared about
equally the benefits of the social migration. Those who refused to admit
that they had become *déclassé*, who clung to the empty shell of gentility,
joined the Nazis and found comfort in blaming their fate on Versailles and
the Jews. Many did not even have that consolation; they lived on pointlessly,
like a great black swarm of tired winterflies crawling over the dim windows
of Europe, members of a class displaced by history.

The other half turned Left, thus confirming the prophecy of the Communist Manifesto: 'Entire sections of the ruling classes are . . . precipitated
into the proletariat, or are at least threatened in their conditions of existence.
They . . . supply the proletariat with fresh elements of enlightenment and
progress'.

That 'fresh element of enlightenment', I discovered to my delight, was I.
As long as I had been nearly starving, I had regarded myself as a temporarily
displaced offspring of the bourgeoisie. In 1931, when at last I had achieved a
comfortable income I found that it was time to join the ranks of the proletariat. But the irony of this sequence only occurred to me in retrospect.

III

The bourgeois family will vanish as a matter of course with the vanishing of
capital. . . . The bourgeois claptrap about the family and education, about the
haloed correlation of parent and child, becomes all the more disgusting the more,
by the action of modern industry, all family ties among the proletarians are torn
asunder. . . .

Thus the Communist Manifesto. Every page of Marx, and even more of
Engels, brought a new revelation, and an intellectual delight which I had
only experienced once before, at my first contact with Freud. Torn from its
context, the above passage sounds ridiculous; as part of a closed system, which
made social philosophy fall into a lucid and comprehensive pattern, the
demonstration of the historical relativity of institutions and ideals—of family,
class, patriotism, bourgeois morality, sexual taboos—had the intoxicating
effect of a sudden liberation from the rusty chains with which a pre-1914
middle-class childhood had cluttered one's mind. To-day, when Marxist
philosophy has degenerated into a Byzantine cult and virtually every single
tenet of the Marxist programme has become twisted into its opposite, it is
difficult to recapture that mood of emotional fervour and intellectual
bliss.

I was ripe to be converted as a result of my personal case-history; thousands
of other members of the intelligentsia and the middle classes of my generation were ripe for it by virtue of other personal case-histories; but however
much these differed from case to case, they had a common denominator: the

rapid disintegration of moral values, of the pre-1914 pattern of life in post-war Europe, and the simultaneous lure of the new revelation which had come from the East.

I joined the Party (which to this day has remained 'the' Party for all of us who once belonged to it) in 1931, at the beginning of that short-lived period of optimism, of that abortive spiritual renaissance, later known as the Pink Decade. The stars of that treacherous dawn were Barbusse, Romain Rolland, Gide and Malraux in France; Piscator, Becher, Renn, Brecht, Eisler, Saeghers in Germany; Auden, Isherwood, Spender in England; Dos Passos, Upton Sinclair, Steinbeck, in the United States. The cultural atmosphere was saturated with Progressive Writers' congresses, experimental theatres, committees for Peace and against Fascism, societies for cultural relations with the U.S.S.R., Russian films and *avant-garde* magazines. It looked indeed as if the Western world, convulsed by the aftermath of war, scourged by inflation, depression, unemployment and the absence of a faith to live for, was at last going to 'clear from the head the masses of impressive rubbish;—Rally the lost and trembling forces of the will—Gather them up and let them loose upon the earth—Till they construct at last a human justice. (Auden.) The new star of Bethlehem had risen in the East; and for a modest sum, Intourist was prepared to allow you a short and well-focused glimpse of the Promised Land.

I lived at that time in Berlin. For the last five years, I had been working for the Ullstein chain of newspapers—first as a foreign correspondent in Palestine and the Middle East, then in Paris. Finally, in 1930, I joined the editorial staff in the Berlin 'House'. For a better understanding of what follows, a few words have to be said about the House of Ullstein, symbol of the Weimar Republic.

Ullstein's was a kind of super-trust; the largest organization of its kind in Europe, and probably in the world. They published four daily papers in Berlin alone, among these the venerable *Vossische Zeitung*, founded in the eighteenth century, and the *B.Z. am Mittag*, an evening paper with a record circulation and a record speed in getting the news out. Apart from these, Ullstein's published more than a dozen weekly and monthly periodicals, ran their own news service, their own travel agency, etc., and were one of the leading book publishers. The firm was owned by the brothers Ullstein—they were five, like the original Rothschild brothers, and like them also, they were Jews. Their policy was liberal and democratic, and in cultural matters progressive to the point of *avant-gardism*. They were anti-militaristic, anti-chauvinistic, and it was largely due to their influence on public opinion that the policy of Franco-German *rapprochement* of the Briand-Stresemann era became a vogue among the progressive part of the German people. The firm of Ullstein was not only a political power in Germany; it was at the same time the embodiment of everything progressive and cosmopolitan in the Weimar

Republic. The atmosphere in the 'House' in the Kochstrasse was more that of a Ministry than of an editorial office.

My transfer from the Paris office to the Berlin house was due to an article I wrote on the occasion of the award of the Nobel Prize for Physics to the Prince de Broglie. My bosses decided that I had a knack for popularizing science (I had been a student of science in Vienna) and offered me the job of Science Editor of the *Vossische* and adviser on matters scientific to the rest of the Ullstein publications. I arrived in Berlin on the fateful day of 14 September 1930—the day of the Reichstag Election in which the National Socialist Party, in one mighty leap, increased the number of its deputies from 4 to 107. The Communists had also registered important gains; the democratic parties of the centre were crushed. It was the beginning of the end of Weimar; the situation was epitomized in the title of Knickerbocker's best-seller: *Germany, Nazi or Communist?* Obviously there was no 'third alternative'.

I did my job, writing about electrons, chromosomes, rocket-ships, Neanderthal men, spiral nebulæ and the universe at large; but the pressure of events increased rapidly. With one-third of its wage-earners unemployed, Germany lived in a state of latent civil war; and if one wasn't prepared to be swept along as a passive victim by the approaching hurricane it became imperative to take sides. Stresemann's party was dead. The Socialists pursued a policy of opportunist compromise. Even by a process of pure elimination the Communists, with the mighty Soviet Union behind them, seemed the only force capable of resisting the onrush of the primitive horde with its swastika totem. But it was not by a process of elimination that I became a Communist. Tired of electrons and wave-mechanics, I began for the first time to read Marx, Engels and Lenin in earnest. By the time I had finished with *Feuerbach* and *State and Revolution*, something had clicked in my brain which shook me like a mental explosion. To say that one had 'seen the light' is a poor description of the mental rapture which only the convert knows (regardless to what faith he has been converted). The new light seems to pour from all directions across the skull; the whole universe falls into pattern like the stray pieces of a jig-saw puzzle assembled by magic at one stroke. There is now an answer to every question; doubts and conflicts are a matter of the tortured past—a past already remote, when one had lived in dismal ignorance in the tasteless, colourless world of those who *don't know*. Nothing henceforth can disturb the convert's inner peace and serenity—except the occasional fear of losing faith again, losing thereby what alone makes life worth living, and falling back into the outer darkness, where there is wailing and gnashing of teeth. This may explain how Communists, with eyes to see and brains to think with, can still act in subjective bona fides, anno Domini 1949. At all times and in all creeds only a minority has been capable of courting excommunication and committing emotional hara-kiri in the name of an abstract truth.

The date on which I applied for membership of the Communist Party of Germany is easy to remember: it was 31 December 1931. The new life was to start with the new calendar-year. I applied by means of a letter addressed to the Central Committee of the K.P.D.;[1] the letter contained a short *curriculum vitæ* and stated my readiness to serve the cause in whatever capacity the Party decided.

It was not usual to apply for membership by writing to the Central Committee; I did it on the advice of friends in close touch with the Party. The normal procedure was to join one of the party-cells, the basic units of the Party's organizational network. There were two types of cells: 'workshop-cells' (*Betriebs-Zellen*), which comprised the Party members of a given factory, workshop, office or any other enterprise; and 'street-cells' (*Strassen-Zellen*), organized according to residential blocks. Most wage-earners belonged both to the workshop-cell of the place where they were employed, and to the street-cell of their homes. This system was universal in all countries where the Party led a legal existence. It was an iron rule that each Party member, however high up in the hierarchy, must belong to a cell. There was, so we were told, a 'workshop-cell' even in the Kremlin, in which members of the Politbureau, sentries and charwomen discussed the policy of the Party in fraternal democracy at the usual weekly meeting, and where Stalin was told off if he forgot to pay his membership fee.

However, my friend N., who had played a decisive part in my conversion, strongly advised me against joining a cell in the usual way (I call him N., for he left the Party years ago and lives now in a country where even a buried and renounced Communist past might mean trouble for a foreigner). N. was a former plumber's apprentice who, through evening classes and dogged night-reading, had made the grade and become a well-known political writer. He knew his Marx and Lenin backwards and forwards and had that absolute, serene faith which exerts a hypnotic power over other people's minds. 'Don't be a fool,' he explained to me, 'once you join a cell and it becomes known that you have become a Party member, you will lose your job with the Ullsteins. And that job is an important asset for the Party.'

I must add that, in the meantime, while retaining my science job at the *Vossische*, I had been appointed Foreign Editor of the *B.Z. am Mittag*; a post which carried a certain political influence and gave access to a good deal of political inside information.

So, on N.'s advice, I wrote direct to the Central Committee.

A week or so later the answer came in the form of a rather puzzling letter. It was typed on a blank sheet of paper without heading, and ran somewhat as follows:

[1] Kommunistiche Partei Deutschlands.

Dear Sir,

   With reference to your esteemed of 31 Dec., we shall be glad if you will meet
a representative of our firm, Herr Schneller, at the offices of the Schneidemühl
paper-mill, ——strasse, next Monday at 3 p.m.

Yours truly,
(illegible signature).

The Schneidermühl paper-mills were well known in Germany, but it had
never occurred to me that they had anything to do with the K.P.D. What
exactly the connection was, I do not know; the fact remains that their Berlin
offices were used as an inconspicuous rendezvous for confidential interviews.
I did not understand the reason for all this conspiratorial secrecy; but I was
thrilled and excited. When, at the appointed time, I arrived at Schneidemühl's and asked for 'Herr Schneller', the girl at the inquiry desk gave me
what is commonly called a 'searching look' but might be more correctly
described as a fish-eyed stare. Since then I have often met that look in similar
situations; whenever the desire for fraternal complicity is checked by distrust
and fear, people exchange glances which are neither 'penetrating' nor
'searching'; they goggle at each other dully, like fish.

'Have you a date with Ernest?' she asked.

'No—with Herr Schneller.'

This stupidity seemed somehow to convince her of my bona fides. She
said Herr Ernest Schneller hadn't arrived yet, and told me to sit down and
wait. I waited—for over half an hour. It was my first experience of that unpunctuality which was *de rigueur* in the higher strata of the Party. The
Russians, as semi-orientals, are congenitally unpunctual; and as, consciously
or unconsciously, every Party bureaucrat tried to live up to Russian style,
the habit gradually filtered down from the top Comintern-bureaucracy into
every national C.P. in Europe.

At last he turned up. He introduced himself, Continental fashion, by bark-
ing out 'Schneller'; I barked 'Koestler'; we shook hands and after a perfunctory apology for being 'a little late' he invited me to a café across the
street. He was a thin, bony man of about thirty-five, with a pinched, taut-
skinned face and an awkward smile. His manner was equally awkward; he
seemed all the time ill at ease. I took him for an insignificant underling in the
Party bureaucracy, and learned only later that his name really was Ernst
Schneller—and that he was *the* Schneller, member of the German Central
Committee and head of the Agitprop (Department for Agitation and Propaganda). Again much later, I learned that he was also the head of the
'Apparat N'[1]—one of the four or five independent and parallel intelligence-
organizations, some of which were run by the German Party, some directly
by the O.G.P.U. What exactly Schneller's 'Apparat' did, whether military

---

[1] I do not actually remember by which letter Schneller's organization was known.

intelligence work or just harmless industrial espionage, I do not know to this day. Schneller himself was sentenced by the Nazis to six years' hard labour, and died, or was killed, in jail.

Of all this of course I knew nothing when I met that insignificant, rather shabby-looking, thin man at the shabby offices of Schneidemühl's, my first contact with the Party. Of our conversation in the little café, I remember that he mentioned that he was a vegetarian and lived mainly on raw vegetables and fruit; it seemed to explain that bony, parched face. I also remember that to my question whether he had read a certain article in a newspaper, he answered that he never read bourgeois papers; the only paper he read was the official Party organ, *Rote Fahne*. This confirmed my opinion that the Central Committee had sent me some narrrow-minded, sectarian petty bureaucrat; the absurdity of a propaganda-chief who only reads his own paper did not dawn on me until later, when I learned of Schneller's official function. He did not ask many questions, but inquired in some detail about the exact position I held at Ullstein's. I told him of my desire to throw up my job and to work for the Party only, as a propagandist or, preferably, as a tractor-driver in the Soviet Union. (This was the period of enforced collectivization, and the Soviet Press was calling desperately for tractor-drivers.) My friend N. had already warned me against this idea, which he called 'typical petty-bourgeois romanticism', and said that, if I talked about it to any Party official, I would make a fool of myself. But I thought him rather cynical and couldn't see what was wrong with being a tractor-driver for a year or two, if that was the most urgent need on the Front of Socialist Reconstruction. Schneller, however, explained to me patiently that the first duty of every Communist was to work for the Revolution in his own country; to be admitted to the Soviet Union, where the Revolution had already triumphed, was a rare privilege, reserved for veterans of the movement. It would be equally wrong to quit my job; I could be much more useful to the Party by carrying on with it and keeping mum about my political convictions. Useful in what way ? I asked. After all, I couldn't turn the *B.Z.* into a Communist paper, or change the policy of the House of Ullstein. Schneller said I was 'putting the question in a mechanistic form'; there were many ways by which I could influence the policy of the paper through small touches; for instance, by featuring more prominently the dangers to world peace which Japanese aggression against China represented (at that time Russia's main fear was a Japanese attack); we could, if I wished, meet once a week to discuss these matters, or even better, he could delegate somebody less busy than himself, who would be at my disposal at practically any time for my political guidance. Besides, through this mutual friend, I could hand on to the Party any political information of special interest which came my way. The Party would probably be forced underground quite soon, and, if that happened, people like myself, in respectable positions, untainted by suspicion, would be even more valuable in the life-and-death struggle against Fascism and imperialistic aggression. All this sounded quite reasonable, and my initial aversion for Schneller soon changed into respect for his simple and astute way of arguing. We agreed to meet in a week's time, when he would introduce me to my future political guide. 'Who is that going to be?' I asked. 'A comrade called Edgar,' said Schneller.

After saying good-bye to him, it suddenly occurred to me that nothing had been said about my formal admission to the Party. The whole thing was left in the air; was I henceforth a real Communist or not? I ran after Schneller and put the question to him. He smiled his awkward smile and said: 'If you insist, we will make you a Party member, but on condition that your membership remains secret. You won't be attached to any Party-cell and you will be known in the Party under a different name.' I agreed to this rather ruefully; for, if debarred from admission to a cell, I would not be able to enter the life, atmosphere and fraternity of the Party. 'Tell me what cover-name you choose,' said Schneller, 'and I'll bring along your Party card the next time.' The name which occurred to me, after the usual blank second, was 'Ivan Steinberg'. 'Ivan', obviously, because it sounded Russian. Steinberg was the name of a friend, a psycho-analyst in Tel Aviv, whom I hadn't seen or heard of for several years. He used to try to persuade me to finish my studies, which I had broken off, at the University in Vienna. 'If you don't graduate,' he once said, 'you will always remain a vagabond. Whatever position you achieve, people will always smell out the tramp in you.'

I met Schneller again one week later at the same place. Instead of Edgar, he had brought a girl along, whom he introduced as Comrade Paula, a collaborator of Edgar's. She was a dark, blowsy girl with a slight squint, about twenty-five. Again we went to the little café, and there Schneller explained that Paula was to function as a liaison between Edgar and me; Edgar was 'difficult to reach' but I could get Paula any time on the telephone and she in turn could always get hold of Edgar. In other words, I was not to be trusted with Edgar's identity and address.

It should be noted that at this time—January 1932—the Communist Party was still legal in Germany; its Deputies, like Schneller, sat in the Reichstag; its newspapers called every morning openly for strife and revolution; its mass-meetings were given the usual police protection; its para-military organization, the R.F.B. (*Roter Frontkämpfer Bund*, League of Red Ex-Servicemen) was one of the four officially recognized private armies in the country (the other three were the Nazi S.A., the Nationalist Stahlhelm, and the Social-Democratic Reichsbanner).

But at the same time the Party was preparing to go underground; and, apart from this contingency, its activities were for the most part of an illegal, underground character. The new recruit to the Party found himself plunged into a strange world, as if he were entering a deep-sea aquarium with its phosphorescent light and fleeting, elusive shapes. It was a world populated by people with Christian names only—Edgars and Paulas and Ivans—without surname or address. This was true not only of the people of the various 'Apparat' nets—and the majority of the Party members had some indirect contact with one Apparat or another—but even of the rank and file in the cells. It was a paradoxical atmosphere—a blend of fraternal comradeship and mutual distrust. Its motto might have been: Love your comrade, but don't trust him an inch—both in your own interest, for he may betray you, and in his, because the less he is tempted to betray, the better for him. This, of course, is true of every underground movement; and it was so much taken for granted in the Party that nobody seemed to realize the transformation of character and of human relationships which a long Party-career infallibly produced.

This second meeting with Schneller was the last one. We again went to the café, where I wrote down Paula's telephone number and arranged to meet her two days later at my flat. Then Schneller produced my Party card, with 'Ivan Steinberg' written on it, and we shook hands awkwardly. Paula gave me the same fish-eyed look as the girl at the reception-desk. I felt it would be a long time before I would be trusted by girls of this type. They were all dowdily dressed, and their faces had a neglected appearance, as if they disdained the effort to be pretty as a bourgeois convention; and they all had that bold stare which proclaimed that they could not be fooled.

Before we parted, Schneller said with his embarrassed smile: 'Now that you are a member of the Party, you must say "thou" to me and Paula, not "you".' I felt like a knight who had just received his accolade.

At the appointed hour, Paula and Edgar appeared at my flat in Neu Westend. They had come by taxi, and Paula had brought her typewriter. Edgar was a smooth and smiling, blond young man of about thirty. We talked about politics. I had qualms about the Party line—why, with Hitler *ante portas*, could we not come to an understanding with the Socialists? Why did we persist in calling them 'Social Fascists', which drove them mad and made any collaboration with them impossible? Edgar explained, with great patience, that the Party desired nothing more than to establish a United Proletarian Front with the social-democratic masses, but unity had to start at the base, not at the top. The Social Democrat leaders were traitors and would betray whatever agreement the Party might conclude with them. The only way to realize the United Front was to unmask the Socialist leaders and to win over the rank and file.

He argued brilliantly, and, after five minutes, I was convinced that only a complete fool could favour collaboration between the two branches of the Workers' Movement against the Nazis. Edgar asked me whether I wanted guidance on any other point; and when I said no, he suggested, with noticeable relief, that I should tell him any bits of political information or confidential gossip that I had picked up in the House of Ullstein. After a minute or two, he asked whether I had any objection to Paula taking down what I said on her typewriter; it would 'save work'. I had no objection.

During the next few weeks, my only Party activities consisted in dictating, once or twice a week, reports to Paula. Sometimes Edgar dropped in too and listened with his smooth, slightly ironical smile, while pacing up and down the room. As I am also in the habit of treading the carpet while dictating, we sometimes both marched at right-angles across my sitting-room, which created an atmosphere of fraternal collaboration. That is about as much warmth as I got out of the Party at this stage.

As for Paula, she hardly ever stepped out of her sulky reticence. Once or twice she spoke on the telephone to comrades of hers—always in half-words and half-hints—and then she became a different person: full of vitality, gay, even giggly. We had no physical attraction for each other, and I knew that spiritually she would not accept me into her world. I was an outsider—useful to the Party, maybe trustworthy, maybe not—but in any case an outsider, a denizen of the world of bourgeois corruption. She never accepted a drink or refreshment: when we met in a café, she insisted on paying for herself; the first time I showed her where to wash, I caught her look of sulky disapproval at my dressing-gown.

Edgar was more smooth and considerate; but whenever I offered him a lift he insisted on being dropped, not at any given address, but at a street-corner. When we met in a café I had to let him leave first, on the understanding that I would leave not less than five minutes later—the implication being that otherwise I might trail him to his home. All this, he said smilingly, was mere formality and Party routine; I would soon get into the habit of it and act automatically in the same way.

But in fact, though I accepted the necessity for conspiratorial vigilance, I felt increasingly frustrated. I was running after the Party, thirsting to throw myself completely into her arms, and the more breathlessly I struggled to possess and be possessed by her, the more elusive and unattainable she became. So, like all rejected suitors, I racked my brains for gifts to make her smile and soften her stony heart. I had offered to sacrifice my job and lead the humble life, driving a tractor in the Russian steppes: that was petty-bourgeois romanticism. I pressed Edgar to let me join a cell where nobody knew me except under my cover-name; he said I might be found out and thereby lose my usefulness to the Party. I asked him what else I could do. He said he would think about it. But weeks passed and nothing happened.

At about that time, a young man was put into my charge at the *B.Z. am Mittag.* Von E. was the son of a former German Ambassador to Turkey. He was twenty-one, and wished to start on a journalistic career. He was to serve a few months of apprenticeship, with only nominal pay, under my tutelage at the foreign desk of the *B.Z.* He had his place opposite mine; when the paper was put to bed, we usually went together to box or work with the medicine-ball at the gymnasium which the Ullsteins had installed for the physical well-being of their staff. With only five years separating us, we soon became friends. I preached the Marxist gospel to him, and as I was his professional tutor, as it were, my arguments were bound to carry added weight. After a fortnight or so, I thought he had made sufficient progress to be roped into the service of the Cause. I did not, of course, tell him that I was a member of the Party; but I told him that I had friends in the Party to whom I occasionally passed on political gossip that came my way. It did not even occur to me that this was a somewhat euphemistic description of my work with Edgar and Paula; I was already reaping the reward of all conversions, a blissfully clean conscience.

The von E.s led a social life and saw a number of German officers and diplomats at their house; so I asked young E. to keep his ears open and report to me, for the good of the common cause, anything of interest—in particular, information relating to the preparation of the war of aggression against the Soviet Union by Germany or other Powers. The young man, rather proud of the trust placed in him, promised to do what he could.

Thus for a while the reports I dictated to Paula became much livelier; they were full of diplomatic gossip, military titbits about rearmament, and information about the complicated and suicidal intrigues between the German parties in this last year of the Weimar Republic. One minor incident has acquired particular vividness in my memory. For weeks the Communist Party Press had sneered at the 'Socialist-Fascist' (Labourite) Prussian Government's unwillingness to take any drastic action against the brownshirts, who were more or less openly preparing for a *putsch*. One day I learnt, off the record, from Reiner, the diplomatic correspondent of the *Vossische Zeitung*, that the Prussian police were to carry out a surprise raid at S.A. headquarters the next morning at 6 a.m., seize their arms and archives, and impose a ban on the wearing of the Nazi uniform. I hurriedly passed on the news to Paula and Edgar. The action was carried out according to plan; but while Berlin feverishly discussed the chances of immediate civil war between Nazis and Socialists, our Communist *Rote Fahne* came out with its usual streamer headline sneer about the Social-Democrat Government's tolerance of the Nazis, thus making a complete fool of itself. I asked Edgar why my warning had been disregarded; he explained that the Party's attitude to the Social-Democrats was a set, long-term policy which could not be reversed by a small incident. 'But every word on the front page is contradicted by the facts,' I objected. Edgar gave me a tolerant smile. 'You still have the mechanistic outlook,' he said, and then proceeded to give me a dialectical interpretation of the facts. The action of the police was merely a feint to cover up their complicity; even if some Socialist leaders were *subjectively* anti-Fascist in their outlook, *objectively* the Socialist Party was a tool of Nazism; in fact the Socialists were the main enemy, for they had split the working class. Already convinced, I objected—to save my face—that, after all, it was the C.P. which had split away from the Socialists in 1919. 'That's the mechanistic outlook again,' said Edgar. 'Formally we were in the minority, but it was we who embodied the revolutionary mission of the proletariat; by refusing to follow our lead, the Socialist leaders split the working class and became lackeys of the reaction.'

Gradually I learnt to distrust my mechanistic preoccupation with facts and to regard the world around me in the light of dialectic interpretation. It was a satisfactory and indeed blissful state; once you had assimilated the technique you were no longer disturbed by facts; they automatically took on the proper colour and fell into their proper place. Both morally and logically, the Party was infallible: morally, because its aims were right, that is, in accord with the Dialectic of History, and these aims justified all means; logically, because the Party was the vanguard of the proletariat, and the proletariat the embodiment of the active principle in History.

Opponents of the Party, from straight reactionaries to Social-Fascists, were products of their environment; their ideas reflected the distortions of bourgeois society. Renegades from the Party were lost souls, fallen out of grace; to argue with them, even to listen to them, meant trafficking with the powers of Evil.

The days of the Weimar Republic were numbered, and each of us members of the German C.P. was earmarked for Dachau, Oranienburg, or some other garish future. But we all moved happily through a haze of dialectical mirages which masked the world of reality. The Fascist beasts were Fascist beasts, but our main preoccupation was the Trotskyite heretics and Socialist schismatics. In 1931, C.P. and Nazis had joined hands in the referendum against the Socialist Prussian Government; in the autumn of 1932 they joined hands again in the Berlin Transport Workers' strike; Heinz Neumann, the brilliant C.P. leader, who had coined the slogan 'Hit the Fascists wherever you meet them', which sounded orthodox enough, was in disgrace prior to his liquidation, and the Party line was wavering dizzily, just as it did prior to the Molotov-Ribbentrop pact. But the Party had decreed that 1932 was to be the year that would see the triumph of the proletarian Revolution in Germany; we had faith—the true faith, which no longer takes divine promises quite seriously—and, the only righteous men in a crooked world, we were happy.

One day Edgar casually asked me whether I had ever been to Japan. I said no. Wouldn't I like to go to Japan? Why, yes, I liked travelling. Couldn't I get Ullstein's to send me as their correspondent to Japan? No—we had our staff there and I did not know the first thing about Japan. 'But to the Party,' Edgar said gently, 'you could be more useful in Japan than here. Could you get some other paper to send you out?' I said that it would be rather difficult; anyway, what was I supposed to do when I got there? Edgar seemed slightly pained by my question. Why, I was to do my job for the paper and earn a good living, just as at present, and continue to pass on information of interest to the Cause to friends with whom I would be put in touch. Would I like to think the matter over? I said there was nothing for me to think over; if the Party wanted me to go, I was prepared to go at once, but the chances of getting a serious newspaper assignment were practically nil. Edgar paused for a moment, then said: 'If we get you the assignment through our connections, would you be prepared to take it?' And again he asked me to take time to think it over. By now I was rather excited. I repeated that there was nothing for me to think over: if the Party wanted me to go, I would go.

Edgar said he would let me know in a few days, and dropped the matter. He never took it up again and, by now thoroughly imbued with Party etiquette, I never asked him.

Another curious incident occurred some time later. One day in the office, a Miss Meyer wanted to see me; on the form which visitors had to fill in she had scrawled as 'object of the visit': 'old friend'. She was a puny, plain girl whom I had never seen before; but the deliberately slatternly way in which she was dressed and her provocative air in walking in, betrayed her at once as a comrade. She had come to ask me to accept the job of 'responsible editor' of a newly founded press agency. According to German law, every publication must have a 'responsible editor' who, like the French *gérant*, is legally responsible for the published contents. In little magazines and mushroom publications, the 'responsible editor' often has nothing at all to do with editing the paper; he is simply a person of some social standing and with a bank reference who lends his name for the purpose. I asked Miss Meyer to explain the aim, background, etc. of this press agency of which I had never heard. She shrugged impatiently: 'But don't you understand—I have been sent by our mutual friends, and it's merely a formality for you to sign.' 'What mutual friends?' I asked with conspiratorial wariness. She became even more impatient, almost rude. She was the neurotic Cinderella type, the frustrated bourgeois girl turned voluntary proletarian, which abounded in the German Party. I asked her to mention the names of the friends who sent her. 'Well, George, of course,' she said reluctantly, scrutinizing my office as if looking for hidden microphones. Now my only Party contacts at that time were Ernst, Edgar and Paula; I knew of no George and told her so. Miss Meyer was furious. 'How dare they make me waste my time with a character like you!' she hissed, and walked out.

The next time I saw Paula, I mentioned the incident to her. She looked puzzled and promised to find out about Miss Meyer. But when we met again she said she had as yet had no time to inquire; and the time after that she shrugged my question off ill-humouredly and said there must have been some mix-up and I had better forget about it. There were more such queer incidents, and all of them were neither here nor there. Maybe Edgar's Tokyo proposition was merely meant as a psychological test; maybe he really wanted to send me to Tokyo, but his superiors did not trust me. Maybe Miss Meyer had really come on behalf of Edgar who was known to her as George (these hyper-conspiratorial hitches occurred constantly); maybe she came from one of the rival Party organs or Apparats which tried to trespass in Edgar's hunting-ground. On this and on many other occasions in Germany and Russia, I found Communist apparat-work much less efficient than its scared opponents presume; and the means at their disposal much more restricted. At the same time there are three factors of a psychological nature which are usually underestimated: the idealism, naivety, and unscrupulousness of the legions of voluntary helpers of the S.S.S.—the Silent Soviet Services.

My contact with Ernst Schneller's Apparat lasted only two or three months. It was a peripheral contact; but the fact that it ended there and that I was not drawn into the vortex to become a full-fledged 'apparatchik' (the homely euphemism used in the Party for agents and spies) was due to no merit of mine. As far as I was concerned, I was quite prepared to become one; I was one of those half-virgins of the Revolution who could be had by the S.S.S., body and soul, for the asking. I mention this, not out of any confessional urge, but because, as a young man of average Central European background, endowed with the average amount of idealism and more than average experience, I consider my case as fairly typical. The Comintern and O.G.P.U. carried on a white-slave traffic whose victims were young idealists flirting with violence.

I was saved from the clutches of the Apparat not, I repeat, by my own insight, but by the innocence of young von E. I have mentioned that he was only twenty-one and that he had for me the affection which one develops at that age for a person who acts both as professional tutor and as Marxist Guru. All went well for a few weeks; then I noticed a certain cooling off in von E.'s attitude to me, but did not give the matter much thought. He mentioned once or twice, timidly, that he would like to have a 'long, thorough talk'; but I was at that time overworked and unhappily in love; besides, I was getting bored with acting the Guru. So I kept putting the 'long, thorough talk' off. This turned out to be one of those mistakes arranged by providence, like missing the aeroplane which is going to crash.

One day, while I was dictating letters to a typist, young von E. burst into the room and asked to talk to me alone at once. He was unshaven, had red, swollen eyes and looked so dramatic that the typist fled in mild panic. 'What's the matter?' I asked, with unpleasant forebodings. 'I have come to the conclusion,' said von E., 'that I have either to shoot myself or to denounce our activities. The decision rests with you.' 'What activities are you talking about?' I asked. 'Activities which are called High Treason,' young von E. said dramatically. Then he blurted out his story. A week before he had been suddenly assailed by doubts about the propriety of what I had induced him to do. During the previous, sleepless night these doubts had become a certainty: he was a traitor and a spy. The choice before him, he repeated, was either to shoot himself or to make a full confession and take the consequences.

I told him that he was talking nonsense; that a spy was a man who stole military documents or sold secrets of State to a foreign power; that all he had done was to pass on some parlour-gossip to a friend.

'And what did you do with the information I gave you?' asked von E. with a new, fierce aggressiveness.

'I told it to my friends, for what it was worth.'

'Friends! You mean foreign agents.'

I told him that the K.P.D. was the Party of the German working class, as German as were the Nazis or the Catholic Centre. No, said von E. hotly; everybody knew that they were tools of Russia.

I wondered what had come over him. Had he turned Nazi overnight? But it transpired that he had not changed his political sympathies. He had merely discovered that to be a Socialist, or Marxist, was one thing, and to pass information to a foreign power another. He admitted with a shrug that technically we were probably not spies; but that, he said, did not alter the fact that we had acted dishonestly and treacherously. It was impossible for him to live on unless he made a full confession. He had actually written it last night. But he would only hand it in with my consent. . . .

With that, he placed a long, handwritten letter on my desk. There were eight pages of it. It was addressed to the *Verlagsdirektor*, the Managing Director of the firm. He asked me to read it.

I read the first two or three lines—'I, the undersigned, hold it be my duty to bring the following facts to your knowledge,' etc., etc.—and then I felt such a reluctance to read on that I stopped. The boy, standing in front of the desk—he had refused to sit down—looked ghastly, with the black stubble on his white face and the swollen, bloodshot eyes. No doubt, he was unconsciously dramatizing the situation and getting an adolescent kick out of it; but few suicides are committed for adult motives, and, for all I knew, he was capable of carrying his self-dramatization to the point of really shooting himself.

The situation struck me as half comic, half disgusting. It was comic, because young von E. seemed to me vastly to exaggerate his own importance and what we had done; I still felt that it merely amounted to half-serious, political busybodying. And yet I felt incapable of arguing with him, or even of reading the letter which, after all, directly involved my future. Later on, when I reported the matter to Edgar, I was unable to explain why I had not read on. This was probably why the Apparat dropped me as a hopeless case. To-day of course the matter is simple to explain: I could not face reading in black and white the factual record of actions which I insisted on regarding through a haze of dialectical euphemisms. Besides, though I was convinced that young von E. was a quixotic ass and myself an earnest worker for the Cause, I felt guilty towards the boy and frightened of the grand gesture, ending in a bang in front of the mirror. So I stuffed the letter back into his pocket and told him to hand it in with my blessing and to go to hell.

'Do you mean that you agree to my doing it?' he asked. He was so surprised, and seized upon his chance with such alacrity, that I thought, for a moment, I was really acting like a fool; maybe with a little arguing and dialectics I could talk him out of his dilemma. But I could not face it; my self-confidence as a Guru had gone. Young von E. came back from the door and shook my hand with solemn sentiment. Then he pushed off, looking already less unshaven.

That was the end of my career with the Ullsteins and the beginning of seven lean years. I had been prepared to throw up my job for the Party; but not to lose it in such an idiotic way.

It was at the same time the end of my connection with the Apparat. Having lost my usefulness for them—in a manner which proved my total unfitness for intelligence work—they dropped me without ceremony. I never saw Edgar or Paula again. Paula, I later learnt, was killed by the Nazis in Ravensbrück; Edgar's identity is unknown to me to this day.

The manner in which the Ullsteins fired me may be called rather decent or an example of bourgeois hypocrisy; it depends on the angle from which you look at it. After von E. had left me, to hand in his eight-page letter, I expected to be called at any minute to *Verlagsdirektor* Müller. I had my defence prepared: yes, I had asked the boy to tell me any political gossip that came to his ears; yes, I occasionally passed such gossip on to friends of mine in the K.P.D.; what on earth was wrong with that? Everybody discussed politics and exchanged gossip with his friends; and my political sympathies were no concern of the firm's as long as they did not interfere with the discharge of my professional duties—etc., etc. This was the line that Edgar suggested; it was all so plausible that, after the initial shock of the scene with von E. had passed, I waited impatiently for the showdown, braced with moral indignation and conscious of being the innocent victim of a witch-hunt. If one lives in the ambiguity of a deep-sea aquarium, it is difficult to distinguish the bodies from the shadows.

However, days passed and nothing happened. Then, a week or ten days after the scene with von E., I found one morning a letter from the firm on my desk. It stated, with extreme courtesy, that, in view of the general reductions of staff made inevitable by the economic crisis, etc., etc., it was necessary to dispense with my services on the editorial staff. It was up to me whether I preferred to continue writing for the Ullstein papers as a free-lance with a guaranteed monthly minimum, or to accept a lump sum in settlement of the remaining term of my five-years' contract. Not a word about von E., the Communist Party, or breach of confidence. The Ullsteins were obviously anxious to avoid a scandal. So was the Party, for Edgar instructed me to accept the settlement and leave it at that. As already mentioned, I never saw him again in my life.

IV

Having lost my job, I was at last free from all fetters of the bourgeois world. The lump sum which Ullstein's paid me I sent to my parents; it was enough to keep them going for two or three years, and thus free me from any obligation, until after the victorious revolution and the dawn of the New Era. I retained, however, 200 marks (about ten pounds), to pay my fare to Soviet Russia, if and when the Party gave me permission to emigrate. I gave up my flat in the expensive district of Neu Westend, and moved into an apartment house on Bonner Platz; it was mainly inhabited by penniless artists of radical views and was known as the Red Block. My three months there were the happiest time in my seven years as a member of the Party.

Now that I had lost my usefulness to the Apparat, there was no longer any objection to my joining a cell and leading the full life of a regular Party member. In actual fact, Edgar had given me permission to join the cell of the Red Block, under my cover name Ivan Steinberg, some time before I was fired by Ullstein's. It had been a kind of reward for being a good boy and dictating those long reports to Paula. I then still lived in Neu Westend, miles away from Bonner Platz; so it was assumed that, if I joined the Red Block cell, nobody would guess the identity of Comrade Ivan Steinberg. It was one of the incredibly crass blunders of the machiavellian Apparat; for, the Red Block being an artists' and writers' colony, the first time I turned up in the cell and was laconically introduced as 'a new member—Comrade Ivan', half-a-dozen familiar faces grinned in welcome.

Having left Ullstein's, I no longer had any reason to keep my Party membership secret. In the Red Block I threw myself body and soul into the fraternal life of the cell. It had about twenty members and met regularly once or twice a week. Like all other Party cells, it was led by a 'triangle': *Pol.-Leiter* (political leader), *Org.-Leiter* (administrative organizer) and *Agit.-Prop.* (the member responsible for agitation and propaganda). Our *Pol.-Leiter* was Alfred Kantorowicz, now editor of a Soviet-sponsored literary magazine in Berlin. He was then about thirty, tall, gaunt, squinting, a free-lance critic and essayist and prospective author of The Novel of Our Time, which never saw the light. But he was an exceptionally warm-hearted comrade and a self-sacrificing friend, and he had both dignity and a rich sense of humour; his only shortcoming was lack of moral courage. We remained friends all through the Paris *emigré* years; when I broke with the Party, he was the only one who did not spit at me. Now he is a literary bigwig under the Soviets—may his innocence and compliance protect him from ever getting caught in the snares of counter-revolutionary formalism, bourgeois cosmopolitanism, neo-Kantian banditry, or just liberal depravity.

Our *Org.-Leiter* was Max Schröder, also a *litterateur*, who lived on the reputation he had earned with several remarkable poems published at the age of nineteen, that is to say fifteen years earlier. But he too was a good egg, the lovable type of Munich bohemian, who had found in his devotion to the Party a compensation for his literary, sexual, pecuniary, and other frustrations. The job of *Agit.-Prop.* fell to me soon after I had joined the cell; some of the leaflets and broadsheets I produced had, I still believe, a truly Jacobine pathos. Among other members of our cell I remember Dr. Wilhelm Reich, Founder and Director of the *Sex.-Pol.* (Institute for Sexual Politics). He was a Freudian Marxist; inspired by Malinovsky, he had just published a book called *The Function of the Orgasm* in which he expounded the theory that the sexual frustration of the proletariat caused a thwarting of its political consciousness; only through a full, uninhibited release of the sexual urge could the working class realize its revolutionary potentialities and historic mission. The whole thing was less cock-eyed than it sounds. After the victory of Hitler, Reich published a brilliant psychological study of Nazi mentality which the Party condemned; he broke with Communism and is now director of a scientific research institute in the U.S.A. We also had two actors from an *avant-garde* theatre called 'The Mouse Trap'; several girls with vaguely intellectual ambitions; an insurance agent; young Ernst, son of a local fruit vendor, and several working men.

Half of the activities of the cell were legal, half illegal. All our meetings started with a political lecture which was delivered either by the *Pol.-Leiter* after he had been briefed at the Party's District H.Q., or by an 'instructor' from H.Q. itself. The purpose of the lecture was to lay down the political line on the various questions of the day. During that fateful spring and summer of 1932, a series of elections took place which shook the country like a succession of earthquakes—the Presidential elections, two Reichstag elections, and an election for the Prussian Diet; all in all four red-hot election campaigns within eight months in a country on the verge of civil war. We participated in the campaigns by door-to-door canvassing, distributing Party literature and turning out leaflets of our own. The canvassing was the most arduous part of it; it was mostly done on Sunday mornings, when people were supposed to be at home. You rang the door bell, wedged your foot between door and post and offered your pamphlets and leaflets, with a genial invitation to engage in a political discussion on the spot. In short, we sold the World Revolution like vacuum cleaners. Reactions were mostly unfriendly, rarely aggressive. I often had the door banged in my face but never a fight. However, we avoided ringing the bell of known Nazis. And the Nazis in and round our block were mostly known to us, just as we were all known to the Nazis, through our rival nets of cells and *Blockwarts*. The whole of Germany, town and countryside, was covered by those two elaborate and fine-meshed dragnets. I still believe that, without the wild jerks from Moscow, which kept entangling our nets and tearing them from our hands, we would have had a fair chance to win. The idea, the readiness for sacrifice, the support of the masses were all there.

We lost the fight because we were not fishermen, as we thought, but bait dangling from the hook. We did not realize this, because our brains had been reconditioned to accept any absurd line of action ordered from above as our innermost wish and conviction. We had refused to nominate a joint candidate with the Socialists for the Presidency, and when the Socialists backed Hindenburg as the lesser evil against Hitler, we nominated Thälmann, though he had no chance whatsoever—except, maybe, to split off enough proletarian votes to bring Hitler immediately into power. Our instructor gave us a lecture proving that there was no such thing as a 'lesser evil', that it was a philosophical, strategical and tactical fallacy; a Trotskyist, diversionist, liquidatorial and counter-revolutionary conception. Henceforth we had only pity and spite for those who as much as mentioned the ominous term; and, moreover, we were convinced that we had always been convinced that it was an invention of the devil. How could anybody fail to see that to have both legs amputated was better than trying to save one, and that the correct revolutionary policy was to kick the crippled Republic's crutches away? Faith is a wondrous thing; it is not only capable of moving mountains, but also of making you believe that a herring is a racehorse.

Not only our thinking, but also our vocabulary was reconditioned. Certain words were taboo—for instance, 'lesser evil' or 'spontaneous'; the latter, because 'spontaneous manifestations of the revolutionary class-consciousness' were part of Trotsky's theory of the Permanent Revolution. Other words and turns of phrase became favourite stocks-in-trade. I mean not only the obvious words of Communist jargon like 'the toiling masses', but words like 'concrete' or 'sectarian' ('you must put your question into a more concrete form, comrade'; 'you are adopting a left-sectarian attitude, comrade'); and even such abstruse words as 'herostratic'. In one of his works Lenin had mentioned Herostratus, the Greek who burnt down a temple because he could think of no other way of achieving fame. Accordingly, one often heard and read phrases like 'the criminally herostratic madness of the counter-revolutionary wreckers of the heroic efforts of the toiling masses in the Fatherland of the Proletariat to achieve the second Five Year Plan in four years.'

According to their vocabulary and favourite clichés, you could smell out at once people with Trotskyite, Reformist, Brandlerite, Blanquist and other deviations. And vice versa, Communists betrayed themselves by their vocabulary to the police, and later to the Gestapo. I know of one girl whom the Gestapo had picked up almost at random, without any evidence against her, and who was caught out on the word 'concrete'. The Gestapo Commissar had listened to her with boredom, half-convinced that his underlings had blundered in arresting her—until she used the fatal word for the second time. The Commissar pricked his ears. 'Where did you pick up that expression?' he asked. The girl, until that moment quite self-possessed, became rattled, and, once rattled, she was lost.

Our literary, artistic and musical tastes were similarly reconditioned. Lenin had said somewhere that he had learnt more about France from Balzac's novels than from all history books put together. Accordingly, Balzac was the greatest writer of all times, whereas other novelists of the past merely reflected 'the distorted values of the decaying society which had produced them'. On the Art Front the guiding principle of the period was Revolutionary Dynamism. A picture without a smoking factory chimney or a tractor in it was escapist; on the other hand, the slogan 'dynamism' left sufficient scope for cubist, expressionist, and other experimental styles. This changed a few years later when Revolutionary Dynamism was superseded by Socialist Realism; henceforth everything modern and experimental became branded as 'bourgeois formalism' expressing 'the putrid corruption of capitalist decay'. In both music and drama, the chorus was regarded at that time as the highest form of expression, because it reflected a collective, as opposed to a bourgeois-individualistic, approach. As individual *personæ* could not be altogether abolished on the stage, they had to be stylized, typified, depersonalized (Meyerhold, Piscator, Brecht, Auden-Isherwood-Spender). Psychology became greatly simplified; there were two recognized emotive impulses: class solidarity and the sexual urge. The rest was 'bourgeois metaphysics'; or, like ambition and the lust for power, 'products of competitive capitalist economy'.

As for the 'sexual urge', though it was officially sanctioned, we were in something of a quandary about it. Monogamy and the whole institution of the family were a product of the economic system; they bred individualism, hypocrisy, an escapist attitude to the class struggle and were altogether to be rejected; bourgeois matrimony was merely a form of prostitution sanctioned by society. But promiscuity was equally a Bad Thing. It had flourished in the Party, both in Russia and abroad, until Lenin made his famous pronouncement against the Glass of Water Theory (that is, against the popular maxim that the sexual act was of no more consequence than the quenching of thirst by a glass of water). Hence bourgeois morality was a Bad Thing. But promiscuity was an equally Bad Thing, and the only correct, concrete attitude towards the sexual urge was Proletarian Morality. This consisted in getting married, being faithful to one's spouse, and producing proletarian babies. But then, was this not the same thing as bourgeois morality? The question, comrade, shows that you are thinking in mechanistic, not in dialectical, terms. What is the difference between a gun in the hands of a policeman and a gun in the hands of a member of the revolutionary working class? The difference between a gun in the hands of a policeman and in the hands of a member of the revolutionary working class is that the policeman is a lackey of the ruling class and his gun an instrument of oppression, whereas the same gun in the hands of a member of the revolutionary working class is an instrument of the liberation of the oppressed masses. Now the same is true of the difference between so-called bourgeois 'morality' and Proletarian Morality. The institution of marriage, which in capitalist society is an aspect of bourgeois decay, is dialectically transformed in a healthy proletarian society. Have you understood, comrade, or shall I repeat my answer in more concrete terms?

Repetitiveness of diction, the catechism technique of asking a rhetorical question and repeating the full question in the answer; the use of stereotyped adjectives and the dismissal of an attitude or fact by the simple expedient of putting words in inverted commas and giving them an ironic inflection (the 'revolutionary' past of Trotsky, the 'humanistic' bleatings of the 'liberal' press, etc.); all these were essential parts of a style of which Josef Djugashvili is the uncontested master, and which, through its very tedium, produced a dull, hypnotic effect. Two hours of this dialectical tom-tom and you didn't know whether you were a boy or a girl, and were ready to believe either as soon as the rejected alternative appeared in inverted commas. You were also ready to believe that the Socialists were (a) your main enemies, (b) your natural allies; that socialist and capitalist countries (a) could live peacefully side by side, and (b) could not live peacefully side by side; and that when Engels had written that Socialism in One Country was impossible, he had meant the exact opposite. You further learnt to prove, by the method of chain-deductions, that anybody who disagreed with you was an agent of Fascism, because (a) by his disagreeing with your line he endangered the unity of the Party; (b) by endangering the unity of the Party he improved the chances of a Fascist victory; hence (c) objectively he acted as an agent of Fascism, even if subjectively he happened to have his kidneys smashed to pulp by the Fascists in Dachau. Generally speaking, words like 'Agent of', 'Democracy', 'Freedom', etc., meant something quite different in Party usage from what they meant in general usage; and, as even their Party meaning changed with each shift of the line, our polemical methods became rather like the croquet game of the Queen of Hearts, in which the hoops moved about the field and the balls were live hedgehogs. With this difference, that when a player missed his turn and the Queen shouted 'off with his head', the order was executed in earnest. To survive, we all had to become virtuosos of Wonderland-croquet.

A special feature of Party life at that period was the cult of the proletarian and abuse of the intelligentsia. It was the obsession, the smarting complex of all Communist intellectuals of middle-class origin. We were in the Movement on sufferance, not by right; this was rubbed into our consciousness night and day. We had to be tolerated, because Lenin had said so, and because Russia could not do without the doctors, engineers and scientists of the pre-revolutionary intelligentsia, and without the hated foreign specialists. But we were no more trusted or respected than the category of Useful Jews in the Third Reich who were allowed to survive and were given distinctive armlets so that they should not by mistake be pushed into a gas-chamber before their span of usefulness expired. The 'Aryans' in the Party were the Proletarians, and the social origin of parents and grandparents was as weighty a factor both when applying for membership and during the bi-annual routine purges as Aryan descent was with the Nazis. The ideal proletarians were the Russian factory workers, and the élite among the latter were those of the Putilov works in Leningrad and of the oilfields in Baku. In all books which we read or wrote the ideal proletarian was always broad-shouldered, with an open face and simple features; he was fully class-conscious, his sexual urge was kept well under control; he was strong and silent, warm-hearted but ruthless when necessary, had big feet, horny hands and a deep baritone voice to sing revolutionary songs with. Proletarians who were not Communists were not real proletarians—they belonged either to the Lumpen-Proletariat or to the Workers' Aristocracy. No movement can exist without a heroic archetype; comrade Ivan Ivanovich of the Putilov works was our Buffalo Bill.

A member of the intelligentsia could never become a real proletarian, but his duty was to become as nearly one as he could. Some tried to achieve this by forsaking neckties, by wearing polo sweaters and black fingernails. This, however, was discouraged: it was imposture and snobbery. The correct way was never to write, say, and above all never to think, anything which could not be understood by the dustman. We cast off our intellectual baggage like passengers on a ship seized by panic, until it became reduced to the strictly necessary minimum of stock-phrases, dialectical clichés and Marxist quotations, which constitute the international jargon of Djugashwilese. To have shared the doubtful privilege of a bourgeois education, to be able to see several aspects of a problem and not only one, became a permanent cause of self-reproach. We craved to become single- and simple-minded. Intellectual self-castration was a small price to pay for achieving some likeness to Comrade Ivan Ivanovich.

V

To come back to life in the cell. The meetings, as I have said, started with one, sometimes two, political lectures which laid down the line. This was followed by discussion, but a discussion of a peculiar kind. It is a basic rule of

Communist discipline that, once the Party has decided to adopt a certain line regarding a given problem, all criticism of that decision becomes deviationist sabotage. In theory discussion is permissible prior to the decision. But as all decisions are imposed from above, out of the blue, without consulting any representative body of the rank and file, the latter is deprived of any influence on policy and even of the chance of expressing an opinion on it: while at the same time the leadership is deprived of the means of gauging the mood of the masses. One of the slogans of the German Party said: 'The front line is no place for discussions.' Another said: 'Wherever a Communist happens to be, he is always in the front line.'

So our discussions always showed a complete unanimity of opinion, and the form they took was that one member of the cell after another got up and recited approving variations in Djugashwilese on the theme set by the lecturer. But 'recited' is probably not the proper word here. We groped painfully in our minds not only to find justifications for the line laid down, but also to find traces of former thoughts which would prove to ourselves that we had always held the required opinion. In this operation we mostly succeeded. I may have been somewhat bewildered when we were told by the instructor that the Party's main slogan in the coming elections to the Prussian Diet was to be not the seven million German unemployed, or the threats of the Brownshirts, but 'the defence of the Chinese proletariat against the aggression of the Japanese pirates'. But if I was bewildered, I no longer remember it. I do remember, however, writing a sincere and eloquent election leaflet, which proved just why events in Shanghai were more important to the German working class than events in Berlin; and the pat on the shoulder I received for it from District H.Q. still makes me feel good—I can't help it.

The proletarian members of the cell usually sat through the lecture with a sleepy expression; they listened, with eyelids slit in mistrust, to the intellectuals expounding the reasons for their agreement; then, after some nudging, one of them would get up and repeat, in a deliberately awkward manner and with an air of defiance, the main slogans from the instructor's speech without bothering to change the words. He would be listened to in solemn silence, sit down amidst a murmur of approval, and the instructor, winding up the proceedings, would point out that of all the speakers Comrade X had formulated the problem in the happiest and most concrete terms.

As I mentioned before, the summer of 1932 was a period of transition; the Party was preparing to go underground and accordingly regrouping its cadres. We might be outlawed overnight; everything had to be ready for this emergency. The moment we were forced into illegality, all Party calls would cease to function and would be superseded by a new, nation-wide structure, the 'Groups of Five'. The cells, whose membership ranged from ten to thirty comrades, were too large for underground work and offered easy opportunities for *agents provocateurs* and informers. The breaking up of the cadres into Groups of Five meant organizational decentralization and a corresponding diminution of risks. Only the leader of the Group was to know the identity and addresses of the other four; and he alone had contact with the next higher level of the Party hierarchy. If he was arrested, he could only betray the four individuals in his group, and his contact man.

So, while the cell still continued to function, each member was secretly allotted to a Group of Five, the idea being that none of the groups should know the composition of any other. In fact, as we were all neighbours in the Block, we each knew which group was secretly meeting in whose flat; and, on the night of the burning of the Reichstag, when Goering dealt his death blow to the Communist Party, the Groups scattered and the whole elaborate structure collapsed all over the Reich. We had marvelled at the conspiratorial ingenuity of our leaders; and, though all of us had read works on the technique of insurrection and civil warfare, our critical faculties had become so numbed that none of us realized the catastrophic implications of the scheme. To prepare for a long underground existence in small decentralized groups meant that our leaders accepted the victory of Nazism as inevitable. And the breaking up of the cadres into small units indicated that the Party would offer no open, armed resistance to the ascent of Hitler to power, but was preparing for sporadic small-scale actions instead.

But we, the rank and file, knew nothing of this. During that long, stifling summer of 1932 we fought our ding-dong battles with the Nazis. Hardly a day passed without one or two dead in Berlin. The main battlefields were the *Bierstuben*, the smoky little taverns of the working-class districts. Some of these served as meeting-places for the Nazis, some as meeting-places (*Verkehrslokale*) for us. To enter the wrong pub was to venture into the enemy lines. From time to time the Nazis would shoot up one of our *Verkehrslokale*. It was done in the classic Chicago tradition: a gang of S.A. men would drive slowly past the tavern firing through the glass panes, then vanish at breakneck speed. We had far fewer motor-cars than the Nazis, and retaliation was mostly carried out in cars either stolen or borrowed from sympathizers. The men who did these jobs were members of the R.F.B., the League of Communist War Veterans. My car was sometimes borrowed by comrades whom I had never seen before, and returned a few hours later with no questions asked and no explanations offered. It was a tiny, red, open Fiat car, model 509, most unsuitable for such purposes; but nobody else in our cell had one. It was the last relic of my bourgeois past; now it served as a vehicle for the proletarian revolution. I spent half my time driving it round on various errands: transporting pamphlets and leaflets, shadowing certain Nazi cars, whose numbers had been notified to us, and acting as a security escort. Once I had to transport the equipment of a complete hand-printing press from a railway station to a cellar under a greengrocer's shop.

The R.F.B. men who came to fetch the car for their guerrilla expeditions were sometimes rather sinister types from the Berlin underworld. They came, announced by a telephone call or verbal message from District H.Q., but the same men rarely turned up twice. Sometimes, on missions of a more harmless nature, I was ordered myself to act as the driver. We would drive slowly past a number of Nazi pubs to watch the goings-on, or patrol a pub of our own when one of our informers in the Nazi camp warned us of an impending attack. This latter kind of mission was unpleasant; we would park, with headlights turned off and engine running, in the proximity of the pub; and at the approach of a car I would hear the click of the safety catch on my passengers' guns, accompanied by the gentle advice 'to keep my chump well down'. But I never saw it come to actual shooting.

Once the R.F.B. men who came to fetch the car disguised themselves in my flat before starting out. They stuck on moustaches, put on glasses, dark jackets and bowler hats. I watched them from the window driving off— four stately, bowler-hatted gents in the ridiculous little red car, looking like a party in a funeral procession. They came back four hours later, changed back to normal, and made off with a silent handshake. My instructions, in case the number of the car was taken by the police during some action, were to say that it had been stolen and that I had found it again in a deserted street.

From time to time a rumour got round that the Nazis were going to attack our Red Block, as they had attacked other notorious Communist agglomerations before. Then we were alerted and some R.F.B. men turned up to mount guard. One critical night some thirty of us kept vigil in my tiny flat, armed with guns, lead-pipes and leather batons. It happened to be the night when Ernst, a friend of mine, arrived from Vienna to stay for a few days. He was a young scientist with a shy, gentle manner and a razor-sharp mind. The flat was dim with cigarette smoke; men were sitting or sleeping all over the place—on the beds, on the floor, under the kitchen sink, amid lead-pipes, beer-glasses and batons. When my turn came to patrol the street, I took Ernst with me. 'What is all this romantic brigandage about?' he asked me. I explained to him. 'I know, I know,' he said, 'but what do you think you are doing with your life?' 'I am helping to prepare the Revolution,' I said cheerfully. 'It doesn't look like it,' he said. 'Why?' 'I don't know,' he said doubtfully. 'I know of course nothing about how revolutions are done. But the whole scene upstairs looked to me like a huddle of stragglers from a beaten army.'

He was right; we thought of ourselves as the vanguard of the Revolution, and were the rear-guard of the disintegrating workers' movement. A few weeks later, von Papen staged his *coup d'état*: one lieutenant and eight men chased the Socialist government of Prussia from office. The Socialist Party, with its eight million followers, did nothing. The Socialist-controlled trade unions did not even call a protest strike. Only we, the Communists, who a

7

year earlier had joined hands with the Nazis against the same Prussian government and who kept repeating that the Socialists were the main enemy of the
working class—we now called for an immediate general strike. The call fell
on deaf ears in the whole of Germany. Our verbiage had lost all real meaning
for the masses, like inflated currency. And so we lost the battle against Hitler
before it was joined. After 20 July 1932, it was evident to all but ourselves
that the K.P.D., strongest among the Communist parties in Europe, was a
castrated giant whose brag and bluster only served to cover its lost virility.

The day after the abortive general strike, the Party Press affirmed that it
had been a resounding victory: by calling for the strike in the face of Socialist
inaction, our Party had definitely unmasked the treachery of the Social-
Fascist leaders.

A few months later everything was over. Years of conspiratorial training
and preparations for the emergency proved within a few hours totally useless.
The giant was swept off his feet and collapsed like a Carnival monster. Thälmann, leader of the Party, and the majority of his lieutenants were found in
their carefully prepared hide-outs and arrested within the first few days. The
Central Committee emigrated. The long night descended over Germany;
to-day, seventeen years later, it has not yet ended.

With Hitler in power, Thälmann in jail, thousands of Party members
murdered and tens of thousands in concentration camps, the Comintern at
last awoke to its responsibilities. The Party tribunals abroad, and the G.P.U.
Collegia in the U.S.S.R., sat in merciless judgment on 'the enemy within'—
the bandits and agents of Fascism, who murdered against the official line,
according to which the Socialist Party remained the enemy No. 1 of the
German working class, and the Communist Party had suffered no defeat,
but merely carried out a strategic retreat.

As a rule, our memory romanticizes the past. But when one has renounced
a creed or been betrayed by a friend, the opposite mechanism sets to work.
In the light of that later knowledge, the original experience loses its innocence, becomes tainted and rancid in recollection. I have tried in these pages
to recapture the mood in which the experiences related were originally
lived—and I know that I have failed. Irony, anger and shame keep intruding;
the passions of that time seem transformed into perversions, its inner certitude
into the closed universe of the drug addict; the shadow of barbed wire lies
across the condemned playground of memory. Those who were caught by
the great illusion of our time, and have lived through its moral and intellectual debauch, either give themselves up to a new addiction of the opposite
type, or are condemned to pay with a lifelong hangover. 'They are the
ambulant cemeteries of their murdered friends; they carry their shrouds as
their banner'.[1]

[1] Manès Sperber, *Et le buisson devint cendre* (Paris, 1949).

Hence the deep, instinctive resistance of the political dope-addicts to the cure.

In the late summer of 1932 my Soviet visa was granted at last. I obtained it on the strength of an invitation from the International Organization of Revolutionary Writers to tour the country and write a book about it. This was to be called *The Soviet Land Through Bourgeois Eyes*. The idea was to describe how Mr. K., a bourgeois reporter with strong anti-Soviet prejudices, is gradually converted by seeing the results of Socialist Reconstruction during the first Five Year Plan, and ends as Comrade K.

I left for the U.S.S.R. six months before Hitler came to power in Germany, armed with a recommendation to Comrade Gopner, at that time head of the *Agit.-Prop.*, E.K.K.I. (Executive Committee of the Communist International), in Moscow. The E.K.K.I., in its turn, provided me with a so-called 'strong' letter asking all Soviet authorities to help me to accomplish my mission 'as a delegate of the Revolutionary Proletarian Writers of Germany'.

A letter of this kind carries in Soviet Russia the weight of a decree. It enabled me to travel unhampered all over the country without a guide, to obtain railway tickets without queuing, sleeping accommodation in government Guest Houses, and food in restaurants reserved for civil servants. It further enabled me to pay for my travels, with several thousand roubles left over at the end of my stay. The procedure was as follows.

When I arrived in a provincial capital, say in Tiflis, I went to the local Writers' Federation where I produced my Komintern letter. The Secretary of the Federation thereupon arranged the usual banquets and meetings with the political leaders and members of the intelligentsia of the town, appointed somebody to look after me, and put me in touch with the editor of the local literary magazine and the director of the State Publishing Trust—in this case the Trust of the Georgian Soviet Republic. The editor of the magazine declared that it had been for many years his dearest wish to publish a story by me. I handed him a copy of a story, published some time ago in Germany; and the same day a cheque for two or three thousand roubles was sent to my hotel. The director of the State Publishing Trust asked for the privilege of publishing a Georgian translation of the book I was going to write; I signed a printed agreement form and was sent another cheque for three or four thousand roubles. (The salary of the average wage-earner was at that time 130 roubles per month.) I thus sold the same short story to eight or ten different literary magazines from Leningrad to Tashkent, and sold the Russian, German, Ukrainian, Georgian, and Armenian rights of my unwritten book against advance payments which amounted to a small fortune. And as I did all this with official encouragement, and as other writers did the same, I could wholeheartedly confirm that Soviet Russia was the writer's paradise and that nowhere else in the world was the creative artist better paid or held in higher esteem. Human nature being what it is, it never occurred to me that my contracts and cash advances had been granted not on the strength of my literary reputation but for reasons of a different nature.

At that time I had not published a single book; my name was completely unknown to those who paid ready cash for a story they had not read, and a book that was not written. They were civil servants, acting on instructions. In a country where all publications are State-owned, editors, publishers and literary critics become *ipso facto* part of the civil service. They will make or break a writer according to orders received: the publishers, by printing vast editions of his new book or by pulping all his previous works; the critics, by calling him a new Tolstoy or a depraved cosmopolitan vermin, or both within an interval of a few months.

The average visiting foreign author knows little about all this; and the little which his intuition makes him guess, his vanity will quickly make him forget. The people whom he meets at banquets and parties seem to know his works by heart; he would have to be a masochist, with a touch of persecution mania, to assume that they have been specially briefed for the occasion. The Central State Publishing Trust offers him a contract for his next book and an advance covering the royalties on a sale of 150,000 copies. If he is very honest, the honoured guest will mention with a blush that this is about fifteen times the number of copies on whose expected sale the cash-advances of well-known European writers are calculated. But that, the director points out to him with a smile, is the practice of capitalist publishers. In the Soviet Union all publishing enterprises are owned by the people, and the average Soviet citizen buys 231.57 per cent more books than the average American; at the end of the second Five Year Plan this quotient will reach and outstrip 365 per cent. So it is only natural that honoured writers in the Soviet Union, instead of living in garrets as in capitalist countries, own two-room flats with a lavatory all of their own, not to mention motor-cars and summer *datshas*. Our visitor is slightly nettled by being suspected of living in a garret; but this, he reassures himself, is petty-bourgeois vanity. He signs the contract and a few days later leaves for home, where he will declare that nowhere else in the world is the creative artist held in higher esteem, etc. Though he can't take his roubles with him, as they are not convertible into foreign currency, he can buy some quite decent Bokhara carpets and leave the rest in the State Bank in Moscow; it is a pleasant feeling to have a nest egg in the Socialist sixth of the earth. In exceptional cases the State Publishing Trust is even authorized to convert part of the sum into the author's home currency and to send it to him in monthly instalments. I know of two famous exiled German authors in France who for years drew monthly royalty cheques of this kind, though one of them never had a book published in Russia. Both were passionate and lucid critics of democratic corruption; neither of them has ever written a word of criticism against the Soviet regime. I do not mean that they have been bribed; we are not concerned here with such crude machinations, but with the dialectics of the unconscious—with that subtle inner voice which whispers that in the capitalist world publishers are sharks, who don't care a damn what you write as long as your books sell, whereas your Soviet publishers are the Soviet people, justifiably resentful of any criticism of their free country.

Russia is indeed the artist's paradise—but alas a paradise of forbidden trees guarded by peak-capped angels with flaming swords.

VI

I stayed in the Soviet Union for one year, half of which I spent travelling, the other half in Kharkov and Moscow, writing my book. A German edition of it was actually published in Kharkov, under a different title.[1] The Russian, Georgian, Armenian, etc., editions have, as far as I know, never seen the light.

My travels led me through the industrial centres along the Volga; then southward through the Ukraine and across the Transcaucasian Republics—Georgia, Armenia and Azerbaijan—to Baku; across the Caspian and through the Central Asiatic Republics—Turkmenistan and Uzbekistan—down to the Afghan frontier; then, via Taskhent and across Kazakstan, back to Moscow. What I saw and experienced came as a shock—but a shock with a delayed-action effect, as it were. My Party education had equipped my mind with such elaborate shock-absorbing buffers and elastic defences that everything seen and heard became automatically transformed to fit the preconceived pattern.

I spoke Russian fairly fluently but, though I travelled alone, I had little occasion to practise it on people other than official acquaintances; the ordinary Soviet citizen knows that to be seen talking to a foreigner is as unhealthy as touching a leper. Those who did talk to me, in restaurants and railway compartments, used the stereotyped clichés of *Pravda* editorials; one would have thought they were reciting conversation pieces from a phrase-book. All this I registered with approval: it was a healthy sign of revolutionary discipline and bolshevik vigilance. I saw the ravages of the famine of 1932–1933 in the Ukraine: hordes of families in rags begging at the railway stations, the women lifting up to the compartment window their starving brats which, with drumstick limbs, big cadaverous heads and puffed bellies, looked like embryos out of alcohol bottles; the old men with frost-bitten toes sticking out of torn slippers. I was told that these were kulaks who had

[1] *Von Weissen Naechten und Roten Tagen*, Ukrdershnazmenwydaw (Kharkov, 1934). The abbreviation stands for 'State Publishing Trust for the National Minorities in the Ukraine'.

resisted the collectivization of the land and I accepted the explanation; they were enemies of the people who preferred begging to work. The maid in the Hotel Regina in Kharkov fainted from hunger while doing my room; the manager explained that she was fresh from the countryside and through a technical hitch had not yet been issued with her ration cards; I accepted the technical hitch.

I could not help noticing the Asiatic backwardness of life, the apathy of the crowds in the streets, tramways and railway stations; the incredible housing conditions which make all industrial towns appear one vast slum (two or three couples sharing one room divided by sheets hanging from washing lines); or the starvation rations handed out by the co-operatives; or the fact that the price of one kilo of butter on the free market equalled the average worker's monthly wage, the price of a pair of shoes two months' wages. But I had learned that facts had to be appreciated not on their face value, not in a static, but in a dynamic way. Living standards were low, but under the Tsarist regime they had been even lower. The working classes in the capitalist countries were better off than in the Soviet Union, but that was a static comparison: for here the level was steadily rising, there steadily falling. At the end of the second Five Year Plan the two levels would be equalized: until that time all comparisons were misleading and bad for the Soviet people's morale. Accordingly, I not only accepted the famine as inevitable, but also the necessity of the ban on foreign travel, foreign newspapers and books, and the dissemination of a grotesquely distorted picture of life in the capitalist world. At first I was shocked when after a lecture I was asked questions like these: 'When you left the bourgeois Press was your ration card withdrawn and were you kicked out at once from your room?' 'What is the average number per day of French working-class families starving to death (a) in rural areas, (b) in the towns?' 'By what means have our comrades in the West succeeded in temporarily staving off the war of intervention which the finance-capitalists are preparing with the aid of the Social-Fascist traitors of the working class?' The questions were always painstakingly formulated in the neo-Russian Djugashvili style. After a while I found them quite natural. There was always a small element of truth in them—this had, of course, been exaggerated and simplified according to the accepted technique of propaganda; but propaganda was indispensable for the survival of the Soviet Union, surrounded by a hostile world.

The necessary lie, the necessary slander; the necessary intimidation of the masses to preserve them from short-sighted errors; the necessary liquidation of oppositional groups and hostile classes; the necessary sacrifice of a whole generation in the interest of the next—it may all sound monstrous and yet it was so easy to accept while rolling along the single track of faith. It had all happened before, in the history of the mediæval churches, in Byzantium, in the hot-houses of mystic sects; but the mental world of the drug addict is difficult to explain to the outsider who has never entered the magic circle and never played Wonderland-croquet with himself.

VII

I left Soviet Russia in the fall of 1933; yet I stayed in the Party for another four and a half years, until the early spring of 1938. My faith had been badly shaken, but, thanks to the elastic shock-absorbers, I was slow in becoming conscious of the damage. A number of external events and inner rationalizations helped me to carry on and delayed the final crack-up.

The most important of these was the Seventh Congress of the Komintern in 1934 which inaugurated a new policy, a complete negation of the previous one—but to be put into effect, as always, by the same leadership. All revolutionary slogans, references to the class struggle and to the Dictatorship of the Proletariat were in one sweep relegated to the lumber room. They were replaced by a brand new façade, with geranium boxes in the windows, called 'Popular Front for Peace and against Fascism'. Its doors were wide open to all men of goodwill—Socialists, Catholics, Conservatives, Nationalists. The notion that we had ever advocated revolution and violence was to be ridiculed as a bogy, refuted as a slander spread by reactionary war-mongers. We no longer referred to ourselves as 'Bolsheviks', nor even as Communists —the public use of the word was now rather frowned at in the Party—we were just simple, honest, peace-loving anti-Fascists and defenders of democracy. On Bastille day 1935, in the Salle Bullier in Paris, acclaimed by a delirious crowd of many thousands, the veteran Communist Party leader Marcel Cachin embraced the Social-Fascist reptile Leon Blum and kissed him on both cheeks. Half of the audience cried, the other half sang the 'Marseillaise' followed by the 'Internationale'. At last, at last, the working class was united again. In the 1936 elections in Spain and France, the Popular Front scored massive victories.

All this was of course a direct consequence of the change in Soviet foreign policy: of Russia's entry into the League of Nations, the victory of the Litvinov line, the pacts with France and Czechoslovakia. Again, in retrospect, one's memories of the Popular Front days are tainted by the ulterior knowledge of the cynical insincerity behind the façade and of the bitter aftermath. But while it lasted, the Popular Front had a strong emotional appeal and a fervent 'mystique' as a mass movement. For me, it was a second honeymoon with the Party.

While I was in Russia, Hitler had come to power in Germany; so, in the autumn of 1933, I joined my Party friends in the Paris exile. The whole Red Block, with the exception of those caught by the Gestapo, was now re-assembled here, in the little hotels of the Left Bank. The next five years were for me years of near-starvation, compensated by hectic political activity. Its centre and motor was Willi Münzenberg, head of the *Agit.-Prop.* for Western Europe and Germany. He was a short, stocky man of proletarian origin; a magnetic personality of immense driving power and a hard, seductive charm. He broke with the Comintern in 1938, six months after myself, and was murdered in the summer of 1940 under the usual lurid and mysterious circumstances; as usual in such cases, the murderers are unknown and there are only indirect clues, all pointing in one direction like magnetic needles to the pole.

Willi was the Red Eminence of the international anti-Fascist movement. He organized the Reichstag Counter-Trial—the public hearings in Paris and London in 1933 which first called the attention of the world to the monstrous happenings in the Third Reich. Then came the series of Brown Books, a flood of pamphlets and *émigré* newspapers which he financed and directed, though his name nowhere appeared. He produced International Committees, Congresses and Movements as a conjurer produces rabbits out of his hat: the Committee of Relief for the Victims of Fascism; Committees of Vigilance and Democratic Control; International Youth Congresses and so on. Each of these 'front organizations' had a panel of highly respectable people, from English duchesses to American columnists and French savants, most of whom had never heard the name of Münzenberg and thought that the Comintern was a bogy invented by Goebbels.

After the change of the general line, decreed by the Seventh Congress and the dawn of the Popular Front, Willi's enterprises became truly dazzling. He organized the Committee for Peace and against Fascism (the so-called Amsterdam-Pleyel movement) presided over by Barbusse; the Writers' Organization for the Defence of Culture; the Committee of Inquiry into alleged Breaches of the Non-Intervention Agreement on Spain, and a series of other international mushroom growths. He was a genius of organization, an inspired propagandist, and no more unscrupulous in his methods than one had to be if one wanted to maintain one's position amidst the poisoned intrigues in the Comintern. A biography of Willi Münzenberg, if it should ever be written, would be one of the most revealing documents of the period between the two wars.

I worked with Willi at the very beginning of the Paris exile, during the Reichstag Trial and Brown Book period; then again during the Spanish War, and finally in 1938, after his break with the Comintern, when we published together a non-Stalinite and anti-Nazi paper, *Die Zukunft*. In between I worked as a free-lance journalist, edited a comic paper for the Party during the Saar Referendum campaign (it was closed down by the Party after the first number as being too frivolous); worked on the staff of a home for children of Communist underground workers in Germany; then on a news agency run by Alex Rado (later on key-man of Soviet Military Intelligence in Switzerland, and after World War II liquidated in Russia); and for one feverish, hungry and happy year was a kind of managing editor of a set-up called I.N.F.A.—*Institut pour l'Étude du Fascisme*. It was an anti-Fascist archive and research bureau, run by Party members and controlled, but not financed, by the Comintern. The idea was to create a centre for serious study of the inner workings of Fascist regimes, independent of the mass-propaganda methods of the Münzenberg enterprises. We were supported by donations from the French trade unions and from French intellectual and academic circles. We all worked unpaid, from ten to twelve hours a day; fortunately our premises, at 25 Rue Buffon, included a kitchen where every day at noon an enormous dish of thick pea soup was produced for the staff. For several weeks this was my only nourishment. At this time, I lived in a hayloft, in an open-air crank colony of pupils of Raymond Duncan in Meudon-Val Fleuri. This was the only place where I could sleep without paying rent, though it meant walking several miles a day on foot to and from the office.

Work is a potent drug: to make oneself feel that one is doing a useful job anonymously and wholeheartedly is the most effective way of bribing one's conscience. The ignominies of the Djugashvili regime and of the Comintern machine faded into the background; the only thing that mattered was to fight against Nazism and the threatening war. I did not know that it was a shadow fight, in which we were the shadows.

A second psychological factor helped me to carry on after my return from Russia. It was a conviction shared by the best among my friends who have now either left the Party or been liquidated. Though we wore blinkers, we were not blind, and even the most fanatical among us could not help noticing that all was not well in our movement. But we never tired of telling each other—and ourselves—that the Party could only be changed from inside, not from outside. You could resign from a club and from the ordinary sort of party if its policy no longer suited you; but the Communist Party was something entirely different: it was the vanguard of the Proletariat, the incarnation of the will of History itself. Once you stepped out of it, you were *extra muros* and nothing which you said or did had the slightest chance of influencing its course. The only dialectically correct attitude was to remain inside, shut your mouth tight, swallow your bile and wait for the day when, after the defeat of the enemy and the victory of World Revolution, Russia and the Comintern were ready to become democratic institutions. Then and only then would the leaders be called to account for their actions: the avoidable defeats, the wanton sacrifices, the mud-stream of slander and denunciation in which the pick of our comrades had perished. Until that day you had to play the game—confirm and deny, denounce and recant, eat your words and lick your vomit; it was the price you had to pay for being allowed to continue feeling useful and thus keep your perverted self-respect.

VIII

On 18 July 1936, General Franco staged his *coup d'état*. I went to see Willi and asked him to help me to join the Spanish Republican Army; this was before the International Brigades were formed. I had brought my passport along; it was a Hungarian passport. Willi looked at it absent-mindedly; as an inveterate propagandist, he was not enthusiastic about writers wasting their time digging trenches. In the passport was my press card as a Paris correspondent of the *Pester Lloyd*. I had never written a word for the *Pester Lloyd*, but every self-respecting Hungarian *émigré* in Paris was equipped with a press card from one Budapest paper or another, to obtain occasional free theatre and movie tickets. Willi's eyes suddenly brightened ; he had an idea.

'Why don't you rather make a trip to Franco's headquarters for the *Pester Lloyd*?' he suggested. 'Hungary is a semi-Fascist country; they will welcome you with open arms.'

I too thought it was an excellent idea, but there were some hitches. Firstly, the *Pester Lloyd* would never agree to sending me; but then why bother to inform them of my going? In the muddle of a civil war, nobody was likely to take the trouble to check my accreditation. Secondly, other foreign correspondents might think it fishy that a poor Hungarian paper was sending a special correspondent to Spain. That difficulty too was overcome. I had friends on the *News Chronicle* in London; the *News Chronicle* was violently anti-Franco and stood no chance of having a staff correspondent of its own admitted to rebel territory; so the Foreign Editor gladly agreed that I should act as his special correspondent, provided that I ever got into Franco Spain.

I did get in, via Lisbon to Seville, but my sojourn was short. On the second day in Seville, which was then Franco's headquarters, I was recognized and denounced as a Communist, but, thanks to the incredible Spanish muddle, managed to get out in the nick of time via Gibraltar. Even during that short visit, however, I had seen the German pilots and German aeroplanes of Franco's army. I published the facts in the *News Chronicle* and in a pamphlet, and thereby incurred the special hostility of the Franco regime. Accordingly when I was captured six months later, as a correspondent with the Republican Army, by Franco's troops, I was convinced that to be shot, without unpleasant preliminaries, was the best I could hope for.

I spent four months in Spanish prisons, in Malaga and Seville, most of the time in solitary confinement and most of the time convinced that I was going to be shot. When, in June 1937, thanks to the intervention of the British Government, I was unexpectedly set free, my hair had not greyed and my features had not changed and I had not developed religious mania; but I had made the acquaintance of a different kind of reality, which had altered my outlook and values; and altered them so profoundly and unconsciously that during the first days of freedom I was not even aware of it. The experiences responsible for this change were fear, pity, and a third one, more difficult to describe. Fear, not of death, but of torture and humiliation and the more unpleasant forms of dying—my companion of patio-exercises, Garcia Atadell, was garrotted shortly after my liberation. Pity for the little Andalusian and Catalan peasants whom I heard crying and calling for their *madres* when they were led out at night to face the firing squad; and finally, a condition of the mind usually referred to in terms borrowed from the vocabulary of mysticism, which would present itself at unexpected moments and induce a state of inner peace which I have known neither before nor since.

The lesson taught by this type of experience, when put into words, always appears under the dowdy guise of perennial commonplaces: that man is a reality, mankind an abstraction; that men cannot be treated as units in operations of political arithmetic because they behave like the symbols for zero and the infinite, which dislocate all mathematical operations; that the end justifies the means only within very narrow limits; that ethics is not a function of social utility, and charity not a petty-bourgeois sentiment but the gravitational force which keeps civilization in its orbit. Nothing can sound more flat-footed than such verbalizations of a knowledge which is not of a verbal nature; yet every single one of these trivial statements was incompatible with the Communist faith which I held.

If this story were fiction, it would end here; the chief character, having undergone a spiritual conversion, takes leave of his comrades of yesterday and goes his own way with a serene smile. But when I was liberated, I did not know that I had ceased to be a Communist. The first thing I did, after the Guardia Civil put me across the frontier at Gibraltar, was to send a cable to the Party. It started with the line from Schiller, '*Seid umschlungen Millionen . . .*'—'I embrace thee, ye millions.' And, even more strange, I added the words 'am cured of all belly-aches'—'belly-ache' being our slang expression for qualms about the Party line.

It was a short euphoria. I spent three quiet months with friends in England, writing a book on Spain; then, after a short trip to the Middle East for the *News Chronicle*, which offered no points of friction with the Party, the conflict began. There was nothing dramatic about it. I made a lecture tour through England for the Left Book Club; whenever a questioner, in the predominantly Communist audiences, asked for details about the treasonable activities of the P.O.U.M.—an independent, left-wing splinter group of Trotskyist leanings in Spain, whom the Party accused of being 'agents of Franco'—I answered that their fractional policy might be bad for the cause, but that they were certainly not traitors. Surprisingly enough, I got away with that; the British C.P. was notoriously lax in denouncing deviations to higher quarters.

Then I learned that, in the Russian mass-purges, my brother-in-law and two of my closest friends had been arrested. My brother-in-law, Dr. Ernst Ascher, was a doctor who worked at a State hospital in the Volga German Republic. Though a member of the German C.P., he was politically naïve and indifferent. The accusation against him, as I later learned, was that he was a saboteur who had injected syphilis into his patients,[1] that he had demoralized the people by pretending that venereal diseases were incurable, and thirdly, as a matter of course, that he was the agent of a foreign power. He has never been heard of since his arrest twelve years ago.

The other two were Alex Weissberg and his wife Eva. For reasons which will appear further on, I have to tell their story in some detail. Alex, a physicist, was employed at the Ukrainian Institute for Physics and Technology (U.F.T.I.); I had known them both for many years and had stayed with them in Kharkov. When I left Russia in 1933, Alex had seen me to the train; his farewell words had been: 'Whatever happens, hold the banner of the Soviet Union high.' He was arrested in 1937, on the charge (as I learned much later) of having hired twenty bandits to ambush Stalin and Kaganovitch on their next hunting trip in the Caucasus. He refused to sign a confession, was kept in various prisons for three years, then, after the Ribbentrop-Molotov pact, was handed over by the G.P.U. to the Gestapo, at Brest-Litovsk, together with a hundred-odd other Austrian, German and Hungarian Communists. (Among them Grete Neumann Buber[2] wife of the German Communist leader Heinz Neumann and sister-in-law of Willi Münzenberg, and the physicist Fiesl Hautermans, a former assistant of Professor Blackett.) He survived the Gestapo, took part in the Warsaw revolt, and has written a book which will be shortly available to English readers.

Alex's wife Eva was a ceramist. She was arrested about a year before Alex and was at first accused of having inserted swastikas into the pattern on the tea-cups which she designed for mass production; then, that she had hidden two pistols under her bed which were to serve to kill Stalin at the next Party Congress. She spent eighteen months in the Lubianka, where the G.P.U. tried to brief her as a repentant sinner for the Bukharin show trial. She cut her veins, was saved, and was released shortly afterwards thanks to the extraordinary exertions of the Austrian Consul in Moscow who happened to be a friend of her mother's.

I met Eva after she had been released and expelled from Russia, in the spring of 1938. Her experiences in Russian prisons, and particularly of the G.P.U.'s methods of obtaining confessions, provided me with part of the material for *Darkness at Noon*. I promised her to do what I could to save Alex. Albert Einstein had already intervened on his behalf; so I wrote a

---

[1] Cf. the charge against Jagoda, former head of the O.G.P.U. and three physicians, that they had poisoned Maxim Gorki by quicksilver fumes.

[2] Cf. *Under Two Dictators* (Gollancz, 1949).

carefully worded cable to Stalin, for which I obtained the signatures of the French Nobel Prize physicists Perrin and Frederic and Irene Joliot-Curie. The cable, a copy of which was sent to State Attorney Vyshinsky, requested that the charges against Weissberg, if any, be made public, and that he be given a public trial. It is characteristic that, although both Joliot-Curies were Soviet sympathizers who shortly afterwards became members of the Party, they obviously did not set great store by the methods of Soviet justice —for, though they had never heard of Alex before, and knew me only slightly, they at once took it for granted that he was innocent. The cable was also signed by Polanyi in Manchester; the only prominent physicist whom I approached and who refused to sign was Professor Blackett. I mention this fact because Blackett did his best to save his former assistant, Hautermans, a close friend of Weissberg's. He was probably afraid that by signing two protests he might spoil the chance of saving at least one victim from the mortal embrace of the Socialist Fatherland.

The moral of this story is that Joliot-Curie, Blackett, and the rest of our nuclear Marxists cannot claim starry-eyed ignorance of the goings-on in Russia. They know in detail the case history of at least these two of their colleagues, both loyal servants of the Soviet Union, arrested on grotesque charges, held for years without trial, and delivered to the Gestapo. They further know that these cases are not exceptional; reliable, second-hand reports of hundreds of similar cases in Russian academic circles are available to them. And the same is true of all Communist or fellow-travelling authors, journalists and intellectuals. Every single one of us knows of at least one friend who perished in the Arctic sub-continent of forced-labour camps, was shot as a spy or vanished without a trace. How our voices boomed with righteous indignation, denouncing flaws in the procedure of justice in our comfortable democracies; and how silent we were when our comrades, without trial and conviction, were liquidated in the Socialist sixth of the earth. Each of us carries a skeleton in the cupboard of his conscience; added together they would form galleries of bones more labyrinthine than the Paris catacombs.

At no time and in no country have more revolutionaries been killed or reduced to slavery than in Soviet Russia. To one who himself for seven years found excuses for every stupidity and crime committed under the Marxist banner, the spectacle of these dialectical tight-rope acts of self-deception, performed by men of goodwill and intelligence, is more disheartening than the barbarities committed by the simple in spirit. Having experienced the almost unlimited possibilities of mental acrobatism on that tight-rope stretched across one's conscience, I know how much stretching it takes to make that elastic rope snap.

About the time when I learned of Alex's arrest, a comrade escaped to Paris from Germany where he had served a term of five years' hard labour. Before his arrest, he had worked for a certain branch of the Apparat whose leaders had meanwhile been liquidated as spies. So, without being given a hearing, without a chance of defending himself, my friend and his wife were de-nounced as agents of the Gestapo and their photographs were printed in the Party press, accompanied by a warning not to have any truck with them. Such cases I had heard of before; I had shrugged them off and continued on the tight-rope. Now these two individuals had become more real to me than the cause in the name of which they were to be sacrificed, and I took their side.[1]

The Party did not react. While I had been in jail, they had used me as a martyr for propaganda purposes; some time must be allowed to lapse before I could be denounced as an agent of Franco and the Mikado.

The end came as a curious anti-climax. Some time during the spring of 1938, I had to give a talk on Spain to the German Emigré Writers' Associa-tion in Paris. Before the talk, a representative of the Party asked me to insert a passage denouncing the P.O.U.M. as agents of Franco; I refused. He shrugged, and asked me whether I cared to show him the text of my speech and 'to discuss it informally'; I refused. The meeting took place in the hall of the Société des Industries Françaises in the Place St. Germain des Prés, before an audience of two to three hundred refugee intellectuals, half of them Communists. I knew it was my last public appearance as a member of the Party. The theme of the speech was the situation in Spain; it contained not a single word of criticism of the Party or of Russia. But it contained three phrases, deliberately chosen, because to normal people they were plati-tudes, to Communists, a declaration of war. The first was: 'No movement, party or person can claim the privilege of infallibility.' The second was: 'Appeasing the enemy is as foolish as persecuting the friend who pursues your own aim by a different road.' The third was a quotation from Thomas Mann: 'A harmful truth is better than a useful lie.'

That settled it. When I had finished, the non-Communist half of the audience applauded, the Communist half sat in heavy silence, most of them with folded arms. This was not done by order, but as a spontaneous reaction to those fatal commonplaces. You might as well have told a Nazi audience that all men are born equal, regardless of race and creed.

A few days later I wrote my letter of resignation to the Central Committee of the Party.

This is the second occasion where the story should end; and yet there was a second anti-climax. My letter was a farewell to the German C.P., the Comin-tern and the Djugashvili regime. But it ended with a declaration of loyalty to the Soviet Union. I stated my opposition to the system, to the cancerous

[1] They have now entered on a new existence, under a different name, in a British Dominion. Incidentally, it was this girl who was caught out by the Gestapo on the word 'concrete'.

growth of the bureaucracy, the suppression of civil liberties. But I professed my belief that the foundations of the Workers' and Peasants' State had remained unshaken, that the nationalization of the means of production was a guarantee for its eventual return to the road of Socialism; and that, in spite of everything, the Soviet Union still 'represented our last and only hope on a planet in rapid decay'.

The tight-rope had snapped, but there was a safety net spread under it. When I landed there, I found myself in a mixed company—veteran acrobats, who had lost their dialectical balance, Trotskyites, critical sympathizers, independent 'cryptos', new statesmen, new republicans, totalitarian liberals, and so on—who were sprawling in the net in various contorted positions. We were all hellishly uncomfortable, suspended in no-man's-land, but at least we did not have to regard ourselves as completely fallen angels. I remained in that state of suspended animation until the day when the swastika was hoisted on Moscow airport, in honour of Ribbentrop's arrival, and the Red Army band broke into the *Horst Wessel Lied*. That was the end; from then onward I no longer cared whether Hitler's allies called me a counter-revolutionary.

Elsewhere I have tried to expose 'the fallacy of the unshaken foundations',[1] the belief that a State-capitalist economy must of necessity lead to a Socialist regime. I shall not repeat the argument; I have only mentioned this epilogue to my Party days, my clinging to the last shred of the torn illusion, because it was typical of that intellectual cowardice which still prevails on the Left. The addiction to the Soviet myth is as tenacious and difficult to cure as any other addiction. After the Lost Week-end in Utopia the temptation is strong to have just one last drop, even if watered down and sold under a different label. And there is always a supply of new labels on the Cominform's black market in ideals. They deal in slogans as bootleggers deal in faked spirits; and the more innocent the customer, the more easily he becomes a victim of the ideological hooch sold under the trademark of Peace, Democracy, Progress, or what have you.

I served the Communist Party for seven years—the length of time Jacob tended Laban's sheep to win Rachel his daughter. When the time was up, the bride was led into his dark tent; only the next morning did he discover that his ardours had been spent not on the lovely Rachel but on the ugly Leah. I wonder whether he ever recovered from the shock of having slept with an illusion. I wonder whether afterwards he believed that he had ever believed in it. I wonder whether the happy end of the legend will be repeated; for, at the price of another seven years of labour, Jacob was given Rachel, and the illusion became flesh. And the seven years seemed unto him but a few days, for the love he had for her.

[1] *The Yogi and the Commissar* (Jonathan Cape, 1945).

THE GHOST IN THE VILLA

BY ALAN MOOREHEAD

from *The Villa Diana* (1951)

THE GHOST IN THE VILLA

I

THE Villa Bruscoli, or as it is now called, the Villa Diana, lies in a ravine about half-way down the steep slope of Fiesole on the cool, north-western side. It is a pleasant house, but the surroundings are strange and even harsh for Tuscany. Directly below the garden the land falls sharply down to the Mugnone River and then rises even more abruptly on the other side, so that the general outlook of the house is upon a wall of brown rocks and over-hanging boulders.

In the winter the wind comes tearing along this valley from the north with an iciness and a persistence beyond anything you would expect in Italy; in the summer this is almost the last house on Fiesole to get the sun in the morning and the first to lose it in the evening.

The Villa itself is approached by a fine sweep of stone steps, very broad and shallow, with two small lions at the bottom standing rampant with their shields. Once you reach the top flight it is possible to look out either end of the ravine, and this is the more reassuring view. To the north the valley breaks out into gentle Tuscan hills towards Cafaggiuolo, which was one of the Medici's summer palaces in the fifteenth and sixteenth centuries. To the south one looks down on Florence with Brunelleschi's great brick-red dome rising from the Cathedral in the centre. To the east, hidden by cypress groves and the curve of the hill, stands the Villa Medici on Fiesole; and Careggi, still another seat of the family, lies in the valley just over the other side of the ravine.

Everything about the countryside is old and it was already old when the Villa Diana was built five hundred years ago or more. These paths were made and these terraces were cultivated in just this way before the Romans arrived, perhaps even before Fiesole was a great Etruscan city in the third century B.C. and Florence was nothing. It is, in fact, one of the oldest inhabited places in Europe.

Above the front door of the Villa Diana a stone plaque has been let into the honey-coloured façade. It says in Italian:

'In this house from 1483 to 1494 lived Agnolo Ambrogini called Poliziano the greatest humanist of his time and the favourite poet of Lorenzo the Magnificent.'

The villa has been altered and enlarged since Poliziano's time, but there is a room where he is said to have slept and water still gushes out of the wall into an old stone basin there. In the last few hundred years the house has passed through many hands—for a long time it was a convent and once it was the country place of a Cardinal—and now no other relics are left except the curious atmosphere of the building and the legend of Poliziano himself. He was an extraordinary man. It was natural enough that I should have grown interested in him since I have been living in the Villa Diana for the past two years; but I became really engrossed one day last summer when I saw the portrait of him painted by Ghirlandaio in the Sassetti Chapel of the Church of Santa Trinita in Florence. It stands fairly high up on the wall behind the altar, but on a fine morning when the sunshine lights upon it from the upper windows, Poliziano comes to life more vividly than he could do in any other way.

He stands in the forefront of the fresco, his long red cloak buttoned up to his neck, emerging from a flight of stairs with his pupil, Giuliano de Medici, Lorenzo's third son, at his side. The portrait of this boy, turning to gaze out of the picture with his confident and trusting eyes, is so enchanting that one immediately fixes one's attention there as though responding instinctively to that innocent and casual glance. Then, with a shock, one looks up into the face of his tutor above. One sees a man with a huge, hooked nose, a fleshy jowl and down-drawn sensual lips. His long dark hair straggles untidily over his shoulders, and he is gazing upwards at his patron Lorenzo the Magnificent with an expression of passionate devotion. It is a startling face, half predatory and half apologetic, extremely intellectual, and in that one squinting black eye there is a look of timidity and cruelty of the most subtle kind.

Nearly everyone else in the painting is gazing at its main subject, Pope Honorius III, giving his benediction to St. Francis. For Poliziano, however, nobody else exists in the room but Lorenzo; and Lorenzo himself, with one hand outstretched, seems to be acknowledging this devotion with a quietly amused air. The story of Poliziano's life is contained in that single, brilliant phrase of painting.

He was born on the 14th of July, 1454, at Montepulciano, the hill town in southern Tuscany where some of the finest Italian wines are grown. At first he was known as Agnolo (or Angelo) Ambrogini, but he changed this later to Poliziano, which is a Latinized version of Montepulciano. The family lived very comfortably in a house on the city walls—one can see it still, a solid fourteenth-century building, in what is now known as the Via Poliziano. Several Italian families are living there at the present time, and except for an inscription over the front door, all evidence of the Ambrogini has long since disappeared.

Poliziano's father, Benedetto Ambrogini, must have been a man of some standing, for he was Gonfaloniere of the city and a judge; but he became involved in a local vendetta and one day he was ambushed and murdered. Little Angelo, then aged nine, saw it happen. He saw the murderers drag his father down to the ground, thrust their pikes into his body, and finally cut his throat.

It has been the custom now for some time—just on five hundred years to be more exact—to regard Poliziano as rather a deplorable character, above all a coward. Yet the chances are that it all began on this summer evening when he saw his father lying bleeding on the ground. From that moment he was oppressed with a nightmarish horror of violence and a deep sense of his personal defencelessness. He never again felt secure, unless there was someone in the background to protect him. He was the opposite of the Benvenuto Cellini sort of character who accepted the violence of the times and made a sport of it. Poliziano was simply frightened. Moreover the other dominating influence on his life—his almost pathological hatred of poverty and his hunger for fame—began to operate immediately after his father's death. He was the eldest of five children all under ten, and Benedetto's widow was quite unable to cope with them all. She packed Angelo off to stay with a poor relation in Florence.

Florence then was a wonderful place in which to live—perhaps more wonderful than any place before or since. It was a city of just one hundred thousand people, spread across both banks of the Arno, the Arno itself spanned by four bridges, and the whole enclosed in a long towered and crenellated wall that sprawled, lizard-like, across the surrounding hills. The Brunelleschi dome, one of the marvels of the world, had been completed twenty-eight years before, and many of the most elegant buildings of Florence were already standing then. Already the palaces and churches were filled with the work of Giotto, Masaccio, Orcagna, Ghiberti, Donatello, Fra Angelico and Lippo Lippi.

Along the narrow streets every other house was a workshop; the place rang with the labour of goldsmiths, weavers, sculptors and other craftsmen, all carrying out works of original design—and in such quantity that even after the city came to be looted and looted again, and half the great houses and institutions of Europe were furnished with its treasures, there would still be enough left over to preserve Florence as one of the chief repositories of the most beautiful things in the world.

It was, of course, the perfect moment to arrive—the height of that brief sunburst of the human intellect in the renaissance when every scholar and artist was hastening to Florence; the Medicis were firmly established in power and the Florentine florin was a harder currency than the dollar is to-day.

A great deal of money was spent on clothes and entertainments: noblemen appeared at their dinners and jousts in marvellous three-decker hats and brilliant cloaks. Their retainers were dressed in parti-coloured padded stockings, pointed shoes and feathered caps. The women used every sort of cosmetic, even for their teeth and eyelids. For both sexes there was a vogue for long hair, even false hair, made of white or yellow silk, and the ideal colour was blond. The love of country life—the 'villa tradition'—had been revived in the surrounding hills; and at this time, when muddy earthen alleys were the usual thing in the other cities of Europe, the streets of Florence were paved and the wealthier people moved about on horseback or in litters and carts.

There was a comfort inside the houses which was unknown in the barbarous cities of France and England—soft beds, carpets, linen, attractive furniture and an enterprising interest in cooking. Centuries after this, it was an odd thing for anyone to take a bath; here in Florence in 1464, the year that Poliziano arrived, people bathed all the time. Diseases like syphilis had not yet arrived (though it did turn up in Naples a few years later, and people were ingenuous enough to think it was a kind of fever in the air). There was, of course, a formidable number of prostitutes, but the Florentines were not especially libertine—they were too busy and too interested in life. In any case the family tradition was very strong and few men would have broken up their households for their mistresses.

All this then was a very fine atmosphere for an ambitious boy about to make a start in life. But Poliziano loathed it. He was lonely and unhappy. When he first arrived, aged ten, he was taken to his uncle's house in the Via Saturnia in one of the poorest districts of the city, on the left bank of the river. The lower part of the building had been let off to some stone masons, and he and his uncle lodged in miserable rooms under the roof. Poliziano spent the next six or seven years in this place and he never could reconcile himself to the poverty and the squalor. All his earliest verses are about it. From them one builds up a picture of a thin and rather ungainly little boy in a threadbare cloak and cracked shoes trudging across the Ponte Vecchio each morning on his way to school at the Compagnia di Dottrina.

But he was a fantastic scholar, far superior to every other boy in the school. At the age of twelve he was writing and eventually publishing letters in Latin. A year or two later he was producing Latin epigrams and at sixteen he embarked on a translation of Homer's *Iliad* into Latin hexameters—an enterprise which had already baffled some of the leading scholars of the day.

He adored his studies, and he was driven on, as he says himself, by a morbid fear that he would have to give them up and go into trade to earn a living. Like most poor and brilliant boys he had a nervous and claustrophobic sense of his own superiority; and a desperate feeling that his talents would never be recognized. All around him he could see that a wonderful life was going on, people were succeeding and enjoying themselves—but how could you break into these enchanted circles if you could not even afford a new pair of shoes? What one needed was a patron. Lorenzo now, in 1469, was aged 21, and he had just opened his reign of the city by winning a notable joust in the Piazza Santa Croce. The chances of a poor student catching his busy eye were not very good; it was much more likely that Angelo would finish up as a stone-cutter's apprentice in the Via Saturnia.

However, it was Homer who saved him. When Poliziano had finished the second book of the *Iliad* he made a parcel of the manuscript, drew a deep breath no doubt, and sent it off to Lorenzo with the following letter written in Latin:

Magnificent Lorenzo, to whom Heaven has given charge of the city and the State, first citizen of Florence, doubly crowned with bays lately for war in San Croce amid the acclamations of the people and for poetry on account of the sweetness of your verses, give ear to me, who drinking at Greek sources, am striving to get Homer into Latin metre. This second book which I have translated (you know we have the first by Messer Carlo d'Arezzo) comes to you and timidly crosses your threshold. If you welcome it I propose to offer you all the 'Iliad'. It rests with you, who can, to help the Poet. I desire no other muse or other gods, but only you; by your help I can do that of which the ancients would not have been ashamed. May it please you, therefore, at your leisure to give audience to Homer . . .

Your servant,

Angelo Poliziano.

Far from being put off by this effusion, Lorenzo read the manuscript, was delighted with it and sent for the author at once. Nobody knows the details of that first interview, but apparently it was a case of something bordering on love at first sight. In the next twenty-three years there was only one major break in their friendship, and Poliziano was with his patron when he died.

Later on, when the reaction against Lorenzo set in, many sinister stories of Poliziano were spread around. At those Lucullan dinner parties on Fiesole—the page boy strumming on the lute, the wine passing rapidly and the lights of Florence shining down below—he was the one who produced the ripest epigrams and the most abandoned songs. He was the courtier who smiled and smiled—and laughed at all Lorenzo's jokes; the sycophant who could never write so much as a carnival ballad without dedicating it to his master saying how brilliant, how generous and how noble he was. Constantly, so the legend runs, Poliziano was begging for something or other in the choicest Latin and with a brand of lick-spittle humility that went beyond flattery into a new and horrible literature of its own.

All of this, if true, seems to overlook the fact that Lorenzo *was* an overwhelming character, a kind of universal man, half gay and half intensely serious. He was a poet, a Latinist and a fabulous collector of manuscripts and works of art. He was a farmer, a huntsman and a lover of music. He had a genius for selecting men and getting the best out of them; and, although he was only 21, he already had the rare gift of seeing politics as a temporary and local thing set against a background of permanent philosophy. He was interested in everything, and he could switch from one mood to another, just as some men can wake or fall asleep at a moment's notice.

He had, too, that vivacity and patient charm of a man who feels at ease with himself and is quite certain of his place in the world. Apparently it did not matter that he had a dark and ugly face with a slightly twisted mouth and a flattened nose: what one noticed was his remarkable eyes. They had an expression that was something between melancholy and laughter; perhaps this came from the fact that there were intervals in his headlong career when he was in great pain.

To come into the presence of this man in his palace—especially if you were a tattered student aged 16—must have been an unusual experience, even rather frightening and exciting. At all events, from the moment of this first meeting Poliziano became the devoted follower. After this he really did have no other gods but Lorenzo, and the rhetorical praises that he started to heap on Lorenzo were no more than the customary thing. At that time when printing was just beginning, a scholar had to have a patron in order to live, and to keep a patron you had to praise him. It was more of a manner of writing than anything else, and in any event, the feeling was genuine in Poliziano's case.

Lorenzo was five years older than he was and all that sense of security and protection which the boy had been hungering for since his father's death now came flowing back into his life again. Since not even Lorenzo's worst enemies have managed to suggest it, there seems to be no question of a homosexual relationship between them; they simply delighted in one another's company.

No doubt Poliziano's teacher, Marsilio Ficino the platonist, did something to pave the way. 'Proceed with the good work, my Lorenzo,' Ficino wrote. 'Homer, the high priest of the muses, under your auspices has come to Italy. By your noble bounty, you maintain that homeric youth, Angelo Poliziano, whom you found wandering a beggar over the face of the earth.'

Lorenzo did more than maintain young Homer; he transformed his life. Poliziano was fitted out with new clothes, the best professors were chosen to teach him at the Studio Fiorentino, and he became a table-companion at the Palazzo Medici. At first he was merely the boy prodigy who was trotted out before the distinguished guests. Later he became a kind of private secretary, helping both Lorenzo and his wife with their correspondence; and in 1473 he was installed in rooms in the palace itself. Soon after this he was made the tutor of Lorenzo's children; later on, with a certain amount of unashamed cadging, he contrived to get possession of the Priory of S. Paolo, a pleasant church that still stands just off the Piazza Santa Maria Novella. This was a snug little benefice, worth a hundred golden florins a year.

Poliziano was not over-taxed in his duties there since, for a small fee, he hired someone else to perform them for him.

By now he was getting up in the world; his mother had married again in Montepulciano, the men who had killed his father had been duly murdered in their turn, and, as tutor to the Medici household, he was in an extremely influential position. When Lorenzo went abroad on his hunting expeditions, it was Poliziano's job to write back to his patron's wife, Clarice, telling her what they were up to. There is a certain unaffected naturalness about these letters which was rare for those days and rarer still for Poliziano.

Magnifica Domina mea, he wrote once from Pisa. I did not write yesterday to Your Magnificence, because Lorenzo sent me to Lucca. I have just come back and take up my pen to keep faith with you. Lorenzo is well and in good spirits. Yesterday there was little wind and he went hawking; but they had not much luck because the young falcon belonging to Pilato, called the Mantuan, was lost. This morning they went out again, but the wind was not favourable; nevertheless, we saw some fine flights, and Maestro Giorgio flew his peregrine falcon which came back to the lure most obediently. Lorenzo is quite in love with it. Of a truth he is not wrong, for Maestro Giorgio says he never saw a handsomer or a better, and declares he will make of him the finest falcon in the world. While we were in the fields, Pilato came back from the river with his lost falcon, so Lorenzo was doubly pleased. If I knew what to write I should be glad; but I can only give you news of this hawking as we do nothing else in the morning and the afternoon. This evening I hear that on Monday Lorenzo intends to hunt roe deer and then return at once to Florence. Please God we may find you well and with a boy in your arms.

(They almost did: Lorenzo's second son, who afterwards became Pope Leo X, was born ten days later.)

I commend myself to Your Magnificence. In Pisa, December 1, 1475.
                                                                Angelo da Montepulciano.

But it is the happy letter written by Poliziano to Clarice from San Miniato that gives the full flavour of these early days.

Magnifica Domina mea, he says. Yesterday, after leaving Florence, we came as far as San Miniato singing all the way, and occasionally talking of holy things so as not to forget Lent. At Lastra we drank zappolino, which tasted much better than I had been told. Lorenzo is brilliant and makes the whole company gay: yesterday I counted twenty-six horses which are with him. When we reached San Miniato last evening we began to read a little of S. Augustine, then the reading resolved itself into music, and looking at and instructing a certain well-known dancer who is here. Lorenzo is just going to Mass. I will finish another time.

At San Miniato. April 8 (1476). Servitor.   *Your Angelo.*

Up to this time there was no sign of the famous row that developed later between Poliziano and Clarice; indeed there were no clouds on Poliziano's

horizon at all. He was an established wit at the Medici dinner table and the
companion of Lorenzo on some of his more worldly adventures in the midnight streets of Florence. He was developing from a student into a poet. And
he was involved in all the elaborate carnivals and parades with which Lorenzo
is supposed to have debauched the Florentines in the early part of his reign.
Many of the songs which were sung by the actors at these performances were
composed by Poliziano and some of the best of them have a charming
quality, reminding one strongly of Herrick, with perhaps a little Spenser
added.

One of the most famous of them begins:

> *Ben venga maggio*
> *E l'gonfalon selvaggio.*

Then there is the ballad about the garden:

> *I' mi trovai un dì tutto soletto*
> *In un bel prato per pigliar diletto . . .*

And such light-hearted lines as *Dagli occhi della bella Leoncina*, which he
wrote in praise of the Florentine girls. There are dozens of ballads like these
and they still sound as spontaneous and artless as a milk boy's whistle in the
morning.

Certainly the theme was slight enough. In all these verses Poliziano is
constantly finding himself in some delectable garden or stretch of the hillside surrounded by spring flowers and dizzy with love. A beautiful and
simple country girl appears (usually referred to as a nymph). He is on fire
at once and it will be madness, says the poet, if the girl resists him. A slight
chase through the woods is permissible, but if she keeps it up too long she
will discover that nobody wants to chase her anyway.

It was Lorenzo himself who set the fashion for this sort of thing with his:

> *Quant 'è bella giovinezza*
> *Che si fugge tuttavia*
> *Chi vuol' esser lieto sia*
> *Di doman non ci è certezza.*

which is probably best translated by Herrick's—

> Gather ye rose-buds while ye may,
> Old Time is still a-flying:
> And this same flower that smiles to-day,
> To-morrow will be dying.

Not all their songs were as innocent as this, and the carnivals themselves
were apt to be hilarious affairs. In the decorated cars that passed down the
streets there were representations of pagan gods and goddesses, devils, imps,

nuns escaping from convents, satyrs pursuing nymphs, clowns, idiots, wild beasts and gypsies. Often there were allegorical figures depicting the four ages of man, the winds and the elements, in addition to fertility rites and phallic symbols. For all these Poliziano wrote songs—ironic, witty or downright bawdy—and a quantity of much more serious verse as well. Presently, he embarked on a much longer piece which was to establish his name as the greatest poet of the day. This was his Stanze.

The Stanze were supposed to be written for the tournament of Giuliano de' Medici, Lorenzo's young brother, but they never arrive at a description of the tournament at all. Instead they are a panegyric in the classical manner—perhaps Pope is the nearest English equivalent—of Giuliano's love for his mistress, Simonetta Vespucci.

The appearance of this girl in Florence somewhere about 1469 apparently caused a sensation, but no amount of research really gets you very far with her story. She remains one of those legends in the Helen of Troy tradition, and it is difficult to find the point where literary figures like Poliziano got hold of the facts and pushed them a good deal further than history will strictly allow.

However, it seems certain that Simonetta was born of a well-connected family in Genoa, about 1453, and the register of the church of Santa Maria Novella in Florence shows that she was married to Marco Vespucci there in 1469, when they were both aged sixteen. Her dowry consisted of a share in some mines at Piombino. At the time of the tournament (when she was twenty-two), she is described as Giuliano's mistress, which may have been true enough for Giuliano had a number of love affairs. But then again she may have been Lorenzo's mistress or even the mistress of Botticelli, for Simonetta was the most beautiful and adored girl in Florence. Half the artists of the time are said to have painted her, every poet sang songs to her, and all the more eligible young men are supposed to have been in love with her. The whole city was charmed and delighted whenever she appeared. There is a possible parallel in the delirious atmosphere that surrounds a film star at the present time.

This was the age of pretty girls in Florence, and it was the fashion to talk and dream about them; Simonetta was the phenomenal flower that suddenly and mysteriously out-matches all the rest. She had blue eyes, golden hair and the most delicate skin. She was unaffected and simple and kind. And in spite of all the talk about her lovers she was chaste as well as beautiful. Lorenzo even said she had the supreme virtue: 'All men praised her and no woman abused her'.

Clearly, at this distance, it is a hopeless business to try and separate the actual girl from the myth; and perhaps even then the myth was almost as real as Simonetta herself. Most of the young poets and artists round Lorenzo were full of their rediscovery of ancient Greece, and it was not long before

La Bella Simonetta was being glamorized into a second Venus—here she was again, the Goddess of Love, the pagan Virgin.

Poliziano, aged twenty-one and full of Hellenic visions, plunged into this mood with gusto, and the Simonetta myth is probably more his creation than that of anybody else. The whole contraption of nymphs, fauns, and woodland groves fascinated him, and at this time, while he was still hewing away at Homer, he was searching about for fresh inspiration. Giuliano's tournament alone would not have been enough, but it was followed by the aesthetically perfect event—Simonetta died.

This happened twelve months after the tournament. Lorenzo had sent his personal physician to attend her. But Simonetta, like so many beautiful girls, was consumptive, and on the night of 26 April 1476, she died at the age of twenty-three.

All Florence went into mourning. In tears great crowds followed the funeral to the Church of the Ognissanti, on the banks of the Arno. The bier was left open and in the springtime sunshine the people looked down for the last time on the blonde curls blowing around the miraculously lovely face.

Poliziano abandoned his Homer and embarked at once on his poem. It consists of one hundred and seventy-three stanzas, divided into two cantos, and it has no set theme or any attempt at reality; it is simply a series of scenes from the Greek myths. Nymphs and satyrs abound, gods and goddesses cavort through classical gardens, with cupids in their wake; and all this is done with a kind of high-polished brilliance that almost comes nearer painting than writing. If you take the verses one by one you get nothing but a stream of starry words, half meaningless in themselves; repeat the whole stanza and it comes perfectly into focus. This kind of exquisite dove-tailing is not the easiest thing to reproduce in English. It is a pity that Rossetti, who translated so many of the earlier Italian poets, never attempted it, for none of the translations made by others have been successful.

Technically the great interest of the poem is that it perfected the eight-line stanza in the Italian language (it rhymes Ababababcc) and in this, as in its general treatment, it set the fashion for verse for the next hundred years or more. It is regarded now as one of the finest lyrical poems in Italian literature, and from the first it had a phenomenal success. Some of the greatest artists of the renaissance—Piero di Cosimo, Leonardo da Vinci, Giulio Romano and even Raphael—are reputed to have painted canvases from scenes in the Stanze. The most famous passages, of course, are those that depict Simonetta in the springtime forest, and the description of Venus riding on a shell towards the shore. From these Botticelli painted his Primavera and his Birth of Venus, which are now practically the best-known possessions of the Uffizi Gallery in Florence. An elaborate controversy still rages among scholars as to just how far Botticelli painted Poliziano's exact words, and how far he simply used them as a spring-board for his own imagination.

However, to the layman's eye, both pictures seem remarkably faithful to the poem. In the Primavera Simonetta is supposed to be the third figure from the right, blonde and enigmatically beautiful. She wears a flowered white robe, precisely as Poliziano described her—*Candida è ella e candida la vesta*. In the Birth of Venus, Simonetta is not supposed to be Venus herself, but the nymph on the right, holding out the robe to her. Neither of these two figures, however, bears much resemblance to the authentic portrait of Simonetta which Ghirlandaio painted in the Ognissanti Church, where she is buried. Ghirlandaio painted a pale and fragile girl with a plucked hair-line—a fashion which was popular at the time, but is slightly repellent to modern taste.

Like the poem itself, with its fantastic mannered brilliance, the Botticelli paintings have undergone an erratic series of ups and downs in popularity during the last five hundred years. There have been times when people discovered that they were the perfect expression of that rose-coloured glow that spread over Renaissance Florence, the romantic paganism and the aching, adolescent sense of beauty. At other moments, and for no given reason, popular taste has swung the other way and Botticelli was regarded as too fanciful and too lyrical, perhaps even decadent. Now, in the Atomic Age, his popularity is immense. If you go into the Uffizi Gallery at any hour of the day you will be sure to find an eager group of tourists gazing up at that shy and delicate figure of Venus as though it were something seen in a dream—not real, but yet conveying so much more than this present mechanical life around us.

Poliziano, no doubt, would have written a good deal more on these themes, had he been given a chance, and, in fact, he was still at work on the poem when, on the morning of 26 April 1478, the anniversary of Simonetta's death, his hero Giuliano was murdered in the Cathedral. After that, there was not much opportunity for Poliziano or anyone else in Florence to feel very romantic for some time to come.

The Pazzi Conspiracy was, of course, a great deal more than a simple vendetta; it was a deliberate plot on the part of Pope Sixtus IV, the Pazzi family and a number of others to murder Lorenzo and Giuliano and seize control of Florence. Its importance in Poliziano's life is that it brought him back into the arena of physical violence and that was where he never showed himself at his best. There is the hint of the frightened man in the way he writes of his events of that drastic morning.

According to Poliziano, the Pazzi brothers and the other plotters decided to make their attack in the Cathedral at Florence, just when Lorenzo and Giuliano were kneeling before the altar at High Mass: and the raising of the Host was to be the signal for them to strike. Since all the plotters were their guests, Lorenzo and Giuliano suspected nothing. But, says Poliziano, Giuliano was ill and failed to turn up at the last moment when everyone else was

filing into the Cathedral. Two of the conspirators then hastened off to
Giuliano's house and persuaded him to come. As they passed into the
Cathedral they affectionately put their arms round Giuliano's shoulders to
make sure that he was not wearing a coat of mail.

Mass began. Lorenzo and Giuliano knelt and the Host was raised. Immediately Giuliano was felled with a terrible dagger thrust in his chest.
Nevertheless, he got up, says Poliziano, 'ran a few steps, but they followed
him. Then, losing consciousness, the poor boy fell to the ground, where
Francesco Pazzi stabbed at him again and again with his dagger and thus
horribly murdered him.'

Meanwhile, Lorenzo too, had been hit in the neck, but not so badly. He
jumped up, wound his cloak round his left arm as a shield and pulled out his
sword. Then with one or two others, he managed to fight his way back into
the sacristy.   Poliziano ran into the sacristy with them, and the heavy doors
were closed and bolted.

By this time the Cathedral was in an uproar, priests, women and children
flying in all directions and crying out that the roof was falling in. Those who
were inside the sacristy with Lorenzo could see nothing, and consequently
had no idea of what was happening.

'While we stood on guard at the door,' Poliziano goes on, 'some of us grew
anxious about Lorenzo's wound, and, fearing that the dagger which made it
was poisoned, Antonio Ridolfo, the son of Jacopo, a brave young man, began
to suck it. Lorenzo, however, paid no attention to it and kept asking: "is
Giuliano safe?" and he angrily threatened and complained against the men
who had betrayed him. Suddenly many young supporters gathered outside
the sacristy door crying out that they were friends and relatives, that Lorenzo,
at all costs, should come out before his opponents could gather strength. We
inside were suspicious, not knowing whether they were friends, or enemies,
but we kept asking them continually if Giuliano was safe. To this they made
no reply.'

In the end, however, one of Lorenzo's attendants climbed the ladders to
the organ loft, where he looked down into the Cathedral. He saw Giuliano's
body lying on the floor and he saw that the men outside the Sacristy were, in
fact, friends. Then he called down to the others to open the doors. Lorenzo's
men posted themselves around him so that he could not see his brother's
body and conducted him home to the Medici Palace.

'I myself,' says Poliziano, 'returning to my house by a direct route, saw
the body full of wounds, all bleeding and horribly dead. Trembling and uncertain and almost out of my mind with the enormity of the tragedy, I was
helped by some friends, who accompanied me to my house.'

According to other accounts, Poliziano was demoralized by the scene and
fainted clean away on the Cathedral floor. At all events, he took no further
part in the happenings for the moment, while fighting continued through the

streets of Florence. A mob gathered outside the Medici Palace and to reassure them Lorenzo appeared on a balcony with his neck bandaged.

When things had quietened down, Poliziano emerged again and went to the Piazza Signoria. There he saw the aftermath of a bloody struggle. Those conspirators who had been chosen to seize the Palazzo Vecchio—the seat of the Government—while the Medicis were being attacked in the Cathedral had been beaten off. Many of them had been captured, hacked to death with pikes and swords, and then hung by their necks from the balconies of the palace. Soldiers were now busy cutting down the bodies and dragging them through the streets. For the moment the victory of the Medici was complete.

There followed through the rest of that catastrophic spring and summer of 1478 the excommunication of Florence by the Pope on 7 June, the plague and the war. On the 13 July a Neapolitan herald arrived at the city gates and on behalf of the Pope and the King of Naples declared war on Florence, unless it chose to expel Lorenzo, 'to which,' says one of the diarists of the time, 'the citizens would not agree; and so war began'.

The principal effect of all this on Poliziano was that he was sent off with Lorenzo's wife and her children to take refuge outside the city on a country estate near Pistoia. No doubt he was glad to go at first. Carnivals, tournaments and the singing of ballads had stopped abruptly and Florence became a dismal city, no place for a poet or a scholar. The long, rose-coloured spring-time of Lorenzo's early reign was over and it seemed to Poliziano, cooped up in the country with nobody to talk to, that the reason for his own existence had vanished as well. He was just twenty-four and he was beginning to discover again what life was like without Lorenzo.

II

One of the surprising things about Angelo Poliziano is that he remained to the end of his life a hopeless politician. Although he lived for more than twenty years with Lorenzo the Magnificent, the shrewdest and most tactful diplomatist of the Renaissance, he apparently learned nothing whatever of the art of dealing with other men. Usually, he had just two reactions: one was adoration and the other was loathing, and he shifted from one to the other with abandon.

When he had arrived as a young man at the Medici Court in Florence, the first thing he wanted to do was to write a triumphal ode in the style of Homer's *Iliad*, in honour of Lorenzo's capture of Volterra. Since this was a cruel and unnecessary campaign, one of the few blunders of Lorenzo's career, it seems hardly likely that the Medicis would have wanted it commemorated in heroic verse; and, in fact, if the poem was ever written, it never appeared. Later on at the height of Poliziano's fame, when he was practically the dictator of Italian letters, he still went on making enemies and taking wrong decisions. At his death, one of his contemporaries remarked tartly: 'The wonder is not that at sixteen Poliziano knew a thousand times more than one usually knows at that age, but that at forty he knew nothing more.'

The worst of these many crises in Poliziano's life, the one that very nearly wrecked his career, occurred in the summer of 1478 when, of all people, he chose to make an enemy of Clarice Orsini, Lorenzo's wife. Apart from everything else, it was a very bad moment to start such a quarrel, since Lorenzo was then deeply involved in his losing struggle against the Pope and the King of Naples.

As wars go, this was not a very bitter affair, since it was fought on both sides by mercenary soldiers, who were none too keen to get to grips with one another. Probably at this stage, Florence was in no real danger, but soon plague broke out in the city and Lorenzo judged it wiser to keep his family out in the country, near Pistoia.

The party which had gone down to Pistoia consisted of Clarice and her six children—the two boys Piero and Giovanni, and the four girls, Lucrezia, Luisa, Maddalena and Contessina. Poliziano's job was to tutor the two boys; and this was where the trouble began. Clarice wanted them taught the scriptures; Poliziano was all for Latin and Greek. She kept interfering. No sooner had Poliziano set the boys an exercise, than Clarice called them off and put them on something else. Already, in August, Poliziano began protesting to Lorenzo that his position was becoming intolerable: he was prepared to put up with it for Lorenzo's sake, he wrote, but it was impossible to avoid constant collisions with Clarice. Surely, now the war was on, Lorenzo could find him some more important job in Florence?

Lorenzo seems to have made no reply to this, and the quarrels dragged on through September. Clarice was pregnant again and often she had to take to her bed. But directly she got up she renewed the attack. Through September there is a rising note of irritation in Poliziano's letters to Lorenzo. Probably he was forced to submit these letters to Clarice's censorship before he sent them off, and he soon began to develop a rather nasty trick of slipping into either Latin or Greek (which Clarice could not read) if he wanted to say anything unpleasant.

'The children play more than usual and are in splendid health,' he says in one of the earlier letters. 'God help them and you. Piero never leaves me or I him. I wish I had to serve you in some more important way, but this has fallen to my lot, and I do it willingly.'

Then he goes on in Latin: 'But I beg you to ensure, either by letter or messenger, that my authority shall not be restricted, so that I can more easily guide the boy and fulfil my duty.'

But the real origins of the row went a good deal deeper than a mere squabble in the children's schoolroom. Clarice and Poliziano were hopelessly ill-adjusted. Poliziano was a nervous, ambitious, highly intellectual character who had jumped into Lorenzo's favour from the obscure back streets of Florence; and he had a sarcastic tongue. Clarice was the daughter of a patrician Roman family with a strictly religious background, and she had an instinctive dislike for these bright young Florentine intellectuals.

There was something desperately pathetic about Clarice. Yet for some reason—perhaps because the list of her worries is too long and too complete— it is difficult to feel as sorry for her as one ought to be. She is the apotheosis of neglected wives. Married to a brilliant man, whose friends she never quite liked or understood, saddled with too many children too quickly, suffering from consumption and probably well aware of Lorenzo's love affairs, there never seems to have been a moment when she could relax with a quiet mind. Lorenzo was always sending her away somewhere or going away himself, and because she loved him, she pursued him with sad little notes: 'There is nothing of importance to tell you except that we are waiting to see you again. When will you come?'

She never felt completely at home among the Florentines; her home was in Rome and her faith was strongly in the Church. Now her husband was not only at war with Rome, but he had been excommunicated by the Pope as well. With her Orsini blood, Clarice was much too proud to submit tamely and there were moments when she was driven beyond endurance (as Poliziano was about to find out); but somehow her protests sounded feeble. She gives the impression of forever trying to catch up, of always being a little uncertain of herself. Lorenzo never humiliated her and his letters are full of affection, but they lack warmth. He treated this marriage for what it was—a political arrangement between two great families—and he was fond of Clarice, but without passion.

She had the misfortune, too, to be over-shadowed by her remarkable mother-in-law, Madonna Lucrezia. It was Lucrezia's cold, shrewd, motherly eye which had first fallen on Clarice when the Medici were hunting about for a wife for Lorenzo eleven years before. At that time, on 27 March 1467, Lucrezia had written to her husband, Piero, from Rome:

On the way to St. Peter's on Thursday morning, I met Madonna Maddalena Orsini, sister to the Cardinal, with her daughter, who is about fifteen or sixteen years old. She was dressed in the Roman fashion with a lenzuolo (a loose shawl). In this dress she seemed to me to be handsome, fair and tall, but being so covered up I could not see her to my satisfaction.

Yesterday I paid a visit to the said Monsignor Orsini in his sister's house, which joins his. When I saluted him in your name, his sister came in with the maiden, who had on a tight frock in the fashion of Rome without the lenzuolo. We talked for some time and I looked closely at the girl. As I said, she is of good height and has a nice complexion, her manners are gentle, though not so winning as those of our girls, but she is very modest and would soon learn our customs. She has not fair hair, because there are no fair women; her

8

hair is reddish and abundant, her face rather round, but it does not displease me. Her throat is fairly elegant, but it seems to me a little meagre, or, so to speak, slight. Her bosom I could not see, as here the women are entirely covered up, but it appeared to me of good proportions. She does not carry her head proudly like our girls, but pokes it forward a little: I think she was shy. Indeed I see no fault in her except shyness.

Her hands are long and delicate. In short, I think, the girl is much above the common, though she cannot compare with Maria, Lucrezia and Bianca (Lucrezia's own daughters). *Lorenzo has seen her and you can find out whether she pleases him. Whatever he and you decide will be well done and I shall be content. Let us leave the issue to God.*

There follows a list of the estates of the Orsini family and a pretty good hint that a substantial dowry could be expected.

Lorenzo and Clarice were married in Florence in June 1469, at a series of ceremonies that went on for five days and nights. Clarice wore a robe of white and gold brocade, and there were over a thousand guests, who danced in a special pavilion in the streets and consumed a hundred barrels of wine a day.

In the nine years since then the long process of disillusionment had set in. Clarice still loved Lorenzo and she missed him terribly at times—especially now that he was in danger in Florence and she was isolated in the country at Pistoia. Poliziano's presence only made matters worse. He was Lorenzo's choice of a tutor, not hers; and no doubt she was irritated by his toadying to Lorenzo and his literary airs.

Poliziano, on his side, was longing to get back to Lorenzo and his gay friends in Florence. He was still young enough and impetuous enough to think that he could laugh at Clarice and occasionally defy her. In fact, he was making the fatal mistake of not only underrating his patron's wife, but all the other people who were also jealous of his intimacy with Lorenzo.

The quarrel was simmering steadily at the end of the summer, when suddenly the family were warned that the enemy was approaching Pistoia itself. They decamped at once to the castle-fortress of Cafaggiuolo, about a day's journey north of Florence. It was already November when they made the trip, and all of them loathed it.

Clarice, Poliziano and the children were now joined by an old friend of the family, Gentile Becchi, and in a long caravan of doctors, attendants, and men-at-arms, they trundled over the mountains in coaches and on horseback.

Even at the present time, when the main road to Bologna runs past the front door and Florence is only an hour away by car, Cafaggiuolo is not a very cheerful place in winter. It lies low down at the head of the Mugello valley among damp river flats. The Medici Castle, which was built by Michelozzo, has been converted into a state agricultural centre in recent years and piles of grain have been dumped into the rooms where Clarice and Poliziano lived and the children used to play. After five hundred years the building is still sound, but damp is creeping in and cracks have begun to develop in the tower.

The rooms are large, square and very lofty, the floors are of stone, and in the fifteenth century no great attention was paid to draughts or heating. There is still no township there—just this one beautiful castle with its out-houses. The Trebbio castle-fortress, another of the Medici possessions, stands a few kilometres away on the crest of a sharp hill overlooking Cafaggiuolo and the valley. To reach either place one has to climb a ridge of mountains from Florence, and in Lorenzo's time the roads were so bad that travellers were often held up for several days. During December and January the icy wind rages for days on end, and it is often accompanied by persistent rain and thunderstorms.

Lorenzo's mother, Madonna Lucrezia, remained in Florence—one can imagine the old lady refusing to budge—and very soon the family were writing to her that they were 'up to their necks in water' and forced to stay indoors all day.

Poliziano enjoyed country life well enough, but he preferred it in the spring, preferably with a nymph sporting about through the wild flowers and the prospect of an amusing dinner party with Lorenzo at the end of the day. Exasperated by the weather and bored to death by the domestic atmosphere of Clarice and her children, he sent off this distraught letter to Madonna Lucrezia in the middle of December:

Magnifica Domina Mea—
The news from this place is that it rains violently and incessantly, so that it is impossible to leave the house, and instead of hunting we have taken to playing ball, so that the children can exercise. We generally play for the soup, the sweet or the meat; and he who loses goes without. Often, when one of my scholars loses, he cries. I have no other news to give you. I sit by the fire in dressing gown and slippers and were you to see me you would think that I was melancholy personified; for that is what I seem to myself. I neither do nor see nor hear anything that gives me pleasure, so much have I taken our calamities to heart. Sleeping and waking they haunt me. Two days ago we began to spread our wings, for we heard the plague had ceased; now we are down again because it is still said to be going about. In Florence we have some sort of comfort, if only that of seeing Lorenzo come home safe and well. Here we are in perpetual anxiety about everything, and I assure you I am dying of melancholy, such is my solitude. I say solitude because Monsignore (Becchi) shuts himself up in his own room with only his thoughts for company, and I always find him so cast down and full of care that my own melancholy is increased in his company.

Ser Alberto di Malerba (a priest who had joined them) mumbles prayers with the children all day long, so I remain alone, and when I am tired of study I ring the changes on plague and war, on grief for the past and fear for the future, and have no one with whom to air my fantasies. I do not find my Madonna Lucrezia in her room, with whom I can unbosom myself and I am bored to death . . . However, I am trying to arm myself with hope and cling to everything in order not to sink to the bottom. I have nothing else to say. I commend myself to Your Magnificence—Cafaggiuolo 18 December 1478. Servitor.
                                                                    Angelus.

Through January 1479, he killed time by composing a Latin ode, keeping a diary of jottings (it is full of nostalgic bright sayings he remembered from Lorenzo's dinner-table), writing his version of the Pazzi conspiracy and bickering with Clarice; and still the rain poured down. Clarice's child was born at last on a brief visit to Florence in February, and they named it Giuliano, after Lorenzo's murdered younger brother. While Clarice was in Florence, Poliziano snatched his pupils away from Ser Alberto, the mumbling priest, and put them back on to the classical languages. But directly Clarice returned to Cafaggiuolo, she reversed all this, and by April things were moving rapidly towards an open breach. Poliziano protested to Lorenzo:

> As for Giovanni (the second boy, who became Pope Leo X), you will have seen for yourself. His mother has taken it upon herself to change his course of reading to the Psalter, a thing I did not approve of. While she was absent he had made wonderful progress.

This was true enough; Poliziano had been pushing both boys through a course of Latin and Greek which would have made a modern schoolboy shudder. Piero, the eldest, was only eight at this time and his letters to his father from Cafaggiuolo have a remarkable maturity.

> Magnificent Father, he wrote, Lucrezia and I are competing to see who can write best. She is writing to grandmother Lucrezia, I, my father, to you. The one who gets what he asks for wins. Until now Lucrezia has had everything she wanted. I, who have always written in Latin, in order to give a more literary tone to my letters, have not had that pony you promised me; and so I am laughed at by everyone. See to it, therefore, Your Magnificence, that she is not always the winner.

This letter was dated 26 May 1479, and it is followed by another, which is undated, except for the year:

> Magnificent Father Mine—That pony does not come, and I am afraid that it will remain so long with you, that Andrea will cause it to change from a beast into a man. We are all well and studying. Giovanni is beginning to spell. By this letter you can judge how I am writing . . . Giuliano laughs and thinks of nothing else; Lucrezia sews, sings and reads; Maddalena knocks her head against the wall, but without hurting herself; Luisa begins to say a few little words; Contessina fills the house with her noise. All the others attend to their duties and we need nothing except your presence. We heard that things are better than last year, and hope that, you being well, there will be nothing but victory in the future. Strong and brave men are not good at subterfuges, but shine in open warfare. Thus we confide in you, as we all know that besides your goodness and valour, you bear in mind the heritage left us by our ancestors and the injury and outrages we have endured. God save you—Your son Piero.

Then this:

> Magnificent Father Mine—I fear that some misfortune has happened to that pony, for

had it been well I know you would have sent it me as you promised. I beg, therefore, as a grace, that you will take this fear away from me; for I think of it day and night, and until the pony comes I shall have no peace. In case the original one cannot come, please send me another. For, as I have already written you, I am here on foot, and sometimes it is necessary for me to go off in the company of my friends. See to this, therefore, Your Magnificence.

Finally:

Magnifico Patrio meo—I cannot tell you, Magnificent Father, how glad I am to have the pony, and how his arrival stimulates me to work. If I desire to praise him, 'Ante diem clause Olympo'. He is so handsome and perfect, that the trumpet of Maronius would hardly be enough to sing his praises. You can imagine how I love him—especially when his joyous neighs resound and rejoice the whole neighbourhood. I owe you and send you many thanks for such a fine gift, and I shall try to repay you by becoming what you wish. Of this you may be sure. I promise that I shall try with all my heart. We are all well: and we long for your arrival. God save you—Your son, Piero.

Meanwhile, Clarice had thrown Poliziano out of the house. The final row must have been bitter, since Clarice, for once, did not wait to consult Lorenzo. Little Piero at one stage appears to have supported his tutor. Much later he declared that his mother was not to blame and that Poliziano used to shout at her. At all events Poliziano left the castle in such a remarkable hurry that he even abandoned his books.

He did not dare to go straight to Florence without Lorenzo's permission, nor did he care to approach Lorenzo until he had prepared the way; and so he made for another of the Medici villas at Careggi, just outside Florence, hoping, no doubt, to find Lorenzo's mother, Madonna Lucrezia, there. Lucrezia was a poet herself, and had always been a good friend of his. It was spring again, the first week in May, the month Poliziano used to sing about so blithely in the old days. This crestfallen little note was delivered to Lorenzo in Florence:

Magnifice mi domine—I am here at Careggi, having left Cafaggiuolo by command of Madonna Clarice. The cause and manner of my departure I desire—indeed I beg—to be allowed to explain by word of mouth, it is too long to write. When you have heard me I think you will admit that the fault is not all mine. For decency's sake and not wishing to go to Florence without your orders, I came here and am waiting till Your Magnificence informs me what I am to do, because I am yours, even if the whole world were against me. If I have had only small success in serving you, it was not that I did not serve with all my heart. I commend myself to Your Magnificence and am entirely at your commands. Careggi 6 May 1479. Ever Your Magnificence's servant.

Angelus Pol.

This put Lorenzo in an awkward position. He was too fond of Poliziano to throw him over entirely; at the same time he could not humiliate Clarice by taking his side. In the end he compromised by installing Poliziano as librarian at the Medici quarters on the hill of Fiesole. Poliziano at once began throwing off epigrams in praise of his patron, and it is not difficult to imagine the sort of gossip he spread about Clarice among his friends. Soon the whole court knew about the quarrel, and Matteo Franco, the poet, permitted himself to make a joke which came to Clarice's ears. She was furious.

> *I should be glad not to be turned into ridicule by Franco . . .* , she wrote to Lorenzo on 28 May, *and also that Messer Angelo should not be able to boast that he lives in your house whether I like it or not; and that you have put him into your own room at Fiesole. You know I told you that if you wished him to remain I was perfectly content, and although I have endured a thousand insults, if it has been by your permission, I am content; but this I can hardly believe.*

In her exasperation Clarice began to put herself in the wrong by refusing to give up Poliziano's books which he had left behind at Cafaggiuolo—they included the Homer, Plato and Demosthenes which he had prepared for Piero, his interpretations and addresses to Lorenzo and a quantity of other private manuscripts. Clarice claimed that since the books were prepared for Piero, they were Medici property, and Poliziano was now complaining loudly; he even got Lorenzo's secretary to demand the books back. Clarice ignored this. Things had reached the point where only Lorenzo himself could pacify her, and at last, at the end of May, he visited Cafaggiuolo. Poliziano, he insisted to Clarice, was to stay at Fiesole and he was to have his books; but she would not be forced to take him back as tutor, and he would see to it that Poliziano did not annoy her. With this Clarice had to be content, and Lorenzo hurried back to Florence and the war again.

The first round then was clearly Poliziano's. But he had won it at the cost of making a permanent enemy of Clarice, and there were a good many others in the Medici household who thought he was getting too big for his boots. In Fiesole, he began to notice a certain coolness in the air. Lorenzo was charming to him whenever they met, but he kept him in suspense about the future. Whenever Poliziano started agitating to be re-appointed as tutor Lorenzo was extremely vague, for by now another man, much more to Clarice's liking, had been appointed in his place.

> '*If he is to remain permanently,*' Poliziano wrote desperately to Madonna Lucrezia, '*then, indeed, I can assume that the bubble has burst. But I cannot believe it and, therefore, I beg you to find out what are Lorenzo's intentions, then I shall know whether to arm myself only for a tournament or for war.*'

Poliziano was young as yet in the arts of courtiership, and was apt to overplay his hand.

> *Yesterday,* he wrote again to Lucrezia, *we were told that Lorenzo was in a somewhat low state. God alone knows how it made me suffer. I am, therefore, sending over Mariotto*

(the Medici's barber) in order to hear how he is. I would have come myself, but I was not sure whether or not I would be intruding. If there is anything I can do . . .

People died suddenly in fifteenth century Florence, and it was all too pain-fully clear to Poliziano that if anything happened to Lorenzo, then it would not take Clarice and her friends very long to turn him out of the Medici Court. In some vague way he could feel himself slipping already: this protector, this new foster-father whom he had grown to love, was turning away from him. Messengers were kept trotting over to Lucrezia's place with anxious inquiries—how was Lorenzo? What was he doing? The answer was that Lorenzo was ill with gout and overwork, and now the war was pushing him towards the major crisis of his life.

Then, too, with the loss of his tutorship, Poliziano was running short of money. Following his success at Florence, his relatives had descended upon him in a body. He put some of them up in rooms in the Via Fossi, near his Priory of San Paulo, and at Fiesole he took in his sister Maria and her family and a certain Tommaso, much given to tavern brawls. With this large house-hold to support, he began manoeuvring for another church benefice; this was a living at Fiesole, in the gift of the Medicis.

I realize, he wrote to Lucrezia, that this is not the moment to ask for anything—first on account of the thunderstorm (the row with Clarice) and then I might be told I have too much already. But the fact is, if I ever needed assistance, it is now. Besides being constantly drained by this sister of mine, the hopes I built on Piero are failing me. The benefice, he adds reflectively, has quite a nice little estate attached to it.

But this time Lucrezia could not help him and the living went to someone else.

Yet, for the rest, it was a profitable summer; he translated the maxims of the Stoic philosopher Epictetus and Plutarch's *Amatoriae narrationes*, in addi-tion to composing some of his best descriptive poems in Latin. Moreover, he began to settle into the work that became the ruling passion of his life—the collection, collation and translation of manuscripts for the Medici Library and the study of old coins and inscriptions. He was just twenty-five and his reputation as a scholar and a poet was now spreading all over Italy.

Up at Fiesole he worked in the Medici Platonic academy in the Badia Fiesolana. The church with its lovely Romanesque façade still remains along with some of the most graceful cloisters in Tuscany that lead off into the monastery. The place has been turned into a school now, and the upper rooms have been converted into dormitories for the boys, but you can still see the rooms where the library was kept before it was removed to Florence, and where Lorenzo, Poliziano, Ficino, Pico della Mirandola and probably Michelangelo, used to discuss philosophy through the night.

No doubt Poliziano might have continued happily at Fiesole, but in

September 1479, the Florentines were overtaken by a major disaster in the war—their headquarters at Poggibonsi, near Siena, were overrun by the Papal and Neapolitan troops. Lorenzo's soldiers managed to struggle on into the winter, but it was obvious that when the enemy renewed their offensive in the spring, Florence itself must fall. Lorenzo made his famous decision to go to Naples and try to negotiate peace there with the King. It was a decision that needed something more than ordinary sangfroid, since the last envoy who had arrived at the King's Court had been immediately murdered. Moreover, it was upon Lorenzo himself—'that ungrateful, excommunicated and heretical Lorenzo de' Medici'—that the Pope had sworn to take vengeance. Only a small party of Lorenzo's closest companions was to go on this dangerous mission.

On 4 December, Poliziano got wind that something was happening and that he was being kept out of it. He went to see his old friend, Madonna Lucrezia, and told her that he wanted to go with Lorenzo, whatever his plans might be. Lucrezia promised to pass this on to the Palazzo Medici. The rumour in Florence on that day was that Lorenzo was going to see the Pope, his principal enemy.

On 5 December, however, Poliziano heard that Lorenzo was not bound for Rome, but for Naples. But he had still not been asked to join the expedition, and so he went back to Lucrezia and repeated his eagerness to go. Then at last, early on the following morning, he was summoned by one of Lorenzo's secretaries, a man named Francesco, and told that he should be ready to leave at a moment's notice. When he asked where they were going, he was told Pisa. This he knew to be untrue; but when he tried to press the matter he got nothing but evasive answers.

This was the point where Poliziano began to make a fuss. He protested that he was being kept in the dark. Why was he being treated as an outsider like this? Were they going to Naples or not? And when? And for how long? He finished by saying that he would never enter into any engagement until he had talked to Lorenzo himself. And he went off to the Palazzo Medici and posted himself outside Lorenzo's door.

There he waited for an hour and a half without being summoned and, not daring to go inside Lorenzo's room without an invitation. That hour and a half was probably the emotional crisis of Poliziano's life. It was one of those moments when one is assailed with dark misgivings about petty things— when there is no real guide to tell one how to act—and yet one feels that the chance of a lifetime may be slipping away. No doubt he was appalled by the dangers of the journey to Naples, but it was worse still that Lorenzo should go without him. Going or staying—they were both intolerable propositions.

It was not much good trying to rationalize the situation by saying that, after all, he was a poet, not a soldier or a politician, and he could not be expected to go; Lorenzo had asked for him and if he refused life in Florence would be impossible. It is not hard to imagine how, as he stood there outside the door, trying to catch attention, his mood of offended dignity began to subside into a welter of doubts and hesitations. Perhaps it was already too late: perhaps he had protested too much and Lorenzo had angrily struck him off the list.

Finally, when he could bear it no longer, he rushed off to see Francesco, and announced that he had changed his mind: he no longer wanted to talk to Lorenzo. He would go without asking more questions.

Leaving Francesco, he went off and got himself a coat for the journey; and then, much agitated, he returned to the Palazzo Medici again. The place was in an uproar. Tailors and embroiderers had been working through the night on Lorenzo's ambassadorial robes. Messengers kept flying in and out and Lorenzo remained closeted with his advisers. This time, however, Poliziano did succeed in getting admitted to his patron and actually had dinner with him. But Lorenzo remained deep in urgent conversation with other people.

Through the long afternoon Poliziano waited anxiously, growing more and more suspicious. One can picture him edging as close as he could to Lorenzo, talking—volubly no doubt—to anyone who looked as though he had any information, but never quite succeeding in drawing Lorenzo to one side.

By evening nobody yet had called him or given him any instructions and Poliziano was appalled to see Lorenzo set off for the Palazzo Vecchio, where forty members of the Government had been gathered in secret session to hear his plans. The expedition was to leave Florence immediately after the meeting. In desperation Poliziano ran after Lorenzo, and was about to tug him by the sleeve, when Francesco called him back and told him that, on Lorenzo's orders, he was not to go. His place had been taken by someone else.

Poliziano says he was bewildered and hurt at this news. He hurried home and composed a letter, a last appeal, and this was sent in to Lorenzo, who was then in conference at the Palazzo Vecchio. It is doubtful if Lorenzo ever read the letter or even received it, for now he was entirely engulfed in his big adventure. He was making the speech, which he later confirmed in a letter, and which brought all his hearers to tears: 'Seeing that all other endeavours have been fruitless, I have determined to run some peril in my own person, rather than expose the city to disaster. Therefore, with the permission of Your Excellencies of the Signoria, I have decided to go openly to Naples. Being the one most hated and persecuted by our enemies, I may, by placing myself in their hands, be the means of restoring peace to our city . . . These are the feelings with which I go for perhaps our Lord God desires that this war, which began with the blood of my brother and my own, should be put an end to by me.'

Late that night Lorenzo left the city for the coast. A week later he set sail by galley for Naples. Utterly deflated, Poliziano roamed about Florence asking himself: 'Where shall I go? What shall I do?' For six years or more he had been the favourite in the Palazzo Medici; everybody had run after Angelo, asking him for favours, telling him how clever he was, and begging him to mention their names to Lorenzo. Now he had been publicly slighted by Lorenzo, and all Florence knew about it. And now, at last, Clarice had her revenge.

There is no record of what Clarice did the day after Lorenzo had gone. Possibly she did nothing, but simply let events take their course. However, the story quickly went around Florence that the favourite had been deposed: he had refused point blank to go to Naples. He had acted like a coward at a moment when the whole city was in danger and Lorenzo was risking his own life.

Technically, Poliziano was still in the pay of the Medici, and he was not at liberty to make any move without permission. No doubt the sensible thing for him to have done was to have gone quietly back to his books at Fiesole and waited there, well out of Clarice's way, until he saw what happened to Lorenzo in Naples. But he was unnerved. He did the foolish and precipitate thing: he quietly packed his clothes and left the city for Bologna in the north, a safe and neutral place.

To those who stayed behind in Florence, and to Lorenzo himself, now fighting for the freedom of the city of Naples, it seemed like the action of a traitor.

III

After he left Florence in 1479, Poliziano spent nearly eight months wandering in the Lombard cities of northern Italy. He drifted through Bologna, Mantua, Verona, Padua and Venice, picking up rich patrons where he could, browsing in libraries and talking to other scholars.

None of this brought him much peace of mind, for he soon realized that he had made a frightful mistake in abandoning Florence and Lorenzo. On 15 March 1480, Lorenzo arrived back from Naples with the news that the war against the Pope was over and Florence was saved. Poliziano lost no time in getting off a couple of complimentary poems to his old patron, together with a strong suggestion that he should be invited back to Florence again. He followed this with a long apologetic letter to Lorenzo, explaining just why he had deserted Florence, and asking for forgiveness. There was no reply either to the poems or the apology. Indeed, a fellow poet, Baccio Ugolini, who took Poliziano's letter down to Florence, reported back to him that he was much out of favour, and it was useless for him to try and return. Lorenzo regarded him as disloyal.

For the time being, then, Poliziano accepted exile. He got an appointment as house chaplain in the Court of Cardinal Gonzaga, at Mantua, and amused himself by writing a play, which he called Orpheus.

Orpheus is not perhaps one of the triumphs of Italian literature but it is a point of new departure in the art of the theatre. Up to this time the only plays shown in Italy were of a religious kind and mostly pantomime and spectacle. Three-decker stages were erected in the public squares—the upper part representing Paradise, the lower Hell, and the Earth lay in between. Devils in hideous masks were apt to come bursting up from Hell below, and angels chanted from Heaven above, while the main action took place on the central stage. There were elaborate contraptions for raising and lowering the actors through the air, and Brunelleschi is credited with once having designed an immense golden ball, out of which the Angel Gabriel sprang at the climax of the show. Usually performances opened with an improving discourse from the saints and angels, followed by a dance; and then one of the biblical parables was acted in dumb show. Garlands and tapestries were hung about, there were songs accompanied by the lute, and the whole thing made a very pretty spectacle against the background of the ancient buildings.

The point about Orpheus is that it was the first straight play to appear with a non-religious theme in the Italian language. You might even argue that it was the forerunner of Italian opera.

'I wrote this play,' Poliziano said later, 'at the request of the Most Reverend the Cardinal of Mantua, in the space of two days, among continual disturbances and in the vulgar tongue that it might be the better understood by the spectators.'

There seems to be no reason to doubt this. The original version of Orpheus consists of barely 400 lines, and it has the simplicity and gusto of a piece composed upon a single inspiration. Years afterwards, Poliziano affected to deplore its publication. 'Let it come out then,' he wrote rather archly to the printer, 'since such is your pleasure; but I suggest your kindness is a cruelty to me.' It is an imperfect child, he goes on, and he would have preferred to expose it, as the Spartans exposed their imperfect children on the hillsides, to destruction.

Even so, Orpheus is a *tour de force*, and has since been printed and played innumerable times. The story is simple, the fable of Orpheus and Eurydice, written in lyrical verse. It has, however, a slightly baffling ending: just at the tragic point where Orpheus turns round and Eurydice is snatched back to Hell, the action suddenly switches from pathos into bathos, and from bathos into a riot. In his rage and disappointment Orpheus declares he will never again love a woman, but instead, indulge himself with 'other (or new) flowers'. Bacchantes then rush upon the stage and tear Orpheus to pieces. The play ends with the bacchantes singing an exultant blood-song, followed by a drunken and orgiastic chant to Bacchus.

To some students that reference to 'other flowers' can mean only one

thing—homosexuality (of which Poliziano is supposed to have been a leading exponent)—and there is some surprise that such a speech should have been
made before a Cardinal. But this was the age of Pope Sixtus IV and the
Borgias—indeed the play is dedicated to the future husband of Vanossa, the
girl who became the mistress of Pope Alexander VI and the mother, by him,
of Cesare and Lucrezia Borgia. A society which knew incest and a fathomless
debauchery in Rome might have been pained but hardly surprised by a
reference to homosexuality in a lyric poem.

Orpheus had an immediate success. It responded, like all of Poliziano's
popular writings, to something in the age itself: that feeling men had then
that they were living in a violent and barbarous time, a contemporary Hades,
which could only be subdued by the Orpheus touch—by music and beauty
and enlightment.

But the poet was still yearning for Florence and Lorenzo. All through
these months he kept up a barrage of epigrams and verses—'I am yours, O
Medici . . . I am yours for ever . . . Give back to me, my Lorenzo, your eyes,
give back to me my happiness.' At last, in August, 1480, Lorenzo called him
back. Possibly the success of Orpheus had something to do with it.

When Lorenzo forgave he forgave handsomely. He reinstated Poliziano as
tutor to his eldest son, Piero, and even appointed him professor of Latin and
Greek eloquence at the Studio Fiorentino.

Poliziano was a tremendous speaker. It is said that he made no great impression when he first came into the lecture room, with that squinting eye and
the huge hooked nose. But when he began to speak he charmed everyone
who heard him, and they would sit spell-bound until he finished. Some of the
ablest scholars of Europe journeyed to Florence to hear him and even his old
professors came and sat as pupils at his feet. He discoursed upon nearly all the
classical authors, explaining and commenting upon the text with a staggering
memory. To anyone who is not passionately interested in squeezing out fine
shades of meaning from a diphthong or an unaccented vowel, these com-
mentaries make pretty heavy going when they are read now. But at that
time, when rhetoric was the fashion, these things were fascinating.

Poliziano spoke for two hours in the morning and two hours in the afternoon, alternating Greek and Latin. He had a trick of introducing his subject
through some very simple and homely idea, and so you get some pretty
surprising things scattered through his lectures. 'They say,' he once began,
'that the female mouse is madly lustful.'

At night he often walked or rode with Lorenzo and discussed with him all
the matters that had been raised in the lecture-room through the day. It was
Lorenzo who had first persuaded Poliziano to write in Italian and they still
composed songs and jingles together. But now, at the age of twenty-six,
Poliziano was turning back to the classics again, and the popular poet was
rapidly becoming lost in the professor. Under his charge the Florentine

library was becoming the most distinguished in Europe. At this time, Lorenzo had agents all over the less barbarous parts of the Continent, and in the Near East, searching for classical manuscripts, and he paid large prices for them. The pearl of his collection was the *Pandects of Justinian*, which was kept under armed guard in the vaults of the Palazzo Vecchio. Since the manuscript was too precious to be moved, Poliziano studied it there, in the light of torches.

Meanwhile, Poliziano's reputation was overflowing. He wrote to his friend Hieronymous Donatus: 'If anyone wants a motto for the hilt of his sword, a phrase for a ring, an inscription for his bedroom or a device for his plate or even his pots and pans, he runs like everybody else to Poliziano. There is hardly a wall I have not besmeared like a snail with the effusions of my brain. One man pesters me for rhymes and drinking songs, another for a grave discourse, a third for a serenade and a fourth for a licentious carnival ballad. This fool tells me his love troubles, which I sit like a fool to hear. Another asks me for a symbol which will baffle the curiosity of the others and which only his mistress will understand. I pass over the unreasonable garrulity of the pedants, the impertinences of the poetasters who are constantly admiring their own productions. These are the plagues I am compelled to endure every day, beside the interruptions I meet with in my walks from the lower classes of this city and its vicinity—they drag me through the streets like an ox through the nose.'

Financially things were going very well indeed with him: he still had his church benefices, to which he added a few more and, in 1483, Lorenzo gave him the Villa Diana, near the little hamlet of Fontelucente (which means 'shining fountain') on the steep north-western side of Fiesole. Here he spent the hot summer months during the remainder of his life and composed his *Sylvae*, one of the most famous of his works. It is a long Latin poem, divided into four books, and is intended to be an introduction to poetry from the time of Hesiod to Dante.

Lorenzo had a habit of bestowing Fiesole villas on his followers and there were now quite a few of them scattered over the hillside. The most notable of these was Poliziano's closest friend, Pico della Mirandola. It was said that a ball of fire appeared in the sky over his mother's bed-chamber when Pico was born; it burnt itself out quickly. Pico was nine years younger than Poliziano, and he died within a month or two of Poliziano at the age of thirty-two. The fire that burned in Pico in those few years was incredible. He was credited with speaking twenty-two languages, he was a poet and a prince, and his vast learning was said to cover all the known philosophies of the East. Pico was one of the first and most distinguished scholars to abandon the luxuries of Renaissance Italy and join Savonarola's crusade for poverty and repentance.

There is a charming description of this conversion by Sir Thomas More, who first introduced Pico to England. 'Before this,' he says, 'Pico had been both desirous of glory and kindled in vain love, and holden in voluptuous use of women. The comeliness of his body, with the lovely favour of his visage, and therewithal his marvellous frame, his excellent learning, great richness and noble kindred, set many women afire on him. From the desire of whom he not abhorring was somewhat fallen into wantoness. But . . . he drew back his mind flowing in riot, and turned it to Christ.'

In an unexplained footnote to his manuscript, Sir Thomas added pleasantly: 'The best of us all hath had a madding time.'

It was mostly with Pico and Lorenzo, and one or two others, that Poliziano used to sit up dreaming, and arguing through the night in a gentle glow of Platonic philosophy, worlds upon worlds opening out before them. The talk was endless. They used to keep a light burning before a bust of Plato and every year there was a banquet to celebrate the great man's birthday. Voltaire goes so far as to suggest that these men were 'superior perhaps to the boasted sages of Greece', which seems extravagant. Yet they did feel that they were on the edge of tremendous things, as in fact they were. Underneath all the heavy-handed rhetoric there is a continuous sense of excitement and discovery, since it was not only the future that was opening up but the past as well.

Every day something new happened and Poliziano's life was a wonderful mixture of the naif and sublime. On Monday he is agog over the discovery of four lost books of Cicero and on Tuesday he is marvelling over the arrival of a giraffe, the gift of the Sultan of Egypt to Lorenzo. He dismisses the discovery of printing with the words: 'The most stupid ideas can now in a moment be transferred into a thousand volumes and spread abroad,' but he is much intrigued by the report that a nest of witches has been found at Fiesole, behind the Villa Diana. Pier Leone, Lorenzo's doctor, announces that he has discovered a wonderful new remedy made of the oil of scorpions and the tongues of asps; and Toscanelli, the geographer, produces a chart which pretends that the world might not, after all, be flat. He has been corresponding about it with a Florentine merchant named Amerigo Vespucci and a young Genovese called Christopher Columbus.

All these things were jumbled up in Poliziano's mind, together with the most advanced scholarship, and a remarkable facility in composing Latin verse. When Michelangelo turned up at the age of sixteen, he was quickly gathered into the Fiesolean circle. Poliziano met him in the Garden of Clarice, the sculptor's school which Lorenzo had established just off the Piazza San Marco, and was enraptured with him. One of the best of Michelangelo's early works, the bas-relief of the battle of the centaurs, was suggested to him by Poliziano.

Through all these years Poliziano worked prodigiously. When he went down to Rome, in 1484, with his pupil Piero de' Medici, he took with him his translation of Herodian, to present to the Pope. He said he had finished it in two days, walking up and down his room dictating to secretaries. The Pope gave him 200 gold crowns for the manuscript, which has since found its way back to the Laurentian Library in Florence. It does indeed appear to have been written down by several copyists and Poliziano has gone over the sheets with his neat handwriting, correcting the work and signing his name at the end.

One has this same impression of haste about most of Poliziano's friends: it is as though they sensed that they had very little time before some terrible and inevitable disaster came bearing down on them and put a stop to all their discoveries. They had the feeling, too, that in the midst of all this exploration, they were losing touch with the ordinary patterns and morals of life. Where were they heading to and what did it all mean? Who was going to control what they created? It was a feeling, in fact, that has a certain familiar ring in the nineteen-fifties.

Meanwhile Lorenzo's family was growing up. Piero, the eldest boy, was now aged seventeen, and in 1488 Poliziano again went down to Rome with him for his marriage to Alfonsina Orsini. Lorenzo's wife, Clarice, Poliziano's old enemy, felt very ill at the wedding, and a few weeks later she returned to Florence to die. She was only thirty-seven.

But Poliziano went triumphantly onward. Now he had Lorenzo to himself, and he even began corresponding on fairly intimate terms with other rulers in Europe. 'By the kindness and liberality of Lorenzo de' Medici,' he wrote to the King of Hungary, 'I have been raised from an obscure birth and humble fortune to the degree of rank and distinction I now enjoy. I have, for a series of years, publicly taught at Florence, not only the Latin language with universal applause, but likewise Greek, which I venture to affirm has been the case with no other Italian for a thousand years past.'

In the same unabashed strain, he wrote to the King of Portugal suggesting he should become the King's historian, lest his doings should 'lie hidden in the vast heap of human frailty'. Only through the minds of learned men, Poliziano said, could kings hope for immortality. The King of Portugal was inclined to agree with him and actually sent off some material for Poliziano to work on; but by then (1492) it was already too late. Lorenzo was dying, Savonarola was looming over Florence, crying 'Repentance: the deluge is coming', and presently Poliziano himself was swept away.

Poliziano was almost the last of Lorenzo's followers to go over to Savonarola. When Pico was converted to austerity, along with Botticelli, Fra Bartolommeo and nearly all the other artists, he still hung back, for it was impossible for him to imagine life without Lorenzo. He saw, perhaps, more clearly than the others, that Savonarola was the real enemy of Lorenzo: his movement meant the end of everything Lorenzo and Poliziano believed in— man's free will, to be elegant, to win fame, to accept good and evil as inevitable in human life, and to have the right, if you chose, to worship Plato as well as Christ.

Life, for Poliziano, was here and now and it was a wonderful thing—not, as this gloomy friar suggested, a brief and sinful interlude, to be got through in the most dismal possible way.

But, in the early spring of 1492, Lorenzo's gout grew worse, and he was in constant pain. On 10 March, after immense contriving, his second son Giovanni was made a Cardinal; but Lorenzo himself had to be carried on a litter into the banquet of celebration in the Medici Palace, and he ate nothing. When Giovanni went off to Rome a few days later Lorenzo collapsed. On 21 March he was taken out to his villa at Careggi, where his father and his grandfather had died before him.

Poliziano was at Careggi when Lorenzo died, and his account of how it happened is probably the authentic one.

'The day before his death,' he says, 'being at Careggi, he grew so weak that all hope of his recovery vanished. Perceiving this, like a wise man, he called for the confessor to purge himself of past sins . . . Rousing himself, he exclaimed, 'It shall never be said that my Lord, who created and saved me, shall come to me—in my room—raise me, I beg you, raise me quickly, so that I may go and meet Him.' Saying this, he raised himself as well as he could and, supported by his servants, advanced to meet the priest in the outer room. There, crying, he knelt down . . . At length the priest ordered that he should be raised from the ground and carried to his bed, so that he could receive the Viaticum in more comfort. For some time he resisted, but at last, out of respect for the priest, he consented. In bed, repeating almost the same prayer as he had before, with much gravity and devotion, he received the body and blood of Christ.'

The doctor then arrived. 'He seemed most learned,' Poliziano says, 'but was summoned too late to be of any use. Yet, to do something, he ordered various precious stones to be pounded together in a mortar, for I know not what kind of medicine. Lorenzo, thereupon asked the servants what the doctor was doing in his room, and what he was preparing, and when I answered that he was composing a remedy to comfort his intestines, he recognized my voice, and looking kindly, as he used to do, he said: 'Oh, Angiolo, are you here?' and, raising his languid arms took both my hands and pressed them tightly. I could not stifle my sobs or hold back my tears, though I tried to hide them by turning my face away. But he showed no emotion and continued to press my hands between his. When he saw I could not speak for crying quite naturally he loosened my hands and I ran into the adjoining room.'

Then Pico arrived and finally Savonarola, who gave Lorenzo his Benediction. 'Bowing his head, immersed in piety and religion, he repeated the words and the prayers of the friar, without paying any attention to the grief now shown openly by his attendants. It seemed that all save Lorenzo were going to die, so calm he was. He gave no signs of anxiety or sorrow: even in that supreme moment he showed his usual strength of mind and his fortitude. The doctors who stood round, not to seem idle, worried him with their remedies and assistance. He submitted to everything they suggested, not because he thought it would save him, but in order not to offend anyone, even in death. To the last he had such mastery over himself that he joked about his own death. Thus, when given something to eat and asked how he liked it he replied: "As well as a dying man can like anything." He embraced us all tenderly and humbly asked pardon if, during his illness, he had caused annoyance to anyone. Then, disposing himself to receive extreme unction, he commended his soul to God.'

Poliziano's life flew to bits. He did not go so far as the doctor, Pier Leone, who, having been terrified of drowning all his life (he once refused to take a job in Venice on account of the canals) committed suicide in a well. But he crept about Florence and Fiesole uttering laments: 'Oh that my head were waters and mine eyes a fountain of tears, that I might weep day and night. So mourns the turtle dove, so mourns the dying swan, so mourns the nightingale. Lightning has struck our laurel tree, beneath whose spreading boughs the God of song himself more sweetly harped and sang. Now all around is dumb, now all is mute and there are none to hear.'

Poliziano hung on for another two years, but he accomplished nothing. There is a feeble moth-like quality about his movements: he still fluttered about Florence and Fiesole, but with a bewildered air as though he could not understand where all the warmth and happiness had gone. He seems to have been surrounded by enemies at the end, for he was known to everyone as Lorenzo's man: and the reaction against Lorenzo was violent. His old pupil Piero, now the head of the State, tried to get him a Cardinal's hat but that fell through; and Piero, himself, on whom Poliziano had poured out all his genius as a teacher, was turning out to be a disastrous failure.

Even the silly business over Alessandra Scala went wrong. Alessandra was a notable blue-stocking in Florence, a poetress and a scholar, and there had been a time when Poliziano imagined he was in love with her. He reached the stage of sending little gifts and exchanging Greek epigrams with her. But Alessandra abruptly broke this off and married, instead, the Greek scholar Marullus, who from a friend had become one of Poliziano's worst enemies. This led to a bitter and abusive quarrel—one of a number of quarrels that bedevilled these last days of his life.

One after another most of his friends vanished—either they died or they crept to Savonarola for repentance. In Florence now there was an almost hysterical reaction towards austerity: it was an emotional excitement for people to make huge public bonfires of their wigs and extravagant carnival clothes. They gathered trembling from early morning at the Cathedral to hear Savonarola and feel their flesh creep as he thundered out his terrible prophecies. But for Poliziano it was meaningless: for him life was over anyway. The best of it evaporated at Lorenzo's death. If there existed a God, then he was some radiant Platonic figure, a benign intellectual, the universal Patron, who was infinitely tolerant and kind.

To Poliziano, Lorenzo's Florence had been heaven, and this monastic, silent, apprehensive city was hell. He wanted no part of it. It had been a wonderful interlude while Lorenzo was alive and now he was the guest who had stayed too long.

Poliziano lived just long enough to see the beginnings of the destruction of everything he had loved and worked for—the looting of the Palazzo Medici and the dispersal of the books in the library, the expulsion of Piero de' Medici, the decline and death of his friends, and the overwhelming of Italy itself by the barbarians coming down from the north. To Poliziano, all this—and he had a glimpse of it before he died—meant nothing less than the return of the dark ages. They had escaped from violence and barbarity for a little—he and Lorenzo and the others. Now they were being sucked back into the darkness again. Poliziano was not a very strong character. He gave up at last. He went down to Savonarola's Church of San Marco and begged to be buried there when he died. His last illness coincides very nearly with the end of the era.

There was one last rather wistful letter written to his old master Ficino, from the Villa Diana:

> I hope when your Careggi becomes too hot in August you will not spurn this little Fiesolan country place of ours. Here we have many springs, and since we are in a narrow valley, there is little sun; certainly we are never without a breeze. The little villa lies hidden away from the road and almost in the middle of a wood, yet even so it has a view over all Florence, and although there are a great many people hereabouts, yet there is always that solitude which the contemplative love. You will also be able to have a twofold pleasure here, for often stealing unannounced from his oak-grove Pico visits me and, having dragged me from my hiding place, takes me with him to dinner which I have indeed known to be frugal but always both sensible and full of delightful conversation and amusement. Nevertheless you had better stay with me because you will not eat worse here and perhaps you will drink better, since in the matter of wines I would be a strong rival even of Pico. Vale.
>
> Angelo Poliziano.

After that he left the Villa and went down to Florence.

There are several versions of his actual death—most of them rather unsavoury. 'Poliziano, that fine genius who spoke Latin so well, was called Angelo,' runs the most popular account, 'but he was far from possessing the purity of one of the angelic choir. The abominable passion he entertained for a youth, Greek by birth, occasioned his death, and has forever dishonoured his memory. For in a paroxysm of amorous fever, he suddenly got up one night while his attendant was asleep, and taking his lute in his hand, went to play and sing under the young Greek's window. He was fetched home half dead, and being put to bed, expired shortly afterwards.'

A second version states that he died 'from knocking his head against the wall in a fury of amorous impatience of the most disgraceful character'. Still another version runs—'He was singing on the staircase some verses he had composed for a former mistress of his (Alessandra?), when he came to a very tender passage, his lute fell from his hand, and he tumbled head foremost downstairs and broke his neck'.

On investigation, there seems not to be a word of truth in any of this: and it is highly probable that the story was put about by Marullus in the first place.

What actually happened, so far as one can judge, was that Poliziano became converted to Savonarola shortly before he died. He had rooms in the Garden of Clarice, just across the street from Savonarola's Church of San Marco, and he used to teach the monks there. One of the monks, Roberto Ubaldini, records that he was often with Poliziano during his last illness and was at his bedside in his rooms when he died. At Poliziano's own request he was received into the Domenican Order just before the end, and he was buried in the habit of a monk. The coffin was placed in the laymen's cemetery by the wall of the Church; and a few weeks later he was joined there by Pico. That marvellous beauty of Pico and his radiant reputation stayed with him to the end.

Up at the Villa Diana not much remains to remind you of Poliziano. We have ghosts, of course, but amiable ones. I personally have never seen anything, but our guests are constantly saying when they come down to breakfast in the morning that they have suddenly woken in the night and heard voices all around them; not menacing or frightening voices, rather pleasant ones, as though a group of friends were having a cheerful conversation. But when the guests put the light on they see nothing. There's another, more prosaic form of haunting too; on a still summer night a cool breeze suddenly comes spiriting through the house and this I *can* vouch for. But whether or not it is due to psychic influence or simply the draught coming through an open window I cannot say.

Down in San Marco in Florence they put up a facetious epitaph after Poliziano's death. It read: 'Poliziano lies in this grave, the angel who had one head and, what is new, three tongues. He died September 24, 1494, aged forty.'

Later on the monks felt that this was hardly adequate for the greatest poet-scholar of the Renaissance. The epitaph, which was engraved on a small rectangular stone, was relegated to a back room and the coffin shifted to a better place. To-day the eager tourist will find that a fine white marble tablet has been let into the wall in the nave just below Pico's tomb. It reads:

Here lie the re-discovered bones of Angelo Ambrogini called Poliziano, 1454–1494, the master and poet of the three most divine languages of Europe, who wanted the Athens of Pericles to rise again in the Florence of the Magnificent.

In 1939 both Pico's and Poliziano's graves were opened. By some chemistry of the elements, as though they wished to confirm the popular reputation of the two men, the body of Pico was found to be excellently preserved. Poliziano, however, had crumbled into bones and dust.

For a time these remains were stowed in a drawer in the sacristy and the old prior of San Marco would show them to visitors there. There was nothing much to evoke the poet in that grey decay. After one curious glance the visitors would turn away and the Prior closed the drawer again.

1848: SEED-PLOT OF HISTORY

BY L. B. NAMIER

from *Avenues of History* (1952)

1848: SEED-PLOT OF HISTORY

THE men of 1848, victorious in Paris, Vienna, and Berlin, stood amazed at their own success and moderation. A revolution had swept over Europe, wider than any before it, but eminently humane in its principles and practice. It had its dead but no victims; it made refugees but no political prisoners. Louis-Philippe crossed the Channel—not the first French ruler nor the last to take to that route. The other sovereigns remained, shaken but not overthrown, Metternich, Guizot, and the Prince of Prussia (the later William I) one by one arrived in London: exponents of three systems, disparate in nature and aims, but seemingly obliterated by the same storm. The strongholds of reaction had fallen, rubble had to be carted away, new structures were to arise; there was a great void, filled by sun and air; and over it brooded a singularly enlightened *Zeitgeist*. Men dreamed dreams and saw visions, and anything the spirit could conceive seemed attainable in that year of unlimited possibilities. Next year the light and the airy visions had faded, and it was as if they had never been.

A gale blows down whatever it encounters, and does not distinguish. Revolutions are anonymous, undenominational, and inarticulate. If there is an inherent program, as in agrarian revolutions, it is of a most primitive character. The elemental forces of a mass movement can be made to do the work of men whose quest is alien to them. Most revolutions are filched or deflected: groups or parties with elaborate programs—panaceas or nostrums —try to stamp them with their own ideology and, if successful, claim to be their spokesmen, or even their makers. But revolutions are not made; they occur. Discontent with government there always is; still, even when grievous and well founded, it seldom engenders revolution till the moral bases of government have rotted away: which are the feeling of community between the masses and their rulers, and, in the rulers, a consciousness of their right and capacity to rule. Revolutions are usually preceded by periods of high intellectual achievement and travail, of critical analysis and doubt, of unrest among the educated classes, and of guilt-consciousness in the rulers: so it was in France in 1789, in Europe in 1848, and in Russia in 1917. If such corrosion of the moral and mental bases of government coincides with a period of social upheaval, and the conviction spreads, even to the rulers themselves, that the ramshackle building cannot last, government disintegrates and revolution ensues. Revolutions, as distinct from mere revolts, usually start at the centre of government, in the capital; but the nature of the actual outbreak and its purpose almost invariably escape analysis. What aim did the labouring poor of Paris pursue in the Great Revolution, and what did they attain? What was it that made them fight in July 1830, or in February 1848? And what would they have done had they been successful in the June Days or in the Paris Commune? Agrarian movements are far more articulate in form and aim, and therefore, if extensive and determined, are usually successful. The village is a living organism and its communal consciousness transcends other loyalties; and the peasants' demand to be relieved of dues, or to be given the land of the nobles and the Church, can be met or enforced overnight. The weakness of agrarian movements usually lies in that they break out sporadically, and therefore can be suppressed. But if linked with a rising in the urban centres and with self-doubt in the upper classes, if fanned by generalizing factors, such as *la grande peur* in 1789, or the effect of war in 1917, they become overpowering; and then urban groups or parties graft on to them their own programs.

The revolution of 1848 followed on a period of intellectual efflorescence such as Europe has never known before or since; it supervened at a time when the Governments themselves came to feel unequal to the new circumstances and problems; in a period of financial crisis and economic distress, but of disjointed, or even contradictory, social movements. A numerous urban proletariat gathered in the rapidly growing capitals; the independent artisans were fighting a long-drawn losing battle against modern industry; the factory workers started their struggle for a human existence; while the incidence of the agrarian problem was uneven and varied. In France it had been solved by the Great Revolution; in Germany it was confined to several large areas; in the Habsburg Monarchy it was general and acute: there the peasants were determined to sweep away the surviving feudal burdens and jurisdictions. Before the first gusts of the revolutionary storm the Governments collapsed without offering serious resistance; there was a paralysis of will and a consciousness of defeat almost before the fight was joined. But there was no uniform or unified social-revolutionary force to continue the struggle; and the educated middle classes, the successors or new partners of the princes, from an exaggerated fear of the Reds, quickly turned counter-revolutionary, though they still counted on preserving the conquests of the initial victory which they had appropriated. The peasants were bought off by timely and extensive concessions; the proletariat was defeated in Paris in the June Days, in Vienna in October, while in Berlin (as in 1933) it succumbed without fighting. In France, where 1789 had done most of the work which still awaited accomplishment elsewhere, 1848 followed a path apart;

in the rest of Europe the conflict was between the principle of dynastic property in countries and that of national sovereignty; from which devolved the problems of self-government and self-determination, of constitutional rights and of national union and independence.

The year 1830 brought a reaction against ingenious solutions which the Congress of Vienna had devised for France, Belgium, and Poland; outside France, 1848 was largely an endeavour to find solutions where the Congress had not seriously attempted any. The movement of 1848 was European, yet consciously French in origin. In 1847 Karl Mathy, a Baden bookseller and publisher, had planned a pamphlet putting forward the demands of the German people, to be distributed broadcast on the death of Louis-Philippe: for this was expected to set the European revolution going. 'Our revolutions, like our fashions, we were wont to receive from Paris,' wrote in 1849 his partner, F. D. Bassermann, a leader of the moderate liberals in the Frankfurt Parliament. The European revolution, when it came, operated within the area of Napoleon's work and influence; for he had sapped inherited forms and loyalties, regrouped territories, established modern administrations, and familiarized tens of millions of men with change in political and social conditions—and new ideas are not nearly as potent as broken habits. When Napoleon was overthrown there had to be restoration. Even had the monarchs and ministers assembled in Vienna wished to reconstruct Europe on a rational basis, how could they by agreement have squared Austrian and Prussian aims and claims in Germany, solved the problem of the Papal State in Italy, or resettled the Habsburg Monarchy on any but dynastic foundations? The failures of 1848 go far to justify 1815. Incapable to devise, men are forced back on to the *status quo ante*; and with the pristine facts return ideas in which men no longer wholly believe: in every restoration there is an element of make-believe. The Vienna Congress reaffirmed the idea of indefeasible monarchical rights—and over wide areas failed to restore the previous rulers. And while, for instance, in *Alt-Preussen* and *Alt-Bayern* the countryside was in 1848 *stock-preussisch* and *bayuvarisch*, and therefore hardly affected by revolution, the Roman Catholic Rhineland felt little allegiance to the Hohenzollern, or Protestant Franconia to the Wittelsbach. Nor were the proprietary and quasi-contractual rights attributed to dynasties or Estates compatible with the new social and economic conditions: for those ideas were connected with the land; they were alien to the *intelligentsia* (including the bureaucracy which supplied a remarkable percentage of members to the Parliaments of 1848) and to the modern cities. With them conceptions of the neo-horde replace those of rooted populations. In 1848 a considerable advance was made towards the State untrammelled by contract and custom; and a non-territorial, linguistic nationality asserted its sway. The privileged orders entered into partnership with the educated middle classes, accepting their intellectual lead. As early as December 12, 1847, the Prince Consort advised the King of Prussia to meet the coming onslaught by attaching 'the well-to-do and intelligent sections of the population—that is, the real people (*das eigentliche Volk*)' to the Government by a share in the administration of the country.

Guizot and Metternich had voluntarily left their countries, conscious of being 'dead above ground'; Prince William had to be persuaded, nay, made to leave in order to put an end to rumours that he was about to march on Berlin. They quitted, and he did not—and all three proved right; their systems were dead, his was to be the foremost beneficiary of 1848. There was philosophic elevation and spiritual pride in the fallen Ministers, while the Prince was single-minded and *borné*. 'Je ne connais guère l'embarras et je ne crains pas la responsabilité,' was Guizot's dictum. 'L'erreur ne s'est jamais approché de mon esprit,' said Metternich with a faint smile when in March 1848 he met Guizot on the steps of the British Museum. But Metternich, on the night of his fall, had replied to his wife: 'Oui, ma chère, nous sommes morts'—and never again did he try to force his way among the living. Nor did Guizot: in France, he wrote, in the great crises, the vanquished *deviennent des morts*. Neither was quite of the country he had governed. Metternich, a Rhinelander, had first come to Vienna at the age of 21: the exponent of a non-national ideal, he tried to uphold the Habsburg Monarchy, that dynastic creation *par excellence*, by tying all Europe to the principle which alone could secure Austria's survival. Internal reform he never seriously contemplated: he apprehended its hopelessness—'je passe ma vie a étayer un édifice ver-moulu'. When asked by Guizot to explain how it was that revolution had spread to Austria, governed by him, he replied: 'J'ai quelquefois gouverné l'Europe, l'Autriche jamais.' Guizot, on the other hand, was a Protestant attracted by British institutions and ideas, and self-nurtured on them, who tried to establish constitutional monarchy in France. Under Louis-Philippe France had enjoyed what the rest of the Continent aspired to in 1848: a Parliamentary regime, equality before the law, civic freedoms. And what Guizot's *toryisme bourgeois* tried to cultivate in France were the civic virtues of Victorian England; 'l'esprit de famille, le goût du travail régulier, le respect des supériorités, des lois et des traditions, les sollicitudes prévoyantes, les habitudes religieuses. . . . ' For him French history neither stopped nor started in 1789; he wanted to secure the achievements of the Revolution and lay its ghosts. He thought of 'ces millions d'existences qui ne font point de bruit mais qui sont la France'. But beyond these were men he combated and feared:

The French Revolution and the Emperor Napoleon I have thrown a certain number of minds, including some of the most distinguished, into a feverish excitement which becomes a moral and, I would almost say, a mental disease. They yearn for events, immense, sudden, and strange; they busy themselves with making and unmaking governments, nations, religions, society, Europe, the world. . . . They are intoxicated with the greatness of their design, and blind to the chances of success. To hear them talk, one might think that they had the elements and ages at their command . . . and that these were the first days of creation or the last days of the world.

And Louis-Philippe would say to Guizot:

You are a thousand times right; it is in the depth of men's minds that the revolutionary spirit must be fought, for it is there that it reigns; *mais pour chasser les démons, il faudrait un prophète.*

Le juste milieu was uninspiring, and no compromise, for neither wing accepted it: to the Legitimists the July Monarchy was a 'profanation of monarchy', to the Republicans a perversion and usurpation of national sovereignty. Sainte-Beuve wrote in 1861:

The Orleans dynasty were neither a principle, nor a national glory; they were a utility, an expedient; and they were taken for what they were.

And this was his account of the period:

I appreciated the joys of that reign of eighteen years, the facilities it afforded to the mind and for study, for all pacific pursuits, its humanity, the pleasures offered, even to those not possessed of a vote, by the wonderful display of Parliamentary talent and of eloquence from the tribune. . . . Yet it was impossible to view that regime, in its spirit and *ensemble*, as in any way grand . . . as something of which one could be proud to have been a contemporary. . . .

Guizot himself writes:

It makes the greatness of our nation . . . that purely material and immediate success does not suffice, and that the mind has to be satisfied as much as the interests.

When the revolution started in the streets of Paris even those who valued the July Monarchy as a 'utility' would not die for it. As de Tocqueville puts it, 'the government was not overthrown, it was allowed to fall'. It flopped.

The February Revolution had been universally expected, and after it had occurred no one could account for it. Its course was meaningless, or at least unproductive of immediate results. Memories were re-lived, and the circle of repetition was completed by the Second Republic, the Presidency of Louis-Napoleon, and the Second Empire. Only in the June Days a new reality pierced through the counterfeit displays; the people of Paris, with a tradition and consciousness of power, but without clear aim, took action. In

1848 the French monarchy was consigned to the grave, and with it an element essential to the proper working of the Parliamentary system was lost. Since then France has faced an uneasy choice between a Parliamentary Republic in which President and Prime Minister to some extent duplicate each other, and a system based on an independent Executive which is a crossing between the American Presidency and the Napoleonic dictatorship. The principles of equality and national sovereignty, bequeathed by the Great Revolution, found in 1848 their logical fulfilment in universal suffrage and the Republic, two principles not contravened even by a plebiscitarian Empire. While British radicals adhered to the tenets of classical economy and free trade, French thought in 1848 moved towards new social concepts: the organization and protection of labour, 'the right to work' (with its concomitant: relief for the unemployed), universal education as a citizen right, a graduated income-tax—most of which were realized in Britain before they were in France. To begin with, the February Revolution was not anti-clerical, still less anti-religious; the revolutionaries were romantics rather than free-thinkers, while the clergy were largely Legitimists. Lammenais and Lacordaire were forerunners of a socially radical Catholicism. It was only after the June Days that the cleavage between the Church and the radicals re-opened, while the big bourgeois drew closer to the Church in a political clericalism. The problem of Church and State was now sharply put, and the battle was joined which was to reach its climax fifty years later.

When Metternich fell, aged seventy-five, he was replaced by Kolowrat, aged seventy, and at the Foreign Office by Ficquelmont, aged seventy-one; in May, Pillersdorf, an official aged only sixty-two, became Prime Minister; but on 8 July he was succeeded by Wessenberg, aged seventy-five, who continued the septuagenarian set-up of Austria's 'rejuvenation' till after the October rising in Vienna. And when Bach (aged thirty-five), a politician of revolutionary origin, attained office, within a few weeks he turned into a heavy-handed reactionary. The Vienna revolution was indeed a peculiar affair. But any radical handling of the situation was bound to endanger Austria, immediately or ultimately. Joseph II, Schwarzenberg and Bach, and the men of 1906–14, were exponents of sharp, centralizing authoritarian systems; Maria Theresa, Metternich, and Francis Joseph in his later years, temporized; *immer fortwurschteln* ('always muddle along') was the precept of the Emperor's most accordant Premier, Count Taaffe. Where historic survival is both *raison d'être* and aim, logical conceptions are a deadly poison. And Austria survived because of the inherent impossibilities and contradictions of the situation. Metternich knew it, but preferred to bedeck the dismal truth with philosophical dissertations.

The pattern of Austria's existence becomes patent in 1848, though it takes time before it is discerned and the consequences are drawn. There were four dominant nationalities within the Habsburg Monarchy whose upper and middle classes covered also the territories of the subject races: Germans, Italians, Magyars, and Poles, versus Czechs, Slovaks, Yugoslavs, Ruthenes, and Rumans. The four master races demanded a united Germany, a united Italy, an independent Hungary, and a reunited Poland, including between them all the territories of the subject races inhabiting the Monarchy. Their programs carried to their logical conclusion implied the complete disruption of the Austrian Empire, and were therefore opposed by the dynasty, and by those among the Austrian Germans who were more Austrian than German. The subject races, too, desired national unity and independence, but they preferred the rule of the non-national Habsburgs to that of the master races. Some of their leaders, especially among the Czechs, went the length of developing a program of 'Austro-Slavism'—of an Austria reconstructed on a Slav basis. But this was a phantasm; for it offered no possible basis for the existence and survival of the Habsburg Monarchy. In the long run the dynasty had to take for partners nationalities which shared their proprietary interest in their territories, as did the Germans, Magyars, and Poles, and which, therefore, were prepared to defend every square mile. But the Germans, inside and outside Austria, would only accept her continued existence in lieu of complete national unity if the German predominance within Austria was maintained and reinforced by a German alliance, which in turn the Habsburgs themselves required to safeguard their dominions; and the Magyars and Poles would only accept it provided it did not touch, and indeed safeguarded, their dominion over Hungary and Galicia. Socially also the German-Magyar-Polish basis best suited the Habsburgs: an ancient dynasty cannot permanently ally itself to peasants against their masters. In 1848–49 the peasant nations supported the dynasty; in 1867 they were abandoned by it to the dominant races. In 1866–67 the German, Italian, and Magyar programs of 1848 were realized in modified forms, and the Polish, in so far as this was possible within the framework of the Habsburg Monarchy alone. In 1918–19 came the time for the subject races of the German and Magyar spheres, and for the Poles; in 1939–45, for the Yugoslavs and Ruthenes in the Italian and Polish spheres. Every idea put forward by the nationalities of the Habsburg Monarchy in 1848 was realized at some juncture, in one form or another. And perhaps even Austro-Slavism will ultimately find its realization in a Danubian Union under Slav aegis.

With 1848 starts the German bid for power, for European predominance, for world dominion: the national movement was the common denominator of the German revolution of 1848, and a mighty Germany, fit to give the law to other nations, its foremost aim. *Einheit, Freiheit, und Macht* ('Unity, Freedom, and Power') was the slogan, with the emphasis on the first and third concepts. 'If I knew that Germany's unity and future greatness demanded a temporary renunciation of all the freedoms (*sämmtlicher Freiheits-rechte*),' declared Bassermann on 16 February, 1849, 'I should be the first to submit to such a dictatorship.' And the line followed by the majority parties of the Frankfurt Assembly in 1849, at Gotha and Erfurt, proves that dictum to have been truly representative. 'Through power to freedom, this is Germany's predestined path,' wrote in April 1848, the outstanding intellectual leader of the Frankfurt assemblies, Professor Dahlmann. Even some of the Republicans were Republicans primarily because they were Nationalists: the existence of thirty-odd dynasties and the rival claims of Habsburgs and Hohenzollern were the foremost obstacles to German unity, easiest removed by proclaiming a German Republic, one and indivisible. The movement for German unity originated in 1848 in the West, South-West, and in the Centre of Germany, in the small States which gave no scope to the German *Wille zur Macht*, and in the newly acquired, disaffected provinces of Prussia and Bavaria. But although the aim of the Frankfurt Parliament was a real Pan-Germany, not a Greater Prussia or Great Austria, one of the two German Great Powers had to be the core of the new German Federal State. And here started the difficulties: Austria was the greatest State within the Federation and its traditional 'head', but of its 36 millions, less than 6 millions were German; while of 16 millions in Prussia, 14 millions were German. Austria obviously could not merge into a German national State, whereas Prussia could—theoretically. It became clear in 1848–49 that a united Greater Germany (*Gross-Deutschland*), comprising the German provinces of Austria, implied the disruption of Austria; otherwise it had to be a Lesser Germany (*Klein-Deutschland*). With an undivided Austria within Germany, the German Confederation could not change into a Federal State; but a Federation of States offered no prospect of real national unity or of power. The Frankfurt Parliament therefore finished by accepting *Klein-Deutschland*, and offered its Crown to the King of Prussia; who refused from respect for Austria and because he could only have accepted the Crown if offered to him by his fellow-sovereigns. Nor would the new Empire as planned at Frankfurt have proved acceptable to the true Prussians: Frankfurt, not Berlin, was to have been its capital, and Prussia was 'to merge into Germany' (there was intense jealousy at Frankfurt against the Berlin Parliament, and as a safeguard against Prussian predominance in a *Klein-Deutschland* it was planned to break up Prussia into her eight provinces, each about the size of a German middle-sized State). When in March 1848, Frederick William IV sported the German tricolour and made his troops assume it, the Second Regiment of the Guards replied by a song about the 'cry which pierced the faithful hearts: you shall be Prussians no longer, you shall be Germans'. When Bismarck showed its text to the Prince of Prussia, tears ran down William's cheeks. But it was his system based on Prussia, her army and administration, which was to be established by the man who showed him the song.

The year 1848 proved in Germany that union could not be achieved through discussion and by agreement; that it could be achieved only by force; that there were not sufficient revolutionary forces in Germany to impose it from below; and that therefore, if it was to be, it had to be imposed by the Prussian army. Again the future was mapped out. There were four programs in 1848–49. That of *Gross-Oesterreich*, a centralized Germanic Austria retaining her traditional preponderance in Germany, was realized by Schwarzenberg in 1850, after Olmütz. That of a Greater Prussia was realized in the North German Confederation of 1866, and was extended in 1870–71 to cover the entire territory of the Frankfurt *Klein-Deutschland*. That program itself, with the capital removed from Berlin, was haltingly attempted under the Weimar Republic; while the other Frankfurt program of *Gross-Deutschland*, including the German and Czech provinces of Austria, was achieved by Hitler in 1938–39.

In 1800, after some forty years in politics, Lord Shelburne wrote in his memoirs:

> It requires experience in government to know the immense distance between planning and executing. All the difficulty is with the last. It requires no small labour to open the eyes of either the public or of individuals, but when that is accomplished, you are not got a third of the way. The real difficulty remains in getting people to apply the principles which they have admitted, and of which they are now so fully convinced. Then springs the mine of private interests and personal animosity. . . . If the Emperor Joseph had been content to sow and not to plant, he would have done more good, and saved a great deal of ill.

Most of the men of 1848 lacked political experience, and before a year was out the 'trees of liberty' planted by them had withered away. None the less, 1848 remains a seed-plot of history. It crystallized ideas and projected the pattern of things to come; it determined the course of the century which followed. It planned, and its schemes have been realized; but—*non vi si pensa quanto sangue costa*.

BENJAMIN CONSTANT AND
ADOLPHE

BY HAROLD NICOLSON

Published in the Novel Library (1949)

BENJAMIN CONSTANT AND ADOLPHE

I

To understand *Adolphe* and to appreciate the mood in which it was written, it is necessary to know something of the life and love-affairs of Benjamin Constant, and to realize the conflict within him between the artist and the man of action. *Adolphe* essentially is an autobiographical novel; but it is neither a complete self-portrait, nor a direct description of the woman by whom, in his middle years, he was dominated and controlled. It represents Constant during that phase of his life when he was torn between pity, subservience, and a desire to escape. Under the transparent disguise of an affair with Anna Lindsay, he describes how the bond which had been forged between him and Madame de Stael had grown, link by link, into a rusted chain of iron.

In *The Red Note-book*—a slim book of 227 written pages, bound in red paper and first published in 1907—Constant has given his own account of the first twenty years of his life. Yet if we are to estimate the curious blending in his character of the purposeful and the haphazard, of the selfish and the self-sacrificing, of ambition and sentiment, of impulsiveness and diffidence; if, that is, we are to acquire any comprehension of his strangely dual temperament; it is necessary to supplement his own account from other and perhaps more objective sources.

Henri Benjamin Constant de Rebecque was born at Lausanne in Switzerland on 25 October 1767. The house, which until 1912 was still standing in the Rue du Grand-Chêne, was a long, low building of two stories with high windows opening upon the chestnuts of a little garden. His mother, Henrietta de Chandieu, died a few days after his birth. His grandmother and his aunt, Madame de Nassau, strove to secure the charge of this motherless infant: his father wished to keep the boy for himself. 'He was,' as his cousin Rosalie wrote in later years, 'regarded by the family as a fragile but precious object, of which each in turn desired to obtain possession.' But the father won.

Colonel Just de Constant is vividly depicted both in the *Cahier Rouge* and in *Adolphe* itself. He combined the tolerance of the eighteenth century with a cold protestantism. While condoning the follies of his son, while encouraging his vices, he was unable (perhaps from secret shyness) to accord him either

245

his confidence or his affection. Although he possessed several different properties in Switzerland, he preferred to take service in the Swiss regiment in
the Low Countries. He was always on the move between the Lake of Geneva,
Brussels, Germany and the garrison towns of the Netherlands. Before his
marriage to Benjamin's mother he had taken charge of a little girl of nine,
whose real name was Jeanne Mangin, but who was subsequently known as
'Marianne'. He educated this child according to his own theories, and eventually she became his housekeeper and his second wife. It was to her simple
care that the young Benjamin was first entrusted. In later years Colonel de
Constant, much to Benjamin's distress, became involved in a lawsuit with the
officers of his own regiment. He failed to win either the lawsuit or the expensive appeal which he thereafter lodged. He lost his job and had to sell most
of his properties. He died a discontented man.

Benjamin's childhood years were spent in one or other of the family
houses which fringed the shores of the Lake of Geneva. He was given French
tutors, German tutors and English tutors; these pedagogues seem to have
been selected almost by chance and without discrimination. Benjamin was
a precocious child; he mastered the rudiments of Greek grammar at the age
of five; the letters which he wrote at the age of ten are so mature that Sainte-
Beuve (who detested Benjamin Constant and sought always to discredit
him) pronounced them to be forgeries. They were, in fact, authentic. 'I
wish,' he wrote while still a little boy, 'that someone could stop my blood
circulating so rapidly and impart to it a calmer rhythm. I have tried to see
whether music could produce this effect; I have been playing adagios and
largos such as would send thirty cardinals to sleep.' The feverish impatience,
which in adult years, amounted to a gambler's recklessness, was a cause of
worry to Benjamin even as a child. His father did little to render him more
quiescent. He dragged him off to Paris, he took him over to Oxford for a
while, he sent him to the German university of Erlangen. From Germany,
on a sudden impulse, Benjamin went to Edinburgh where he enrolled himself as a student. The year and a half which he spent in Scotland appeared to
him in later life as the happiest of all his many interludes. In 1786, at the age
of nineteen, he crossed again to Paris; there followed a period of gaming and
debauchery; and it was then that he met the first of the three women who
were to dominate his life.

Madame de Charrière at that date was forty-seven years of age: she is the
'Zélide' of Geoffrey Scott's delicate biography. As a girl of some beauty and
great gifts she had had many suitors, including James Boswell and Benjamin's uncle. But in the end she married M. de Charrière, her brother's
dull but worthy tutor, and with him she retired to the estate of Colombiers,
near Neuchâtel. She acquired a certain literary reputation by her novel *Caliste*
and her *Lettres de Lausanne*; she possessed a logical eighteenth-century mind,
considerable powers of conversation, a taste for opium, and a capacity for deep

maternal affection. Constant accompanied her from Paris to Colombiers, where he started writing his *History of Religion*, the final version of which was not published for forty years. At Colombiers Constant found many of the things that he needed; seclusion, since at that time he was suffering from an unfortunate malady which developed into skin disease; that maternal affection of which fate had deprived him; and infinite opportunities for conversation. They would sit there by the stove in Madame de Charrière's drawing-room, under the heavy Pompeian decoration of the domed ceiling, and exchange general ideas until the dawn showed through the shutters. She became his mentor and his confidante: in *Adolphe* she appears as a peaceful memory in the passages which occur in Chapter I.

Constant's platonic, but not unemotional, friendship with Madame de Charrière lasted for almost ten years, from 1786 to 1795. With her he found protection without captivity, firmness without rage. While she ruled his life he was free to indulge in other employments and to contract other affections. There was Mrs. Trevor, the wife of the British Minister at Turin, a coquette of mature years who rejected his vigorous but timid advances. There was Jenny Pourras, a young heiress who refused to marry him, at which, and not for the last time, he staged a mock suicide. In 1788, while he was still suffering from herpes, his father, resenting what he imagined to be the idleness of Colombiers, packed him off to the Court of Brunswick, having obtained for him a post of junior chamberlain. The next year Benjamin startled them all by marrying Baroness Minna von Cramm, one of the ladies of the ducal court, who possessed neither beauty, charm, nor character. After a few months of bitter wrangling they agreed to separate; Minna was not only unfaithful to him, she also disclosed to the Duke of Brunswick certain writings of Constant in which his employers were exposed to ridicule; he thus lost his job and his wife at the same time. They were divorced in March 1793 and Constant returned to Colombiers to nurse his wounds.

Madame de Charrière had always realized that the influence which she exercised upon the young Constant was protective and intellectual; she called it her 'intellectual maternity'. She had not, for this reason, been jealous of Mrs. Trevor, or Jenny Pourras, or even of Minna von Cramm; she knew that she could provide him with something which they could never supply. But she was terrified of Madame de Stael. Here was a potential rival, twenty-six years younger than herself, abounding in vitality, rich, managing, famous, and endowed with a capacity for conversation in comparison to which the talks at Colombiers would seem but faint logical murmurs beside a stove. In her letters she sought to discredit her formidable successor in the eyes of Benjamin. How vulgar was Madame de Stael, how inelegant, how snobbish, how essentially silly. 'She is not,' wrote Zélide, 'authentic.' But in her lonely, unhappy heart, Madame de Charrière knew that in the end the two must meet; and that her Benjamin would at once be captured and enslaved.

On a September morning in 1794 Madame de Stael was driving along the
road from Coppet to Mézery. Her carriage was intercepted by a young man
on horseback who explained that he had just been to Coppet and had been
told by her servants that she had left but an hour before; he had thus cantered
along the road to catch her up. She invited him to enter her carriage; at
once they embarked upon a tremendous discussion regarding the liberty of
the press.

Benjamin Constant at that date was twenty-seven years of age. His appearance was not prepossessing. His carroty hair hung over his forehead in wisps,
his white face was blotched with yellow patches; his little eyes glinted within
half-closed eyelids and behind green spectacles; his lips were mobile and slim.
He had a weedy body, and white freckled hands which jerked nervously; his
finger was constantly in his mouth. He had a thin, rather effeminate voice,
and when he uttered his epigrams, the sibilants hissed and whistled.

Constant returned to Coppet with Madame de Stael. Madame de Charrière
sought for a moment to brave it out. 'What fun we shall have,' she wrote
pathetically, 'laughing at her when you return.' 'It seems to me,' replied
Constant, 'that you judge her too severely.' This letter had been written on
a paper scented with ambergris. Madame de Charrière was too intelligent a
woman not to realize that she was beaten. 'Benjamin,' she replied, 'you are
beginning to take pains about your personal appearance; you no longer love
me.' Constant, in a mood of ruthless impatience, decided to confess that he
had fallen in love with Madame de Stael. 'She is,' he wrote to Zélide, 'the
second woman in my life who could fill my whole universe; you know who
was the first.' The reign of Madame de Charrière had ended: the tyranny of
Germaine de Stael had begun.

The subsequent stages of Constant's enslavement are comprehensible; we
can find in them a combination of mixed motives and emotions: intellectual
admiration and enjoyment, habit, convenience, vanity, a need for mental
excitement, gratitude, duty, worldly ambition, compassion, and sheer
physical and nervous terror. It is the sudden and overwhelming infatuation
of the first months that is so difficult to explain. Madame de Stael, even at the
age of twenty-eight, was not an attractive woman. Her figure was ungainly,
her skin tawny, her gestures violent, her voice loud and hoarse. It may be
that, like Adolphe, Constant possessed the gambler's reckless desire for
immediate acquisition. It may be also that, as so often happens with neurotics,
he was less in love with an individual than in love with love. It may be
that, being conscious of his own sexual timidity, he forced himself into
positions more extreme and inevitable than a less cerebral sensualist would
need to adopt. And it may be again that, mortified as he was by his own

lack of physical attraction, detecting in the eyes of Madame de Stael the repulsion which he inspired, he forced himself to stake everything on win or lose.

He was certainly impulsive. A few hours only after his arrival at Coppet he began to display marked symptoms of physical passion. Madame de Stael rejected his advances. He resorted to his former trick of attempted suicide; he swallowed opium, roused the household, and insisted that Madame de Stael should come to him before he expired. 'Tell her,' he panted, 'that it is from love of her that I die.' Madame de Stael, roused from her slumbers, hurried to his bedside; he covered her hand with kisses and almost immediately recovered. When she returned to her own room she plunged into scented water the hand that he had kissed. 'I feel for that man,' she confessed, 'a physical antipathy which nothing can surmount.'

Within a few days Constant was convalescent. She allowed him to sit up with her until midnight had struck. One night he overstayed the time allotted to him and she told him to consult his watch. It was ten minutes after midnight. He took the watch and smashed it against the marble mantelpiece. This gesture seems to have had more effect upon the Baroness than the attempted suicide. Next morning Constant notes in his diary: 'I shall not buy another watch. I have no longer any need of it.'

Madame de Stael was the most possessive woman that ever lived. None of her victims was ever allowed to leave the gilded cage. She forced them to sign acts of capitulation under which they bound themselves to eternal fidelity and obedience. If any of them managed to escape for a moment one of the other victims, or even her own son, was sent after the renegade to fetch him back. The discipline she imposed was ferocious; the scenes she enacted were uncontrolled; she would rush like a maenad along the passages with foam upon her lips; the placid waters of Lac Leman echoed to her hoarse and frenzied cries. The prisoners themselves, in spite of their mutual antipathy, huddled like cows together in a common fear.

The Coppet establishment has often been described. The permanent prisoners, apart from Constant himself, were Mathieu de Montmorency, Schlegel, the banker Sismondi, Elzear de Sabran and Prosper de Barante. The only women inhabitants were Madame Necker de Saussure and Madame Récamier. They all met at breakfast at eight in the morning; conversation then continued for three-and-a-half hours until the midday meal; there was a pause till dinner when conversation was resumed. From time to time there would be amateur theatricals, at which Madame de Stael excelled in the part of Phèdre. The lack of privacy must have been appalling; there were no locks to the doors and Madame de Stael, armed with her green morocco writing case, would burst into the rooms of her victims at any hour of the day and night, shouting incessantly, often in rage. Occasionally they would all go on expeditions together or undertake voyages to Germany or France.

Vociferous and untiring, Madame de Stael lashed out at her troop of galley slaves. They bowed their head in admiration, anger and shame.

III

In May 1795 Madame de Stael had felt that it was safe to return to Paris and to re-open her salon. She brought Benjamin with her. When the Directory was established a few months later they imagined that their opportunity had come. The frenzy of the Revolution had spent itself; a new epoch of philosophic liberalism was about to open; and under such a system they would both, with their intellectual energies and their uncompromised pasts, find scope for their ambitions. Benjamin would play the part of a liberal politician, perhaps even of a statesman; and Madame de Stael from her salon would become the tutelary goddess of the whole movement. Their hopes were disappointed. Benjamin presented himself to the electors, but, owing to his Swiss origin, he was not returned; and Madame de Stael aroused hostility by her arrogance, and suspicion by her unbridled tactlessness. 'One is no more,' she confessed, 'than a pebble thrown into an enormous wheel.'

And then came the 18 Brumaire and the advent of Bonaparte. Madame de Stael loved liberty, but she worshipped power. She spared no pains to flatter Bonaparte and to obtain a place for Benjamin. Somewhat contemptuously the First Consul appointed Benjamin Constant as the representative in the Tribunate for the Department of Leman. 'After all,' he is reported to have said, 'why not?' But Madame de Stael was unable to keep silent as Constant was unable to refrain from criticism. Bonaparte soon lost his patience. In 1802 Constant was deprived of his job in the Tribunate and Madame de Stael was ordered to leave Paris. So far from having assisted him in his ambitions, Madame de Stael, by her chatter and self-assertion, had ruined his political career. They returned to Coppet, mortified and resentful. The only function that remained to them was to become the twin martyrs of Bonapartism.

The infatuation which had swept Constant off his balance in 1794 had not been of long duration; within a few months the lover had become the servant. So long ago as May 1797 he had confessed to his aunt, Madame de Nassau, that 'a bond by which I am held, owing to a sense of duty, or, if you prefer it, from weakness, renders me profoundly unhappy'. With the destruction of his political ambitions, this bond became increasingly irksome. Moreover, while in Paris in 1800, he had fallen in love with someone else.

Anna Lindsay, known officially as Madame Lindsay, had been born in 1764, the daughter of an Irish innkeeper at Calais of the name of Jeremy O'Dwyer. While still a girl she had attracted the attention of the Duchess of Fitz-James who had removed her from her father's inn, given her some education and a taste for elegance and then left her to her own devices. After an early life of varied gallantry, she had formed in 1788 a serious connection with Auguste de Lamoignon, by whom she had two children. She possessed a domestic nature and a longing to become respectable; her personal charm, the services which during the Revolution she had been able to render to the *émigrés*, and her long fidelity to Lamoignon, enabled her to create a place for herself on the fringes of the tolerant society of the Directory. It was Julie Talma, Constant's devoted friend, who brought the two together in October 1800. Benjamin was thirty-two at that date and Madame Lindsay was thirty-six; he had always preferred women older than himself. He fell in love with her and she gave herself to him within a few days of their first meeting. It was customary for Constant to tire of a thing the moment he had come to possess it; the honeymoon with Anna Lindsay was prolonged by the stimulating circumstances that possession could not be absolute. She was tied by her duty towards Lamoignon; he by his service to Madame de Stael. An element of uncertainty was thus introduced into their relationship; and this tension postponed for Benjamin the advent of satiety. This early period is described in the famous, and indeed striking, opening to Chapter 4. Constant, during the blaze of his early passion, urged Madame Lindsay to break with Lamoignon, and promised that if she did so, he would sever his connection with Madame de Stael. Within a few months, however, he had thought much better of this proposal. Not only would it be difficult, and even dangerous, to escape from Madame de Stael's clutches, but if Lamoignon ceased to be responsible for Anna Lindsay, then Constant might have to support both her and the two children himself. He poured out his perplexity to Madame Talma. She was sympathetic, helpful, but a shade too frank. Julie Talma was a penetrating woman. She understood Benjamin Constant better even than he understood himself. Her nickname for him was '*la vieille coquette*'. Behind all his ecstatics she detected the exasperation wrought in him by the conflict between his artistic sensibility and his desire to appear as the man of action, irresistible and passionate. She foresaw the reaction which possession was bound to produce. 'What you would like to do,' she wrote to him a trifle harshly, 'is to seduce women; but you can only charm them.' The letters which Constant wrote to Madame Lindsay did not seem to Madame Talma to be honest or fair. 'They are a mixture,' she wrote, 'of passion and indifference; of the outspoken and the sly; half of what they contain induces despair; the other half inspires hope.' So long as Madame Talma was alive the affair between Constant and Madame Lindsay pursued its complicated and neurotic course. But Madame Talma died in May 1805; and thereafter Constant returned to Coppet and did not see Anna Lindsay for a space of ten years. Mortified, unhappy, and disgusted with his own wretched weakness, he resumed his former servitude. And it was in such a mood, in the late autumn of 1806, that he wrote *Adolphe*.

In 1801, Monsieur de Stael, the dim but official husband of the Baroness, had died of apoplexy. Constant felt that it was obligatory to suggest marriage to his widow. She refused, on the sensible ground that it would be foolish at her age to change a name which she had rendered so famous. In 1804 a further entanglement occurred. Monsieur Necker, the father for whom Madame de Stael entertained so extravagant a passion, died at Coppet. Her desolation at this misfortune was not feigned; Constant felt obliged to comfort and assuage her by any means in his power. This added a further link to his chain. By 1806, however, this link also had become rusted. It must be realized that *Adolphe* was written at a moment when Constant was ruminating, was even planning, the most intricate and excruciating manœuvres for escape. 'I am tired,' he wrote, 'of being always necessary and never adequate.' 'Benjamin,' wrote Madame de Stael, 'is too incomplete, both in feeling and in character, to suffice me wholly.'

He began to write *Adolphe* in the autumn of 1806. 'Benjamin,' Madame de Stael informed Bonstetten on 15 November of that year, 'has begun a novel, which is the most original and the most moving of any I have read.' It may be, as M. Rudler suggests, that this first sketch represented Adolphe as torn between the love of two women, Ellénore and a less worthy person of the type of Mrs. Trevor. He abandons Ellénore for the coquette; Ellénore dies of a broken heart and Adolphe refuses to see Mrs. Trevor again. It may well have been this first draft to which Madame de Stael refers in her letter to Bonstetten. We know from the *Journal Intime* that Constant realized thereafter that if a second woman were introduced into the novel, Ellénore would lose her central position and the weakness of Adolphe himself would become too odious. In the first fortnight of January 1807 he therefore rewrote the novel, more or less in its present form, and finished it within fifteen days. He read it aloud on repeated occasions and in different circles; the final draft was not written out until 1810; the novel was not printed until 1816. Two manuscript copies exist, the one in the library at Geneva, the other in the Monamy-Valin archives.

To us Anglo-Saxons, with our congenital reticence in all such matters, it may seem strange that Benjamin Constant should so frequently have indulged in the exhibitionism of reading aloud to strangers the story of his own amours. There was an element in his sensibility which added relish to such self-humiliation. He would have called it an act of conscience. There exist several records of these public readings. On 19 April 1815, we learn from the memoirs of the Duc de Broglie, Constant was feeling weary and exhausted; when he came to the death of Ellénore his voice broke; the whole audience dissolved into tears; and then as a reaction everybody started to laugh wildly.

Constant notes this incident in his diary. '*Lu mon roman: fou rire.*' A few weeks later, on 20 June 1815, he went to the Rue Cerutti to read the novel to Queen Hortense. Before they had reached the death of Ellénore, the Duke of Rovigo entered the room hurriedly and took the Queen aside. He told her that Napoleon had been decisively defeated within a few miles of Brussels. The following February Miss Berry, in her journal, mentions a similar reading in London:

'Wednesday, February 14, 1816. In the evening at the Bourkes (the Danish Minister), where there had been a dinner. Lady Holland, Madame de Lieven etc., and where Benjamin Constant read his romance, or history; I do not know what to call it as he has not given it a name. It is very well written: —a sad, and much too true, history of the human heart; but almost ridiculously so, with the company before whom it was read. It lasted two hours and a half. The end was so touching that it was scarcely possible to restrain one's tears and the effort I made to do so made me positively ill. Agnes and I both burst into tears on our return home.'

The fame of these readings spread through London society. Constant decided to have the novel published. It was issued in French under the title '*Adolphe; an anecdote found among the papers of an unknown person and published by Monsieur Benjamin de Constant*'. It bears the double imprint of 'London, Colburn, Bookseller' and 'Paris, Tröttel and Wurtz'. On 17 August 1816, Constant wrote to his cousin from London: 'I only published the thing in order to save myself the trouble of reading it in company. Having given four readings in a single week, I thought it would be more worth while to allow others to have the trouble of reading it themselves.' Moreover, he received from Messrs. Colburn a welcome advance payment of £70. A second edition, with a new preface, was published in Paris a few weeks later. A third edition, with yet another preface, was published by Brissot-Thivers in Paris in 1824. The last edition to be published in Constant's lifetime appeared in 1828.

V

I have brought the story of Benjamin Constant's loves and servitude up to that fortnight in January 1807 when he composed the basic draft of *Adolphe*. Before I examine how far the novel must be regarded as autobiographical, it may be well to sketch the outlines of Constant's subsequent career.

When in Germany in 1793, he had had an affair with Charlotte von Hardenberg which lasted for two months. He found her 'romantic and tiresome', and he went his way. At the time she made no attempt to recapture his affections; he discovered, characteristically, 'that something that escapes one is wholly different from something that pursues one'. Often, when lacerated by the claws of Madame de Stael, he had thought back upon Charlotte's gentle pliancy, her soothing hands. In 1807, when his hatred of Madame de Stael had reached its aching climax, he entered into correspondence with Charlotte who in the interval had married a Monsieur Dutertre. He asked her to obtain a divorce and to become his wife. Pliant, as usual, she travelled to Germany in order to institute divorce proceedings against the unfortunate Monsieur Dutertre. Constant had not, of course, dared to reveal these stratagems to Madame de Stael; in fact, to ease his conscience, he again begged her to become his wife. A scene followed in which she accused him, in front of her children, of seeking either to obtain her fortune or to destroy her life. As usual, he capitulated and returned submissively to Coppet. The old relations were resumed.

Meanwhile Charlotte had obtained her divorce from Monsieur Dutertre, and was expecting Benjamin to make the next move. At that very moment Madame de Stael went on a journey to Austria where she found a new lover in the shape of Maurice O'Donnell. Benjamin quickly seized this opportunity for escape. He married Charlotte at Brévans on 5 June 1808. Madame de Stael returned from Austria, having tired of O'Donnell, and re-established her court at Coppet. Benjamin did not dare to disclose to her his secret marriage: he remained at Coppet for almost a year, during which his only encounter with Charlotte was one frightened conversation conducted through the railings of the park. After months of further servitude he at last came to a decision. Charlotte herself must reveal to Madame de Stael the guilty secret which was theirs. The scene that followed had all the swift intensity of a typhoon. Madame de Stael imposed unconditional surrender. The marriage must remain a secret: Charlotte must disappear; and Benjamin must return to Coppet as if nothing had occurred. Charlotte thereupon attempted to commit suicide but recovered within a few days; and Benjamin remained a prisoner at Coppet until February 1811. It was then that John Rocca, a cavalry captain of the age of twenty-three, appeared as the deliverer. He was passionate and handsome; he was violent; he was sensual; he was a romantic and male. Moreover, he was not a conversationalist. 'Speech,' admitted Madame de Stael, 'is not his language.' He challenged Benjamin to a duel because he objected to the attentions which he paid to Madame de Stael. The latter stopped the duel, but was entranced by the episode. At last Benjamin plucked up his courage. The final scene, and it was extravagant, took place on the staircase of the Hôtel de la Couronne at Lausanne at 11 a.m. on the morning of 10 May 1811. The chain at last was broken. Constant retired to Göttingen with Charlotte, where he settled down to a life of domestic austerity, studiously working at the twelve volumes of his *History of Religion*.

Then came Leipzig and the collapse of the Napoleonic Empire. The time for action had at last arrived. Constant, impulsive as ever, was whirled off his

feet by a wind of political opportunism. He established relations with Bernadotte who, he imagined, was the most likely candidate for the Napoleonic
succession. He went to Paris. By then Louis XVIII was established on the
throne of his fathers and Constant, having rapidly severed his connection
with Bernadotte, rallied to the Bourbon regime. When Napoleon landed at
Fréjus, Constant publicly announced that he was prepared to sacrifice his life
in order to repel the usurper and the tyrant; even when Napoleon had
reached Auxerre, and Louis XVIII was preparing his escape to Ghent, Constant published in the *Journal des Débats* a wild manifesto of defiance. This
juvenile conduct may have been due to his desire to impress Madame
Récamier, with whom, since August 1814, he had fallen desperately in love.
In the old Coppet days, Constant had scarcely noticed Juliette Récamier; 'not
a single wrinkle,' he had written of her, 'not a single idea'; but by 1814
Madame Récamier was approaching her fortieth year, and Constant, who
liked his fruit to be slightly over-ripe, entered upon the most unsuccessful,
and therefore the most lasting, of his many love-affairs.

When Napoleon entered Paris, Constant escaped to the country where he
remained for a few weeks in hiding. Having been assured that his life was in
no danger, he crept back to Paris. Napoleon, realizing that the enthusiasm
which had greeted his return could not be of long duration, was by then
seeking to pose as a liberal. He sent for Benjamin Constant, appointed him a
Councillor of State, and charged him with drafting the 'Additional Act to
the Imperial Constitution'. When Napoleon returned from Waterloo he
accorded Constant an audience of three hours which took place in the garden
of the Elysée. But the allies by then were advancing inexorably on Paris:
Napoleon retired to Malmaison and thereafter to St. Helena; and Constant
made his escape to London.

Having changed sides three times within one year, Constant then prepared
to change sides once again. He had always believed that principles were more
than parties; and it must be accorded to him in justice that, whatever may
have been the colour of the successive cockades which in those breathless
months he affixed to his buttonhole, he always remained a liberal at heart.
He therefore made his peace with the Bourbons and returned to France. In
1819 he was elected for the Department of the Sarthe and, owing to a succession of trenchant speeches and pamphlets, became the acknowledged leader
of the liberal opposition to the royalist reactionaries. He was unseated in
1822, but thereafter was elected for the Department of the Vosges amid
scenes of popular rejoicing. With the Revolution of July it seemed that the
road was at last opened to him for high office. But Louis-Philippe, who was
too shrewd a man not to realize Constant's inherent instability, merely
accorded him the honorary post of President of the Council of State. Having
failed as a politician, he endeavoured to confirm his reputation as a writer.
In the autumn of 1830 he sought admission to the French Academy; he was

not elected. On 10 December 1830 he died a disappointed man. His funeral
acquired the proportions of a popular demonstration. But by posterity he is
remembered, not as the author of the *History of Religion*, not as the able
parliamentarian and the champion of liberalism, but as the man who, in that
January fortnight of 1807, wrote the story of *Adolphe*.

VI

Benjamin Constant adopted many devices in the hope of concealing from
the public the fact that his novel was a record of personal experience. He
pretended that the manuscript had come into his hands by chance, having
been left behind by an unknown traveller in a Calabrian tavern. In the preface to the second edition he states expressly that 'none of the characters in
Adolphe bears any relation to any person that I have ever known'. To identify
the characters in the novel with any single individual was to indulge in 'a
form of malignity which, aspiring to the merit of penetration, discovers
allusions which are in fact based upon absurd conjectures'. He claimed that
his novel had been written with a moral purpose; that it was a cautionary
tale, devised to warn young men that it is a mistake to suppose that 'one can
easily break attachments which one has formed lightheartedly'. In the third
edition of 1824 he adopted an even more specious device. He contended that
Adolphe was no more than a literary exercise, written 'with the sole idea of
convincing several friends, who were staying together in the country, that
it would be feasible to give some sort of interest to a story in which the
characters would be restricted to two, and in which the situation would
always remain the same'.

In private conversation, Constant was less obscurantist. We find the
following in Samuel Rogers's diary for 14 July 1816: 'Benjamin Constant to
breakfast. . . . *Adolphe*, many parts, he will confess, from his own experience.
He had often in his mind an Englishwoman,—still living with a Frenchman
in Paris—a Mrs. Lindsay.'

It is quite evident that the external circumstances, the factual apparatus,
of the story were based—and deliberately based—upon the affair between
Constant and Anna Lindsay. Ellénore was Polish by origin and Anna Irish:
to the French mind in the early nineteenth century these two oppressed
nationalities were analogous. The relations between Ellénore and the Comte
de P—— are identical with those which had for so long existed between
Anna Lindsay and Auguste de Lamoignon. The connection in each case had
lasted for some twelve years and had acquired a tone of domestic respectability; two children had been born; and Ellénore had remained faithful to
the Comte de P——, even as Anna Lindsay had remained faithful to Lamoignon, during the hard days of poverty and exile. Ellénore, like Anna, 'attached

the greatest importance to regularity of conduct, precisely because hers was not regular according to conventional notions'. Even the minor characters—Juste de Constant, Madame de Charrière and Julie Talma—can readily be identified. In fact, the only fictional character in the whole novel is the Baron de T—— who would seem to be an idealization of Benjamin's father, in his more reflective moods.

There can be little doubt that Constant adopted this factual framework in order that Madame de Stael could at least pretend that the whole story was about someone else. If any awful doubt assailed her, she could always point to the key-sentence which Constant had introduced into Chapter 2. 'Ellénore,' he had written, 'was not a woman of exceptional intelligence'. Obviously, such a phrase could not, by any stretch of malignity, be applied to Germaine de Stael. She adopted the only attitude which was open to her to adopt; she accepted the story at its face value, and she pressed it upon her friends as a remarkable account of an episode which had occurred when Benjamin was on leave. 'The first time I ever read it,' wrote Byron in sending the book to Lady Blessington, 'was at the desire of Madame de Stael, who was supposed by the good-natured world to be the heroine . . . which she was not, and was furious at the supposition.'

Madame de Stael possessed, it is true, unlimited powers of self-deception: with a sweep of the wing she could hurl any unwanted fledgeling from the cluttered bird's-nest of her mind. Yet it is difficult to believe that when she read and re-read the pages of *Adolphe* some suspicion did not occur to her that here, transparently disguised, was a tortured protest and an agonized appeal.

There were in the first place certain events, certain circumstances, certain psychological states, which could not possibly apply to the Benjamin–Anna relation and which certainly applied to the Benjamin–de Stael relation. There was the death of M. Necker; there was Madame de Stael's expulsion by Napoleon's police; there was the financial obligation into which Benjamin had entered both to M. Necker and to Germaine herself, and which envenomed his dependence. She must have realized that the affair between Benjamin and Anna had not lasted quite long enough to produce that sense of intimacy, that deep familiarity, which could justify the words 'We were living on the memories of our hearts'. She must have known that when he wrote of Caden he was thinking of Coppet. She was too intelligent a woman not to see that the 'destructive passion', the actual rage and violence, manifested by Ellénore were inconsistent with her comparatively placid character, or that the reckless indiscretion which she displayed was out of harmony with her prim and calculating nature. Some fibre of self-reproach must surely have been set vibrating in Madame de Stael's egoism when she read the phrase 'I recognized in Ellénore the denial of all the success to which I might have aspired'. She must have known that when he wrote of this inexorable

chain, this horrible incarceration, this 'fantastic despotism', he was not really
thinking of Anna Lindsay but of the ruthless tyranny which she herself had
exercised for all those years. And it must have been with anguish—or was
it only with seething rage?—that her eyes lighted upon the implied but
piteous appeal. 'What have I not sacrificed for Ellénore? For her sake I left
my home and family; for her sake I am living in this place, where my youth
slips away in solitude, without glory, without honour, and without delight.
. . . Yet it is time that I embarked on a career, began a life of action, acquired
some claim to the esteem of my fellow men and put my faculties to some
worthy use.' This supposition must have occurred to her; she may perhaps,
as Byron said, have thereby been rendered 'furious'; I hope she was also
rendered ashamed.

VII

It is useless to pretend that the character of Benjamin Constant as he portrays
it in the pages of *Adolphe* is an estimable character. He was an intelligent but
unattractive man. 'He does not manage even,' wrote Pauline de Beaumont to
Joubert, 'to like himself.' 'I possess excellent qualities,' confessed Constant to
his diary, 'such as pride, generosity and devotion, but I am not quite a real
person.' M. du Bos denies the latter accusation. 'Never,' he writes, 'has any
man been more authentic.' There was, as so many have recognized, a dualism
in Constant's character which enabled him to observe with lucidity and
detachment the vagaries and the results of his own actions. And perhaps his
vanity, his ruthlessness, and his appalling weakness are redeemed by the fact
that he possessed an unlimited fund of human pity; he suffered atrociously—
as Byron did not suffer—from the pain which he caused.

It may be interesting, in conclusion, to refer to the effect produced by
Adolphe upon successive generations. Constant's contemporaries and com-
patriots, versed as they were in the doctrine of 'sensibility', trained as they
had been in the self-expository novel by *René* and *Corinne*, and even Madame
de Krüdener's *Valérie*, found in it a highly romantic exposition of the conflict
between personal emotion and the social conventions. Yet even in 1816
Byron (who had some knowledge of similar situations) remarked that 'it
leaves an unpleasant impression'. Succeeding generations, fortified as they
were by moral earnestness, regarded *Adolphe* as ethically and artistically
abhorrent; as M. Fabre-Luce has noted, Sismondi, who had been swept off
his feet by *Adolphe* in 1816, found it detestable when he re-read it in 1837.
Between 1840 and 1870 *Adolphe* was repudiated and ignored. With the
revival of individualism in the early eighties, with the spread of the analytical
spirit, it was suddenly discovered that *Adolphe* possessed the unique virtue of
'sincerity'. 'People used to find fault with Adolphe,' wrote Anatole France,
'but now we pity him.' For Paul Bourget, Constant was a man who despised

hypocrisy and who became virtuous through self-revelation; Barrès saw in him the intellectual, toying with his own sensations; for him Constant became the 'Great Saint' of the *culte de moi*. And what of to-day? The present generation can read *Adolphe* with interest, partly because of its importance in the development of the French analytical novel, partly because of the excellence of its style and the subtlety of its interpretation of character, and partly because it describes what actually happens in life, rather than what ought ideally to occur. It responds to the realism of our present age, to our dislike of all synthetic formulas, and to the sad fatalism which leads so many young people to imagine that the fortunes of men are determined, not by their strength or virtues, but by their weakness and their faults.

hypocrisy and who became virtuous through self-revelation; Barrès says in him the intellectual, toying with his own sensations; for him Constant became the 'Great Saint' of the culte du moi. And what of to-day? The present generation can read Adolphe with interest, partly because of its importance in the development of the French analytical novel, partly because of the excellence of its style and the subtlety of its interpretation of character; and partly because it describes what actually happens in life, rather than what ought ideally to occur. It responds to the realism of our present age, to our dislike of all synthetic formulas, and to the sad fatalism which leads so many young people to imagine that the fortunes of men are determined, not by their strength or virtues, but by their weakness and their faults.

THE UNQUIET GRAVE

A WORD CYCLE

BY 'PALINURUS'

WITH AN INTRODUCTION BY
CYRIL CONNOLLY

(*Revised Edition*, 1951)

CONTENTS

		Page
	INTRODUCTION	265
Part I	ECCE GUBERNATOR	269
Part II	TE PALINURE PETENS	298
Part III	LA CLE DES CHANTS	321

'Palinurus, a skilful pilot of the ship of Æneas, fell into the sea in his sleep, was three days exposed to the tempests and waves of the sea and at last came safe to the seashore near Velia, where the cruel inhabitants of the place murdered him to obtain his clothes: his body was left unburied on the seashore.'

LEMPRIÈRE

Mox vero Lucanis pestilentia laborantibus respondit oraculum, Manes Palinuri esse placandos: ob quam rem non longe a Velia et lucum et cenotaphium ei dederunt.'[1]

SERVIUS, Commentary on
the Æneid, Bk. vi, l. 378

'A shelfy Coast,
Long infamous for Ships, and Sailors lost;
And white with Bones':

Dryden's Virgil

---

[1] Soon the Oracle gave this answer to the Lucanians, who were suffering from an epidemic: 'The shade of Palinurus must be appeased!' Whereupon they dedicated to him not far from Velia, a Cenotaph and a Sacred Grove.

THE UNQUIET GRAVE

INTRODUCTION

It is nearly ten years since *The Unquiet Grave* was begun, long enough for a book to cease to be contemporary, and to start settling down to a position in time. With this new and revised edition, an opportunity is presented to show how and why it came to be written and to take on its present form. This may answer some of the criticisms to which Palinurus has not had a chance to reply; such as that *The Unquiet Grave* is merely an anthology, a collection of extracts chosen with 'outremer' snobbery and masquerading as a book or that, if book it be, then it is both morbid and depressing.

The Unquiet Grave is inevitably a war-book. Although the author tried to extricate himself from the war and to escape from his time and place into the bright empyrean of European thought, he could not long remain above the clouds. He was an editor living in Bedford Square who kept a journal in three little notebooks provided by his wise printer between the autumn of 1942 and the autumn of 1943. As a man, he was suffering from a private grief,—a separation for which he felt to blame; as an editor, he was struggling against propaganda (the genial guidance of thought by the state which undermines the love of truth and beauty); as a Londoner, he was affected by the dirt and weariness, the gradual draining away under war conditions of light and colour from the former capital of the world and, lastly, as a European, he was acutely aware of being cut off from France. And so in keeping a journal for what a Russian peasant would have called his 'back thoughts', he was determined to quote as many passages as he could from the French to show the affinity between their thought and ours, and to prove how near and necessary to us were the minds and culture of those across the channel who then seemed quite cut off from us, perhaps for ever. To evoke a French beach at that time was to be reminded that beaches did not exist for mines and pill-boxes and barbed wire but for us to bathe from and that, one day, we would enjoy them again.

We must understand the author's obsession with pleasure at a time when nearly all pleasures were forbidden. Besides his love of France, Palinurus also wished to proclaim his faith in the unity and continuity of Western culture in its moment of crisis. He chose his quotations to illustrate how we have gone on thinking the same things since the days of the ancient Greeks, how the present can always be illuminated by the past. He looked for sanctions rather than originality.

Meanwhile the three notebooks filled up, while the personal sorrow came to a head and disappeared into a long false lull, like an illness. Working on the manuscript for another year, Palinurus began to see that there was a pattern to be brought out; in the diaries an art-form slumbered,—an initiation, a descent into hell, a purification and cure. The various themes could be given symphonic structure and be made to lead into and suggest each other until every paragraph became fitted into an inevitable position in the pilot's periplus (or intellectual voyage) from which it could not be moved. Stained by the juice of time, the second autumn was not quite like the first; the returns of grief or pleasure or religion acquired a richer orchestration, the writing had developed the writer. There was so much to cut or to improve; the exploration of the Palinurus myth (which is mentioned incidentally in the first article the author published) led on to others, until one seemed always to be pursuing some new clue. It seemed also the moment to collate once and for all the findings of depth-psychology with subjective feelings even if a loss to literature were the result. Finally the whole book had to be re-set. *The Unquiet Grave* by now consisted of thirty long galley-proofs scissored into little pieces like a string of clown's black sausages, covered with insertions and deletions and spread out on the floor to be arranged and re-arranged into a mosaic. The coils of print seemed to move with a life of their own. With incomparable devotion, Lys Lubbock and Sonia Brownell, the two secretaries at *Horizon*, had typed the whole manuscript out twice and at last it was published from here in December 1944 with four collotype plates in a limited edition of a thousand. Lys and Sonia sold copies over the counter, the demand grew and the expenses of the two printings were recovered. The identity of the author-publisher was never regarded as a top secret. By publishing the book without his name, however, more reality was given to the Palinurus myth and the anonymity acted as a coat of varnish to protect what might otherwise seem too personal a confession.

The plot of the book is contained in the title. *The Unquiet Grave* first suggests the tomb of Palinurus, pilot of Æneas; it is the cenotaph from which he haunts us. 'The ghost of Palinurus must be appeased'. He is the core of melancholy and guilt that works destruction on us from within. But the title is also that of an old border ballad in which a lover haunts the grave of his mistress and troubles her sleep.

> 'The wind doth blow to-night, my love,
> And a few small drops of rain,
> I never had but one true love,
> In cold grave she was lain.'

He remains by her grave for a year and a day (the period of the diary) until she dismisses him,

> 'The stalk is withered dry my love,
> So will our hearts decay,
> So make yourself content my love,
> Till God calls you away.

In the first part, Ecce Gubernator ('Behold the pilot'), we are presented with a self-portrait of Palinurus, with his views on literature, love and religion, his bitter doubting attitude. Something is badly wrong; he has lost touch with his sub-conscious self, the well is obstructed; he is reminded of a gull fouled with oil. The presiding genius of this section is Pascal whose terrible sayings penetrate the mask and cause Palinurus to reveal himself and so allude for the first time to his private sorrow, 'Revisit pale Chelsea's nook-shotten Cythera'. Cythera was the Island of love, Shakespeare's word 'nook-shotten' can mean full of indentations, the 'shelfy coast' of the title-page or else full of nooks and alcoves. There follows the first allusion to Paris, 'lost love, lost youth, lost Paris; remorse and folly. Aïe!' Pascal and Leopardi dominate because when they died they were the same age as Palinurus (thirty-nine). Will he survive them? After considering opium as a remedy the pilot continues his downward rush towards the notion of suicide with which the section ends. 'Te Palinure Petens' (looking for you, Palinurus) begins with the worst period of the nightmare journey. The names of four friends who took their own lives are evoked, one, who shoots herself at this very moment, was the companion of the 'dark face' from the Ile-Saint-Louis, most sacred of the holy places. Palinurus is soon driven to admit that all his trouble comes from Paris, and he mentions the Rue Delambre, the Quai d'Anjou (on the Island) and the Rue de Vaugirard as connected with his deepest feelings. Two new Genii preside over this section, Sainte-Beuve and Chamfort who bring respectively philo-sophic resignation and cynical courage to dispel the pessimism of Pascal and Leopardi or the suicidal raving of Nerval. On page 308 comes the first ray of hope. 'Streets of Paris, pray for me; beaches in the sun, pray for me; ghosts of the Lemurs, intercede for me; plane-tree and laurel-rose, shade me; summer rain on quais of Toulon, wash me away.' In the last section this prayer is literally answered. The title 'La clé des chants' (the key to the songs) also suggests Grandville's 'la clé des champs'. The nature-cure. The ferrets and lemurs who represent the strength and beauty of the healthy libido as well as the innocent paradise, the happy pagan honeymoon of the doomed relationship make their appearance in a kind of litany. Here the presiding genius is Flaubert who enriches the sensibility and stoical courage which he shares with the others, with the joy of creation.

Baudelaire, one-time dweller in the Ile-Saint-Louis, also haunts this section and their mutual friend Sainte-Beuve makes a farewell appearance.

The last movement opens with a series of alternating passages on the theme 'Streets of Paris', recalled by autumn mist in London, and 'Beaches in the sun' suggested by the late summer radiance. Mediterranean harbour scenes are followed by Atlantic sea-scapes, with allusions to Baudelaire at Honfleur, Proust at Houlgate and Flaubert at Trouville, where he met his 'fantôme' and dark inspirer, Madame Schlesinger. About the fortieth birthday of Palinurus the catharsis occurs; he re-lives the early stages of his love-affair: the walk to the apartment on the Ile-Saint-Louis, the Paris of the ex-patriates, and the year in the South of France, the villa *Les Lauriers Roses*. Describing this Paradise Lost brings Eden up from the dark world of the sub-conscious where it has been festering into the daylight of art. The ghosts are laid and the avenging 'Lemures' become the affectionate lemurs, until the book closes with a long and reasoned apology for the pursuit of happiness, an affirmation of the values of humanism. Placated and placating, the soul of Palinurus drifts away; his body is washed up on a favourite shore.

As a signal of distress from one human being to another *The Unquiet Grave* went unanswered, but the suffering was alleviated. As a demonstration of the power of words, however, of the obsessional impetus in an aesthetic form to fulfil its destiny, the work was an object-lesson. All grief, once made known to the mind, can be cured by the mind, the manuscript proclaimed; the human brain, once it is fully functioning, as in the making of a poem, is outside time and place and immune from sorrow. 'La pensée console de tout'. If *The Unquiet Grave*, therefore, should leave an impression of being morbid and gloomy then its intention has not been fulfilled.

CYRIL CONNOLLY

London
December 1950

PART I

ECCE GUBERNATOR

THE more books we read, the clearer it becomes that the true function of a writer is to produce a masterpiece and that no other task is of any consequence. Obvious though this should be, how few writers will admit it, or having drawn the conclusion, will be prepared to lay aside the piece of iridescent mediocrity on which they have embarked! Writers always hope that their next book is going to be their best, and will not acknowledge that they are prevented by their present way of life from ever creating anything different.

Every excursion into journalism, broadcasting, propaganda and writing for the films, however grandiose, will be doomed to disappointment. To put our best into these is another folly, since thereby we condemn good ideas as well as bad to oblivion. It is in the nature of such work not to last, and it should never be undertaken. Writers engrossed in any literary task which is not an assault on perfection are their own dupes and, unless these self-flatterers are content to dismiss such activity as their contribution to the war effort, they might as well be peeling potatoes.

'Les plus forts y ont péri. L'art est un luxe; il veut des mains blanches et calmes. On fait d'abord une petite concession, puis deux, puis vingt. On s'illusionne sur sa moralité pendant longtemps. Puis on s'en fout complètement et puis on devient imbécile.'—FLAUBERT

Poets arguing about wartime poetry: jackals snarling over a dried-up well.

How many books did Renoir write on how to paint?

To fashion a golden book, to weave a suit that will last some hundred years, it is necessary to feel, to think, and to write. These three activities must be co-ordinated. 'Bien écrire c'est à la fois bien sentir, bien penser et bien dire.'—BUFFON.

We cannot think if we have no time to read, nor feel if we are emotionally exhausted, nor out of cheap material create what is permanent. We cannot co-ordinate what is not there.

What is a masterpiece? Let me name a few. The *Odes* and *Epistles* of Horace, the *Eclogues* and *Georgics* of Virgil, the *Testament* of Villon, the Essays of

Montaigne, the Fables of La Fontaine, the Maxims of La Rochefoucauld and La Bruyère, the *Fleurs du Mal* and Intimate Journals of Baudelaire, the Poems of Pope and Leopardi, the *Illuminations* of Rimbaud, and Byron's *Don Juan*.

Such a catalogue reveals the maker. What is common in thought to these twelve writers? Love of life and nature; lack of belief in the idea of progress; interest in, mingled with contempt for humanity. All are what Palinurus has been called by a critic: 'Earthbound'! Yet all are more adult and less romantic than he. These masterpieces then (mostly high peaks of the secondary range), reflect either what he would like to be, or a self to which he is afraid of confessing. He would like to have written *Les Fleurs du Mal* or the *Saison en Enfer* without being Rimbaud or Baudelaire, that is without undergoing their mental suffering and without being diseased and poor.

In feeling, these works of art contain the maximum of emotion compatible with a classical sense of form.

Observe how they are written; many are short and compressed, fruit of reflective and contemplative natures, prose or poetry of great formal beauty and economy of phrase. There are no novels, plays or biographies included in the list and the poetry is of a kind which speculates about life. They have been chosen by one who most values the art which is distilled and crystallized out of a lucid, curious and passionate imagination. All these writers enjoy something in common, 'jusqu'au sombre plaisir d'un cœur mélancolique': a sense of perfection and a faith in human dignity, combined with a tragic apprehending of our mortal situation, and our nearness to the Abyss.

We can deduce then that the compiler should set himself to write after these models. However unfavourable the conditions for the birth of a classic, he can at least attempt to work at the same level of intention as the Sacred Twelve. Spiritualize the Earthbound, Palinurus, and don't aim too high!

What follow are the doubts and reflections of a year, a word-cycle in three or four rhythms; art, love, nature and religion: an experiment in self-dismantling, a search for the obstruction which is blocking the flow from the well and whereby the name of Palinurus is becoming an archetype of frustration.

As we grow older we discover that what seemed at the time an absorbing interest or preoccupation which we had taken up and thrown over, was in reality an appetite or passion which had swept over us and passed on, until at last we come to see that our life has no more continuity than a pool in the rocks filled by the tide with foam and flotsam and then emptied. Nothing remains of the self but the sediment which this flux deposits; ambergris valuable only to those who know its use.

'Dry again?' said the Crab to the Rock-Pool. 'So would you be,' replied the Rock-Pool, 'if you had to satisfy, twice a day, the insatiable sea.'

As we grow older, in fact, we discover that the lives of most human beings are worthless except in so far as they contribute to the enrichment and emancipation of the spirit. However attractive in our youth the animal graces may seem, if by our maturity they have not led us to emend one character in the corrupt text of existence, then our time has been wasted. No one over thirty-five is worth meeting who has not something to teach us,—something more than we could learn by ourselves, from a book.

LOVE AND ANXIETY

A lover's warning:

'The sixth age is ascribed to Jupiter, in which we begin to take account of our time, to judge of ourselves, and grow to the perfection of our under-standing; the last and seventh age to Saturn, wherein our days are sad and overcast and in which we find by dear and lamentable experience, and by the loss which can never be repaired, that of all our vain passions and affections past, the sorrow only abideth.'—SIR WALTER RALEIGH.

There is no pain equal to that which two lovers can inflict on one another. This should be made clear to all who contemplate such a union. The avoidance of this pain is the beginning of wisdom, for it is strong enough to contaminate the rest of our lives: and since it can be minimized by obeying a few simple rules, rules which approximate to Christian marriage, they provide, even to the unbeliever, its *de facto* justification. It is when we begin to hurt those whom we love that the guilt with which we are born becomes intolerable, and since all those whom we love intensely and continuously grow part of us and as we hate ourselves in them, so we torture ourselves and them together.

The object of Loving is a release from Love. We achieve this through a series of unfortunate love affairs or, without a death-rattle, through one that is happy.

Complete physical union between two people is the rarest sensation which life can provide—and yet not quite real, for it stops when the telephone rings. Such a passion can be maintained at full strength only by the admixture of more unhappiness (jealousy, rows, renunciation) or more and more artificiality (alcohol and other technical illusions). Who escapes this heaven may never have lived, who exists for it alone is soon extinguished.

We pay for vice by the knowledge that we are wicked: we pay for pleasure when we find out, too late, that we are disappearing.

'Pleasure seizes the whole man who addicts himself to it, and will not give him leisure for any good office in life which contradicts the gaiety of the present hour. You may indeed observe in people of pleasure a certain complacency and absence of all severity, which the habit of a loose and unconcerned life gives them; but tell the man of pleasure your secret wants, cares, or sorrows, and you will find that he has given up the delicacy of his passions to the craving of his appetites.'—STEELE.

Beneath a mask of selfish tranquillity nothing exists except bitterness and boredom. I am one of those whom suffering has made empty and frivolous: each night in my dreams I pull the scab off a wound; each day, vacuous and habit-ridden, I help it re-form.

When I contemplate the accumulation of guilt and remorse which, like a garbage-can, I carry through life, and which is fed not only by the lightest action but by the most harmless pleasure, I feel Man to be of all living things the most biologically incompetent and ill-organized. Why has he acquired a seventy-years' life-span only to poison it incurably by the mere being of himself? Why has he thrown Conscience, like a dead rat, to putrefy in the well?

It is no answer to say that we are meant to rid ourselves of the self: religions like Christianity and Buddhism are desperate stratagems of failure, the failure of men to be men. As escapes from the problem, as flights from guilt, they may be welcome, but they cannot turn out to be the revelation of our destiny. What should we think of dogs' monasteries, hermit cats, vegetarian tigers? Of birds who tore off their wings or bulls weeping with remorse? Surely it is in our nature to realize ourselves, yet there remains the deadly flaw by which we feel most guilty when we are most confidently human and are most to be pitied when most successful. Is this because Christianity is true? Or is it an ungrained effect of propaganda for the under-dog? When did the ego begin to stink? Those of us who were brought up as Christians and have lost our faith have retained the sense of sin without the saving belief in redemption. This poisons our thought and so paralyses us in action.

Communism is the new religion which denies original sin, though seldom do we meet a real Communist who seems either complete or happy. And yet Original Sin, what rubbish! The Expulsion from Eden is an act of vindictive womanish spite; the Fall of Man, as recounted in the Bible, comes nearer to the Fall of God.

When I consider what I believe, which I can do only by proceeding from what I do not, I seem in a minority of one,—and yet I know that there are thousands like me: Liberals without a belief in progress, Democrats who despise their fellow-men, Pagans who must live by Christian morals, Intellectuals who cannot find the intellect sufficient,—unsatisfied Materialists, we are as common as clay.

But there can be no going back to Christianity nor can I inhabit an edifice of truth which seems built upon a base of falsehood. The contradictions will out; hence the terrible record of the Church, which 'brings not peace, but a sword'—her persecutions, her cupidity, her hypocrisy, her reaction. These are inherent in her nature as a jealous, worldly, and dogmatic body; and because of these the Church, whenever strong enough to do so, has always belied her spiritual claims.

How privileged are Mahommedans! Small wonder there are more of them than of any other religion and that they are still making converts; for their creed is extroverted,—the more fanatical they become, the faster they relieve themselves by killing other people. They observe a dignified ritual, a congenial marriage code and appear to be without the sense of guilt.

In my religion all believers would stop work at sundown and have a drink together 'pour chasser la honte du jour.' This would be taken in remembrance of the first sunset when man must have thought the oncoming night would prove eternal, and in honour of the gift of wine to Noah as a relief from the abysmal boredom of the brave new world after the flood. Hence the institution of my 'Sundowner' with which all believers, whether acquainted or not, would render holy that moment of nostalgia and evening apprehension. *Brevis hic est fructus homullis*. In my religion there would be no exclusive doctrine; all would be love, poetry and doubt. Life would be sacred, because it is all we have and death, our common denominator, the fountain of consideration. The Cycle of the Seasons would be rhythmically celebrated together with the Seven Ages of Man, his Identity with all living things, his glorious Reason, and his sacred Instinctual Drives.

Ah, see how on lonely airfield and hill petrol-station the images of Freud and Frazer are wreathed in flowers! From Wabash to Humber the girls are launching their fast-perishing gardens of Adonis far out on to the stream; with sacred rumbas and boogie-woogies the Id is being honoured in all the Hangars, the Priestess intones long passages of the liturgy to which it is most partial; boastful genealogies and anecdotes of the Pornocrats, voodoo incantations, oceans of gibberish from Maldoror and Finnegans Wake! In a rapture of kisses the river-gods return, till Pan and Priapus in their red bowler-hats give way to Human Reason, Human Reason to Divine Love, 'Caelestis Venus', and Divine Love to the gyrations of the Planets through the bright selfless wastes of the Aether.

'The ideal, cheerful, sensuous, pagan life is not sick or sorry. No; yet its natural end is the sort of life which Pompeii and Herculaneum bring so vividly before us,—a life which by no means in itself suggests the thought of horror and misery, which even, in many ways, gratifies the senses and the understanding; but by the very intensity and unremittingness of its appeal to the senses and the understanding, by its stimulating a single side of us too absolutely, ends by fatiguing and revolting us; ends by leaving us with a sense of confinement, of oppression,—with a desire for an utter change, for clouds, storms, effusion and relief.'—MATTHEW ARNOLD

This argument is often used against Paganism. It is no more true to say that Pompeii and Herculaneum express what is finest in paganism, than that Blackpool and Juan-les-Pins represent the best in Christianity. A life based on reason will always require to be balanced by an occasional bout of violent and irrational emotion, for the instinctual drives must be satisfied. In the past this gratification was provided by the mystery religions, somewhat grossly by the cults of the Great Mother, more spiritually by the Eleusinian and Orphic mysteries. Where Apollo reigns, Dionysus will follow.

Ancestor, my old incarnation, O *Palinurus Vulgaris*, the Venetian red craw-fish, langouste, or rock-lobster, whether feeding on the spumy Mauretanian Banks, or undulating—southward to Teneriffe, northward to Scilly—in the systole and diastole of the wave: free me from guilt and fear, free me from guilt and fear, dapple-plated scavenger of the resounding sea!

My previous incarnations: a melon, a lobster, a lemur, a bottle of wine, Aristippus.

Periods when I lived: the Augustan age in Rome, in Paris and London from 1660 to 1740, and lastly from 1770 to 1850.

My friends in the first were Horace, Tibullus, Petronius and Virgil; in the second: Rochester, Congreve, La Fontaine, La Bruyère, La Rochefoucauld, Saint Evremond, Dryden, Halifax, Pope, Swift, Racine, Hume, Voltaire; while in the last avatar I frequented Walpole and Gibbon; Byron, Fox, Beckford, and Stendhal, Tennyson, Baudelaire, Nerval and Flaubert.— Afternoons at Holland House, dinners chez Magny.

There are some fruits which awaken in me feelings deeper than appetite. When I contemplate the musky golden orb of the sugar-melon or the green and brown seaweed markings of the tiger cantaloup, the scales of the pine-apple or the texture of figs and nectarines, the disposition of oranges and lemons on the tree or the feign-death coils of the old vine-serpent, I swell in unity with them, I ripen with the ripe sugar-cane, the banana in flower, I graft myself on certain trees,—the stone or umbrella-pine, the sun-loving Norfolk Island pine, the leaning bamboo, the squat carob, the rusty cork-oak and the plane. For the hundredth time I remark with wonder how the leaves and sprays of the plane-tree forge the pendulous signature of the vine! 'Evincet ulmos platanus coelebs.' The bachelor plane shall drive out the elms. . . .

My desire is for wisdom, not for the exercise of the will. 'The will is the strong blind man who carries on his shoulders the lame man who can see.'—SCHOPENHAUER.

For me success in life means survival. I believe that a ripe old age is nature's reward to those who have grasped her secret. I do not wish to die young or mad. The true pattern of existence can best be studied in a long life like Goethe's,—a life of reason interrupted at intervals by emotional outbursts, displacements, passions, follies. In youth the life of reason is not in itself sufficient; afterwards the life of emotion, except for short periods, becomes unbearable.

Sometimes at night I get a feeling of claustrophobia; of being smothered by my own personality, of choking through being in the world. During these moments the universe seems a prison wherein I lie fettered by the chains of my senses and blinded through being myself.

It is like being pinned underneath the hull of a capsized boat, yet being afraid to dive deeper and get clear. In those moments it seems that there must be a way out, and that through sloughing off the personality alone can it be taken.

We love but once, for once only are we perfectly equipped for loving: we may appear to ourselves to be as much in love at other times—so will a day in early September, though it be six hours shorter, seem as hot as one in June. And on how that first true love-affair will shape depends the pattern of our lives.

Two fears alternate in marriage, of loneliness and of bondage. The dread of loneliness being keener than the fear of bondage, we get married. For one person who fears being thus tied there are four who dread being set free. Yet the love of liberty is a noble passion and one to which most married people secretly aspire,—in moments when they are not neurotically dependent—but by then it is too late; the ox does not become a bull, nor the hen a falcon.

The fear of loneliness can be overcome, for it springs from weakness; human beings are intended to be free, and to be free is to be lonely, but the fear of bondage is the apprehension of a real danger, and so I find it all the more pathetic to watch young men and beautiful girls taking refuge in marriage from an imaginary danger, a sad loss to their friends and a sore trial to each other. First love is the one most worth having, yet the best marriage is often the second, for we should marry only when the desire for freedom be spent; not till then does a man know whether he is the kind who can settle down. The most tragic breakings-up are of those couples who have married young and who have enjoyed seven years of happiness, after which the banked fires of passion and independence explode—and without knowing why, for they still love each other, they set about accomplishing their common destruction.

When a love-affair is broken off, the heaviest blow is to the vanity of the one who is left. It is therefore reasonable to assume that, when a love-affair is beginning, the greatest source of satisfaction is also to the vanity. The first signs of a mutual attraction will induce even the inconsolable to live in the present.

Cracking tawny nuts, looking out at the tawny planes with their dappled festoons of yellow and green, reading the Tao Tê Ching by a log fire: such is the wisdom of October: autumn bliss; the equinoctial study of religions.

Jesus was a petulant man: his malediction on the barren fig tree was sheer spite, his attitude towards the Pharisees one of paranoiac wrath. He speaks of them as Hitler of the men who made the League of Nations. Those parables which all end 'There shall be wailing and gnashing of teeth',—what a tone for a Redeemer! I find such incidents as the violence used on the man without a wedding garment or the praise of usury in the parable of the talents to be understandable only as outbursts of arrogance and bad temper. Though an inspired genius as a mystic and an ethical reformer, Jesus is also completely a Jew; he does not wish to break away from the Jewish framework of the Old Testament, the Law and the Prophets, but to enrich their ethical content; consequently he imitates the intolerance of the Pharisees whom he condemns ('O ye generation of vipers') and maintains the avenging rôle of God the Father which he claims to have superseded.

Impression of Jesus Christ after re-reading the Gospels: He *thought* he was the son of God, he disliked his parents, was a prig, a high-spirited and serious young man (where was he, what was he doing, between the ages of twelve and twenty-nine?). He felt an especial hatred for the Pharisees, the family, his hometown and adultery, and he may have been illegitimate (Ben Pandere);[1]

---

[1] The Jewish tradition was that he was the son of a Roman Centurion, Pantheras, the Panther. Hence his aloofness to his 'father' and 'brethren', his ambivalent attitude to his mother and to adultery. (His definition of adultery is very sharp, and he sets 'Thou shalt not commit adultery' as the only commandment beside 'Thou shalt love thy neighbour as thyself'. The question about the woman taken in adultery may have been put to him as a trap by those who believed this

he had a macabre sense of humour; was overwhelmingly grateful to those who believed in him ('Thou art Peter'), and extremely close to his elder cousin John, but though moulding himself on him, he was less ascetic. He was fond of wine and very partial to grapes and figs. More civilized than his cousin, he was yet deeply affected by his end, which warned him of what would be his own if he persisted. The death of John and the revelation of Messiahship at Cæsarea Philippi completely changed him: impatient, ironical and short-tempered, he was a true faith-healer, inspired by his sublime belief in himself and tragically betrayed by it. I can't believe in his divinity, yet it is impossible not to admire his greatness, his majesty, his fatalistic intuition and that mixture of practical wisdom with sublime vision which alone can save our world. His faith carried him through to the end, then wavered. Was there a secret understanding with John the Baptist? John the Baptist, I feel, holds many clues. About the miracles I suspend judgment. But not about the sermon on the Mount. Those loving dazzling teasing-tender promises are like lifting of the human horror, the bursting of a great dam. How different he is from Buddha!

Buddha though a philosopher-king is too oriental. His courage in living to a great age, among ageing disciples, confers a pedagogic monotony on his teaching. Besides, we can never absorb his titles; they are ill-accommodated to the Western ear. The Chinese wisdom alone has a natural affinity for the West, the Chinese are always practical. And Tao—a religion without words, without a saviour, without a doubt a God or a future life, whose truth is in a hoof-mark filled with water—what more dare we ask?[1]

'Repose, tranquillity, stillness, inaction—these were the levels of the universe, the ultimate perfection of Tao.'—CHUANG TZU

Forty,—sombre anniversary to the hedonist,—in seekers after truth like Buddha, Mahomet, Mencius, St. Ignatius, the turning-point of their lives.

The secret of happiness (and therefore of success) is to be in harmony with existence, to be always calm, always lucid, always willing, 'to be joined to the universe without being more conscious of it than an idiot', to let each wave of life wash us a little farther up the shore.

story.) I have heard a friend say that the German scholar Von Domaszewski claimed to have found on our Roman Wall the gravestone of Pantheras which showed that his legion had been in Judaea about 4 B.C. The Christians maintained that 'Pantherou', son of the Panther, was a corruption of 'Parthenou', of the Virgin. There is a strange poem by Hardy on this theme.

[1] Taoism (pronounced Dowism) is a Monist reconciliation of the human being to the inhuman, inactive harmony of the universe. In return for such an adaption the Taoist resolves his conflict, and gains a sensation of power and tranquillity which he is loth to disturb. His quietism is akin to that of Zeno, Epicurus, Molinos and St. John of the Cross, but dangerously exposed to the corruption of *laisser-aller*.

But the secret of art? There have been so many Infernos and so few Paradises in European art that the Infernos would seem our true climate. Yet those who have survived Satanism, war or passion have cared only for Paradise. In that sense Religion is the sequel to art and the sequel to love, as *Paradise Regained* follows half-heartedly after *Paradise Lost*.

TWO MODERN TAOISTS

'I have never seen a man who had such creative quiet. It radiated from him as from the sun. His face was that of a man who knows about day and night, sky and sea and air. He did not speak about these things. He had no tongue to tell of them ...'

'I have often seen Klee's window from the street, with his pale oval face, like a large egg, and his open eyes pressed to the window pane.'—J. ADLER

'The only thing in all my experience I cling to is my coolness and leisurely exhilarated contemplation. If I could influence you to achieve that *je t'aurais rendu un peu de service. J'y tiens TELLEMENT—si tu savais comme j'y tiens.* Let this advice be my perpetual and most solemn legacy to you.'— W. SICKERT (to Nina Hamnett).

'The mind of the sage in repose becomes the mirror of the universe, the speculum of all creation.'—CHUANG TZU

Whether or not he produce anything this contemplation is the hall-mark of the artist. It is his gelatine, his queen-bee jelly, the compost round his roots: the violent are drawn to such a man by the violence of his serenity.

'Points upon which the Yellow Emperor doubted, how can Confucius know?'[1]

Palinurus says: 'It is better to be the lichen on a rock than the President's carnation. Only by avoiding the beginning of things can we escape their ending.' Thus every friendship closes in the quarrel which is a conflict of wills, and every love-affair must reach a point where it will attain marriage, and be changed, or decline it, and wither.

The friendships which last are those wherein each friend respects the other's dignity to the point of not wanting anything from him. Therefore a man with a will to power can have no friends. He is like a boy with a chopper.

[1] A proverb which the Taoists coined to discredit their bustling rival. The Yellow Emperor or Ancestor, revered by the Taoists, flourished *circa* 2700–2600 B.C. 'The close of his long reign was made glorious by the appearance of the Phœnix and the mysterious animal known as the Chi Lin, in token of his wise and humane administration.'—GILES: *Chinese Biographical Dictionary.*

He tries it on flowers, then on sticks, then on furniture, and at last he breaks it on a stone.

There cannot be a personal God without a pessimistic religion. A personal God is a disappointing God; and Job, Omar Khayyam, Euripides, Palladas, Voltaire and Professor Housman will denounce him. With Buddhism, Taoism, Quietism, and the God of Spinoza there can be no disappointment, because there is no Appointment.

Yet no one can achieve Serenity until the glare of passion is past the meridian. There is no certain way of preserving chastity against the will of the body. Lao-Tsu succeeded. But then he was eighty and a Librarian. So he inveighed against books and book-learning, and left but one, shorter than the shortest gospel—a Kaleidoscope of the Void.

Action is the true end of Western religion, contemplation of Eastern; therefore the West is in need of Buddhism (or Taoism or Yoga) and the East of Communism (or muscular Christianity)—and this is just what both are getting. Undergoing the attraction of opposites, we translate the Tao Tê Ching and the Bhagavad-Gita, they learn the Communist Manifesto.

The moment a writer puts his pen to paper he is of his time; the moment he becomes of his time he ceases to appeal to other periods and so will be forgotten. He who would write a book that would last for ever must learn to use invisible ink. Yet if an author is of his age, parallel situations will recur which he may return to haunt. He will obsess the minds of living writers, prevent them from sleeping, crowd them out like the *Horla* and snatch the bread from their mouths.

Our minds do not come of age until we discover that the great writers of the past whom we patronize, dead though they be, are none the less far more intelligent than ourselves—Proust, James, Voltaire, Donne, Lucretius—how we would have bored them!

Fallen leaves lying on the grass in the November sun bring more happiness than daffodils. Spring is a call to action, hence to disillusion, therefore is April called 'the cruellest month'. Autumn is the mind's true Spring; what is there we have, 'quidquid promiserat annus' and it is more than we expected.

WOMEN

There is no fury like an ex-wife searching for a new lover. When we see a woman chewing the cud meekly beside her second husband, it is hard to imagine how brutally, implacably and pettily she got rid of the others. There are two great moments in a woman's life: when first she finds herself to be deeply in love with her man and when she leaves him. Leaving him enables her to be both sadist and masochist, to be stony when he implores her to stay and to weep because she has decided to go. Women differ from men in that to break with the past and mangle their mate in the process fulfils a dark need. Thus a wife's woman-friends will derive an almost equal satisfaction from her impending departure. Together they prepare the brief against the husband which will strip him of his friends. They love to know the date, to fan the flames, and when the Monster is alone to rush round and inspect him. They will hear the clump of suit-cases a hundred streets away.

Beware of a woman with too many girl-friends, for they will always try to destroy the conjugal WE. One girl-friend is worse, unless afterwards we marry her. In America every woman has her set of girl-friends; some are cousins, the rest are gained at school. These form a permanent committee who sit on each other's affairs, who come out together, marry and divorce together, and who end as those groups of bustling, heartless well-informed club-women who govern society. Against them the Couple or Ehepaar is helpless and Man in their eyes but a biological interlude.

In the sex-war thoughtlessness is the weapon of the male, vindictiveness of the female. Both are reciprocally generated, but a woman's desire for revenge outlasts all other emotion.

> 'And their revenge is as the tiger's spring,
> Deadly, and quick, and crushing; yet as real
> Torture is theirs, what they inflict they feel.'

When every unkind word about women has been said, we have still to admit, with Byron, that they are nicer than men. They are more devoted, more unselfish and more emotionally sincere. When the long fuse of cruelty, deceit and revenge is set alight, it is male thoughtlessness which has fired it.

A woman who will not feign submission can never make a man happy and so never be happy herself. There has never been a happy suffragette. In a perfect union the man and woman are like a strung bow. Who is to say whether the string bend the bow, or the bow tighten the string? Yet male bow and female string are in harmony with each other and an arrow can be fitted. Unstrung, the bow hangs aimless, the cord flaps idly.

A man who has nothing to do with women is incomplete. A puritan is incomplete because he excludes that half of himself of which he is afraid and so the deeper he imprisons himself in his fastidiousness, the more difficulty he has in finding a woman who is brave enough to simulate the vulgarity by which he can be released.

'Sabba dukkha, sabba anatta, sabba anikka.'[1]

A stone lies in a river; a piece of wood is jammed against it; dead leaves, drifting logs, and branches caked with mud collect; weeds settle there, and soon birds have made a nest and are feeding their young among the blossoming water plants. Then the river rises and the earth is washed away. The birds depart, the flowers wither, the branches are dislodged and drift downward; no trace is left of the floating island but a stone submerged by the water;—such is our personality.

If (as Christians, Buddhists, Mystics, Yogis, Platonists, believe), our life is vanity, the world unreal, personality non-existent, the senses deceivers, their perceptions and even reason and imagination false; then how tragic that from the Flesh are such deductions always made! If our mission in life is to evolve spiritually, then why are we provided with bodies so refractory that in many thousands of years we have not been able to improve them? Not one lust of the flesh, not one single illusion, not even our male nipples have been bred out of us; and still our new-born babies roll about in paroxysms of sensual cupidity and egomaniac wrath.

Three faults, which are found together and which infect every activity: laziness, vanity, cowardice. If one is too lazy to think, too vain to do a thing badly, too cowardly to admit it, one will never attain wisdom. Yet it is only the thinking which begins when habit-thinking leaves off, which is ignited by the logic of the train of thought, that is worth pursuing. A comfortable person can seldom follow up an original idea any further than a London pigeon can fly.

Complacent mental laziness is our national disease.

To-day our literature is suffering from the decay of poetry and the decline of fiction, yet never have there been so many novelists and poets; this is because neither will overcome the difficulties of their medium. Irresponsible poets who simulate inspiration trample down the flower of a language as brutally as politician and journalist blunt and enfeeble with their slovenliness the common run of words. Many war poets don't try; they are like boys playing about on a billiard table who wonder what the cues and pockets are for. Nor is it easier for novelists, who can no longer develop character, situation or plot.

[1] Sorrow is everywhere
   In man is no abiding entity
   In things no abiding reality.'—BUDDHA ('a dirge that still resounds mournfully in ten thousand monasteries').

Flaubert, Henry James, Proust, Joyce and Virginia Woolf have finished off the novel. Now all will have to be re-invented as from the beginning.

Let us reflect whether there be any living writer whose silence we would consider a literary disaster: one who, with three centuries more of art and history to draw from, can sustain a comparison with, for example, Pascal.

Pascal's *Pensées* were written about 1660. Many of them are modern not merely in thought, but in expression and force; they would be of over-whelming importance if they were now published for the first time. Such a genius must invalidate the usual conception of human progress. Particularly modern are his rapidity, detachment and intellectual impatience.

Resemblance. Pascal: Leopardi: Baudelaire.

WISDOM OF PASCAL 1623–1662

'Tout le malheur des hommes vient d'une seule chose, qui est de ne savoir pas demeurer en repos, dans une chambre.'

'Notre nature est dans le mouvement; le repos entier est la mort.'

Ennui: 'Rien n'est si insupportable à l'homme que d'être dans un plein repos, sans passions, sans affaire, sans divertissement, sans application. Il sent alors son néant, son insuffisance, sa dépendance, son impuissance, son vide. Incon-tinent il sortira du fond de son âme l'ennui, la noirceur, la tristesse, le chagrin, le dépit, le désespoir.'

Misère: 'La seule chose qui nous console de nos misères est le divertissement, et cependant c'est la plus grande de nos misères, car c'est cela qui nous empêche principalement de songer à nous, et qui nous fait perdre insensible-ment.'

La Gloire: 'L'admiration gâte tout dès l'enfance: Oh! que cela est bien dit! Oh! qu'il a bien fait! Qu'il est sage, etc. . . .'

'Les enfants de Port-Royal, auxquels on ne donne point cet aiguillon d'envie et de gloire, tombent dans la nonchalance.'

Pascal and Leopardi (both died aged thirty-nine), depress and frighten one because they were ill, almost deformed, and therefore because their deformity renders suspect so much of their pessimism. They are the Grand Inquisitors who break down our alibis of health and happiness. Are they pessimistic because they are ill? Or does their illness act as a short cut to reality—which is intrinsically tragic? [1] Or did their deformities encourage the herd to treat them thoughtlessly, and so create in them a catastrophic impression of human nature?

In many of Pascal's reflections one detects not only the scientific accuracy, but the morbidity and peevishness, the *injustice* of Proust.

How was La Rochefoucauld's health?

Pascal's 'moi' is Freud's 'Id'. Thus Pascal writes, 'Le *moi* est haïssable . . . le *moi* a deux qualités: il est injuste en soi, en ce qu'il se fait centre du tout; il est incommode aux autres, en ce qu'il les veut asservir: car chaque *moi* est l'ennemi et voudrait être le tyran de tous les autres'.

This is Freud. But though babies are born *all* 'Id', we do not for that condemn the human race.

We may consider that we are born as 'Id' and that the object of life is to sublimate the 'Id',—the 'Id' is all greed, anger, fear, vanity and lust. Our task is to purge it, to shed it gradually as an insect sheds its larval form.

Life is a maze in which we take the wrong turning before we have learnt to walk.

Pascal says: 'Death should infallibly put them [the pleasure-lovers] very soon in the horrible necessity of being eternally unhappy . . .' We keep forgetting his belief in Hell, because we can accept so much else that he believes. Yet believing in Hell must distort every judgment on this life. However much a Christian may claim that the central doctrine of the Church is the Incarnation and nothing else, he is led on inevitably to exclusive salvation, to Heaven and Hell, to censorship and the persecution of heresy, till he finds himself among the brothel-owning Jesuits and cannon-blessing bishops of the Spanish war.

Pascal (or Hemingway, Sartre, or Malraux).

'Qu'on s'imagine un nombre d'hommes dans les chaînes, et tous condamnés à la mort, dont les uns étant chaque jour égorgés à la vue des autres, ceux qui restent voient leur propre condition dans celle de leurs semblables, et, se regardant les uns et les autres avec douleur et sans espérance, attendent à leur tour. C'est l'image de la condition des hommes.'

---

[1] 'For aught we know to the contrary, 103 or 104 degrees Fahrenheit might be a much more favourable temperature for truths to germinate and sprout in, than the more ordinary blood-heat of 97 or 98 degrees.'—WILLIAM JAMES.

December 12th: Revisit pale Chelsea's nook-shotten Cythera.

Christmas Eve: Dégouté de tout. Midwinter cafard.

> La Nochebuena se viene
> la Nochebuena se va
> y nosotros nos iremos
> y no volveremos más.[1]

No opinions, no ideas, no true knowledge of anything, no ideals, no inspiration; a fat slothful, querulous, greedy, impotent carcass; a stump, a decaying belly washed up on the shore. 'Manes Palinuri esse placandos!' Always tired, always bored, always hurt, always hating.

Sacred names: Rue de Chanaleilles. Summer night, limes in flower; old houses, with large gardens enclosed by high walls; silent heart of the leafy Faubourg: sensation of what is lost: lost love, lost youth, lost Paris,—remorse and folly. Aïe!

A love affair is a grafting operation. 'What has once been joined, never forgets.' There is a moment when the graft takes; up to then is possible without difficulty the separation which afterwards comes only through breaking off a great hunk of oneself, the ingrown fibre of hours, days, years.

New-year resolution: lose a stone, then all the rest will follow. Obesity is a mental state, a disease brought on by boredom and disappointment; greed, like the love of comfort, is a kind of fear. The one way to get thin is to re-establish a purpose in life.

Thus a good writer must be in training: if he is a stone too heavy, then that fourteen pounds represents for him so much extra indulgence, so much clogging laziness; in fact a coarsening of sensibility. There are but two ways to be a good writer: like Homer, Shakespeare or Goethe, to accept life completely, or like Pascal, Proust, Leopardi, Baudelaire, to refuse ever to lose sight of its horror.

When we reflect on life we perceive that only through solitary communion with nature can we gain an idea of its richness and meaning. We know that in such contemplation lies our true personality, and yet we live in an age when we are told exactly the opposite and asked to believe that the social and co-operative activity of humanity is the one way through which life can be developed. Am I an exception, a herd-outcast? There are also solitary bees, and it is not claimed that they are biologically inferior. A planet of

---

[1] Christmas eve comes, Christmas eve goes and we too shall pass and never more return. Old Spanish carol.

contemplators, each sunning himself before his doorstep like the mason-wasp; no one would help another, and no one would need help!

Marriage: 'An experience everyone should go through and then live his own life' *or* 'living one's own life—an experience everyone should go through and then marry'?

The tragedy of modern marriage is that married couples no longer enjoy the support of society, although marriage, difficult enough at any time, requires social sanction. Thus, in the past, married women censured the unmarried; the constant punished the inconstant; society outlawed the divorced and the dwellers-in-sin. Now it does the opposite. The State harries the human couple and takes both man and wife for its wars, society quests impatiently for the first suspicion of mistress or lover, and neurotic three-in-a-bedders, lonely and envious, make the young ménage their prey.

'In wise love each divines the high secret self of the other, and, refusing to believe in the mere daily self, creates a mirror where the lover or the beloved sees an image to copy in daily life.'—YEATS

Human life is understandable only as a state of transition, as part of an evolutionary process; we can take it to be a transition between the animal world and some other form which we assume to be spiritual. Anxiety and remorse are the results of failing to advance spiritually. For this reason they follow close on pleasure, which is not necessarily harmful, but which, since it does not bring advancement with it, outrages that part of us which is concerned with growth. Such ways of passing time as chess, bridge, drink and motoring accumulate guilt. But what constitutes the spiritual ideal? Is it the Nietzschean Superman or his opposite, the Buddha? The spiritual trend of human beings would seem to be towards pacifism, vegetarianism, contemplative mysticism, the elimination of violent emotion and even of self-reproduction. But is it impossible to improve animal-man so that instead of being made to renounce his animal nature, he refines it? Can anxiety and remorse be avoided in that way? Imagine a cow or a pig which rejected the body for a 'noble eight-fold way of self-enlightenment'. One would feel that the beast had made a false calculation. If our elaborate and dominating bodies are given us to be denied at every turn, if our nature is always wrong and wicked, how ineffectual we are—like fishes not meant to swim. Have the solitary, the chaste, the ascetic who have been with us now for six thousand years, ever been proved to be right? Has humanity shown any sign of evolving in their direction? As well as Diogenes and the Stylite, there is also Aristippus and Epicurus as alternative to the Beast.[1]

---

[1] The Middle Way.

'Aristippus parlant à des jeunes gens qui rougissaient de le voir entrer chez une courtisane: "Le vice est de n'en pas sortir, non pas d'y entrer." '—MONTAIGNE (*Essais*, III, v).

And now we have a new conception: the Group Man. Man's spiritual evolution, about which I prate, taking the form of a leap from the poorly organized wolf-pack and sheep-flock into an insect society, a community in which the individual is not merely a gregarious unit, but a cell in the body itself. Community and individual are, in fact, indistinguishable. How will you enjoy that, Palinurus?

A charm against the Group Man

The Magic Circle

Peace-aims: (1) yellow manor farm inside this magic circle;
(2) a helicopter to take me to
(3) an office in London or Paris and
(4) to my cabin at Almuñecar or Ramatuelle.

Daydream: A golden classical house, three stories high, with *œil de bœuf* attic windows looking out over water. A magnolia Delavayi growing up the wall, a terrace for winter, a great tree for summer and a lawn for games; a wooded hill behind and a river below, then a sheltered garden, indulgent to fig and nectarine, and at an angle of the wall, a belvedere, book-lined like that of Montaigne, wizard of the magic circle, with this motto from him: 'La liberté et l'oisiveté qui sont mes maîtresses qualités'.

As I waddle along in thick black overcoat and dark suit with a leather brief-case under my arm, I smile to think how this costume officially disguises the wild and storm-tossed figure of Palinurus; who knows that a poet is masquerading here as a whey-faced bureaucrat? And who should ever know?

The secret of happiness lies in the avoidance of Angst (anxiety, spleen, noia, fear, remorse, cafard). It is a mistake to consider happiness as a positive state. By removing Angst, the condition of all unhappiness, we are then prepared to receive such blessings as may come our way. We know very little about Angst, which may even proceed from the birth trauma, or be a primitive version of the sense of original sin, but we can try to find out what makes it worse.[1]

Angst can take the form of remorse about the past, guilt about the present, anxiety about the future. Often it is due to our acceptance through an imperfect knowledge of ourselves of conventional habits of living. Thus to keep someone waiting or to be kept waiting is a cause of Angst which is out of all proportion to the minor fault of unpunctuality. Therefore we may assume that we keep people waiting symbolically because we do not wish to see them and that our anxiety is due not to being late, but lest our hostility be detected. The chronically unpunctual should cancel all engagements for a definite period. Similarly, anxiety at being kept waiting is a form of jealousy, a fear that we are not liked.

Fatigue is one cause of Angst which may disappear if the tired person is able to lie down; bad air is another, or seeing a tube train move out as one reaches the platform.

To sit late in a restaurant (especially when one has to pay the bill) or over a long meal after a cocktail party is particularly conducive to Angst, which does not affect us after snacks taken in an armchair with a book. The business lunch is another meal from which we would prefer to be driven away in a coffin. Certainly a frequent cause of Angst is an awareness of the waste of our time and ability, such as may be witnessed among people kept waiting by a hairdresser.

Further considerations on cowardice, sloth and vanity; vices which do small harm to other people but which prevent one from doing any good and which poison and enfeeble all the virtues. Sloth rots the intelligence, cowardice destroys all power at the source, while vanity inhibits us from facing any fact which might teach us something; it dulls all other sensation.

---

[1] Freudians consider anxiety to arise from the repression of anger or love. Kretschmer thinks there is an obscure somatic relation between anxiety and sex. Theologians associate it with the Fall, Behaviourists with undigested food in the stomach, Kierkegaard with the vertigo that precedes sin. Buddha and many philosophers regarded it as concurrent with Desire. Thus Bacon quotes Epicurus: 'Use not that you may not wish, wish not that you may not fear.'

Home Truth from La Bruyère: 'L'expérience confirme que la mollesse ou l'indulgence pour soi et la dureté pour les autres n'est qu'un seul et même vice'.

I see the world as a kind of Black Hole of Calcutta, where we are all milling about in darkness and slime; now and then the mere being in the world is enough to cause violent claustrophobia (or is it a physical shortness of breath which creates the sensation of claustrophobia and therefore the image of the Black Hole?) And then I know that it is only by some desperate escape, like Pascal's, that I can breathe; but cowardice and sloth prevent me from escaping.

Who have escaped?
> 'Those who know don't speak;
> Those who speak don't know.'

On the American desert are horses which eat locoweed and some are driven mad by it; their vision is affected, they take enormous leaps to cross a tuft of grass or tumble blindly into rivers. The horses which have become thus addicted are shunned by the rest and will never rejoin the herd. So is it with human beings: those who are conscious of another world, the world of the spirit, acquire an outlook which distorts the values of ordinary life; they are consumed by the weed of non-attachment. Curiosity is their one excess and therefore they are recognized not by what they do but by what they refrain from doing, like those Araphants or disciples of Buddha who were pledged to the 'Nine Incapabilities'. Thus they do not take life, they do not compete, they do not boast, they do not join groups of more than six, they do not condemn others; they are 'abandoners of revels, mute, contemplative' who are depressed by gossip, gaiety and equals, who wait to be telephoned to, who neither speak in public nor keep up with their friends nor take revenge on their enemies. Self-knowledge has taught them to abandon hate and blame and envy in their lives until they look sadder than they are. They seldom make positive assertions because they see, outlined against any statement (as a painter sees a complementary colour), the image of its opposite. Most psychological questionnaires are designed to search out these moonlings and ensure their non-employment. They divine each other by a warm indifference for they know that they are not intended to foregather, but, like stumps of phosphorus in the world's wood, each to give forth his misleading radiance.

The two errors: We can either have a spiritual or a materialist view of life. If we believe in the spirit then we make an assumption which permits a whole chain down to a belief in fairies, witches, astrology, black magic, ghosts, and treasure-divining; the point at which we stop believing is dictated by our temperament or by our mood at a given moment. Thus the early Christians believed in the miracles of false prophets, and regarded the pagan gods as devils who had entrenched themselves in secure positions. They were more pagan than I am. On the other hand a completely materialist view leads to its own excesses, such as a belief in Behaviourism, in the economic basis of art, in the social foundation of ethics and the biological nature of psychology, in fact to the justification of expediency and therefore ultimately to the Ends-Means fallacy of which our civilization is perishing.

If we believe in a supernatural or superhuman intelligence creating the universe, then we end by stocking our library with the prophecies of Nostradamus and the calculations on the Great Pyramid. If instead we choose to travel viâ Montaigne and Voltaire, then we choke among the brimstone aridities of the Left Book Club.

It is a significant comment on the victory of science over magic that were someone to say 'if I put this pill in your beer it will explode,' we might believe them; but were they to cry 'if I pronounce this spell over your beer it will go flat', we should remain incredulous and Paracelsus, the Alchemists, Aleister Crowley and all the Magi have lived in vain. Yet when I read science I turn magical; when I study magic, scientific.

We cannot say that truth lies in the centre between the spiritual and material conception, since life must be one thing or the other. But can it be both? Supposing life were created by an act of God willing the accidental combination of chemicals to form a cell; created in fact by deliberate accident. Then, in the confidence of youth when the body seems self-sufficing, it would be natural to emphasize the materialist nature of phenomena, and in old age, when the body begins to betray us, to abandon our sensual outlook for a more spiritual cosmorama,—and both times we should be right.

Sunshine streams through the room, the dove grinds her love-song on the roof, out in the square the grass turns green, the earth has been cleared round the daffodils as a stage is cleared for the dancers, and under a rinsed blue sky the streets remember Canaletto; London spring is on its way.

Spring, season of massacre and offensives, of warm days and flowing blood, of flowers and bombs. Out with the hyacinths, on with the slaughter! Glorious weather for tanks and land-mines!

The creative moment of a writer comes with the autumn. The winter is the time for reading, revision, preparation of the soil; the spring for thawing back to life; the summer is for the open air, for satiating the body with health and action, but from October to Christmas for the release of mental energy, the hard crown of the year.

The duality of man is the heresy of Paul and Plato, heresy because the concept of soul and body is bound to imply a struggle between them which leads on the one hand to ascetism and puritanism, on the other to excess of materialism and sensuality. The greatness of Christ and Buddha sprang from the abandonment of asceticism for the Middle Path.

The spiritual life of man is the flowering of his bodily existence: there is a physical life which remains the perfect way of living for natural man, a life in close contact with nature, with the sun and the passage of the seasons, and one rich in opportunities for equinoctial migrations and home-comings. This life has now become artificial, out of reach of all but the rich or the obstinately free, yet until we can return to it we are unable to appreciate the potentialities of living. (Whales, branded in the Arctic, are found cruising in Antarctic waters; men, ringed in childhood, are observed, seventy years later, under the same stone.) We may compare a human being to a fruit-tree whose purpose is its fruit, fruit out of all proportion to the tree's value; yet, unless the tree receives its years of leisure, its requirements of sun and rain, the fruit will not ripen. So it is with the spiritual virtues of man, for we have divided man into two kinds; those whose soil is so poor or the climate of whose lives so unsuitable that they can never bear, or those who are forced and cramped under glass, whose lives are so constricted by responsibility that they become all fruit; hasty, artificial and without flavour.

We progress through an intensifying of the power generated by the physical satisfaction of natural man, whose two worst enemies are apathy and delirium; the apathy which spreads outward from the mechanical life, the delirium which results from the violent methods we use to escape.

Happiness lies in the fulfilment of the spirit through the body. Thus humanity has already evolved from an animal life to one more civilized. There can be no complete return to nature, to nudism or desert-islandry: city life is the subtlest ingredient in the human climate. But we have gone wrong over the size of our cities and over the kind of life we lead in them; in the past the clods were the peasants, now the brute mass of ignorance is urban. The village idiot walks in Leicester Square. To live according to nature we should pass a considerable time in cities for they are the glory of human nature, but they should never contain more than two hundred thousand inhabitants; it is our artificial enslavement to the large city, too sprawling to leave, too enormous for human dignity, which is responsible for half our sickness and misery. Slums may well be breeding-grounds of crime, but middle-class sudurbs are incubators of apathy and delirium. No city should be too large for a man to walk out of in a morning.[1]

---

[1] 'We are not yet ripe for growing up in the streets . . . has any good ever come out of the foul-clustering town-proletariat, beloved of humanitarians? Nothing—never; they are only

Surrealism is a typical city-delirium movement, a violent explosion of urban claustrophobia; one cannot imagine Surrealists except in vast cities, 'paysans de Paris' or New York. The nihilism of Céline and Miller is another by-product, and so are those mass-movers, Marx with his carbuncles, Hitler with his Beer-Hall. The English masses are lovable: they are kind, decent, tolerant, practical and not stupid. The tragedy is that there are too many of them, and that they are aimless, having outgrown the servile functions for which they were encouraged to multiply. One day these huge crowds will have to seize power because there will be nothing else for them to do, and yet they neither demand power nor are ready to make use of it; they will learn only to be bored in a new way. Sooner or later the population of England will turn Communist, and then take over. Some form of State Socialism is the only effective religion for the working class; its coming is therefore as inevitable as was that of Christianity. The Liberal Die-hard then grows to occupy historically the same position as the 'good Pagan': he is doomed to extinction.

While we re-live the horrors of the Dark Ages, of absolute States and ideological wars, the old platitudes of liberalism loom up in all their glory, familiar streets as we reel home furious in the dawn.

Wisdom of de Quincey
de Quincey: decadent English essayist who, at the age of seventy-five, was carried off by half a century of opium-eating.

'Marriage had corrupted itself through the facility of divorce and through the consequences of that facility (viz. levity in choosing and fickleness in adhering to the choice) into so exquisite a traffic of selfishness that it could not yield so much as a phantom model of sanctity.'

'By the law I came to know sin.'

On the first time he took opium in 1804: 'It was Sunday afternoon, wet and cheerless; and a duller spectacle this earth of ours has not to show than a rainy Sunday in London.'

The mystery of drugs: How did savages all over the world, in every climate, discover in frozen tundras or remote jungles the one plant, indistinguishable from so many others of the same species, which could, by a most elaborate process, bring them fantasies, intoxication, and freedom from care? How unless by help from the plants themselves? Opium-smokers in the East become surrounded by cats, dogs, birds and even spiders, who are attracted

waiting for a leader, some "inspired idiot" to rend to pieces our poor civilization.'—NORMAN DOUGLAS: *Siren Land*, 1911.

by the smell. The craving for the drug proceeds from the brain-cells which revolt and overrule the will. The Siberian tribes who eat Agaric say, 'The Agaric orders me to do this or that'—the Hashish chewers experience a like sensation. Horses and cattle which become 'indigo eaters' continue to gorge till they drop dead. Though one of the rarest and most obscure drugs, Peotl gave its name to a range of uninhabited mountains where it is found.

The Greeks and Romans looked on alcohol and opium as lovely twin reconcilers to living and dying presented to man by Dionysus and Morpheus, —God-given because of their extraordinary sympathy to us and because of the mystery attending their discovery. If man be part of nature, then his parasites may well understand him better than he knows.

Since there are flowers whose fertilization is impossible except by means of an insect, flowers which eat insects and therefore understand them, since so low and unconscious an order has these correspondences with the one above, may there not be animals and birds who make use of man and study his habits and if they do, why not insects and vegetables? What grape, to keep its place in the sun, taught our ancestors to make wine?

Everything is a dangerous drug to me except reality, which is unendurable. Happiness is in the imagination. What we perform is always inferior to what we imagine; yet day-dreaming brings guilt; there is no happiness except through freedom from Angst and only creative work, communion with nature and helping others are Anxiety-free.

Fraternity is the State's bribe to the individual; it is the one virtue which can bring courage to members of a materialist society. All State propaganda exalts comradeship for it is this gregarious herd-sense and herd-smell which keep people from thinking and so reconcile them to the destruction of their private lives. A problem for government writers or for the war artists in their war cemeteries: how to convert Fraternity into an æsthetic emotion?

Subversive thought for the year: 'Every man is to be respected as an absolute end in himself; and it is a crime against the dignity that belongs to him to use him as a mere means to some external purpose.'—KANT.

'If I had to choose between betraying my country and betraying my friend, I hope I should have the guts to betray my country.' This statement by Mr. E. M. Forster reminds us how far we have wandered from the ancient conception of friendship, of treating a kindred soul as an end not a means. 'The Chinese poet recommends himself as a friend, the Western poet as a lover,' writes Arthur Waley; but the Western prose-writer also used to recommend himself as a friend; the seventeenth and eighteenth centuries elaborated friendship and all but made it their religion. In the circle of Johnson, of Walpole and Madame du Deffand or of the Encyclopædists nobody could live without his friend. They loved them and even a misanthropic philosopher like La Bruyère could grow sentimental over the theme. Only the invalid Pascal demolished friendship on the ground that if we could read each other's thoughts it would disappear.

Now the industrialization of the world, the totalitarian State, and the egotism of materialism have made an end to friendship; the first through speeding up the tempo of human communication to the point where no one is indispensable, the second by making such demands on the individual that comradeship can be practised between workers and colleagues only for the period of their co-operation and the last by emphasizing whatever is fundamentally selfish and nasty in people, so that we are unkind about our friends and resentful of their intimacy because of something which is rotting in ourselves. We have developed sympathy at the expense of loyalty.

How many people drop in on us? That is a criterion of friendship. Or may tell us our faults? To how many do we give unexpected presents? With whom can we remain silent? The egocentric personality requires, alas, a changing audience, not a constant scrutiny. Romantic lovers are disloyal and, by making fun of old friends, they hit upon a congenial way of entertaining each other.

Voltaire on Friendship: 'C'est un contrat tacite entre deux personnes sensibles et vertueuses. Je dis *sensibles* car un moine, un solitaire peut n'être point méchant et vivre sans connaître l'amitié. Je dis *vertueuses*, car les méchants n'ont que des complices, les voluptueux ont des compagnons de débauche, les intéressés ont des associés, les politiques assemblent des fâcheux, le commun des hommes oisifs a des liaisons, les princes ont des courtisans: les hommes vertueux ont seuls des amis.' When we see someone living alone, like a beech-tree in a clearing, with no other signs of life around him yet proclaiming his freedom, displaying his possessions and maintaining his devotion to his friends, we can be sure that such a person is an ogre and that human bone-meal lies buried under his roots.

MASTERPLAY

Three requisites for a work of art: validity of the myth, vigour of belief, intensity of vocation. Examples of valid myths: The Gods of Olympus in Ancient Greece; the City of Rome and afterwards the Roman Empire; Christianity; the discovery of Man in the Renaissance with its consequence, the Age of Reason; the myths of Romanticism and of Material Progress (how powerful is the myth of bourgeois life in the work of the Impressionist painters!) The belief in a myth whose validity is diminishing will not produce such great art as the belief in one which is valid, and none are valid to-day.

Yet no myth is ever quite worthless as long as there remains one artist to honour it with his faith.

O for the past, when a masterpiece was enough to maintain a reputation for life! All Catullus, Tibullus and Propertius fit into the same volume; Horace and Virgil require but one tome, so do La Fontaine and La Bruyère. One book for each lifetime and the rest is fame, ease and freedom from Angst. Nature was so indulgent; if we could but write one good book every twelve years we would have done as well as Flaubert. Voltaire wrote *Candide* when he was sixty-five, Peacock wrote *Gryll Grange* at seventy-five, at eighty Joinville began his *Life of St. Louis*. Waste is a law of art as it is of nature. There is always time.

Every good writer must discover the yawning crevasse which separates Man's finite destiny from his infinite potentialities. It is afterwards that he will reveal his artistic courage and so register the protest which is a final plea for order, his *Gulliver's Travels*, his *Maxims*, his *Songs of Experience*, his *Saison en Enfer*, his *Fleurs du Mal*. The rest either pretend that they have seen nothing, and that all is well, or else howl with self-pity. Optimism and self-pity are the positive and negative poles of contemporary cowardice.

What makes the great writers of the past vivid to us is the extent of their misery; the despair of Pascal, the bitterness of La Rochefoucauld, the ennui of Flaubert, the 'noia' of Leopardi, the 'spleen' of Baudelaire,—none but the truths which have been extracted under mental torture appeal to us. We live in so desperate an age that any happiness which we possess must be hidden like a deformity, for we know that, though all our nature revolt, we can create only through what we suffer.

'We are all conceived in close prison . . . and then all our life is but a going out to the place of execution, to death. Nor was there any man seen to sleep in the cart between Newgate and Tyburn—between prison and the place of execution, does any man sleep? But we sleep all the way; from the womb to the grave we are never thoroughly awake.'—DONNE

A modern Rune: 'Pooey on the war!' No one can pronounce these four words and not feel a tremor of earth-shaking dimension. And not until the two thousand and fifty million belligerents can thunder them in unison, will the war be over.

A Rune for the very bored: When very bored recite: 'It was during the next twenty minutes that there occurred one of those tiny incidents which revolutionize the whole course of our life and alter the face of history. Truly we are the playthings of enormous fates.'

The ten-year torture of two faces. 'The tyranny of the human face.' When we see a friend in the depth of despair because they have been left by some-one whom we know to be insignificant, we must remember that there is a way of leaving and yet of not leaving; of hinting that one loves and is willing to return, yet never coming back and so preserving a relationship in a linger-ing decay. This technique can be learnt like a hold in jiu-jitsu. The person who has been abandoned is always psychologically groggy; the ego is wounded in its most tender part and is forced back on the separation and rejection phobias of infancy. Someone who knows how to prolong this state and to reproduce it at will can be quite insignificant,—so is the sand-wasp which stings a grub in the nerve-centre where it will be paralysed, yet remain alive.

Axiom: There is no happiness to be obtained by the destruction of another's. To take wife away from husband or husband from wife, is a kind of murder; guilt turns lovers into bad accomplices and the wrecking of a home destroys the wreckers. As we leave others, so shall we be left.

There is immunity in reading, immunity in formal society, in office routine, in the company of old friends and in the giving of officious help to strangers, but there is no sanctuary in one bed from the memory of another. The past with its anguish will break through every defence-line of custom and habit; we must sleep and therefore we must dream.

And in our dreams, as in the vacant afternoons of London week-ends, there enter the excluded, the disinherited, the heartbroken, the heart-breakers, the saboteurs and wrecking crews of our daylight selves. Θύραζε κῆρες.[1] Bone-crunching hyenas!

The harbour of Cassis on a bright winter morning; a gull is floating a few yards from the quay, unable to rise because its wings are fouled with oil. The fisher-children pelt it with stones. I drive them off; laughing they run across to the farther side and begin again, the stones falling around the dying bird as it bobs on the water like a painted decoy.

> 'While under its storm-beaten breast
> Cried out the hollows of the sea.'

Causes of Angst: Angst is inherent in the uncoiling of the ego, the tapeworm, the *ver solitaire*. It dwells in the *Lacrimæ Rerum*, in the contrasting of the Past with the present. It lurks in old loves and old letters or in our despair at the complexity of modern life.

Effect: Misery, disgust, tears, guilt.

Temporary cures: (1) Lunch with a new friend, gossip, literary talk, i.e.

[1] 'Spectres avaunt!' Ancient Greek spell.

appeals to vanity; (2) Art (Renoir landscapes), the true escape into *Timelessness*; (3) The office personality (Alibi Ike); (4) Old friends (relationships which date from before the Fall.)

Angoisse des Gares: A particularly violent form of Angst. Bad when we meet someone at the station, but worse when we are seeing them off; not present when we are departing ourselves, but unbearable when arriving in London, if only from a day in Brighton. Since all Angst is identical, we may learn something from these station-fears: Arrival-Angst is closely connected with guilt, with the dread of something terrible having happened during our absence. Death of parents. Entry of bailiffs. Flight of loved one. Sensation worse at arriving in the evening than in the morning, and much worse at Victoria and Waterloo than at Paddington. This may have been due in my case to my way of going abroad every vacation and therefore returning to London with guilt-feelings about having spent my money or not written to my parents, and to endless worry over work and debt.[1] Going to London as a schoolboy was a treat, as an undergraduate an ordeal, a surrender to justice. Later on the trips abroad grew longer, and returns were painful because of neglected household worries, and through a particularly strong guilt-feeling about not being at work, out-distanced by successful stay-at-home friends. But this is not all, for much of our anxiety is caused by horror of London itself; of the hideous entrails seen from the southern approaches, the high cost of living, the slums where we may die, embodiment of ugly and unnatural urban existence. When living in France, I began to have a similar feeling about Paris, though it has none of the same associations. I therefore deduce, that though it is wrong for us to live and work in great cities, to live away from them *without working* is worse. Angst begins at Reading, Woking or Croydon, or even in Paris, when we see the first grisly English faces homeward bound at the Gare du Nord.

If, instead of Time's notorious and incompetent remedy, there was an operation by which we could be cured of loving, how many of us would not rush to have it!

To be kept for six months in a refrigerator or to hibernate in deep narcotic sleep, to be given new drugs, new glands, a new heart, and then to wake up with the memory swept clear of farewells and accusations, never more to be haunted by the grief-stricken eyes of our assassinated murderers!

But Angst descends; I wake up in anxiety; like a fog it overlays all my action, and my days are muffled with anguish. Somewhere in the mind are crossed the wires of fear and lust and all day long nature's burglar-alarm shrills out

---

[1] But why was I extravagant, why couldn' I write to them?—A deeper level of anxiety becomes apparent.

in confusion. I dread the bell, the post, the telephone, the sight of an acquaintance. Anguish, anxiety, remorse and guilt: TOUT EST DÉGOÛT ET MISÈRE.
When even despair ceases to serve any creative purpose, then surely we are
justified in suicide. For what better ground for self-destruction can there be
than to go on making the same series of false moves which invariably lead
to the same disaster, and to repeat a pattern without knowing what it is or
wherein lies the flaw? And yet to perceive that in ourselves there revolves a
cycle of activity which is certain to end in paralysis of the will, desertion,
panic and despair—always to go on loving those who have ceased to love us,
those who have quite lost all resemblance to the beings whom once we loved!
Suicide is catching: what if the agony which self-murderers go through while
being driven to take their own lives, the conviction that all is lost, be infectious also? And if you have contracted it, Palinurus, if it has sought you
out?

TE PALINURE PETENS, TIBI SOMNIA TRISTIA PORTANS INSONTI?[1]

Madame du Deffand to Horace Walpole:

'Ennui. C'est une maladie de l'âme dont nous afflige la nature en nous
donnant l'existence; c'est le ver solitaire qui absorbe tout . . . "Ah! je le répète
sans cesse, il n'y a qu'un malheur, celui d'être né."

Comment est-il possible qu'on craigne la fin d'une vie aussi triste . . .
Divertissez-vous, mon ami, le plus que vous pourrez; ne vous affligez point
de mon état, nous étions presque perdus l'un pour l'autre; nous ne nous
devions jamais revoir; vous me regretterez, parce qu'on est bien aise de se
savoir aimé.'

[1] Looking for you, Palinurus, bringing you sad visions which you have not deserved.

PART II

TE PALINURE PETENS

'YOU are very wise, very understanding and really very kindly. I wonder that you remain the critic. You can go beyond. You must have great fears and doubts, and you have overlaid another personality on the original one, a protective masked being which deals with what you imagine to be a harsh, cruel world.'—HENRY MILLER to Palinurus.

'Had I followed my pleasure and chosen what I plainly have a decided talent for: police spy, I should have been much happier than I afterwards became.'—KIERKEGAARD—*Journals*, 1843.

'Ne cherchez plus mon cœur; les bêtes l'ont mangé.'

APRIL MESSAGE

Pack up, Your situation is untenable, your loss irretrievable *y no hay remedio.* CHANGE YOUR BEDDING![1]

ORATE PRO NOBIS

Philip Heseltine, Harry Crosby, René Crevel, Mara Andrews.[2]

Spring in the Square, when the nile-green tendrils of the plane uncurl against the blue and the Tree of Heaven prepares a book-plate entry; a soldier and his girl come in to kiss because the gate is open, it locks as they close it behind them and, hours later, they still wander around and round the empty garden like insects trying to escape from a pitcher plant. Lying on the fresh grass in the sun I read about opium as one would inquire about a new religion. Confessions of an opium-reader! Opium made de Quincey great and

---

[1] Lamas do not die, but on reincarnation, are said to 'change their bedding'. 'And there is no remedy.' From a drawing of a dead man by Goya.

[2] Philip Heseltine (Peter Warlock) took his life by gas 17 December 1930, aged thirty-six. The coroner read out part of a letter: 'I would very much rather visit you at some other time than Christmas. It is a season of the year which I dislike more and more as time goes on.'

Harry Crosby (according to Mr. Cowley in *Exile's Return*) planned his 'felo de se' 31 October 1942, at the end of his fortieth year, by flying his plane till it crashed, 'a sun death into sun'. Unable to wait, he shot himself in New York in 1929.

René Crevel, surrealist poet, shot himself in Paris in 1935, aged thirty-four. He left a note: 'Je suis dégouté de tout.'

Mara Andrews, once of the Ile Saint-Louis, committed suicide in New York while this was being written, aged thirty-two.

Cocteau serious. Would it prove the remedy, the 'Heart-balm'? To take a drug which exploded all the minefields of memory! And afterwards to come out not knowing who we are, not even being able to read and then to learn, and to discover some writers to whom we were strangely attracted,—as if we had known them in another life! And then as a fresh start to develop an Adult Personality, to attest that the one way to be happy is to make other people happy; that virtue is social. 'Happiness lies in the approval of our fellow-men, unhappiness in their disapproval, to earn one is virtue, the other vice.' That is what I should teach, and if sometimes it sounded rather dull, that could only mean I was a little constipated.

Civilization is an active deposit which is formed by the combustion of the Present with the Past. Neither in countries without a Present nor in those without a Past is it to be encountered. Proust in Venice, Matisse's birdcages overlooking the flower market at Nice, Gide on the seventeenth-century quais of Toulon, Lorca in Granada, Picasso by Saint-Germain-des-Prés: there lies civilization and for me it can exist only under those liberal regimes in which the Present is alive and therefore capable of assimilating the Past. Civilization is maintained by a very few people in a small number of places and we need only some bombs and a few prisons to blot it out altogether.

The civilized are those who get more out of life than the uncivilized, and for this we are not likely to be forgiven. One by one, the Golden Apples of the West are shaken from the tree.

The quince, coing, membrillo, marmellata, pyrus cydonia or portugalensis; emblem of love and happiness to the Ancients, was the golden fruit of the Hesperides and the love-apple which Greek maidens used to give their boys. It was also a Chinese symbol of long life and passion. I behold in it an emblem of the civilization of Europe with its hard flesh, bright colour and unearthly savour. The simple flower, the astringent fruit which ripens only in the south, the mysterious pips full of emulgent oil—all are significant. There are artists like quinces, 'of quaint and loose habit', whose fragrance does not cloy.

Mysteries of nature: The properties of the quince, of the truffle (a truffle placed near a fresh egg will impregnate it with its odour), of the opium poppy and the peotl bud; the stormy life of wine; the cry of the cicada and the death's-head moth, the flight of the stag-beetle, the philoparasitism of the ant, the gaze of the mantis[1]; lemons and the scent of lemon-verbena and lemon-scented magnolia, the colour of gentians, the texture of water-lilies, the vegetable view of man. The smell of cigar-smoke, of coffee being roasted

[1] 'Elle épouse, elle tue et elle n'est que plus belle.'—BINET (on the Mantis).

or of wine-barrels and of herbs in cooking is irresistible and demonstrates how intense and mutual is our collaboration.

Never would it occur to a child that a sheep, a pig, a cow or a chicken was good to eat, while, like Milton's *Adam*, he would eagerly make a meal off fruit, nuts, thyme, mint, peas and broad beans which penetrate further and stimulate not only the appetite but other vague and deep nostalgias. We are closer to the Vegetable Kingdom than we know; is it not for man alone that mint, thyme, sage, and rosemary exhale 'crush me and eat me!'— for us that opium poppy, coffee-berry, tea-plant and vine perfect themselves? Their aim is to be absorbed by us, even if it can only be achieved by attaching themselves to roast mutton.

'Les hommes et les insectes font partie de la même nature.'—CAILLOIS

Why do ants alone have parasites whose intoxicating moistures they drink and for whom they will sacrifice even their young? Because as they are the most highly socialized of insects, so their lives are the most intolerable.

Protective colouring in insects represents not only their defence against the creatures who prey on them but their homage to the vegetables by whom they are guarded. The insect resembles a leaf at the wish of a tree. The vast vegetable world governs the tiny animal world by letting itself be assimilated. Why do sole and turbot borrow the colours and even the contours of the sea-bottom? Out of self-protection? No, out of self-disgust.

The civilization of the nineteenth century was founded on Coal, Electricity and Central Heating. These brought to the northern countries continuous industrial energy and a corresponding increase of population. With air-conditioning the civilization of the twentieth century can move south. This invention, by restoring their dynamic to the Mediterranean countries, may yet save Europe. We may even abolish the desert and the siesta as far south as Khartoum and Dakar, we may live to see the Mediterranean become as industrialized as the Great Lakes with Barcelona as Chicago and Athens as Detroit. England will appeal to these new and ventilated Carthaginians as a summer resort: a grey little fey little island.

The goal of every culture is to decay through over-civilization; the factors of decadence,—luxury, scepticism, weariness and superstition,—are constant. The civilization of one epoch becomes the manure of the next. Everything over-ripens in the same way. The disasters of the world are due to its inhabitants not being able to grow old simultaneously. There is always a raw and intolerant nation eager to destroy the tolerant and mellow. With the

Brave New World we may hope to see whole populations on an equal footing, until all the nations wither in unison. We may say with Fontenelle 'Il faut du temps pour ruiner un monde, mais enfin, il ne faut que du temps.'

There was once a man (reputed to be the wisest in the world) who, although living to an untold age, confined his teaching to the one command: 'Endure!' At length a rival arose who challenged him to a debate which took place before a large assembly. 'You say "Endure",' cried his competitor, 'but I don't want to endure. I wish to love and to be loved, to conquer and create, I wish to know what is right, then do it and be happy.' There was no reply from his opponent, and, on looking more closely at the old creature, his adversary found him to consist of an odd-shaped rock on which had taken root a battered thorn that represented, by an optical illusion, the impression of hair and a beard. Triumphantly he pointed out the mistake to the authorities but they were not intimidated. 'Man or rock,' they answered, 'does it really matter?' And at that moment the wind, reverberating through the sage's moss-grown orifice, repeated with a hollow sound: 'Endure!'

A love-affair can prosper only when both parties enter free. If one lover is free and the other not, then in the process of destroying their rival or the memory of their rival, the one who is free will destroy the illusion of their own virtue. A couple jointly possess so much of their two selves that to hurt one is to wound the other, and, even if they are wounded willingly, resentment is set up. When we want a house we go to the house-agent and inquire what is on the market; we do not pick on the first one we like and force the tenant to leave. The romantic prestige of adultery comes from exaggerating the importance of chastity in the unmarried. If fornication were no sin, then adultery would be condemned, for it is a token form of murder. We do not murder the rival husband or wife but we murder their image in the eyes of those whom they love and so prepare for the cancer of the ego and the slow death by desertion. If our society allowed promiscuity only to the free, that is to the unmarried or to those who had both agreed on separation, and if it punished the breaking-up of homes as it punishes robbery-with-violence, then the nervous breakdowns, the resort to alcohol and drugs, would disappear with much of the incurable unhappiness of the betrayed and forsaken.

The particular charm of marriage, which may grow irresistible to those who once have tasted it, is the duologue, the permanent conversation, between two people who talk over everything and everyone till death breaks the record. It is this back-chat which, in the long run, makes a reciprocal equality more intoxicating than any form of servitude or domination. But for the artist it may prove dangerous; he is one of those who must look alone out of the window and for him to enter into the duologue, the non-stop per-

formance of a lifetime, is a kind of exquisite dissipation which, despite the
pleasure of a joint understanding of the human comedy, is likely to deprive
him of those much rarer moments which are particularly his own. For this
reason great artists are not always those who repose the most entire confidence in their wives (this is why second wives are sometimes best) and the
relation of many an artist to his wife is apt to puzzle the spectator.

1 May: To-day we begin a new pincer movement against Angst, Melancholia and Memory's ever-festering wound: a sleeping-pill to pass the night
and a Benzedrine to get through the day. The sleeping-pill produces a thick
sleep, rich in dreams that are not so much dreams as tangible experiences,
the Benzedrine a kind of gluttonous mental anger through which the sadness
persists—O how sad,—but very much farther off. Whether they can ever
combine in the mind to produce a new energy remains to be proven.

When I take Vitamin B, Metatone or other tonics, they render me calm,
coarse and sensual; the voice becomes deeper, the manner more robust.
Yet I am aware that this is not my real personality, but a toned-up film
version, an escape from the serious ego, and soon I return to my true diffident and dyspeptic self. Confidence does not become me.

Ennui is the condition of not fulfilling our potentialities; remorse of not
having fulfilled them; anxiety of not being able to fulfil them,—but what
are they?

Let us take such a simple idea as the desire to improve, to become better.
Is it a natural human instinct or is it the result of early conditioning? Croco-
diles, kingcrabs, eagles, do not evolve and yet they seem perfectly content
with their humble status. And many human beings enjoy a quiet existence
without feeling themselves obliged to expand or develop. With the desire to
evolve arises the fear of remaining static, or guilt. If there were no parents
to make us try to be good, no school-masters to persuade us to learn, no one
who wished to be proud of us, would not we be happier? Promise is the
white child's burden of which the savage, in his pre-mental bliss, has never
heard. When we are sick we revert to our childhood patterns. Do we not
live according to them in some degree when we are well? Heard, for
example, is the son of a puritan clergyman, Huxley is by birth a public-
spirited Victorian; what is their evolutionary zeal but a duty-reflex conditioned by their upbringing? Does Nature care in the least whether we
evolve or not? Her instincts are for the gratification of hunger and sex, the
destruction of rivals and the protection of offspring. What monster first
slipped in the idea of progress? Who destroyed our conception of happiness
with these growing-pains?

MASTERPLAY

The triple decadence: Decadence of the material; of the writer's language.
The virgin snow where Shakespeare and Montaigne used to cut their deep
furrows, is now but a slope flattened by innumerable tracks until it is unable
to receive an impression. Decadence of the myth, for there is no longer a
unifying belief (as in Christianity or in Renaissance Man) to permit a writer
a sense of awe and of awe which he shares with the mass of humanity. And
even the last myth of all, the myth of the artist's vocation, of 'l'homme c'est
rien, l'œuvre c'est tout', is destroyed by the times, by the third decadence,
that of society. In our lifetime we have seen the arts advance further and
further into an obscure and sterile cul-de-sac. Science has done little to help
the artist, beyond contributing radio, linotype and the cinema; inventions
which enormously extend his scope, but which commit him more than ever
to the policy of the State and the demands of the ignorant. Disney is the
tenth-rate Shakespeare of our age, forced by his universal audience to
elaborate his new-world sentimentality with increasing slickness. There may
arise Leonardos of the screen and microphone who will astound us but not
until the other arts have declined into regional or luxury crafts, like book-
binding, cabinet-making, thatching or pargetting. To-day an artist must
expect to write in water and to cast in sand.

Yet to live in a decadence need not make us despair; it is but one technical
problem the more which a writer has to solve.

Even in the most socialized community, there must always be a few who
best serve it by being kept isolated. The artist, like the mystic, naturalist,
mathematician or 'leader', makes his contribution out of his solitude. This
solitude the State is now attempting to destroy, and a time may come when
it will no more tolerate private inspiration. State Socialism in politics is
bound to lead to social realism in the arts, until the position is reached that
whatever the common man does not understand is treason. Yet it is a mistake
completely to identify the State with a philistine father-figure and so to
react blindly against it. For the State includes its own critics and their
objections may lead to change. To-day the State shows a benevolent face to
Culture-Diffusion but to those who produce culture no trace of sympathy
or indulgence, with the result that we are becoming a nation of commentators, of critics and hack-explainers, most of whom are ex-artists. Everything for the Milk-bar, nothing for the cow! Patiently and obstinately the
artist must convince the State that, in the long run, it will be judged by its
art and that, if the State is to replace the private patron, then it must imitate
and even surpass that patron's tolerance, humility and liberality. When will

the State say, 'Here is a thousand pounds, young man; go anywhere you like for six months, and bring me back something beautiful'?

A great artist is like a fig-tree whose roots run a hundred feet underground in search of tea-leaves, cinders and old boots. Art which is directly produced for the Community can never have the same withdrawn quality as that which is made out of the artist's solitude. For this possesses the integrity and bleak exhilaration that are to be gained only from the absence of an audience and from communion with the primal sources of unconscious life. One cannot serve both beauty and power: 'Le pouvoir est essentiellement stupide.' A public figure can never be an artist and no artist should ever become one unless, his work being done, he should choose to retire into public life.

An artist grows into a public figure through being always willing to address strangers. 'Pauvre et sans honneurs,' wrote Valéry of Mallarmé, 'la nudité de sa condition avilissait tous les avantages des autres. . . . Tout leur semblait naïf et lâche après qu'ils l'avaient lu.'

A Chinese Parallel: Hui Tzu was prime minister in the Liang State. Chuang Tzu went thither to visit him.

Someone remarked: 'Chuang Tzu has come. He wants to be minister in your place.'

Thereupon Hui Tzu was afraid, and searched all over the State for three days and three nights to find him.

Then Chuang Tzu went to see Hui Tzu and said: 'In the south there is a bird. It is a kind of phœnix. Do you know it? It started from the south sea to fly to the north sea. Except on the wu-t'ung tree it would not alight. It would eat nothing but the fruit of the bamboo, drink nothing but the purest spring water. An owl which had got the rotten carcass of a rat looked up as the phœnix flew by, and screeched. Are you not screeching at me over your kingdom of Liang?' (*Musings of a Chinese Mystic*.)

4 May: Failure of pincer movement. Am unwilling to take sleeping pills which are used up by my friends. Benzedrine has lost effect. Apathy, sluggishness and morning tears return with the sense of 'All-is-lost' and the torture of two faces.

> '. . . et me laissez enfin
> Dans ce petit coin sombre avec mon noir chagrin.'

What is the use of useless suffering? Where is the escape? What can one ever make out of the *nessun maggior dolore*, the stranglehold of the past, the heart broken but never dead? 'Je le répète sans cesse, il n'y a qu'un malheur, celui d'être né.'

Is it possible to love any human being without being torn limb from limb? No one was ever made wretched in a brothel; there need be nothing angst-forming about the sexual act. Yet a face seen in the tube can destroy our peace for the rest of the day, and once a mutual attraction develops it is too late; for when sexual emotion increases to passion, then something starts growing which possesses a life of its own and which, easily though it may be destroyed by ignorance and neglect, will die in agony and go on dying after it is dead.

As bees their sting, so the promiscuous leave behind them in each encounter something of themselves by which they are made to suffer.

It is the fear of middle-age in the young, and of old-age in the middle-aged, which is the prime cause of infidelity, that infallible rejuvenator.

When young we are faithful to individuals, older we grow more loyal to a situation or a type. Confronted by such specimens, we seem to know all about them in an instant (which is true) and thus in spite of our decreasing charm we sweep them off their feet, for young people do not understand themselves and, fortunately for us, can still be hypnotized by those who do.

The mind has its own womb to which, baffled by speculation, it longs to return; the womb of Homer and Herodotus, of the pastoral world where men and gods were ruled by the same passions and where all our personal problems seemed easy of solution. Then the womb fills with the Middle Ages, with the Popes, the Crusades and the Renaissance. For some it stretches to include the court of Charles II, or the writers of the reign of Anne; it is the Hôtel des Grands Hommes, the Pantheon of mythical or historical figures who were masters of their surroundings, arbiters of their destiny and who went through life bundled together in a well-documented cats'-cradle of loving intimacy.

Desire to smoke opium comes back. 'It dulls the moral sense.'

> In blackest noon the shutter falls
> That folds me from the slanting day.
> Before the night a Stranger calls
> Who strikes the fearless and the gay.
>
> There is no love however deep
> Can stay the verdict in his eye,
> There is no laugh however sweet
> Can drown the moment's passing sigh.

'L'obésité a une influence fâcheuse sur les deux sexes, en ce qu'elle nuit à la force et à la beauté . . . L'obésité nuit à la beauté en détruisant l'harmonie de proportion primitivement établie.'

'Proposer à des obèses de se lever le matin, c'est leur percer le cœur.'—
BRILLAT-SAVARIN

Imprisoned in every fat man a thin one is wildly signalling to be let out.

A lazy person, whatever the talents with which he set out, will have condemned himself to second-hand thoughts and to second-rate friends.

Intense emotion, a mixture of relief and despair, at reading Sainte-Beuve's notebook *Mes Poisons*, and discovering 'This is me'. This Elegiac, as he styled himself, who quotes my favourite lines of Latin poetry and who sums up happiness as reading Tibullus in the country 'avec une femme qu'on aime', who calls himself 'le dernier des délicats', who loved, suffered and was disillusioned, and yet who recognizes love as the true source of happiness, who is sceptical of everyone and everything, a smaller man though a better artist than his romantic contemporaries; who loves the eighteenth century but was never taken in, who hated puritans and prigs and pedants but knew how the wine of remorse is trodden from the grapes of pleasure, and who, with all his scholarship and self-analysis, was at heart a Taoist, respecting the essential mystery ('le vrai c'est le secret de quelques-uns') and what he calls his 'âme pastorale',—how deeply moving to listen to such a voice from the past which in the present becomes an inspiration! I feel like a cringing cur kicked about in a crowd, which, running down an alley, finds there silence, an apprehension of revelation, and then, round a corner, comes suddenly upon a huge dark doggy statue, a canine colossus from another age; awe-inspiring and faith-restoring, lending him courage and wishing him well.

WISDOM OF SAINTE-BEUVE 1804-69

'L'épicuréisme bien compris est la fin de tout.'

'Que m'importe, pourvu que je fasse *quelque chose* le matin, et que je sois *quelque part* le soir.'

'La saturation, il y a un moment où cela vient dans ce repas qu'on appelle la vie: il ne faut qu'une goutte alors pour faire déborder la coupe du dégoût.'

'Il y a des moments où la vie, le fond de la vie se rouvre au dedans de nous comme une plaie qui saigne et ne veut pas se fermer.'

'Je suis resté avant tout un Elégiaque et un rêveur. Une grande et solide partie des jours, même aux années réputées graves, s'est passée pour moi dans les regrets stériles, dans les vagues désirs de l'attente, dans les mélancolies et les langueurs qui suivent le plaisir.'

'Je n'ai jamais conçu l'amour sans le mystère, et là où était le mystère, là pour moi déjà était l'amour.'

'Ne me demandez pas ce que j'aime et ce que je crois, n'allez pas au fond de mon âme.'

EPICTETUS: 'When God fails to provide for you, then He is giving the signal of retreat. He has opened the door and says to you, "Come"—"Where?"— "To nothing fearful, but thither whence you were born, to things friendly and akin to you, the Elements".'

Illumination: Tout mon mal vient de Paris. Rue Delambre, Quai d'Anjou, Rue de Vaugirard. Aïe!
   'Ahi tu passasti, eterno sospiro mio.'

The hard black ball of suicidal despair. The door is open.
NERVAL: 'Arrivé sur la Place de la Concorde, ma pensée était de me détruire.' Bad moment; the door is open, Paris 'ma plaie et ma fatalité'.

> 'The wind doth blow to-day my love
> And a few small drops of rain.'

                    .   .   .

As the lights in the penitentiary grow dim when the current is switched on for the electric chair, so we quiver in our hearts at a suicide, for there is no human life self-taken for which all society is not to blame.

WISDOM OF CHAMFORT (1741–1794)

'L'indécision, l'anxiété sont à l'esprit et à l'âme ce que la question est au corps.'

'Les passions font *vivre* l'homme; la sagesse le fait seulement *durer*.'

'Quand on a été bien tourmenté, bien fatigué par sa propre sensibilité, on s'aperçoit qu'il faut vivre au jour le jour, oublier beaucoup, enfin *éponger la vie* à mesure qu'elle s'écoule.'

'Otez l'amour-propre de l'amour, il en reste trop peu de chose . . . l'amour,

                    11

tel qu'il existe dans la société, n'est que l'échange de deux fantaisies et le contact de deux épidermes.'

'Un homme amoureux qui plaint l'homme raisonnable me paraît ressembler à un homme qui lit des contes de fées, et qui raille ceux qui lisent l'histoire.'

'Presque tous les hommes sont esclaves, par le raison que les Spartiates donnaient de la servitude des Perses, faute de savoir prononcer la syllabe *non*. Savoir prononcer ce mot et savoir vivre seul sont les deux seuls moyens de conserver sa liberté et son caractère.'

In the jungles of South America grows a trumpet flower fourteen inches deep, and there too is found a moth with a proboscis of the same length, the one creature able to penetrate to the honey and so ensure the plant's fertilization. I, Palinurus, am such an orchid, growing daily more untempting as I await the Visitor who never comes.

> 'On a pour ma personne une aversion grande
> et quelqu'un de ces jours il faut que je me pende.'

Yet there are many who dare not kill themselves for fear of what the neighbours will say.

In the small hours when the acrid stench of existence rises like sewer gas from everything created, the emptiness of life seems more terrible than its misery, 'Inferum deplorata silentia' . . .

Streets of Paris, pray for me; beaches in the sun, pray for me; ghosts of the lemurs, intercede for me; plane-tree and laurel-rose, shade me; summer rain on quays of Toulon, wash me away.

A young man who wished to marry consulted his uncle, an old courtier of the Prince of Wales's set. 'No one will want to marry you as you are,' said his uncle. 'You must get polish, your own particular aroma. Take a house, get to know about furniture and painting, buy the new books, listen to music, know whom to entertain and how to shake a dry Martini. Then you'll have something to offer and all the right mothers will snap you up.' The young man did as he was told and, some fifteen years later, he called again on the ancient week-ender of Fort Belvedere, whose old eyes now were seldom far from tears or alcohol.

'My house is perfect,' squeaked the brittle youth, 'the pictures are pure bliss, the bindings of green morocco catch the light of the evening sun; my *Louis Seize* commodes belly out in the alcoves, there are Malvern water and biscuits by every bed and in each lavatory the toilet-paper, loosely arranged

in scented sheets, is weighted down by a coloured stone. Ladies cry themselves into my life, then cough their way out of it; nobody who comes to
luncheon remembers afterwards anything they have said. I am at last perfectly eligible. What shall I do?'

The old Beau laughed and lit his third cigar. 'Just carry on,' he chuckled;
'I think we've got *you* out of the wood.'

Bournemouth. Branksome Towers Hotel. Steamy tropical atmosphere,
avenues of villas hidden in evergreens; the hotel with long vine-hung
veranda and lawn sloping to the sea, dimly visible through a group of leaning pine-trees. The pines here with their undergrowth of rhododendron and
arbutus form the northernmost tip of the maritime forest which stretches
from Hossegor, near Bayonne, by the Landes and Royan, the Ile d'Oleron,
La Rochelle, the Vendean coast, La Baule and the Landes of Brittany, to
expire at Bournemouth and Le Touquet. Across the sea lies the unspoilt,
uninhabited paradise of the Isle of Purbeck with its sandy beaches and chalk
promontories.

Led by chance to discover the hanging foot-bridge over Alum Chine.
Walking over the quivering planks I felt rooted, as in a nightmare, to the
spot in the centre where the asphalt road lies directly underneath, a leaden
water-snake uncurling through pine and giant hemlock. To drag one's sticky
feet across was like plunging through a bog. What a place to make away
with oneself or some loved one!

L'ennui de la campagne; l'angoisse des villes. Chaque fois que je rentre à
Londres, j'assiste à un crime.

I am now forced to admit that anxiety is my true condition, occasionally
intruded on by work, pleasure, melancholy or despair.

STEKEL: 'All neurotics are at heart religious. Their ideal is pleasure without
guilt. The neurotic is a criminal without the courage to commit a crime. . . .
Every neurotic is an actor playing a particular scene. . . . Anxiety is repressed
desire. Every individual who cannot find a form of sex-satisfaction adequate
to himself suffers from an anxiety neurosis. . . . It is the disease of a bad
conscience.'

A mistake which is commonly made about neurotics is to suppose that
they are interesting. It is not interesting to be always unhappy, engrossed
with oneself, malignant or ungrateful, and never quite in touch with reality.
Neurotics are heartless: as Baudelaire wrote 'tout homme qui n'accepte pas
les conditions de la vie vend son âme'.

The true index of a man's character is the health of his wife.

'Aimer et haïr, ce n'est qu'éprouver avec une passion singulière l'être d'un être.'

'Quand l'univers considère avec indifférence l'être que nous aimons, qui est dans la vérité?'—JOUHANDEAU

We think we recognize someone in passing. A mistake, but a moment later we run into them. This pre-view was our arrival on their wavelength, within their magnetic orbit.

Like the glow-worm; dowdy, minute, passive, yet full of mystery to the poet and erotic significance to its fellows; so everything and everybody eternally radiate a dim light for those who care to seek. The strawberry hidden under the last leaf cries, 'Pick me'; the forgotten book, in the forgotten bookshop, screams to be discovered. The old house hidden in the hollow agitates itself violently at the approach of its pre-destined admirer. Dead authors cry 'Read me'; dead friends say 'Remember me'; dead ancestors whisper, 'Unearth me'; dead places, 'Revisit me'; and sympathetic spirits, living and dead, are continually trying to enter into communion. Physical or intellectual attraction between two people is a constant communication. Underneath the rational and voluntary world lies the involuntary, impulsive, integrated world, the world of Relation in which everything is one; where sympathy and antipathy are engrossed in their selective tug-of-war.

We learn a new word for the first time. Then it turns up within the next hour. Why? Because words are living organisms impelled by a crystallizing process to mysterious agglutinative matings at which the word-fancier is sometimes privileged to assist. The glow-worms light up.... The individual also is like a moving mirror or screen which reflects in its motion an ever-changing panorama of thoughts, sensations, faces and places, and yet the screen is always being guided to reflect one film rather than another, always seeking a chosen *querencia*. In the warm sea of experience we blob around like plankton, we love-absorb or hate-avoid each other or are avoided or are absorbed, devoured and devouring. Yet we are no more free than the cells in a plant or the microbes in a drop of water but are all held firmly in tension by the pull of the future and the tug of the past.

'Du moment que je me fus assuré de ce point que j'étais soumis aux épreuves de l'initiation sacrée, une force invincible entra dans mon esprit. Je me jugeais un héros vivant sous le regard des dieux; tout dans la nature prenait des aspects nouveaux, et des voix secrètes sortaient de la plante, de l'arbre, des animaux, des plus humbles insectes, pour m'avertir et m'encourager. Le langage de mes compagnons avait des tour mystérieux dont je comprenais le sens, les objets sans forme et sans vie se prêtaient eux-mêmes aux calculs de mon esprit; des combinaisons de cailloux, des figures d'angles, de fentes ou d'ouvertures, des découpures de feuilles, des couleurs, des odeurs et des sons, je voyais ressortir des harmonies jusqu'alors inconnues. "Comment", me disais-je, "ai-je pu exister si longtemps hors de la nature et sans m'identifier à elle? Tout vit, tout agit, tout se correspond; les rayons magnétiques émanés de moi-même ou des autres traversent sans obstacle la chaîne infinie des choses créées; c'est un réseau transparent qui couvre le monde, et dont les fils déliés se communiquent de proche en proche aux planètes et aux étoiles." Captif en ce moment sur la terre, je m'entretiens avec le chœur des astres qui prend part à mes joies et à mes douleurs!'—G. DE NERVAL; Aurélia.[1]

In the break-up of religions and creeds there is but one deity whose worshippers have multiplied without a set-back. The Sun. In a few years there will be a stampede towards this supreme anæsthetic. Scotland will pour itself into Southern England, Canada into the U.S.A., the U.S.A. dwindle to Florida, California and New Mexico, while Southern Englanders will have migrated en masse to the Mediterranean. The temperate zone, especially for women, is becoming uninhabitable. Let us leave England to retired Generals and culture-diffusionists, goose-fleshed politicians and bureaucrats, while the rest of us heliotropes cluster nearer to the great bronze disc of church-emptying Apollo, hardener of heart and skin.

July: Once more the bold Dragonfly of pleasure has brushed me with its wing. Divine Sainte-Beuve,—'L'épicuréisme bien compris',—and Hume, the Northern Epicurus. Late June, July and early August—fruit-eating months when the English become callous, pleasure-ridden, amorous and Elizabethan. It is necessary.

After the long suicidal winter Pleasure comes to rescue us from the desert island of the ego and allow us two months' grace. Good-bye sick Pascal and his mouldy troupe; gaunt Kierkegaard, hunch-backed Leopardi, wheezing Proust and limping Epictetus with his Open Door! Midsummer greeting to La Fontaine, Congreve, Aristippus, Horace and Voltaire! Good-bye morning tears, 'All-is-lost', never-again, doubt, despair! Welcome cheese-breathing hang-over, tipsy mornings for gargling poetry, asparagus afternoons,

[1] This piece, written by Nerval in his madness, resembles a late landscape of Van Gogh. The intense associations of atomical pantheism become what mental doctors call 'Delusions of Reference'. In manic elation communication seems to exist between inanimate objects and the Observer. Flowers signal to him, stones cry out, and all nature approves. In suicidal depression the same phenomena arise, but in this case nature seems to pass a vote of censure; inanimate objects urge the Observer to make a thorough good job of it. Are both fatigue and ecstasy poisons which distort our relation to external reality? Or do they liberate deep-buried instinctive perceptions of relationship to which normally we are blind?

gull's-egg evenings, affection slopping over into gossip, who-was-there and ring-a-ling! Taoism at last rewarded! 'Flower o' the Quince', . . . Hour of the Broad Bean.

If all the world loved pleasure as much as Palinurus there would be no war.

THE PLAY-BOY PERMIT

I

'Le plaisir crée une franc-maçonnerie charmante. Ceux qui y sont profès se reconnaissent d'un clin d'œil, s'entendent sans avoir besoin de paroles, et il se passe là de ces choses imprévues, sans prélude et sans suites, de ces hasards de rencontre et de mystère qui échappent au récit, mais qui remplissent l'imagination et qui sont un des enchantements de la vie. Ceux qui y ont goûté n'en veulent plus d'autres.'—SAINTE-BEUVE

II

'Les hommes trouveront toujours que la chose la plus sérieuse de leur existence, c'est jouir.'—FLAUBERT

Dining-out is a vice, a dissipation of spirit punished by remorse. We eat, drink and talk a little too much, abuse all our friends, belch out our literary preferences and are egged on by accomplices in the audience to acts of mental exhibitionism. Such evenings cannot fail to diminish those who take part in them. They end on Monkey Hill.

Society: A perfect dinner-party for sixteen. Each person as carefully chosen as an instrument in an orchestra,—yet how many of the guests would rather be engaged that evening in tête-à-tête? Or be glad to leave early for a brothel?

MESSAGE FROM THE ID

'If you would collect women instead of books, I think I could help you.'

'And there came thunder and lightning and pestilence and famine and the people were sore afraid. And the Lord spake out of the tempest and out of the whirlwind and the earth quaked and all the people trembled with fear, and the Lord cried with a mighty voice: "When thou goest away for weekends thou shalt not stay over Monday; over thy luncheon not long shalt thou squat, nor shalt thou take taxis, nor buy books; third class thou shalt travel, not first; neither shalt thou drink wine nor giggle nor spoon; but thou shalt sorrow and sweat wherever thou goest,—for I the Lord thy God am a jealous God and behold I will crush thee as a slimy worm." And lo, there fell a silence over the earth and the land lay barren a thousand years.'

Anxiety again, *en grande tenue*. The two faces. Everything connected with them is excruciating: people, places, sounds, smells, habits. An old letter coils up and explodes like a land-mine, an inscription in a book pronounces a life-sentence, gramophone records screech from the grave; even the harmless sunbeam and the green surge of summer out of doors are decoys which ambush the heart at a sultry corner. *Da dextram misero*! O, never to have met or never to have parted! Living in the present (the one escape) can only be contrived by drugs, by an injection of work or pleasure or by the giving 'which plays you least false'. The past is a festering wound; the present the compress vainly applied, painfully torn off. Paris, Chelsea, Cannes—*misère*! We are all serving a life-sentence in the dungeon of self.

Sainte-Beuve's poem, 'Dans l'île Saint-Louis'. He knew.

Imagination = nostalgia for the past, the absent; it is the liquid solution in which art develops the snapshots of reality. The artist secretes nostalgia round life, as a worm plasters its tunnel, a caterpillar spins a cocoon or as a sea-swallow masticates her nest. Art without imagination is as life without hope.

Egotism sucks us down like the law of gravity. In the small hours this law is somewhat weakened, we are less subject to it and even the self-centredness with which the earth rotates on its axis, seems to fade. As egotism subsides we grow more conscious of the meagre foundation of our lives, of the true nature of the Authorities whom we try to please and by whom we wish to be loved—those who feed our lost selves with their admiration.

For a dark play-girl in a night-club I have pined away, for a dead school boy, for a bright angel-vixen I have wept in vain. If this thoughtless woman were to die there would be nothing to live for, if this faithless girl forgot me there would be no one for whom to write. These two unseen and otherwise occupied figures composed the fragile arch of my being and constitute a Tribunal which they have long ceased to attend.

Miserable Orpheus who, turning to lose his Eurydice, beholds her for the first time as well as the last.

'The self-torments of melancholiacs, which are without doubt pleasurable, signify a gratification of sadistic tendencies and of hate, both of which relate to an object and in this way have both been turned round upon the self. In the end the sufferers usually succeed in taking revenge, by the circuitous path of self-punishment, on the original object who occasioned the injury and who is usually to be found in their near neighbourhood. No neurotic harbours thoughts of suicide which are not murderous impulses against others redirected upon himself.'—FREUD.

The cycle of the hours. 'The Lars and Lemures moan with midnight plaint.' 1 a.m.: Anger turns to Misery. 2 a.m.: Misery to Panic. The low tide and nadir of hope about 2 a.m. to 4. Magical Euphoria wells from 4 a.m. to 6— the thalamic 'All Clear'; Peace and Certainty arrive through Despair. All morning the tide of confidence rolls in with high water of egotism from 2 p.m. to 3. (We are farthest then from the idea of death as in the nocturnal small hours we are nearest.) Momentary depression at sunset, though often at my best from 6 o'clock to 10. Then the bilges begin to empty.

Thought can be made to take liberties by artificial stimulation of the brain. The cortex is a machine for thinking. It can be 'revved up', slowed down, choked, fed various types of fuel according to the ideas it is required to produce. When the mixture is too rich, as in the small hours, the engine pinks, whence the manic symptom, 'Flight of Ideas'.

Thus tea, coffee, alcohol stimulate.

So do heights, wet days, south-west gales, hotel bedrooms in Paris and windows overlooking harbours. Also snow, frost, the electric bell outside a cinema at night, sex-life and fever.

Cigars, tisanes, long draughts of water and fruit-juice have a clearing, calming effect. They 'rev' down the motor and overcome stoppages. And so do sitting still, relaxing climates, luxury, constipation, music, sun-bathing, hang-overs, listening to fountains, waves and waterfalls.

A thorough knowledge of opium, benzedrine, phosphorus and other drugs should make it possible for us to feed the brain the right mixture according to the effect desired; whether we contemplate a work of the imagination (putting ideas into our heads) or of the intellect (analysis, reasoning, memory).

When we decide to write, we should first consider the ingredients involved. Proportions of heart and head, of judgment and imagination. 'A peach of an essay', 'a melon of a poem', 'a quince of a book',—we must let ourselves be impregnated by an archetypal form. Then we should treat the personality with the right mixture till the glaze (style) is suitable,—'for my philosophical novel with a milligramme of nostalgia, I am taking ephedrine twice a week, opium once—with a little mescaline to loosen up my imagery and a massage on the nape of the neck to stimulate the thalamus after the monthly orgy. I am writing two-thirds standing up in the early morning, one-third in the afternoon lying down. My supervisor is a Jungian.'

LAST WORDS ON OPIUM-READING

'L'opium est la seule substance végétale qui nous communique l'état végétal. Par lui nous avons une idée de cette autre vitesse des plantes.'

'L'opium apprivoisé adoucira le mal des villes.'—COCTEAU.

'Here were the hopes which blossom in the paths of life reconciled with the peace which is in the grave.'—DE QUINCEY.

Others merely live; I vegetate.

O sacred solitary empty mornings, tranquil meditation—fruit of book-case and clock-tick, of note-book and armchair; golden and rewarding silence, influence of sun-dappled plane-trees, far-off noises of birds and horses, possession beyond price of a few cubic feet of air and an hour of leisure! This vacuum of peace is the state from which art should proceed, for art is made by the alone for the alone, and now this cerulean atmosphere, which we should all be able to take for granted, has become an unattainable end.

The reward of art is not fame or success but intoxication: that is why so many bad artists are unable to give it up.

What fathers would I like to vindicate? Who, on reading Palinurus in the Asphodel Club will say, 'I told you so'? Aristippus, Horace, Tibullus, Montaigne, Saint Flaubert and Sainte-Beuve. But Pascal? He frightens me,— and Chamfort? I don't think so.

I have much more in common with Chamfort than with Pascal; sometimes I feel that I was Chamfort, for there is nothing of his that I might not, with luck, have written, yet it is by reading the thoughts of Pascal (which I never could have written) that I change and grow. Literary charm, arising out of the desire to please, excludes those flights of intellectual power which are more rewarding than pleasure.

THE PREDICAMENT OF CHAMFORT, 1741-94

His mother was a 'dame de compagnie', his father unknown, and he was christened merely 'Nicolas'. Mother and son came from Auvergne to Paris where Nicolas was a brilliant schoolboy. After dallying with the Church, he plunged into the world of letters. A love-child, Chamfort was swept to success by the favours of women, a success which exhausted him physically and led to serious disorders; however, he obtained a well-paid sinecure, a literary prize, and a stage triumph through his wit, his gallantry, and the love of his friends, until at forty he retired to Boileau's old home at Auteuil; there he fell in love with a 'dame de compagnie' to the Duchesse de Maine, aged forty-eight, who died six months later. After her loss, he returned to Paris to become the cynical jester and licensed darling of the Court. 'My sentiments are republican, yet I live with courtiers. I love poverty, my friends are all rich; I believe that illusions are a necessary luxury of life, yet I live without any; I believe that passions are more useful to us than reason, yet I have destroyed my capacity for feeling.' When the Revolution broke out, Chamfort, a genuine republican, sided with his friend and admirer Mirabeau. He spoke at street corners and was one of the first to enter the Bastille. Though he lost all his pensions he plunged with enthusiasm into politics and contributed such slogans as 'Guerre aux châteaux, Paix aux chaumières'! and 'Moi, tout; le reste rien! Voilà le despotisme. Moi, c'est un autre; un autre c'est moi: voilà la démocratie'. In spite of a warning that his sallies would not be tolerated as indulgently as under the old regime, he soon began to mimic and satirize the new personages of the Revolution. In 1793 he sealed his fate with his description of Jacobin ethics: 'Sois mon frère ou je te tue'. 'I am not afraid,' he said, 'Je n'ai pas peur; n'ai-je pas toujours marché au premier rang de la phalange républicaine?' Denounced anonymously, he was taken to prison. He was released but almost immediately rearrested. Rather than lose his liberty at the hands of the Party to which he was convinced he belonged, he made an excuse to leave the room, and shot himself. The bullet broke his nose and went into his eye. He next tried to cut his throat with a razor. He partially recovered from his wounds but died soon afterwards from pneumonia. His last words were: 'Je m'en vais enfin de ce monde, où il faut que le cœur se brise ou se bronze.'

The complexity of Chamfort's character would seem to be due to his temperament as a love-child; he transmuted his passionate love for his mother into a general desire for affection which he concentrated at last on the elderly lady-in-waiting who resembled her. With this need for love went that equally violent feeling, so familiar to bastards, of a grievance against society. The warmth of his affections combined with his sense of injustice and his clear mind to propel him to the crest of the Revolution, but he was one of those observers who cannot blind themselves to the defects of men who logically carry out an ideal in action. Though he himself believed in their cause, he was a philosopher without hope and without pity.[1] Physically Chamfort was tall and handsome, an Adonis in youth, pale and exhausted in later life; he was a man who lived in spurts, and who seemed kept alive by the fire of his intelligence. Mirabeau called him 'noble et digne' and admired his 'tête électrique', Chateaubriand praised his cold blue eye. His predicament is one with which we are all familiar and there is every danger that it

---

[1] 'All literature might be ransacked in vain for a more repulsive saying than this (of Chamfort): "A man must swallow a toad every morning if he wishes to be sure of finding nothing still more disgusting before the day is over." '—MORLEY: Studies of Literature, p. 95.

will soon become only too common; that of the revolutionary whose manners and way of life are attached to the old regime, whose ideals and loyalties belong to the new, and who, by a kind of courageous exhibitionism, is impelled to tell the truth about both, and to expect from the commissars of King Stork the applause for his sallies which they received from the courtiers of King Log. Most lovable of Chamfort's sayings which, remarkable though they be for splenetic violence, are apt to grow irritating through an excess of point, a somewhat vulgar urbanity, is his final outburst, just after he had attempted his life. He is speaking to a friend in his usual quiet tone of familiar irony: 'Que voulez-vous? Voilà ce que c'est que d'être maladroit de la main: on ne réussit à rien, pas même à se tuer.' He began to explain how, instead of blowing out his brains, he had punctured his eye and the lower part of his forehead, then, instead of cutting his throat, he had gashed his neck and even hacked his chest without succeeding in stabbing his heart. 'Enfin,' he concludes, 'je me suis souvenu de Sénèque, et, en l'honneur de Sénèque, j'ai voulu m'ouvrir les veines; mais il était riche, lui; il avait tout à souhait, un bain bien chaud, enfin toutes ses aises; moi, je suis un pauvre diable, je n'ai rien de tout cela. Je me suis fait un mal horrible, et me voilà encore; mais j'ai la balle dans la tête, c'est là le principal. Un peu plus tôt, un peu plus tard, voilà tout.'

WISDOM OF CHAMFORT II

C'est un grand malheur de perdre, par notre caractère, les droits que nos talents nous donnent sur la société.

Il y a une certaine énergie ardente, mère ou compagne nécessaire de telle espèce de talents, laquelle pour l'ordinaire condamne ceux qui les possèdent au malheur. C'est une âpreté dévorante dont ils ne sont pas maîtres et qui les rend très-odieux.

En renonçant au monde et à la fortune, j'ai trouvé le bonheur, le calme, la santé, même la richesse; et, en dépit du proverbe, je m'aperçois que 'qui quitte la partie la gagne'.

La vie contemplative est souvent misérable. Il faut agir davantage, penser moins, et ne pas se regarder vivre.

Il faut recommencer la société humaine.

. . . . . .

Les fléaux physiques et les calamités de la nature humaine ont rendu la société nécessaire. La société a ajouté aux malheurs de la nature. Les incon-

vénients de la société ont amené la nécessité du gouvernement, et le gouvernement ajoute aux malheurs de la société. Voilà l'histoire de la nature humaine.

Les pauvres sont les nègres de l'Europe.

Quand un homme et une femme ont l'un pour l'autre une passion violente, il
me semble toujours que . . . les deux amants sont l'un à l'autre *de par la nature*,
qu'ils s'appartiennent *de droit divin*.

'Les prétentions sont une source de peines, et l'époque du bonheur de la vie
commence au moment où elles finissent.'

'La pensée console de tout.'

When I turn to see what Sainte-Beuve thinks of Chamfort, how the old love
will greet the new, I find him somewhat severe, the Superego judging the
Ego. One would have expected him to feel more sympathy for a man so
melancholy and disillusioned, one to whom, like himself, people were 'as
those insects whose transparent tissue lets us see the veins and all the different
shades of the blood'; instead he is over-critical, and a little alarmed by him.
He admits that Chamfort's aphorisms are like 'des flèches acérées qui arrivent brusquement et sifflent encore', but he reproaches him with being a
bachelor and therefore a recluse on whom Nature took her revenge. With
equivocal serenity this other bachelor, the dubious monk of letters of the Rue
de Montparnasse, finds fault with Chamfort for two of his maxims—'Je ne
veux point me marier, dans la crainte d'avoir un fils qui me ressemble', and
'Quiconque n'est pas misanthrope à quarante ans n'a jamais aimé les hommes'.

Unwillingly one has to admit the justice of Sainte-Beuve's profound,
stern, yet not unsympathetic analysis. Compared to him, Chamfort is a
Byronic adolescent. 'J'ai du Tacite dans la tête et du Tibulle dans le cœur,'
writes Chamfort. 'Ni le Tibulle ni le Tacite,' cracks Sainte-Beuve, 'n'ont pu
en sortir pour la postérité'. What makes Sainte-Beuve superior? He detected
Chamfort's tragedy; that he was a moralist whose credentials have never
quite been accepted, that there was too much egotism in his judgment
(which reflects the guilty self-hatred of those who know that they are
neglecting their talent through indolence and hedonism). Chamfort detested humanity, but, unlike Sainte-Beuve, he could find no compensation
in the love of nature. Chamfort was a classical pagan, Sainte-Beuve a double-
minded critic who had passed through the mystical experience and the
Romantic Movement to a scepticism infinitely enriched by both.

Another view: 'I believe only in French culture, and I regard everything else
in Europe which calls itself culture as a misunderstanding. . . . When one
reads Montaigne, La Rochefoucauld, Vauvenargues and Chamfort, one is

nearer to antiquity than with any group of authors in any other nation.'—
NIETZSCHE.

And with Baudelaire, Flaubert, Sainte-Beuve, nearer to ourselves.

Those who are consumed with curiosity about other people but who do not
love them should write maxims, for no one can become a novelist unless he
love his fellow-men. Being myself contaminated by oriental philosophy, I
cannot take people seriously, (Sabba dukka! 'In those countries human life is
but a weed'). They all seem replaceable except for the few who carry away
sections of ourselves which cannot be replaced. Once we believe that the
ego is like a cell which by over-assertion of itself causes cancer, the cancer of
developing at the expense of society or at the expense of the self's natural
harmony with the order of things, a harmony which it drowns by its own
din, then we can only dislike the pushing, confident extroverts who, with
their petty ambitions, form the backbone of fiction. If we have no appetite
for the idiosyncrasies of minor personalities, then we must fight shy of the
novel which will end by seeming as grotesque to us as the portrait of an
alderman to a Tibetan Lama.

> 'When the bells justle in the tower
> The hollow night amid,
> Then on my tongue the taste is sour
> Of all I ever did.'[1]

Vanished symptoms of health: early rising, early shaving, briskness in
lavatory and bath, alacrity in crossing the street, care for personal appearance,
horror of possessions, indifference to the newspaper, kindness to strangers,
Folie des Maures.

7 August: the first autumn day. For once I have lived in the present!
Walked to the book-shop at closing time. Raining. A girl tried to get into
the shop but the doors were bolted. Went out and followed her past the
Zwemmer Gallery and through the streets towards St. Giles's, only to lose
her by the Cambridge Theatre, cursing the upbringing which has left me
after all these years unable to address a stranger. Much disturbed by the
incident, for this girl, with her high forehead, pointed nose, full lips and fine
eyes, her dark hair and her unhappy and sullen expression, personified both
intelligence and beauty in distress. She was bare-legged and wore sandals, a
green corduroy suit under a linen coat. With a feeling of intolerable frustration I watched her out of sight: 'o toi que j'eusse aimée'.

From my violent reaction to this encounter I was able to learn a little more
about the nature of my emotions.

[1] Stanza dreamt by Professor Housman.

I. To fall in love at first sight there has to be what Sainte-Beuve called '*le mystère*'. In my case the mystery must take the form of a rejection of the industrial system and of the twentieth century. It is an aloofness, a suggestion of the primitive that I crave. Hence the appeal of sandals, which alone permit human beings to hold themselves naturally. This air of aloofness is incompatible with happiness since it springs from a feeling of isolation, a sense of rebellion and hostility towards society which cannot in these days make for contentment. Indeed, I think that women, when they achieve domestic happiness at the price of independence, forfeit most of their appeal.

II. This primitive and untamed expression is not enough; it must be illuminated by an interest in the arts, especially in modern painting and surrealism. The gipsy-look must correspond to the chaos of our time, to the spiritual wilderness of modern art. This taste is shared, I believe, by others who have made their peace with society. We are captivated by the feminine shadow of the self we might have been; in my case by that counterpart of the romantic writer who should have had the courage to reject society and to accept poverty for the sake of the development of his true personality. Now when I see such things I hope that I can somehow be free from my shortcomings by union with them. Hence the recurrent longing to forsake external reality for a dream and to plunge into a ritual flight.

Some fall in love with women who are rich, aristocratic or stupid. I am attracted by those who mysteriously hold out a promise of the integrity which I have lost; unsubdued daughters of Isis, beautiful as night, tumultuous as the moon-stirred Atlantic.[1]

III. Recognition takes place at the turn of the year and must be followed at once by the ritual flight and consummation in a cave.

To banish the rainy evening, the dripping plane-trees, the depression of Fitzroy Square and Charlotte Street and the afternoon's disappointment, I asked some friends round to drink a bottle of rum. Since old friends are almost indistinguishable from enemies, we talked about each other's vices. One said the vice of Palinurus was inconstancy. But is it not rather constancy? Fidelity to the experience of abandoning all the world for a new face with an invitation to ecstasy? Or is it that but one more autumn ruse for self-destruction?

> 'Shall I believe the *Syren* South again
> And, oft-betray'd, not know the Monster Main?'

[1] Isis was represented as the moon rising from the sea: 'ista luce feminea collustrans cuncta moenia et udis ignibus nutriens laeta semina.—APULEIUS. MET. XI. [With her feminine light sharply bringing out the city walls, and with her damp fires nourishing the happy seed]

PART III

LA CLÉ DES CHANTS

ILLUMINATION: 'La mélancolie elle-même n'est qu'un souvenir qui s'ignore.'—FLAUBERT.

The Sun warms out old memories, the Mist exhumes others, as they intensify the fragrance of trees or the smell of ferns.

First faint impression of urban autumn. There are memories which are brought into play by certain sounds, smells or changes in temperature; like those tunes which recur in the mind at a given time of year. With the sweeping up of the dead leaves in the square, the first misty morning, the first yellowing of the planes, I remember Paris and the old excitement of looking for autumn lodgings in an hotel. Streets round the Rue de l'Université, Rue Jacob, Rue de Bourgogne and Rue de Beaune, with their hotel signs and hall-ways where the concierge sits walled in by steamer trunks. A stuffy salon full of novels by Edith Wharton, the purple wall-paper which we will grow to hate as we lie in bed with grippe, the chintz screen round the bidet, the tall grey panelling with a cupboard four inches deep. . . .

Hôtel de l'Université for American college girls, Hôtel de Londres with a chestnut tree in the courtyard, Hôtel Jacob for wasting much time; Hôtel de Savoie, Hôtel Delambre, Hôtel de la Louisiane; central-heated Stations of the Cross: names that stir the lees within me.

For an angora pullover, for a red scarf, for a beret and some brown shoes I am bleeding to death; my heart is dry as a kidney.

Peeling off the kilometres to the tune of 'Blue Skies', sizzling down the long black liquid reaches of Nationale Sept, the plane trees going sha-sha-sha through the open window, the windscreen yellowing with crushed midges, she with the Michelin beside me, a handkerchief binding her hair. . . .

'Le cœur a ses raisons',—and so have rheumatism and 'flu. The sole of the foot, the nape of the neck still recollect the embrace of the Mediterranean— pale water streaked with sapphirine sea-shadow, translucent under the Esterel.

Paris afternoons; the quiet of hotel bedroom and of empty lounge; the bed covered with clothes and magazines, the *Chicago Tribune*, the *Crapouillot*, the *Semaine à Paris*; programmes of the Pagoda Cinema, The Ursulines, Studio

Vingt-huit; faraway cries of 'voici l'Intran' answered by the honking of horns. . . .

Early morning on the Mediterranean: bright air resinous with Aleppo pine, water spraying over the gleaming tarmac of the Route Nationale and darkly reflecting the spring-summer green of the planes; swifts wheeling round the oleander, waiters unpiling the wicker chairs and scrubbing the café tables; armfuls of carnation on the flower-stall, pyramids of lemon and aubergine, rascasses on the fishmonger's slab goggling among the wine-dark urchins; smell of brioches from the bakers, sound of reed curtains jingling in the barber shop, clang of the tin kiosk opening for Le Petit Var. Our rope-soles warm up on the cobbles by the harbour where the Jean d'Agrève prepares for a trip to the Islands and the Annamese boy scrubs her brass. Now cooks from many yachts step ashore with their market-baskets, one-eyed cats scrounge among the fish-heads, while the hot sun refracts the dancing sea-glitter on the café awning, until the sea becomes a green gin-fizz of stillness in whose depth a quiver of sprats charges and counter-charges in the pleasure of fishes.

Dead leaves, coffee grounds, grenadine, tabac Maryland, mental expectation, —perfumes of the Nord-Sud; autumn arrival at Pigalle or the sortie from Notre-Dame-des-Champs into the lights of Montparnasse where the chestnuts, glowing red by the métro entrance, live in a warmer climate than their fellows. . . .

Our memories are card-indexes consulted and then returned in disorder by authorities whom we do not control.

Back-streets of Cannes; tuberoses in the window, the book-shop over the railway bridge which we comb for memoirs and detective stories while the cushions of the car deflate in the afternoon sun. Petit Marseillais. Eclaireur de Nice: head-lines about the Spanish war soaked in sun-bathing oil, torn maps, the wet bathing-dress wrapped in a towel,—and now we bring home memoirs, detective stories, tuberoses, round the dangerous corner of the Rue d'Antibes and along the road by the milky evening sea.

The boredom of Sunday afternoon, which drove de Quincey to smoke opium, also gave birth to surrealism: hours propitious for making bombs.

15 August: Wet Sunday recalling many others. 'Fantômes de Trouville', 'Sea-scape with frieze of girls'.

Beaches of the West: Houlgate, Royan, Saint-Jean-de-Luz. A red digue, colour of porphyry. In the shops hang buckets, toy yachts, shrimping-nets and string-bags enclosing rubber balls with a dull bloom, of the same porphyry colour. Children in the shop are choosing their sandals and gym-shoes, girls are walking arm-in-arm along the promenade; the west wind from the sea spatters the jetty; old bills of casino galas with their faded 'Attractions' roll flapping among the tamarisks. Prowling from the Marquise de Sévigné tea room to the Potinière bar, dark and smelling of gin, we lie in wait for one more glimpse of the sea-side girls in their impregnable adolescence—before the Atlantic sun fades angrily over enormous sands, coloured like the under-belly of soles.

Saint-Jean-de-Luz. Buying a melon in the morning market and eating it for breakfast in a café on the Bidassoa; pursuing a macintosh, a beret and a strand of wet curls round the sea-wall in the rain. Maize and pimento, light-footed Basques with round lean faces dancing Fandango and Arin-Arin, playing pelota against the church wall while a huge green sunset agonizes through plate-glass windows. Angoisse des digues. . . .

Hemingway is great in that alone of living writers he has saturated his work with the memory of physical pleasure, with sunshine and salt water, with food, wine and making love and the remorse which is the shadow of that sun.

30 August: Morning tears return; spirits at their lowest ebb. Approaching forty, sense of total failure: not a writer but a ham actor whose performance is clotted with egotism; dust and ashes; 'brilliant',—that is, not worth doing. Never will I make that extra effort to live according to reality which alone makes good writing possible: hence the manic-depressiveness of my style,—which is either bright, cruel and superficial; or pessimistic; moth-eaten with self-pity.

Everything I have written seems to date except the last lines I set down. These appear quite different, absolute exceptions to the law—and yet what dates in them does not vary but remains the same—a kind of auto-intoxication which is brought out by the act of writing.

Approaching forty, I am about to heave my carcass of vanity, boredom, guilt and remorse into another decade.

> Lusisti satis, edisti satis, atque bibisti[1]
> Tempus abire tibi est.

Both my happiness and unhappiness I owe to the love of pleasure; of sex, travel, reading, conversation (hearing oneself talk), food, drink, cigars and lying in warm water.

Reality is what remains when these pleasures, together with hope for the

[1] You have played enough, you have eaten and drunk enough. It's time you went home.' —HORACE.

future, regret for the past, vanity of the present, and all that composes the aroma of the self are pumped out of the air-bubble in which I shelter.

When we have ceased to love the stench of the human animal, either in others or in ourselves, then are we condemned to misery, and clear thinking can begin. 'Le seule réalité, c'est le souci (*sorge*) dans toute l'échelle des êtres. Pour l'homme perdu dans le monde et ses divertissements, ce souci est une peur brève et fuyante. Mais que cette peur prenne conscience d'elle-même et elle devient l'angoisse (*angst*), climat perpetuel de l'homme lucide "dans lequel existence se retrouve".'—HEIDEGGER.

O, qu'elle est belle l'étoile de mer! The starfish sprawling on an Atlantic beach streaked with shallow pools; ridges of mackerel sand taut under the bare foot; the sun on the split water-beads which mark the tide by streamers of bladder-wrack and melting jelly-fish; all these will return and the leisure to enjoy them, to paddle under a razor-shell sky among rocks where the transparent prawn leans up against the weed like an old man reading in a public library, feathering with his legs and feelers and rocketing backwards with a flick of the tail. And there will be time to observe the blenny where it lies half out of the water, the hermit-crab and anemone, the pin-pointed urchin, the sea-slug on her green sea-salad, the swaying zoster.

> O litus vita mihi dulcius, O mare! felix[1]
> qui licet ad terras ire subinde meas!

Midnight harbours of France, O rain-swept lights on the quay!

Approaching forty, a singular dream in which I almost grasped the meaning and understood the nature of what it is that wastes in wasted time.

Present pleasure kills time, it is like sleep, a harmless anæsthetic: harmless when once we have recognized that our life is so painful as to need what otherwise would distil both guilt and remorse. If, however, we understand that the love of pleasure can be increased or decreased according to need, then as the pleasure fades into the past it will leave behind only a sense of nostalgia and this nostalgia can be converted into art, and, once so converted, all trace of guilt is washed away.

Art is memory: memory is re-enacted desire.

The body remembers pleasure past and on being made aware of it, floods the mind with sweetness. Thus the smell of sun-warmed pine-needles and the bloom on ripe whortle-berries re-open the file marked Kitzbühel and bring

---

[1] O sea shore sweeter to me than life, O sea, happy am I who may come at last to go to my own lands.—PETRONIUS.

back the lake with its muddy water, raft conversations and pink water-lilies; the drive over the white Alpine road through the black fir-wood or the walk over the meadow where runnels of water sing in wooden troughs beside the châlets. Remembering all this communicates several varieties of pleasure; those which, like lying in a thick peat-bath on a rainy evening, are purely sensual, which are social like playing bridge in the afternoon or intellectual like talking to Pierre; pleasures of vanity like flirting in the Tiefenbrünner or buying local jackets and *lederhosen*,—and ever present, as the bald peak of the Kitzbühlerhorn, the unpunished delights of health; of mountain air, good food and natural living. The Wooden Age, where bed and wall and door and house are made of pine-logs, where night is always cold, morning loud with rivers and cow-bells and existence balsam-sharp.

To-day my deepest wish is to go to sleep for six months, if not for ever; it is an admission that life has become almost unendurable and that I must look to pleasure as a waking substitute for sleep. We cannot sleep twenty-four hours a day but we can at least make sleep and pleasure alternate, if once we will admit that, like deep narcotic treatment for nervous breakdown, they are remedies for the very sick. Reality, union with reality, is the true state of the soul when confident and healthy. Thus when Pope wrote:

'So slow the unprofitable Moments roll
    That lock up all the Functions of my soul;
        That keep me from Myself;'

he stated a profound truth. Unreality is what keeps us from ourselves and most pleasure is unreal.

In that dream of approaching forty I felt that I was about to die and became aware that I was no longer myself, but a creature inhabited entirely by para-sites, a caterpillar infested by grubs of the ichneumon fly. Gin, whisky, sloth, fear, guilt, tobacco, had been appointed my inquilines; alcohol sloshed about within, while tendrils of melon and vine spread out from ear and nostril. My mind was a worn gramophone record, my true self was such a shadow as to seem non-existent and all this had taken place in the last three years.

Approaching forty. A glimpse of wisdom. 'Live in the present, Palinurus; you are too unbalanced to brood upon the past. One day you will remember nothing but its essence; now you must expel it from your mind.'

'The twelvemonth and a day being up,
    The dead began to speak:

"Oh who sits weeping on my grave,
  And will not let me sleep?"—

' "'Tis I, my love, sits on your grave,
    And will not let you sleep;
  For I crave one kiss of your clay-cold lips,
    And that is all I seek."—

' "You crave one kiss of my clay-cold lips;
    But my breath smells earthy strong;
  If you have one kiss of my clay-cold lips,
    Your time will not be long.

' "'Tis down in yonder garden green,
    Love, where we used to walk,
  The finest flower that ere was seen
    Is wither'd to a stalk.

' "The stalk is wither'd dry, my love
    So will our hearts decay;
  So make yourself content, my love,
    Till God calls you away." '[1]

Paris afternoons: The book-stall on the quai with old prints that nobody wants, naughty novels corseted in cellophane; the animal shop on the Quai de Gesvres; ferrets, squirming and clucking in the straw, with red eyes and little yawns which reveal their fine white teeth; marmosets chattering over their stump of rotten banana, moulting parrots; the mysterious ailing nocturnal creature that I was always tempted to buy—'c'est un binturong, monsieur'—and then the walk back over the bridge; poplar leaves eddying in the yellow river; misty black-and-grey streets of the Left Bank; discreet shops full of *bibelots*, bad modern paintings, Empire clocks.

Disorder of the hotel bedroom; books, drawings, clothes and red plush; shadows lengthening, the desirable afternoon sleep with its bewildering nightmare-starts and awakenings, its flash-backs to the past. Then the purple neon sign shining in at the window and the concierge on the telephone: 'Il y a quelqu'en en bas qui vous demande'. 'Voulez-vous lui dire de monter.'

In youth the animal world obsessed me; I saw life through creatures which were in a state of grace, creatures without remorse, without duties, without a past or a future owning nothing but the intense present and their eternal rhythm of hunger, sleep and play. The ring-tailed lemurs with their reverence for the sun, their leaps through the air and their howls of loneliness, were dark Immortals of a primitive race; the ferrets with their passionate

[1] *Oxford Book of Ballads*: 'The Unquiet Grave.'

blood-thirst and their tunnelling mania; the beautiful mute genette, the pine-marten, the racoons, the pitiful coati, the dying ocelot, the slow loris,—even the animals which I never owned, the beaver, otter, palm-civet and linsang,—these bright-fanged, saffron-throated aristocrats held the secret of life for me; they were clues to an existence without thought, guilt or ugliness wherein all was grace, appetite and immediate sensation: Impressionist masterpieces which Nature flung upon the canvas of a day.

Now I care only for the Vegetable world; my day-dreams are no longer of otter-pool and sunny lemurarium, but of slobbering melon, downy quince and dew-dusted nectarine. I feel fruit trees to be an even stranger form of life and therefore more rewarding. Nothing is so alien, so unexpected in a tree as its fruit and yet by the fruit it is known; leaves, height and blossom are sacrificed; so by thinking, reading and maintaining an inner calm we too mature and ripen until the life which once flowered in such careless profusion is concentrated into husks, husks, that, like pomegranates or the tomato on our window-sill, continue to mellow long after the leaf has fallen and the plant that bore them rotted to the ground.

'Good is the passive that obeys reason. Evil is the active springing from energy.'—BLAKE. It is more important, in fact, to be good than to do good because being, rather than doing, is the state which keeps us in tune with the order of things. Hence Pascal's reflection that all the evil of the world comes from men not being able to sit quietly in a room. Good is the retention of energy; evil a waste of it, energy which is taken away from growth. Like water, we are truest to our nature in repose.

'Tao is in the emptiness. Emptiness is the fast of the mind.'—CHUANG-TZU.

MASTERPLAY

Three thoughts from Eliot:

'Someone said: "The dead writers are remote from us because we *know* so much more than they did." Precisely, and they are that which we know.'

'What is to be insisted upon is that the poet must develop or procure the consciousness of the past and that he should continue to develop this consciousness throughout his career. What happens is a continual surrender of himself as he is at the moment to some thing which is more valuable. The progress of an artist is a continual self-sacrifice, a continual extinction of personality.'

'The more perfect the artist, the more completely separate in him will be the man who suffers and the mind which creates.'

The supreme liberty is liberty from the body, the last freedom is freedom from time; the true work of art the one which the seventh wave of genius throws far up the beach where the under-tow of time cannot drag it back. When all the motives that lead artists to create have fallen away, and the satisfactions of vanity and the play-instinct been exhausted, there remains the desire to construct that which has its own order, as a protest against the chaos to which all else appears condemned. While thought exists, words are alive and literature becomes an escape, not from, but into living.

Works of art which survive must all be indebted to the spirit of their age. Thus though Virgil and Horace copied Greek models, they imitated them at a time when the flowering of Roman civilization demanded just such a refinement, a taking over of the trusteeship of the past by the swelling Latin genius. In that sense every writer refashions the literature of the past and produces his tiny commentary, nothing is ever quite new; but there comes a moment when a whole culture ripens and prepares to make its own version of the great art of its predecessors.

The masterpieces appropriate to our time are in the style of the early Chirico, the later Rouault and Picasso's Guernica; sombre, magnificent yet personal statements of our tragedy; work of strong and noble architecture austerely coloured by loneliness and despair. Flaubert spoke true: to succeed a great artist must have both character and fanaticism and few in this country are willing to pay the price. Our writers have either no personality and therefore no style or a false personality and therefore a bad style; they mistake prejudice for energy and accept the sensation of material well-being as a system of thought.

The English language is like a broad river on whose bank a few patient anglers are sitting, while, higher up, the stream is being polluted by a string of refuse-barges tipping out their muck. The English language has, in fact, so contracted to our own littleness that it is no longer possible to make a good book out of words alone. A writer must concentrate on his vocabulary but must also depend on the order, the timing and spacing of his words, and try to arrange them in a form which is seemingly artless, yet perfectly proportioned. He must let a hiatus suggest that which the language will no longer accomplish. Words to-day are like the shells and rope of seaweed which a child brings home glistening from the beach and which in an hour have lost their lustre.

It is right proportion combined with simplicity of expression and seriousness of thought that enables a book to stand the test of time. To construct from the mind and to colour with the imagination a work which the judgment of unborn arbiters will consider perfect is the one immortality of which we can be sure. When we read the books of a favourite writer together with all that has been written about him, then his personality will take shape and leave his work to materialize through our own. The page will liberate its author; he will rise from the dead and become our friend. So is it with Horace, Montaigne, Sainte-Beuve, with Flaubert and Henry James: they survive in us, as we increase through them.

But these intimacies can be dangerous. For there are writers who lay siege to our personality, then storm the feeble garrison and occupy the citadel. Thus Flaubert, who appears at first our ally becomes, as we venture further into his work, the terrible Christos Pantocrator of our age with Sainte-Beuve his John the Baptist and George Sand his Magdalene. We relive his Passion with him, his Temptation, his Agony at Croisset, his Betrayal and Crucifixion by the Bourgeois; his letters become the Sermon on the Mount— 'Tout est là; l'amour de l'Art'—and so we falter and faint and deny him thrice, in the Press, in the Ministry or on the Air,—until he rises before us in cold Norman wrath to pronounce 'Justice not mercy!' 'Un homme qui s'est institué artiste n'a plus le droit de vivre comme les autres.'

Flaubert on the Masterpiece

'Je me demande si un livre, indépendamment de ce qu'il dit, ne peut pas produire le même effet? (as the base of the Parthenon). Dans la précision des assemblages, la rareté des éléments, le poli de la surface, l'harmonie de l'ensemble, n'y a-t-il pas une vertu intrinsèque, une espèce de force divine, quelque chose d'éternel comme un principe? (Je parle en platonicien.) Ainsi pourquoi y a-t-il un rapport nécessaire entre le mot juste et le mot musical? Pourquoi arrive-t-on toujours à faire un vers quand on resserre trop sa pensée? La loi des nombres gouverne donc les sentiments et les images, et ce qui paraît être l'extérieur est tout bonnement le dedans?'

10 September: Full autumn magnificence; the green and gold streamers of the plane-tree waving transparently against the high sunlit sky. Birthday resolution: From now on specialize; never again make any concession to the ninety-nine parts of you which are like everybody else at the expense of the one which is unique. Never listen to the False Self talking.

'Le néant d'avoir quarante ans.'

15 September: Entrée des coings.

Pomifer autumnus fruges effuderit, et mox
Bruma recurrit iners.[1]

[1] Horace Odes, Book IV: 'Autumn, bringer of fruit, has poured out her riches, and soon sluggish winter returns.'

ENEMIES OF ANGST

Flight to the country: the morning awakening of a house, noise of women in a courtyard, the chickens, ducks, geese and dogs being let out; the parrot stropping its beak on the bars of the cage; the smell of breakfast, the gardener bringing in tomatoes and lettuces; Sunday papers, taps running; and the drone of fighter-squadrons overhead. Lunch out of doors.

The afternoon nap, so rich in disturbances of memory; the bath in the fading daylight with hot-water pipes rumbling and shrieks of children going to bed, while the cold elmy sunshine westers over liquid fields. The sharp bed-time sortie into the night air.

It is only in the country that we can get to know a fellow-being or a book.

The mill where I sometimes stay provides another cure for Angst; the red lane through the Spanish chestnut wood, the apple trees on the lawn, the bees in the roof, the geese on the pond, the black sun-lit marsh marigolds, the wood-fire crackling in the low bedroom, the creak of the cellar-door and the recurrent monotonies of the silver-whispering weir,—what could be more womb-like or reassuring? Yet always the anxious owner is flying from it as from the scene of a crime.

Romantic surrealism and classical humanism, however antagonistic, are akin; they breed each other and the artist must contrive a synthesis. Blake and Pope or Flaubert and his mad 'Garçon' are complementary. The classical humanist is the parent, the surrealist the rebellious adolescent. Both are mother-fixed; only 'Social Realism' lies outside the family.

Surrealist and humanist differ as to what proportion of 'strangeness' (*le merveilleux*) is necessary as an ingredient of beauty and what proportion of violence is best suited to creative emotion.

Surrealism, the last international movement in the arts, is now in its decadence. Why? Because it borrowed the Communist idea of a small iron-disciplined élite without the appeal to the masses by which such discipline tries to justify itself. An æsthetic movement with a revolutionary dynamism and no popular appeal should proceed quite otherwise than by public scandal, publicity stunt, noisy expulsion and excommunication.

For twenty years political mass-movements have absorbed the mounting sap of humanity. Surrealism, like its rival, classical humanism, is too romantic and too anti-industrial for the times. Our world has no use for liberal father or rebellious anarchist son. *Le merveilleux*, with the Sublime of the Humanists, belongs to the nineteenth-century past.

This is a pity, for as time goes on we see how Surrealism was revolutionary not only in the sense that all could take it home and practise there but as the last convulsion necessary to complete the French artistic-cycle, to tie the strands of classicism and romanticism, reason and imagination into a final knot, and so restore the clear head to the rebel heart.

Classical and romantic: private language of a family quarrel, a dead dispute over the distribution of emphasis between man and nature.

Abstract art denies both man and nature and thrives on the machine age; Naturalism refuses man all place while in Social Realism he dominates the picture.

Beware nevertheless of false dualities: classical and romantic, real and ideal, reason and instinct, mind and matter, male and female,—all should be merged into each other (as the Taoists merged their Yin and Yang into the Tao) and should be regarded as two aspects of one idea. Dualities which are defined at the same moment (stoic and epicurean, Whig and Tory) become united by the historical process, and end by having more, not less, in common. In a hundred years Science and Ethics (power and love), the present-day duality, may seem as dead as the iota controversy, together with good and evil, free will and determinism, even space and time. Ideas which have for long divided individuals will become meaningless in the light of the forces that will separate groups.

Yet ridiculous as may seem the dualities in conflict at a given time, it does not follow that dualism is a worthless process. The river of truth is always splitting up into arms that reunite. Islanded between them the inhabitants argue for a lifetime as to which is the main-stream.

EARTH-LOVES OF THE EARTH BOUND: ENNOIA

Three or four people whom I have loved seem utterly set apart from all the rest; angelic, ageless creatures more alive than the living, embalmed perpetually in their all-devouring myth.

Ile de Gavrinis: Montagne de la Margeride: Auberge de Peyrebeilhe. 'Mar of murmury mermers in the mind . . .'

Clumps of rushes, brackish water, marram-grass, sea-thistles, *flore des dunes*, —Ile de Gavrinis over the green and violet ocean of the Morbihan. The dinghy grounds on white sand printed with the tails of lizards, the ancient lime avenue leads up to the lonely farm where a path winds among gorse and asphodel to the Presence of the Dead. There, in his Tumulus, lies the last Celtic prince, wrapped in his race's age-long death-wish; his great vault-stone carved with indecipherable warnings; runes of serpents and oak-leaves, of wave-eddies and wind-patterns, finger prints of giant hands,—O powerless to save! And that night in Vannes, the cave-wedding—*Summoque ulularunt vertice Nymphæ.*[1] She with sad grave gem-like beauty and happiness soon to be thrown away.

Leaving Bellac after crossing for two days the plains of the sandy Loire, we enter the Bocage Limousin, traverse a country of tall tree-hedges blueing into the pale spring sky and reach the first hills, the Blond mountains, forest beginnings of the Châtaigneraie. A new strip of maps and the sun always warmer; mountain nights in stone buildings, melted snow in the running water, darker wine in the inns, deeper beds. Rivers tumbling through towns; rain-drenched chestnuts green in the swinging lights of Tulle; Mauriac, Sainte-Flour, Saint-Chély-d'Apcher; snow-driven moorlands of the Margeride, pine-forests of Velay and Vivarais; cloud-shadows over the Gerbier de Jonc. There on the edge of the tableland stands the haunted Auberge de Peyrebeilhe, (where once so few came out who went in.)[2] But now the low room with blackened ceiling has grown less dangerous to lovers than the almond-blossom airs of the warm Ardéche, than the limestone chasm leading down to civilization where the Furies are awaiting Ennoia and happiness is thrown away.

'Courage is not simply *one* of the virtues but the form of every virtue at the testing point, which means at the point of highest reality.'—C. S. LEWIS

Cowardice in living: without health and courage we cannot face the present or the germ of the future in the present and take refuge in evasion. Evasion through comfort, society, through acquisitiveness, through the book-bed-bath defence system, above all through the flight to the romantic womb of history, into primitive myth-making. The refusal to include the great mass-movements of the twentieth century in our art or our myth will drive us to take refuge in the past; in surrealism, magic, primitive religion or eighteenth-century wonderlands. We fly to Mediterranean womb-pockets and dream-islands, into dead controversy and ancient hermetic bric-à-brac, like a child who sits hugging his toys and who screams with rage when told to put on his boots.

Realities of our time.

> History constructed out of global blocks.
> The Decline of Europe.
> Anglo-American rivalry and imperialism.
> Russian Managerial imperialism.

---

[1] The nymphs wailed from the top of the hill. (An air-raid warning.)
[2] The innkeeper and his coloured wife used to murder their guests.

Chinese or Japanese imperialism.

English National Suburbanism.

The Great American Vacuum.

Massacres and atrocities, poverty, famine.

'Well, which side are you on? The Corn-Goddess or the Tractor? The Womb or the Bulldozer? Christ, Freud, Buddha, Baudelaire, Bakunin, or Marx, Watson, Pavlov, Stalin, Shaw? Come clean, moody Palinurus, no synthesis this time and no Magic Circle either? We need men like you in the Group Age. Will you take your turn at the helm as you used to? Remember?

> Princeps gubernator densum Palinurus agebat
> Agmen?[1]

or do you prefer to daydream in the lavatory, *petit coin sombre* of the Bourgeois Formalist, while a new world is being born?

How do you react to our slogan 'Total Everybody Always?' Have you at last understood that your miserable failure as an individual is proof that you pursue a lost cause? Man invents God when he loses his Party Card. He is neither angel, nor beast, nor as you with your mystique of sloth would make him even a vegetable, but a social unit, a cell, and as such will find fulfilment only through participation in the communal life of an organized group.'

Answer: 'In my beginning is my end.' As the acorn contains the oak or the folded kernel of the Spanish chestnut implies the great whorled bole and serrated leaf of the full-grown tree, so each human being possesses a form appropriate to him which time will educate and ripen. 'Tout est dans la semence': the acorns will not make a hedge nor the chestnuts an avenue; we are born with certain shapes ahead of us, certain ideas to fulfil; to seek unity or bring out diversity; to attack tradition or perpetuate lost causes; to build the future or to exhume our spiritual ancestors, and derive hope and inspiration from them; to discover certain places, to love and lose certain faces or to develop an immediate antipathy to others. If I had been a true product of the age your question could never have arisen. My role is not of the future but, like Eliot's poet, 'to live in what is not merely the present, but the present moment of the past'. I believe that a conscious affinity with Nature forms the shield of Perseus through which man can affront the Gorgon of his fate and that, in the termitaries of the future where humanity cements itself up from the light of the sun, this dragon-slaying mirror will rust and tarnish. So I have nothing to say to the masses or to the machines, to bosses

[1] 'Ahead of all the Master Pilot steer'd.'

or bureaucrats, States or statistics, Nations or Parties. I am but a link in the chain of individual heretics and failures, a woodwind solo in the interminable symphony, drowned at once by the brass and percussion but necessary to the composer's score. An interpreter between intellect and imagination, between reason and the physical world, I tend the graves,—*sapientum templa serena*— of Horace and Tibullus, of Pythagoras and Aristippus, of Montaigne and Lao-Tsu; I speak the language of animals and enjoy the confidence of the vegetable powers.

And I answer a seven-fold 'No' to your question: A physiological no, because I am not a cell, but myself. A biological no, because a specialized mutation from the norm indicates the richness and vitality of the species. A sociological no, because those who lack the herd-instinct are generally in advance of the herd which is conservative, stupid, intolerant and bourgeois. A psychological no, because those who have been all their lives used to intellectual isolation are the ones best fitted to remain isolated; they grow adjusted to their mal-adjustment. A political no, for England will remain the smallest of the great powers and so must depend for her survival on qualitative standards. An æsthetic no, because the practice of literature is still best carried through the individual unit. An ethical no, because I do not 'find fulfilment through participation in the communal life of an organized group',—that is tyranny,—but in the pursuit of art and knowledge and by communion with the Bourgeois Formalism of Nature. To sum up: I agree with Flaubert, 'A mesure que l'humanité se perfectionne, l'homme se dégrade.'

October, Quince days. Io Lemuria![1]

Departure of my tormentors. Philosophic calm, soaring Hope, manic exaltation, mysterious freedom from Angst. Dare I suppose that a cure has been accomplished, the bones of Palinurus buried and his ghost laid? For once it seems that the past has fallen away like the mantle of snow from a creaking fir-tree.

> 'As for the Dog, the Furies and their Snakes
> The gloomy Caverns or the burning Lakes
> And all the vain infernal trumpery
> They neither are, nor were, nor e'er can be.'

There is no hate without fear. Hate is crystallized fear, fear's dividend, fear objectivized. We hate what we fear and so where hate is, fear will be lurking.

[1] Roman festival designed to propitiate the Lemures or wandering evil spirits of the dead. Once a year as on our All Souls Eve, they hungrily revisit their loved ones. Broad Beans (a most suggestive vegetable) were thrown to them as an appeasement offering after which they were requested to leave. 'Manes exite Paterni!' Ovid. Fasti, Bk. v.

Thus we hate what threatens our person, our liberty, our privacy, our income, our popularity, our vanity and our dreams and plans for ourselves. If we can isolate this element in what we hate we may be able to cease from hating. Analyse in this way the hatred of ideas or of the kind of people whom we have once loved and whose faces are preserved in Spirits of Anger. Hate is the consequence of fear; we fear something before we hate; the child who fears noises becomes the man who hates them.

'Whatever you blame, that you have done yourself.'—GRODDECK.

Dark saying of La Rochefoucauld: 'Le seul honnête homme est celui qui ne se pique de rien'.

'Ce serait avoir gagné beaucoup dans la vie que de savoir rester toujours parfaitement naturel et sincère avec soi-même, de ne croire aimer que ce qu'on aime véritablement, et de ne pas prolonger par amour-propre et par émulation vaine des passions déjà expirées.'—SAINTE-BEUVE.

FAREWELL TO SAINTE-BEUVE

'Le souvenir est comme une plante qu'il faut avoir plantée de bonne heure ensemble; sans quoi elle ne s'enracine pas.'

'Les lieux les plus vantés de la terre sont tristes et désenchantés lorsqu'on n'y porte plus ses espérances.'

'Quelle que soit la diversité des points de départ les esprits des capables de mûrir arrivent, plus qu'on ne croit, aux mêmes résultats; combien de gens meurent avant d'avoir fait le tour d'eux-mêmes.'

'Je ne suis complètement moi que plume en main et dans le silence du cabinet.'

A child, left to play alone, says of quite an easy thing, 'Now I am going to do something very difficult'. Soon, out of vanity, fear and emptiness, he builds up a world of custom, convention and myth in which everything must be just so; certain doors are one-way streets, certain trees sacred, certain paths taboo. Then along comes a grown-up or a more robust child; they kick over the imaginary wall, climb the forbidden tree, regard the difficult as easy and the private world is destroyed. The instinct to create myth, to colonize reality with the emotions, remains. The myths become tyrannies until they are swept away, when we invent new tyrannies to hide our suddenly perceived nakedness. Like caddis-worms or like those crabs which dress themselves with seaweed, we wear belief and custom.

Taoists believe that devotion to anything except Nature ages them and therefore live simply on hill-sides or near forests, like the sage whose wants were so few that when he decided to leave his cottage he found the brambles round it had grown too high for him to pass. But what becomes of loving Nature if Nature does not want us? Let us go for a walk on the moors; at first the high pure air, the solitude under the hot sun where the burns splash and the grouse shrieks, purge us of our city poison until art and civilization seem oppressive and vulgar, rainbow hues on the dying mullet, occupations which cut man off from his primitive vegetation-cult. Then as the day gets hotter and we stumble on over scruffy heather and bubbling bog there is a change; Nature would seem not to share in our communion and to prefer her own backward progeny; the grouse's cackle, raven, falcon, mountain hare, the noisy burn, the whole hill-side in the hot afternoon become ominous and hostile—archaic emblems of Ennui—something we have long grown out of. Once more the craving revives for architecture, art and the intellect. By the evening it is raining and, after the visit to our great, gross, unappreciative Mother, we are glad to be back with our books and fire-side conversation. It is to Civilization, not to Nature that man must return.

The Vegetable Conspiracy: Man is now on his guard against insect parasites; against liver-flukes, termites, Colorado beetles, but has he given thought to the possibility that he has been selected as the target of vegetable attack, marked down by the vine, hop, juniper, the tobacco plant, tea-leaf and coffee-berry for destruction? What willing converts these Jesuits of the gastric juices make,—and how cleverly they retain them! Does a smoker consider the menace of the weed spreading in his garden, will a drunkard read the warning of the ivy round the oak? What populations fear the seed-strangling rubber or have recorded the increasing mortality caused by punctures from the rose? And what of gold, that slow mineral poison?

Money talks through the rich as alcohol swaggers in the drunken, calling softly to itself to unite into the lava flow which petrifies all it touches.

No one would start to play a game without knowing the rules. Yet most of us play the interminable game of life without any because we have no idea what they are. But there are only two possible systems according to whether or not we believe in God. If we believe that the universe is an accident and life an accident contingent on the universe and man an accident contingent on life; then rules are made for men to be happy and it has been found by generations of exponents that happiness consists in fulfilment of the personality—in former days through the family, now by rendering more and more services to a group—in fact through the happiness of the greatest number. This is the game as played by Epicurus, Holbach, Marx, Mill, Bentham, Comte, and William James.

If, however, we believe in God, then our duty is to do His will and not our own and our conception of the rules varies with our conception of His nature. But whatever this conception is we are united in the belief that the success or failure of our life as such cannot be estimated by any utilitarian standard.

Faced, then, with these completely different systems for this all-important game, can we not find out once and for all whether there is a God; whether He had strewn clues over the universe for man to pick up or whether we ourselves have invented Him, as a useful three-letter expression for anything which remains outside our knowledge?

The answer seems to rest with three categories of thinkers; the physicists, who incline to believe in God but are now all busy making explosives; the biologists and chemists who can produce almost everything except life and who, if they could create life, would prove that it might once have arisen accidentally; and the psychologists and physiologists, who are struggling to discover the relation of mind to brain, the nature of consciousness.

A baby, after an exhibition on the pot, with much anger and howling, stretches out her arms with a little cry, as when her pram is passing under trees, to reveal an immense wonder and love for life,—a Soul. I have read that the cuckoo enters the world with two advantages over other birds; a special muscle on its back for throwing them from the nest; and a cry which is irresistible to the foster-parents. This sudden cry of recognition and pleasure is what keeps us all on the go from grab-all to grave. *Volupté*! The eternal cuckoo call.

'O fins d'automne, hivers, printemps trempés de boue, Endormeuses saisons' . . .

Tout mon mal vient de Paris. There befell the original sin and the original ecstasy; there were the holy places—the Cross-Roads and the Island. Quai Bourbon, Rue de Vaugirard, Quai d'Anjou.

Air: *Transfrétons la Sequane*!

'Nous transfrétons le Sequane au dilicule et crepuscule; nous déambulons par les compites et quadriviers de l'urbe, nous déspumons la verbocination latiale'.

Evening in June: walking down the Rue Vavin, past the shop with ivory canes in the window, away from the polyglot bedlam of Montparnasse into the Luxembourg garden where children are playing croquet under the black-trunked chestnuts and wool-green catalpas, then out at the corner where the Rue Servandoni's leaning mansards join the sombre Rue de Vaugirard. On by the book-booths of the Odéon, by the shimmering Fontaine de Medicis and the diners in the open air, then through the broad melancholy twilight of the Rue Soufflot to the cold splendour of the Panthéon, past the blistered shutters of the Hôtel des Grands Hommes. There, behind the church, the Rue de la Montagne Sainte-Geneviève, Via Sacra of the Latin Quarter, winds steeply down the Founder's holy hill.

In the doorways sit families on their wooden chairs, while from the Bal Musette where *Fiesta* began the Java fades on the sultry air; then across the Rue des Ecoles with its groaning trams, and so by the stews and noisy wine-shops of the Place Maubert to meet the Seine at the Quai de la Tournelle.

Quai Bourbon, Miserere. The Ile Saint-Louis strains at her moorings, the river eddies round the stone prow where tall poplars stand like masts, and mist rises about the decaying houses which seventeenth-century nobles raised on their meadows. Yielding asphalt, sliding waters; long windows with iron bars set in damp walls; anguish and fear. Rendez-vous des Mariniers, Hôtel de Lauzun: moment of the night when the saint's blood liquefies, when the leaves shiver and presentiments of loss stir within the dark coil of our fatality.

'Porque sabes que siempre te he querido.'

Quai Bourbon, Quai d'Orléans, Quai d'Anjou.

Then came the days of ferrets with ribs like wish-bones for whom we bought raw liver from the horse-butcher in the Rue de Seine while they tunnelled round the octagonal room in the Hôtel de la Louisiane. They pursued oranges, eggs and ping-pong balls and wore harness with little bells; and from their number came forth a queen, the tawny, docile Norfolk beauty whom we named the English Rose, who performed her cycle of eating, playing, sleeping and relieving herself and who saw three continents from a warm sleeve. She hunted the Rue Monge and the Rue Mouffetard, the courts of the Val de Grace and the gardens of the Observatoire, the Passage des Princes and the Place de Fürstenberg. She searched the Parc Montsouris and the Buttes-Chaumont, the doss-houses of the Rue Quincampoix and the Boulevard de la Chapelle; she visited the tattered buildings in the Rue de la Goutte d'Or and heard the prostitutes calling to each other from their beds in the Rue de la Charbonnière; she explored the gilt, the plush, the columns and flaking ceilings of the Deuxième Arrondissement, the arcades of the Palais-Royal and the Place des Victoires, the corner-houses, razor-sharp, in the Rue de la Lune. She sniffed at all the gates of Paris: Porte Saint-Denis, Porte d'Orléans, Porte des Lilas; pocket gardens of the Gobelin workers along the Bièvre, exposed tendons of the Nord railway by the Boulevard Barbès and warehouses on the Saint-Martin Canal. Yet most she loved, a short walk from her couch of straw, the stony public garden by Saint-Germain-des-Prés.

And many bars where sad-eyed barmen told the seasons by clipping chits for 'grogs-américains' and 'champagne-oranges', and many restaurants, now closed and forgotten, understood her favourite diet of raw egg. The Moine Gourmet, the Restaurant de la Chaise with its Burgundy and Lesbians, Montagné's perfection, Foyot's dying autumnal grandeur, Madame Genot's austere bistro with her home-grown wines. Rosalie's fresh corn, Lafon's pâté, Marius' pellucid Beaujolais,—in all of these she clucked approval.

And many boîtes once made her welcome: the Bateau Ivre in the Place de l'Odéon, the old Bœuf, Melody's and the Grand Ecart, the trellised galleries of the Bal Blomet and the Stygian reaches of the Magic River in Luna-Park. Love came to her in Hampshire and she was covered, and in Toulon gave birth to nine fine youngsters in the hotel bath. She would wash them and clean up their droppings till ambivalence was engendered when, to escape their demands, she would climb on to my lap, looking up at us with pale golden eyes and yawning to show that nothing was changed. Then one day, being hungry, she strayed from the garden and entered a cottage kitchen, where she sat up to beg as we had taught her—until the ignorant peasants kicked her to death and brought back her limp body; filthy-hearted women; 'Oui, monsieur, on a bien vu qu'elle n'a pas voulu mourir.'

It was after the reign of the English Rose that our days were darkened by the graves of the lemurs; on distant shores they lie,—far from Madagascar, yet never far from the rocks where the flowering cistus out-blanches the salt-encrusting spray.

'Living for beauty',—October on the Mediterranean; blue sky scoured by the mistral, red and golden vine branches, wind-fretted waves chopping round the empty yachts; plane-trees peeling; palms rearing up their dingy under-linen; mud in the streets and from doorways at night the smell of burning oil. Through the dark evening I used to bicycle in to fetch our dinner, past the harbour with its bobbing launches and the cafés with their signs banging. At the local restaurant there would be one or two 'plats à emporter', to which I would add some wine, sausage and Gruyère cheese, a couple of 'Diplomates' to smoke and a new 'Detective' or 'Chasseur Français'; then I would bowl back heavy-laden with the mistral behind me, a lemur buttoned up inside my jacket with his head sticking out. Up the steep drive it was easy to be blown off into the rosemary, then dinner would be spoilt. We ate it with our fingers beside the fire,—true beauty lovers,—then plunged into the advertisements in *Country Life*, dreaming of that Priory at Wareham where we would end our days. 'Living for Beauty' entailed a busy life of answering advertisements, writing for prospectuses, for information about cottages in Hampstead, small manors in the West—or else for portable canoes, converted Dutch barges 'that could go through the Canals', second-hand yachts, caravans and cars. Homesick, we liked best the detective stories, because they reeked of whisky, beefsteaks, expresses from Paddington, winter landscapes, old inns and Georgian houses that screen large gardens off the main street of country towns. There live the solicitors and doctors and clever spinsters who brew home-made poison and who come into their own in these exacting tales, there arrive for summer the artist from London and the much-consulted military man. At last we would go to bed, bolting the doors while the lemurs cried in the moonlight, house-ghosts bounding from the mulberries to the palms, from the palms to the tall pines whose cones the dormice nibble from the pines to the roof, and so to our bedroom window where they would press their eager faces to the pane. In the bathroom one of us would be washing while the other crammed fir-cones in the stove. The stove roars, the water is heated and the room fills with steamy fragrance. The two lemurs are admitted and worm their way down to sleep in the bottom of the bed. In the early morning, while we dream of Wareham, they will creep out round our feet, seize the aromatic tooth-paste in their long black gloves, jump through the window and spring with it down to the sunny earth.

When I think of lemurs depression engulfs me 'à peu que le cœur ne me fend'. As W. H. Hudson says, 'they have angel's eyes' and they die of 'flu.

GRAVES OF THE LEMURS

Whoopee. Gentle and fearless, he passed four leafy years in the South of France. He would chase large dogs, advancing backwards and glaring through his hind legs, then jump chittering at them and pull their tails. He died through eating a poisoned fig laid down for rats. The children who saw him take the fruit tried to coax it from him, but he ran up a tree with it. There they watched him eat and die.

Polyp. Most gifted of lemurs, who hated aeroplanes in the sky, on the screen and even on the wireless. How he would have hated this war! He could play in the snow or swim in a river or conduct himself in a nightclub; he judged human beings by their voices; biting some, purring over others, while for one or two well-seasoned old ladies he would brandish a black prickle-studded penis, shaped like an eucalyptus seed. Using his tail as an aerial, he would lollop through long grass to welcome his owners, embracing them with little cries and offering them a lustration from his purple tongue and currycomb teeth. His manners were those of some spoiled young Maharajah, his intelligence not inferior, his heart all delicacy,—women, gin and muscats were his only weaknesses. Alas, he died of pneumonia while we scolded him for coughing, and with him vanished the sea-purple cicada kingdom of calanque and stone-pine and the concept of life as an arrogant private dream shared by two.

.   .   .

As the French soldier said of the Chleuhs in Morocco, 'Je les aime et je les tue'. So it is with the lemurs, black and grey bundles of vitality, eocene ancestors from whom we are all descended, whose sun-greeting call some hold to be the origin of the word 'Ra' and thus of human language,—we have treated these kings in exile as we used Maoris and Marquesas islanders or the whistling Guanches of Teneriffe,—all those golden islandraces, famous for beauty, whom Europe has taken to its shabby heart to exploit and ruin.

To have set foot in Lemuria is to have been close to the mysterious sources of existence, to have known what it is to live wholly in the present, to soar through the green world four yards above the ground, to experience sun, warmth, love and pleasure as intolerably as we glimpse them in a waking dream, and to have heard that heart-rending cry of the lonely or abandoned which goes back to our primaeval dawn. Wild ghost faces from a lost continent who soon will be extinct. . . .

And 'living for beauty': in one lovely place always pining for another; with the perfect woman imagining one more perfect; with a bad book unfinished beginning a second, while the almond tree is in blossom, the grasshopper fat and the winter night disquieted by the plock and gurgle of the sea,—that too would seem extinct for ever.

'Your time is short, watery Palinurus. What do you believe?'

I believe in two-faced truth, in the Either, the Or and the Holy Both. I believe that if a statement is true then its opposite must be true. (Aristotle: "The knowledge of opposites is one.") Thus now (November the eleventh) I am again interested in philosophy, psychology, and religion and am reading about Gnosticism, most exquisite and insidious of heresies and once more find myself among its charms and amulets; its snake-god ABRASAX, and the Gnostic theory that Adam in the Garden of Eden was the babe in the womb fed by four rivers (arteries from the navel), and expelled from his mother into the world at the Fall. This time a year ago I was interested in these same ideas, reading Lao-Tsu with as much passion as I now read Epicurus (and now I find that Lao-Tsu was called "The Chinese Epicurus"), so that it is more true to say that this is the time of year when religions are interested in me. Or is it that in late autumn the season forbids an active existence, and so we are forced back on reading and contemplation, on those schemes of thought which imply a corresponding rejection of the world?

To attain two-faced truth we must be able to resolve all our dualities, simultaneously to perceive life as comedy and tragedy, to see the mental side of the physical and the reverse. We must learn to be at the same time objective and subjective—like Flaubert, who enjoyed what Thibaudet called 'la pleine logique artistique de la vision binoculaire', or with that 'double focus' which Auden beautifully describes in *New Year Letter*.

To-day the function of the artist is to bring imagination to science and science to imagination, where they meet, in the myth.[1]

Now that I seem to have attained a temporary calm, I understand how valuable unhappiness can be; melancholy and remorse form the deep leaden keel which enables us to sail into the wind of reality; we run aground sooner than the flat-bottomed pleasure-lovers but we venture out in weather that would sink them and we choose our direction. What distinguishes true civilization from the mass-fabricated substitutes except that tap-root to the Unconscious, the sense of original sin? What artist-philosopher except Voltaire and Goethe has been without it?

'Voilà ce que tous les socialistes du monde n'ont pas voulu voir avec leur éternelle prédication matérialiste, ils ont nié la *douleur*, ils ont blasphémé les trois quarts de la poésie moderne; le sang du Christ qui se remue en nous, rien ne l'extirpera, rien ne le tarira, il ne s'agit pas de le dessécher, mais de lui faire des ruisseaux. Si le sentiment de l'insuffisance humaine, du néant de la vie, venait à périr (ce qui serait la conséquence de leur hypothèse) nous serions plus bêtes que les oiseaux qui au moins perchent sur les arbres.'— FLAUBERT.

If we apply depth-psychology to our own lives we see how enslaved we remain to the womb and the mother. Womb of Mother Church, of Europe, mother of continents, of horseshoe harbour and valley, of the lap of earth,

---

[1] Gide gives the perfect two-faced myth-truth about religion (*Attendu que . . .* Algiers 1943): 'Il ne peut être question de deux Dieux. Mais je me garde, sous ce nom de Dieu, de confondre deux choses très différentes; différentes jusqu'à s'opposer: D'une part l'ensemble du Cosmos et des lois naturelles qui le régissent; matière et forces, énergies; cela c'est le côté Zeus; et l'on peut bien appeler cela Dieu, mais c'est en enlevant à ce mot toute signification personnelle et morale. D'autre part le faisceau de tous les efforts humains vers le bien, vers le beau, la lente maîtrisation de ces forces brutales et leur mise en service pour réaliser le bien et le beau sur la terre; ceci, c'est le côté Prométhée; et c'est le côté Christ aussi bien; c'est l'épanouissement de l'homme et toutes les vertus y concourent. Mais ce Dieu n'habite nullement la nature; il n'existe que dans l'homme et par l'homme; il est créé par l'homme, ou si vous préférez, c'est à travers l'homme qu'il se crée; et tout effort reste vain, pour l'extérioriser par la prière.'

of the bed, the arm-chair and the bath or of the Court of Charles II, of
Augustan London, or the Rome of Cicero; of the bow-window of the club,
of the house by the lake or water-front sacred to Venus;—all our lives
seeking a womb with a view. Knowing this weakness we can make allowance for it in our thinking, aware that these reassuring apron-symbols
have their parallel in certain sets of ideas; particularly in the half-mystical
and theological, half-legendary beliefs and prejudices which we derive from
the classical world and which form a kind of old wives' tale or maternal
substitute for the vigour and audacity of constructive thought. Thus I fulfil
the childhood pattern of making little expeditions into the world outside
my myth-mother and then running back to her warmth. Yet in these days
it is important for an artist to grasp that the logical exploratory voyage of
reason is the finest process of the mind. Every other activity is a form of
regression,—'Penser fait la grandeur de l'homme'. Thus the much vaunted
'night-mind', the subconscious world of myth and nostalgia, of child-
imagination and instinctual drives, though richer, stranger and more absorbing than the world of reason, as Isis than Apollo, nevertheless owes its
strength to our falling back on all that is primitive and infantile; it is an
act of cowardice to the God in Man.

Man exudes a sense of reverence like a secretion. He smears it over everything and so renders a place like Stonehenge or the lake of Nemi (Diana's
mirror) particularly sacred,—yet the one can become a petrol-station and
the other be drained by a megalomaniac; no grove is too holy to be cut down.
When we are tired or ill, our capacity for reverence, like our capacity for
seeing the difficulty of things, increases till it becomes a kind of compulsion-
neurosis or superstition; therefore it would seem that the mythoclasts are
always right,—until we know what these mother-haters, these savages of
the breast, will worship in their turn. Lenin, the father figure mummified,
replaces the Byzantine Christ. Reverence and destruction alternate; therefore
the wise two-faced man will reverence destructively, like Alaric or Akbar,
and like Gibbon, Renan, Gide, reverently destroy.

Example of destructive reverence: *Un Chien Andalou*.[1]

Studio Vingt-Huit—high up a winding street of Montmartre in the full
blasphemy of a freezing Sunday; taxis arriving, friends greeting each other,
an excitable afternoon audience. In the hall stands a surrealist bookstall,
behind is a bar where a gramophone plays 'Ombres Blanches' and disturbing
sardanas while beyond is a small modern theatre. The lights are lowered and
the film begins: 'Prologue'; 'Once upon a time' [I quote from the script], 'a
balcony was in the dark. Indoors a man was whetting his razor. He looked

---

[1] 'Un Chien Andalou was the film of adolescence and death which I was going to plunge right
into the heart of Paris with all the weight of an Iberian dagger.'—DALI: *Autobiography*.

up through the window at the sky and saw a fleecy cloud drawing near to the full moon. Then a young girl's head with staring eyes. Now the fleecy cloud passes over the moon. And the razor-blade passes through the girl's eye, slicing it in two.—End of Prologue.' The audience gasp—and there appear the beautiful haunted creatures,—Pierre Batchef as the young man, the cyclist, with his intellectual distinction and romantic depravity, then his Spanish-looking heroine. And the lovely girl in the street, who picks up the severed hand with the painted fingers! 'She must at that very moment register an extraordinary emotion which completely distracts her. She is as if entranced by echoes of some far-off church music, perhaps it is the music she has heard in earliest childhood. . . . She remains rooted to the spot in utter contrition. Motor-cars flash by at break-neck speed. Suddenly she is run over by one and horribly mutilated. Thereupon, with the firmness of one doing what he is fully entitled to do, the cyclist comes up to the other and, having gazed lecherously straight into her eyes, puts his hand on her jumper over her breasts. Close-up of the eager hands touching the breasts. These themselves appear through the jumper. Thereupon the cyclist's face is seen to take on a look of terrible, almost mortal anguish, and blood dribbles from his mouth on to the girl's bared breast.'

So the film hurries to its end where the woman and her cyclist lover 'lie buried up to their necks in the limitless desert, blind and ragged, roasted by the sun and eaten by a swarm of insects'. This contemptuous private world of jealousy and lust, of passion and aridity, whose beautiful occupants patter about like stoats in search of blood, produced an indescribable effect, a tremendous feeling of excitement and liberation. The Id had spoken and,—through the obsolete medium of the silent film,—the spectators had been treated to their first glimpse of the fires of despair and frenzy which were smouldering beneath the complacent post-war world.

The picture was received with shouts and boos and when a pale young man tried to make a speech, hats and sticks were flung at the screen. In one corner a woman was chanting 'Salopes, salopes, salopes!' and soon the audience began to join in. With the impression of having witnessed some infinitely ancient horror, Saturn swallowing his sons, we made our way out into the cold of February 1929, that unique and dazzling cold.[1]

Why does this strong impression still persist? Because *Un Chien Andalou* brought out the grandeur of the conflict inherent in romantic love, the truth that the heart is made to be broken, and after it has mended, to be broken again. For romantic love, the supreme intoxication of which we are capable, is more than an intensifying of life; it is a defiance of it and belongs to those evasions of reality through excessive stimulus which Spinoza called 'titivations'. By the law of diminishing returns our desperate century forfeits the

[1] 'A date in the history of the Cinema, a date marked in blood.'—*Montes* (Dali: *Autobiography*)·

chance of being happy and, because it finds happiness insipid, our world is regressing to chaos.

Why? Because, as in the days of the Delphic Oracle, happiness consists in temperance and self-knowledge, and these are now beyond the reach of ordinary people who, owing to the pursuit of violent sensation, can no longer distinguish between pleasure and pain.

'Happiness is the only sanction of life; where happiness fails, existence remains a mad and lamentable experiment,' writes Santayana, which is but a restatement of Aristotle's definition that happiness, not goodness, is the end of life: 'we choose happiness for itself, and never with a view to anything further; whereas we choose honour, pleasure, intellect, because we believe that through them we shall be made happy.' Yet at once the ring of the words 'mad and lamentable' drowns the definition. A 'mad and lamentable experiment' seems to us more compulsive, more beguiling, and more profound in its appeal. Compare Aristotle and Santayana with a mental specialist, Doctor Devine. I quote from his *Recent Advances in Psychiatry:*

'Sometimes the development of a delusion leads to a cessation of tension, and is associated with a feeling of tranquillity and certainty, such as the patient had not hitherto experienced. A study of the past history of these cases sometimes creates the impression that the whole life had been converging to its solution in the psychosis in an inevitable kind of way. It is not unusual for a patient to say that his whole life had been like a dream and that now he feels awake for the first time. The delusion is, as it were, the inspiration for which he had long been waiting. . . . Something altogether unique is created in a psychosis; the mind is invaded by morbid mental growths.'

Thus in opposition to Aristotle's definition of happiness as an intensifying of the life of reason, we can oppose the existence of these illusion-ridden patients, the paraphrenics who have 'achieved a state of permanent bio-psychic equilibrium at the expense of their reason'—and there are also schizophrenes and manic-depressives whose lives are rich and crowded above the normal. To quote Dr. Devine: 'The schizophrenic does not suffer from a loss of something, he suffers from a surfeit, psychologically his consciousness is fuller than normal consciousness and the reality which it embraces is more thickly populated than that comprehended by the normal mind. . . . The conscious personality plays a passive role as far as the development of his psychosis is concerned and can do nothing to control what is happening within his organism.'

This moth-and-candle preoccupation with the Morbid Mind is but one of the Approaches to Pain which nowadays seem so rich in glamour. Insanity beckons us to fulfil high destinies and to recognize our paraphrenic vocation. Milder forms of manic-depression withdraw the over-sensitive from circulation to let them off lightly with an anxiety-neurosis or nervous breakdown; tuberculosis offers some a prolonged ecstasy; alcohol clowns others into oblivion; stomach-ulcers, piles and colitis provide us with honourable excuses; impotence or frigidity can always be relied upon to stop the cheque and every degree of fever is at hand to send up our emotional temperature. And what illness performs for the individual, war accomplishes for the mass, until total war succeeds in plunging the two thousand million inhabitants of the globe into a common nightmare.

Why? 'Because,' says the priests, 'men have forgotten God'; 'wanting the Pilot and Palinure of reason and religion they runne themselves upon the rocks'; 'because,' say the materialists, 'they have neglected economic principles'; 'because,' says a philosopher, 'a madman at Sils Maria once wrote a book which, fifty years later, inspired another in Munich'. Or because we blindly enjoy destruction and can think of nothing better, since for us

'Le printemps adorable a perdu son odeur'?

Why do we like war? Is it that all men would revenge themselves for their betrayal by their mothers and of their mothers, hitting out blindly to efface the memory of the triple expulsion—expulsion from the sovereignty of the womb, from the sanctuary of the breast, from the intoxication of the bed and the lap?

No, it is not just through our weaning that we learn to use our teeth on one another, nor even from the terrible rebuff which we can still remember when our mother began to reject our advances and we were packed off to the living death of school, so much as by that more subtle conditioning which Freud analyses in *Beyond the Pleasure Principle*. There he argues that certain patterns of childhood unhappiness and separation are re-enacted in later life. 'Thus one knows people with whom every relationship ends in the same way: benefactors whose protégés invariably after a time desert them in ill-will, men with whom every friendship ends in the friend's treachery, lovers whose tender relationships with women each and all run through the same phases and come to the same end . . . in the light of such observations as these, we may venture to make the assumption that there really exists in psychic-life a repetition-compulsion which goes beyond the pleasure principle'. In *Civilization and Its Discontents* Freud considers all prevailing nostrums for happiness and finds them wanting; in our culture Eros and the Death-wish fight it out; in our civilization there is a Superego which makes us all feel guilty and a repressive and anal element in the bureaucratic tidiness, caution, and frugality of the society which we have made.

Yet to blame society or the tyranny of the herd is but to distribute the blame on the individual in a more general way. If we had all enjoyed happy childhoods with happy parents, then prisons, barracks and asylums would be empty. The herd would be kinder, society wiser, the world would be changed. Man, however, is complete not only through being well adjusted to humanity; humanity must also be adjusted to the non-human, to the Nature which it perpetually thwarts and outrages, to the indifferent Universe. In Gide's use of the myth, Prometheus must come to terms with Zeus. If we return to our fortunate madmen, not to the remorse-stricken melancholiacs, but to those who are happier for their renunciation of the external world, we find that they are happy because 'they have achieved permanent bio-psychic equilibrium at the expense of their reason'.

In other words, bio-psychic equilibrium is such an intense and unfailing source of happiness that the loss of their reason and of all personal contact with reality are a small price for these Taoists to pay. Now this bio-psychic equilibrium is but that sensation of harmony with the universe, of accepting life and of being part of nature which we experience in childhood and which afterwards we discover through love, artistic creation, the pursuit of wisdom, through mystical elation or luminous calm.

'The greatest good,' wrote Spinoza, 'is the knowledge of the union which the mind has with the whole nature', and those who have found this out, who have opened Nature's Dictionary of Synonyms, do not wish for any other. But we live in a civilization in which so few can experience it, where 'Le vrai, c'est le secret de quelques-uns', where those who have been fortunate are like competitors in a treasure hunt who, while the others are still elbowing each other about and knocking things over, in silence discover the clue, know that they are right and sit down.

Moreover, even as obscure poisons, foci of infection, septic teeth and germ-crowded colons play a part in the origins of insanity, so do slums, great cities, proletarian poverty and bourgeois boredom or tyrannies of family and herd contribute to obscure our sense of union with the physical world. 'The misery of mankind is manifold' and breeds everywhere the despair, fear, hate and destruction which ulcerate our peace. Nature is banished from our civilization, the seasons lose their rhythm, the fruits of the earth their savour, the animals, co-heirs of our planet, are wantonly exterminated, the God within us is denied and the God without. Wisdom and serenity become treasures to be concealed and happiness a lost art. Resentment triumphs; the frustrated 'Have-nots' massacre the 'Haves'. We are in fact within sight of achieving a world neurosis, a world in which atrophy of the instincts (except that of herd-slaughter), abuse of the intellect and perversion of the heart will obliterate our knowledge of the purpose of life: humanity will choke in its own bile.

When the present slaughter terminates humanity can survive only through a return to the idea of happiness as the highest good, happiness which lies not in Power or in the exercise of the Will, but in the flowering of the spirit, and which in an unwarped society should coincide with consciousness. The justification for the State therefore will consist in rendering the individuals who compose it happier than they can make themselves by helping them to fulfil their potentialities, to control their Promethean environment and to revere the Zeus-environment which they cannot master. When once we have discovered how pain and suffering diminish the personality and how joy alone increases it, then the morbid attraction which is felt for evil, pain and abnormality will have lost its power. Why do we reward our men of genius, our suicides, our madmen and the generally maladjusted with the melancholy honours of a posthumous curiosity? Because we know that it is our society which has condemned these men to death and which is guilty because, out of its own ignorance and malformation, it has persecuted those who were potential saviours; smiters of the rock who might have touched the spring of healing and brought us back into harmony with ourselves.

Somehow, then, and without going mad, we must learn from these madmen to reconcile fanaticism with serenity. Either one, taken alone, is disastrous, yet except through the integration of these two opposites there can be no great art and no profound happiness—and what else is worth having? For nothing can be accomplished without fanaticism and without serenity nothing can be enjoyed. Perfection of form or increase of knowledge, pursuit of fame or service to the community, love of God or god of Love,—we must select the Illusion which appeals to our temperament and embrace it with passion, if we want to be happy. This is the farewell autumn precept with which Palinurus takes leave of his fast-fading nightmare. 'J'ai cueilli ce brin de bruyère.'

And now one more year of knowing nothing has gone by: once more the Pleiads are sinking; the plane-tree is bare; the bowstring relaxed. Exorcized is the dark face from the island poplars, drowned in the swirl of the moon-tarnished river; dishonoured are the graves of the lemurs; untended the sepulchre of the Prince on Gavrinis, forgotten as an Andalusian dog.

But thou, mimosa-shaded Siagne, flowing clear between the two Saint-Cassiens, receive Palinurus,—gently bear him under the scented Tanneron, past Auribeau and Mandelieu and the shrine on the tufted mount of Venus to his tomb by the shore.[1]

[1] Palinurus enters the Siagne by the deserted village of Saint-Cassien des Bois; from there he floats some ten miles down to the wooded mound of Arluc, where stands the chapel of Saint-Cassien, scene of a pilgrimage and other nocturnal festivities on 23 July. The chapel, which is surrounded by ancient elms and cypresses, overlooks the old delta of the Siagne from the site

There, in the harsh sunshine, among the sea-holly and the midday plant, eringo and mesembrianthemum, where the tide prints its colophon of burnt drift-wood and the last susurrus of the wave expires on the sand,—naked under his watery sign shall he come to rest; a man too trustful in the calm of sky and sea.

'O nimium coelo et pelago confise sereno
Nudus in ignota, Palinure, jacebis harena.'

of a pagan temple dedicated by Roman sailors to Venus. 'Nazarius, vir stenuus et pius, non ferens animas hominum illudi fraude diabolica, delubrum et aram impudicae Veneri prope pontem fluminis nunc vulgo nuncupati *Siagnia*, omnino eliminare curavit . . .'—(*Chronol. Lerin.*, II, p. 80).

(The pious and energetic Nazarius would not permit men's minds to be deceived by a fraud of the Devil, and so he caused the ruined altar, dedicated to licentious Venus, to be utterly destroyed; that 'altar of the grove' on the mound called Arluc, by the bridge over the river now commonly known as the Siagne.)

Palinurus thus completes his periplus among the stone-pines on the beach by La Napoule. This is at variance with Virgil's account in which Æneas names after him Capo Palinuro on the Gulf of Policastro, and marks one more of the discrepancies which lead one to question the author's veracity.

STANDARD ENGLISH

WAR ADOPTIONS

BY ERIC PARTRIDGE

from *Usage and Abusage* (1947)

STANDARD ENGLISH

AND

STANDARD AMERICAN

I. HISTORY

OLD English had a standard (witness Old English literature), but that standard disappeared with the Norman Conquest. In the victorious reigns of Edward I (1272–1307) and Edward III (1327–77), there was a strong growth of national feeling; national consciousness was certainly accompanied by, and probably it was in part the source of, an increasing hostility to the use of French in England and consequently an increasingly favourable attitude towards the use of English. 'In the second half of the Fourteenth Century', says McKnight, 'the English language came once more to its own, into use not only in Parliament and the law courts and in schools, but in the literary productions composed for English cultured society.'

In this revival of English as a literary language, after it had so long been a merely spoken language, the particular kind of English adopted was the East Midland dialect. The reasons for this adoption, says McKnight, are these: 'The dialect of the East Midland district lay between Northern and Southern dialects and, as the Northern differed considerably from the Southern, the Midland served as a midway compromise understandable by all; it formed the speech of Oxford and Cambridge, the two great centres of higher education and of a culture more profound and mellow than that of London; it formed also the dialect of London itself, the centre of the political, official and commercial life of the country. And thus it was the speech of Chaucer, who, the greatest English writer until the sixteenth century and, during the eleventh to fourteenth centuries, the only great writer to employ English at all, passed most of his life in London; as the dialect spoken at Oxford, it was used by Wycliffe, who discarded his native Yorkshire for this smoother speech; as the dialect of London and hence of the Court, it was used by Gower, who might have been expected to employ the Kentish dialect.' Chaucer's and Gower's best work appeared in the last twenty years of the fourteenth century; in the fifteenth, their disciples—and

353

others—followed their lead and wrote in the East Midland dialect. Standard English, then, began in the second half of the fourteenth century as the East Midland dialect; and in the fifteenth century that dialect was established as the correct one to use for general literary purposes. It was the more readily adopted because it had not the harshness of the Northern dialects, very little of the rather drawling softness of the Southern. The supremacy of the East Midland dialect was unquestioned by the dramatists and the poets of the Elizabethan age.

The language of the sixteenth and early seventeenth century, however, was far from being so fixed and regularized as that of the nineteenth and, though less, the twentieth century. Spelling was idiosyncratic, syntax experimental, and vocabulary a glorious uncertainty; these features and tendencies were counter-balanced by 'the freedom enjoyed by the writers of that period in the adoption of new words and the combination of existing words in word-compound and in phrase'. Regularity in spelling and vocabulary, along with order in accidence and syntax, came in the approximate period, 1660–1800. 'In the eighteenth century, especially near the end, the influence of grammars and dictionaries made itself fully felt. Words admissible into literary use were registered with their meanings in dictionaries, which also more and more undertook to indicate the pronunciation. English grammar became a subject for school study, and conformity to the use authorized by dictionary and grammar became the test of [culture] in language.'

For more than three hundred years the East Midland dialect, 'at first, no doubt, merely held to be the fashionable mode of speech, has gained in prestige, until, at the present day, it is spreading all over [Great Britain], and among all classes' (Wyld, *The Growth of English*). This dialect has become Standard English: the criteria of that standard are the choice of words and phrases, the syntax, the pronunciation. Of Standard English as we know it in the twentieth century, we may say that it 'is a kind of English which is tinged neither with the Northern, nor Midland, nor Southern peculiarities of speech [and] which gives no indication . . . of where the speaker comes from. . . . It is the ambition of all educated persons in [Great Britain and Northern Ireland] to acquire this manner of speaking, and this is the form of our language which foreigners wish to learn' (*ibid.*).

But it is important to bear in mind that 'no form of language is, *in itself*, [originally] better than any other form. A dialect gains whatever place of superiority it enjoys solely from the estimation in which it is commonly held. It is natural that the language of the Court should come to be regarded as the most elegant and refined type of English, and that those who do not speak that dialect naturally'—that is, as birthright or as environmental training—'should be at the pains of acquiring it. This is what has happened, and is still happening, to the dialect which is called Standard English',—although Standard English is to be no longer regarded as a dialect properly so called.

'Of course, since this form of English is used in the conversation of the refined, the brilliant and the learned, it has become a better instrument for the expression of ideas than any other [variety] of speech now spoken.'

'When', continues Professor Wyld, 'we speak of Good English, or Standard English, or Pure English, as distinct from . . . Provincial English [the dialects proper], we must remember that there is nothing in the original nature of these . . . dialects which is in itself inferior, or reprehensible, or contemptible. In a word, the other dialects are in reality and apart from fashion and custom, quite as good as Standard English [—the same holds, of course, for Standard American in relation to American dialects—], considered simply as forms of language; but they have not the same place in general estimation, they have not been so highly cultivated' (nor have they become so subtle and delicate), 'and they have not the same wide currency.'

II. STANDARD ENGLISH: DEGREES AND KINDS

There are, however, different kinds of Standard English: The best of these is Received Standard[1], for it fulfils all the requirements of good speech; Modified Standard is Standard English that differs from Received mainly in pronunciation; and Literary Standard lies beyond any matter of pronunciation, and is confined to written English,—and should it be used in speech, it is too bookish to be Received.

Of Literary English—Literary Standard—it is necessary only to say that it is the more conventional, stylized, and dignified, more accurate and logical, sometimes the more beautiful form that Received Standard assumes, like evening dress, for important occasions; it is also more rhythmical and musical. The prose of Sir Thomas Browne, Gibbon, De Quincey, The Landors, Pater is in Literary English. With dialect, colloquialism, slang, cant it has nothing to do unless they possess a long pedigree—and then only in rare instances.

What then of Received Standard and Modified Standard? 'It is proposed', says Wyld in his *Short History of English*, 'to use the term *Received Standard* for that form which all would probably agree in considering the best, that form which has the widest currency and is heard with practically no variation among speakers of the better class all over the country. This type might be called Public School English.' (The stress here, you see, is on pronunciation and enunciation.) 'It is proposed to call the vulgar English of the Towns, and the English of the Villager who has abandoned his native Regional Dialect'—dialect in the ordinary sense of the term—'*Modified Standard*. That

---

[1] 'Received Standard' and 'Modified Standard' are Professor Wyld's designations, whereas 'Literary Standard' is a designation proposed—after due thought—by myself.

is, it is Standard English, modified, altered, differentiated, by various influences, regional and social. Modified Standard differs from class to class,
and from locality to locality; it has no uniformity, and no single form of it
is heard outside a particular class or a particular area.' Very obvious, as
Professor Wyld is the first to admit; very important, as he was the first to
emphasize.

III. THE LIMITS OF PURE (or, RECEIVED STANDARD) ENGLISH[1]

There is a perhaps startling difference between pure English and the
English spoken by the uncultured.[2] In the American 'Them guys ain't got
no pep' and the English 'Them blokes ain't got no go', not even a single
word satisfies the standard exacted by pure English, whether American
English or British English. In both versions, the first word (*them*) is un-
grammatical (for 'these' or 'those'); the second is slang (for 'men'); the
third (*ain't*) is illiterate; the fourth (*got*) is unnecessary—and colloquial; the
fifth (*no*) is illogical, the sense demanding *any*; and the sixth (*pep*: *go*) is
slang. Both versions are not merely uncultured but illiterate; yet the speech
is straight from the shoulder, the meaning unmistakable.

There are, however, inestimable advantages to be obtained from uniformity of vocabulary and from regularity of syntax: that uniformity and
that regularity do at least make understanding much easier: and com-
municability is the primary requisite of both speech and writing.

Since the seventeenth century, English has gained tremendously in precision. Language has not been evolved to be the sport of the illiterate, any
more than to be the plaything of the highbrow or the chopping-block of
the journalist. Language is a means—the chief means—of communication,
not merely between two Chicago gangsters or two Soho toughs, but among
all the members of a nation; internationally too. 'It is important that
the language medium should offer as little as possible resistance to the
thought current, and this end is attained only when the symbols of
language are ones that convey precisely the same meaning to all who use
the language.'

But we may raise a question concerning the degree to which a language
can be healthily standardized. Too often are spoken English and spoken
American criticized as though it were impossible for them to have any laws
of their own—a freedom not shackled at every turn by the rules explicit
or implicit in Literary Standard.

---

[1] In this section I draw heavily on G. H. McKnight's *English Words and Their Background*.

[2] Dialect is considered as of an essentially different order from illiterate speech—as indeed it is.

A language cannot be at the same time entirely standardized and truly vital: a rigorously regimented language would die from stiffness of the joints and atrophy of the spirit. 'Ideas inherited from the past . . . may find adequate expression in the idiom of the past. . . . The shifting, developing forms assumed by living thought, however, demand the plastic medium of a living language.' It is only natural that new systems of thought and new modes of living should, by the very strength of their processes and by their widespread currency, generate new words, new compounds, new phrases and even new modes of expression: in linguistics, as in politics, the will of the nation is all-powerful; it is of no use for the pedants to deplore and lament the misuses implicit in (say) *aggravating* or *the psychological moment*, for usage has consecrated the original errors and turned them into correct currency.

On this question of the limits of pure English (Received Standard), Logan Pearsall Smith, an American long resident in England, has, in 'Popular Speech and Standard English' (an admirable article to be read in full), in *Words and Idioms*, written as follows: 'Since our language seems to be growing year by year more foreign, abstract and colourless in character, it stands in greater need than ever of this vigorous and native reinforcement' which we could obtain from dialect in particular and popular speech in general. This reinforcement could be enlisted and fruitfully employed by all of us, 'were we not paralysed by that superstitious feeling of awe and respect for standard English [i.e., Received Standard] which is now [1925] spread by the diffusion of education'. We are enslaved by the tyrant Correctitude.

But why should Standard English have to resort to dialectal and popular speech for vitality and picturesqueness instead of drawing on its own resources? 'It is inevitable', Pearsall Smith continues, 'that when any form of speech becomes a standard and written language, it should as a conse-quence lose much of its linguistic freedom. All forms of speech have of course their rules and usages, but in a written language these rules and usages become much more settled and stereotyped': so that, finally, words and phrases are adjudged to be good or bad, not by their strength, clarity and aptness of expression, but by the external criterion of correctness. 'Such an attitude . . . tends . . . to fix grammar and pronunciation, to discourage assimilation [of picturesque or vigorous outsiders], and to cripple the free and spontaneous powers of word-creation.' Then, too, 'a standard language, in modern conditions, tends to be rather a written than a spoken language. The printed word becomes more and more the reality, the spoken word an echo or [a] faint copy of it. This inversion of the normal relation between speech and writing, this predominance'—almost, tyranny—'of the eye over the ear, of the written symbol over its audible'—i.e., spoken—'equivalent, tends to deprive the language of that vigour and reality which comes, and can only come, from its intimate association with the acts and passions of men, as they vividly describe and express them in their speech.'

The foregoing, however, is not to be taken as an attack on, nor as a depreciation of, the *virtues and the advantages* of Standard English, for this, the accepted form of English, with its national scope and its national use, with its rich and varied vocabulary, with its often subtle and, for the most part, flexible syntax, with all the historical associations inevitably and naturally garnered in the course of centuries, and these and other associations enriched by successive generations, is the inestimably precious inheritance of the English people, as any such language is of any ancient people. The position of good (or pure) English is, in essentials, impregnable: for as it arises from, so does it serve, a social need. The danger lies, not in its being set aside (with the result of linguistic chaos, and hence of a lack of national unity), but in its being so unreflectingly and blindly respected that we may forget the very existence of popular speech and widespread colloquialism, of slang and dialect, and thus forget both their intrinsic value and their value as readily available sources of freshness and invigoration.

No standard language exists on its own capital; no standard language can thus exist,—if it is to continue to be a language and not become a mausoleum. Standard English, sprung from a dialect, has never, for long, disregarded the other dialects, over which, by a geographical, political and social accident, it has been exalted: those others have always had too much to offer in potential enrichment of the triumphant dialect. Like dialect, popular speech abounds in uncouth phrases and low words and absurd (or, at the least, hasty) perversions and inaccuracies; but it also abounds in vivid phrases, in racy and vigorous words, in strong monosyllables and picturesque compounds, and also in ancient words that have, unfortunately for us, dropped out of cultured speech. How useful, how valuable, how fitting it would be if many of these words and phrases were to be admitted, or re-admitted, to standard speech and were, in their turn, to become Received Standard, whence there would duly be expelled those learned terms which had become synonyms of these racier or stronger or more musical terms adopted from dialect and from the popular speech of the towns. Their adoption would not merely enrich but also improve the material stock, hence the cultural and spiritual value and potentialities, of Standard English, which they would strengthen and render less standardized.

'Human speech', as Pearsall Smith has remarked in that work which we have already quoted, 'is after all a democratic product, the creation, not of scholars and grammarians, but of . . . unlettered people. Scholars and men of education may cultivate and enrich it, and make it flower into all the beauty of a literary language', but they should not, in their efforts to keep the language pure, forget that it should also be kept vigorous; they are too apt to forget that the 'rarest blooms are grafted on a wild stock, and [that] its roots are deep-buried in the common soil. From that soil it must still draw its sap and nourishment, if it is not to perish [from inanition], as the other standard languages of the past have perished, when . . . they have been . . . cut off from the popular vernacular.'

Nevertheless, as McKnight has excellently said in his excellent *Modern English in the Making*, 'the standardization of modern English is not as nearly complete as is sometimes supposed. The language ideal of philosophers like [Wilkins and] Locke has never been realized. Idealistic efforts . . . have been only partially successful. The English language has not been subjected to absolute rule. . . . In other words, English is not yet a dead language. . . . "Law," says Roscoe Pound, "must be stable and yet cannot stand still." The statement applies with little modification to . . . language. Language though regulated, . . . must change in company with changing conditions of life.'

Let us, therefore, have purity, so far as possible. But not to the detriment of raciness and vigour.

IV. STANDARD ENGLISH IN THE DOMINIONS AND COLONIES

Except among Public School men and women resident there, the Dominions and Colonies have not a Received Standard pronunciation, although the vocabulary is, among the cultured and the well educated, that of Received Standard. They may be said to speak Modified Standard. One may hope that, in the Dominions (especially perhaps, Canada and Australia), the clarity and subtlety of the best Standard English will always exercise a beneficent influence. Certainly it would be idle to fear that these Dominion writers might be unduly cramped thereby.

Colonial scorn of Public School English, like English scorn of Colonial accents, should be allowed to die. There is a reason for Colonial accents; much virtue in Public School English.

V. STANDARD AMERICAN SPEECH AND WRITING

The United States presents a knottier problem, for, there, a much larger population is concerned than that of the English-speakers in the Dominions.

In writing, there is an American Literary Standard, which so closely resembles English Literary Standard as to establish no basic, no important difference. But is there, in American speech, a Received Standard? Or is there nothing but a number of Modified Standards? One might, on first thought, say that there are only Modified Standards, although one might add that some of these modifications are more pleasing to the British ear or more widely used than others. But the fact remains that, although there is, in the United States, no speech that can be classified as Received Standard with the same feeling of certainty as Public School speech can be said to be Received Standard in England, yet the speech of the cultured elements of American society is as close to being a Received Standard as can be expected in so vast and many-peopled a land as the United States. That the criterion is neither so severe nor so rigid as that of English Received Standard does not make it any the less a genuine criterion.[1] But in America even more than in Great Britain, the speakers of Modified Standard are more numerous than the speakers of Received Standard.

It must, however, be remembered that the differentiation between Standard and popular speech, between Standard and slang, between slang and cant, is, on the whole, less marked in the United States than in the British Empire.

---

[1] [The best account of American pronunciation is Professor Kenyon's admirable 'Guide to Pronunciation', *Webster's New International Dictionary*, Second Edition.]

WAR ADOPTIONS AND ADAPTATIONS

THE Second World War, both by its actual course and by its antecedent alarms and rumours, occupations and penetrations, has exercised a considerable influence upon the English language. The popularization of technicalities was almost startling; even children talked knowledgeably of aircraft and submarines, Forts and Stormoviks, and they still do. But of such popularization and such dissemination of knowledge, nothing further will be said in an article that concerns itself with unmistakable acquisitions: adoptions, adaptations, equivalents; and with only such of these as have come to us from abroad: Spain, Germany, Norway, France, Russia, Japan, America.

These acquisitions fall into two main groups: words and phrases well known, some even thoroughly acclimatized, before 1 September 1939; and those which have become well and widely known only since the date on which the Germans, previously content with propaganda, Anschluss, peaceful penetrations, protective occupations, finally decided to substitute a huge conflagration for the bonfires of the preceding two years—to come out into the open—and to institute their long-planned policy of world-domination by methods no longer political but military; military on the three planes of air, land and sea.

The pre-war acquisitions are all German, with the exception of *Fifth Column* and its derivative *fifth-columnist*, which originated during the Spanish Civil War of the middle 'thirties. A fifth column (the capital letters are applicable only in connection with that civil war) consists of an organized body of persons that, within a country at war, or in danger of being at war, not merely sympathize with but work for the enemy or prospective enemy; such a column had been operating in every European country, including Britain, since 1933.

Fascist and *Nazi* have been established too long for justifiable inclusion here, and the same exclusion applies to *Führer*. But from a list of pre-war adoptions, adaptations, and equivalents of or for German terms, the following could hardly be omitted: *Aryan, Herrenvolk, Führerprinzip, Lebensraum,*

361

Weltpolitik, totalitarian, strength through joy; *Axis, appeasement, encirclement, peaceful penetration, Gestapo, preventive custody, concentration camp.*

Until Hitler imposed upon the word a racial sense, *Aryan* was applied only to languages. Witness Professor Ernest Weekley, who says, 'From Sanskrit *arya*, noble. Hence also Greek *Areia*, Eastern Persia, and Persian languages . . . Divided into West *Aryan*, i.e. most European languages (except Basque, Finnish, Hungarian, Turkish) and East *Aryan*, i.e. Persian, Sanskrit, and the Hindu vernaculars related to the latter. . . . Some use *Aryan* of the Asiatic group only.' In Hitler's eyes, the greatest sin of the Jews was that they are non-Aryan.

The 'noble' origin of *Aryan* influenced the birth of the term *Herrenvolk*, 'the master race', into which crept, early enough, something of the grandiosely Teutonic idea of the *superman*. *Superman* is Mr. G. B. Shaw's felicitous imitation of Nietzsche's *Übermensch*, which Goethe, and Herder before him, had already used. How could a race never master of itself become the rulers of the world?

But even Herrenvolk require a ruler—euphemistically called a *Führer*. Of the *Führerprinzip* ('leader principle'), Lord Samuel, in *Belief and Action*, 1937, acutely and prophetically wrote, 'The aura surrounding the State is extended to the spokesman. Here the new philosophy pursues earlier tendencies. Frequently recurring in both German and Italian history is the cult of the Hero. The present *Führerprinzip* is the formulation of old practice.'

Obviously these supermen, this master race, this Führer needed *Lebensraum* or 'living-space', or such territory as the Reich believed it required for its full development; such space is to the State what the French *place au soleil* (itself from German *Platz an der Sonne*) or 'place in the sun' is to the individual. The Germans needed rather too much; more than was implied in some wag's rendering of *Lebensraum* as 'national elbow-room'. But much was implied in Hitler's dream of world-domination and in that ideology which was partly expressed in *Weltpolitik* or 'world politics', although this term had been current in Germany since the first lustrum of the twentieth century; by the way, *world-domination* is a mistranslation of *Weltmacht*, which properly means 'colonial power' and in this sense antedates the First World War.

Totalitarian and *Axis* go together, for the Axis powers (Germany and Italy; and by extension *the tripartite Axis* or *the Berlin–Rome–Tokyo Axis*) were totalitarian, 'permissive of rivals neither in political parties nor in policies', i.e. State-dictatorial; *totalitarian* apes *authoritarian*, not only in form but in sense ('favouring or inculcating or exacting obedience to authority, instead of favouring individual liberty'). But only the Germans spoke of *strength through joy*, that pretentious phrase which, in the fact, implies a regimented, Boy-Scoutish joy and an athlete's strength.

Appeasement, in the nuance 'pacification' (Latin *ad pacem*, Old French *à pais*, 'at peace', hence *apaiser*, with noun-ending *-ment*), was the tragic, though often circumstance-enforced, policy of those states which sought to satisfy Germany's appetite for domination by surrender to Germany's mail-fisted needs: Olaf Stapledon, in *Beyond the Isms*, 1942, spoke feelingly of the 'appeasement of international brigandage'; too late, several European countries perceived that, instead of glutting that appetite, they had merely whetted it and that *peaceful penetration* meant warlike penetration and preparation by 'the peaceful'; that in the guise of cultural and commercial agreements and negotiations, Germany was securely establishing herself inside the country of the prospective victims; and that the *co-operation* so glibly and attractively pretexted by that country signified, at the least, submission and political enslavement.

Almost as cynical in its implications was Germany's frantic cry that she was being encircled. As though *encirclement* had not always been her lot, and *Lebensraum* her slogan!

Pretending to act in accordance with a racial and political *ideology* (system of ideas; originally, science of ideas), Germany preferred, in fact, to rely upon such coercions as had, ever since its inception, been applied by the *Gestapo* (or secret police), an 'initials-formed' word like *Nazi* and *Ogpu*. *Gestapo*, by the way, has, in the Royal Air Force, become a jocose and slangy synonym of 'Service (later: R.A.F.) Police'. One of its more clement activities, in pre-War days, was to take suspects into *protective custody* or 'police safe-keeping': *quis custodiet ipsos custodes?* Many a person so detained, ostensibly for his own good, found that the only good involved was that of the *Reich* (literally, 'empire'; from Latin *regere*, 'to rule'—compare *rajah*). One of its less clement activities consisted in the establishment and maintenance and staffing of *concentration camps*, where the disaffected and the often imaginedly dangerous were imprisoned and whence they too seldom emerged at all or, if they did emerge, only as broken men and women. Another Nazi amenity was the *purge*, so much more drastic than any aperient: more than once, it became a *blood-bath*.

Thus we arrive at those words and phrases which the war itself either popularized or engendered. The Norwegian *quisling*: the German *Blitzkrieg* and its derivative *blitz*; *total war(fare)*; *Luftwaffe*, (to) *Rotterdam* and (to) *Coventrate*; *Panzer*; *defence in depth, fluid* (front), *elasticity*: the French *Maginot Line*, *do a Dunkirk*; *the Underground* and the *Maquis*: the Russian *scorched earth*: and the American *jeep* and *pursuit plane*; *G.I.* and *Rangers*.

Quisling, 'a fifth-columnist; hence, a traitor', now written *quisling*,[1] so generalized has it become, derives from that Vidkun Quisling who poisonously and effectually worked for Norway's rapid subjugation by Germany: his ambition has rendered him Judas-infamous and internationally execrable.

---

[1] For Proper Names that have yielded common nouns and ordinary adjectives (*platonic* love) or verbs (*macadamize*), see my dictionary *Name into Word* (Secker & Warburg).

The crop of German words is perhaps smaller than one might have expected; but its smallness is more than compensated by its dread significance and its deathful connotations.

Blitzkrieg, 'lightning war' or the war of rapid movement and swift coups, was a term most aptly descriptive of Germany's conquest of Europe in May–June, 1940; four years later, we showed that we were good learners. From *Blitz* (lightning) came *blitz* for an 'air raid', and the verb soon became a colloquialism; by the end of 1944, they ranked as Familiar English. Blitzkrieg formed but one aspect of *total war*, another of those felicitous inventions and concepts of the totalitarian states: war in which civilians, so far from having protective rights and prescriptive privileges, were employed as pawns in a diabolical chessmanship—for instance, to block the roads and thus impede the combatant forces of the foe; war in which cities were mercilessly bombed in order to reduce morale.

The *Luftwaffe* (literally, Air Force) presented an unwilling world with two words, 'to *Rotterdam*' and its near-synonym, 'to *Coventrate*': the former means, 'utterly to bomb-destroy a predetermined area of (a city)', the latter 'thus to destroy, or attempt to destroy the entirety (of a city)': the people of Coventry, like those of Rotterdam, will not forget, nor will they soon forgive, their atrocious ordeal.

The German army sprang a surprise with the panther-like speed, the armament and the armour of its *Panzer*[1] divisions: 'Churchills' and 'Shermans', however, constituted an admirable counter. Having exploited the novel virtues of swift attack, the Germans were, from 1943 onwards, compelled to develop the almost equally useful virtues of the self-explanatory *defence in depth*; it must be admitted that they always have excelled in defensive fighting. But *fluid front* and *elasticity* were virtues born, like the 'withdrawal according to plan' of 1918, of necessity: fine words to cover a disorganization rather less fine, the elasticity resulting from an enforced mobility, the fluidity from uncertainty.

The *Maginot Line*, built in 1927—35 and named after the French War Minister (who had apparently failed to hear of the formation of German 'paratroops'), has come to synonymize *white elephant*, with the further connotation of military delusion: the Germans, countering with the Siegfried Line, encouraged the French to fool themselves as never a nation had been fooled. To *do a Dunkirk* is to make a seaborne, air-bombarded escape from a country that has been militarily occupied by the departing troops; in the latter half of 1945, the repatriation of prisoners-of-war by sea was described as 'a Dunkirk in reverse'. *The Underground (Movement)*, French *le mouvement souterrain*, is a picturesque name for that grim and secret organized resistance planned and prosecuted by the patriots within an occupied country. The

---

[1] *Panzer*, by the way, means not 'panther' but simply 'armour', as in *Panzerzug*, 'armoured train'.

Maquis were those armed French resisters who, in France, sheltered and drilled in and harryingly issued from those wild, bushy, mountainous or, at the least, hilly regions of eastern France which took their generic name, *makis* or *maquis*, from the Corsican *macchia*.

Scorched earth was the fiery devastation practised by the Russians[1] in 1941–42, against the advancing Germans, on hamlets and towns, on granaries and crops and even pasture-lands.

Japan, in late 1941–45, familiarized us with *bushido* and re-familiarized us with *hara-kiri*. *Hara-kiri* is suicide by disembowelment: *hara*, 'belly', and *kiri*, 'to cut'. Ceremonial suicide by this means is properly known as *seppuku*, but the newspapers, in the latter half of 1945, failed to make contact with this fact, and so the public know not *seppuku*. *Bushido*, the Samurai code of honour, is *bu-shi-do*, literally 'military-knight ways': the code of the well-born soldier; hence, to the British and American public, the code of military honour—loosely, the code of national honour, or the national code of honour. It is, therefore, hardly surprising that *honourable*, so often issuing from Japanese lips, has taken to itself a somewhat ironic tinge.

The adoptions from America are much less grim than those from Germany, France, Russia. *A pursuit plane* is a fighter; *Rangers*, the equivalent of British commando troops. *Jeep* is the originally slang, by 1943 generally accepted, name of the small general-purposes motorized truck; *G.I.*, 'general issue', is the no-longer-slang term for the American 'Tommy'. Both jeep and G.I. have notably contributed to the gaiety of the nations.

---

[1] A Russian term that, although—mainly in the translations of the Russian communiqués—it gained some sort of currency in British newspapers, never properly 'caught on', was *Hitlerite* for 'a German soldier' or 'any Nazi'.

OF ELLEN TERRY:
OUR LADY OF THE LYCEUM

BY W. GRAHAM ROBERTSON

from *Time Was* (1931)

OF ELLEN TERRY:
OUR LADY OF THE LYCEUM

T HOUGH for many years I had worshipped from afar and had been, so to speak, brought up in the shadow of the Lyceum Theatre, it was not until a memorable evening in the winter of '87 that I first met Ellen Terry.

I was at a dance, and I remember that it was a dull dance, and I was making preparations to leave it when there was a sudden stir at the door—something was happening—something in the nature of a sunrise.

At the entry stood a golden figure which seemed actually to diffuse light, the golden figure which I had first beheld in the palace of Belmont.

A fairer vision than Ellen Terry, then at the zenith of her loveliness, cannot be imagined: she shone with no shallow sparkle or glitter, but with a steady radiance that filled the room and had the peculiar quality of making everybody else invisible.

From after experience I feel sure that she was in act of whispering to her hostess, 'Now don't you bother about me and I'll just slip in without being noticed and sit down somewhere'—a feat which might have been performed with equal ease by the sun at noonday.

Somehow or another I got myself presented and indeed, though I did not at the moment realize it, the meeting must have been arranged by Providence expressly for my benefit, for neither before nor after have I ever again seen Ellen Terry at a dance—except at her sister's house, which does not count.

Though I could only secure a few words I at once fell completely under the matchless charm of her personality; the stuffy room and the jigging music faded, leaving only Ellen Terry, who might have stepped in from some dim garden, her arms full of lavender and lad's-love and bringing with her a freshness, a breeze from the open sky.

What was it that made her so unlike any other actress; why had the stage left no mark upon her, for never was woman less stagy or artificial? I think it was because, at the most critical and receptive age of nineteen, when most young players are working up towards their first success and living wholly in the world behind the footlights, she left the stage and gave what would be considered her best years to a real life, away in the country, far from theatres and all concerning them.

369

During these six years, which I have often heard called the lost years of Ellen Terry, she lived through those emotions which she was to portray later on; she knew great happiness and keen suffering, glad tranquillity, fear, loneliness, and even actual want; she learned in her sorrow to creep close to the heart of Nature and to draw from it help and comfort, in her joy to turn to Nature for an answering smile.

That quiet but eventful time was very sacred to her. She spoke of it seldom, to me not at all during the first years of our friendship, but I know that it was often in her thoughts, and later on, especially when we were together in the country, perhaps jogging along the lanes in a donkey-cart or sitting in the spring copses among the bluebells, she would often say, 'This is like Harpenden days', and would tell me tales of those hidden years which had so developed her character and her art. Most of the tales were sad, yet like Sophie Arnould, she held in loving memory 'les beaux jours quand j'étais si malheureuse'.

Often, during that period, she had felt the pinch of poverty and had not known where to look for supplies. She had sat up many a night doing copies of elaborate architectural drawings for which, when finished, she would get a guinea, and this fine work, done by very insufficient light, strained her eyes and produced a weakness in them which ever afterwards troubled her.

One dismal evening, she told me, everything had looked unusually black. She had been alone for many days, funds were very low, she was ill and anxious. She had harnessed the little rough pony and driven to meet the last train, hoping that someone, half expected, would come by it and put an end to the fears and the loneliness.

But the last train played her false as it had often done before, and she drove back through the dark lanes wearied out in body and brain. She would not trouble about supper, she would creep into bed and rest—rest was all she could think of. She would go straight to bed—but there was the pony. The pony must be unharnessed and rubbed down, and though she wanted no supper, the pony must have his. So the weary girl led the weary pony into his stall and made him comfortable; shook up his bed, gave him his drink of water, and finally, raising herself on tiptoe, began to pull down his supper of hay into the manger from the rack above her head. As she did so, out of the hay and straight down her back fell a mouse.

We have heard of the patience of Job, but it is not on record that the patriarch at the supreme crisis of his afflictions had a mouse down his back. Had this been so we might have heard less of his patience. It was the Thing Too Much: the girl's brave spirit for once was conquered. Never had she been so tired, never so unhappy, never so utterly alone; here was the darkest hour of her life—and she had a mouse down her back. It was her nadir. Never, before or after, did she touch the misery of that moment.

On another night, returning from one of those forlorn expeditions to the station, her lamp had gone out and the night was pitch dark. In a lonely lane a man's rough voice suddenly called out some obviously useless question. She answered shortly, heard the rough voice mutter, 'My God, it's a gal!' and the next minute a man had sprung into the cart beside her—she felt his hot, whisky-laden breath on her cheek.

Drawing back as far as she could, she clubbed the whip and brought down the handle with all her might upon the place where she judged his head ought to be. It was evidently there—for after a minute's pause something dropped heavily upon the road and she, whipping up the pony, fled away into the darkness.

She never heard anything more of the matter, so the man must have quickly recovered, but he probably remembered his meeting with the 'gal' in the dark lane for some time to come.

A third dismal tale was of returning home through a wood, late on a dark night, ill and nervous, starting at the snapping of a twig or at the tall shadows cast by her lantern. As she reached the middle of the wood a shining object in her way attracted her attention; she lowered the lantern and found herself looking into the bright eyes of a large frog. Behind him sat another frog, also solemnly staring, beyond him still more; she was in the midst of a circle of frogs which swarmed over the path in all directions. When she had thoroughly taken in these details she dropped the lantern, which immediately went out, leaving her in pitch darkness.

Even afterwards, in broad daylight, she was never able to make up her mind as to what she ought to have done. If she stepped forward—no, that did not bear thinking of. But the way back presented equal difficulties. What she finally did was to feel about for a clear space and then to sit down and wait shiveringly through the long hours of darkness until dawn began to steal between the branches and the frog party broke up.

Against the misery of this enforced vigil may be set the joy of another, entered upon willingly.

She had been talking with one whose opinion carried great weight for her and he had objected to some trivial remark as unworthy.

'That thought is small,' he had said, 'and you should have no room for small thoughts. Thought should be great.'

'How can I make my thoughts great?' asked Ellen Terry. 'What must I do?'

'For one whole night,' he said, 'you must lie out in the fields alone and watch the sky from dusk to dawn.'

So all night long the girl lay on the short grass of the common looking up into the great mystery of the night. No sleep came to her, but the stillness and the awe and the beauty sank into her and brought rest and knowledge.

13

The wonderful pageant of the heavens passed over her from its rising to its setting, the moon drifted away behind the coppice and the stars shrank and grew pale in the dark hour before the dawn, but the watcher still lay there, wide-eyed and happy, until in the grey of the morning she crept to her room and fell asleep.

What she had learnt that night she could not tell; she could not remember, but she *knew*, and the knowledge remained with her. What she had learnt was something of proportion, something of rhythm, of reverence, of melody—she could not formulate, only feel, but the memory never faded, and all through her life she found courage and peace in a vision of stars passing across the sky above Fallows Green.

And I think it was then that she first fell in love with night, for, though golden Portia and dazzling Beatrice might suggest the sun at his height, yet Ellen Terry was a daughter of the night, happy in its shadow and mystery and loving the moon with a strange ecstasy which I have never met with in another.

She was weary, the moon rested her; she was sad, the moon consoled her; she was anxious, the moon gave her peace; like the Princess Daylight of the fairy-tale she seemed to wax and to wane with it, and only at the full of the moon was the true Ellen Terry at her very best.

The moon magic stayed with her all her life, and I have a letter in which she rejoices that her youngest grandson is able to share it with her.

'—Good Lord, that November moon! I had to pull little Teddy out of his bed one night so that he should not miss the teeming loveliness. His face in the pale light I shall never forget. The delicacy of it—so grave and so adoring! His morning reading has been a great bond between us, but the Moon—He made me promise to wake him up once a month to see the sight. . . .'

Yet I know that, however sympathetic might be her companion, the moon spell always drew her back to Harpenden and Fallows Green. Once, in the after-years, I was sitting with her in an orchard under the full moon: she had been silent for a long while, quietly content and peaceful.

Suddenly I turned to look at her, thinking she spoke. Beside me sat a girl of eighteen or nineteen, the wistful face, half child, half woman, which we know in the pictures of Watts, gazed up at the moon between the apple branches, the lips moved in whispered speech.

I got up softly and left her—three are always an awkward number.

It is seldom given to any of us to step back across the years and to re-live even a few moments of the past, yet Ellen Terry experienced something akin to this in 1912.

Her thoughts had been dwelling much upon early days—I think the moon must have been unusually bright and near the full—and she felt a sudden longing to revisit the place of memories. She would go by herself that she might walk alone with her dreams and reconstruct old times out of what she might find left of old places.

She found much, for the world had stood very still at Harpenden, the countryside had escaped development and 'improvement' and still kept its rustic quiet and peace.

She passed along the well-remembered lanes, repeopling the farms and cottages with the folk of the past, now, she supposed, all swept away: she had been very young in her Harpenden days and the neighbours had seemed to her, for the most part, well stricken in years.

A farm gate stood open and she looked along the path into the dim old house. This used to be—ah, yes—Thrales's. The Thrales, two old men and a still older sister, had lived there—all that were left of the famous Thrales of Streatham.

They had fired the imagination of the young Ellen Terry. Here were undoubted Thrales. Not exactly the right Thrales perhaps, but still Thrales— and old—and if they had not personally known Doctor Johnson and Sir Joshua and Mrs. Siddons, or made Sophy Streatfield cry for the benefit of Fanny Burney, one could pretend they had, which would be very satisfying.

But the Thrales had proved uninspiring. They were heavy and slow, admitting to vague 'papers' concerning the family stored in an attic, but taking no interest in them.

They were wholly bucolic, had gone back to the land for good, and were far less alive than dear, bright, dead and gone Mrs. Thrale of Streatham.

No, it must be confessed that the Thrales had conspicuously failed to make good from the Dreamland point of view; still—the gate was open—no one was about—Ellen Terry would look once more into the low, dark kitchen.

As she passed into its shadow she seemed to leave the present outside. Within the room all was unchanged. The old furniture stood in the old places, the old clock ticked in the corner, but the big old Thrale men no longer strode about; the house was silent and empty—she started as she realized that it was not empty.

There, on a chair by the fire, sat what seemed the oldest thing of all: shrivelled and bent as it sat there; its claw-like hands folded, its eyes fixed curiously upon her, the shadow of what once had been a woman.

The two gazed at each other silently until from the old, old creature in the chair came a far-away voice. 'Well, Nelly,' she said.

'Well, Miss Thrale,' whispered Nelly, for Ellen Terry had vanished, leaving little Nelly from Mackery End standing there half afraid of the dim room and the shadow in the chair.

The old woman sat still, looking across the gulf of the years which to her seemed the space of a day and a night. She had, as the neighbours said, 'touched her hundred' a few days before and Time had passed her by. So

Nelly had run in again. She had been in yesterday, had she not? So why——?

Old Miss Thrale still gazed, searching her memory. What was Nelly doing in her kitchen again so soon? Suddenly her face brightened.

'You want to see the Tiger?' she said.

'The—the *Tiger*?'

'Yes,' said Miss Thrale. 'You may run upstairs by yourself and look at it.'

Ellen Terry gasped slightly. She had been searching for the Gate of Dreams, and behold it stood wide.

'The Tiger? Upstairs?' she faltered.

'Yes,' said Miss Thrale, more sharply. '*You* know where it is. In the cupboard on the landing.'

In the cupboard—of course! The long-forgotten Tiger, once escaped from a menagerie and shot by one of the Thrales as it prowled along the lane! The long-forgotten cupboard where its stuffed but fearsome presence lurked, mysterious and mothy!

'I don't think I'll look at the Tiger to-day, thank you, Miss Thrale. I only wanted——' But it was evident that Miss Thrale took no further interest in what was wanted.

The spark of recognition had leaped up quickly, to be as quickly extinguished; the little scene from the long-ago was played out and Ellen Terry passed softly out again into the sunlight and the world of To-day.

All her life the atmosphere of the open country was about her: though she never played the part upon the stage, her favourite role in private was The Country Girl. For the town and all the town could give she cared not a jot, she delighted in her friends but hated what is called Society, she loved companionship but shrank from the crowd and contrived a thousand ways of escape from it.

She had a collection of odd little cottages in unlikely places within reach of London and was perpetually disappearing into one or another of these burrows.

The first one to which I was admitted was a tiny public-house on the outskirts of Uxbridge, on the road leading to Chalfont St. Giles, and thither I was bidden one day in early spring for 'a breath of fresh air'.

The Audrey Arms stood in a row of cottages and next to another little 'pub' which sold much better beer and drew most of the custom. Ellen Terry was obliged by her lease to keep the business going, but had established a reputation for 'swipes' at the Audrey Arms which filled the coffers of the establishment next door. Only one customer dropped in during my visit when we were at luncheon in the bar parlour and I stepped out to serve him. It was my sole experience as potman and I trust that I gave satisfaction and good measure.

Later on I was admitted to other retreats: the funny little cottage in King-

ston Vale, the Tower Cottage, Winchelsea, a house built into the ivied wall
of the ancient Town Gate, and, best of all, the lovely old farm at Small
Hythe, with its huge timbers and cool low rooms full of the scent from a
great bed of Madonna lilies which blew through and through the knot
holes of the wooden walls.

The perfect simplicity of Ellen Terry's life and mind was in curious
contrast to the exotic complexities of her great sister artist, Sarah Bernhardt,
but I noticed that, in their relations to each other, while Sarah knew little
or nothing about Ellen, Ellen understood Sarah completely and, as a natural
result, liked her greatly.

Once, during a performance of Sarah's, I was taking the air outside the
theatre for a minute. The play was *L'Aiglon*, during which I often required
air. I was still under the golden spell of Sarah, impressed by the solemn
ritual that surrounded her, the bowing servitors, the *jeune premier* in waiting
to lead her from the stage; I was reflecting that I had never met anyone else
outside the classic drama who required to be 'led'.

Bump! A large basket collided abruptly with my back; behind it was the
lovely wistful face of Ellen Terry.

'What have you got there?' I inquired.

'Eggs,' replied Miss Terry, as if it were the most natural thing in the
world for England's leading actress to struggle along Charles Street at
11 p.m. laden with eggs. 'I'm out early. Is Sally B. dead yet?'

I gathered that she wished to know if Madame Bernhardt had finished
her last act and replied in the negative.

'Then let's try for the back row of the pit.'

We obtained admission for ourselves and the eggs and found Madame
Sarah by no means moribund but still haranguing the ghosts in the interminable vision scene.

At its close we went round to see her and she inquired where we were
sitting. 'In the pit,' said Ellen Terry. Madame Sarah was really shocked.
That a sister goddess should watch her from the pit pained her: what, she
wondered, were goddesses coming to in these levelling days. She would
give us stalls—a box. Ellen Terry didn't want a box. '*Il faut que nous*—go
on, you tell her,' she said. 'We've left the eggs in the pit and we *must* go
back,' said I in the French tongue.

Madame Sarah was accustomed to my French and sometimes understood
quite a lot of it, but now she looked hopelessly at me. 'Eggs?' she repeated
vaguely, and really seemed relieved when we left, evidently anticipating a
mental crisis.

A woman friend of Ellen Terry's, who knew her perhaps better than anyone else, once gave a wonderfully true description of her.

'She is like a garden of spring flowers,' she said, 'a garden without a hedge
round it. And cheap excursion trains come in and the trippers swarm over

the paths, stubbing up the flowers and strewing the grass with orange-peel and ginger-beer bottles. We think that the garden can bloom no more, but next morning there is not a footmark on the grass, not a flower disturbed, not a single drop of dew brushed away.'

Of Ellen Terry, the actress, Our Lady of the Lyceum as Oscar Wilde used to style her, what a series of wonderful pictures lives in the memory. Ophelia, a pale shadow with bright hair, the perfect Portia, effulgent, golden, Camma of *The Cup*, beautiful exceedingly, but too frail for the great scene of denunciation in the Temple of Artemis, Juliet, Viola, Beatrice, Imogen, a very pageant of fair women shown in the likeness of one fair woman.

Who shall say which part became her best?

As Portia I think she must have realized almost everyone's ideal—she *was* Portia; as Beatrice she realized something so far above *my* ideal that I could hardly recognize the character, for I have the bad taste not to admire Beatrice.

For the (in my eyes) noisy, pushing, unmannerly, Messinine minx Ellen Terry contrived to substitute a wholly delightful creature whose bubbling and infectious high spirits were never allowed to hide her gentle kindliness and well-bred grace of manner.

From what she evolved her I have never made out; I cannot find her in the play, even with the aid of the crib supplied by Miss Terry, but I hope that my blindness is at fault and that Shakespeare really wrote the part as she played it.

Many people said that her Beatrice was a foretaste of what her Rosalind might be, and surely this supports my theory, for what has Beatrice in common with 'heavenly Rosalind'? Dear me, how intensely Rosalind would have disliked the woman!

About the Lady Macbeth of Ellen Terry there was much diversity of opinion because she did not conform to the accepted Siddons tradition, but her view of the character was an entirely legitimate and logical one and supported by every line of the part. Driven on by love and ambition for her husband she determines at all costs to sweep away the one obstacle that bars his way to power; she sees no further than the murder of Duncan and until this is accomplished she is steel and adamant, allowing no thoughts of pity or honour to weaken her purpose. The murder done, her strength fails; she cannot support Macbeth in his lying tale or act out the scene of hypo-critical grief; she faints and is carried away and thenceforward is but a weary, broken creature, flashing into action for a moment at the interrupted banquet but almost at once sinking back into apathy.

I can hear now the dull hopelessness of Ellen Terry's voice as she mechanically answered Macbeth's, 'What is the night?'—

'Almost at odds with morning, which is which.'

while from her throne she watched the chill dawn-light creep into the hall of feasting.

While she was studying the part a copy of the play was lent to her annotated by Sarah Siddons, and she was much interested to find that the great actress had cut out the swoon after Duncan's murder as 'too terribly hypocritical', her theory being that the faint was feigned in order to show the grief of the hostess. This, of course, may be the right reading, but Ellen Terry's led more naturally to the rapid breakdown of mind and body which followed the crime.

One note by Mrs. Siddons recorded what must have been a marvellous effect. Against the great apostrophe to the spirits of evil in Lady Macbeth's first scene she had written, 'All this in a whisper.'

'Would it not be wonderful and terrible?' said Ellen Terry. 'Of course it ought to be in a whisper but *I* couldn't do it. There would be no use in my trying. I have to get at it another way—but the whisper is *right*!'

She was always more than ready to admire another's work. As Lady Macbeth her appearance was magnificent: long plaits of deep red hair fell from under a purple veil over a robe of green upon which iridescent wings of beetles glittered like emeralds, and a great wine-coloured cloak, gold embroidered, swept from her shoulders.

The effect was barbaric and exactly right, though whence the wife of an ancient Scottish chieftain obtained so many oriental beetles' wings was not explained, and I remember Oscar Wilde remarking, 'Judging from the banquet, Lady Macbeth seems an economical housekeeper and evidently patronizes local industries for her husband's clothes and the servants' liveries, but she takes care to do all her own shopping in Byzantium.'

As Queen Katherine, Ellen Terry again measured herself against the greatest of the Kembles and again was found by many to be wanting in force and weight.

In this play, both she and her great fellow-actor seemed to be a little misplaced; Irving's Wolsey was a magnificent representation of a haughty Prince of the Church, but history gives us a very clear outline of Wolsey's appearance and personality and it is in direct opposition to Irving's. The great actor's pride, which seemed a consuming flame, was the pride of Lucifer, the rebel archangel, not the pride of the Ipswich butcher's son; his ascetic face was that of a religious fanatic, pale with fasting and spiritual strife; Wolsey loved good living and display, he was very much a man and a man of the world.

Irving's great moment, for me, was when, in his first passing across the stage, he turned and looked for a long moment at Buckingham. How Buckingham survived that moment I could never understand—I used to feel quite anxious for Johnston Forbes-Robertson. Luckily, in the part of Buckingham, the actor is unhampered by historical tradition. Buckingham may have been like a mediæval saint whose beautiful face above his black death robe recalled an exquisite early Italian carving in ivory, whose grand voice, ringing out between the strokes of the passing bell, drew all hearts towards him—he may or he may not. But Forbes-Robertson's Buckingham, possessing all these advantages, challenged no comparison and his scene of farewell was the triumph of the production.

Always nervous on a first night, Miss Terry was more than usually so in *Henry VIII* and suddenly swept in upon me on the very day of the production in a highly distraught condition, exclaiming, 'I've just come in to tell you that I'm going to break down to-night. I can tell you the very line—it's in the scene with the two cardinals. I'm going to dry up—dead!'

'But if you know the line—why dry up?'

'I can't tell you why, but I know I shall,' she said.

And she did.

Her Cordelia captured all hearts. Lovely and gracious, she *was* Cordelia as she had been Portia, though I regret to say that, when studying the character, she wrote 'FOOL' in large letters against the young lady's refusal to admit her love for her old father. Yet I am not sure that it was not as Imogen, the last great Shakespearean part played by her at the Lyceum, that she outdid all former achievements. Her scene of joy, on receiving the false letter, a joy so great that sorrow must needs be close behind, was absolutely overwhelming; it moved to tears.

It is of course as a Shakespearean actress that her name will live, yet those who truly loved her unique genius will perhaps recall her most often as Olivia—the Olivia of Goldsmith. Here was a character after her own heart —so much like herself that, as she has told me, before going upon the stage, she had but to think herself back into certain periods of her own life to become the actual Olivia. Pretty Olivia, laughing with the Squire under the old apple-tree in the Vicarage garden, Olivia on the eve of her flight dividing her poor possessions among her dear ones and taking the farewell which she must not speak, Olivia in the wayside inn, looking with innocent eyes at her betrayer, unable to take in the brutal meaning of his words, Olivia at every turn of her pitiful little story lived and breathed before us.

In many of these parts she dominated the play or at least shone at Henry Irving's side with an equal lustre, but there were other minor roles in which it was interesting to watch her loyal support of her great colleague and her capacity for making something out of nothing.

From a technical point of view it is almost more instructive to see a fine actor or actress in a bad part than a good one, and I never realized the art of Ellen Terry more clearly than in the part of Rosamund in Tennyson's *Becket*. The character fairly puzzled her as she studied it.

'I don't know what to do with her,' she said to me. 'She is not there. She does not exist. I don't think that Tennyson ever knew very much about women, and now he is old and has forgotten the little that he knew. She is not a woman at all.'

But she did her best for Rosamund and played her for all she was worth and more.

I was particularly struck one night by her absolute identification (for the moment) with the character.

In the last scene Rosamund sees the murder of Becket in the cathedral from a gallery above and rushes down a stairway to kneel beside the body. Behind the scenes, Rosamund gained her watch-tower with the help of a ladder which led to a little platform overlooking the stage.

I had come in to arrange with her some plan for the next day—we were going somewhere to show somebody something, I recall, but memory gives no further details.

She was already on her perch waiting for her last entrance and I climbed the ladder and sat with her quietly discussing our business when I asked some question and received no answer. I looked round and found Rosamund de Clifford beside me, pale and breathless, her eyes fixed and full of a gradually growing horror, deaf and blind to everything but the mimic murder on the dark stage below. The dying words of Becket floated up— 'Into Thy hands, O Lord, into Thy hands'—she clutched my shoulder tightly, seeming to struggle for speech which would not come, until at last a long gasping cry broke from her lips as she tottered forward and began to run down the steps. Even as she ran the moment of identity with Rosamund passed, and Ellen Terry whispered back, 'Missed it again! I never can *time* that cry right.'

'Fair Rosamund,' as represented by her, was indeed fair. She looked her loveliest, especially in the rich gown of her first entrance, a wonderful, Rossettian effect of dim gold and glowing colour veiled in black, her masses of bright hair in a net of gold and golden hearts embroidered on her robe.

I wonder what a leading lady of the present day would think of that dress, could she examine it closely. The foundation was an old pink gown, worn with stage service and reprieved for the occasion from the rag-bag. The mysterious veiling was the coarsest and cheapest black net, the glory of hair through golden meshes was a bag of gold tinsel stuffed with crumpled paper, and the broidered hearts were cut out of gold paper and gummed on, The whole costume would have been dear at ten shillings and was one of the finest stage dresses that I have ever seen.

Lucy Ashton in *Ravenswood* was another small part which in Ellen Terry's hands became a great one; the almost wordless mad scene was of her very best, and deeply moving.

Her effects seemed so natural that it was difficult to believe they had ever been studied and I remember that she herself was surprised to find how exactly she repeated her performance each night. One evening, after the scene at the Wolf's Crag in which Lucy is seized by a fit of half-hysterical laughter at the excuses made by Cabel Balderstone for her frugal entertainment, Henry Irving came up evidently much annoyed.

'Why did you alter the laugh?' he asked. 'It put me out altogether—I was waiting for you to finish.'

'I laughed as usual,' said Ellen Terry.

'No, you didn't,' said Irving. 'You always say Ha! ha! seventeen times—you only said it fourteen times to-night.'

'I knew nothing about those seventeen Ha! ha's!' said Ellen when telling me about it. 'It was pure luck my getting the same number every night. I try to time the laugh, of course, but as to how many Ha, ha's!—— Now I am *sure* to get it wrong; I shall see Henry standing there counting.'

Ravenswood also dwells in my memory as the play in which I very nearly appeared with Miss Terry in an unrehearsed scene.

At the close of the last act, the craggy coast disappeared for a few moments in gloom, the stage, strewn with rocks, the dead body of William Terris and other objects of interest, miraculously cleared itself, and when the shadow lifted the final tableau was revealed—the incoming tide rippling over the Kelpie's Flow under a sky full of the glory of dawn.

It was a wonderful illusion; the empty stage looked limitless, the scene was almost entirely a transparency, the effect being produced by the gradual turning up of concealed lights.

Lucy Ashton had died distraught, to the keen distress of the audience and her own complete satisfaction. It was one of the few scenes in which she really admired herself and she now stood, bunching up her trailing satin robes, quite unwearied and full of the youthful desire to be where she ought not to be and to see what was not intended for inspection.

'Let us watch the change to the Kelpie's Flow *on* the stage,' she whispered to me. 'It's so interesting to see how it all works. We can hide behind that rock.'

We hid. The play was ending, the lights began to fade; Edgar of Ravenswood had ridden off to his fate and the witch woman's prophetic chant rang out in the shadows.

> 'He shall stable his steed in the Kelpie's Flow
> And his name shall be lost for ever mo——'

Darkness fell and things began to stir curiously; trees and rocks developed strange activity and slid silently away in all directions. Hayston of Bucklaw's dead body glided by, skidding comfortably along on a sliding plank. As it passed, the corpse giggled audibly and remarked, 'Look out. Your rock's going next'.

Our rock! Our solid, immovable rock in whose shelter we crouched? Impossible. Nevertheless, after a preliminary shiver, our rock got into motion, sailing slowly across the stage bound for the far-distant O.P. wings. Other smaller rocks which would have masked our retreat had already deserted us—in another moment the deceased Bride of Lammermuir in all the glories of her wedding toilette would be discovered sitting in the middle of the Kelpie's Flow!

We did our best, and the progress of Miss Ashton and friend on all fours across the Lyceum stage must have been an impressive sight which was at any rate much appreciated by the late Bucklaw, who had drifted into haven and was now sitting up, absorbed in our Odyssey and trying to shout advice in a whisper. It was a race between us and the rock and a close one at the finish but luckily ending in a dead heat. 'Where—where was my train?' panted Lucy Ashton.

'Most of it was in my mouth,' I puffed—I was very hot and dusty; 'the rest was bunched up between my knees.'

'Thank goodness that Henry went straight up to his room,' exclaimed Miss Ashton piously, and I thanked goodness from a full heart.

One of the most beautiful scenes ever put upon the stage was in *Ravenswood*; a dell in a spring coppice where sunbeams sifted faintly through the tender green and where the Mermaidens' Well bubbled up amidst sheets of bluebells. It was by Hawes Craven and was an almost perfect illusion as well as an admirable background for figures. It was repainted and used again as the hawthorn brake in *King Arthur*, but at the loss of much of its original charm.

For the *King Arthur* scenery and costumes Irving had gone to Burne-Jones, who made lovely and elaborate designs for both.

Ellen Terry was so absolutely of the legendary period, those mythical, mystical days which never were and never could have been, that her Queen Guinevere had been looked forward to for years: when it came it was a disappointment.

It was not her fault; she looked lovely and played well.

It was not precisely the author's fault, for J. Comyns Carr had pieced together a very workmanlike frame in which to set the series of Burne-Jones pictures which formed the real attraction of the play. It was the fault of Tennyson, whose 'blameless king' of the Idylls has taken such root in the public mind that Mr. Carr no doubt feared to dig him up.

Unfortunately, a blameless Arthur knocks all meaning out of the Arthurian legends, and Arthur became Fortune's fool upon whose haloed head unmerited misfortunes were heaped by a freakish Providence, while Guinevere, no longer the instrument of Fate, was merely a frisky matron, 'no better than she should be'. No awkward questions were raised as to the parentage of Modred, he had apparently 'just growed', like Topsy, and Johnston Forbes-Robertson, as Launcelot, played and looked Galahad to perfection.

Under these circumstances there was little chance for Guinevere and it is curious how little I can recall of the whole production beyond Irving's figure in black armour, which seemed as though it had stepped from the canvas of Burne-Jones.

One would have thought that this ideal knight and the two 'blessed damozels', Ellen Terry and Sarah Bernhardt, would inevitably have been seized upon as models by the Painter-in-Ordinary to the Court of King Arthur; but, as far as I know, he never made even a sketch of one of them. It is even more strange that Ellen Terry, who was the accepted type of the Pre-Raphaelite School and an embodiment of all the romance and glamour of their favourite literature, should never have been painted by any member of the band.

Yet she has been fortunate in her painters; the Watts studies have caught much of the wistful charm of her girlhood, and the splendid Sargent portrait (Lady Macbeth) will be an enduring memorial of her maturity.

Irving secured the 'Lady Macbeth' and it hung for many years in his room at the theatre, in company with his own portrait by Whistler, which chance had delivered into his hands.

One evening he announced with some diffidence to Ellen Terry that he had bought a picture: he knew that picture dealing was not in his line and, as a rule, consulted her before committing himself.

Ellen looked anxious. 'A picture?'

'Yes. As I was passing a frame-shop I saw that thing that Whistler did of me—Philip of Spain—do you remember it?'

'I should think I *did*. Well?'

'Well, I thought I'd ask the price and the man said a hundred pounds.'

'A hundred pounds?'

'Yes. Was that too much?'

'A hundred pounds! There weren't any *other* Whistler pictures in the shop, were there?'

'Oh yes, lots. I didn't look at 'em—I only wanted the portrait.'

All the next day Ellen Terry was hopelessly busy but on the day after she flew to the frame-shop: not a Whistler canvas was to be seen—the great chance was lost.

In spite of his luck, Irving never cared for the 'Philip' picture. Applauded for his cleverness in finding and buying it, he conceded it a place in the Beef Steak Room at the Lyceum but never hesitated to say that he thought little of it. And, from his point of view, he was right. He had no concern with it as a design and did not value its tone and quality: he regarded it solely as a portrait and as such it is of little importance. It is a mere rub in of the wonderful face, a fine start as to tone and with promise of character in the expression but hardly carried further than the preliminary stage. Irving was a bad sitter, impatient and uninterested, and this may have had something to do with the incomplete state of the picture. Whistler demanded full measure from his models both of time and patience and certainly would not have got much of either out of Henry Irving.

Ellen Terry, on the contrary, was a good sitter, her love of art and real understanding of pictures giving her far more sympathy and consideration for the artist than is usually accorded to that downtrodden person.

I myself victimized her several times, though only once—from an unexpected sitting—did I get anything like a satisfactory result.

On one dark, foggy morning a ring had come at my studio bell. I opened the door—there stood Ophelia, wraith-like in the mist, an aureole of pale hair clinging about her face and shoulders.

'I've washed my head,' announced the apparition, resolving itself into Ellen Terry. 'May I come in and dry it? All the fires at home seemed to have gone out,' she continued, as she drifted into the room, 'and I remembered that you usually have a good one so—here I am. You haven't got a model, have you?'

'Yes,' said I, 'if you don't mind being one.'

'No, I don't mind,' said Ellen with resignation: she knew the ways of studios and seldom escaped from one without paying toll, 'but you must let me sit by the fire so that my hair may dry.'

So she sat by the fire and her hair dried beautifully and I made a pastel study which, by happy accident, turned out a good likeness, catching a rapt expression which I had tried for before but never succeeded in fixing. Irving used to call the head 'Ellen in Heaven', and there was something appropriate in the title, though she had but been drawn to the skies by a warm fire and the satisfactory drying of her hair.

When that ceremony was at an end and my sketch finished, she rose to go. 'I don't sit badly, do I?' she said. 'I dare say I could have made something as a model. Are there men painting away behind each of those doors?' she inquired, as we came out into the dark passage. 'Do I know any of them?'

'You know Phil Burne-Jones—the end door,' said I. 'None of the others, I think.'

'Then I shall call on them and see if they'll engage me,' said Ellen firmly, and rang the nearest bell.

'No, no. Go away,' bellowed the artist, bursting forth for a second, then slamming the door.

I coughed discreetly.

'Pooh, he didn't look at me. That doesn't count,' said Ellen, moving to the next bell.

'Perhaps this one *will*,' I murmured, 'and what are you going to do then?' But the door was already open.

'Please, do you want a model?' said Miss Terry.

'No,' said the man, peering at her in the dimness, 'that is—here, you'd better come in.'

The model hesitated, then came inspiration.

'I ought to tell you that I only sit for Scriptural subjects,' she observed. 'The Infant Samuel and so on.'

She posed and I thought we were lost, the Infant Samuel was most attractive; but luckily the light was dim, the poor man missed his chance and, casting a distrustful look at the infant, hastily shut himself in.

'He was rather better,' said Ellen hopefully.

'*He* thought you were a bit off it,' said I. 'Goodness knows what the next one will think.'

She rang at a third door with no result.

'I can't get hold of this one,' she complained, applying herself afresh to the bell.

'No more can the police,' I observed. 'He has been "wanted" for the last three weeks.'

Ellen seemed suddenly discouraged.

'I don't think I'll try any more of them,' she said. 'They don't seem very interesting so far—perhaps I had better stick to my present job.'

And I agreed with her.

CHARLES DICKENS AND
GREAT EXPECTATIONS

BY BERNARD SHAW

Published in *The Novel Library* (1947)

CHARLES DICKENS AND
GREAT EXPECTATIONS

'GREAT EXPECTATIONS' is the last of the three full-length stories written by Dickens in the form of an autobiography. Of the three, *Bleak House*, as the autobiography of Miss Esther Summerson, is naturally the least personal, as Esther is not only a woman but a maddening prig, though we are forced to admit that such paragons exist and are perhaps worthy of the reverent admiration with which Dickens regarded them. Ruling her out, we have *David Copperfield* and *Great Expectations*. David was, for a time at least, Dickens's favourite child, perhaps because he had used him to express the bitterness of that episode in his own experience which had wounded his boyish self-respect most deeply. For Dickens, in spite of his exuberance, was a deeply reserved man: the exuberance was imagination and acting (his imagination was ceaseless, and his outward life a feat of acting from beginning to end); and we shall never know whether in that immensely broadened outlook and knowledge of the world which began with *Hard Times* and *Little Dorrit*, and left all his earlier works behind, he may not have come to see that making his living by sticking labels on blacking bottles and rubbing shoulders with boys who were not gentlemen, was as little shameful as being the genteel apprentice in the office of Mr. Spenlow, or the shorthand writer recording the unending twaddle of the House of Commons and electioneering bunk on the hustings of all the Eatanswills in the country.

That there was a tragic change in his valuations can be shown by contrasting Micawber with William Dorrit, in which light Micawber suddenly becomes a mere marionette pantaloon with a funny bag of tricks which he repeats until we can bear no more of him, and Dorrit a portrait of the deadliest and deepest truth to nature. Now contrast David with Pip; and believe, if you can, that there was no revision of his estimate of the favourite child David as a work of art and even as a vehicle of experience. The adult David fades into what stage managers call a walking gentleman. The reappearance of Mr. Dickens in the character of a blacksmith's boy may be regarded as an apology to Mealy Potatoes.

Dickens did in fact know that *Great Expectations* was his most compactly perfect book. In all the other books, there are episodes of wild extravagance, extraordinarily funny if they catch you at the right age, but recklessly grotesque as nature studies. Even in *Little Dorrit*, Dickens's masterpiece among many masterpieces, it is impossible to believe that the perfectly authentic Mr. Pancks really stopped the equally authentic Mr. Casby in a crowded street in London and cut his hair; and though Mr. F.'s aunt is a first-rate clinical study of senile deficiency in a shrewd old woman, her collisions with Arthur Clennam are too funny to be taken seriously. We cannot say of Casby, Pancks, and the aunt, as we can say of Sam Weller, that such people never existed; for most of us have met their counterparts in real life; but we can say tht Dickens's sense of fun ran away with him over them. If we have absolutely no fun in us we may even state gravely that there has been a lapse from the artistic integrity of the tragic picture of English society which is the subject of the book.

In *Great Expectations* we have Wopsle and Trabb's boy; but they have their part and purpose in the story and do not overstep the immodesty of nature. It is hardly decent to compare Mr. F.'s aunt with Miss Havisham; but as contrasted studies of madwomen they make you shudder at the thought of what Dickens might have made of Miss Havisham if he had seen her as a comic personage. For life is no laughing matter in *Great Expectations*; the book is all of one piece and consistently truthful as none of the other books are, not even the compact *Tale of Two Cities*, which is pure sentimental melodrama from beginning to end, and shockingly wanting in any philosophy of history in its view of the French Revolution.

Dickens never regarded himself as a revolutionist, though he certainly was one. His implacable contempt for the House of Commons, founded on his experience as a parliamentary reporter, never wavered from the account of the Eatanswill election and of Nicholas Nickleby's interview with Pugstyles to the Veneering election in *Our Mutual Friend*, his last book (*Edwin Drood* is only a gesture by a man three-quarters dead). And this was not mere satire, of which there had been plenty. Dickens was the first writer to perceive and state definitely that the House of Commons, working on the Party system, is an extraordinarily efficient device for dissipating all our reforming energy and ability in Party debate and when anything urgently needs to be done, finding out 'how not to do it'. It took very little time to get an ineffective Factory Act. It took fifty years to make it effective, though the labour conditions in the factories and mines were horrible. After Dickens's death, it took thirty years to pass an Irish Home Rule Bill, which was promptly repudiated by the military plutocracy, leaving the question to be settled by a competition in slaughter and house burning, just as it would have been between two tribes of savages. Liberty under the British parliamentary system means slavery for nine-tenths of the people, and slave exploitation or parasitic idolatry and snobbery for the rest. Parliament men

—one cannot call them statesmen—and even historians, keep declaring that the British parliamentary system is one of the greatest blessings British political genius has given to the world; and the world has taken it at its self-valuation and set up imitations of it all over Europe and America, always with the same result: political students outside Parliament exposing the most frightful social evils and prescribing their remedies, and Parliament ignoring them as long as possible and then engulfing their disciples and changing them from reformers into partisans with time for nothing but keeping their party in power or opposing the Government, rightly or wrongly ('it is the duty of the Opposition to oppose'), as the case might be. In the middle of the nineteenth century Dickens saw this and said it. He had to be ignored, as he would not stand for Parliament and be paralysed.

Europe has had to learn from hard experience what it would not learn from Dickens. The Fascist and Communist revolutions which swept the great parliamentary sham into the dustbin after it had produced a colossal Anarchist war, made no mention of Dickens; but on the parliamentary point he was as much their prophet as Marx was the economic prophet of the Soviets. Yet a recent reactionist against Dickens worship declares that he 'never went ahead of his public'.

Marx and Dickens were contemporaries living in the same city and pursuing the same profession of literature; yet they seem to us like creatures of a different species living in different worlds. Dickens, if he had ever become conscious of Karl Marx, would have been classed with him as a revolutionist. The difference between a revolutionist and what Marx called a bourgeois is that the bourgeois regards the existing social order as the permanent and natural order of human society, needing reforms now and then and here and there, but essentially good and sane and right and respectable and proper and everlasting. To the revolutionist it is transitory, mistaken, objectionable, and pathological: a social disease to be cured, not to be endured. We have only to compare Thackeray and Trollope with Dickens to perceive this contrast. Thackeray reviled the dominant classses with a savagery which would have been unchivalrous in Dickens: he denied to his governing class characters even the common good qualities and accomplishments of ladies and gentleman, making them mean, illiterate, dishonest, ignorant, sycophantic to an inhuman degree, whilst Dickens, even when making his aristocrats ridiculous and futile, at least made gentlemen of them. Trollope, who regarded Thackeray as his master and exemplar, had none of his venom, and has left us a far better balanced and more truthful picture of Victorian well-off society, never consciously whitewashing it, though allowing it its full complement of black sheep of both sexes. But Trollope's politics were those of the country house and the hunting field just as were Thackeray's. Accordingly, Thackeray and Trollope were received and approved by fashionable society with complete confidence. Dickens, though able to fascinate all classes, was never so received or approved except by quite good-natured or stupid ladies and gentlemen who were incapable of criticizing anyone who could make them laugh and cry. He was told that he could not describe a gentleman and that *Little Dorrit* is twaddle. And the reason was that in his books the west-end heaven appears as a fool's paradise that must pass away instead of being an indispensable preparatory school for the New Jerusalem of Revelation. A leading encyclopedia tells us that Dickens had 'no knowledge of country gentlemen'. It would have been nearer the mark to say that Dickens knew all that really mattered about Sir Leicester Dedlock and that Trollope knew nothing that really mattered about him. Trollope and Thackeray could see Chesney Wold; but Dickens could see through it. And this was no joke to Dickens. He was deeply concerned about it, and understood how revolutions begin with burning the chateaux.

The difference between Marx and Dickens was that Marx knew that he was a revolutionist whilst Dickens had not the faintest suspicion of that part of his calling. Compare the young Dickens looking for a job in a lawyer's office and teaching himself shorthand to escape from his office stool to the reporters' gallery, with the young Trotsky, the young Lenin, quite deliberately facing disreputable poverty and adopting revolution as their profession with every alternative of bourgeois security and respectability much more fully open to them than to Dickens.

And this brings us to Dickens's position as a member of the educated and cultured classes who had neither education nor culture. This was fortunate for him and for the world in one way, as he escaped the school and university routine which complicates cultural Philistinism with the mentality of a Red Indian brave. Better no schooling at all than the schooling of Rudyard Kipling and Winston Churchill. But there are homes in which a mentally acquisitive boy can make contact with the fine arts. I myself learnt nothing at school, but gained in my home an extensive and highly educational knowledge of music. I had access to illustrated books on painting which sent me to the National Gallery; so that I was able to support myself as a critic of music and painting as Dickens supported himself by shorthand. I devoured books on science and on the religious controversies of the day. It is in this way, and not in our public schools and universities that such culture as there is in England is kept alive.

Now the Dickenses seem to have been complete barbarians. Dickens mentions the delight with which he discovered in an attic a heap of eighteenth-century novels. But Smollett was a grosser barbarian than Dickens himself; and *Don Quixote* and *The Arabian Nights*, though they gave the cue to his eager imagination, left him quite in the dark as to the philosophy and art of his day. To him a philosopher, an intellectual, was a figure of fun. Count Smorltork is the creation of a street Arab: Dickens did not even know that the Count's method of studying Chinese metaphysics by studying metaphysics and China and 'combining the information' was not only sensible and correct, but the only possible method. To Dickens as to most Victorian Englishmen metaphysics were ridiculous, useless, unpractical, and the mark of a fool. He was musical enough to have a repertory of popular ballads which he sang all over the house to keep his voice in order; and he made Tom Pinch play the organ in church as an amiable accomplishment; but I cannot remember hearing that he ever went to a classical concert, or even knew of the existence of such entertainments. The articles on the National Gallery in *All the Year Round*, though extremely funny in their descriptions of 'The Apotheosis' of 'William the Silent' (the title alone would make a cat laugh), and on some profane points sensible enough, are those of a complete Philistine. One cannot say that he disliked all painters in the face of his friendship with Maclise and Clarkson Stanfield; but it was not a cultural friendship: Stanfield was a scene painter who appealed to that English love of landscape which is so often confused with a love of art; and Maclise was a pictorial anecdotist who presented scenes from Shakespeare's plays exactly as they were presented on the stage. When Dickens introduced in his stories a character whom he intensely disliked he chose an artistic profession for him. Henry Gowan in *Little Dorrit* is a painter. Pecksniff is an architect. Harold Skimpole is a musician. There is real hatred in his treatment of them.

Now far be it from me to imply that they are false to nature. Artists are often detestable human beings; and the famous Anti-Scrape, officially The Society for the Protection of Ancient Buildings, was founded by William Morris and his friends to protect ancient buildings from architects. What is more, the ultra-artistic sets, the Pre-Raphaelites and the aesthetes grouped round Rossetti and Morris and Ruskin, were all Dickens worshippers who made a sort of cult of Trabb's boy and would have regarded me as a traitor if they had read what I am now writing. They knew better than anyone else that Leigh Hunt deserved all he got as Harold Skimpole, that Gowan's shallow sort of painting was a nuisance, and that architecture was just the right profession for a parasite on Salisbury Cathedral like Pecksniff. But all their Dickensian enthusiasm, and all the truth to life of Dickens's portraiture cannot extenuate the fact that the cultural side of art was as little known to Dickens as it is possible for a thing so public to remain to a man so apprehensive. You may read the stories of Dickens from beginning to end without ever learning that he lived through a period of fierce revivals and revolutionary movements in art, in philosophy, in sociology, in religion: in short, in culture. Dean Inge's remark that 'the number of great subjects in which Dickens took no interest whatever is amazing' hits the nail exactly on the head. As to finding such a person as Karl Marx among his characters, one would as soon look for a nautilus in a nursery.

Yet *Little Dorrit* is a more seditious book than *Das Kapital*. All over Europe

men and women are in prison for pamphlets and speeches which are to
Little Dorrit as red pepper to dynamite. Fortunately for social evolution
Governments never know where to strike. Barnacle and Stiltstalking were
far too conceited to recognize their own portraits. Parliament, wearying its
leaders out in a few years in the ceaseless drudgery of finding out how not to
do it, and smothering it in talk, could not conceive that its heartbreaking
industry could have any relation to the ridiculous fiction of the Coodle-
Doodle discussions in Sir Leicester Dedlock's drawing-room. As to the
Circumlocution Office, well, perhaps the staffs, owing their posts to
patronage and regarding them as sinecures, were a bit too insolent to the
public, and would be none the worse for a little chaff from a funny fellow
like Dickens; but their inefficiency as a public service was actually a good
thing, as it provided a standing object lesson in the superiority of private
enterprise. Mr. Sparkler was not offended: he stuck to his job and never read
anything. *Little Dorrit* and *Das Kapital* were all the same to him: they never
entered his world; and to him that world was the whole world.

The mass of Dickens readers, finding all these people too funny to be
credible, continued to idolize Coodle and Doodle as great statesmen, and
made no distinction between John Stuart Mill at the India Office and Mr.
Sparkler. In fact the picture was not only too funny to be credible: it was
too truthful to be credible. But the fun was no fun to Dickens: the truth was
too bitter. When you laugh at Jack Bunsby, or at The Orfling when the
handle of her corkscrew came off and smote her on the chin, you have no
doubt that Dickens is laughing with you like a street boy, despite Bunsby's
tragic end. But whilst you laugh at Sparkler or young Barnacle, Dickens is
in deadly earnest: he means that both of them must go into the dustbin
if England is to survive.

And yet Dickens never saw himself as a revolutionist. It never occurred
to him to found a Red International, as Marx did, not even to join one out
of the dozens of political reform societies that were about him. He was an
English gentleman of the professional class, who would not allow his
daughter to go on the stage because it was not respectable. He knew so little
about revolutionists that when Mazzini called on him and sent in his card,
Dickens, much puzzled, concluded that the unknown foreign gentleman
wanted money, and very kindly sent him down a sovereign to get rid of him.
He discovered for himself all the grievances he exposed, and had no sense of
belonging to a movement, nor any desire to combine with others who
shared his subversive views. To educate his children religiously and historically he wrote *A Child's History of England* which had not even the excuse of
being childish, and a paraphrase of the gospel biography which is only a
belittling of it for little children. He had much better have left the history to
Little Arthur and Mrs. Markham and Goldsmith, and taken into account
the extraordinary educational value of the Authorized Version as a work of

literary art. He probably thought as seldom of himself as a literary artist as of himself as a revolutionist; and he had his share in the revolt against the supernatural pretensions of the Bible which was to end in the vogue of Agnosticism and the pontificate of Darwin. It blinded that generation to the artistic importance of the fact that at a moment when all the literary energy in England was in full eruption, when Shakespeare was just dead and Milton just born, a picked body of scholars undertook the task of translating into English what they believed to be the words of God himself. Under the strain of that conviction they surpassed all their normal powers, transfiguring the original texts into literary masterpieces of a splendour that no merely mortal writers can ever again hope to achieve. But the nineteenth century either did not dare think of the Bible in that way, it being fetish, or else it was in such furious reaction against the fetishisms that it would not allow the so-called Holy Scriptures even an artistic merit. At all events Dickens thought his Little Nell style better for his children than the English of King James's inspired scribes. He took them (for a time at least) to churches of the Unitarian persuasion, where they could be both sceptical and respectable; but it is hard to say what Dickens believed or did not believe metaphysically or metapolitically, though he left us in no doubt as to his opinion of the Lords, the Commons, and the ante-Crimean Civil Service.

On the positive side he had nothing to say. Marxism and Darwinism came too late for him. He might have been a Comtist—perhaps ought to have been a Comtist, but was not. He was an independent Dickensian, a sort of unphilosophic Radical, with a complete disbelief in government by the people and an equally complete hostility to government in any other interest than theirs. He exposed many abuses and called passionately on the rulers of the people to remedy them; but he never called on the people themselves. He would as soon have thought of calling on them to write their own novels.

Meanwhile he overloaded himself and his unfortunate wife with such a host of children that he was forced to work himself to death prematurely to provide for them and for the well-to-do life he led. The reading public cannot bear to think of its pet authors as struggling with the economic pressures that often conflict so cruelly with the urge of genius. This pressure was harder on Dickens than on many poorer men. He had a solid bourgeois conscience which made it impossible for him to let wife and children starve whilst he followed the path of destiny. Marx let his wife go crazy with prolonged poverty whilst he wrote a book which changed the mind of the world. But then Marx had been comfortably brought up and thoroughly educated in the German manner. Dickens knew far too much of the horrors of impecuniosity to put his wife through what his mother had gone through, or have his children pasting labels on blacking bottles. He had to please his public or lapse into that sort of poverty. Under such circumstances the domestic conscience inevitably pushes the artistic conscience into the second place. We shall never know how much of Dickens's cheery optimism belied his real outlook on life. He went his own way far enough to make it clear that when he was not infectiously laughing he was a melancholy fellow. Arthur Clennam is one of the Dismal Jemmies of literature. For any gaiety of heart we have to turn to the impossible Dick Swiveller, who by the way, was designed as a revoltingly coarse fortune hunter, and still appears in that character in the single scene which precedes his sudden appeal to Dickens's sense of fun, and consequent transformation into a highly entertaining and entirely fantastic clown. This was a genuine conversion and not a concession to public taste; but the case of Walter Gay in *Dombey and Son*, whose high spirits were planned as a prelude to his degeneration and ruin, is a flagrant case of a manufactured happy ending to save a painful one. Martin Chuzzlewit begins as a study in selfishness and ends nowhere. Mr. Boffin, corrupted by riches, gets discharged without a stain on his character by explaining that he was only pretending for benevolent purposes, but leaves us with a feeling that some of his pretences were highly suspicious. Jarndyce, a violently good man, keeps on doing generous things, yet ends by practising a heartlessly cruel and indelicate deception on Esther Summerson for the sake of giving her a pleasant melodramatic surprise. I will not go so far as to say that Dickens's novels are full of melancholy intentions which he dares not carry through to their unhappy conclusions; but he gave us no vitally happy heroes and heroines after Pickwick (begun, like Don Quixote, as a contemptible butt). Their happy endings are manufactured to make the books pleasant. Nobody who has endured the novels of our twentieth-century emancipated women, enormously cleverer and better informed than the novels of Dickens, and ruthlessly calculated to leave their readers hopelessly discouraged and miserable, will feel anything but gratitude to Dickens for his humanity in speeding his parting guests with happy faces by turning from the world of destiny to the world of accidental good luck; but as our minds grow stronger some of his consolations become unnecessary and even irritating. And it happens that it is with just such a consolation that *Great Expectations* ends.

It did not always end so. Dickens wrote two endings, and made a mess of both. In the first ending, which Bulwer Lytton persuaded him to discard, Pip takes little Pip for a walk in Piccadilly and is stopped by Estella, who is passing in her carriage. She is comfortably married to a Shropshire doctor, and just says how d'y'do to Pip and kisses the little boy before they both pass on out of one another's lives. This, though it is marred by Pip's pious hope that her husband may have thrashed into her some understanding of how much she has made him suffer, is true to nature. But it is much too matter-of-fact to be the right ending to a tragedy. Piccadilly was impossible in such a context; and the passing carriage was unconsciously borrowed from

A Day's Ride: A Life's Romance, the novel by Lever which was so unpopular that *Great Expectations* had to be written to replace it in *All The Year Round*. But in Lever's story it is the man who stops the carriage, only to be cut dead by the lady. Dickens must have felt that there was something wrong with this ending; and Bulwer's objection confirmed his doubt. Accordingly, he wrote a new ending, in which he got rid of Piccadilly and substituted a perfectly congruous and beautifully touching scene and hour and atmosphere for the meeting. He abolished the Shropshire doctor and left out the little boy. So far the new ending was in every way better than the first one.

Unfortunately, what Bulwer wanted was what is called a happy ending, presenting Pip and Estella as reunited lovers who were going to marry and live happily ever after; and Dickens, though he could not bring himself to be quite so explicit in sentimental falsehood, did, at the end of the very last line, allow himself to say that there was 'no shadow of parting' between them. If Pip had said 'Since that parting I have been able to think of her without the old unhappiness; but I have never tried to see her again, and I know I never shall' he would have been left with at least the prospect of a bearable life. But the notion that he could ever have been happy with Estella: indeed that anyone could ever have been happy with Estella, is positively unpleasant. I can remember when the Cowden Clarks ventured to hint a doubt whether Benedick and Beatrice had a very delightful union to look forward to; but that did not greatly matter, as Benedick and Beatrice have none of the reality of Pip and Estella. Shakespeare could afford to trifle with *Much Ado About Nothing*, which is avowedly a potboiler; but *Great Expectations* is a different matter. Dickens put nearly all his thought into it. It is too serious a book to be a trivially happy one. Its beginning is unhappy; its middle is unhappy; and the conventional happy ending is an outrage on it.

Estella is a curious addition to the gallery of unamiable women painted by Dickens. In my youth it was commonly said that Dickens could not draw women. The people who said this were thinking of Agnes Wickfield and Esther Summerson, of Little Dorrit and Florence Dombey, and thinking of them as ridiculous idealizations of their sex. Gissing put a stop to that by asking whether shrews like Mrs. Raddle, Mrs. Macstinger, Mrs. Gargery, fools like Mrs. Nickleby and Flora Finching, warped spinsters like Rosa Dartle and Miss Wade, were not masterpieces of women drawing. And they are all unamiable. But for Betsy Trotwood, who is a very lovable fairy godmother and yet a genuine nature study, and an old dear like Mrs. Boffin, one would be tempted to ask whether Dickens had ever in his life met an amiable female. The transformation of Dora into Flora is diabolical, but frightfully true to nature. Of course Dickens with his imagination could invent amiable women by the dozen; but somehow he could not or would not bring them to life as he brought the others. We doubt whether he ever knew a Little

Dorrit; but Fanny Dorrit is from the life unmistakably. So is Estella. She is a much more elaborate study than Fanny, and, I should guess, a recent one.

Dickens, when he let himself go in *Great Expectations*, was separated from his wife and free to make more intimate acquaintances with women than a domesticated man can. I know nothing of his adventures in this phase of his career, though I daresay a good deal of it will be dug out by the little sect of anti-Dickensites whose fanaticism has been provoked by the Dickens Fellow-ships. It is not necessary to suggest a love affair; for Dickens could get from a passing glance a hint which he could expand into a full-grown character. The point concerns us here only because it is the point on which the ending of *Great Expectations* turns: namely, that Estella is a born tormentor. She deliberately torments Pip all through for the fun of it; and in the little we hear of her intercourse with others there is no suggestion of a moment of kindness: in fact her tormenting of Pip is almost affectionate in contrast to the cold disdain of her attitude towards the people who were not worth tormenting. It is not surprising that the unfortunate Bentley Drummle, whom she marries in the stupidity of sheer perversity, is obliged to defend himself from her clever malice with his fists: a consolation to us for Pip's broken heart, but not altogether a credible one; for the real Estellas can usually intimidate the real Bentley Drummles. At all events the final sugary suggestion of Estella redeemed by Bentley's thrashings and waste of her money, and living happily with Pip for ever after, provoked even Dickens's eldest son to rebel against it, most justly.

Apart from this the story is the most perfect of Dickens's works. In it he does not muddle himself with the ridiculous plots that appear like vestiges of the stone age in many of his books, from *Oliver Twist* to the end. The story is built round a single and simple catastrophe: the revelation to Pip of the source of his great expectations. There is, it is true, a trace of the old plot superstition in Estella turning out to be Magwitch's daughter, but it provides a touchingly happy ending for that heroic Warmint. Who could have the heart to grudge it to him?

As our social conscience expands and makes the intense class snobbery of the nineteenth century seem less natural to us, the tragedy of *Great Expectations* will lose some of its appeal. I have already wondered whether Dickens himself ever came to see that his agonizing sensitiveness about the blacking bottles and his resentment of his mother's opposition to his escape from them was not too snobbish to deserve all the sympathy he claimed for it. Compare the case of H. G. Wells, our nearest to a twentieth-century Dickens. Wells hated being a draper's assistant as much as Dickens hated being a warehouse boy; but he was not in the least ashamed of it, and did not blame his mother for regarding it as the summit of her ambition for him. Fate having imposed on that engaging cricketer Mr. Wells's father an incongruous means of livelihood in the shape of a small shop, shop-keeping did not present itself to the young Wells as beneath him, whereas to the genteel Dickens being a warehouse boy was an unbearable comedown. Still, I cannot help speculating on whether if Dickens had not killed himself prematurely to pile up money for that excessive family of his, he might not have reached a stage at which he could have got as much fun out of the blacking bottles as Mr. Wells got out of his abhorred draper's counter.

Dickens never reached that stage; and there is no prevision of it in *Great Expectations*; for in it he never raises the question why Pip should refuse Magwitch's endowment and shrink from him with such inhuman loathing. Magwitch no doubt was a Warmint from the point of view of the genteel Dickens family and even from his own; but Victor Hugo would have made him a magnificent hero, another Valjean. Inspired by an altogether noble fixed idea, he had lifted himself out of his rut of crime and honestly made a fortune for the child who had fed him when he was starving. If Pip had no objection to be a parasite instead of an honest blacksmith, at least he had a better claim to be a parasite on Magwitch's earnings than, as he imagined, on Miss Havisham's property. It is curious that this should not have occurred to Dickens; for nothing could exceed the bitterness of his exposure of the futility of Pip's parasitism. If all that came of sponging on Miss Havisham (as he thought) was the privilege of being one of the Finches of the Grove, he need not have felt his dependence on Magwitch to be incompatible with his entirely baseless self-respect. But Pip—and I am afraid Pip must be to this extent identified with Dickens—could not see Magwitch as an animal of the same species as himself or Miss Havisham. His feeling is true to the nature of snobbery; but his creator says no word in criticism of that ephemeral limitation.

The basic truth of the situation is that Pip, like his creator, has no culture and no religion. Joe Gargery, when Pip tells a monstrous string of lies about Miss Havisham, advises him to say a repentant word about it in his prayers; but Pip never prays; and church means nothing to him but Mr. Wopsle's orotundity. In this he resembles David Copperfield, who has gentility but neither culture nor religion. Pip's world is therefore a very melancholy place, and his conduct, good or bad, always helpless. This is why Dickens worked against so black a background after he was roused from his ignorant middle-class cheery optimism by Carlyle. When he lost his belief in bourgeois society and with it his lightness of heart he had neither an economic Utopia nor a credible religion to hitch on to. His world becomes a world of great expectations cruelly disappointed. The Wells world is a world of greater and greater expectations continually being fulfilled. This is a huge improvement. Dickens never had time to form a philosophy or define a faith; and his later and greater books are saddened by the evil that is done under the sun; but at least he preserved his intellectual innocence sufficiently to escape the dismal pseudo-scientific fatalism that was descending on the world in his latter days, founded on the preposterous error as to causation in which the future is determined by the present, which has been determined by the past. The true causation, of course, is always the incessant irresistible activity of the evolutionary appetite.

BERLIN AND BLOOMSBURY
IN THE THIRTIES

BY STEPHEN SPENDER

from *World Within World* (1951)

BERLIN AND BLOOMSBURY
IN THE THIRTIES

AT the side of a lake there is a city which in the gloom suggests a vast construction of many forms, all shaped like gallows. Buildings, some of which are only blackened façades with broken windows, rise from its shores. An outline of the town's centre still exists, with churches, offices and hotels. Indeed, some of the buildings are remarkably unscathed, just as in a corpse some flesh seems perfect and even flushed with life. But that astonishing and total change, that incalculable shift from a soaring to a sinking motion which distinguishes a dead body, has taken place in Hamburg.

This is Hamburg as I saw it in August 1945. All legends of the living city have been superseded by the legend of the dead one. In a great air raid, when fire bombs were dropped in a ring around the centre of the city, the immense heat of the fire caused a whirlwind in which flames rushed from building to building, and thousands of people were roasted alive.

Dusk fell as I walked along the end of the lake in the late August evening. The water of the lake became a soft blue gauze wrapped round the plough of stars reflected in its surface.

In all my memories of Germany these great wrecks rise up between me and my past. They are the more insistent because they were implicit in their own past: and now it is difficult for me to think of my first evening in Hamburg (which now seems joined to present evenings by an axle of bright stars reflected in the diaphanous lake) without remembering that then I was conscious of a wrecked city in the future, as now I am conscious of an un-damaged one behind to-day's ruins.

In July 1929, I walked along the shore of the lake with my host whom I had met in Oxford and who invited me to stay with him at Hamburg—the pale, rather intent, young Jew, Dr. Jessell—and he made a watchful, attentive guide. As we walked I started whistling. 'What tune are you whistling?' he asked. 'The scherzo of the Eighth Symphony.' 'So. Then you like music. We have many tastes in common.'

For the first time I noticed the scent of lime trees, which in Hamburg is like a screen along the roads by the lake. Sixteen years later it was a running trail, nostalgic scent of a past life, through the ruins. Between the road and the

lake were grassy banks planted with occasional weeping willows. Their
trailing branches made a Chinese calligraphy upon the paper-blue lake.
Triangular sails floated across the water as softly as petals. It was like the
music of Debussy. 'I have written poems in French and German, but I do
not quite know whether my English is idiomatic enough,' said Dr. Jessell at
my side. 'You can help me a great deal in things like that. I anticipate much
from our friendship.'

My host introduced me to his friends, who invited me to parties in their
bed-sitting-rooms and studios. We went swimming in the lake and for
excursions in canoes. To these young Germans, who had little money and
who spent what they had immediately, the life of the senses was a sunlit
garden from which sin was excluded. Perhaps they thought that their
generation had been purged of the bourgeois ideal of accumulated property
by the great inflation of 1923. Now their aims were simply to live from day
to day, and to enjoy to the utmost everything that was free: sun, water,
friendship, their bodies.

The sun—symbol of the great wealth of nature within the poverty of man
—was a primary social force in this Germany. Thousands of people went to
the open-air swimming baths or lay down on the shores of the rivers and
lakes, almost nude, and sometimes quite nude, and the boys who had turned
the deepest mahogany walked amongst those people with paler skins, like
kings among their courtiers.

The sun healed their bodies of the years of war, and made them conscious
of the quivering, fluttering life of blood and muscles covering their exhausted
spirits like the pelt of an animal: and their minds were filled with an abstraction of the sun, a huge circle of fire, an intense whiteness blotting out the
sharp outlines of all other forms of consciousness, burning out even the sense
of time. During their leisure, all their powers of thought were sucked up,
absorbed into the sun, as moisture evaporates from the soil.

I went to the bathing places, and I went to parties which ended at dawn
with the young people lying in one another's arms. This life appeared to me
innocuous, being led by people who seemed naked in body and soul, in the
desert of white bones which was post-war Germany. Yet I walked through
all this curiously unscathed. There was something about my appearance at
this time, so inhibited, pre-occupied, and physically nervous, that it prevented these young Germans from being drawn to me as they were to one
another. They looked at me and said: '*Nicht schön, sondern interessant*', or
'*unschuldig*'.

Their lives flowed easily into the movements of art, literature and painting,
which surrounded them. Everything was 'new', deceptively so. There were
buildings, with broad clean vertical lines crossed by strong horizontals,
which drove into the sky like railroads. There were experiments in the theatre
and opera, all in a style which expressed with facility the fusion of naked

liberation with a kind of bitter pathos, which was characteristic of this Germany. I once saw a movie which contained sequences of scenes with trams and bicycles going along the street. Music had been used to give these sequences a certain unreality. The bells of the trams and bicycles, the noises of the traffic, were woven into themes expressing a kind of tragic yet gay recklessness. This skilfully conveyed the nihilism, sophistication and primitive vitality which was so dangerously attractive in the beginning of the Weimar Republic.

Modernism in this Germany was (within certain limits of which I was not then aware) a popular mass-movement. Roofless houses, expressionist painting, atonal music, bars for homosexuals, nudism, sun-bathing, camping, all were accepted, and became like bright, gaudy, superficial colours in which the whole country was painted. Surrounded by this superficiality there were also serious artists, indignant Protestants, vengeful nationalists, Communists, many private tragedies, and much suffering. But such intense expressions of will and feeling were obscured by the predominant fashionableness of advanced attitudes. It was easy to be advanced. You had only to take off your clothes.

I was so intoxicated by my first weeks in Hamburg that I felt too creative to write very much: as when the conception of a book so overwhelms a writer that he can scarcely bring himself to work on it. I used often to leave the house of the Jessells with whom I was staying, and walk along the shore of the lake, with the grass and willow trees on one side of the broad road, the clean fronts of houses behind lime and plane trees on the other, whilst the road surface itself throbbed like a drum-skin under the traffic. On these walks I had a tremendous sense of release, of having got away from Oxford and home. Drums and flags seemed to march through my brain: it was as though my blood were a river of music. An embrace of recognition seemed celebrated between my inner life and the hot, green, throbbing world outside. When I had reached the centre of the town, I would go to some café and look at the poem or the novel I was then engaged on. I would drink an iced coffee crowned with thick cream.

Dr. Jessell had introduced me to several of his friends. Gradually I found myself detaching myself from him and spending more and more time with them. The two I liked most were called Joachim and Willi. Joachim had a large studio flat, of which he was extremely proud, on the outskirts of Hamburg. One night he invited my host and me to a party.

We climbed up four flights of stairs and I found myself in a large simple, airy room, like an attic, lit by a skylight and by slits of windows looking over Hamburg. The room was L-shaped, so that one part of it could not be seen from the other. At each end were beds which were mattresses, and bare modernist tables and chairs made of tubes of steel and bent plywood. The main part of the room formed a large space which had been cleared for

14

dancing. The room was lit by lamps of tubular and rectangular ground glass.

We arrived late for the party. The other guests were already there. Joachim was tall, with a rather Mexican appearance, a sallow complexion, black eyes, raised, sensual, expressive nostrils, brushed back hair. As soon as he saw me, he took my arm and showed me all the objects in the room: the bowl of rough-cut glass, the Mexican mat, the modernist crockery, and the massive books printed in heavy clear-cut modern types which indented the rag paper pages. He talked English with a faint American accent, telling me he had bought these books shortly after he had left school, but that he didn't read much now. He liked beautiful things, but he preferred 'living' to having things. Living was bathing, friendship, travelling, lying in the sun. 'I like the sun mostly and doing things with my friends: not reading.' I admired a drawing pinned on the wall. He said that he had done it long ago but that now he had given up drawing. He did, however, take photographs, and giving me a handful from a shelf under the Finnish table, he strolled off to greet other arrivals.

The photographs were like an enormous efflorescence of Joachim's taste for 'living', a great stream of magnificent young people, mostly young men, lying on the sand, standing with their heads enshadowed and pressed back as though leaning against the sun, rising from bulrushes and grasses, swimming in seas and rivers, laughing from verandas, embracing one another. (I imagine all these photographs now, sodden under sweet-smelling rubbish from which weeds grow behind broken window frames: and where is this army of the young?) About the appearance of them all and about the very technique of the photography, there was the same glaze and gleam of the 'modern' as in the room itself and the people in it: something making them seem released and uninhibited yet anonymous, as they asserted themselves by the mere force of their undistinguishable instincts.

A door out of the main room led to a little scullery, and here I found Joachim's friend Willi preparing drinks. He was quite different from Joachim, blond, blue-eyed, Scandinavian and always smiling. A lock of his hair flopped over his blue eyes. He pushed this back from time to time across his forehead with his hand. His conversation showed his utter devotion to his friend, whose tastes and furniture and photographs he thought the most wonderful in the world. There was a kind of sadness, though, about this admiration. When I left Willi and went back to the main room it was filled with other guests. They were bronze-skinned and they dressed with a simplicity which suggested leaves and summer. The boys seemed girlish whilst the girls seemed masculine.

There was dancing, and when I danced with a girl called Irmi, who was slim and boyish, she danced in an inviting way, pressing her body close to mine, and holding her warm brown face almost against my lips. This seemed natural and so simple that the questions which would have arisen before me at Oxford did not arise.

After the dance, she left me and went towards Joachim, threw her arms around his neck and kissed him: that she should do this after having just embraced me also seemed natural. I seemed to be moving in a trance of sensuous freedom where everything was possible and plausible and easy. Irmi wore a short skirt like a kilt, and plaid socks with little tabs stuck into them. Her knees were bare.

A film was shown of another party just like the one at which I was now present and with some of the same people. Then there were pictures of sunbathing, swimming. It was as though this Germany were a series of boxes fitting into one another, and all of them the same.

In the picture Joachim was now on board ship under a sky almost black with heat. Iron shadows lay on the sun-bright deck. Joachim leaned on the railings as he stared out to sea, his brow corrugated in a squinting smile which seemed to carry a great burden of pleasure. An instant later he was playing deck-tennis, laughing and gesticulating in a gayer mood than I had yet seen him in. Now on the screen there was a party here in this very room and people dancing. The camera passed through moving figures, surveying the room, occasionally pausing as it were to examine someone's dress or figure. Boys and girls were lying on the ground embracing and then rolling away from one another to turn their faces towards the camera's lens. Willi lay stroking the head of a girl beside him. He turned, his face white in the light, and then he kissed her, the shadow first, and then his head, covering the light on her lips. I heard Willi laugh beside me.

After the film was over, people rose up with gestures as though they were yawning, and then stood quietly around with a strained excitement. Only one light, in the centre of the room, was turned on. The corners of the room were in darkness. Two or three couples started dancing, softly, to no music in the half-darkness, and then they seemed to swoon away together, prostrated in silence and shadow of corners of the room.

Dr. Jessell came up to me and said: 'I think it's about time we went home.' 'All right,' I said. 'But I want first of all to say good night to Willi.' 'He's just gone out of the room, I think.'

Dr. Jessell gazed at me with a scrutinizing smile which seemed posted like a sentry at the outskirts of his face, ready to open fire at a sign from me. He went away and came back with Willi. 'What do you want, Stephen?' Willi asked, smiling broadly. 'I only want to say good night to you, Willi.' 'Oh, is that all!' he burst out laughing and took my hand. 'How very funny! Good night!'

I walked back through the streets with Dr. Jessell, whose presence always forced me behind barriers of impassivity. I stopped walking when we came to a bridge over a stream flowing sluggishly into the lake. As I looked down on to the lake I noticed that something was happening in the sky. Dawn was beginning. There was no sun as yet, but the sky was no longer quite dark. A faint light seemed to cover the town, slowly filling it like water filling a tank. Below the liquid air I saw the heavy foliage, massive, without detail, over the river and the lake.

In the evenings in Hamburg, I used sometimes to go down to the district of San Pauli near the port, where there were cafés and bars for sailors, labourers, and tourists. Most of these *Lokalen* were situated on either side of a broad road brightly lit with signs, opposite a park dominated by an enormous statue of Prince Bismarck, looking like a monstrous pepper-pot carved out of granite.

Deep down by the quays of the harbour, as though plunged below the city into its black waters, there was the strangest of these places, a den kept by an old sailor who had a square unshaven chin, bristling hair and bulging Mussolini eyes. He had collected in his den the souvenirs of Arabian Nights' Voyages. From the ceiling hung stuffed alligators. Huge bats were clamped like escutcheons to the wall. One end of the bar was fenced with prairie grass and bamboo, overgrown with withered poison ivy. Under the chair on which Joachim sat, a porcupine spread its quills.

Another *Lokal* had the air of a parish hall decorated for Christmas with tinsel stars, paper ribbons, coloured crêpe and brightly lit coloured electric bulbs. The dancers here were poorly dressed, and men danced with men. Several freakish febrile men were dressed as women. Singing weirdly, rolling their eyes, chucking staid citizens seated at their tables under the chin, these lolled from table to table. Most of the guests sat quietly at their tables drinking their beer, taking all this quite for granted. Leaning against the platform at one end of the room, or standing together in talkative groups, were working boys wearing their peaked caps, and a few sailors.

At one table not far distant from ours was an old man with a long beard, staring with eyes of unwavering desire at a young couple dancing together, whilst with young-seeming nervous fingers he touched the rim of his glass. There were men who stared into the centre of the room as if from a drugged sleep.

Amongst the dancers was a young man who danced alone. He had pale features. He wore pince-nez and the drab clothes of a bank clerk. He seemed, from the way in which he held himself, to suffer from some kind of partial paralysis. He was a little drunk now, as he threaded his way through the dancing couples waving his hands to and fro with an angular distorted movement like a parody of wings.

None of this seemed to me ugly or terrible or shocking. I saw it, rather, as a kind of play in which the ways in which people sought for happiness—and suffered—were revealed. And the fact that everything was bare and there were no pretences made even ugliness seem beautiful and exhilarating to me.

The reverse aspect of this decadence was the swimming, the sun-bathing, the rather facile pleasure in beautiful things. Once some friends drove me in their little car to a small modern house in the countryside near Hamburg. After dinner, we lay in the garden listening to gramophone records of Mozart's flute concerto played on a portable gramophone. I have never before or since heard this music sound at once so ethereal and yet so earthly, as though the flute passages moved amongst the orchestra like a white and secret stream pouring through roots of plants in dark, scented flower-beds, on a summer night. When it was quite dark we lit a bonfire in the garden, and as the light shone on to the house and wandering sparks drifted with the smoke into the warm upper air, the wife of our host came out on to the veranda. She was a beautiful young woman, far advanced in a pregnancy which added radiance to her beauty. In the light reflecting upwards from the fire she looked Rembrandtesque, a ripe glowing figure painted in shadows and gold, bathed in flickering light.

But even here, in one of the most beautiful moments of my first visit to Germany, a certain heartlessness at the centre of it all raised questions in my mind. Our host, a very Nordic-looking blond young man with self-consciously liberated and advanced views which were almost an orthodoxy here, explained that he had determined to go for a long bicycling tour by himself in Holland during the last days of his wife's pregnancy, as it was quite unnecessary for a modern husband to be near his wife at the time of child-birth. What happened in the hearts of these people who gave themselves so easily to so many things? If any of them had deep feelings, were these not bound to be hurt and disappointed?

Joachim was a dominating character who drew me into his orbit. He regarded himself as the commanding predatory captain of his own world, one who knew what he wanted, was not influenced by others, ruled over a court of those who loved him. He had organized his life in a way which seemed to him admirable. He worked for several hours a day in the great Hanseatic business of his family, which was selling coffee. He prided himself on being a good businessman: yet at the same time not dominated by busi-ness. He assiduously organized every moment of his day towards the pleasure which he called 'living'. The luncheon hour, which for him extended from one to four, was devoted to a simple vegetarian meal with friends, followed by swimming in one of the baths at the centre of the town. In the evening he went to the *Lokal* of San Pauli, or canoeing on the lake with friends, or to some party. The most intense experience of his life was what he called '*Une grande passion*'. By this he meant a passion which to some extent was outside his control, for someone whom he might want to see when that person did not want to see him. It was a variant on his feeling that people were willing objects invoked to satisfy a temporary state of desire.

He regarded me as an ally. He would meet me at luncheon at Hamburg's vegetarian restaurant (which was rather fashionable) and discuss his affairs, and explain his philosophy of 'living'. He often had stories to tell which were amusing, and although what he took for smartness in his dress was a little vulgar, his self-confidence gave him a certain style. His black eyes shone, he had the big slow smile of the cowboy, and he wore broad-brimmed hats which recalled American travels.

In the late summer, Joachim invited me to go with him for a walking tour on the Rhine. In beautiful weather we walked along that part of the river where the shores are most mountainous. At nights we would stop in some little town with a boulevard looking out over the wide river. Here the people, dressed in their fancy dress costumes, seemed to have gaping mouths into which grapes were pressed. The boys in leather shorts and the girls in their billowing skirts stood gazing out over the river in the evening, when the darkness seemed inwoven with heavy scent, and it was as though they dissolved into the dragonish sensuality of the Rhine landscape.

Joachim in his dynamic arrogant way strode amongst the groups of girls and boys, with an expression as though one magnetic look could extract any-one of his choice from a crowd and bind him to Joachim for ever. One evening, when I had gone by myself for a walk after dinner, I returned to the inn where we were staying, to find Joachim drinking with one of the youths who stared across the waters as though waiting for an arm to rise out of them with a gleaming sword. Joachim gave me a burning look and said: 'Heinrich, this is Stephen.'

The next morning he told me that Heinrich was to accompany us on our tour. Heinrich and Joachim walked along in an exalted mood, singing in turn the songs of Hamburg and of Bavaria. (Heinrich was Bavarian.) I could not join in these songs and I realized that after all there was something exclusive about this Germany which included the bronzed, the athletic, the good-looking and the smart, but shut out the old, the intellectual and the ugly.

Heinrich, though, was very friendly. During the next days, often he came to me as though with a message from Joachim, put his arm round my shoulders and said in broken English: 'I like you; you must like me.' His body was like carved polished wood, rather emaciated and yet strong and lithe. He seemed some saint made by an artist who has fallen sensually in love with his own carving, and produced a pagan instead of a Christian image. Forehead, mouth, chin, and even hair, gave the same impression of carved wood, varnished by many suns, a product of Bavarian folk-art. Yet in this carved face there were almond-shaped, greenish, extremely watchful eyes, which did not leave your face when he was talking to you.

Joachim soon told me that his relationship with Heinrich was the great attachment of his life, as, indeed, rather surprisingly, it almost proved to be. Even in those first few days I would sometimes notice a strange expression in Heinrich's eyes: not just shrewd or calculating, but vengeful and spiteful. At the same time I learned something of his history—the folk story of the workless wanderers in the Germany of 1929. It was nothing more than a story of wanderings, misfortunes, bad beginnings, in which his own disasters were inseparably confused with those of all the other boys who were his comrades. It was a fragment of the saga of all this German youth which had been born into war, starved in the blockade, stripped in the inflation—and which now, with no money and no beliefs and an extraordinary anonymous beauty, sprang like a breed of dragon's teeth waiting for its leader, into the centre of Europe.

So impressed was I that I wrote a poem in which I described the young bank clerk with 'world-offended eyes' who stood naked with the 'new German', and 'myself, being English', prepared to build his world out of our bones.

We ended our walking tour at Cologne, which in the light of that summer lay on each side of the river, like two great turbines, one the cathedral, the other the modern concrete buildings of the exhibition: the two of them connected by arches of great bridges like folded wings. (When I crossed the river at Cologne sixteen years later, in 1945, it was on a pontoon because the bridges had fallen into the river. Two uniformed public-school boys were with me: and the city, where it had not been completely broken, was torn and scratched over as if by claws.)

After this walking tour I returned to England for my last year at Oxford. As I have explained, I simply neglected my studies during this last year. I spent the remaining part of the long vacation printing a little volume of the *Poems* of W. H. Auden, an edition of thirty copies which is sought after to-day.

When I had left the University, I returned to Hamburg. But I no longer lived in the great house of the Jessells at the end of the lake. I had a bed-sitting-room in a boarding-house. At one *Lokal* I met an unemployed young man called Walter, in whom I rather arbitrarily decided to take an interest. Walter had large clumsy hands, an intent expression of his eyes in his pale face, under the cloth cap which he nearly always wore. I used often to go with him to the amusements arcade. He would put his heavy fingers on the handles which controlled silver balls, in those games where illuminated numbers appear, bells ring, balls disappear down holes, and if you achieve a victory reckoned in an enormous sum, you get some money back. Walter was for ever explaining to me that he needed money for some journey which would take him to his mother or a brother or an aunt from whom he had been separated for many years. Several times I gave him the money, but his journey was one of those frustrated voyages which are never made, because it always happened that he lost his money before he got on to the train: and then, when I was lying on the bed of my bed-sitting-room, my bell would ring and there he would be, with gravely shining eyes under his peaked cap, explaining in his Hamburg dialect that before taking his ticket to the station he had been so tired that he had lain down to sleep in the waiting-room, where he had been robbed: or that he had lent his money to that friend, of whom I had already been told, whose girl must have the abortion. At the advice of Joachim, I finally bought Walter a ticket and put him on to a train which presumably took him to his relatives.

Now I look back with amusement at the episode of Walter. Yet at the time I took his problem seriously, and I tried to believe the stories he told me. If I had not tried to believe him, or if I had not thought that his stories were ways of expressing a need for money with which I could sympathize, the relationship would have been more cynical. Because it was not so, I can still think of it as a friendship in which there was something more significant than a kind of mutual exploitation. I cannot just dismiss Walter as part of my very gullible past when I allowed myself to be victimized by a tramp. For in this relationship there was a grain of real affection of a kind which I had not had before. It is as though I was in need of some precious ore and had been driven to seek it in the smallest quantities and the roughest places. What my friends—and even I myself, at moments, saw—was that I returned with clothes tattered, and having been robbed and degraded. But as a matter of fact I did have a little of the precious ore: there were moments when in the middle of cheating me Walter trusted me, and when I gave him more than money. With him I escaped to some extent from the over-spiritualized, puritan, competitive atmosphere in which I had been brought up, to something denser, less pure, but out of which I could extract and refine little granules of affection. From such experiences I gradually learned a feeling which I could later bring to the highest relationships.

Through Walter, I imagined the helplessness, the moral weakness, the drift, of unemployment. I imagined, I suppose, that something which I was now beginning to call in my mind 'the revolution' would alter his lot, and I felt that as a member of a more fortunate social class I owed him a debt. If he had robbed me I would have felt that he could never rob me sufficiently of advantages which society had given me over him: for I was a member of a class whose money enabled me to benefit automatically from its institutions of robbery, to assume automatically its disguises of respectability. To my mind, it appeared that there are two classes of robbers: the social and the anti-social.

Although this attitude embodied a certain truth, I was being sentimental. I had allowed a sense of social guilt to put me in a position where I was unable to criticize a thief or a blackmailer. This meant that I was a potential exploitee, because I could never feel within myself the rightness of a social situation which would rebuke the wrongness of others. So I allowed my time, energy and money, all of which I should have spent to the advantage of my talent, to be wasted. Or did I? For after all, what seemed, and may still seem, inexcusable wasting was at least in part a flowing in of life through silted, muddy channels. What was really bad, was that my attitude prevented me from being able seriously to help Walter. For I saw his faults as projections of my own guilt, and not as problems which he must deal with for his own interests, within his own situation. I should have been tougher and more cynical, accepting my own position in the world, and expecting others to accept theirs, or more prudent, or else perhaps more fanatically idealistic, giving up my advantages, so that I was able to speak to outcasts as one who had made himself an outcast. But although I had comparatively little money, my whole position of independence depended on it. Without it, I would not ever have gone to Germany and lived the life in a bed-sitting-room. It was not the quantity of what I had which was striking, but the quality of what I could do and be by virtue of having a little. The difference between having twenty thousand a year and three hundred is as nothing compared with that between having three hundred and none.

Because I projected my own weakness on to those around me, I was fascinated by those with no qualifications for adapting themselves to their circumstances. Such people are forced into a certain detachment from aims and conventions by being neither rulers nor workers, but victims. Their existences are marginal, registering as delicately as the needle of an instrument, booms and slumps, when they are unemployed or thrown into unemployment: periods of social decadence, when they are demoralized: of upheaval, when they become the crude material of revolution: wars, when they may suddenly become heroes. The unemployment of the 1930's produced tens of thousands of such hapless, workless people, all over the world.

At this time my prevalent social attitude was one of pity. This, and sympathy with weakness, showed in my work and behaviour. These were attitudes of what Yeats calls 'passive suffering'. They were the projections of a mixture of strength and weakness: strength, to the extent to which I was master of my own kingdom of the creative imagination, my own work wherein I might create as I chose. Within this inner world even weakness could become a kind of strength. It isolated me and disqualified me from other kinds of work than poetic writing. I needed only the strength of my own weakness to say that I had no other responsibilities than simply to exist in order to write. It enlarged my sympathies by leading me down paths where people were insulted, oppressed, or vicious. It saved me from having to judge them by conventional rules of conduct, since I did not observe these myself.

The danger, which I did not avoid, was of identifying the weakness of him who really does nothing, with that of the poet who sometimes appears to do nothing, but who, in a way which mystifies his fellows, redeems himself by turning a meaningless or depraved or idle life around him into the significant material of his poem. I detected in others qualities which I shared, and I thought they might share mine, so that there were moments when it would not have surprised me if someone like Walter or Joachim had produced from his pocket a poem, magical with the mystery of the lights and silver balls of amusement arcades, or smouldering with the passion which chooses a different bed-mate from the pavements every night. I held back my energies, in order not to disturb the precarious happiness of those whose lives I shared by revealing that there was in me this difference, this *deus ex machina*: the poem.

During these months in Hamburg, I discovered a terrifying mystery of cities which fascinated me in the way that one reads of people in the past being fascinated by the Eleusinian Rites. This is that a great city is a kind of labyrinth within which at every moment of the day the most hidden wishes of every human being are performed by people who devote their whole existences to doing this and nothing else. Along a road there walks a man with a desire repressed in his heart. But a few doors away there are people utterly devoted to accomplishing nothing but this desire. What has been crushed, never spoken of for generations by his family, revolves there night and day like the wheels of a machine. He has only to know a secret word, open a door, and he may enter into this continuity of things which are elsewhere forbidden. He has only to shut the door again and walk out of the house and he is again in the locked street where things are scarcely mentioned and unseen. Yet he has in his hands this magic key of entrance into a perpetual stream of fulfilment which he can use whenever he wills. When he even no longer feels desire, he can in an idle, abstract and unwishing kind of way prove to himself, almost for no reason except a mysterious and remote compulsion to reaffirm that it is so, that the hidden life of forbidden wishes exists in extravagant nakedness behind mazes of walls.

When I discovered this, I was almost tempted to think that I had stripped bare my deepest wishes and found that others shared them and that even if this were a kind of hell, perhaps it was my destiny.

At the same time there was a desire to save myself for work. I realized the danger of there being a place beyond which the fulfilment of the senses becomes an automatic activity too complete and devouring in itself for one to want anything else or be able to work.

Nevertheless, during the year or so when I was living a life dangerous to myself and impossible to justify to others, I was writing my best early poems.

After I had been in Hamburg only a few months, Christopher Isherwood, who was in Berlin, invited me to live near him there.

At this time he was not the successful writer and well-known personality he has subsequently become. He was comparatively poor and almost unrecognized. His novel, *All the Conspirators*, had been remaindered, and he was working on a second, *The Memorial*. During the years when I was often in Berlin, he lived in various poor parts of the town, of which the best was in the neighbourhood of the Nollendorfplatz—a grand-shabby square dominated by a station of the overhead railway—the worst, that of the Hallesches Tor, an area of slum tenements. He lived very poorly, scarcely ever spending more than sixty pfennigs (about eightpence) on a meal. During this time, when I had meals almost every day with him, we ate food such as horse flesh and lung soup, which for some years ruined my digestion, and for all time my teeth, as they had long ago ruined his.

Very soon my relationship with Christopher fell into a routine. I would leave my bed-sitting-room, situated in the slightly more luxurious Motzstrasse, and walk past its grey houses whose façades seemed out of moulds made for pressing enormous concrete biscuits. Then I would come to the Nollendorfplatz, an eyrie of concrete eagles, with verandas like breasts shedding stony flakes of whatever glory they once had into the grime of soot which caked the walls of this part of Berlin. The bridges, arches, stations and commanding noise of the overhead railway had taken possession of the square and of the streets leading westwards through Tauenzienstrasse and Wittembergplatz, and eastwards to the ever more sordid tenements which never yet quite lost some claim to represent the Prussian spirit, by virtue of their display of eagles, helmets, shields and prodigious buttocks of armoured babies. A peculiar all-pervading smell of hopeless decay (rather like the smell of the inside of an old cardboard box) came out of the interiors of these grandiose houses now converted into pretentious slums.

I turned out of the Nollendorfplatz down the Nollendorfstrasse, yellowing parody of the Motzstrasse, to the still more sordid street in which Christopher lived. I climbed up two or three flights of stairs, the walls of which had an even stronger odour than the street outside. Then I rang the door-bell of the flat where Christopher had his room. The front door was opened by Christopher's landlady, Fräulein Thurau, with pendulous jaws and hanging breasts, the watch-dog of the Herr Issyvoo world; and now I had entered one of Christopher's stories, Fräulein Thurau, with a '*Guten Tag, Herr Spender*' of a cordial kind which recognized that I was one of those friends of Christopher whom she did not reckon a blackmailer or a wastrel, perhaps even that I was a 'good influence', would add '*Herr Issyvoo ist noch nicht fertig*' with a rolling of her eyes, or '*Herr Issyvoo hat Besuch*', with a sombre humorousness which suggested a double meaning. I would then be shown into the room which was the very centre of the Fräulein Thurau universe, reception room, dining-room, entrance hall, as one might choose to regard it, with faded tapestried and oaken furniture, out of which the doors of other rooms opened. Here on a wide chair large enough to seat two people, in front of the table covered with a wine-coloured velvet table-cloth which had been affected by a kind of mange so that it looked like a skin of a huge cat of the same colour, I would sit amongst the tassels, the pictures of Blücher's yellowing victories, the wreckage of Fräulein Thurau's mythical grandeur, waiting an unconscionably long time for Christopher to appear. Whilst I was waiting, one or other of the characters of his as yet unwritten novels would dart out of one of the rooms opening into this one. Perhaps Bobbi the bar-tender would shoot fish-like through this central tank and escape into another room, or perhaps Sally Bowles would appear, her clothes dishevelled, her eyes large onyxes fringed by eyelashes like enamelled wire, in a face of carved ivory. Christopher lived in this apartment surrounded by the models for his creations, like one of those portraits of a writer by a bad painter, in which the writer is depicted meditating in his chair whilst the characters of his novels radiate round him under a glowing cloud of dirty varnish, not unlike the mote-laden lighting of Fräulein Thurau's apartment.

After some time Christopher would appear, probably in his shirt-sleeves, razor in hand, to say that he was extremely sorry but last night had been terrible, he had not slept, but now he would be ready in a few minutes. Ten minutes later he would reappear, remarkably transformed, with a neatness of the cuffs emphasized by the way in which he often held his hands extended, slightly apart from his body. His hair was brushed in a boyish lick over his forehead, below which his round shining eyes had a steadiness which seemed to come from the strain of effort, as though their feat of balancing themselves in Christopher's face at the same time balanced the whole world which they saw. They were the eyes of someone who, when he is a passenger in an aeroplane, thinks that the machine is kept in the air by an act of his will, and that unless he continues to look steadily in front of him it will fall instantly to the ground. These eyes were under sharp-angled eyebrows which added to the impression of his being a strained school leader. The mouth, with its deep vertical lines at the corners, was that of a tragi-comic Christ. He was well aware of these effects. Perhaps if we decided to go to Insel Ruegen from Berlin in the summer, after discussing other possibilities, he would say: 'Well, to the North', and assume the bleak wrinkled look of a pilot steering through arctic seas with icicles hanging from sandy eyebrows. Once when we were eating an execrable meal, I implored him, with that exaggerated concern I had in those days for any annoyance to a friend with whom I was, to eat something better. But he waved the suggestion away in bad German which, with his gesture, absurdly recalled the Greek of the New Testament: '*Was ich habe gegessen ich habe gegessen.*'

My morning call at Fräulein Thurau's was always the time for grave pronouncements. 'That is the last time I ever go to *that* place I went to last night again. They can sink or swim without me.' Or: 'Do you know what that bitch Sally said to me last night?' 'No.' 'Perhaps, one day, Christopher darling, you will write something really great, like Noel Coward.' Or:

'Mr. Norris has been caught.' Or: 'I have given Fräulein Thurau notice. I will not live under the same roof as Bobbi an instant longer.'

I entered so completely into Christopher's moods that, although I was in part entertained by these pronouncements, they also filled me with a certain apprehension, and, as we went down the stairs into the street, I felt the oppression of the silence which follows fateful news. Secretly I was disappointed that Christopher's dramas rarely ended with complete catharsis. All the people who had fallen into disgrace were sooner or later taken back into favour, for Christopher, so far from being the self-effacing spectator he depicts in his novels, was really the centre of his characters, and neither could they exist without him nor he without them.

We would then have a meal consisting of watery soup followed by some frightful meat. Eating such food was a penance for Christopher to which he attached an unstated but disciplinary importance. When sometimes, if I was alone, I went to one of those pleasant restaurants with outdoor gardens in the Kurfurstendamm, and had a meal costing one mark fifty, or if, still more self-indulgent, I went to one of the excellent Russian restaurants which were a feature of Berlin, with my friend the American composer, Roger Sessions, or my brother Michael, I felt as though I had betrayed him.

After lunch there was a relaxation of our regime, for we then walked to a shop near the Bahnhof-am-Zoo where we bought a packet of toffee. So regular were our appearances at this shop, that on seeing us enter a girl assistant would rush behind the counter, fetch the packet of sweets, hand it to us and receive one mark in payment, all without a word. Perhaps it was the influence of Christopher which had this effect, because I do not believe it would have happened to me had I been alone. In fact, in his own neighbourhood, Christopher had trained most of the shop people to spring into automatic, swift, silent action as soon as he appeared at the shop door, as though he were a switch and they machines running on electric rails. When a certain grocer refused to act in this way, Christopher took revenge by buying his groceries at a store a few doors away, having them packed as bulkily as possible, and, thus laden, walking slowly, bowed down with his purchases, past the erring grocer's shop, hoping thus to break his spirit.

It may seem that there was an inconsistency about his extreme economies and the purchase of the sweets. This is true. But I think that Christopher regarded the sweets as being in their way another penance, an excess ruining his teeth. What he would have regarded as inexcusable would have been a 'balanced diet', for at that time Auden and he were in full revolt against all forms of hygiene. If you were 'pure in heart' you would not catch a disease with which you came in contact. But iced coffees and toffee had an exorbitant place in our budget, so that once Christopher said to me when he was complaining about money: 'If I could suddenly see now in front of me the

Niagara of iced coffees which I have drunk during the past year, then I would understand where all my money goes.'

Eating our toffee, we would then, if the weather were fine, take a train to the Grünewald where we would walk among the pine trees or along the shores of the lake. We walked a great deal, and my memories of the stories which Christopher told me—of his family in the house near Manchester, of Chalmers, of meeting Auden when they were both at the same preparatory school—are mingled with impressions of the sandy Grünewald and the streets of Berlin. The architecture of Berlin was unlike that of any other town. It had a unity amid its diversity, and was like (as it was meant to be) an ideological expression in stone, granite, and concrete, of certain ideas. The streets were straight, long, grey, uniform, and all their ornaments expressed the idea of Prussian domination. There were a good many squares, but these had little positive character. They were just places .where several streets halted and had a rest before going on with their uniformed march, at the exact opposite side of the square from where they had left off. They were more like spaces in time than in place, intervals in which the passer-by was able to breathe before resuming the logic of the street. Certain parts of Berlin were characterized by what seemed a relaxation of regime, or by a rise into higher ranks, rather than by a change of style. The streets grew wider, there were more frequent intervals between houses, more trees and gardens, and the squares, when one came to them, were larger. Other parts of Berlin represented wild fantasies, as though the architects who had restrained themselves when they designed the more austere neo-classical buildings of the Unter den Linden had gone mad when they came to design the cathedral and the palace. Moreover, Unter den Linden and its environments were connected to the West End of the Kurfurstendamm by roads and bridges laid like twisting cables over chaotic parts of the city, consisting of railway lines, stations and canals. Lastly, nothing expressed the cynical relationship between the grim architecture and the feckless population more than the belief of the Berlin population that one of the stone lions outside the palace at the end of the Unter den Linden roared whenever a virgin walked by.

When we had got out of our train and were walking through the Grünewald with the flat, white, Moroccan-looking modernist houses gleaming behind the brown and green pine trees, and with the sun-bathers lying in profusion on the flint-grey grass—the relentlessly handsome German youths with their arms round their doughy girls—Christopher talked. He told me the plot of a novel he was planning, to be called *The Lost*. Day after day, against the background of the pine trees, lakes or street, I witnessed that transformation taking place in his mind, where the real becomes the malleable, the people who are garrulous and shabby in life become the crystal entertainers of fiction.

Like most vital people, Christopher could be depressive, silent, or petulant.

Sometimes he would sit in a room with Sally Bowles or Mr. Norris without saying a word, as though refusing to bring his characters to life. Sometimes he was in a Dostoevskian mood of gloom, or a Baudelairean one of debt and failure. About once a fortnight he was hypochondriac and I would accompany him to the doctor, both of us imagining that he was about to be sentenced to a fatal disease. Sometimes he was broke and we would force ourselves to think up ways of earning money. He gave English lessons, he translated, occasionally he even did a little journalism, but in Berlin in 1930 you not only had to work very hard to earn very little, you also had to be a financial genius to get paid.

In the early stages of our friendship I was drawn to him by the adventurousness of his life. His renunciation of England, his poverty, his friendship, his independence, his work, all struck me as heroic. During months in the winter of 1930, when I went back to England, I corresponded with him in the spirit of writing letters to a Polar explorer. I thought of him in the centre of the northern European plain, gripped in icy cold, across the stormy and black channel. His letters were of a besieged person, facing creditors, the elements, and the breakdown of a civilization, surrounded by a little loyal crew: 'the position is absurdly terrible. The ice is cracking on the capitalist Wannsee like pistol shots and the doomed skaters in tights and Hessian boots are at least a kilometre from the beer house on the shore.' And: 'My financial troubles are worse than ever before. Chalmers left the sinking ship this morning,' he wrote. I was sometimes an emissary from Isherwood in Berlin to editors and publishers in London. We both thought of London as a kind of province on which we unfortunately depended, to which I had been sent. 'I am praying to God to soften the heart of Virginia Woolf,' he writes. 'An appropriate greeting to Mr. Lehmann if he is still with you.' Then there is the bulletin of Berlin disasters: 'Sally goes into the clinic to-morrow. Last night I was drunk.' And there is always the note of his consciously overacting his own role: 'A telegram handed to a porter at Liverpool Street is sufficient notice for me.'

About three years of my life, I realize now, were lived precariously off the excitement of being with Isherwood. I told him everything, I showed him every letter of any interest I received, I looked to his judgment of my friends and activities.

Sometimes, as in the case of my friendship with a girl called Gisa Soloweitschik, I seemed to be offering my own feelings on an altar of Christopher's domination. Thus I encouraged, even if I did not provoke, in him characteristics which he probably did not care for in himself. Gisa Soloweitschik was of Lithuanian origin. I was an undergraduate and she was seventeen when I first met her whilst ski-ing in Switzerland. I introduced Christopher to her in Berlin. Her parents used most generously to invite us each Sunday to their flat in Wilmersdorf where they gave us a large meal, at the end of which they used to send us away with our pockets stuffed with fruit. They called Christopher Shakespeare and me Byron. Gisa was studying *Kunstgeschichte*. She would fill her rooms with volumes opened at pictures which she showed us, saying: 'Look! That is beautiful. Isn't it? Yes!' Or she would suddenly stop the conversation with a command: 'Listen! This is beautiful! I think you need it!' And play what was her then favourite piece, the adagio of the Beethoven Violin Concerto, on her portable gramophone. Christopher would listen to the music in silence, a polite but sour smile on his face. Gisa said: 'But do you not find it beautiful?' 'Oh, yes. Beautiful. Exquisite,' Christopher said and then sighed, leaning back against his chair. 'I understand!' exclaimed Gisa. 'You do not like music! You are stone-deaf. Stone-deaf or tone-deaf, do you say? Which?' 'I like music very much, and particularly that concerto, which I happen to know very well. As a matter of fact, it may interest you to know that I was secretary for some time to a violinist. André Mangeot. You may have heard of him,' said Christopher rather acidly. Somewhat on these lines a struggle went on between them, with Gisa standing for Art and the things of the spirit, Christopher for human relationships and for war against all self-conscious æsthetic and intellectual pretensions. In his mood of hating intellectualism, he disapproved of my going to concerts, was bored when I attempted to discuss ideas, and was cold about friends with whom I shared intellectual interests.

He soon found out that there was an Oriental sense of untouchability in Gisa. She could not drink from a glass if anyone else had drunk from it; she hated even to be touched. The result of the conflict was that although Gisa and Christopher were always at one another's throats, within a few weeks he knew her better than I had done in seven years. I realize now that I myself had engineered this result, so great was my desire to know people through his knowing them. Partly I was surrendering my relationships to him; partly I just wanted to see my friends live in his conversation.

Perhaps my greatest debt to Christopher is the confidence he gave me in my work. He was more than a young rebel passing through a phase of revolt against parents, conventional morality and orthodox religion. He also recognized that nearly everyone wanted something out of life which he or she had been taught to conceal. He was on the side of the forces which make a work of art, even more than he was interested in art itself, and on the side of the struggle towards self-realization more than he was interested in the happy ending or the success story. He simply believed in his friends and their work, and in his own judgment of them. His judgment might be wrong but it would be himself who would decide this. No institutions with their standards or examinations, no citing of convention and past examples, no criticism, would affect this. His hatred of institutions of learning and even of the reputation attached to some past work of art, was really hatred of the fact that they came between people and their direct unprejudiced approach to one another. Of course Christopher's judgments were not always just. But what is true is that a creative writer can be enormously encouraged by the complete support, without conditions and without reference to any other judgment, of a fellow writer.

Meanwhile the background of our lives in Germany was falling to pieces. There was a sensation of doom to be felt in the Berlin streets. For years the newspapers contained little news but of growing unemployment and increased taxation necessary to pay reparations and doles. The Nazis at the one extreme, and the Communists at the other, with their meetings, their declamatory newspapers, their uniformed armies of youths, their violence against the Republic and against one another, did all in their power to exacerbate the situation.

Brüning had abandoned the attempt to govern through the yelling mob of members of twenty-nine different political parties, which was the Reichstag (broadcasts of whose howling debates, punctuated by a tinkling bell, were a feature of the German wireless), and, using emergency powers under the Constitution, governed by decree. Every decree, accompanied by dissenting cries of 'dictatorship' from the extreme Right and the extreme Left, produced an impression of the Brüning Cabinet as a little boat manned by a hopeless crew, trying to navigate an unending storm.

The feeling of unrest in Berlin went deeper than any crisis. It was a permanent unrest, the result of nothing being fixed and settled. The Brüning regime was neither democracy nor dictatorship, socialism or conservatism, it represented no group nor class, only a common fear of the overwhelming disorder, which formed a kind of rallying place of frightened people. It was the *Weimardaemmerung*. Tugged by forces within and without, by foreign powers and foreign moneylenders, industrialist plotters, embittered generals, impoverished landed gentry, potential dictators, refugees from Eastern Europe, it reeled from crisis to crisis within a permanent crisis.

In this Berlin, the poverty, the agitation, the propaganda, witnessed by us in the streets and cafés, seemed more and more to represent the whole life of the town, as though there were almost no privacy behind doors. Berlin was the tension, the poverty, the anger, the prostitution, the hope and despair thrown out on to the streets. It was the blatant rich at the smart restaurants, the prostitutes in army top boots at corners, the grim, submerged-looking Communists in processions, and the violent youths who suddenly emerged from nowhere into the Wittembergplatz and shouted: '*Deutschland Erwache!*'

Germany had been pushed down to that level where the members of every group were conscious of themselves as a political interest. The prosperity of some was the direct result of the inflation (there was a row of luxurious new houses in Hamburg, known to the population as *Inflationstrasse*) which had been the ruin of others. Almost no one had interests above and outside the immediate day-to-day political situation. Not only were nearly all thus conscious of being politically involved, persecuting and persecuted, but events wore the same political aspect. When, for example, the Darmstadter National Bank failed, there was an atmosphere of general collapse in Berlin for a few days. The Nazi newspaper *Der Angriff*, trying to push the Republic over the abyss, came out with the headline: '*Alles bricht zusammen.*' A spell of intensely cold weather, by increasing misery, throwing workers out of employment, and thus adding a burden to the dole, became a political crisis threatening the Government, and welcomed by the Nazis and Communists.

Thus the whole of Germany was politicized in a way which divided it against itself. The depressed and partly ruined middle classes attributed their downfall to the Jews and to the Polish refugees who had poured into Berlin after 1918. The aristocrats and generals considered themselves to be fighting for the survival of the noblest German tradition against foreign elements and proletarianization. In the course of their self-righteous struggle, General Schleicher, the Hindenburg family, von Papen and the rest, made strange allies and corrupting compromises. The Jews and intellectuals, attacked by the Nazis and Nationalists, were fighting for survival. The workers were class-conscious, but wooed by Communists and Nazis: and some of them remained staunch Social Democrats. The young, finding themselves thrust into a world of unemployment, were enlisted by Parties which promised them a future of work and prosperity, and which even gave them present opportunities to strut about in uniforms and feel important.

Christopher and I, leading our life in which we used Germany as a kind of cure for our personal problems, became ever more aware that the carefree personal lives of our friends were façades in front of the immense social chaos. There was more and more a feeling that this life would be swept away. When we were on holiday at Insel Ruegen, where the naked bathers in their hundreds lay stretched on the beach under the drugging sun, sometimes we heard orders rapped out, and even shots, from the forest whose edges skirted the shore, where the Storm Troopers were training like executioners waiting to martyr the naked and self-disarmed.

In 1929 I had first heard of Hitler when, in between the singing of Bavarian songs, Joachim had told me of an orator from Austria, who had a power of speech which those who listened to him called hypnotic, whilst realizing that he talked nonsense. Hitler was regarded as a kind of wonder whom one did not have to take seriously. But two years later in Berlin, the Soloweitschiks were beginning to make grimly comforting jokes to the effect that the Jews had nothing to fear; for every Nazi, although an anti-semite, had his favourite Jew whom he wished to spare from persecution, and that made up as many Jews as all the Nazis. In the summer of 1932, a friend of Christopher's, Wilfrid Israel, came to stay with us in Sellin. One day, he and I went for a walk together through the forest. He was an elegant, distinguished, dark-eyed young man, whose family owned one of the great department stores in East Berlin. Wilfrid Israel surprised me, during our walk, by outlining a plan of action for the Jews when Hitler seized Germany—an event which he seemed to anticipate as certain. The Jews, he said, should close their businesses and go out into the streets, remaining there, as a protest, and refusing to go home even if the Storm Troopers fired on them. It was only such a united action, within a hopeless situation, which would arouse the conscience of the world.

Nearly all the German intellectuals whom we knew accepted and practised a kind of orthodoxy of the Left. This attitude influenced the theatre, the novel, the cinema, and even music and painting. So great was the unanimity of opinion that it occurred to me once that perhaps these people, just because they appeared to have arrived at their political views so easily, might be wrong. After all, the Nazis, whom they so hated, claimed to be socialists and were opposed to the treatment of Germany by the Allies, which I was opposed to also. Possibly Germany was in a position where socialism could only be achieved by a virulently nationalist party. I decided that I must study the Nazi point of view: so I bought the Nazi programme and a good deal of the literature of Goebbels and the other Nazi propagandists. I found that they were written with a blatant cynicism and brutality which could deceive no one. So far from pretending to believe their own propaganda, or even doing their followers the service of trying to deceive them, the Nazis openly proclaimed that the purpose of propaganda was to state, without any regard for truth, lies which served their cause. After I had read this literature, I knew that I hated the Nazis.

One day Isherwood told me that he had received a letter from his greatest Cambridge friend (whom he has called Chalmers in his autobiographical sketch, *Lions and Shadows*), saying that Chalmers had joined the Communist Party. We regarded this as an extraordinary action. Communism to us was an extremist, almost unnatural cause, and we found it hard to believe that any of our friends could be Communists. However, Chalmers's action deepened our interest in Berlin politics. We discussed them with our friends, went to political meetings, read the newspapers and a good deal of political literature attentively. Whenever we could, we went to see those Russian films which were shown often in Berlin at this period: *Earth*, *The General Line*, *The Mother*, *Potemkin*, *Ten Days that Shook the World*, *The Way into Life*, etc. These films, which form a curiously isolated episode in the æsthetic history of this century, excited us because they had the modernism, the poetic sensibility, the satire, the visual beauty, all those qualities we found most exciting in other forms of modern art, but they also conveyed a message of hope like an answer to *The Waste Land*. They extolled a heroic attitude which had not yet become officialized; in this they foreshadowed the defiant individualism of the Spanish Republicans. We used to go long journeys to little cinemas in the outer suburbs of Berlin, and there among the grimy tenements we saw the images of the New Life of the workers building with machine tools and tractors their socially just world under the shadows of baroque statues reflected in ruffled waters of Leningrad, or against waving, shadow-pencilled plains of corn.

Upon us in this restless and awakening mood came Isherwood's friend Chalmers, on his way back to England from an Intourist Tour of Moscow. Very much the emissary of a Cause he seemed, with his miniature sensitive beauty of features, his keen-smiling yet dark glance, his way of holding the stem of his pipe with his finely formed fingers of a chiseller's or wood-engraver's hand. He was not unlike the smiling young Comsomol hero who saves the boys in the reform school in one of our favourite films—*The Way into Life*. Two days after his arrival, he and I went for a walk. I remember that we went through that part of Berlin where roads connect the Tiergarten, the Bahnhof-am-Zoo, and the Gedaechtniskirche—a church on a road island, with the traffic streaming all round it. The pressure of what Chalmers said to me was not just his words, but a consciousness of Berlin, of unemployment and Fascism, and, dimly beyond that day, of the day fifteen years later when I would walk along the same road and see the Gedaechtniskirche, which had looked (on the occasion of our walk) like an absurdly ornate over-large inkstand set down in the middle of the traffic, transformed into a neo-Gothic ruin, having about it something of senile dignity. What Chalmers was really asking me was (as though we both looked through the transparent traffic on to the ruin) how to stop this happening? How prevent this Europe being destroyed in the war which—as he analysed the situation—was certain to arise from recrudescent German nationalism, supported by American and British capitalism, and flung (as he thought it would be) against Russia? I gave my stumbling answers: I desired social justice; I abhorred war; I could not accept the proposition that to resist evil we must renounce freedom, and accept dictatorship and methods of revolutionary violence. Chalmers who had listened intently, smiling slightly to himself, observed quietly, when I had finished speaking: 'Gandhi.'

My vaguely distressed consciousness now began to formulate itself along lines laid down by Marxist arguments. The essential ideas which moved me were: firstly, the inevitable development of social situations resulting from analysable material conditions; secondly, the division of the world into two interests, the bourgeois and the proletarian, which represented not just political views, but also influenced the whole pattern of behaviour and thought and culture of everyone who belonged to them.

Until now I had, I suppose, thought of myself as being a member of society in the same way as a passenger thinks of himself belonging to the ship on which he is carried. The very fact of my being in Germany, a country where

I was a foreigner, emphasized my outside position to myself. I pitied the unemployed, deplored social injustices, wished for peace, and held socialist views. These attitudes were emotional, and I used them as a way of proving my own values to myself and testing my sincerity in some hypothetical situation. The opposite feelings to pity and sympathy and well-wishing would not have done me credit in my own eyes. The hypothetical test was to ask myself whether I was really prepared to make sacrifices if socialism 'happened', and I found myself a member of a classless society. The answer to this question was that, on the whole, I thought I would. But a more significant fact was that I thought of socialism as 'happening' outside me within a society of which I did not think of myself as a part.

In general, I thought of public events as happening more or less incalculably, as the result of clashes of interests, economic factors, the influence of outstanding personalities in political life. The future was always uncertain: and this made it unreal to me. For example, I could not think that in 1931 a war which would take place eight years later existed within the structure of events, like the foundation stone beneath a building or like past history; that unless the structure was altered the war would inevitably take place; and that, in order to alter it, methods would have to be used which could really achieve the alteration. As all political events, solid as they might seem to-day, appeared to liquefy in the uncertainty of to-morrow, it seemed to me enough that I should preserve a guileless attitude in relation to them.

But during the coming years I began to appreciate the seriousness of the political situation: that within to-day there were not only all the injustices of the day—producing unemployment, poverty and exploitation—but also the victims of to-morrow, buried as it were within its structure, all the shot-down pilots, the inmates of concentration camps, and participants in war—a generation then at school, training, if one viewed things in this way, to be shot down by machine guns. This Berlin contained within a pattern, partly its own and partly imposed on it by the folly of the victors of the war of 1914–18, its own ruins and the ruins of the European cities, exactly as if buildings and their ruins co-existed; for they already were within the political situation. And now I saw that a personal self-righteousness whereby I secretly washed my hands of social guilt had no objective value.

A debate which still continues had begun in my mind. I was impressed by the overwhelming accusation made by Communism against bourgeois society, an accusation not only against all its institutions but also reaching deep into the individual soul.

When I considered the existing injustices and the future destruction which were involved in the system in which I lived, I longed to be on the side of the accusers, the setters-up of world socialism. But at this stage, having shifted the centre of the struggle within myself from the bourgeois camp to the communist one, I failed to find myself convinced by Communism.

Even when I had accepted in my own mind the possibility of having to sacrifice everything I gained by living in a bourgeois society, I still could not abandon my liberal concepts of freedom and truth. The Marxist challenge, thrown out in the Communist Manifesto, that the opponents of Communism were concerned only with *their* freedom, *their* truth, and that all their ideas were rationalizations of their interests, made me think out for myself the position of the freedom of the individual. It became extremely important to answer the question—was my sense of my own individuality simply an expression of the class interest which I, unknowingly and instinctively in everything I thought and wrote and did, represented? If this was so, must I accept the argument that to alter my position I must make myself its exact opposite—a function of the proletariat?

When I had admitted to myself the force behind the Marxist arguments, I still found in myself a core of resistance to the idea that if I was a Marxist my conceptions of freedom and truth must simply be behaviour and facts dictated by Marxist expediency. This hard core was the point in my self-examination when the rather abstract phrase 'freedom of the individual' became replaced by the more concrete one, 'independent witnessing'. However much a projection of class interest the mind of the individual may be, I was persuaded there was a point where he chose simply to witness truths which served no interest.

Another objection to Communism which I could never overcome was to what I called in my own mind the world-provincialism of Marxism. I can explain this best by a hypothetical illustration. Suppose that in a corner of Africa there are two tribes, A and B, interlocked in a historic struggle. In such a conflict, Marxism assumes that each must think entirely in terms of its own interest in asserting itself and overcoming the other. Suppose that tribe B is in a state of historic decline, has been wasting its own resources and compensating for this by raiding and enslaving tribe A, so that historically it is doomed to exhaust not only itself but, owing to its internal contradictions, tribe A as well. Then the historic task of tribe A is to throw off tribe B and establish a system with a political and economic future. This means that the whole view of life of everyone in tribe A must be directed towards this aim. Whatever does not serve this end, is not truth for tribe A. The story that there are white men living beyond the furthest mountain ranges and having factories and great ships is only a myth serving the interests of tribe B, by distracting the attention of the warriors of tribe A from their historic task.

This stifling provincialism is the communist attitude applied to the class struggle of the whole world within history and the universe. Philosophic speculation, unpropagandist art, and even scientific research which do not serve the interest of the workers, are labelled idealistic, untruthful, escapist, and reactionary.

The insistent philosophic materialism of the communist dogmatists struck me as characteristic of their way of over-reaching themselves, in order to achieve concentration of purpose on immediate aims, by depriving their followers of a moral attitude which has anything in common with that of the rest of humanity. To divide humanity into irreconcilable groups with irreconcilable attitudes, having no common language of truth and morality, is, ultimately, to rob both groups of their humanity. They will be inhuman first to one another, and lastly to their own followers.

From 1931 onwards, in common with many other people, I felt hounded by external events. There was ever-increasing unemployment in America, Great Britain, and on the Continent. The old world seemed incapable of solving its problems, and out of the disorder Fascist regimes were rising.

There was the feeling through all these years of having to race against time to produce a book or a poem. Not only was this disturbing to the stillness of attention necessary for creative work, but the life itself out of which the work grew was being borne away from under us. No wonder that the literature of this period is time-obsessed, time-tormented, as though beaten with rods of restless days.

From notes which I kept at this time—notes of such urgency that they even interrupt the manuscript sketches of poems—I find that there were two things which incessantly preoccupied me. One was the problem of the freedom of the individual, which I have just discussed. The other was the problem of the sense of guilt. For if, on the one hand, the Communists told me that my sense of freedom was only a projection of the interest of the bourgeois class, there was also a Freudian argument which told me that I only troubled about these things out of a sense of guilt. Rid myself of guilt, and I would no longer worry about my privileged position in society.

What I gradually came to see is that there is not just one guilt but many guilts, and that we must learn to distinguish between these, discarding useless guilt and making use of that kind of guilt which, so far from inhibiting us, releases us. For example, it was useless guilt which prevented me criticizing my Hamburg friend Walter, because, feeling myself involved in a gigantic lie of my whole social heritage, I could not criticize his small dishonesties. On the other hand, in discarding the attitude which prevented me from helping Walter, I would have been mistaken to discard also what was valuable in this attitude: the realization that my own position did rest on a social injustice.

Thus although guilt may create for us a kind of stumbling darkness in which we cannot act, it is also the thread leading us out of a labyrinth into places where we accept, instead of being overwhelmed by, the responsibility of action.

In 1932, Michael Roberts edited an anthology of poems called *New Signatures*, published by the Hogarth Press. This he followed a year later with a second volume, containing prose as well as poetry, called *New Country*. These two anthologies revealed the existence of a new, for the most part socially conscious, group of young writers. Of these, W. H. Auden, William Empson, Cecil Day Lewis, Rex Warner, William Plomer, A. J. S. Tessimond, John Lehmann, Julian Bell and myself made the greatest impression. These writers wrote with a near-unanimity, surprising when one considers that most of them were strangers to one another, of a society coming to an end and of revolutionary change.

In 1933 my volume, *Poems*, was published. It followed on Auden's *Poems* and Day Lewis's volume, *Transitional Poem*. Immediately, the names of Auden, Day Lewis and Spender were linked together by the critics. In fact, we were very different talents. Auden was a highly intellectual poet, an arranger of his world into intellectual patterns, illustrated with the brilliant imagery of his experience and observation. His special achievement was that he seized on the crude material of the unconscious mind which had been made bare by psycho-analysts, and transformed it into a powerful poetic imagery. He showed great technical virtuosity. Day Lewis was a more traditional talent, a writer steeped in the work of his immediate predecessors, the 'Georgians', much as Yeats had, when a young man, been steeped in the *fin de siècle*. Day Lewis to some extent corrected the blurred quality of the Georgians by introducing images drawn from factories and slums and machinery into his poetry. This modernism had a slightly willed quality in his early work, and as he developed further he tended to drop it. He had a metrical strictness and an intellectual sternness which were impressive and refreshing. As for me, I was an autobiographer restlessly searching for forms in which to express the stages of my development.

Why then should the work of these three poets have been linked together? Partly, I think, on account of the influence of Auden, which was responsible, for example, for much subject matter of the early poems of Day Lewis. My own work showed his influence in certain imagery, the tone of certain lines. What we had, then, in common was in part Auden's influence, in part also not so much our relationship to one another, as to what had gone immediately before us. The writing of the 1920's had been characterized variously by despair, cynicism, self-conscious æstheticism, and by the prevalence of French influences. Although it was perhaps symptomatic of the political post-war era, it was consciously anti-political. If there was one principle the writers of this generation shared, it was that they considered politics alien to literature. During the First World War, some English poets, for instance Osbert Sitwell and Siegfried Sassoon, had satirized war, and after it they had turned to Left-wing politics. But this phase had been followed by one of abandoning political faith entirely.

Perhaps, after all, the qualities which distinguished us from the writers of the previous decade lay not in ourselves, but in the events to which we reacted.

These were unemployment, economic crisis, nascent fascism, approaching war, which I have described. The older writers were reacting in the 'twenties to the exhaustion and hopelessness of a Europe in which the old regimes were falling to pieces. We were a 'new generation', but it took me some time to appreciate the meaning of this phrase. It amounted to meaning that we had begun to write in circumstances strikingly different from those of our immediate predecessors and that a consciousness of this was shown in our writing. According to this familiar use of the phrase 'new generation', every important historic change produces its generation of young talent whose sensitive reactions to a new set of circumstances separate their work from what has gone before. In this century, generation succeeds generation with a rapidity which parallels the development of events. The Georgian poets were a pre-1914 generation. The war of 1914–18 produced a generation of War Poets, many of whom were either killed by the war or unable to develop beyond it. The 1920's were a generation to themselves. We were the 1930's.

Rather apart from both the 1920's and the 1930's, was the group of writers and artists labelled 'Bloomsbury'. Bloomsbury has been derided by some people and has attracted the snobbish admiration of others: but I think it was the most constructive and creative influence on English taste between the two wars.

The label 'Bloomsbury' was applied to people more by others than by themselves. Nevertheless if one examines the reasons for regarding Bloomsbury as a serious tendency, if not as a self-conscious movement, the label is meaningful.

The names most usually associated with Bloomsbury are Virginia Woolf, Roger Fry, Lytton Strachey, Clive Bell, Vanessa Bell, Duncan Grant, Raymond Mortimer, and perhaps David Garnett. E. M. Forster and T. S. Eliot are associated with it rather than 'belonging' to it, if 'belonging' may be said of a free association of people with similar tastes and talents.

Bloomsbury represented a meeting of certain influences and an adoption of certain attitudes which became almost a cult.

Not to regard the French impressionist and post-impressionist painters as sacrosanct, not to be an agnostic and in politics a Liberal with Socialist leanings, was to be put oneself outside Bloomsbury. For this reason Eliot was too dogmatic in religion and too Conservative in politics to fit in. It is more difficult to say why Forster does not quite fit. He was perhaps too impish, too mystical, too moralizing.

But the positive qualities of Bloomsbury were shared not only by Forster and Eliot, but by nearly all the best talent of this period. Roger Fry, Lytton Strachey and T. S. Eliot, in their different ways, introduced the influences of French impressionism, French prose, and in poetry the French symbolists. All these writers were preoccupied with re-examining and restating the principles and aims of art and criticism. They were interested in experiment, and were amongst the first to discuss and defend James Joyce and Proust. Their attitude towards an easy-going conventionality masquerading as traditionalism was critical: at the same time, they were deeply concerned with traditional values which they studied and restated with a vigour which made the old often have the force of the revolutionary. They insisted on the necessity of expressing past values in the imagery and idiom of to-day.

Most of these writers had begun writing before 1914, though they did not become widely known until after the war. They had sympathized with pacifism. Leonard Woolf, an intellectual Socialist who was at heart a Liberal, Maynard Keynes, the economist who denounced the Treaty of Versailles, Bertrand Russell and Harold Nicolson, were amongst their friends and colleagues who discussed politics, economics, philosophy, history and literature with them. In this way Bloomsbury was like the last kick of an enlightened aristocratic tradition. Its purism was founded on a wide interest in ideas and knowledge of affairs. Reading the essays of Lytton Strachey, Virginia Woolf, Clive Bell, Raymond Mortimer, and even Forster, one sees how inevitably they interested themselves in the eighteenth-century French salons and the English Whig aristocrats.

Like a watered-down aristocracy they made moderate but distinct claims on society. They were individualists who asked for themselves (and usually by their own efforts, from themselves) the independence in which to do their best work, leisure for reading, and pleasure. In order to produce a few works which seem likely to live, and a great many witty, intelligent and graceful conversation pieces, they needed to nourish themselves on a diet of the arts, learning, amusement, travel, and good living. They certainly were not malicious exploiters of their fellow men, and they expected less reward than the bureaucratically favoured Soviet writer receives to-day. At the same time, their standard of 'five hundred pounds a year and a room of one's own' (Virginia Woolf's formula in a well-known essay) made them decidedly unwilling to sacrifice their independence to the cause of the working-class struggle. They were class-conscious, conscious even of a social gulf which divided them from one of their most talented contemporaries—D. H. Lawrence, the miner's son. Despite their Leftist sympathies the atmosphere of Bloomsbury was nevertheless snobbish. They were tolerant in their attitude towards sexual morals, scrupulous in their personal relationships with each other.

To them there was something barbarous about our generation. It seemed that with us the thin wall which surrounded their little situation of independence and which enabled them to retain their air of being the last of the Romans had broken down. A new generation had arisen which proclaimed that bourgeois civilization was at an end, and which assumed the certainty of revolution, which took sides and which was exposed even within its art to the flooding-in of outside public events, which cared but little for style and knew nothing of Paris.

I spent about six months of each year from 1930–1933 in Germany, and the remainder in London. When my book of poems was published I began to lead a literary-social life of luncheons, teas, and week-ends at country houses.

Nothing could have been more different from the atmosphere of Berlin than this way of living, which had hardly been shaken by the war or even by the economic crisis. It is true that the Slump had caused a certain uneasiness, and the fall of the pound still more. But with the recovery from these disasters, during the years of the Baldwin Government, not only were these forgotten, but English middle-class life was characterized by a refusal to contemplate further disasters. The middle years of the 1930's were symbolized in England not by Hitlerism or even the Spanish war, but by the Royal Jubilee.

Most of the writers I knew regarded the Continent as a refreshing well of culture, not as a storm centre. My friends deplored my spending so much time in Germany and wished that I went more often to France: but to them France was still the France of Proust and the French Impressionists, not the France of the Front Populaire.

The English were passing through a phase of isolation not just of place but also of time, so that there was a refusal to recognize problems which affected England very deeply if these appeared disturbing to the very narrow vision imposed by Baldwinism and the Jubilee. All that the English permitted themselves to see of Europe was characterized by the Salzburg Music Festival, French Impressionism, the Lake of Geneva, and of course the museums and art galleries.

The idea that the future of the British Empire was being decided in Europe between 1933 and 1939 was absolutely intolerable to all classes. It was characteristic of the English attitude that when I published in 1936 a book called *The Destructive Element* in which I analysed the deep consciousness of destructive forces threatening our civilization, which was to be found in the work of Henry James, James Joyce, T. S. Eliot and some more recent writers, a reviewer wrote that if I had not gone abroad so much, but had stayed in England during the year of the Royal Jubilee, I would realize that England could not possibly be affected by forces of chaos which disturbed continental countries.

One of the writers with whom I often stayed was Rosamond Lehmann, whom I had met already while I was an undergraduate. She had then the beautiful Ipsden House in the Chilterns, which had once belonged to Charles Reade, the novelist. It had a garden partly surrounded by a screen of trees, through gaps in which the whale-like grey-green Berkshire downs could be seen. The house and garden sheltered by the trees had their own closed-in atmosphere of lawn and paths and old brick walls, in which some windows survived from the Elizabethan period, in a Georgian façade.

Rosamond was one of the most beautiful women of her generation. Tall, and holding herself with a sense of her presence, her warmth and vitality prevented her from seeming coldly statuesque. She had almond-shaped eyes, a firm mouth which contradicted the impression of uncontrolled spontaneity given by her cheeks, which often blushed. Her manner was warm, impulsive, and yet like her mouth it concealed a cool self-control, and the egoism of the artist. At this age she seemed at the height of her beauty: yet when I look at photographs of her then it seems to me that her features were in fact too rounded, too girlish, and that years confirmed a sculptural quality which one felt then in her presence but which later showed in her features. So that she was one of those women in whom even greying hair was a kind of triumph, a fulfilment of maturity which her youth had promised.

Wogan Philipps—to whom Rosamond was then married—was at this period a painter. He used to paint with a fanaticism which later he brought to politics. The house was full of his wild, somewhat childish paintings, amongst which were many portraits of Rosamond Although these were not good portraits they brought out something grandiose, almost Byzantine, mosaic-like about her appearance.

Rosamond and Wogan would often take me with them when they drove to see friends in the country or at Oxford. One of their not-too-distant neighbours was Lytton Strachey. Strachey, with his long russet-brown beard and his high squeaky voice, was certainly the most astonishing of the Bloomsbury group. He combined strikingly their gaiety with their intermittent chilliness. Sometimes he would play childish games such as 'Up Jenkins', which we played one Christmas. Often he would gossip brilliantly and maliciously. At times there was something insidious about his giggling manner; at times he would sit in his chair without saying a word. He was delicate and hypochondriacal. Wogan Philipps, who was given to Celtic exaggeration, told me once that Strachey had an arrangement by which the wires of his bed under the mattress were electrically heated: so that lying in bed he was agreeably grilled all night long.

Thus I began to enter into this civilized world of people who lived in country houses, pleasantly modernized, with walls covered with areas of pale green, egg-shell blue, or pale pink distempering, upon which were hung their paintings and drawings of the modern French school, and a Roger Fry, Vanessa Bell, or Duncan Grant. They had libraries and good food and wine. They discussed few topics outside literature, and they gossiped endlessly and entertainingly about their friends. In my mind these houses in the south and south-west of England, belonging to people who knew one another and who maintained approximately the same standards of living well, talking well, and believing passionately in their own kind of individualism, were connected by drives along roads which often went between hedges. At night the head-lamps would project a hundred yards in front of us an image of what looked like a luminous grotto made of crystal leaves, coloured agate or jade. This moved always in front of us on the leaves and branches. Delight in a vision familiar yet mysterious of this kind was the object of much of their painting, writing and conversation, so that when we drove in the country at night, and I watched that moving brilliant core of light, I felt often that I was looking into the eyes of their sensibility.

One house where I stayed sometimes was Long Barn in Kent, where Harold Nicolson and his wife, Victoria Sackville-West, then lived. Nicolson had interested himself in a small volume by me called *Twenty Poems*, which Blackwell published at the end of my last year at Oxford, selling all the copies of a limited edition to cover the cost of other copies which I gave to friends. At that time he was reviewing for the *Daily Express* and he kindly asked me whether I would care for him to notice this book in his columns. This offer I refused on the grounds that the book was only a limited edition and not for public sale, but really out of pride and for no other reason.

Nicolson was a strange combination of contradictory qualities: idealism and cynicism; unworldliness and love of the world; satire and sentiment. When he told me that he had kept a diary every day of his life since his boyhood, I thought these contradictions were exactly those which make a diarist. For he never lost his passionate desire to enter into other people's lives, to be with people who were at the centre of events, nor his capacity to be affected personally by these. I was reminded of what Auden had said about the poet thriving on humiliation.

Now when I look back on these days when I was twenty-one, I see that I missed opportunities of friendship which were offered to me. I had so strong a sense of the busy, filled lives of people like the Nicolsons that unless they asked to see me I never dared ask to see them. But to them it perhaps seemed that I did not respond to their kindnesses. But one unspoken friendship I always felt confident in, though little was said between us: this was with Vita Sackville-West. Working always in her garden, caring for her friends, her flowers and her poetry, modest and never interesting herself in literary disputes, her friendship had the freedom of silence and watchfulness about it, and I often think of it with gratitude.

Nicolson discussed Communism with me (as he did other problems of my life) sensibly and seriously, recommending me to see a Labour M.P. of the extreme Left who had disagreed with the Communists, for reasons which Nicolson thought I would take seriously. To the Nicolsons I confided the kind of discouragement I sometimes felt which made me think I would not go on writing, and they said: 'You are describing exactly what every creative writer feels.' When I sent to Vita Nicolson the copy of a poem which began,

'O young men, O young comrades', she wrote back saying that she was dazzled by it, that nevertheless my attitude horrified her.

When I was twenty a friend had sent some of my poems to T. S. Eliot, and a few weeks later I met him for the first time at one of those London clubs where I have met him so often since. His appearance was grave, slightly bowed, aquiline, ceremonious, and there was something withdrawn and yet benevolent about his glance. When Eliot orders a drink or inclines over the menu to consider a meal the effect is such as to produce a hush. It is a priestly act as he says in a grave voice: 'Now will you have a turtle soup (I doubt whether it will be made from *real* turtle) or green pea soup?' But he is also a connoisseur who has strong views about wines, and still more, cheese.

On the occasion of one of our first meals, I disturbed him a little by announcing that I would choose smoked eel to eat. I was surprised to hear him say: 'I don't think I dare eat smoked eel', thus unconsciously para-phrasing Mr. Prufrock who asks himself: 'Do I dare to eat a peach?' This incident suddenly became illuminating for me shortly after I had recorded it in a draft of this book when, having tea one day with Eliot, he refused cake and jam, saying: 'I daren't take cake, and jam's too much trouble.' Then I noticed that the effectiveness of the line, 'Shall I part my hair behind? Do I dare to eat a peach?' is precisely that it is in the poet's own idiomatic voice.

Eliot's conversation is gravely insistent. It does not give the impression of exceptional energy, but it has a kind of drive all its own, as it proceeds along its rigid lines. He cannot easily be interrupted or made to change the subject. I say it is a fine day, and Eliot replies gravely: 'Yes, it is a fine day, but it was still finer yesterday—' with a faint hint in his voice that when I used the word 'fine' of to-day I was not choosing the word altogether exactly. However, he continues about the weather: 'If I remember, this time last year the lilac——' and then it is quite likely that if I have gone on listening carefully, out of this dry climate, there will suddenly flash a few words of poetry like a kingfisher's wing across the club room conversation. His voice alone, grave, suggesting a bowed gesture, almost trembling at moments, and yet strangely strong and sustained—his voice alone is Eliot. Again, the observation of the obvious becomes here suggested. For despite its intensity the line of Eliot's poetry is relaxed and natural. It is near to conversation made rhythmic.

At our first luncheon he asked me what I wanted to do. I said: 'Be a poet.' 'I can understand your wanting to write poems, but I don't quite know what you mean by "being a poet",' he objected. I said I didn't only want to write poems, but also perhaps novels and short stories. He said that poetry was a task which required the fullest attention of a man during his whole lifetime. I said I wished to be poet and novelist like, say, Thomas Hardy. He ob-served dryly that the poems of Hardy had always struck him as being those of a novelist. 'What about Goethe?' I asked. He replied that he thought the case of Goethe was rather like that of Hardy, only on a greater scale.

This dismayed me, in part because it gave me a sudden moment of insight in which I realized that I could not devote myself entirely to poetry. My problem is that which this book must make apparent: what I write are fragments of autobiography: sometimes they are poems, sometimes stories, and the longer passages may take the form of novels.

At this first meeting I asked him a crude question such as I suppose only someone as young would confront him with so soon. 'What,' I asked, 'do you think is the future of Western civilization?' He indicated that politically he thought there was no future 'except'—I remember the phrase because I did not quite understand it—'internecine conflict'. I asked him what exactly he meant by this, and he said: 'People killing one another in the streets.'

This marked a difference in our attitudes. Towards social and political action his was one of negation and despair, or, at best, he thought that one should do what one could within a conviction of despair. I think he continued to feel like this until the war, but the war modified his attitude by convincing him that there was a Western cause to be positively defended. And after the war there was a Germany to be brought back within the Western tradition.

I am now forty, the same age as Eliot was when, at the age of twenty, I first met him. He seemed to me then exactly as old as he does now. I am not so much surprised that he should seem no older now as that he should not have seemed younger then. Perhaps we do not notice people who are older than ourselves getting older, but only our contemporaries or those who are younger. Yet perhaps being mentally old, being adult, living always a few years beyond his age, has been part of his art of living and writing. For at the age of twenty he was writing the Prufrock poems which surely express the sensibility of a man of forty. Shortly after the time I met him, when he was in his early forties, he was to liken himself in *Ash Wednesday* to an 'agèd eagle'. He has always exercised some privilege of post-dating his age. This must have helped him to elude his contemporaries and perhaps even to avoid some of the problems which arise from people being the age they are.

Eliot, in his capacity of a director of the firm of Faber and Faber, was one of my publishers. Just as we conducted a relationship which, after all, meant a good deal more than I realized, under the surface of meetings in clubs, so we conducted a correspondence under the surface of business letters. Looking over these now, I am surprised by a considerateness, a friendliness, a concern, which at the time I must have ignored because I could not believe it to be there, in the same way as I failed to cultivate the kindness of the Nicolsons. Occasionally I wrote questioning Eliot's views on his religion, which I crudely imagined to be an 'escape' from social tasks. I attacked him because I felt that in doing so I was discussing a public issue where he himself met his public. I would not have dared approach him on some more private matter.

He replied that religion was not such an effective escape as I seemed to

think: and he pointed out that the great majority of people find their escape
in easier ways, by reading novels, looking at films, or driving very fast on
land or in the air, 'which makes even dreams unnecessary'. He went on to
say that 'what matters is whether I believe in Original Sin'.

This letter I remember reading in the bright spring sunlight in the Hof-
garten at Munich. There I felt sure that I did not believe in 'Original Sin'. I
supposed, even, that it was wrong to do so. Nevertheless, I felt guilty and
disturbed at the back of my mind when I read this letter, which was an answer
to mine disputing his pamphlet, *Thoughts after Lambeth*, in which he maintained that what the young need is to be taught 'chastity, humility, austerity,
and discipline'.

Quite early in our relationship I wrote a review of Eliot's essays, criticizing his political attitudes and certain implications of his traditionalism. After
this had been published, it grieved me, and I sent a copy of the review to
him, together with a letter of explanation. Eliot wrote back an answer
which, while disagreeing with one or two points in my review, was gentle.
He ended by saying that I must always write exactly what I felt when I
criticized his work and that our public relationship had no connection with
our private one.

At about the same time as I received this letter, Harold Nicolson told me
of a painful experience he had after unfavourably reviewing the novel of a
friend. Grieving as I had done, he wrote a letter of explanation and apology.
A few days later he got the answer which ran (as I remember) something
like this: 'Little as I can forgive you for stabbing me in the back in public, I
can forgive still less that you should apologize in private.'

William Plomer, whom I have already mentioned meeting when I was
English Club secretary at Oxford, became my close neighbour when we
both lived in Maida Vale. This was a part of London which almost rivals
Berlin in its atmosphere of decay. Along the banks of the canal were the rows
of stucco houses, whose doors and windows, flanked with yellowing, peeling
Corinthian or Ionic columns, 'tactfully struck a soft Egyptian note, varied
by a Greek one', as Plomer pointed out to me. Steam rose from the canal,
covering the lower parts of the houses and washing everything in sweat,
as though this part of London were a Turkish bath. But at the back of the
sinister row of houses (drawn out like a bow directing an arrow against
Paddington) called Randolph Crescent, in which I lived, there was a very
large garden with lawns and trees and flowers, stretching for hundreds of
yards and totally unknown to all except the inhabitants of the houses around
it, by which it was completely surrounded.

Often people relate the most revealing things about themselves when one
first meets them, so that the subsequent relationship becomes the development of a theme already indicated at its opening. I first met William Plomer
(before I had invited him to Oxford) at the flat of my friend, Réné Janin. I

remember how that 'evening I said little, but listened to Plomer tell Janin stories of life in Japan. Plomer spoke of the necessity of presenting a mask to the world, and his clear-cut features, his smoothly brushed-back fair hair, the faintly ironical yet sparkling smile on his lips, had something of the mask, a certain impassivity imposed on most unoriental features. Through that slightly bronzed face, hewn as it were from a hard light-coloured wood, very clear blue eyes looked out at the world. During the coming years I was to see how the effect of his 'mask', which concealed his feelings, was to give him exceptional sympathy for the difficulties of others and a capacity to ignore his own troubles or, if they were discussed, to treat them with a lightness which had the effect of objectifying them.

Plomer, when he came to Oxford for the English Club Meeting, was accompanied by his friend Anthony Butts. Tony Butts looked like a malicious and naughty boy who had gone completely bald. He had eyes of a china blue which stared out of their façade of a slapstick face, with a solemnity which would suddenly collapse in laughter. A portrait of one of his ancestors in an eighteenth-century family group, which hangs in the National Gallery, contains a boy who looks exactly like him. One could fancy that his head was bald, because, belonging so much to the eighteenth century, his skin instinctively anticipated a wig. Tony Butts was a master of the absurd who when he was at Oxford, bought a large motor-cycle, got on to it without having learnt how to drive, managed to start it and then could not stop. He drove straight out of Oxford, and found no place where he could turn until he got to Blenheim. The story runs that there he drove round the back of the palace, past the private grounds in which a tea party was taking place. The guests were extremely surprised to see a young man on a motor-cycle rushing along the private drive. Noting their astonishment, Tony Butts waved his hand with a courteous gesture and continued—as he had to—on his way. This story, like most of those which depend on the vivacity of the protagonist who relates it himself, now has a somewhat faded air. In any case it would be impossible for anyone to tell it with the baroque extravagance, the ribbons and trimmings, of Tony's conversation. His one book, published anonymously after his death and edited by William Plomer, contains some of his stories about his family. It is a book which has found a small band of enthusiasts, in the way that Firbank found admirers. Some critics complained that the incredibility of the adornments to the stories robs them of a good deal of interest. However this may be, I have indicated—all too briefly and flatly—the story about the motor-cycle, because the picture of the wigless young eighteenth-century beau rushing through the country on a motor-cycle which he cannot stop is so like Tony Butts's own life. He was one of those extremely talented people who do not know how to direct their gifts. During one promising period of his life he became a painter, and was for a time a pupil of Sickert. Sickert told Plomer that Butts was the best talker he had known since Degas. Later he stopped painting and began writing plays (I never knew what happened to these). He wrote also the memoir, from whose disordered drafts Plomer edited the volume I have mentioned. At a time when fashions were becoming surrealist, he and William Edmiston, a young man with ideas almost as extravagant as his own, started a business for designing fantastic hats. At an early age he contracted a serious illness, and he died during the war, leaving a few paintings and manuscripts.

The group of people whom I describe here, look, at this distance of time, and through this frame of European ruins, like a large loosely knit family, most of them under the rather remote guardianship of their parent of Bloomsbury. At the centre of Bloomsbury was Virginia Woolf, whom I constantly heard discussed by the Nicolsons, and Rosamond Lehmann and Wogan Philipps.

Sometimes I dined with Leonard and Virginia Woolf at their house in Tavistock Square. They lived in the upper half of this, the lower half being occupied by the offices of their publishing firm, the Hogarth Press. Their drawing-room was large, tall, pleasant, square-shaped, with rather large and simple furniture, giving, as I recollect it now, an impression of greys and greens. Painted panels by Duncan Grant and Vanessa Bell represented mandolins, fruit, and perhaps a view of the Mediterranean through an open window or a curtain drawn aside. These were painted thickly and opaquely in browns and terra-cottas, reds and pale blue, with a hatch work effect in the foreground with shadows of the folds of a curtain. These decorations were almost a hall-mark of Bloomsbury. Similar ones were to be found in the house of Lytton Strachey. They represented a fusion of Mediterranean release with a certain restraint and austerity. Looking at them, one recollected that Roger Fry was of a family of Quakers, and that Virginia Woolf was the daughter of Leslie Stephen.

When her guests arrived, Virginia Woolf would be perhaps nervous, preoccupied with serving out the drink. Her handshake and her smile of welcome would be a little distraught. Now when I recall her face it seems to me that there was something about the tension of the muscles over the fine bones of the skin which was like an instrument tautly strung. The greyish eyes had a sometimes limpid, sometimes wandering, sometimes laughing, concentration or distractedness.

When we had gone upstairs and had sat down to dinner, she would say to William Plomer (we were often invited together): 'If you and Stephen insist on talking about Bloomsbury, I shall label you "the Maida Vale group".' 'Really,' Plomer said, raising his eyebrows and laughing, 'I am not aware of having talked of Bloomsbury, but you know how much one has to write these days. . . .' 'Well, then, if it's not you, it's Stephen!' 'Oh, Stephen.

How like him! But still, please don't include him with me; I can assure you we are very different kettles of fish! Still, I can imagine nothing more charming than an essay by you, Virginia, on the Maida Vale group.' Then the conversation wandered a little. Perhaps the name of a critic who ran a small literary magazine in which he had made a scurrilous attack on her would be mentioned, and she would say aciduously: 'Why do you mention that name? Surely we have more interesting things to discuss.' The uncomfortable moment passed and she answered, with a warmer interest, someone's question whether adverse criticism annoyed her: 'Of course it annoys me for the moment. It is as though someone broke a china vase I was fond of. But I forget about it afterwards.' Then another name was dropped into the conversation, that of a poet, later to become a supporter of General Franco, who had written a satire directed at two friends whose crime was that they had lent him for an indefinite period a small house in their garden where he might work. 'What ungrateful people writers are!' she said. 'They always bite the hand that feeds them.' She looked pensive. As I write this it suddenly occurs to me, by the kind of intuition which remembering things across a gulf of years brings in the very act of writing, what she may have been thinking at that moment. For the people who had been ungratefully attacked were the Nicolsons: and her novel *Orlando* is a fantastic meditation on a portrait of Victoria Sackville-West; and in this novel there is an account of a poet who comes to stay with Orlando, accepting his/her hospitality and then writing a cruel satire on the visit.

Did she say that when she wrote *Orlando* she began writing the first sentences without at all knowing how she would continue? Or am I thinking of something else? How Julian Green told me that he wrote his novels without in the least knowing how the story would develop? Or how Vita Sackville-West, who owned the manuscript of *Orlando*, showed me, written across the first page, a brief note explaining the idea for a novel, whose hero-heroine should live for three hundred years of English history, experiencing half-way through this life a change of sex, from hero into heroine. The excitement with which she embarked straight from this note on to her voyage of three centuries of English history, is shown by the letter which she wrote to Victoria Sackville-West the same day: 'I dipped my pen in the ink, and wrote these words, as if automatically, on a clean sheet: *Orlando, A Biography*. No sooner had I done this than my body was filled with rapture and my brain with ideas. I wrote rapidly till 12.'

In recalling Virginia Woolf there is something which causes my memory to become even more a kind of reverie than most of what I write here. It is necessary to remind myself that often she served the meal herself efficiently, and that she cooked it well. The dining-room was a lighter, perhaps more successful, room than the drawing-room. There was a pleasant table of painted wood, the work of her sister, Vanessa Bell, who also had designed the dishes. The pink blodges, small black dots, lines like brackets, characteristic of this style of decoration, were extremely successful on the creamy white surface of the china. Then Virginia described the beginning of the Hogarth Press, and at the age I then was, I listened like a child entranced. Her husband, Leonard Woolf, had won a prize in the Calcutta Sweepstake. With this they had bought a printing press and some type, and in the house where they then lived at Richmond they had printed stories by Virginia herself and by Leonard Woolf, T. S. Eliot's *The Waste Land*, and several other small volumes. She described how they had done this with little thought except to please themselves, and then one book (I think it was her own *Kew Gardens*) had been well reviewed in the *Times Literary Supplement*. She described running downstairs and seeing the door-mat deep in letters bringing orders for more copies. They then had to farm out the printing of a second edition with a local printer, and hence they found that they had become not amateur printers who sold their own work privately, but The Hogarth Press, a small but flourishing firm which even produced a few best-sellers.

From publishing the conversation turned to writing. She asked: 'How do you write, William?' 'How do I write?' 'Yes, what do you do when you write? Do you look out of the window? Do you write while you are walking in the street? Do you cross out a lot? Do you smoke when you are writing? Do you start by thinking of one phrase?'

When William and I had both been examined, we would ask her how she wrote. She came out with something like this: 'I don't think there's any form in which the novel has to be written. My idea is to make use of every form and bring it within a unity, which is that particular novel. There's no reason why a novel shouldn't be written partly in verse, partly in prose, and with scenes in it like those in a play. I would like to write a novel which is a fusion of poetry and dialogue as in a play. I would like to experiment with every form and bring it within the scope of the novel.'

She said that no one should publish before he or she is thirty. 'Write till then, but scrap it or put it aside.' She herself had covered reams of paper with that she called 'just writing for the sake of writing', and she had scrapped it all. She said she believed that prose was more difficult to write than poetry.

Then after dinner we would go down to the drawing-room again, and Virginia would smoke a cheroot. There would be talk perhaps of politics, that is to say, of war. For Leonard and Virginia were among the very few people in England who had a profound understanding of the state of the world in the 1930's; Leonard, because he was a political thinker and historian with an almost fatalistic understanding of the consequences of actions. So that when, in 1934, I asked him whether he thought there would be a war he replied: 'Yes, of course. Because when the nations enter into an armaments race, as they are doing at present, no other end is possible. The arms have to be used before they become completely out of date.' Virginia had also a profound political insight, because the imaginative power which she shows in her novels, although it is concentrated often on small things—the light on the branches of the tree, a mark upon a whitewashed wall—nevertheless held at bay vast waters, madness, wars, destructive forces.

While Leonard was talking about war, labour, League of Nations, Virginia would fall silent. There was often after dinner this kind of political intermezzo. She had a little the air of letting the men talk: still more that of listening to Leonard.

The conversation passed from politics to gossip about personalities, quite possibly to Hugh Walpole. Now some stories seem so familiar to me that they have become inseparable from this life of literary London, as though it were woven out of them. For example, the story of how Hugh Walpole sat up all of one night reading an advance copy of Somerset Maugham's *Cakes and Ale*, to recognize himself in the cruel analysis of the career of the best-selling novelist.

Virginia had a passionate social curiosity, about the 'upper', the 'middle', and the 'lower' (I think these distinctions of class were sharply present in her mind). The Royal Family was a topic of intense interest to her. This preoccupation could be embarrassing—if one is embarrassed by snobbishness. Yet her interest in royalty was largely due to the fact that royalty, surrounded by an atmosphere of radiant adoration as though bathed in a tank of lambent water, were peculiar and exotic in precisely the way in which people are strange and luminous in her writing. The little episode in *Mrs. Dalloway* where a chauffeur extends a small disc to a policeman, and the car shoots on ahead of the stopped traffic, exactly expresses like a minute phrase in a descriptive symphony what fascinated her—the privileged special life sealed off in the limousine whose driver has a pass. Indeed, her Mrs. Dalloways and Mrs. Ramsays are by nature queens shut off from other people who gaze at them with wonder, as through a window. The wonder of life is a wonder of royal self-realization, which has something akin to a gaping crowd staring at a lady dressed in ermine. When she writes—in her essay in *The Common Reader*—of Dr. Johnson, and Fanny Burney, and the Elizabethans—one is staring at exotic fish swimming in their tank.

'Why are we so interested in them—they aren't so different from us?' she would exclaim after the talk on the Royal Family had bordered almost on tedium. The answer was 'because they are held up to our gaze', or 'because they are like a living museum of flesh and blood dressed in the clothes of past history', or 'because after all, their heredity does make them extraordinary'.

There was a division between her and other people which she attempted—not quite satisfactorily perhaps—to bridge by questions. She inquired of everyone endlessly about his or her life: of writers how and why they wrote, of a newly-married young woman how it felt to be a bride, of a bus con-

ductor where he lived and when he went home, of a charwoman how it felt
to scrub floors. Her strength and her limitations were that she didn't really
know how it felt to be someone else. What she did know was how it felt
to be alone, unique, isolated, and since to some extent this is part of universal
experience, to express this was to express what many feel. But she was lacking in the sense of a solid communal life, divided arbitrarily into separate
bodies, which all nevertheless share. What bound people together escaped
her. What separated them was an object of wonder, delight and despair.

She seemed as detached from herself as from everyone else. Thus she would
talk about herself with an objectivity which was unambiguous in her but
which in others would have seemed uneasy. She was simply interested in the
point she was making or the story she was telling, and the fact that she herself might be deeply involved in it seemed irrelevant. Once the conversation
having turned to Rupert Brooke, she said: 'He was very keen on living "the
free life". One day he said, "Let's go swimming, quite naked".' 'And did you,
Virginia?' William asked. 'Of course,' she answered, and then she added:
'Lytton always said that Rupert had bandy legs. But I don't think that was
so.' She said that Rupert Brooke was writing at this time his poem which
begins 'These have I loved', in which he lists a catalogue of sensations which
had given him pleasure. She said that he was quite external in his way of
making this list and that he surprised her by asking what was the brightest
thing in nature, as he needed a dazzling image for his poem. She looked up
at the sky and saw a poplar tree with white underleaves rotating to shimmer
against the light. She said: 'Bright leaves against the sky.'

She seemed to hate her dinner parties to come to an end. Sometimes they
would go on until 2 a.m. She gave her guests an impression of gaiety which
could plunge at any moment into the deepest seriousness. She would tell
stories of things which amused her until the tears ran down her cheeks.
Usually these stories concerned one or two people who played a kind of
jester's role in her life. There was a trace of cruelty in her feeling towards
them. One of these was Hugh Walpole, concerning whom I have quoted one
of her stories, and another, Dame Ethel Smyth. There was always some new
item about Dame Ethel. Once, when Dame Ethel was already eighty-four,
Virginia had just received a letter from her, announcing that she had become
attached to a lady aged eighty who lived next door. 'And to think that we
have been close neighbours for five years,' Dame Ethel's letter complained,
'and that we might have met when she was seventy-five and I only seventy-
nine.' Dame Ethel was a highly eccentric character. On one occasion the
Woolfs invited her to dine at their house at Rodmell near Lewes, Sussex.
Dame Ethel bicycled the twenty miles from the village where she lived to
Rodmell, dressed in rough tweeds. About two miles from her destination
she decided that perhaps she was not suitably dressed for a dinner party. She
thought that possibly corsets were required to smarten up her figure. Accord-

ingly, she went into a village shop and asked for some corsets. There were none. Distressed, she looked round the shop and her eye lighted on a bird cage, which she purchased. About twenty minutes later, Virginia went into her garden to discover Dame Ethel in a state of undress in the shrubbery struggling with the bird cage, which she was wrenching into the shape of corsets and forcing under her tweeds.

Virginia Woolf was a most scrupulous artist who demanded high standards of artistic integrity from others. Once I submitted to The Hogarth Press a novel which was rejected. It interested her and she spent some part of an afternoon discussing it with me. As she made several favourable comments I asked how I could re-write it. 'Scrap it!' she exclaimed with force. 'Scrap it, and write something completely different.' When she said 'Scrap it!' I had a glimpse of the years during which she had destroyed her own failures.

She composed, I imagine, like a poet. That is to say, her writing proceeds from the organic development of images growing out of her subject matter. These become symbols in a discussion which often takes her beyond the subject itself. I have in front of me an essay called The Leaning Tower, which is the written version of a lecture given in 1939. The essay develops from the apparently simple image of a writer sitting in a chair at his desk. This image proliferates into further ones of the pen, the paper, and the writer's chair even: and these all become symbols of the writer's high calling, expressed in terms of the simple machinery of his trade, scarcely altering through the ages, and joining him to past writers. Within this symbolism there is a further symbol of the hand holding a pen: and through the veins of the hand there flows the blood which is the whole life of the literary tradition joining the writer, sitting at his desk, with Shakespeare. Such writing, dependent for its truth on the inter-relation of ideas in the structure of thought, developed parallel with the inter-relation of the images: the chair, the desk, the pen, etc., can only 'grow' like a poem. And I have heard that there were as many drafts of some of Virginia Woolf's essays as most poets make of a poem.

But just as my lack of belief in Original Sin divided me from the views of Eliot, so my attitude to politics divided me from Virginia Woolf. Not that we disagreed about the political issues themselves: for she hated Fascism, sympathized with the Spanish Republicans, and held much the same political views as we did. But she objected to the way in which our writing was put to the service of our views, and she discerned that my generation were 'sold' to a public sometimes more on account of their views than for the merit of their writing. Indeed all of us irritated her in this respect, and she sometimes showed her irritation. It occurs first in the Letter to a Young Poet, where she quotes Auden, Day Lewis, John Lehmann and myself in order to criticize us for our impatience, our preoccupation with external social factors, and with our desire to set the world right. She returns to the assault, less directly, in *A Room of One's Own*, where she discerns in George Eliot and Charlotte Brontë a desire to preach (though she excuses this as being the result of the position of women in their time). At the beginning of the war, in the essay I have mentioned, *The Leaning Tower*, she returns to the attack more directly. She felt that though we were aware of the calamitous condition of the world, we reacted to it with our intellects and wills, before we had experienced it fully through our sensibilities. 'You have to be beaten and broken by things before you can write about them,' she once said to me. To hold strong views and feel deeply about what, however significant and important, was outside the range of one's experience, was not enough. I might have replied—though I did not—that, often passing Edith Cavell's monument near Charing Cross, with its inscription of *Patriotism is not enough*, I reflected that I would like to have *Sensibility is not enough* engraved on my tombstone.

She and her circle formed a group of friends who shared the same ideas and who, within a common appreciation of high values, had a deep loyalty for one another. Living in their small country houses, their London flats, full of taste, meeting at week-ends and at small parties, discussing history, painting, literature, gossiping greatly, and producing a few very good stories, they resembled those friends who at the time of the Plague in Florence withdrew into the countryside and told the stories of Boccaccio. Our generation, unable to withdraw into exquisite tale-telling and beautiful scenery, resembled rather the *Sturm und Drang* generation of Goethe's contemporaries, terribly involved in events and oppressed by them, reacting to them at first enthusiastically and violently, later with difficulty and disgust.

This Boccaccio-like group, together with others who did not belong to it, had a pre-eminent hostess in whose house and garden they often met. This was Lady Ottoline Morrell. The house was Garsington, near Oxford. At the time I knew her she no longer lived in Garsington, but only in Gower Street in London. Long before I had been invited to her London drawing-room, the Nicolsons, who were exact prophets of my future, told me that I would inevitably meet this extraordinary great lady who dyed her hair purple (I think they said purple, though when I met her it seemed dark red). She had, they said, made the most bizarre impression on those who accepted her hospitality: as was shown by the portraits of her in books by D. H. Lawrence, Graham Greene, Aldous Huxley, and several others.

She interested herself in the work, plans and ideas of these friends, helped them, interfered with their personal lives, was loved and hated by them.

Bertrand Russell, Augustus John and D. H. Lawrence were the means by which she had escaped from the Dukeries and discovered and entered into a world of exciting ideas, ideals, and passions. An evangelist fervour went into her social life, and to say that she was a great hostess and patroness would be to give an inadequate idea of the role she played in the lives of her friends. Her guests undoubtedly revealed to her the highest quality of friendship.

She had an exalted devotion to what she took to be the True, the Good, and the Beautiful.

Her intensive idealism was complicated by a great inquisitiveness. Thoroughly incapable of being shocked by anything human, she wished her friends to contribute their most intimately dramatic qualities to the *commedia* which was her home. 'Does your friend have *no* Love-Life?' she complained once to a poet who had brought a somewhat reticent friend to tea.

Early in 1934 an invitation arrived for me on hand-made writing paper, scented with a powder which she used for drying ink. This ink itself was of a rust colour, as though it had been manufactured out of nails left a long time in water. The hand-writing was almost vertical—perhaps it sloped a little backwards—and very fine. It was prolific in shoots, tendrils, and loops which blossomed at every curve or even with the crossing of a 't'. These forms were purely ornamental, having an extraordinary natural grace and no utilitarian purpose whatever. They must have made writing a slow process and they did not help towards deciphering it.

When I entered Lady Ottoline's drawing-room, I saw an enormous quantity of objects: pictures, looking-glasses, small boxes, vases, armchairs, sofas, large and small tables, beautifully bound books. On some tables, bowls were placed which contained heaps of pomanders. These gave out a musty odour, making the room smell like the inside of an Oriental cedar box. Long damask curtains hung on either side of tall windows which, at the back of the house, looked out on to a garden. In a prominent position on the wall there was a misty spiritualist painting by the Irish poet A.E., and there were other paintings by Sickert and Henry Lamb, and early Augustus Johns of figures in front of landscape.

In the dining-room, which had a long table, was a large portrait of Lady Ottoline by John. The pose recalled Reynolds' portrait of Mrs. Siddons, whilst the head itself with smudged lips was like a Velasquez portrait of one of the Hapsburgs.

The eighteenth-century style which Augustus John had indicated was most evident in her dress. She affected the tradition of its aristocratic eighteenth century shepherdesses. She wore creaking silks and satins and she carried a crook when she walked in the Bloomsbury squares.

In the last years of her life (which was when I knew her) she always had the air of falling apart, with hair like a curtain suddenly dropping over one eye, or a bodice bursting open. On one occasion, when she was in the middle of a sentence, a large ear-ring fell off the lobe of one ear and dropped into her tea-cup. Without interrupting what she was saying, she fished it out and attached it to her ear again. I once or twice saw far worse things happen, but she was not at all embarrassed as, with a diving, pulling motion, she set herself to rights. Sometimes her lipstick was askew: and she had rheumy eyes. Yet all these things were incidental to her grand manner, and they even partook of her grandeur. Had not Augustus John smeared the line of the lips in his portrait of her? What would have been slovenly in others, acquired in her a kind of audacity.

When Lady Ottoline went out, she had attached to her, or to her shepherdess's crook, by ribbons, two or three pekinese dogs. She never ceased to be surprised that people stared at her in the street. Having heard of my socialist sympathies, she explained to me once that she had much sympathy for the workers—was prepared to love them—but there was this difficulty— they would stare so. For example, only two days previously, she had boarded a tram (Bloomsbury was a district where trams were indigenous)—she loved sailing through the streets in a tram—such a beautiful, billowing motion—on a London tram she felt like Queen Elizabeth floating down the Thames in the royal barge. But, of course, she had to be helped with her pekinese on to the top by the conductor, and then of course she liked the front (or was it the back?) seat . . . and everyone had stared so . . . and 'there was a man who I think must have been slightly under the weather who made a *rude* remark, and some rather silly children. . . .' She was prepared to be *most friendly*, but she had met with *such concentrated hostility* that it was impossible not to be impressed by the fact that she was *not* welcome among them.

She talked with many underlinings, in that way which is so consciously verbal with some women that it is their idiom, as a special timbre of blank verse distinguishes each Elizabethan dramatist. My Aunt May, for example, had a style which underlined certain words with an effect of hammering spikes into each sentence with great blows. But Lady Ottoline's underlinings were often only of syllables. The syllables which she unerringly chose to emphasize changed speech into horn-like blasts which were peculiarly her own. Her conversation was interrupted by these significant trumpetings. One listened to her not so much for words as for an operatic aria, where the real meaning is in the music, though the words may also be understood.

Just as the opera demands that the idiom of the libretto should be adapted to the musical expression, so she had created for her own music a librettist's form, with a syntax different from prose. Sentences consisting of single words, whose separate syllables were trumpeted, were a feature of this special language. But where there were sequences of words, these were broken by dashes and pauses, a use of punctuation which was really the libretto modifying itself to musical notation and phrasing.

Even her letters were written in a style which reflected the demands restricting her conversation to very short sentences. Her handwriting, which I have already mentioned, in a way echoed her style of talking. For, just as in talking, her words became swallowed up in a sound like amplified sighing, so in writing, her more expressive words passed beyond mere letters into a realm of pure ornament where the words which look most beautiful on a page are in fact the most illegible, becoming a mass of waving tendrils and exquisite loops like convolvuli. On the written page, a sentence such as the following resembles the effect of her conversation:

'*Venice needs sun . . . & shadow . . . & creeping round corners–and sunsets & Barges . . . with pomegranates and grapes. And Melons.*'

Greece, Italy, Plato, Phidias, Michelangelo, Shelley were for her pure evocations of Truth, Goodness and Beauty. Eliot's dislike of Shelley and paganism were to her more distressingly blasphemous than her own pantheism would seem to most Christians.

'*I saw T.S.E. again . . . he was ever so Nice—but—I think he is very queer. . . . I showed him photographs of Greek IVth and Vth Century Statues and he said they gave him The Creeps. They were so akin to "Snake Worship". Now of all Art. Phidias / the Time of . . . seems to me to be Sublime—&—Not Corrupt. Don't you think it odd of him—I feel he has Demons . . . on the Brain——*'

Lady Ottoline's Thursdays were often very crowded. Some of the guests attended them regularly, in particular two Irish poets, George Russell (A.E.) and James Stephens. George Russell gave the impression of living within his brown bushy beard like a luminous spirit haunting a dark forest. He talked of Indian mysticism, but paradoxically, what made people speak of him with awe was that he was supposed to be an excellent economist. James Stephens was gnomelike and very loquacious. Not only did the Irish as well as the English writers and poets attend on Ottoline, but the scientists and philosophers as well. Julian Huxley and his wife Juliette came often. Bertrand Russell was one of her oldest friends. Here I met Aldous Huxley, who, remarking that I was about the same height as himself, looked at me meditatively and said: 'You and I are the wrong height for the work we wish to do. The great creative geniuses are short and robust "pyknic" types with almost no neck to divide the nerves of the body from the centres of the brain. Balzac, Beethoven, Picasso, did not have great stooping bodies to lug around. There was no gulf to divide their minds from the immediate communication of their physical senses.'

There were also teas on days other than Thursday, for smaller groups. On one of these occasions I was invited to meet W. B. Yeats. Yeats, at the age of seventy, had something of the appearance of an overgrown art student, with shaggy, hanging head and a dazed, grey, blind gaze. On the occasion of our first meeting he looked at me fixedly and said: 'What, young man, do you think of the Sayers?' This took me aback and I murmured that I had not read any. 'The Sayers,' he repeated, 'the Sayers.' Lady Ottoline then explained that he was speaking of a certain troup of speakers who recited poetry in chorus. I knew even less of these than of detective fiction and had to admit so. Lady Ottoline, who had arranged for us to have tea with very few people present, saw that I was a failure. She left the room and telephoned to Virginia Woolf to get into a taxi and come round from Tavistock Square *at once*. Virginia, highly amused, arrived a few minutes later.

After tea, I listened, relieved not to have to take part in the conversation, while Yeats sat on the sofa with Virginia Woolf and explained to her that her novel, *The Waves*, expressed in fiction the idea of pulsations of energy throughout the universe which was common to the modern theories of physicists and to recent discoveries in psychic research.

I heard no more of this, as other guests arrived, but later Yeats was kind enough to talk to me again, and this time we discussed his attitude towards the writing of poetry. He told me how, when he had written *The Tower*, he took the manuscript to Rapallo. From his hotel there he sent it to Ezra Pound, with a note explaining that he had not written poetry for some years, that he was writing in a new style; that if this were not an improvement on his past work, he was too old now to hope to develop in another direction. For these reasons he was very anxious to know Pound's opinion of them. A day or so later he received a post-card with written on it the one word: 'Putrid, E.P.' Yeats told me this story with amusement, and he went on to talk of Pound's kindness which resulted in his discovery at all too-frequent intervals of new literary geniuses, and his introduction into his house of many stray cats.

(Fifteen years later, at the hospital where he was confined at Washington, D.C., I went to visit Pound. The American poet Robert Lowell and I were allowed to talk to him, seated round a table in the ward of the hospital. As we talked, other patients wandered through the ward. Here, amongst the lunatics, Pound seemed a genial and benevolent host, receiving us with the same courtesy as he might have done at his home in Italy, and talking of literature and personalities. I asked him whether he remembered the visit of Yeats to Rapallo. He looked at me and said: 'If you want me to talk about Yeats I shall do so, but you must give me twenty-four hours' notice, as the top layer of my mind is gone.')

Yeats went on to criticize the Imagist poets for the lack of movement in their poetry. Pound's own poetry, he said, when I asked him for his opinion of it, was static, like a tapestry. For his part, he felt that poetry should always have an underlying lilt, as simple as Byron's: 'So we'll go no more a-roving, / So late into the night.' He said he was brought up in an environment of æstheticism and artificiality. He had striven all his life to simplify his diction. Yet he did not think that to write free verse was a solution of the problem. He wanted to write starkly and yet not sacrifice the Byronic lilt.

Then he spoke about the political views in the writing of my friends and myself, contrasting it with his own interest in spiritualism. 'We are entering,' he said, 'the political era, dominated by considerations of political necessity which belong to *your* people. That will be bad enough, but there will be worse to come. For after that there will be an age dominated by the psychologists, which will be based on the complete understanding by everyone of all his own motives at every stage of his life. After that, there will be the worst age of all: the age of *our* people, the spiritualists. That will be a time when the separation of the living from the dead, and the dead from the living, will be completely broken down, and the world of the living will be in full communication with that of the dead.'

Yeats expressed these ideas in a half-prophetic, half-humorous vein, and I may have distorted them in recording them. But certainly he spoke of the three ages to come, of the political, the psychological, and the spiritual: and he affirmed that the last would be 'the worst'. It is difficult to understand how seriously to take such a prophecy. What is clear though, is that he saw spiritualism as a revolutionary social form as important in its power to influence the world, as politics, psychology, or science.

Of all that Yeats said, I remembered most his words about Shakespeare. 'In the end,' he said, 'Shakespeare's mind is terrible.' When I asked him to expand this, he said: 'The final reality of existence in Shakespeare's poetry is of a terrible kind.'

There were other occasions when I met Yeats at Lady Ottoline's. Once he came to a 'Thursday' when there were even more people than usual on those crowded afternoons. He told amusing stories of George Moore and Edward Martyn. His worst malice was directed against George Moore who, in *Ave atque Vale*, brings out the most ridiculous (as well as the best) aspects of Yeats. But to some extent he also saw himself in a ludicrous as well as a noble light. In his poem he refers often to his own folly and absurdity. Also, he was conscious of a pose, a mask, which it was necessary to assume for the purpose of meeting other people. After one of these parties Anthony Butts, who had been there, said: 'I didn't realize that Yeats had a——' 'Shanghai belly', did he say? or 'Singapore belly'?—at any rate some soubriquet to describe the curious way in which the poet's stomach jutted out. Another irreverent spirit—Mark Gertler—used to entertain his friends with descriptions of the hush which Lady Ottoline imposed on her guests at Garsington, when Yeats, seated in the drawing-room, was supposed to be composing. This also shocked me a little at the time. Yet now it seems to me that there was certainly something in Yeats which called out to be mocked at. Virginia, on the way back from the party I have described where I first met him, said that when he had finished talking about *The Waves* he went on to speak of the carved wooden head of a baby on a pillar at the foot of a staircase, which Yeats said had spouted Greek to him. She went home impressed and elated and amused and mocking. When, many years later, I read a poem describing a meeting with Yeats by a solemn poet who had recorded with the utmost seriousness some of Yeats's most nonsensical generalizations—I suddenly thought of Anthony Butts laughing at Yeats's protruding figure—then the vision of Yeats blazed vividly before me.

There was a sense of fulfilment in meeting these people. I was accepted by writers whose names were still surrounded for me by a sacred glow. Although I became used to meeting them, I never lost the feeling of awe for those who had written work which I continued to admire. A sentence of Virginia Woolf's, beginning 'A great beast stamps its foot', a line of Eliot, 'The awful daring of a moment's surrender', and, at a later date, a description of a rock pool by Cyril Connolly—all these seemed to be beyond the writers themselves, as the sceptre and crown lie beyond the man who is a king. To know the writers themselves was never to give me an insight deeper than that which had come to me through their single lines, but there were moments when I saw in the conversation of Virginia Woolf, Eliot, Isherwood, Auden, or Cyril Connolly, the working of the characteristic sensibility of each.

What can I feel but gratitude that I was taken into this great wave of the talent of my time? When I had been bathed in it, I was imperceptibly changed. That strange feeling which I had had at the age of eighteen when I walked down a crowded road and felt a wall of ice surrounding me and shutting me out from the people who shared my own preoccupations was now melted away. There are moments when one can be grateful for disaster. At this moment I am almost grateful for the war and the losses which followed, because they have put a part of my own life into a distant perspective, where I can praise wholly the lives of the people I knew then.

Really, I suppose, this life gave me what I had failed to obtain from the University. For Bloomsbury was largely a product of King's, and its interests had already begun among a group of people who were together at Cambridge. I should add to those whom I praise the name of E. M. Forster, the best English novelist of this century, and one of the most acute of its moralists. But Forster's strange mixture of qualities—his self-effacingness combined with a positive assertion of his views, his whimsicality combined with a great precision, his almost pagan amorality combined with his minute preoccupation with moral issues, his love of freedom combined with an impressive self-discipline, would make it wrong to describe him in connection with a group, even of his friends. He is one of the most comforting of modern writers, and at the same time one of the most uncomfortable.

The London meetings I have here described were part of a literary social life, which inevitably consisted of week-end parties, luncheons, dinners, teas. I fairly soon fell into a manner of living in which whole days were wasted. In London it often takes an hour to get to a luncheon, which lasts perhaps till three-thirty. It then takes an hour to return home, and at six-thirty you may have to leave again for a dinner engagement. I was always extremely bad at saying 'No'. If I was asked whether I was free at a certain time, my response was to look in my diary, and if I had no engagement to say truthfully 'Yes'. Having once said 'Yes' I felt it would be terrible to let my hosts down by excusing myself, or in the case of a cocktail party, simply not appearing. I had an exaggerated sense of social obligation. To this day it still torments me to remember an occasion when I forgot a dinner party. I did not actually enjoy social life, but I felt a strong compulsion towards it. As I have said, I never lost the sense that to meet certain people was a wonderful privilege. Moreover, I had always the romantic hope that one day I should meet someone, perhaps at such a party, who would alter my whole life.

Meeting people, receiving a large number of letters and invitations, and feeling under an obligation to reply to them, these are perhaps greater dangers to the writer than debauchery. For debauchery is a sleep-walker's activity, an attempt to act out fantasies within an obscure reality. Its danger is that it may become an end in itself more significant than creative activity, and more exhausting, and therefore destructive. However, this is a problem which lies within the writer's own personal development, whereas social life and public life are external factors which easily get outside his control. They mean entering into obligations with other people to fulfil engagements, undertaking loyalties which may prevent him saying what he feels about this very life which has become so large a part of his experience, and accepting the standards of some kind of social group. The fact that these may be lax, or eccentric, or Bohemian, does not make any difference to the confusion which they may cause in his pursuit of his own standards.

Social life is all the more dangerous because it is to some extent necessary to him. It is one of his main doors of entrance into the life of other people; unless indeed he happens to be one of those solitaries who can gain nothing from others. Of course, there is no great problem for those who have sound judgment and strong wills. But one can be talented without having either. And the writer is peculiarly dependent on his own judgment and will—made dependent by his very freedom. He is not protected by having an office and office hours. Unless he fights hard against them he is constantly exposed to interruptions.

Another danger of social life is that it is exhausting. People who move energetically in society put a greater strain on themselves than many of those who work. All the hostesses I have ever known have had something about them of the athletic champion—the Channel swimmer or the Olympic runner. The hot rooms, the standing up, the dinning of voices, the alcohol, the late hours, all absorb time and energy.

Thus whilst I met people in London whom I wanted to know, I also worked less than when I was leading an unrespectable life in Berlin. Several of my friends realized what was happening and reproached me for being so sociable. William Plomer, in his affectionate, mocking way, chided me for going out so much. He himself controlled every moment of his day, refused to be on the telephone, only saw a small number of people, and made all his friends conscious of the value of his time. My friends always seemed to think that all my time was available to them; and I myself wished them to think this. For a matter of principle was really involved. I did not want to wear a mask, to exert my will, to choose among people, to judge before I knew them, whom I should see and whom not see; I felt that any such attitude would inevitably result in a kind of hardness from which my work would suffer, and which would be a far more serious sacrifice than the loss of time.

Therefore I solved the problem by simply running away from England. I went abroad six months a year and during these months I lived a more solitary life.

Shortly after my half-dozen poems appeared in *New Signatures*, a publisher wrote asking me to contribute an essay on Coventry Patmore in a collection discussing Nineteenth-Century Poets. This reached me when I was at Sellin on Insel Ruegen. The publisher offered me what then seemed the large sum of ten pounds for an essay of 3,500 words. I regretfully replied that I knew nothing of Patmore and was far from libraries. The publisher wrote that Patmore's poems could be sent to me, and that I could then form an opinion of them. But I was in that state of literary innocence when I thought that even if I read Patmore I might have nothing to say about him, so I refused. How little I knew myself.

After this, editors wrote asking me to review books, and publishers to write a biography. There was a great hunt after biographies at the beginning of the 'thirties, and the only question was to find some past figure who had not already been debunked in the manner of Lytton Strachey. The candidature of Lady Hester Stanhope was pressed on me. I thought (quite rightly) that I would never know enough about anyone to write a biography, so I refused.

However, I got into the habit of writing reviews. I do not think I reviewed much better or much worse than most reviewers, and I tried to be fair. On looking back, I see that often in reviewing a book I was too ready to take up certain points I agreed or disagreed with, and make them the subject of my review, instead of considering the book as a whole. If I read a book with the idea of writing a review, I approached it with a different attitude of mind from when I read it out of simple curiosity. As a reviewer, when reading I was, as it were, interrupting what the writer had to say, with the pressure of my need to write my few hundred words, and this had much the same effect as not listening to someone's remarks because one is thinking how to answer them.

Once I had become deeply involved in the literary profession, I could not help approaching the works of all but a very few of my contemporaries either in a spirit of rivalry or in one of identification of my aims with theirs. Gone were the days when I read every new book which had been recommended to me, as it were, open-mouthed, and expecting manna to fall. Now that I myself had appeared in print, my attitude began to resemble that of the owner of a race-horse, who watches the field not only with an eye on the performance of his own entrant, but also with a sharp sense of the methods of other trainers, which he often judges as mistakes into which he has avoided falling.

It never occurred to me that anything I wrote might annoy the author I was reviewing. That he or anyone else should attach importance to my opinions appeared to me so unlikely that in my early days I often overstated them. But at a later date I knew so many writers and had experienced their hurt sensibilities so often that I had a kind of loss of nerve, and found myself unwilling to criticize the work of those I knew personally, not that I was frightened, but because I did not see how to do so without a certain awareness of the writer's personality entering into my writing which would destroy its objectivity.

A part of my literary experience was not just reviewing but being reviewed. Here I showed all the vulnerability which I believed other writers could not show. The good reviews which I received sometimes gave me a sense of being recognized with that warmth which is truly encouraging, but more often that of having scraped, with all my glaring faults, by the reviewer's defences. Adverse criticism was a terrible blow to me in my early days, and I still find it extremely discouraging when it is made of my poetry. In fact, I think that it is more difficult for a poet than for other kinds of writer to 'take' criticism. It is impossible to 'prove' that a poem is good, and a refusal to enter into the illusion created by a poem demonstrates that there is a failure of the poet to communicate, at least with the reviewer. A poem succeeds completely or not at all. Every weak place in a poet's armour is an opening for a fatal thrust.

Gradually I came to realize that the reviews which a writer receives are less his business than that of anyone else. They are a kind of conversation which goes on behind his back, which happens, though, to be published. Reviewers do not address themselves to writers but to readers. To overhear conversations behind his back is more disconcerting than useful to the writer; though he can perhaps search for criticism which may really help him to remedy faults in style. But he should remember that the tendency of reviewers is to criticize work not for what it is but for what it fails to be, and it is not necessarily true that he should remedy this by trying to become other than he is. Thus, in my own experience, I have wasted time by paying heed to criticism that I had no skill in employing rhyme. This led me to try rhyme, whereas I should have seen that the moral for me was to avoid it.

At first the money I earned from writing was only useful pocket money, for I found my three hundred a year enough to live on. But soon, with increased responsibilities, my earnings became an addition to my income which I could not do without, until at last I became almost completely dependent on what I earned, for supporting a family.

Economically, I found that there is much in common between the career of a writer and that of a gambler. Work of the same quality and even about the same subject-matter sometimes does not pay at all or sometimes pays extremely well. A poem of mine, 'I think continually of those who were truly great', which was refused by several literary editors to whom I sent it, was subsequently chosen to represent me in every anthology, and has made more money than any other poem I have written. On the whole, it holds true that a writer is paid best for doing his worst work: although sometimes, as in the case of the poem I have just mentioned, he may, almost accidentally, express in a form which attracts a wide public, some idea which is very significant to him. To-day, a special temptation of writers is that they can live largely by giving their views about subjects of which they know nothing. Because there is a popular idea that the writers are 'wise', and since the public is not interested in the particular form in which this wisdom is best expressed, they are expected to be omniscient about those subjects, such as Higher Education, Euthanasia, and the Atom Bomb, which interest the public. A Brains Trust of misapplied Brains is the prevalent idea of the function of writers, and this is encouraged by editors, Talks' Directors of Broadcasting, governmental organizations for cultural propaganda, and an enormous machinery for misdirecting creative energy.

I became involved in obligations to editors and publishers, accepting suggestions as to what I should write, instead of carrying out my original plan for novels, poems and stories. I began in my own mind to divide my work into three categories: poetry, my vocation; books about things which interested me, the subjects of which were sometimes suggested by publishers; journalism, which I often wrote hurriedly.

This division of labour was not really satisfactory, for the reason that a creative writer should always write out of the inner necessity of a unique occasion. Not to do this is to risk paying a price. The labour which he puts into studies not essential to his inner development, and the shoddiness of journalism, overflow into his creative work by widening his experience too much and confusing his sensibility. Or if these things do not happen, his best work becomes too obviously hedged off and separated from the rest.

Circumstances combined to make me attach too much importance to my opinions. For my views as critic, as journalistic observer, and as amateur politician, were all in demand, and sometimes the pressure to express them was not just economic, but came from events themselves, such as the need to take sides against Fascism.

I found that my own views, however strongly held, bored me as soon as they were uttered. I realized that they concerned things which other people could express better, or that they arose out of the irritation of the moment, like an angry telegram. The effect of publishing too many opinions was like an inflation of the currency of my reputation, not only before others, but—which was more serious—to myself. Before I published a line I felt a kind of awe at the idea of my own writing. Later I lost a good deal of this, and only recently have I determined to act so as to regain it. My resolution was rather banal: to take much greater pains over everything, including journalism, and to publish no poems for several years, so that I could keep my poetry in a kind of isolation away from my other activities.

There is something about the literary life which, although it offers the writer freedom and honour enjoyed by very few, at the same time brings him a cup of bitterness with every meal. There is too much betrayal, there is a general atmosphere of intellectual disgrace, writers have to make too many concessions in order to support themselves and their families, the successful acquire an air of being elevated into public figures and therefore having lost their own personalities, the unsuccessful are too spiteful and vindictive and cliquey, and even the greatest, when they are attacked, reveal themselves often as touchy and vain. I think that almost every writer secretly feels that the literary career is not worthy of the writer's vocation. For this vocation resembles that of the religious.

Perhaps, though, the writers belong to an order which is not only plunged in the world, but actually belongs to it and has to do so. Literature has its purists, both in work and life, but it would grow devitalized with more than a few of these in each generation, and some of the greatest writers (Dostoevsky, Balzac, even Yeats) have involved themselves in controversy and journalism in their time.

If success is corrupting, failure is narrowing. What a writer really needs is a success of which he then purges himself. The writer's life should, in fact, be one of entering into external things and then withdrawing himself from them. Without entering in, he lacks experience of the world; and if he cannot withdraw, he is carried away on the impulse of literary politics, success, and the literary career.

My London life was the occasion of a break with Christopher Isherwood, which led to my leaving Berlin.

In the winter of 1932, Christopher came to London at the same time as myself. He met most of my friends, shortly before or after I had met them. He found that I had already told them most of his stories, and that I had been indiscreet. Moreover, he disliked seeing me transformed from his Berlin disciple into a London literary figure. Our quarrel was, on the surface, as simple as this. Underneath, Christopher had better reasons than these for being annoyed. I had lived vicariously on his life in Berlin, and later in

London I had taken up a proprietary attitude towards it. He had accepted my dependence in Berlin, only to discover that all the while I had a life of my own in London. He felt cheated, irritated and even betrayed.

One day Christopher and I were together at the house which William Plomer then shared with Anthony Butts. At this party, Christopher showed so clearly his irritation with me that I decided I must lead a life which was far more independent of his. So the next day I called on him at his mother's house in Kensington, where he was staying. I explained that I had noticed I was getting on his nerves, and that when we returned to Berlin we should see nothing, or very little of each other. He said that he was quite unaware of any strain, and that of course we should meet, exactly as before. I went away not at all relieved, because I thought he was refusing, more out of pride than friendship, to face a situation which he himself had made obvious. Moreover, he had expressed his views in the accents of ironic correctitude with which Auden, Chalmers and he could sometimes be insulting. Next day I received a letter from him saying that if I returned to Berlin he would not do so, that my life was poison to him, that I lived on publicity, that I was intolerably indiscreet, etc.

The result of this letter was that I decided not to return to Berlin. It made me break with my habit of dependence on Christopher. Most important of all, it made me realize that at the age of twenty-four I had still succeeded in forming no intimate human relationship. It was true that I had new friends, but it was clear that in every case they had friends in their lives who played a more significant role than I. There was no one whom I could ask to travel with me or share a flat.

Christopher went back to Berlin. We immediately made up the quarrel by writing to one another frequently, and by meeting often when we happened to be in the same place. All that occurred was a slight readjustment of our relationship, in a way that was inevitable. Christopher was at fault, perhaps, in not simply accepting my offer that we should agree to see less of one another. But I had been seriously at fault long before this, and doubtless my attempt to manipulate a change in our relationship, after my prolonged and deceptive docility, was irritating. The way in which people recognize a change which is inevitable, can often be the cause of quarrel, and at this distance of time I can assume that my way was a bad one.

I did not want to live alone and I did not consider marrying. I was in the mood when people advertise for a companion in the newspapers. I used to inquire of my friends of their friends in case they knew anyone suitable. So when by chance I met a young man who was unemployed, called Jimmy Younger, I asked him to live in my flat and work for me.

Jimmy came from a small town near Cardiff where his father kept an hotel. He had run away from home at the age of eighteen, and been in various jobs, including, for three years, the Army.

He was pleasant-looking, friendly, quickly intelligent in certain ways, and capable of learning. He read a good deal and had a response to poetry which often astonished me. For example, he understood without apparent effort, by a kind of immediate apprehension, passages in Auden which I found difficult. When I had known him a short time, I was also surprised to find that he knew most of my own poems by heart. He wrote excellent letters, and at a time which I will describe later, when he was in the Spanish war, moving ones.

When we first met, there was a certain mutual suspicion of employer and employed between us. He was accustomed to be treated rough, and he expected that I would behave like his past employers. When I did not do so he was disconcerted and felt that in some way I was gaining power over him as no one had done before. Quite early in our relationship, when we were at Levanto on the Italian coast, he said: 'I want to go away. You are very nice to me, but I feel that I am becoming completely your property. I have never felt like that before with anyone, and I can't bear it.' I said that he could go away at once, if he wished to, that he could leave me entirely, or he could go back to London, and when I returned continue to work for me. Actually, when I said this I was stating what I was giving him, and how little I expected in return. Inevitably, this made it difficult for him to leave me. I realize now that this was one of the most important moments in our relationship. He knew that what I said was true, and he did not notice the element of self-deception in it. He could leave at any moment he wished, and he was under no obligation to me. By saying this, I had deprived him of any reason for wishing to leave.

I really did not need a secretary, and I find it difficult to force someone who is living on equal terms with me to work. Moreover, to make Jimmy work seriously, meant attempting to discipline a person who had already been disciplined by harsher employers than I could ever hope to be. He had been shouted at by sergeant-majors, locked up in guard rooms for some trivial offence, and so on. As with most soldiers, the Army had disciplined him at the price of breaking down any power of self-discipline which he might once have possessed. Outside the Army he seemed lacking in will and purpose, because these had been forced upon him by punishments and drills.

We painted our Maida Vale flat, Jimmy cooked, I worked, we entertained and were entertained. Occasionally we quarrelled, largely because I was furious with him for having so little to do—then I repented because I realized that there really was very little he could do. There were days when I did not notice him, and then when I looked up and saw him moving about the flat, I felt extraordinarily touched, and I felt also a kind of pity for the burdens which my way of life imposed on him—the weight of which he could surely scarcely understand. There was real affection, real happiness, real interest in our life together, but also a sterility which sometimes affected me so much that I would lie down on my bed with a sensation I have never known before or since, as though my mouth were full of ashes.

At this period, I sometimes asked myself whether I shouldn't be doing him more good by turning him out, than by keeping him with me. In ordinary circumstances it would certainly have been better to force him to stand on his own feet. But the question was made rather theoretical by the fact that if he had left me he would simply have been thrown amongst the millions of the unemployed.

I asked it partly because our life together, despite our bonds of affection, was a strain. Often I realized that the pressure was greater on him than on me. For it was he who was living my life, not I his. He met my friends, listened to our conversation, entered a world which was alien to him. He was successful when he simply drew on his natural intelligence. He was sympathetic and amusing, and he could tell a story well. Yet for him this life was a kind of perpetual examination in which he felt that he ought to be answering the questions which he did not understand. There came moments when he was involved in some fairly difficult argument about politics or literature. He had the Welsh passion for arguing about things of which he knew little. This, coupled with the fact that he was out of his depth sometimes, made him lose his head. It was then that I would be at first most irritated with him, and finally most sorry. The irritation and the sorrow cancelled one another out. For if I started to blame him I recollected that I had much more than he to blame myself for.

The strain on my side came from the impression of being with someone whose life was empty, and who was living in a way which seemed to lead to no better future. The uncreativeness of Jimmy's life often left me with a feeling that my own work was a kind of disloyalty to him, the exercise of an unfair advantage. The emptiness of his day filled my imagination. If his restless desire to amuse himself made me impatient, what really depressed me was the realization that he had no other way of filling his time, which without me would have been even more wasted. There was certainly a sense in which I could see that this very arbitrary decision of mine to take him as a companion, having once been made, became a social phenomenon, as though in him I had taken into my home the purposelessness of the life of the Depression outside.

In the spring of 1933 we travelled in Italy. After a few days in Florence, we went to the beautiful little town of Levanto which I have mentioned. In the following year and the year after that we stayed at a small village called Mlini, near Dubrovnik on the Jugoslav coast. Mlini consisted simply of two or three pensions, a church, and a pier for steamers. It had one enormous tree which created a monumental effect of shade and quiet, and gave the village a curious quality as though it had brought within a few yards from the coast, the peace of a place far in the interior. The pension where we stayed had tables out of doors a few yards from the water. Opposite Mlini was one of the many islands of which there are hundreds in this part of the Adriatic.

Dubrovnik, a few miles from Mlini, is a little off-shoot of Venice, with marble streets, Venetian palaces and a wall surrounding it. Two other walls stretch out into the sea like a mailed hand, opened out to form the harbour.

There was a walk along the coast from Mlini to a ruined palace in a garden where all the flowers ran wild. Above the village was the coastal road, and beyond it the mountain-side rose to a jagged crest of jutting rock, from which one saw range after range, all the stony mountains of the interior. The coastal road led to Montenegro where it twisted with many hair-pin bends to the top of the mountain, from which there was a great view of the Bay of Kotor like an immense mirror under the mountain.

This country with a riviera which is still wild, where many villages in the valleys lie half in ruins from Turkish invasion, where in the mountains a field is like a jewel set in a ring of stones, where there are half a dozen races, fascinated me. Some of them, the blonde, often tall and blue-eyed Montenegrins, were among the most beautiful people in the world. But when, in 1935, we sailed south to Greece, I saw how Jugoslavia, though beautiful, was perennially savage, whereas Greece, though wild, was intrinsically civilized. Jugoslavia lifted against the sky its cargo of crags and ruins. Occasionally the light and the sea wonderfully made many islands look like transparent scattered agates; this happened one afternoon when I looked northwards from the hill on which there is the famous cemetery of Cavtat. Nevertheless Jugoslavia remained Balkan, stormy, resistant of light, heaped with the wrecks of past quarrels and populated with dissident races. Greece was a country chiselled out of its own light. For what is that architecture, that columnar marble, except an invocation of light? The stone is cut into, with the aim of making a column look subtly straight against the sky, and shadows lift their darkness upwards like wings.

It seems to me now, thinking about our travels, that I could almost describe Jimmy Younger's character by recording his reaction to the places we visited. Levanto passed off almost without incident. He liked the life of swimming, bathing, and the conversation of pensions both there and at Mlini. He enjoyed the adventure of journeys in ships and motor-buses in Greece. In Austria he was probably happiest, because the architecture of Vienna was dramatic in a way which raised no question in his mind, and because the scenery of green mountains and lakes, like solid rock-crystal, pleased him. There was also something close to the Austrian in his *gemuetlich*, easy-going, lax temperament, which entered easily into enjoyment and conversations, and was easily discouraged.

But his reaction to two places, Venice and Toledo, was something like panic. Venice he was mentally unprepared for. This overwhelming flesh of marble with arteries of water, which he had been told was the most beautiful place in the world, simply dismayed and depressed him. All he noticed was the dirt and the smells. Toledo discouraged him in a different way. We took a bus across the great plain outside Madrid, which had the quality of miles and miles of leather, like the hide of a great slaughtered bull. Then we came to that extraordinary river-encircled, mountain-cresting city of Toledo, of a merciless perfection with a cathedral rising from it like a great embossed candlestick. There was something about the city itself as alien and uncompromising as its inhabitants, whose attitude to tourists was either to stare at them with hostility or to beg from them with an insulting flagrancy.

Even the idea of certain places fills the minds of most people with a kind of sacred joy, not unconnected with the sense of prestige of having been there. To say therefore that Jimmy did not enjoy Venice and Toledo may sound like accusing him of an inability to comprehend the obviously beautiful. But actually going to places is not like appreciating diamonds into which all that is valuable has been concentrated into the hardest possible stone: nor even paintings in which the painter has selected his visual experiences in order to create his form. Travel is an art which has to be created by the traveller. It requires the piecing together of experiences of the places visited, until we have discovered for ourselves Paris in Paris, Vienna in Vienna, Rome in Rome, Athens in Athens. A re-creation of these places in our minds is an art by which we fuse our conception of their pasts with our scrappy experience of their present. To do this we have to reconcile with the past a great deal of fragmentary contemporary material.

How well I know the dirty brick and rusted iron railway station, situated amid a desert of sidings and sheds, which is like a projection from many hundreds of miles away of an equally sad point of departure: the stuffy bed-sitting-room smelling of bugs and looking out on to a narrow courtyard in a district which seems to be situated nowhere, and refuses absolutely to offer the serene comforting assurance, 'You arrived where you set out to be; the architecture stretches out its cool, classic, famous arms to take you in'; the smell of homesickness which rises from nostalgic gutters even in the most beautiful places; the lamps in tenement windows seen from the gliding window of a train, which seem to say, 'Stranger, this is not your home——' —the glimpse of double beds and then the drawing down of blinds; the untidy, squalid secrets of tins and bits of wood and rubber, laid out on the wide sand of the famous resort when it is 'out of season'; the immensely serious and purposeful buildings in the centre of famous cities, which shut out with their hard edges glimpses of the crumbling Crusaders' tower or the cathedral; the hurrying contemporaries in dark suits and Homburg hats who pursue the affairs and politics which rise from all cities like a dense smoke enveloping the modern world; the squinting mountaineers in leather shorts and with flowers embroidered on their braces, with their minds like little caves of calculating darkness which the light-reflecting snow has never penetrated; the dismay felt at the edge of deserts and glaciers; the beggars who show their sores on the steps of buildings which are the wonders of the world, diseases which have not been cured by the most privileged scenery; the pimps who offer their sisters, so insolently sure are they that the traveller is a hypocrite who has come for this and not for the sake of art; and the guide who offers dirty post-cards to those who have travelled across the world to see a statue or a painting or a building.

How thoroughly I learned this lesson; that everywhere I went I took myself dressed in my clothes which at home were ordinary, but abroad were the uniform of the English tourist. Arrived at my room, I first propped my books up on the mantelpiece and set my notebooks out on to the table, and then I went out into the streets to start on the chase of the historic town through the modern town. But then I often was in turn chased through these by my fears and my desires; these demons had more in common with what I had left behind than with anything new which I found. And always the threat of war lay over all these places like the meshes of one huge net.

Is travel then the mirage where the real itself becomes mirage, a mirage of mirages? When we are in Rome or Athens, do they evade us, lost under the scurrying modern life imposed on them, an ancient ghost behind a modern ghost? Do we meet always and everywhere nothing but ourselves? Or are there, in Florence, for example, moments when the emanation of the past stamped on stone and bronze surges up above the present, with a greater order perhaps than it ever had in the past? This is surely so when, from Fiesole, we see the dome of the cathedral like a shield made of rust-coloured petals guarding the city. Or is travel only a collecting of distinct memories, shade by shade, and colour by colour, like the paints upon a palette, so that on the canvas of the mind we paint for ourselves a picture of the world, laying the ruggedness of Jugoslavia against the clear light of Greece, or the transparency of Italy, where each olive tree stands up, minutely observed leaf by leaf, against a terraced hillside reflecting light?

Certainly I think the chief purpose of my own travelling was to form a gradually enlarging picture in which the countries were the paints which went to form the world.

Several years after the time of which I am now writing, I added, as it were, the sky to my picture of the world. For in travelling frequently to and from and across the United States, I went almost always by air. Then I discovered the great joy of being high above the clouds, where the flat outstretched wings of shining silver metal move in an enormous calm space of blue, alone with the sun I came to understand the far longer time through which an immensely fast aeroplane seems to move than the slower trains and cars on land, so that in the air there seems to be an almost unchanging scene of sky and clouds, and sea, mountains or fields below. The highest mountains, or the jagged lines of coasts, or the curves of great rivers, provide all the scenery: except when the atmosphere itself displays range on range of cloud, through whose summits the aeroplane moves, as though an alpinist swum through a mountain peak which had suddenly become a river.

I can well understand now that the journeys which were also an escape from London and a search for a place where I could work, as well as an education, were a strain on Jimmy. Sometimes they brought out attractive aspects of his character. As when we first went to Italy, he wrapped his great-coat round him and dossed down on the floor of the compartment, or when in our room of the hotel on the island of Tinos, he burned hundreds of pieces of paper in an effort to discourage the mosquitoes.

I have never had so many quarrels with anyone as with Jimmy. They went on because he was completely unable to give way in an argument, because he liked arguing for its own sake, and because I was equally unable to give way on what I thought to be a matter of principle, and nearly everything between us became for me a matter of principle. These quarrels arose from unbelievably trivial causes. One of the worst was because I told him one day to buy a tin of roast chicken. Immediately he denied with indignation that one could possibly buy such a thing; that I should have thought so became a symbol to him of a certain vagueness in me which irritated him. So years before, as a boy lying in my bedroom at home, I had been irritated by the vague way in which my father shuffled his feet as he ran down the path in front of our house. For Jimmy had really become the son whom I attempted to console, but of whom I was the maddening father. However, I was convinced that I had in fact seen a picture of a sizzling farmhouse chicken entire on the outside of a chicken-sized oblong can. Therefore Jimmy's assumption that I was being vague in a particular instance, when I thought I wasn't, outraged me. Thus the smallest differences rapidly became illustrations of the weaknesses which annoyed us in each other. There was, of course, a further reason for these quarrels. They were the means by which Jimmy broke through the barriers of self-protection surrounding me. At such moments we really were ferociously together, revealed to one another, with all defences down. What we heard was Jimmy's real voice, under his irrelevant angry voice, saying: 'You have helped me at the price of taking away all possibility of my having any self-respect. I have been moved into your world where everyone must think of me as your creation, and no one as having an existence independently of you. When I realize this, I want to get away from you.' And mine, which said: 'Your complete dependence on me, your lack of any life of your own, your indolence, sap my work. When I write, I am away from you. I only exist when I am free of you.'

Yet the morning after such a scene he would insist that he had not meant a word of what he said, that I should forget it all, that he could imagine no happiness apart from his life with me. This was indeed quite true; for his mind spoke with two voices; one was the voice of the enjoyment of living from day to day, of adjusting himself to situations as they arose; the other was the voice of an inner despair which told him his life with me was hopeless. But even if, as I came to think, the despairing voice was the true one, casting him out into a society where he had already been unemployed did not solve the problem. His position with me was perhaps the best he could get in any case; and now it once more sometimes seemed to me that the most eccentric and intimate factor in Jimmy's life—his hopeless dependence on me—for which I was responsible, was also a social phenomenon with an entirely public aspect.

Though I was not reassured by Jimmy's telling me that everything was all right, I had my own faith which was perhaps almost as shallowly optimistic. This was that our affection, our need of one another, formed a situation in which there was a meeting of two human beings, and this transcended our separate characteristics, which I regarded as superficial. But gradually I came to see that in the moments of our quarrels and the making up of them, when we were most completely and terribly together, there was something in each which wanted to destroy the other. My character undermined his belief in himself; his dependence and lack of anything to do threatened my creativeness.

There was perhaps another reason for the failure of our relationship. We had come against the difficulty which confronts two men who endeavour to set up house together. Because they are of the same sex, they arrive at a point where they know everything about each other and it therefore seems impossible for the relationship to develop beyond this. Further development being impossible, all they can do is to keep their friendship static and not revert to a stage of ignorance or indifference. This meant in our case that loyalty demanded, since the relationship itself could not develop, that neither of us should develop his own individuality in a way that excluded the other. Thus a kind of sterility was the result of the loyalty of each to the other; or rather of his loyalty to the relationship itself which he did not wish to grow beyond.

It might be said (and indeed I often argued this with myself) that if Jimmy and I had had interests in common, we ought to have been able to grow side by side, without this feeling that having arrived at the furthest place of knowing one another we had reached sterility. Yet—superficially at least—it seemed to me that a relationship with an intellectual equal would have been even more open to the same objection. For the differences of class and interest between Jimmy and me certainly did provide some element of mystery which corresponded almost to a difference of sex. I was in love, as it were, with his background, his soldiering, his working-class home. Nothing moved me more than to hear him tell stories of the Cardiff streets of Tiger Bay, of his uncle who was in the Salvation Army and who asked for his trumpet to be buried beside him in his grave, so that when he awoke on the day of judgment he might blow a great blast of hallelujah on it. When Jimmy talked of such things, I was perhaps nearer poetry than talking to most of my fellow poets. At such moments, too, I was very close to certain emotions awakened in childhood by the workers, who to us seemed at the same time coarse, unclean, and yet with something about them of forbidden fruit, and also of warm-heartedness which suddenly flashed across the cold gulf of class, secret and unspoken. As I write, many instances of this unfold before me in all their original unsullied excitement. One especially, of an air-raid alarm on the Norfolk coast when I was seven. A soldier carried me in his arms from our house at Sheringham to some dug-out on the cliffs. As he did this, he held me to his heart with a simplicity which my parents with their fears for health and morals, and their view that any uninhibited feeling was dangerous, could scarcely show.

My relationship with Jimmy had therefore made me realize that if I were to live with anyone it could not be with a man. Through this very relationship I began to discover a need for women, to think about them, to look for them. At the same time I did not lose my fundamental need for the friendship of a man with whom I could identify my own work and development, even the need for women. But I did not now need this friendship on the same terms as before. Then, when I thought I had arrived at a goal, I was only at an early stage of a difficult journey.

The things I am now writing of are difficult to explain. Very few people dare to have a clear view of their own complexity. They would prefer to simplify themselves even at the expense of condemning their way of life rather than maintain complex and perhaps contradictory attitudes towards it, from which a harmony might finally be achieved.

At this time, then, I became vividly aware of an ambivalence in my attitudes towards men and women. Love for a friend expressed a need for self-identification. Love for a woman, the need for a relationship with some-one different, indeed opposite, to myself. I realized that self-identification leads to frustration if it be not realized; destruction, perhaps, if it be half-realized; a certain sterility if it be realized. The relationship of a man with the 'otherness' of a woman is a relationship of opposite poles. They complete, yet never become one another, never reach a static situation where every-thing which is possible to be known between two people is known, every gesture a repetition of one already performed, where little development, except the loss of youth, seems possible beyond this. As I understand Goethe, he defined creative human energy as the action of male force, energizing, intelligent, constructive, upon the receptive body of that which is outside it—*das Ewigweibliche*—the eternally feminine. I could not develop beyond a certain point unless I were able to enter a stream of nature through human contacts, that is to say, through experience of women. Yet I never lost the need for camaraderie also, my desire to share my creative and intellectual adventures with a man, whose search was the same as mine.

The two needs, while existing side by side, seemed to some extent to be mutually exclusive, so that whilst I was with a friend it might seem that I had renounced a whole world, of marriage, of responsibilities, and I had been received into another where everything was understood, where work, ideas, play and physical beauty corresponded in the friend's life with my own. On the other hand, when I was with a woman, it was as though I had shed my other personality, left it in some other room, and that instead of reflecting and being reflected by my physical-spiritual comrade, I had entered into the wholeness of a life outside me, giving to the woman that in myself which was not contained in her, and taking from her what was not in me. At the same time, I was afraid of losing too much by this exchange, afraid of becoming something different from what I was. One curious result of this was that I felt less immediately present with a woman than with a man. So that when I had shared some experience with her, there was a time-lag, and my moments of deepest feeling often occurred after I had left her.

CARMICHAELS
ARNOLD BENNETT

BY FRANK SWINNERTON

from *Tokefield Papers, Old and New* (1949)

CARMICHAELS

EVERY family has its Carmichaels. Most families have several of them. They are as universal as clever children. And yet as far as I know they have never been publicly named and classified until this moment. It was not I who first called the species 'Carmichael', or observed the full enormity of the vast body of Carmichaels who infest the earth; but I have long gladly described Carmichaels as Carmichaels, and shall continue to do so. The word came into being in this way. Friends of mine who wished to talk with impunity before their children of what Dick Deadeye called 'a certain intimate relation' hit upon the alias of 'Mrs. Carmichael'. Having so named her, and having discussed between themselves various of Mrs. Carmichael's characteristics, they looked about the world, and found innumerable other Carmichaels dwelling in it. And, indeed, the explanation of 'Carmichaelism' being once made, we perceive ourselves to be completely surrounded by Carmichaels of the first order. They fill our homes, they fill our businesses, our streets, our omnibuses and shopping-stores, they owe us money, they distress us in all sorts of indescribable ways. Members of the inventors' family, making political speeches of 'progressive tendency', have gone so far as to beg the nation not to let itself be 'Carmichaeled by the Government'. As for common life, one finds Carmichaels by the score in all varieties of circumstance, from the slum to the Cabinet, from the bench to the Bar, the forecastle to the Royal Academy, and beyond even the Royal Academy.

The first, and essential, feature of the Carmichael is the gift of being pathetic. Cats and dogs can be Carmichaels. Cats that mope when they are left, and cause us to stay at home because they will miss us, are Carmichaels. Dogs that by their glee at the sight of our hats and walking-sticks make us take them inconveniently upon journeys which we would rather make alone are Carmichaels. Children who dissolve into tears at a hasty word, or who believe themselves to be misunderstood, or who cannot play by themselves, are Carmichaels. Older people whose feelings are easily wounded, who successfully wear a strained expression when we meet them after a short absence, during which we have written no letters, or when we part with them upon an excursion of pleasure to which they are not bidden, so that we are filled by the knowledge of their deprivation with shame and self-reproach, are Carmichaels. All parents whose sons and daughters dare not marry for fear of the gap they would leave at home are Carmichaels. Grand-parents who show us that they feel rather neglected but that of course they are nobody at all, sniff, are Carmichaels. In fact, all those living creatures who make us feel absolutely and brutally selfish are Carmichaels.

Carmichaels may be meddlers and sensationalists. They may drink or suffer from paralysis or melancholia; but they are not Carmichaels in virtue of these habits or infirmities. They may lie, they may be hypocritical, they may feign illness—I knew one Carmichael who had an extraordinary gift for losing all control of her limbs in such an emergency, as the late George Grossmith is said to have done in the part of Ko-Ko; but these aspects of character in themselves are not prima facie evidence of Carmichaelism. They are what scientific people (especially weather experts) would call 'second-aries', but the true Carmichael goes farther back than such manifest ailments and deceptions. The real Carmichaels can be known by their moral effects upon us, and by no other test. Nobody is a Carmichael unless he or she makes us feel inhumanly cruel and vilely selfish.

It must be realized that Carmichaels thrive and fatten upon the tender-hearted only. Really rugged egotists and bluff manly fellows with rude health and obtuse intellects are not conscious of them. It is the pedestrian who cannot escape the beggar, while his rich brother, the motorist, sails past un-molested. In the same way, only the sensitive can be Carmichaeled. But which of us is not sensitive in relation to those we love? Which of us in the Anglo-Saxon civilization, based as it is upon conscience and the opinion of others (these two terms being often interchangeable), cannot be Car-michaeled? Few indeed. Our hearts are easily lacerated. Shame, with us, is a potent force. We stand and deliver more readily to the appealing mother at the kerb than to the importunate hustler who looks strong enough to trounce us if we refuse his demand for alms.

I have heard of one Carmichael who called upon the hardest-hearted and most resolute of her daughters, protested against the behaviour of one of her grandchildren, and proceeded to deliver a lament upon the subject. Her daughter was obdurate, and made it clear that she did not think her son's deportment was any business of his grandmother's. The Carmichael became violently distressed at such cruelty to herself, and showed signs of fainting. The hard-hearted daughter remained unmoved. The Carmichael rose, staggered. . . . Still her daughter was inflexible. With pathetic dignity the Carmichael proposed, as her counsels were not needed, to leave the house for ever. She was not begged to remain. She left the house, but as soon as she was beyond the front door the horror of the scene in which she had just played a part had such an effect upon her that she sank weakly to the door-step, and lost consciousness. Her brutal daughter, witnessing the scene through the coloured glass which formed the upper half of the front door, and dissembling her tremors, opened the door. A faint groan came from the Carmichael, who lay otherwise perfectly still, with her eyes closed. 'Go,' said the callous daughter loudly to her ill-mannered son. 'Go and get a pail of water. That is the best thing for people who have fainted. Go and get a pail of water. We'll throw it over her.' And with that the daughter and her son retired to the house. When they returned in two minutes' time, with such a pail of restorative water as had been threatened, the fainting Carmichael had disappeared.

But not all of this Carmichael's daughters are so cruel. The others are of gentler disposition. With them the conviction of sin (for, after all, this wicked daughter of whom I have told the above true story had been married very young and had been subjected to the mental debauchery of a stern and methodical husband, a Civil Servant) was constant. The second, it is true, married; but for years was harrowed by weekly visits from her mother and by subjection to her own sympathetic dread of giving pain. As for the third, the youngest, marriage for her was out of the question. She was a pretty and intelligent and healthy girl; and in the course of a number of years she could have married any one of several agreeable young men who sought her company. But the thought of what the loss of her would mean to a delicate and sensitive elderly lady, whose heart became unmanageable at any sugges- tion that she might be left alone with her husband, deprived of a daughter's care, kept this girl single. She had in full measure the sense of wickedness which Carmichaels create in those they love. Desiring another kind of life than the one she led at home, she knew that in even conceiving such desire she was revealed as selfish to the core. Not only that. It was clear to this girl that if she married—even though it be for love, and to sacrifice herself to a husband—the knowledge of her mother's suffering would spoil any happi- ness the marriage might bring. Accordingly, she remained unmarried, cherishing the Carmichael, and struggling to quell the eagerness for other life which from time to time the Devil aroused in her heart. Until one evening this abandoned girl lost all sense of propriety. At the age of twenty- eight or twenty-nine she suddenly and hysterically fled from her parents' house. The Devil had won. But she had been Carmichaeled for so many years that she arrived at the home of one of her sisters in a state of incoherence and collapse. She was ill. She was oppressed with all the consciousness of guilt which we suppose a murderess to feel.

Nevertheless, she had escaped. She had broken the bonds of Carmichael- ism. She never returned to her old home. For weeks conscience struggled in her breast with selfishness, and selfishness won. She took a situation, she found her mind and nature growing and flowering, she at length married, she achieved happiness. Nobody, seeing her now the loving and devoted wife of a poor man and the absorbed mother of a small and delightful family, could realize the wickedness of her selfish flight. The Carmichael, deserted, was a piteous figure. She had never been so ill, so pathetic, so bereft of love.

All the illnesses of a medical dictionary attacked her simultaneously, and her husband would really have called in the doctor if she had not assured him that she was past all medical aid. But she is still alive, ten years after her bereavement, and her Carmichaeling talents are being surreptitiously exercised upon a younger generation.

The best of people have at times a touch of the Carmichael in them; and I must not be thought unmindful of the mother or father who genuinely suffers from the loss of a loved child. If we are forsaken, or dread that we may be forgotten, we do—all of us—strive to make ourselves more interesting to the beloved. For the time we are sick persons engrossed in our own ego. A cat will pluck the sleeve of one who plays with a puppy, a dog will lick a hand and whine for unaccorded notice, a child will make an appeal— in face of the admired exhibition of a younger child—which only a hard heart could ignore. How much more, then, a grown-up person, one who has a thousand endangered links with her child, and one who has proved the short memory and heedlessness of other humans, may feel a ghastly sense of loneliness or of being ignored! It is a disloyalty, a failure of confidence in the beloved, but how natural! It is only human—it is only canine and feline —to feel slight jealousy—jealousy that is no jealousy of an individual, no basely motived hostility, although it arises from perhaps a similar cause. The cause of all jealousy is the feeling of powerlessness or inferiority. As jealousy arises when somebody does something that we should like to be able to do, and suspect ourselves of being unable to do, so this fear comes from conviction that love for ourselves is incompatible with love for the highly superior being who has won our darling's heart. We touch her sleeve, as does the cat; we do whatever is the human equivalent for licking his hand as the dog does; we strive to remind him or her of our existence, our claim to love, to attention. We soften our tone, as lovers grow gentle. Having gained momentary notice, we expatiate upon our own doings and our own helplessness. Ever so little, we yield to the temptation to appeal for sympathy. We do not beg—no! A wistful note, a glance, a pressure—so slight as hardly to wound our self-esteem—and the pathetic approach is made. Pity is what we crave. Pity—it is Carmichaelism, to be controlled! The poison is working in our systems. It is natural; it is pathetic; but we ought not to ask for pity. What we want is love, freely given. If we cannot keep it by fair means, let us not seek to keep it by foul! There is the world of difference between love and pity, for all that the poet said; and if we are wise and proud we shall be silent for the sake of the loved one's happiness rather than noisy and appealing for the sake of our own. What if he or she does forget us for a time? Will the tide of love not return? Then let our dearest ones come back to us as freely as they go, to love and understanding and not to the reproach of loneliness and neglect. For us the duty is clear. It is to hold our heads high. Death to the Carmichaelistic tendencies of our fainting hearts!

Often, of two friends, or of two who marry, there is one who begins thus, through some weakness or inferiority of character or strangling tenacity of affection, to exercise unscrupulous or unconscious power. In each case the battle is between weakness upon the one hand, making claims, and pity upon the other, yielding ever, and through love permitting a tyranny to arise. Who has not seen a young wife or a young husband 'giving in', because 'it means so much' to the other member of the partnership? A petulant husband, or a sulky one, who does not like his wife to dance with other men, so that she eventually stays at home and gives up dancing altogether. Or a husband who forsakes his friends because his wife must not be left alone, because she is tired in the evening, and so pathetically needs to be petted. Beware! Carmichael is awake! Carmichael is busy! With such a beginning, the end is only a question of time. A husband who grows ill-used, a wife whose mouth puckers—into whose eyes tears start. . . . Carmichael is very near. Tears are always ready to fill the Carmichael's eyes. Tears must be watched. They are a danger-signal. So must objectless staring upon the part of a male Carmichael, a fondness for the solitary bottle, sighs, any sudden fierce caress, or indisposition for caress. Headaches. Shrinking from society. . . .

For Carmichael is not only to be found within almost every home, in the affairs of fathers and mothers of advanced age, or of aunts and uncles, and such like human impedimenta. Once measure and judgment in affection are tinged with pity, and the pity is accepted, Carmichael has his clutch upon the household. Pity accepted is pity exploited. Carmichael is in possession. Thereafter the kind and gentle will be Carmichaeled (there is no other word to suggest a tyranny of supplication) to death. Carmichaelism grows before our eyes. It is contagious. I have known families where the husband and father has been Carmichaeled by his children until he has given them mildly and amiably the whole of his care and energy, and has kept nothing for himself. He has fed them by pecking his own breast, as does that celebrated bird the name of which I have forgotten. We all know wives and mothers who have reared Carmichaels in this way. We have watched them yielding to the greedy, to the over-demonstratively affectionate, the tragically mis-understood, in exactly this way. They do it, some of them, because their own youth has been hard, or because they are silly and pleased with demon-strative affection, without counting how much of their own life is appro-priated by youthful Carmichaels. I have been told of one mother who once murmured over her Carmichael, 'She's such a little tragedy queen!' The Carmichael was young then. She is now old. She is at this moment more sorry for herself, more the recipient of pity and the flowers of pity, than anybody I ever met. She weeps readily. She groans. She is constantly afflicted with faintness and sickness if those at hand should appear disposed to thwart her. And she is as tough as leather. She is a true parasite. In a word, she is a Carmichael.

And there is this to be said. Every community has the Carmichaels it deserves. Carmichaels are born, but they can be subdued. Their inclination to Carmichael their own families can be repressed. It only needs alertness to the danger. But those of us who first yield to the impulse of pity, who are hampered and shackled and paralysed by the pathos of the incipient Carmichael, have a grave responsibility to mankind. We are the ones who deserve blame, because it is our tenderness that enables the Carmichael to flourish. We cannot bring ourselves to say 'No!' although we know that we ought to refuse. We yield, and the consequences are such as to create terror in the observer. We are made the prey of weakness greater than our own—weakness that is a malignant growth. The doctrine of pity is a beautiful one (if by 'pity' we mean 'mercy'), but pity as it is involuntarily practised by most unselfish people is more than the sacrifice of a momentary impulse. It is a betrayal of life to the Carmichaels. It is nothing less than moral ruin to them and to ourselves. For Carmichaels live upon the tenderness of others, as slugs live upon the most tender shoots in the garden. Carmichaelism is an instinctive thing, like the turning of a flower's face to the sun. The Carmichael could not imagine himself or herself to be a parasite, although hypochondria (the power to be miserable about one's own misery) is not unknown to Carmichaels. Carmichaels are not bullies or conscious hypocrites. They are possessors of the unique gift, which gives them their power, of making us feel remorseful, hideously selfish, hard, brutal, callous, thoughtless, and disgusting. They are like those aunts who sit in pain while a cheerful boy, at first noisy and full of life, is frowned into abashed silence. They are the cuckoos in the hedge-sparrow's nest. They are the moral invalids of our day. They are death and destruction to our peace of mind. They have no life without us; their tyranny is inscrutable and incessant; and they strangle our happiness and vitality as surely as any convolvulus strangles the self-supporting flower around which it subtly entwines itself. Woe to the Carmichaels! They are the enemies of the good.

ARNOLD BENNETT

ARNOLD BENNETT was the best, the kindest, the most generous, and the
greatest man with whom I have ever come into close contact. He had great
sagacity, great simplicity, a good deal of most lovable vanity; and he was
astoundingly modest. The better one knew him the more one loved him,
and the more impressive his quality as a man became.

All his friends will agree with me as to his character, even if they deny
greatness to his literary work. And all will agree that to a powerful personality, in which resoluteness, integrity, and a love of plain speaking had their
obvious place, he united a charm at once mischievous and benign which
many of his readers must have missed.

Strangers often formed very different opinions from these. They were
sometimes a little frightened by his reputation. They misconstrued his
abruptness of manner. They found him assertive and inflexible. And they
believed the legend that he was a man who had mapped out his life with
the sole object of amassing money. Many of them resented his success. But
I do not know anybody who was indifferent to him.

Let me try to give some notion of what Arnold Bennett looked like. He
was stoutly built and about five feet ten inches in height. He held himself
very erect and his shoulders very rigid, so that his body had no natural swing
as he walked, but rather swayed stiffly from side to side. He always walked
slowly and with great seriousness.

His brow was square and rose straight from eyes that looked tired, because
of rather heavy eyelids, to the small flourish of hair which latterly replaced
the famous coif made fun of by caricaturists. His cheeks were clear and
showed a faint colour. His mouth was irregular and his upper teeth were also
irregular.

The eyes, once the first impression of tiredness had passed, were a warm
brown, and smiled. Bennett was a master of the wink. When some effusive
stranger buttonholed him to express admiration, Bennett was at all times
courteous; but, if he caught a friendly eye beyond his enthusiast, one of
those heavy lids would irresistibly quiver.

In repose his expression I should have said, represented calm melancholy.
But his smile was very sweet, and the aura of kindness which surrounded

him was such that he was extremely popular with children. Odd as it may seem to some, he could converse with children very effectively. But he was a shy and sensitive man, who normally talked little.

When I first knew him, he once referred to Mr. H. G. Wells's unlimited brilliance as a conversationalist by saying briefly: 'He talks, you know. I can't do that.' And in those days he could not, or did not, talk. When pressed for an opinion by guests at his own table, he would often jerk his head in my direction, and say: '*He'll* tell you.'

One day I said to him: 'I talk too much.' He said: 'Yes; but from politeness.' It was politeness that caused Bennett to talk more freely in later years. He did not really enjoy talking. But he talked to entertain his guests, to 'make things go', and he did this very well, though sometimes with exaggeration of his own mannerisms.

And I am here reminded to mention a fact which explains much about Bennett which has puzzled and irritated his less sympathetic readers. I have said that he was exceptionally shy and sensitive. He stammered. It was not a slight stammer; but when he was at all agitated the stammer became a complete inhibition of speech.

So strong was his will that he always persisted in fighting the stammer until he could pronounce the word he had in mind; but these struggles often caused disconcerting delays and silences, and their possibility was ever present in his mind. Hence his abruptness, which communicated itself to his writing, and gave that writing an air of dogmatism.

He would say, if his opinion were challenged: 'I can't argue.' It was often thought that he disdained argument. This was not the case. He argued with his intimates; but with his intimates he rarely stammered, unless he had something painful to tell them.

His voice was rather harsh, and gave the impression of being high-pitched. His manner was, to friends, genial. Very often, one would catch sight of him from a little distance, seated, very carefully smoking a cigarette. Probably making a note in a tiny notebook which he always carried. His expression would be grave.

But as one approached he would look up. 'Hello, boss,' he would say, saluting with a finger to his forelock. Or, if one had a surname which he liked to pronounce, but which offered difficulties to his tongue, he would *say* the first letters with mock ceremoniousness—as 'Well, Mister S-W-I-innerton.' Comparatively few people, except in company, called him 'Arnold'. To innumerable friends, old and young, he was 'A.B.' It was as if they used a diminutive.

And his friends really were innumerable. They were absolutely sure of his interest and his integrity. They went to him with all sorts of petitions, troubles, confessions. He listened to them at length; then he gave his advice. He corresponded with them—hundreds of them. He was always ready to help them, and did so, with money, encouragement, and sympathy.

Sometimes he would refer to one of them as 'he'. 'That chap,' he would say. A pause. A jerk of the head. Then: 'He has to be *helped*.' And he *was* helped. Once, when I had received an appeal, and had shown him the letter, he said (though he did not know the applicant): 'What are you going to send! I should like to do the same!' And out popped one of the odd cheques which he always carried for emergencies.

He came, as is well known, from Staffordshire; and I think his first interest in myself (otherwise a literary interest) arose from the fact that mine is a Staffordshire name. He was born a Methodist. And in spite of the fact that intellectually he was an agnostic he remained essentially a Methodist (and a Midlander) all his life.

The sneers of some people (who had not learned courtesy in the course of an otherwise elaborate curriculum) at his 'provincialism' had no truth so far as his intellect and his imagination were concerned. He was provincial in the sense that the Provinces, the backbone of England, are provincial. He also retained certain provincialisms of speech and pronunciation (I only mean in such words as 'bath' or 'ask', in which he used the light 'a', and such phrases as his favourite 'We shall look a bit soft').

He was easily impressed by magnificence or by a display of knowledge. I think he could at times be caught by the second-rate. But only for a time, for his judgment was in constant repair, and his scrutiny was very unsentimental. Otherwise, when he was thought 'provincial', he was often just humorous. As for example when he moved into a house where the panels of all the doors had been decorated by a former tenant with mirrors. At my first visit to this house I said, 'Oh, Lord! I couldn't stand all this looking-glass!' He replied, blandly, 'I was born for it!'

He dressed with great care. His shirts were always superfine. Once, when he dined in company with a very great personage, the personage broke a long silence by saying: 'Mr. Bennett; do you mind if I ask you something?' Bennett agreed to be asked something. 'Do you mind telling me where you get your shirts?'

It was a great moment. I can imagine the wave of Bennett's hand—for he used, deliberately, a good deal of not always graceful gesture—as he responded. That was what I meant in referring to his lovable vanity. He could be, and was, teased endlessly as to his clothes; but he did give them a great deal of thought. As a consequence he was always described by *The Tailor and Cutter* as 'the best-dressed author in London'.

What interested him most of all, however, was not clothes. Nor was it talk. He had a really passionate interest in human nature; and a really passionate love of the fine arts. You had only to look at his beautiful and sensitive hands (of which I never knew him to be conscious) to realize a delicacy for which his manner might not have prepared you; only to be in his company during the performance of music or before pictures, to realize that power he had of yielding himself completely to beauty.

He was not a systematic critic, but was purely intuitive. As a result, some of the opinions he expressed on particular artists or particular works were erratic. The elegant often shivered at his judgments. On the whole, however, these judgments (unless they were roundly stated, when it was wise to suspect them) wore well, and will wear well.

He was a little bitten with the desire to be up to date. Not in private. Some of his friends used to tease him about his pronouncements. He was always ready for such gibes; and equal to them. And at the end of a bout of opposed statements either the opinions did not seem so eccentric, or Bennett would remark: 'Well, there may be something in what you say.' Immediately afterwards, recovering himself, he would add: 'But not much.' He would never yield to argument; but he would listen to it 'with due respect'.

Not always, though. Several years ago, the date of Marie Lloyd's birth became a subject of dispute between us. I said she was born in 1870. Bennett said I was wrong; that she must have been born much earlier. I insisted. He said: 'We'll soon settle it. I've got all the reference books in my study.' He disappeared. Ten minutes later, he returned. 'Extraordinary!' said he. 'I've looked in a dozen books. And they're ALL wrong!'

But he was laughing as he spoke. His downrightness—when not due to his stammer—was largely an innocent pose. He was also, as I have said (the remark may have caused some rubbing of eyes), an excessively modest man. He never spoke of his own books, though often of the number of words he had written that day. He accepted printed criticism (though it was sometimes violent) better than any other author I have ever known. His response to private praise, when he took it seriously, was one of surprise and pleasure.

Indeed, as a proof of his modesty, I recall that once, when somebody not myself had repeated quite reasonable praise of his work, he meditatively said: 'Well, it's odd, but I can't see it!' This was the truth. In public he always pretended to be delighted with his own performance.

His greatest vanity was that he was a man-of-the-world. He was never a man-of-the-world. He had not the pulpy sentimentality veneered with cynicism that is characteristic of that species. He was, on the contrary, once he went outside his own shrewd, practical genius, simple almost to naïveté.

He had the loving heart of a good man, plus the sensitiveness of the artist, the efficient mind of the practical thinker, the timidity of the stammerer, the determination of the Midlander, the rigour of the moralist, and the generosity of greatness. I think he was a great writer, but he was a greater man.

As for his personality, it is not without significance that he came from the same county as Doctor Johnson. It was his habit to say that 'nine out of every ten people improve on acquaintance', and the more one knew Arnold Bennett the more one marvelled at the sympathy, the patience, the large tolerance, and the essential sweetness and simplicity which were the sources of his strength and of the affection of his friends.

28 *March* 1931

THE RULER IN BERLIN
THE SUPERMEN

BY A. J. P. TAYLOR

from *From Napoleon to Stalin* (1950)

THE RULER IN BERLIN

ON 31 July 1914, Berchtold, Austro-Hungarian Foreign Minister, was dismayed by advice from Bethmann, the German Chancellor, to act with restraint and not to give the signal for war. His distraction was interrupted by Conrad, Chief of the Austrian General Staff. Conrad showed him a telegram from Moltke, Chief of the German General Staff, which urged that Austria-Hungary should at once mobilize against Russia and so launch a European war. Berchtold, with his irresponsible giggle, exclaimed: 'That beats everything. Who rules then in Berlin?' This flippant remark was a profound judgment on the Germany of William II, and for that matter on the work of Bismarck. The question baffled contemporaries and has baffled later observers.

Between 1871 and 1890 it had seemed possible to answer the question. Bismarck ruled in Berlin. He devised legislation, determined policy, controlled even the military leaders; his decisions settled Germany's course. Yet Bismarck himself did not give this answer. He always insisted that Germany was ruled by the King of Prussia; and claimed that this was the core of his achievement. Bismarck's answer was not a mere pretence; even he, the greatest of political Germans, shrank from ultimate responsibility and shouldered it on to a 'King by the Grace of God'. All the same, the version was nonsense in practice, and largely even in theory. Germany could not be ruled by the King-Emperor, as Prussia had been ruled by Frederick the Great or even by Frederick William IV. Men may obey their king, even in a period when monarchical sentiment is declining; they will not obey someone else's king, and the King of Prussia was the king of others for the majority of Germans. The King of Prussia was German Emperor by conquest, by invitation of the German princes, by political intrigue, by constitutional arrangement, by everything except 'the Grace of God'. The German Emperor had no coronation—hence no religious sanction. Right still counted for much in Germany; and the Emperor's right rested on national sentiment, not on divine appointment.

Bismarck's creation deserved its name of 'the second Empire'; its spirit was, in truth, nearer to the demagogy of Napoleon III than to the mystic tradition of 'the Holy Roman Empire of the German Nation'. After 1806, when the Holy Roman Empire ended, German authority could rest only

on the masses. Bismarck had concealed this fact, as the titanic figure of
Napoleon I had concealed it in France in similar circumstances. With the
fall of Bismarck it could be concealed no longer. The question, 'Who rules
in Berlin?' was stated with ever-increasing urgency, until it found an answer
in 1933.

William II had perhaps supposed in 1890 that he himself would rule in
Berlin. This view was held later by those who wished 'to hang the Kaiser'.
The fault of William was his failure to rule, not that he ruled wrongly.
Dr. Eyck, his latest historian,[1] is nearer the truth when he draws a parallel
with the system of English government in the reign of George III. George III,
too, used to be accused of personal rule; this is a myth no longer believed
by anyone. On the personal side it is unfair to compare William II with
George III. William had considerable political gifts, to say nothing of his
gift for phrase-making. Theodore Roosevelt said to him in 1910: 'In America
you would have your ward behind you and would lead your delegation at
your party's national convention.' In fact, William was a first-rate 'key-note'
speaker. On the great issues of politics he often saw farther than his professional advisers. In 1890 he was right to reject Bismarck's programme of
a *coup d'état* in favour of reconciling the working-classes to the Reich; in
1905 he was right in opposing Holstein's policy of the Tangier visit; he was
right (from the German point of view) in promoting the Baghdad railway;
he was right in distrusting the moribund Habsburg monarchy and, at the
end, in advocating concessions to Rumania as the one way of staving off
disaster; even his advances to both Russia and England did more good than
harm—without such a gesture, for example, as his visit to the deathbed of
Queen Victoria, estrangement between England and Germany would have
come even sooner than it did. While the German Foreign Office was confidently snubbing all the Great Powers in turn, William II saw the dangers
of 'the free hand' and never ceased, though by erratic impulses, to seek for
some great political combination.

His immediate reactions, no doubt, were often as wild as his longer vision
was sound. He would scribble, 'We must mobilize at once' on the news of
some colonial dispute; and even proposed to arrest the transference of the
British Fleet to the North Sea by an ultimatum. He exploded repeatedly
against Austrian failure to destroy Serbia; yet he realized more clearly than
any German diplomatist that this was a futile programme and, in his serious
moments, urged reconciliation. His marginal notes, which made so much
stir when published, were written for pleasure, not for action; and no action
ever followed from them. They were the outbreaks of a man knowing himself, and known to be, irresponsible. The Kruger telegram is a case in point.
This was certainly a watering-down of William's original idea of landing

---

[1] *Das Persönliche Regiment Wilhelms II*. Politische Geschichte des deutschen Kaiserreiches von
1890 bis 1914. By Erich Eyck.

marines at Delagoa Bay. All the same, it would never have been sent, had it not suited Holstein's scheme of frightening England with the shadow of a Continental League. When this scheme failed, Marschall and Holstein shifted the blame to William, though the policy underlying it was theirs. So later, in the great crisis of the reign, Germans of all classes, from Bülow downwards, used the *Daily Telegraph* affair as a means for shifting on to William II all the consequences of German arrogance and power.

William II was not a ruler; he was a medium. He reflected the political mind of Germany and expressed it with genius. Contemporary observers were much at fault when they attributed the great German Navy to a personal whim of William II. The Navy was a demagogic cause, promoted by liberal professors and popular even among Socialist and Roman Catholic voters. Had William surrendered altogether to his demagogic impulses, he would have anticipated Hitler's undisputed power. As it was, his upbringing and conscience reined him in; the King of Prussia restrained the German Emperor, as Prussia, in Bismarck's conception, restrained Germany. These negations were not a solution; and since William failed to lead, the problem was returned to the Chancellors. Here, indeed, is the profound political interest of the reign of William II—the search for a principle of authority and responsibility when this could no longer be provided by the Crown. To return to the analogy with George III: Dr. Eyck supposes that George III was defeated by 'the opposition of Charles Fox', and blames the Germans for not producing a liberal figure of similar eminence. This does that charming gambler too much honour. Growth of a sense of responsibility, not of an opposition, transformed the British Constitution; and this responsibility rested on a governing class which was truly representative of 'the political nation'. In Bismarckian Germany the governing classes, military and civil, were not merely out of touch with the masses who had now become the nation: they were actively and consciously opposed to everything that was dearest to national ambition. Bismarck's greatest achievement was his defeat of Greater Germany: he preserved the Habsburg monarchy and insisted that his truncated Germany was a 'satiated State'. This flew in the face of national sentiment. The only binding force in the governing classes was resistance to the popular will. Liberal observers, misled by Western analogies, thought that this implied principally resistance to a constitutional system; but the national masses demanded most of all a truly united Germany.

The reign of William II saw two attempts to break the deadlock between the governing classes and the nation; in different ways both Caprivi and Bülow aspired 'to rule in Berlin'. Caprivi took the way of liberalism; Bülow attempted to wield the bow of Bismarck and to create a new Bismarckian compromise by agility and intrigue. Caprivi, who followed Bismarck as Chancellor, has been neglected by historians; yet he was the most significant of Bismarck's successors, for he conducted the experiment in liberalism which later writers often suggested as the 'solution' of the German problem. In fact Caprivi was the only parliamentary Chancellor of Imperial Germany. Though appointed by the Emperor, he thought in terms of a parliamentary majority, and this could be created only by means of a 'national' programme. Hence Caprivi gave up Bismarck's negative foreign policy and supported the German cause in south-eastern Europe: domestic and foreign demagogy went hand in hand. Caprivi justified the imperial military programme by reference to Russia, instead of to France; and the climax of his policy came in 1893 when he carried the increased Army grant with the votes of Roman Catholics, Poles and some Progressives. As Dr. Eyck rightly says, the split in the Progressive party which followed this vote marked the end of liberalism as a political force in Germany. Dr. Eyck calls it suicide; suicide is sometimes the only solution. Liberalism had no future if it failed to support Caprivi; equally it had no future if it supported him. For Caprivi himself had no future. In 1894 he ran into conflict with Botho Eulenburg, Prime Minister of Prussia. Caprivi wanted a democratic reform of the Prussian suffrage, Eulenburg a revival of the anti-Socialist laws. William II took the only course and dismissed them both. The decisive answer was given: no one could rule in Berlin.

This answer was accepted by Hohenlohe, the next Chancellor. Dr. Eyck speaks contemptuously of his age and feebleness; these were the necessary conditions of his existence. As a Bavarian, he would not restrain Germany for the sake of Prussia; as a Conservative, he would not break Prussia for the sake of Germany. With little power over events and no influence in the Reichstag, he tolerated all the decisive lurches in German policy: the Baghdad railway, the great Navy, the establishment in China were all Hohenlohe's doing, or rather consequences of his lack of doing. He deliberately avoided asking the great question, let alone attempting to answer it. Yet it was a question which demanded an answer. The man who attempted to answer it in the reign of William II was Bülow, Chancellor from 1900 to 1909. Bülow's name is weighed down by his *Memoirs*, the most trivial record ever left by a man who has occupied high position. Nevertheless he dominated the history of Wilhelmine Germany. Bülow was the only Imperial Chancellor after Bismarck to count in German politics—the only one who made effective speeches and to whom men looked for a 'policy'. Still more, 'the Bülow *bloc*' of 1906 was the first stable parliamentary combination behind the Chancellor since Bismarck broke with the National Liberals in 1879, and it was a more reliable coalition than any created under the Weimar republic. Finally, in 1908, Bülow—whether deliberately or not—used the *Daily Telegraph* affair to eject William II from politics and to impose upon him the limitations of a constitutional monarch. William II never recovered from this blow; it ended whatever fragments of 'personal rule' remained.

Bülow's success was barren. It served only to reveal that the problem of

German government lay deeper than in William's character; it was rooted in the foundations of Bismarck's Reich. The humiliation of William II left Bülow face to face with the Prussian Conservatives; and once more, as with Caprivi, it became clear that the twin causes of 'world policy' and internal democracy could be achieved only after the defeat of the classes which Bismarck had preserved, the forces of old Prussia. Bülow declared to the Conservatives who brought him down: 'We shall meet again at Philippi.' The engagement was not fought in Bülow's lifetime; it was won by his demagogic heir in 1933 and completed by the massacres which followed 20 July 1944. Bülow's fall led to another, more fateful, interregnum, the Chancellorship of Bethmann Hollweg. Hohenlohe had allowed policy to be made without him; Bethmann Hollweg had it made against him. It was a grotesque, though inevitable, conclusion to Bismarck's work that the Chancellor should be helpless both in the Reichstag and in the Prussian Landtag; universal suffrage and privileged class-franchise alike rejected him. Yet for this very reason he was the only possible Chancellor. As in Metternich's Austria, 'administration had taken the place of government'.

A solution of a sort was found, perhaps against Bethmann Hollweg's will: a solution of foreign policy. German foreign policy of the 1890's had been 'cabinet diplomacy', even though it made an occasional demagogic gesture. The last display of this 'cabinet diplomacy' was the first Moroccan crisis of 1905, a crisis deliberately engineered by Holstein without any preparation of public opinion and hence ending in failure for Germany. Once more, in the Bosnian crisis, Bülow was the man of the transition: demagogue enough to back the German cause in south-eastern Europe, Bismarckian enough to regret having done so. In 1911 national opinion came into its own: the Agadir crisis was fought with public backing from start to finish. Nevertheless, Agadir was a false start, a red herring: it was deliberately designed by Kiderlen, last of the Bismarckians, to distract German chauvinism from eastern Europe and so from the mortal conflict with Russia. Until Agadir, Germany had remained a Power which, if not 'satiated', could still be satisfied with colonial gains; after Agadir, Germany had to bid for the mastery of Europe. This inescapable fate determined the diplomacy of 1913 and 1914, which Dr. Eyck describes in full detail: German policy sought in vain to avoid the mission of conquest which was being thrust upon it. Few historians will quarrel with Dr. Eyck's verdict that the German statesmen and generals did not deliberately plan the outbreak of world war in July 1914; yet a war of conquest was the only possible outcome of German history. Bethmann Hollweg had been the only Imperial Chancellor to be censured by the Reichstag; he was also the only Chancellor to receive from the Reichstag a unanimous vote of confidence. Certainly in August 1914 Bethmann Hollweg did not 'rule in Berlin'; what ruled at last in Berlin was the will of the German people for power.

The German problem, past and present, is the problem of German unity. Though this does not exist now, we are tempted to think that it existed in some Golden Age of the past. Dr. Eyck's book is a reminder that this Golden Age cannot be found in the age of William II. Imperial Germany was never a united national State, in the sense that France was united and made a nation by the great revolution. In Imperial Germany, almost as much as in the Holy Roman Empire, there was a balance of authorities and classes; instead of authoritarian rule there was 'organized anarchy'. Germany had, in some sort, a 'governing class'—the Prussian army officers and Prussian administrators. Though this class held Germany together, it was even more concerned to hold Germany back; while offering Germany a corset, it strapped on a strait-jacket. The first German war weakened this class; the Hitler revolution completed its destruction. There are now no forces within Germany to resist the full programme of German unification, and the present partition rests solely on the occupying armies. This gives it a unique and precarious character. A Germany free from foreign control will seek to restore the united Greater Germany which Hitler achieved in 1938; nor will democracy provide an automatic safeguard against a new German aggression. In the reign of William II every step towards democracy was a step towards general war. The Navy was popular, 'world policy' was popular, support for the German cause in eastern Europe was popular. Attempts at reconciliation with others were unpopular; and William's prestige was ruined in 1908 when it became known that he favoured friendship with England.

The harsh truth of German history is that the solution of the German question cannot be found within Germany. Partition cannot be maintained as a permanent policy; yet a united Germany will keep Europe in apprehension, and would be tolerable only in a world of United Nations. Wilhelmine Germany overshadowed her neighbours by playing off East and West; any future Germany will seek to do the same. If the Great Powers were on friendly terms, there would even now be no German problem; so long as they remain estranged, Germany will offer the occasion, and may be the originator of future wars. 'Who rules in Berlin?' The question once dominated German history; now it torments all the world. In our impatience and anxiety we are led to hope that one day the German people may rule in Berlin. That outcome is, in the long run, unavoidable; it will be tolerable only if there also rules in Berlin awareness of a community of nations. It is for the Germans to seek unity on a democratic and pacific basis; the Great Powers must ensure that the Germans do not promote unity by a programme of foreign aggression. At the present time, both the Germans and the Great Powers are failing in their task; and the question, 'Who rules in Berlin?' has lost nothing of its menacing character.

THE SUPERMEN: HITLER AND MUSSOLINI

A GREAT idea seldom gets a free run. The scientist in his laboratory can concentrate on a single line of research and work it to fruition—or to death. In the world of real life experiments are always being interrupted or broken off half-way. Thus, the policy of treating the Germans resolutely was broken off by the French in 1923 just when it was succeeding: and the policy of co-operating with the Russians was broken off in 1945 before the rewards (and difficulties) of this policy became plain. The great question of the future is whether mankind will turn against the scientists before they succeed in blowing up the planet—certainly an experiment of great interest. One idea has had a real run for its money—tried out without restriction and carried to its extreme. This is the idea of the Hero or Superman, the political saviour for whom many Europeans have been craving ever since the time of Napoleon. The myth was launched by Napoleon himself and took his own nephew prisoner; Carlyle preached it with religious frenzy; Wagner dressed it up in musical form for the Germans; and in the early twentieth century practically every writer offered some form of anti-democratic, superman doctrine.

Twenty years later the superman arrived—or rather two supermen arrived, Mussolini and Hitler, Napoleons of the twentieth century, the heroes of our time. Both were pure-hero types, without any of the adventitious aids of their predecessors. Frederick the Great inherited his crown; Napoleon had a background of military success; Cromwell and Lenin rested on a compact revolutionary class. Hitler and Mussolini made themselves. Except as heroes, they were nobodies. Before they attained power, they had achieved nothing; and the supposed class-basis of their rule (Fascism as the last stage of capitalism) was arrant nonsense. Their real supporters were men as classless as themselves, not great capitalists or even the petty *bourgeoisie*. General Beck said of Hitler, 'this man has no country', and one could add—no class, no past, no family. Mussolini had a family and even a mistress: this did not prevent his ordering the execution of his son-in-law. Certainly he sometimes repeated 'proletarian' echoes of his past, as Hitler lived on the Greater German rhetoric that he had picked up in Vienna. These were merely incantations, phrases to produce the popular roar; not genuine beliefs, still less the motives of their action. These heroes believed only in themselves.

487

Like all men in public life, they craved for power. The exceptional thing in them was the addition of intense personal vanity: they wished both to stand in the limelight and to control the switchboard, to be actor, producer and playwright. In short, they wished to be God; and mankind having lost its faith in God, acquiesced in their wish.

Heroes are not of mortal clay; that we know of all supermen from Siegfried to Jack Tanner. We cannot expect them to act according to normal standards or even to notice the human beings around them. But how do they get on with each other? This is the fascinating topic of Miss Wiskemann's book[1]: the relations of the two supermen. According to all authorities, heroes recognize each other instinctively: they keep faith with each other, though they betray all the world besides. Miss Wiskemann attributes to Hitler and Mussolini a common intellectual ancestry: she puts all the blame on Nietzsche. This seems to me too narrow a basis: there is little to it except that Hitler once fell into a trance before the bust of the master. It leaves out of account the long hero-tradition in modern Europe. Mussolini summed up the Latin line of that tradition from Bonaparte to Georges Sorel; Hitler sprang directly from Carlyle and Wagner. More deeply (and this is the sense in the hero-idea) each in his way expressed the 'genius' of his people—a parody, no doubt, as summaries always are, but no more a parody than Churchill, say, if of the British people. One can safely adapt for both Hitler and Mussolini Gardiner's phrase about Cromwell: 'the greatest, because the most typical Englishman of all time.' Of course both men were lunatics, as Miss Wiskemann firmly establishes of Hitler, though doubtfully of Mussolini (such is her soft-heartedness for all Italians). The point is not of moment. All men are mad who devote themselves to the pursuit of power when they could be fishing, painting pictures, or simply sitting in the sun. If men were sane, there would be no history. Though lunatics do not follow the rules of sane behaviour, they have rules of their own. The task of the historian is to discover these rules. No man acts out of character; and, as Machiavelli said, a man has only one character, as he has only one face. Hitler's rules and character ran true to a form that is easily mapped; Mussolini's behaviour was more complicated and therefore Miss Wiskemann inclines to believe him sane—or suffering from a duodenal ulcer, which comes to the same thing. There is a more profound explanation: even the hero cannot escape reality, even he remains rooted in the ground from which he has sprung.

Miss Wiskemann disapproves of such high subjects as Hitler and Mussolini being treated by 'witty Oxford dons' (alas! this is not a reference to the present writer). Wit has its advantages: it puts the hero in his historic setting. The difference between Hitler and Mussolini was the difference between their two countries. In Miss Wiskemann's book Germany and Italy come in

[1] *The Rome-Berlin Axis.* By Elizabeth Wiskemann.

too little. They are treated as two sovereign States of comparable importance; there is no analysis of their historic background or (apart from a table of Italy's coal imports) of their economic strength. The coal statistics give the game away. Coal is the most important index of power. Italy has no coal; therefore she is dependent for her power on others, condemned to a jackal diplomacy—or to none at all. The hesitations and manœuvres of Mussolini were not, as Miss Wiskemann thinks, the results of doubt so much as a hero's resentment against the limitations of real life—truly, Mussolini was a hero of the suburbs. Vain and arrogant as he was, he yet had the sense to see that Italy could simulate greatness only by hunting with Hitler: he never shared the futile misjudgment of those western diplomats who thought that Italy could take the place of Russia in an anti-Hitler coalition (a favourite idea of the British foreign office), and he never accepted for a moment the ambition of Italian diplomats, from Ciano downwards, to play fast-and-loose with Germany and yet swagger among the great. Hitler saw the dilemma just as clearly. He wrote to Mussolini on 6 March 1940:

> The outcome of this war will also decide the future of Italy. If this future is considered in your country in terms of merely perpetuating the existence of a European state of modest pretensions, then I am wrong. But if this future is considered in terms of a guarantee of the existence of the Italian people from a historical, geopolitical and moral point of view, or according to the rights of your people, those who are fighting Germany to-day will be your enemies too.

Against this profound analysis, Miss Wiskemann concludes: 'It was not mere rhetoric to say that one Italian alone forced Italy into the war in June 1940.' It is all very well to like Italians better than Germans. Who doesn't? This does not alter the fact that Germany was (and is) the only country on the European continent of Great Power stature; and that Italy could be carried to greatness only on Germany's back. Miss Wiskemann writes as though the Axis was an aberration of Mussolini's; in reality it came at the end of a tradition which includes Charlemagne and Napoleon, Metternich and Bismarck.

This, indeed, is the most curious thing about these heroes. According to the prophets, they were to be men without a past, beyond good and evil, and—what is more important—beyond tradition and habit. Both Hitler and Mussolini tried to follow the teachings of the prophetic books. They invented their uniforms and their methods of address—Duce and Fuehrer, titles never heard before. They wrote each other interminable letters, which were meant to be the correspondence of gods. Miss Wiskemann quotes a description by Shirer of the signing of the Pact with Japan: 'Three loud knocks on the giant door are heard. There is a tense hush in the great hall. The Japanese hold their breath. The door swings slowly open and in strides Hitler.' It is like a scene from The Great Dictator, except that no one is allowed to laugh. Yet as soon as it comes to practical affairs, these heroes turn out to be creatures of history like anyone else. Hitler's ideas were the commonplace of pan-Germans in Vienna; Mussolini's policy is what one would expect from a countryman of Cavour and Crispi. Thus the history of the Axis is a story on two planes. On one level it expressed merely the personality of two lunatics; on the other it was a profoundly important chapter in the diplomacy of Germany and Italy, the two revolutionary nations of 1848. This contradiction baffled the two heroes themselves. As the only gods in Europe, they ought to have been on terms of peculiar confidence, faithfully united against all others. This was the impression they tried to give to the world and even to themselves: each believed in the other—Mussolini was hypnotized by Hitler, and Hitler was genuinely taken in by Mussolini. All the same, the pull of real life was too strong for them. Hitler despised Mussolini at the very moment of believing in him; Mussolini knew that Hitler was leading him to disaster, even though he followed him with conviction. Each tricked the other and intrigued against the other though each knew that this was a sin against the hero in himself. Thus Mussolini encouraged the Czechs to become Communists in the autumn of 1939 in order to make things difficult between Moscow and Berlin; he protected Polish refugees and even hoped that Yugoslavia would be a barrier against German expansion in the Balkans. Hitler kept German irredentism in Tyrol up his sleeve, cut down Italy's share of Yugoslavia after its conquest, rejected Italy's claims against France. As a final oddity, though both were liars without restraint or scruple, each swallowed the other's lies and then was genuinely hurt at having been deceived. Probably each was happiest in the last phase, securely divorced from reality, Mussolini rattling the bones of the Fascist Republic and dreaming of St. Helena, Hitler reading Carlyle and preparing a stupendous *Gotterdämmerung*. Both ran true to form to the end. Hitler's last letter reproached Mussolini for having lost the war by invading Greece; Mussolini carried this letter in his pocket to show that he had been the first of the resisters. In these last acts each expressed national character as well as his own—the hard-luck story of the German, the smart intrigue of the Italian. They were a very nasty and ridiculous pair. The worst part of the story is that millions of people believed in them and applauded their every action. No doubt men deserved what they got, when they went around crying for a hero, a human saviour, a superman, instead of making the best of their own virtues and defects. Perhaps the Axis will sicken humanity with heroes for a long time to come. But I doubt it. Despite Miss Wiskemann, despite witty Oxford dons, Hitler and Mussolini seem safe for Valhalla.

MRS. GASKELL AND *CRANFORD*

BY ANGELA THIRKELL

published in *The Novel Library* (1951)

MRS. GASKELL AND CRANFORD

ELIZABETH CLEGHORN GASKELL was the daughter of William Stevenson and Elizabeth Holland. It is very often found that talent springs from families which have a religious background. In Scotland the 'son of the manse' is almost proverbial in his success in any walk of life. In England the Church or the Ministry has produced many brilliant children. If combined with this background there is also a solid country ancestry of industry and good stock, one may expect talent if not genius to show itself sooner or later. Mrs. Gaskell's father came of a Border family, had his schooling at Berwick-on-Tweed and was then trained for the Unitarian Ministry. Like many ministers of those days he held two appointments, preaching on Sunday and teaching classics in the Manchester Academy during the week. He gave up professional Arianism not so much, we gather, from a return to orthodoxy as a conviction of the impropriety of a paid ministry, and took to farming in East Lothian, where agricultural experiments were being made on scientific lines. It still remains one of the best farming parts of Scotland. This was not altogether a success. Perhaps the farmer's mother in one of Mrs. Gaskell's short stories who says, 'If on twelve acres he managed to lose a hundred pounds a year, what would he lose on one hundred and fifty?' gives the reason. In any case he gave up his farm and went to Edinburgh where he established a boarding house for students and coached at the University, proving once more that 'When land is gone and money spent, Then learning is most excellent'. In Edinburgh he made the acquaintance of a young medical student from Cheshire, Henry Holland (afterwards Sir Henry Holland, a Royal physician). Both men were Unitarians, both were interested in the land, and their friendship led later to Stevenson's marriage. In about 1806 the Earl of Lauderdale, Governor-General designate of India, who had a very high opinion of Stevenson's abilities, offered him the post of private secretary, and when owing to the opposition of the East India Company Stevenson withdrew his claim, he compensated his secretary with a rare generosity by obtaining for him the vacant post of Keeper of the Records to the Treasury. All that we know to Stevenson's discredit, and it is highly to his discredit, is that he wrote 'Some Remarks on the very inferior Utility of Classical Learning'. It may or may not stand to his credit that the Czar offered him a professorship of technology at the University of Kharkov.

At about this time he married Elizabeth Holland, a relation of his friend
Henry Holland. She again had a good country and professional background.
Her people on both sides were of good blood and her father, Peter Holland,
was a surgeon; not in the narrow sense of the word as used to-day, but in
the older sense of doctor as well. That noble type of universal physician is
now only a remembrance. Specialization and the advance of science have
driven it away. There are doubtless advantages and certainly disadvantages
in this increasing division between separate branches of the healing art. Not
that doctors now are less skilful, less kind, less devoted in their aims and
their lives, but that loved friend the Family Physician becomes rarer as
medicine ramifies. All readers of Dr. John Brown's works (he who wrote
among other things of Marjorie Fleming, Sir Walter Scott's 'Pet Marjorie')
will remember his descriptions of the Scotch country doctor called out in
the midwinter nights to a farm or a shepherd's cottage away in the hills or
across river and moorland, sometimes driving in his gig, shawled and great-
coated against the storm; sometimes walking against the northern blast and
driving snow that the horse would not face; helping a woman in childbirth,
or the herd (*anglicè* shepherd) who had broken a leg or arm, and often getting home cold and exhausted in the dark hours of an early winter morning
to find fresh calls, settling his hat more firmly on his head, pulling his plaid
more tightly round him and going out again into the dark storm. There was
then no such thing as a professional dispensing chemist. The doctor, aided
in some cases by the 'young gentlemen' who were studying under him,
made and dispensed his own medicines in the surgery; and if the pupils fell
in love with the doctor's daughter, as in the case of Molly Gibson in *Wives
and Daughters*, the doctor might have unwillingly to dispense with his
dispenser.

This patriarchal state of master and prentice still had echoes in my childhood. As a very little girl I used to stay with an uncle and aunt at Uxbridge,
then so pretty and small a town that I cannot bear to think of it now as a
suburb of London. Both were Scotch, like Mrs. Gaskell's Dr. Gibson and
his first wife. My Aunt Nan was my father's elder and only sister and the
house was called St. Andrews. The long garden where apricots ripened
against a red brick wall and the large attic where the garden apples were
stored are among my earliest and dearest recollections. In the surgery which
had an entrance from the house and a separate entrance for patients from the
street (a room strictly forbidden to me) the medicines were compounded
on the spot by an assistant. In fair weather Uncle John would visit his
patients in a high dog-cart, with a servant sitting behind; in bad weather in
a closed carriage driven by the groom, just as Dr. Gibson did in *Wives and
Daughters* nearly a hundred years earlier. An old family doctor in London,
now also dead for many years, told my mother when motors came in that
he would not have one. The time spent in his brougham, he said, between

patient and patient, gave him time to think over the last case and to prepare his mind for the next case. All this is altered now, but this type of Beloved Physician (not without a sharp tongue and a strong hand when required) was part of the background of Elizabeth Stevenson's youth and has been quietly immortalized by the daughter she hardly knew, for she died when her little Elizabeth was only a few weeks old.

The Chelsea to which Stevenson had brought his bride and where their elder child, a boy, was also born survives here and there. There is now a tablet on the house recording the writer's birthplace, but Chelsea is sadly altered since William Stevenson took his wife to 12, Lindsey Row, now numbered 93, Cheyne Walk. The heavy hand of prosperous mid-Victorianism, the German bombs, have altered and defaced so much of that lovely irregular row of houses that runs from the bottom of Flood Street to where Cheyne Walk comes to an unrespected end near the Lots Road Power Station. Old Chelsea Church was almost totally destroyed by fire and explosives during the last war (by which we mean the 1939–45 war, for it seems highly improbable at the moment that it will be the last, nor is there yet any accurate system of nomenclature for differentiating between this and the 1914–18 war). Of the mellow irregular red-brick structure, some four hundred years old, rich in monuments, full of memories of nobles, statesmen, poets and preachers, only a fragment next to the river remains. Here pious ladies have cleared the ground of debris and planted flowers with loving care. The remaining part of the church with a few monuments has been made sound and reconsecrated, but the church itself has perished for ever. How lovely Chelsea must have been then (so alive is Mrs. Gaskell to-day that one hardly believes it is nearly a hundred and fifty years since she was born and more than eighty since she died) when the Thames still flowed clear and the foreshore was the happy playground of children; mudlarks as we used to call them. Here, where a part of the mid-Victorian Embankment stonily bounds the river, used to be little houses, their backs to the water, their gardens or yards sloping towards it, just across the narrow roadway from Lindsey Row, so narrow in one place that an arch ran from house to house over the road as in pictures of the old City before the Fire of London. Half-way up Church Street, about where the south side of Paulton Square now stands, was still to be seen the decaying fabric of Essex House (also known as Church Place, or Queen Elizabeth's House), once the property of Henry VIII's Thomas Cromwell during his power. On the further side of the river, across the ferry, were fields and trees and the windmill immortalized by Girtin in one of his loveliest water-colour drawings.

To see Chelsea as it was then, read Henry Kingsley's The Hillyars and the Burtons, that strange, enchanting novel. His father was the second Vicar of Chelsea, and Henry as a boy knew every street and stone of it and has described them with nostalgic affection and their inhabitants, with 'Church

Street at feud with Danvers Street on the west and Lawrence Street on the east'. The last two streets stand (Danvers Street rather damaged at the south end); they keep their names, but their character has gone, and Lawrence Street in particular is as depressing an example of piecemeal rebuilding in various bad periods as you would wish to see. The south or river end of Church Street was destroyed with the church, though every effort had already been made to ruin it by the re-erection of Crosbie Hall, taken from the City and set down by the river where, with one end still unfinished and bricked up, it looks like a District Visitor poking its nose in where it is not wanted with intent to improve anyone who is about; a Mrs. Pardiggle of a place.

To the east the heavy hand of the mid-Victorian Improver is in evidence in the hospital and the block of flats which stand at the bottom of Cheyne Row with its dignified little eighteenth-century houses. Their hideous hot-coloured red-purply bricks and graceless aimless ornament cannot be excused even by their being well and solidly built. They in their unpleasing hideousness stood the bombing well, but even this is no defence, even post-dated, for their outward appearance. Enough of Chelsea. To read *The Hillyars and the Burtons* is to wring one's heart all to no purpose.

The motherless child was taken by stage-coach to her mother's home at Knutsford in Cheshire, where her mother's sister, Mrs. Lumb, took kindly charge of her, and her uncle Dr. Peter Holland became the guardian of her health. Mrs. Lumb's house, described by Lady Ritchie (Anne Thackeray) as 'a tall red house on the Heath, with a wide spreading view, and with a pretty carved staircase and many light windows both back and front', must have been a good, comfortable middle-class home. Mrs. Lumb had been obliged to part from a husband whose habits made domestic life impossible, and had one little daughter, a cripple, who did not live very long. To part with a husband then meant something very serious, and we can only guess that Mrs. Lumb had every reason to do so, for apparently there was no criticism of her action. Luckily there seems to have been money enough and little Elizabeth was well cared for. And here she came into a family circle of brains and talents, for a Wedgwood was her Uncle Peter Holland's wife, and through the Wedgwoods Charles Darwin the naturalist was a cousin. Not till I began to read about Mrs. Gaskell's life did I realize that Darwin had been deeply interested in her novels, and was apparently rather confused to find himself drawn, recognizably he thought, as Roger Hamley in *Wives and Daughters*; not that anyone could have minded the comparison, except that Roger is just a little too worthy for us to love. Another and unusual connection came later from Knutsford through her husband, for a Gaskell was the mother of Clive of India who, when not climbing the church spire at Market Drayton, might have been found at Knutsford, where he went to school, jumping from one ball on the top of the pillars of a gate to the other 'to the great danger of his arms and legs', and at another time helping his school-fellows to dam the mill-stream by making a coffer-dam of his own body against which they could pile stones. Not that any of Clive's blood ran in the Stevenson veins, but one cannot help being amused by these things.

When Elizabeth was about fifteen she was sent to a boarding school at Stratford-on-Avon, where she stayed (as did Esther Summerson in *Bleak House*) during the holidays (and, we may add, as did the parents at the school for grown-ups in Dickens's mock-serious *Mrs. Orange and Mrs. Lemon*). She was seventeen and her father seems to have felt the need of having his daughter with him, but he had married again and had a son and a daughter, so that her father's house was far less home to her than her aunt's house at Knutsford. He was not a wealthy man, and seems to have decided that his daughter should be prepared to earn her living; a far kinder attitude than that of the Victorian father who spent his own fortune (and possibly his wife's) and felt that somehow the girls would be provided for. Concerning this time she says that she was 'very, very unhappy' and that 'her child's heart was ready to break'; but it did not last long (when one is young time can be very, very long though in days it is short) and within two years he died. For a time she lived with a Holland uncle in Park Lane and then to her great joy was able to go back to her aunt Mrs. Lumb at Knutsford. Later she went to Newcastle for two years to study under the Rev. William Turner, a Unitarian minister and lecturer in Natural and Experimental Philosophy at Newcastle, who is partly described as Thurstan Benson in Mrs. Gaskell's novel *Ruth*, presumably to fit herself for teaching. While she was working under him she went to visit Mr. Turner's elder daughter, married to a Unitarian colleague in Manchester, and here she met the Rev. William Gaskell, junior minister at the Cross Street Unitarian Chapel. After their engagement she went for a time to Edinburgh, partly because of a cholera scare in Newcastle and possibly also to know the country where her father had farmed and studied. Their marriage took place at the parish church of Knutsford in 1832.

'Nothing but good was ever known of William Gaskell,' said an old Manchester Unitarian, who had known him for many years. 'He was a man after God's own heart, modest, cultured, religious in the truest sense of the word.' They settled in a small house near the chapel and her life's work had begun.

This is not the place to write her life. She was for the rest of her days a wife, a mother, foremost; then a worker among her husband's flock and a friend to the poor and outcast. Her books were written, as so much good work is, as and when she could find time. No writer has yet, I firmly believe, really suffered from not being able to 'devote' him or herself to writing. Possibly men—in many ways the weaker vessel—require the sacred hours that may not be impinged upon, the shelter from outside interference, the feeling (which must be highly satisfying) of MY WORK. But this splendid isolation is not possible for many women, and they do remarkably well without it. As a well-known novelist once said, when asked by an interviewer what her hours of work were, 'I have no intention of letting my writing get the upper hand of me; it just has to fit itself in where it can'. So did Mrs. Gaskell, writing far into the night, or getting up early, never letting the daily tasks of housemother and minister's wife be neglected: *ohne Hast, ohne Rast*.

Their fourth child was a boy, after three girls, and the little creature died at ten months old from scarlet fever. It was her husband who suggested that writing might help her to forget her grief and pass the time, for she was temporarily an invalid after the grief and strain of the baby's illness and death. The born writer's mind, seizing incidents or fragments of talk without knowing why, often reveals something which is unsuspected even to itself. The words of the old servant Betty in *Cousin Phillis* are like a rougher reflection of Mr. Gaskell's quiet advice to his wife. After the light-hearted, faithless Holdsworth has left Phillis she droops and languishes and succumbs to a fever from which she has not the energy to rally, though the illness has left her.

'Now, Phillis,' says Betty, coming to her side, 'we ha' done all we can for you, and th' doctors has done a' they can for you, and I think the Lord has done all He can for you, and more than you deserve, too, if you don't do something for yourself. If I were you, I'd rise up and snuff the moon sooner than break your father's and your mother's heart wi' watching and waiting till it pleases you to fight your own way back to cheerfulness. There, I never favoured long preachings and I've said my say.'

In very different words must her husband have spoken, but he had, luckily for us, touched the right chord, and it led her to *Mary Barton* and so to the rest of her work and to the friendship of Dickens, Thackeray, Charlotte Brontë, Madame Mohl, and circles in London and Paris to which the minister's wife would never have had the key. Both Dickens and Thackeray admired her work, and Thackeray's daughter Anne became a firm friend. But who that came within Anne Thackeray's charm did not also become a firm friend? Like Pope's General Oglethorpe, 'driven by strong benevolence of soul', it was impossible for anyone to come within talking distance of her and not be a lifelong friend. I cannot think of an unkind word from her. I only knew her in her later life, in the kind of widow's bonnet with black strings in which Sargent drew her, but her children and grandchildren and I have been friends for a lifetime. I was born in the little house, 27, Young Street, just off Kensington Square, opposite Thackeray's own house with its bow windows; the Ritchies were our landlords, and my brother was named after Thackeray's Denis Duval. That also is part of time lost. Number twenty-seven was next to the Greyhound public-house where Esmond spent the night before his ill-starred attempt to bring in the Stuarts after Queen Anne's death, and the Greyhound was then much as Esmond must have seen it, a modest house, just like ours except that it had a little porch with two stone greyhounds couched on it; which greyhounds were to be seen in Judge Lushington's front garden in Kensington Square till time and the Germans swept all away. Then from our house with its long garden we could look north to the trees of Kensington Gardens, where now all is red-brick flats and shops. Lady Ritchie describes it in her *Old Kensington* as the house of the curate Mr. Morgan and his mother and family, and there was a swing at the end of the garden, just as there was for us when we were small. All this has reached the appointed term of its life. The little house and its neighbours have been bought by 'big business' and are being allowed to rot and decay till they can he condemned and destroyed. Beauty vanishes, beauty passes. Thackeray's own house is saved for the time being, but it will soon be lost among huge senseless commercial buildings where hundreds of men and women work all day with never a gleam of daylight, like some horrible dream of things to come. Let us return to an age where we are more at home.

Mrs. Gaskell's contemporaries perhaps admired and respected most her books about social problems: *Ruth*, *Mary Barton*, *Lizzie Leigh*, *North and South*. Her work was also much admired by Dickens who published many of her stories in *Household Words*, but I do not think they are much read now. Nor is her last, delightful, unfinished book, *Wives and Daughters*, which appeared serially in the *Cornhill* in 1863 and 1864, though doubtless it will come to the surface again with time. She would perhaps have been amused and surprised to know that the book which keeps her name loved is a little book with no plot at all, with no social problem but that of etiquette in a small provincial town, about people who beyond being gentlefolk have no special distinction and know very little outside what goes on in the High Street and the houses where they cautiously visit, well wrapped up at night and guarded by a maid with a lantern. It is almost ninety-nine years since it made its first appearance, coming out in parts in *Household Words*, and its hold on the reading public is as strong as ever. There is nothing 'strong' in it, the character drawing is low in tone and almost uniformly kind, nothing particular ever happens—so little, in fact, that one is sometimes tempted to disbelieve in anything so dramatic as the reappearance of Miss Matty's brother—there is little in the way of descriptions of scenery, most of the characters are nearing middle-age or older; yet it has kept its hold on our hearts. If the question were put in any company, 'For what is Mrs. Gaskell known?' the odds are that ninety-nine out of a hundred would answer *Cranford*.

In what does this peculiar attraction lie? There are a thousand answers and not one of them wholly satisfactory. It is peculiarly English for one. The English spinster of good birth and often narrow means is a remarkable character and Mrs. Gaskell saw her in all her aspects. One has often observed that more life lies seething behind the one street of a little country town than in all a great metropolis—or one is more conscious of it. *Cranford* has no plot, which has been characteristic of a number of English novels, but it inspires strong if reserved affections. To us now it has the charm of the past; yet to the readers of *Household Words* that past was but little removed from their present. Landscape hardly exists; the country is simply there as a background, and roads are things for people to walk on. No one but the narrator is young. Yet when we come to the end we emerge from a country we know and love.

It seems to me impossible and indeed unnecessary to find a formula for anything in literature; we may hunt for it, but *cependant ces choses existent*. An attempt was made by a contemporary French writer Emile Montégut to explain Mrs. Gaskell's popularity; and as he translated Shakespeare we may allow him some familiarity with the English language, though with reservations when we reflect upon the intransigent attitude of our formerly lively neighbours the Gauls towards our language, and remember Scott's old French aristocrat who admired Shakespeare, but insisted that 'chewing the cud of sweet and bitter fancy' should be read as 'showing the code' because Shakespeare could not have perpetrated so barbarous a phrase. He theorized that each century has a special force of its own; that the sixteenth century was characterized by will, so that the characters of the men of that time were in value far beyond their convictions; the seventeenth I forget; in the eighteenth ideas were of more importance than lives; books and pamphlets better than the men that wrote them. And the prevailing force of the nineteenth century, he says, is the force of sentiment, and a man who is not obliged to be right in order to guard his vanity has only to describe in simple words some fact or some moral wrong that needs redressing and see the effect that follows. As far as Mrs. Gaskell's moral books go, this thesis is not far out. She never ranted against evils; she described with clear, simple English what happened and its result, and left her readers to ponder on the causes that produced such effects. I doubt whether her touching stories of such men and women as Ruth, Lizzie Leigh, Mary Barton, Philip Hepburn, did any immediate and active good, but they spoke of the 'hungry forties' and the agony of women betrayed and parents watching a child 'clem to death'; and England read them and a kind of universal consciousness was roused, reaching perhaps people whom Dickens's glorious rage had not touched: the doctrinaires whose faith in works only needed to be practically canalized. Perhaps we are attributing too much importance to M. Montégut's theories. He was not, however, the only Frenchman to think along those lines. Louis Cazamian in his rather exhausting (and I do not mean exhaustive) study of Mrs. Gaskell in *Le Roman Social en Angleterre* (*Dickens, Disraeli, Mrs. Gaskell, Kingsley*) describes her quality as *L'Intervention Chrétien*, which is not unlike Montégut's idea. But as his chapter on Dickens has the sub-title *Le Philosophe de Noel* and the author concentrates on *Les Christmas* (sic) *Books, Le Cantique de Noel, Le Grillon du Foyer, La Bataille de la Vie* and *Le Possédé*, having thrown this passing glance on him we will not argue further but continue our way.

It is almost impossible to think of *Cranford* without also remembering Anne Thackeray, whose *Old Kensington* made the past live for us as *Cranford* does, only a generation later. Her words about it in her own easy inimitable style are worth quoting:

'One scene in *Cranford* always comes back to me, because I saw my father reading it. I can still remember him coming through the doorway just as I had finished the chapter, when not without some excitement and agitation I put the close-printed number of *Household Words* into his hands. It was in the little dining-room of his house in Young Street, by gas light, just before dinner time. The story was that of Captain Brown, and he sat down and read it then and there, and afterwards told me the writer's name. But indeed I did not think of it as a story at all, it seemed to me rather that I had wit-nessed some touching and heroic deed, some sad disaster, and though I was a grown girl at the time I had a foolish wish for my father's sympathy, and a feeling that even yet he might avoid the catastrophe. Dear Captain Brown! in his shabby wig and faded coat, loved and remembered far beyond the narrow boundaries of Cranford—the city of the Amazons, the home of Miss Pole and Miss Matty and Miss Jenkyns, the place where economy was always "elegant" where "though some might be poor we were all aristo-cratic".'

Nor was Anne Thackeray alone among writers in her enthusiasm. Charlotte Brontë writes to Mrs. Gaskell in 1853, 'Thank you for your letter. It was as pleasant as a quiet chat, as welcome as spring showers, as reviving as a friend's visit; in short, it was very like a page of *Cranford*.' One cannot think that Charlotte Brontë would have spoken otherwise than from the heart in this case.

Again Anne Thackeray speaks: 'Cranford chooses its own inhabitants, and is everywhere, where people have individuality and kindliness, and where oddities are tolerated, nay, greatly loved, for the sake of the individuals. I am sure Cranford existed in the corner of Paris where my own early youth was passed. I can remember it in Kensington also, though we did not quite go the length of putting our cows into grey flannel dressing-gowns, as Miss Betsy Barker did. . . . Miss Deborah belongs to an altogether bygone type, but all the rest of the ladies in Cranford are as modern and as much alive as if they had been born in the 'sixties.'

I am not quite sure whether I agree with Lady Ritchie about Miss
Deborah. The type of elderly spinster of narrow means and far from narrow
character is so English that it will take more than two wars and a social
revolution to do away with her. People who live in London and write books
(as I do) may think that she is dead. But let them get down to the West, or
up to the North, or into the still unravished fastnesses of East Anglia, and
they will find that Miss Deborah being dead, still liveth. There may be an
outward difference. She does not wear a cravat and a little bonnet like a
jockey cap, but she is very likely to wear a good but shabby suit, a manly
shirt and a manly tie, and instead of a bonnet she may have grey hair, neatly
cropped or madly straggling, and she will deal with any emergency even if
the sufferer would really rather not be dealt with. She may tell the sufferer
what she thinks about it with devastating sincerity, but she will help from
her deep heart and her thin purse.

I have stayed in Knutsford, long ago before the 1914 war, but have sadly
little recollection of it. I knew it was Cranford, but when you are young as
I was then and your whole life is suddenly bound up with music, Manchester
and a concert have more importance than a little town which has been in a
book. And I visited Mrs. Gaskell's surviving daughter, Miss Meta Gaskell,
in their old home in Plymouth Grove. I regret now that I did not observe
with a more seeing eye, but these regrets like most others are vain. To
refresh my memory I have to turn to books.

The setting of *Cranford* is dated by the publication of the *Pickwick Papers*
in 1836, coming out in numbers. As we sadly remember, Captain Brown
was 'deeply engaged in the perusal of a number of *Pickwick* which he
had just received' when the child strayed on to the 'nasty cruel railroad'
and he was killed in rescuing it. Lord Melbourne was Prime Minister, Free
Trade and Protection were at daggers drawn, Daniel O'Connor was exer-
cising the favourite sport of his nation in making himself an intolerable
nuisance to everyone, young Disraeli had challenged him after a fine exchange of contumelious epithets on both sides and the challenge, after so
much coat trailing, had been declined. But of all this and a thousand things
more, Cranford very properly took no notice. Miss Betsy Barker's cow was
far more important; and rightly, we think, for by giving the cow who
had fallen into a lime-pit and lost her hair a grey flannel 'waistcoat and
drawers' Cranford became part of history. It is delightful to find that this
cow was a real person, if I may so put it. The Rev. H. Green, minister at
Brook Street Chapel, Knutsford (it was he who read Mrs. Gaskell's funeral
service at which, in accordance with the wishes of the family, only five
mourners including her husband were present), wrote a pleasant and unpretentious *History of Knutsford*, with many anecdotes. Among them is the
following: 'Mrs. Gaskell, the author of *Mary Barton* and of several other
tales of deep interest, may be claimed as belonging to this town during her

infancy and early life up to the time of her marriage. . . . There is one work of hers—*Cranford*—which, in my judgment, while depicting life in almost any country town is specially descriptive of some of the past and present social characteristics of Knutsford. I know that the work was not intended to delineate this place chiefly or especially, but a little incident within my own experience will show the accuracy of the pictures as applied to our town. A woman of advanced age, who was confined to her house through illness, about three years ago, asked me to lend her an amusing or cheerful book. I lent her *Cranford*, without telling her what it was supposed to relate. She read the tale of "Life in a Country Town", and when I called again she was full of eagerness to say, "Why, sir! that *Cranford* is all about Knutsford; my old mistress, Miss Harker, is mentioned in it; and our poor cow she did go to the field in a large flannel waistcoat, because she had burned herself in a lime-pit".'

It does not do to push analogies too far. I may say from personal experience that readers of novels appear to have a passion for telling the writer who her characters really are. I have—if I may for a moment divagate to personal experiences—been accused quite a number of times of 'taking' or 'copying' people in my books from some well-known public character, or someone like Aunt Eliza. I suppose one must do so in a way; that is, no one could absolutely invent a character, for he or she would be something in a vacuum, a Frankenstein's monster, a mere invention which could not be real or alive. Certain traits—a look, a way of speaking, a way of turning a head or walking —these unconsidered trifles are snapped up by the writer's mind and used as required, often without the faintest idea where they originally came from. But the kind reader at once pounces on Aunt Jane, or the Vicar of Spiffton-extra-Sooper, or the local M.P. and with joy writes to tell the author how the character has been recognized. These are our crosses. I imagine that Mrs. Gaskell may have drawn some of her *Cranford* 'Amazons', with no unloving hand, from several originals, but not from one person. One person does not make good fiction; the writer must add something of his or her self. I may say with truth, as far as one ever knows what the truth is, a question which has been in search of an answer since Pilate, that only once have I deliberately copied a character, in indignation at that person's deliberate slighting of people in a dependent position. Many other people who have passed through my pages have this or that of some friend or acquaintance in them, without which, as I have just said, they could not be alive; but only one has had a living original. When accused sometimes of having 'taken' this or that person I feel inclined to answer in the words of Mrs. Morland that if one put that person into a book, the book would fall dead of its own weight.

This is a digression, but it bears on *Cranford*, in which I feel certain that Mrs. Gaskell, with gentle amusement to herself, must have used various amiable eccentricities in various characters but never drawn a whole-length picture. A lady would not.

One of the prettiest compliments a writer can have is when a reader protests against the death of a character, a death which had by nature or by art to occur simply because, as the writer sees it, it *did* occur. The death of Captain Brown is an example of this. Ruskin wrote: 'I flew into a passion at Captain Brown being killed, and would not go any further', while Dickens's friend John Forster, one of her most helpful critics, wrote, 'I could quarrel with you for killing the poor Captain'. It does strike one now that the Captain Brown episode is rather unrelated to the rest of the book. He is rather like Solomon Grundy, Born on Monday—the rhyme will be familiar to all educated people—and finally Died on Saturday, Buried on Sunday, And that was the end of Solomon Grundy. But there is a reason for this which I did not before know. Mrs. Gaskell's explanation was that the first two chapters of *Cranford* were only meant to be one complete sketch in *Household Words* and therefore (the word therefore needs a little more explaining!) she killed Captain Brown much against her own wishes. 'It was her duty, and she did.' But after this Dickens was so delighted with the first instalment that he begged for more, and so Miss Jenkyns was also killed, off-stage, and *Cranford* continued its equable way.

We may laugh a little now, or smile quietly at some of the *Cranford* ladies' ways and their 'elegant economy', but it must be with an under-current of nostalgia. For their economy was forced upon them by their worldly circumstances, and though the Honourable Mrs. Jamieson was sister-in-law to the late Earl of Glenmire, all she could give at her little evening parties were wafer bread-and-butter and sponge-biscuits. And do not let us turn up our noses at this. How long is it since we saw a loaf from which one could cut the 'wafer-thin' bread? How long is it since we had the fresh butter, the white flour, the new-laid eggs from which to confect those sponge-biscuits? As for Miss Barker's party, Miss Barker who had sold 'select millinery' to her 'aristocratic connection', and her little supper after a game of 'Preference', what can we say of it? We must not forget the tea which preceded it, brought in by the little maidservant 'tottering under the weight of the tea-tray', which was so abundantly loaded. 'I was pleased to see it, I was so hungry,' says the narrator who was much younger than the rest of the party, 'but I was afraid the ladies present might think it vulgarly heaped up. I know they would have done at their own houses; but some-how the heaps disappeared here. I saw Mrs. Jamieson eating seed-cake, slowly and considerately, as she did everything; and I was rather surprised, for I knew she had told us, on the occasion of her last party, that she never had it in her house, it reminded her so much of scented soap. She always gave us Savoy biscuits. However, Mrs. Jamieson was kindly indulgent to Miss Barker's want of knowledge of the customs of high life; and, to spare her feelings, ate three large pieces of seed-cake, with a placid, ruminating expression of countenance, not unlike a cow's.'

After the cards, another tray! 'Scalloped oysters, potted lobsters, jelly, a dish called "little Cupids" (which was in great favour with the Cranford ladies, although too expensive to be given, except on solemn occasions— macaroons sopped in brandy, I should have called it, if I had not known its more refined and classical name). And then cherry-brandy. We none of us had ever seen such a thing, and rather shrank back when she proffered it to us—"just a little, leetle glass, ladies; after the oysters and lobsters, you know. Shell-fish are sometimes thought not very wholesome." . . . It was not exactly unpalatable, though so hot and strong that we thought ourselves bound to give evidence that we were not accustomed to such things by coughing terribly. . . .

' "It's very strong," said Miss Pole, as she put down her empty glass; "I do believe there's spirit in it."

' "Only a little drop—just necessary to make it keep," said Miss Barker. "You know we put brandy-pepper over our preserves to make them keep. I often feel tipsy myself from eating damson tart." '

Alas! alas! oft in the stilly night when slumber's chains have bound us, Fond memory brings the light of other food around us. But let us leave this too painful subject.

Side by side with Mrs. Gaskell's gentle way of poking fun at the people she loves is a gift for irrelevant talk almost worthy of Mrs. Finching, which could easily lead me into a digression as to whether Dickens and Mrs. Gaskell ever had any influence on one another's writing. Her first important book, *Mary Barton*, was published before Dickens's great mature books were written and his admiration for her was profound and sincere. *Cranford* was appearing in *Household Words* between 1851 and 1853, before *Little Dorrit*. We know that Mrs. Finching is the product of Genius, but there are pages in *Cranford* showing a genius for inspired irrelevance that the great man himself might have envied.

When, through the conjuror Signor Brunoni alias Samuel Brown, there is hope of some news of Miss Matty's long-lost brother, the ladies of Cranford form themselves into a kind of informal committee about it. 'In my search after facts, I was often reminded of a description my father had once given of a ladies' committee he had had to preside over. He said he could not help thinking of a passage in Dickens, which spoke of a chorus in which every man took the tune he knew best, and sang it to his own satisfaction. So, at this charitable committee, every lady took the subject uppermost in her mind, and talked about it to her own great contentment, but not much to the advancement of the subject they had met to discuss. But even that committee could have been nothing to the Cranford ladies when I attempted to get some clear and definite information as to poor Peter's height, appearance, and when and where he was seen and heard of last. For instance, I remember asking Miss Pole (and I thought the question was very opportune, for I put it when I met her at a call at Mrs. Forrester's, and both ladies had known Peter, and I imagined that they might refresh each other's memories)—I asked Miss Pole what was the very last thing they had ever heard about him; and then she named the absurd report to which I have alluded, about his having been elected Great Lama of Thibet; and this was a signal for each lady to go off on her separate idea. Mrs. Forrester's start was made on the veiled prophet in *Lalla Rookh*—whether I thought he was meant for the Great Lama, though Peter was not so ugly, indeed rather handsome, if he had not been freckled. I was thankful to see her double upon Peter; but, in a moment, the delusive lady was off upon Rowland's Kalydor, and the merits of cosmetics and hair oils in general, and holding forth so fluently that I turned to listen to Miss Pole who (through the llamas, the beasts of burden) had got to Peruvian bonds, and the share market, and her poor opinion of joint-stock banks in general, and of that one in particular in which Miss Matty's money was invested. In vain I put in, "When was it —in what year was it that you heard that Mr. Peter was the Great Lama?" They only joined issue to dispute whether llamas were carnivorous animals or not; in which dispute they were not quite on fair grounds, as Mrs. Forrester (after they had grown warm and cool again) acknowledged that she always confused carnivorous and graminivorous together, just as she did horizontal and perpendicular; but then she apologized for it very prettily, by saying that in her day the only use people made of four-syllabled words was to teach how they should be spelt.

'The only fact I gained from this conversation was that certainly Peter had last been heard of in India, "or that neighbourhood"; and that this scanty intelligence of his whereabouts had reached Cranford in the year in which Miss Pole had bought her Indian muslin gown, long since worn out (we washed it and mended it, and traced its decline and fall into a window-blind before we could go on); and in a year when Wombwell came to Cranford, because Miss Matty had wanted to see an elephant in order that she might the better imagine Peter riding on one; and had seen a boa-constrictor too, which was more than she wished to imagine in her fancy-pictures of Peter's locality; and in a year when Miss Jenkyns had learnt some piece of poetry off by heart, and used to say, at all the Cranford parties, how Peter was "surveying mankind from China to Peru", which everybody had thought very grand and rather appropriate, because India was between China and Peru, if you took care to turn the globe to the left instead of the right,' which breathless piece of prose is almost worthy of Flora herself.

It is interesting to know that in a letter to Ruskin she confessed that *Cranford* was the only one of her books that she could bear to read over and over again, taking her back as it did to the scenes of her girlhood.

Many suggestions have been made about the possible originals of the *Cranford* characters. As we said before, probably no writer draws exactly from nature, but there are traits that can often be recognized. Miss Deborah and Miss Matty Jenkyns are said to be like her elder cousins, Miss Mary and Miss Lucy Holland, and the Honourable Mrs. Jamieson may have been inspired by Lady Jane Stanley, of Brook House, where the story of the cat who swallowed the lace, as told by the Honourable Mrs. Jamieson, is said actually to have happened. But it is not particularly profitable to look for originals. Mrs. Gaskell's pen could draw a full-blown character from one trait as well as a scientist can reconstruct a prehistoric animal from one bone —and far more probably.

How perceptive are her words about the little foibles that we all have, especially those hoarding and saving ways that the war forced upon us and from which many of us will never recover. Speaking for myself, I can never again cut string or throw away the paper from a parcel. During the war, as many of us will remember, paper became a serious problem, and there was a moment at which so august a place as the London Library was glad to have a present of brown paper from an American parcel and string from the same quarter, string used with a lavishness that almost appalled one; 'we were so unacquainted with string that its presence was shocking to us.' Mrs. Gaskell had not experienced this particular want herself, but she writes of it with delightful understanding:

'I have often noticed that almost everyone has his own individual small economies . . . any disturbance of which annoys him more than spending shillings or pounds on some real extravagance. An old gentleman of my acquaintance, who took the intelligence of the failure of a Joint-Stock Bank, in which some of his money was invested, with stoical mildness, worried his family all through a long summer's day because one of them had torn (instead of cutting) out the written leaves of his now useless bank-book; of course, the corresponding pages at the other end came out as well, and this little unnecessary waste of paper (his private economy) chafed him more than all the loss of his money. Envelopes fretted his soul terribly when they first came in; the only way in which he could reconcile himself to such waste of his cherished article was by patiently turning inside out all that were sent to him, and so making them serve again.' (I have sometimes done that myself, during the war, and found it a most maddening and unprofitable task.) 'Even now, though tamed by age, I see him casting wistful glances at his daughters when they send a whole instead of a half sheet of paper, with the three lines of acceptance to an invitation, written on only one of the sides. I am not above owning that I have this human weakness myself. String is my foible. My pockets get full of little hanks of it, picked up and twisted together, ready for uses that never come. I am seriously annoyed if anyone cuts the string of a parcel instead of patiently and faithfully undoing it fold by fold. How people can bring themselves to use india-rubber rings, which are a sort of deification of string, as lightly as they do, I cannot imagine. To me an india-rubber ring is a precious treasure. I have one which is not new—one that I picked up off the floor nearly six years ago. I have really tried to use it, but my heart failed me, and I could not commit the extravagance.

'Small pieces of butter grieve others. They cannot attend to conversation because of the annoyance occasioned by the habit which some people have of invariably taking more butter than they want. Have you not seen the anxious look (almost mesmeric) which such persons fix on the article? They would feel it a relief if they might bury it out of their sight by popping it into their own mouths and swallowing it down; and they are really made happy if the person on whose plate it lies unused suddenly breaks off a piece of toast (which he does not want at all) and eats up his butter. They think that this is not waste.'

I defy anyone to find a better definition of waste, and the delightful thing is that we all do much the same ourselves in different ways and think we are being economical. I must confess to string and butter, and I still (though this is a war inhibition) keep any envelope which has come with a penny stamp and not licked up, though it costs me more money and trouble in so-called Economy Labels than in buying some new envelopes for myself. 'That which we are, we are,' and Mrs. Gaskell knew it very well.

One thing we would very much like to know: what Mary Smith, the 'I' of the story, was like. Was she Mrs. Gaskell in disguise? Was she some friend of hers? Was she pure invention? She is a charming narrator, but we never get to know much about her. She had a father whose shirts she made during her long visits to Cranford, and who came over to help when Miss Matty's little fortune was lost in the failure of the Town and County Bank, a kind man, full of business and rather peremptory.

'Miss Matty and I sat assenting to accounts, and schemes, and reports, and documents, of which I do not believe either of us understood a word; for my father was clear-headed and decisive, and a capital man of business, and if we made the slightest inquiry, or expressed the slightest want of comprehension, he had a sharp way of saying, "Eh? eh? it's as clear as daylight. What's your objection?" And as we had not comprehended anything of what he had proposed, we found it rather difficult to shape our objections; in fact we were never sure if we had any. So presently Miss Matty got into a nervously acquiescent state, and said "Yes", and "Certainly", at every pause, whether required or not; but when I once joined in as chorus to a "Decidedly", pronounced by Miss Matty in a tremblingly dubious tone, my father fired round at me and asked me "What there was to decide?" And I am sure to this day I have never known. But, in justice to him, I must say he had come over from Drumble to help Miss Matty when he could ill spare the time, and when his own affairs were in a very anxious state.'

Was he at all like Mr. Stevenson? Or like Mr. Gaskell? Or an invention? At any rate 'I' must have been a most delightful creature, and our only sorrow is that we never hear of any likelihood of her being married. But perhaps in Cranford one did not talk of such things.

And there were a great many things about which one did not talk in Cranford. Perhaps one of the most charming scenes is the meeting in Miss Pole's drawing-room when Miss Matty's friends suggest that they might contribute to her income, but find it almost impossible to talk about money. The amount that each can contribute is written on a paper, signed and sealed, and then Mary Smith is taken aside by each lady in turn; one to apologize for the little she can afford, though she is giving more than a twentieth of her little hundred pounds a year; another to apologize for putting down less than she could afford because 'she thought she could never look Miss Matty in the face again if she presumed to be giving her so much as she should like to do', because Miss Matty had been the rector's daughter. Which mention of the rector reminds me that there is as far as I can remember hardly a mention of church or chapel in *Cranford*, a curious omission when one thinks how bound up the author's life had been with her husband's work. Miss Matty's father, the old rector, is mentioned with tender amusement and her mother's delightful letter when her husband sent her a Latin *carmen*, which she endorsed, 'Hebrew verses sent me by my honoured husband. I thowt to have had a letter about the killing the pig, but must wait'. And there is the charming letter from the rector's young wife about her baby, 'Dear mother, I wish you could see her! Without any pershality, I do think she will grow up a regular bewty!'

' "We must burn them, I suppose," said Miss Matty, looking doubtfully at me. "No one will care for them when I am gone." And one by one she dropped them into the middle of the fire, watching each blaze up, die out, and rise away, in faint, white, ghostly semblance, up the chimney, before she gave another to the same fate.'

But the genius of Mrs. Gaskell has kept the memories of Cranford and its Amazons fragrant for us. 'Even in their ashes live their wonted fires', and at this little, brightly burning, well-tended fire we may warm our hearts and think gratefully of the hand that wrote *Cranford*.

MARCEL PROUST

BY MARTIN TURNELL

from *The Novel in France* (1950)

Pour ce qui me concerne tout au moins, Proust aura été
le révélateur le plus effrayant que je pouvais rencontrer sur
moi-même.

Jacques Rivière

*English quotations, except where otherwise stated, are
from C. K. Scott Moncrieff's translation of 'Remembrance of Things past', by kind permission of Messrs.
Chatto and Windus.*

MARCEL PROUST

I. A NEW VISION

'UN univers nouveau s'ouvrait à moi,' wrote Léon Pierre-Quint of his discovery of Proust. He spoke not only for himself, but for a whole generation. To those of us who grew up between the wars, Proust's work was a revelation, an unforgettable experience which modified our sensibility. It introduced us to a world whose existence we had barely even suspected, gave us a new insight into the depth and complexity of the human heart and offered us an interpretation of man which seemed at first to be totally different from that of the classic novelists. This world may appear remote from our own, but by identifying ourselves with it, as we must in reading Proust, we are liberated from our stereotyped ways of seeing and feeling. His vision has been compared to looking at life through a microscope, but its effect is more lasting. Once we have shared it, nothing can ever look exactly the same again.

It is not easy to define this vision. Ortega y Gasset has described Proust as 'the inventor of a new distance between ourselves and the world of things'. This puts the emphasis in the right place. He has had a good deal of attention from professional philosophers who have written absorbing studies of the importance of his contribution to philosophy. Proust may have provided the philosopher with valuable data, but his novel is an experience and not an epistemological problem. His conception of reality and his theory of knowledge are only interesting to the critic in so far as they illuminate the tensions and stresses of his book. For his revelation is *psychological* and not *metaphysical*. His search for *la vraie vie*—the reality which he believed was concealed behind the transitory world of appearances—may sometimes remind us of K's attempts to gain admission to 'the castle' in Kafka's novel, but the resemblances are superficial. He had little in common with a novelist like Kafka who invented a world where the ordinary laws governing human conduct seem suddenly to have been suspended, leaving us with a sense that events are at once fatally predetermined and unpredictable. Proust plays havoc with time and place; the order of our emotional reactions is often reversed; but we know that his characters could never be called upon to defend themselves against unknown charges in the presence of invisible judges.

Proust's art is immensely subtle, but it is firmly rooted in the soil of France. He himself speaks of

> . . . une tradition à la fois antique et directe, ininterrompue, orale, déformée, méconnaissable et vivante.
>
> [. . . a tradition at once ancient and direct, unbroken, oral, deformed, unrecognizable, and alive.]

We are aware on almost every page he wrote of that ancient France with its thousand years of civilization, its cathedrals, its village churches, the wide undulating plains with the peasants working in the fields, the orchards and the apple blossom, the châteaux in their parks dimly visible behind the hedges of lilac, of that France which is symbolized by the one word: 'Combray.'

For in spite of the extraordinary impact of his sensibility, in many ways Proust's world resembles our own. It is simply that we are looking at everything from a new and unexpected angle. This is how he describes a shower of rain:

> Un petit coup au carreau, comme si quelque chose l'avait heurté, suivi d'une ample chute légère comme de grains de sable qu'on eût laissé tomber d'une fenêtre au-dessus, puis la chute s'étendant, se réglant, adoptant un rythme, devenant fluide, sonore, musicale, innombrable, universelle: c'était la pluie.
>
> [A little tap at the window, as though some missile had struck it, followed by a plentiful, falling sound, as light, though, as if a shower of sand were being sprinkled from a window overhead; then the fall spread, took on an order, a rhythm, became liquid, loud, drumming, musical, innumerable, universal. It was the rain.]

Although this is a description of a common phenomenon which we have all observed, Proust manages to convey an impression of freshness and novelty. We hear a small tap on the window as though something had knocked lightly against it. It is followed by a shower of light, dry taps like grains of sand, and we wonder vaguely whether the people above have upset something. The sound seems to spread, becomes regular instead of intermittent, acquires a rhythm—Proust's use of the present participles swimming into one another to give a sensation of immediacy and continuity was clearly learnt from Flaubert—the 'dry' sound gives place to a 'fluid' sound which is 'sonore, musicale, innombrable, universelle'. The piled adjectives make us feel the isolated taps merging relentlessly into a single sound which swells into a roar and seems to envelop us. Then, with a shock, we realize—'It's the rain'. The last clause has been described by one critic as a *phrase-détonation*. At a stroke the charged, stifling atmosphere, which has become intolerable, clears. We experience an immense sense of release.

In another place he looks at a sunbeam playing on a balcony and this is what he sees:

Devant la fenêtre, le balcon était gris. Tout d'un coup, sur sa pierre maussade je ne voyais pas une couleur moins terne, mais je sentais comme un effort vers une couleur moins terne, la pulsation d'un rayon hésitant qui voudrait libérer sa lumière.

[Outside the window, the balcony was grey. Suddenly, on its sullen stone, I did not indeed see a less negative colour, but I felt as it were an effort towards a less negative colour, the pulsation of a hesitating ray that struggled to discharge its light.]

Only a writer belonging to the age of Impressionism would have described the dull stone as *maussade* and have written of colour as Proust does here. It is not a mere 'impression'. We feel him trying to penetrate the composition of the colours, giving the scene a strange poetic life of its own.

An old lady is out walking in the park and suddenly she has a stroke:

Elle était apparue, bien qu'à côté de moi, plongée dans ce monde inconnu au sein duquel elle avait déjà reçu les coups dont elle portait les traces quand je l'avais vue tout à l'heure aux Champs-Elysées, son chapeau, son visage, son manteau dérangés par la main de l'ange invisible avec lequel elle avait lutté.

[She had appeared to them, although I was still by her side, submerged in that unknown world somewhere in which she had already received the blows, traces of which she still bore when I looked up at her a few minutes earlier in the Champs-Elysées, her hat, her face, her cloak left in disorder by the hand of the invisible angel with whom she had wrestled.]

We are suddenly aware that we are all prisoners in our private worlds which are separated from one another by almost insurmountable barriers. The *monde inconnu* is a psychological world. The child knows that his grandmother is battling alone on the other side of one of these barriers with *l'ange invisible* and trying to conceal from him the ravages of her stroke.

Then the grandmother dies:

. . . ainsi, dans un désir fou de me précipiter dans ses bras, ce n'était qu'à l'instant, plus d'une année après son enterrement, à cause de cet anachronisme qui empêche si souvent le calendrier des faits de coïncider avec celui des sentiments, que je venais d'apprendre qu'elle était morte.

[. . . and so, in my insane desire to fling myself into her arms, it was not until this moment, more than a year after her burial, because of that anachronism which so often prevents the calendar of facts from corresponding to that of our feelings, that I became conscious that she was dead.]

It is only a year later that he 'realizes'. It is an example of the way in which Proust reverses the conventional order of our emotions and substitutes the rhythm of our real feelings for time.

He writes of Swann's love for Odette de Crécy:

> . . . son amour s'étendait bien au delà des régions du désir physique. La personne même d'Odette n'y tenait plus une grande place.

> [. . . his love extended a long way beyond the province of physical desire. Odette's person, indeed, no longer held any great place in it.]

The ready-made categories are again brushed aside. We have to adjust ourselves to a 'love' where there is scarcely room for the *person* of the beloved.

Yet when we return to Proust in middle life, it is often with a sense of disenchantment. We no longer seem to enjoy him as much as we did in the past; the vision which once illuminated his pages appears to have vanished or grown dim; we are so oppressed by the *longueurs* and complexities of the later volumes that we may even cease to be receptive to the poetry of *Swann* or to a *trouvaille* like this:

> Le temps des lilas approchait de sa fin; quelques-uns effusaient encore en hauts lustres mauves les bulles délicates de leurs fleurs, mais dans bien des parties du feuillage où déferlait, il y avait seulement une semaine, leur mousse embaumée, se flétrissait diminuée, et noircie, une écume creuse, sèche et sans parfum.

> [Lilac-time was nearly over; some of the trees still thrust aloft, in tall purple chandeliers, their tiny balls of blossom, but in many places among their foliage where, only a week before, they had still been breaking in waves of fragrant foam, these were now spent and shrivelled and discoloured, a hollow scum, dry and scentless.]

There is no mistaking the debt to the *Mémoires d'outre-tombe*, but Proust has transformed what he borrowed into something new and achieved an effect which was beyond the powers of Chateaubriand. For Chateaubriand was very much the product of the Romantic Movement. We often feel in reading him that 'Nature' was largely a pretext for turning loose feelings which somehow float unattached on the page. There is nothing of the sort in Proust. On the contrary, we are impressed by the complex organization of the passage, by the acuteness of his perceptions and by a hard intellectual core underneath. We have an almost painful sensation of the fragile beauty of the lilacs which comes to stand symbolically for the fading of childhood and of life itself. 'Combray', the first section of the novel, is indeed an account of the childish paradise which is gradually lost, and it is not for nothing that the description of the lilacs occurs some forty pages before the incident at Montjouvain. Nor are the three adjectives at the end of the passage there for euphony or emphasis. The winding sentence makes us feel that life is being slowly throttled, that its gleam is fading, as it moves inevitably to its dying fall. We find ourselves looking all round the shattered blooms and seeing that in fact no life remains, only a dry, shrunken, blackened, scentless mass.

It is even possible to become so submerged in the apparently endless paragraphs and the interminable subordinate clauses that we are blind to the remarkable virtuoso in prose who could write:

. . . les phrases, au long col sinueux et démesuré, de Chopin, si libres, si tactiles, qui commencent à chercher leur place en dehors et bien loin de la direction de leur départ, bien loin du point où on avait pu espérer qu'atteindrait leur attouchement, et qui ne se jouent dans cet écart de fantaisie que pour revenir plus délibérément,— dans un retour plus prémédité, avec plus de précision, comme sur un cristal qui résonnerait jusqu'à faire crier,—vous frapper au cœur.

[. . . those long-necked, sinuous creatures, the phrases of Chopin, so free, so flexible, so tactile, which begin by seeking their ultimate resting-place somewhere beyond and far wide of the direction in which they started, the point which one might have expected them to reach, phrases which divert themselves in those fantastic by-paths only to return more deliberately—with a more premeditated reaction, with more precision, as on a crystal bowl which, if you strike it, will ring and throb until you cry aloud in anguish—to clutch at one's heart.]

The sentence seems to *perform* the curve which it describes. It reaches its culminating point at the word *délibérément*, pauses, then turns menacingly towards us, and, with a ruthlessness punctuated by the words *prémédité*, *précision* and *crier*, swoops down upon us and buries itself, with a shock, in our 'heart'.

We have to decide whether the reason for our disenchantment lies in ourselves or in the work, whether *A la Recherche du temps perdu* is the great novel it once was thought to be or is simply a repertoire of astonishing phrases buried in an inert, unreadable mass of words.

Hostile critics have been quick to allege that Proust was the product of a dying aristocracy, the laureate of a society which vanished at the outbreak of the second world war and that his attitude is no longer capable of interesting us, is indeed incomprehensible. The truth seems to me to be less simple than that. It is always difficult to judge a contemporary and almost impossible in the case of a writer of the bulk and complexity of Proust. Now that he has been dead nearly thirty years, however, we are in a better position to see his work in perspective.

Violent changes in taste are usually due to one of two causes. They may be the result of the snobbish depreciation from which D. H. Lawrence has suffered or they may be due to the fact that the writer was overrated in his lifetime as Virginia Woolf undoubtedly was in hers.

There is, however, a third alternative. The appearance of a really original work of art produces three separate reactions in the public: perplexity, enthusiasm, neglect. The perplexity is caused by the difficulty of accustoming ourselves to a new vision; enthusiasm is the reward of perseverance; and neglect follows when we have absorbed it, or as much of it as we can for the time being. It may be that Proust's vision was as original as it once appeared, but that we have grown so used to it that it has become part of our make-up and needs to be rediscovered.

That, broadly, is the thesis which I propose to defend here, but the part played by non-literary factors in Proust's sudden eclipse and his early revival must not be overlooked. 'There is an egalitarian bias native to this age,' wrote Professor Brogan during the last war, 'that must be overcome if Proust is to be approached in a proper spirit of willingness to listen, to be converted. His characters are, for the most part, rich and idle and vicious.' In the nineteen-thirties these words would have been damning: to-day they are a positive commendation. Now that levelling down has been elevated into a political first principle, we are more conscious of what was valuable in the aristocratic societies of the past. We are growing weary, too, of the *littérature engagée*. It is a relief to turn to a writer who doesn't take sides and who has virtually nothing to say of political and economic problems. That is why there is something immensely fascinating about Proust's world, about the fabulous creatures—'rich and idle and vicious'—of whom he wrote. The bustle and gaiety of the age, the parties and the spectacle of the gorgeous Laure Hayman, the famous *cocotte*, passing, as someone put it, 'dans sa gloire impure', offer a momentary escape from our own sordid plight.

This has, to be sure, little to do with the literary merits of the novel, but it is of great importance. It predisposes the reader in favour of Proust. He feels better able to face the *longueurs*, more capable of making the effort to delve beneath the surface and to recapture the strange charm of his first reading.

II. THE NOAH'S ARK

> When I was very small, there was no character in the Bible whose lot seemed to me to be as wretched as Noah's because of the flood which kept him a prisoner in the ark for forty days. Later on I was often ill and for days on end I, too, had to stay in the ark. I understood then that Noah was never able to see the world so well as he did from the ark in spite of the fact that it was closed and darkness covered the earth.
>
> *Les Plaisirs et les jours*

MARCEL PROUST was born in Paris on 10 July 1871, and was the elder of two sons. His father came of a middle-class provincial Catholic family. Dr. Adrien Proust was the first of the family to leave his native Illiers and seek his fortune in Paris where he became a distinguished surgeon. Proust's mother belonged to the prosperous Jewish family of Weil.

'This little being,' writes Mme de Gramont of the novelist, 'was to contain at once all the earthly savour of the Prousts of Illiers and the whole of the Biblical soul of his maternal ancestors.' There can be little doubt that the mixture of races played a decisive part in the formation of his character and the development of his art. From his father he derived his feeling for the historic France which gives his novel its strength and solidity; from his mother his exceptionally delicate nervous sensibility, and possibly his interest in clans and coteries.

In spite of pronounced differences of opinion, Proust was devoted to both his parents and did not leave the parental home until his mother died in 1905, two years after his father. He was, however, essentially his mother's son as his brother, Robert, was his father's; and it is the influence of her family which is preponderant in the novel.[1] At the age of fourteen he was asked in a questionnaire: 'What is your idea of misery?' He replied: 'To be separated from *maman*.' He was passionately fond of his mother and her death was the greatest sorrow of his life.

At the age of nine he had the first of the attacks of asthma from which he suffered all his life. Proust's ill-health has always been something of a mystery. There has been a tendency to regard him in some quarters as a lifelong martyr to asthma, but it may be doubted whether this view is entirely correct.

> Doubtless [writes an American critic] this asthma was a nervous disorder and one is permitted to suspect that it was a sympathetic device rather than a cause of the peculiarities of his temperament. It enabled him in childhood to claim, from

---

[1] Mme de Gramont, who knew the family, describes Robert, who followed his father's profession, as 'l'image de la force, de la santé et de l'équilibre'. She may be right in suggesting that the fact that Marcel was born in the anxious days following the French defeat tipped the scales in favour of his mother.

his mother especially, the extravagant affection which he demanded, and in later life it served as an excuse for fantastic habits which he doubtless did not want to give up. But it was real enough nevertheless and it marked the first step in that progressive retirement from active life which was to constitute the course of his outward existence. The little Marcel—it was thus that he continued until his dying day to be known—must make a life of his own since he obviously could not share the life of his fellows.

There seems to be a good deal of truth in this diagnosis. Proust was certainly a sick man, but one cannot help feeling that the development, if not the origin, of his sickness was in some way *voulu*. For it must be remembered that his isolation from the world was essential for writing the sort of masterpiece that he did in fact write and that from a very early age he regarded himself as a dedicated man. He loved the social world, but once he had collected his material he may have felt the need to justify his retirement from it to himself.

This view appears to be supported by the opinion of one of the specialists who attended him.

I consulted Mohlen [we find him writing in one of his letters], the doctor who with Faisan is considered the best. He told me that my asthma has become a nervous habit and that the only way of curing it would be to go to an anti-asthmatic establishment in Germany where they would break the habit of my asthma—[I say would] for I shall certainly not go—as one breaks the habit of morphine in a morphine-addict.

Proust was educated at the Lycée Condorcet and the Sorbonne. The Lycée Condorcet seems to have been much more civilized than the other famous French lycées. The discipline was mild—too mild for the parents of some of the pupils—the masters were intelligent and there was plenty of intellectual life. It was here that Proust made friends with Robert de Flers, Jacques Bizet, Daniel Halévy and Léon Brunschwicg, and launched a college magazine with them. According to his biographers, he had already begun to form his famous style while still at school to the delight of an intelligent master and the scandal of a stuffy school inspector when Proust was invited, as the prize pupil, to read aloud his weekly essay during the visitation. It was also at the lycée that Proust first became interested in natural history— an interest which had a considerable influence on his mature style.

Proust's father wanted him to take up law or diplomacy and at the University he read law and political science. He displayed little interest in those subjects, and in spite of some opposition from his parents it was eventually agreed that he need not follow a profession.

It can hardly be said that the University played as important a part in his intellectual formation as the lycée, but he did make one valuable acquaintance there. He met Bergson, whose *Essai sur les données immédiates de la conscience* had appeared in 1889, and went to some of his lectures which stimulated his interest in philosophical problems. The link between the two men was strengthened when, a little later, Bergson married Mlle Neuberger, a relative of Proust's on his mother's side.

Proust's family was very well off and from adolescence he showed an immense relish for social life.

At fifteen [writes Léon Pierre-Quint] we find him in the *salon* of Mme Straus sitting like a faithful little page at her feet on a great plush footstool. The prominent personalities of the Third Republic who came to visit the lady of the house did not fail to bestow a few minutes' attention on her youthful favourite. They compared him to the handsome Italian princes in Paul Bourget's novels. At home his mirror was framed with invitation cards; and a famous courtesan sent him a book bound in silk from one of her petticoats.[1]

The same writer provides us with another glimpse of him at the age of twenty:

He had large, bright black eyes with heavy lids which slanted a little to one side. His expression was one of extreme gentleness which fastened itself for long moments on any object at which he looked. His voice was still gentler, a little out of breath with a slight drawl which bordered on affectation yet managed to avoid it. He had long thin black hair which sometimes obscured his forehead and which never turned white. But it was the eyes which held one's attention—those immense eyes with mauve circles, tired, nostalgic, extremely mobile, which seemed to move and follow the secret thoughts of the speaker. On his lips was a continual smile, amused, welcoming, hesitating, then fixing itself unmoving on his lips. His complexion was matt, but at that time fresh and rosy. In spite of his small black moustache, he reminded you of a great lazy child who was too knowing for his years.

As a young man he entertained his friends on a lavish scale either at his parents' house or at the most expensive restaurants. On these occasions he used to have his own meal before the dinner so that he could talk more freely and he would move round the table, sitting first beside one guest, then another. 'His imagination,' said Pierre-Quint, 'worked on concrete data and was controlled by his observation.' He had already adopted the practice of minute observation of the appearance and gestures of his friends, which was to serve him in writing his novel. He used to make notes on tiny scraps of paper for future use. He also became as a young man a famous mimic and often delighted the company with his impersonations of friends. Among the victims was the writer, Comte Robert de Montesquiou, who provided some

[1] The courtesan was Laure Hayman and the book Bourget's *Gladys Harvey*, of which she was the heroine.

—but only some—of the material for Charlus.[1] It is recorded that on one occasion Proust went to a party simply to observe the Comte de Sagan's monocle; that on another he visited a woman friend to ask her to let him see a hat which she had worn twenty years before and was very surprised to learn that she no longer had it.

Proust's first book was published in 1896.[2] *Les Plaisirs et les jours* is a collection of stories, poems and sketches. It seems to have been influenced by Baudelaire—the poems on painters and musicians are a pastiche of *Les Phares* —and by the prose of Jules Laforgue, Huysmans and the later Symbolists.[3] There has been some difference of opinion about its value. Proust's contemporaries dismissed it as the work of a youthful dilettante, but later critics have emphasized its importance for an understanding of the novel and have claimed to detect a distinctive note which points to the future author of *A la Recherche du temps perdu*. If Proust had written nothing else the book would probably have long since been forgotten, but it is certainly not without merit. It was not perhaps altogether an exaggeration to write, as Anatole France did in his preface:

> He displays a sureness of aim which is surprising in so young an archer. He is by no means an innocent, but he is so sincere and so true that he becomes naïve and in this way he pleases us. There is in him something of a depraved Bernardin de Saint-Pierre and an ingenuous Petronius.[4]

For underneath the period décors and the preciosity we are conscious of the writer's gift of analysis, a very intense sensibility and the unrest which we shall meet again and again in the novel. We also recognize some of the main themes of the novel. 'La Mort de Baldassare Silvandre, Vicomte de Sylvanie' is the story of a handsome and wealthy aristocrat who is slowly dying of an unnamed disease, and it introduces the character of the prisoner-invalid. 'La Confession d'une Jeune Fille' is the death-bed confession of a girl who takes the wrong turning, drives her mother to her death and then shoots herself. It is probably the most interesting piece of work in the book. I think that those critics are right who have argued that it is a portrait of the artist as a *jeune fille* and it certainly looks forward to Mlle Vinteuil. 'La Fin

---

[1] On the genesis of the characters, see André Maurois, *A la Recherche de Marcel Proust* (Paris, 1949), pp. 147–66. It appears that one of the other models for Charlus was a certain Baron Jacques Doazan. J-E. Blanche records that Montesquiou and Doazan were 'at daggers drawn' because the Count had stolen the *baron de l'empire's* 'boy-friend'.

There are strange discrepancies in the spelling of proper names in the works of Proust's French critics. In cases of doubt I have followed M. Maurois who seems to be the most reliable of the novelist's biographers in this respect.

[2] It was also the year in which *Matière et mémoire* was published.

[3] Laforgue's *Moralités légendaires* had been collected in 1887.

[4] It was Mme Straus who persuaded France to write the preface and it is thought that it was in part her handiwork.

de la Jalousie' deals with a subject whose importance needs no emphasis while other sketches describe fashionable life. Over them all broods a personal nostalgia and a sense of personal guilt which breaks through again and again in Proust's accounts of the different *amours* of his hero and his characters in *A la Recherche du temps perdu*.

In 1900 Proust's parents left the Boulevard Malesherbes and went to live at 45 Rue de Courcelles. It was the year in which John Ruskin died. Proust had already become interested in him and he paid his tribute to the dead writer by publishing a short essay called 'Pélerinages Ruskiniens en France' in the *Figaro*.[1] Although Proust could only read English with considerable difficulty, he set to work with the help of his mother and friends to translate Ruskin into French. His translation of *The Bible of Amiens* with an introduction and notes appeared in 1904 and *Sesame and Lilies* two years later.[2] It has been said that Proust's mother and grandmother introduced him to the great French classics of the seventeenth century and that Ruskin introduced him to the Middle Ages. That is undoubtedly true, but critics who claim that he was directly influenced by Ruskin's æsthetic theories and his prose style are on less certain ground. Ruskin certainly played an important part in Proust's formation, but his real influence was probably indirect. He awakened something that was already latent in Proust, and it was through him that Proust became aware of his true vocation.

On the death of his mother, Proust went to live at the flat at 102 Boulevard Haussmann where much of his novel was written.[3] It was the end of the society man and the beginning of the recluse. The famous cork-lined room was constructed. It was decorated by a portrait of Proust at the age of twenty by Jacques-Émile Blanche and an Infanta by Velasquez. Proust had always been extremely sensitive to noise. When, as a young man, he had spent his summer holidays by the sea at Cabourg—the Balbec of the novel—he had engaged not only a room for himself, but the four rooms above, below and on either side so that he would not be disturbed by the sound of other guests in the adjoining rooms. In the Boulevard Haussmann the windows were kept permanently closed. The long room was lighted by a single globe and the walls retained their musty brown colour because Proust, who was completely unadapted to the needs of practical life, never managed to find a decorator to do them in up some more attractive colour. He seldom left his prison except at night. When he was seized with a nostalgic desire to

---

[1] Reprinted in *Chroniques*.

[2] The two introductions were rewritten and combined in the long essay called 'Journées de Lecture' in *Pastiches et mélanges*.

[3] He remained there until 1919 when he was turned out by the new landlord to whom his aunt, Mme Catusse, had sold the freehold without telling her nephew. He then spent some months in a flat in the Rue Laurent-Pichat before going to live in a furnished flat on the fourth floor at 44 Rue Hamelin which, as he said, 'costs 16,000 francs and is more or less like a servant's room'.

see the hawthorn blossom or the water-lilies, he would drive into the country in a carriage which was completely closed to prevent the scent of the flowers from bringing on an attack of asthma, and looked at the countryside through the windows.

Yet the work went on. He used to send for his friends—usually at night—and interrogate them minutely about fashions, clothes and social events. On the rare occasions on which he ventured out to attend some reception at which he felt that he would obtain valuable material for his book, the strain was so great that the outing was often paid for by weeks of prostration.

His practice of questioning people about the world was not confined to his friends. He would spend hours—sometimes as much as two or three hours at a stretch—with the head waiters of the Ritz, the Wéber and the Hôtel des Réservoirs at Versailles, documenting himself on the appearance and behaviour of the guests.

In his own home Proust was looked after by his devoted servant Céleste. Later, members of her family and her husband, Odilon Albaret the taxi-driver, were added to his staff.

In spite of his wealth, he spent practically nothing on himself. He wore his suits for three years. As he grew older, he spent more and more time in bed, writing his book propped up on his pillows and scattering the finished sheets over the room. When he got up, he usually wore an old dressing-gown which he only replaced when it was literally falling to pieces. His wealth and his modest requirements did not prevent him from constantly imagining—it is another neurotic trait—that some disaster on the Stock Exchange had reduced him to penury.

The writing of the novel and visits from friends were not the only occupations of his later years. Prince Antoine Bibesco has suggested that in his reclusion Proust felt the need of greater contact with the outside world than was provided by either of these activities and that this made him an indefatigable correspondent. His view is supported by the letters themselves. A few—a very few—contain precious information about the composition of the novel, but the vast majority are concerned with other matters or deal only with the surface of literary life. He kept his friends carefully informed about the disastrous state of his health. He would have liked to arrange a little dinner at the Ritz; but after the previous one he was poorly for weeks, so it will have to be a bedside dinner. He really feels that he is on his last legs; he nearly killed himself the other day by getting in a muddle with his pills and taking the wrong dose. There are little tiffs and misunderstandings. Proust is terribly upset about that preface he was going to write for a book of Jacques-Émile Blanche's; he goes into the most elaborate details which greatly adds to the confusion. He also directs literary operations from his bed. He writes to Souday about his review of the latest volume of the novel or angles for favourable notices of a book by one of his friends. Naturally, everything goes wrong and to his horror the *Nouvelle Revue Française* prints a notice which is little short of an *éreintement*. He chides Gallimard over his slowness in reprinting *A l'Ombre des jeunes filles en fleurs* and goes into a frenzy when his brother reports that none of the provincial booksellers has ever heard of *Sodome et Gomorrhe*. And why will that wretched printer persist in putting a circumflex on the word 'Sodome'!

Those of Proust's friends who have written biographies or memoirs of him have all spoken warmly of his extraordinary charm of manner, his gentleness and his generosity. On one occasion, for example, M. Paul Morand happened to tell him that he was about to consult a well-known and very expensive Paris specialist. The following day he was surprised to receive a large sum—much larger than the consultant's fee—from the novelist. It was useless for him to say that he did not need it. After a protracted correspondence, he was obliged to accept to avoid giving mortal offence to the donor and had to resort to all sorts of ruses in order to be allowed to repay it. Nor was Proust's generosity restricted to his friends. The munificence of his tips was legendary and an embarrassment to the guests whom he entertained in restaurants. When, at the end of one of these dinners, Proust had distributed lavish rewards to all the waiters who had served him, he suddenly beckoned to a boy who had been watching the proceedings. 'Come, Marcel,' said one of the guests. 'He's done nothing for us.' 'Never mind,' came the answer, 'he looked so sad standing there seeing what the others were getting.'

In spite of these tributes, when we consider the different portraits of the man which have come down to us, we feel that there is something missing, something which eludes us, a gap between Proust and his book. Can this gentle suffering recluse, this generous and warm-hearted if exacting friend, really be the same person who wrote those extraordinary accounts of jealousy and vice? Can there be any connection between him and the exasperating hero of the novel who seems bent on torturing himself and his friends with his horrifying suspicions, who employs friends and servants to spy on his mistress and who finally nags her into suicide?

The glimpses that we have of Proust sometimes remind us of the manner in which he presents his own characters. We have the impression that we are turning over the pages of a family album, glancing at the faded photographs of the novelist at different periods of his life. There are gaps in the collection. We see him clearly enough at the age of fifteen sitting at Mme Straus's feet and again at the age of twenty; but the later pictures, instead of being clearer, are more conventional. Then we come across this:

Illness had profoundly changed him. His face was pale, the ends of his moustache were of unequal length. His nose had a pinched appearance, his cheeks were sunken and his eyes more brilliant. When he was not in bed, he received his visitors in a snuff-coloured dressing-gown. He felt the cold more than ever and wore strips of cotton wool over his shirt collar, cotton gloves on his hands and woollen slippers on his feet. His fumigating apparatus gave out a suffocating smell. He looked like some fabulous necromancer in his laboratory. The dead whom he raised were people whom he had known and whom he brought back to life in his novel.[1]

It is still the portrait of the recluse, but by using the word 'necromancer' Proust's biographer has, probably without realizing it, introduced a fresh and slightly sinister impression. Another observer actually uses the word 'sinister'.

I see again that sinister room in the Rue Hamelin, that black hearth, that bed with an overcoat for a blanket, that waxen mask out of which you would have said that our host was watching us eat and of which only the hair seemed to be alive. . . . Proust seemed already to be more than half engaged in the realm of non-being, turning into that enormous, proliferating mushroom which was nourished by his own substance, by his work—*Le Temps retrouvé*.[2]

The impression is confirmed by two other accounts of Proust written towards the end of his life:

From time to time he strokes the sides of his nose with the edge of a hand which appears dead, whose fingers are oddly stiff and extended. Nothing is more striking than this clumsy, insane gesture which seems like the movement of an animal or a madman.[3]

His face is fixed like a mask against the wall as though refusing to allow the soft, fallen features and the eyes circled by the vampire of solitude to be reflected in the mirrors. When he stood up, his shirt front and dress coat gave him the appearance of a dead man propped upright in his coffin. Without appearing to see anything, was he ramming everything down into his laboratory of decomposition?[4]

M. Buchet describes these as the portraits of a 'monster', but the term needs qualifying.

I seemed to discover in the cruelties of the man [wrote Maurice Sachs] the cruelties of the child and to understand that the whole of *A la Recherche du temps perdu* is the work of a sort of child-monster whose mind possessed the whole of man's experience and whose soul was only ten years old.

There is something monstrous about the man which is reflected in the more sombre parts of the novel, but we are somehow aware of the *enfant-monstre* behind it. Proust was almost a dual personality. The gentle suffering

[1] Pierre-Quint, *Marcel Proust: sa vie, son œuvre* (Paris, 1935).

[2] François Mauriac, *Du Côté de chez Proust* (Paris, 1947), pp. 41-2.

[3] André Gide, *Journal*, p. 694.

[4] Clifford Barney in a letter quoted by Édmond Buchet, *Écrivains intelligents du XXe siècle* (Paris, 1945), p. 41.

recluse was real, but so was the unsavoury being who haunted the slaughter-houses in the hope of seeing a calf killed, who would have rats pricked with hatpins in his presence and who indulged in other peculiarities which will be discussed in their proper place.

Swann was published by Grasset at the author's expense in 1913 and attracted little attention. Proust went on working on his novel throughout the war, but published nothing more until Swann was reissued by Gallimard in 1917. A l'Ombre des jeunes filles en fleurs followed in 1918 and was awarded the Prix Goncourt the next year. This was the beginning of Proust's gloire. In spite of a good deal of detraction, particularly in his own country, he became almost overnight a European celebrity.

Le Côté de Guermantes and the first part of Sodome et Gomorrhe appeared in 1920. The second part of Sodome et Gomorrhe came out in 1922 and was the last part of the novel to be published during its author's lifetime. He died on 18 November 1922. La Prisonnière was published in 1923, Albertine disparue in 1925, and Le Temps retrouvé in 1927.

To most of us Proust's life must appear depressing and in some ways repellent. Yet artistically there is a curious rightness about it. We have the impression that everything in it conspired to help him to write the book which he had been born to write, transforming this life into what M. Sartre would call a 'destiny'. He enjoyed the economic independence which was essential to the writing of that particular book. Whatever the causes of his mysterious illness, that too was essential to the undertaking; and his parents died at exactly the right time. In 1905 he was already fully conscious of his vocation, had amassed a great deal of material for the novel and was ready to begin writing it. He realized, however, that his parents would have been profoundly grieved by its content, and if they had lived his affection for them might very well have led him to postpone the start until it was too late.

III. A LA RECHERCHE DU TEMPS PERDU

1. Structure

WHEN we look up at the sixteen volumes of A la Recherche du temps perdu standing in a row on our shelves, their white covers worn and tattered or neatly bound in yellow buckram, we find ourselves wondering what Proust wrote about, what he was trying to do, what sort of a book this is and what is its 'message'.

We know that he brought 'a new vision' to the novel, but this recognition is only the first step in the exploration of his work. There have been plenty of attempts to define his aims and genius, some provided by the novelist himself or by his narrator and others by his critics: 'The story of an invisible vocation.' 'A new sensibility.' 'Analysis pushed to the point at which it becomes creative.' 'An intimate diary.' 'The views, the generalizations of the most *penetrating* moralist who has ever existed in literature.' 'The book is written in the form of a novel, but it belongs rather to the category of memoirs.' 'Situated half-way between the novel and memoirs, the population of Proust's world belongs to both.' 'The memoirs of Saint-Simon of another period.'[1]

It is a tribute to the richness and variety of Proust's work that all these definitions contain a measure of truth and that, with two possible exceptions, they do not contradict one another. Yet it must be confessed that when we first approach it, the novel presents an appearance of considerable confusion. It opens with the narrator's recollections of his childhood at Combray, switches towards the close of the first volume to a long account of Swann's love affair with Odette de Crécy which took place before the narrator was born; returns in volume three to his childhood memories and his first love affair with Swann's daughter Gilberte, and describes a seaside holiday at Balbec where he meets Albertine Simonet and the *jeunes filles en fleurs*. Two volumes are devoted to the Guermantes family and to Marcel's infatuation for the Duchess, three more to the world of the homosexuals and the love affair with Albertine.[2] At the end of *Sodome et Gomorrhe* his attention is largely concentrated on Albertine. Her death and his jealousy occupy four more volumes. *Le Temps retrouvé* deals with the changes that have taken place in society since the war and with the theory of art which underlies the whole work. All through the sixteen volumes there are elaborate accounts of dinner parties, receptions and the life of the 'worldlings'.

The principal difficulty is to discover the connection between the brilliant social life and the private love affairs of the individuals which are described with an even greater wealth of detail.

Proust's critics have been very conscious of the difficulty. It was fashionable at one time—particularly among critics writing before publication of the novel was complete—to pretend that it was formless, was as loosely constructed as Saint-Simon's Memoirs and its content determined by the evolution of the society in which it was written.[3] When *Le Temps retrouvé* appeared, opinion swung to the other extreme and we were invited to admire the extraordinary artistry of the book's construction.

---

[1] The authors of these comments are Proust, Middleton Murry, Conrad, Pierre Abraham, Mauriac, Albert Feuillerat, Pierre Abraham, Proust.

[2] In future I shall refer to the narrator as Marcel.

[3] Some of the most discerning, however, liked Benjamin Crémieux and Pierre-Quint, foretold that a plan would emerge when publication was complete.

A further change of opinion occurred in 1934 when M. Albert Feuillerat published a book called *Comment Marcel Proust a composé son roman*. When he first planned his novel, Proust intended it to be complete in two volumes of six or seven hundred pages each, but the work swelled to such proportions that it actually contains over four thousand pages and would almost certainly have been much longer had he lived.[1] It is well known that he practically re-wrote large parts of it in proof. M. Feuillerat succeeded in examining proofs of the early volumes and compared them with the published text. He argued that Proust's revisions, which sometimes involved substantial alterations in the personality of his characters and other inconsistencies, completely disrupted the classic proportions of the original plan and destroyed the unity of tone and atmosphere which is one of the most remarkable and attractive qualities of *Swann*. There was also a pronounced change of style. M. Feuillerat, indeed, speaks of two distinct styles. There is the poetic, evocative style of *Swann* and the intellectual, analytical style of the later volumes in which, significantly, phrases like *Je sentis* are replaced by *Je compris*, in which direct experience is overlaid or interlarded with the wisdom and reflections of a lifetime, is interspersed with treatises and maxims on life, love and art which are worthy of the greatest moralists. This gives them an extraordinary richness, but it also confuses the reader. For he is never sure whether Marcel is a boy or a man, and a good many incidents which clearly belong to childhood are accompanied by reflections which could only have been made by a grown man with a wealth of worldly experience behind him.

When he came to draw up his balance sheet, M. Feuillerat decided that though there had undoubtedly been considerable loss, it was outweighed by the gain. It was these changes, however, which made him conclude that the finished work should be described as memoirs rather than as a novel.

The book is certainly an outstanding contribution to the study of Proust, but it seems to me that M. Feuillerat goes further than is warranted by the facts. There are undoubtedly inconsistencies, but the main alterations in the personality of the characters were very far from being fortuitous. They sprang from the novelist's theory of the immense difficulty of ever knowing another person.[2] Nor was Proust's method of composition altogether as haphazard as M. Feuillerat seems to suggest. In a letter written to Paul Souday in 1922, he could declare that the novel was so 'meticulously composed' that the last chapter of the last volume was written immediately after the first chapter of the first volume. The truth is that Proust was not a writer who produced 'social criticism', a sociological treatise or memoirs in the

---

[1] The estimate varied. See *Correspondance générale*, IV, pp. 39–41.

[2] See the very interesting letter in *Lettres de Marcel Proust à Bibesco* (La Guilde du Livre, Lausanne, 1949), pp. 175–7. (This book was originally issued to members of a Swiss book society and was not available to the general public when this was written. I am indebted to Mr. Harold Nicolson for his kindness in lending me his copy.)

form of a novel; he succeeded, as practically no other novelist has done, in *combining* the methods as well as the findings of the novelist and the memoir-writer. His characters do, as Abraham suggested, belong to the world of both and this makes him unique among twentieth-century novelists.

Although we must concede that the later volumes do not possess the formal beauty of *Swann* or its strange, haunting poetry, this should not prevent us from doing justice to the skilful construction of the first two volumes. For they are as carefully and elaborately constructed as Joyce's *Ulysses*. 'It is so complex,' said Proust himself, 'that its meaning will not be revealed until all the themes have begun to combine.' The word 'theme' is an important one. The construction of the book is largely musical and Mr. Edmund Wilson has well described the famous first sentence—'Longtemps, je me suis couché de bonne heure'—as the opening chord in a vast symphony. In the first three pages, Proust refers to nearly all the principal 'themes' of the book: childhood, memory, time, love, music, art, sleep, society, the historic France. In these first two volumes each of the principal themes is picked up again, isolated, examined, dropped, then taken up again in the later volumes and 'combined'. The description of the magic lantern, with Golo advancing towards the castle of Geneviève de Brabant, at the beginning of *Swann*, looks at first like a random childhood memory, but it turns out to be a complex image which keeps on recurring.[1] It introduces the Guermantes who, as we are told later in the book, were descended from Geneviève de Brabant. It also introduces the theme of the 'prisoner' and appears to be the first direct reference to art. It thus prepares the way for the famous incident of the *madeleine* which marks the end of the 'Overture' and the beginning of the symphony proper. In the volumes which follow Marcel's experience in eating the *madeleine* is frequently referred to and compared with similar experiences; in *Le Temps retrouvé* the experience is finally and fully analysed. It is in *Swann*, too, that we first hear the *petite phrase* of Vinteuil's sonata which becomes the *air national* first of Swann's love for Odette, then of Marcel's for Albertine.[2] The incident of Vinteuil's daughter and her friend is suddenly and apparently gratuitously introduced, but Montjouvain becomes the symbol of the homosexual relationships which occupy so much of the book and might almost be described as the entrance to the cities of the plain. When we reach the end of the second volume of *Swann*, we see that it had to come where it does because Swann suspects Odette of homosexuality as Marcel later suspects Albertine.

Un Amour de Swann sometimes appears to be an admirable short novel

---

[1] It turns up, significantly, as we shall see, at the end of *Le Temps retrouvé*.

[2] In one of his letters Proust tells us that Vinteuil's sonata, in which the *petite phrase* occurs, was based among other works on a sonata of Saint-Saens' for piano and violin, a prelude of Wagner's, a sonata of Franck's and a *ballade* of Fauré's. (*Lettres de Marcel Proust à Bibesco*, pp. 153–154.)

which has little to do with the rest of the book, but Proust himself was careful to draw attention to the parallel between Swann's affair with Odette and the coming one between Marcel and Albertine. One critic has declared that Swann is Proust's Jewish and Marcel his Catholic side, but I suspect that the connection is deeper than that.[1] The story of Swann's liaison is used partly to cover the period preceding Marcel's birth, but its main purpose is to facilitate Proust's peculiar angle of vision. For Swann is in a sense the base of the pyramid. Proust tells, from an objective point of view, the story of a cultured man of the world in society and shows how he allows a love affair with a courtesan to cut him off from his own circle. He follows Odette into the narrower circle of the Verdurins' *petit clan*, is eventually ostracized by them and driven back into himself. In the case of Marcel and Albertine the story is re-told from a subjective point of view, or rather re-told from inside at much greater length and with much greater wealth of detail. For Marcel's pursuit of Albertine takes him through the narrowing circles of the cities of the plain until he, too, finds himself alone in his room brooding over the infidelities of his dead mistress as Swann had brooded over the connection between Odette and Forcheville long after he had ceased to love her. With Marcel and Albertine the focus shifts from society to the effect of love on the individual. The feeling that we are approaching the top of the spiral or the pyramid from inside explains the peculiar sense of oppressiveness, of life unfolding and feelings evolving with greater and greater intensity in a smaller and smaller physical space.

I have spoken of the apparent difficulty of perceiving the connection between the personal lives of Proust's characters and the social life which occupies so much of their time. A glance at the definitions of his genius shows that the list divides into two groups. One stresses the personal, the other the social element in his experience; and his critics do tend as a rule to give slightly greater prominence to one or other of these factors. The novelist himself avoided doing so. Marcel describes the novel as 'the story of an invisible vocation'; but he also calls it 'the memoirs of Saint-Simon of another period'; and unless we realize that it is both, we shall not appreciate it to the full. It is, indeed, the story of an artistic vocation, but of a vocation which manifested itself at a particular moment of history in a particular society and which tempts me to call it the vocation of the twentieth-century artist. Now you cannot have an artistic vocation without a subject, and the evolution of society is just as much Proust's subject as Swann's love affair with Odette de Crécy or Marcel's with Albertine.

[1] Marcel speaks of 'ce premier Swann dans lequel je retrouve les erreurs charmantes de ma jeunesse'. 'We know,' writes Spitzer, 'that Swann is nothing but a variant of the narrator (*eine Variante des erzählenden Ich*).'

In Proust's world—a world in which, significantly, religion has no place —art represents the spiritual element and society what Fernandez calls 'a sort of counter-spirituality'. Thus we are told that Albertine and Andrée symbolized 'the incapacity of people of the world to make a valid judgment in intellectual matters'. And the thing that wrecked Mme de Villeparisis's social position was not her liaison with M. de Norpois; it was, says Proust, her intelligence, 'an intelligence which was almost that of a writer of the second order far more than that of a woman of the world'. Proust used the word 'vocation', and he meant exactly what he said. The novel describes the conflict between a genuine vocation and a series of false vocations represented by social life, love and friendship. This helps us to grasp the full significance of Swann. The contrast between Marcel and Swann is not confined to their love affairs. Marcel's vocation is a true one: Swann is the 'socialite', the dilettante who is always going to write that book on Vermeer—Proust's 'favourite painter'—and dies without doing so. And as the story unfolds we come to see that Swann belongs to the past, that he is submerged in 'lost time' while Marcel moves forward by virtue of his vocation towards 'time regained' which is identified with *la vraie vie*.

2. *The Memoirs of Saint-Simon of Another Period*

It is one of the inherent difficulties of Proust's conception of time that all the events in his book seem to take place on the same plane and that we have practically no sense of succession. When we reach *Le Temps retrouvé*, we realize with a shock that all the characters have suddenly changed, have become old, battered and semi-idiotic. Yet the book is a study of French society from 1880 to 1919 or, as Crémieux put it, it is an essay on the transformation of that society. The word 'transformation' is important. The society which Proust describes is in no sense static; it is in a perpetual state of evolution, and his greatness does not consist least in the way in which he shows the connection between the changes in manners, sensibility and human relationships. Elstir, whose art is analysed in a masterly passage, stands for Impressionism or the 'new painting', Vinteuil for the 'new music'. Berma, the celebrated actress, and Bergotte do not stand merely for the 'old' and the 'new' literature, but for the continuity between them. Proust is at pains to underline this continuity by making Berma play Phèdre and Bergotte write a book on Racine and by the innumerable references in the novel to the French classics, particularly to Mme de Sévigné, Saint-Simon, Racine and the great nineteenth-century authors, who are seen to be a living force.[1]

[1] M. Feuillerat shows that Bergotte is one of the characters who underwent 'revision' in a very unfavourable sense. He suggests that when the character was first invented Proust had in

The same is true in less exalted spheres. 'He introduces into his work all the novelties of the period,' said Crémieux: 'modern military theories, the telephone, the motor-car . . . with the result that it assumes the appearance of a *summa* of French life.'

These are what may be called the *grandes lignes* of Proust's work and we need to keep them constantly in mind in reading him.

We are inclined to think of him exclusively as the historian of the aristocracy and the upper classes. The society of *A la Recherche du temps perdu* certainly seems strange and remote from our own preoccupations. There is not a sentence in the book to suggest that economic problems even exist or that, with the exception of an ageing courtesan, anyone could possibly have *ennuis d'argent*. In an age of department stores, we feel inclined to rub our eyes when we read of Swann's birthday present of fruit to the Princesse de Parme. He was not, we are told, very experienced in choosing fruit and asked a cousin of his mother's to do it for him. She explains with pride that she did not buy all the fruit from the same shop, but from different shops each specializing in a particular fruit—the grapes from Crapote, the strawberries from Jauret and the pears from Chevet.

It is these things which gave rise to the legend that Proust was a snob who only knew one section of society. Nothing could be further from the truth. He had good reasons for concentrating on the Faubourg Saint-Germain:

> Whether we like it or not [wrote Ramon Fernandez] as soon as a society is formed in France, whatever the rank and ideas of its members, it reproduces the characteristics in a more or less modified form and more or less caricatured of the society of the Faubourg Saint-Germain which it sometimes claims like the members of the *petit clan* to despise. . . . In order to acquire a social sense . . . it is therefore opportune to frequent the milieu which provides the key and the syntax of fashionable social life. . . . The frequentation of the Faubourg Saint-Germain enables us to reconstruct in their true perspective and their hierarchy all the French *salons* including Jupien's shop and the concierge's flat.

Proust does indeed see French society as a hierarchy with the Faubourg Saint-Germain at the top imposing its pattern on society as a whole. The salons themselves form a hierarchy within this hierarchy which begins with Mme Verdurin, the symbol of the vulgar aggressive middle class which emerged from the industrial revolution, goes on to Mme de Saint-Euverte, then to the Duchesse de Guermantes and reaches the pinnacle with the Princesse de Guermantes. It is not difficult to see that Proust's picture is by no means a favourable one. This is how he describes the Duc de Guermantes:

mind Anatole France who had, as we know, written a Preface for *Les Plaisirs et les jours*, and that he modified it because his subsequent relations with that writer were a good deal less cordial.

. . . dans les manières de M. de Guermantes, homme attendrissant de gentillesse et révoltant de dureté, esclave des plus petites obligations et délié des pactes les plus sacrés, je retrouve encore intacte après plus de deux siècles écoulés cette déviation particulière à la vie de cour sous Louis XIV et qui transporte les scrupules de conscience du domaine des affections et de la moralité aux questions de pure forme.

[. . . in the manners of M. de Guermantes, a man who melted one's heart by his courtesy and revolted it by his harshness, I found still intact after the lapse of more than two centuries that deviation typical of court life under Louis XIV which transfers all scruples of conscience from matters of the affections and morality and applies them to purely formal questions.]

It is a criticism not simply of an individual or even of a period, but of the representative of an ancient line whose weaknesses are at least as old as its fame. In this world Marcel's grandmother and his mother are certainly intended to represent genuine human values—the values of decency, kindness and uprightness—in contrast to the 'socialites'; and there is no mistaking the writer's intention when the woman who keeps the public lavatory in the Champs-Elysées speaks to the grandmother of 'my salon', and emphasizes the care with which the 'guests' are chosen; or again when the Duke and Duchess give the dying Swann his congé because the Duke suddenly discovers that his wife is wearing the wrong-coloured shoes which she must change at once or they will be late for somebody's soirée.

The working classes and the peasantry are not studied with the same minute care as the aristocracy, but they are undeniably there and they play an important part in the construction of the novel. Françoise, the old servant, stands as surely as Molière's servants for the robust common sense of the peasants and she fits into the background of the feudal France which is constantly evoked. There are moments when she is expressing her disapproval of Albertine in which she reminds us of the *confidents* of the classical tragedians who warn their masters and mistresses against some hazardous undertaking. This does not mean that Proust merely provides glimpses of the different strata of society. One writer has used the expression 'human flora' to describe his approach and the society which he portrays is seen as a living organism. The close relations between the different strata are suggested by his fondness for metaphors drawn from natural science, geology and above all from botany which give the impression of human solidarity, of an immensely complex network of social relationships. This impression is heightened by Proust's flair—it was helped by his prodigious memory and his histrionic gifts—for the peculiarities of speech which belong not merely to the different classes, but to people in the different subdivisions of those classes.

It is time now to examine some concrete examples of Proust's method.

We know that Rivière regarded him as the heir of the classical tradition
and Mr. Edmund Wilson as the first important novelist to apply the principles of Symbolism in fiction. The account of Swann's visit to Mme de
Saint-Euverte's is an illustration not merely of the way in which he blends
classicism and Symbolism, but of the way in which the methods of the
classical dramatist are adapted to criticize contemporary society. Proust
reveals himself as a master of social comedy and the emphasis on word and
gesture is used to balance his subjectivism. Swann arrives somewhat late for
the party:

> . . . pour la première fois il remarqua, réveillée par l'arrivée inopinée d'un invité
> aussi tardif, la meute éparse, magnifique et désœuvrée de grands valets de pied qui
> dormaient çà et là sur des banquettes et des coffres et qui, soulevant leurs nobles
> profils aigus de lévriers, se dressèrent et, rassemblés, formèrent le cercle autour
> de lui.

> [. . . he now noticed, for the first time, roused by the unexpected arrival of so
> belated a guest, the scattered pack of splendid effortless animals, the enormous
> footmen who were drowsing here and there upon benches and chests, until, point-
> ing their noble greyhound profiles, they towered upon their feet and gathered in
> a circle round about him.]

The writing is deliberately stylized. The tone recalls the 'heroic comedies'
of the seventeenth century with its ironic contrast between 'la meute éparse,
magnifique et désœuvrée' and 'leurs nobles profils aigus de lévriers'. For
Proust works at two contrasted levels. We are conscious at once of the
surface décor, the *magnifique*, *désœuvrée* and *nobles*, and the animals underneath. The impression we have is like that of a circus, but a circus with
'human' animals. Nor should we miss the significance of the 'greyhounds'
crowding in on the belated guest and forming a slightly oppressive circle
round him as though he were a vanquished 'prey'; it is intended to bring
out the peculiar atmosphere of the salons which is at once perceptible to
Swann. The allusion is continued in the brilliantly comic passage which
follows:

> L'un d'eux, d'aspect particulièrement féroce et assez semblable à l'exécuteur
> dans certains tableaux de la Renaissance qui figurent des supplices, s'avança vers lui
> d'un air implacable pour lui prendre ses affaires. Mais la dureté de son regard d'acier
> était compensée par la douceur de ses gants de fil, si bien qu'en approchant de
> Swann il semblait témoigner du mépris pour sa personne et des égards pour son
> chapeau.

> [One of them, of a particularly ferocious aspect, and not unlike the headsman
> in certain Renaissance pictures which represent executions, tortures, and the like,
> advanced upon him with an implacable air to take his 'things'. But the harshness

of his steely glare was compensated by the softness of his cotton gloves, so effectively that, as he approached Swann, he seemed to be exhibiting at once an utter
contempt for his person and the most tender regard for his hat.]

The comic greyhounds lead naturally to the comic executioner. It is
characteristic of Swann's mode of thought that he always sees life in terms
of art and it is, perhaps, the secret cause of his ineffectualness. There is an
undercurrent of disillusionment here which looks forward to the moment
when, mounting the elaborate staircase, Swann will tell himself that he is
entering a world from which Odette is excluded. The footman is an
'executioner' because he is felt to be the person who divides Swann from
Odette. The masterly final sentence stresses the importance which the world
he is entering attaches to externals and its disregard for the serious, human
feelings which are the source of Swann's distress.

> A quelques pas, un grand gaillard en livrée rêvait, immobile, sculptural, inutile,
> comme ce guerrier purement décoratif qu'on voit dans les tableaux le plus tumul-
> tueux de Mantegna, songer, appuyé sur son bouclier, tandis qu'on se précipite et
> qu'on s'égorge à côté de lui.

> [A few feet away, a strapping great lad in livery stood musing, motionless,
> statuesque, useless, like that purely decorative warrior whom one sees in the most
> tumultuous of Mantegna's paintings, lost in dreams, leaning upon his shield, while
> all around him are fighting, bloodshed and death.]

As Swann begins to mount the staircase which leads up to the rooms
where the reception is being held, the prose takes on a ceremonial, ritual
tone. The words *immobile, sculptural, inutile* stress once again the uselessness
and the artificiality of social life which is contrasted with the 'tumultuous'
life of the emotions. For everything depends on weight and size:

> D'autres encore, colossaux aussi, se tenaient sur les degrés d'un escalier monu-
> mental que leur présence décorative et leur immobilité marmoréenne auraient pu
> faire nommer comme celui du Palais Ducal 'l'Escalier des Géants' et dans lequel
> Swann s'engagea avec la tristesse de penser qu'Odette ne l'avait jamais gravi.

> [Others again, no less colossal, were disposed upon the steps of a monumental
> staircase which, by their decorative presence and marmorean immobility, was
> made worthy to be named, like the god-crowned ascent in the Palace of the Doges,
> the 'Staircase of the Giants', and on which Swann now set foot, saddened by the
> thought that Odette had never climbed it.]

The point is driven home when we learn, a page or two later, that the
expensive, liveried servants do not form part of the hostess's normal establishment, but are simply engaged for the evening in the hope that her recep-

tion will make the right impression on the condescending aristocrats who look in for a few moments.

Swann thinks longingly of another staircase and another world which are less splendid but more real than this:

> Ah! avec quelle joie au contraire il eût grimpé les étages noirs, malodorants et casse-cou de la petite couturière retirée, dans le 'cinquième' de laquelle il aurait été si heureux de payer plus cher qu'une avant-scène hebdomadaire à l'Opéra le droit de passer la soirée quand Odette venait. . . .

> [Ah, with what joy would he, on the other hand, have raced up the dark, evil-smelling, breakneck flights to the little dressmaker's, in whose attic he would so gladly have paid the price of a weekly stage-box at the Opera for the right to spend the evening there when Odette came. . . .]

The extreme virtuosity of the writing is admirably maintained:

> Parvenu en haut de l'escalier . . . Swann passa devant un bureau où des valets, assis comme des notaires devant de grands registres, se levèrent et inscrivirent son nom.
>
> Il ne restait plus à Swann qu'à pénétrer dans la salle du concert dont un huissier chargé de chaînes lui ouvrit les portes, en s'inclinant, comme il lui aurait remis les clefs d'une ville.

> [Coming to the top of the staircase . . . Swann passed by an office in which the lackeys, seated like notaries before their massive registers, rose solemnly to their feet and inscribed his name.
>
> Swann had now only to enter the concert-room, the doors of which were thrown open to him by an usher loaded with chains, who bowed low before him as though tendering to him the keys of a conquered city.]

The point of the story is still to come. The elaborate ceremonial is finished at last. The doors open and this is what Swann sees:

> Swann retrouva rapidement le sentiment de la laideur masculine, quand, au delà de la tenture de tapisserie, au spectacle des domestiques, succéda celui des invités.

> [He speedily recovered his sense of the general ugliness of the human male when, on the other side of the tapestry curtain, the spectacle of the servants gave place to that of the guests.]

The 'ugliness' of the guests is a symbol of moral corruption and the ceremonial which leads up to the discovery is aimed at displaying their worthless, frivolous lives.

Proust makes brilliant use of the impressionist method when he goes on to describe the different monocles worn by the men:

. . . le monocle du général, resté entre ses paupières comme un éclat d'obus dans sa figure vulgaire, balafrée et triomphale, au milieu du front qu'il éborgnait comme l'œil unique du cyclope, apparut à Swann comme une blessure monstrueuse qu'il pouvait être glorieux d'avoir reçue, mais qu'il était indécent d'exhiber. . . .

[. . . the General's monocle, stuck like a shell-splinter in his common, scarred, victorious, overbearing face, in the middle of a forehead which it left half-blinded, like the single-eyed flashing front of the Cyclops, appeared to Swann as a monstrous wound which it might have been glorious to receive but which it was certainly not decent to expose. . . .]

The allusion to the Cyclops suggests that all these people are 'one-eyed'. Then the novelist turns on the *romancier mondain*

qui venait d'installer au coin de son œil un monocle, son seul organe d'investigation psychologique et d'impitoyable analyse.

Le monocle du marquis de Forestelle était minuscule, n'avait aucune bordure et obligeant à une crispation incessante et douloureuse l'œil où il s'incrustait comme un cartilage superflu dont la présence est inexplicable et la matière recherchée. . . .

. . . M. de Palancy qui avec sa grosse tête de carpe aux yeux ronds, se déplaçait lentement au milieu des fêtes, en desservant d'instant en instant ses mandibules comme pour chercher son orientation, avait l'air de transporter seulement avec lui un fragment accidentel, et peut-être purement symbolique du vitrage de son aquarium. . . .

[who had just fitted into the angle of eyebrow and cheek his own monocle, the sole instrument that he used in his psychological investigations and remorseless analyses of character.

The Marquis de Forestelle's monocle was minute and rimless, and, by enforcing an incessant and painful contraction of the eye over which it was encrusted like a superfluous cartilage, the presence of which there was inexplicable and its substance unimaginable. . . .

. . . M. de Palancy, who with his huge carp's head and goggling eyes moved slowly up and down the stream of festive gatherings, unlocking his great mandibles at every moment as though in search of his orientation, had the air of carrying about upon his person only an accidental and perhaps purely symbolical fragment of the glass wall of his aquarium. . . .]

The description of M. de Palancy is a reference back to the 'greyhounds', but the comparison is all in favour of the servants with their *nobles profils aigus*. It is not simply that his monocle reminds us of an aquarium; the whole building is suddenly seen as an aquarium in which hideous fish circle round and round, hopelessly shut off from *la vraie vie*. For in this scene Proust accomplishes two things. He makes us feel that through his liaison with Odette Swann's old milieu has become strange and foreign to him; but we also see that its strangeness and unpleasantness, which Swann perceives for the first time, are real.

From this we must turn to a remarkable passage in *Le Temps retrouvé*:

Ainsi, dans le faubourg Saint-Germain, ces positions en apparence imprenables du duc et de la duchesse de Guermantes, du baron de Charlus avaient perdu leur inviolabilité, comme toutes choses changent en ce monde, par l'action d'un principe intérieur auquel on n'avait pas pensé, chez M. de Charlus l'amour de Charlie qui l'avait rendu esclave des Verdurin, puis le ramollissement, chez Mme de Guermantes, un goût de nouveauté et d'art, chez M. de Guermantes un amour exclusif comme il en avait déjà eu de pareils dans sa vie que la faiblesse de l'âge rendait plus tyrannique. . . .

[Thus, in the Faubourg Saint-Germain, the positions in appearance impregnable of the Duc and Duchesse de Guermantes, of the Baron de Charlus had lost their inviolability, as everything changes in this world by the action of an interior principle to which no one had given thought—with M. de Charlus the love of Charlie, which had made him the slave of the Verdurins, then a softening of the brain, with Mme de Guermantes a taste for novelty and art, with M. de Guermantes an exclusive love of a kind of which he had already known similar examples in his life and which age had rendered more tyrannical. . . .][1]

In the account of Swann's visit to Mme de Saint-Euverte's Proust uses the method of the *novelist* to expose the corruption of high society; in the passage from *Le Temps retrouvé* he is deliberately using the method of the *memoir-writer* to sum up the decline and fall of the exclusive world of the Faubourg Saint-Germain.[2]

The last passage is a lucid statement of Proust's aims as a social critic. He records the disintegration of the old aristocracy, the invasion of the Faubourg Saint-Germain by the bourgeoisie and the beginning of the general levelling down between all classes which followed the First World War. His novel is, indeed, the account of an immense *déclassement* which is the result—this is the important point—of 'the action of an interior principle' and which has some unusual features.[3]

The world to which we are introduced at the beginning of the novel is as rigidly organized as the world of the *ancien régime*, is in fact a survival of feudal times.

The bourgeois [writes Proust in the first chapter of *Swann*] considered society as though it were composed of closed castes where everyone, as soon as he was born, found himself assigned to the same rank as that occupied by his parents.

---

[1] My translation.

[2] Compare: 'Proust exaggerates to the point of improbability this vision of the reversal of values and takes the same malign pleasure, displays the same vindictive insistence in smirching the social purity of this world that he brought to the denunciation of the silliness and selfishness of the Guermantes.' (Feuillerat.)

[3] 'Ce qui caractérisait le plus cette société, c'était sa prodigieuse aptitude au déclassement' (*Le Temps retrouvé*, II, p. 137.)

Any attempt to move out of one's sphere, whether upwards or downwards, was regarded with the utmost disapproval. The different castes are isolated from one another and know nothing of one another's lives. Marcel's parents have no idea that Swann, whom they patronize, is an intimate friend of the Prince of Wales, and when something of the truth leaks out, they regard his social activities with a mixture of incredulity and disapproval. The contrast between 'Swann's way' and the 'Guermantes' way' is intentional; they stand for two different social spheres which are normally shut off from one another and which lie in 'opposite directions':

For there were, in the environs of Combray, two 'ways' which we used to take for our walks, and so diametrically opposed that we would actually leave the house by a different door, according to the way we had chosen: the way towards Méséglise-la-Vineuse, which we called also 'Swann's way', because to get there, one had to pass along the boundary of M. Swann's estate, and the 'Guermantes way'. Of Méséglise-la-Vineuse, to tell the truth, I never knew anything more than the way there, and the strange people who would come over on Sundays to take the air in Combray. . . . As for Guermantes, I was to know it well enough one day, but that day had still to come; and, during the whole of my boyhood, if Méséglise was to me something as inaccessible as the horizon, which remained hidden from sight, however far one went, by the folds of a country which no longer bore the least resemblance to the country round Combray; Guermantes, on the other hand, meant no more than the ultimate goal, ideal rather than real, of the 'Guermantes way', a sort of abstract geographical term like the North Pole or the Equator. And so to 'take the Guermantes way' in order to get to Méséglise, or vice versa, would have seemed to me as nonsensical a proceeding as to turn to the east in order to reach the west. . . .

But, above all, I set between them, far more distinctly than the mere distance in miles and yards and inches which separated one from the other, the distance that there was between the two parts of my brain in which I used to think of them, one of those distances of the mind which time serves only to lengthen, which separate things irremediably from one another, keeping them for ever on separate planes. And this distinction was rendered still more absolute because the habit we had of never going both ways on the same day, or in the course of the same walk, but the 'Méséglise way' one time and the 'Guermantes way' another, shut them up, so to speak, far apart and unaware of each other's existence, in the sealed vessels—between which there could be no communication—of separate afternoons.

When we had decided to go the 'Méséglise way' we would start (without undue haste, and even if the sky were clouded over, since the walk was not very long, and did not take us too far from home), as though we were not going anywhere in particular, by the front door of my aunt's house, which opened on to the Rue du Saint-Esprit. . . .

If the 'Méséglise way' was so easy, it was a very different matter when we took the 'Guermantes way', for that meant a long walk, and we must make sure, first, of the weather.

These passages illustrate the care with which Proust originally planned his novel. 'Swann's way' is easy because people are moving in their own social sphere; the difficulty and distance of 'Guermantes' way' look forward to the 'impregnable positions' which fall in the last volume. Social distances are expressed here in terms of spatial distances, but they are also seen to involve 'mental' distances 'which separate things irremediably from one another' and lives which are so different that they might be enclosed 'in sealed vessels'.

It is true that, as Crémieux suggests, these distances are finally overcome and the book closes with the fusion of the Guermantes and Swann worlds, but Proust's interpretation is a subtle one. He is not interested merely in one form of *déclassement* which belongs to a particular epoch, but in something much older and much more complex. For society is not divided simply into the aristocracy, the bourgeoisie and the *peuple*. Within the main social classes, we detect a tendency to form other groups. We read of the Verdurins' *petit noyau*, *petit clan*, *petit groupe*, as we read of the *bande* of the *jeunes filles en fleurs*. These groups are the reverse of the natural groups like the family— we are told of Mme Verdurin that 'elle haïssait les familles (ce dissolvant du petit noyau)'—and they have their 'orthodoxy' and their 'faithful'. In order to belong to the Verdurins, 'one thing was sufficient, but it was necessary: a tacit assent to a *credo* . . . the Verdurins felt . . . that this spirit of inquiry and the demon of frivolity might through contagion prove fatal to the orthodoxy of the little church. . . .'

The Verdurins' orthodoxy rests on snobbery, but there is a much more potent factor at work in the other groups. The overmastering interest which transcends the ordinary class-distinctions and which is responsible for the formation of the 'band' of *jeunes filles* is the sexual connection whether in its normal or its abnormal form. We can say therefore that one of the principal themes of Proust's novel is not merely a *déclassement*, but a *déclassement* in which the sexual factor is either the agent of destruction or the means of social advancement.

Nearly all the main characters have a foot in more than one world, but Swann's position is unusual. For Swann, the connoisseur and the friend of the Prince of Wales, does not owe his position to birth or directly to the fortune amassed by his father on the Stock Exchange. He is the patrician, the intellectual aristocrat who is admitted to the highest circles on account of his intellectual and social gifts. It is in this respect that his position most closely resembles Marcel's, but his race seems to count for something in his ascension. The exclusive caste, which assumes the proportions of an obsession in the book, is characteristic of the Jews, but their rootlessness is a no less pronounced characteristic. Swann mixes with the highest society because he is not attached to the commercial middle class into which he was born by any of the normal social ties, but it is precisely his rootlessness which tempts him to make the return journey, to separate himself from his aristocratic friends for the sake of his taste in women. He shares with Marcel himself a tendency—it is another and a very unpleasant racial characteristic—to regard women as a 'commodity' which has its price:

> ... these were, as often as not, women whose beauty was of a distinctly 'common' type, for the physical qualities which attracted him instinctively, and without reason, were the direct opposite of those that he admired in the women painted or sculptured by his favourite masters. Depth of character, or a melancholy expression on a woman's face would freeze his senses, which would, however, immediately melt at the sight of healthy, abundant, rosy human flesh.

When he stops going to the house of a society friend, she only discovers by accident that she has been 'dropped' when she comes across a letter of farewell to her cook who was the reigning mistress; and in the end he completes his social ruin by marrying Odette.

His daughter, Gilberte, outstrips the triumphs of her father, marries Robert de Saint-Loup and becomes a Guermantes by marriage. Saint-Loup has an extraordinary love affair with a woman named Rachel whom Marcel has met in a brothel. After his marriage he shares the tastes of his aristocratic uncle, Baron de Charlus, and even takes up with the Baron's lower-class 'boy-friend'. Charlus, who must rank as one of the great characters of fiction, is in the same position.

One of the funniest scenes in the book is the evening at the Verdurins when Charlus agrees to bring some of his aristocratic friends. He usurps the functions of his hostess and receives the guests himself. They behave with an insolence which is characteristic of their ancient line and, pointing a finger at the wretched lady of the house, ask: 'Who's that? Is that woman Mme Verdurin?' These social triumphs are not confined to the middle classes. The lift-boy at Balbec confides in Marcel that his sister is well placed with a 'rich gentleman', learns the piano and adopts very peculiar methods of showing her contempt for the class which she has abandoned. The informant goes on to add that the enterprising father has also succeeded in placing his younger brother with an Indian prince where he has embarked on an elegant career as *tapette*. But the greatest *déclassement* of all is reserved for the last volume where we learn with shocked surprise that Mme Verdurin has become by her third marriage—the Princesse de Guermantes. The last, the most 'impregnable' position of all in the Faubourg Saint-Germain has fallen.

We have observed the tendency in Proust's work of society to subdivide into a vast number of sects, groups, cells, clans and bands; and we have also seen that in many cases the common interest which binds them together is sexual, as it certainly is with the *jeunes filles en fleurs*. One of the most curious achievements of the book is the novelist's anatomy of homosexuality. He speaks of the homosexuals as forming

a freemasonry far more extensive, more powerful and less suspected than that of the Lodges, for it rests upon an identity of tastes, needs, habits, dangers, apprenticeship, knowledge, traffic, glossary, and one in which the members themselves, who intend not to know one another, recognize one another immediately by natural or conventional, involuntary or deliberate signs which indicate one of his cogeners to the beggar in the street, in the great nobleman whose carriage door he is shutting, to the father in the suitor for his daughter's hand, to him who has sought healing, absolution, defence, in the doctor, the barrister to whom he has had recourse. . . .

These volumes are a remarkable contribution to sociology. Proust describes with minute care the behaviour, dress and even the peculiar manner of speaking of the homosexuals, giving us the impression of a vast secret society or, to use his own word, a vast 'freemasonry', whose tentacles extend into every corner of society and produce the strangest *déclassements* of all.

When we read of the disreputable diplomat, M. de Vaugoubert:

Ayant passé d'une débauche presque infantile à la continence absolue datant du jour où il avait pensé au quai d'Orsay et voulu faire une grande carrière, il avait l'air d'une bête en cage, jetant dans tous les sens des regards qui exprimaient la peur, l'appétance et la stupidité.

[Having passed from an almost infantile corruption to an absolute continence dating from the day on which his thoughts had turned to the Quai d'Orsay and he had begun to plan a great career for himself, he had the air of a caged animal, casting in every direction glances expressive of fear, appetite and stupidity.]

we might reasonably take it for a piece of social criticism in the manner of Saint-Simon, the master with whom Proust is most often compared. When the same criticism is repeated in slightly different words thirty pages later:

La carrière diplomatique avait eu sur sa vie l'effet d'une entrée dans les ordres. Combinée avec l'assiduité à l'École des Sciences Politiques, elle l'avait voué depuis ses vingt ans à la chasteté du chrétien.

[The career of diplomacy had had the same effect upon his life as a monastic profession. Combined with his assiduous frequentation of the School of Political Sciences, it had vowed him from his twentieth year to the chastity of a professing Christian.]

a doubt arises. What might pass in the earlier passage for a detached irony now appears as a note of frustration, as though the writer were trying to solve a personal problem by caricaturing it in one of his characters. The suspicion is strengthened by the crude description at the same party of Marcel's enthusiastic acceptance of a friend's invitation to visit some time in the future a particularly 'smart' brothel. This note of frustration is really the clue to the interpretation of the later volumes of *A la Recherche du temps perdu.*

Proust's biographers have been curiously reticent about their hero's sexual life. It is true that they hint that, during the years when he was a brilliant young man of the world before his work and his illness turned him into a recluse, he had considerable success with women; but to read them one might suppose that after 'sowing his wild oats' he was vowed to a chastity as absolute as M. de Vaugoubert's and for nobler reasons. Now it does not call for great powers of divination to see that the author of *A la Recherche du temps perdu* was profoundly homosexual, but unless this is realized a great deal of the later volumes are meaningless. It has often been hinted that 'Albertine' was a boy, but it is only very recently that the story of Proust's personal peculiarities has been made public. It is by no means an edifying story, but it has an obvious bearing on the novel.

It will be recalled that in the novel Charlus set up a male brothel in the name of Jupien—a former paramour and his servant and companion during his dotage—who acted as manager. In some of the least agreeable pages in the novel, Marcel describes a visit to this establishment and his view of the proprietor chained to a bed being flagellated. According to Sachs, the facts on which Proust drew were somewhat different. The brothel, or, as it was called, the *établissement de bains*, certainly existed, but its proprietor was none other than Proust himself and the nominee his devoted servant Albert.

Sachs is certainly not an unimpeachable witness, but his account of Proust's clandestine activities and their effect on his work is highly plausible. We do not know to what extent Proust himself was *pratiquant*, but he appears to have been a *voyeur* which perhaps explains why Marcel always observes the most scandalous incidents in the book—they are invariably homosexual incidents—from a concealed position. Proust's establishment, which was known as Les Bains du Ballon d'Alsace, is said to have been frequented by some of the highest personages in the land. Proust, who had often seen them at the Ritz, saw a very different side when they visited the Bains, which has an obvious bearing on his presentation of character and on his attitude towards the aristocracy which becomes more and more hostile as the novel progresses.

Very few of Proust's characters are healthy or even normal beings [writes M. Buchet]. Even those who appear to be at first—Albertine and her friends, Gilberte and Saint-Loup—turn out in the end to be inverts. The story is told that one day Proust was discovered on his knees in his room collecting the manuscripts of his work, giving a final look at his characters and crying out in tears, as though he had just made a discovery which horrified him: 'They're all like that.'[1]

The later volumes of the novel certainly record a universal drift towards the Cities of the Plain. Mr. Edmund Wilson has compared Proust's supposed denunciation of the homosexuals to the tone of the Old Testament prophets and puts it down to his Jewish blood. This seems to me to be a simplification. Proust's attitude is much more complex. The truth is that there is no denunciation, that on the pretext of explaining sexual aberrations Proust contrives, indirectly, to excuse them and is never tired of expatiating on Charlus' 'moral qualities'.[2] This does not mean that his attitude was wholly indulgent or that there was no conflict in the presentation of his material. Nearly everything that he writes about homosexuality betrays a profound sense of guilt, and what Mr. Wilson takes for 'denunciation' might more accurately be described as a tone of 'lamentation'. Yet even here his attitude is ambivalent. In one place he writes:

> . . . rapprochant la mort de ma grand'mère et celle d'Albertine, il me semblait que ma vie était souillée d'un double assassinat. . . .

> [. . . thinking at once of my grandmother's death and of Albertine's, it seemed to me that my life was stained with a double murder. . . .]

The intention of this passage is only fully apparent when we place it beside another from *Sodome et Gomorrhe*:

> Au reste peut-on séparer entièrement l'aspect de M. de Charlus du fait que les fils n'ayant pas toujours la ressemblance paternelle, même sans être invertis et en recherchant des femmes, ils consomment dans leur visage la Profanation de leur mère. Mais laissons ici ce qui mériterait un chapitre à part: les mères profanées.

> [Not that there need be any connection between the appearance of M. de Charlus and the fact that sons, who do not always take after their fathers, even without being inverts, and though they go after women, may consummate upon their faces the profanation of their mothers. But we need not consider here a subject that deserves a chapter to itself: the Profanation of the Mother.]

It is a pity that Proust never wrote his chapter on the *mères profanées*, but he

---

[1] The one notable exception is the narrator. In the remarkable conversation recorded in his *Journal*, Gide reports Proust as saying to him in 1921: 'You can tell everything . . . but on condition that you never say: *I*.'

'Far from denying or hiding his uranism,' writes Gide of the same meeting, 'he displays it, and I might almost say: prides himself on it. He said that he had never loved women except spiritually and had never experienced love except with men.' (*Journal*, p. 692.)

[2] He seems to have taken the view that the causes of homosexuality were purely physiological and that it should therefore be regarded as a misfortune rather than a vice. In spite of the admissions to Gide, however, his attitude was disingenuous. (See Maurois, *loc. cit.*)

has said enough to reveal his line of thought. In all love, he thinks, particularly in its unnatural forms, man is driven on by the urge to destroy the person he loves. The man who loves women feels obscurely that possession is a violation of the mother-figure and this feeling is enormously intensified in the case of the homosexual who outrages not only his mother, but Woman herself. This is also true of the Lesbians who feel that they are profaning the father-figure. In the account of Mlle Vinteuil and her friend at Monjouvain, the desire of profanation assumes a ritual form and relations between the two women are preceded by Mlle Vinteuil spitting on the photograph of the father to whom she was devoted and whose death had been hastened by the discovery of his daughter's tastes.[1] Finally, in the description of Marcel's visit to Charlus' establishment we are shown a priest, who was among the clients, about to leave without paying. Jupien introduces a note of grisly comedy by shaking his purse and crying: 'Pour les frais du culte, monsieur l'abbé.'

Proust speaks constantly of 'prisons', 'prisoners', 'captives' and 'cages'. The words are of great significance, but their significance is only apparent when they are considered in relation to the little 'groups', 'clans' and 'bands'. For these sects are at once cells and secret societies which are founded on mutual interest and 'prisons' because they cut the 'faithful' off from intercourse with the rest of society, as Mme Verdurin is always at pains to keep her faithful away from people of a higher social sphere whom she calls the *ennuyeux*.[2] For Vaugoubert diplomacy was a 'prison' because it prevented him from joining the homosexuals; but the strangest example is the imprisonment of Albertine.[3] Consider the following passages from *La Prisonnière*:

. . . Albertine, que d'ailleurs je ne trouvais plus guère jolie et avec laquelle je m'ennuyais, que j'avais la sensation nette de ne pas aimer. . . .

Son charme un peu incommode était ainsi d'être à la maison moins comme une jeune fille, que comme une bête domestique qui entre dans une pièce, qui en sort, qui se trouve partout où on ne s'y attend pas. . . .

Je n'aimais plus Albertine.

Albertine s'était étonnamment développée, ce qui m'était entièrement égal. . . .

[. . . Albertine, in whom for that matter I could no longer see any beauty and who was beginning to bore me, with whom I was clearly conscious that I was not in love. . . .

[1] He explains that Mlle Vinteuil's 'sadism' is not the result of vice, but of 'sentimentality', and argues that sadists are really sentimentalists.

[2] Swann is 'expelled' from the *petit clan* for defending some of his aristocratic friends whom Mme Verdurin classed as *ennuyeux*.

[3] According to Maurois there was a succession of 'prisoners' at Proust's home—well-favoured but not very competent male secretaries, the last of whom was 'released' on the eve of the publication of *Sodome et Gomorrhe*. (*Op. cit.*, pp. 211–12.)

Her somewhat disturbing charm was, in fact, that of taking the place in the household not so much of a girl as of a domestic animal which comes into a room, goes out, is to be found wherever one does not expect to find it. . . .

I was no longer in love with Albertine.

Albertine had developed in an astonishing way, a thing that was a matter of indifference to me.]

When we ask why he was so determined to keep prisoner a woman whom he neither loved nor found attractive, this is the answer:

J'avais pu séparer Albertine de ses complices et, par là, exorciser mes hallucinations.

[I had been able to separate Albertine from her accomplices and in that way exorcize my hallucinations.]

The whole story of this enforced detention of the woman is a curious and sinister myth of a crumbling society trying desperately to convince itself of its own normality, to stop its drift towards perversion and collapse. The writer invents a woman whose vices are his own; he congratulates himself on his forcible prevention of practices which in secret he envies and, at the same time, by changing the object of desire into a woman, tries to conceal the roots of the evil from himself. Nor should we overlook the significance of the consultations with the Duchesse de Guermantes over Albertine's clothes. It is not the adornment of the bride, but a form of fetishism, a solemn incensing of the twofold being who is at once the symbol of normality and perversity.

There has been a good deal of speculation about Albertine's sex, but Sachs is certainly right in saying that 'the sex of Proust's heroine is not clearly defined. She is love itself and anyone can invest her with the image of the person who is dearest to him.' But this comment overlooks one important point. Proust speaks somewhere of the *néant* which is behind all love. His interest in homosexuality was dictated largely but not wholly by personal factors. For homosexuality is essentially a symbol of sterility and frustration, of that nihilism which colours much of the novel.

The figure of M. de Charlus has been rightly praised as a great comic creation in which Proust outdoes Dickens and Balzac on their own ground. There is, indeed, a savage farce about his account of the dissolution of the middle-aged homosexual; but when we look into it, we find that the irony is seldom disinterested. It seems to me that Proust displays the same ambiguous attitude towards him as he does towards Albertine and that these two characters are really complementary. He invests another with his own vices and shows how ugly they are; but Charlus inspires in his creator the same conflict as Albertine, the same mixture of dislike and envy. For there

is little doubt that secretly he envied both Charlus and Morel who, under
cover of an engagement to a very normal young woman, carries on his
appalling intrigue with Charlus as well as with Saint-Loup and Albertine
whom he supplies with *petites filles* after first corrupting them—he seems to
have been very versatile—does in short what Proust would like to have done
himself. That is why the novelist was determined to punish the pair of them.

When we come to the end of the novel, we find that though Proust's
characters still cling to 'class' and 'family', these things have lost much of
their importance and have been replaced by the 'groups', 'cells' and 'bands'
which did so much to undermine them. And no doubt the final glimpse of
Charlus who has fallen into a state of idiocy—he is ironically compared to
King Lear—demonstrates, and is intended to demonstrate, the decline and
fall of the aristocracy through a vice which is sometimes said to belong
peculiarly to periods of decadence; but we are forced to admit that Proust's
criticism is largely neutralized by his own complicity and by the absence of
'moral values' with which he is often reproached. When we compare this
part of his novel with the end of Baudelaire's *femmes damnées*, where the
moral attitude is completely fused into the poetic image, we realize why
Baudelaire's poetry has in this respect a maturity, a finality, for which we
shall look in vain in Proust's novel.[1]

We observe the same failings in his views of society as a whole. His study
of society is undoubtedly an impressive performance. He possessed an extraordinary insight into the workings of the social organism, and his account
of the impact of the Dreyfus Affair and the war on it is particularly impressive; but this is no reason for minimizing his deficiencies. I have described
him as a 'social critic', but I feel that the proper term is 'social analyst'. He
records the disintegration of the aristocratic élite and its absorption by the
bourgeoisie. He himself attributed it to 'the action of an interior principle',
but the truth is that the aristocracy succumbed to the absence of any constructive principle, to a moral inertia which assumed the forms of perversion,
frivolity, snobbery and unintelligence. M. Feuillerat comments on Proust's
growing rancour towards the aristocracy, but he does not explore its causes.
They are not difficult to discover and they are very important. Compared
with the urbanity of Stendhal or the extreme moral rectitude of Constant,
Proust's attitude is often no more than a lamentable exhibition of petty
spite. He disliked the aristocracy because he thought that they had let the
side down and the Verdurins in. His acrimony was probably intensified by
the fact that his health condemned him to reclusion, missing what fun was
still to be had. Nor are his positive standards impressive. It is true that the
grandmother, the mother and Françoise stand for decency, but they do so

---

[1] Gide reports Proust as asserting that Baudelaire was a homosexual and displaying indignant
surprise when Gide denied it. (*Journal, loc. cit.*)

at an elementary level. They represent the human qualities which are an indispensable minimum in any reasonable society. Although Proust spoke contemptuously of the 'néant de la vie de salon' and of society as 'un spectacle sans cause', there is no reason to suppose that he had any higher ideal or that he would not have been perfectly at home in the 'social aquarium'. That is why 'social analyst' rather than 'social critic', which implies a different scale of values, seems the proper term for him.

3. An Invisible Vocation

Nearly all the great French masters have been men who liked to discuss and explain their art, to discover how their effects were achieved; but I cannot think of any writer who has gone as far as Proust. The artist's vocation is a recurrent theme in the novel; a substantial part of *Le Temps retrouvé* is devoted to the analysis of his own method, his peculiar vision and the place of art in life. Yet there is a marked difference between his approach and that of other writers. The pages of *Le Temps retrouvé* in which he discusses his art are not an abstract treatise on æsthetics like Joyce's at the end of *A Portrait of the Artist as a Young Man* and Marcel's treatment of his vocation is far more impressive than Gide's in the *Faux-Monnayeurs*. Art is not merely one of the principal themes of the novel; the theories on which it is based and indeed the actual writing of the book are part of the novelist's experience.

It is therefore necessary at this point to say something of the incident of the *petite madeleine* and the *mémoire involontaire* which is the pivot of the whole theory:

> Il y avait déjà bien des années que, de Combray, tout ce qui n'était pas le théâtre et le drame de mon coucher, n'existait plus pour moi, quand un jour d'hiver, comme je rentrais à la maison, ma mère, voyant que j'avais froid, me proposa de me faire prendre, contre mon habitude, un peu de thé. Je refusai d'abord et, je ne sais pourquoi, me ravisai. Elle envoya chercher un de ces gâteaux courts et dodus appelés Petites Madeleines qui semblent avoir été moulés dans la valve rainurée d'une coquille de Saint-Jacques.

> [Many years had elapsed during which nothing of Combray, save what was comprised in the theatre and the drama of my going to bed there, had any existence for me, when one day in winter, as I came home, my mother, seeing that I was cold, offered me some tea, a thing I did not ordinarily take. I declined at first, and then, for no particular reason, changed my mind. She sent out for one of those short, plump little cakes called *petites madeleines*, which look as though they had been moulded in the fluted scallop of a pilgrim's shell.]

He then goes on to relate the strange experience which he had when he dipped the *madeleine* into his tea and put it in his mouth. We feel the resistance—the unconscious resistance—when his mother persuades him to have some tea *contre mon habitude*. We feel, too, his mental weariness in the slow, dragging sentence

> Et bientôt, machinalement, accablé par la morne journée et la perspective d'un triste lendemain, je portais à mes lèvres une cuillerée du thé où j'avais laissé s'amollir un morceau de madeleine.

> [And soon, mechanically, weary after a dull day with the prospect of a depressing morrow, I raised to my lips a spoonful of the tea in which I had soaked a morsel of the cake.]

Then there is a sudden change of tone, a sense of immense excitement coupled with great watchfulness:

> Mais à l'instant même où la gorgée mêlée des miettes du gâteau toucha mon palais, je tressaillis, attentif à ce qui se passait d'extraordinaire en moi. Un plaisir délicieux m'avait envahi, isolé, sans la notion de sa cause.

> [No sooner had the warm liquid, and the crumbs with it, touched my palate than a shudder ran through my whole body, and I stopped, intent upon the extraordinary changes that were taking place. An exquisite pleasure had invaded my senses, but individual, detached, with no suggestion of its origin.]

The experience takes the form at first of a feeling of intense but inexplicable happiness:

> Il m'avait aussitôt rendu les vicissitudes de la vie indifférentes, ses désastres inoffensifs, sa brièveté illusoire, de la même façon qu'opère l'amour, en me remplissant d'une essence précieuse: ou plutôt cette essence n'était pas en moi, elle était moi.

> [And at once the vicissitudes of life had become indifferent to me, its disasters innocuous, its brevity illusory—this new sensation having had on me the effect which love has of filling me with a precious essence; or rather the essence was not in me, it was myself.]

He begins to speculate about the source of his experience and to analyse it. It is linked to the taste of the *madeleine*. He eats another spoonful. Then he realizes that the source lies not in the cake, but in himself:

> Il est clair que la vérité que je cherche n'est pas en lui, mais en moi.

Although the experience is started by the mechanical action of eating the cake soaked in tea, the artist is *passive*:

> Un plaisir délicieux m'avait envahi . . . je sens tressaillir en moi quelque chose

qui se déplace, voudrait s'élever, quelque chose qu'on aurait désancré à une grande profondeur; je ne sais ce que c'est, mais cela monte lentement; j'éprouve la résistance et j'entends la rumeur des distances traversées.

[An exquisite pleasure had invaded my senses. . . . I feel something start within me, something that leaves its resting-place and attempts to rise, something that has been embedded like an anchor at a great depth; I do not know yet what it is, but I can feel it mounting slowly; I can measure the resistance, I can hear the echo of great spaces traversed.]

The close of the passage is perhaps the most remarkable part of it. We feel the strange forces stirring at a level far below that of the conscious mind, struggling to reach the surface from the *grande profondeur* where they are 'anchored'; and we are also aware of the immense *psychological* distances which they must traverse. The 'meaning' of the experience suddenly becomes clear to him:

Certes, ce qui palpite ainsi au fond de moi, ce doit être l'image, le souvenir visuel, qui, lié à cette saveur, tente de la suivre jusqu'à moi.

[Undoubtedly what is thus palpitating in the depths of my being must be the image, the visual memory which, being linked to the taste, has tried to follow it into the conscious mind.]

The experience originates in an association of ideas. The taste of the *madeleine* recalls the taste of the *madeleine* which his aunt Léonie used to give him when he was a child at Combray. He had temporarily 'forgotten' the past except for the nightly drama of his mother's kiss, and it is this past which is suddenly recreated and is trying to escape from the depths of his being where it is imprisoned.

The focal words of the passage are *souvenir visuel*. He sees the old grey house in which his aunt lived, and with the house the town, its square, its streets:

Comme dans ce jeu où les Japonais s'amusent à tremper dans un bol de porcelaine rempli d'eau, de petits morceaux de papier jusque-là indistincts qui, à peine y sont-ils plongés s'étirent, se contournent, se colorent, se différencient, deviennent des fleurs, des maisons, des personnages consistants et reconnaissables, de même maintenant toutes les fleurs de notre jardin et celles du parc de M. Swann, et les nymphéas de la Vivonne, et les bonnes gens du village et leurs petits logis et l'église et tout Combray et ses environs, tout cela qui prend forme et solidité, est sorti, ville et jardins, de ma tasse de thé.

[And just as the Japanese amuse themselves by filling a porcelain bowl with water and steeping in it little crumbs of paper which until then are without character or form, but, the moment they become wet, stretch themselves and bend, take on colour and distinctive shape, become flowers or houses or people, permanent and recognizable, so in that moment all the flowers in our garden and in M. Swann's park, and the water-lilies on the Vivonne and the good folk of the village and their little dwellings and the parish church and the whole of Combray and of its surroundings, taking their proper shapes and growing solid, sprang into being, town and gardens alike, from my cup of tea.]

The Japanese flowers were no doubt suggested by the sight of the tea-leaves floating round the cup. The accumulation of the four verbs, 's'étirent, se contournent, se colorent, se différencient', seems to be another device borrowed from Flaubert, but Proust uses it with greater artistry. He gives us a deliberately 'indistinct' picture of the dried paper flowers falling into the bowl, opening, revolving, revealing their colours, assuming separate shapes. With the switch to the three substantives, the 'indistinct' image suddenly becomes sharp and precise. We have a vivid sensation of 'flowers, town, people' tumbling pell-mell out of the cup. 'Consistants et reconnais-sables' looks back to 'indistincts' and forward to 'prend forme et solidité'. We see every detail of the picture—Swann's park, the water-lilies in the Vivonne, the people, the church. These details merge again into the general-ized image of 'tout Combray et ses environs', making us feel the landscape unfolding before us; while the repeated 'ville et jardins' deftly emphasizes the contrast between the wide panorama and the cup from which it has emerged.

The whole passage is a remarkable piece of psychological observation, a description of the creative act as it takes place in certain writers. It is repeated at intervals throughout the book; but though the content is always similar, the incident which starts it is always different. On one occasion it is the sight of the three belfries at Martinville, on another the scent of the hawthorn or of the mouldering wood. Finally, in *Le Temps retrouvé*, it is the unequal paving-stones and the rough towel on which Marcel dries his hands.

Proust does not claim that his experience is unique. On the contrary, he states explicitly that he has observed the same phenomenon in Chateau-briand's *Mémoires d'outre-tombe*, in Gérard de Nerval's *Sylvie* and in Baude-laire's poetry. He might, indeed, have quoted the famous passage from Baudelaire's diaries:

Dans certain états de l'âme presque surnaturels, la profondeur de la vie se révèle dans le spectacle, si ordinaire qu'il soit, qu'on a sous les yeux. Il en devient le Symbole.

For in what Dandieu calls his *états privilégiés*, it is precisely this that happens. The inner meaning of life becomes clear to him. Incidents, which seemed to belong to the world of time and chance and to which he had paid little attention, are abstracted from that world and become part of a timeless world in which they acquire immense significance.

The fruits of Proust's experience are certainly impressive and the pages in which he describes Aunt Léonie are among the most memorable in the book. Yet we sometimes have the impression that he tried to use the theory of the *mémoire involontaire* to prove too much and that it could not really have been the staple of the novel as he contrived to suggest. His conception of time and all that it implies was very different from Bergson's *durée*. It was of the essence of his experience that it was fragmentary, intermittent, discontinuous. The extraordinary novelty of his vision depends very largely on sudden switches from the surface of experience to a deeper level and back again. That is why the magic lantern, the Japanese flowers, snapshots and 'photographs taken by our sensibility' are key-images, or what Proust himself called *phrase-types*, in the novel. It must be remembered, however, that the book is concerned not so much with isolated experiences as with a particular attitude of mind. Proust deliberately adopted a passive standpoint towards the phenomena of experience and played down intelligence because he was convinced that intelligence distorted experience by imposing artificial categories, and that what we call 'personality' was very largely an abstract construction which excluded too much.

There are naturally grounds on which he can legitimately be criticized. He does tend in the final volume to surround his experience with an aura of mystery and it is his own fault if this has led to misunderstanding and encouraged bad habits on the part of his critics. For some of them have used the word 'mystic' to describe his experience. It is a technical term borrowed from theology which has no application to art and might with advantage be removed from the vocabulary of literary criticism. But though there appears to be no resemblance between the *content* of Proust's experience and that of the religious mystics, there is one important parallel. The religious mystic believes that he has had an immediate experience of the Absolute—theologians speak of an experimental knowledge of God without the intermediary of a concept—but Proust pursued a *psychological* absolute. It was, as we shall see, precisely because he sought an absolute in those realms of experience in which there can be no absolute and no finality, that all his work has a perpetual underlying tension.

4. People

Proust's scepticism was largely responsible for his peculiar method of presenting 'character' which is different not merely from that of the classic novelists, but of his own contemporaries. In the classic novelists character is in general one of the *données*. The novelist begins by 'creating' characters, but once they have been created they do not undergo any fundamental change. All their adventures or experiences are the outcome of character and of the friction of one character on another. The modern writer has no doubt discarded the theory of fixed unchanging character and instead portrays the psychological development of characters who are completely different at the end of the book from the beginning. It should be emphasized that the change is real; it is not, as it sometimes is with the classic writers, that different facets of the main characters are only revealed as the result of the experiences which are described in the book.

The concept of a fixed unchanging character is common to the writers of classical antiquity, the Middle Ages and the English and French novelists of the eighteenth century. In Fielding and Smollett, in Marivaux and Laclos, there is, properly speaking, no development of character. The novelist starts with a special knowledge of his character and he reveals it to the reader by inventing a series of situations in which they become involved.

A different approach, however, can already be discerned in the dramatists as well as in the principal French novelists of the seventeenth century. Although strictly limited, there is development in Corneille, Molière, Racine and Mme de La Fayette. The Alceste who abandons society in search of an *endroit écarté* in the fifth act of *Le Misanthrope* is certainly different from the fiery reformer of Act I, though his 'change of heart' is the logical outcome of the *données*. Corneille's characters undergo a moral growth and become 'integrated'; Racine's and Mme de La Fayette's suffer complete moral collapse.

Another change occurs at the close of the eighteenth century. There is a strong autobiographical element in Constant and Stendhal, but comparatively little development. Their characters are all trying to discover what sort of people they are and their discoveries are the outcome not so much of action, situation and their relations with other people as of solitary analysis in a silent room or in prison.

Proust's approach differs from all these writers or rather he combines a number of different approaches and produces a new standpoint and a new method. The classical novelists were convinced that in spite of his changing moods, man was essentially *one*. Proust was equally convinced that he was *many*. His characters are composed in layers or, if one prefers, they are all to some degree multiple personalities. The only way of bringing out this complexity and of dealing with the very real problem of our knowledge of other people was to apply the method of the memoir-writer to his characters. They are constructed by direct observation, by encounters between Marcel and the other characters at different periods of their lives and in different situations, but also by gossip and hearsay. This enables Proust to present them from a large number of different angles and to show that the same person may appear completely different to different people. We remember the incident of Saint-Loup's mistress:

Suddenly Saint-Loup appeared, accompanied by his mistress, and then, in this woman who was for him all the love, every possible delight in life, whose personality, mysteriously enshrined in a body as in a tabernacle, was the object that still occupied incessantly the toiling imagination of my friend, whom he felt that he would never really know, as to whom he was perpetually asking himself what could be her secret self, behind the veil of eyes and flesh, in this woman I recognized at once 'Rachel when from the Lord', her who, but a few years since—women change their position so rapidly in that world, when they do change—used to say to the procuress: 'To-morrow evening, then, if you want me for anyone, you will send round, won't you. . . .'

I realized also then all that the human imagination can put behind a little scrap of face, such as this girl's face was, if it is the imagination that was the first to know it; and conversely into what wretched elements, crudely material and utterly without value, might be decomposed what had been the inspiration of countless dreams if, on the contrary, it should be so to speak controverted by the slightest actual acquaintance. I saw that what had appeared to me to be not worth twenty francs in the house of ill fame, where it was then for me simply a woman desirous of earning twenty francs, might be worth more than a million, more than one's family, more than all the most coveted positions in life if one had begun by imagining her to embody a strange creature, interesting to know, difficult to seize and to hold. No doubt it was the same thin and narrow face that we saw, Robert and I. But we had arrived at it by two opposite ways, between which there was no communication, and we should never both see it from the same side.

At the end of his Memoirs Saint-Simon describes his book, with the superb confidence of his century, as a *miroir de vérité* which he could not publish during the lifetime of his victims because of the 'universal convulsion' which so strong a dose of truth would cause. Proust was always trying to arrive at 'truth', but it would never have occurred to him to make the same claim for his book as Saint-Simon. On the contrary, he is at pains to emphasize that our knowledge of other people is always relative. In one of his letters he compares his presentation of character to a town seen from a train. While the train follows its winding track, the town sometimes appears on our right and sometimes on our left. In the same way, he says, the different aspects of the same character will appear like a succession of different people. Such characters, he adds, will later reveal that they are very different from the people for whom we took them, as often happens in life for that matter. The account of Saint-Loup's mistress shows how closely Proust's practice followed his theories:

No doubt it was the same thin face that we saw, Robert and I. But we had arrived at it by two opposite ways, between which there was no communication, and we should never both see it from the same side.

This seems to me to be a complete answer to those critics who have

claimed that Proust's presentation of character was inconsistent and uncon-
vincing. It is no accident that we often have the impression that we are in a
vast room of distorting mirrors which reflect the same person simultaneously
from different and often contradictory angles. All of them give us a glimpse
of the truth, but none of them the whole truth. In this way Proust subjects
us to a series of shocks. We are introduced to Saint-Loup as the sympathetic
representative of the old aristocracy, the hero who at once rejoins his old
regiment on the outbreak of war only to discover that he either is or has
become a rabid homosexual. The effect of this is not merely to emphasize
the complexity of human nature and the elusiveness of 'personality', but to
introduce a moral relativity. Proust is very careful not to judge his main
characters. They simply appear in a series of different guises, some of them
creditable, others highly discreditable. The *jeune héros* who eventually dies
gloriously on the field of battle is the same man who carries on the nefarious
traffic with Morel and visits Charlus' *établissement*.

Proust employs a different method still with Marcel and to a certain extent
with Swann. It looks at first like the method of Constant. He is certainly
trying to answer the same question as the nineteenth-century novelist: 'What
sort of a man am *I*?' But he is also trying to answer a number of still more
urgent and still more searching questions: 'What is love?' 'What is jealousy?'
'What is personality?' 'What is time?' 'What is reality?' It is one of the signs
of Proust's greatness that his problems are always treated concretely. His
analysis of love and jealousy is very profound, but it could never be said of
him as it was—mistakenly in my opinion—of Racine and Molière that he
dealt with the 'abstract emotions' or that he shows us the Lover and the
Jealous Man as generalized figures. For in his novel, the correspondence between the lover and the jealous man and the individual who is in love and
is jealous is absolute.

5. The Prisoner

It will be apparent from what has already been said that Proust's art is
largely subjective. He is constantly telling us of his attempts to reach *la vraie
vie* and it is a struggle in which all his characters in a greater or lesser degree
are engaged. His work with its arguments, its method of trial and error,
sometimes reminds us a little oddly of Descartes' *doute méthodique*, but there
is one great difference between the seventeenth-century philosopher and the
twentieth-century novelist. Descartes' 'doubt' is a means of arriving at a
truth which he knows exists; but from the first Proust makes us doubt the
very existence of *la vraie vie* or, if we do not actually doubt its existence,
we certainly doubt whether it is attainable. For in this world values are
necessarily relative to the person who suffers the experience. Our interest

lies less in the goal than in the pursuit—the *recherche*—and its vicissitudes. The nature of the struggle is evident from a passage in *Swann*:

> Si mes parents m'avaient permis, quand je lisais un livre, d'aller visiter la région qu'il décrivait, j'aurais cru faire un pas inestimable dans la conquête de la vérité. Car si on a la sensation d'être toujours entouré de son âme, ce n'est pas comme d'une prison immobile; plutôt on est comme emporté avec elle dans un perpétuel élan pour la dépasser, pour atteindre à l'extérieur, avec une sorte de découragement, entendant toujours autour de soi cette sonorité identique qui n'est pas écho du dehors mais retentissement d'une vibration interne.

> [Had my parents allowed me, when I read a book, to pay a visit to the country it described, I should have felt that I was making an enormous advance towards the ultimate conquest of truth. For even if we have the sensation of being always enveloped in, surrounded by our own soul, still it does not seem a fixed and immovable prison; rather do we seem to be borne away with it, and perpetually struggling to pass beyond it to break, out into the world, with a perpetual discouragement as we hear endlessly, all around us, that unvarying sound which is no echo from without, but the resonance of a vibration from within.]

This passage explains the peculiar *angoisse* which is always throbbing just below the surface of Proust's novel. Then, from time to time, it suddenly, unexpectedly produces an eruption. We feel a note of hope behind 'la conquête de la vérité' which is at once stifled by 'entouré de son âme'. It is not a tangible prison from which he can escape; the prison itself is mobile and just at the moment when his *élan* seems about to carry him outside the closed circle, when he is on the point of reaching freedom, he hears 'cette sonorité identique' and realizes, with fresh discouragement, that there is no escape. For the 'echo' is not even a sound from the outside world, but the 'retentissement d'une vibration interne'.

We can begin to appreciate now how closely the two sides of Proust's world are connected. We have already seen that when he describes, or appears to describe, society objectively, the principal characters always turn out to be 'prisoners'—prisoners of a social class, prisoners of the little 'groups' or 'bands' into which they have formed themselves or simply prisoners of their own vices.

The great myth of the nineteenth century was the 'outsider' myth; the great myth of the twentieth century is the myth of the 'prisoner'. The real hero of *A la Recherche du temps perdu* is the Prisoner. The Prisoner is not Swann or Charlus or even Albertine, but Marcel himself. The heroes of Stendhal are cut off from society by their own exceptional gifts of intelligence and sensibility; but they are always attacking. Julien Sorel disrupts the precarious balance of French society in 1830 and Fabrice del Dongo disorganizes the eighteenth-century political pattern which in the miniature

police state of Parma has become rigid and hard. Proust's hero, too, is
endowed with exceptional gifts of intelligence and sensibility. He, too, is in
a sense an 'outsider', but he is the outsider who failed to make his escape and
was trapped in his extraordinary mobile prison. Stendhal's view of life
implies a philosophy of action, Proust's a highly personal form of quietism.
Marcel does not possess the power of attack which is common to Julien and
Fabrice; he is the passive victim who is exposed to almost every conceivable
kind of pressure and obsession known to human society. For he is the prisoner
not so much of 'clans' and 'groups' as of emotions, habits, of his own sensibility and, ultimately, of time. I think we can add that the symbolical figure
who dominates the novel is not simply the Prisoner, but the Artist-Prisoner
who after many false starts and misfortunes comes to see that the only hope
of escape lies in his 'vocation'. That is why Proust's withdrawal from the
world to meditate on time and memory stamps him as the twentieth-century
artist.

M. Maurice Muller has described the book with felicity as

> This psychological comedy in which the characters are Love, Jealousy, Falsehood,
> Habit, Forgetting, Memory which are incarnate in a being who is very much alive,
> the narrator—a comedy which is subject to laws which are subtle, but implac-
> able. . . .

The main drama is of course the Prisoner's attempts to escape from himself, from a prison which seems to have no exit, to attain a truth which will
make him free. Now inside this main drama there is a series of 'psychological
comedies' which are endlessly repeated. They are played out between
M. Muller's six characters who assume the proportions of obsessions. When
Proust tells us that what is dangerous in love 'is not the woman but the
habit', we know that we are witnessing the scene between Love and Habit
which merges into the scene between Love and Forgetting or Love and
Memory. Then there is a sudden switch:

> L'amour n'est provoqué que par le mensonge et consiste seulement dans le
> besoin de voir nos souffrances apaisées par l'être qui nous a fait souffrir.

> [Love is provoked only by falsehood, and consists merely in our need to see
> our sufferings appeased by the person who has made us suffer.]

The tension always rises steeply in the scenes between Love and Falsehood.
For Falsehood is one of the principal characters in the novel.

It has been pointed out that Proust displayed a particular interest in doctors,
diplomats and servants. His interest is very understandable. They are people
who are obliged to adopt a professional attitude, are constantly telling
'diplomatic lies'. They therefore become for the novelist incarnations of

Falsehood. Then we gradually realize that social relations are simply 'a tissue of lies'. Falsehood exists at different levels, appearing sometimes as a series of concentric circles and at others as the mental obstacle which hinders the search for 'truth' and maintains *angoisse*. The doctors, diplomats and servants are minor characters in Proust's comedy. They underline the main theme and give Marcel an opportunity of studying their 'technique' so that he will have a better chance of catching his mistress out. Charlus plays many roles, but in this particular context he represents the Lie at a rather higher level than the 'professional liars'. His whole life has become an elaborate lie in order to conceal his sexual aberrations and he provides Marcel with a still better example of the way in which the liar goes about his business. At the centre of the circle stands Albertine. We suspect that the whole of her life, too, is a lie and that she is trying to conceal the same anomaly as Charlus. The drama now becomes much more complex. Jealousy enters the scene. In his endeavours to discover whether Albertine was or was not a Lesbian, Marcel himself is driven to lying; and we find in the end that he is playing a sort of triple role: *Amour—Jalousie—Mensonge*. This is the point at which the drama reaches its maximum intensity.

When we look back to the sentence on lies—

L'amour n'est provoqué que par le mensonge et consiste seulement dans le besoin de voir nos souffrances apaisées par l'être qui nous a fait souffrir.

we are aware of the vicious circle. Love is aroused by a falsehood. It can only be assuaged by the person who aroused it, but the person who aroused it is Falsehood. There is no way out. The most that we can hope for is one of those comfortable sayings in which Proust's work abounds. 'L'amour est un mal inguérissable.' The best moments in love contain 'la possibilité insoupçonnée du désastre'.

It is not difficult to see the bearing of this on human relations as a whole. It is commonly assumed or believed that when two people 'fall in love' they suddenly become aware of one another's personality in a new way, discover something in the personality of the loved one which is not apparent to others and makes him or her particularly sympathetic, becomes the foundation of a lifelong attachment. Now Proust's psychology is a reversal of the traditional view. You do not get to know a person to see whether you love her; you love her in order to get to know her or, to use a term which conveys Proust's double purpose, to 'possess' her. We are told, for example, of the relations between Swann and Odette that she was

Plus désireuse peut-être de connaître ce qu'il était que désireuse d'être sa maîtresse.

[More desirous perhaps to know what sort of a man he was than desirous to be his mistress.]

According to this conception, love is one of the ways of trying to break out of 'prison', to reach 'truth' or to still the *angoisse* which continually afflicts you. It is naturally fraught with every kind of difficulty. It is difficult to know all those different beings who are collectively labelled 'Odette' or 'Albertine'; a profound scepticism makes you doubt whether you can ever really get to know another human being at all even if there is goodwill on both sides. Goodwill is naturally extremely rare in a world of 'lies'. You are almost certain to have a rival. Your mistress is probably a Lesbian or has spent her youth in a brothel or has some other shameful secret to conceal. At this point the comedy of Love and Falsehood turns to tragedy.

It is now possible to go on to examine in more detail Proust's conception of love and personality.

6. *L'Amour*

'For the medieval author of *Tristan et Iseult*,' said Ortega y Gasset, 'love is a sentiment which possesses a sharp profile. For the primitive exponent of the psychological novel, love is love and nothing more. Proust, on the contrary, describes a love affair of Swann's which is completely without the form of love. . . . Only one thing is lacking—love.

'No doubt,' he goes on, 'Proust belongs to the lineage of Stendhal, "the investigator of the human heart"; but while for Stendhal the human heart is a solid body with plastic and rigid lines, for Proust it is a diffused vapour which varies from one moment to another with meteorological versatility.

It is impossible in writing of Proust to avoid the word 'love', but one cannot use it without a sense of misgiving, without feeling that some other expression like 'sexual connection' would be more accurate. Proust employs it as a blanket term to describe an emotional situation, or better an emotional equation, which is capable of almost endless variations. Its only resemblance to traditional love seems at first to lie in the fact that two people are necessary, but we shall see that even this is an exaggeration.

Proust has been criticized by conservative writers for destroying the unity of personality. I have shown that his conception of personality was largely determined by historical changes, but though history can explain, it cannot justify. The only justification is artistic. He shared Laforgue's hostility to *l'homme absolu* which he would have regarded as an abstract intellectual construction; he would have approved of the substitution of *innombrables claviers humains*; but he did not intend any more than Laforge to launch a frivolous attack on the unity of the human person. On the contrary, his work is a plea for a more profound conception of the self which would give him a better chance of reaching the elusive *vraie vie* and revealing its mysteries. It is one of his great merits that he avoided the mistake of the nineteenth-century novelists who achieved a specious unity by 'imagining the moral qualities of their characters before the characters themselves'. Yet, ironically, his determination to be absolutely honest and not to be deceived by appearances led to the tragic discovery that he was pursuing a chimera. The fascination and horror of his love affairs depend, indeed, on the reduction of 'the human heart' to 'a diffused vapour which varies from one moment to another with meteorological versatility':[1]

> . . . notre amour, notre jalousie . . . se composent d'une infinité d'amours successifs, de jalousies différentes et qui sont éphémères, mais par leur multitude uninterrompue, donnent l'impression de la continuité, l'illusion de l'unité.

> [. . . our love, our jealousy . . . are composed of an infinity of successive loves, of different jealousies, each of which is ephemeral, although by their uninterrupted multitude they give us the impression of continuity, the illusion of unity.]

It follows that if the continuity and unity of emotion is an illusion, the unity of the person who suffers the emotion must be an illusion too:

> Je n'étais pas un seul homme, mais le défilé heure pas heure d'une armée compacte où il y avait selon le moment des passionnés, des indifférents, des jaloux—des jaloux dont pas un n'était jaloux de la même femme.

> [I was not one man only, but the steady advance hour after hour of an army in close formation, in which there appeared, according to the moment, impassioned men, indifferent men, jealous men—jealous men no two of whom were jealous of the same woman.]

They are not 'jealous of the same woman' because she is nothing but a figment of the imagination:

> C'est la terrible tromperie de l'amour qu'il commence par nous faire jouer avec une femme non du monde extérieur, mais avec une poupée intérieure à notre cerveau, la seule d'ailleurs que nous ayons toujours à notre disposition, la seule que nous posséderons, que l'arbitraire du souvenir, presque aussi absolu que celui de l'imagination, peut avoir fait aussi différente de la femme réelle, que du Balbec réel avait été pour moi le Balbec rêvé; création factice à laquelle, peu à peu pour notre souffrance, nous forcerons la femme réelle, à ressembler.

> [It is the terrible deception of love that begins by engaging us in play not with a woman of the external world but with a puppet fashioned and kept in our brain, the only form of her moreover that we have always at our disposal, the only one that we shall ever possess, one which the arbitrary power of memory, almost as

[1] I naturally do not include Señor Ortega y Gasset among 'conservative' writers. For an interesting criticism from a philosophical point of view of Proust's conception of personality, see Fernandez, *Messages* (Paris, 1926), pp. 147–69.

absolute as that of imagination, may have made as different from the real woman
as had been from the real Balbec the Balbec of my dreams; an artificial creation
to which by degrees, and to our own hurt, we shall force the real woman into
resemblance.]

Here is the explanation:

C'est que cette femme n'a fait que susciter par des sortes d'appels magiques
mille éléments de tendresse existant en nous à l'état fragmentaire et qu'elle a
assemblés, unis, effaçant toute cassure entre eux, c'est nous-mêmes qui en lui
donnant ses traits avons fourni toute la matière solide de la personne aimée.

[The truth is that the woman has only raised to life by a sort of magic spell a
thousand elements of affection existing in us already in a fragmentary state, which
she has assembled, joined together, bridging every gap between them, it is ourself
who by giving her her features have supplied all the solid matter of the beloved
object.]

The result of this view of personality is that love can only end in disaster,
in the sudden shattering discovery that behind the innumerable illusions
which it creates there is nothing but the void. Thus, in a sentence which
gives the heart of his experience, Proust speaks of

L'acte de possession physique—où d'ailleurs l'on ne possède rien.

[The act of physical possession (in which, paradoxically, the possessor possesses
nothing).]

He speaks in another place of 'le caractère purement subjectif du phéno-
mène qu'est l'amour'. It is clearly inaccurate even to use the expression
'sexual connection' in writing of Proust because all his characters fail to
'connect':

Les liens entre un être et nous n'existent que dans notre pensée.

[The bonds that unite another person to ourself exist only in our mind.]

There is no direct contact between the lovers; they never do succeed in
knowing one another. The beloved is nothing but *une poupée intérieure*, the
exteriorization of our own personal needs and desires which we contrive
to graft on to a completely anonymous being. We like to imagine that love
is an exclusive attachment for a particular woman, but we realize that

Bien souvent un amour n'est que l'association d'une image de jeune fille (qui
sans cela nous eût été vite insupportable) avec les battements de cœur inséparables
d'une attente interminable, vaine, et d'un 'lapin' que la demoiselle nous a posé.

[As often as not love is nothing more than the association of the face of a girl (whom otherwise we should soon have found intolerable) with the heartbeats inseparable from an endless, vain expectation, and from some trick that she has played upon us.]

The anonymity of the beloved is constantly underlined:

Quand on aime, l'amour est trop grand pour pouvoir être contenu tout entier en nous; il irradie vers la personne aimée, rencontre en elle une surface qui l'arrête, le force à revenir vers son point de départ et c'est ce choc en retour de notre propre tendresse que nous appelons les sentiments de l'autre et qui nous charme plus qu'à l'aller, parce que nous ne connaissons pas qu'elle vient de nous.

[When we are in love, our love is too big a thing for us to be able altogether to contain it within us. It radiates towards the beloved object, finds in her a surface which arrests it, forcing it to return to its starting-point, and it is this shock of the repercussion of our own affection which we call the other's regard for ourselves, and which pleases us more then than on its outward journey because we do not recognize it as having originated in ourselves.]

We engage in the pursuit of an *amour exclusif*, but the beloved is not a person who satisfies the same needs and desires. She is a 'surface' which refracts our own *tendresse* as another surface might refract the light. The Prisoner is a psychological hermaphrodite trying in vain to 'possess' himself. What we call 'love' is simply a hideous, sickening see-saw between states of 'joy' and 'suffering'. He speaks of 'l'amour et la souffrance qui fait un avec lui'.

Again:

En réalité, dans l'amour il y a une souffrance permanente, que la joie neutralise, rend virtuelle, ajourne, mais qui peut à tout moment devenir ce qu'elle serait depuis longtemps si l'on n'avait pas obtenu ce qu'on souhaitait, atroce.

[Actually, there is in love a permanent strain of suffering which happiness neutralizes, makes conditional only, procrastinates, but which may at any moment become what it would long since have been had we not obtained what we were seeking, sheer agony.]

For Proust therefore love can only mean *l'amour-maladie* and he analyses it in an extraordinary passage on Swann's attitude towards Odette:

... cette maladie qu'était l'amour de Swann avait tellement multiplié, il était si étroitement mêlé à toutes les habitudes de Swann, à tous ses actes, à sa pensée, à sa santé, à son sommeil, à sa vie, même à ce qu'il désirait pour après sa mort; il ne faisait tellement plus qu'un avec lui, qu'on n'aurait pas pu l'arracher de lui, sans le détruire lui-même à peu près tout entier: comme on dit en chirurgie, son amour n'était plus opérable.

[. . . this malady, which was Swann's love, had so far multiplied, was so closely interwoven with all his habits, with all his actions, with his thoughts, his health, his sleep, his life, even with what he hoped for after his death, was so entirely one with him that it would have been impossible to wrest it away without almost entirely destroying him; as surgeons say, his case was past operation.]

When at length his love dies and Swann quietly marries the mistress for whom he no longer cares to give a name to their child, this is his comment on it to himself:

Dire que j'ai gâché des années de ma vie, que j'ai voulu mourir, que j'ai eu mon plus grand amour pour une femme qui ne me plaisait pas, qui n'était pas mon genre!

[To think that I have wasted years of my life, that I have longed for death, that the greatest love that I have ever known has been for a woman who did not please me, who was not in my style!]

The truth is that his characters cannot do without love; it is the one absorbing activity of their lives, the one thing which enables them to focus this activity and which gives an appearance of unity to their personality; but once they indulge in it, they are doomed to destruction—the victims of 'un mal inguérissable' '[qui n'est] plus opérable'.

While the story of Swann in love has been generally admired in Anglo-Saxon countries, Marcel's affair with Albertine has been decidedly less popular. It looks at first like a repetition of Swann's story in which the experience is analysed in much greater detail and is much more intensely felt. In a sense this is true, but only in a sense. The difference between Swann and Marcel is not simply a difference of degree, but a difference of kind. For, writes M. Feuillerat,

Instead of the regular movements of a pendulum which accompany the anguish of a Swann or a Saint-Loup, in the case of the narrator the alternatives are complicated by a multitude of secondary movements which are themselves regulated by a contradiction. . . . So that the movements which distinguish the principal oscillations almost always subdivide producing a new play of opposites from which will emerge in turn fresh alternatives.

The greater part of the account of Marcel's affair with Albertine is written in what M. Feuillerat calls Proust's 'second manner'. In place of the comparatively straightforward style of *Swann*, the analysis of almost every mood is accompanied by an elaborate disquisition on the nature of sexual passion. One could, observes M. Feuillerat, construct a whole *Art of Love* out of the passages in which the narrator, who is supposed to be a naïve and inexperienced man, skilfully analyses the feelings that he experiences for Albertine. We only need to turn up the word *amour* in M. Celly's fascinating compendium to appreciate the truth of this observation.[1] It would indeed be possible to construct an *Art of Love* which would make some of the classic moralists look like children.

No people have displayed more diligence and more ingenuity than the French in analysing, classifying and labelling the different kinds and degrees of sexual passion. What is fascinating in the story of Albertine is not the account of Marcel falling in love with her, but the account of his falling out of love or what a French writer has lately called *le désamour*. The story is also a horrifying one. What is horrifying to many Anglo-Saxon readers is the fact that he is on his own admission 'l'artisan volontaire, impitoyable et patient' of his own grief. For he does not discover suddenly that he no longer cares for either Gilberte or Albertine. He makes a conscious and deliberate attempt to wreck his own happiness and he describes it with a clairvoyance which is worthy of the greatest French writers.

'La jalousie,' said La Rochefoucauld, 'naît toujours avec l'amour; elle ne meurt pas toujours avec lui.' Jealousy is a *maladie des sentiments*. The discovery that it may survive the emotion on which it is founded is not new. What is new in Proust is to have shown the extent to which the *sentiment* can become engulfed in the *maladie* and the extraordinary way in which the *maladie* can survive the total destruction of the *sentiment*. We are told of Swann that

> Il était depuis longtemps insoucieux qu'Odette l'eût trompé et le trompât encore. Et pourtant il avait continué pendant quelques années à rechercher d'anciens domestiques d'Odette, tant avait persisté chez lui la douloureuse curiosité de savoir si ce jour-là, tellement ancien, à six heures, Odette était couchée avec Forcheville.

> [For a long time now it had made no matter to him that Odette had been false to him, and was false still. And yet he had continued for some years to seek out old servants of Odette, so strongly in him persisted the painful curiosity to know whether on that day, so long ago, at six o'clock, Odette had been in bed with Forcheville.]

The emotional life is composed of strands of feeling which one by one come undone and disappear. Swann has grown 'indifferent' to Odette and her unfaithfulness, but one spot in his personality still remains painfully *sensible*—his desire to know whether at a certain hour on a certain day many years ago she was or was not in bed with the boring Forcheville. It is a remarkable description of the way in which Swann's love has disintegrated, but it is simple compared with the startling aphorism which he introduces into the account of his liaison with Albertine:

> On n'a pas besoin d'être deux, il suffit d'être seul dans sa chambre, à penser, pour que de nouvelles trahisons de votre maîtresse se produisent, fût-elle morte.

[1] *Répertoire des thèmes de Marcel Proust* (Les Cahiers Marcel Proust, 7), Paris, 1935.

[We have no need of her company, it is enough to be alone in our room, think-ing, for fresh betrayal of us by our mistress to come to light, even though she be dead.]

We can see now why it is an exaggeration to say that the existence of two people, of the couple, is necessary to Proust's conception of love. The different characters in the 'psychological comedy' may very well be played by a single performer, or rather the drama takes place between the solitary protagonist and the phantoms which haunt his own mind.

Proust's revelation depends on the existence of a mind which was pre-occupied with its own workings to an extent that is almost undreamed of in the textbooks of the professors. He distinguished between 'notre moi permanent qui se prolonge pendant toute la durée de notre vie' and what he calls 'nos moi successifs qui en somme le composent en partie'. The *moi successifs* look at first like a succession of moods, but that is not what he meant. It is obvious that man is a person, that there is in him some principle of identity which corresponds to Descartes' 'thinking substance'; but round this *moi permanent* Proust groups the subsidiary *moi*. They are not moods; they are the different people that I have been at different moments of my life. It is here that Proust's theory of memory plays its part. The incident of the *madeleine* shows that memory is not something which I recall and which I see as belonging to the past. It is essentially a recreation of the past and a logical part of Proust's conception of time. Instead of simply surviving as memories, the people that I have been at different periods of my career come to life again and take on an independent existence of their own. The *moi permanent* is the core round which they are grouped. When my mistress abandons me, my *chagrin* is not simply heightened by a memory of a night spent with her at Balbec, a walk in the Luxembourg or the time when she was my 'prisoner' at my parents' flat. The person I was at each of those moments is resurrected in me as a separate being which intensifies my present suffering:

. . . ainsi à chaque instant, il y avait quelqu'un des innombrables et humbles 'moi' qui nous composent qui était ignorant encore du départ d'Albertine et à qui il fallait le notifier; il fallait—ce qui était plus cruel que s'ils avaient été des étrangers et n'avaient pas emprunté ma sensibilité pour souffrir,—annoncer le malheur qui venait d'arriver à tous ces êtres, à tous ces 'moi' qui ne le savaient pas encore. . . .

[. . . thus, at every moment there was one more of those innumerable and humble 'selves' that compose our personality which was still unaware of Albertine's departure and must be informed of it; I was obliged—and this was more cruel than if they had been strangers and had not borrowed my sensibility to pain—to describe to all these 'selves' who did not yet know of it, the calamity that had just occurred. . . .]

It is apparent from this that instead of providing the unity which he sought, the *moi permanent* is simply a precarious position which is continually undermined by the painful experiences of the *moi successifs*.

It is of the essence of Proust's experience that there is no absolute discontinuity between the events of the external world and those of the mental world. It is rather as though life were developing on parallel lines on either side of a partition:

> Pour que la mort d'Albertine eût pu supprimer mes souffrances, il eût fallu que le choc l'eût tuée non seulement en Touraine, mais en moi. Jamais elle n'y avait été plus vivante.

> [For the death of Albertine to be able to suppress my suffering, the shock of the fall would have had to kill her not only in Touraine but in myself. There, never had she been more alive.]

These two sentences bring out the full horror of the Prisoner alone with his obsessions. For not even the destruction of the cause or the apparent cause of his obsession can release him from it. We are told of an elderly Jewish homosexual:

> Il aimait d'ailleurs tout le labyrinthe de couloirs, de cabinets secrets, de salons, de vestiaires, de garde-mangers, de galeries qu'était l'hôtel de Balbec. Par atavisme d'oriental il aimait les sérails et quand il sortait le soir, on le voyait en explorer furtivement les détours.

> [He loved moreover all the labyrinth of corridors, private offices, reception rooms, cloakrooms, larders, galleries which composed the hotel at Balbec. With a strain of Oriental atavism he loved a seraglio, and when he went out at night might be seen furtively exploring its purlieus.]

This description of the fascination of the winding corridors and secret rooms of the old-fashioned hotel corresponds closely to Proust's conception of the mind. For Proust the mind is indeed a labyrinth where the Prisoner is condemned to wander unceasingly, pursuing his phantoms and looking for an outlet which does not exist. The longer he spends there, the more thoroughly he explores the galleries of the labyrinth, the more desperate his position and the more terrifying his obsessions become:

> J'étais torturé pas l'incessante reprise du désir toujours plus anxieux, et jamais accompli, d'un bruit d'appel; arrivé au point culminant d'une ascension tourmentée —dans les spirales de mon angoisse solitaire. . . .

> [I was tortured by the incessant recurrence of my longing, ever more anxious and never to be gratified, for the sound of a call; arrived at the culminating point of a tortuous ascent through the coils of my lonely anguish. . . .]

It is a perfect example of the 'spiral movement' of the latter part of the novel. We are aware of the Prisoner's progressive withdrawal further and further into his 'prison' until in a passage like this we have an almost frightening sense of mental claustrophobia. Proust's strength and weakness are inseparable because the sense of revolving more and more rapidly in a smaller and smaller physical space is only made possible by his very acute and very limited sensibility.

It will be remembered that in the fairy-tale of the Prince and the Sleeping Beauty it is the 'outsider' who sets the 'prisoner' free. There is nothing of the sort in Proust. In his first chapter he describes the lantern slide showing the sinister figure of Golo advancing towards the Princess's castle. In the last chapter he evokes the same image; but Golo is still in the same place outside the castle, a symbol of the terrors which haunt the Prisoner's mind, of the hallucinations which he is incapable of exorcizing.

'This part of *A la Recherche du temps perdu*,' writes M. Feuillerat of the affair between Marcel and Albertine, 'is the richest and most tormented love story in literature.' It deserves the praise that he gives it, but as usual there is a reservation to be made. Ortega y Gasset's comment applies even more forcibly to Marcel than to Swann. 'Only one thing is lacking—love.' For Marcel's 'love' is purely cerebral. He describes Albertine somewhere as *un être de fuite*, and this puts the matter very neatly. The characters remind us of beings on opposite sides of a glass partition. They are continually moving desperately towards one another, flattening their faces longingly against the glass, trying frantically to 'connect'. For just as they are unable to enter into one another's minds, so there is no physical contact between them, no warmth, no kindliness, no satisfaction. The mental isolation—the impossibility of really knowing the woman whom we imagine that we love—is accompanied by a shattering physical isolation.[1]

Would Albertine have come back to him? Did she go away because he did not see that she was a *jeune fille à marier*, did not offer her the one chance of escape from her vice? Was he or was he not responsible for her suicide? They are questions to which he can find no answer.

Rapprochant la mort de ma grand'mère et celle d'Albertine, il me semblait que ma vie était souillée d'un double assassinat.

Weighed down by guilt, he collapses and goes away from Paris to 'forget'. When, some years later, he emerges from his retirement, it is to find that all at once the world he knew has grown old and that he too is an old man. Albertine is at last 'forgotten'. He turns his attention to his novel. We

---

[1] 'Il se passait entre Albertine et moi la chose suivante (j'entends la chose vue par moi, de mon côté du verre qui n'était nullement transparent et sans que je puisse savoir ce qu'il y avait de vrai de l'autre côté). . . .'

remember that 'the last chapter of the last volume was written immediately after the first chapter of the first volume'. When we take leave of Marcel he is about to sit down and write the novel which we have just read. He has explained the theory on which it is based and his one fear seems to be that he may die before the book is written, that he may like Swann disappear into 'lost time'.

It is probable that Proust himself was haunted by the fear of dying before he had time to finish his novel, but Marcel's fear does not arise solely from the fact that death may deprive the world of a masterpiece. I have spoken of the part played by the actual writing of the novel in the artist's experience. I think that we can now go on to say that in this world the act of writing possesses a moral function. Art is the Prisoner's one chance of escape, the one chance of 'exorcizing his hallucinations'. Redemption lies in transmuting his experience—his guilty experience—into timeless art; it is his way of making amends to the *mère profanée* as Mlle Vinteuil's friend makes amends to the *père profané* by establishing the text of his unpublished works which would otherwise have been lost to the world.

The aim of the final volume is therefore to explain how 'lost time' is transformed into 'time regained'. It is scarcely an exaggeration to say that the novelist introduces a new 'hero' in the closing pages. This hero is *le Temps retrouvé* which is invested with a capital letter. The final paragraph is one of Proust's outstanding achievements as a master of French prose:

> Si du moins il m'était laissé assez de temps pour accomplir mon œuvre, je ne manquerais pas de la marquer au sceau de ce Temps dont l'idée s'imposait à moi avec tant de force aujourd'hui, et j'y décrirais les hommes, cela dût-il les faire ressembler à des êtres monstrueux, comme occupant dans le Temps une place autrement considérable que celle si restreinte qui leur est réservée dans l'espace, une place, au contraire, prolongée sans mesure, puisqu'ils touchent simultanément, comme des géants, plongés dans les années, à des époques vécues par eux, si distantes,—entre lesquelles tant de jours sont venus se placer—dans le Temps.

> [If at least, time enough were allotted to me to accomplish my work, I would not fail to mark it with the seal of Time, the idea of which imposed itself upon me with so much force to-day, and I would therein describe men, if need be, as monsters occupying a place in Time infinitely more important than the restricted one reserved for them in space, a place, on the contrary, prolonged immeasurably since, simultaneously touching widely separated years and the distant periods they have lived through—between which so many days have ranged themselves—they stand like giants immersed in Time.]

The word 'time' occurs in the opening sentence of the novel and we hear it all through the book, now softly and now more loudly; but in the closing paragraph—the climax of the whole novel—it sounds like a great bell; a bell warning the writer that his end is drawing near, but at the same moment transfiguring events, giving them an importance outside the petty 'time' of everyday experience and placing them in the eternal Time which transcends time. The passage begins gently reminding us of an invocation or a prayer addressed to 'Time' to spare him and closes with the final chord—the final chord of the 'symphony' which began at Combray—*dans le Temps*. And the sound reverberates in the mind long after we have shut the book.

That at any rate seems to have been Proust's intention, but we must not be misled by his consummate virtuosity. His theory of time and art is very fascinating, but in spite of its immense psychological interest, *Le Temps retrouvé* is something of a tour de force. Marcel was overcome with guilt, was horrified by a life 'souillée d'un double assassinat'. He felt the need to make reparation even if it were only to a false god; he tries to invest his experience with some transcendental significance in order to remove the *souillure* and resorts to a sleight of hand. We are grateful for the new vision, for his psychological revelation and for what is undoubtedly a very great achievement; but we do not need to accept this personal profession of faith. The conflict between art and life, the spiritual and 'counter-spirituality', and the conception of the artist as prisoner are a restatement of a perennial problem. The contemporary artist is necessarily a prisoner who attempts to transform the *données* of the actual world and his success does not depend on 'escape', still less on the highly personal interpretation which Proust appears to impose on experience in this last volume. His apotheosis therefore remains the final, dramatic attempt of the Prisoner to escape. And it fails.

PLAYS AND POETRY

THE BROWNING VERSION

BY TERENCE RATTIGAN

from *Playbill* (1949)

CHARACTERS IN THE PLAY

JOHN TAPLOW

FRANK HUNTER

MILLIE CROCKER-HARRIS

ANDREW CROCKER-HARRIS

DR. FROBISHER

PETER GILBERT

MRS. GILBERT

THE BROWNING VERSION

SCENE: *The sitting-room of the Crocker-Harrises' rooms in a public school in the South of England. It is between six and seven o'clock on a July evening. The building in which the rooms are situated is large and Victorian, and at some fairly recent date has been converted into flats of varying size for masters, married and unmarried. The Crocker-Harrises have the ground floor and their sitting-room is probably the biggest—and gloomiest—room in the house. It boasts, however, access [through a stained glass door L.] to a small garden, and is furnished with chintzy and genteel cheerfulness. Another door, back R. leads into the hall and he rest of the flat. This door is concealed by a screen.*

The room is empty at the rise of the curtain, but we hear the front door opening and closing and immediately after a timorous knock on the door, repeated after a pause.

Finally the door opens and JOHN TAPLOW *makes his appearance. He is a plain, moon-faced boy of about sixteen, with glasses. He stands in doubt at the door for a moment, then goes back into the hall, where we hear him calling.*

TAPLOW [calling off]: Sir! Sir!

After a pause, he re-enters. He is dressed in grey flannels, a dark blue coat and white scarf. He goes to the garden door and opens it.

[Calling.] Sir!

There is no reply. TAPLOW, *standing in the bright sunshine at the door, emits a plaintive sigh, then closes it firmly and goes to a table on which he places a book, a notebook and a pen.*

On the table is a small box of chocolates, probably the Crocker-Harrises' ration for the month. TAPLOW *opens the box, counts the number inside, and removes two. One of these he eats and the other, after a second's struggle, either with his conscience or his judgment of what he might be able to get away with, he virtuously replaces in the box. Finally he picks up a walking stick with a crooked handle and makes a couple of golf-swings, with an air of great concentration.*

FRANK HUNTER *appears from behind the screen covering the door. He is a rugged young man—not perhaps quite as rugged as his deliberately-cultivated manner of ruthless honesty makes him appear, but wrapped in all the self-confidence of the popular master. He watches* TAPLOW, *whose back is to the door, making his swing.*

FRANK: Roll the wrists away from the ball. Don't break them like that.

575

He walks over quickly and puts his large hands over the abashed TAPLOW'S. Now swing.

TAPLOW, *guided by* FRANK'S *evidently expert hands, succeeds in hitting the carpet with more effect than before.*

Too quick. Slow back and stiff left arm. It's no good just whacking the ball as if you were the headmaster and the ball was you. It'll never go more than fifty yards if you do. Get a rhythm. A good golf swing is a matter of aesthetics, not of brute strength.

TAPLOW, *only half listening, is gazing at the carpet.*

FRANK: What's the matter?

TAPLOW: I think we've made a tear in the carpet, sir.

FRANK *examines the spot perfunctorily.*

FRANK: Nonsense. That was there already. [*He puts the stick in a corner of the room.*] Do I know you?

TAPLOW: No, sir.

FRANK: What's your name?

TAPLOW: Taplow.

FRANK: Taplow? No, I don't. You're not a scientist I gather.

TAPLOW: No, sir. I'm still in the lower fifth. I can't specialize until next term—that's to say if I've got my remove all right.

FRANK: Don't you know yet if you've got your remove?

TAPLOW: No, sir. Mr. Crocker-Harris doesn't tell us the results like the other masters.

FRANK: Why not?

TAPLOW: Well, you know what he's like, sir.

FRANK: I believe there *is* a rule that form results should only be announced by the headmaster on the last day of term.

TAPLOW: Yes—but who else pays any attention to it—except Mr. Crocker-Harris?

FRANK: I don't, I admit—but that's no criterion. So you've got to wait until to-morrow to know your fate, have you?

TAPLOW: Yes, sir.

FRANK: Supposing the answer is favourable—what then?

TAPLOW: Oh—science, sir, of course.

FRANK [*sadly*]: Yes. We get all the slackers.

TAPLOW [*protestingly*]: I'm extremely interested in science, sir.

FRANK: Are you? I'm not. Not at least in the science I have to teach.

TAPLOW: Well, anyway, sir, it's a good deal more exciting than this muck. [*Indicating his book.*]

FRANK: What is this muck?

TAPLOW: Aeschylus, sir. The *Agamemnon.*

FRANK: And your considered view is that the *Agamemnon* of Aeschylus is muck, is it?

TAPLOW: Well, no, sir. I don't think the play is muck—exactly. I suppose, in a way, it's rather a good plot, really, a wife murdering her husband and having a lover and all that. I only meant the way it's taught to us—just a lot of Greek words strung together and fifty lines if you get them wrong.

FRANK: You sound a little bitter, Taplow.

TAPLOW: I am rather, sir.

FRANK: Kept in, eh?

TAPLOW: No, sir. Extra work.

FRANK: Extra work—on the last day of school?

TAPLOW: Yes, sir—and I might be playing golf. You'd think *he'd* have enough to do anyway himself, considering he's leaving to-morrow for good—but oh no. I missed a day last week when I had 'flu—so here I am—and look at the weather, sir.

FRANK: Bad luck. Still, there's one consolation. You're pretty well bound to get your remove to-morrow for being a good boy in taking extra work.

TAPLOW: Well, I'm not so sure, sir. That would be true of the ordinary masters, all right. They just wouldn't dare not give a chap a remove after his taking extra work—it would be such a bad advertisement for them. But those sort of rules don't apply to the Crock—Mr. Crocker-Harris. I asked him yesterday outright if he'd given me a remove and do you know what he said, sir?

FRANK: No. What?

TAPLOW [*mimicking a very gentle, rather throaty voice*]: 'My dear Taplow, I have given you exactly what you deserve. No less; and certainly no more.' Do you know, sir, I think he may have marked me down, rather than up, for taking extra work. I mean, the man's barely human. [*He breaks off quickly.*] Sorry, sir. Have I gone too far?

FRANK: Yes. Much too far.

TAPLOW: Sorry, sir. I got sort of carried away.

FRANK: Evidently. [*He picks up* The Times *and opens it.*] Er—Taplow.

TAPLOW: Yes, sir?

FRANK: What was that Mr. Crocker-Harris said to you? Just—er—repeat it, would you?

TAPLOW [*mimicking again*]: 'My dear Taplow, I have given you exactly what you deserve. No less; and certainly no more.'

FRANK *snorts, then looks stern.*

FRANK: Not in the least like him. Read your nice Aeschylus and be quiet.

TAPLOW [*with weary disgust*]: Aeschylus.

FRANK: Look, what time did Mr. Crocker-Harris tell you to be here?

TAPLOW: Six-thirty, sir.

FRANK: Well, he's ten minutes late. Why don't you cut? You could still get nine holes in before lock-up.

TAPLOW [*genuinely shocked*]: Oh, no, I couldn't cut. Cut the Crock—Mr.

Crocker-Harris? I shouldn't think it's ever been done in the whole time he's been here. God knows what would happen if I did. He'd probably follow me home, or something——

FRANK: I must admit I envy him the effect he seems to have on you boys in his form. You all seem scared to death of him. What does he do—beat you all, or something?

TAPLOW: Good Lord, no. He's not a sadist, like one or two of the others.

FRANK: I beg your pardon?

TAPLOW: A sadist, sir, is someone who gets pleasure out of giving pain.

FRANK: Indeed? But I think you went on to say that some other masters——

TAPLOW: Well, of course they are, sir. I won't mention names, but you know them as well as I do. Of course I know most masters think we boys don't understand a thing—but dash it, sir, you're different. You're young —well comparatively anyway—and you're science and you canvassed for Labour in the last election. You must know what sadism is.

FRANK [after a pause]: Good Lord! What are public schools coming to?

TAPLOW: Anyway the Crock isn't a sadist. That's what I'm saying. He wouldn't be so frightening if he were—because at least it would show he had some feelings. But he hasn't. He's all shrivelled up inside like a nut and he seems to hate people to like him. It's funny, that. I don't know any other master who doesn't like being liked——

FRANK: And I don't know any boy who doesn't trade on that very foible.

TAPLOW: Well, it's natural, sir. But not with the Crock——

FRANK [making a feeble attempt at re-establishing the correct relationship]: Mr. Crocker-Harris.

TAPLOW: Mr. Crocker-Harris. The funny thing is that in spite of everything, I do rather like him. I can't help it. And sometimes I think he sees it and that seems to shrivel him up even more——

FRANK: I'm sure you're exaggerating.

TAPLOW: No, sir, I'm not. In form the other day he made one of his little classical jokes. Of course nobody laughed because nobody understood it, myself included. Still, I knew he'd meant it as funny, so I laughed. Not out of sucking-up, sir, I swear, but ordinary common politeness, and feeling a bit sorry for him having made a dud joke. [He goes to the table and sits down]. Now I can't remember what the joke was—but let's say it was [adopting his imitative voice again] benedictus, benedicatur, benedictine . . . Now, you laugh, sir——

FRANK laughs. TAPLOW looks at him over an imaginary pair of spectacles, and then, very gently crooks his fore-finger to him in indication to approach the table. FRANK does so—simply, not clowning. He is genuinely interested in the incident. [In a gentle, throaty voice.] 'Taplow—you laughed at my little pun, I noticed. I must confess I am flattered at the evident advance your Latinity has made that you should so readily have understood what the rest of the form did not. Perhaps, now, you would be good enough to explain it to them, so that they too can share your pleasure.'

The door behind the screen is pushed open and MILLIE CROCKER-HARRIS *appears. She is a thin woman in the late thirties, rather more smartly dressed than the general run of schoolmasters' wives. She stands by the screen pulling off her gloves and watching* TAPLOW *and* FRANK. *It is a few seconds before they notice her.*

'Come along, Taplow. Do not be so selfish as to keep a good joke to yourself. Tell the others——' [*he breaks off suddenly, seeing* MILLIE]. Oh Lord!

FRANK *turns quickly, and seems infinitely relieved at seeing* MILLIE.

FRANK: Oh, hullo.

MILLIE [*without expression*]: Hullo.

She puts down a couple of parcels she has been carrrying, and goes back into the hall to take off her hat.

TAPLOW [*frantically whispering to* FRANK]: Do you think she heard?

FRANK *shakes his head comfortingly.*

I think she did. She was standing there quite a time. If she did and she tells him, there goes my remove——

FRANK: Nonsense——

MILLIE *comes back into the room.*

MILLIE [*to* TAPLOW]: Waiting for my husband?

TAPLOW: Er—yes.

MILLIE: He's at the Bursar's and might be there quite a time. If I were you I'd go.

TAPLOW [*doubtfully*]: He said most particularly I was to come——

MILLIE: Well, why don't you run away for a quarter of an hour and come back?

TAPLOW: Supposing he gets here before me?

MILLIE [*smiling*]: I'll take the blame. I tell you what—you can do a job for him. Take this prescription to the chemist and get it made up.

TAPLOW: All right, Mrs. Crocker-Harris.

MILLIE: And while you're there you might as well slip into Stewarts and have an ice. Here. Catch. [*She takes a shilling from her bag and throws it to him.*]

TAPLOW: Thanks awfully. [*He passes* FRANK *on his way to the door. In a whisper.*] See she doesn't tell him.

FRANK: O.K.

MILLIE [*turning as* TAPLOW *is going*]: Oh, Taplow——

TAPLOW: Yes, Mrs. Crocker-Harris.

MILLIE: I had a letter from my father to-day in which he says he once had the pleasure of meeting your mother——

TAPLOW [*uninterested, but polite*]: Oh, really?

MILLIE: Yes. It was at some fête or other in Bradford. My uncle—that's Sir William Bartop, you know—made a speech and so did your mother. My father met her afterwards at tea——

TAPLOW: Oh, really?

MILLIE: He said he found her quite charming.

TAPLOW: Yes, she's jolly good at those sort of functions. [*Aware of his lack of tact.*] I mean—I'm sure she found him charming, too. Well, I'd better get going. So long.

TAPLOW *goes out.*

MILLIE: Thank you for coming round.

FRANK: That's all right.

MILLIE: You're staying for dinner?

FRANK: If I may.

MILLIE: If you may! Give me a cigarette.

He extends his case. She takes a cigarette.

[*Indicating case.*] You haven't given it away yet, I see.

FRANK: Do you think I would?

MILLIE: Frankly, yes. Luckily it's a man's case. I don't suppose any of your girl friends would want it——

FRANK: Don't be silly.

MILLIE: Where have you been all this week?

FRANK: Correcting exam papers—making reports. You know what end of term is like——

MILLIE: I do know what end of term is like. But even Andrew has managed this last week to take a few hours off to say good-bye to people——

FRANK: I really have been appallingly busy. Besides I'm coming to stay with you in Bradford——

MILLIE: Not for over a month. Andrew doesn't start his new job until September first. That's one of the things I had to tell you.

FRANK: Oh. I had meant to be in Devonshire in September.

MILLIE [*quickly*]: Who with?

FRANK: My family.

MILLIE: Surely you can go earlier, can't you? Go in August.

FRANK: It'll be difficult.

MILLIE: Then you'd better come to me in August.

FRANK: But Andrew will still be there.

MILLIE: Yes.

Pause.

FRANK: I think I can manage September.

MILLIE: That'd be better—from every point of view. Except that it means I shan't see you for six weeks.

FRANK [*lightly*]: You'll survive that, all right.

MILLIE: Yes, I'll survive it—but not as easily as you will.

FRANK *says nothing.*

I haven't much pride, have I? [*She approaches him.*] Frank, darling, I love you so much——

He kisses her, on the mouth, but a trifle perfunctorily, and then breaks quickly away, as if afraid someone had come into the room.

[*Laughing.*] You're very nervous.

FRANK: I'm afraid of that screen arrangement. You can't see people coming in——

MILLIE: Oh, yes. That reminds me. What were you and Taplow up to when I came in just now? Making fun of my husband?

FRANK: Afraid so. Yes.

MILLIE: It sounded rather a good imitation. I must get him to do it for me sometime. It was very naughty of you to encourage him.

FRANK: I know. It was.

MILLIE [*ironically*]: Bad for discipline.

FRANK: Exactly. Currying favour with the boys, too. My God, how easy it is to be popular. I've only been a master three years but I've already slipped into an act and a vernacular that I just can't get out of. Why can't anyone ever be natural with the little blighters?

MILLIE: They probably wouldn't like it if you were.

FRANK: I don't see why not. No one seems to have tried it yet, anyway. I suppose the trouble is—we're all too scared of them. Either one gets forced into an attitude of false and hearty and jocular bonhomie like myself, or into the sort of petty, soulless tyranny which your husband uses to protect himself against the lower fifth.

MILLIE [*rather bored with this*]: He'd never be popular whatever he did——

FRANK: Possibly not. He ought never to have become a schoolmaster, really. Why did he?

MILLIE: It was his vocation, he said. He was sure he'd make a big success of it, especially when he got his job here first go off. [*Bitterly.*] Fine success he's made, hasn't he?

FRANK: You should have stopped him.

MILLIE: How was I to know? He talked about getting a house, then a headmastership.

FRANK: The Crock a headmaster! That's a pretty thought.

MILLIE: Yes, it's funny to think of now, all right. Still he wasn't always the Crock, you know. He had a bit more gumption once. At least I thought he had. Don't let's talk any more about him—it's too depressing.

FRANK: I'm sorry for him.

MILLIE [*indifferently*]: He's not sorry for himself, so why should you be? It's me you should be sorry for.

FRANK: I am.

MILLIE [*smiling*]: Then show me.

She stretches out her arms to him. He kisses her again quickly and lightly, but she holds him hungrily. He has to free himself almost roughly.

FRANK: What have you been doing all day?

MILLIE: Calling on the other masters' wives—saying fond farewells. I've worked off twelve. I've another seven to do to-morrow.

FRANK: You poor thing! I don't envy you.

MILLIE: It's the housemasters' wives that are the worst. They're all so damn patronizing. You should have heard Betty Carstairs. 'My dear—it's such terrible bad luck on you both—that your husband should get this heart trouble just when, if only he'd stayed on, he'd have been bound to get a house. I mean, he's considerably senior to my Arthur as it is, and they simply couldn't have gone on passing him over, could they?'

FRANK: There's a word for Betty Carstairs, my dear, that I would hesitate to employ before a lady.

MILLIE: She's got her eye on you, anyway.

FRANK: Betty Carstairs? What utter rot!

MILLIE: Oh, yes, she has. I saw you at that concert. Don't think I didn't notice.

FRANK: Millie, darling! Really! I detest the woman.

MILLIE: Then what were you doing in her box at Lord's?

FRANK: Carstairs invited me. I went there because it was a good place to see the match from.

MILLIE: Yes, I'm sure it was. Much better than the grandstand, anyway.

FRANK [*as if remembering something suddenly*]: Oh, my God!

MILLIE: It's all right, my dear. Don't bother to apologize. We gave the seat away, as it happens——

FRANK: I'm most terribly sorry.

MILLIE: It's all right. We couldn't afford a box, you see——

FRANK: It wasn't that. You know it wasn't that. It's just that I—well, I clean forgot.

MILLIE: Funny you didn't forget the Carstairs' invitation——

FRANK: Millie—don't be a fool.

MILLIE: It's you who are the fool. [*Appealingly.*] Frank—have you never been in love? I know you're not in love with me—but haven't you ever been in love with anyone? Don't you realize what torture you inflict on someone who loves you when you do a thing like that?

FRANK: I've told you I'm sorry—I don't know what more I can say.

MILLIE: Why not the truth?

FRANK: The truth is—I clean forgot.

MILLIE: The truth is—you had something better to do—and why not say it?

FRANK: All right. Believe that if you like. It happens to be a lie, but believe it all the same. Only for God's sake stop this——

MILLIE: Then for God's sake show me some pity. Do you think it's any pleasanter for me to believe that you cut me because you forgot? Do you think that doesn't hurt either?

FRANK *turns away.*

Oh, damn! I was so determined to be brave and not mention Lord's. Why did I? Frank, just tell me one thing. Just tell me you're not running away from me—that's all I want to hear.

FRANK: I'm coming to Bradford.

MILLIE: I think, if you don't, I'll kill myself.

FRANK: I'm coming to Bradford.

The door is pushed open. FRANK *has made a move towards* MILLIE, *but stops at the sound.* MILLIE *has recovered herself as* ANDREW CROCKER-HARRIS *appears by the screen. Despite the summer sun he wears a serge suit and a stiff collar. He carries a portfolio and looks, as ever, neat, complacent and unruffled. He speaks in a very gentle voice which he rarely raises.*

ANDREW: Is Taplow here?

MILLIE: I sent him to the chemist to get your prescription made up——

ANDREW: What prescription?

MILLIE: Your heart medicine. Don't you remember? You told me this morning it had run out——

ANDREW: Of course I remember, my dear, but there was no need to send Taplow for it. If you had telephoned the chemist he would have sent it round in plenty of time. He knows the prescription. Now Taplow will be late and I am so pressed for time I hardly know how to fit him in.

This colloquy has taken place near the door, the screen and MILLIE *blocking* ANDREW'S *view of the room. As he now comes in he sees* FRANK.

Ah, Hunter! How are you?

FRANK: Very well, thanks.

They shake hands.

ANDREW: Most kind of you to drop in, but, as Millie should have warned you I am expecting a pupil for extra work and——

MILLIE: He's staying to dinner, Andrew.

ANDREW: Good. Then I shall see something of you. However, when Taplow returns I'm sure you won't mind——

FRANK [*making a move*]: No, of course not. I'll make myself scarce now, if you'd rather—I mean, if you're busy——

ANDREW: Oh, no. There is no need for that. Sit down, do. Will you smoke? I don't, as you know, but Millie does. Millie, give our guest a cigarette——

MILLIE: I haven't any, I'm afraid. I've had to cadge from him.

FRANK *takes out his cigarette case and offers it to* MILLIE *who exchanges a glance with him as she takes one.*

ANDREW: We expected you at Lord's, Hunter.

FRANK: What? Oh, yes. I'm most terribly sorry. I——

MILLIE: He clean forgot, Andrew. Imagine.

ANDREW: Forgot?

MILLIE: Not everyone is blessed with your superhuman memory, you see.

FRANK: I really can't apologize enough——

ANDREW: Please don't bother to mention it. On the second day we managed to sell the seat to a certain Dr. Lambert, who wore, I regret to say, the colours of the opposing faction, but who otherwise seemed a passably agreeable person. You liked him, didn't you, Millie?

MILLIE [*looking at* FRANK]: Very much, indeed. I thought him quite charming.

ANDREW: A charming old gentleman. [*To* FRANK.] You have had tea?

FRANK: Yes—thank you——

ANDREW: Is there any other refreshment I can offer you?

FRANK: No, thank you.

ANDREW: Would it interest you to see the new timetable I have drafted for next term?

FRANK: Yes, very much.

ANDREW *has taken out a long roll of paper, made by pasting pieces of foolscap together and which is entirely covered by his meticulous writing.*

I never knew you drafted our timetables——

ANDREW: Didn't you? I have done so for the last fifteen years. Of course they are always issued in mimeograph under the headmaster's signature— Now what form do you take? Upper fifth Science—there you are—that's the general picture, but on the back you will see each form specified under separate headings—there—that's a new idea of mine—Millie, this might interest you——

MILLIE [*suddenly harsh*]: You know it bores me to death——

FRANK *looks up, surprised and uncomfortable.* ANDREW *does not remove his eyes from the timetable.*

ANDREW: Millie has no head for this sort of work. There you see. Now here you can follow the upper fifth Science throughout every day of the week.

FRANK [*indicating timetable*]: I must say, I think this is a really wonderful job.

ANDREW: Thank you. It has the merit of clarity, I think.

FRANK: I don't know what they'll do without you.

ANDREW [*without expression*]: They'll find somebody else, I expect.

Pause.

FRANK: What sort of job is this you're going to?

ANDREW [*looking at his wife for the first time*]: Hasn't Millie told you?

FRANK: She said it was a cr—— a private school.

ANDREW: A crammer's—for backward boys. It is run by an old Oxford contemporary of mine who lives in Dorset. The work will not be so arduous as here and my doctor seems to think I will be able to undertake it without—er—danger——

FRANK [*with genuine sympathy*]: It's the most rotten bad luck for you. I'm awfully sorry.

ANDREW [*raising his voice a little*]: My dear Hunter, there is nothing whatever to be sorry for. I am looking forward to the change——

There is a knock at the door.

ANDREW: Come in.

TAPLOW *appears, a trifle breathless and guilty looking. He carries a medicine bottle wrapped and sealed.*

Ah, Taplow, Good. You have been running, I see.

TAPLOW: Yes, sir. [*He hands the bottle to* MILLIE.]

ANDREW: There was a queue at the chemist's, I suppose?

TAPLOW: Yes, sir.

ANDREW: And doubtless an even longer one at Stewarts?

TAPLOW: Yes, sir—I mean—no, sir—I mean—[*he looks at* MILLIE] yes, sir.

MILLIE: You were late, yourself, Andrew.

ANDREW: Exactly. And for that I apologize, Taplow.

TAPLOW: That's all right, sir.

ANDREW: Luckily we have still a good hour before lock-up, so nothing has been lost——

FRANK [*to* MILLIE]: May I use the short cut? I'm going back to my digs.

MILLIE: Yes. Go ahead. Come back soon. If Andrew hasn't finished we can sit in the garden. [*Moving to door.*] I'd better go and see about dinner.

She goes out at back.

ANDREW [*to* FRANK]: Taplow is desirous of obtaining a remove from my form, Hunter, so that he can spend the rest of his career here playing happily with the crucibles, retorts and bunsen burners of your science fifth.

FRANK [*at door*]: Oh. Has he?

ANDREW: Has he what?

FRANK: Obtained his remove?

ANDREW [*after a pause*]: He has obtained exactly what he deserves. No less; and certainly no more.

TAPLOW *utters an explosion of mirth.*

FRANK *nods, thoughtfully, and goes out through the garden door.*

ANDREW *has caught sight of* TAPLOW's *contorted face, but passes no remark on it. He sits at the table and makes a sign for* TAPLOW *to sit beside him. He picks up a text of the* Agamemnon *and* TAPLOW *does the same.*

Line thirteen hundred and ninety-nine. Begin.

TAPLOW: Chorus. We—are surprised at——

ANDREW [*automatically*]: We marvel at.

TAPLOW: We marvel at—thy tongue—how bold thou art—that you——

ANDREW: Thou [ANDREW's *interruptions are automatic. His thoughts are evidently far distant.*]

TAPLOW: Thou—can——

ANDREW: Canst——

TAPLOW: Canst—boastfully speak——

ANDREW: Utter such a boastful speech——

TAPLOW: Utter such a boastful speech—over—[*in a sudden rush of inspiration*] the bloody corpse of the husband you have slain——

ANDREW *looks down at his text for the first time.* TAPLOW *looks apprehensive.*

ANDREW: Taplow—I presume you are using a different text from mine——

TAPLOW: No, sir.

ANDREW: That is strange for the line as I have it reads: ἥτις τοιόνδ' ἐπ' ἀνδρὶ κομπάζεις λόγον. However diligently I search I can discover no 'bloody'—no 'corpse'—no 'you have slain'. Simply 'husband'——

TAPLOW: Yes, sir. That's right.

ANDREW: Then why do you invent words that simply are not there?

TAPLOW: I thought they sounded better, sir. More exciting. After all she did kill her husband, sir. [*With relish.*] She's just been revealed with his dead body and Cassandra's weltering in gore——

ANDREW: I am delighted at this evidence, Taplow, of your interest in the rather more lurid aspects of dramaturgy, but I feel I must remind you that you are supposed to be construing Greek, not collaborating with Aeschylus.

TAPLOW [*greatly daring*]: Yes, but still, sir, translator's licence, sir—I didn't get anything wrong—and after all it *is* a play and not just a bit of Greek construe.

ANDREW [*momentarily at a loss*]: I seem to detect a note of end of term in your remarks. I am not denying that the *Agamemnon* is a play. It is perhaps the greatest play ever written——

TAPLOW [*quickly*]: I wonder how many people in the form think that?

Pause. TAPLOW *is instantly frightened of what he has said.*

Sorry, sir. Shall I go on?

ANDREW *does not answer. He sits motionless staring at his book.*

Shall I go on, sir?

There is another pause. ANDREW *raises his head slowly from his book.*

ANDREW [*murmuring gently, not looking at* TAPLOW]: When I was a very young man, only two years older than you are now, Taplow, I wrote, for my own pleasure, a translation of the *Agamemnon*—a very free translation—I remember—in rhyming couplets.

TAPLOW: The whole *Agamemnon*—in verse? That must have been hard work, sir.

ANDREW: It was hard work; but I derived great joy from it. The play had so excited and moved me that I wished to communicate, however imperfectly, some of that emotion to others. When I had finished it, I remember, I thought it very beautiful—almost more beautiful than the original.

TAPLOW: Was it ever published, sir?

ANDREW: No. Yesterday I looked for the manuscript while I was packing my papers. I was unable to find it. I fear it is lost—like so many other things. Lost for good.

TAPLOW: Hard luck, sir.

ANDREW *is silent again.* TAPLOW *steals a timid glance at him.*

Shall I go on, sir?

ANDREW, *with a slight effort, lowers his eyes again to his text.*

ANDREW [*raising his voice slightly*]: No. Go back and get that last line right.

TAPLOW, *out of* ANDREW'S *vision, as he thinks, makes a disgusted grimace in his direction.*

TAPLOW: That—thou canst utter such a boastful speech over thy husband——

ANDREW: Yes. And, now, if you would be so kind, you will do the line again, without the facial contortion which you just found necessary to accompany it——

TAPLOW *is just beginning the line again, when* MILLIE *appears hurriedly. She has on an apron.*

MILLIE: The headmaster's just coming up the drive. Don't tell him I'm in. The fish pie isn't in the oven yet.

She disappears.

TAPLOW, *who has jumped up on* MILLIE'S *entrance, turns hopefully to* ANDREW.

TAPLOW: I'd better go, hadn't I, sir? I mean—I don't want to be in the way——

ANDREW: We do not yet know that it is I the headmaster wishes to see. Other people live in this building.

There is a knock at the door.

ANDREW: Come in.

DR. FROBISHER *comes in. He looks more like a distinguished diplomat than a doctor of literature and classical scholar. He is in the middle fifties and goes to a very good tailor.*

FROBISHER: Ah. Crocker-Harris. I've caught you in. I'm so glad. I hope I'm not disturbing you?

ANDREW: I have been taking a pupil in extra work——

FROBISHER: On the penultimate day of term? That argues either great conscientiousness on your part or considerable backwardness on his.

ANDREW: Perhaps a combination of both——

FROBISHER: Quite so, but as this is my only chance of speaking to you before to-morrow, I think that perhaps your pupil will be good enough to excuse us—[*he turns politely to* TAPLOW].

TAPLOW: Oh, yes, sir. That's really quite all right. [*He collects his books and dashes to the door.*]

ANDREW: I'm extremely sorry, Taplow. You will please explain to your

father exactly what occurred over this lost hour and tell him that I shall
in due course be writing to him to return the money involved——

TAPLOW [*hurriedly*]: Yes, sir. But please don't bother, sir. I know it's all
right, sir. Thank you, sir.

He darts out.

FROBISHER: Have the Gilberts called on you, yet?

ANDREW: The Gilberts, sir? Who are they?

FROBISHER: Gilbert is your successor with the lower fifth. He is down here
to-day with his wife, and as they will be taking over this flat I thought
perhaps you wouldn't mind if they came in to look it over.

ANDREW: Of course not.

FROBISHER: I've told you about him, I think. He is a very brilliant young
man and won exceptionally high honours at Oxford.

ANDREW: So I understand, sir.

FROBISHER: Not, of course, as high as the honours you yourself won there.
He didn't, for instance, win the Chancellor's prize for Latin verse or the
Gainsford.

ANDREW: He won the Hertford Latin, then?

FROBISHER: No. [*Mildly surprised.*] Did you win that, too?

ANDREW *nods.*

It's sometimes rather hard to remember that you are perhaps the most
brilliant classical scholar we have ever had at the school——

ANDREW: You are very kind.

FROBISHER [*urbanely corrects his gaffe*]: Hard to remember, I mean—because
of your other activities—your brilliant work on the school timetable, for
instance, and also for your heroic battle for so long and against such odds
with the soul destroying lower fifth.

ANDREW: I have not found that my soul has been destroyed by the lower
fifth, headmaster.

FROBISHER: I was joking, of course.

ANDREW: Oh, I see.

FROBISHER: Is your wife in?

ANDREW: Er—no. Not at the moment.

FROBISHER: I shall have a chance of saying good-bye to her to-morrow.
I am rather glad I have got you to myself. I have a delicate matter—two
rather delicate matters—to broach.

ANDREW: Please sit down.

FROBISHER: Thank you. [*He sits.*] Now you have been with us, in all,
eighteen years, haven't you?

ANDREW *nods.*

It is extremely unlucky that you should have had to retire at so comparatively an early age and so short a time before you would have been eligible
for a pension.

The HEADMASTER *is regarding his nails, as he speaks, studiously avoiding* ANDREW'S *gaze.*

ANDREW: Pension? [*After a pause.*] You have decided, then, not to award me a pension?

FROBISHER: Not I, my dear fellow. It has nothing at all to do with me. It's the governors who, I'm afraid, have been forced to turn down your application. I put your case to them as well as I could, but they decided with great regret, that they couldn't make an exception to the rule.

ANDREW: But I thought—my wife thought, that an exception was made some five years ago——

FROBISHER: Ah. In the case of Buller, you mean? True. But the circumstances with Buller were quite remarkable. It was, after all, in playing rugger against the school that he received that injury——

ANDREW: Yes. I remember.

FROBISHER: And then the governors received a petition from boys, old boys and parents with over five hundred signatures.

ANDREW: I would have signed that petition myself, but through some oversight I was not asked——

FROBISHER: He was a splendid fellow, Buller. Splendid. Doing very well, too, now, I gather.

ANDREW: I'm delighted to hear it.

FROBISHER: Your own case, of course, is equally deserving. If not more so— for Buller was a younger man. Unfortunately—rules are rules—and are not made to be broken every few years; at any rate that is the governors' view.

ANDREW: I quite understand.

FROBISHER: I knew you would. Now might I ask you a rather impertinent question.

ANDREW: Certainly.

FROBISHER: You have, I take it, private means?

ANDREW: My wife has some.

FROBISHER: Ah, yes. Your wife has often told me of her family connections. I understand her father has a business in—Bradford—isn't it?

ANDREW: Yes. He runs a men's clothing shop in the Arcade.

FROBISHER: Indeed? Your wife's remarks had led me to imagine something a little more—extensive.

ANDREW: My father-in-law made a settlement on my wife at the time of our marriage. She has about three hundred a year of her own. I have nothing. Is that the answer to your question, headmaster?

FROBISHER: Yes. Thank you for your frankness. Now, this private school you are going to——

ANDREW: My salary at the crammer's is to be two hundred pounds a year.

FROBISHER: Quite so. With board and lodging, of course?

ANDREW: For eight months of the year.

FROBISHER: Yes, I see. [*He ponders a second.*] Of course, you know, there is the School Benevolent Fund that deals with cases of actual hardship——

ANDREW: There will be no actual hardship, headmaster.

FROBISHER: No. I am glad you take that view. I must admit, though, I had hoped that your own means had proved a little more ample. Your wife had certainly led me to suppose——

ANDREW: I am not denying that a pension would have been very welcome, headmaster, but I see no reason to quarrel with the governors' decision. What is the other delicate matter you have to discuss?

FROBISHER: Well, it concerns the arrangements at prize-giving to-morrow. You are, of course, prepared to say a few words?

ANDREW: I had assumed you would call on me to do so.

FROBISHER: Of course. It is always done, and I know the boys appreciate the custom.

ANDREW: I have already made a few notes of what I am going to say. Perhaps you would care——

FROBISHER: No, no. That isn't necessary at all. I know I can trust your discretion—not to say your wit. It will be, I know, a very moving moment for you—indeed for us all—but, as I'm sure you realize, it is far better to keep these occasions from becoming too heavy and distressing. You know how little the boys appreciate sentiment——

ANDREW: I do.

FROBISHER: That is why I've planned my own reference to you at the end of my speech to be rather more light and jocular than I would otherwise have made it.

ANDREW: I quite understand. I too have prepared a few little jokes and puns for my speech. One—a play of words on *vale*, farewell, and Wally, the Christian name of a backward boy in my class, is, I think, rather happy.

FROBISHER: Yes. [*He laughs belatedly*]: Very neat. That should go down extremely well.

ANDREW: I'm glad you like it.

FROBISHER: Well, now—there is a particular favour I have to ask of you in connection with the ceremony, and I know I shall not have to ask in vain. Fletcher, as you know, is leaving, too.

ANDREW: Yes. He is going into the city, they tell me.

FROBISHER: Yes. Now he is, of course, considerably junior to you. He has only been here—let me see—five years. But, as you know, he has done great things for our cricket—positive wonders, when you remember what doldrums we were in before he came——

ANDREW: Our win at Lord's this year was certainly most inspiriting——

FROBISHER: Exactly. Now I'm sure that to-morrow the boys will make the occasion of his farewell speech a tremendous demonstration of gratitude. The applause might go on for minutes—you know what the boys feel about Lord's—and I seriously doubt my ability to cut it short or even, I admit, the propriety of trying to do so—Now, you see the quandary in which I am placed?

ANDREW: Perfectly. You wish to refer to me and for me to make my speech before you come to Fletcher?

FROBISHER: It's extremely awkward, and I feel wretched about asking it of you—but it's more for your own sake than for mine or Fletcher's that I do. After all, a climax is what one must try to work up to on these occasions.

ANDREW: Naturally, headmaster, I wouldn't wish to provide an anti-climax.

FROBISHER: You really mustn't take it amiss, my dear fellow. The boys, in applauding Fletcher for several minutes and yourself say—for—well, for not quite so long—won't be making any personal demonstration between you. It will be quite impersonal—I assure you—quite impersonal.

ANDREW: I understand.

FROBISHER [warmly]: I knew you would, and I can hardly tell you how wisely I think you have chosen. Well now—as that is all my business, I think perhaps I had better be getting along. This has been a terribly busy day for me—for you too, I imagine.

ANDREW: Yes.

MILLIE comes in. She has taken off her apron, and tidied herself up.

MILLIE [her social manner]: Ah, headmaster. How good of you to drop in.

FROBISHER [more at home with her than with Andrew]: Mrs. Crocker-Harris. How are you?

They shake hands.

You're looking extremely well, I must say. Has anyone ever told you, Crocker-Harris, that you have a very attractive wife?

ANDREW: Many people, sir. But then I hardly need to be told.

MILLIE: Can I persuade you to stay a few moments and have a drink, head-master. It's so rarely we have the pleasure of seeing you——

FROBISHER: Unfortunately, dear lady, I was just on the point of leaving. I have two frantic parents waiting for me at home. You are dining with us to-morrow—both of you, aren't you?

MILLIE: Yes, indeed—and so looking forward to it.

FROBISHER: I'm so glad. We can say our sad farewells then. [To ANDREW.] Au revoir, Crocker-Harris, and thank you very much.

ANDREW bows.

MILLIE holds the door open for FROBISHER and follows him out into the hall.

MILLIE [to ANDREW as she goes out with FROBISHER]: Don't forget to take your medicine, dear, will you?

ANDREW: No.

FROBISHER [*in the hall*]: Lucky invalid! To have such a very charming nurse——

MILLIE [*also in the hall*]: I really don't know what to say to all these compliments, headmaster. I don't believe you mean a word of them.

FROBISHER: Every word. Till to-morrow, then? Good-bye.

We hear the door slam. ANDREW *is staring out of the window.* MILLIE *reappears.*

MILLIE: Well? Do we get it?

ANDREW [*absently*]: Get what?

MILLIE: The pension, of course. Do we get it?

ANDREW: No.

MILLIE: My God? Why not!

ANDREW: It's against the rules.

MILLIE: Buller got it, didn't he? Buller got it? What's the idea of giving it to him and not to us?

ANDREW: The governors are afraid of establishing a precedent.

MILLIE: The mean old brutes! My God, what I wouldn't like to say to them! [*Rounding on* ANDREW.] And what did you say? Just sat there and made a joke in Latin, I suppose?

ANDREW: There wasn't very much I could say, in Latin or any other language.

MILLIE: Oh, wasn't there? I'd have said it all right. I wouldn't just have sat there twiddling my thumbs and taking it from that old phoney of a headmaster. But then, of course, I'm not a man.

ANDREW *is turning the pages of the* Agamemnon, *not looking at her.*

What do they expect you to do? Live on my money, I suppose.

ANDREW: There has never been any question of that. I shall be perfectly able to support myself.

MILLIE: Yourself? Doesn't the marriage service say something about the husband supporting his wife? Doesn't it? You ought to know?

ANDREW: Yes, it does.

MILLIE: And how do you think you're going to do that on two hundred a year?

ANDREW: I shall do my utmost to save some of it. You're welcome to it, if I can.

MILLIE: Thank you for precisely nothing.

ANDREW *underlines a word in the text he is reading.*

What else did the old fool have to say?

ANDREW: The headmaster? He wants me to make my speech to-morrow before instead of after Fletcher.

MILLIE: Yes. I knew he was going to ask that.

ANDREW [*without surprise*]: You knew?

MILLIE: Yes. He asked my advice about it a week ago. I told him to go ahead. I knew you wouldn't mind, and as there isn't a Mrs. Fletcher to make *me* look a fool, I didn't give two hoots.

There is a knock on the door.

Come in.

MR. and MRS. GILBERT come in. He is about twenty-two, and his wife a year or so younger.

GILBERT: Mr. Crocker-Harris?

ANDREW [*rising*]: Yes. Is it Mr. and Mrs. Gilbert? The headmaster told me you might look in.

MRS. GILBERT: I do hope we're not disturbing you.

ANDREW: Not at all. This is my wife.

MRS. GILBERT: How do you do.

ANDREW: Mr. and Mrs. Gilbert are our successors to this flat, my dear.

MILLIE: Oh, yes. How nice to meet you both.

GILBERT: How do you do? We really won't keep you more than a second— my wife thought as we were here you wouldn't mind us taking a squint at our future home.

MRS. GILBERT [*unnecessarily*]: This is the drawing-room, I suppose?

MILLIE: That's right. Well, it's really a living-room. Andrew uses it as a study.

MRS. GILBERT: How charmingly you've done it!

MILLIE: Oh, do you think so? I'm afraid it isn't nearly as nice as I'd like to make it—but a schoolmaster's wife has to think of so many other things besides curtains and covers. Boys with dirty boots and a husband with leaky fountain pens, for instance.

MRS. GILBERT: Yes, I suppose so. Of course I haven't been a schoolmaster's wife for very long, you know.

GILBERT: Don't swank, darling. You haven't been a schoolmaster's wife at all yet.

MRS. GILBERT: Oh yes, I have—for two months. You were a schoolmaster when I married you.

GILBERT: Prep school doesn't count.

MILLIE: Have you only been married two months?

MRS. GILBERT: Two months and sixteen days.

GILBERT: Seventeen.

MILLIE [*sentimentally*]: Andrew, did you hear? They've only been married two months.

ANDREW: Indeed? Is that all?

MRS. GILBERT [*at the garden door*]: Oh, look, darling. They've got a garden. It is yours, isn't it?

MILLIE: Oh, yes. It's only a pocket handkerchief, I'm afraid, but it's very useful to Andrew. He often works out there, don't you, dear?

ANDREW: Yes, indeed. I find it very agreeable.

MILLIE: Shall I show you the rest of the flat? It's a bit untidy, I'm afraid, but you must forgive that.

MRS. GILBERT: Oh, of course.

MILLIE [*as they move to the door*]: And the kitchen is in a terrible mess. I'm in the middle of cooking dinner——

MRS. GILBERT [*breathlessly*]: Oh. . . Do you cook?

MILLIE: Oh, yes. I have to. We haven't had a maid for five years.

MRS. GILBERT: Oh. I do think that's wonderful of you. I'm scared stiff of having to do it for Peter—I know the first dinner I have to cook for him will wreck our married life——

GILBERT: Highly probable.

MILLIE [*following* MRS. GILBERT *out*]: Well, these days we've all got to try and do things we weren't really brought up to do.

They disappear.

ANDREW [*to* GILBERT]: Don't you want to see the rest of the flat?

GILBERT: No. I leave all that sort of thing to my wife. She's the boss. I thought perhaps you could tell me something about the lower fifth.

ANDREW: What would you like to know?

GILBERT: Well, sir, quite frankly, I'm petrified.

ANDREW: I don't think you need to be. May I give you some sherry?

GILBERT: Thank you.

ANDREW: They are mostly boys of about fifteen or sixteen. They are not very difficult to handle.

GILBERT: The headmaster said you ruled them with a rod of iron. He called you the Himmler of the lower fifth.

ANDREW: Did he? The Himmler of the lower fifth? I think he exaggerated. I hope he exaggerated. The Himmler of the lower fifth?

GILBERT [*puzzled*]: He only meant that you kept the most wonderful discipline. I must say I do admire you for that. I couldn't even manage that with eleven-year-olds, so what I'll be like with fifteens and sixteens I shudder to think.

ANDREW: It is not so difficult. They aren't bad boys. Sometimes—a little wild and unfeeling, perhaps—but not bad. The Himmler of the lower fifth? Dear me!

GILBERT: Perhaps I shouldn't have said that. I've been tactless, I'm afraid.

ANDREW: Oh, no, please sit down.

GILBERT: Thank you, sir.

ANDREW: From the very beginning I realized that I didn't possess the knack of making myself liked—a knack that you will find you do possess.

GILBERT: Do you think so?

ANDREW: Oh, yes. I am quite sure of it. It is not a quality of great importance to a schoolmaster, though, for too much of it, as you may also find, is as great a danger as the total lack of it. Forgive me lecturing, won't you?

GILBERT: I want to learn.

ANDREW: I can only teach you from my own experience. For two or three years I tried very hard to communicate to the boys some of my own joy in the great literature of the past. Of course, I failed, as you will fail, nine hundred and ninety-nine times out of a thousand. But a single success can atone and more than atone for all the failures in the world. And sometimes—very rarely, it is true—but sometimes I had that success. That was in the early years.

GILBERT [*eagerly listening*]: Please go on, sir.

ANDREW: In early years, too, I discovered an easy substitute for popularity. I had, of course, acquired—we all do—many little mannerisms and tricks of speech, and I found that the boys were beginning to laugh at me. I was very happy at that, and encouraged the boys' laughter by playing up to it. It made our relationship so very much easier. They didn't like me as a man, but they found me funny as a character, and you can teach more things by laughter than by earnestness—for I never did have much sense of humour. So, for a time, you see, I was quite a success as a schoolmaster— [*he stops*] I fear this is all very personal and embarrassing to you. Forgive me. You need have no fears about the lower fifth.

GILBERT [*after a pause*]: I'm afraid I said something that hurt you very much. It's myself you must forgive, sir. Believe me, I'm desperately sorry.

ANDREW: There's no need. You were merely telling me what I should have known for myself. Perhaps I did in my heart, and hadn't the courage to acknowledge it. I knew, of course, that I was not only not liked, but now positively disliked. I had realized, too, that the boys—for many long years now—had ceased to laugh at me. I don't know why they no longer found me a joke. Perhaps it was my illness. No, I don't think it was that. Something deeper than that. Not a sickness of the body, but a sickness of the soul. At all events it didn't take much discernment on my part to realize I had become an utter failure as a schoolmaster. Still, stupidly enough, I hadn't realized that I was also feared. The Himmler of the lower fifth! I suppose that will become my epitaph.

GILBERT *is now deeply embarrassed and rather upset, but he remains silent.* [*With a mild laugh.*] I cannot for the life of me imagine why I should choose to unburden myself to you—a total stranger—when I have been silent to others for so long. Perhaps it is because my very unworthy mantle is about to fall on your shoulders. If that is so I shall take a prophet's privilege and foretell that you will have a very great success with the lower fifth.

GILBERT: Thank you, sir. I shall do my best.

ANDREW: I can't offer you a cigarette. I'm afraid, I don't smoke.

GILBERT: That's all right, sir. Nor do I.

MILLIE *and* MRS. GILBERT *can be heard in the hall outside.*

MRS. GILBERT: Thank you so much for showing me round.

ANDREW: I trust your wife has found no major snags in your new flat.

MRS. GILBERT: No. None at all.

MILLIE *and* MRS. GILBERT *come in.*

MRS. GILBERT: Just imagine, Peter. Mr. and Mrs. Crocker-Harris first met each other on a holiday in the Lake District. Isn't that a coincidence?

GILBERT [*a little distrait*]: Yes. Yes, it certainly is. On a walking tour, too?

MILLIE: Andrew was on a walking tour. No walking for me. I can't abide it. I was staying with my uncle—that's Sir William Bartop, you know—you may have heard of him.

GILBERT *and* MRS. GILBERT *try to look as though they had heard of him constantly.*

He'd taken a house near Windermere—quite a mansion it was really—rather silly for an old gentleman living alone—and Andrew knocked on our front door one day and asked the footman for a glass of water. So my uncle invited him in to tea.

MRS. GILBERT: Our meeting wasn't quite as romantic as that.

GILBERT: I knocked her flat on her face.

MRS. GILBERT: Not with love at first sight. With the swing doors of our hotel bar. So, of course, then he apologized and——

GILBERT [*brusquely*]: Darling. The Crocker-Harrises, I'm sure, have far more important things to do than to listen to your detailed but inaccurate account of our very sordid little encounter. Why not just say I married you for your money and leave it at that? Come on, we must go.

MRS. GILBERT [*to* MILLIE]: Isn't he awful to me?

MILLIE: Men have no souls, my dear. My husband is just as bad.

MRS. GILBERT: Good-bye, Mr. Crocker-Harris.

ANDREW [*bowing*]: Good-bye.

MRS. GILBERT [*as she goes out with* MILLIE]: I think your idea about the dining-room is awfully good—if only I can get the permit——

MILLIE *and* MRS. GILBERT *go out.* GILBERT *has dallied to say good-bye alone to* ANDREW.

GILBERT: Good-bye, sir.

ANDREW: Er—you will, I know, respect the confidences I have just made to you——

GILBERT: I should hate you to think I wouldn't.

ANDREW: I am sorry to have embarrassed you. I don't know what came over me. I have not been very well, you know. Good-bye, my dear fellow, and my best wishes.

GILBERT: Thank you. The very best of good luck to you too, sir, in your future career.

ANDREW: My future career? Yes. Thank you.

GILBERT: Well, good-bye, sir.

GILBERT *goes out.*

We hear voices in the hall, cut short as the front door closes. MILLIE *comes back.*

MILLIE: Good-looking couple.

ANDREW: Very.

MILLIE: He looks as if he'd got what it takes. I should think he'll be a success all right.

ANDREW: That's what I thought.

MILLIE: I don't think it's much of a career, though—a schoolmaster—for a likely young chap like that.

ANDREW: I know you don't.

MILLIE: Still I bet when he leaves this place it won't be without a pension. It'll be roses, roses all the way, and tears and cheers and good-bye, Mr. Chips.

ANDREW: I expect so.

MILLIE: What's the matter with you?

ANDREW: Nothing.

MILLIE: You're not going to have another of your attacks, are you? You look dreadful.

ANDREW: I'm perfectly all right.

MILLIE [*indifferently*]: You know best. Your medicine's there, anyway, if you want it.

She goes out.

ANDREW, *left alone, continues for a time staring at the text he has been pretending to read. Then he puts one hand over his eyes. There is a knock on the door.*

ANDREW: Come in.

TAPLOW *appears timidly from behind the screen.*

[*sharply*]. Yes, Taplow? What is it?

TAPLOW: Nothing, sir.

ANDREW: What do you mean, nothing?

TAPLOW [*timidly*]: I just came back to say good-bye, sir.

ANDREW: Oh. [*He gets up.*]

TAPLOW: I didn't have a chance with the head here. I rather dashed out, I'm afraid. I thought I'd just come back and—and wish you luck, sir.

ANDREW: Thank you, Taplow. That's good of you.

TAPLOW: I—er—thought this might interest you, sir. [*He quickly thrusts a small book into* ANDREW'S *hand.*]

ANDREW: What is it?

TAPLOW: Verse translation of the *Agamemnon*, sir. The Browning Version. It's not much good. I've been reading it in the Chapel gardens.

ANDREW *very deliberately turns over the pages of the book.*

ANDREW: Very interesting, Taplow. [*He seems to have a little difficulty in speaking. He clears his throat and then goes on in his level, gentle voice.*] I know the translation, of course. It has its faults, I agree, but I think you will enjoy it more when you get used to the metre he employs.

He hands it to TAPLOW *who brusquely thrusts it back to him.*

TAPLOW: It's for you, sir.

ANDREW: For me?

TAPLOW: Yes, sir. I've written in it.

ANDREW *opens the fly-leaf and reads whatever is written there.*

ANDREW: Did you buy this?

TAPLOW: Yes, sir. It was only second-hand.

ANDREW: You shouldn't have spent your pocket-money this way.

TAPLOW: That's all right, sir. It wasn't very much. The price isn't still inside, is it?

ANDREW *carefully wipes his glasses and puts them on again.*

ANDREW [*at length*]: No. Just what you've written. Nothing else.

TAPLOW: Good. I'm sorry you've got it already. I thought you probably would have——

ANDREW: I haven't got it already. I may have had it once. I can't remember. But I haven't got it now.

TAPLOW: That's all right, then.

ANDREW *continues to stare at* TAPLOW'S *inscription on the fly-leaf.*

[*Suspiciously.*] What's the matter, sir? Have I got the accent wrong on εὐμενῶς?

ANDREW: No. The perispomenon is perfectly correct.

He lowers the book and we notice his hands are shaking from some intense inner effort as he takes off his spectacles.

Taplow, would you be good enough to take that bottle of medicine, which you so kindly brought in, and pour me out one dose in a glass which you will find in the bathroom?

TAPLOW [*seeing something is wrong*]: Yes, sir.

ANDREW *sits at his seat by the table.*

ANDREW: The doses are clearly marked on the bottle. I usually put a little water with it.

TAPLOW: Yes, sir.

He takes the bottle and darts out.

ANDREW, *the moment he is gone, breaks down and begins to sob uncontrollably. He makes a desperate attempt, after a moment, to control himself, but when* TAPLOW *comes back his emotion is still very apparent.*

ANDREW [*taking the glass*]: Thank you. [*He drinks it, turning his back on* TAPLOW *as he does so. At length.*] You must forgive this exhibition of weakness, Taplow. The truth is I have been going through rather a strain lately.

TAPLOW: Of course, sir. I quite understand.

There is a knock on the garden door.

ANDREW: Come in.

FRANK *comes in.*

FRANK: Oh, sorry. I thought you'd be finished by now——

ANDREW: Come in, Hunter, do. It's perfectly all right. Our lesson was over some time ago, but Taplow most kindly came back to say good-bye.

FRANK, *taking in* TAPLOW'*s rather startled face and* ANDREW'*s obvious emotion, looks a little puzzled.*

FRANK: Are you sure I'm not intruding?

ANDREW: No, no. I want you to see this book that Taplow has given me, Hunter. Look. [*He hands it to* HUNTER.] A translation of the *Agamemnon* by Robert Browning. Do you see the inscription he has put into it?

FRANK: Yes, but it's no use to me, I'm afraid. I never learnt Greek.

ANDREW: Then we'll have to translate it for him, won't we, Taplow. [*Reciting by heart.*] τὸν κρατοῦντα ἡαλθακῶς θεὸς πρόσωθεν εὐμενῶς προσδέρχεται. That means—in a rough translation: 'God from afar looks graciously upon a gentle master.' It comes from a speech of Agamemnon's to Clytaemnestra.

FRANK: I see. Very pleasant and very apt. [*He hands the book back to* ANDREW.]

ANDREW: Very pleasant. But perhaps not, after all, so very apt.

He turns quickly away from both of them as emotion once more seems about to overcome him. FRANK *brusquely jerks his head to the bewildered* TAPLOW *to get out.* TAPLOW *nods.*

TAPLOW: Good-bye, sir, and the best of luck.

ANDREW: Good-bye, Taplow, and thank you very much.

TAPLOW *flees quickly.*

FRANK *watches* ANDREW'*s back with a mixture of embarrassment and sympathy.* [*Turning at length, slightly recovered.*] Dear me, what a fool I made of myself in front of that boy. And in front of you, Hunter. I can't imagine what you must think of me.

FRANK: Nonsense.

ANDREW: I am not a very emotional person, as you know, but there was something so very touching and kindly about his action, and coming as it did just after—— [*he stops, then glances at the book in his hand.*] This is a very delightful thing to have, don't you think?

FRANK: Delightful.

ANDREW: The quotation, of course, he didn't find entirely by himself. I happened to make some little joke about the line in form the other day. But he must have remembered it all the same to have found it so readily— and perhaps he means it.

FRANK: I'm sure he does, or he wouldn't have written it.

MILLIE *comes in.*

MILLIE: Hullo, Frank. I'm glad you're in time. [*She picks up the medicine bottle and the glass from the table and puts them aside. To* FRANK.] Lend me a cigarette. I've been gasping for one for an hour.

FRANK *once more extends his case and* MILLIE *takes a cigarette which he lights.*

FRANK: Your husband has just had a very nice present.

MILLIE: Oh? Who from?

FRANK: Taplow.

MILLIE [*smiling*]: Oh, Taplow. Let's see. [*She takes the book from* ANDREW.]

ANDREW: He bought it with his own pocket-money, Millie, and wrote a very charming inscription inside.

FRANK: God looks kindly upon a gracious master.

ANDREW: No—not gracious—gentle I think—τὸν κρατοῦντα ηαλθακῶς— yes I think gentle is the better translation. I would rather have had this present than almost anything I can think of.

Pause. MILLIE *laughs suddenly.*

MILLIE: The artful little beast——

FRANK [*urgently*]: Millie——

ANDREW: Artful? Why artful?

MILLIE *looks at* FRANK *who is staring meaningly at her.*

Why artful, Millie?

MILLIE *laughs again, quite lightly, and turns from* FRANK *to* ANDREW.

MILLIE: My dear, because I came into this room this afternoon to find him giving an imitation of you to Frank here. Obviously he was scared stiff I was going to tell you, and you'd ditch his remove or something. I don't blame him for trying a few bobs' worth of appeasement.

She hands the book back to ANDREW *who stands quite still looking down at it.*

ANDREW [*nodding, at length*]: I see. [*He puts the book gently on the table and walks to the door.*]

MILLIE: Where are you going, dear? Dinner's nearly ready.

ANDREW: Only to my room for a moment. I won't be long.

He takes the medicine bottle and a glass.

MILLIE: You've just had a dose of that, dear. I shouldn't have another, if I were you.

ANDREW: I am allowed two at a time.

MILLIE: Well, see it is two and no more, won't you?

ANDREW *meets her eye for a moment, at the door, then goes out quietly.*

MILLIE *turns to* FRANK *with an expression half defiant and half ashamed.*

FRANK [*with a note of real repulsion in his voice*]: Millie! My God! How could you?

MILLIE: Well, why not? Why should he be allowed his comforting little illusions? I'm not.

FRANK [*advancing on her*]: Listen. You're to go to his room now and tell him that was a lie.

MILLIE: Certainly not. It wasn't a lie.

FRANK: If you don't, I will.

MILLIE: I shouldn't, if I were you. It'll only make things worse. He won't believe you.

FRANK [*moving*]: We'll see about that.

MILLIE: Go ahead. See what happens. He knows I don't lie to him. He knows what I told him was the truth, and he won't like your sympathy. He'll think you're making fun of him, like Taplow.

FRANK *hesitates at the door then comes slowly back into the room.* MILLIE *watches him, a little frightened.*

FRANK [*at length*]: We're finished, Millie—you and I.

MILLIE [*laughing*]: Frank really! Don't be hysterical.

FRANK: I'm not. I mean it.

MILLIE [*lightly*]: Oh, yes, you mean it. Of course you mean it. Now just sit down, dear, and relax and forget all about artful little boys and their five bob presents, and talk to me.

She touches his arm. He moves away from her brusquely.

FRANK: Forget? If I live to be a hundred I shall never forget that little glimpse you've just given me of yourself.

MILLIE: Frank—you're making a frightening mountain out of an absurd little molehill.

FRANK: Of course, but the mountain I'm making in my imagination is so frightening that I'd rather try to forget both it and the repulsive little molehill that gave it birth. But as I know I never can, I tell you, Millie—from this moment you and I are finished.

MILLIE [*quietly*]: You can't scare me, Frank. I know that's what you're trying to do, but you can't do it.

FRANK [*quietly*]: I'm not trying to scare you, Millie. I'm telling you the simple truth. I'm not coming to Bradford.

MILLIE [*after a pause, with an attempt at bravado*]: All right, my dear, if that's the way you feel about it. Don't come to Bradford.

FRANK: Right. Now I think you ought to go to your room and look after Andrew. I'm leaving.

MILLIE *runs quickly to stop him.*

MILLIE: What is this? Frank, I don't understand, really I don't. What have I done?

FRANK: I think you know what you've done, Millie. Go and look after Andrew.

MILLIE: Andrew? Why this sudden concern for Andrew?

FRANK: Because I think he's just been about as badly hurt as a human being can be; and as he's a sick man and in a rather hysterical state it might be a good plan to go and see how he is.

MILLIE [*scornfully*]: Hurt? Andrew hurt? You can't hurt Andrew. He's dead.

FRANK: Why do you hate him so much, Millie?

MILLIE: Because he keeps me from you.

FRANK: That isn't true.

MILLIE: Because he's not a man at all.

FRANK: He's a human being.

MILLIE: You've got a fine right to be so noble about him, after deceiving him for six months.

FRANK: Twice in six months—at your urgent invitation.

MILLIE *slaps his face, in a violent paroxysm of rage.*

Thank you for that. I deserved it. I deserve a lot worse than that, too——

MILLIE [*running to him*]: Frank, forgive me—I didn't mean it——

FRANK [*quietly*]: You'd better have the truth, Millie. It had to come some time. I've never loved you. I've never told you I loved you.

MILLIE: I know, Frank, I know—I've always accepted that.

FRANK: You asked me just now if I was running away from you. Well, I was.

MILLIE: I knew that too.

FRANK: But I was coming to Bradford. It was going to be the very last time I was ever going to see you and at Bradford I would have told you that.

MILLIE: You wouldn't. You wouldn't. You've tried to tell me that so often before—and I've always stopped you somehow—somehow. I would have stopped you again.

FRANK [*quietly*]: I don't think so, Millie. Not this time.

MILLIE: Frank, I don't care what humiliations you heap on me. I know you don't give two hoots for me as a person. I've always known that. I've never minded so long as you cared for me as a woman. And you do, Frank. You do. You do, don't you?

FRANK *is silent.*

It'll be all right at Bradford, you see. It'll be all right, there——

FRANK: I'm not coming to Bradford, Millie.

The door opens slowly and ANDREW *comes in, carrying the bottle of medicine. He hands it to* MILLIE *and passes on.* MILLIE *quickly holds the bottle up to the light.* ANDREW *turns and sees her.*

ANDREW [*gently*]: You should know me well enough by now, my dear, to realize how unlikely it is that I should ever take an overdose.

MILLIE, *without a word, puts the bottle down and goes out.*

ANDREW *goes to a cupboard at back and produces a decanter of sherry and a glass.*

FRANK: I'm not staying to dinner, I'm afraid.

ANDREW: Indeed? I'm sorry to hear that. You'll have a glass of sherry?

FRANK: No, thank you.

ANDREW: You will forgive me if I do.

FRANK: Of course.

ANDREW *pours himself a glass.*

Perhaps I'll change my mind.

ANDREW *pours* FRANK *a glass.*

About Taplow——

ANDREW: Oh, yes?

FRANK: It *is* perfectly true that he was imitating you. I, of course, was mostly to blame in that, and I'm very sorry.

ANDREW: That is perfectly all right. Was it a good imitation?

FRANK: No.

ANDREW: I expect it was. Boys are often very clever mimics.

FRANK: We talked about you, of course, before that. He said—you probably won't believe this, but I thought I ought to tell you—he said he liked you very much.

ANDREW *smiles slightly.*

ANDREW: Indeed?

FRANK: I can remember very clearly his exact words. He said: 'He doesn't seem to like people to like him—but in spite of that, I do—very much.' [*Lightly.*] So you see it looks after all as if the book might not have been a mere question of—appeasement.

ANDREW: The book? [*He picks it up.*] Dear me! What a lot of fuss about a little book—and a not very good little book at that. [*He drops it on the table.*]

FRANK: I would like you to believe me.

ANDREW: Possibly you would, my dear Hunter; but I can assure you I am not particularly concerned about Taplow's views of my character; or about yours either, if it comes to that.

FRANK [*hopelessly*]: I think you should keep that book all the same. You may find it'll mean something to you after all.

ANDREW: Exactly. It will mean a perpetual reminder to myself of the story with which Taplow is at this very moment regaling his friends in the House. 'I gave the Crock a book, to buy him off, and he blubbed. The Crock blubbed. I tell you I was there. I saw it. The Crock blubbed.' My mimicry is not as good as his, I fear. Forgive me. And now let us leave this idiotic subject and talk of more pleasant things. Do you like this sherry? I got it on my last visit to London——

FRANK: If Taplow ever breathes a word of that story to anyone at all, I'll murder him. But he won't. And if you think I will you greatly underestimate my character as well as his. [*He drains his glass.*] Good-bye.

ANDREW: Are you leaving so soon? Good-bye, my dear fellow.

He does not get up nor offer to shake hands. FRANK *goes to the window.*

FRANK: As this is the last time I shall probably ever see you I'm going to offer you a word of advice.

ANDREW [*politely*]: I shall be glad to listen to it.

FRANK: Leave your wife.

Pause. ANDREW *takes a sip of his sherry.*

ANDREW [*at length*[: So that you may the more easily carry on your intrigue with her?

FRANK *stares at him, then comes back into the room.*

FRANK: How long have you known that?

ANDREW: Since it first began.

FRANK: How did you find out?

ANDREW: By information.

FRANK: By whose information?

ANDREW: By someone's whose word I could hardly discredit.

Pause.

FRANK [*slowly, with repulsion*]: No! That's too horrible to think of.

ANDREW: Nothing is ever too horrible to think of, Hunter. It is simply a question of facing facts.

FRANK: She might have told you a lie. Have you faced that fact?

ANDREW: She never tells me a lie. In twenty years she has never told me a lie. Only the truth.

FRANK: This was a lie.

ANDREW: No, my dear Hunter. Do you wish me to quote you dates?

FRANK [*still unable to believe it*]: And she told you six months ago.

ANDREW: Isn't it seven?

FRANK [*savagely*]: Then why have you allowed me inside your home? Why haven't you done something—reported me to the governors—anything— made a scene, knocked me down?

ANDREW: Knocked you down?

FRANK: You didn't have to invite me to dinner.

ANDREW: My dear Hunter, if, over the last twenty years, I had allowed such petty considerations to influence my choice of dinner guests I would have found it increasingly hard to remember which master to invite and which to refuse. You see, Hunter, you mustn't flatter yourself you are the first. My information is a good deal better than yours, you understand. It's authentic.

Pause.

FRANK: She's evil.

ANDREW: That's hardly a kindly epithet to apply to a lady whom, I gather, you have asked to marry.

FRANK: Did she tell you that?

ANDREW: She's a dutiful wife. She tells me everything.

FRANK: That, at least, was a lie.

ANDREW: She never lies.

FRANK: That was a lie. Do you want the truth? Can you bear the truth?

ANDREW: I can bear anything.

FRANK: What I did, I did cold-bloodedly out of weakness and ignorance and crass stupidity. I'm bitterly, bitterly ashamed of myself, but, in a sense, I'm glad you know, though I'd rather a thousand times that you'd heard it from me than from your wife. I won't ask you to forgive me. I can only tell you, with complete truth, that the only emotion she has ever succeeded

in arousing in me she aroused in me for the first time ten minutes ago—
an intense and passionate disgust.

ANDREW: What a delightfully chivalrous statement——

FRANK: Forget chivalry, Crock, for God's sake. Forget all your fine mosaic
scruples. You must leave her—it's your only chance.

ANDREW: She's my wife, Hunter. You seem to forget that. As long as she
wishes to remain my wife, she may.

FRANK: She's out to kill you.

ANDREW: My dear Hunter, if that was indeed her purpose, you should
know by now that she fulfilled it long ago.

FRANK: Why won't you leave her?

ANDREW: Because I wouldn't wish to add another grave wrong to one I
have already done her.

FRANK: What wrong have you done her?

ANDREW: To marry her.

Pause. FRANK *stares at him in silence.*

You see, my dear Hunter, she is really quite as much to be pitied as I.
We are both of us interesting subjects for your microscope. Both of us
needing from the other something that would make life supportable for
us, and neither of us able to give it. Two kinds of love. Hers and mine.
Worlds apart, as I know now, though when I married her I didn't think
they were incompatible. In those days I hadn't thought that her kind of
love—the love she requires and which I was unable to give her—was so
important that its absence would drive out the other kind of love—the
kind of love that I require and which I thought, in my folly, was by far
the greater part of love. I may have been, you see, Hunter, a brilliant
classical scholar, but I was woefully ignorant of the facts of life. I know
better now, of course. I know that in both of us, the love that we should
have borne each other has turned to bitter hatred. That's all the problem
is. Not a very unusual one, I venture to think—nor nearly as tragic as you
seem to imagine. Merely the problem of an unsatisfied wife and a hen-
pecked husband. You'll find it all over the world. It is usually, I believe, a
subject for farce. And now, if you have to leave us, my dear fellow, please
don't let me detain you any longer.

He turns his back deliberately on FRANK, *who makes no move to go.*

FRANK: Don't go to Bradford. Stay here, until you take up your new job.

ANDREW: I think I've already told you I'm not interested in your advice.

FRANK: Leave her. It's the only way.

ANDREW [*violently*]: Will you please go!

FRANK: All right. I'd just like you to say good-bye to me, properly, though.
Will you? I shan't see you again.

ANDREW *rises and walks slowly over to him.*

I know you don't want my pity, but I would like to be of some help.

ANDREW: If you think, by this expression of kindness, Hunter, that you can get me to repeat the shameful exhibition of emotion I made to Taplow a moment ago, I must tell you that you have no chance. My hysteria over that book just now was no more than a sort of reflex action of the spirit. The muscular twitchings of a corpse. It can never happen again.

FRANK: A corpse can be revived.

ANDREW: I don't believe in miracles.

FRANK: Don't you? Funnily enough, as a scientist, I do.

ANDREW: Your faith would be touching, if I were capable of being touched by it.

FRANK: You are, I think. [*After a pause.*] I'd like to come and visit you at this crammer's.

ANDREW: That is an absurd suggestion.

FRANK: I suppose it is rather, but all the same I'd like to do it. May I?

ANDREW: Of course not.

FRANK: Your term begins on the first of September, doesn't it?

ANDREW: I tell you the idea is quite childish——

FRANK: I could come about the second week.

ANDREW: You would be bored to death. So, probably, would I.

FRANK [*glancing at pocket calendar*]: Let's say Monday the twelfth, then.

ANDREW [*his hands beginning to tremble again*]: Say anything you like, only please go. Please go, Hunter.

FRANK [*writing in his book and not looking at* ANDREW]: That's fixed, then. Monday, September the twelfth. Will you remember that?

ANDREW [*after a pause, speaking with difficulty*]: I suppose I'm at least as likely to remember it as you are.

FRANK: That's fixed then. [*He slips the book into his pocket and puts out his hand.*] Good-bye, until then.

ANDREW, *after hesitation, shakes his hand.*

ANDREW: Good-bye.

FRANK: May I go out through your garden?

ANDREW [*nodding*]: Of course.

FRANK: I'm off to have a quick word with Taplow. By the way, may I take him a message from you?

ANDREW: What message?

FRANK: Has he or has he not got his remove?

ANDREW: He has.

FRANK: May I tell him?

ANDREW: It is highly irregular. Yes, you may.

FRANK: Good. [*He turns to go then turns back.*] Oh, by the way, I'd better have the address of that crammer's. [*He takes out his notebook and points his pencil, ready to write.*]

MILLIE *comes in with tray, dishes and cutlery. She starts to set the table.*

MILLIE: Dinner's ready. You're staying, Frank, aren't you?

FRANK [*politely*]: No, I'm afraid not. [*To* ANDREW.] What's that address?

ANDREW [*after great hesitation*]: The Old Deanery, Malcombe, Dorset.

FRANK: I'll write to you and you can let me know about trains. [*To* MILLIE.] Good-bye. [*To* ANDREW.] Good-bye.

He goes out.

MILLIE *is silent for a moment. Then she laughs.*

MILLIE: That's a laugh, I must say.

ANDREW: What's a laugh, my dear?

MILLIE: You inviting him to stay with you.

ANDREW: I didn't. He suggested it.

MILLIE: He's coming to Bradford.

ANDREW: Yes. I remember your telling me so.

MILLIE *comes close to* ANDREW.

MILLIE: He's coming to Bradford. He's not going to you.

ANDREW: The likeliest contingency is, that he's not going to either of us. Shall we have dinner?

MILLIE: He's coming to Bradford.

ANDREW: I expect so. Oh, by the way, I'm not. I shall be staying here until I go to Dorset.

MILLIE [*indifferently*]: Suit yourself—what makes you think I'll join you there?

ANDREW: I don't.

MILLIE: You needn't expect me.

ANDREW: I don't think either of us has the right to expect anything further from the other.

The telephone rings.

ANDREW: I don't. Excuse me. [*He picks up the receiver.*] Hullo . . . Yes, headmaster . . . The timetable? . . . It's perfectly simple. The middle fourth B division will take a ten-minute break on Tuesdays and a fifteen-minute break on alternate Wednesdays; while exactly the reverse procedure will apply to the lower Shell, C division. I thought I had sufficiently explained that on my chart . . . Oh, I see . . . Thank you, that is very good of you . . . yes, I think you will find it will work out quite satisfactorily . . . Oh, by the way, headmaster. I have changed my mind about the prize-giving ceremony. I intend to speak after, instead of before, Fletcher, as is my privilege. . . . Yes, I quite understand, but I am now seeing the matter in a different light. . . . I know, but I am of opinion that occasionally an anti-climax can be surprisingly effective. Good-bye. [*He rings off and goes and sits at the table.*] Come along, my dear. We mustn't let our dinner get cold.

MILLIE *slowly sits and begins to serve dinner.*

CURTAIN

IN CAMERA
(Huis Clos)

A Play in one Act

BY JEAN-PAUL SARTRE
TRANSLATED BY STUART GILBERT

from *In Camera* and *The Flies* (1946)

———————

CHARACTERS IN THE PLAY

VALET

GARCIN

ESTELLE

INEZ

IN CAMERA

A drawing-room in Second Empire style. A massive bronze group stands on the mantelpiece.

GARCIN *enters, accompanied by the* ROOM-VALET, *and glances round him.*

GARCIN: Hm! So here we are?

VALET: Yes, Mr. Garcin.

GARCIN: And this is what it looks like?

VALET: Yes.

GARCIN: Second Empire furniture, I observe. . . . Well, well, I dare say one gets used to it in time.

VALET: Some do. Some don't.

GARCIN: Are all the other rooms like this one?

VALET: How could they be? We cater for all sorts: Chinamen and Indians, for instance. What use would they have for a Second Empire chair?

GARCIN: And what use do you suppose *I* have for one? Do you know who I was? . . . Oh, well, it's no great matter. And, to tell the truth, I'd quite a habit of living amongst furniture that I didn't relish, and in false positions. I'd even come to like it. A false position in a Louis-Philippe dining-room —you know the style?—well, that had its points, you know. Bogus in bogus, so to speak.

VALET: And you'll find that living in a Second Empire drawing-room has its points.

GARCIN: Really? . . . Yes, yes, I dare say. . . . [*He takes another look round.*] Still, I certainly didn't expect—this! You know what they tell us down there?

VALET: What about?

GARCIN: About [*makes a sweeping gesture*] this—er—residence.

VALET: Really, sir, how could you believe such cock-and-bull stories? Told by people who'd never set foot here. For, of course, if they had . . .

GARCIN: Quite so. [*Both laugh. Abruptly the laugh dies from* GARCIN's *face.*] But, I say, where are the instruments of torture?

VALET: The what?

GARCIN: The racks and red-hot pincers and all the other paraphernalia?

VALET: Ah, you must have your little joke, sir!

GARCIN: My little joke? Oh, I see. No, I wasn't joking. [*A short silence. He*

611

strolls round the room.] No mirrors, I notice. No windows. Only to be expected. And nothing breakable. [*Bursts out angrily.*] But, damn it all, they might have left me my toothbrush!

VALET: That's good! So you haven't yet got over your—what-do-you-call-it?—sense of human dignity? Excuse me smiling.

GARCIN [*thumping ragefully the arm of an armchair*]: I'll ask you to be more polite. I quite realize the position I'm in, but I won't tolerate . . .

VALET: Sorry, sir. No offence meant. But all our guests ask me the same questions. Silly questions, if you'll pardon me saying so. Where's the torture-chamber? That's the first thing they ask, all of them. They don't bother their heads about the bathroom-requisites, that I can assure you. But, after a bit, when they've got their nerve back, they start in about their toothbrushes and what-not. Good heavens, Mr. Garcin, can't you use your brains? What, I ask you, would be the point of brushing your teeth?

GARCIN [*more calmly*]: Yes, of course you're right. [*He looks round again.*] And why should one want to see oneself in a looking-glass? But that bronze contraption on the mantelpiece, that's another story. I suppose there will be times when I stare my eyes out at it. Stare my eyes out—see what I mean? . . . All right, let's put our cards on the table. I assure you I'm quite conscious of my position. Shall I tell you what it feels like? A man's drowning, choking, sinking by inches, till only his eyes are just above water. And what does he see? A bronze atrocity by—what's the fellow's name?—Barbedienne. A collector's piece. Like in a nightmare. That's their idea, isn't it? . . . No, I suppose you're under orders not to answer questions; and I won't insist. But don't forget, my man, I've a shrewd notion of what's coming to me, so don't you boast you've caught me off my guard. I'm facing up to the situation, facing up. [*He starts pacing the room again.*] So that's that; no toothbrush. And no bed, either. One never sleeps, I take it?

VALET: That's so.

GARCIN: Just as I expected. *Why* should one sleep? A sort of drowsiness steals on you, tickles you behind the ears, and you feel your eyes closing—but why sleep? You lie down on the sofa and . . . in a flash, sleep flies away. Miles and miles away. So you rub your eyes, get up, and it starts all over again.

VALET: Romantic, that's what you are.

GARCIN: Will you keep quiet, please! . . . I won't make a scene, I shan't be sorry for myself, I'll face up to the situation, as I said just now. Face it fairly and squarely. I won't have it springing at me from behind, before I've time to size it up. And you call that being 'romantic'! . . . So it comes to this; one doesn't need rest. Why bother about sleep if one isn't sleepy? That stands to reason, doesn't it? Wait a bit, there's a snag somewhere;

something disagreeable. Why, now, should it be disagreeable? . . . Ah, I
see; it's life without a break.

VALET: What do you mean by that?

GARCIN: What do I mean? [*Eyes the* VALET *suspiciously.*] I thought as much.
That's why there's something so beastly, so damn' bad-mannered, in the
way you stare at me. They're paralysed.

VALET: What are you talking about?

GARCIN: Your eyelids. We move ours up and down. Blinking, we call it.
It's like a small black shutter that clicks down, and makes a break. Everything goes black; one's eyes are moistened. You can't imagine how restful,
refreshing, it is. Four thousand little rests per hour. Four thousand little
respites—just think! . . . So that's the idea. I'm to live without eyelids.
Don't act the fool, you know what I mean. No eyelids, no sleep; it follows,
doesn't it? I shall never sleep again. But then—how shall I endure my own
company? Try to understand. You see, I'm fond of teasing, it's a second
nature with me—and I'm used to teasing myself. Plaguing myself, if you
prefer; I don't tease nicely. But I can't go on doing that without a break.
Down there I had my nights. I slept. I always had good nights. By way
of compensation, I suppose. And happy little dreams. There was a
green field. Just an ordinary field. I used to stroll in it. . . . Is it daytime
now?

VALET: Can't you see? The lights are on.

GARCIN: Ah yes, I've got it. It's *your* daytime. And outside?

VALET: Outside?

GARCIN: Damn it, you know what I mean. Beyond that wall.

VALET: There's a passage.

GARCIN: And at the end of the passage?

VALET: There's more rooms, more passages and stairs.

GARCIN: And what lies beyond them?

VALET: That's all.

GARCIN: But surely you have a day off sometimes. Where do you go?

VALET: To my uncle's place. He's the head valet here. He has a room on
the third floor.

GARCIN: I should have guessed as much. Where's the light-switch?

VALET: There isn't any.

GARCIN: What? Can't one turn off the light?

VALET: Oh, the management can cut off the current, if they want to. But
I can't remember their having done so on this floor. We have all the
electricity we want.

GARCIN: So one has to live with one's eyes open all the time?

VALET: To *live*, did you say?

GARCIN: Don't let's quibble over words. With one's eyes open. For ever.
Always broad daylight in my eyes . . . and in my head. [*Short silence.*] And

suppose I took that contraption on the mantelpiece and dropped it on the lamp—wouldn't it go out?

VALET: You can't move it. It's too heavy.

GARCIN [*seizing the bronze ornament and trying to lift it*]: You're right. It's too heavy.

A short silence follows.

VALET: Very well, sir, if you don't need me any more, I'll be off.

GARCIN: What? You're going? [*The* VALET *goes up to the door.*] Wait. [VALET *looks round.*] That's a bell, isn't it? [VALET *nods.*] And if I ring, you're bound to come?

VALET: Well, yes, that's so—in a way. But you can never be sure about that bell. There's something wrong with the wiring, and it doesn't always work.

GARCIN *goes to the bell-push and presses the button. A bell purrs outside.*

GARCIN: It's working all right.

VALET [*looking surprised*]: So it is. [*He, too, presses the button.*] But I shouldn't count on it too much if I were you. It's . . . capricious. Well, I really must go now. [GARCIN *makes a gesture to detain him.*] Yes, sir?

GARCIN: No, never mind. [*He goes to the mantelpiece and picks up a paper-knife.*] What's this?

VALET: Can't you see? An ordinary paper-knife.

GARCIN: Are there books here?

VALET: No.

GARCIN: Then what's the use of this? [VALET *shrugs his shoulders.*] Very well. You can go. [VALET *goes out.*]

GARCIN *is by himself. He goes to the bronze ornament and strokes it reflectively. He sits down: then gets up, goes to the bell-push and presses the button. The bell remains silent. He tries two or three times, without success. Then he tries to open the door, also without success. He calls the* VALET *several times, but gets no result. He beats the door with his fists, still calling. Suddenly he grows calm and sits down again. At the same moment the door opens and* INEZ *enters, followed by the* VALET.

VALET: Did you call, sir?

GARCIN [*on the point of answering 'Yes'—but then his eyes fall on* INEZ]: No.

VALET [*turning to* INEZ]: This is your room, Madam. [INEZ *says nothing.*] If there's any information you require . . . ? [INEZ *still keeps silent, and the* VALET *looks slightly huffed.*] Most of our guests have quite a lot to ask me. But I won't insist. Anyhow, as regards the toothbrush, and the electric bell, and that thing on the mantelshelf, this gentleman can tell you anything you want to know, as well as I could. We've had a little chat, him and me. [VALET *goes out.*] [GARCIN *refrains from looking at* INEZ, *who is inspecting the room. Abruptly she turns to* GARCIN.]

INEZ: Where's Florence? [GARCIN *does not reply.*] Didn't you hear? I asked you about Florence. Where is she?

GARCIN: I haven't an idea.

INEZ: Ah, that's the way it works, is it? Torture by separation. Well, as far as I'm concerned, you won't get anywhere. Florence was a tiresome little fool, and I shan't miss her in the least.

GARCIN: I beg your pardon. Who do you suppose I am?

INEZ: You? Why, the torturer, of course.

GARCIN *looks startled, then bursts out laughing.*

GARCIN: Well, that's a good one! Too comic for words. I, the torturer! So you came in, had a look at me, and thought I was—er—one of the staff. Of course it's that silly fellow's fault; he should have introduced us. A torturer indeed! I'm Joseph Garcin, journalist and man of letters by profession. And as we're both in the same boat, so to speak, might I ask you, Mrs. . . . ?

INEZ [*testily*]: Not 'Mrs.' I'm unmarried.

GARCIN: Right. That's a start, anyway. Well, now that we've broken the ice, do you *really* think I look like a torturer . . . ? And, by the way, how does one recognize torturers when one sees them? Evidently you've ideas on the subject.

INEZ: They look frightened.

GARCIN: Frightened! But how ridiculous! Of whom should they be frightened? Of their victims?

INEZ: Laugh away, but I know what I'm talking about. I've often watched my face in the glass.

GARCIN: In the glass? [*He looks round him.*] How beastly of them! They've removed everything in the least resembling a glass. [*Short silence.*] Anyhow, I can assure you I'm not frightened. Not that I take my position lightly; I realize its gravity only too well. But I'm not afraid.

INEZ [*shrugging her shoulders*]: That's your affair. [*Silence.*] Must you be here all the time, or do you take a stroll outside, now and then?

GARCIN: The door's locked.

INEZ: Oh! . . . That's too bad.

GARCIN: I can quite understand that it bores you having me here. And I, too—well, quite frankly, I'd rather be alone. I want to think things out, you know; to set my life in order, and one does that better by oneself. But I'm sure we'll manage to pull along together somehow. I'm no talker, I don't move much; in fact I'm a peaceful sort of fellow. Only, if I may venture on a suggestion, we should make a point of being extremely courteous to each other. That will ease the situation for us both.

INEZ: I'm not polite.

GARCIN: Then I must be polite for two.

A longish silence. GARCIN *is sitting on a sofa, while* INEZ *paces up and down the room.*

INEZ [*fixing her eyes on him*]: Your mouth!

GARCIN [*as if waking from a dream*]: I beg your pardon.

INEZ: Can't you keep your mouth still? You keep twisting it about all the time. It's grotesque.

GARCIN: So sorry. I wasn't aware of it.

INEZ: That's just what I reproach you with. [GARCIN's *mouth twitches.*] There you are! You talk about politeness, and you don't even try to control your face. Remember you're not alone; you've no right to inflict the sight of your fear on me.

GARCIN [*getting up and going towards her*]: How about you? Aren't you afraid?

INEZ: What would be the use? There was some point in being afraid *before*; while one still had hope.

GARCIN [*in a low voice*]: There's no more hope—but it's still 'before'. We haven't yet begun to suffer.

INEZ: That's so. [*A short silence.*] Well? What's going to happen?

GARCIN: I don't know. I'm waiting.

Silence again. GARCIN *sits down and* INEZ *resumes her pacing up and down the room.* GARCIN'S *mouth twitches; after a glance at* INEZ *he buries his face in his hands. Enter* ESTELLE *with the* VALET. ESTELLE *looks at* GARCIN, *whose face is still hidden by his hands.*

ESTELLE [*to* GARCIN]: No! Don't look up. I know what you're hiding with your hands. I know you've no face left. [GARCIN *removes his hands.*] What? [*A short pause. Then, in a tone of surprise*]: But I don't know you!

GARCIN: I'm not the torturer, Madam.

ESTELLE: I never thought you were. I . . . I thought someone was trying to play a rather nasty trick oh me. [*To the* VALET.] Is anyone else coming?

VALET: No, Madam. No one else is coming.

ESTELLE: Oh! Then we're to stay by ourselves, the three of us, this gentleman, this lady, and myself. [*She starts laughing.*]

GARCIN [*angrily*]: There's nothing to laugh about.

ESTELLE [*still laughing*]: It's those sofas. They're so hideous. And just look how they've been arranged. It makes me think of New Year's Day—when I used to visit that boring old aunt of mine, Aunt Mary. Her house is full of horrors like that. . . . I suppose each of us has a sofa of his own. Is that one mine? [*To the* VALET.] But you can't expect me to sit on that one. It would be too horrible for words. I'm in pale blue and it's vivid green.

INEZ: Would you prefer mine?

ESTELLE: That claret-coloured one, you mean? That's very sweet of you, but really—no, I don't think it'd be so much better. What's the good of worrying, anyhow? We've got to take what comes to us, and I'll stick to the green one. [*Pauses.*] The only one which might do, at a pinch, is that gentleman's. [*Another pause.*]

INEZ: Did you hear, Mr. Garcin?

GARCIN [*with a slight start*]: Oh . . . the sofa, you mean. So sorry. [*He rises.*] Please take it, Madam.

ESTELLE: Thanks. [*She takes off her coat and drops it on the sofa. A short silence.*] Well, as we're to live together, I suppose we'd better introduce ourselves. My name's Rigault. Estelle Rigault. [GARCIN *bows and is going to announce his name, but* INEZ *steps in front of him.*]

INEZ: And I'm Inez Serrano. Very pleased to meet you.

GARCIN [*bowing again*]: Joseph Garcin.

VALET: Do you require me any longer?

ESTELLE: No, you can go. I'll ring when I want you.

Exit VALET, *with polite bows to everyone.*

INEZ: You're very pretty. I wish we'd had some flowers to welcome you with.

ESTELLE: Flowers? Yes, I loved flowers. Only they'd fade so quickly here, wouldn't they? It's so stuffy. Oh, well, the great thing is to keep as cheerful as we can, don't you agree? Of course, you, too, are . . .

INEZ: Yes. Last week. What about you?

ESTELLE: I'm . . . quite recent. Yesterday. As a matter of fact, the ceremony's not quite over. [*Her tone is natural enough, but she seems to be seeing what she describes.*] The wind's blowing my sister's veil all over the place. She's trying her best to cry. Come, dear! Make another effort. That's better. Two tears, two teeny little tears are twinkling under the black veil. Oh dear! What a sight Olga looks this morning! She's holding my sister's arm, helping her along. She's not crying, and I don't blame her; tears always mess one's face up, don't they? Olga was my bosom friend, you know.

INEZ: Did you suffer much?

ESTELLE: No. I was only half conscious, mostly.

INEZ: What was it?

ESTELLE: Pneumonia. [*In the same tone as before.*] It's over now, they're leaving the cemetery. Good-bye. Good-bye. Quite a crowd they are. My husband's stayed at home. Prostrated with grief, poor man. [*To* INEZ.] How about you?

INEZ: The gas-stove.

ESTELLE: And you, Mr. Garcin?

GARCIN: Twelve bullets through my chest. [ESTELLE *makes a horrified gesture.*] Sorry! I fear I'm not good company amongst the dead.

ESTELLE: Please, please don't use that word. It's so . . . so crude. In terribly bad taste, really. It doesn't mean much, anyhow. Somehow I feel we've never been so much alive as now. If we've absolutely got to mention this . . . this state of things, I suggest we call ourselves—wait!—absentees. Have you been . . . been absent for long?

GARCIN: About a month.

ESTELLE: Where do you come from?

GARCIN: From Rio.

ESTELLE: I'm from Paris. Have you anyone left down there?

GARCIN: Yes, my wife. [*In the same tone as* ESTELLE *has been using.*] She's waiting at the entrance of the barracks. She comes there every day. But they won't let her in. Now she's trying to peep between the bars. She doesn't yet know I'm . . . absent, but she suspects it. Now she's going away. She's wearing her black dress. So much the better, she won't need to change. She isn't crying, but she never did cry, anyhow. It's a bright sunny day and she's like a black shadow creeping down the empty street. Those big tragic eyes of hers—with that martyred look they always had. Oh, how she got on my nerves!

A short silence. GARCIN *sits on the central sofa, and buries his head in his hands.*

INEZ: Estelle!

ESTELLE: Please, Mr. Garcin!

GARCIN: What is it?

ESTELLE: You're sitting on my sofa.

GARCIN: I beg your pardon. [*He gets up.*]

ESTELLE: You looked so . . . so far away. Sorry I disturbed you.

GARCIN: I was setting my life in order. [INEZ *starts laughing.*] You may laugh, but you'd do better to follow my example.

INEZ: No need. My life's in perfect order. It tidied itself up nicely of its own accord. So I needn't bother about it now.

GARCIN: Really? You imagine it's so simple as that. [*He runs his hand over his forehead.*] Whew! How hot it is here! Do you mind if . . .? [*He begins taking off his coat.*]

ESTELLE: How dare you! [*More gently.*] No, please don't. I loathe men in their shirt-sleeves.

GARCIN [*putting on his coat again*]: All right. [*A short pause.*] Of course I used to spend my nights in the newspaper office, and it was a regular Black Hole, so we never kept our coats on. Stiflingly hot it could be. [*Short pause. In the same tone as previously.*] Stifling, that *is*. It's night now.

ESTELLE: That's so. Olga's undressing; it must be after midnight. How quickly the time passes, on earth!

INEZ: Yes, after midnight. They've sealed up my room. It's dark, pitch dark, and empty.

GARCIN: They've slung their coats on the backs of the chairs and rolled up their shirt-sleeves above the elbow. The air stinks of men and cigar-smoke. [*A short silence.*] I used to like living among men in their shirt-sleeves.

ESTELLE [*aggressively*]: Well, in that case our tastes differ. That's all it proves. [*Turning to* INEZ.] What about you? Do you like men in their shirt-sleeves?

INEZ: Oh, I don't care much for men, any way.

ESTELLE [*looking at the other two with a puzzled air*]: Really I can't imagine why they put us three together. It doesn't make sense.

INEZ [*stifling a laugh*]: What's that you said?

ESTELLE: I'm looking at you two and thinking that we're going to live together. . . . It's so absurd. I expected to meet old friends, or relatives.

INEZ: Yes, a charming old friend—with a hole in the middle of his face.

ESTELLE: Yes, him, too. He danced the tango so divinely. Like a professional. . . . But why, why should we of all people be put together?

GARCIN: A pure fluke, I should say. They lodge folks as they can, in the order of their coming. [*To* INEZ.] Why are you laughing?

INEZ: Because you amuse me with your 'flukes'. As if they left anything to chance. But I suppose you've got to reassure yourself somehow.

ESTELLE [*hesitantly*]: I wonder now. Don't you think we may have met each other at some time in our lives?

INEZ: Never. I shouldn't have forgotten you.

ESTELLE: Or perhaps we have friends in common. I wonder if you know the Dubois-Seymours?

INEZ: Not likely.

ESTELLE: But *everyone* went to their parties.

INEZ: What's their job?

ESTELLE: Oh, they don't do anything. But they have a lovely house in the country, and hosts of people visit them.

INEZ: I didn't. I was a post-office clerk.

ESTELLE [*recoiling a little*]: Ah, yes . . . Of course, in that case . . . [*A pause.*] And you, Mr. Garcin?

GARCIN: We've never met. I always lived in Rio.

ESTELLE: Then you must be right. It's mere chance that has brought us together.

INEZ: Mere chance? Then it's by chance this room is furnished as we see it. It's an accident that the sofa on the right is a livid green, and that one on the left's wine-red. Mere chance? Well, just try to shift the sofas and you'll see the difference quick enough. And that thing on the mantelpiece, do you think it's there by accident? And what about the heat here? How about that? [*A short silence.*] I tell you they've thought it all out. Down to the last detail. Nothing was left to chance. This room was all set for us.

ESTELLE: But really! Everything here's so hideous; all in angles, so uncomfortable. I always loathed angles.

INEZ [*shrugging her shoulders*]: And do you think *I* lived in a Second Empire drawing-room?

ESTELLE: So it was all fixed up beforehand?

INEZ: Yes. And they've put us together deliberately.

ESTELLE: Then it's not mere chance that *you* precisely are sitting opposite *me*? But what can be the idea behind it?

INEZ: Ask me another! I only know they're waiting.

ESTELLE: I never could bear the idea of anyone's expecting something from me. It always made me want to do just the opposite.

INEZ: Well, do it. Do it, if you can. You don't even know what they expect.

ESTELLE [*stamping her foot*]: It's outrageous! So something's coming to me from you two? [*She eyes each in turn.*] Something nasty, I suppose. There are some faces that tell me everything at once. Yours don't convey anything.

GARCIN [*turning abruptly towards* INEZ]: Look here! Why are we together? You've given us quite enough hints, you may as well come out with it.

INEZ [*in a surprised tone*]: But I know nothing, absolutely nothing about it. I'm as much in the dark as you are.

GARCIN: We've *got* to know. [*Ponders for a while.*]

INEZ: If only each of us had the guts to tell . . .

GARCIN: Tell what?

INEZ: Estelle!

ESTELLE: Yes?

INEZ: What have you done? I mean, why have they sent you here?

ESTELLE [*quickly*]: That's just it. I haven't a notion, not the foggiest. In fact I'm wondering if there hasn't been some ghastly mistake. [*To* INEZ.] Don't smile. Just think of the number of people who . . . who become absentees every day. There must be thousands and thousands, and probably they're sorted out by—by understrappers, you know what I mean. Stupid employees who don't know their job. So they're bound to make mistakes sometimes. . . . Do stop smiling. [*To* GARCIN.] Why don't you speak? If they made a mistake in my case, they may have done the same about you. [*To* INEZ.] And you, too. Anyhow, isn't it better to think we've got here by mistake?

INEZ: Is that all you have to tell us?

ESTELLE: What else should I tell? I've nothing to hide. I lost my parents when I was a kid, and I had my young brother to bring up. We were terribly poor and when an old friend of my people asked me to marry him I said 'Yes'. He was very well off, and quite nice. My brother was a very delicate child and needed all sorts of attention, so really that was the right thing for me to do, don't you agree? My husband was old enough to be my father, but for six years we had a happy married life. Then two years ago I met the man I was fated to love. We knew it the moment we set eyes on each other. He asked me to run away with him, and I refused. Then I got pneumonia and it finished me. That's the whole story. No doubt, by certain standards, I did wrong to sacrifice my youth to a man nearly three times my age. [*To* GARCIN.] Do *you* think that could be called a sin?

GARCIN: Certainly not. [*A short silence.*] And now, tell me, do you think it's a crime to stand by one's principles?

ESTELLE: Of course not. Surely no one could blame a man for that!

GARCIN: Wait a bit! I ran a pacifist newspaper. Then war broke out. What was I to do? Everyone was watching me, wondering, 'Will he dare?' Well, I dared. I folded my arms and they shot me. Had I done anything wrong?

ESTELLE [*laying her hand on his arm*]: Wrong? On the contrary. You were . . .

INEZ [*breaks in ironically*]: . . . a hero! And how about your wife, Mr. Garcin?

GARCIN: That's simple. I'd rescued her from . . . from the gutter.

ESTELLE [*to* INEZ]: You see! You see!

INEZ: Yes, I see. [*A pause.*] Look here! What's the point of play-acting, trying to throw dust in each other's eyes? We're all tarred with the same brush.

ESTELLE [*indignantly*]: How dare you!

INEZ: Yes, we are criminals—murderers—all three of us. We're in hell, my pets, they never make mistakes, and people aren't damned for nothing.

ESTELLE: Stop! For heaven's sake . . .

INEZ: In hell! Damned souls—that's us, all three!

ESTELLE: Keep quiet! I forbid you to use such disgusting words.

INEZ: A damned soul—that's you, my little plaster saint. And ditto our friend there, the noble pacifist. We've had our hour of pleasure, haven't we? There have been people who burnt their lives out for our sakes—and we chuckled over it. So now we have to pay the reckoning.

GARCIN [*raising his fist*]: Will you keep your mouth shut, damn it!

INEZ [*confronting him fearlessly, but with a look of vast surprise*]: Well, well! [*A pause.*] Ah, I understand now. I know why they've put us three together.

GARCIN: I advise you to . . . to think twice before you say any more.

INEZ: Wait! You'll see how simple it is. Childishly simple. Obviously there aren't any physical torments—you agree, don't you? And yet we're in hell. And no one else will come here. We'll stay in this room together, the three of us, for ever and ever. . . . In short, there's someone absent here, the official torturer.

GARCIN [*sotto voce*]: I'd noticed that.

INEZ: It's obvious what they're after—an economy of man-power . . . or devil-power, if you prefer. The same idea as in the cafeteria where customers serve themselves.

ESTELLE: What ever do you mean?

INEZ: I mean that each of us will act as torturer of the two others.
There is a short silence, while they digest this information.

GARCIN [*gently*]: No, I shall never be your torturer. I wish neither of you any harm, and I've no concern with you. None at all. So the solution's easy enough; each of us stays put in his or her corner, and takes no notice of the others. You here, you here, and I there. Like soldiers at our posts. Also, we mustn't speak. Not one word. That won't be difficult; each of us has plenty of material for self-communings. I think I could stay ten thousand years with only my thoughts for company.

ESTELLE: Have *I* got to keep silent, too?

GARCIN: Yes. And that way we . . . we'll work out our salvation. Looking into ourselves, never raising our heads. Agreed?

INEZ: Agreed.

ESTELLE [*after some hesitation*]: I agree.

GARCIN: Then . . . Good-bye.

He goes to his sofa, and buries his head in his hands. There is a long silence; then INEZ *begins singing to herself.*

INEZ [*singing*]:

> What a crowd in Whitefriars Lane!
> They've set trestles in a row,
> With a scaffold and the knife,
> And a pail of bran below.
> Come, good folks, to Whitefriars Lane,
> Come to see the merry show!
>
> The headsman rose at crack of dawn,
> He'd a long day's work in hand,
> Chopping heads off generals,
> Priests and peers and admirals,
> All the highest in the land.
> What a crowd in Whitefriars Lane!
>
> See them standing in a line,
> Ladies all dressed up so fine.
> But their heads have got to go,
> Heads and hats roll down below.
> Come, good folks, to Whitefriars Lane,
> Come to see the merry show!

Meanwhile ESTELLE *has been plying her powder-puff and lipstick. She looks round for a mirror, fumbles in her bag, then turns towards* GARCIN.

ESTELLE: Excuse me, have you a glass? [GARCIN *does not answer.*] Any sort of glass, a pocket-mirror will do. [GARCIN *remains silent.*] Even if you won't speak to me, you might lend me a glass.

His head still buried in his hands, GARCIN *ignores her.*

INEZ [*eagerly*]: Don't worry! I've a glass in my bag. [*She opens her bag. Angrily.*] It's gone! They must have taken it from me at the entrance.

ESTELLE: How tiresome!

A short silence. ESTELLE *shuts her eyes and sways, as if about to faint.* INEZ *runs forward and holds her up.*

INEZ: What's the matter?

ESTELLE *opens her eyes and smiles.*

ESTELLE: I feel so queer. [*She pats herself.*] Don't you ever get taken that way? When I can't see myself I begin to wonder if I really and truly exist. I pat myself just to make sure, but it doesn't help much.

INEZ: You're lucky. I'm always conscious of myself—in my mind. Painfully conscious.

ESTELLE: Ah yes, in your mind. But everything that goes on in one's head is so vague, isn't it? It makes one want to sleep. [*She is silent for a while.*] I've six big mirrors in my bedroom. There they are. I can see them. But they don't see me. They're reflecting the carpet, the settee, the window . . . but how empty it is, a glass in which I'm absent. When I talked to people I always made sure there was one near by in which I could see myself. I watched myself talking. And somehow it kept me alert, seeing myself as others saw me. . . . Oh dear! My lipstick! I'm sure I've put it on all crooked. No, I can't do without a looking-glass for ever and ever, I simply can't.

INEZ: Suppose I try to be your glass? Come and pay me a visit, dear. Here's a place for you on my sofa.

ESTELLE: But—— [*Points to* GARCIN.]

INEZ: Oh, he doesn't count.

ESTELLE: But we're going to . . . to hurt each other. You said it yourself.

INEZ: Do I look as if I wanted to hurt you?

ESTELLE: One can never tell.

INEZ: Much more likely *you*'ll hurt *me*. Still, what does it matter? If I've got to suffer, it may as well be at your hands, your pretty hands. Sit down. Come closer. Closer. Look into my eyes. What do you see?

ESTELLE: Oh, I'm there! But so tiny I can't see myself properly.

INEZ: But *I* can. Every inch of you. Now ask me questions. I'll be as candid as any looking-glass.

ESTELLE *seems rather embarrassed and turns to* GARCIN, *as if appealing to him for help.*

ESTELLE: Please, Mr. Garcin. Sure our chatter isn't boring you?

GARCIN *makes no reply.*

INEZ: Don't worry about him. As I said, he doesn't count. We're by ourselves. . . . Ask away.

ESTELLE: Are my lips all right?

INEZ: Show! No, they're a bit smudgy.

ESTELLE: I thought as much. Luckily [*throws a quick glance at* GARCIN] no one's seen me. I'll try again.

INEZ: That's better. No. Follow the line of your lips. Wait! I'll guide your hand. There. That's quite good.

ESTELLE: As good as when I came in?

INEZ: Far better. Crueller. Your mouth looks quite diabolical that way.

ESTELLE: Good gracious! And you say you like it! How maddening, not being able to see for myself! You're quite sure, Miss Serrano, that it's all right now?

INEZ: Won't you call me Inez?

ESTELLE: Are you sure it looks all right?

INEZ: You're lovely, Estelle.

ESTELLE: But how can I rely upon your taste? Is it the same as *my* taste? Oh, how sickening it all is, enough to drive one crazy!

INEZ: I *have* your taste, my dear, because I like you so much. Look at me. No, straight. Now smile. I'm not so ugly, either. Aren't I nicer than your glass?

ESTELLE: Oh, I don't know. You scare me rather. My reflection in the glass never did that; of course I knew it so well. Like something I had tamed. . . . I'm going to smile, and my smile will sink down into your pupils, and heaven knows what it will become.

INEZ: And why shouldn't you 'tame' me? [*The women gaze at each other,* ESTELLE *with a sort of fearful fascination.*] Listen! I want you to call me 'Inez'. We must be great friends.

ESTELLE: I don't make friends with women very easily.

INEZ: Not with postal clerks, you mean? Hullo, what's that—that nasty red spot at the bottom of your cheek? A pimple?

ESTELLE: A pimple? Oh, how simply foul! Where?

INEZ: There . . . You know the way they catch larks—with a mirror? I'm your lark-mirror, my dear, and you can't escape me. . . . There isn't any pimple, not a trace of one. So what about it? Suppose the mirror started telling lies? Or suppose I covered my eyes—as he is doing—and refused to look at you, all that loveliness of yours would be wasted on the desert air. No, don't be afraid, I can't help looking at you, I shan't turn my eyes away. And I'll be nice to you, ever so nice. Only you must be nice to me, too.

A short silence.

ESTELLE: Are you really . . . attracted by me?

INEZ: Very much indeed.

Another short silence.

ESTELLE [*indicating* GARCIN *by a slight movement of her head*]: But I wish he'd notice me, too.

INEZ: Of course! Because he's a Man! [*To* GARCIN.] You've won. [GARCIN *says nothing.*] But look at her, damn it! [*Still no reply from* GARCIN.] Don't pretend. You haven't missed a word of what we've said.

GARCIN: Quite so; not a word. I stuck my fingers in my ears, but your voices thudded in my brain. Silly chatter. Now will you leave me in peace, you two? I'm not interested in you.

INEZ: Not in me, perhaps—but how about this child? Aren't you interested in her? Oh, I saw through your game; you got on your high horse just to impress her.

GARCIN: I asked you to leave me in peace. There's someone talking about me in the newspaper office and I want to listen. And, if it'll make you any happier, let me tell you that I've no use for the 'child', as you call her.

ESTELLE: Thanks.

GARCIN: Oh, I didn't mean it rudely.

ESTELLE: You cad!

They confront each other in silence for some moments.

GARCIN: So that's that. [*Pause.*] You know I begged you not to speak.

ESTELLE: It's *her* fault; she started. I didn't ask anything of her and she came and offered me her . . . her glass.

INEZ: So you say. But all the time you were making up to him, trying every trick to catch his attention.

ESTELLE: Well, why shouldn't I?

GARCIN: You're crazy, both of you. Don't you see where this is leading us? For pity's sake, keep your mouths shut. [*Pause.*] Now let's all sit down again quite quietly; we'll look at the floor and each must try to forget the others are there.

A longish silence. GARCIN *sits down. The women return hesitantly to their places. Suddenly* INEZ *swings round on him.*

INEZ: To forget about the others? How utterly absurd! I *feel* you there, down to my marrow. Your silence clamours in my ears. You can nail up your mouth, cut your tongue out—but you can't prevent your *being there.* Can you stop your thoughts? I hear them ticking away like a clock, tick-tock, tick-tock, and I'm certain you hear mine. It's all very well skulking on your sofa, but you're everywhere, and every sound comes to me soiled, because you've intercepted it on its way. Why, you've even stolen my face; you know it and I don't! And what about her, about Estelle? You've stolen her from me, too; if she and I were alone do you suppose she'd treat me as she does? No, take your hands from your face, I won't leave you in peace—that would suit your book too well. You'd go on sitting there, in a sort of trance, like a Yogi, and even if I didn't see her I'd feel it in my bones—that she was making every sound, even the rustle of her dress, for your benefit, throwing you smiles you didn't see. . . . Well, I won't stand for that, I prefer to choose my hell; I prefer to look you in the eyes, and fight it out face to face.

GARCIN: Have it your own way. I suppose we were bound to come to this; they knew what they were about, and we're easy game. If they'd put me in a room with men . . . men can keep their mouths shut. But it's no use wanting the impossible. [*He goes to* ESTELLE *and lightly fondles her neck.*] So I attract you, little girl? It seems you were making eyes at me?

ESTELLE: Don't touch me.

GARCIN: Why not? We might, anyhow, be natural. . . . Do you know, I used to be mad keen on women? And some were fond of me. So we may as well stop posing, we've nothing to lose. Why trouble about politeness, and decorum, and the rest of it? We're between ourselves. And presently we shall be naked as—as new-born babes.

ESTELLE: Oh, let me be!

GARCIN: As new-born babes. Well, I'd warned you, anyhow. I asked so little of you, nothing but peace and a little silence. I'd put my fingers in my ears. Gomez was spouting away as usual, standing in the centre of the room, with all the pressmen listening. In their shirt-sleeves. I tried to hear, but it wasn't too easy. Things on earth move so quickly, you know. Couldn't you have held your tongues? Now it's over, he's stopped talking, and what he thinks of me has gone back into his head. Well, we've got to see it through somehow. . . . Naked as we were born. So much the better; I want to know whom I have to deal with.

INEZ: You know already. There's nothing more to learn.

GARCIN: You're wrong. So long as each of us hasn't made a clean breast of it—why they've damned him or her—we know nothing. Nothing that counts. You, young lady, you shall begin. Why? Tell us why. If you are frank, if we bring our spectres into the open, it may save us from disaster. So—out with it! Why?

ESTELLE: I tell you I haven't a notion. They wouldn't tell me why.

GARCIN: That's so. They wouldn't tell me, either. But I've a pretty shrewd idea. . . . Perhaps you're shy of speaking first? Right. I'll lead off. [*A short silence.*] I'm not a very estimable person.

INEZ: No need to tell us that. We know you were a deserter.

GARCIN: Let that be. It's only a side-issue. I'm here because I treated my wife abominably. That's all. For five years. Naturally, she's suffering still. There she is; the moment I mention her, I see her. It's Gomez who interests me, and it's she I see. Where's Gomez got to? For five years. There! They've given her back my things; she's sitting by the window, with my coat on her knees. The coat with the twelve bullet-holes. The blood's like rust; a brown ring round each hole. It's quite a museum-piece, that coat; scarred with history. And I used to wear it, fancy! . . . Now, can't you shed a tear, my love? Surely you'll squeeze one out—at last? No? You can't manage it? . . . Night after night I came home blind drunk; stinking of wine and women. She'd sat up for me, of course. But she never cried, never uttered a word of reproach. Only her eyes spoke. Big, tragic eyes. I don't regret anything. I must pay the price, but I shan't whine. . . . It's snowing in the street. Won't you cry, confound you! That woman was a born martyr, you know; a victim by vocation.

INEZ [*almost tenderly*]: Why did you hurt her like that?

GARCIN: It was so easy. A word was enough to make her flinch. Like a sensitive plant. But never, never a reproach. I'm fond of teasing. I watched and waited. But no, not a tear, not a protest. I'd picked her up out of the gutter, you understand. . . . Now she's stroking the coat. Her eyes are shut and she's feeling with her fingers for the bullet-holes. What are you after? What do you expect? I tell you I regret nothing. The truth is, she admired me too much. Does that mean anything to you?

INEZ: No. Nobody admired *me*.

GARCIN: So much the better. So much the better for you. I suppose all this strikes you as very vague. Well, here's something you can get your teeth into. I brought a half-caste girl to stay in our house. My wife slept upstairs; she must have heard . . . everything. She was an early riser and, as I and the girl stayed in bed late, she served us our morning coffee.

INEZ: You brute!

GARCIN: Yes, a brute, if you like. But a well-beloved brute. [*A far-away look comes to his eyes.*] No, it's nothing. Only Gomez, and he's not talking about *me*. . . . What were you saying? Yes, a brute. Certainly. Else why should I be here? [*To* INEZ.] Your turn.

INEZ: Well, I was what some people down there called 'a damned bitch'. Damned already. So it's no surprise, being here.

GARCIN: Is that all you have to say?

INEZ: No. There was that affair with Florence. A dead men's tale. With three corpses to it. He to start with; then she and I. So there's no one left, I've nothing to worry about; it was a clean sweep. Only that room. I see it now and then. Empty, with the doors locked. . . . No, they've just unlocked them. 'To Let.' It's to let; there's a notice on the door. That's . . . too ridiculous.

GARCIN: Three. Three deaths, you said?

INEZ: Three.

GARCIN: One man and two women?

INEZ: Yes.

GARCIN: Well, well. [*A pause.*] Did he kill himself?

INEZ: He? No, he hadn't the guts for that. Still, he'd every reason; we led him a dog's life. As a matter of fact he was run over by a tram. A silly sort of end . . . I was living with them; he was my cousin.

GARCIN: Was Florence fair?

INEZ: Fair? [*Glances at* ESTELLE.] You know, I don't regret a thing; still, I'm not so very keen on telling you the story.

GARCIN: That's all right. . . . So you got sick of him?

INEZ: Quite gradually. All sorts of little things got on my nerves. For instance, he made a noise when he was drinking—a sort of gurgle. Trifles like that. He was rather pathetic really. Vulnerable. Why are you smiling?

GARCIN: Because, I, anyhow, am *not* vulnerable.

INEZ: Don't be too sure. . . . I crept inside her skin, she saw the world through my eyes. When she left him, I had her on my hands. We shared a bed-sitting-room at the other end of the town.

GARCIN: And then?

INEZ: Then that tram did its job. I used to remind her every day: 'Yes, my pet, we killed him between us.' [*A pause.*] I'm rather cruel, really.

GARCIN: So am I.

INEZ: No, you're not cruel. It's something else.

GARCIN: What?

INEZ: I'll tell you later. When I say I'm cruel, I mean I can't get on without making people suffer. Like a live coal. A live coal in others' hearts. When I'm alone I flicker out. For six months I flamed away in her heart, till there was nothing but a cinder. One night she got up and turned on the gas while I was asleep. Then she crept back into bed. So now you know.

GARCIN: Well! Well!

INEZ: Yes? What's in your mind?

GARCIN: Nothing. Only that it's not a pretty story.

INEZ: Obviously. But what matter?

GARCIN: As you say, what matter? [*To* ESTELLE.] Your turn. What have you done?

ESTELLE: As I told you, I haven't a notion. I rack my brain, but it's no use.

GARCIN: Right. Then we'll give you a hand. That fellow with the smashed face, who was he?

ESTELLE: Who . . . who do you mean?

INEZ: You know quite well. The man you were so scared of seeing when you came in.

ESTELLE: Oh, him! A friend of mine.

GARCIN: Why were you afraid of him?

ESTELLE: That's my business, Mr. Garcin.

INEZ: Did he shoot himself on your account?

ESTELLE: Of course not. How absurd you are!

GARCIN: Then why should you have been so scared? He blew his brains out, didn't he? That's how his face got smashed.

ESTELLE: Don't! Please don't go on.

GARCIN: Because of you. Because of you.

INEZ: He shot himself because of you.

ESTELLE: Leave me alone! It's . . . it's not fair, bullying me like that. I want to go! I want to go!

She runs to the door and shakes it.

GARCIN: Go, if you can. Personally, I ask for nothing better. Unfortunately the door's locked.

ESTELLE *presses the bell-push, but the bell does not ring.* INEZ *and* GARCIN *laugh.* ESTELLE *swings round on them, her back to the door.*

ESTELLE [*in a muffled voice*]: You're hateful, both of you.

INEZ: Hateful? Yes, that's the word. Now, get on with it. That fellow who killed himself on your account—you were his mistress, eh?

GARCIN: Of course she was. And he wanted to have her to himself alone. That's so, isn't it?

INEZ: He danced the tango like a professional, but he was poor as a church mouse—that's right, isn't it?

A short silence.

GARCIN: Was he poor or not? Give a straight answer.

ESTELLE: Yes, he was poor.

GARCIN: And then you had your reputation to keep up. One day he came and implored you to run away with him, and you laughed in his face.

INEZ: That's it. You laughed at him. And so he killed himself.

ESTELLE: Used you to look at Florence in that way?

INEZ: Yes.

A short pause, then ESTELLE *bursts out laughing.*

ESTELLE: You've got it all wrong, you two. [*She stiffens her shoulders, still leaning against the door, and faces them. Her voice grows shrill, truculent.*] He wanted me to have a baby. So there!

GARCIN: And you didn't want one?

ESTELLE: I certainly didn't. But the baby came, worse luck. I went to Switzerland for five months. No one knew anything. It was a girl. Roger was with me when she was born. It pleased him no end, having a daughter. It didn't please *me*!

GARCIN: And then?

ESTELLE: There was a balcony overlooking the lake. I brought a big stone. He could see what I was up to, and he kept on shouting, 'Estelle, for God's sake, don't!' I hated him then. He saw it all. He was leaning over the balcony and he saw the rings spreading on the water . . .

GARCIN: Yes? And then?

ESTELLE: That's all. I came back to Paris—and he did as he wished.

GARCIN: You mean, he blew his brains out?

ESTELLE: It was absurd of him, really; my husband never suspected anything. [*A pause.*] Oh, how I loathe you! [*She sobs tearlessly.*]

GARCIN: Nothing doing. Tears don't flow in this place.

ESTELLE: I'm a coward. A coward! [*Pause.*] If you knew how I hate you!

INEZ [*taking her in her arms*]: Poor child! [*To* GARCIN.] So the hearing's over. But there's no need to look like a hanging judge.

GARCIN: A hanging judge? [*He glances round him.*] I'd give a lot to be able to see myself in a glass. [*Pause.*] How hot it is! [*Unthinkingly he takes off his coat.*] Oh, sorry! [*He starts putting it on again.*]

ESTELLE: Don't bother. You can stay in your shirt-sleeves. As things are . . .

GARCIN: Just so. [*He drops his coat on the sofa.*] You mustn't be angry with me, Estelle.

ESTELLE: I'm not angry with you.

INEZ: And what about me? Are you angry with me?

ESTELLE: Yes.

A short silence.

INEZ: Well, Mr. Garcin, now you have us in the nude all right. Do you understand things any better for that?

GARCIN: I wonder. Yes, perhaps a trifle better. [*Timidly.*] And now suppose we start trying to help each other?

INEZ: I don't need help.

GARCIN: Inez, they've laid their snare damned cunningly—like a cobweb. If you make any movement, if you raise your hand to fan yourself, Estelle and I feel a little tug. Alone, none of us can save himself or herself; we're linked together inextricably. So you can take your choice. [*A pause.*] Hullo? What's happening?

INEZ: They've let it. The windows are wide open, a man is sitting on my bed. *My* bed, if you please! They've let it, let it! Step in, step in, make yourself at home, you brute! Ah, there's a woman, too. She's going up to him, putting her hands on his shoulders. . . . Damn it, why don't they turn the lights on? It's getting dark. Now he's going to kiss her. But that's my room, *my* room! Pitch dark now. I can't see anything, but I hear them whispering, whispering. Is he going to make love to her on *my* bed? What's that she said? That it's noon and the sun is shining? I must be going blind. [*A pause.*] Blacked out. I can't see or hear a thing. So I'm done with the earth, it seems. No more alibis for me! [*She shudders.*] I feel so empty, desiccated—really dead at last. All of me's here, in this room. [*A pause.*] What were you saying? Something about helping me, wasn't it?

GARCIN: Yes.

INEZ: Helping me to do what?

GARCIN: To defeat their devilish tricks.

INEZ: And what do you expect me to do, in return?

GARCIN: To help *me*. It only needs a little effort, Inez; just a spark of human feeling.

INEZ: Human feeling. That's beyond my range. I'm rotten to the core.

GARCIN: And how about me? [*A pause.*] All the same, suppose we try?

INEZ: It's no use. I'm all dried up. I can't give and I can't receive. How could

I help you? A dead twig, ready for the burning. [*She falls silent, gazing at* ESTELLE, *who has buried her head in her hands.*] Florence was fair, a natural blonde.

GARCIN: Do you realize that this young woman's fated to be your torturer?

INEZ: Perhaps I've guessed it.

GARCIN: It's through her they'll get you. I, of course, I'm different . . . aloof. I take no notice of her. Suppose you had a try . . .

INEZ: Yes?

GARCIN: It's a trap. They're watching you, to see if you'll fall into it.

INEZ: I know. And you're another trap. Do you think they haven't fore-known every word you say? And of course there's a whole nest of pitfalls that we can't see. Everything here's a booby-trap. But what do I care? I'm a pitfall, too. For her, obviously. And perhaps I'll catch her.

GARCIN: You won't catch anything. We're chasing after each other, round and round in a vicious circle, like the horses on a roundabout. That's part of their plan, of course. . . . Drop it, Inez. Open your hands and let go of everything. Or else you'll bring disaster on all three of us.

INEZ: Do I look the sort of person who lets go? I know what's coming to me. I'm going to burn, and it's to last for ever. Yes, I *know* everything. But do you think I'll let go? I'll catch her, she'll see you through my eyes, as Florence saw that other man. What's the good of trying to enlist my sympathy? I assure you I know everything, and I can't feel sorry even for myself. A trap! Don't I know it, and that I'm in a trap myself, up to the neck, and there's nothing to be done about it. And, if it suits their book, so much the better!

GARCIN [*gripping her shoulders*]: Well, *I*, anyhow, can feel sorry for you, too. Look at me, we're naked, naked right through and I can see into your heart. That's one link between us. Do you think I'd want to hurt you? I don't regret anything, I'm dried up, too. But for you I can still feel pity.

INEZ, *who has let him keep his hands on her shoulders until now, shakes herself loose.*

INEZ: Don't. I hate being pawed about. And keep your pity for yourself. Don't forget, Garcin, that there are traps for you, too, in this room. All nicely set for you. You'd do better to watch your own interests. [*A pause.*] But, if you will leave us in peace, this child and me, I'll see I don't do you any harm.

GARCIN *gazes at her for a moment, then shrugs his shoulders.*

GARCIN: Very well.

ESTELLE [*raising her head*]: Please, Garcin.

GARCIN: What do you want of me?

ESTELLE *rises and goes up to him.*

ESTELLE: You can help *me*, anyhow.

GARCIN: If you want help, apply to her.

[INEZ *has come up and is standing behind* ESTELLE, *but without touching her.*
During the dialogue that follows she speaks almost in her ear. But ESTELLE *keeps*
her eyes on GARCIN, *who observes her without speaking, and she addresses her*
answers to him, as if it were he who is questioning her.]

ESTELLE: I implore you, Garcin . . . you gave me your promise, didn't you?
Help me quick. I don't want to be left alone. Olga's taken him to a
cabaret.

INEZ: Taken whom?

ESTELLE: Peter. . . . Oh, now they're dancing together.

INEZ: Who's Peter?

ESTELLE: Such a silly boy. He called me his glancing stream—just fancy!
He was terribly in love with me. . . . She's persuaded him to come out
with her to-night.

INEZ: Do you love him?

ESTELLE: They're sitting down now. She's puffing like a grampus. What a
fool the girl is to insist on dancing! But I dare say she does it to reduce.
. . . No, of course I don't love him; he's only eighteen, and I'm not a baby-
snatcher.

INEZ: Then why bother about them? What difference can it make?

ESTELLE: He belonged to me.

INEZ: Nothing on earth belongs to you any more.

ESTELLE: I tell you he was mine. All mine.

INEZ: Yes, he *was* yours—once. But now—— Try to make him hear, try
to touch him. Olga can touch him, talk to him as much as she likes. That's
so, isn't it? She can squeeze his hands, rub herself against him . . .

ESTELLE: Yes, look! She's pressing her great fat chest against him, puffing
and blowing in his face. But, my poor little lamb, can't you see how ridiculous she is, why don't you laugh at her? Oh, once I'd have only had to
glance at them, and she'd have slunk away. Is there really nothing, nothing
left of me?

INEZ: Nothing whatever. Nothing of you's left on earth—not even a
shadow. All you own is here. Would you like that paper-knife? Or that
ornament on the mantelpiece? That blue sofa's yours. And I, my dear,
am yours for ever.

ESTELLE: You mine! That's good. Well, which of you two would dare to
call me his glancing stream, his crystal girl? You know too much about
me, you know I'm rotten through and through . . . Peter dear, think of
me, fix your thoughts on me, and save me. All the time you're thinking
'my glancing stream, my crystal girl', I'm only half here, I'm only half
wicked, and half of me is down there with you, clean and bright and
crystal-clear as running water. . . . Oh, just look at her face, all scarlet, like
a tomato! No, it's absurd, we've laughed at her together, you and I, often
and often. . . . What's that tune, I always loved it? Yes, the St. Louis

Blues . . . All right, dance away, dance away. Garcin, I wish you could see her, you'd die of laughing. Only—she'll never know I *see* her. Yes, I see you, Olga, with your hair all anyhow, and you do look a dope, my dear. Oh, now you're treading on his toes. It's a scream! Hurry up! Quicker! Quicker! He's dragging her along, bundling her round and round—it's too ghastly! He always said I was so light, he loved to dance with me. [*She is dancing as she speaks.*] I tell you, Olga, I can see you. No, she doesn't care, she's dancing through my gaze. What's that? What's that you said? 'Our poor dear Estelle?' Oh, don't be such a humbug! You didn't even shed a tear at the funeral. . . . And she has the nerve to talk to him about her poor dear friend Estelle! How dare she discuss me with Peter? Now then, keep time. She never could dance and talk at once. Oh, what's that . . . ? No, no. Don't tell him. Please, please don't tell him. You can keep him, do what you like with him, but please don't tell him about— that! [*She has stopped dancing.*] All right. You can have him now. Isn't it *foul*, Garcin? She's told him everything, about Roger, my trip to Switzerland, the baby. 'Poor Estelle wasn't exactly . . .' No, I wasn't exactly . . . True enough. He's looking grave, shaking his head, but he doesn't seem so very much surprised, not what one'd expect. Keep him then—I won't haggle with you over his long eyelashes, his pretty girlish face. They're yours for the asking. His glancing stream, his crystal. Well, the crystal's shattered into bits. 'Poor Estelle!' Dance, dance, dance. On with it. But do keep time. One, two. One, two. How I'd love to go down to earth just for a moment, and dance with him again. [*She dances again for some moments.*] The music's growing fainter. They've turned down the lights, like they do for a tango. Why are they playing so softly? Louder, please. I can't hear. It's so far away, so far away. I . . . I can't hear a sound. [*She stops dancing.*] All over. It's the end. The earth has left me. [*To* GARCIN.] Don't turn from me . . . please. Take me in your arms.

Behind ESTELLE'S *back,* INEZ *signs to* GARCIN *to move away.*

INEZ [*commandingly*]: Now then, Garcin!

GARCIN *moves back a step, and, glancing at* ESTELLE, *points to* INEZ.

GARCIN: It's to her you should say that.

ESTELLE [*clinging to him*]: Don't turn away. You're a man, aren't you, and surely I'm not such a fright as all that! Everyone says I've lovely hair and, after all, a man killed himself on my account. You have to look at something, and there's nothing here to see except the sofas and that awful ornament and the table. Surely I'm better to look at than a lot of stupid furniture. Listen! I've dropped out of their hearts like a little sparrow fallen from its nest. So gather me up, dear, fold me to your heart—and you'll see how nice I can be.

GARCIN [*freeing himself from her, after a short struggle*]: I tell you it's to that lady you should speak.

ESTELLE: To her? But she doesn't count, she's a woman.

INEZ: Oh, I don't count? Is that what you think? But, my poor little fallen nestling, you've been sheltering in my heart for ages, though you didn't realize it. Don't be afraid; I'll keep looking at you for ever and ever, without a flutter of my eyelids, and you'll live in my gaze like a mote in a sunbeam.

ESTELLE: A sunbeam indeed! Don't talk such rubbish! You've tried that trick already, and you should know it doesn't work.

INEZ: Estelle! My glancing stream. My crystal!

ESTELLE: *Your* crystal? It's grotesque. Do you think you can fool me with that sort of talk? Everyone knows by now what I did to my baby. The crystal's shattered, but I don't care. I'm just a hollow dummy, all that's left of me is the outside—but it's not for you.

INEZ: Come to me, Estelle. You shall be whatever you like: a glancing stream, a muddy stream. And deep down in my eyes you'll see yourself just as you want to be.

ESTELLE: Oh, leave me in peace. You haven't any eyes. Oh, damn it, isn't there anything I can do to get rid of you? I've an idea. [*She spits in* INEZ' *face.*] There!

INEZ: Garcin, you shall pay for this.

A pause. GARCIN *shrugs his shoulders and goes to* ESTELLE.

GARCIN: So it's a man you need?

ESTELLE: Not *any* man. You.

GARCIN: No humbug now. Any man would do your business. As I happen to be here, you want me. Right! [*He grips her shoulders.*] Mind, I'm not your sort at all, really; I'm not a young nincompoop and I don't dance the tango.

ESTELLE: I'll take you as you are. And perhaps I shall change you.

GARCIN: I doubt it. I shan't pay much attention; I've other things to think about.

ESTELLE: What things?

GARCIN: They wouldn't interest you.

ESTELLE: I'll sit on your sofa and wait for you to take some notice of me. I promise not to bother you at all.

INEZ [*with a shrill laugh*]: That's right, fawn on him, like the silly bitch you are. Grovel and cringe! And he hasn't even good looks to commend him!

ESTELLE [*to* GARCIN]: Don't listen to her. She has no eyes, no ears. She's—nothing.

GARCIN: I'll give you what I can. It doesn't amount to much. I shan't love you; I know you too well.

ESTELLE: Do you want me, anyhow?

GARCIN: Yes.

ESTELLE: I ask no more.

GARCIN: In that case . . . [*He bends over her.*]

INEZ: Estelle! Garcin! You must be going crazy. You're not alone. I'm here too.

GARCIN: Of course—but what does it matter?

INEZ: Under my eyes? You couldn't . . . couldn't do it.

ESTELLE: Why not? I often undressed with my maid looking on.

INEZ [*gripping* GARCIN'S *arm*]: Let her alone. Don't paw her with your dirty man's hands.

GARCIN [*thrusting her away roughly*]: Take care. I'm no gentleman, and I'd have no compunction about striking a woman.

INEZ: But you promised me; you promised. I'm only asking you to keep your word.

GARCIN: Why should I, considering you were the first to break our agreement?

INEZ *turns her back on him and retreats to the far end of the room.*

INEZ: Very well, have it your own way. I'm the weaker party, one against two. But don't forget I'm here, and watching. I shan't take my eyes off you, Garcin; when you're kissing her, you'll feel them boring into you. Yes, have it your own way, make love and get it over. We're in hell; my turn will come.

During the following scene she watches them without speaking.

GARCIN [*coming back to* ESTELLE *and grasping her shoulders*]: Now then. Your lips. Give me your lips.

A pause. He bends to kiss her; then abruptly straightens up.

ESTELLE [*indignantly*]: Really! [*A pause.*] Didn't I tell you not to pay any attention to her?

GARCIN: You've got it wrong. [*Short silence.*] It's Gomez; he's back in the press-room. They've shut the windows; it must be winter down there. Six months. Six months since I . . . Well, I warned you I'd be absent-minded sometimes, didn't I? They're shivering, they've kept their coats on. Funny they should feel the cold like that, when I'm feeling so hot. Ah, this time he's talking about me.

ESTELLE: Is it going to last long? [*Short silence.*] You might at least tell me what he's saying.

GARCIN: Nothing. Nothing worth repeating. He's a swine, that's all. [*He listens attentively.*] A god-damned, bloody swine. [*He turns to* ESTELLE.] Let's come back to—to ourselves. Are you going to love me?

ESTELLE [*smiling*]: I wonder now!

GARCIN: Will you trust me?

ESTELLE: What a quaint thing to ask! Considering you'll be under my eyes all the time, and I don't think I've much to fear from Inez, so far as you're concerned.

GARCIN: Obviously. [*A pause. He takes his hands off* ESTELLE'S *shoulders.*] I was thinking of another kind of trust. [*Listens.*] Talk away, talk away, you swine. I'm not there to defend myself. [*To* ESTELLE.] Estelle, you *must* give me your trust.

ESTELLE: Oh, what a nuisance you are! I'm giving you my mouth, my arms, my whole body—and everything could be so simple. . . . My trust! I haven't any to give, I'm afraid, and you're making me terribly embarrassed. You must have something pretty ghastly on your conscience to make such a fuss about my trusting you.

GARCIN: They shot me.

ESTELLE: I know. Because you refused to fight. Well, why shouldn't you?

GARCIN: I . . . I didn't exactly refuse. [*In a far-away voice.*] I must say he talks well, he makes out a good case against me, but he never says what I should have done, instead. Should I have gone to the General and said, 'General, I decline to fight'? A mug's game; they'd have promptly locked me up. But I wanted to show my colours, my true colours, do you understand? I wasn't going to be silenced. [*To* ESTELLE.] So I . . . I took the train. . . . They caught me at the frontier.

ESTELLE: Where were you trying to go?

GARCIN: To Mexico. I meant to launch a pacifist newspaper down there. [*A short silence.*] Well, why don't you speak?

ESTELLE: What could I say? You acted quite rightly, as you didn't want to fight. [GARCIN *makes a fretful gesture.*] But, darling, how on earth can I guess what you want me to answer?

INEZ: Can't you guess? Well, *I* can. He wants you to tell him that he bolted like a lion. For 'bolt' he did, and that's what's biting him.

GARCIN: 'Bolted,' 'went away'—we won't quarrel over words.

ESTELLE: But you *had* to run away. If you'd stayed they'd have sent you to jail, wouldn't they?

GARCIN: Of course. [*A pause.*] Well, Estelle, am I a coward?

ESTELLE: How can I say? Don't be so unreasonable, darling. I can't put myself in your skin. You must decide that for yourself.

GARCIN [*wearily*]: I can't decide.

ESTELLE: Anyhow, you must remember. You must have had reasons for acting as you did.

GARCIN: I had.

ESTELLE: Well?

GARCIN: But were they the real reasons?

ESTELLE: You've a twisted mind, that's your trouble. Plaguing yourself over such trifles!

GARCIN: I'd thought it all out, and I wanted to make a stand. But was that my real motive?

INEZ: Exactly. That's the question. Was that your real motive? No doubt you argued it out with yourself, you weighed the pros and cons, you found good reasons for acting as you did. But fear and hatred and all the dirty little instincts one keeps dark—they're motives too. So carry on, Mr. Garcin, and try to be honest with yourself—for once.

GARCIN: Do I need you to tell me that? Day and night I paced my cell, from the window to the door, from the door to the window. I pried into my heart, I sleuthed myself like a detective. By the end of it I felt as if I'd given my whole life to introspection. But always I harked back to the one thing certain—that I had acted as I did, I'd taken that train to the frontier. But why? Why? Finally I thought: My death will settle it. If I face death courageously, I'll prove I am no coward.

INEZ: And how did you face death?

GARCIN: Miserably. Rottenly. [INEZ *laughs*.] Oh, it was only a physical lapse—that might happen to anyone; I'm not ashamed of it. Only everything's been left in suspense, for ever. [*To* ESTELLE.] Come here, Estelle. Look at me. I want to feel someone looking at me while they're talking about me on earth . . . I like green eyes.

INEZ: Green eyes! Just hark to him! And you, Estelle, do you like cowards?

ESTELLE: If you knew how little I care! Coward or hero, it's all one—provided he kisses well.

GARCIN: There they are, slumped in their chairs, sucking at their cigars. Bored they look. Half-asleep. They're thinking: Garcin's a coward. But only vaguely, dreamily. One's got to think of something. 'That chap Garcin was a coward.' That's what they've decided, those dear friends of mine. In six months' time they'll be saying, 'Cowardly as that skunk Garcin.' You're lucky, you two; no one on earth is giving you another thought. But I—I'm long in dying.

INEZ: What about your wife, Garcin?

GARCIN: Oh, didn't I tell you? She's dead.

INEZ: Dead?

GARCIN: Yes, she died just now. About two months ago.

INEZ: Of grief?

GARCIN: What else should she die of? So all is for the best, you see; the war's over, my wife's dead, and I've carved out my place in history.

He gives a choking sob and passes his hand over his face. ESTELLE *catches his arm.*

ESTELLE: My poor darling! Look at me. Please look. Touch me. Touch me. [*She takes his hand and puts it on her neck.*] There. Keep your hand there. [GARCIN *makes a fretful movement.*] No, don't move. Why trouble what those men are thinking? They'll die off one by one. Forget them. There's only me, now.

GARCIN: But *they* won't forget *me*, not they! They'll die, but others will come after them to carry on the legend. I've left my fate in their hands.

ESTELLE: You think too much, that's your trouble.

GARCIN: What else is there to do now? I was a man of action once. . . .

Oh, if only I could be with them again, for just one day—I'd fling their lie in their teeth. But I'm locked out; they're passing judgment on my life without troubling about me, and they're right, because I'm dead. Dead and done with. [*Laughs.*] A back number.

A short pause.

ESTELLE [*gently*]: Garcin.

GARCIN: Still there? Now listen! I want you to do me a service. No, don't shrink away. I know it must seem strange to you, having someone asking you for help; you're not used to that. But if you'll make the effort, if you'll only *will* it hard enough, I dare say we can really love each other. Look at it this way. A thousand of them are proclaiming I'm a coward; but what do numbers matter? If there's someone, just one person, to say quite positively I did not run away, that I'm not the sort who runs away, that I'm brave and decent and the rest of it—well, that one person's faith would save me. Will you have that faith in me? Then I shall love you and cherish you for ever. Estelle—will you?

ESTELLE [*laughing*]: Oh, you dear silly man, do you think I could love a coward?

GARCIN: But just now you said——

ESTELLE: I was only teasing you. I like men, my dear, who're real men, with tough skin and strong hands. You haven't a coward's chin, or a coward's mouth, or a coward's voice, or a coward's hair. And it's for your mouth, your hair, your voice, I love you.

GARCIN: Do you mean this? *Really* mean it?

ESTELLE: Shall I swear it?

GARCIN: Then I snap my fingers at them all, those below and those in here. Estelle, we shall climb out of hell. [INEZ *gives a shrill laugh. He breaks off and stares at her.*] What's that?

INEZ [*still laughing*]: But she doesn't mean a word of what she says. How can you be such a simpleton? 'Estelle, am I a coward?' As if she cared a damn either way.

ESTELLE: Inez, how dare you? [*To* GARCIN.] Don't listen to her. If you want me to have faith in you, you must begin by trusting me.

INEZ: That's right! That's right! Trust away! She wants a man—that far you can trust her—she wants a man's arm round her waist, a man's smell, a man's eyes glowing with desire. And that's all she wants. She'd assure you you were God Almighty if she thought it would give you pleasure.

GARCIN: Estelle, is this true? Answer me. Is it true?

ESTELLE: What do you expect me to say? Don't you realize how maddening it is to have to answer questions one can't make head or tail of? [*She stamps her foot.*] You do make things difficult. . . . Anyhow, I'd love you just the same, even if you were a coward. Isn't that enough?

A short pause.

GARCIN [to the two women]: You disgust me, both of you. [He goes towards the door.]

ESTELLE: What are you up to?

GARCIN: I'm going.

INEZ [quickly]: You won't get far. The door is locked.

GARCIN: I'll make them open it. [He presses the bell-push. The bell does not ring.]

ESTELLE: Please! Please!

INEZ [to ESTELLE]: Don't worry, my pet. The bell doesn't work.

GARCIN: I tell you they shall open. [Drums on the door.] I can't endure it any longer, I'm through with you both. [ESTELLE runs to him; he pushes her away.] Go away. You're even fouler than she. I won't let myself get bogged in your eyes. You're soft and slimy. Ugh! [Bangs on the door again.] Like an octopus. Like a quagmire.

ESTELLE: I beg you, oh I beg you not to leave me. I'll promise not to speak again, I won't trouble you in any way—but don't go. I daren't be left alone with Inez, now she's shown her claws.

GARCIN: Look after yourself. I never asked you to come here.

ESTELLE: Oh, how mean you are! Yes, it's quite true you're a coward.

INEZ [going up to ESTELLE]: Well, my little sparrow fallen from the nest, I hope you're satisfied now. You spat in my face—playing up to him, of course—and we had a tiff on his account. But he's going, and a good riddance it will be. We two women will have the place to ourselves.

ESTELLE: You won't gain anything. If that door opens, I'm going, too.

INEZ: Where?

ESTELLE: I don't care where. As far from you as I can.

GARCIN has been drumming on the door while they talk.

GARCIN: Open the door! Open, blast you! I'll endure anything, your red-hot tongs and molten lead, your racks and prongs and garrots—all your fiendish gadgets, everything that burns and flays and tears—I'll put up with any torture you impose. Anything, anything would be better than this agony of mind, this creeping pain that gnaws and fumbles and caresses one, and never hurts quite enough. [He grips the door-knob and rattles it.] Now will you open? [The door flies open with a jerk, and he nearly falls on the floor.] Ah! A long silence.

INEZ: Well, Garcin? . . . You're free to go.

GARCIN [meditatively]: Now I wonder why that door opened.

INEZ: What are you waiting for? Hurry up and go.

GARCIN: I shall not go.

INEZ: And you, Estelle? [ESTELLE does not move. INEZ bursts out laughing.] So what? Which shall it be? Which of the three of us will leave? The barrier's down, why are we waiting? . . . But what a situation! It's a scream! We're . . . inseparables!

ESTELLE *springs at her from behind.*

ESTELLE: Inseparables? Garcin, come and lend a hand. Quickly. We'll push
her out and slam the door on her. That'll teach her a lesson.

INEZ [*struggling with* ESTELLE]: Estelle! I beg you, let me stay. I won't go,
I won't go. Not into the passage.

GARCIN: Let go of her.

ESTELLE: You're crazy. She hates you.

GARCIN: It's because of her I'm staying here.

ESTELLE *releases* INEZ *and stares dumbfoundedly at* GARCIN.

INEZ: Because of me? [*Pause.*] All right, shut the door. It's ten times hotter
here since it opened. [GARCIN *goes to the door and shuts it.*] Because of me,
you said?

GARCIN: Yes. *You,* anyhow, know what it means to be a coward.

INEZ: Yes, I know.

GARCIN: And you know what wickedness is, and shame, and fear. There
were days when you peered into yourself, into the secret places of your
heart, and what you saw there made you faint with horror. And then,
next day, you didn't know what to make of it, you couldn't interpret the
horror you had glimpsed the day before. Yes, you know what evil *costs.*
And when you say I'm a coward, you know from experience what that
means. Is that so?

INEZ: Yes.

GARCIN: So it's you whom I have to convince; you are of my kind. Did
you suppose I meant to go? No, I couldn't leave you here, gloating over
my defeat, with all those thoughts about me running in your head.

INEZ: Do you really wish to convince me?

GARCIN: That's the one and only thing I wish for now. I can't hear them
any longer, you know. Probably that means they're through with me.
For good and all. The curtain's down, nothing of me is left on earth—not
even the name of coward. So, Inez, we're alone. Only you two remain to
give a thought to me. She—she doesn't count. It's you who matter; you
you hate me. If you'll have faith in me I'm saved.

INEZ: It won't be easy. Have a look at me. I'm a hard-headed woman.

GARCIN: I'll give you all the time that's needed.

INEZ: Yes, we've lots of time in hand. *All* time.

GARCIN [*putting his hands on her shoulders*]: Listen! Each man has an aim in
life, a leading motive; that's so, isn't it? Well, I didn't give a damn for
wealth, or for love. I aimed at being a real man. A tough, as they say.
I staked everything on the same horse. . . . Can one possibly be a coward
when one's deliberately courted danger at every turn? And can one judge
a life by a single action?

INEZ: Why not? For thirty years you dreamt you were a hero, and condoned
a thousand petty lapses—because a hero, of course, can do no wrong. An

easy method, obviously. Then a day came when you were up against it, the red light of real danger—and you took the train to Mexico.

GARCIN: I 'dreamt', you say. It was no dream. When I chose the hardest path, I made my choice deliberately. A man is what he wills himself to be.

INEZ: Prove it. Prove it was no dream. It's what one does, and nothing else, that shows the stuff one's made of.

GARCIN: I died too soon. I wasn't allowed time to . . . to do my deeds.

INEZ: One always dies too soon—or too late. And yet one's whole life is complete at that moment, with a line drawn neatly under it, ready for the summing up. You are—your life, and nothing else.

GARCIN: What a poisonous woman you are! With an answer for everything.

INEZ: Now then! Don't lose heart. It shouldn't be so hard, convincing me. Pull yourself together, man, rake up some arguments. [GARCIN *shrugs his shoulders.*] Ah, wasn't I right when I said you were vulnerable? Now you're going to pay the price, and what a price! You're a coward, Garcin, because I wish it. I wish it—do you hear?—I wish it. And yet, just look at me, see how weak I am, a mere breath on the air, a gaze observing you, a formless thought that thinks you. [*He walks towards her, opening his hands.*] Ah, they're open now, those big hands, those coarse, man's hands! But what do you hope to do? You can't throttle thoughts with hands. So you've no choice, you must convince me, and you're at my mercy.

ESTELLE: Garcin!

GARCIN: What?

ESTELLE: Revenge yourself.

GARCIN: How?

ESTELLE: Kiss me, darling—then you'll hear her squeal.

GARCIN: That's true, Inez. I'm at your mercy, but you're at mine as well.

He bends over ESTELLE. INEZ *gives a little cry.*

INEZ: Oh, you coward, you weakling, running to women to console you!

ESTELLE: That's right, Inez. Squeal away.

INEZ: What a lovely pair you make! If you could see his big paw splayed out on your back, rucking up your skin and creasing the silk. Be careful, though! He's perspiring, his hand will leave a blue stain on your dress.

ESTELLE: Squeal away, Inez, squeal away! . . . Hug me tight, darling; tighter still—that'll finish her off, and a good thing too!

INEZ: Yes, Garcin, she's right. Carry on with it, press her to you till you feel your bodies melting into each other; a lump of warm, throbbing flesh. . . . Love's a grand solace, isn't it, my friend? Deep and dark as sleep. But I'll see you don't sleep.

GARCIN *makes a slight movement.*

ESTELLE: Don't listen to her. Press your lips to my mouth. Oh, I'm yours, yours, yours.

INEZ: Well, what are you waiting for? Do as you're told. What a lovely scene: coward Garcin holding baby-killer Estelle in his manly arms! Make your stakes, everyone. Will coward Garcin kiss the lady, or won't he dare? What's the betting? I'm watching you, everybody's watching, I'm a crowd all by myself. Do you hear the crowd? Do you hear them muttering, Garcin? Mumbling and muttering. 'Coward! Coward! Coward! Coward!'—that's what they're saying. . . . It's no use trying to escape, I'll never let you go. What do you hope to get from her silly lips? Forgetfulness? But I shan't forget you, not I! 'It's I you must convince.' So come to me. I'm waiting. Come along now. . . . Look how obedient he is, like a well-trained dog who comes when his mistress calls. You can't hold him, and you never will.

GARCIN: Will night never come?

INEZ: Never.

GARCIN: You will always see me?

INEZ: Always.

GARCIN *moves away from* ESTELLE *and takes some steps across the room. He goes to the bronze ornament.*

GARCIN: This bronze. [*Strokes it thoughtfully.*] Yes, now's the moment; I'm looking at this thing on the mantelpiece, and I understand that I'm in hell. I tell you, everything's been thought out beforehand. They knew I'd stand at the fireplace stroking this thing of bronze, with all those eyes intent on me. Devouring me. [*He swings round abruptly.*] What? Only two of you? I thought there were more; many more. [*Laughs.*] So this is hell. I'd never have believed it. You remember all we were told about the torture-chambers, the fire and brimstone, the 'burning marl'. Old wives' tales! There's no need for red-hot pokers. Hell is . . . other people!

ESTELLE: My darling! Please . . .

GARCIN [*thrusting her away*]: No, let me be. She is between us. I cannot love you when she's watching.

ESTELLE: Right! In that case, I'll stop her watching us.

She picks up the paper-knife from the table, rushes at INEZ, *and stabs her several times.*

INEZ [*struggling and laughing*]: But, you crazy creature, what do you think you're doing? You know quite well I'm dead.

ESTELLE: Dead?

She drops the knife. A pause. INEZ *picks up the knife and jabs herself with it regretfully.*

INEZ: Dead! Dead! Dead! Knives, poison, ropes—all useless. It has happened *already*, do you understand? Once and for all. So here we are, for ever. [*Laughs.*]

ESTELLE [*with a peal of laughter*]: For ever. My God, how funny! For ever.

GARCIN *looks at the two women, and joins in the laughter.*

GARCIN: For ever, and ever, and ever.

They slump on to their respective sofas. A long silence. Their laughter dies away, and they gaze at each other.

GARCIN: Well, well, let's get on with it. . . .

CURTAIN

SIX POEMS

BY PAUL DEHN

from *The Day's Alarm* (1949)

SIX POEMS

─────────

CHEZ M. PRIEUR

The still rain drops; the raindrops still
Navigate my window-sill,
Where I watched them yesterday;
And still beyond the dripping eaves
By tanglewood and willow-leaves
The river bears the rain away.

From willow-tree to window-pane
Between the river and the rain
The garden's green asylum goes.
Here, the indecent toadstools sprout
And bryony that twists about
The thorny ropes of rambler rose.

Burdock, bindweed, barley-grass,
Razor-blade and broken glass
Constrict the worm that never dies.
Look! where maternal marrows sprawl.
The penitential raindrops fall
From chicory with wet blue eyes.

A flat, black boat, its bloat, fat back
Aground among the garden wrack
Lies where it has always lain,
Though yarrow-foam and sorrel-sand
Weave a slipway overland
To meet the river and the rain.

Though sorrel-sand and yarrow-foam
Call the stranded exile home,
The garden whispers: 'Peace! Be still.'

And still the river sings beyond
The seven catfish in the pond
Who may not wander where they will.

.   .   .

Another time, another day
(I sit and dream the rain away)
The wind sang, the sun shone.
O visionary weather-vane,
Point the west wind home again
And let the prisoners be gone.

Let convolvulus at dawn
Creep across a ghostly lawn
In flight from the captivity.
Shift the wind, unfix the star
Till the fever-swamps, that are,
Were not and will never be;

Till the boat in sunlight rides
With water slapping both its sides
On a noonday pleasure-cruise,
In the green shadow of whose wake
Voluptuary catfish take
Their dappled ease among the ooze.

Here, beyond my boyhood's eye,
Where salmon-coloured sandbanks lie,
The white birds whistle to the sea;
And fish and boat and bird are one,
Moving seaward in the sun.
O God of Gardens, set them free.

The still rain drops; the raindrops still
Navigate my window-sill,
Where I watched them yesterday;
And still beyond the dripping eaves
By tanglewood and willow-leaves
The river bears the rain away.

NEW AGE

To-night the wind comes screaming up the road
Like a train in the tube. Over my cringing head
Gas-lamps are ghosts of the still-marching Dead
Whose butchered eyes, blown open,
Pity our cold condition.
Here, in this rotting air,
The traffic lights ripen
From green to yellow, from yellow to red;
And I, with a cobweb of rain in my hair,
Trudge between tram-lines, seeking a world's salvation.

Only the lost are with me, only the late
And the last, lonely stragglers in the street:
A drunkard in the lamplight, on whose coat
Something still glistens;
The frosted whore who marks
My footfall on the stone,
Sniffs in the wind and listens
Under the red lamp of the traffic light;
And a flash boy, adrift in the pin-stripe rain,
Edging towards the privacy of parks.

These, my cold company; whose nailed feet
Scrape on the pavements of eternal night;
The down-at-heel, who drift in the wet light,
Seeking a wind to blow
The spent leaf from its stalk;
Who long for death,
As the leaf longs for snow.
These only are unafraid, who throng to meet
The wind that bears a world's end in its breath.
O Christ, have pity on them, where they walk.

Raise Your nailed hand! Unwedge the window-frame
Of the sleek man in bed. Shiver the dream
That muffles his drugged ear to the crack of doom
And let him hear the shriek
Of the relentless wind
And the loose casement, rattling.

Listen. The clocks strike,
Heard by the lost; unheard in the locked room
Under the sheet where the sly hands go shuttling,
This night and evermore, world without end.

AT THE BUCA DI BACCO

Over and over, to-night,
The pianist plays by the reef
In the sea-green light
Of lamp under leaf.
His fingers are fish,
Leaping
The surf of a glimmering keyboard;
And over and over the drummer is keeping
Time, with the swing and the swish
Of waves on the seaboard.

Over and over the moon,
Drifting from key to key,
Fingers an endless tune
Of light on the sea;
Whose virginal air,
Meeting
The sensuous air of the summer,
Sounds over and over to breakers beating
Time, with the whisk and the whirr
Of a lazy drummer.

LAMENT FOR A SAILOR

Here, where the night is clear as sea-water
And stones are white and the sticks are spars,
Swims on a windless, mackerel tide
The dolphin moon in a shoal of stars.

Here, in the limbo, where moths are spinners
And clouds like hulls drift overhead,
Move we must for our colder comfort,
I the living and you the dead.

Each on our way, my ghost, my grayling,
You to the water, the land for me;
I am the fat-knuckled, noisy diver
But you are the quietest fish in the sea.

AT THE DARK HOUR

(To A.)

Our love was conceived in silence and must live silently.
This only our sorrow, and this until the end.
Listen, did we not lie all of one evening
Your heart under my hand

And no word spoken, no, not even the sighing
Of pain made comfortable, not the heart's beat
Nor sound of urgency, but a fire dying
And the cold sheet?

The sailor goes home singing, the sleepy soldier
May pin to the lit wall his lover's face.
Boys whistle under windows, and are answered;
But we must hold our peace.

Day, too, broke silently. Before the blackbird,
Before the trouble of traffic and the mist unrolled,
I shall remember at the dark hour turning to you
For comfort in the cold.

AN EXPLANATION

When the pillars of smoke, that towered between heaven and earth
On the day we died, have thinned in the wind and drifted
And the hooded crow flaps home across the volcanic sky,
Somewhere beyond and below the littered horizon
(O from what green and golden island?)
Man, I suppose, will emerge and grow wise and read
What we have written in guilt, again with an innocent eye.

Then, if the desperate song we sang like storm-cocks
At the first flash, survives the ultimate thunder
To be dreamily misunderstood by the children of quieter men,
Remember that we who lived in the creeping shadow
(Dark over woodland, cloud and water)
Looked upon Beauty always as though for the last time
And loved all things the more, that might never be seen again;

Who chewed the leaf, uncertain of seeing the hawthorn
Scatter its stars the length of a lane in summer,
Or fingered the sparrow's egg that might never be born a bird;
And wondered, even, whether the windflaw moving
Silently over the water's surface
Should gain the distant edge of the lake in safety
Before the inferno struck, whose echoes shall never be heard.

I sing to a boy unborn and unbegotten,
Who have no war-song, now, for his huddled fathers
In the lost light awaiting their time of eternal cold.
I know, I know that a legion of singers before us
Looked their last on much that was lovely
And perished as we must perish. But who will remember
That most of them wept and died only because they were old?

EIGHT POEMS

BY KATHLEEN RAINE

from *The Pythoness and Other Poems* (1949)

EIGHT POEMS

THE WORLD

It burns in the void,
Nothing upholds it.
Still it travels.

Travelling the void
Upheld by burning
Nothing is still.

Burning it travels.
The void upholds it.
Still it is nothing.

Nothing it travels
A burning void
Upheld by stillness.

THE TRAVELLER

A hundred years I slept beneath a thorn
Until the tree was root and branches of my thought,
Until white petals blossomed in my crown.

A thousand years I floated in a lake
Until my brimful eye could hold
The scattered moonlight and the burning cloud.

Mine is the gaze that knows
Eyebright, asphodel, and briar rose.
I have seen the rainbow open, the sun close.

A wind that blows about the land
I have raised temples of snow, castles of sand
And left them empty as a dead hand.

A winged ephemerid I am born
With myriad eyes and glittering wings
That flames must wither or waters drown.

I must live, I must die,
I am the memory of all desire,
I am the world's ashes, and the kindling fire.

THE JOURNEY

(*For Winifred Nicholson*)

As I went over fossil hill
I gathered up small jointed stones,
And I remembered the archaic sea
Where once these pebbles were my bones.

As I walked on the Roman wall
The wind blew southward from the pole.
O I have been that violence hurled
Against the ramparts of the world.

At nightfall in an empty kirk
I felt the fear of all my deaths:
Shapes I had seen with animal eyes
Crowded the dark with mysteries.

I stood beside a tumbling beck
Where thistles grew upon a mound
That many a day had been my home,
Where now my heart rots in the ground.

I was the trout that haunts the pool,
The shadowy presence of the stream.
Of many many lives I leave
The scattered bone and broken wing.

I was the dying animal
Whose cold eye closes on a jagged thorn,
Whose carcass soon is choked with moss,
Whose skull is hidden by the fern.

My footprints sink in shifting sand
And barley-fields have drunk my blood,
My wisdom traced the spiral of a shell,
My labour raised a cairn upon a fell.

Far I have come and far must go,
In many a grave my sorrow lies,
But always from dead fingers grow
Flowers that I bless with living eyes.

THE INVISIBLE SPECTRUM

Learn, if I dare, the order of the wind,
Fire, tempest and the sea.
Learn if I dare into what mode of being
The leaf falls from the tree.

Everywhere
There are holes in the air,
Graves open to receive us,

After the seventh colour
And before the first
Lies darkness.

Beyond sound, silence
Audible to bats
And deep-sea fish that feel the throb of waves,

Beyond sense, the spinning spheres,
Atoms and stars
That weave our lives.

Lovers seek sanctuary
In the abyss
From which they fly,

For in love's depths we sound
The void
Beyond mortality

And through our sleep
Move latent powers
Strange as nebulae,
Dreams not ours.

THE PYTHONESS

(For John Hayward)

I am that serpent-haunted cave
Whose navel breeds the fates of men.
All wisdom issues from a hole in the earth:
The gods form in my darkness, and dissolve again.

From my blind womb all kingdoms come,
And from my grave seven sleepers prophesy.
No babe unborn but wakens to my dream,
No lover but at last entombed in me shall lie.

I am that feared and longed-for burning place
Where man and phoenix are consumed away,
And from my low polluted bed arise
New sons, new suns, new skies.

SELF

Who am I, who
Speaks from the dust,
Who looks from the clay?

Who hears
For the mute stone,
For fragile water feels
With finger and bone?

Who for the forest breathes the evening,
Sees for the rose,
Who knows
What the bird sings?

Who am I, who for the sun fears
The demon dark,
In order holds
Atom and chaos?

Who out of nothingness has gazed
On the beloved face?

WORD MADE FLESH

Word whose breath is the world-circling atmosphere,
Word that utters the world that turns the wind,
Word that articulates the bird that speeds upon the air,

Word that blazes out the trumpet of the sun,
Whose silence is the violin-music of the stars,
Whose melody is the dawn, and harmony the night,

Word traced in water of lakes, and light on water,
Light on still water, moving water, waterfall
And water colours of cloud, of dew, of spectral rain,

Word inscribed on stone, mountain range upon range of stone,
Word that is fire of the sun and fire within
Order of atoms, crystalline symmetry,

Grammar of five-fold rose and six-fold lily,
Spiral of leaves on a bough, helix of shells,
Rotation of twining plants on axes of darkness and light,

Instinctive wisdom of fish and lion and ram,
Rhythm of generation in flagellate and fern,
Flash of fin, beat of wing, heartbeat, beat of the dance,

22

Hieroglyph in whose exact precision is defined
Feather and insect-wing, refraction of multiple eyes,
Eyes of the creatures, oh myriadfold vision of the world,

Statement of mystery, how shall we name
A spirit clothed in world, a world made man?

PEACE OF MIND

If the pool were still
The reflected world
Of tottering houses
The falling cities,
The quaking mountains
Would cohere on the surface

And stars invisible
To the troubled mind
Be seen in water
Drawn from the soul's
Bottomless well.

FICTION

THE PURSUIT OF LOVE

BY NANCY MITFORD

(1945)

THE PURSUIT OF LOVE

CHAPTER I

THERE is a photograph in existence of Aunt Sadie and her six children sitting round the tea-table at Alconleigh. The table is situated, as it was, is now, and ever shall be, in the hall, in front of a huge open fire of logs. Over the chimney-piece plainly visible in the photograph, hangs an entrenching tool, with which, in 1915, Uncle Matthew had whacked to death eight Germans one by one as they crawled out of a dug-out. It is still covered with blood and hairs, an object of fascination to us as children. In the photograph Aunt Sadie's face, always beautiful, appears strangely round, her hair strangely fluffy, and her clothes strangely dowdy, but it is unmistakably she who sits there with Robin, in oceans of lace, lolling on her knee. She seems uncertain what to do with his head, and the presence of Nanny waiting to take him away is felt though not seen. The other children, between Louisa's eleven and Matt's two years, sit round the table in party dresses or frilly bibs, holding cups or mugs according to age, all of them gazing at the camera with large eyes opened wide by the flash, and all looking as if butter would not melt in their round pursed-up mouths. There they are, held like flies in the amber of that moment—click goes the camera and on goes life; the minutes, the days, the years, the decades, taking them further and further from that happiness and promise of youth, from the hopes Aunt Sadie must have had for them, and from the dreams they dreamed for themselves. I often think there is nothing quite so poignantly sad as old family groups.

When a child I spent my Christmas holidays at Alconleigh, it was a regular feature of my life, and, while some of them slipped by with nothing much to remember, others were distinguished by violent occurrences and had a definite character of their own. There was the time, for example, when the servants' wing caught fire, the time when my pony lay on me in the brook and nearly drowned me (not very nearly, he was soon dragged off, but meanwhile bubbles were said to have been observed). There was drama when Linda, aged ten, attempted suicide in order to rejoin an old smelly Border Terrier which Uncle Matthew had had put down. She collected and ate a basketful of yew-berries, was discovered by Nanny and given mustard and water to make her sick. She was then 'spoken to' by Aunt Sadie, clipped

over the ear by Uncle Matthew, put to bed for two days and given a
Labrador puppy, which soon took the place of the old Border in her affections. There was much worse drama when Linda, aged twelve, told the
daughters of neighbours, who had come to tea, what she supposed to be
the facts of life. Linda's presentation of the 'facts' had been so gruesome that
the children left Alconleigh howling dismally, their nerves permanently im-
paired, their future chances of a sane and happy sex life much reduced. This
resulted in a series of dreadful punishments, from a real beating, administered
by Uncle Matthew, to luncheon upstairs for a week. There was the unforgettable holiday when Uncle Matthew and Aunt Sadie went to Canada. The
Radlett children would rush for the newspapers every day hoping to see
that their parents' ship had gone down with all aboard; they yearned to be
total orphans—especially Linda, who saw herself as Katie in *What Katie Did*,
the reins of the household gathered into small but capable hands. The ship
met with no iceberg and weathered the Atlantic storms, but meanwhile we
had a wonderful holiday, free from rules.

But the Christmas I remember most clearly of all was when I was fourteen
and Aunt Emily became engaged. Aunt Emily was Aunt Sadie's sister, and
she had brought me up from babyhood, my own mother, their youngest
sister, having felt herself too beautiful and too gay to be burdened with a
child at the age of nineteen. She left my father when I was a month old, and
subsequently ran away so often, and with so many different people, that she
became known to her family and friends as the Bolter; while my father's
second, and presently his third, fourth and fifth wives, very naturally had
no great wish to look after me. Occasionally one of these impetuous parents
would appear like a rocket, casting an unnatural glow upon my horizon.
They had great glamour, and I longed to be caught up in their fiery trails
and be carried away, though in my heart I knew how lucky I was to have
Aunt Emily. By degrees, as I grew up, they lost all charm for me; the cold
grey rocket cases mouldered where they had happened to fall, my mother
with a major in the South of France, my father, his estates sold up to pay his
debts, with an old Rumanian countess in the Bahamas. Even before I was
grown up much of the glamour with which they had been surrounded had
faded, and finally there was nothing left, no foundation of childish memories
to make them seem any different from other middle-aged people. Aunt
Emily was never glamorous but she was always my mother, and I loved
her.

At the time of which I write, however, I was at an age when the least
imaginative child supposes itself to be a changeling, a Princess of Indian
blood, Joan of Arc, or the future Empress of Russia. I hankered after my
parents, put on an idiotic face which was intended to convey mingled suffering and pride when their names were mentioned, and thought of them as
engulfed in deep, romantic, deadly sin.

Linda and I were very much preoccupied with sin, and our great hero was Oscar Wilde.

'But what did he *do*?'

'I asked Fa once and he roared at me—goodness, it was terrifying. He said: "If you mention that sewer's name again in this house I'll thrash you, do you hear, damn you?" So I asked Sadie and she looked awfully vague and said: "Oh, duck, I never really quite knew, but whatever it was was worse than murder, fearfully bad. And, darling, don't talk about him at meals, will you?" '

'We must find out.'

'Bob says he will, when he goes to Eton.'

'Oh, good! Do you think he was worse than Mummy and Daddy?'

'Surely he couldn't be. Oh, you are so lucky, to have wicked parents.'

This Christmas-time, aged fourteen, I stumbled into the hall at Alconleigh blinded by the light after a six-mile drive from Merlinford station. It was always the same every year, I always came down by the same train, arriving at tea-time, and always found Aunt Sadie and the children round the table underneath the entrenching tool, just as they were in the photograph. It was always the same table and the same tea-things; the china with large roses on it, the tea-kettle and the silver dish for scones simmering over little flames— the human beings of course were getting imperceptibly older, the babies were becoming children, the children were growing up, and there had been an addition in the shape of Victoria now aged two. She was waddling about with a chocolate biscuit clenched in her fist, her face was smothered in chocolate and was a horrible sight, but through the sticky mask shone un- mistakably the blue of two steady Radlett eyes.

There was a tremendous scraping of chairs as I came in, and a pack of Radletts hurled themselves upon me with the intensity and almost the ferocity of a pack of hounds hurling itself upon a fox. All except Linda. She was the most pleased to see me, but determined not to show it. When the din had quieted down and I was seated before a scone and a cup of tea, she said:

'Where's Brenda?' Brenda was my white mouse.

'She got a sore back and died,' I said. Aunt Sadie looked anxiously at Linda.

'Had you been riding her?' said Louisa, facetiously. Matt, who had recently come under the care of a French nursery governess, said in a high-pitched imitation of her voice: '*C'était, comme d'habitude, les voies urinaires.*'

'Oh, dear,' said Aunt Sadie, under her breath.

Enormous tears were pouring into Linda's plate. Nobody cried so much or so often as she; anything, but especially anything sad about animals, would set her off, and, once begun, it was a job to stop her. She was a delicate, as

well as a highly nervous child, and even Aunt Sadie, who lived in a dream
as far as the health of her children was concerned, was aware that too much
crying kept her awake at night, put her off her food, and did her harm. The
other children, and especially Louisa and Bob, who loved to tease, went as
far as they dared with her, and were periodically punished for making her
cry. *Black Beauty, Owd Bob, The Story of a Red Deer*, and all the Seton
Thompson books were on the nursery index because of Linda, who, at one
time or another, had been prostrated by them. They had to be hidden away,
as, if they were left lying about, she could not be trusted not to indulge in
an orgy of self-torture.

Wicked Louisa had invented a poem which never failed to induce rivers
of tears:

> 'A little, houseless match, it has no roof, no thatch,
> It lies alone, it makes no moan, that little, houseless match.'

When Aunt Sadie was not around the children would chant this in a
gloomy chorus. In certain moods one had only to glance at a match-box to
dissolve poor Linda; when, however, she was feeling stronger, more fit to
cope with life, this sort of teasing would force out of her very stomach an
unwilling guffaw. Linda was not only my favourite cousin, but, then and
for many years, my favourite human being. I adored all my cousins, and
Linda distilled, mentally and physically, the very essence of the Radlett
family. Her straight features, straight brown hair and large blue eyes were a
theme upon which the faces of the others were a variation; all pretty, but
none so absolutely distinctive as hers. There was something furious about
her, even when she laughed, which she did a great deal, and always as if
forced to against her will. Something reminiscent of pictures of Napoleon
in youth, a sort of scowling intensity.

I could see that she was really minding much more about Brenda than I
did. The truth was that my honeymoon days with the mouse were long since
over; we had settled down to an uninspiring relationship, a form, as it were,
of married blight, and, when she had developed a disgusting sore patch on
her back, it had been all I could do to behave decently and treat her with
common humanity. Apart from the shock it always is to find somebody stiff
and cold in their cage in the morning, it had been a very great relief to me
when Brenda's sufferings finally came to an end.

'Where is she buried?' Linda muttered furiously, looking at her plate.

'Beside the robin. She's got a dear little cross and her coffin was lined with
pink satin.'

'Now, Linda darling,' said Aunt Sadie, 'if Fanny has finished her tea why
don't you show her your toad?'

'He's upstairs asleep,' said Linda. But she stopped crying.

'Have some nice hot toast, then.'

'Can I have Gentleman's Relish on it?' she said, quick to make capital out of Aunt Sadie's mood, for Gentleman's Relish was kept strictly for Uncle Matthew, and supposed not to be good for children. The others made a great show of exchanging significant looks. These were intercepted, as they were meant to be, by Linda, who gave a tremendous bellowing boo-hoo and rushed upstairs.

'I wish you children wouldn't tease Linda,' said Aunt Sadie, irritated out of her usual gentleness, and followed her.

The staircase led out of the hall. When Aunt Sadie was beyond earshot, Louisa said: 'If wishes were horses beggars would ride. Child hunt to-morrow, Fanny.'

'Yes, Josh told me. He was in the car—been to see the vet.'

My Uncle Matthew had four magnificent bloodhounds, with which he used to hunt his children. Two of us would go off with a good start to lay the trail, and Uncle Matthew and the rest would follow the hounds on horse-back. It was great fun. Once he came to my home and hunted Linda and me over Shenley Common. This caused the most tremendous stir locally, the Kentish week-enders on their way to church were appalled by the sight of four great hounds in full cry after two little girls. My uncle seemed to them like a wicked lord of fiction, and I became more than ever surrounded with an aura of madness, badness, and dangerousness for their children to know.

The child hunt on the first day of this Christmas visit was a great success. Louisa and I were chosen as hares. We ran across country, the beautiful bleak Cotswold uplands, starting soon after breakfast when the sun was still a red globe, hardly over the horizon, and the trees were etched in dark blue against a pale blue, mauve and pinkish sky. The sun rose as we stumbled on, longing for our second wind; it shone, and there dawned a beautiful day, more like late autumn in its feeling than Christmas-time.

We managed to check the bloodhounds once by running through a flock of sheep, but Uncle Matthew soon got them on the scent again, and, after about two hours of hard running on our part, when we were only half a mile from home, the baying slavering creatures caught up with us, to be rewarded with lumps of meat and many caresses. Uncle Matthew was in a radiantly good temper, he got off his horse and walked home with us, chatting agreeably. What was most unusual, he was even quite affable to me.

'I hear Brenda has died,' he said, 'no great loss I should say. That mouse stank like merry hell. I expect you kept her cage too near the radiator, I always told you it was unhealthy, or did she die of old age?'

'She was only two,' I said, timidly.

Uncle Matthew's charm, when he chose to turn it on, was considerable, but at that time I was always mortally afraid of him, and made the mistake of letting him see that I was.

'You ought to have a dormouse, Fanny, or a rat. They are much more interesting than white mice—though I must frankly say, of all the mice I ever knew, Brenda was the most utterly dismal.'

'She was dull,' I said, sycophantically.

'When I go to London after Christmas, I'll get you a dormouse. Saw one the other day at the Army & Navy.'

'Oh Fa, it *is* unfair,' said Linda, who was walking her pony along beside us. 'You know how I've always longed for a dormouse.'

'It is unfair' was a perpetual cry of the Radletts when young. The great advantage of living in a large family is that early lesson of life's essential unfairness. With them I must say it nearly always operated in favour of Linda, who was the adored of Uncle Matthew.

To-day, however, my uncle was angry with her, and I saw in a flash that this affability to me, this genial chat about mice, was simply designed as a tease for her.

'You've got enough animals, miss,' he said, sharply. 'You can't control the ones you have got. And don't forget what I told you—that dog of yours goes straight to the kennel when we get back, and stays there.'

Linda's face crumpled, tears poured, she kicked her pony into a canter and made for home. It seemed that her dog Labby had been sick in Uncle Matthew's business-room after breakfast. Uncle Matthew was unable to bear dirtiness in dogs, he flew into a rage, and, in his rage, had made a rule that never again was Labby to set foot in the house. This was always happening, for one reason or another, to one animal or another, and, Uncle Matthew's bark being invariably much worse than his bite, the ban seldom lasted more than a day or two, after which would begin what he called the Thin End of the Wedge.

'Can I bring him in just while I fetch my gloves?'

'I'm so tired—I can't go to the stables—do let him stay just till after tea.'

'Oh, I see—the thin end of the wedge. All right, this time he can stay, but if he makes another mess—or I catch him on your bed—or he chews up the good furniture (according to whichever crime it was that had resulted in banishment), I'll have him destroyed, and don't say I didn't warn you.'

All the same, every time sentence of banishment was pronounced, the owner of the condemned would envisage her beloved moping his life away in the solitary confinement of a cold and gloomy kennel.

'Even if I take him out for three hours every day, and go and chat to him for another hour, that leaves twenty hours for him all alone with nothing to do. Oh, why can't dogs read?'

The Radlett children, it will be observed, took a highly anthropomorphic view of their pets.

To-day, however, Uncle Matthew was in a wonderfully good temper, and, as we left the stables, he said to Linda, who was sitting crying with Labby in his kennel:

'Are you going to leave that poor brute of yours in there all day?'

Her tears forgotten as if they had never been, Linda rushed into the house with Labby at her heels. The Radletts were always either on a peak of happiness or drowning in black waters of despair; their emotions were on no ordinary plane, they loved or they loathed, they laughed or they cried, they lived in a world of superlatives. Their life with Uncle Matthew was a sort of perpetual Tom Tiddler's ground. They went as far as they dared, sometimes very far indeed, while sometimes, for no apparent reason, he would pounce almost before they had crossed the boundary. Had they been poor children they would probably have been removed from their roaring, raging, whacking papa and sent to an approved home, or, indeed, he himself would have been removed from them and sent to prison for refusing to educate them. Nature, however, provides her own remedies, and no doubt the Radletts had enough of Uncle Matthew in them to enable them to weather storms in which ordinary children like me would have lost their nerve completely.

CHAPTER II

IT was an accepted fact at Alconleigh that Uncle Matthew loathed me. This violent, uncontrolled man, like his children, knew no middle course, he either loved or he hated, and generally, it must be said, he hated. His reason for hating me was that he hated my father; they were old Eton enemies. When it became obvious, and obvious it was from the hour of my conception, that my parents intended to doorstep me, Aunt Sadie had wanted to being me up with Linda. We were the same age, and it had seemed a sensible plan. Uncle Matthew had categorically refused. He hated my father, he said, he hated me, but, above all, he hated children, it was bad enough to have two of his own. (He evidently had not envisaged so soon having seven, and indeed both he and Aunt Sadie lived in a perpetual state of surprise at having filled so many cradles, about the future of whose occupants they seemed to have no particular policy.) So dear Aunt Emily, whose heart had once been broken by some wicked dallying monster, and who intended on this account never to marry, took me on and made a life's work of me, and I am very thankful that she did. For she believed passionately in the education of women, she took immense pains to have me properly taught, even going to live at Shenley on purpose to be near a good day school. The Radlett daughters did practically no lessons. They were taught by Lucille, the

French nursery governess, to read and write, they were obliged, though utterly unmusical, to 'practise' in the freezing ballroom for one hour a day each, when, their eyes glued to the clock, they would thump out the 'Merry Peasant' and a few scales, they were made to go for a French walk with Lucille on all except hunting days, and that was the extent of their education. Uncle Matthew loathed clever females, but he considered that gentlewomen ought, as well as being able to ride, to know French and play the piano. Although as a child I rather naturally envied them their freedom from thrall and bondage, from sums and science, I felt, nevertheless, a priggish satisfaction that I was not growing up unlettered, as they were.

Aunt Emily did not often come with me to Alconleigh. Perhaps she had an idea that it was more fun for me to be there on my own, and no doubt it was a change for her to get away and spend Christmas with the friends of her youth, and leave for a bit the responsibilities of her old age. Aunt Emily at this time was forty, and we children had long ago renounced on her behalf the world, the flesh, and the devil. This year, however, she had gone away from Shenley before the holidays began, saying that she would see me at Alconleigh in January.

On the afternoon of the child hunt Linda called a meeting of the Hons. The Hons was the Radlett secret society, anybody who was not a friend to the Hons was a Counter-Hon, and their battle-cry was 'Death to the horrible Counter-Hons'. I was a Hon, since my father, like theirs, was a lord.

There were also, however, many honorary Hons; it was not necessary to have been born a Hon in order to be one. As Linda once remarked: 'Kind hearts are more than coronets, and simple faith than Norman blood.' I'm not sure how much we really believed this, we were wicked snobs in those days, but we subscribed to the general idea. Head of the hon. Hons was Josh, the groom, who was greatly beloved by us all and worth buckets of Norman blood; chief of the horrible Counter-Hons was Craven, the gamekeeper, against whom a perpetual war to the knife was waged. The Hons would creep into the woods and hide Craven's steel traps, let out the chaffinches which, in wire cages without food or water, he used as bait for hawks, give decent burial to the victims of his gamekeeper's larder, and, before a meet of the hounds, unblock the earths which Craven had so carefully stopped.

The poor Hons were tormented by the cruelties of the countryside, while, to me, holidays at Alconleigh were a perfect revelation of beastliness. Aunt Emily's little house was in a village; it was a Queen Anne box; red brick, white panelling, a magnolia tree and a delicious fresh smell. Between it and the country were a neat little garden, an ironwork fence, a village green and a village. The country one then came to was very different from Gloucestershire, it was emasculated, sheltered, over-cultivated, almost a suburban garden. At Alconleigh the cruel woods crept right up to the house; it was not unusual to be awoken by the screams of a rabbit running in horrified circles round a stoat, by the strange and awful cry of the dog-fox, or to see from one's bedroom a live hen being carried away in the mouth of a vixen; while the roosting pheasant and the waking owl filled every night with wild primeval noise. In the winter, when snow covered the ground, we could trace the footprints of many creatures. These often ended in a pool of blood, a mass of fur or feathers, bearing witness to successful hunting by the carnivores.

On the other side of the house, within a stone's throw, was the Home Farm. Here the slaughtering of poultry and pigs, the castration of lambs and the branding of cattle, took place as a matter of course, out in the open for whoever might be passing by to see. Even dear old Josh made nothing of firing, with red-hot irons, a favourite horse after the hunting season.

'You can only do two legs at a time,' he would say, hissing through his teeth as though one were a horse and he grooming one, 'otherwise they can't stand the pain.'

Linda and I were bad at standing pain ourselves, and found it intolerable that animals should have to lead such tormented lives and tortured deaths. (I still do mind, very much indeed, but in those days at Alconleigh it was an absolute obsession with us all.)

The humanitarian activities of the Hons were forbidden, on pain of punishment, by Uncle Matthew, who was always and entirely on the side of Craven, his favourite servant. Pheasants and partridges must be preserved, vermin must be put down rigorously, all except the fox, for whom a more exciting death was in store. Many and many a whacking did the poor Hons suffer, week after week their pocket-money was stopped, they were sent to bed early, given extra practising to do; nevertheless they bravely persisted with their discouraged and discouraging activities. Huge cases full of new steel traps would arrive periodically from the Army & Navy Stores, and lie stacked until required round Craven's hut in the middle of the wood (an old railway carriage was his headquarters, situated, most inappropriately, among the primroses and blackberry bushes of a charming little glade); hundreds of traps, making one feel the futility of burying, at great risk to life and property, a paltry three or four. Sometimes we would find a screaming animal held in one; it would take all our reserves of courage to go up to it and let it out, to see it run away with three legs and a dangling mangled horror. We knew that it then probably died of blood-poisoning in its lair; Uncle Matthew would rub in this fact, sparing no agonizing detail of the long-drawn-out ordeal, but, though we knew it would be kinder, we could never bring ourselves to kill them; it was asking too much. Often, as it was, we had to go away and be sick after these episodes.

The Hons' meeting-place was a disused linen cupboard at the top of the

house, small, dark, and intensely hot. As in so many country houses, the
central-heating apparatus at Alconleigh had been installed in the early days
of the invention, at enormous expense, and was now thoroughly out of date.
In spite of a boiler which would not have been too large for an Atlantic
liner, in spite of the tons of coke which it consumed daily, the temperature
of the living-rooms was hardly affected, and all the heat there was seemed
to concentrate in the Hons' cupboard, which was always stifling. Here we
would sit, huddled up on the slatted shelves, and talk for hours about life
and death.

Last holidays our great obsession had been childbirth, on which entrancing
subject we were informed remarkably late, having supposed for a long time
that a mother's stomach swelled up for nine months and then burst open like
a ripe pumpkin, shooting out the infant. When the real truth dawned upon
us it seemed rather an anticlimax, until Linda produced, from some novel,
and read out loud in ghoulish tones, the description of a woman in labour.

'Her breath comes in great gulps—sweat pours down her brow like water
—screams as of a tortured animal rend the air—and can this face, twisted
with agony, be that of my darling Rhona—can this torture-chamber really
be our bedroom, this rack our marriage-bed? "Doctor, doctor," I cried,
"do something"—I rushed out into the night——' and so on.

We were rather disturbed by this, realizing that too probably we in our
turn would have to endure these fearful agonies. Aunt Sadie, who had only
just finished having her seven children, when appealed to, was not very
reassuring.

'Yes,' she said, vaguely. 'It is the worst pain in the world. But the funny
thing is, you always forget in between what it's like. Each time, when it
began, I felt like saying, "Oh, now I can remember, stop it, stop it." And,
of course, by then it was nine months too late to stop it.'

At this point Linda began to cry, saying how dreadful it must be for cows,
which brought the conversation to an end.

It was difficult to talk to Aunt Sadie about sex; something always seemed
to prevent one; babies were the nearest we ever got to it. She and Aunt
Emily, feeling at one moment that we ought to know more, and being, I
suspect, too embarrassed to enlighten us themselves, gave us a modern text-
book on the subject.

We got hold of some curious ideas.

'Jassy,' said Linda one day, scornfully, 'is obsessed, poor thing, with sex.'

'Obsessed with sex!' said Jassy, 'there's nobody so obsessed as you, Linda.
Why if I so much as look at a picture you say I'm a pygmalionist.'

In the end we got far more information out of a book called *Ducks and
Duck Breeding*.

'Ducks can only copulate,' said Linda, after studying this for a while, 'in
running water. Good luck to them.'

This Christmas Eve we all packed into the Hons' meeting-place to hear what Linda had to say—Louisa, Jassy, Bob, Matt and I.

'Talk about back-to-the-womb,' said Jassy.

'Poor Aunt Sadie,' I said. 'I shouldn't think she'd want you all back in hers.'

'You never know. Now rabbits eat their children—somebody ought to explain to them how it's only a complex.'

'How can one *explain* to *rabbits*? That's what is so worrying about animals, they simply don't understand when they're spoken to, poor angels. I'll tell you what about Sadie though, she'd like to be back in one herself, she's got a thing for boxes and that always shows. Who else—Fanny, what about you?'

'I don't think I would, but then I imagine the one I was in wasn't very comfortable at the time you know, and nobody else has ever been allowed to stay there.'

'Abortions?' said Linda with interest.

'Well, tremendous jumpings and hot baths anyway.'

'How *do* you know?'

'I once heard Aunt Emily and Aunt Sadie talking about it when I was very little, and afterwards I remembered. Aunt Sadie said: "How does she manage it?" and Aunt Emily said: "Skiing, or hunting, or just jumping off the kitchen table."'

'You are so lucky, having wicked parents.'

This was the perpetual refrain of the Radletts, and, indeed, my wicked parents constituted my chief interest in their eyes—I was really a very dull little girl in other respects.

'The news I have for the Hons to-day,' said Linda, clearing her throat like a grown-up person, 'while of considerable Hon interest generally, particularly concerns Fanny. I won't ask you to guess, because it's nearly tea-time and you never could, so I'll tell straight out. Aunt Emily is engaged.'

There was a gasp from the Hons in chorus.

'Linda,' I said, furiously, 'you've made it up.' But I knew she couldn't have.

Linda brought a piece of paper out of her pocket. It was a half-sheet of writing-paper, evidently the end of a letter, covered with Aunt Emily's large babyish handwriting, and I looked over Linda's shoulder as she read it out:

"... not tell the children we're engaged, what d'you think, darling, just at first? But then suppose Fanny takes a dislike to him, though I don't see how she could, but children are so funny, won't it be more of a shock? Oh, dear, I can't decide. Anyway, do what you think best, darling, we'll arrive on Thursday, and I'll telephone on Wednesday evening and see what's happened. All love from Emily.'

Sensation in the Hons' cupboard.

CHAPTER III

'BUT why?' I said, for the hundredth time.

Linda, Louisa and I were packed into Louisa's bed, with Bob sitting on the end of it, chatting in whispers. These midnight talks were most strictly forbidden, but it was safer, at Alconleigh, to disobey rules during the early part of the night than at any other time in the twenty-four hours. Uncle Matthew fell asleep practically at the dinner-table. He would then doze in his business-room for an hour or so before dragging himself, in a somnambulist trance, to bed, where he slept the profound sleep of one who has been out of doors all day until cockcrow the following morning, when he became very much awake. This was the time for his never-ending warfare with the housemaids over wood-ash. The rooms at Alconleigh were heated by wood fires, and Uncle Matthew maintained, rightly, that if these were to function properly, all the ash ought to be left in the fireplaces in a great hot smouldering heap. Every housemaid, however, for some reason (an early training with coal fires probably) was bent on removing this ash altogether. When shakings, imprecations, and being pounced out at by Uncle Matthew in his paisley dressing-gown at 6 a.m., had convinced them that this was really not feasible, they became absolutely determined to remove, by hook or by crook, just a little, a shovelful or so, every morning. I can only suppose they felt that like this they were asserting their personalities.

The result was guerrilla warfare at its most exciting. Housemaids are notoriously early risers, and can usually count upon three clear hours when a house belongs to them alone. But not at Alconleigh. Uncle Matthew was always, winter and summer alike, out of his bed by 5 a.m., and it was then his habit to wander about, looking like Great Agrippa in his dressing-gown, and drinking endless cups of tea out of a thermos flask, until about seven, when he would have his bath. Breakfast for my uncle, my aunt, family and guests alike, was sharp at eight, and unpunctuality was not tolerated. Uncle Matthew was no respecter of other people's early morning sleep, and, after five o'clock one could not count on any, for he raged round the house, clanking cups of tea, shouting at his dogs, roaring at the housemaids, cracking the stock whips which he had brought back from Canada on the lawn with a noise greater than gun-fire, and all to the accompaniment of Galli-Curci on his gramophone, an abnormally loud one with an enormous horn, through which would be shrieked 'Una voce poco fa'—'The Mad Song' from *Lucia*—'Lo, here the gen-tel lar-ha-hark'—and so on, played at top speed, thus rendering them even higher and more screeching than they ought to be.

Nothing reminds me of my childhood days at Alconleigh so much as

those songs. Uncle Matthew played them incessantly for years, until the spell
was broken when he went all the way to Liverpool to hear Galli-Curci in
person. The disillusionment caused by her appearance was so great that the
records remained ever after silent, and were replaced by the deepest bass
voices that money could buy.

> 'Fearful the death of the diver must be,
> Walking alone in the de-he-he-he-he-epths of the sea'

or 'Drake is going West, lads'.

These were, on the whole, welcomed by the family, as rather less piercing
at early dawn.

'Why should she want to be married?'

'It's not as though she could be in love. She's forty.'

Like all the very young we took it for granted that making love is child's
play.

'How old do you suppose he is?'

'Fifty or sixty I guess. Perhaps she thinks it would be nice to be a widow.
Weeds, you know.'

'Perhaps she thinks Fanny ought to have a man's influence.'

'Man's influence!' said Louisa. 'I foresee trouble. Supposing he falls in love
with Fanny, that'll be a pretty kettle of fish, like Somerset and Princess
Elizabeth—he'll be playing rough games and pinching you in bed, see if he
doesn't.'

'Surely not, at his age.'

'Old men love little girls.'

'And little boys,' said Bob.

'It looks as if Aunt Sadie isn't going to say anything about it before they
come,' I said.

'There's nearly a week to go—she may be deciding. She'll talk it over
with Fa. Might be worth listening next time she has a bath. You can,
Bob.'

Christmas Day was spent, as usual at Alconleigh, between alternate bursts
of sunshine and showers. I put, as children can, the disturbing news about
Aunt Emily out of my mind, and concentrated upon enjoyment. At about
six o'clock Linda and I unstuck our sleepy eyes and started on our stockings.
Our real presents came later, at breakfast and on the tree, but the stockings
were a wonderful *hors d'œuvre* and full of treasures. Presently Jassy came in
and started selling us things out of hers. Jassy only cared about money because
she was saving up to run away—she carried her post office book about with
her everywhere, and always knew to a farthing what she had got. This was

then translated by a miracle of determination, as Jassy was very bad at sums, into so many days in a bed-sitting-room.

'How are you getting on, Jassy?'

'My fare to London and a month and two days and an hour and a half in a bed-sitter, with basin and breakfast.'

Where the other meals would come from was left to the imagination. Jassy studied advertisements of bed-sitters in *The Times* every morning. The cheapest she had found so far was in Clapham. So eager was she for the cash that would transform her dream into reality, that one could be certain of picking up a few bargains round about Christmas and her birthday. Jassy at this time was aged eight.

I must admit that my wicked parents turned up trumps at Christmas, and my presents from them were always the envy of the entire household. This year my mother, who was in Paris, sent a gilded bird-cage full of stuffed humming-birds which, when wound up, twittered and hopped about and drank at a fountain. She also sent a fur hat and a gold and topaz bracelet, whose glamour was enhanced by the fact that Aunt Sadie considered them unsuitable for a child, and said so. My father sent a pony and cart, a very smart and beautiful little outfit, which had arrived some days before, and been secreted by Josh in the stables.

'So typical of that damned fool Edward to send it here,' Uncle Matthew said, 'and give us all the trouble of getting it to Shenley. And I bet poor old Emily won't be too pleased. Who on earth is going to look after it?'

Linda cried with envy. 'It *is* unfair,' she kept saying, 'that you should have wicked parents and not me.'

We persuaded Josh to take us for a drive after luncheon. The pony was an angel and the whole thing easily managed by a child, even the harnessing. Linda wore my hat and drove the pony. We got back late for the Tree—the house was already full of tenants and their children; Uncle Matthew, who was struggling into his Father Christmas clothes, roared at us so violently that Linda had to go and cry upstairs, and was not there to collect her own present from him. Uncle Matthew had taken some trouble to get her a longed-for dormouse and was greatly put out by this; he roared at everybody in turns, and ground his dentures. There was a legend in the family that he had already ground away four pairs in his rages.

The evening came to a climax of violence when Matt produced a box of fireworks which my mother had sent him from Paris. On the box they were called *pêtards*. Somebody said to Matt: 'What do they do?' to which he replied: '*Ben, ça pête, quoi?*' This remark, overheard by Uncle Matthew, was rewarded with a first-class hiding, which was actually most unfair, as poor Matt was only repeating what Lucille had said to him earlier in the day. Matt however, regarded hidings as a sort of natural phenomenon, unconnected with any actions of his own, and submitted to them philosophically enough.

I have often wondered since how it was that Aunt Sadie could have chosen Lucille, who was the very acme of vulgarity, to look after her children. We all loved her, she was gay and spirited and read aloud to us without cease, but her language really was extraordinary, and provided dreadful pitfalls for the unwary.

'Qu'est-ce que c'est ce custard, qu'on fout partout?'

I shall never forget Matt quite innocently making this remark in Fullers at Oxford, where Uncle Matthew had taken us for a treat. The consequences were awful.

It never seemed to occur to Uncle Matthew that Matt could not know these words by nature, and that it would really have been more fair to check them at their source.

CHAPTER IV

I NATURALLY awaited the arrival of Aunt Emily and her future intended with some agitation. She was, after all, my real mother, and, greatly as I might hanker after that glittering evil person who bore me, it was to Aunt Emily that I turned for the solid, sustaining, though on the face of it uninteresting, relationship that is provided by motherhood at its best. Our little household at Shenley was calm and happy and afforded an absolute contrast to the agitations and tearing emotions of Alconleigh. It may have been dull, but it was a sheltering harbour, and I was always glad to get back to it. I think I was beginning dimly to realize how much it all centred upon me; the very timetable, with its early luncheon and high tea, was arranged to fit in with my lessons and bedtime. Only during those holidays when I went to Alconleigh did Aunt Emily have any life of her own, and even these breaks were infrequent, as she had an idea that Uncle Matthew and the whole stormy set-up there were bad for my nerves. I may not have been consciously aware of the extent to which Aunt Emily had regulated her existence round mine, but I saw, only too clearly, that the addition of a man to our establishment was going to change everything. Hardly knowing any men outside the family, I imagined them all to be modelled on the lines of Uncle Matthew, or of my own seldom seen, violently emotional papa, either of whom, plunging about in that neat little house, would have been sadly out of place. I was filled with apprehension, almost with horror, and, greatly assisted by the workings of Louisa's and Linda's vivid imaginations, had got myself into a real state of nerves. Louisa was now teasing me with the Constant Nymph. She read aloud the last chapters, and soon I was dying at a Brussels boarding-house, in the arms of Aunt Emily's husband.

On Wednesday Aunt Emily rang up Aunt Sadie, and they talked for ages.

The telephone at Alconleigh was, in those days, situated in a glass cupboard halfway down the brilliantly lighted back passage; there was no extension, and eavesdropping was thus rendered impossible. (In later years it was moved to Uncle Matthew's business-room, with an extension, after which all privacy was at an end.) When Aunt Sadie returned to the drawing-room she said nothing except: 'Emily is coming to-morrow on the three-five. She sends you her love, Fanny.'

The next day we all went out hunting. The Radletts loved animals, they loved foxes, they risked dreadful beatings in order to unstop their earths, they read and cried and rejoiced over Reynard the Fox, in summer they got up at four to go and see the cubs playing in the pale-green light of the woods; nevertheless, more than anything in the world, they loved hunting. It was in their blood and bones and in my blood and bones, and nothing could eradicate it, though we knew it for a kind of original sin. For three hours that day I forgot everything except my body and my pony's body; the rushing, the scrambling, the splashing, struggling up the hills, sliding down them again, the tugging, the bucketing, the earth and the sky. I forget everything, I could hardly have told you my name. That must be the great hold that hunting has over people, especially stupid people; it enforces an absolute concentration, both mental and physical.

After three hours Josh took me home. I was never allowed to stay out long or I got tired and would be sick all night. Josh was out on Uncle Matthew's second horse; at about two o'clock they changed over, and he started home on the lathered, sweating first horse, taking me with him. I came out of my trance, and saw that the day, which had begun with brilliant sunshine, was now cold and dark, threatening rain.

'And where's her ladyship hunting this year?' said Josh, as we started on a ten-mile jog along the Merlinford road, a sort of hog's back, more cruelly exposed than any road I have ever known, without a scrap of shelter or windscreen the whole of its fifteen miles. Uncle Matthew would never allow motor-cars, either to take us to the meet or to fetch us home; he regarded this habit as despicably soft.

I knew that Josh meant my mother. He had been with my grandfather when she and her sisters were girls, and my mother was his heroine, he adored her.

'She's in Paris, Josh.'

'In Paris—what for?'

'I suppose she likes it.'

'Ho,' said Josh, furiously, and we rode for about half a mile in silence. The rain had begun, a thin cold rain, sweeping over the wide views on each side of the road; we trotted along, the weather in our faces. My back was not strong, and trotting on a side-saddle for any length of time was agony to me. I edged my pony on to the grass, and cantered for a bit, but I knew how much

Josh disapproved of this, it was supposed to bring the horses back too hot; walking, on the other hand, chilled them. It had to be jog, jog, back-breaking jog, all the way.

'It's my opinion,' said Josh at last, 'that her ladyship is wasted, downright wasted, every minute of her life that she's not on a 'oss.'

'She's a wonderful rider, isn't she?'

I had had all this before from Josh, many times, and could never have enough of it.

'There's no human being like her, that I've ever seen,' said Josh, hissing through his teeth. 'Hands like velvet, but strong like iron, and her seat——! Now look at you, jostling about on that saddle, first here, then there—we shall have a sore back to-night, that's one thing certain we shall.'

'Oh, Josh—trotting. And I'm so tired.'

'Never saw her tired. I've seen 'er change 'osses after a ten-mile point, get on to a fresh young five-year-old what hadn't been out for a week—up like a bird—never know you had 'er foot in your hand, pick up the reins in a jiffy, catch up its head, and off and over a post and rails and bucking over the ridge and furrow, sitting like a rock. Now his lordship (he meant Uncle Matthew) he can ride, I don't say the contrary, but look how he sends the 'osses home, so darned tired they can't drink their gruel. He can ride all right, but he doesn't study his 'oss. I never knew your mother bring them home like this, she'd know when they'd had enough, and then heads for home and no looking back. Mind you, his lordship's a great big man, I don't say the contrary, rides every bit of sixteen stone, but he has great big 'osses and half kills them, and then who has to stop up with them all night? Me!'

The rain was pouring down by now. An icy trickle was feeling its way past my left shoulder, and my right boot was slowly filling with water, the pain in my back was like a knife. I felt that I couldn't bear another moment of this misery, and yet I knew I must bear another five miles, another forty minutes. Josh gave me scornful looks as my back bent more and more double; I could see that he was wondering how it was that I could be my mother's child.

'Miss Linda,' he said, 'takes after her ladyship something wonderful.'

At last, at last, we were off the Merlinford road, coming down the valley into Alconleigh village, turning up the hill to Alconleigh house, through the lodge gates, up the drive, and into the stable yard. I got stiffly down, gave the pony to one of Josh's stable boys, and stumped away, walking like an old man. I was nearly at the front door before I remembered, with a sudden leap of my heart, that Aunt Emily would have arrived by now, with HIM. — It was quite a minute before I could summon up enough courage to open the front door.

Sure enough, standing with their backs to the hall fire, were Aunt Sadie, Aunt Emily, and a small, fair, and apparently young man. My immediate impression was that he did not seem at all like a husband. He looked kind and gentle.

'Here is Fanny,' said my aunts in chorus.

'Darling,' said Aunt Sadie, 'can I introduce Captain Warbeck?'

I shook hands in the abrupt graceless way of little girls of fourteen, and thought that he did not seem at all like a captain either.

'Oh, darling, how wet you are. I suppose the others won't be back for ages—where have you come from?'

'I left them drawing the spinney by the Old Rose.'

Then I remembered, being after all a female in the presence of a male, how dreadful I always looked when I got home from hunting, splashed from head to foot, my bowler all askew, my hair a bird's nest, my stock a flapping flag, and, muttering something, I made for the back stairs, towards my bath and my rest. After hunting we were kept in bed for at least two hours. Soon Linda returned, even wetter than I had been, and got into bed with me. She, too, had seen the Captain, and agreed that he looked neither like a marrying nor like a military man.

'Can't see him killing Germans with an entrenching tool,' she said, scornfully.

Much as we feared, much as we disapproved of, passionately as we sometimes hated Uncle Matthew, he still remained for us a sort of criterion of English manhood; there seemed something not quite right about any man who greatly differed from him.

'I bet Uncle Matthew gives him rat week,' I said, apprehensive for Aunt Emily's sake.

'Poor Aunt Emily, perhaps he'll make her keep him in the stables,' said Linda with a gust of giggles.

'Still, he looks rather nice you know, and, considering her age, I should think she's lucky to get anybody.'

'I can't wait to see him with Fa.'

However, our expectations of blood and thunder were disappointed, for it was evident at once that Uncle Matthew had taken an enormous fancy to Captain Warbeck. As he never altered his first opinion of people, and as his few favourites could commit nameless crimes without doing wrong in his eyes, Captain Warbeck was, henceforward, on a good wicket with Uncle Matthew.

'He's such a frightfully clever cove, literary you know, you wouldn't believe the things he does. He writes books, and criticizes pictures, and whacks hell out of the piano, though the pieces he plays aren't up to much. Still, you can see what it would be like, if he learnt some of the tunes out of the *Country Girl*, for instance. Nothing would be too difficult for him, you can see that.'

At dinner Captain Warbeck sitting next to Aunt Sadie, and Aunt Emily next to Uncle Matthew, were separated from each other, not only by four of us children (Bob was allowed to dine down, as he was going to Eton next half), but also by pools of darkness. The dining-room table was lit by three electric bulbs hanging in a bunch from the ceiling, and screened by a curtain of dark-red jap silk with a gold fringe. One spot of brilliant light was thus cast into the middle of the table, while the diners themselves, and their plates, sat outside it in total gloom. We all, naturally, had our eyes fixed upon the shadowy figure of the fiancé, and found a great deal in his behaviour to interest us. He talked to Aunt Sadie at first about gardens, plants and flowering shrubs, a topic which was unknown at Alconleigh. The gardener saw to the garden, and that was that. It was quite half a mile from the house, and nobody went near it, except as a little walk sometimes in the summer. It seemed strange that a man who lived in London should know the names, the habits, and the medicinal properties of so many plants. Aunt Sadie politely tried to keep up with him, but could not altogether conceal her ignorance, though she partly veiled it in a mist of absent-mindedness.

'And what is your soil here?' asked Captain Warbeck.

Aunt Sadie came down from the clouds with a happy smile, and said, triumphantly, for here was something she did know, 'Clay'.

'Ah, yes,' said the Captain.

He produced a little jewelled box, took from it an enormous pill, swallowed it, to our amazement, without one sip to help it down, and said, as though to himself, but quite distinctly,

'Then the water here will be madly binding.'

When Logan, the butler, offered him shepherd's pie (the food at Alconleigh was always good and plentiful, but of the homely schoolroom description) he said, again so that one did not quite know whether he meant to be overheard or not.

'No, thank you, no twice-cooked meat. I am a wretched invalid. I must be careful, or I pay.'

Aunt Sadie, who so much disliked hearing about health that people often took her for a Christian Scientist, which, indeed, she might have become had she not disliked hearing about religion even more, took absolutely no notice, but Bob asked with interest, what it was that twice-cooked meat did to one.

'Oh, it imposes a most fearful strain on the juices, you might as well eat leather,' replied Captain Warbeck, faintly, heaping on to his plate the whole of the salad. He said, again in that withdrawn voice:

'Raw lettuce, anti-scorbutic,' and, opening another box of even larger pills, he took two, murmuring, 'Protein.'

'How delicious your bread is,' he said to Aunt Sadie, as though to make up for his rudeness in refusing the twice-cooked meat. 'I'm sure it has the germ.'

'What?' said Aunt Sadie, turning from a whispered confabulation with Logan ('ask Mrs. Crabbe if she could quickly make some more salad').

'I was saying that I feel sure your delicious bread is made of stone-ground flour, containing a high proportion of the germ. In my bedroom at home I have a picture of a grain of wheat (magnified, naturally) which shows the germ. As you know, in white bread the germ, with its wonderful health-giving properties, is eliminated—extracted, I should say—and put into chicken food. As a result the human race is becoming enfeebled, while hens grow larger and stronger with every generation.'

'So in the end,' said Linda, listening all agog, unlike Aunt Sadie, who had retired into a cloud of boredom, 'Hens will be Hons and Hons will be Hens. Oh, how I should love to live in a dear little Hon-house.'

'You wouldn't like your work,' said Bob. 'I once saw a hen laying an egg, and she had a most terrible expression on her face.'

'Only about like going to the lav,' said Linda.

'Now, Linda,' said Aunt Sadie, sharply, 'that's quite unnecessary. Get on with your supper and don't talk so much.'

Vague as she was, Aunt Sadie could not always be counted on to ignore everything that was happening around her.

'What were you telling me, Captain Warbeck, something about germs?'

'Oh, not germs—the germ——'

At this point I became aware that, in the shadows at the other end of the table, Uncle Matthew and Aunt Emily were having one of their usual set-tos, and that it concerned me. Whenever Aunt Emily came to Alconleigh these tussles with Uncle Matthew would occur, but, all the same, one could see that he was fond of her. He always liked people who stood up to him, and also he probably saw in her a reflection of Aunt Sadie, whom he adored. Aunt Emily was more positive than Aunt Sadie, she had more character and less beauty, and she was not worn out with childbirth, but they were very much sisters. My mother was utterly different in every respect, but then she, poor thing, was, as Linda would have said, obsessed with sex.

Uncle Matthew and Aunt Emily were now engaged upon an argument we had all heard many times before. It concerned the education of females.

Uncle Matthew: 'I hope poor Fanny's school (the word school pronounced in tones of withering scorn) is doing her all the good you think it is. Certainly she picks up some dreadful expressions there.'

Aunt Emily, calmly, but on the defensive: 'Very likely she does. She also picks up a good deal of education.'

Uncle Matthew: 'Education! I was always led to suppose that no educated person ever spoke of notepaper, and yet I hear poor Fanny asking Sadie for notepaper. What is this education? Fanny talks about mirrors and mantel-pieces, handbags and perfume, she takes sugar in her coffee, has a tassel on her umbrella, and I have no doubt that, if she is ever fortunate enough to catch a husband, she will call his father and mother Father and Mother. Will the wonderful education she is getting make up to the unhappy brute for all these endless pinpricks? Fancy hearing one's wife talk about notepaper—the irritation!'

Aunt Emily: 'A lot of men would find it more irritating to have a wife who had never heard of George III. (All the same, Fanny darling, it is called writing-paper you know—don't let's hear any more about note, please.) That is where you and I come in you see, Matthew, home influence is admitted to be a most important part of education.'

Uncle Matthew: 'There you are——'

Aunt Emily: 'A most important, but not by any means the most important.'

Uncle Matthew: 'You don't have to go to some awful middle-class establishment in order to know who George III was. Anyway, who was he, Fanny?'

Alas, I always failed to shine on these occasions. My wits scattered to the four winds by my terror of Uncle Matthew, I said, scarlet in the face:

'He was king. He went mad.'

'Most original, full of information,' said Uncle Matthew, sarcastically. 'Well worth losing every ounce of feminine charm to find that out, I must say. Legs like gateposts from playing hockey, and the worst seat on a horse of any woman I ever knew. Give a horse a sore back as soon as look at it. Linda, you're uneducated, thank God, what have you got to say about George III?'

'Well,' said Linda, her mouth full, 'he was the son of poor Fred and the father of Beau Brummel's fat friend, and he was one of those vacillators you know. "I am his Highness's dog at Kew, pray tell me, sir, whose dog are you?"' she added, inconsequently. 'Oh, how sweet!'

Uncle Matthew shot a look of cruel triumph at Aunt Emily. I saw that I had let down the side and began to cry, inspiring Uncle Matthew to fresh bouts of beastliness.

'It's a lucky thing that Fanny will have £15,000 a year of her own,' he said, 'not to speak of any settlements the Bolter may have picked up in the course of her career. She'll get a husband all right, even if she does talk about lunch, and *en*velope, and put the milk in first. I'm not afraid of that, I only say she'll drive the poor devil to drink when she has hooked him.'

Aunt Emily gave Uncle Matthew a furious frown. She had always tried to conceal from me the fact that I was an heiress, and, indeed, I only was one until such time as my father, hale and hearty and in the prime of life, should marry somebody of an age to bear children. It so happened that, like the Hanoverian family, he only cared for women when they were over forty; after my mother had left him he had embarked upon a succession of middle-aged wives whom even the miracles of modern science were unable to render fruitful. It was also believed, wrongly, by the grown-ups that we children were ignorant of the fact that my mamma was called the Bolter.

'All this,' said Aunt Emily, 'is quite beside the point. Fanny may possibly, in the far future, have a little money of her own (though it is ludicrous to talk of £15,000). Whether she does, or does not, the man she marries may be able to support her—on the other hand, the modern world being what it is, she may have to earn her own living. In any case she will be a more mature, a happier, a more interested and interesting person if she——'

'If she knows that George III was a king and went mad.'

All the same, my aunt was right, and I knew it and she knew it. The Radlett children read enormously by fits and starts in the library at Alconleigh, a good representative nineteenth-century library, which had been made by their grandfather, a most cultivated man. But, while they picked up a great deal of heterogeneous information, and gilded it with their own originality, while they bridged gulfs of ignorance with their charm and high spirits, they never acquired any habit of concentration, they were incapable of solid hard work. One result, in later life, was that they could not stand boredom. Storms and difficulties left them unmoved, but day after day of ordinary existence produced an unbearable torture of ennui, because they completely lacked any form of mental discipline.

As we trailed out of the dining-room after dinner, we heard Captain Warbeck say:

'No port, no, thank you. Such a delicious drink, but I must refuse. It's the acid from port that makes one so delicate now.'

'Ah—you've been a great port drinker, have you?' said Uncle Matthew.

'Oh, not me, I've never touched it. My ancestors——'

Presently, when they joined us in the drawing-room, Aunt Sadie said: 'The children know the news now.'

'I suppose they think it's a great joke,' said Davey Warbeck, 'old people like us being married.'

'Oh, no, of course not,' we said, politely, blushing.

'He's an extraordinary fellow,' said Uncle Matthew, 'knows everything. He says those Charles II sugar casters are only a Georgian imitation of Charles II, just fancy, not valuable at all. To-morrow we'll go round the house and I'll show you all our things and you can tell us what's what. Quite useful to have a fella like you in the family, I must say.'

'That will be very nice,' said Davey, faintly, 'and now I think, if you don't mind, I'll go to bed. Yes, please, early morning tea—so necessary to replace the evaporation of the night.'

He shook hands with us all, and hurried from the room, saying to himself: 'Wooing, so tiring.'

'Davey Warbeck is a Hon,' said Bob as we were all coming down to break-fast next day.

'Yes, he seems a terrific Hon,' said Linda, sleepily.

'No, I mean he's a real one. Look, there's a letter for him, The Hon. David Warbeck. I've looked him up, and it's true.'

Bob's favourite book at this time was Debrett, his nose was never out of it. As a result of his researches he was once heard informing Lucille that *'les origines de la famille Radlett sont perdues dans les brumes de l'antiquité'.*

'He's only a second son, and the eldest has got an heir, so I'm afraid Aunt Emily won't be a lady. And his father's only the second Baron, created 1860, and they only start in 1720, before that it's the female line.' Bob's voice was trailing off. 'Still——' he said.

We heard Davey Warbeck, as he was coming down the stairs, say to Uncle Matthew:

'Oh no, that couldn't be a Reynolds. Prince Hoare, at his very worst, if you're lucky.'

'Pig's thinkers, Davey?' Uncle Matthew lifted the lid of a hot dish.

'Oh, yes please, Matthew, if you mean brains. So digestible.'

'And after breakfast I'm going to show you our collection of minerals in the north passage. I bet you'll agree we've got something worth having there, it's supposed to be the finest collection in England—left me by an old uncle, who spent his life making it. Meanwhile, what'd you think of my eagle?'

'Ah, if that were Chinese now, it would be a treasure. But Jap I'm afraid, not worth the bronze it's cast in. Cooper's Oxford, please, Linda.'

After breakfast we all flocked to the north passage, where there were hundreds of stones in glass-fronted cupboards. Petrified this and fossilized that, blue-john and lapis were the most exciting, large flints which looked as if they had been picked up by the side of the road, the least. Valuable, unique, they were a family legend. 'The minerals in the north passage are good enough for a museum.' We children revered them. Davey looked at them carefully, taking some over to the window and peering into them. Finally, he heaved a great sigh and said:

'What a beautiful collection. I suppose you know they're all diseased?'

'Diseased?'

'Badly, and too far gone for treatment. In a year or two they'll all be dead—you might as well throw the whole lot away.'

Uncle Matthew was delighted.

'Damned fella,' he said, 'nothing's right for him, I never saw such a fella. Even the minerals have got foot-and-mouth, according to him.'

CHAPTER V

THE year which followed Aunt Emily's marriage transformed Linda and me from children, young for our ages, into lounging adolescents waiting for love. One result of the marriage was that I now spent nearly all my holidays at Alconleigh. Davey, like all Uncle Matthew's favourites, simply could not see that he was in the least bit frightening, and scouted Aunt Emily's theory that to be too much with him was bad for my nerves.

'You're just a lot of little crybabies,' he said, scornfully, 'if you allow yourselves to be upset by that old cardboard ogre.'

Davey had given up his flat in London and lived with us at Shenley, where, during term-time, he made but little difference to our life, except in so far as a male presence in a female household is always salutary (the curtains, the covers, and Aunt Emily's clothes underwent an enormous change for the better), but, in the holidays, he liked to carry her off, to his own relations or on trips abroad, and I was parked at Alconleigh. Aunt Emily probably felt that, if she had to choose between her husband's wishes and my nervous system, the former should win the day. In spite of her being forty they were, I believe, very much in love; it must have been a perfect bore having me about at all, and it speaks volumes for their characters that never, for one moment, did they allow me to be aware of this. Davey, in fact was, and has been ever since, a perfect stepfather to me, affectionate, understanding, never in any way interfering. He accepted me at once as belonging to Aunt Emily, and never questioned the inevitability of my presence in his household.

By the Christmas holidays Louisa was officially 'out', and going to hunt balls, a source of bitter envy to us, though Linda said scornfully that she did not appear to have many suitors. We were not coming out for another two years—it seemed an eternity, and especially for Linda, who was paralysed by her longing for love, and had no lessons or work to do which could take her mind off it. In fact, she had no other interest now except hunting, even the animals seemed to have lost all charm for her. She and I did nothing on non-hunting days but sit about, too large for our tweed suits, whose hooks and eyes were always popping off at the waist, and play endless games of patience; or we lolled in the Hons' cupboard, and 'measured'. We had a tape-measure and competed as to the largeness of our eyes, the smallness of wrists, ankles, waist and neck, length of legs and fingers, and so on. Linda always won. When we had finished 'measuring' we talked of romance. These were most innocent talks, for to us, at that time, love and marriage were synonymous, we knew that they lasted for ever, to the grave and far, far beyond. Our preoccupation with sin was finished; Bob, back from Eton, had been able to tell us all about Oscar Wilde, and, now that his crime was no longer a mystery, it seemed dull, unromantic, and incomprehensible.

We were, of course, both in love, but with people we had never met; Linda with the Prince of Wales, and I with a fat, red-faced, middle-aged farmer, whom I sometimes saw riding through Shenley. These loves were strong, and painfully delicious; they occupied all our thoughts, but I think we half realized that they would be superseded in time by real people. They were to keep the house warm, so to speak, for its eventual occupant. What we never would admit was the possibility of lovers after marriage. We were looking for real love, and that could only come once in a lifetime; it hurried to consecration, and thereafter never wavered. Husbands, we knew, were not always faithful, this we must be prepared for, we must understand and forgive. 'I have been faithful to thee, Cynara, in my fashion' seemed to explain it beautifully. But women—that was different; only the lowest of the sex could love or give themselves more than once. I do not quite know how I reconciled these sentiments with the great hero-worship I still had for my mother, that adulterous doll. I suppose I put her in an entirely different category, in the face that launched a thousand ships class. A few historical characters must be allowed to have belonged to this, but Linda and I were perfectionists where love was concerned, and did not ourselves aspire to that kind of fame.

This winter Uncle Matthew had a new tune on his gramophone, called 'Thora'. 'I live in a land of roses,' boomed a deep male voice, 'but dream of a land of snow. Speak, speak, SPEAK to me, Thora.' He played it morning, noon and night; it suited our mood exactly, and Thora seemed the most poignantly beautiful of names.

Aunt Sadie was giving a ball for Louisa soon after Christmas, and to this we pinned great hopes. True, neither the Prince of Wales nor my farmer was invited, but, as Linda said, you never could tell in the country. Somebody might bring them. The Prince might break down in his motor-car, perhaps on his way to Badminton; what could be more natural than that he should while away the time by looking in on the revelry?

'Pray, who is that beautiful young lady?'

'My daughter Louisa, sir.'

'Ah, yes, very charming, but I really meant the one in white taffeta.'

'That is my younger daughter Linda, Your Royal Highness.'

'Please present her to me.'

They would then whirl away in a waltz so accomplished that the other dancers would stand aside to admire. When they could dance no more they would sit for the rest of the evening absorbed in witty conversation.

The following day an A.D.C., asking for her hand——

'But she is so young!'

'His Royal Highness is prepared to wait a year. He reminds you that Her

Majesty the Empress Elizabeth of Austria was married at sixteen. Meanwhile, he sends this jewel.'

A golden casket, a pink white cushion, a diamond rose.

My daydreams were less exalted, equally improbable, and quite as real to me. I imagined my farmer carrying me away from Alconleigh, like young Lochinvar, on a pillion behind him to the nearest smith, who then declared us man and wife. Linda kindly said that we could have one of the royal farms, but I thought this would be a great bore, and that it would be much more fun to have one of our own.

Meanwhile, preparations for the ball went forward, occupying every single member of the household. Linda's and my dresses, white taffeta with floating panels and embroidered bead belts, were being made by Mrs. Josh, whose cottage was besieged at all hours to see how they were getting on. Louisa's came from Reville, it was silver lamé in tiny frills, each frill edged with blue net. Dangling on the left shoulder, and strangely unrelated to the dress, was a large pink silk overblown rose. Aunt Sadie, shaken out of her accustomed languor, was in a state of exaggerated preoccupation and worry over the whole thing; we had never seen her like this before. For the first time, too, that any of us could remember, she found herself in opposition to Uncle Matthew. It was over the following question: The nearest neighbour to Alconleigh was Lord Merlin; his estate marched with that of my uncle, and his house at Merlinford was about five miles away. Uncle Matthew loathed him, while, as for Lord Merlin, not for nothing was his telegraphic address Neighbourtease. There had, however, been no open breach between them; the fact that they never saw each other meant nothing, for Lord Merlin neither hunted, shot, nor fished, while Uncle Matthew had never in his life been known to eat a meal in anybody else's house. 'Perfectly good food at home,' he would say, and people had long ago stopped asking him. The two men, and indeed their two houses and estates, afforded an absolute contrast. Alconleigh was a large, ugly, north-facing, Georgian house, built with only one intention, that of sheltering, when the weather was too bad to be out of doors, a succession of bucolic squires, their wives, their enormous families, their dogs, their horses, their father's relict, and their unmarried sisters. There was no attempt at decoration, at softening the lines, no apology for a façade, it was all as grim and as bare as a barracks, stuck up on the high hillside. Within, the keynote, the theme, was death. Not death of maidens, not death romantically accoutred with urns and weeping willows, cypresses and vale-dictory odes, but the death of warriors and of animals, stark, real. On the walls halberds and pikes and ancient muskets were arranged in crude patterns with the heads of beasts slaughtered in many lands, with the flags and uniforms of bygone Radletts. Glass-topped cases contained, not miniatures of ladies, but miniatures of the medals of their lords, badges, penholders made of tigers' teeth, the hoof of a favourite horse, telegrams announcing casualties in battle and commissions written out on parchment scrolls, all lying together in a timeless jumble.

Merlinford nestled in a valley of south-westerly aspect, among orchards and old mellow farmhouses. It was a villa, built at about the same time as Alconleigh, but by a very different architect, and with a very different end in view. It was a house to live in, not to rush out from all day to kill enemies and animals. It was suitable for a bachelor, or a married couple with one, or at most two, beautiful, clever, delicate children. It had Angelica Kauffmann ceilings, a Chippendale staircase, furniture by Sheraton and Hepplewhite; in the hall there hung two Watteaus; there was no entrenching tool to be seen, nor the head of any animal.

Lord Merlin added continually to its beauties. He was a great collector, and not only Merlinford, but also his houses in London and Rome flowed over with treasures. Indeed, a well-known antique dealer from St. James's had found it worth his while to open a branch in the little town of Merlinford, to tempt his lordship with choice objects during his morning walk, and was soon followed there by a Bond Street jeweller. Lord Merlin loved jewels; his two black whippets wore diamond necklaces designed for whiter, but not slimmer or more graceful necks than theirs. This was a neighbour-tease of long standing; there was a feeling among the local gentry that it incited the good burghers of Merlinford to dishonesty. The neighbours were doubly teased, when year after year went by and the brilliants still sparkled on those furry necks intact.

His taste was by no means confined to antiques; he was an artist and a musician himself, and the patron of all the young. Modern music streamed perpetually from Merlinford, and he had built a small but exquisite play-house in the garden, where his astonished neighbours were sometimes invited to attend such puzzlers as Cocteau plays, the opera 'Mahagonny', or the latest Dada extravagances from Paris. As Lord Merlin was a famous practical joker, it was sometimes difficult to know where jokes ended and culture began. I think he was not always perfectly certain himself.

A marble folly on a nearby hill was topped with a gold angel which blew a trumpet every evening at the hour of Lord Merlin's birth (that this happened to be 9.30 p.m., just too late to remind one of the B.B.C. news, was to be a great local grievance in years to come). The folly glittered by day with semi-precious stones, by night a powerful blue beam was trained upon it.

Such a man was bound to become a sort of legend to the bluff Cotswold squires among whom he lived. But, although they could not approve of an existence which left out of account the killing, though by no means the eating, of delicious game, and though they were puzzled beyond words by the æstheticism and the teases, they accepted him without question as one of themselves. Their families had always known his family, and his father, many years ago, had been a most popular M.F.H.; he was no upstart, no new rich, but simply a sport of all that was most normal in English country life. Indeed, the very folly itself, while considered absolutely hideous, was welcomed as a landmark by those lost on their way home from hunting.

The difference between Aunt Sadie and Uncle Matthew was not as to whether Lord Merlin should or should not be asked to the ball (that question did not arise, since all neighbours were automatically invited), but whether he should be asked to bring a house party. Aunt Sadie thought he should. Since her marriage the least worldly of women, she had known the world as a girl, and she knew that Lord Merlin's house party, if he consented to bring one, would have great decorative value. She also knew that, apart from this, the general note of her ball would be utter and unrelieved dowdiness, and she became aware of a longing to look once more upon young women with well brushed hair, London complexions, and Paris clothes. Uncle Matthew said: 'If we ask that brute Merlin to bring his friends, we shall get a lot of æsthetics, sewers from Oxford, and I wouldn't put it past him to bring some foreigners. I hear he sometimes has Frogs and even Wops to stay with him. I will not have my house filled with Wops.'

In the end, however, as usual, Aunt Sadie had her way, and sat down to write:

> 'Dear Lord Merlin,
> We are having a little dance for Louisa, etc. . . .'

while Uncle Matthew went gloomily off, having said his piece, and put on 'Thora'.

Lord Merlin accepted, and said he would bring a party of twelve people, whose names he would presently submit to Aunt Sadie. Very correct, perfectly normal behaviour. Aunt Sadie was quite agreeably surprised that his letter, when opened, did not contain some clockwork joke to hit her in the eye. The writing-paper did actually have a picture of his house on it, and this she concealed from Uncle Matthew. It was the kind of thing he despised.

A few days later there was another surprise. Lord Merlin wrote another letter, still jokeless, still polite, asking Uncle Matthew, Aunt Sadie and Louisa to dine with him for the Merlinford Cottage Hospital Ball. Uncle Matthew naturally could not be persuaded, but Aunt Sadie and Louisa went. They came back with their eyes popping out of their heads. The house, they said, had been boiling hot, so hot that one never felt cold for a single moment, not even getting out of one's coat in the hall. They had arrived very early, long before anyone else was down, as it was the custom at Alconleigh always to leave a quarter of an hour too soon when motoring, in case there should be a puncture. This gave them the opportunity to have a good look round. The house was full of spring flowers, and smelt wonderful. The hot-houses at Alconleigh were full of spring flowers too, but somehow they never found their way into the house, and certainly would have died of cold if they had. The whippets did wear diamond necklaces, far grander ones than Aunt Sadie's, she said, and she was forced to admit that they looked very beautiful in them. Birds of paradise flew about the house, quite tame, and one of the young men told Louisa that, if she came in the daytime, she would see a flock of multi-coloured pigeons tumbling about like a cloud of confetti in the sky.

'Merlin dyes them every year, and they are dried in the linen cupboard.'

'But isn't that frightfully cruel?' said Louisa, horrified.

'Oh, no, they love it. It makes their husbands and wives look so pretty when they come out.'

'What about their poor eyes?'

'Oh, they soon learn to shut them.'

The house party, when they finally appeared (some of them shockingly late) from their bedrooms, smelt even more delicious than the flowers, and looked even more exotic than the birds of paradise. Everybody had been very nice, very kind to Louisa. She sat between two beautiful young men at dinner, and turned upon them the usual gambit:

'Where do you hunt?'

'We don't,' they said.

'Oh, then why do you wear pink coats?'

'Because we think they are so pretty.'

We all thought this dazzlingly funny, but agreed that Uncle Matthew must never hear of it, or he might easily, even now, forbid the Merlinford party his ball.

After dinner the girls had taken Louisa upstairs. She was rather startled at first to see printed notices in the guest rooms:

OWING TO AN UNIDENTIFIED CORPSE IN THE CISTERN VISITORS ARE RE-QUESTED NOT TO DRINK THE BATH WATER.

VISITORS ARE REQUESTED NOT TO LET OFF FIREARMS, BLOW BUGLES, SCREAM OR HOOT, BETWEEN THE HOURS OF MIDNIGHT AND SIX A.M.

and, on one bedroom door:

MANGLING DONE HERE

But it was soon explained to her that these were jokes.

The girls had offered to lend her powder and lipstick, but Louisa had not quite dared to accept, for fear Aunt Sadie would notice. She said it made the others look simply too lovely.

As the great day of the Alconleigh ball approached, it became obvious that Aunt Sadie had something on her mind. Everything appeared to be

going smoothly, the champagne had arrived, the band, Clifford Essex's third
string, had been ordered, and would spend the few hours of its rest in Mrs.
Craven's cottage. Mrs. Crabbe, in conjunction with the Home Farm,
Craven, and three women from the village who were coming in to help,
was planning a supper to end all suppers. Uncle Matthew had been persuaded
to get twenty oil-stoves, with which to emulate the caressing warmth of
Merlinford, and the gardener was preparing to transfer to the house every
pot-plant that he could lay his hands on. ('You'll be dyeing the White
Leghorns next,' said Uncle Matthew, scornfully.)

But, in spite of the fact that the preparations seemed to be going forward
without a single hitch, Aunt Sadie's brow was still furrowed with anxiety,
because she had collected a large house-party of girls and their mammas, but
not one single young man. The fact was that those of her own contemporaries
who had daughters were glad to bring them, but sons were another matter.
Dancing partners, sated with invitations at this time of year, knew better
than to go all the way down to Gloucestershire to a house as yet untried,
where they were by no means certain of finding the warmth, the luxury and
fine wines which they looked upon as their due, where there was no known
female charmer to tempt them, where they had not been offered a mount,
and where no mention had been made of a shoot, not even a day with the
cocks.

Uncle Matthew had far too much respect for his horses and his pheasants
to offer them up to be messed about by any callow unknown boy.

So here was a horrible situation. Ten females, four mothers and six girls,
were advancing from various parts of England, to arrive at a household
consisting of four more females (not that Linda and I counted, still, we wore
skirts and not trousers, and were really too old to be kept all the time in the
schoolroom) and only two males, one of whom was not yet in tails.

The telephone now became red-hot, telegrams flew in every direction.
Aunt Sadie abandoned all pride, all pretence that things were as they should
be, that people were asked for themselves alone, and launched a series of
desperate appeals. Mr. Wills, the vicar, consented to leave Mrs. Wills at
home, and dine, *en garçon*, at Alconleigh. It would be the first time they had
been separated for forty years. Mrs. Aster, the agent's wife, also made the
same sacrifice, and Master Aster, the agent's son, aged not quite seventeen,
was hurried off to Oxford to get himself a ready-made dress suit.

Davey Warbeck was ordered to leave Aunt Emily and come. He said he
would, but unwillingly, and only after the full extent of the crisis had been
divulged. Elderly cousins, and uncles who had been for many years forgotten
as ghosts, were recalled from oblivion and urged to materialize. They nearly
all refused, some of them quite rudely—they had, nearly all, at one time or
another, been so deeply and bitterly insulted by Uncle Matthew that forgiveness was impossible.

At last Uncle Matthew saw that the situation would have to be taken in hand. He did not care two hoots about the ball, he felt no particular responsibility for the amusement of his guests, whom he seemed to regard as an onrushing horde of barbarians who could not be kept out, rather than as a group of delightful friends summoned for mutual entertainment and joyous revelry. But he did care for Aunt Sadie's peace of mind, he could not bear to see her looking so worried, and he decided to take steps. He went up to London and attended the last sitting of the House of Lords before the recess. His journey was entirely fruitful.

'Stromboli, Paddington, Fort William and Curtley have accepted,' he told Aunt Sadie, with the air of a conjurer producing four wonderful fat rabbits out of one small wine-glass.

'But I had to promise them a shoot—Bob, go and tell Craven I want to see him in the morning.'

By these complicated devices the numbers at the dinner-table would now be even, and Aunt Sadie was infinitely relieved, though inclined to be giggly over Uncle Matthew's rabbits. Lord Stromboli, Lord Fort William and the Duke of Paddington were old dancing partners of her own. Sir Archibald Curtley, Librarian of the House, was a well-known diner-out in the smart intellectual world, he was over seventy and very arthritic. After dinner, of course, the dance would be another matter. Mr. Wills would then be joined by Mrs. Wills, Captain Aster by Mrs. Aster, Uncle Matthew and Bob could hardly be counted as partners, while the House of Lords contingent were more likely to head for the bridge table than for the dancing floor.

'I fear it will be sink or swim for the girls,' said Aunt Sadie, dreamily.

In one way, however, it was all to the good. These old boys were Uncle Matthew's own choice, his own friends, and he would probably be polite to them; in any case they would know what he was like before they came. To have filled the house with strange young men would, she knew, have been taking a great risk. Uncle Matthew hated strangers, he hated the young, and he hated the idea of possible suitors for his daughters; Aunt Sadie saw rocks ahead, but this time they had been circumnavigated.

This then is a ball. This is life, what we have been waiting for all these years, here we are and here it is, a ball, actually going on now, actually in progress round us. How extraordinary it feels, such unreality, like a dream. But, alas, so utterly different from what one had imagined and expected; it must be admitted, not a good dream. The men so small and ugly, the women so frowsty, their clothes so messy and their faces so red, the oil-stoves so smelly, and not really very warm, but, above all, the men, either so old or so ugly. And when they ask one to dance (pushed to it, one cannot but suspect, by kind Davey, who is trying to see that we have a good time at our first party), it is not at all like floating away into a delicious cloud, pressed by a manly arm to a manly bosom, but stumble, stumble, kick, kick. They balance, like King Stork, on one leg, while, with the other, they come down, like King Log, on to one's toe. As for witty conversation, it is wonderful if any conversation, even of the most banal and jerky description, lasts through a whole dance and the sitting out. It is mostly: 'Oh, sorry—oh, my fault', though Linda did get as far as taking one of her partners to see the diseased stones.

We had never learnt to dance, and, for some reason, we had supposed it to be a thing which everybody could do quite easily and naturally. I think Linda realized there and then what it took me years to learn, that the behaviour of civilized man really has nothing to do with nature, that all is artificiality and art more or less perfected.

The evening was saved from being an utter disillusionment by the Merlinford house party. They came immensely late, we had all forgotten about them in fact, but, when they had said how do you do to Aunt Sadie and taken the floor, they seemed at once to give the party a new atmosphere. They flourished and shone with jewels, lovely clothes, brilliant hair and dazzling complexions; when they danced they really did seem to float, except when it was the Charleston, and that, though angular, was so accomplished that it made us gasp with admiration. Their conversation was quite evidently both daring and witty, one could see it ran like a river, splashing, dashing and glittering in the sun. Linda was entranced by them, and decided then and there that she would become one of these brilliant beings and live in their world, even if it took her a lifetime to accomplish. I did not aspire to this. I saw that they were admirable, but they were far removed from me and my orbit, belonging more to that of my parents; my back had been towards them from the day Aunt Emily had taken me home, and there was no return—nor did I wish for it. All the same, I found them fascinating as a spectacle, and, whether I sat out with Linda or stumped round the room with kind Davey, who, unable to persuade any more young men to take us on, gave us an occasional turn himself, my eyes were glued to them. Davey seemed to know them all quite well, and was evidently great friends with Lord Merlin. When he was not being kind to Linda and me, he attached himself to them, and joined in their accomplished chatter. He even offered to introduce us to them, but, alas, the floating panels of taffeta, which had seemed so original and pretty in Mrs. Josh's cottage, looked queerly stiff beside their printed chiffons, so soft and supple; also, our experiences earlier in the evening had made us feel inferior, and we begged him not to.

That night in bed, I thought more than ever of the safe sheltering arms of my Shenley farmer. The next morning Linda told me that she had renounced the Prince of Wales.

'I have come to the conclusion,' she said, 'that Court circles would be rather dull. Lady Dorothy is a lady-in-waiting and look at her.'

CHAPTER VI

THE ball had a very unexpected sequel. Lord Fort William's mother invited Aunt Sadie and Louisa to stay at their place in Sussex for a hunt ball, and, shortly afterwards, his married sister asked them to a shoot and an Infirmary Ball. During this visit, Lord Fort William proposed to Louisa and was accepted. She came back to Alconleigh a fiancée, to find herself the centre of attention there for the first time since the birth of Linda had put her nose for ever out of joint. This was indeed an excitement, and tremendous chats took place in the Hons' cupboard, both with and without Louisa. She had a nice little diamond ring on her fourth finger, but was not as communicative as we could have wished on the subject of Lord (John now to us, but how could we remember that?) Fort William's love-making, retiring, with many blushes, behind the smoke-screen of such things being too sacred to speak of. He soon appeared again in person, and we were able to observe him as an individual, instead of part, with Lord Stromboli and the Duke of Paddington, of a venerable trinity. Linda pronounced the summing-up. 'Poor old thing, I suppose she likes him, but, I must say, if he was one's dog one would have him put down.' Lord Fort William was thirty-nine, but he certainly looked much more. His hair seemed to be slipping off backwards, like an eiderdown in the night, Linda said, and he had a generally uncared-for middle-aged appearance. Louisa, however, loved him, and was happy for the first time in her life. She had always been more frightened of Uncle Matthew than any of the others, and with good reason; he thought she was a fool and was never at all nice to her, and she was in heaven at the prospect of getting away from Alconleigh for ever.

I think Linda, in spite of the poor old dog and the eiderdown, was really very jealous. She went off for long rides by herself, and spun more and more fantastic daydreams; her longing for love had become an obsession. Two whole years would have to be made away with somehow before she would come out in the world, but oh the days went dragging by. Linda would flop about in the drawing-room, playing (or beginning and then not finishing) endless games of patience, sometimes by herself, sometimes with Jassy, whom she had infected with her own restlessness.

'What's the time, darling?'

'Guess.'

'A quarter to six?'

'Better than that.'

'Six!'

'Not quite so good.'

'Five to?'

'Yes.'

'If this comes out I shall marry the man I love. If this comes out I shall marry at eighteen.'

If this comes out—shuffle—if this comes out—deal. A queen at the bottom of the pack, it can't come out, begin again.

Louisa was married in the spring. Her wedding dress, of tulle frills and sprays of orange blossom, was short to the knee and had a train, as was the hideous fashion then. Jassy got very worked up about it.

'So unsuitable.'

'Why, Jassy?'

'To be buried in, I mean. Women are always buried in their wedding dresses, aren't they? Think of your poor old dead legs sticking out.'

'Oh, Jassy, don't be such a ghoul. I'll wrap them up in my train.'

'Not very nice for the undertakers.'

Louisa refused to have bridesmaids. I think she felt that it would be agreeable, for once in her life, to be more looked at than Linda.

'You can't think how stupid you'll look from behind,' Linda said, 'without any. Still, have it your own way. I'm sure we don't want to be guyed up in blue chiffon, I'm only thinking what would be kinder for you.'

On Louisa's birthday, John Fort William, an ardent antiquarian, gave her a replica of King Alfred's jewel. Linda, whose disagreeableness at this time knew no bounds, said that it simply looked like a chicken's mess. 'Same shape, same size, same colour. Not my idea of a jewel.'

'I think it's lovely,' said Aunt Sadie, but Linda's words had left their sting all the same.

Aunt Sadie had a canary then, which sang all day, rivalling even Galli Curci in the pureness and loudness of its trills. Whenever I hear a canary sing so immoderately it recalls that happy visit, the endless flow of wedding presents, unpacking them, arranging them in the ballroom with shrieks of admiration or of horror, the hustle, the bustle, and Uncle Matthew's good temper, which went on, as fine weather sometimes does, day after unbelievable day.

Louisa was to have two houses, one in London, Connaught Square, and one in Scotland. Her dress allowance would be three hundred a year, she would possess a diamond tiara, a pearl necklace, a motor car of her own and a fur cape. In fact, granted that she could bear John Fort William, her lot was an enviable one. He was terribly dull.

The wedding day was fine and balmy, and, when we went in the morning to see how Mrs. Wills and Mrs. Josh were getting on with the decorations, we found the light little church bunchy with spring flowers. Later, its well-known outlines blurred with a most unaccustomed throng of human beings, it looked quite different. I thought that I personally should have liked better to be married in it when it was so empty and flowery and full of the Holy Ghost.

Neither Linda nor I had ever been to a wedding before, as Aunt Emily, most unfairly we thought at the time, had been married privately in the chapel at Davey's home in the North of England, and we were hardly prepared for the sudden transformation on this day of dear old Louisa, of terribly dull John, into eternal types of Bride and Bridegroom, Heroine and Hero of romance.

From the moment when we left Louisa alone at Alconleigh with Uncle Matthew, to follow us in the Daimler in exactly eleven minutes, the atmosphere became positively dramatic. Louisa, enveloped from head to knee in tulle, sat gingerly on the edge of a chair, while Uncle Matthew, watch in hand, strode up and down the hall. We walked, as we always did, to the church, and arranged ourselves in the family pew at the back of it, from which vantage point we were able to observe with fascination, the unusual appearance of our neighbours, all tricked out in their best. The only person in the whole congregation who looked exactly as usual was Lord Merlin.

Suddenly there was a stir. John and his best man, Lord Stromboli, appearing like two jacks-in-the-box from nowhere, stood beside the altar steps. In their morning coats, their hair heavily brilliantined, they looked quite glamorous, but we hardly had time to notice this fact before Mrs. Wills struck up 'Here comes the Bride', with all the stops out, and Louisa, her veil over her face, was being dragged up the aisle at double quick time by Uncle Matthew. At this moment I think Linda would gladly have changed places with Louisa, even at the cost—the heavy cost—of being happy for ever after with John Fort William. In what seemed no time at all Louisa was being dragged down the aisle again by John, with her veil back, while Mrs. Wills nearly broke the windows, so loud and so triumphant was her 'Wedding March'.

Everything had gone like clockwork, and there was only one small incident. Davey slipped out of the family pew almost unobserved, in the middle of 'As pants the hart' (Louisa's favourite hymn) and went straight to London, making one of the wedding cars take him to Merlinford station. That evening he telephoned to say that he had twisted his tonsil, singing, and had thought it better to go immediately to Sir Andrew Macpherson, the nose, throat and ear man, who was keeping him in bed for a week. The most extraordinary accidents always seemed to overtake poor Davey.

When Louisa had gone away and the wedding guests had left Alconleigh, a sense of flatness descended upon the house, as always happens on these occasions. Linda then became plunged into such despairing gloom that even Aunt Sadie was alarmed. Linda told me afterwards that she thought a great deal about killing herself, and would most likely have done so had the material difficulties not been so great.

'You know what it is,' she said, 'trying to kill rabbits. Well, think of *oneself*!'

Two years seemed an absolute eternity, not worth ploughing through even with the prospect (which she never doubted, just as a religious person does not doubt the existence of heaven) of blissful love at the end of it. Of course, this was the time when Linda should have been made to work, as I was, all day and hard, with no time for silly dreaming except the few minutes before one went to sleep at night. I think Aunt Sadie dimly perceived this fact, she urged her to learn cooking, to occupy herself in the garden, to be prepared for confirmation. Linda furiously refused, nor would she do jobs in the village, nor help Aunt Sadie in the hundred and one chores which fall to the lot of a country squire's wife. She was, in fact, and Uncle Matthew told her so countless times every day, glaring at her with angry blue eyes, thoroughly bloody-minded.

Lord Merlin came to her rescue. He had taken a fancy to her at Louisa's wedding, and asked Aunt Sadie to bring her over to Merlinford some time. A few days later he rang up. Uncle Matthew answered the telephone, and shouted to Aunt Sadie, without taking his mouth away from the receiver:

'That hog Merlin wants to speak to you.'

Lord Merlin, who must have heard, was quite unmoved by this. He was an eccentric himself, and had a fellow feeling for the idiosyncrasies of others. Poor Aunt Sadie, however, was very much flustered, and, as a result, she accepted an invitation which she would otherwise most probably have refused, to take Linda over to Merlinford for luncheon.

Lord Merlin seemed to become immediately aware of Linda's state of mind, was really shocked to discover that she was doing no lessons at all, and did what he could to provide some interests for her. He showed her his pictures, explained them to her, talked at length about art and literature, and gave her books to read. He let fall the suggestion, which was taken up by Aunt Sadie, that she and Linda should attend a course of lectures in Oxford, and he also mentioned that the Shakespeare Festival was now in progress at Stratford-on-Avon.

Outings of this kind, which Aunt Sadie herself very much enjoyed, soon became a regular feature of life at Alconleigh. Uncle Matthew scoffed a bit, but he never interfered with anything Aunt Sadie wanted to do; besides, it was not so much education that he dreaded for his daughters, as the vulgarizing effect that a boarding-school might have upon them. As for governesses, they had been tried, but none had ever been able to endure for more than a few days the terror of Uncle Matthew's grinding dentures, the piercing furious blue flash of his eyes, the stock whips cracking under their bedroom windows at dawn. Their nerves, they said, and made for the station, often before they had had time to unpack enormous trunks, heavy as though full of stones, by which they were always accompanied.

Uncle Mattthew went with Aunt Sadie and Linda on one occasion to a Shakespeare play, *Romeo and Juliet*. It was not a success. He cried copiously, and went into a furious rage because it ended badly. 'All the fault of that damned padre,' he kept saying on the way home, still wiping his eyes. 'That fella, what's 'is name, Romeo, might have known a blasted papist would mess up the whole thing. Silly old fool of a nurse too, I bet she was an R.C., dismal old bitch.'

So Linda's life, instead of being on one flat level plain of tedium, was now, to some extent, filled with outside interests. She perceived that the world she wanted to be in, the witty, sparkling world of Lord Merlin and his friends, was interested in things of the mind, and that she would only be able to shine in it if she became in some sort educated. The futile games of patience were abandoned, and she sat all day hunched up in a corner of the library sofa, reading until her eyes gave out. She often rode over to Merlinford, and, unbeknownst to her parents, who never would have allowed her to go there, or indeed anywhere, alone, left Josh in the stable yard where he had congenial friends, and chatted for hours with Lord Merlin on all sorts of subjects. He knew that she had an intensely romantic character, he foresaw much trouble ahead, and he continually urged upon her the necessity for an intellectual background.

CHAPTER VII

WHAT could possibly have induced Linda to marry Anthony Kroesig? During the nine years of their life together people asked this question with irritating regularity, almost every time their names were mentioned. What was she after, surely she could never possibly have been in love with him, what was the idea, how could it have happened? He was admittedly very rich, but so were others and surely the fascinating Linda had only to choose? The answer was, of course, that, quite simply, she was in love with him. Linda was far too romantic to marry without love and indeed I, who was present at their first meeting and during most of their courtship, always understood why it had happened. Tony, in those days, and to unsophisticated country girls like us, seemed a glorious and glamorous creature. When we first saw him, at Linda's and my coming-out ball, he was in his last year at Oxford, a member of Bullingdon, a splendid young man with a Rolls-Royce, plenty of beautiful horses, exquisite clothes, and large luxurious rooms, where he entertained on a lavish scale. In person he was tall and fair, on the heavy side, but with a well-proportioned figure; he had already a faint touch of pomposity, a thing which Linda had never come across before, and which she found not unattractive. She took him, in short, at his own valuation.

What immediately gave him great prestige in her eyes was that he came to the ball with Lord Merlin. It was really most unlucky, especially as it happened that he had only been asked at the eleventh hour, as a stopgap.

Linda's ball was not nearly such a fiasco as Louisa's had been. Louisa, a married London lady now, produced a lot of young men for Aunt Sadie's house-party, dull, fair Scotch boys mostly, with nice manners; nothing to which Uncle Matthew could possibly take exception. They got on quite well with the various dull dark girls invited by Aunt Sadie, and the house-party seemed to 'go' very nicely, though Linda had her head in the air, saying they were all too impossibly dreary for words. Uncle Matthew had been implored by Aunt Sadie for weeks past to be kind to the young and not to shout at anybody, and he was quite subdued, almost pathetic in his wish to please, creeping about as though there were an invalid upstairs and straw in the street.

Davey and Aunt Emily were staying in the house to see me come out (Aunt Sadie had offered to bring me out with Linda and give us a London season together, an offer which was most gratefully accepted by Aunt Emily) and Davey constituted himself a sort of bodyguard to Uncle Matthew, hoping to stand as much as possible between him and the more unbearable forms of irritation.

'I'll be simply wonderful to everybody, but I won't have the sewers in my business-room, that's all,' Uncle Matthew had said, after one of Aunt Sadie's prolonged exhortations, and, indeed, spent most of the week-end (the ball was on a Friday and the house-party stayed on until Monday) locked into it, playing '1812' and the 'Haunted Ballroom' on the gramophone. He was rather off the human voice this year.

'What a pity,' said Linda, as we struggled into our ball dresses (proper London ones this time, with no floating panels), 'that we are dressing up like this, and looking so pretty, and all for those terrible productions of Louisa's. Waste, I call it.'

'You never know in the country,' I said, 'somebody may bring the Prince of Wales.'

Linda shot me a furious look under her eyelashes.

'Actually,' she said, 'I am pinning great hopes on Lord Merlin's party. I'm sure he'll bring some really interesting people.'

Lord Merlin's party arrived, as before, very late, and in very high spirits. Linda immediately noticed a large, blond young man in a beautiful pink coat. He was dancing with a girl who often stayed at Merlinford, called Baby Fairweather, and she introduced him to Linda. He asked her to dance the next, and she abandoned one of Louisa's Scotch boys, to whom she had promised it, and strutted off with him in a quick one-step. Linda and I had both been having dancing lessons, and, if we did not exactly float round the room, our progress was by no means so embarrassing as it had been before.

Tony was in a happy mood, induced by Lord Merlin's excellent brandy, and Linda was pleased to find how well and easily she was getting on with this member of the Merlinford set. Everything she said seemed to make him laugh; presently they went to sit out, she chattered away, and Tony roared with laughter. This was the royal road to Linda's good books; she liked people who laughed easily more than anything; it naturally did not occur to her that Tony was a bit drunk. They sat out the next dance together. This was immediately noticed by Uncle Matthew, who began to walk up and down in front of them, giving them furious looks, until Davey, observing this danger signal, came up and hurried him away, saying that one of the oil-stoves in the hall was smoking.

'Who is that sewer with Linda?'

'Kroesig, Governor of the Bank of England, you know; his son.'

'Good God, I never expected to harbour a full-blooded Hun in this house—who on earth asked him?'

'Now, Matthew dear, don't get excited. The Kroesigs aren't Huns, they've been over here for generations, they are a very highly respected family of English bankers.'

'Once a Hun always a Hun,' said Uncle Matthew, 'and I'm not too set on bankers myself. Besides, the fella must be a gate-crasher.'

'No, he's not. He came with Merlin.'

'I knew that bloody Merlin would start bringing foreigners here sooner or later, I always said he would, but I didn't think even he would land one with a German.'

'Don't you think it's time somebody took some champagne to the band?' said Davey.

But Uncle Matthew stumped down to the boiler room, where he had a long soothing talk with Timb, the odd man, about coke.

Tony, meanwhile, thought Linda ravishingly pretty, and great fun, which indeed she was. He told her so, and danced with her again and again, until Lord Merlin, quite as much put out as Uncle Matthew by what was happening, firmly and very early took his party home.

'See you at the meet to-morrow,' said Tony, winding a white silk scarf round his neck.

Linda was silent and preoccupied for the rest of the evening.

'You're not to go hunting, Linda,' said Aunt Sadie the next day, when Linda came downstairs in her riding-habit, 'it's too rude, you must stay and look after your guests. You can't leave them like that.'

'Darling, darling Mummie,' said Linda, 'the meet's at Cock's Barn, and

you know how one can't resist. And Flora hasn't been out for a week, she'll
go mad. Be a love and take them to see the Roman villa or something, and
I swear to come back early. And they've got Fanny and Louisa after all.'

It was this unlucky hunt that clinched matters as far as Linda was concerned. The first person she saw at the meet was Tony, on a splendid chestnut
horse. Linda herself was always beautifully mounted. Uncle Matthew was
proud of her horsemanship, and had given her two pretty, lively little
horses. They found at once, and there was a short sharp run, during which
Linda and Tony, both in a somewhat showing-off mood, rode side by side
over the stone walls. Presently, on a village green, they checked. One or two
hounds put up a hare, which lost its head, jumped into a duckpond, and
began to swim about in a hopeless sort of way. Linda's eyes were filled with
tears.

'Oh, the poor hare!'

Tony got off his horse, and plunged into the pond. He rescued the hare,
waded out again, his fine white breeches covered with green muck, and put
it, wet and gasping, into Linda's lap. It was the one romantic gesture of his
life.

At the end of the day Linda left hounds to take a short cut home across
country. Tony opened a gate for her, took off his hat, and said:

'You are a most beautiful rider, you know. Good night, when I'm back in
Oxford I'll ring you up.'

When Linda got home she rushed me off to the Hons' cupboard and told
me all this. She was in love.

Given Linda's frame of mind during the past two endless years, she was
obviously destined to fall in love with the first young man who came along.
It could hardly have been otherwise; she need not, however, have married
him. This was made inevitable by the behaviour of Uncle Matthew. Most
unfortunately Lord Merlin, the one person who might perhaps have been
able to make Linda see that Tony was not all she thought him, went to Rome
the week after the ball, and remained abroad for a year.

Tony went back to Oxford when he left Merlinford, and Linda sat about
waiting, waiting, waiting for the telephone bell. Patience again. If this
comes out he is thinking of me now this very minute—if this comes out he'll
ring up to-morrow—if this comes out he'll be at the meet. But Tony hunted
with the Bicester, and never appeared on our side of the country. Three
weeks passed, and Linda began to feel in despair. Then one evening, after
dinner, the telephone bell rang; by a lucky chance Uncle Matthew had gone
down to the stables to see Josh about a horse that had colic, the business-
room was empty, and Linda answered the telephone herself. It was Tony.
Her heart was choking her, she could scarcely speak.

'Hullo, is that Linda? It's Tony Kroesig here. Will you come to lunch next
Thursday?'

'Oh! But I should never be allowed to.'

'Oh, rot,' very impatiently, 'several other girls are coming down from London—bring your cousin if you like.'

'All right, that will be lovely.'

'See you then—about one—7 King Edward Street, I expect you know the rooms. Altringham had them when he was up.'

Linda came away from the telephone trembling, and whispered to me to come quick to the Hons' cupboard. We were absolutely forbidden to see young men at any hour unchaperoned, and other girls did not count as chaperons. We knew quite well, though such a remote eventuality had never even been mooted at Alconleigh, that we would not be allowed to have luncheon with a young man in his lodgings with any chaperon at all, short of Aunt Sadie herself. The Alconleigh standards of chaperonage were medieval; they did not vary in the slightest degree from those applied to Uncle Matthew's sister, and to Aunt Sadie in youth. The principle was that one never saw any young man alone, under any circumstances, until one was engaged to him. The only people who could be counted on to enforce this rule were one's mother or one's aunts, therefore one must not be allowed beyond the reach of their ever-watchful eyes. The argument, often put forward by Linda, that young men were not very likely to propose to girls they hardly knew, was brushed aside as nonsense. Uncle Matthew had proposed, had he not? to Aunt Sadie, the very first time he ever saw her, by the cage of a two-headed nightingale at an Exhibition at the White City. 'They respect you all the more.' It never seemed to dawn upon the Alconleighs that respect is not an attitude of mind indulged in by modern young men, who look for other qualities in their wives than respectability. Aunt Emily, under the enlightened influence of Davey, was far more reasonable, but, of course, when staying with the Radletts, I had to obey the same rules.

In the Hons' cupboard we talked and talked. There was no question in our minds but that we must go, not to do so would be death for Linda, she would never get over it. But how to escape? There was only one way that we could devise, and it was full of risk. A very dull girl of exactly our age called Lavender Davis lived with her very dull parents about five miles away, and once in a blue moon, Linda, complaining vociferously, was sent over to luncheon with them, driving herself in Aunt Sadie's little car. We must pretend that we were going to do that, hoping that Aunt Sadie would not see Mrs. Davis, that pillar of the Women's Institute, for months and months, hoping also that Perkins, the chauffeur, would not remark on the fact that we had driven sixty miles and not ten.

As we were going upstairs to bed, Linda said to Aunt Sadie, in what she hoped was an offhand voice, but one which seemed to me vibrant with guilt: 'That was Lavender ringing up. She wants Fanny and me to lunch there on Thursday.'

'Oh, duck,' said Aunt Sadie, 'you can't have my car, I'm afraid.'

Linda became very white, and leant against the wall.

'Oh, please, Mummy, oh please do let me, I do so terribly want to go.'

'To the Davises,' said Aunt Sadie in astonishment, 'but, darling, last time you said you'd never go again as long as you lived—great haunches of cod you said, don't you remember? Anyhow, I'm sure they'll have you another day, you know.'

'Oh, Mummy, you don't understand. The whole point is, a man is coming who brought up a baby badger, and I do so want to meet him.'

It was known to be one of Linda's greatest ambitions, to bring up a baby badger.

'Yes, I see. Well, couldn't you ride over?'

'Staggers and ringworm,' said Linda, her large blue eyes slowly filling with tears.

'What did you say, darling?'

'In their stables—staggers and ringworm. You wouldn't want me to expose poor Flora to that.'

'Are you sure? Their horses always look so wonderful.'

'Ask Josh.'

'Well, I'll see. Perhaps I can borrow Fa's Morris, and if not, perhaps Perkins can take me in the Daimler. It's a meeting I must go to, though.'

'Oh, you are kind, you are kind. Oh, do try. I do so long for a badger.'

'If we go to London for the season you'll be far too busy to think of a badger. Good night then, ducks.'

'We must get hold of some powder.'

'And rouge.'

These commodities were utterly forbidden by Uncle Matthew, who liked to see female complexions in a state of nature, and often pronounced that paint was for whores and not for his daughters.

'I once read in a book that you can use geranium juice for rouge.'

'Geraniums aren't out at this time of year, silly.'

'We can blue our eyelids out of Jassy's paint-box.'

'And sleep in curlers.'

'I'll get the verbena soap out of Mummy's bathroom. If we let it melt in the bath, and soak for hours in it, we shall smell delicious.'

'I thought you loathed Lavender Davis.'

'Oh, shut up, Jassy.'

'Last time you went you said she was a horrible Counter-Hon, and you would like to bash in her silly face with the Hons' mallet.'

'I never said so. Don't invent lies.'

'Why have you got your London suit on for Lavender Davis?'

'Do go away, Matt.'

'Why are you starting already, you'll be hours too early.'

'We're going to see the badger before luncheon.'

'How red your face is, Linda. Oh, oh you do look so funny!'

'If you don't shut up and go away, Jassy, I swear I'll put your newt back in the pond.'

Persecution, however, continued until we were in the car and out of the garage yard.

'Why don't you bring Lavender back for a nice long cosy visit?' was Jassy's parting shot.

'Not very Honnish of them,' said Linda, 'do you think they can possibly have guessed?'

We left our car in the Clarendon yard, and, as we were very early, having allowed half an hour in case of two punctures, we made for Elliston & Cavell's ladies-room, and gazed at ourselves, with a tiny feeling of uncertainty, in the looking-glasses there. Our cheeks had round scarlet patches, our lips were the same colour, but only at the edges, inside it had already worn off, and our eyelids were blue, all out of Jassy's paint-box. Our noses were white, Nanny having produced some powder with which, years ago, she used to dust Robin's bottom. In short, we looked like a couple of Dutch dolls.

'We must keep our ends up,' said Linda, uncertainly.

'Oh, dear,' I said, 'the thing about me is, I always feel so much happier with my end down.'

We gazed and gazed, hoping thus, in some magical way, to make ourselves feel less peculiar. Presently we did a little work with damp handkerchiefs, and toned our faces down a bit. We then sallied forth into the street, looking at ourselves in every shop window that we passed. (I have often noticed that when women look at themselves in every reflection, and take furtive peeps into their hand looking-glasses, it is hardly ever, as is generally supposed, from vanity, but much more often from a feeling that all is not quite as it should be.)

Now that we had actually achieved our objective, we were beginning to feel horribly nervous, not only wicked, guilty and frightened, but also filled with social terrors. I think we would both gladly have got back into the car and made for home.

On the stroke of one o'clock we arrived in Tony's room. He was alone, but evidently a large party was expected, the table, a square one with a coarse white linen cloth, seemed to have a great many places. We refused sherry and cigarettes, and an awkward silence fell.

'Been hunting at all?' he asked Linda.

'Oh, yes, we were out yesterday.'

'Good day?'

'Yes, very.' We found at once, and had a five-mile point and then——'
Linda suddenly remembered that Lord Merlin had once said to her: 'Hunt
as much as you like, but never talk about it, it's the most boring subject in
the world.'

'But that's marvellous, a five-mile point. I must come out with the Hey-
throp again soon, they are doing awfully well this season, I hear. We had a
good day yesterday, too.'

He embarked on a detailed account of every minute of it, where they
found, where they ran to, how his first horse had gone lame, how, luckily,
he had then come upon his second horse, and so on. I saw just what
Lord Merlin meant. Linda, however, hung upon his words with breathless
interest.

At last noises were heard in the street, and he went to the window.

'Good,' he said, 'here are the others.'

The others had come down from London in a huge Daimler, and poured,
chattering, into the room. Four pretty girls and a young man. Presently
some undergraduates appeared, and completed the party. It was not really
very enjoyable from our point of view, they all knew each other too well.
They gossiped away, roared with laughter at private jokes, and showed off;
still, we felt that this was Life, and would have been quite happy just looking
on had it not been for that ghastly feeling of guilt, which was now beginning
to give us a pain rather like indigestion. Linda turned quite pale every time
the door opened. I think she really felt that Uncle Matthew might appear at
any moment, cracking a whip. As soon as we decently could, which was not
very soon, because nobody moved from the table until after Tom had struck
four, we said good-bye, and fled for home.

The miserable Matt and Jassy were swinging on the garage gate.

'So how was Lavender? Did she roar at your eyelids? Better go and wash
before Fa sees you. You have been hours. Was it cod? Did you see the
badger?'

Linda burst into tears.

'Leave me alone, you horrible Counter-Hons,' she cried, and rushed upstairs to her bedroom.

Love had increased threefold in one short day.

On Saturday the blow fell.

'Linda and Fanny, Fa wants you in the business-room. And sooner you
than me by the look of him,' said Jassy, meeting us in the drive as we came
in from riding. Our hearts plunged into our boots. We looked at each other
with apprehension.

'Better get it over,' said Linda, and we hurried to the business-room,
where we saw at once that the worst had occurred.

Aunt Sadie, looking unhappy, and Uncle Matthew, grinding his teeth, confronted us with our crime. The room was full of blue lightning flashing from his eyes, and Jove's thunder was not more awful than what he now roared at us:

'Do you realize,' he said, 'that, if you were married women, your husbands could divorce you for doing this?'

Linda began to say no they couldn't. She knew the laws of divorce from having read the whole of the Russell case off newspapers with which the fires in the spare bedrooms were laid.

'Don't interrupt your father,' said Aunt Sadie, with a warning look.

Uncle Matthew, however, did not even notice. He was in the full flood and violence of his storm.

'Now we know you can't be trusted to behave yourselves, we shall have to take certain steps. Fanny can go straight home to-morrow, and I never want you here again, do you understand? Emily will have to control you in future, if she can, but you'll go the same way as your mother, sure as eggs is eggs. As for you, miss, there's no more question of a London season now—we shall have to watch you in future every minute of the day—not very agreeable, to have a child one can't trust—and there would be too many opportunities in London for slipping off. You can stew in your own juice here. And no more hunting this year. You're damned lucky not to be thrashed; most fathers would give you a good hiding, do you hear? Now you can both go to bed, and you're not to speak to each other before Fanny leaves. I'm sending her over in the car to-morrow.'

It was months before we knew how they found out. It seemed like magic, but the explanation was simple. Somebody had left a scarf in Tony Kroesig's rooms, and he had rung up to ask whether it belonged to either of us.

CHAPTER VIII

As always, Uncle Matthew's bark was worse than his bite, though, while it lasted, it was the most terrible row within living memory at Alconleigh. I was sent back to Aunt Emily the next day, Linda waving and crying out of her bedroom window: 'Oh, you *are* lucky, not to be me' (most unlike her, her usual cry being 'Isn't it lovely to be lovely *me*'); and she was stopped from hunting once or twice. Then relaxation began, the thin end of the wedge, and gradually things returned to normal, though it was reckoned in the family that Uncle Matthew had got through a pair of dentures in record time.

Plans for the London season went on being made, and went on including me. I heard afterwards that both Davey and John Fort William took it upon themselves to tell Aunt Sadie and Uncle Matthew (especially Uncle

Matthew) that, according to modern ideas, what we had done was absolutely normal, though, of course, they were obliged to own that it was very wrong of us to have told so many and such shameless lies.

We both said we were very sorry, and promised faithfully that we would never act in such an underhand way again, but always ask Aunt Sadie if there was something we specially wanted to do.

'Only then, of course, it will always be no,' as Linda said, giving me a hopeless look.

Aunt Sadie took a furnished house for the summer near Belgrave Square. It was a house with so little character that I can remember absolutely nothing about it, except that my bedroom had a view over chimney-pots, and that on hot summer evenings I used to sit and watch the swallow, always in pairs, and wish sentimentally that I too could be a pair with somebody.

We really had great fun, although I don't think it was dancing that we enjoyed so much as the fact of being grown up and in London. At the dances the great bar to enjoyment was what Linda called the chaps. They were terribly dull, all on the lines of the ones Louisa had brought to Alconleigh; Linda, still in her dream of love for Tony, could not distinguish between them, and never even knew their names. I looked about hopefully for a possible life-partner, but, though I honestly tried to see the best in them, nothing remotely approximating to my requirements turned up.

Tony was at Oxford for his last term, and did not come to London until quite the end of the season.

We were chaperoned, as was to be expected, with Victorian severity. Aunt Sadie or Uncle Matthew literally never let us out of the sight of one or the other; as Aunt Sadie liked to rest in the afternoon, Uncle Matthew would solemnly take us off to the House of Lords, park us in the Peeresses' Gallery, and take his own forty winks on a back bench opposite. When he was awake in the house, which was not often, he was a perfect nuisance to the Whips, never voting with the same party twice running; nor were the workings of his mind too easy to follow. He voted, for instance, in favour of steel traps, of blood sports and of steeplechasing, but against vivisection and the exporting of old horses to Belgium. No doubt he had his reasons, as Aunt Sadie would remark, with finality, when we commented on this inconsistency. I rather liked those drowsy afternoons in the dark Gothic chamber, fascinated by the mutterings and antics that went on the whole time, and besides, the occasional speech one was able to hear was generally rather interesting. Linda liked it too, she was far away, thinking her own thoughts. Uncle Matthew would wake up at tea-time, conduct us to the Peers' dining-room for tea and buttered buns, and then take us home to rest and dress for the dance.

Saturday to Monday was spent by the Radlett family at Alconleigh; they rolled down in their huge, rather sick-making Daimler; and by me at

Shenley, where Aunt Emily and Davey were always longing to hear every detail of our week.

Clothes were probably our chief preoccupation at this time. Once Linda had been to a few dress shows, and got her eye in, she had all hers made by Mrs. Josh, and, somehow, they had a sort of originality and prettiness that I never achieved, although mine, which were bought at expensive shops, cost about five times as much. This showed, said Davey, who used to come and see us whenever he was in London, that either you get your clothes in Paris or it is a toss-up. Linda had one particularly ravishing ball-dress made of masses of pale grey tulle down to her feet. Most of the dresses were still short that summer, and Linda made a sensation whenever she appeared in her yards of tulle, very much disapproved of by Uncle Matthew, on the grounds that he had known three women burnt to death in tulle ball-dresses.

She was wearing this dress when Tony proposed to her in the Berkeley Square summer-house at six o'clock on a fine July morning. He had been down from Oxford about a fortnight, and it was soon obvious that he had eyes for nobody but her. He went to all the same dances, and, after stumping round with a few other girls, would take Linda to supper, and thereafter spend the evening glued to her side. Aunt Sadie seemed to notice nothing, but to the whole rest of the debutante world the outcome was a foregone conclusion, the only question being when and where Tony would propose.

The ball from which they had emerged (it was in a lovely old house on the east side of Berkeley Square, since demolished) was only just alive, the band sleepily thump-thumped its tunes through the nearly empty rooms; poor Aunt Sadie sat on a little gold chair trying to keep her eyes open and passionately longing for bed, with me beside her, dead tired and very cold, my partners all gone home. It was broad daylight. Linda had been away for hours, nobody seemed to have set eyes on her since supper-time, and Aunt Sadie, though dominated by her fearful sleepiness, was apprehensive, and rather angry. She was beginning to wonder whether Linda had not committed the unforgivable sin, and gone off to a night club.

Suddenly the band perked up and began to play 'John Peel' as a prelude to 'God Save the King'; Linda, in a grey cloud, was galloping up and down the room with Tony; one look at her face told all. We climbed into a taxi behind Aunt Sadie (she never would keep a chauffeur up at night), we splashed away past the great hoses that were washing the streets, we climbed the stairs to our rooms, without a word being spoken by any of us. A thin oblique sunlight was striking the chimney-pots as I opened my window. I was too tired to think, I fell into bed.

We were allowed to be late after dances, though Aunt Sadie was always up and seeing to the household arrangements by nine o'clock. As Linda came sleepily downstairs the next morning, Uncle Matthew shouted furiously at her from the hall:

'That bloody Hun Kroesig has just telephoned, he wanted to speak to you. I told him to get to hell out of it. I don't want you mixed up with any Germans, do you understand?'

'Well, I am mixed up,' said Linda, in an offhand, would-be casual voice, 'as it happens I'm engaged to him.'

At this point Aunt Sadie dashed out of her little morning-room on the ground floor, took Uncle Matthew by the arm, and led him away. Linda locked herself into her bedroom and cried for an hour, while Jassy, Matt, Robin, and I speculated upon future developments in the nursery.

There was a great deal of opposition to the engagement, not only from Uncle Matthew, who was beside himself with disappointment and disgust at Linda's choice, but also quite as much from Sir Leicester Kroesig. He did not want Tony to marry at all until he was well settled in his career in the City, and then he had hoped for an alliance with one of the other big banking families. He despised the landed gentry, whom he regarded as feckless, finished and done with in the modern world, he also knew that the vast, the enviable capital sums which such families undoubtedly still possessed, and of which they made so foolishly little use, were always entailed upon the eldest son, and that very small provision, if any, was made for the dowries of daughters. Sir Leicester and Uncle Matthew met, disliked each other on sight, and were at one in their determination to stop the marriage. Tony was sent off to America, to work in a bank house in New York, and poor Linda, the season now being at an end, was taken home to eat her heart out at Alconleigh.

'Oh, Jassy, darling Jassy, lend me your running-away money to go to New York with.'

'No, Linda, I've saved and scraped for five years, ever since I was seven, I simply can't begin all over again now. Besides I shall want it for when I run away myself.'

'But, darling, I'll give it you back, Tony will, when we're married.'

'I know men,' said Jassy, darkly.

She was adamant.

'If only Lord Merlin were here,' Linda wailed. 'He would help me.' But Lord Merlin awas still in Rome.

She had 15s. 6d. in the world, and was obliged to content herself with writing immense screeds to Tony every day. She carried about in her pocket a quantity of short, dull letters in an immature handwriting and with a New York postmark.

After a few months Tony came back, and told his father that he could not settle down to business or banking, or think about his future career at all, until the date for his marriage had been fixed. This was quite the proper line to take with Sir Leicester. Anything that interfered with making money must be regulated at once. If Tony, who was a sensible fellow, and had never given his father one moment's anxiety in his life, assured him that he could only be serious about banking after marriage, then married he must be, the sooner the better. Sir Leicester explained at length what he considered the disadvantages of the union. Tony agreed in principle, but said that Linda was young, intelligent, energetic, that he had great influence with her, and did not doubt that she could be made into a tremendous asset. Sir Leicester finally gave his consent.

'It might have been worse,' he said, 'after all, she is a lady.'

Lady Kroesig opened negotiations with Aunt Sadie. As Linda had virtually worked herself into a decline, and was poisoning the lives of all around her by her intense disagreeableness, Aunt Sadie, secretly much relieved by the turn things had taken, persuaded Uncle Matthew that the marriage, though by no means ideal, was inevitable, and that, if he did not wish to alienate for ever his favourite child, he had better put a good face on it.

'I suppose it might have been worse,' Uncle Matthew said doubtfully, 'at least the fella's not a Roman Catholic.'

CHAPTER IX

THE engagement was duly announced in *The Times*. The Kroesigs now invited the Alconleighs to spend a Saturday to Monday at their house near Guildford. Lady Kroesig, in her letter to Aunt Sadie, called it a week-end, and said it would be nice to get to know each other better. Uncle Matthew flew into a furious temper. It was one of his idiosyncrasies that, not only did he never stay in other people's houses (except, very occasionally, with relations), but he regarded it as a positive insult that he should be invited to do so. He despised the expression 'week-end', and gave a sarcastic snort at the idea that it would be nice to know the Kroesigs better. When Aunt Sadie had calmed him down a bit, she put forward the suggestion that the Kroesig family, father, mother, daughter Marjorie and Tony, should be asked instead if they would spend Saturday to Monday at Alconleigh. Poor Uncle Matthew, having swallowed the great evil of Linda's engagement, had, to do him justice, resolved to put the best face he could on it, and had no wish to make trouble for her with her future in-laws. He had at heart a great respect for family connections, and once, when Bob and Jassy were slanging a cousin whom the whole family, including Uncle Matthew himself, very much disliked, he had turned upon them, knocked their heads together sharply, and said:

'In the first place he's a relation, and in the second place he's a clergyman, so shut up.'

It had become a classical saying with the Radletts.

So the Kroesigs were duly invited. They accepted, and the date was fixed. Aunt Sadie then got into a panic, and summoned Aunt Emily and Davey. (I was staying at Alconleigh anyhow, for a few weeks' hunting.) Louisa was feeding her second baby in Scotland, but hoped to come south for the wedding later on.

The arrival at Alconleigh of the four Kroesigs was not auspicious. As the car which had met them at the station was heard humming up the drive, every single light in the whole house fused—Davey had brought a new ultra-violet lamp with him, which had done the trick. The guests had to be led into the hall in pitch darkness, while Logan fumbled about in the pantry for a candle, and Uncle Matthew rushed off to the fuse box. Lady Kroesig and Aunt Sadie chatted politely about this and that, Linda and Tony giggled in the corner, and Sir Leicester hit his gouty foot on the edge of a refectory table, while the voice of an invisible Davey could be heard, apologizing in a high wail, from the top of the staircase. It was really very embarrassing.

At last the lights went up, and the Kroesigs were revealed. Sir Leicester was a tall fair man with grey hair, whose undeniable good looks were marred by a sort of silliness in his face; his wife and daughter were two dumpy little fluffy females. Tony evidently took after his father, and Marjorie after her mother. Aunt Sadie, thrown out of her stride by the sudden transformation of what had been mere voices in the dark into flesh and blood, and feeling herself unable to produce more topics of conversation, hurried them upstairs to rest, and dress for dinner. It was always considered at Alconleigh that the journey from London was an experience involving great exhaustion, and people were supposed to be in need of rest after it.

'What is this lamp?' Uncle Matthew asked Davey, who was still saying how sorry he was, still clad in the exiguous dressing-gown which he had put on for his sun-bath.

'Well, you know how one never can digest anything in the winter months.'

'I can, damn you,' said Uncle Matthew. This, addressed to Davey, could be interpreted as a term of endearment.

'You think you can, but you can't really. Now this lamp pours its rays into the system, your glands begin to work, and your food does you good again.'

'Well, don't pour any more rays until we have had the voltage altered. When the house is full of bloody Huns one wants to be able to see what the hell they're up to.'

For dinner, Linda wore a white chintz dress with an enormous skirt, and a black lace scarf. She looked entirely ravishing, and it was obvious that Sir

Leicester was much taken with her appearance—Lady Kroesig and Miss Marjorie, in bits of georgette and lace, seemed not to notice it. Marjorie was an intensely dreary girl, a few years older than Tony, who had failed so far to marry, and seemed to have no biological reason for existing.

'Have you read *Brothers*?' Lady Kroesig asked Uncle Matthew, conversationally, as they settled down to their soup.

'What's that?'

'The new Ursula Langdok—*Brothers*—it's about two brothers. You ought to read it.'

'My dear Lady Kroesig, I have only ever read one book in my life, and that is *White Fang*. It's so frightfully good I've never bothered to read another. But Davey here reads books—you've read *Brothers*, Davey, I bet.'

'Indeed, I have not,' said Davey petulantly.

'I'll lend it to you,' said Lady Kroesig, 'I have it with me, and I finished it in the train.'

'You shouldn't,' said Davey, 'read in trains, ever. It's madly wearing to the optic nerve centres, it imposes a most fearful strain. May I see the menu, please? I must explain that I'm on a new diet, one meal white, one meal red. It's doing me so much good. Oh, dear, what a pity, Sadie—oh, she's not listening—Logan, could I ask for an egg, very lightly boiled, you know. This is my white meal, and we are having saddle of mutton I see.'

'Well, Davey, have your red meal now and your white meal for breakfast,' said Uncle Matthew. 'I've opened some Mouton Rothschild, and I know how much you like that—I opened it specially for you.'

'Oh, it is too bad,' said Davey, 'because I happen to know that there are kippers for breakfast, and I do so love them. What a ghastly decision. No! it must be an egg now, with a little hock. I could never forgo the kippers, so delicious, so digestible, but, above all, so full of proteins.'

'Kippers,' said Bob, 'are brown.'

'Brown counts as red. Surely you can see that.'

But when a chocolate cream, in generous supply, but never quite enough when the boys were at home, came round, it was seen to count as white. The Radletts often had cause to observe that you could never entirely rely upon Davey to refuse food, however unwholesome, if it was really delicious.

Aunt Sadie was making heavy weather with Sir Leicester. He was full of boring herbaceous enthusiasms, and took it for granted that she was too.

'What a lot you London people always know about gardens,' she said. 'You must talk to Davey, he is a great gardener.'

'I am not really a London person,' said Sir Leicester, reproachfully. 'I work in London, but my home is in Surrey.'

'I count that,' Aunt Sadie said, gently but firmly, 'as the same.'

The evening seemed endless. The Kroesigs obviously longed for bridge, and did not seem to care so much for racing demon when it was offered as a

substitute. Sir Leicester said he had had a tiring week, and really should go to bed early.

'Don't know how you chaps can stand it,' said Uncle Matthew, sympathetically. 'I was saying to the bank manager at Merlinford only yesterday, it must be the hell of a life fussing about with other blokes' money all day, indoors.'

Linda went to ring up Lord Merlin, who had just returned from abroad. Tony followed her, they were gone a long time, and came back looking flushed and rather self-conscious.

The next morning, as we were hanging about in the hall waiting for the kippers, which had already announced themselves with a heavenly smell, two breakfast trays were seen going upstairs, for Sir Leicester and Lady Kroesig.

'No, really, that beats everything, dammit,' said Uncle Matthew. 'I never heard of a *man* having breakfast in bed before.' And he looked wistfully at his entrenching tool.

He was slightly mollified, however, when they came downstairs, just before eleven, all ready to go to church. Uncle Matthew was a great pillar of the church, read the lessons, chose the hymns, and took round the bag, and he liked his household to attend. Alas, the Kroesigs turned out to be blasted idolaters, as was proved when they turned sharply to the east during the creed. In short, they were of the company of those who could do no right, and sighs of relief echoed through the house when they decided to catch an evening train back to London.

'Tony is Bottom to Linda, isn't he?' I said, sadly.

Davey and I were walking together through Hen's Grove the next day. Davey always knew what you meant, it was one of the nice things about him.

'Bottom,' he said sadly. He adored Linda.

'And nothing will wake her up?'

'Not before it's too late,' I fear. Poor Linda, she has an intensely romantic character, which is fatal for a woman. Fortunately for them, and for all of us, most women are madly *terre à terre*, otherwise the world could hardly carry on.'

Lord Merlin was braver than the rest of us, and said right out what he thought. Linda went over to see him and asked him.

'Are you pleased about my engagement?' to which he replied:

'No, of course not. Why are you doing it?'

'I'm in love,' said Linda proudly.

'What makes you think so?'

'One doesn't think, one knows,' she said.

'Fiddlesticks.'

'Oh, you evidently don't understand about love, so what's the use of talking to you.'

Lord Merlin got very cross, and said that neither did immature little girls understand about love.

'Love,' he said, 'is for grown-up people, as you will discover one day. You will also discover that it has nothing to do with marriage. I'm all in favour of you marrying soon, in a year or two, but for God's sake, and all of our sakes, don't go and marry a bore like Tony Kroesig.'

'If he's such a bore, why did you ask him to stay?'

'I didn't ask him. Baby brought him, because Cecil had 'flu and couldn't come. Besides, I can't guess you'll go and marry every stopgap I have in my house.'

'You ought to be more careful. Anyhow, I can't think why you say Tony's a bore, he knows everything.'

'Yes, that's exactly it, he does. And what about Sir Leicester? And have you seen Lady Kroesig?'

But the Kroesig family was illuminated for Linda by the great glow of perfection which shone around Tony, and she would hear nothing against them. She parted rather coldly from Lord Merlin, came home, and abused him roundly. As for him, he waited to see what Sir Leicester was giving her for a wedding present. It was a pigskin dressing-case with dark tortoiseshell fittings and her initials on them in gold. Lord Merlin sent her a morocco one double the size, fitted with blonde tortoiseshell, and instead of initials, LINDA in diamonds.

He had embarked upon an elaborate series of Kroesig-teases of which this was to be the first.

The arrangements for the wedding did not go smoothly. There was trouble without end over settlements. Uncle Matthew, whose estate provided a certain sum of money for younger children, to be allocated by him as he thought best, very naturally did not wish to settle anything on Linda, at the expense of the others, in view of the fact that she was marrying the son of a millionaire. Sir Leicester, however, refused to settle a penny unless Uncle Matthew did—he had no great wish to make a settlement in any case, saying that it was against the policy of his family to tie up capital sums. In the end, by sheer persistence, Uncle Matthew got a beggarly amount for Linda. The whole thing worried and upset him very much, and confirmed him, if need be, in his hatred of the Teutonic race.

Tony and his parents wanted a London wedding, Uncle Matthew said he had never heard of anything so common and vulgar in his life. Women were married from their homes; he thought fashionable weddings the height of degradation, and refused to lead one of his daughters up the aisle of St. Margaret's through a crowd of gaping strangers. The Kroesigs explained to Linda that, if she had a country wedding, she would only get half the amount of wedding presents, and also that the important, influential people, who would be of use, later, to Tony, would never come down to Gloucestershire in the depth of winter. All these arguments were lost on Linda. Since the days when she was planning to marry the Prince of Wales she had had a mental picture of what her wedding would be like, that is, as much like a wedding in a pantomime as possible, in a large church, with crowds both outside and in, with photographers, arum lilies, tulle, bridesmaids, and an enormous choir singing her favourite tune, 'The Lost Chord'. So she sided with the Kroesigs against poor Uncle Matthew, and, when fate tipped the scales in their favour by putting out of action the heating in Alconleigh church, Aunt Sadie took a London house, and the wedding was duly celebrated with every circumstance of publicized vulgarity at St. Margaret's.

What with one thing and another, by the time Linda was married, her parents and her parents-in-law were no longer on speaking terms. Uncle Matthew cried without restraint all through the ceremony; Sir Leicester seemed to be beyond tears.

CHAPTER X

I THINK Linda's marriage was a failure almost from the beginning, but I really never knew much about it. Nobody did. She had married in the face of a good deal of opposition; the opposition proved to have been entirely well founded, and, Linda being what she was, maintained, for as long as possible, a perfect shop-front.

They were married in February, had a hunting honeymoon from a house they took at Melton, and settled down for good in Bryanston Square, after Easter. Tony then started work in his father's old bank, and prepared to step into a safe Conservative seat in the House of Commons, an ambition which was very soon realized.

Closer acquaintanceship with their new in-laws did not make either the Radlett or the Kroesig families change their minds about each other. The Kroesigs thought Linda eccentric, affected, and extravagant. Worst of all, she was supposed not to be useful to Tony in his career. The Radletts considered that Tony was a first-class bore. He had a habit of choosing a subject, and then droning round and round it like an inaccurate bomb-aimer round his target, ever unable to hit; he knew vast quantities of utterly dreary facts, of which he did not hesitate to inform his companions, at great length and in great detail, whether they appeared to be interested or not. He was infinitely serious, he no longer laughed at Linda's jokes, and the high spirits which, when she first knew him, he had seemed to possess, must have been due to youth, drink, and good health. Now that he was grown up and married he put all three resolutely behind him, spending his days in the bank house and his evenings at Westminster, never having any fun or breathing fresh air: his true self emerged, and he was revealed as a pompous, money-grubbing ass, more like his father every day.

He did not succeed in making an asset out of Linda. Poor Linda was incapable of understanding the Kroesig point of view; try as she might (and in the beginning she tried very hard, having an infinite desire to please) it remained mysterious to her. The fact is that, for the first time in her life, she found herself face to face with the bourgeois attitude of mind; and the fate often foreseen for me by Uncle Matthew as a result of my middle-class education had actually befallen her. The outward and visible signs which he so deprecated were all there—the Kroesigs said notepaper, perfume, mirror and mantelpiece, they even invited her to call them Father and Mother, which, in the first flush of love, she did, only to spend the rest of her married life trying to get out of it by addressing them to their faces as 'you', and communicating with them by postcard or telegram. Inwardly their spirit was utterly commercial, everything was seen by them in terms of money. It was their barrier, their defence, their hope for the future, their support for the present, it raised them above their fellowmen, and with it they warded off evil. The only mental qualities that they respected were those which produced money in substantial quantities, it was their one criterion of success, it was power and it was glory. To say that a man was poor was to label him a rotter, bad at his job, idle, feckless, immoral. If it was somebody whom they really rather liked, in spite of this cancer, they could add that he had been unlucky. They had taken care to insure against this deadly evil in many ways. That it should not overwhelm them through such cataclysms beyond their control as war or revolution they had placed huge sums of money in a dozen different countries; they owned ranches, and estancias, and South African farms, an hotel in Switzerland, a plantation in Malaya, and they possessed many fine diamonds, not sparkling round Linda's lovely neck to be sure, but lying in banks, stone by stone, easily portable.

Linda's upbringing had made all this incomprehensible to her; for money was a subject that was absolutely never mentioned at Alconleigh. Uncle Matthew had no doubt a large income, but it was derived from, tied up in, and a good percentage of it went back into, his land. His land was to him something sacred, and, sacred above that, was England. Should evil befall his country he would stay and share it, or die, never would the notion have entered his head that he might save himself, and leave old England in any sort of lurch. He, his family, and his estates were part of her and she was part of him, for ever and ever. Later on, when war appeared to be looming upon the horizon, Tony tried to persuade him to send some money to America.

'What for?' said Uncle Matthew.

'You might be glad to go there yourself, or send the children. It's always a good thing to have——'

'I may be old, but I can still shoot,' said Uncle Matthew, furiously, 'and I haven't got any children—for the purposes of fighting they are all grown up.'

'Victoria——'

'Victoria is thirteen. She would do her duty. I hope, if any bloody foreigners ever got here, that every man, woman and child would go on fighting them until one side or the other was wiped out. Anyhow, I loathe abroad, nothing would induce me to live there, I'd rather live in the game-keeper's hut in Hen's Grove, and, as for foreigners, they are all the same, and they all make me sick,' he said, pointedly, glowering at Tony, who took no notice, but went droning on about how clever he had been in transferring various funds to various places. He had always remained perfectly unaware of Uncle Matthew's dislike for him, and, indeed, such was my uncle's eccentricity of behaviour, that it was not very easy for somebody as thick-skinned as Tony to differentiate between Uncle Matthew's behaviour towards those he loved and those he did not.

On the first birthday she had after her marriage, Sir Leicester gave Linda a cheque for £1,000. Linda was delighted and spent it that very day on a necklace of large half pearls surrounded by rubies, which she had been admiring for some time in a Bond Street shop. The Kroesigs had a small family dinner party for her, Tony was to meet her there, having been kept late at his office. Linda arrived, wearing a very plain white satin dress cut very low, and her necklace, went straight up to Sir Leicester, and said: 'Oh, you were kind to give me such a wonderful present—look——'

Sir Leicester was stupefied.

'Did it cost all I sent you?' he said.

'Yes,' said Linda. 'I thought you would like me to buy one thing with it, and always remember it was you who gave it to me.'

'No, dear. That wasn't at all what I intended. £1,000 is what you might call a capital sum, that means something on which you expect a return. You should not just spend it on a trinket which you wear three or four times a year, and which is most unlikely to appreciate in value. (And, by the way, if you buy jewels, let it always be diamonds—rubies and pearls are too easy to copy, they won't keep their price.) But, as I was saying, one hopes for a return. So you could either have asked Tony to invest it for you, or, which is what I really intended, you could have spent it on entertaining important people who would be of use to Tony in his career.'

These important people were a continual thorn in poor Linda's side. She was always supposed by the Kroesigs to be a great hindrance to Tony, both in politics and in the City, because, try as she might, she could not disguise how tedious they seemed to her. Like Aunt Sadie, she was apt to retire into a

cloud of boredom on the smallest provocation, a vague look would come into her eyes, and her spirit would absent itself. Important people did not like
this; they were not accustomed to it; they like to be listened and attended to
by the young with concentrated deference when they were so kind as to
bestow their company. What with Linda's yawns, and Tony informing
them how many harbour-masters there were in the British Isles, important
people were inclined to eschew the young Kroesigs. The old Kroesigs deeply
deplored this state of affairs, for which they blamed Linda. They saw that
she did not take the slightest interest in Tony's work. She tried to at first but
it was beyond her; she simply could not understand how somebody who
already had plenty of money could go and shut himself away from God's
fresh air and blue skies, from the spring, the summer, the autumn, the winter, letting them merge into each other unaware that they were passing,
simply in order to make more. She was far too young to be interested in
politics, which were anyhow, in those days before Hitler came along to
brighten them up, a very esoteric amusement.

'Your father was cross,' she said to Tony, as they walked home after
dinner. Sir Leicester lived in Hyde Park Gardens; it was a beautiful night,
so they walked.

'I don't wonder,' said Tony shortly.

'But look, darling, how pretty is it. Don't you see how one couldn't
resist it?'

'You are so affected. Do try and behave like an adult, won't you?'

The autumn after Linda's marriage Aunt Emily took a little house in St.
Leonard's Terrace, where she, Davey and I installed ourselves. She had been
rather unwell, and Davey thought it would be a good thing to get her away
from all her country duties and to make her rest, as no woman ever can at
home. His novel, *The Abrasive Tube*, had just appeared, and was having a
great success in intellectual circles, It was a psychological and physiological
study of a South Polar explorer, snowed up in a hut where he knows he must
eventually die, with enough rations to keep him going for a few months.
In the end he dies. Davey was fascinated by Polar expeditions; he liked to
observe, from a safe distance, how far the body can go when driven upon
thoroughly indigestible foodstuffs deficient in vitamins.

'Pemmican,' he would say, gleefully falling upon the delicious food for
which Aunt Emily's cook was renowned, 'must have been so bad for them.'

Aunt Emily, shaken out of the routine of her life at Shenley, took up with
old friends again, entertained for us, and enjoyed herself so much that she
talked of living half the year in London. As for me, I have never, before or
since, been happier. The London season I had with Linda had been the
greatest possible fun; it would be untrue and ungrateful to Aunt Sadie to
deny that; I had even quite enjoyed the long dark hours we spent in the

Peeresses' gallery; but there had been a curious unreality about it all, it was not related, one felt, to life. Now I had my feet firmly planted on the ground. I was allowed to do what I liked, see whom I chose, at any hour, peacefully, naturally, and without breaking rules, and it was wonderful to bring my friends home and have them greeted in a friendly, if somewhat detached manner, by Davey, instead of smuggling them up the back stairs for fear of a raging scene in the hall.

During this happy time I became happily engaged to Alfred Wincham, then a young don at, now Warden of, St. Peter's College, Oxford. With this kindly scholarly man I have been perfectly happy ever since, finding in our home at Oxford that refuge from the storms and puzzles of life which I had always wanted. I say no more about him here; this is Linda's story, not mine.

We saw a great deal of Linda just then; she would come and chat for hours on end. She did not seem to be unhappy, though I felt sure she was already waking from her Titania-trance, but was obviously lonely, as her husband was at his work all day and at the House in the evening. Lord Merlin was abroad, and she had, as yet, no other very intimate friends; she missed the comings and goings, the cheerful bustle and hours of pointless chatter which had made up the family life at Alconleigh. I reminded her how much, when she was there, she had longed to escape, and she agreed, rather doubtfully, that it was wonderful to be on one's own. She was much pleased by my engagement, and liked Alfred.

'He has such a serious, clever look,' she said. 'What pretty little black babies you'll have, both of you so dark.'

He only quite liked her; he suspected that she was a tough nut, and rather, I must own, to my relief, she never exercised over him the spell in which she had entranced Davey and Lord Merlin.

One day, as we were busy with wedding invitations, she came in and announced:

'I am in pig, what d'you think of that?'

'A most hideous expression, Linda dear,' said Aunt Emily, 'but I suppose we must congratulate you.'

'I suppose so,' said Linda. She sank into a chair with an enormous sigh. 'I feel awfully ill, I must say.'

'But think how much good it will do you in the long run,' said Davey, enviously, 'such a wonderful clear-out.'

'I see just what you mean,' said Linda. 'Oh, we've got such a ghastly evening ahead of us. Some important Americans. It seems Tony wants to do a deal or something, and these Americans will only do the deal if they take a fancy to me. Now can you explain that? I know I shall be sick all over them, and my father-in-law will be so cross. Oh, the horror of important people— you are lucky not to know any.'

Linda's child, a girl, was born in May. She was ill for a long time before, and very ill indeed at her confinement. The doctors told her that she must never have another child, as it would almost certainly kill her if she did. This was a blow to the Kroesigs, as bankers, it seems, like kings, require many sons, but Linda did not appear to mind at all. She took no interest whatever in the baby she had got. I went to see her as soon as I was allowed to. She lay in a bower of blossom and pink roses, and looked like a corpse. I was expecting a baby myself, and naturally took a great interest in Linda's.

'What are you going to call her—where is she, anyway?'

'In Sister's room—it shrieks. Moira, I believe.'

'Not Moira, darling, you can't. I never heard such an awful name.'

'Tony likes it, he had a sister called Moira who died, and what d'you think I found out (not from him, but from their old nanny)? She died because Marjorie whacked her on the head with a hammer when she was four months old. Do you call that interesting? And then they say we are an uncontrolled family—why even Fa has never actually murdered anybody, or do you count that beater?'

'All the same, I don't see how you can saddle the poor little thing with a name like Moira, it's too unkind.'

'Not really, if you think. It'll have to grow up a Moira if the Kroesigs are to like it (people always grow up to their names I've noticed) and they might as well like it because frankly, I don't.'

'Linda, how can you be so naughty, and, anyway, you can't possibly tell whether you like her or not, yet.'

'Oh, yes I can. I can always tell if I like people from the start, and I don't like Moira, that's all. She's a fearful Counter-Hon, wait till you see her.'

At this point the Sister came in, and Linda introduced us.

'Oh, you are the cousin I hear so much about,' she said. 'You'll want to see the baby.'

She went away and presently returned carrying a Moses basket full of wails.

'Poor thing,' said Linda indifferently. 'It's really kinder not to look.'

'Don't pay any attention to her,' said the Sister. 'She pretends to be a wicked woman, but it's all put on.'

I did look, and, deep down among the frills and lace, there was the usual horrid sight of a howling orange in a fine black wig.

'Isn't she sweet,' said the Sister. 'Look at her little hands.'

I shuddered slightly, and said:

'Well, I know it's dreadful of me, but I don't much like them as small as that; I'm sure she'll be divine in a year or two.'

The wails now entered on a crescendo, and the whole room was filled with hideous noise.

'Poor soul,' said Linda. 'I think it must have caught sight of itself in a glass. Do take it away, Sister.'

24

Davey now came into the room. He was meeting me there to drive me down to Shenley for the night. The Sister came back and shooed us both off, saying that Linda had had enough. Outside her room, which was in the largest and most expensive nursing home in London, I paused, looking for the lift.

'This way,' said Davey, and then, with a slightly self-conscious giggle: '*Nourri dans le sérail, j'en connais les détours.* Oh, how are you, Sister Thesiger? How very nice to see you.'

'Captain Warbeck—I must tell Matron you are here.'

And it was nearly an hour before I could drag Davey out of this home from home. I hope I am not giving the impression that Davey's whole life was centred round his health. He was fully occupied with his work, writing, and editing a literary review, but his health was his hobby, and, as such, more in evidence during his spare time, the time when I saw most of him. How he enjoyed it! He seemed to regard his body with the affectionate preoccupation of a farmer towards a pig—not a good doer, the small one of the litter, which must somehow be made to be a credit to the farm. He weighed it, sunned it, aired it, exercised it, and gave it special diets, new kinds of patent food and medicine, but all in vain. It never put on so much as a single ounce of weight, it never became a credit to the farm, but, somehow it lived, enjoying good things, enjoying its life, though falling victim to the ills that flesh is heir to, and other, imaginary ills as well, through which it was nursed with unfailing care, with concentrated attention, by the good farmer and his wife.

Aunt Emily said at once, when I told her about Linda and poor Moira:

'She's too young. I don't believe very young mothers ever get wrapped up in their babies. It's when women are older that they so adore their children, and maybe it's better for the children to have young unadoring mothers and to lead more detached lives.'

'But Linda seems to loathe her.'

'That's so like Linda,' said Davey. 'She has to do things by extremes.'

'But she seemed so gloomy. You must say that's not very like her.'

'She's been terribly ill,' said Aunt Emily. 'Sadie was in despair. Twice they thought she would die.'

'Don't talk of it,' said Davey. 'I can't imagine the world without Linda.'

CHAPTER XI

LIVING in Oxford, engrossed with my husband and young family, I saw less of Linda during the next few years than at any time in her life. This, however, did not affect the intimacy of our relationship, which remained absolute, and, when we did meet, it was still as though we were seeing each other every day. I stayed with her in London from time to time, and she with me in Oxford, and we corresponded regularly. I may as well say here that the one thing she never discussed with me was the deterioration of her marriage; in any case it would not have been necessary, the whole thing being as plain as relations between married people ever can be. Tony was, quite obviously, not good enough as a lover to make up, even at first, for his shortcomings in other respects, the boredom of his company and the mediocrity of his character. Linda was out of love with him by the time the child was born, and, thereafter, could not care a rap for the one or the other. The young man she had fallen in love with, handsome, gay, intellectual and domineering, melted away upon closer acquaintance, and proved to have been a chimera, never to have existed outside her imagination. Linda did not commit the usual fault of blaming Tony for what was entirely her own mistake, she merely turned from him in absolute indifference. This was made easier by the fact that she saw so little of him.

Lord Merlin now launched a tremendous Kroesig-tease. The Kroesigs were always complaining that Linda never went out, would not entertain, unless absolutely forced to, and did not care for society. They told their friends that she was a country girl, entirely sporting, that if you went into her drawing-room she would be found training a retriever with dead rabbits hidden behind the sofa cushions. They pretended that she was an amiable, half-witted, beautiful rustic, incapable of helping poor Tony, who was obliged to battle his way through life alone. There was a grain of truth in all this, the fact being that the Kroesig circle of acquaintances was too ineffably boring; poor Linda, having been unable to make any headway at all in it, had given up the struggle, and retired to the more congenial company of retrievers and dormice.

Lord Merlin, in London for the first time since Linda's marriage, at once introduced her into his world, the world towards which she had always looked, that of smart bohemianism; and here she found her feet, was entirely happy, and had an immediate and great success. She became very gay and went everywhere. There is no more popular unit in London society than a young, beautiful, but perfectly respectable woman who can be asked to dinner without her husband, and Linda was soon well on the way to having her head turned. Photographers and gossip writers dogged her footsteps, and indeed one could not escape the impression, until half an hour of her company put one right again, that she was becoming a bit of a bore. Her house was full of people from morning till night, chatting. Linda, who loved to chat, found many congenial spirits in the carefree, pleasure-seeking London of those days, when unemployment was rife as much among the upper as the lower classes. Young men, pensioned off by their relations, who would sometimes suggest in a perfunctory manner that it might be a good thing if they found some work, but without seriously helping them to do so (and, anyhow, what work was there for such as they?) clustered round Linda like bees round honey, buzz, buzz, buzz, chat, chat, chat. In her bedroom, on her bed, sitting on the stairs outside while she had a bath, in the kitchen while she ordered the food, shopping, walking round the park, cinema, theatre, opera, ballet, dinner, supper, night clubs, parties, dances, all day, all night— endless, endless, chat.

'But what do you suppose they talk about?' Aunt Sadie, disapproving, used to wonder. What, indeed?

Tony went early to his bank, hurrying out of the house with an air of infinite importance, an attaché case in one hand and a sheaf of newspapers under his arm. His departure heralded the swarm of chatterers, almost as if they had been waiting round the street corner to see him leave, and there- after the house was filled with them. They were very nice, very good-look- ing, and great fun—their manners were perfect. I never was able, during my short visits, to distinguish them much one from another, but I saw their attraction, the unfailing attraction of vitality and high spirits. By no stretch of the imagination, however, could they have been called 'important', and the Kroesigs were beside themselves at this turn of affairs.

Tony did not seem to mind; he had long given up Linda as hopeless from the point of view of his career, and was rather pleased and flattered by the publicity which now launched her as a beauty. 'The beautiful wife of a clever young M.P.' Besides, he found that they were invited to large parties and balls, to which it suited him very well to go, coming late after the House, and where there were often to be found not only Linda's unimportant friends, with whom she would amuse herself, but also colleagues of his own, and by no means unimportant ones, whom he could buttonhole and bore at the bar. It would have been useless, however, to explain this to the old Kroesigs, who had a deeply rooted mistrust of smart society, of dancing, and of any kind of fun, all of which led, in their opinion, to extravagance, without compensating material advantages. Fortunately for Linda, Tony at this time was not on good terms with his father, owing to a conflict of policies in the bank; they did not go to Hyde Park Gardens as much as when they were first married, and visits to Planes, the Kroesig house in Surrey, were, for the time being, off. When they did meet, however, the old Kroesigs made it clear to Linda that she was not proving a satisfactory daughter-in-law. Even Tony's divergence of views was put down to her, and Lady Kroesig told her friends, with a sad shake of the head, that Linda did not bring out the best in him.

Linda now proceeded to fritter away years of her youth, with nothing whatever to show for them. If she had had an intellectual upbringing the place of all this pointless chatter, jokes and parties might have been taken by a serious interest in the arts, or by reading; if she had been happy in her marriage that side of her nature which craved for company could have found its fulfilment by the nursery fender; things being as they were, however, all was frippery and silliness.

Alfred and I once had an argument with Davey about her, during which we said all this. Davey accused us of being prigs, though at heart he must have known that we were right.

'But Linda gives one so much pleasure,' he kept saying, 'she is like a bunch of flowers. You don't want people like that to bury themselves in serious reading; what would be the good?'

However, even he was forced to admit that her behaviour to poor little Moira was not what it should be. (The child was fat, fair, placid, dull and backward, and Linda still did not like her; the Kroesigs, on the other hand, adored her, and she spent more and more time, with her nanny, at Planes. They loved having her there, but that did not stop them from ceaseless criticism of Linda's behaviour. They now told everybody that she was a silly society butterfly, hard-hearted neglecter of her child.)

Alfred said, almost angrily:

'It's so odd that she doesn't even have love affairs. I don't see what she gets out of her life, it must be dreadfully empty.'

Alfred likes people to be filed neatly away under some heading that he can understand; careerist, social climber, virtuous wife and mother, or adulteress.

Linda's social life was completely aimless; she simply collected around her an assortment of cosy people who had the leisure to chat all day; whether they were millionaires or paupers, princes or refugee Rumanians, was a matter of complete indifference to her. In spite of the fact that, except for me and her sisters, nearly all her friends were men, she had such a reputation for virtue that she was currently suspected of being in love with her husband.

'Linda believes in love,' said Davey, 'she is passionately romantic. At the moment I am sure she is, subconsciously, waiting for an irresistible temptation. Casual affairs would not interest her in the least. One must hope that when it comes it will not prove to be another Bottom.'

'I suppose she is really rather like my mother,' I said, 'and all of hers have been Bottoms.'

'Poor Bolter!' said Davey, 'but she's happy now, isn't she, with her white hunter?'

Tony soon became, as was to be expected, a perfect mountain of pomposity, more like his father every day. He was full of large, clear-sighted ideas for bettering the condition of the capitalist classes, and made no bones of his hatred and distrust of the workers.

'I hate the lower classes,' he said one day, when Linda and I were having tea with him on the terrace of the House of Commons. 'Ravening beasts, trying to get my money. Let them try, that's all.'

'Oh, shut up, Tony,' said Linda, bringing a dormouse out of her pocket, and feeding it with crumbs. 'I love them, anyway I was brought up with them. The trouble with you is you don't know the lower classes and you don't belong to the upper classes, you're just a rich foreigner who happens to live here. Nobody ought to be in Parliament who hasn't lived in the country, anyhow part of their life—why, my old Fa knows more what he's talking about, when he does talk in the House, than you do.'

'I have lived in the country,' said Tony. 'Put that dormouse away, people are looking.'

He never got cross, he was far too pompous.

'Surrey,' said Linda, with infinite contempt.

'Anyhow, last time your Fa made a speech, about the Peeresses in their own right, his only argument for keeping them out of the House was that, if once they got in, they might use the Peers' lavatory.'

'Isn't he a love?' said Linda. 'It's what they all thought, you know, but he was the only one who dared to say it.'

'That's the worst of the House of Lords,' said Tony. 'These backwoodsmen come along just when they think they will, and bring the whole place into disrepute with a few dotty remarks, which get an enormous amount of publicity and give people the impression that we are governed by a lot of lunatics. These old peers ought to realize that it's their duty to their class to stay at home and keep quiet. The amount of excellent, solid, necessary work done in the House of Lords is quite unknown to the man in the street.'

Sir Leicester was expecting soon to become a peer, so this was a subject close to Tony's heart. His general attitude to what he called the man in the street was that he ought constantly to be covered by machine-guns; this having become impossible, owing to the weakness, in the past, of the great Whig families, he must be doped into submission with the fiction that huge reforms, to be engineered by the Conservative party, were always just round the next corner. Like this he could be kept quiet indefinitely, as long as there was no war. War brings people together and opens their eyes, it must be avoided at all costs, and especially war with Germany, where the Kroesigs had financial interests and many relations. (They were originally a Junkers family, and snubbed their Prussian connections as much as the latter looked down on them for being in trade.)

Both Sir Leicester and his son were great admirers of Herr Hitler; Sir Leicester had been to see him during a visit to Germany, and had been taken for a drive in a Mercedes-Benz by Dr. Schacht.

Linda took no interest in politics, but she was instinctively and unreasonably English. She knew that one Englishman was worth a hundred foreigners, whereas Tony thought that one capitalist was worth a hundred workers. Their outlook upon this, as upon most subjects, differed fundamentally.

CHAPTER XII

By a curious irony of fate it was at her father-in-law's house in Surrey that Linda met Christian Talbot. The little Moira, aged six, now lived permanently at Planes; it seemed a good arrangement as it saved Linda, who disliked housekeeping, the trouble of running two establishments, while Moira was given the benefit of country air and food. Linda and Tony were supposed to spend a couple of nights there every week, and Tony generally did so. Linda, in fact, went down for Sunday about once a month.

Planes was a horrible house. It was an overgrown cottage, that is to say, the rooms were large, with all the disadvantages of a cottage, low ceilings, small windows with diamond panes, uneven floorboards, and a great deal of naked knotted wood. It was furnished neither in good nor in bad taste, but simply with no attempt at taste at all, and was not even very comfortable. The garden which lay around it would be a lady water-colourist's heaven, herbaceous borders, rockeries and water-gardens were carried to a perfection of vulgarity, and flaunted a riot of huge and hideous flowers, each individual bloom appearing twice as large, three times as brilliant as it ought to have been and if possible of a different colour from that which nature intended. It would be hard to say whether it was more frightful, more like glorious Technicolor, in spring, in summer, or in autumn. Only in the depth of winter, covered by the kindly snow, did it melt into the landscape and become tolerable.

One April Saturday morning, in 1937, Linda, with whom I had been staying in London, took me down there for the night, as she sometimes did. I think she liked to have a buffer between herself and the Kroesigs, perhaps especially between herself and Moira. The old Kroesigs were by way of being very fond of me, and Sir Leicester sometimes took me for walks and hinted how much he wished that it had been me, so serious, so well educated, such a good wife and mother, whom Tony had married.

We motored down past acres of blossom.

'The great difference,' said Linda, 'between Surrey and proper, real country, is that in Surrey, when you see blossom, you know there will be no fruit. Think of the Vale of Evesham, and then look at all this pointless pink stuff—it gives you quite a different feeling. The garden at Planes will be a riot of sterility, just you wait.'

It was. You could hardly see any beautiful, pale, bright, yellow-green of spring, every tree appeared to be entirely covered with a waving mass of pink or mauve tissue-paper. The daffodils were so thick on the ground that they too obscured the green, they were new varieties of a terrifying size, either dead white or dark yellow, thick and fleshy; they did not look at all like the fragile friends of one's childhood. The whole effect was of a scene for musical comedy, and it exactly suited Sir Leicester, who, in the country, gave a surprisingly adequate performance of the old English squire. Picturesque. Delightful.

He was pottering in the garden as we drove up, in an old pair of corduroy trousers, so much designed as an old pair that it seemed improbable that they had ever been new, an old tweed coat on the same lines, secateurs in his hand, a depressed Corgi at his heels, and a mellow smile on his face.

'Here you are,' he said, heartily. (One could almost see, as in the strip advertisements, a bubble coming out of his head—thinks—'You are a most unsatisfactory daughter-in-law, but nobody can say it's our fault, we always have a welcome and a kind smile for you.') 'Car going well, I hope? Tony and Moira have gone out riding, I thought you might have passed them. Isn't the garden looking grand just now, I can hardly bear to go to London and leave all this beauty with no one to see it. Come for a stroll before lunch—Foster will see to your gear—just ring the front-door bell, Fanny, he may not have heard the car.'

He led us off into Madam Butterfly-land.

'I must warn you,' he said, 'that we have got rather a rough diamond coming to lunch. I don't know if you've ever met old Talbot who lives in the village, the old professor? Well, his son, Christian. He's by way of being rather a Communist, a clever chap gone all wrong, and a journalist on some daily rag. Tony can't bear him, never could as a child, and he's very cross with me for asking him to-day, but I always think it's as well to see something of these Left-wing fellows. If people like us are nice to them they can be tamed wonderfully.'

He said this in the tone of one who might have saved the life of a Communist in the war, and, by this act, turned him, through gratitude, into a true blue Tory. But in the first world war Sir Leicester had considered that, with his superior brain, he would have been wasted as cannon fodder, and had fixed himself in an office in Cairo. He neither saved nor took any lives, nor did he risk his own, but built up many valuable business contacts, became a major and got an O.B.E., thus making the best of all worlds.

So Christian came to luncheon, and behaved with the utmost intransigence. He was an extraordinarily handsome young man, tall and fair, in a completely different way from that of Tony, thin and very English-looking. His clothes were outrageous—he wore a really old pair of grey flannel trousers, full of little round moth-holes in the most embarrassing places, no coat, and a flannel shirt, one of the sleeves of which had a tattered tear from wrist to elbow.

'Has your father been writing anything lately?' Lady Kroesig asked, as they sat down to luncheon.

'I suppose so,' said Christian, 'as it's his profession. I can't say I've asked him, but one assumes he has, just as one assumes that Tony has been banking something lately.'

He then planted his elbow, bare through the rent, on to the table between himself and Lady Kroesig and swivelling right round to Linda, who was on his other side, he told her, at length and in immense detail, of a production of *Hamlet* he had seen lately in Moscow. The cultured Kroesigs listened attentively, throwing off occasional comments calculated to show that they knew *Hamlet* well—'I don't think that quite fits in with my idea of Ophelia', or 'But Polonius was a very old man', to all of which Christian turned an utterly deaf ear, gobbling his food with one hand, his elbow on the table, his eyes on Linda.

After luncheon he said to Linda:

'Come back and have tea with my father, you'd like him', and they went off together, leaving the Kroesigs to behave for the rest of the afternoon like a lot of hens who have seen a fox.

Sir Leicester took me to his water-garden, which was full of enormous pink forget-me-nots, and dark-brown irises, and said:

'It is really rather too bad of Linda, little Moira has been so much looking forward to showing her the ponies. That child idolizes her mother.'

She didn't, actually, in the least. She was fond of Tony and quite indifferent to Linda, calm and stolid and not given to idolatry, but it was part of the Kroesigs' creed that children should idolize their mothers.

'Do you know Pixie Townsend?' he asked me, suddenly.

'No,' I said, which was true, nor did I then know anything about her. 'Who is she?'

'She's a very delightful person.' He changed the subject.

Linda returned just in time to dress for dinner, looking extremely beautiful. She made me come and chat while she had her bath—Tony was reading to Moira upstairs in the night nursery. Linda was perfectly enchanted with her outing. Christian's father, she said, lived in the smallest house imaginable, an absolute contrast to what Christian called the Kroesighof, because, although absolutely tiny, it had nothing whatever of a cottage about it—it was in the grand manner, and full of books. Every available wall space was covered with books, they lay stacked on tables and chairs and in heaps on the floor. Mr. Talbot was the exact opposite of Sir Leicester, there was nothing picturesque about him, or anything to indicate that he was a learned man, he was brisk and matter-of-fact, and had made some very funny jokes about Davey, whom he knew well.

'He's perfect heaven,' Linda kept saying, her eyes shining. What she really meant, as I could see too clearly, was that Christian was perfect heaven. She was dazzled by him. It seemed that he had talked without cease, and his talk consisted of variations upon a single theme—the betterment of the world through political change. Linda, since her marriage, had heard no end of political shop talked by Tony and his friends, but this related politics entirely to personalities and jobs. As the persons all seemed to her infinitely old and dull, and as it was quite immaterial to her whether they got jobs or not, Linda had classed politics as a boring subject, and used to go off into a dream when they were discussed. But Christian's politics did not bore her. As they walked back from his father's house that evening he had taken her for a tour of the world. He showed her Fascism in Italy, Nazism in Germany, civil war in Spain, inadequate Socialism in France, tyranny in Africa, starvation in Asia, reaction in America and Right-wing blight in England. Only the U.S.S.R., Norway and Mexico came in for a modicum of praise.

Linda was a plum ripe for shaking. The tree was now shaken, and down she came. Intelligent and energetic, but with no outlet for her energies, unhappy in her marriage, uninterested in her child, and inwardly oppressed with a sense of futility, she was in the mood either to take up some cause, or to embark upon a love affair. That a cause should now be presented by an attractive young man made both it and him irresistible.

CHAPTER XIII

THE poor Alconleighs were now presented with crises in the lives of three of their children almost simultaneously. Linda ran away from Tony, Jassy ran away from home, and Matt ran away from Eton. The Alconleighs were obliged to face the fact, as parents must sooner or later, that their children had broken loose from control and had taken charge of their own lives. Distracted, disapproving, worried to death, there was nothing they could do; they had become mere spectators of a spectacle which did not please them in the least. This was the year when the parents of our contemporaries would console themselves, if things did not go quite as they hoped for their own children, by saying: 'Never mind, just think of the poor Alconleighs!'

Linda threw discretion, and what worldly wisdom she may have picked up during her years in London society, to the winds; she became an out-and-out Communist, bored and embarrassed everybody to death by preaching her new-found doctrine, not only at the dinner-table, but also from a soap-box in Hyde Park, and other equally squalid rostra, and finally, to the infinite relief of the Kroesig family, she went off to live with Christian. Tony started proceedings for divorce. This was a great blow to my aunt and uncle. It is true that they had never liked Tony, but they were infinitely old-fashioned in their ideas; marriage, to their way of thinking, was marriage, and adultery was wrong. Aunt Sadie was, in particular, profoundly shocked by the light-hearted way in which Linda had abandoned the little Moira. I think it all reminded her too much of my mother, and that she envisaged Linda's future from now on as a series of uncontrollable bolts.

Linda came to see me in Oxford. She was on her way back to London after having broken the news at Alconleigh. I thought it was really very brave of her to do it in person, and indeed, the first thing she asked for (most unlike her) was a drink. She was quite unnerved.

'Goodness,' she said. 'I'd forgotten how terrifying Fa can be—even now, when he's got no power over one. It was just like after we lunched with Tony; in the business-room just the same, and he simply roared, and poor Mummy looked miserable, but she was pretty furious too, and you know how sarcastic she can be. Oh, well, that's over. Darling, it's heaven to see you again.'

I hadn't seen her since the Sunday at Planes when she met Christian, so I wanted to hear all about her life.

'Well,' she said, 'I'm living with Christian in his flat, but it's very small, I must say, but perhaps that is just as well, because I'm doing the housework, and I don't seem to be very good at it, but luckily he is.'

'He'll need to be,' I said.

Linda was notorious in the family for her unhandiness, she could never even tie her own stock, and on hunting days either Uncle Matthew or Josh always had to do it for her. I so well remember her standing in front of a looking-glass in the hall, with Uncle Matthew tying it from behind, both the very picture of concentration, Linda saying: 'Oh, now I see. Next time I know I shall be able to manage.' As she had never in her life done so much as make her own bed, I could not imagine that Christian's flat could be very tidy or comfortable if it was being run by her.

'You are horrid. But oh how dreadful it is, cooking, I mean. That oven—Christian puts things in and says: "Now you take it out in about half an hour". I don't dare tell him how terrified I am, and at the end of half an hour I summon up all my courage and open the oven, and there is that awful hot blast hitting one in the face. I don't wonder people sometimes put their heads in and leave them out of sheer misery. Oh, dear, and I wish you could have seen the Hoover running away with me, it suddenly took the bit between its teeth and made for the lift shaft. How I shrieked—Christian only just rescued me in time. I think housework is far more tiring and frightening than hunting is, no comparison, and yet after hunting we had eggs for tea and were made to rest for hours, but after housework people expect one to go on just as if nothing special had happened.' She sighed.

'Christian is very strong,' she said, 'and very brave. He doesn't like it when I shriek.'

She seemed tired I thought and rather worried, and I looked in vain for signs of great happiness or great love.

'So what about Tony—how has he taken it?'

'Oh, he's awfully pleased, actually, because he can now marry his mistress without having a scandal, or being divorced, or upsetting the Conservative Association.'

It was so like Linda never to have hinted, even to me, that Tony had a mistress.

'Who is she?' I said.

'Called Pixie Townsend. You know, the sort, young face, with white hair dyed blue. She adores Moira, lives near Planes, and takes her out riding every day. She's a terrific Counter-Hon, but I'm only too thankful now that she exists, because I needn't feel in the least bit guilty—they'll all get on so much better without me.'

'Married?'

'Oh, yes, and divorced her husband years ago. She's frightfully good at all poor Tony's things, golf and business and Conservatism, just like I wasn't, and Sir Leicester thinks she's perfect. Goodness, they'll be happy.'

'Now I want to hear more about Christian, please.'

'Well, he's heaven. He's a frightfully serious man, you know, a Communist, and so am I now, and we are surrounded by comrades all day, and they are terrific Hons, and there's an anarchist. The comrades don't like anarchists, isn't it queer? I always thought they were the same thing, but Christian likes this one because he threw a bomb at the King of Spain; you must say it's romantic. He's called Ramon, and he sits about all day and broods over the miners at Oviedo because his brother is one.'

'Yes, but, darling, tell about Christian.'

'Oh, he's perfect heaven—you must come and stay—or perhaps that wouldn't be very comfortable—come and see us. You can't think what an extraordinary man he is, so detached from other human beings that he hardly notices whether they are there or not. He only cares for ideas.'

'I hope he cares for you.'

'Well, I think he does, but he is very strange and absent-minded. I must tell you, the evening before I ran away with him (I only moved down to Pimlico in a taxi, but running away sounds romantic) he dined with his brother, so naturally I thought they'd talk about me and discuss the whole thing, so I couldn't resist ringing him up at about midnight and saying "Hullo, darling, did you have a nice evening, and what did you talk about?" and he said: "I can't remember—oh, guerrilla warfare, I think".'

'Is his brother a Communist too?'

'Oh, no, he's in the Foreign Office. Fearfully grand, looks like a deep-sea monster—you know.'

'Oh, that Talbot—yes, I see. I hadn't connected them. So now what are your plans?'

'Well, he says he's going to marry me when I'm divorced. I think it's rather silly. I rather agree with Mummy that once is enough, for marriage, but he says I'm the kind of person one marries if one's living with them, and the thing is it would be bliss not to be called Kroesig any more. Anyway, we'll see.'

'Then what's your life? I suppose you don't go to parties and things now, do you?'

'Darling, such killing parties, you can't think—he won't let us go to ordinary ones at all. Grandi had a dinner-dance last week, and he rang me up himself and asked me to bring Christian, which I thought was awfully nice of him actually—he always has been nice to me—but Christian got into quite a temper and said if I couldn't see any reason against going I'd better go, but nothing would induce him to. So in the end, of course, neither of us went, and I heard afterwards it was the greatest fun. And we mayn't go to the Ribs or to . . . .' and she mentioned several families known as much for their hospitality as for their Right-wing convictions.

'The worst of being a Communist is that the parties you may go to are—well—awfully funny and touching, but not very gay, and they're always in such gloomy places. Next week, for instance, we've got three, some Czechs at the Sacco and Vanzetti Memorial Hall at Golders Green, Ethiopians at the Paddington Baths, and the Scotsboro' boys at some boring old rooms or other. You know.'

'The Scotsboro' boys,' I said. 'Are they really still going? They must be getting on.'

'Yes, and they've gone downhill socially,' said Linda, with a giggle. 'I remember a perfectly divine party Brian gave for them—it was the first party Merlin ever took me to so I remember it well. Oh, dear, it was fun. But next Thursday won't be the least like that. (Darling, I am being disloyal, but it is such heaven to have a chat after all these months. The comrades are sweet, but they never chat, they make speeches all the time.) But I'm always saying to Christian how much I wish his buddies would either brighten up their parties a bit or else stop giving them, because I don't see the point of sad parties, do you? And Left-wing people are always sad because they mind dreadfully about their causes, and the causes are always going so badly. You see, I bet the Scotsboro' boys will be electrocuted in the end, if they don't die of old age first, that is. One does feel so much on their side, but it's no good, people like Sir Leicester always come out on top, so what can one do? However, the comrades don't seem to realize that, and, luckily for them, they don't know Sir Leicester, so they feel they must go on giving these sad parties.'

'What do you wear at them?' I asked, with some interest, thinking that Linda, in her expensive-looking clothes, must seem very much out of place at these baths and halls.

'You know, that was a great tease at first, it worried me dreadfully, but I've discovered that, so long as one wears wool or cotton, everything is all right. Silk and satin would be the blunder. But I only ever do wear wool and cotton, so I'm on a good wicket. No jewels, of course, but then I left them behind at Bryanston Square, it's the way I was brought up but I must say it gave me a pang. Christian doesn't know about jewellery—I told him, because I thought he'd be rather pleased I'd given them all up for him, but he only said: "Well, there's always the Burma Jewel Company." Oh, dear, he is such a funny man, you must meet him again soon. I must go, darling, it has so cheered me up to see you.'

I don't quite know why, but I felt somehow that Linda had been once more deceived in her emotions, that this explorer in the sandy waste had only seen another mirage. The lake was there, the trees were there, the thirsty camels had gone down to have their evening drink; alas, a few steps forward would reveal nothing but dust and desert as before.

A few minutes only after Linda had left me to go back to London, Christian and the comrades, I had another caller. This time it was Lord Merlin. I liked Lord Merlin very much, I admired him, I was predisposed in his favour, but I was by no means on such intimate terms with him as Linda was. To tell the real truth he frightened me. I felt that, in my company, boredom was for him only just round the corner, and that, anyhow, I was merely regarded as pertaining to Linda, not existing on my own except as a dull little don's wife. I was nothing but the confidante in white linen.

'This is a bad business,' he said, abruptly, and without preamble, though I had not seen him for several years. 'I'm just back from Rome, and what do I find—Linda and Christian Talbot. It's an extraordinary thing that I can't ever leave England without Linda getting herself mixed up with some thoroughly undesirable character. This is a disaster—how far has it gone? Can nothing be done?'

I told him that he had just missed Linda, and said something about her marriage with Tony having been unhappy. Lord Merlin waved this remark aside—it was a disconcerting gesture and made me feel a fool.

'Naturally she never would have stayed with Tony—nobody expected that. The point is that she's out of the frying-pan into an empty grate. How long has it been going on?'

I said I thought it was partly the Communism that had attracted her.

'Linda has always felt the need of a cause.'

'Cause,' he said, scornfully. 'My dear Fanny, I think you are mixing up cause with effect. No, Christian is an attractive fellow, and I quite see that he would provide a perfect reaction from Tony, but it is a disaster. If she is in love with him he will make her miserable, and, if not, it means she has embarked upon a career like your mother's, and that, for Linda, would be very bad indeed. I don't see a ray of comfort anywhere. No money either, of course, and she needs money, she ought to have it.'

He went to the window, and looked across the street at Christ Church gilded by the westerly sun.

'I've known Christian,' he said, 'from a child—his father is a great friend of mine. Christian is a man who goes through the world attached to nobody—people are nothing in his life. The women who have been in love with him have suffered bitterly because he has not even noticed that they are there. I expect he is hardly aware that Linda has moved in on him—his head is in the clouds and he is always chasing after some new idea.'

'This is rather what Linda has just been saying.'

'Oh, she's noticed it already? Well, she is not stupid, and, of course, at first it adds to the attraction—when he comes out of the clouds he is irresistible, I quite see that. But how can they ever settle down? Christian has never had a home, or felt the need for one; he wouldn't know what to do with it—it would hamper him. He'll never sit and chat to Linda, or concentrate upon her in any way, and she is a woman who requires, above all things, a great deal of concentration. Really it is too provoking that I should have been away when this happened, I'm sure I could have stopped it. Now, of course, nobody can.'

He turned from the window and looked at me so angrily that I felt it had all been my fault—actually I think he was unaware of my presence.

'What are they living on?' he said.

'Very little. Linda has a small allowance from Uncle Matthew, I believe, and I suppose Christian makes something from his journalism. I hear the Kroesigs go about saying that there is one good thing, she is sure to starve.'

'Oh, they do, do they?' said Lord Merlin, taking out his notebook, 'can I have Linda's address, please, I am on my way to London now.'

Alfred came in, as usual unaware of exterior events and buried in some pamphlet he was writing.

'You don't happen to know,' he said to Lord Merlin, 'what the daily consumption of milk is in the Vatican City?'

'No, of course not,' said Lord Merlin angrily. 'Ask Tony Kroesig, he'll be sure to. Well, good-bye, Fanny, I'll have to see what I can do.'

What he did was to present Linda with the freehold of a tiny house far down Cheyne Walk. It was the prettiest little dolls' house that ever was seen, on that great bend of the river where Whistler had lived. The rooms were full of reflections of water and full of south and west sunlight; it had a vine and a Trafalgar balcony. Linda adored it. The Bryanston Square house, with an easterly outlook, had been originally dark, cold, and pompous. When Linda had had it done up by some decorating friend, it had become white, cold, and tomblike. The only thing of beauty that she had possessed was a picture, a fat tomato-coloured bathing-woman, which had been given her

by Lord Merlin to annoy the Kroesigs. It had annoyed them, very much.
This picture looked wonderful in the Cheyne Walk house, you could hardly
tell where the real water-reflections ended and the Renoir ones began. The
pleasure which Linda derived from her new surroundings, the relief which
she felt at having once and for all got rid of the Kroesigs, were, I think, laid
by her at Christian's door, and seemed to come from him. Thus the discovery that real love and happiness had once more eluded her was delayed
for quite a long time.

CHAPTER XIV

THE Alconleighs were shocked and horrified over the whole Linda affair,
but they had their other children to think of, and were, just now, making
plans for the coming out of Jassy, who was as pretty as a peach. She, they
hoped, would make up to them for their disappointment with Linda. It was
most unfair, but very typical of them, that Louisa, who had married entirely
in accordance with their wishes and had been a faithful wife and most prolific
mother, having now some five children, hardly seemed to count any more.
They were really rather bored by her.

Jassy went with Aunt Sadie to a few London dances at the end of the
season, just after Linda had left Tony. She was thought to be rather delicate,
and Aunt Sadie had an idea that it would be better for her to come out
properly in the less strenuous autumn season, and, accordingly, in October
took a little house in London into which she prepared to move with a few
servants, leaving Uncle Matthew in the country, to kill various birds and
animals. Jassy complained very much that the young men she had met so far
were dull and hideous, but Aunt Sadie took no notice. She said that all girls
thought this at first, until they fell in love.

A few days before they were to have moved to London Jassy ran away.
She was to have spent a fortnight with Louisa in Scotland, had put Louisa off
without telling Aunt Sadie, had cashed her savings, and, before anybody even
knew that she was missing, had arrived in America. Poor Aunt Sadie
received, out of the blue, a cable saying: 'On way to Hollywood. Don't
worry, Jassy.'

At first the Alconleighs were completely mystified. Jassy had never shown
the smallest interest in stage or cinema, they felt certain she had no wish to
become a film star, and yet, why Hollywood? Then it occurred to them that
Matt might know something, he and Jassy being the two inseparables of the
family, and Aunt Sadie got into the Daimler and rolled over to Eton. Matt
was able to explain everything. He told Aunt Sadie that Jassy was in love with
a film star called Gary Coon (or Carey Coon, he could not remember
which), and that she had written to Hollywood to ask him if he were

married, telling Matt that if he proved not to be she was going straight out there to marry him herself. Matt said all this, in his wobbling half grown-up, half little-boy voice, as if it were the most ordinary situation imaginable.

'So I suppose,' he ended up, 'that she got a letter saying he's not married and just went off. Lucky she had her running away money. What about some tea, Mum?'

Aunt Sadie, deeply preoccupied as she was, knew the rules of behaviour and what was expected of her, and stayed with Matt while he consumed sausages, lobsters, eggs, bacon, fried sole, banana mess and a chocolate sundae.

As always in times of crisis, the Alconleighs now sent for Davey, and, as always, Davey displayed a perfect competence to deal with the situation. He found out in no time that Cary Goon was a second-rate film actor whom Jassy must have seen when she was in London for the last parties of the summer. He had been in a film then showing called *One Splendid Hour*. Davey got hold of the film, and Lord Merlin put it on in his private cinema for the benefit of the family. It was about pirates, and Cary Goon was not even the hero, he was just a pirate and seemed to have nothing in particular to recommend him; no good looks, talent, or visible charm, though he did display a certain agility shinning up and down ropes. He also killed a man with a weapon not unlike the entrenching tool, and this, we felt, may have awakened some hereditary emotion in Jassy's bosom. The film itself was one of those of which it is very difficult for the ordinary English person, as opposed to the film fan, to make head or tail, and every time Cary Goon appeared the scene had to be played over again for Uncle Matthew, who had come determined that no detail should escape him. He absolutely identified the actor with his part, and kept saying:

'What does the fella want to do that for? Bloody fool, he might know there would be an ambush there. I can't hear a word the fella says—put that bit on again, Merlin.'

At the end he said he didn't think much of the cove, he appeared to have no discipline and had been most impertinent to his commanding officer. 'Needs a haircut! and I shouldn't wonder if he drinks.'

Uncle Matthew said how-do-you-do and good-bye quite civilly to Lord Merlin. He really seemed to be mellowing with age and misfortune.

After great consultations it was decided that some member of the family, not Aunt Sadie or Uncle Matthew, would have to go to Hollywood and bring Jassy home. But who? Linda, of course, would have been the obvious person, had she not been under a cloud and, furthermore, engrossed with her own life. But it would be of no use to send one bolter to fetch back another bolter, so somebody else must be found. In the end, after some persuasion ('madly inconvenient just now that I have started this course of *piqûres*') Davey consented to go with Louisa—the good, the sensible Louisa.

By the time this had been decided, Jassy had arrived in Hollywood, had broadcast her matrimonial intentions to all and sundry, and the whole thing appeared in the newspapers, which devoted pages of space to it, and (it was a silly season with nothing else to occupy their readers) turned it into a sort of serial story. Alconleigh now entered upon a state of siege. Journalists braved Uncle Matthew's stock-whips, his bloodhounds, his terrifying blue flashes, and hung around the village, penetrating even into the house itself in their search for local colour. Their stories were a daily delight. Uncle Matthew was made into something between Heathcliff, Dracula, and the Earl of Dorincourt, Alconleigh a sort of Nightmare Abbey or House of Usher, and Aunt Sadie a character not unlike David Copperfield's mother. Such courage, ingenuity and toughness were displayed by these correspondents that it came as no surprise to any of us when, later on, they did so well in the war. 'War report by So-and-So——'

Uncle Matthew would then say:

'Isn't that the damned sewer I found hiding under my bed?'

He greatly enjoyed the whole affair. Here were opponents worthy of him, not jumpy housemaids, and lachrymose governesses with wounded feelings, but tough young men who did not care what methods they used so long as they could get inside his house and produce a story.

He also seemed greatly to enjoy reading about himself in the newspapers and we all began to suspect that Uncle Matthew had a hidden passion for publicity. Aunt Sadie, on the other hand, found the whole thing very distasteful indeed.

It was thought most vital to keep it from the press that Davey and Louisa were leaving on a voyage of rescue, as the sudden surprise of seeing them might prove an important element in influencing Jassy to return. Unfortunately, Davey could not embark on so long and so trying a journey without a medicine chest, specially designed. While this was being made they missed one boat, and, by the time it was ready, the sleuths were on their track—this unlucky medicine chest having played the same part that Marie Antoinette's *nécessaire* did in the escape to Varennes.

Several journalists accompanied them on the crossing, but did not reap much of a reward, as Louisa was prostrated with sea-sickness and Davey spent his whole time closeted with the ship's doctor, who asserted that his trouble was a cramped intestine, which could easily be cured by manipulation, rays, diet, exercises and injections, all of which, or resting after which, occupied every moment of his day.

On their arrival in New York, however, they were nearly torn to pieces, and we were able, in common with the whole of the two great English-speaking nations, to follow their every move. They even appeared on the newsreel, looking worried and hiding their faces behind books.

It proved to have been a useless trip. Two days after their arrival in

Hollywood Jassy became Mrs. Carey Goon. Louisa telegraphed this news home, adding, 'Carey is a terrific Hon'.

There was one comfort, the marriage killed the story.

'He's a perfect dear,' said Davey, on his return. 'A little man like a nut. I'm sure Jassy will be madly happy with him.'

Aunt Sadie, however, was neither reassured nor consoled. It seemed hard luck to have reared a pretty love of a daughter in order for her to marry a little man like a nut, and live with him thousands of miles away. The house in London was cancelled, and the Alconleighs lapsed into such a state of gloom that the next blow, when it fell, was received with fatalism.

Matt, aged sixteen, ran away from Eton, also in a blaze of newspaper publicity, to the Spanish war. Aunt Sadie minded this very much, but I don't think Uncle Matthew did. The desire to fight seemed to him entirely natural, though, of course, he deplored the fact that Matt was fighting for foreigners. He did not take a particular line against the Spanish reds, they were brave boys and had had the good sense to bump off a lot of idolatrous monks, nuns and priests, a proceeding of which he approved, but it was surely a pity to fight in a second-class war when there would so soon be a first-class one available. It was decided that no steps should be taken to retrieve Matt.

Christmas that year was a very sad one at Alconleigh. The children seemed to be melting away like the ten little nigger boys. Bob and Louisa, neither of whom had given their parents one moment of disquiet in their lives, John Fort William, as dull as a man could be, Louisa's children, so good, so pretty, but lacking in any sort of originality, could not make up for the absence of Linda, Matt and Jassy, while Robin and Victoria, full as they were of jokes and fun, were swamped by the general atmosphere, and kept themselves to themselves as much as possible in the Hons' cupboard.

Linda was married in the Caxton Hall as soon as her divorce was through. The wedding was as different from her first as the Left-wing parties were different from the other kind. It was not exactly sad, but dismal, uncheerful, and with no feeling of happiness. Few of Linda's friends, and none of her relations except Davey and me were there; Lord Merlin sent two Aubusson rugs and some orchids but did not turn up himself. The pre-Christian chatters had faded out of Linda's life, discouraged, loudly bewailing the great loss she was in theirs.

Christian arrived late, and hurried in, followed by several comrades.

'I must say he is wonderful-looking,' Davey hissed in my ear, 'but oh, bother it all!'

There was no wedding breakfast, and, after a few moments of aimless and rather embarrassed hanging about in the street outside the hall, Linda and Christian went off home. Feeling provincial, up in London for the day and determined to see a little life, I made Davey give me luncheon at the Ritz. This had a still further depressing effect on my spirits. My clothes, so nice and suitable for the George, so much admired by the other dons' wives ('My dear, where did you get that lovely tweed?'), were, I now realized, almost bizarre in their dowdiness; it was the floating panels of taffeta all over again. I thought of those dear little black children, three of them now, in their nursery at home, and of dear Alfred in his study, but just for the moment this thought was no consolation. I passionately longed to have a tiny fur hat, or a tiny ostrich hat, like the two ladies at the next table. I longed for a neat black dress, diamond clips and a dark mink coat, shoes like surgical boots, long crinkly black suède gloves, and smooth polished hair. When I tried to explain all this to Davey, he remarked, absentmindedly:

'Oh, but it doesn't matter a bit for you, Fanny, and, after all, how can you have time for *les petits soins de la personne* with so many other, more important things to think of.'

I suppose he thought this would cheer me up.

Soon after her marriage the Alconleighs took Linda back into the fold. They did not count second weddings of divorced people, and Victoria had been severely reprimanded for saying that Linda was engaged to Christian.

'You can't be engaged when you're married.'

It was not the fact of the ceremony which had mollified them, in their eyes Linda would be living from now on in a state of adultery, but they felt the need of her too strongly to keep up a quarrel. The thin end of the wedge (luncheon with Aunt Sadie at Gunters) was inserted, and soon everything was all right again between them. Linda went quite often to Alconleigh, though she never took Christian there, feeling that it would benefit nobody were she to do so.

Linda and Christian lived in their house in Cheyne Walk, and, if Linda was not as happy as she had hoped to be, she exhibited, as usual, a wonderful shop-front. Christian was certainly very fond of her, and, in his way, he tried to be kind to her, but, as Lord Merlin had prophesied, he was much too detached to make any ordinary woman happy. He seemed, for weeks on end, hardly to be aware of her presence; at other times he would wander off and not reappear for days, too much engrossed in whatever he was doing to let her know where he was or when she might expect to see him again. He would eat and sleep where he happened to find himself—on a bench at St. Pancras station, or just sitting on the doorstep of some empty house. Cheyne Walk was always full of comrades, not chatting to Linda, but making speeches to each other, restlessly rushing about, telephoning, typewriting, drinking, quite often sleeping in their clothes, but without their boots, on Linda's drawing-room sofa.

Money troubles accrued. Christian, though he never appeared to spend any money, had a disconcerting way of scattering it. He had few, but expensive amusements, one of his favourites being to ring up the Nazi leaders in Berlin, and other European politicians, and have long teasing talks with them, costing pounds a minute. 'They never can resist a call from London,' he would say, nor, unfortunately, could they. At last, greatly to Linda's relief, the telephone was cut off, as the bill could not be paid.

I must say that Alfred and I both liked Christian very much. We are intellectual pinks ourselves, enthusiastic agreers with the *New Statesman*, so that his views, while rather more advanced than ours, had the same foundation of civilized humanity, and he seemed to us a great improvement on Tony. All the same, he was a hopeless husband for Linda. Her craving was for love, personal and particular, centred upon herself; wider love, for the poor, the sad, and the unattractive, had no appeal for her, though she honestly tried to believe that it had. The more I saw of Linda at this time, the more certain I felt that another bolt could not be very far ahead.

Twice a week Linda worked in a Red bookshop. It was run by a huge, perfectly silent comrade, called Boris. Boris liked to get drunk from Thursday afternoon, which was closing day in that district, to Monday morning, so Linda said she would take it over on Friday and Saturday. An extraordinary transformation would then occur. The books and tracts which mouldered there month after month, getting damper and dustier until at last they had to be thrown away, were hurried into the background, and their place taken by Linda's own few but well-loved favourites. Thus for *Whither British Airways* was substituted *Round the World in Forty Days*, *Karl Marx, the Formative Years* was replaced by *The Making of a Marchioness*, and *The Giant of the Kremlin* by *Diary of a Nobody*, while *A Challenge to Coal-Owners* made way for *King Solomon's Mines*.

Hardly would Linda have arrived in the morning on her days there, and taken down the shutters, than the slummy little street would fill with motor cars, headed by Lord Merlin's electric brougham. Lord Merlin did great propaganda for the shop, saying that Linda was the only person who had ever succeeded in finding him *Froggie's Little Brother* and *Le Père Goriot*. The chatters came back in force, delighted to find Linda so easily accessible again, and without Christian, but sometimes there were embarrassing moments when they came face to face with comrades. Then they would buy a book and beat a hasty retreat, all except Lord Merlin, who had never felt disconcerted in his life. He took a perfectly firm line with the comrades.

'How are you to-day?' he would say with great emphasis, and then glower furiously at them until they left the shop.

All this had an excellent effect upon the financial side of the business. Instead of showing, week by week, an enormous loss, to be refunded from one could guess where, it now became the only Red bookshop in England to make a profit. Boris was greatly praised by his employers, the shop received a medal, which was stuck upon the sign, and the comrades all said that Linda was a good girl and a credit to the Party.

The rest of her time was spent in keeping house for Christian and the comrades, an occupation which entailed trying to induce a series of maids to stay with them, and making sincere, but sadly futile, efforts to take their place when they had left, which they usually did at the end of the first week. The comrades were not very nice or very thoughtful to maids.

'You know, being a Conservative is much more restful,' Linda said to me once in a moment of confidence, when she was being unusually frank about her life, 'though one must remember that it is bad, not good. But it does take place within certain hours, and then finish, whereas Communism seems to eat up all one's life and energy. And the comrades are such Hons, but sometimes they make me awfully cross, just as Tony used to make one furious when he talked about the workers. I often feel rather the same when they talk about us—you see, just like Tony, they've got it all wrong. I'm all for them stringing up Sir Leicester, but if they started on Aunt Emily and Davey, or even on Fa, I don't think I could stand by and watch. I suppose one is neither fish, flesh, nor good red herring, that's the worst of it.'

'But there is a difference,' I said, 'between Sir Leicester and Uncle Matthew.'

'Well, that's what I'm always trying to explain. Sir Leicester grubs up his money in London, goodness knows how, but Fa gets it from his land, and he puts a great deal back into the land, not only money, but work. Look at all the things he does for no pay—all those boring meetings, County Council, J.P., and so on. And he's a good landlord, he takes trouble. You see, the comrades don't know the country—they didn't know you could get a lovely cottage with a huge garden for 2s. 6d. a week until I told them, and then they hardly believed it. Christian knows, but he says the system is wrong, and I expect it is.'

'What exactly does Christian do?' I said.

'Oh, everything you can think of. Just at the moment he's writing a book on famine—goodness! it's sad—and there's a dear little Chinese comrade who comes and tells him what famine is like, you never saw such a fat man in your life.'

I laughed.

Linda said, hurriedly and guiltily:

'Well, I may seem to laugh at the comrades, but at least one does know they are doing good not harm, and not living on other people's slavery like Sir Leicester, and really you know I do simply love them, though I sometimes wish they were a little more fond of chatting, and not quite so sad and earnest and down on everybody.'

CHAPTER XV

EARLY in 1939, the population of Catalonia streamed over the Pyrenees into the Roussillon, a poor and little-known province of France, which now, in a few days, found itself inhabited by more Spaniards than French-men. Just as the lemmings suddenly pour themselves in mass suicide off the coast of Norway, knowing neither whence they come nor whither bound, so great is the compulsion that hurls them into the Atlantic, thus half a million men, women and children suddenly took flight into the bitter moun-tain weather, without pausing for thought. It was the greatest movement of population, in the time it took, that had ever hitherto been seen. Over the mountains they found no promised land; the French government, vacillat-ing in its policy, neither turned them back with machine-guns at the frontier, nor welcomed them as brothers-in-arms against Fascism. It drove them like a herd of beasts down to the cruel salty marshes of that coast, enclosed them, like a herd of beasts, behind barbed-wire fences, and forgot all about them.

Christian, who had always, I think, had a half-guilty feeling about not having fought in Spain, immediately rushed off to Perpignan to see what was happening, and what, if anything, could be done. He wrote an endless series of reports, memoranda, articles and private letters about the conditions he had found in the camps, and then settled down to work in an office financed by various English humanitarians with the object of improving the camps, put-ting refugee families in touch again, and getting as many as possible out of France. This office was run by a young man who had lived many years in Spain called Robert Parker. As soon as it became clear that there would not be, as at first was expected, an outbreak of typhus, Christian sent for Linda to join him in Perpignan.

It so happened that Linda had never before been abroad in her life. Tony had found all his pleasures, hunting, shooting, and golf, in England, and had grudged the extra days out of his holiday which would have been spent in travelling; while it would never have occurred to the Alconleighs to visit the Continent for any other purpose than that of fighting. Uncle Matthew's four years in France and Italy between 1914 and 1918 had given him no great opinion of foreigners.

'Frogs,' he would say, 'are slightly better than Huns or Wops, but abroad is unutterably bloody and foreigners are fiends.'

The bloodiness of abroad, the fiendishness of foreigners, had, in fact, be-come such a tenet of the Radlett family creed that Linda set forth on her journey with no little trepidation. I went to see her off at Victoria, she was looking intensely English in her long blond mink coat, the *Tatler* under her arm, and Lord Merlin's morocco dressing-case, with a canvas cover, in her hand.

'I hope you have sent your jewels to the bank,' I said.

'Oh, darling, don't tease, you know how I haven't got any now. But my money,' she said with a self-conscious giggle, 'is sewn into my stays. Fa rang up and begged me to, and I must say it did seem quite an idea. Oh, why aren't you coming? I do feel so terrified—think of sleeping in the train, all alone.'

'Perhaps you won't be alone,' I said. 'Foreigners are greatly given, I believe, to rape.'

'Yes, that would be nice, so long as they didn't find my stays. Oh, we are off—good-bye, darling, do think of me,' she said, and, clenching her suède-covered fist, she shook it out of the window in a Communist salute.

I must explain that I know everything that now happened to Linda, although I did not see her for another year, because afterwards, as will be shown, we spent a long quiet time together, during which she told it all to me, over and over again. It was her way of re-living happiness.

Of course the journey was an enchantment to her. The porters in their blue overalls, the loud, high conversations, of which, although she thought she knew French quite well, she did not understand a single word, the steamy, garlic-smelling heat of the French train, the delicious food, to which she was summoned by a little hurried bell, it was all from another world, like a dream.

She looked out of the window and saw chateaux, lime avenues, ponds and villages exactly like those in the *Bibliothèque Rose*—she thought she must, at any moment, see Sophie in her white dress and unnaturally small black pumps cutting up goldfish, gorging herself on new bread and cream, or scratching the face of good, uncomplaining Paul. Her very stilted, very English French, got her across Paris and into the train for Perpignan without a hitch. Paris. She looked out of the window at the lighted dusky streets, and thought that never could any town have been so hauntingly beautiful. A strange stray thought came into her head that, one day, she would come back here and be very happy, but she knew that it was not likely, Christian would never want to live in Paris. Happiness and Christian were still linked together in her mind at this time.

At Perpignan she found him in a whirl of business. Funds had been raised, a ship had been chartered, and plans were on foot for sending six thousand Spaniards out of the camps to Mexico. This entailed an enormous amount of staff work, as families (no Spaniard would think of moving without his entire family) had to be reunited from camps all over the place, assembled in a camp in Perpignan, and taken by train to the port of Cette, whence they finally embarked. The work was greatly complicated by the fact that Spanish husbands and wives do not share a surname. Christian explained all this to

Linda almost before she was out of the train; he gave her an absent-minded peck on the forehead and rushed her to his office, hardly giving her time to deposit her luggage at an hotel on the way and scouting the idea that she might like a bath. He did not ask how she was or whether she had had a good journey—Christian always assumed that people were all right unless they told him to the contrary, when, except in the case of destitute, coloured, oppressed, leprous, or otherwise unattractive strangers, he would take absolutely no notice. He was really only interested in mass wretchedness, and never much cared for individual cases, however genuine their misery, while the idea that it is possible to have three square meals a day and a roof and yet be unhappy or unwell, seemed to him intolerable nonsense.

The office was a large shed with a yard round it. This yard was permanently full of refugees with mountains of luggage and quantities of children, dogs, donkeys, goats, and other appurtenances, who had just struggled over the mountains in their flight from Fascism, and were hoping that the English would be able to prevent them being put into camps. In certain cases they could be lent money, or given railway tickets enabling them to join relations in France and French Morocco, but the vast majority waited hours for an interview, only to be told that there was no hope for them. They would then, with great and heart-breaking politeness, apologize for having been a nuisance and withdraw. Spaniards have a highly developed sense of human dignity.

Linda was now introduced to Robert Parker and to Randolph Pine, a young writer who, having led a more or less playboy existence in the South of France, had gone to fight in Spain, and was now working in Perpignan from a certain feeling of responsibility towards those who had once been fellow soldiers. They seemed pleased that Linda had arrived, and were most friendly and welcoming, saying that it was nice to see a new face.

'You must give me some work to do,' said Linda.

'Yes, now what can we think of for you?' said Robert. 'There's masses of work, never fear, it's just a question of finding the right kind. Can you speak Spanish?'

'No.'

'Oh, well, you'll soon pick it up.'

'I'm quite sure I shan't,' said Linda doubtfully.

'What do you know about welfare work?'

'Oh, dear, how hopeless I seem to be. Nothing, I'm afraid.'

'Lavender will find her a job,' said Christian, who had settled down at his table and was flapping over a card index.

'Lavender?'

'A girl called Lavender Davis.'

'No! I know her quite well, she used to live near us in the country. In fact she was one of my bridesmaids.'

'That's it,' said Robert, 'she said she knew you. I'd forgotten. She's wonderful, she really works with the Quakers in the camps, but she helps us a great deal too. There's absolutely nothing she doesn't know about calories and babies' nappies, and expectant mummies, and so on, and she's the hardest worker I've ever come across.'

'I'll tell you,' said Randolph Pine, 'what you can do. There's a job simply waiting for you, and that is to arrange the accommodation on this ship that's going off next week.'

'Oh, yes, of course,' said Robert, 'the very thing. She can have this table and start at once.'

'Now look,' said Randolph. 'I'll show you. (What delicious scent you have, Après l'Ondée? I thought so.) Now here is a map of the ship—see—best cabins, not such good cabins, lousy cabins, and battened down under the hatches. And here is a list of the families who are going. All you have to do is to allocate each family its cabin—when you have decided which they are to have, you put the number of the cabin against the family—here—you see? And the number of the family on the cabin here, like that. Quite easy, but it takes time, and must be done so that when they arrive on the boat they will know exactly where to go with their things.'

'But how do I decide who gets the good ones and who is battened? Awfully tricky, isn't it?'

'Not really. The point is it's a strictly democratic ship run on republican principles, class doesn't enter into it. I should give decent cabins to families where there are small children or babies. Apart from that do it any way you like. Take a pin if you like. The only thing that matters is that it should be done, otherwise there'll be a wild scramble for the best places when they get on board.'

Linda looked at the list of families. It took the form of a card index, the head of each family having a card on which was written the number and names of his dependants.

'It doesn't give their ages,' said Linda. 'How am I to know if there are young babies?'

'That's a point,' said Robert. 'How is she to?'

'Quite easy,' said Christian. 'With Spaniards you can always tell. Before the war they were called either after saints or after episodes in the life of the Virgin—Anunciacion, Asuncion, Purificacion, Concepcion, Consvelo, etc. Since the Civil War they are all called Carlos after Charlie Marx, Federigo after Freddie Engels or Estalina (very popular until the Russians let them down with a wallop), or else nice slogans like Solidaredad-Obrera, Libertad, and so on. Then you know the children are under three. Couldn't be simpler, really.'

Lavender Davis now appeared. She was indeed the same Lavender, dowdy, healthy and plain, wearing an English country tweed and brogues. Her short brown hair curled over her head, and she had no make-up. She greeted Linda with enthusiasm, indeed, it had always been a fiction in the Davis family that Lavender and Linda were each other's greatest friends. Linda was delighted to see her, as one always is delighted to see a familiar face, abroad.

'Come on,' said Randolph, 'now we're all here let's go and have a drink at the Palmarium.'

For the next weeks, until her private life began to occupy Linda's attention, she lived in an atmosphere of alternate fascination and horror. She grew to love Perpignan, a strange little old town, so different from anything she had ever known, with its river and broad quays, its network of narrow streets, its huge wild-looking plane trees, and all around it the bleak vine-growing country of the Roussillon bursting into summery green under her very eyes. Spring came late and slowly, but when it came it was hand-in-hand with summer, and almost at once everything was baking and warm and in the villages the people danced every night on concrete dancing floors under the plane trees. At week-ends the English, unable to eradicate such a national habit, shut up the office and made for Collioure on the coast, where they bathed and sunbathed and went for Pyrenean picnics.

But all this had nothing to do with the reason for their presence in these charming surroundings—the camps. Linda went to the camps nearly every day, and they filled her soul with despair. As she could not help very much in the office owing to her lack of Spanish, nor with the children, since she knew nothing about calories, she was employed as a driver, and was always on the road in a Ford van full of supplies, or of refugees, or just taking messages to and from the camps. Often she had to sit and wait for hours on end while a certain man was found and his case dealt with; she would quickly be surrounded by a perfect concourse of men talking to her in their heavy guttural French. By this time the camps were quite decently organized; there were rows of orderly though depressing huts, and the men were getting regular meals, which, if not very appetizing, did at least keep body and soul together. But the sight of these thousands of human beings, young and healthy, herded behind wire away from their womenfolk, with nothing on earth to do day after dismal day, was a recurring torture to Linda. She began to think that Uncle Matthew had been right—that abroad, where such things could happen, was indeed unutterably bloody, and that foreigners, who could inflict them upon each other, must be fiends.

One day as she sat in her van, the centre, as usual, of a crowd of Spaniards, a voice said:

'Linda, what on earth are you doing here?'

And it was Matt.

He looked ten years older than when she had last seen him, grown up, in fact, and extremely handsome, his Radlett eyes infinitely blue in a dark-brown face.

'I've seen you several times,' he said, 'and I thought you had been sent to fetch me away so I made off, but then I found out you are married to that Christian fellow. Was he the one you ran away from Tony with?'

'Yes,' said Linda, 'I'd no idea, Matt. I thought you'd have been sure to go back to England.'

'Well, no,' said Matt. 'I'm an officer, you see—must stay with the boys.'

'Does Mummy know you're all right?'

'Yes, I told her—at least if Christian posted a letter I gave him.'

'I don't suppose so—he's never been known to post a letter in his life. He is funny, he might have told me.'

'He didn't know—I sent it under cover to a friend of mine to forward. Didn't want any of the English to find out I was here, or they would start trying to get me home, I know.'

'Christian wouldn't,' said Linda. 'He's all for people doing what they want to in life. You're very thin, Matt, is there anything you'd like?'

'Yes,' said Matt, 'some cigarettes and a couple of thrillers.'

After this Linda saw him most days. She told Christian, who merely grunted and said: 'He'll have to be got out before the world war begins, I'll see to that,' and she wrote and told her parents. The result was a parcel of clothes from Aunt Sadie, which Matt refused to accept, and a packing-case full of vitamin pills from Davey, which Linda did not even dare to show him. He was cheerful and full of jokes and high spirits, but then there is a difference, as Christian said, between staying in a place because you are obliged to, and staying there because you think it right. But in any case, with the Radlett family, cheerfulness was never far below the surface.

The only other cheerful prospect was the ship. It was only going to rescue from hell a few thousand of the refugees, a mere fraction of the total amount, but, at any rate, they would be rescued, and taken to a better world, with happy and useful future prospects.

When she was not driving the van Linda worked hard over the cabin arrangements, and finally got the whole thing fixed and finished in time for the embarkation.

All the English except Linda went to Cette for the great day, taking with them two M.P.s and a duchess, who had helped the enterprise in London and had come out to see the fruit of their work. Linda went over by bus to Argelès to see Matt.

'How odd the Spanish upper classes must be,' she said, 'they don't raise a finger to help their own people, but leave it all to strangers like us.'

'You don't know Fascists,' Matt said, gloomily.

'I was thinking yesterday when I was taking the Duchess round Barcarès— yes, but why an English duchess, aren't there any Spanish ones, and, come to that, why is it nothing but English working in Perpignan? I knew several

Spaniards in London, why don't they come and help a bit? They'd be awfully useful. I suppose they speak Spanish.'

'Fa was quite right about foreigners being fiends,' said Matt, 'upper-class ones are, at least. All these boys are terrific Hons, I must say.'

'Well, I can't see the English leaving each other in the lurch like this, even if they did belong to different parties. I think it's shameful.'

Christian and Robert came back from Cette, in a cheerful mood. The arrangements had gone like clockwork, and a baby which had been born during the first half-hour on the ship was named Embarcacion. It was the kind of joke Christian very much enjoyed. Robert said to Linda:

'Did you work on any special plan when you were arranging the cabins, or how did you do it?'

'Why? Wasn't it all right?'

'Perfect. Everybody had a place, and made for it. But I just wondered what you went by when you allocated the good cabins, that's all.'

'Well, I simply,' said Linda, 'gave the best cabins to the people who had *Labrador* on their card, because I used to have one when I was little and he was such a terrific . . . so sweet, you know.'

'Ah,' said Robert, gravely, 'all is now explained. '*Labrador* in Spanish happens to mean labourer. So you see under your scheme (excellent by the way, most democratic) the farm hands all found themselves in luxury while the intellectuals were battened. That'll teach them not to be so clever. You did very well, Linda, we were all most grateful.'

'He was such a sweet Labrador,' said Linda dreamily. 'I wish you could have seen him. I do miss not having pets.'

'Can't think why you don't make an offer for the *sangsue*,' said Robert.

One of the features of Perpignan was a leech in a bottle in the window of a chemist's shop, with a typewritten notice saying: 'SI LA SANGSUE MONTE DANS LA BOUTEILLE IL FERA BEAU TEMPS. SI LA SANGSUE DESCEND—L'ORAGE.'

'It might be nice,' said Linda, 'but I can't somehow imagine her getting very fond of one—too busy fussing about the weather all day, up and down, up and down—no time for human relationships.'

CHAPTER XVI

LINDA never could remember afterwards whether she had really minded when she discovered that Christian was in love with Lavender Davis, and, if so, how much. She could not at all remember her emotions at that time. Certainly wounded pride must have played a part, though perhaps less so with Linda than it would have with many women, as she did not suffer from much inferiority feeling. She must have seen that the past two years, her running away from Tony, all now went for nothing—but was she stricken at the heart, was she still in love with Christian, did she suffer the ordinary pangs of jealousy? I think not.

All the same, it was not a flattering choice. Lavender had seemed, for years and years, stretching back into childhood, to epitomize everything that the Radletts considered most unromantic : a keen girl guide, hockey player, tree climber, head girl at her school, rider astride. She had never lived in a dream of love; the sentiment was, quite obviously, far removed from her thoughts, although Louisa and Linda, unable to imagine that anybody could exist without some tiny spark of it, used to invent romances for Lavender—the games mistress at her school or Dr. Simpson of Merlinford (of whom Louisa had made up one of her nonsense rhymes—'He's doctor and king's proctor too, and she's in love with him but he's in love with you'). Since those days she had trained as a nurse and as a welfare worker, had taken a course of law and political economy, and, indeed, might have done it all, Linda saw only too well, with the express intention of fitting herself to be a mate for Christian. The result was that in their present surroundings, with her calm assured confidence in her own ability, she easily outshone poor Linda. There was no competition, it was a walk-over.

Linda did not discover their love in any vulgar way—surprising a kiss, or finding them in bed together. It was all far more subtle, more dangerous than that, being quite simply borne in upon her week after week that they found perfect happiness in each other, and that Christian depended entirely on Lavender for comfort and encouragement in his work. As this work now absorbed him heart and soul, as he thought of nothing else and never relaxed for a moment, dependence upon Lavender involved the absolute exclusion of Linda. She felt uncertain what to do. She could not have it out with Christian; there was nothing tangible to have out, and, in any case, such a proceeding would have been absolutely foreign to Linda's character. She dreaded scenes and rows more than anything else in the world, and she had no illusions about what Christian thought of her. She felt that he really rather despised her for having left Tony and her child so easily, and that, in his opinion, she took a silly, light-hearted and superficial view of life. He liked serious, educated women, especially those who had made a study of welfare, especially Lavender. She had no desire to hear all this said. On the other hand she began to think that it would be as well for her to get away from Perpignan herself before Christian and Lavender went off together, as it seemed to her most probable that they would, wandering off hand in hand to search for and relieve other forms of human misery. Already she felt embarrassed when she was with Robert and Randolph, who were obviously very sorry for her and were always making little manœuvres to prevent her noticing that Christian was spending every minute of the day with Lavender.

One afternoon, looking idly out of the window of her hotel bedroom, she saw them walking up the Quai Sadi Carnot together, completely absorbed, utterly contented in each other's company, radiating happiness. Linda was seized by an impulse and acted on it. She packed her things, wrote a hasty letter to Christian saying that she was leaving him for good, as she realized that their marriage had been a failure. She asked him to look after Matt. She then burnt her boats by adding a postscript (a fatal feminine practice), 'I think you had much better marry Lavender'. She bundled herself and her luggage into a taxi and took the night train for Paris.

The journey this time was horrible. She was, after all, very fond of Christian, and as soon as the train had left the station, she began to ask herself whether she had not in fact behaved stupidly and badly. He probably had a passing fancy for Lavender, based on common interests, which would fade away as soon as he got back to London. Possibly it was not even that, but simply that he was obliged, for his work, to be with Lavender all the time. His absentminded treatment of Linda was, after all, nothing new, it had begun almost as soon as he had got her under his roof. She began to feel that she had done wrong to write that letter.

She had her return ticket, but very little money, indeed just enough, she reckoned, for dinner on the train and some food the next day. Linda always had to translate French money into pounds, shillings and pence before she knew where she was with it. She seemed to have about 18s. 6d. with her, so there could be no question of a sleeper. She had never before sat up all night in a train, and the experience appalled her; it was like some dreadful feverish illness, when the painful hours drag by, each one longer than a week. Her thoughts brought her no comfort. She had torn up her life of the past two years, all that she had tried to put into her relationship with Christian, and thrown it away like so much waste-paper. If this was to be the outcome why had she ever left Tony, her real husband for better for worse, and her child? That was where her duty had lain, and well she knew it. She thought of my mother and shuddered. Could it be that she, Linda, was from now on doomed to a life that she utterly despised, that of a bolter?

And in London what would she find? A little empty, dusty house. Perhaps, she thought, Christian would pursue her, come and insist that she belonged to him. But in her heart she knew that he would not, and that she did not, and that this was the end. Christian believed too sincerely that people must be allowed to do as they wish in life, without interference. He was fond of Linda, she knew, but disappointed in her, she also knew; he would not himself have made the first move to separate, but would not much regret the fact that she had done so. Soon he would have some new scheme in his head, some new plan for suffering mortals, any mortals, anywhere, so long as there were enough of them and their misery was great. Then he would forget Linda, and possibly also Lavender, as if they had never been. Christian was not in passionate quest of love, he had other interests, other aims, and it mattered very little to him what woman happened to be in his life at a given moment. But in his nature, she knew, there was a certain ruthlessness. She felt that he would not forgive what she had done, or try to persuade her to go back on it, nor, indeed, was there any reason why he should do so.

It could not be said, thought Linda, as the train pursued its way through the blackness, that her life so far had been a marked success. She had found neither great love nor great happiness, and she had not inspired them in others. Parting with her would have been no death blow to either of her husbands; on the contrary, they would both have turned with relief to a much preferred mistress, who was more suited to them in every way. Whatever quality it is that can hold indefinitely the love and affection of a man she plainly did not possess, and now she was doomed to the lonely, hunted life of a beautiful but unattached woman. Where now was love that would last to the grave and far beyond? What had she done with her youth? Tears for her lost hopes and ideals, tears of self-pity in fact, began to pour down her cheeks. The three fat Frenchmen who shared the carriage with her were in a snoring sleep, she wept alone.

Sad and tired as Linda was, she could not but perceive the beauty of Paris that summer morning as she drove across it to the Gare du Nord. Paris in the early morning has a cheerful, bustling aspect, a promise of delicious things to come, a positive smell of coffee and croissants, quite peculiar to itself.

The people welcome a new day as if they were certain of liking it, the shopkeepers pull up their blinds serene in the expectation of good trade, the workers go happily to their work, the people who have sat up all night in night-clubs go happily to their rest, the orchestra of motor-car horns, of clanking trams, of whistling policemen tunes up for the daily symphony, and everywhere is joy. This joy, this life, this beauty did but underline poor Linda's fatigue and sadness, she felt it but was not of it. She turned her thoughts to old familiar London, she longed above all for her own bed, feeling as does a wounded beast when it crawls home to its lair. She only wanted to sleep undisturbed in her own bedroom.

But when she presented her return ticket at the Gare du Nord she was told, furiously, loudly and unsympathetically, that it had expired.

'*Voyons, madame—le 29 Mai. C'est aujourd'hui le 30, n'est ce pas? Donc——!*' Tremendous shruggings.

Linda was paralysed with horror. Her 18s. 6d. was by now down to 6s. 3d., hardly enough for a meal. She knew nobody in Paris, she had absolutely no idea what she ought to do, she was too tired and too hungry to think clearly. She stood like a statue of despair. Her porter, tired of waiting beside a statue of despair, deposited the luggage at its feet and went grumbling off. Linda sank on to her suitcase and began to cry; nothing so dreadful had ever happened to her before. She cried bitterly, she could not stop. People passed to and fro as if weeping ladies were the most ordinary phenomenon at the Gare du Nord. 'Fiends! fiends!' she sobbed. Why had she not listened to her father, why had she ever come to this bloody abroad? Who would help her? In London there was a society, she knew, which looked after ladies stranded at railway stations; here, more likely, there would be one for shipping them off to South America. At any moment now somebody, some genial-looking old woman might come up and give her an injection, after which she would disappear for ever.

She became aware that somebody was standing beside her, not an old lady, but a short, stocky, very dark Frenchman in a black Homburg hat. He was laughing. Linda took no notice, but went on crying. The more she cried the more he laughed. Her tears were tears of rage now, no longer of self-pity.

At last she said, in a voice which was meant to be angrily impressive, but which squeaked and shook through her handkerchief:

'*Allez-vous en.*'

For answer he took her hand and pulled her to her feet.

'*Bonjour, bonjour,*' he said.

'*Voulez-vous vous en aller?*' said Linda, rather more doubtfully, here at least was a human being who showed signs of taking some interest in her. Then she thought of South America.

'*Il faut expliquer que je ne suis pas,*' she said, '*une esclave blanche. Je suis la fille d'un très important lord anglais.*'

The Frenchman gave a great bellow of laughter.

'One does not,' he said in the nearly perfect English of somebody who has spoken it from a child, 'have to be Sherlock Holmes to guess that.'

Linda was rather annoyed. An Englishwoman abroad may be proud of her nationality and her virtue without wishing them to jump so conclusively to the eye.

'French ladies,' he went on, 'covered with *les marques extérieures de la richesse* never never sit crying on their suitcases at the Gare du Nord in the very early morning, while *esclaves blanches* always have protectors, and it is only too clear that you are unprotected just now.'

This sounded all right, and Linda was mollified.

'Now,' he said, 'I invite you to luncheon with me, but first you must have a bath and rest and a cold compress on your face.'

He picked up her luggage and walked to a taxi.

'Get in, please.'

Linda got in. She was far from certain that this was not the road to Buenos Aires, but something made her do as he said. Her powers of resistance were at an end, and she really saw no alternative.

'Hotel Montalembert,' he told the taxi man. 'Rue du Bac. *Je m'excuse,*

25

madame, for not taking you to the Ritz, but I have a feeling for the Hotel Montalembert just now, that it will suit your mood this morning.'

Linda sat upright in her corner of the taxi, looking, she hoped, very prim. As she could not think of anything pertinent to say she remained silent. Her companion hummed a little tune, and seemed vastly amused. When they arrived at the hotel, he took a room for her, told the liftman to show her to it, told the *concierge* to send her up a *café complet*, kissed her hand, and said:

'*A tout à l'heure*—I will fetch you a little before one o'clock and we will go out to luncheon.'

Linda had her bath and breakfast and got into bed. When the telephone bell rang she was so sound asleep that it was a struggle to wake up.

'*Un monsieur qui demande madame.*'

'*Je descends tout de suite*,' said Linda, but it took her quite half an hour to get ready.

CHAPTER XVII

'AH! You keep me waiting,' he said, kissing her hand, or at least making a gesture of raising her hand towards his lips and then dropping it rather suddenly. 'That is a very good sign.'

'Sign of what?' said Linda. He had a two-seater outside the hotel and she got into it. She was feeling more like herself again.

'Oh, of this and that,' he said, letting in the clutch, 'a good augury for our affair, that it will be happy and last long.'

Linda became intensely stiff, English and embarrassed, and said, self-consciously:

'We are not having an affair.'

'My name is Fabrice—may one ask yours?'

'Linda.'

'Linda. *Comme c'est joli.* With me, it usually lasts five years.'

He drove to a restaurant where they were shown, with some deference, to a table in a red plush corner. He ordered the luncheon and the wine in rapid French, the sort of French that Linda frankly could not follow, then, putting his hands on his knees, he turned to her and said:

'*Allons, racontez, madame.*'

'*Racontez* what?'

'Well, but of course, the story? Who was it that left you to cry on that suitcase?'

'He didn't. I left him. It was my second husband and I have left him for ever because he has fallen in love with another woman—a welfare worker, not that you'd know what that is, because I'm sure they don't exist in France. It just makes it worse, that's all.'

'What a very curious reason for leaving one's second husband. Surely with your experience of husbands you must have noticed that falling in love with other women is one of the things they do? However, it's an ill wind, and I don't complain. But why the suitcase? Why didn't you put yourself in the train and go back to Monsieur the important lord, your father?'

'That's what I was doing until they told me that my return ticket had expired. I only had 6s. 3d., and I don't know anybody in Paris, and I was awfully tired, so I cried.'

'The second husband—why not borrow some money from him? Or had you left a note on his pillow—women never can resist these little essays in literature, and they do make it rather embarrassing to go back, I know.'

'Well, anyhow he's in Perpignan, so I couldn't have.'

'Ah, you come from Perpignan. And what were you doing there, in the name of heaven?'

'In the name of heaven we were trying to stop you frogs from teasing the poor Epagnards,' said Linda with some spirit.

'E-spa-gnols! So we are teasing them, are we?'

'Not so badly now—terribly at the beginning.'

'What were we supposed to do with them? We never invited them to come, you know.'

'You drove them into camps in that cruel wind, and gave them no shelter for weeks. Hundreds died.'

'It is quite a job to provide shelter, at a moment's notice, for half a million people. We did what we could—we fed them—the fact is that most of them are still alive.'

'Still herded in camps.'

'My dear Linda, you could hardly expect us to turn them loose on the countryside with no money—what would be the result? Do use your common sense.'

'You should mobilize them to fight in the war against Fascism that's coming any day now.'

'Talk about what you know and you won't get so angry. We haven't enough equipment for our own soldiers in the war against Germany that's coming—not any day, but after the harvest, probably in August. Now go on telling me about your husbands. It's so very much more interesting.'

'Only two. My first was a Conservative, and my second is a Communist.'

'Just as I guessed, your first is rich, your second is poor. I could see you once had a rich husband, the dressing-case and the fur coat, though it is a hideous colour, and no doubt, as far as one could see, with it bundled over your arm, a hideous shape. Still, *vison* usually betokens a rich husband somewhere. Then this dreadful linen suit you are wearing has ready-made written all over it.'

'You are rude, it's a very pretty suit.'

'And last year's. Jackets are getting longer you will find. I'll get you some clothes—if you were well dressed you would be quite good-looking, though it's true your eyes are small. Blue, a good colour, but small.'

'In England,' said Linda, 'I am considered a beauty.'

'Well, you have points.'

So this silly conversation went on and on, but it was only froth on the surface. Linda was feeling, what she had never so far felt for any man, an overwhelming physical attraction. It made her quite giddy, it terrified her. She could see that Fabrice was perfectly certain of the outcome, so was she perfectly certain, and that was what frightened her. How could she, Linda, with the horror and contempt she had always felt for casual affairs, allow herself to be picked up by any stray foreigner, and, having seen him only for an hour, long and long and long to be in bed with him? He was not even good-looking, he was exactly like dozens of other dark men in Homburgs that can be seen in the streets of any French town. But there was something about the way he looked at her which seemed to be depriving her of all balance. She was profoundly shocked, and, at the same time, intensely excited.

After luncheon they strolled out of the restaurant into brilliant sunshine.

'Come and see my flat,' said Fabrice.

'I would rather see Paris,' said Linda.

'Do you know Paris well?'

'I've never been here before in my life.'

Fabrice was really startled.

'Never been here before?' he could not believe it. 'What a pleasure for me, to show it all to you. There is so much to show, it will take weeks.'

'Unfortunately,' said Linda, 'I leave for England to-morrow.'

'Yes, of course. Then we must see it all this afternoon.'

They drove slowly round a few streets and squares, and then went for a stroll in the Bois. Linda could not believe that she had only just arrived there, that this was still the very day which she had seen unfolding itself, so full of promise, through her mist of morning tears.

'How fortunate you are to live in such a town,' she said to Fabrice. 'It would be impossible to be very unhappy here.'

'Not impossible,' he said. 'One's emotions are intensified in Paris—one can be more happy and also more unhappy here than in any other place. But it is always a positive source of joy to live here, and there is nobody so miserable as a Parisian in exile from his town. The rest of the world seems unbearably cold and bleak to us, hardly worth living in.' He spoke with great feeling.

After tea, which they had out of doors in the Bois, he drove slowly back into Paris. He stopped the car outside an old house in the Rue Bonaparte, and said, again:

'Come and see my flat.'

'No, no,' said Linda. 'The time has now come for me to point out that I am *une femme sérieuse.*'

Fabrice gave his great bellow of laughter.

'Oh,' he said, shaking helplessly, 'how funny you are. What a phrase, *femme sérieuse,* where did you find it? And if so serious, how do you explain the second husband?'

'Yes, I admit that I did wrong, very wrong indeed, and made a great mistake. But that is no reason for losing control, for sliding down the hill altogether, for being picked up by strange gentlemen at the Gare du Nord and then immediately going with them to see their flat. And please, if you will be so kind as to lend me some money. I want to catch the London train to-morrow morning.'

'Of course, by all means,' said Fabrice.

He thrust a roll of banknotes into her hand, and drove her to the Hotel Montalembert. He seemed quite unmoved by her speech, and announced he would come back at eight o'clock to take her out to dinner.

Linda's bedroom was full of roses, it reminded her of when Moira was born.

'Really,' she thought with a giggle, 'this is a very penny-novelettish seduction, how can I be taken in by it?'

But she was filled with a strange, wild, unfamiliar happiness, and knew that this was love. Twice in her life she had mistaken something else for it; it was like seeing somebody in the street who you think is a friend, you whistle and wave and run after him, and it is not only not the friend, but not even very like him. A few minutes later the real friend appears in view, and then you can't imagine how you ever mistook that other person for him. Linda was now looking upon the authentic face of love, and she knew it, but it frightened her. That it should come so casually, so much by a series of accidents, was frightening. She tried to remember how she had felt when she had first loved her two husbands. There must have been strong and impelling emotion; in both cases she had disrupted her own life, upset her parents and friends remorselessly, in order to marry them, but she could not recall it. Only she knew that never before, not even in dreams, and she was a great dreamer of love, had she felt anything remotely like this. She told herself, over and over again, that to-morrow she must go back to London, but she had no intention of going back, and she knew it.

Fabrice took her out to dinner and then to a night club, where they did not dance, but chatted endlessly. She told him about Uncle Matthew, Aunt Sadie and Louisa and Jassy and Matt, and he could not hear enough, and egged her on to excesses of exaggeration about her family and all their various idiosyncrasies.

'*Et* Jassy—*et* Matt—*alors, racontez.*'

And she recounted, for hours.

In the taxi on their way home she refused again to go back with him or to let him come into the hotel with her. He did not insist, he did not try to hold her hand, or touch her at all. He merely said:

'*C'est une résistance magnifique, je vous félicite de tout mon cœur, madame.*'

Outside the hotel she gave him her hand to say good night. He took it in both of his and really kissed it.

'*A demain*,' he said, and got back into the taxi.

'*Allô—allô.*'

'Hullo.'

'Good morning. Are you having your breakfast?'

'Yes.'

'I thought I heard a coffee-cup clattering. Is it good?'

'It's so delicious that I have to keep stopping, for fear of finishing it too quickly. Are you having yours?'

'Had it. I must tell you that I like very long conversations in the morning, and I shall expect you to *raconter des histoires*.'

'Like Schéhérazade?'

'Yes, just like. And you're not to get that note in your voice of "now I'm going to ring off", as English people always do.'

'What English people do you know?'

'I know some. I was at school in England, and at Oxford.'

'No! When?'

'1920.'

'When I was nine. Fancy, perhaps I saw you in the street—we used to do all our shopping in Oxford.'

'Elliston & Cavell?'

'Oh, yes, and Webbers.'

There was a silence.

'Go on,' he said.

'Go on, what?'

'I mean don't ring off. Go on telling.'

'I shan't ring off. As a matter of fact I adore chatting. It's my favourite thing, and I expect you will want to ring off ages before I do.'

They had a long and very silly conversation, and, at the end of it, Fabrice said:

'Now get up, and in an hour I will fetch you and we will go to Versailles.'

At Versailles, which was an enchantment to Linda, she was reminded of a story she had once read about two English ladies who had seen the ghost of Marie Antoinette sitting in her garden at the Little Trianon. Fabrice found this intensely boring, and said so.

'*Histoires*,' he said, 'are only of interest when they are true, or when you have made them up specially to amuse me. *Histoires de revenants*, made up by some dim old English virgins, are neither true nor interesting. *Donc plus d'histoires de revenants, madame, s'il vous plaît.*'

'All right,' said Linda, crossly. 'I'm doing my best to please—you tell me a story.'

'Yes, I will—and this story is true. My grandmother was very beautiful and had many lovers all her life, even when she was quite old. A short time before she died she was in Venice with my mother, her daughter, and one day, floating up some canal in their gondola, they saw a little palazzo of pink marble, very exquisite. They stopped the gondola to look at it, and my mother said: "I don't believe anybody lives there, what about trying to see the inside?"

'So they rang the bell, and an old servant came and said that nobody had lived there for many, many years, and he would show it to them if they liked. So they went in and upstairs to the *salone*, which had three windows looking over the canal and was decorated with fifteenth-century plaster work, white on a pale blue background. It was a perfect room. My grandmother seemed strangely moved, and stood for a long time in silence. At last she said to my mother:

' "If, in the third drawer of that bureau there is a filigree box containing a small gold key on a black velvet ribbon, this house belongs to me."

'And my mother looked, and there was, and it did. One of my grandmother's lovers had given it to her years and years before, when she was quite young, and she had forgotten all about it.'

'Goodness,' said Linda, 'what fascinating lives you foreigners do lead.'

'And it belongs to me now.'

He put his hand up to Linda's forehead and stroked back a strand of hair which was loose:

'And I would take you there to-morrow if——'

'If what?'

'One must wait here now, you see, for the war.'

'Oh, I keep forgetting the war,' said Linda.

'Yes, let's forget it. *Comme vous êtes mal coiffée, ma chère.*'

'If you don't like my clothes and don't like my hair and think my eyes are so small, I don't know what you see in me.'

'*Quand-même j'avoue qu'il y a quelque-chose,*' said Fabrice.

Again they dined together.

Linda said: 'Haven't you any other engagements?'

'Yes, of course, I have cancelled them.'

'Who are your friends?'

'*Les gens du monde.* And yours?'

'When I was married to Tony, that is, my first husband, I used to go out in the *monde*, it was my life. In those days I loved it. But then Christian didn't approve of it, he stopped me going to parties and frightened away my friends, whom he considered frivolous and idiotic, and we saw nothing but serious people trying to put the world right. I used to laugh at them, and rather long for my other friends, but now I don't know. Since I was at Perpignan perhaps I have become more serious myself.'

'Everybody is getting more serious, that's the way things are going. But, whatever one may be in politics, right, left, Fascist, Communist, *les gens du monde* are the only possible ones for friends. You see, they have made a fine art of personal relationships and of all that pertains to them—manners, clothes, beautiful houses, good food, everything that makes life agreeable. It would be silly not to take advantage of that. Friendship is something to be built up carefully, by people with leisure, it is an art, nature does not enter into it. You should never despise social life—*de la haute société*—I mean, it can be a very satisfying one, entirely artificial of course, but absorbing. Apart from the life of the intellect and the contemplative religious life, which few people are qualified to enjoy, what else is there to distinguish man from the animals but his social life? And who understands it so well and who can make it so smooth and so amusing as *les gens du monde*? But one cannot have it at the same time as a love affair, one must be whole-hearted to enjoy it, so I have cancelled all my engagements.'

'What a pity,' said Linda, 'because I'm going back to London to-morrow morning.'

'Ah yes, I had forgotten. What a pity.'

'*Allô—allô.*'
'Hullo.'
'Were you asleep?'
'Yes, of course. What's the time?'
'About two. Shall I come round and see you?'
'Do you mean now?'
'Yes.'
'I must say it would be very nice, but the only thing is, what would the night porter think?'
'*Ma chère,* how English you are. *Eh bien, je vais vous le dire—il ne se fera aucune illusion.*'
'No, I suppose not.'
'But I don't imagine he's under any illusion as it is. After all, I come here for you three times every day—you've seen nobody else, and French people are quite quick at noticing these things, you know.'
'Yes—I see——'
'*Alors, c'est entendu—à tout à l'heure.*'

The next day Fabrice installed her in a flat, he said it was *plus commode*. He said, 'When I was young I liked to be very romantic and run all kinds of risks. I used to hide in wardrobes, be brought into the house in a trunk, disguise myself as a footman, and climb in at windows. How I used to climb! I remember once halfway up a creeper there was a wasps' nest—oh the agony—I wore a Kestos *soutien-gorge* for a week afterwards. But now I prefer to be comfortable, to follow a certain routine, and have my own key.'

Indeed, Linda thought, nobody could be less romantic and more practical than Fabrice, no nonsense about him. A little nonsense, she thought, would have been rather nice.

It was a beautiful flat, large and sunny, and decorated in the most expensive kind of modern taste. It faced south and west over the Bois de Boulogne, and was on a level with the tree-tops. Tree-tops and sky made up the view. The enormous windows worked like windows of a motor car, the whole of the glass disappearing into the wall. This was a great joy to Linda, who loved the open air and loved to sunbathe for hours with no clothes on, until she was hot and brown and sleepy and happy. Belonging to the flat, belonging, it was evident, to Fabrice, was a charming elderly *femme de ménage* called Germaine. She was assisted by various other elderly women who came and went in a bewildering succession. She was obviously most efficient, she had all Linda's things out of her suitcase, ironed and folded away, in a moment, and then went off to the kitchen, where she began to prepare dinner. Linda could not help wondering how many other people Fabrice had kept in this flat; however, as she was unlikely to find out, and, indeed, had no wish to know, she put the thought from her. There was no trace of any former occupant, not so much as a scribbled telephone number or the mark of a lipstick anywhere to be seen; the flat might have been done up yesterday.

In her bath, before dinner, Linda thought rather wistfully of Aunt Sadie. She, Linda, was now a kept woman and an adulteress, and Aunt Sadie, she knew, wouldn't like that. She hadn't liked it when Linda had committed adultery with Christian, but he, at least, was English, and Linda had been properly introduced to him and knew his surname. Also, Christian had all along intended to marry her. But how much less would Aunt Sadie like her daughter to pick up an unknown, nameless foreigner and go off to live with him in luxury. It was a long step from lunching in Oxford to this, though Uncle Matthew would, no doubt, have considered it a step down the same road if he knew her situation, and he would disown her for ever, throw her out into the snow, shoot Fabrice, or take any other violent action which might occur to him. Then something would happen to make him laugh, and all would be well again. Aunt Sadie was a different matter. She would not say very much, but she would brood over it and take it to heart, and wonder if there had not been something wrong about her method of bringiug up Linda which had led to this; Linda most profoundly hoped that she would never find out.

In the middle of this reverie the telephone bell rang. Germaine answered it, tapped on the bathroom door, and said:

'*M. le duc sera légèrement en retard, madame.*'

'All right—thank you,' said Linda.

At dinner she said:

'Could one know your name?'

'Oh,' said Fabrice. 'Hadn't you discovered that? What an extraordinary lack of curiosity. My name is Sauveterre. In short, *madame*, I am happy to tell you that I am a very rich duke, a most agreeable thing to be, even in these days.'

'How lovely for you. And, while we are on the subject of your private life, are you married?'

'No.'

'Why not?'

'My fiancée died.'

'Oh, how sad—what was she like?'

'Very pretty.'

'Prettier than me?'

'Much prettier. Very correct.'

'More correct than me?'

'*Vous—vous êtes une folle, madame, aucune correction. Et elle était gentille—mais d'une gentillesse, la pauvre.*'

For the first time since she knew him, Fabrice had become infinitely sentimental, and Linda was suddenly shaken by the pangs of a terrible jealousy, so terrible that she felt quite faint. If she had not already recognized the fact, she would have known now, for certain and always, that this was to be the great love of her life.

'Five years,' she said, 'is quite a long time when it's all in front of you.'

But Fabrice was still thinking of the fiancée.

'She died much more than five years ago—fifteen years in the autumn. I always go and put late roses on her grave, those little tight roses with very dark green leaves that never open properly—they remind me of her. *Dieu, que c'est triste.*'

'And what was her name?' said Linda.

'Louise. *Enfant unique du dernier Rancé.* I often go and see her mother, who is still alive, a remarkable old woman. She was brought up in England at the court of the Empress Eugénie, and Rancé married her in spite of that, for love. You can imagine how strange everybody found it.'

A deep melancholy settled on them both. Linda saw too clearly that she could not hope to compete with a fiancée who was not only prettier and more correct than she was, but also dead. It seemed most unfair. Had she remained alive her prettiness would surely, after fifteen years of marriage, have faded away, her correctness have become a bore; dead, she was embalmed for ever in her youth, her beauty, and her *gentillesse*.

After dinner, however, Linda was restored to happiness. Being made love to by Fabrice was an intoxication, quite different from anything she had hitherto experienced.

('I was forced to the conclusion,' she said, when telling me about this time, 'that neither Tony nor Christian had an inkling of what we used to call the facts of life. But I suppose all Englishmen are hopeless as lovers.'

'Not all,' I said, 'the trouble with most of them is that their minds are not on it, and it happens to require a very great deal of application. Alfred,' I told her, 'is wonderful.'

'Oh, good,' she said, but she sounded unconvinced I thought.)

They sat until late looking out of the open window. It was a hot evening, and, when the sun had gone, a green light lingered behind the black bunches of the trees until complete darkness fell.

'Do you always laugh when you make love?' said Fabrice.

'I hadn't thought about it, but I suppose I do. I generally laugh when I'm happy and cry when I'm not. I am a simple character, you know. Do you find it odd?'

'Very disconcerting at first, I must say.'

'But why—don't most women laugh?'

'Indeed, they do not. More often they cry.'

'How extraordinary—don't they enjoy it?'

'It has nothing to do with enjoyment. If they are young they call on their mothers, if they are religious they call on the Virgin to forgive them. But I have never known one who laughed except you. *Mais qu'est ce que vous voulez, vous êtes une folle.*'

Linda was fascinated.

'What else do they do?'

'What they all do, except you, is to say: "*Comme vous devez me mépriser*".'

'But why should you despise them?'

'Oh, really, my dear, one does, that's all.'

'Well, I call that most unfair. First you seduce them, then you despise them, poor things. What a monster you are.'

'They like it. They like grovelling about and saying "*Qu'est ce que j'ai fait? Mon Dieu, hélas Fabrice, que pouvez-bien penser de moi? O, que j'ai honte*". It's all part of the thing to them. But you, you seem unaware of your shame, you just roar with laughter. It is very strange. *Pas désagréable, il faut avouer.*'

'Then what about the fiancée,' said Linda, 'did you despise her?'

'*Mais non, voyons*, of course not. She was a virtuous woman.'

'Do you mean to say you never went to bed with her?'

'Never. Never would such a thing have crossed my mind in a thousand thousand years.'

'Goodness,' said Linda. 'In England we always do.'

'*Ma chère, c'est bien connu, le côté animal des anglais.* The English are a drunken and an incontinent race, it is well known.'

'They don't know it. They think it's foreigners who are all those things.'

'French women are the most virtuous in the world,' said Fabrice, in the tones of exaggerated pride with which Frenchmen always talk about their women.

'Oh, dear,' said Linda, sadly. 'I was so virtuous once. I wonder what happened to me. I went wrong when I married my first husband, but how was I to know? I thought he was a god and that I should love him for ever. Then I went wrong again when I ran away with Christian, but I thought I loved him, and I did too, very much more than Tony, but he never really loved me, and very soon I bored him, I wasn't serious enough, I suppose. Anyhow, if I hadn't done these things, I shouldn't have ended up on a suitcase at the Gare du Nord and I would never have met you, so, really, I'm glad. And in my next life, wherever I happen to be born, I must remember to fly to the boulevards as soon as I'm of marriageable age, and find a husband there.'

'*Comme c'est gentil,*' said Fabrice, '*et, en effet,* French marriages are generally very very happy you know. My father and mother had a cloudless life together, they loved each other so much that they hardly went out in society at all. My mother still lives in a sort of afterglow of happiness from it. What a good woman she is!'

'I must tell you,' Linda went on, 'that my mother and one of my aunts, one of my sisters and my cousin, are virtuous women, so virtue is not unknown in my family. And anyway, Fabrice, what about your grandmother?'

'Yes,' said Fabrice, with a sigh. 'I admit that she was a great sinner. But she was also *très grande dame,* and she died fully redeemed by the rites of the Church.'

CHAPTER XVIII

THEIR life now began to acquire a routine. Fabrice dined with her every night in the flat—he never took her out to a restaurant again—and stayed with her until seven o'clock the following morning. '*J'ai horreur de coucher seul,*' he said. At seven he would get up, dress, and go home, in time to be in his bed at eight o'clock, when his breakfast was brought in. He would have his breakfast, read the newspapers, and, at nine, ring up Linda and talk nonsense for half an hour, as though he had not seen her for days.

'Go on,' he would say, if she showed any signs of flagging. '*Allons, des histoires!*'

During the day she hardly ever saw him. He always lunched with his mother, who had the first-floor flat in the house where he lived on the ground floor. Sometimes he took Linda sightseeing in the afternoon, but generally he did not appear until about half-past seven, soon after which they dined.

Linda occupied her days buying clothes, which she paid for with great wads of banknotes given her by Fabrice.

'Might as well be hanged for a sheep as a lamb,' she thought. 'And as he despises me anyway it can't make very much difference.'

Fabrice was delighted. He took an intense interest in her clothes, looked them up and down, made her parade round her drawing-room in them, forced her to take them back to the shops for alterations which seemed to her quite unnecessary, but which proved in the end to have made all the difference. Linda had never before fully realized the superiority of French clothes to English. In London she had been considered exceptionally well dressed, when she was married to Tony; she now realized that never could she have had, by French standards, the smallest pretensions to *chic*. The things she had with her seemed to her so appallingly dowdy, so skimpy and miserable and without line, that she went to the Galeries Lafayette and bought herself a ready-made dress there before she dared to venture into the big houses. When she did finally emerge from them with a few clothes, Fabrice advised her to get a great many more. Her taste, he said, was not at all bad, for an Englishwoman, though he doubted whether she would really become *élégante* in the true sense of the word.

'Only by trial and error,' he said, 'can you find out your *genre*, can you see where you are going. *Continuez, donc, ma chère, allez-y. Jusqu'à présent, ça ne va pas mal du tout.*'

The weather now became hot and sultry, holiday, seaside weather. But this was 1939, and men's thoughts were not of relaxation but of death, not of bathing-suits but of uniforms, not of dance music but of trumpets, while beaches for the next few years were to be battle and not pleasure grounds. Fabrice said every day how much he longed to take Linda to the Riviera, to Venice and to his beautiful chateau in the Dauphiné. But he was a reservist, and would be called up any day now. Linda did not mind staying in Paris at all. She could sunbathe in her flat as much as she wanted to. She felt no particular apprehensions about the coming war, she was essentially a person who lived in the present.

'I couldn't sunbathe naked like this anywhere else,' she said, 'and it's the only holiday thing I enjoy. I don't like swimming, or tennis, or dancing, or gambling, so you see I'm just as well off here sunbathing and shopping, two perfect occupations for the day, and you, my darling love, at night. I should think I'm the happiest woman in the world.'

One boiling hot afternoon in July she arrived home wearing a new and particularly ravishing straw hat. It was large and simple, with a wreath of flowers and two blue bows. Her right arm was full of roses and carnations, and in her left hand was a striped bandbox, containing another exquisite hat. She let herself in with her latchkey, and stumped, on the high cork soles of her sandals, to the drawing-room.

The green venetian blinds were down, and the room was full of warm shadows, two of which suddenly resolved themselves into a thin man and a not so thin man—Davey and Lord Merlin.

'Good heavens,' said Linda, and she flopped down on to a sofa, scattering the roses at her feet.

'Well,' said Davey, 'you do look pretty.'

Linda felt really frightened, like a child caught out in some misdeed, like a child whose new toy is going to be taken away. She looked from one to the other. Lord Merlin was wearing black spectacles.

'Are you in disguise?' said Linda.

'No, what do you mean? Oh, the spectacles—I have to wear them when I go abroad, I have such kind eyes you see, beggars and things cluster round and annoy me.'

He took them off and blinked.

'What have you come for?'

'You don't seem very pleased to see us,' said Davey. 'We came, actually, to see if you were all right. As it's only too obvious that you are, we may as well go away again.'

'How did you find out? Do Mummy and Fa know?' she added, faintly.

'No, absolutely nothing. They think you're still with Christian. We haven't come in the spirit of two Victorian uncles, my dear Linda, if that's what you're thinking. I happened to see a man I know who had been to Perpignan, and he mentioned that Christian was living with Lavender Davis——'

'Oh good,' said Linda.

'What? And that you had left six weeks ago. I went round to Cheyne Walk and there you obviously weren't, and then Mer and I got faintly worried to think of you wandering about the Continent, so ill suited (we thought, how wrong we were) to look after yourself, and at the same time madly curious to know your whereabouts and present circumstances, so we put in motion a little discreet detective work, which revealed your whereabouts—your circumstances are now as clear as daylight, and I, for one, feel most relieved.'

'You gave us a fright,' said Lord Merlin, crossly. 'Another time, when you are putting on this Cléo de Mérode act, you might send a postcard. For one thing, it is a great pleasure to see you in the part. I wouldn't have missed it for worlds. I hadn't realized, Linda, that you were such a beautiful woman.'

Davey was laughing quietly to himself.

'Oh, goodness, how funny it all is—so wonderfully old-fashioned. The shopping! The parcels! The flowers! So tremendously Victorian. People have been delivering cardboard boxes every five minutes since we arrived. What an interest you are in one's life, Linda dear. Have you told him he must give you up and marry a pure young girl yet?'

Linda said disarmingly: 'Don't tease, Dave. I'm so happy you can't think.'

'Yes, you look happy I must say. Oh, this flat is such a joke.'

'I was just thinking,' said Lord Merlin, 'that, however much taste may change, it always follows a stereotyped plan. Frenchmen used to keep their mistresses in *appartements*, each exactly like the other, in which the dominant note, you might say, was lace and velvet. The walls, the bed, the dressing table, the very bath itself were hung with lace, and everything else was velvet. Nowadays for lace you substitute glass, and everything else is satin. I bet you've got a glass bed, Linda?'

'Yes—but——'

'And a glass dressing-table, and bathroom, and I wouldn't be surprised if your bath were made of glass, with goldfish swimming about in the sides of it. Goldfish are a prevailing motif all down the ages.'

'You've looked,' said Linda sulkily. 'Very clever.'

'Oh, what heaven,' said Davey. 'So it's true! He hasn't looked, I swear, but you see it's not beyond the bounds of human ingenuity to guess.'

'But there are some things here,' said Lord Merlin, 'which do raise the level, all the same. A Gauguin, those two Matisses (chintzy, but accomplished) and this Savonnerie carpet. Your protector must be very rich.'

'He is,' said Linda.

'Then, Linda dear, could one ask for a cup of tea?'

She rang the bell, and soon Davey was falling upon *éclairs* and *mille feuilles* with all the abandon of a schoolboy.

'I shall pay for this,' he said, with a devil-may-care smile, 'but never mind, one's not in Paris every day.'

Lord Merlin wandered round with his tea-cup. He picked up a book which Fabrice had given Linda the day before, of romantic nineteenth-century poetry:

'Is this what you're reading now?' he said. ' "*Dieu, que le son du cor est triste au fond des bois*". I had a friend, when I lived in Paris, who had a boa constrictor as a pet, and this boa constrictor got itself inside a French horn. My friend rang me up in a fearful state, saying: "*Dieu, que le son du boa est triste au fond du cor*". I've never forgotten it.'

'What time does your lover generally arrive?' said Davey, taking out his watch.

'Not till about seven. Do stay and see him, he's such a terrific Hon.'

'No, thank you, not for the world.'

'Who is he?' said Lord Merlin.

'He's called the Duke of Sauveterre.'

A look of great surprise, mingled with horrified amusement, passed between Davey and Lord Merlin.

'Fabrice de Sauveterre?'

'Yes. Do you know him?'

'Darling Linda, one always forgets, under that look of great sophistication, what a little provincial you really are. Of course we know him, and all about him, and, what's more, so does everyone except you.'

'Well, don't you think he's a terrific Hon?'

'Fabrice,' said Lord Merlin with emphasis, 'is undoubtedly one of the wickedest men in Europe, as far as women are concerned. But I must admit that he's an extremely agreeable companion.'

'Do you remember in Venice,' said Davey, 'one used to see him at work in that gondola, one after another, bowling them over like rabbits, poor dears?'

'Please remember,' said Linda, 'that you are eating his tea at this moment.'

'Yes, indeed, and so delicious. Another *éclair*, please, Linda. That summer,' he went on, 'when he made off with Ciano's girl friend, what a fuss there was, I never shall forget, and then, a week later, he *plaqué*'d her in Cannes and went to Salzburg with Martha Birmingham, and poor old Claud shot at him four times, and always missed him.'

'Fabrice has a charmed life,' said Lord Merlin. 'I suppose he has been shot at more than anybody, and, as far as I know, he's never had a scratch.'

Linda was unmoved by these revelations, which had been forestalled by Fabrice himself. Anyhow, no woman really minds hearing of the past affairs of her lover, it is the future alone that has the power to terrify.

'Come on, Mer,' said Davey. 'Time the *petite femme* got herself into a *négligée*. Goodness, what a scene there'll be when he smells Mer's cigar, there'll be a *crime passionel*, I shouldn't wonder. Good-bye, Linda darling, we're off to dine with our intellectual friends, you know, will you be lunching with us at the Ritz to-morrow? About one, then. Good-bye—give our love to Fabrice.'

When Fabrice came in he sniffed about, and asked whose cigar. Linda explained.

'They say they know you?'

'*Mais bien sûr—Merlin tellement gentil, et l'autre Warbeck, toujours si malade, le pauvre. Je les connaissais à Venise.* What did they think of all this?'

'Well, they roared at the flat.'

'Yes, I can imagine. It is quite unsuitable for you, this flat, but it's convenient, and with the war coming——'

'Oh, but I love it, I wouldn't like anything else half so much. Wasn't it clever of them, though, to find me?'

'Do you mean to say you never told anybody where you were?'

'I really didn't think of it—the days go by, you know—one simply doesn't remember these things.'

'And it was six weeks before they thought of looking for you? As a family you seem to me strangely *décousu*.'

Linda suddenly threw herself into his arms, and said, with great passion: 'Never, never let me go back to them.'

'My darling—but you love them. Mummy and Fa, Matt and Robin and Victoria and Fanny. What is all this?'

'I never want to leave you again as long as I live.'

'Aha! But you know you will probably have to, soon. The war is going to begin, you know.'

'Why can't I stay here? I could work—I could become a nurse—well, perhaps not a nurse, actually, but something.'

'If you promise to do what I tell you, you may stay here for a time. At the beginning we shall sit and look at the Germans across the Maginot Line, then I shall be a great deal in Paris, between Paris and the front, but mostly here. At that time I shall want you here. Then somebody, we or the Germans, but I am very much afraid the Germans, will pour across the line, and a war of movement will begin. I shall have notice of that *étape*, and what you must promise me is that the very minute I tell you to leave for London you will leave, even if you can see no reason for doing so. I should be hampered beyond words in my duties if you were still here. So will you solemnly promise, now?'

'All right,' said Linda. 'Solemnly. I don't believe anything so dreadful could happen to me, but I promise to do as you say. Now will you promise that you will come to London as soon as it's all over and find me again. Promise?'

'Yes,' said Fabrice. 'I will do that.'

Luncheon with Davey and Lord Merlin was a gloomy meal. Preoccupation reigned. The two men had stayed up late and merrily with their literary friends, and showed every sign of having done so. Davey was beginning to be aware of the cruel pangs of dyspepsia. Lord Merlin was suffering badly from an ordinary straightforward hangover, and, when he removed his spectacles, his eyes were seen to be not kind at all. But Linda was far the most wretched of the three, she was, in fact, perfectly distracted by having over-heard two French ladies in the foyer talking about Fabrice. She had arrived, as, from old habits of punctuality drummed into her by Uncle Matthew she always did, rather early. Fabrice had never taken her to the Ritz, she thought it delightful, she knew she was looking quite as pretty, and nearly as well dressed, as anybody there, and settled herself happily to await the others. Suddenly she heard, with that pang which the heart receives when the loved one's name is mentioned by strangers:

'And have you seen Fabrice at all?'

'Well, I have, because I quite often see him at Mme de Sauveterre's, but he never goes out anywhere, as you know.'

'Then what about Jacqueline?'

'Still in England. He is utterly lost without her, poor Fabrice, he is like a dog looking for its master. He sits sadly at home, never goes to parties, never goes to the club, sees nobody. His mother is really worried about him.'

'Who would ever have expected Fabrice to be so faithful? How long is it?'

'Five years, I believe. A wonderfully happy *ménage*.'

'Surely Jacqueline will come back soon.'

'Not until the old aunt has died. It seems she changes her will incessantly, and Jacqueline feels she must be there all the time—after all, she has her husband and children to consider.'

'Rather hard on Fabrice?'

'*Qu'est-ce que vous voulez?* His mother says he rings her up every morning and talks for an hour——'

It was at this point that Davey and Lord Merlin, looking tired and cross, arrived, and took Linda off to luncheon with them. She was longing to stay and hear more of this torturing conversation, but, eschewing cocktails with a shudder, they hurried her off to the dining-room, where they were only fairly nice to her, and frankly disagreeable to each other.

She thought the meal would never come to an end, and, when at last it did, she threw herself into a taxi and drove to Fabrice's house. She must find out about Jacqueline, she must know his intentions. When Jacqueline returned would that be the moment for her, Linda, to leave as she had promised? War of movement indeed!

The servant said that M. le Duc had just gone out with Madame la Duchesse, but that he would be back in about an hour. Linda said she would wait, and he showed her into Fabrice's sitting-room. She took off her hat, and wandered restlessly about. She had been here several times before, with Fabrice, and it had seemed, after her brilliantly sunny flat, a little dismal. Now that she was alone in it she began to be aware of the extreme beauty of the room, a grave and solemn beauty which penetrated her. It was very high, rectangular in shape, with grey boiseries and cherry-coloured brocade curtains. It looked into a courtyard and never could get a ray of sunshine, that was not the plan. This was a civilized interior, it had nothing to do with out-of-doors. Every object in it was perfect. The furniture had the severe lines and excellent proportions of 1780, there was a portrait by Lancret of a lady with a parrot on her wrist, a bust of the same lady by Bouchardon, a carpet like the one in Linda's flat, but larger and grander, with a huge coat of arms in the middle. A high carved bookcase contained nothing but French classics bound in contemporary morocco, with the Sauveterre crest, and open on a map table lay a copy of Redouté's roses.

Linda began to feel much more calm, but, at the same time, very sad. She saw that this room indicated a side of Fabrice's character which she had hardly been allowed to apprehend, and which had its roots in old civilized French grandeur. It was the essential Fabrice, something in which she could never have a share—she would always be outside in her sunny modern flat, kept away from all this, kept rigidly away even if their liaison were to go on for ever. The origins of the Radlett family were lost in the mists of antiquity, but the origins of Fabrice's family were not lost at all, there they were, each generation clutching at the next. The English, she thought, throw off their ancestors. It is the great strength of our aristocracy, but Fabrice has his round his neck, and he will never get away from them.

She began to realize that here were her competitors, her enemies, and that Jacqueline was nothing in comparison. Here, and in the grave of Louise. To come here and make a scene about a rival mistress would be utterly meaningless, she would be one unreality complaining about another. Fabrice would be annoyed, as men always are annoyed on these occasions, and she would get no satisfaction. She could hear his voice, dry and sarcastic:

'Ah! *Vous me grondez, madame?*'

Better go, better ignore the whole affair. Her only hope was to keep things on their present footing, to keep the happiness which she was enjoying day by day, hour by hour, and not to think about the future at all. It held nothing for her, leave it alone. Besides, everybody's future was in jeopardy now the war was coming, this war which she always forgot about.

She was reminded of it, however, when, that evening, Fabrice appeared in uniform.

'Another month I should think,' he said. 'As soon as they have got the harvest in.'

'If it depended on the English,' said Linda, 'they would wait until after the Christmas shopping. Oh, Fabrice, it won't last very long, will it?'

'It will be very disagreeable while it does last,' said Fabrice. 'Did you come to my flat to-day?'

'Yes, after lunching with those two old cross-patches I suddenly felt I wanted to see you very much.'

'*Comme c'est gentil,*' he looked at her quizzically, as though something had occurred to him, 'but why didn't you wait?'

'Your ancestors frightened me off.'

'Oh, they did? But you have ancestors yourself I believe, *madame?*'

'Yes, but they don't hang about in the same way as yours do.'

'You should have waited,' said Fabrice, 'it is always a very great pleasure to see you, both for me and for my ancestors. It cheers us all up.'

Germaine now came into the room with huge armfuls of flowers and a note from Lord Merlin, saying:

'Here are some coals for Newcastle. We are tottering home by the ferry-boat. Do you think I shall get Davey back alive? I enclose something which might, one day, be useful.'

It was a note for 20,000 francs.

'I must say,' said Linda, 'considering what cruel eyes he has, he does think of everything.'

She felt sentimental after the occurrences of the day.

'Tell me, Fabrice,' she said, 'what did you think the first moment you ever saw me?'

'If you really want to know, I thought: "*Tiens, elle ressemble à la petite Bosquet*".'

'Who is that?'

'There are two Bosquet sisters, the elder, who is a beauty, and a little one who looks like you.'

'*Merci beaucoup*,' said Linda. '*J'aimerais autant ressembler à l'autre.*'

Fabrice laughed. '*Ensuite, je me suis dit, comme c'est amusant, le côté demodé de tout ça——*'

When the war, which had for so long been pending, did actually break out some six weeks later, Linda was strangely unmoved by the fact. She was enveloped in the present, in her own detached and futureless life, which, anyhow, seemed so precarious, so much from one hour to another: exterior events hardly impinged on her consciousness. When she thought about the war it seemed to her almost a relief that it had actually begun, in so far as a beginning is the first step towards an end. That it had only begun in name and not in fact did not occur to her. Of course, had Fabrice been taken away by it her attitude would have been very different, but his job, an intelligence one, kept him mostly in Paris, and, indeed, she now saw rather more of him than formerly, as he moved into her flat, shutting up his own and sending his mother to the country. He would appear and disappear at all sorts of odd moments of the night and day, and, as the sight of him was a constant joy to Linda, as she could imagine no greater happiness than she always felt when the empty space in front of her eyes became filled by his form, these sudden apparitions kept her in a state of happy suspense and their relationship at fever point.

Since Davey's visit Linda had been getting letters from her family. He had given Aunt Sadie her address and told her that Linda was doing war work in Paris, providing comforts for the French army, he said vaguely, and with some degree of truth. Aunt Sadie was pleased about this, she thought it very good of Linda to work so hard (all night sometimes, Davey said), and was glad to hear that she earned her keep. Voluntary work was often unsatisfactory and expensive. Uncle Matthew thought it a pity to work for foreigners, and deplored the fact that his children were so fond of crossing oceans, but he also was very much in favour of war work. He was himself utterly disgusted that the War Office were not able to offer him the opportunity of repeating his exploit with the entrenching tool, or, indeed, any job at all, and he went about like a bear with a sore head, full of unsatisfied desire to fight for his King and country.

I wrote to Linda and told her about Christian, who was back in London, had left the Communist party and had joined up. Lavender had also returned: she was now in the A.T.S.

Christian did not show the slightest curiosity about what had happened to Linda, he did not seem to want to divorce her or to marry Lavender, he had thrown himself heart and soul into army life and thought of nothing but the war.

Before leaving Perpignan he had extricated Matt, who, after a good deal of persuasion, had consented to leave his Spanish comrades in order to join the battle against Fascism on another front. He went into Uncle Matthew's old regiment, and was said to bore his brother officers in the mess very much by arguing that they were training the men all wrong, and that, during the battle of the Ebro, things had been done thus and thus. In the end his colonel, who was rather brighter in the head than some of the others, hit upon the obvious reply, which was, 'Well, anyway, your side lost!' This shut Matt up on tactics, but got him going on statistics—'30,000 Germans and Italians, 500 German planes', and so forth—which were almost equally dull and boring.

Linda heard no more about Jacqueline, and the wretchedness into which she had been thrown by those few chance words overheard at the Ritz was gradually forgotten. She reminded herself that nobody ever really knew the state of a man's heart, not even, perhaps specially not, his mother, and that in love it is actions that count. Fabrice had no time now for two women, he spent every spare moment with her and that in itself reassured her. Besides, just as her marriages with Tony and Christian had been necessary in order to lead up to her meeting with Fabrice, so this affair had led up to his meeting with her: undoubtedly he must have been seeing Jacqueline off at the Gare du Nord when he found Linda crying on her suitcase. Putting herself in Jacqueline's shoes, she realized how much preferable it was to be in her own: in any case it was not Jacqueline who was her dangerous rival, but that dim, virtuous figure from the past, Louise. Whenever Fabrice showed signs of becoming a little less practical, a little more nonsensical and romantic, it was of his fiancée that he would speak, dwelling with a gentle sadness upon her beauty, her noble birth, her vast estates and her religious mania. Linda once suggested that, had the fiancée lived to become a wife, she might not have been a very happy one.

'All that climbing,' she said, 'in at other people's bedroom windows, might it not have upset her?'

Fabrice looked intensely shocked and reproachful and said that there never would have been any climbing, that, where marriage was concerned, he had the very highest ideals, and that his whole life would have been devoted to making Louise happy. Linda felt herself rebuked, but was not entirely convinced.

All this time Linda watched the tree-tops from her window. They had changed, since she had been in the flat, from bright green against a bright blue sky, to dark green against a lavender sky, to yellow against a cerulean sky, until now they were black skeletons against a sky of moleskin, and it was Christmas Day. The windows could no longer be opened until they disappeared, but, whenever the sun did come out, it shone into her rooms, and the flat was always as warm as a toast. On this Christmas morning Fabrice arrived, quite unexpectedly, before she was up, his arms full of parcels, and soon the floor of her bedroom was covered with waves of tissue paper through which, like wrecks and monsters half submerged beneath a shallow sea, appeared fur coats, hats, real mimosa, artificial flowers, feathers, scent, gloves, stockings, underclothes and a bulldog puppy.

Linda had spent Lord Merlin's 20,000 francs on a tiny Renoir for Fabrice: six inches of seascape, a little patch of brilliant blue, which she thought would look just right in his room in the Rue Bonaparte. Fabrice was the most difficult person to buy presents for, he possessed a larger assortment of jewels, knick-knacks and rare objects of all kinds than anybody she had ever known. He was delighted with the Renoir, nothing, he said, could have pleased him more, and Linda felt that he really meant it.

'Oh, such a cold day,' he said. 'I've just been to church.'

'Fabrice, how can you go to church when there's me?'

'Well, why not.'

'You're a Roman Catholic, aren't you?'

'Of course I am. What do you suppose? Do you think I look like a Calvinist?'

'But then aren't you living in mortal sin? So what about when you confess?'

'On ne précise pas,' said Fabrice, carelessly, 'and, in any case, these little sins of the body are quite unimportant.'

Linda would have liked to think that she was more in Fabrice's life than a little sin of the body, but she was used to coming up against these closed doors in her relationship with him, and had learnt to be philosophical about it and thankful for the happiness that she did receive.

'In England,' she said, 'people are always renouncing each other on account of being Roman Catholics. It's sometimes very sad for them. A lot of English books are about this, you know.'

'Les Anglais sont des insensés, je l'ai toujours dit. You almost sound as if you want to be given up. What has happened since Saturday? Not tired of your war work, I hope?'

'No, no, Fabrice. I just wondered, that's all.'

'But you look so sad, *ma chérie*, what is it?'

'I was thinking of Christmas Day at home. I always feel sentimental at Christmas.'

'If what I said might happen does happen and I have to send you back to England, shall you go home to your father?'

'Oh, no,' said Linda, 'anyway, it won't happen. All the English papers say we are killing Germany with our blockade.'

'*Le blocus*,' said Fabrice impatiently, '*quelle blague! Je vais vous dire, madame, ils ne se fichent pas mal de votre blocus.* So where would you go?'

'To my own house in Chelsea, and wait for you to come.'

'It might be months, or years.'

'I shall wait,' she said.

The skeleton tree-tops began to fill out, they acquired a pinkish tinge, which gradually changed to golden-green. The sky was often blue, and, on some days, Linda could once more open her windows and lie naked in the sun, whose rays by now had a certain strength. She always loved the spring, she loved the sudden changes of temperature, the dips backward into winter and forward into summer, and, this year, living in beautiful Paris, her perceptions heightened by great emotion, she was profoundly affected by it. There was now a curious feeling in the air, very different from and much more nervous than that which had been current before Christmas, and the town was full of rumours. Linda often thought of the expression '*fin de siècle*'. There was a certain analogy, she thought, between the state of mind which it denoted and that prevailing now, only now it was more like '*fin de vie*'. It was as though everybody around her, and she herself, were living out the last few days of their lives, but this curious feeling did not disturb her, she was possessed by a calm and happy fatalism. She occupied the hours of waiting between Fabrice's visits by lying in the sun, when there was any, and playing with her puppy. On Fabrice's advice she even began to order some new clothes for the summer. He seemed to regard the acquisition of clothes as one of the chief duties of woman, to be pursued through war and revolution, through sickness, and up to death. It was as one who might say, 'whatever happens the fields must be tilled, the cattle tended, life must go on'. He was so essentially urban that to him the slow roll of the seasons was marked by the spring *tailleurs*, the summer *imprimés*, the autumn *ensembles*, and the winter furs of his mistress.

On a beautiful windy blue and white day in April the blow fell. Fabrice, whom Linda had not seen for nearly a week, arrived from the front looking grave and worried, and told her that she must go back to England at once.

'I've got a place for you in the aeroplane,' he said, 'for this afternoon. You must pack a small suitcase, and the rest of your things must go after you by train. Germaine will see to them. I have to go to the Ministère de la Guerre, I'll be back as soon as possible, and anyhow in time to take you to Le Bourget. Come on,' he added, 'just time for a little war work.' He was in his most practical and least romantic mood.

When he returned he looked more preoccupied than ever. Linda was waiting for him, her box was packed, she was wearing the blue suit in which he had first seen her, and had her old mink coat over her arm.

'*Tiens*,' said Fabrice, who always at once noticed what she had on, 'what is this? A fancy-dress party?'

'Fabrice, you must understand that I can't take away the things you have given me. I loved having them while I was here, and while they gave you pleasure seeing me in them, but, after all, I have some pride. *Je n'étais quand-même pas élevée dans un bordel.*'

'*Ma chère*, try not to be so middle-class, it doesn't suit you at all. There's no time for you to change—wait, though——' He went into her bedroom, and came out again with a long sable coat, one of his Christmas presents. He took her mink coat, rolled it up, threw it into the waste-paper basket, and put the other over her arm in its place.

'Germaine will send your things after you,' he said. 'Come now, we must go.'

Linda said good-bye to Germaine, picked up the bulldog puppy, and followed Fabrice into the lift, out into the street. She did not fully understand that she was leaving that happy life behind her for ever.

CHAPTER XIX

AT first, back in Cheyne Walk, she still did not understand. The world was grey and cold certainly, the sun had gone behind a cloud, but only for a time: it would come out again, she would soon once more be enveloped in that heat and light which had left her in so warm a glow, there was still much blue in the sky, this little cloud would pass. Then, as sometimes happens, the cloud, which had seemed at first such a little one, grew and grew, until it became a thick grey blanket smothering the horizon. The bad news began, the terrible days, the unforgettable weeks. A great horror of steel was rolling over France, was rolling towards England, swallowing on its way the puny beings who tried to stop it, swallowing Fabrice, Germaine, the flat, and the past months of Linda's life, swallowing Alfred, Bob, Matt, and little Robin, coming to swallow us all. London people cried openly in the buses, in the streets, for the English army which was lost.

Then, suddenly one day, the English army turned up again. There was a feeling of such intense relief, it was as if the war were over and won. Alfred and Bob and Matt and little Robin all reappeared, and, as a lot of French soldiers also arrived, Linda had a wild hope that Fabrice might be with them. She sat all day by the telephone, and when it rang and was not Fabrice she was furious with the unlucky telephone—I know, because it happened to me. She was so furious that I dropped the receiver and went straight round to Cheyne Walk.

I found her unpacking a huge trunk, which had just arrived from France. I had never seen her looking so beautiful. It made me gasp, and I remembered how Davey had said, when he got back from Paris, that at last Linda was fulfilling the promise of her childhood, and had become a beauty.

'How do you imagine this got here?' she said, between tears and laughter. 'What an extraordinary war. The Southern Railway people brought it just now and I signed for it, all as though nothing peculiar were happening—I don't understand a word of it. What are you doing in London, darling?'

She seemed unaware of the fact that half an hour ago she had spoken to me, and indeed bitten my head off, on the telephone.

'I'm with Alfred. He's got to get a lot of new equipment and see all sorts of people. I believe he's going abroad again very soon.'

'Awfully good of him,' said Linda, 'when he needn't have joined up at all, I imagine. What does he say about Dunkirk?'

'He says it was like something out of the Boy's Own—he seems to have had a most fascinating time.'

'They all did, the boys were here yesterday and you never heard anything like their stories. Of course they never quite realized how desperate it all was until they got to the coast. Oh, isn't it wonderful to have them back. If only—if only one knew what had happened to one's French buddies——'

She looked at me under her eyelashes, and I thought she was going to tell me about her life, but, if so, she changed her mind and went on unpacking.

'I shall have to put these winter things back in their boxes really,' she said. 'I simply haven't any cupboards that will hold them all, but it's something to do, and I like to see them again.'

'You should shake them,' I said, 'and put them in the sun. They may be damp.'

'Darling, you are wonderful, you always know.'

'Where did you get that puppy?' I said enviously. I had wanted a bulldog for years, but Alfred never would let me have one because of the snoring.

'Brought him back with me. He's the nicest puppy I ever had, so anxious to oblige, you can't think.'

'What about quarantine then?'

'Under my coat,' said Linda, laconically. 'You should have heard him grunting and snuffling, it shook the whole place, I was terrified, but he was so good. He never budged. And talking of puppies, those ghastly Kroesigs are sending Moira to America, isn't it typical of them? I've made a great thing with Tony about seeing her before she goes, after all I am her mother.'

'That's what I can't ever understand about you, Linda.'

'What?'

'How you could have been so dreadful to Moira.'

'Dull,' said Linda. 'Uninteresting.'

'I know, but the point is that children are like puppies, and if you never see puppies, if you give them to the groom or the gamekeeper to bring up, look how dull and uninteresting they always are. Children are just the same—you must give them much more than their life if they are to be any good. Poor little Moira—all you gave her was that awful name.'

'Oh, Fanny, I do know. To tell you the truth I believe it was always in the back of my mind that, sooner or later, I should have to run away from Tony, and I didn't want to get too fond of Moira, or make her too fond of me. She might have become an anchor, and I simply didn't dare let myself be anchored to the Kroesigs.'

'Poor Linda.'

'Oh, don't pity me. I've had eleven months of perfect and unalloyed happiness, very few people can say that, in the course of long long lives, I imagine.'

I imagined so too. Alfred and I are happy, as happy as married people can be. We are in love, we are intellectually and physically suited in every possible way, we rejoice in each other's company, we have no money troubles and three delightful children. And yet, when I consider my life, day by day, hour by hour, it seemed to be composed of a series of pinpricks. Nannies, cooks, the endless drudgery of housekeeping, the nerve-racking noise and boring repetitive conversation of small children (boring in the sense that it bores into one's very brain), their absolute incapacity to amuse themselves, their sudden and terrifying illnesses. Alfred's not infrequent bouts of moodiness, his invariable complaints at meals about the pudding, the way he will always use my tooth-paste and will always squeeze the tube in the middle. These are the components of marriage, the wholemeal bread of life, rough, ordinary, but sustaining; Linda had been feeding upon honey-dew, and that is an incomparable diet.

The old woman who had opened the door to me came in and said was that everything, because, if so, she would be going home.

'Everything,' said Linda. 'Mrs. Hunt,' she said to me, when she had gone. 'A terrific Hon—she comes daily.'

'Why don't you go to Alconleigh,' I said, 'or to Shenley? Aunt Emily and Davey would love to have you, and I'm going there with the children as soon as Alfred is off again.'

'I'd like to come for a visit some time, when I know a little more what is happening, but at the moment I must stop here. Give them my love though.

I've got such masses to tell you, Fanny, what we really need is hours and hours in the Hons' cupboard.'

After a good deal of hesitation Tony Kroesig and his wife, Pixie, allowed Moira to go and see her mother before leaving England. She arrived at Cheyne Walk in Tony's car, still driven by a chauffeur in uniform not the King's. She was a plain, stodgy, shy little girl, with no echo of the Radletts about her; not to put too fine a point on it she was a real little Gretchen.

'What a sweet puppy,' she said, awkwardly, when Linda had kissed her. She was clearly very much embarrassed.

'What's his name?'

'Plon-plon.'

'Oh. Is that a French name?'

'Yes, it is. He's a French dog, you see.'

'Daddy says the French are terrible.'

'I expect he does.'

'He says they have let us down, and what can we expect if we have anything to do with such people.'

'Yes, he would.'

'Daddy thinks we ought to fight with the Germans and not against them.'

'M'm. But Daddy doesn't seem to be fighting very much with anybody, or against anybody, or at all, as far as I can see. Now, Moira, before you go I have got two things for you, one is a present and the other is a little talk. The talk is very dull, so we'll get that over first, shall we?'

'Yes,' said Moira, apathetically. She lugged the puppy on to the sofa beside her.

'I want you to know,' said Linda, 'and to remember, please, Moira (stop playing with the puppy a minute and listen carefully to what I am saying) that I don't at all approve of you running away like this, I think it most dreadfully wrong. When you have a country which has given you as much as England has given all of us, you ought to stick to it, and not go wandering off as soon as it looks like being in trouble.'

'But it's not my fault,' said Moira, her forehead puckering. 'I'm only a child and Pixie is taking me. I have to do what I'm told, don't I?'

'Yes, of course, I know that's true. But you'd much rather stay, wouldn't you?' said Linda hopefully.

'Oh no, I don't think so. There might be air-raids.'

At this Linda gave up. Children might or might not enjoy air-raids actually in progress, but a child who was not thrilled by the idea of them was incomprehensible to her, and she could not imagine having conceived such a being. Useless to waste any more time and breath on this unnatural little girl. She sighed and said:

'Now wait a moment and I'll get your present.'

She had in her pocket, in a velvet box, a coral hand holding a diamond arrow, which Fabrice had given her, but she could not bear to waste anything so pretty on this besotted little coward. She went to her bedroom and found a sports wristwatch, one of her wedding presents when she had married Tony and which she had never worn, and gave this to Moira, who seemed quite pleased by it, and left the house as politely and unenthusiastically as she had arrived.

Linda rang me up at Shenley and told me about this interview.

'I'm in such a temper,' she said, 'I must talk to somebody. To think I ruined nine months of my life in order to have that. What do your children think about air-raids, Fanny?'

'I must say they simply long for them, and I am sorry to say they also long for the Germans to arrive. They spend the whole day making booby-traps for them in the orchard.'

'Well that's a relief anyhow—I thought perhaps it was the generation. Actually of course, it's not Moira's fault, it's all that bloody Pixie—I can see the form only too clearly, can't you? Pixie is frightened to death and she has found out that going to America is like the children's concert, you can only make it if you have a child in tow. So she's using Moira—well, it does serve one right for doing wrong.' Linda was evidently very much put out. 'And I hear Tony is going too, some Parliamentary mission or something. All I can say is what a set.'

All through those terrible months of May, June and July, Linda waited for a sign from Fabrice, but no sign came. She did not doubt that he was still alive, it was not in Linda's nature to imagine that anyone might be dead. She knew that thousands of Frenchmen were in German hands, but felt certain that, had Fabrice been taken prisoner (a thing which she did not at all approve of, incidentally, taking the old-fashioned view that, unless in exceptional circumstances, it is a disgrace), he would undoubtedly manage to escape. She would hear from him before long, and, meanwhile, there was nothing to be done, she must simply wait. All the same, as the days went by with no news, and as all the news there was from France was bad, she did become exceedingly restless. She was really more concerned with his attitude than with his safety—his attitude towards events and his attitude towards her. She felt sure that he would never be associated with the armistice, she felt sure that he would want to communicate with her, but she had no proof, and, in moments of great loneliness and depression, she allowed herself to lose faith. She realized how little she really knew of Fabrice, he had seldom talked seriously to her, their relationship having been primarily physical while their conversations and chat had all been based on jokes.

They had laughed and made love and laughed again, and the months had slipped by with no time for anything but laughter and love. Enough to satisfy her, but what about him? Now that life had become so serious, and, for a Frenchman, so tragic, would he not have forgotten that meal of whipped cream as something so utterly unimportant that it might never have existed? She began to think, more and more, to tell herself over and over again, to force herself to realize, that it was probably all finished, that Fabrice might never be anything for her now but a memory.

At the same time the few people she saw never failed when talking, as everybody talked then, about France, to emphasize that the French 'one knew', the families who were '*bien*', were all behaving very badly, convinced Pétainists. Fabrice was not one of them, she thought, she felt, but she wished she knew, she longed for evidence.

In fact, she alternated between hope and despair, but as the months went by without a word, a word that she was sure he could have sent if he had really wanted to, despair began to prevail.

Then, on a sunny Sunday morning in August, very early, her telephone bell rang. She woke up with a start, aware that it had been ringing already for several moments, and she knew with absolute certainty that this was Fabrice.

'Are you Flaxman 2815?'

'Yes.'

'I've got a call for you. You're through.'

'*Allô—allô?*'

'Fabrice?'

'*Oui.*'

'Oh! Fabrice—*on vous attend depuis si longtemps.*'

'*Comme c'est gentil. Alors, on peut venir tout de suite chez vous?*'

'Oh, wait—yes, you can come at once, but don't go for a minute, go on talking. I want to hear the sound of your voice.'

'No, no, I have a taxi outside, I shall be with you in five minutes. There's too much one can't do on the telephone, *ma chère, voyons*——' Click.

She lay back, and all was light and warmth. Life, she thought, is sometimes sad and often dull, but there are currants in the cake and here is one of them. The early morning sun shone past her window on to the river, her ceiling danced with water-reflections. The Sunday silence was broken by two swans winging slowly upstream, and then by the chugging of a little barge, while she waited for that other sound, a sound more intimately connected with the urban love affair than any except the telephone bell, that of a stopping taxicab. Sun, silence, and happiness. Presently she heard it in the street, slowly, slower, it stopped, the flag went up with a ring, the door slammed, voices, clinking coins, footsteps. She rushed downstairs.

Hours later Linda made some coffee.

'So lucky,' she said, 'that it happens to be Sunday, and Mrs. Hunt isn't here. What would she have thought?'

'Just about the same as the night porter at the Hotel Montalembert, I expect,' said Fabrice.

'Why did you come, Fabrice? To join General de Gaulle?'

'No, that was not necessary, because I have joined him already. I was with him in Bordeaux. My work has to be in France, but we have ways of communicating when we want to. I shall go and see him, of course, he expects me at midday, but actually I came on a private mission.'

He looked at her for a long time.

'I came to tell you that I love you,' he said, at last.

Linda felt giddy.

'You never said that to me in Paris.'

'No.'

'You always seemed so practical.'

'Yes, I suppose so. I had said it so often and often before in my life, I had been so romantic with so many women, that when I felt this to be different I really could not bring out all those stale old phrases again, I couldn't utter them. I never said I loved you, I never tutoyé'd you, on purpose. Because from the first moment I knew that this was as real as all the others were false, it was like recognizing somebody—there, I can't explain.'

'But that is exactly how I felt too,' said Linda, 'don't try to explain, you needn't, I know.'

'Then, when you had gone, I felt I had to tell you, and it became an obsession with me to tell you. All those dreadful weeks were made more dreadful because I was being prevented from telling you.'

'How ever did you get here?'

'On circule,' said Fabrice, vaguely. 'I must leave again to-morrow morning, very early, and I shan't come back until the war is over, but you'll wait for me, Linda, and nothing matters so much now that you know. I was tormented, I couldn't concentrate on anything, I was becoming useless in my work. In future I may have much to bear, but I shan't have to bear you going away without knowing what a great great love I have for you.'

'Oh, Fabrice, I feel—well, I suppose religious people sometimes feel like this.'

She put her head on his shoulder, and they sat for a long time in silence.

When he had paid his visit to Carlton Gardens they lunched at the Ritz. It was full of people Linda knew, all very smart, very gay, and talking with the greatest flippancy about the imminent arrival of the Germans. Had it not been for the fact that all the young men there had fought bravely in Flanders, and would, no doubt, soon be fighting bravely again, and this time with more experience, on other fields of battle, the general tone might have been considered shocking. Even Fabrice looked grave, and said they did not seem to realize——

Davey and Lord Merlin appeared. Their eyebrows went up when they saw Fabrice.

'Poor Merlin has the wrong kind,' Davey said to Linda.

'The wrong kind of what?'

'Pill to take when the Germans come. He's just got the sort you give to dogs.'

Davey brought out a jewelled box containing two pills, one white and one black.

'You take the white one first and then the black one—he really must go to my doctor.'

'I think one should let the Germans do the killing,' said Linda. 'Make them add to their own crimes and use up a bullet. Why should one smooth their path in any way? Besides, I back myself to do in at least two before they get me.'

'Oh, you're so tough, Linda, but I'm afraid it wouldn't be a bullet for me, they would torture me, look at the things I've said about them in the *Gazette*.'

'No worse than you've said about all of us,' Lord Merlin remarked.

Davey was known to be a most savage reviewer, a perfect butcher, never sparing even his dearest friends. He wrote under several pseudonyms, which in no way disguised his unmistakable style, his cruellest essays appearing over the name Little Nell.

'Are you here for long, Sauveterre?'

'No, not for long.'

Linda and Fabrice went in to luncheon. They talked of this and that, mostly jokes. Fabrice told her scandalous stories about some of the other lunchers known to him of old, with a wealth of unlikely detail. He spoke only once about France, only to say that the struggle must be carried on, everything would be all right in the end. Linda thought how different it would have been with Tony or Christian. Tony would have held forth about his experiences and made boring arrangements for his own future. Christian would have launched a monologue on world conditions subsequent to the recent fall of France, its probable repercussions in Araby and far Cashmere, the inadequacy of Pétain to deal with such a wealth of displaced persons, the steps that he, Christian, would have taken had he found himself in his, the Marshal's, shoes. Both would have spoken to her exactly, in every respect, as if she had been some chap in their club. Fabrice talked to her, at her, and for only her, it was absolutely personal talk, scattered with jokes and allusions private to them both. She had a feeling that he would not allow himself to be serious, that if he did he would have to embark on tragedy, and that he wanted her to carry away a happy memory of his visit. But he also gave an impression of boundless optimism and faith, very cheering at that dark time.

Early the next morning, another beautiful, hot, sunny morning, Linda lay back on her pillows and watched Fabrice while he dressed, as she had so often watched him in Paris. He made a certain kind of face when he was pulling his tie into a knot, she had quite forgotten it in the months between, and it brought back their Paris life to her suddenly and vividly.

'Fabrice,' she said. 'Do you think we shall ever live together again?'

'But of course we shall, for years and years and years, until I am ninety. I have a very faithful nature.'

'You weren't very faithful to Jacqueline.'

'Aha—so you know about Jacqueline, do you? *La pauvre, elle était si gentille—gentille, élégante, mais assommante, mon Dieu! Enfin*, I was immensely faithful to her and it lasted five years, it always does with me (either five days or five years). But as I love you ten times more than the others that brings it to when I am ninety, and, by then, *j'en aurai tellement l'habitude*——'

'And how soon shall I see you again?'

'*On fera la navette.*' He went to the window. 'I thought I heard a car—oh yes, it is turning round. There, I must go. *Au revoir*, Linda.'

He kissed her hand politely, almost absentmindedly, it was as if he had already gone, and walked quickly from the room. Linda went to the open window and leaned out. He was getting into a large motor car with two French soldiers on the box and a Free French flag waving from the bonnet. As it moved away he looked up.

'*Navette—navette*——' cried Linda with a brilliant smile. Then she got back into bed and cried very much. She felt utterly in despair at this second parting.

CHAPTER XX

THE air-raids on London now began. Early in September, just as I had moved there with my family, a bomb fell in the garden of Aunt Emily's little house in Kent. It was a small bomb compared with what one saw later, and none of us were hurt, but the house was more or less wrecked. Aunt Emily, Davey, my children and I, then took refuge at Alconleigh, where Aunt Sadie welcomed us with open arms, begging us to make it our home for the war. Louisa had already arrived there with her children, John Fort William had gone back to his regiment and their Scotch home had been taken over by the Navy.

'The more the merrier,' said Aunt Sadie. 'I should like to fill the house, and, besides, it's better for rations. Nice, too, for your children to be brought up all together, just like old times. With the boys away and Victoria in the Wrens Matthew and I would be a very dreary old couple here all alone.'

The big rooms at Alconleigh were filled with the contents of some science museum and no evacuees had been billeted there, I think it was felt that nobody who had not been brought up to such rigours could stand the cold of that house.

Soon the party received a very unexpected addition. I was upstairs in the nursery bathroom doing some washing for Nanny, measuring out the soap-flakes with wartime parsimony and wishing that the water at Alconleigh were not so dreadfully hard, when Louisa burst in.

'You'll never guess,' she said, 'in a thousand thousand years who has arrived.'

'Hitler,' I said, stupidly.

'Your mother, Auntie Bolter. She just walked up the drive and walked in.'

'Alone?'

'No, with a man.'

'The Major?'

'He doesn't look like a major. He's got a musical instrument with him and he's very dirty. Come on, Fanny, leave those to soak——'

And so it was. My mother sat in the hall drinking a whisky-and-soda and recounting in her birdlike voice with what incredible adventures she had escaped from the Riviera. The major with whom she had been living for some years, always having greatly preferred the Germans to the French, had remained behind to collaborate, and the man who now accompanied my mother was a ruffianly-looking Spaniard called Juan, whom she had picked up during her travels, and without whom, she said, she could never have got away from a ghastly prison camp in Spain. She spoke of him exactly as though he were not there at all, which produced rather a curious effect, and indeed seemed most embarrassing until we realized that Juan understood no word of any language except Spanish. He sat staring blankly into space, clutching a guitar and gulping down great draughts of whisky. Their relationship was only too obvious, Juan was undoubtedly (nobody doubted for a moment, not even Aunt Sadie), the Bolter's lover, but they were quite incapable of verbal exchange, my mother being no linguist.

Presently Uncle Matthew appeared, and the Bolter told her adventures all over again to him. He said he was delighted to see her, and hoped she would stay as long as she liked, he then turned his blue eyes upon Juan in a most terrifying and uncompromising stare. Aunt Sadie led him off to the business room, whispering, and we heard him say:

'All right then, but only for a few days.'

One person who was off his head with joy at the sight of her was dear old Josh.

'We must get her ladyship up on to a horse,' he said, hissing with pleasure.

My mother had not been her ladyship since three husbands (four if one were to include the Major), but Josh took no account of this, she would

26

always be her ladyship to him. He found a horse, not worthy of her, in his eyes, but not an absolute dud either, and had her out cub-hunting within a week of her arrival.

As for me it was the first time in my life that I had really found myself face to face with my mother. When a small child I had been obsessed by her and the few appearances she had made had absolutely dazzled me, though, as I have said, I never had any wish to emulate her career. Davey and Aunt Emily had been very clever in their approach to her, they, and especially Davey, had gradually and gently and without in any way hurting my feelings, turned her into a sort of joke. Since I was grown up I had seen her a few times, and had taken Alfred to visit her on our honeymoon, but the fact that, in spite of our intimate relationship, we had no past life in common put a great strain upon us and these meetings were not a success. At Alconleigh, in contact with her morning, noon and night, I studied her with the greatest curiosity, apart from anything else she was, after all, the grandmother of my children. I couldn't help rather liking her. Though she was silliness personified there was something engaging about her frankness and high spirits and endless good nature. The children adored her, Louisa's as well as mine, and she soon became an extra unofficial nurserymaid, and was very useful to us in that capacity.

She was curiously dated in her manner, and seemed still to be living in the 1920's. It was as though, at the age of thirty-five, having refused to grow any older, she had pickled herself, both mentally and physically, ignoring the fact that the world was changing and that she was withering fast. She had a short canary-coloured shingle (windswept) and wore trousers with the air of one still flouting the conventions, ignorant that every suburban shopgirl was doing the same. Her conversation, her point of view, the very slang she used, all belonged to the late 'twenties, that period now deader than the dodo. She was intensely unpractical, foolish, and apparently fragile, and yet she must have been quite a tough little person really, to have walked over the Pyrenees, to have escaped from a Spanish camp, and to have arrived at Alconleigh looking as if she had stepped out of the chorus of *No, No, Nanette*.

Some confusion was caused in the household at first by the fact that none of us could remember whether she had, in the end, actually married the Major (a married man himself and father of six) or not, and, in consequence, nobody knew whether her name was now Mrs. Rawl or Mrs. Plugge. Rawl had been a white hunter, the only husband she had ever lost respectably through death, having shot him by accident in the head during a safari. The question of names was soon solved, however, by her ration book, which proclaimed her to be Mrs. Plugge.

'This Gewan,' said Uncle Matthew, when they had been at Alconleigh a week or so, 'what's going to be done about him?'

'Well, Matthew dulling,' she larded her phrases with the word darling, and that is how she pronounced it. 'Hoo-arn saved my life, you know, over and over again, and I can't very well tear him up and throw him away, now can I, my sweet?'

'I can't keep a lot of dagoes here, you know,' Uncle Matthew said this in the same voice with which he used to tell Linda that she couldn't have any more pets, or if she did they must be kept in the stables. 'You'll have to make some other arrangements for him, Bolter, I'm afraid.'

'Oh, dulling, keep him a little longer, please, just a few more days, Matthew dulling,' she sounded just like Linda, pleading for some smelly old dog, 'and then I promise I'll find some place for him and tiny me to go to. You can't think what a lousy time we had together. I must stick to him now, I really must.'

'Well, another week if you like, but it's not to be the thin end of the wedge, Bolter, and after that he must go. You can stay as long as you want to, of course, but I do draw the line at Gewan.'

Louisa said to me, her eyes as big as saucers: 'He rushes into her room before tea and lives with her.' Louisa always describes the act of love as living with. 'Before tea, Fanny, can you imagine it?'

'Sadie, dear,' said Davey. 'I am going to do an unpardonable thing. It is for the general good, for your own good too, but it is unpardonable. If you feel you can't forgive me when I've said my say, Emily and I will have to leave, that's all.'

'Davey,' said Aunt Sadie in astonishment, 'what can be coming?'

'The food, Sadie, it's the food. I know how difficult it is for you in war-time, but we are all, in turns, being poisoned. I was sick for hours last night, the day before Emily had diarrhoea, Fanny has that great spot on her nose, and I'm sure the children aren't putting on the weight they should. The fact is, dear, that if Mrs. Beecher were a Borgia she could hardly be more success-ful—all that sausage mince is poison, Sadie. I wouldn't complain if it were merely nasty, or insufficient, or too starchy, one expects that in the war, but actual poison does, I feel, call for comment. Look at the menus this week—Monday, poison pie; Tuesday, poison burger steak; Wednesday, Cornish poison——'

Aunt Sadie looked intensely worried.

'Oh, dear, yes, she is an awful cook, I know, but Davey, what can one do? The meat ration only lasts about two meals, and there are fourteen meals in a week, you must remember. If she minces it up with a little sausage meat—poison meat (I do so agree with you really)—it goes much further, you see.'

'But in the country surely one can supplement the ration with game and farm produce? Yes, I know the home farm is let, but surely you could keep a pig and some hens? And what about game? There always used to be such a lot here.'

'The trouble is Matthew thinks they'll be needing all their ammunition for the Germans, and he refuses to waste a single shot on hares or partridges. Then you see Mrs. Beecher (oh, what a dreadful woman she is, though of course, we are lucky to have her) is the kind of cook who is quite good at a cut off the joint and two veg., but she simply hasn't an idea of how to make up delicious foreign oddments out of little bits of nothing at all. But you are quite, absolutely right, Davey, it's not wholesome. I really will make an effort to see what can be done.'

'You always used to be such a wonderful housekeeper, Sadie dear, it used to do one so much good, coming here. I remember one Christmas I put on four and a half ounces. But now I am losing steadily, my wretched frame is hardly more than a skeleton and I fear that, if I were to catch anything, I might peter out altogether. I take every precaution against that, everything is drenched in T.C.P., I gargle at least six times a day, but I can't disguise from you that my resistance is very low, very.'

Aunt Sadie said: 'It's quite easy to be a wonderful housekeeper when there are a first-rate cook, two kitchenmaids, a scullerymaid, and when you can get all the food you want. I'm afraid I am dreadfully stupid at managing on rations, but I really will try and take a pull. I'm very glad indeed that you mentioned it, Davey, it was absolutely right of you, and of course, I don't mind at all.'

But no real improvement resulted. Mrs. Beecher said 'yes, yes' to all suggestions, and continued to send up Hamburger steaks, Cornish pasty and shepherd pie, which continued to be full of poison sausage. It was very nasty and very unwholesome, and, for once, we all felt that Davey had not gone a bit too far. Meals were no pleasure to anybody and a positive ordeal to Davey, who sat, a pinched expression on his face, refusing food and resorting more and more often to the vitamin pills with which his place at the table was surrounded—too many by far even for his collection of jewelled boxes—a little forest of bottles, Vitamin A, vitamin B, vitamins A and C, vitamins B_3 and D, one tablet equals two pounds of summer butter—ten times the strength of a gallon of cod-liver oil—for the blood—for the brain—for muscle—for energy—anti this and protection against that—all but one bore a pretty legend.

'And what's in this, Davey?'

'Oh, that's what the panzer troops have before going into action.'

Davey gave a series of little sniffs. This usually denoted that his nose was about to bleed, pints of valuable red and white corpuscles so assiduously filled with vitamins would be wasted, his resistance still further lowered.

Aunt Emily and I looked up in some anxiety from the rissoles we were sadly pushing round our plates.

'Bolter,' he said severely, 'you've been at my Mary Chess again.'

'Oh, Davey dulling, such a tiny droppie.'

'A tiny drop doesn't stink out the whole room. I'm sure you have been pouring it into the bath with the stopper out. It is a shame. That bottle is my quota for a month, it is too bad of you, Bolter.'

'Dulling, I swear I'll get you some more—I've got to go to London next week, to have my wiggie washed, and I'll bring back a bottle, I swear.'

'And I very much hope you'll take Gewan with you and leave him there,' growled Uncle Matthew. 'Because I won't have him in this house much longer, you know. I've warned you, Bolter.'

Uncle Matthew was busy from morning to night with his Home Guard. He was happy and interested and in a particularly mellow mood, for it looked as if his favourite hobby, that of clocking Germans, might be available again at any moment. So he only noticed Juan from time to time, and, whereas in the old days he would have had him out of the house in the twinkling of an eye, Juan had now been an inmate of Alconleigh for nearly a month. However, it was beginning to be obvious that my uncle had no intention of putting up with his presence for ever and things were clearly coming to a head where Juan was concerned. As for the Spaniard himself, I never saw a man so wretched. He wandered about miserably, with nothing whatever to do all day, unable to talk to anybody, while at mealtimes the disgust on his face fully equalled that of Davey. He hadn't even the spirit to play his guitar.

'Davey, you must talk to him,' said Aunt Sadie.

My mother had gone to London to have her hair dyed, and a family council was gathered in her absence to decide upon the fate of Juan.

'We obviously can't turn him out to starve, as the Bolter says he saved her life, and, anyhow, one has human feelings.'

'Not towards Dagoes,' said Uncle Matthew, grinding his dentures.

'But what we can do is to get him a job, only first we must find out what his profession is. Now, Davey, you're good at languages, and you're so clever, I'm sure if you had a look at the Spanish dictionary in the library you could just manage to ask him what he used to do before the war. Do try, Davey.'

'Yes, darling, do,' said Aunt Emily. 'The poor fellow looks too miserable for words at present, I expect he'd love to have some work.'

Uncle Matthew snorted.

'Just give me the Spanish dictionary,' he muttered. 'I'll soon find the word for "get out".'

'I'll try,' said Davey, 'but I can guess what it will be, I'm afraid. G for gigolo.'

'Or something equally useless, like M for matador or H for hidalgo,' said Louisa.

'Yes. Then what?'

'Then B for be off,' said Uncle Matthew, 'and the Bolter will have to support him, but not anywhere near me, I beg. It must be made perfectly clear to both of them that I can't stand the sight of the sewer lounging about here any longer.'

When Davey takes on a job he does it thoroughly. He shut himself up for several hours with the Spanish dictionary, and wrote down a great many words and phrases on a piece of paper. Then he beckoned Juan into Uncle Matthew's business room and shut the door.

They were only there a short time, and, when they emerged, both were wreathed in happy smiles.

'You've sacked him, I hope?' Uncle Matthew said, suspiciously.

'No, indeed, I've not sacked him,' said Davey, 'on the contrary, I've engaged him. My dears, you'll never guess, it's too absolutely glamorous for words, Juan is a cook, he was the cook, I gather, of some cardinal before the Civil War. You don't mind, I hope, Sadie. I look upon this as an absolute lifeline—Spanish food, so delicious, so unconstipating, so digestible, so full of glorious garlic. Oh, the joy, no more poison-burger—how soon can we get rid of Mrs. Beecher?'

Davey's enthusiasm was fully justified, and Juan in the kitchen was the very greatest possible success. He was more than a first-class cook, he had an extraordinary talent for organization, and soon, I suspect, became king of the local black market. There was no nonsense about foreign dishes made out of little bits of nothing at all; succulent birds, beasts, and crustaceans appeared at every meal, the vegetables ran with extravagant sauces, the puddings were obviously based upon real ice-cream.

'Juan is wonderful,' Aunt Sadie would remark in her vague manner, 'at making the rations go round. When I think of Mrs. Beecher—really, Davey, you were so clever.'

One day she said: 'I hope the food isn't too rich for you now, Davey?'

'Oh no,' said Davey. 'I never mind rich food, it's poor food that does one such an infinity of harm.'

Juan also pickled and bottled and preserved from morning till night, until the store cupboard, which he had found bare except for a few tins of soup, began to look like a pre-war grocer's shop. Davey called it Aladdin's Cave, or Aladdin for short, and spent a lot of his time there, gloating. Months of tasty vitamins stood there in neat rows, a barrier between him and that starvation which had seemed, under Mrs. Beecher's regime, only just round the corner.

Juan himself was now a very different fellow from the dirty and disgruntled refugee fellow who had sat about so miserably. He was clean, he wore a white coat and hat, he seemed to have grown in stature, and he soon acquired a manner of great authority in his kitchen. Even Uncle Matthew acknowledged the change.

'If I were the Bolter,' he said, 'I should marry him.'

'Knowing the Bolter,' said Davey, 'I've no doubt at all that she will.'

Early in November I had to go to London for the day, on business for Alfred, who was now in the Middle East, and to see my doctor. I went by the eight o'clock train, and, having heard nothing of Linda for some weeks, I took a taxi and drove straight to Cheyne Walk. There had been a heavy raid the night before, and I passed through streets which glistened with broken glass. Many fires still smouldered, and fire engines, ambulances, and rescue men hurried to and fro, streets were blocked, and several times we had to drive quite a long way round. There seemed to be a great deal of excitement in the air. Little groups of people were gathered outside shops and houses, as if to compare notes; my taxi-driver talked incessantly to me over his shoulder. He had been up all night, he said, helping the rescue workers. He described what he had found.

'It was a spongy mass of red,' he said, ghoulishly, 'covered with feathers.'

'Feathers?' I said, horrified.

'Yes. A feather bed, you see. It was still breathing, so I takes it to the hospital, but they says that no good to us, take it to the mortuary. So I sews it in a sack and takes it to the mortuary.'

'Goodness,' I said.

'Oh, that's nothing to what I have seen.'

Linda's nice daily woman, Mrs. Hunt, opened the door to me at Cheyne Walk.

'She's very poorly, ma'am, can't you take her back to the country with you? It's not right for her to be here, in her condition. I hate to see her like this.'

Linda was in her bathroom, being sick. When she came out she said:

'Don't think it's the raid that's upset me. I like them. I'm in the family way, that's what it is.'

'Darling, I thought you weren't supposed to have another baby.'

'Oh, doctors! They don't know anything, they are such fearful idiots. Of course I can, and I'm simply longing for it, this baby won't be the least bit like Moira, you'll see.'

'I'm going to have one too.'

'No—how lovely—when?'

'About the end of May.'

'Oh, just the same as me.'

'And Louisa, in March.'

'Haven't we been busy? I do call that nice, they can all be Hons together.'

'Now, Linda, why don't you come back with me to Alconleigh? Whatever is the sense of stopping here in all this? It can't be good for you or the baby.'

'I like it,' said Linda. 'It's my home, and I like to be in it. And besides, somebody might turn up, just for a few hours you know, and want to see me, and he knows where to find me here.'

'You'll be killed,' I said, 'and then he won't know where to find you.'

'Darling Fanny, don't be so silly. There are seven million people living in London, do you really imagine they are all killed every night? Nobody is killed in air-raids, there is a great deal of noise and a great deal of mess, but people really don't seem to get killed much.'

'Don't—don't——' I said. 'Touch wood. Apart from being killed or not it doesn't suit you. You look awful, Linda.'

'Not so bad when I'm made up. I'm so fearfully sick, that's the trouble, but it's nothing to do with the raids, and that part will soon be over now and I shall be quite all right again.'

'Well, think about it,' I said, 'it's very nice at Alconleigh, wonderful food——'

'Yes, so I hear. Merlin came to see me, and his stories of caramelized carrots swimming in cream made my mouth water. He said he was preparing to throw morality to the winds and bribe this Juan to go to Merlinford, but he found out it would mean having the Bolter too and he couldn't quite face that.'

'I must go,' I said uncertainly. 'I don't like to leave you, darling, I do wish you'd come back with me.'

'Perhaps I will later on, we'll see.'

I went down to the kitchen and found Mrs. Hunt. I gave her some money in case of emergency, and the Alconleigh telephone number, and begged her to ring me up if she thought there was anything I could do.

'She won't budge,' I said. 'I've done all I can to make her, but it doesn't seem to be any good, she's as obstinate as a donkey.'

'I know, ma'am. She won't even leave the house for a breath of air, sits by that telephone day in day out playing cards with herself. It ain't hardly right she should sleep here all alone in my opinion, either, but you can't get her to listen to sense. Last night, ma'am, whew! it was terrible, walloping down all night, and those wretched guns never got a single one, whatever they may tell you in the papers. It's my opinion they must have got women on those guns, and, if so, no wonder. Women!'

A week later Mrs. Hunt rang me up at Alconleigh. Linda's house had received a direct hit and they were still digging for her.

Aunt Sadie had gone on an early bus to Cheltenham to do some shopping. Uncle Matthew was nowhere to be found, so Davey and I simply took his car, full of Home Guard petrol, and drove to London, hell for leather. The little house was an absolute ruin, but Linda and her bulldog were unhurt, they had just been got out and put to bed in the house of a neighbour. Linda was flushed and excited, and couldn't stop talking.

'You see,' she said. 'What did I tell you, Fanny about air-raids not killing people. Here we are, right as rain. My bed simply went through the floor, Plon-plon and I went on it, most comfortable.'

Presently a doctor arrived and gave her a sedative. He told us she would probably go to sleep and that when she woke up we could drive her down to Alconleigh. I telephoned to Aunt Sadie and told her to have a room ready.

The rest of the day was spent by Davey in salvaging what he could of Linda's things. Her house and furniture, her beautiful Renoir, and everything in her bedroom was completely wrecked, but he was able to rescue a few oddments from the splintered, twisted remains of her cupboards, and in the basement he found, untouched, the two trunks full of clothes which Fabrice had sent after her from Paris. He came out looking like a miller, covered with white dust from head to foot, and Mrs. Hunt took us round to her own little house and gave us some food.

'I suppose Linda may miscarry,' I said to Davey, 'and I'm sure it's to be hoped she will. It's most dangerous for her to have this child—my doctor is horrified.'

However, she did not; in fact she said that the experience had done her a great deal of good, and had quite stopped her from feeling sick. She demurred again at leaving London, but without much conviction. I pointed out that if anybody was looking for her and found the Cheyne Walk house a total wreck they would be certain at once to get into touch with Alconleigh. She saw that this was so, and agreed to come with us.

CHAPTER XXI

WINTER now set in with its usual severity on those Cotswold uplands. The air was sharp and bracing, like cold water; most agreeable if one only goes out for short brisk walks or rides, and if there is a warm house to go back to. But the central-heating apparatus at Alconleigh had never been really satisfactory and I suppose that by now the pipes, through old age, had become thoroughly furred up—in any case they were hardly more than tepid. On coming into the hall from the bitter outside air one did feel a momentary glow of warmth; this soon lessened, and gradually, as circulation died down, one's body became pervaded by a cruel numbness. The men on the estate, the old ones that is, who were not in the army, had no time to chop up logs for the fires; they were occupied from morning till night, under the leadership of Uncle Matthew, in drilling, constructing barricades and blockhouses, and otherwise preparing to make themselves a nuisance to the German army before ending up as cannon-fodder.

'I reckon,' Uncle Matthew would say proudly, 'that we shall be able to stop them for two hours—possibly three—before we are all killed. Not bad for such a little place.'

We made our children go out and collect wood. Davey became an assiduous and surprisingly efficient woodman (he had refused to join the Home Guard, he said he always fought better out of uniform), but somehow, they only produced enough to keep the nursery fire going, and the one in the brown sitting-room, if it was lit after tea, and, as the wood was pretty wet, this only really got warm just when it was time to tear oneself away and go up the freezing stairs to bed. After dinner the two armchairs on each side of the fire were always occupied by Davey and my mother. Davey pointed out that it would be more trouble for everybody in the end if he got one of his chills; the Bolter just dumped herself down. The rest of us sat in a semi-circle well beyond the limits of any real warmth, and looked longingly at the little flickering yellow flames, which often subsided into sulky smoke. Linda had an evening coat, a sort of robe from head to foot, of white fox lined with white ermine. She wrapped herself in this for dinner, and suffered less than we others did. In the daytime she either wore her sable coat and a pair of black velvet boots lined with sable to match, or lay on the sofa tucked up in an enormous mink bedspread lined with white velvet quilting.

'It used to make me so laugh when Fabrice said he was getting me all these things because they would be useful in the war, the war would be fearfully cold he always said, but I see now how right he was.'

Linda's possessions filled the other females in the house with a sort of furious admiration.

'It does seem rather unfair,' Louisa said to me one afternoon when we were pushing our two youngest children out in their prams together. We were both dressed in stiff Scotch tweeds, so different from supple flattering French ones, in woollen stockings, brogues, and jerseys, knitted by ourselves, of shades carefully chosen to 'go with' though not 'to match' our coats and skirts. 'Linda goes off and has this glorious time in Paris, and comes back covered with rich furs, while you and I—what do we get for sticking all our lives to the same dreary old husbands? Three-quarter-length shorn lamb.'

'Alfred isn't a dreary old husband,' I said loyally. But of course I knew exactly what she meant.

Aunt Sadie thought Linda's clothes too pretty.

'What lovely taste, darling,' she would say when another ravishing garment was brought out. 'Did that come from Paris too? It's really wonderful what you can get there, on no money, if you're clever.'

At this my mother would give tremendous winks in the direction of anybody whose eye she might happen to catch, including Linda herself. Linda's face would then become absolutely stony. She could not bear my mother; she felt that, before she met Fabrice, she had been heading down the same road herself, and she was appalled to see what lay at the end of it. My mother started off by trying a 'let's face it, dear, we are nothing but two fallen women' method of approach to Linda, which was most unsuccessful. Linda became not only stiff and cold, but positively rude to the poor Bolter, who, unable to see what she could have done to offend, was at first very much hurt. Then she began to be on her dignity, and said it was great nonsense for Linda to go on like this; in fact, considering she was nothing but a high-class tart, it was most pretentious and hypocritical of her. I tried to explain Linda's intensely romantic attitude towards Fabrice and the months she had spent with him, but the Bolter's own feelings had been dulled by time, and she either could not or would not understand.

'It was Sauveterre she was living with, wasn't it?' my mother said to me, soon after Linda arrived at Alconleigh.

'How do you know?'

'Everybody knew on the Riviera. One always knew about Sauveterre somehow. And it was rather a thing, because he seemed to have settled down for life with that boring Lamballe woman; then she had to go to England on business and clever little Linda nabbed him. A very good cop for her, dulling, but I don't see why she has to be so high-hat about it. Sadie doesn't know, I quite realize that, and of course wild horses wouldn't make me tell her, I'm not that kind of a girl, but I do think, when we're all together, Linda might be a tiny bit more jolly.'

The Alconleighs still believed that Linda was the devoted wife of Christian, who was now in Cairo, and, of course, it had never occurred to them for a moment that the child might not be his. They had quite forgiven her for leaving Tony, though they thought themselves distinctly broad-minded for having done so. They would ask her from time to time what Christian was doing, not because they were interested, but so that Linda shouldn't feel out of it when Louisa and I talked about our husbands. She would then be obliged to invent bits of news out of imaginary letters from Christian.

'He doesn't like his Brigadier very much,' or,

'He says Cairo is great fun, but one can have enough of it.'

In point of fact Linda never got any letters at all. She had not seen her English friends now for so long, they were scattered in the war to the ends of the earth, and, though they might not have forgotten about Linda, she was no longer in their lives. But, of course, there was only one thing she wanted, a letter, a line even, from Fabrice. Just after Christmas it came. It was forwarded in a typewritten envelope from Carlton Gardens with General de Gaulle's stamp on it. Linda, when she saw it lying on the hall table, became perfectly white. She seized it and rushed up to her bedroom.

About an hour later she came to find me.

'Oh, darling,' she said, her eyes full of tears. 'I've been all this time and I can't read one word. Isn't it torture? Could you have a look?'

She gave me a sheet of the thinnest paper I ever saw, on which were scratched, apparently with a rusty pin, a series of perfectly incomprehensible hieroglyphics. I could not make out one single word either, it seemed to bear no relation to handwriting, the marks in no way resembled letters.

'What can I do?' said poor Linda. 'Oh, Fanny.'

'Let's ask Davey,' I said.

She hesitated a little over this, but feeling that it would be better, however intimate the message, to share it with Davey than not to have it at all, she finally agreed.

Davey said she was quite right to ask him.

'I am very good at French handwriting.'

'Only you wouldn't laugh at it?' Linda said, in a breathless voice like a child.

'No, Linda, I don't regard it as a laughing matter any longer,' Davey replied, looking with love and anxiety at her face, which had become very drawn of late. But when he had studied the paper for some time, he too was obliged to confess himself absolutely stumped by it.

'I've seen a lot of difficult French writings in my life,' he said, 'and this beats them all.'

In the end Linda had to give up. She went about with the piece of paper, like a talisman, in her pocket, but never knew what Fabrice had written to her on it. It was cruelly tantalizing. She wrote to him at Carlton Gardens, but this letter came back with a note regretting that it could not be forwarded.

'Never mind,' she said. 'One day the telephone bell will ring again and he'll be there.'

Louisa and I were busy from morning to night. We now had one Nanny (mine) between eight children. Fortunately they were not at home all the time. Louisa's two eldest were at a private school, and two of hers and two of mine went for lessons to a convent Lord Merlin had most providentially found for us at Merlinford. Louisa got a little petrol for this, and she or I or Davey drove them there in Aunt Sadie's car every day. It can be imagined what Uncle Matthew thought of this arrangement. He ground his teeth, flashed his eyes, and always referred to the poor good nuns as 'those damned parachutists'. He was absolutely convinced that whatever time they could spare from making machine-gun nests for other nuns, who would presently descend from the skies, like birds, to occupy the nests, was given to the seduction of the souls of his grandchildren and great-nieces.

'They get a prize you know for anybody they can catch—of course you can see they are men, you've only got to look at their boots.'

Every Sunday he watched the children like a lynx for genuflexions, making the sign of the Cross, and other Papist antics, or even for undue interest in the service, and when none of these symptoms was to be observed he was hardly reassured.

'These Romans are so damned artful.'

He thought it most subversive of Lord Merlin to harbour such an establishment on his property, but only really what one might expect of a man who brought Germans to one's ball and was known to admire foreign music. Uncle Matthew had most conveniently forgotten all about 'Una voce poco fa', and now played, from morning to night, a record called 'The Turkish Patrol', which started piano, became forte, and ended up pianissimo.

'You see,' he would say, 'they come out of a wood, and then you can hear them go back into the wood. Don't know why it's called Turkish, you can't imagine Turks playing a tune like that, and of course there aren't any woods in Turkey. It's just the name, that's all.'

I think it reminded him of his Home Guard, who were always going into woods and coming out of them again, poor dears, often covering themselves with branches as when Birnam Wood came to Dunsinane.

So we worked hard, mending and making and washing, doing any chores for Nanny rather than actually look after the children ourselves. I have seen too many children brought up without Nannies to think this at all desirable. In Oxford, the wives of progressive dons did it often as a matter of principle; they would gradually become morons themselves, while the children looked like slum children and behaved like barbarians.

As well as looking after the clothes of our existing families we also had to make for the babies we were expecting, though they did inherit a good deal from brothers and sisters. Linda, who naturally had no store of baby clothes, did nothing of all this. She arranged one of the slatted shelves in the Hons' cupboard as a sort of bunk, with pillows and quilts from spare bedrooms, and here, wrapped in her mink bedspread, she would lie all day with Plonplon beside her, reading fairy stories. The Hons' cupboard, as of old, was the warmest, the one really warm place in the house. Whenever I could I brought my sewing and sat with her there, and then she would put down the blue or the green fairy book, Andersen or Grimm, and tell me at length about Fabrice and her happy life with him in Paris. Louisa sometimes joined us there, and then Linda would break off and we would talk about John Fort William and the children. But Louisa was a restless busy creature, not much of a chatter, and, besides, she was irritated to see how Linda did absolutely nothing, day after day.

'Whatever is the baby going to wear, poor thing,' she would say crossly to me, 'and who is going to look after it, Fanny? It's quite plain already that you and I will have to, and really, you know, we've got enough to do as it is. And another thing, Linda lies there covered in sables or whatever they are, but she's got no money at all, she's a pauper—I don't believe she realizes that in the least. And what is Christian going to say when he hears about the baby, after all, legally his, he'll have to bring a suit to illegitimize it, and then there'll be such a scandal. None of these things seem to have occurred to Linda. She ought to be beside herself with worry, instead of which she is behaving like the wife of a millionaire in peacetime. I've no patience with her.'

All the same, Louisa was a good soul. In the end it was she who went to London and bought a layette for the baby. Linda sold Tony's engagement ring, at a horribly low price, to pay for it.

'Do you ever think about your husbands?' I asked her one day, after she had been talking for hours about Fabrice.

'Well, funnily enough, I do quite often think of Tony. Christian, you see, was such an interlude, he hardly counts in my life at all, because, for one thing, our marriage lasted a very short time, and then it was quite over-shadowed by what came after. I don't know, I find these things hard to remember, but I think that my feelings for him were only really intense for a few weeks, just at the very beginning. He's a noble character, a man you can respect, I don't blame myself for marrying him, but he has no talent for love.

'But Tony was my husband for so long, more than a quarter of my life, if you come to think of it. He certainly made an impression. And I see now that the thing going wrong was hardly his fault, poor Tony, I don't believe it would have gone right with anybody (unless I had happened to meet Fabrice) because in those days I was so extremely nasty. The really important thing, if a marriage is to go well, without much love, is very very great niceness—*gentillesse*—and wonderful good manners. I was never *gentille* with Tony, and often I was hardly polite to him, and, very soon after our honeymoon, I became exceedingly disagreeable. I'm ashamed now to think what I was like. And poor old Tony was so good-natured, he never snapped back, he put up with it all for years and then just ambled off to Pixie. I can't blame him. It was my fault from beginning to end.'

'Well, he wasn't very nice really, darling, I shouldn't worry yourself about it too much, and look how he's behaving now.'

'Oh, he's the weakest character in the world, it's Pixie and his parents who made him do that. If he'd still been married to me he would have been a Guards officer by now, I bet you.'

One thing Linda never thought about, I'm quite sure, was the future. Some day the telephone bell would ring and it would be Fabrice, and that was as far as she got. Whether he would marry her, and what would happen about the child, were questions which not only did not preoccupy her, but which never seemed to enter her head. Her mind was entirely on the past.

'It's rather sad,' she said one day, 'to belong, as we do, to a lost generation.

I'm sure in history the two wars will count as one war and that we shall be squashed out of it altogether, and people will forget that we ever existed. We might just as well never have lived at all, I do think it's a shame.'

'It may become a sort of literary curiosity,' Davey said. He sometimes crept, shivering, into the Hons' cupboard to get up a little circulation before he went back to his writing. 'People will be interested in it for all the wrong reasons, and collect Lalique dressing-table sets and shagreen boxes and cock-tail cabinets lined with looking-glass and find them very amusing. Oh good,' he said, peering out of the window, 'that wonderful Juan is bringing in another pheasant.'

(Juan had an invaluable talent, he was expert with a catapult. He spent all his odd moments—how he had odd moments was a mystery, but he had—creeping about the woods or down by the river armed with this weapon. As he was an infallible shot, and moreover, held back by no sporting inhibitions, that a pheasant or a hare should be sitting or a swan the property of the King being immaterial to Juan, the results of these sallies were excellent from the point of view of larder and stock-pot. When Davey really wanted to relish his food to the full he would recite, half to himself, a sort of little grace, which began: 'Remember Mrs. Beecher's tinned tomato soup.'

The unfortunate Craven was, of course, tortured by these goings on, which he regarded as little better than poaching. But his nose, poor man, was kept well to the grindstone by Uncle Matthew, and, when he was not on sentry-go, or fastening the trunks of trees to bicycle-wheels across the lanes to make barricades against tanks, he was on parade. Uncle Matthew was a byword in the county for the smartness of his parades. Juan, as an alien, was luckily excluded from these activities, and was able to devote all his time to making us comfortable and happy, in which he very notably succeeded.)

'I don't want to be a literary curiosity,' said Linda. 'I should like to have been a living part of a really great generation. I think it's too dismal to have been born in 1911.'

'Never mind, Linda, you will be a wonderful old lady.'

'You will be a wonderful old gentleman, Davey,' said Linda.

'Oh, me? I fear I shall never make old bones,' replied Davey, in accents of the greatest satisfaction.

And, indeed, there was a quality of agelessness about him. Although he was quite twenty years older than we and only about five years younger than Aunt Emily, he had always seemed much nearer to our generation than to hers, nor had he altered in any respect since the day when he had stood by the hall fire looking unlike a captain and unlike a husband.

'Come on, dears, tea, and I happen to know that Juan has made a layer-cake, so let's go down before the Bolter gets it all.'

Davey carried on a great meal-time feud with the Bolter. Her table manners had always been casual, but certain of her habits, such as eating jam with a spoon which she put back into the jam-pot, and stubbing out her cigarette in the sugar-basin, drove poor Davey, who was very ration-conscious, to a frenzy of irritation, and he would speak sharply to her, like a governess to a maddening child.

He might have spared himself the trouble. The Bolter took absolutely no notice whatever, and went on spoiling food with insouciance.

'Dulling,' she would say, 'whatever does it matter, my perfectly divine Hoo-arn has got plenty more up his tiny sleeve, I promise you.'

At this time there was a particularly alarming invasion scare. The arrival of the Germans, with full paraphernalia of airborne troops dressed as priests, ballet dancers, or what you will, was expected from one day to the next. Some unkind person put it about that they would all be the doubles of Mrs. Davis, in W.V.S. uniform. She had such a knack of being in several places at once that it already seemed as if there were a dozen Mrs. Davises parachuting about the countryside. Uncle Matthew took the invasion very seriously indeed, and one day he gathered us all together, in the business room, and told us in detail the part that we were expected to play.

'You women, with the children, must go to the cellar while the battle is on,' he said, 'there is an excellent tap, and I have provisioned you with bully-beef for a week. Yes, you may be there several days, I warn you.'

'Nanny won't like that,' Louisa began, but was quelled by a furious look.

'While we are on the subject of Nanny,' Uncle Matthew said, 'I warn you, there's to be no question of cluttering up the roads with your prams, mind, no evacuation under any circumstances at all. Now, there is one very important job to be done, and that I am entrusting to you, Davey. You won't mind it I know, old boy, if I say that you are a very poor shot—as you know, we are short of ammunition, and what there is must, under no circumstances, be wasted—every bullet must tell. So I don't intend to give you a gun, at first, anyhow. But I've got a fuse, and a charge of dynamite (I will show you, in a moment), and I shall want you to blow up the store cupboard for me.'

'Blow up Aladdin,' said Davey. He turned quite pale. 'Matthew, you must be mad.'

'I would let Gewan do it, but the fact is, though I rather like old Gewan now, I don't altogether trust the fella. Once a foreigner always a foreigner in my opinion. Now I must explain to you why I regard this as a most vital part of the operations. When Josh and Craven and I and all the rest of us have been killed there is only one way in which you civilians can help, and that is by becoming a charge on the German army. You must make it their business to feed you—never fear, they'll do so, they don't want typhus along their lines of communication—but you must see that it's as difficult as possible for them. Now that store cupboard would keep you going for weeks, I've just had a look at it; why, it would feed the entire village. All wrong. Make them

THE PURSUIT OF LOVE

bring in the food and muck up their transport, that's what we want, to be a perfect nuisance to them. It's all you'll be able to do, by then, just be a nuisance, so the store cupboard will have to go, and Davey must blow it up.'

Davey opened his mouth to make another observation, but Uncle Matthew was in a very frightening mood and he thought better of it.

'Very well, dear Matthew,' he said, sadly, 'you must show me what to do.'

But as soon as Uncle Matthew's back was turned he gave utterance to loud complaints.

'No, really, it is too bad of Matthew to insist on blowing up Aladdin,' he said. 'It's all right for him, he'll be dead, but he really should consider us a little more.'

'But I thought you were going to take those black and white pills,' said Linda.

'Emily doesn't like the idea, and I had decided only to take them if I were arrested, but now I don't know. Matthew says the German army will have to feed us, but he must know as well as I do that if they feed us at all, which is extremely problematical, it will be on nothing but starch—it will be Mrs. Beecher again, only worse, and I can't digest starch especially in the winter months. It is such a shame. Horrid old Matthew, he's so thoughtless.'

'Well, but Davey,' said Linda, 'how about us? We're all in the same boat, but we don't grumble.'

'Nanny will,' said Louisa with a sniff, which plainly said, 'and I wish to associate myself with Nanny.'

'Nanny! She lives in a world of her own,' said Linda. 'But we're all supposed to know why we're fighting, and, speaking for myself, I think Fa is absolutely right. And if I think that, in my condition——'

'Oh, you'll be looked after,' said Davey, bitterly, 'pregnant women always are. They'll send you vitamins and things from America, you'll see. But nobody will bother about me, and I am so delicate, it simply won't do for me to be fed by the German army, and I shall never be able to make them understand about my inside. I know Germans.'

'You always said nobody understood as much about your inside as Dr. Meyerstein.'

'Use your common sense, Linda. Are they likely to drop Dr. Meyerstein over Alconleigh? You know perfectly well he's been in a camp for years. No, I must make up my mind to a lingering death—not a very pleasant prospect, I must say.'

Linda took Uncle Matthew aside after that, and made him show her how to blow up Aladdin.

'Davey's spirit is not so frightfully willing,' she said, 'and his flesh is definitely weak.'

There was a certain coldness between Linda and Davey for a little while after this, each thought the other had been quite unreasonable. It did not last, however. They were much too fond of each other (in fact, I am sure that Davey really loved Linda most in the world) and, as Aunt Sadie said, 'Who knows, perhaps the necessity for these dreadful decisions will not arise'.

So the winter slowly passed. The spring came with extraordinary beauty, as always at Alconleigh, with a brilliance of colouring, a richness of life, that one had forgotten to expect during the cold grey winter months. All the animals were giving birth, there were young creatures everywhere, and we now waited with longing and impatience for our babies to be born. The days, the very hours, dragged slowly by, and Linda began to say 'better than that' when asked the time.

'What's the time, darling?'

'Guess.'

'Half-past twelve?'

'Better than that— a quarter to one.'

We three pregnant women had all become enormous, we dragged ourselves about the house like great figures of fertility, heaving tremendous sighs, and feeling the heat of the first warm days with exaggerated discomfort.

Useless to her now were Linda's beautiful Paris clothes, she was down to the level of Louisa and me in a cotton smock, maternity skirt and sandals. She abandoned the Hons' cupboard, and spent her days, when it was fine weather, sitting by the edge of the wood, while Plon-plon, who had become an enthusiastic, though unsuccessful, rabbiter, plunged panting to and fro in the green mists of the undergrowth.

'If anything happens to me, darling, you will look after Plon-plon,' she said. 'He has been such a comfort to me all this time.'

But she spoke idly, as one who knows, in fact, that she will live for ever, and she mentioned neither Fabrice nor the child, as surely she would have done had she been touched by any premonition.

Louisa's baby, Angus, was born at the beginning of April. It was her sixth child and third boy, and we envied her from the bottom of our hearts for having got it over.

On 28 May both ours were born—both boys. The doctors who said that Linda ought never to have another child were not such idiots after all. It killed her. She died, I think, completely happy, and without having suffered very much, but for us at Alconleigh, for her father and mother, brothers and sisters, for Davey and for Lord Merlin a light went out, a great deal of joy that never could be replaced.

At about the same time as Linda's death Fabrice was caught by the Gestapo and subsequently shot. He was a hero of the Resistance, and his name has become a legend in France.

I have adopted the little Fabrice, with the consent of Christian, his legal father. He has black eyes, the same shape as Linda's blue ones, and is a most beautiful and enchanting child. I love him quite as much as, and perhaps more than, I do my own.

The Bolter came to see me while I was still in the Oxford nursing home where my baby had been born and where Linda had died.

'Poor Linda,' she said, with feeling, 'poor little thing. But Fanny, don't you think perhaps it's just as well? The lives of women like Linda and me are not so much fun when one begins to grow older.'

I didn't want to hurt my mother's feelings by protesting that Linda was not that sort of woman.

'But I think she would have been happy with Fabrice,' I said. 'He was the great love of her life, you know.'

'Oh, dulling,' said my mother, sadly. 'One always thinks that. Every, every time.'

THE OUTSIDER
(L'Etranger)

BY ALBERT CAMUS

TRANSLATED BY STUART GILBERT

(1946)

THE OUTSIDER

INTRODUCTION

THE OUTSIDER is the first book of a writer, now in his middle thirties, who played a notable part in the French Resistance Movement, who edited the daily paper, *Combat*, and whose name has been closely linked with Jean-Paul Sartre in the forefront of the new philosophical and realistic school of French literature. As well as this novel, Albert Camus has produced between 1942 and 1944 two plays, *Caligula* and *Le Malentendu*, and a book of essays, *Le Mythe de Sisyphe*. But he has an even more distinctive quality which colours all his work. He is an Algerian.

What is an Algerian? He is not a French colonial, but a citizen of France domiciled in North Africa, a man of the Mediterranean, an *homme du midi* yet one who hardly partakes of the traditional Mediterranean culture, unlike Valéry whose roots spread from Sète by way of Montpellier to Genoa; for him there is no eighteenth century, no baroque, no renaissance, no crusades or troubadours in the past of the Barbary Coast; nothing but the Roman Empire, decaying dynasties of Turk and Moor, the French Conquest and the imposition of the laws and commerce of the Third Republic on the ruins of Islam. It is from a sultry and African corner of Latin civilization that *The Outsider* emerges, the flower of a pagan and barrenly philistine culture. This *milieu* has a certain affinity with the Key West of Hemingway, or Deep South of Faulkner and Caldwell, with those torrid American cities where 'poor whites' exist uneasily beside poor blacks; in fact the neo-paganism which is common to both civilizations, together with Camus's rapid and somewhat colloquial style, have caused some critics to consider *The Outsider* merely as a French exercise in the American 'tough guy' manner. But the atmosphere is not really similar. *The Outsider* is not at all a morbid book, it is a violent affirmation of health and sanity, there are no monsters, no rapes, no incest, no lynchings in it; it is the reflection, on the whole, of a happier society. Monsieur Sartre asked, in a recent interview, if his friend Camus is also an 'existentialist', replied 'No. That's a grave misconception. Although he owes something to Kierkegaard, Jaspers, and Heidegger, his true masters are the French moralists of the seventeenth century. He is a classical Mediterranean. I would call his pessimism "solar" if you remember how much black there is in the sun. The philosophy of Camus is a philosophy of the absurd, and for him the absurd springs from the relation of man to the world, of his legitimate aspirations to the vanity and futility of human wishes. The conclusions which he draws from it are those of classical pessimism.'

We possess a valuable piece of evidence which bears out this theory. In 1936 and 1937 Camus wrote two or three essays which have since been reprinted as *Les Noces*. No writer can avoid in his first essays the mention of the themes which are crystallizing for his later work. Two melodies emerge in these papers, a passionate love for Algiers and for the harsh meridional ecstasy which youth enjoys there, and also an anger and defiance of death and of our northern emphasis upon it. These are the two keys to *The Outsider*.

'Le bourreau étrangla le Cardinal Carrafa avec un cordon de soie qui se rompit —il fallut y revenir deux fois. Le Cardinal regarda le bourreau sans daigner prononcer un mot.'

STENDHAL: *La Duchesse de Palliano.*

This quotation at the head of *Les Noces* might stand as a motto for the novel.

In his essay in *Summer in Algiers* Camus introduces us to the kind of *milieu* we will meet in the later book.

'Men find here throughout all their youth a way of living commensurate with their beauty. After that, decay and oblivion. They've staked all on the body and they know that they must lose. In Algiers, for those who are young and alive, everything is their haven and an occasion for excelling—the bay, the sun, the red and white checkerboard of terraces going down to the sea, the flowers and stadiums, the fresh brown bodies . . . But for those whose youth is past no place exists, no sanctuary to absorb their melancholy.'

Farther on he gives a brief account of the ethics of these athletes. 'The notion of hell, for instance, is here no more than a silly joke. Such imaginings are only for the very virtuous. And I am convinced that the word virtue is entirely meaningless throughout Algeria. Not that its men are without principles. They have their moral code. We don't "chuck" our mothers, we make our wife respected in the street, we are considerate to the pregnant, we don't attack an enemy two against one, because it's "cheap". Whoever doesn't keep these elementary commandments "is not a man" and the business is settled.'

'There are words whose meaning I have never clearly understood,' he continues, 'such as the word sin. I know enough, however, to see that these men have never sinned against life, for if there is a sin against life, it is not perhaps so much to despair of life, as to hope for another life and to lose sight of the implacable grandeur of this one. These men have not cheated; lords of the Summer at twenty through their joy of living, though deprived of all hope they are gods still. I have seen two die, horrified but silent. It is better so. That is the rude lesson of the Algerian dog-days.'

So much for the ambience of *The Outsider*. When we study its philosophy, the limpid style disguises a certain confusion. According to one critic, the Outsider himself represents the drying up of all bourgeois sources of sensation, and the complete decadence of renaissance man; he is a 'poor white'. According to another, Maurice Blanchot, he grows out of character in the last pages, when he becomes too articulate, and thus destroys the unity of the book. I don't agree with either. Meursault represents the neo-pagan, a reversion to Mediterranean man as once he was in Corinth or Carthage or Alexandria or Tarshish, as he is to-day in Casablanca or Southern California. He is sensual and well-meaning, profoundly in love with life, whose least pleasures, from a bathe to a yawn, afford him complete and silent gratification. He lives without anxiety in a continuous present and has no need to think or to express himself; there is no Nordic why-clause in his pact with nature. The misfortunes into which he is led by his lazy desire to please and by his stubborn truthfulness gradually force the felt but unspoken philosophy of his existence to emerge into the open, and finally to express itself in words. To understand this last outburst we must study Camus's attitude to death. In his essay on the Roman ruins of Djemila he makes clear how much he admires the fortitude of the pagan ending, even as he shares the sure-set pagan passion for life. 'What does eternity matter to me? To lose the touch of flowers and women's hands is the supreme separation.' In his long essay on suicide in *The Myth of Sisyphus* he introduces his conceptions of the Absurd. 'Everything which exalts life adds at the same time to its absurdity,' he says in *Summer in Algiers*, and comes to the conclusion in the *Myth* that 'the Man under Sentence of Death is freer than the suicide—than the man who takes his own life'. The Suicide is a coward, he is one who abandons the struggle with fate; the Condemned Man, however, has the chance to rise above the society which has condemned him and by his courage and intellectual liberation to nullify it. The egotism of suicides with their farewells and resentments is sometimes grotesque, the dignity of a brave man on the Scaffold never. In his own words, 'The precise opposite of the suicide is the man who is condemned to death . . . The God-like disponibility of the condemned man before whom the prison gates open one day just before dawn, his incredible disinterestedness about everything except the pure flame of life within him, here I am quite sure that Death and Absurdity are the principles which generate the only rational Liberty—that which a human being can experience with body and soul.'

Having said all this, I will leave the reader to form his judgment. The Bourgeois Machinery with its decaying Christian morality, and bureaucratic self-righteousness which condemns the Outsider just because he is so foreign to it, is typical of a European code of Justice applied to a non-European people. A few hundred miles farther south and 'a touch of the Sun' would have been readily recognized, no doubt, as a cause for acquittal, in case of a white man accused of murdering a native, but part of the rigidity of the moribund French court is the pompous assumption that Algiers is France. On the other hand it is a failure of sensibility on the part of Camus that the other sufferer in his story, the Moorish girl whose lover beats her up and whose brother is killed when trying to avenge her, is totally forgotten. She too may have been 'privileged' to love life just as much, so may her murdered brother, for they too were 'foreigners' to the Colonial System, and a great deal besides. But the new paganism, I am afraid, is no kinder to women than the old.

Nevertheless something will have to happen soon and a new creed of happiness, charity and justice be brought to men. *The Outsider* is only a stage. He is a negative destructive force who shows up the unreality of bourgeois ethics. It is not enough to love life, we must teach everyone else to love it, we must appreciate that that happiness is consciousness, and consciousness is one, that all its manifestations are sacred, and it is from these newer schools of novelists and poets in all countries that one day we will learn it.

CYRIL CONNOLLY

MOTHER died to-day. Or, maybe, yesterday; I can't be sure. The telegram from the Home says: *Your mother passed away. Funeral to-morrow. Deep sympathy.* Which leaves the matter doubtful; it could have been yesterday.

The Home for Aged Persons is at Marengo, some fifty miles from Algiers. With the two-o'clock bus I should get there well before nightfall. Then I can spend the night there, keeping the usual vigil beside the body, and be back here by to-morrow evening. I have fixed up with my employer for two days' leave; obviously, under the circumstances, he couldn't refuse. Still, I had an idea he looked annoyed, and I said, without thinking: 'Sorry, sir, but it's not my fault, you know.'

Afterwards it struck me I needn't have said that. I had no reason to excuse myself; it was up to him to express his sympathy and so forth. Probably he will do so the day after to-morrow, when he sees me in black. For the present, it's almost as if Mother weren't really dead. The funeral will bring it home to one, put an official seal on it, so to speak. . . .

I took the two-o'clock bus. It was a blazing hot afternoon. I'd lunched, as usual, at Céleste's restaurant. Everyone was most kind, and Céleste said to me, 'There's no one like a mother'. When I left they came with me to the door. It was something of a rush, getting away, as at the last moment I had to call in at Emmanuel's place to borrow his black tie and mourning-band. He lost his uncle a few months ago.

I had to run to catch the bus. I suppose it was my hurrying like that, what with the glare off the road and from the sky, the reek of petrol and the jolts, that made me feel so drowsy. Anyhow, I slept most of the way. When I woke I was leaning up against a soldier; he grinned and asked me if I'd come from a long way off, and I just nodded, to cut things short. I wasn't in a mood for talking.

The Home is a little over a mile from the village. I went there on foot. I asked to be allowed to see Mother at once, but the door-porter told me I must see the Warden first. He wasn't free, and I had to wait a bit. The porter chatted with me while I waited; then he led me to the office. The Warden was a very small man, with grey hair and a Legion of Honour rosette in his buttonhole. He gave me a long look with his watery blue eyes. Then we shook hands, and he held mine so long that I began to feel embarrassed. After that he consulted a register on his table, and said:

'Madame Meursault entered the Home three years ago. She had no private means and depended entirely on you.'

I had a feeling he was blaming me for something, and started to explain. But he cut me short.

'There's no need to excuse yourself, my boy. I've looked up the record and obviously you weren't in a position to see that she was properly cared for. She needed someone to be with her all the time, and young men in jobs like yours don't get too much pay. In any case she was much happier in the Home.'

I said: 'Yes, sir; I'm sure of that.'

Then he added: 'She had good friends here, you know, old folks like herself, and one gets on better with people of one's own generation. You're much too young, you couldn't have been much of a companion to her.'

That was so. When we lived together, Mother was always watching me, but we hardly ever talked. During her first few weeks at the Home she used to cry a good deal. But that was only because she hadn't settled down. After a month or two she'd have cried if she'd been told to leave the Home. Because this, too, would have been a wrench. That was why, during the last year, I seldom went to see her. Also, it would have meant losing my Sunday—not to mention the fag of going to the bus, getting my ticket, and spending two hours on the journey, each way.

The Warden went on talking, but I didn't pay much attention. Finally he said:

'Now, I suppose you'd like to see your mother?'

I rose without replying and he led the way to the door. As we were going down the stairs he explained:

'I've had the body moved to our little mortuary—so as not to upset the other old people, you understand. Every time there's a death here, they're in a nervous state for two or three days. Which means, of course, extra work and worry for our staff.'

We crossed a courtyard where there were a number of old men, talking amongst themselves in little groups. They fell silent as we came up with them. Then, behind our backs, the chattering began again. Their voices reminded me of parakeets in a cage, only the sound wasn't quite so shrill. The Warden stopped outside the entrance of a small, low building.

'So here I leave you, Monsieur Meursault. If you want me for anything, you'll find me in my office. We propose to have the funeral to-morrow morning. That will enable you to spend the night beside your mother's coffin, as no doubt you would wish to do. Just one more thing; I gathered from your mother's friends that she wished to be buried with the rites of the Church. I've made arrangements for this; but I thought I should let you know.'

I thanked him. So far as I knew, my mother, though not a professed atheist, had never given a thought to religion in her life.

I entered the mortuary. It was a bright, spotlessly clean room, with whitewashed walls and a big skylight. The furniture consisted of some chairs and trestles. Two of the latter stood open in the centre of the room and the coffin rested on them. The lid was in place, but the screws had been given only a few turns and their nickelled heads stuck out above the wood, which was stained dark walnut. An Arab woman, a nurse I supposed, was sitting beside the bier; she was wearing a blue smock and had a rather gaudy scarf wound round her hair.

Just then the porter came up behind me. He'd evidently been running, as he was a little out of breath.

'We put the lid on, but I was told to unscrew it when you came, so that you could see her.'

While he was going up to the coffin I told him not to trouble.

'Eh? What's that?' he exclaimed. 'You don't want me to . . . ?'

'No,' I said.

He put back the screwdriver in his pocket and stared at me. I realized then that I shouldn't have said 'No', and it made me rather embarrassed. After eyeing me for some moments he asked:

'Why not?' But he didn't sound reproachful; he simply wanted to know.

'Well, really I couldn't say,' I answered.

He began twiddling his white moustache; then, without looking at me, said gently:

'I understand.'

He was a pleasant-looking man, with blue eyes and ruddy cheeks. He drew up a chair for me near the coffin, and seated himself just behind. The nurse got up and moved towards the door. As she was going by the porter whispered in my ear:

'It's a tumour she has, poor thing.'

I looked at her more carefully and I noticed that she had a bandage round her head, just below her eyes. It lay quite flat across the bridge of her nose, and one saw hardly anything of her face except that strip of whiteness.

As soon as she had gone, the porter rose.

'Now I'll leave you to yourself.'

I don't know whether I made some gesture, but instead of going he halted behind my chair. The sensation of someone posted at my back made me uncomfortable. The sun was getting low and the whole room was flooded with a pleasant, mellow light. Two hornets were buzzing overhead, against the skylight. I was so sleepy I could hardly keep my eyes open. Without looking round I asked the porter how long he'd been at the Home. 'Five years.' The answer came so pat that one could have thought he'd been expecting my question.

That started him off, and he became quite chatty. If anyone had told him ten years ago that he'd end his days as door-porter at a Home at Marengo, he'd never have believed it. He was sixty-four, he said, and hailed from Paris.

When he said that, I broke in without thinking, 'Ah, you don't come from here?'

I remembered then that, before taking me to the Warden, he'd told me something about Mother. He said she'd have to be buried mighty quickly because of the heat in these parts, especially down in the plain. 'At Paris they keep the body for three days, sometimes four.' After that he mentioned that he'd spent the best part of his life in Paris, and could never manage to forget it. 'Here,' he said, 'things have to go with a rush, like. You've hardly time to get used to the idea that somebody's dead, before you're hauled off to the funeral.' 'That's enough,' his wife put in. 'You didn't ought to say such things to the poor young gentleman.' The old fellow blushed and began to apologize. I told him it was quite all right. As a matter of fact I found it rather interesting, what he'd been telling me; I hadn't thought of that before.

Now he went on to say that he'd entered the Home as an ordinary inmate. But he was still quite hale and hearty, so when the porter's job fell vacant, he offered to take it on.

I pointed out that, even so, he was really an inmate like the others, but he wouldn't hear of it. He was 'an official, like'. I'd been struck before that by his habit of saying 'they' or, less often, 'them old folks', when referring to inmates no older than himself. Still, I could see his point of view. As door-porter he had a certain standing, and some authority over the rest of them.

Just then the nurse returned. Night had fallen very quickly; all of a sudden, it seemed, the sky went black above the skylight. The porter switched on the lamps, and I was almost blinded by the blaze of light.

He suggested I should go to the refectory for dinner, but I wasn't hungry. Then he proposed bringing me a mug of *café au lait*. As I am very fond of *café au lait* I said 'Thanks', and a few minutes later he came back with a tray. I drank the coffee, and then I wanted a cigarette. But I wasn't sure if I should smoke, under the circumstances—in Mother's presence. I thought it over; really it didn't seem to matter, so I offered the porter a cigarette and we both smoked.

After a while he started talking again.

'You know, your mother's friends will be coming soon, to keep vigil with you beside the body. We always have a "vigil" here, when anyone dies. I'd better go and get some chairs and a pot of black coffee.'

The glare from the white walls was making my eyes smart, and I asked him if he couldn't turn off one of the lamps. 'Nothing doing,' he said. They'd arranged the lights like that; either one had them all on or none at all. After that I didn't pay much more attention to him. He went away, brought some chairs and set them out round the coffin. On one he placed a coffee-pot and ten or a dozen cups. Then he sat down facing me, on the far side of Mother.

The nurse was at the other end of the room, with her back to me. I couldn't see what she was doing, but by the way her arms moved I guessed that she was knitting. I was feeling very comfortable; the coffee had warmed me up, and through the open door came scents of flowers, and breaths of cool night air. I think I dozed off for a while.

I was awakened by an odd rustling in my ears. After having had my eyes closed, I had a feeling that the light had grown even stronger than before. There wasn't a trace of shadow anywhere, and every object, each curve or angle, scored its outline on one's eyes. The old people, Mother's friends, were coming in. I counted ten in all, gliding almost soundlessly through the bleak white glare. None of the chairs creaked when they sat down. Never in my life had I seen anyone so clearly as I saw these people; not a detail of their clothes or features escaped me. And yet I couldn't hear them, and it was hard to believe they really existed.

Nearly all the women wore aprons, and the strings drawn tight round their waists made their big stomachs bulge still more. I'd never yet noticed what big paunches old women usually have. Most of the men, however, were thin as rakes, and they all carried sticks. What struck me most about their faces was that one couldn't see their eyes, only a dull glow in a sort of nest of wrinkles.

On sitting down, they looked at me, and wagged their heads awkwardly, sucking their lips in between their toothless gums. I couldn't decide if they were greeting me and trying to say something, or if it was due to some infirmity of age. I inclined to think that they were greeting me, after their fashion, but it had a queer effect, seeing all those old fellows grouped round the porter, solemnly eyeing me and dandling their heads from side to side. For a moment I had an absurd impression that they had come to sit in judgment on me.

A few minutes later one of the women started weeping. She was in the second row and I couldn't see her face because of another woman in front. At regular intervals she emitted a little choking sob; one had a feeling she would never stop. The others didn't seem to notice. They sat in silence, slumped in their chairs, staring at the coffin or at their walking-sticks or any other object just in front of them, and never took their eyes off it. And still the woman sobbed. I was rather surprised, as I didn't know who she was. I wanted her to stop crying, but dared not speak to her. After a while the porter bent towards her and whispered in her ear; but she merely shook her head, mumbled something I couldn't catch, and went on sobbing as steadily as before.

The porter got up and moved his chair beside mine. At first he kept silent; then, without looking at me, he explained.

'She was devoted to your mother. She says your mother was her only friend in the world, and now she's all alone.'

I had nothing to say, and the silence lasted quite a while. Presently the woman's sighs and sobs became less frequent, and, after blowing her nose and snuffling for some minutes, she, too, fell silent.

I'd ceased feeling sleepy, but I was very tired and my legs were aching badly. And now I realized that the silence of these people was telling on my nerves. The only sound was a rather queer one; it came at longish intervals, and at first I was puzzled by it. However, after listening attentively, I guessed what it was; the old men were sucking at the insides of their cheeks, and this caused the odd, wheezing noises that had mystified me. They were so much absorbed in their thoughts that they didn't know what they were up to. I even had an impression that the dead body in their midst meant nothing at all to them. But now I suspect that I was mistaken about this.

We all drank the coffee, which the porter handed round. After that, I can't remember much; somehow the night went by. I can recall only one moment; I had opened my eyes and I saw the old men sleeping hunched up on their chairs, with one exception. Resting his chin on his hands clasped round his stick, he was staring hard at me, as if he had been waiting for me to wake. Then I fell asleep again. I woke up after a bit, because the ache in my legs had developed into a sort of cramp.

There was a glimmer of dawn above the skylight. A minute or two later one of the old men woke up and coughed repeatedly. He spat into a big check handkerchief and each time he spat, it sounded as if he was retching. This woke the others, and the porter told them it was time to make a move. They all got up at once. Their faces were ashen-grey after the long, uneasy vigil. To my surprise each of them shook hands with me, as though this night together, in which we hadn't exchanged a word, had created a kind of intimacy between us.

I was quite done in. The porter took me to his room and I tidied myself up a bit. He gave me some more white coffee, and it seemed to do me good. When I went out the sun was up and the sky mottled red above the hills between Marengo and the sea. A morning breeze was blowing and it had a pleasant salty tang. There was the promise of a very fine day. I hadn't been in the country for ages, and I caught myself thinking what an agreeable walk I might have had, if it hadn't been for Mother.

As it was, I waited in the courtyard under a plane-tree. I sniffed the smells of the cool earth and found I wasn't sleepy any more. Then I thought of the other fellows in the office. At this hour they'd be getting up, preparing to go to work; for me this was always the worst hour of the day. I went on thinking, like this, for ten minutes or so; then the sound of a bell inside the building attracted my attention. I could see movements behind the windows; then all was calm again. The sun had risen a little higher and was beginning to warm my feet. The porter came across the yard and said the Warden wished to see me. I went to his office and he got me to sign some document.

I noticed that he was in black, with pin-stripe trousers. He picked up the telephone-receiver and looked at me.

'The undertaker's men arrived some moments ago, and they will be going to the mortuary to screw down the coffin. Shall I tell them to wait, for you to have a last glimpse of your mother?'

'No,' I said.

He spoke into the receiver, lowering his voice.

'That's all right, Figeac. Tell the men to go there now.'

He then informed me that he was going to attend the funeral, and I thanked him. Sitting down behind his desk, he crossed his short legs and leant back. Besides the nurse on duty, he told me, he and I would be the only mourners at the funeral. It was a rule of the Home that inmates shouldn't attend funerals, though there was no objection to letting some of them sit up beside the coffin, the night before.

'It's for their own sakes,' he explained, 'to spare their feelings. But in this particular instance I've given permission for an old friend of your mother to come with us. His name is Thomas Pérez.' The Warden smiled. 'It's a rather touching little story in its way. He and your mother had become almost inseparable. The other old people used to tease Pérez about having a "fiancée". "When are you going to marry her?" they'd ask. He'd turn it with a laugh. It was a standing joke, in fact. So, you can guess, he feels very badly about your mother's death. I thought I couldn't decently refuse him permission to attend the funeral. But, on our medical officer's advice, I forbade him to sit up beside the body last night.'

For some time we stayed without speaking. Then the Warden got up and went to the window. Presently he said:

'Ah, there's the padre from Marengo. He's a bit ahead of time.'

He warned me that it would take us a good three-quarters of an hour, walking to the church, which was in the village. Then we went downstairs.

The priest was waiting just outside the mortuary door. With him were two acolytes, one of whom had a censer. The priest was stooping over him, adjusting the length of the silver chain on which it hung. When he saw us he straightened up and said a few words to me, addressing me as 'My son'. Then he led the way into the mortuary.

I noticed at once that four men in black were standing behind the coffin and the screws in the lid had now been driven home. At the same moment I heard the Warden remark that the hearse had arrived, and the priest started his prayers. Then everybody made a move. Holding a strip of black cloth, the four men approached the coffin, while the priest, the boys and myself filed out. A lady I hadn't seen before was standing by the door. 'This is Monsieur Meursault,' the Warden said to her. I didn't catch her name, but I gathered she was a nursing sister attached to the Home. When I was introduced, she bowed, without the trace of a smile on her long, gaunt face. We stood aside from the doorway to let the coffin by; then, following the bearers down a corridor, we came to the front entrance, where a hearse was waiting. Oblong, glossy, varnished black all over, it vaguely reminded me of the pen-trays in the office.

Beside the hearse stood a quaintly dressed little man, whose duty it was, I understood, to supervise the funeral, as a sort of master of ceremonies. Near him, looking constrained, almost bashful, was old M. Pérez, my mother's special friend. He wore a soft felt hat with a pudding-basin crown and a very wide brim—he whisked it off the moment the coffin emerged from the doorway—trousers that concertina'd on his shoes, a black tie much too small for his high white double-collar. Under a bulbous, pimply nose, his lips were trembling. But what caught my attention most was his ears; pendulous, scarlet ears that showed up like blobs of sealing-wax on the pallor of his cheeks and were framed in wisps of silky white hair.

The undertaker's factotum shepherded us to our places, with the priest in front of the hearse, and the four men in black on each side of it. The Warden and myself came next, and, bringing up the rear, old Pérez and the nurse.

The sky was already a blaze of light, and the air stoking up rapidly. I felt the first waves of heat lapping my back, and my dark suit made things worse. I couldn't imagine why we waited so long for getting under way. Old Pérez, who had put on his hat, took it off again. I had turned slightly in his direction and was looking at him when the Warden started telling me more about him. I remember his saying that old Pérez and my mother used often to have a longish stroll together in the cool of the evening; sometimes they went as far as the village, accompanied by a nurse, of course.

I looked at the countryside, at the long lines of cypresses sloping up towards the skyline and the hills, the hot red soil dappled with vivid green, and here and there a lonely house sharply outlined against the light—and I could understand Mother's feelings. Evenings in these parts must be a sort of mournful solace. Now, in the full glare of the morning sun, with everything shimmering in the heat-haze, there was something inhuman, discouraging, about this landscape.

At last we made a move. Only then I noticed that Pérez had a slight limp. The old chap steadily lost ground as the hearse gained speed. One of the men beside it, too, fell back and drew level with me. I was surprised to see how quickly the sun was climbing up the sky, and just then it struck me that for quite a while the air had been throbbing with the hum of insects and the rustle of grass warming up. Sweat was trickling down my face. As I had no hat I tried to fan myself with my handkerchief.

The undertaker's man turned to me and said something that I didn't catch. At the same time he wiped the crown of his head with a handkerchief that he held in his left hand, while with his right he tilted up his hat. I asked him what he'd said. He pointed upwards.

'Sun's pretty bad to-day, ain't it?'

'Yes,' I said.

After a while he asked: 'Is it your mother we're burying?'

'Yes,' I said again.

'What was her age?'

'Well, she was getting on.' As a matter of fact I didn't know exactly how old she was.

After that he kept silent. Looking back, I saw Pérez limping along some fifty yards behind. He was swinging his big felt hat at arm's length, trying to make the pace. I also had a look at the Warden. He was walking with carefully measured steps, economizing every gesture. Beads of perspiration glistened on his forehead, but he didn't wipe them off.

I had an impression that our little procession was moving slightly faster. Wherever I looked I saw the same sun-drenched countryside, and the sky was so dazzling that I dared not raise my eyes. Presently we struck a patch of freshly tarred road. A shimmer of heat played over it and one's feet squelched at each step, leaving bright black gashes. In front, the coachman's glossy black hat looked like a lump of the same sticky substance, poised above the hearse. It gave one a queer, dreamlike impression, that bluey-white glare overhead and all this blackness round one: the sleek black of the hearse, the dull black of the men's clothes and the silvery black gashes in the road. And then there were the smells, smells of hot leather and horse-dung from the hearse, veined with whiffs of incense-smoke. What with these and the hangover from a poor night's sleep, I found my eyes and thoughts growing blurred.

I looked back again. Pérez seemed very far away now, almost hidden by the heat-haze; then, abruptly, he disappeared altogether. After puzzling over it for a bit, I guessed that he had turned off the road into the fields. Then I noticed that there was a bend of the road a little way ahead. Obviously Pérez, who knew the district well, had taken a short cut, so as to catch us up. He rejoined us soon after we were round the bend; then began to lose ground again. He took another short cut and met us again farther on; in fact this happened several times during the next half-hour. But soon I lost interest in his movements; my temples were throbbing and I could hardly drag myself along.

After that everything went with a rush; and also with such precision and matter-of-factness that I remember hardly any details. Except that when we were on the outskirts of the village the nurse said something to me. Her voice took me by surprise, it didn't match her face at all; it was musical and slightly tremulous. What she said was: 'If one goes too slowly there's the risk of a heat-stroke. But, if one goes too fast, one perspires, and the cold air in the church gives one a chill.' I saw her point; either way one was for it.

Some other memories of the funeral have stuck in my mind. The old boy's face, for instance, when he caught us up for the last time, just outside the village. His eyes were streaming with tears, of exhaustion or distress, or both together. But because of the wrinkles they couldn't flow down. They spread out, criss-crossed, and formed a sort of glaze over the old, worn face.

And I can remember the look of the church, the villagers in the street, the red geraniums on the graves, Pérez's fainting-fit—he crumpled up like a rag doll—the tawny red earth pattering on Mother's coffin, the bits of white roots mixed up with it; then more people, voices, the wait outside a café for the bus, the rumble of the engine, and my little thrill of pleasure when we entered the first brightly lit streets of Algiers, and I pictured myself going straight to bed and sleeping twelve hours at a stretch.

2

ON waking I understood why my employer had looked rather glum when I asked for my two days off; it was a Saturday to-day. I hadn't thought of this at the time; it only struck me when I was getting out of bed. Obviously he had seen that it would mean my getting four days' holiday straight off, and one couldn't expect him to like that. Still, for one thing, it wasn't my fault if Mother was buried yesterday and not to-day; and then, again, I'd have had my Saturday and Sunday off in any case. But naturally this didn't prevent me from seeing my employer's point.

Getting up was an effort, as I'd been really exhausted by the previous day's experiences. While shaving, I wondered how to spend the morning, and decided that a swim would do me good. So I caught the tram that goes down to the harbour.

It was quite like old times; a lot of young people were in the swimming-pool, amongst them Marie Cardona who used to be a typist at the office. I was rather keen on her in those days, and I fancy she liked me too. But she was with us so short a time that nothing came of it.

While I was helping her to climb on to a raft, I let my hand stray over her breasts. Then she lay flat on the raft, while I trod water. After a moment she turned and looked at me. Her hair was over her eyes and she was laughing. I clambered up on to the raft, beside her. The air was pleasantly warm and, half jokingly, I let my head sink back upon her lap. She didn't seem to mind, so I let it stay there. I had the sky full in my eyes, all blue and gold, and I could feel Marie's stomach rising and falling gently under my head. We must have stayed a good half-hour on the raft, both of us half asleep. When the sun got too hot she dived off and I followed. I caught her up, put my arm round her waist and we swam side by side. She was still laughing.

While we were drying ourselves on the edge of the swimming-pool she said: 'I'm browner than you.' I asked her if she'd come to the cinema with me that evening. She laughed again and said 'Yes', if I'd take her to the comic everybody was talking about, the one with Fernandel in it.

When we had dressed, she stared at my black tie and asked if I was in mourning. I explained that my mother had died. 'When?' she asked, and I said, 'Yesterday'. She made no remark, though I thought she shrank away a little. I was just going to explain to her that it wasn't my fault, but I checked myself, as I remembered having said the same thing to my employer, and realizing then it sounded rather foolish. Still, foolish or not—somehow one can't help feeling a bit guilty, I suppose, about things like that.

Anyhow, by the evening Marie had forgotten all about it. The film was funny in parts, but much of it downright stupid. She pressed her leg against mine while we were in the picture-house, and I was fondling her breast. Towards the end of the show I kissed her, but rather clumsily. Afterwards she came back with me to my place.

When I woke up Marie had gone. She'd told me her aunt expected her first thing in the morning. I remembered it was a Sunday, and that put me off; I've never cared for Sundays. So I turned my head and lazily sniffed the smell of brine that Marie's head had left on the pillow. I slept until ten. After that I stayed in bed until noon, smoking cigarettes. I decided not to lunch at Céleste's restaurant as I usually did; they'd be sure to pester me with questions, and I dislike being questioned. So I fried some eggs, and ate them off the pan. I did without bread as there wasn't any left, and I couldn't be bothered going down to buy it.

After lunch I felt at a loose end and roamed about the little flat. It suited us well enough when Mother was with me, but now I was by myself it was too large and I'd moved the dining-table into my bedroom. That was now the only room I used; it had all the furniture I needed: a brass bedstead, a dressing-table, some cane chairs whose seats had more or less caved in, a wardrobe with a tarnished mirror. The rest of the flat was never used, so I didn't trouble to look after it.

A bit later, for want of anything better to do, I picked up an old news-paper that was lying on the floor and read it. There was an advertisement of Kruschen Salts and I cut it out and pasted it into an album where I keep things that amuse me in the papers. Then I washed my hands and, as a last resource, went out on to the balcony.

My bedroom overlooks the main street of our district. Though it was a fine afternoon the paving-blocks were black and glistening. What few people were about seemed in an absurd hurry. First of all there came a family going for their Sunday afternoon walk; two small boys in sailor suits, with short trousers hardly down to their knees, and looking rather uneasy in their Sunday best; then a little girl with a big pink bow and black patent-leather shoes. Behind them was their mother, an enormously fat woman in a brown silk dress, and their father, a dapper little man, whom I knew by sight. He had a straw hat, a walking-stick, and a butterfly tie. Seeing him beside his wife, I understood why people said he came of a good family and had married beneath him.

Next came a group of young fellows, the local 'bloods', with sleek oiled hair, red ties, coats cut very tight at the waist, braided pockets, and square-toed shoes. I guessed they were going to one of the big cinemas in the centre of the town. That was why they had started out so early and were hurrying to the tram-stop, laughing and talking at the top of their voices.

After they had passed the street gradually emptied. By this time all the matinées must have begun. Only a few shopkeepers and cats remained about. Above the sycamores bordering the road the sky was cloudless, but the light was soft. The tobacconist on the other side of the street brought a chair out on to the pavement in front of his door and sat astride it, resting his arms on the back. The trams which a few minutes before had been crowded were now almost empty. In the little café, *Chez Pierrot*, beside the tobacconist's, the waiter was sweeping up the sawdust in the empty restaurant. A typical Sunday afternoon. . . .

I turned my chair round and seated myself like the tobacconist, as it was more comfortable that way. After smoking a couple of cigarettes I went back to the room, got a tablet of chocolate and returned to the window to eat it. Soon after, the sky clouded over and I thought a summer storm was coming. However, the clouds gradually lifted. All the same they had left in the street a sort of threat of rain, which made it darker. I stayed watching the sky for quite a while.

At five there was a loud clanging of trams. They were coming from the stadium in our suburb where there had been a football match. Even the back platforms were crowded and people were standing on the steps. Then another tram brought back the teams. I knew they were the players by the little suitcase each man carried. They were bawling out their team-song, 'Keep the ball rolling, boys'. One of them looked up at me and shouted, 'We licked them!' I waved my hand and called back, 'Good work!' From now on there was a steady stream of private cars.

The sky had changed again; a reddish glow was spreading up beyond the housetops. As dusk set in the street grew more crowded. People were returning from their walks, and I noticed the dapper little man with the fat wife amongst the passers-by. Children were whimpering and trailing wearily after their parents. After some minutes the local cinemas disgorged their audiences. I noticed that the young fellows coming from them were taking longer strides and gesturing more vigorously than at ordinary times; doubtless the picture they'd been seeing was of the Wild West variety. Those who had been to the picture-houses in the middle of the town came a little later, and looked more sedate, though a few were still laughing. On the whole, however, they seemed languid and exhausted. Some of them remained loitering in the street under my window. A group of girls came by, walking arm in arm. The young men under my window swerved so as to brush against them, and shouted humorous remarks, which made the girls turn their heads and giggle. I recognized them as girls from my part of the town, and two or three of them, whom I knew, looked up and waved to me.

Just then the street-lamps came on, all together, and they made the stars that were beginning to glimmer in the night sky paler still. I felt my eyes getting tired, what with the lights and all the movement I'd been watching in the street. There were little pools of brightness under the lamps, and now and then a tramcar passed, lighting up a girl's hair, or a smile, or a silver bangle.

Soon after this, as the trams became fewer and the sky showed velvety black above the trees and lamps, the street grew emptier, almost imperceptibly, until a time came when there was nobody to be seen and a cat, the first of the evening, crossed unhurrying the deserted street.

It struck me that I'd better see about some dinner. I had been leaning so long on the back of my chair, looking down, that my neck hurt when I straightened myself up. I went down, bought some bread and spaghetti, did my cooking and ate my meal standing. I'd intended to smoke another cigarette at my window, but the night had turned rather chilly and I decided against it. As I was coming back, after shutting the window, I glanced at the mirror and saw reflected in it a corner of my table with my spirit-lamp and some bits of bread beside it. It occurred to me that somehow I'd got through another Sunday, that Mother now was buried, and to-morrow I'd be going back to work as usual. Really, nothing in my life had changed.

3

I HAD a busy morning in the office. My employer was in a good humour. He even inquired if I wasn't too tired, and followed it up by asking what Mother's age was. I thought a bit, then answered, 'Round about sixty', as I didn't want to make a blunder. At which he looked relieved—why, I can't imagine—and seemed to think that closed the matter.

There was a pile of bills of lading waiting on my desk and I had to go through them all. Before leaving for lunch I washed my hands. I always enjoyed doing this at midday. In the evening it was less pleasant, as the roller-towel after being used by so many people was sopping wet. I once brought this to my employer's notice. It was regrettable, he agreed—but, to his mind, a mere detail. I left the office building a little later than usual, at half-past twelve, with Emmanuel, who works in the Forwarding Department. Our building overlooks the sea, and we paused for a moment on the steps to look at the shipping in the harbour. The sun was scorching hot. Just then a big truck came up, with a din of chains and backfires from the engine, and Emmanuel suggested we should try to jump it. I started to run. The truck was well away, and we had to chase it for quite a distance. What with the heat and the noise from the engine, I felt half dazed. All I was conscious of was our mad rush along the waterfront, amongst cranes and winches, with dark hulls of ships alongside and masts swaying in the offing. I was the first to catch up with the truck. I took a flying jump, landed safely, and helped Emmanuel to scramble in beside me. We were both of us out of breath and the bumps of the truck on the roughly laid cobbles made things worse. Emmanuel chuckled, and panted in my ear, 'We've made it!'

By the time we reached Céleste's restaurant we were dripping with sweat. Céleste was at his usual place beside the entrance, with his apron bulging on his paunch, his white moustache well to the fore. When he saw me he was sympathetic and 'hoped I wasn't feeling too badly'. I said 'No', but I was extremely hungry. I ate very quickly and had some coffee, to finish up. Then I went to my place and took a short nap, as I'd drunk a glass of wine too many. When I woke I smoked a cigarette before getting off my bed. I was a bit late and had to run for the tram. The office was stifling, and I was kept hard at it all the afternoon. So it came as a relief when we closed down and I was strolling slowly along the wharves in the coolness. The sky was green, and it was pleasant to be out of doors after the stuffy office. However, I went straight home as I had to put some potatoes on to boil.

The hall was dark and, when I was starting up the stairs, I almost bumped into old Salamano, who lived on the same floor as I. As usual, he had his dog with him. For eight years the two had been inseparable. Salamano's spaniel is an ugly brute, afflicted with some skin disease—mange, I expect; anyhow it has lost all its hair and its body is covered with brown scabs. Perhaps through living in one small room, cooped up with his dog, Salamano has come to resemble it. His towy hair has gone very thin, and he has reddish blotches on his face. And the dog has developed something of its master's queer hunched-up gait; it always has its muzzle stretched far forward and its nose to the ground. But, oddly enough, though so much alike, they detest each other.

Twice a day, at eleven and six, the old fellow takes his dog for a walk, and for eight years that walk has never varied. You can see them in the Rue de Lyon, the dog pulling his master along as hard as he can, till finally the old chap misses a step and nearly falls. Then he beats his dog and calls it names. The dog cowers and lags behind, and it's his master's turn to drag him along. Presently the dog forgets, starts tugging at the leash again, gets another hiding and more abuse. Then they halt on the pavement, the pair of them, and glare at each other; the dog with terror and the man with hatred in his eyes. Every time they're out this happens. When the dog wants to stop at a lamp-post, the old boy won't let him, and drags him on, and the wretched spaniel leaves behind him a trail of little drops. But, if he does it in the room, it means another hiding.

It's been going on like this for eight years, and Céleste always says it's a 'crying shame', and something should be done about it; but really one can't be sure. When I met him in the hall, Salamano was bawling at his dog, calling him a bastard, a lousy mongrel, and so forth, and the dog was whining. I said, 'Good evening', but the old fellow took no notice and went on cursing. So I thought I'd ask him what the dog had done. Again, he didn't answer, but went on shouting, 'You bloody cur!' and the rest of it. I couldn't see very clearly, but he seemed to be fixing something on the dog's collar. I raised my voice a little. Without looking round, he mumbled in a sort of suppressed fury: 'He's always in the way, blast him!' Then he started up the stairs, but the dog tried to resist and flattened itself out on the floor, so he had to haul it up on the leash, step by step.

Just then the man who lives on my floor came in from the street. The general idea hereabouts is that he's a pimp. But if one asks him what his job is, he says he's a warehouseman. One thing's sure: he isn't popular in our street. Still, he often has a word for me, and drops in sometimes for a short talk in my room, because I listen to him. As a matter of fact, I find what he says quite interesting. So, really, I've no reason for freezing him off. His name is Sintès: Raymond Sintès. He's short and thick-set, has a nose like a boxer's, and always dresses very sprucely. He, too, once said to me, referring to Salamano, that it was 'a bloody shame', and asked me if I wasn't disgusted by the way the old man served his dog. I answered: 'No.'

We went up the stairs together, Sintès and I, and when I was turning in at my door, he said:

'Look here! How about having some grub with me? I've a black-pudding and some wine.'

It struck me that this would save my having to cook my dinner, so I said, 'Thanks very much'.

He, too, has only one room, and a little kitchen without a window. I saw a pink-and-white plaster angel above his bed, and some photos of sporting champions and naked girls pinned to the opposite wall. The bed hadn't been made and the room was dirty. He began by lighting a paraffin lamp; then fumbled in his pocket and produced a rather grimy bandage, which he wrapped round his right hand. I asked him what the trouble was. He told me he'd been having a rough house with a fellow who'd annoyed him.

'I'm not one who looks for trouble,' he explained, 'only I'm a bit short-tempered. That fellow said to me, challenging, like, "Come down off that tram, if you're a man". I says, "You keep quiet, I ain't done nothing to you". Then he said I hadn't any guts. Well, that settled it. I got down off the tram and I said to him, "You better keep your mouth shut, or I'll shut it for you"—"I'd like to see you try!" says he. Then I gave him one across the face and laid him out good and proper. After a bit I started to help him to get up, but all he did was to kick at me from where he lay. So I gave him one with my knee and a couple more swipes. He was bleeding like a pig when I'd done with him. I asked him if he'd had enough, and he said "Yes".'

Sintès was busy fixing his bandage while he talked, and I was sitting on the bed.

'So you see,' he said, 'it wasn't my fault; he was asking for it, wasn't he?' I nodded, and he added:

'As a matter of fact, I rather want to ask your advice about something; it's connected with this business. You've knocked about the world a bit, and I dare say you can help me. And then I'll be your pal for life; I never forget anyone who does me a good turn.'

When I made no comment, he asked me if I'd like us to be pals. I replied that I had no objection, and that appeared to satisfy him. He got out the black-pudding, cooked it in a frying-pan, then laid the table, putting out two bottles of wine. While he was doing this he didn't speak.

We started dinner, and then he began telling me the whole story, hesitating a bit at first.

'There's a girl behind it—as usual. We slept together pretty regular. I was keeping her, as a matter of fact, and she cost me a tidy sum. That fellow I knocked down is her brother.'

Noticing that I said nothing, he added that he knew what the neighbours said about him, but it was a filthy lie. He had his principles like everybody else, and a job in a warehouse.

'Well,' he said, 'to go on with my story. . . . I found out one day that she was letting me down.' He gave her enough money to keep her going, without extravagance, though; he paid the rent of her room and twenty francs a day for food. 'Three hundred francs for rent, and six hundred for her grub, with a little present thrown in now and then, a pair of stockings or what not. Say, a thousand francs a month. But that wasn't enough for my fine lady; she was always grumbling that she couldn't make both ends meet with what I gave. So one day I says to her, "Look here, why not get a job for a few hours a day? That'd make things easier for me, too. I bought you a new frock this month, I pay your rent and give you twenty francs a day. But you go and waste your money at the café with a pack of girls. You give them coffee and sugar. And of course the money comes out of my pocket. I treat you on the square, and that's how you pay me back." But she wouldn't hear of working, though she kept on saying she couldn't make do with what I gave her. And then one day I found out she was doing the dirty on me.'

He went on to explain that he'd discovered a lottery ticket in her bag, and, when he asked where the money'd come from to buy it, she wouldn't tell him. Then, another time, he'd found a pawn-ticket for two bracelets which he'd never set eyes on before.

'So I knew there was dirty work going on, and I told her I'd have nothing more to do with her. But, first, I gave her a good hiding, and I told her some home-truths. I said that there was only one thing interested her and that was getting into bed with men whenever she'd the chance. And I warned her straight, "You'll be sorry one day, my girl, and wish you'd got me back. All the girls in the street, they're jealous of your luck in having me to keep you".'

He'd beaten her till the blood came. Before that he'd never beaten her. 'Well, not hard, anyhow; only affectionately, like. She'd howl a bit, and I had to shut the window. Then, of course, it ended as per usual. But this time I'm done with her. Only, to my mind, I ain't punished her enough. See what I mean?'

He explained that it was about this he wanted my advice. The lamp was smoking, and he stopped pacing up and down the room, to lower the wick. I just listened, without speaking. I'd had a whole bottle of wine to myself and my head was buzzing. As I'd used up my cigarettes I was smoking Raymond's. Some late trams passed, and the last noises of the street died off with them. Raymond went on talking. What bored him was that he had 'a sort of lech on her' as he called it. But he was quite determined to teach her a lesson.

His first idea, he said, had been to take her to an hotel, and then call in the special police. He'd persuade them to put her on the register as a 'common prostitute' and that would make her wild. Then he'd looked up some friends of his in the underworld, fellows who kept tarts for what they could make out of them, but they had practically nothing to suggest. Still, as he pointed out, that sort of thing should have been right up their street; what's the good of being in that line if you don't know how to treat a girl who's let you down? When he told them that, they suggested he should 'brand' her. But that wasn't what he wanted, either. It would need a lot of thinking out. . . . But, first, he'd like to ask me something. Before he asked it, though, he'd like to have my opinion of the story he'd been telling, in a general way.

I said I hadn't any, but I'd found it interesting.

Did I think she really had done the dirty on him?

I had to admit it looked like that. Then he asked me if I didn't think she should be punished, and what I'd do if I were in his shoes. I told him one could never be quite sure how to act in such cases, but I quite understood his wanting her to suffer for it.

I drank some more wine, while Raymond lit another cigarette and began explaining what he proposed to do. He wanted to write her a letter, 'a real stinker, that'll get her on the raw', and at the same time make her repent of what she'd done. Then, when she came back, he'd go to bed with her and, just when she was 'properly primed up', he'd spit in her face and throw her out of the room. I agreed it wasn't a bad plan; it would punish her all right.

But, Raymond told me, he didn't feel up to writing the kind of letter that was needed, and that was where I could help. When I didn't say anything, he asked me if I'd mind doing it right away, and I said 'No', I'd have a shot at it.

He drank off a glass of wine and stood up. Then he pushed aside the plates and the bit of cold pudding that was left, to make room on the table. After carefully wiping the oilcloth, he got a sheet of squared paper from the drawer of his bedside table; after that, an envelope, a small red wooden penholder and a square inkpot with purple ink in it. The moment he mentioned the girl's name I knew she was a Moor.

I wrote the letter. I didn't take much trouble over it, but I wanted to satisfy Raymond, as I'd no reason not to satisfy him. Then I read out what I'd written. Puffing at his cigarette, he listened, nodding now and then. 'Read it again, please,' he said. He seemed delighted. 'That's the stuff,' he chuckled. 'I could tell you was a brainy sort, old boy, and you know what's what.'

At first I hardly noticed that 'old boy'. It came back to me when he slapped me on the shoulder and said, 'So now we're pals, ain't we?' I kept silence and he said it again. I didn't care one way or the other, but as he seemed so set on it, I nodded and said, 'Yes'.

He put the letter in the envelope and we finished off the wine. Then both of us smoked for some minutes, without speaking. The street was quite quiet, except when now and again a car passed. Finally I remarked that it was getting late, and Raymond agreed. 'Time's gone mighty fast this evening,' he added, and in a way that was true. I wanted to be in bed, only it was such an effort making a move. I must have looked tired, for Raymond told me 'one mustn't let things get one down'. At first I didn't catch his meaning. Then he explained that he had heard of my mother's death; any-how, he said, that was something bound to happen one day or another. I appreciated that, and told him so.

When I rose Raymond shook hands very warmly, remarking that men always understood each other. After closing the door behind me I lingered for some moments on the landing. The whole building was quiet as the grave, a dank, dark smell rising from the well-hole of the stairs. I could hear nothing but the blood throbbing in my ears, and for a while I stood listening to it. Then the dog began to moan in old Salamano's room, and through the sleep-bound house the little plaintive sound rose slowly, like a flower growing out of the silence and the darkness.

4

I HAD a busy time in the office throughout the week. Raymond dropped in once to tell me he'd sent off the letter. I went to the pictures twice with Emmanuel, who doesn't always understand what's happening on the screen and asks one to explain it. Yesterday was Saturday, and Marie came as we'd arranged. She had a very pretty dress, with red and white stripes, and leather sandals, and I couldn't take my eyes off her. One could see the outline of her firm little breasts, and her sun-tanned face was like a velvety brown flower. We took the bus and went to a beach I know, some miles out of Algiers. It's just a strip of sand between two rocky spurs, with a line of rushes at the back, along the tide-line. At four o'clock the sun wasn't too hot, but the water was pleasantly tepid, and small, languid ripples were creeping up the sand.

Marie taught me a new game. The idea was, while one swam, to suck in the spray off the waves and, when one's mouth was full of foam, to lie on one's back and spout it out against the sky. It made a sort of frothy haze that melted into the air or fell back in a warm shower on one's cheeks. But very soon my mouth was smarting with all the salt I'd drawn in; then Marie came up and hugged me in the water, and pressed her mouth to mine. Her tongue cooled my lips, and we let the waves roll us about for a minute or two before swimming back to the beach.

When we had finished dressing, Marie looked hard at me. Her eyes were sparkling. I kissed her; after that neither of us spoke for quite a while. I pressed her to my side as we scrambled up the foreshore. Both of us were in a hurry to catch the bus, get back to my place and tumble on to the bed. I'd left my window open and it was pleasant to feel the cool night air flowing over our sunburnt bodies.

Marie said she was free next morning so I proposed she should have luncheon with me. She agreed, and I went down to buy some meat. On my way back I heard a woman's voice in Raymond's room. A little later old Salamano started grumbling at his dog and presently there was a sound of boots and paws on the wooden stairs; then, 'Filthy brute! Get on, you cur!' and the two of them went out into the street. I told Marie about the old chap's habits, and it made her laugh. She was wearing one of my pyjama suits, and had the sleeves rolled up. When she laughed I wanted her again. A moment later she asked me if I loved her. I said that sort of question had no meaning, really; but I supposed I didn't. She looked sad for a bit, but when we were getting our lunch ready she brightened up and started laughing, and when she laughs I always want to kiss her. It was just then that the row started in Raymond's room.

First we heard a woman saying something in a high-pitched voice; then Raymond bawling at her, 'You let me down, you bitch! I'll learn you to let me down!' There came some thuds, then a piercing scream—it made one's blood run cold—and in a moment there was a crowd of people on the landing. Marie and I went out to see. The woman was still screaming and Raymond still knocking her about. Marie said, wasn't it horrible! I didn't answer anything. Then she asked me to go and fetch a policeman, but I told her I didn't like policemen. However, one turned up presently; the lodger on the second floor, a plumber, came up with him. When he banged on the door the noise stopped inside the room. He knocked again and, after a moment, the woman started crying, and Raymond opened the door. He had a cigarette dangling from his underlip and a rather sickly smile. 'Your name?' Raymond gave his name. 'Take that cigarette out of your mouth when you're talking to me,' the policeman said gruffly. Raymond hesitated, glanced at me, and kept the cigarette in his mouth. The policeman promptly swung his arm and gave him a good hard smack on the left cheek. The cigarette shot from his lips and dropped a yard away. Raymond made a wry face, but said nothing for a moment. Then in a humble tone he asked if he mightn't pick up his fag.

The officer said 'Yes', and added: 'But don't you forget next time that we don't stand for any nonsense, not from blokes like you.'

Meanwhile the girl went on sobbing and repeating: 'He hit me, the coward. He's a pimp.'

'Excuse me, officer,' Raymond put in, 'but is that in order, calling a man a pimp in the presence of witnesses?'

The policeman told him to 'shut his trap'.

Raymond then turned to the girl. 'Don't you worry, my pet. We'll meet again.'

'That's enough,' the policeman said, and told the girl to go away. Raymond was to stay in his room till summoned to the police-station. 'You ought to be ashamed of yourself,' the policeman added, 'getting so tight you can't stand steady. Why, you're shaking all over!'

'I'm not tight,' Raymond explained. 'Only when I see you standing there and looking at me, I can't help trembling. That's only natural.'

Then he closed his door, and we all went away. Marie and I finished getting our lunch ready. But she hadn't any appetite, and I ate nearly all. She left at one, and then I had a nap.

Towards three there was a knock at my door and Raymond came in. He sat down on the edge of my bed and for a minute or two said nothing. I asked him how it had gone off. He said it had all gone quite smoothly at first, as per programme; only then she'd slapped his face and he'd seen red, and started thrashing her. As for what happened after that, he needn't tell me, as I was there.

'Well,' I said, 'you taught her a lesson all right, and that's what you wanted, isn't it?'

He agreed, and pointed out that whatever the police did, that wouldn't change the fact she'd had her punishment. As for the police, he knew exactly how to handle them. But he'd like to know if I'd expected him to return the blow when the policeman hit him.

I told him I hadn't expected anything whatsoever and, anyhow, I had no use for the police. Raymond seemed pleased and asked if I'd like to come out for a stroll with him. I got up from the bed and started brushing my hair. Then Raymond said that what he really wanted was for me to act as his witness. I told him I had no objection; only I didn't know what he expected me to say.

'It's quite simple,' he replied. 'You've only got to tell them that the girl had let me down.'

So I agreed to be his witness.

We went out together and Raymond stood me a brandy in a café. Then we had a game of billiards; it was a close game and I lost by only a few points. After that he proposed going to a brothel, but I refused; I didn't feel like it. As we were walking slowly back he told me how pleased he was at having paid out his mistress so satisfactorily. He made himself extremely amiable to me and I quite enjoyed our walk.

When we were nearly home I saw old Salamano on the doorstep; he seemed very excited. I noticed that his dog wasn't with him. He was turning like a teetotum, looking in all directions, and sometimes peering into the darkness of the hall with his little bloodshot eyes. Then he'd mutter something to himself and start gazing up and down the street again.

Raymond asked him what was wrong, but he didn't answer at once. Then I heard him grunt, 'The bastard! The filthy cur!' When I asked him where his dog was, he scowled at me and snapped out, 'Gone!' A moment later, all of a sudden, he launched out into it.

'I'd taken him to the Parade Ground as usual. There was a fair on, and one could hardly move for the crowd. I stopped at one of the booths to look at the Handcuff King. When I turned to go, the dog was gone. I'd been meaning to get a smaller collar, but I never thought the brute could slip it and get away like that.'

Raymond assured him the dog would find its way home, and told him stories of dogs that had travelled miles and miles to get back to their masters. But this seemed to make the old fellow even more worried than before.

'Don't you understand, they'll do away with him; the police, I mean. It's not likely anyone will take him in and look after him; with all those scabs he puts everybody off.'

I told him that there was a Pound at the police station, where stray dogs are taken. His dog was certain to be there, and he could get it back on payment of a small charge. He asked me how much the charge was, but there I couldn't help him. Then he flew into a rage again.

'Is it likely I'd give money for a tyke like that? No bloody fear! They can kill him for all I care.' And he went on calling his dog the usual names.

Raymond gave a laugh and turned into the hall. I followed him upstairs, and we parted on the landing. A minute or two later I heard Salamano's footsteps and a knock on my door.

When I opened it, he halted for a moment in the doorway.

'Excuse me . . . I hope I'm not disturbing you.'

I asked him in, but he shook his head. He was staring at his toe-caps, and the gnarled old hands were trembling. Without meeting my eyes, he started talking.

'They won't really take him from me, will they, Monsieur Meursault? Surely they wouldn't do a thing like that. If they do—I don't know what will become of me.'

I told him that, so far as I knew, they kept stray dogs in the Pound for three days, waiting for their owners to call for them. After that they disposed of the dogs as they thought fit.

He stared at me in silence for a moment, then said, 'Good evening'. After that I heard him pacing up and down his room for quite a while. Then his bed creaked. Through the wall there came to me a little wheezing sound, and I guessed that he was weeping. For some reason, I don't know what, I began thinking of Mother. But I had to get up early next day; so, as I wasn't feeling hungry, I did without supper, and went straight to bed.

5

RAYMOND rang me up at the office. He said that a friend of his—to whom he'd spoken about me—invited me to spend next Sunday at his little seaside bungalow just outside Algiers. I told him I'd have been delighted; only I had promised to spend Sunday with a girl. Raymond promptly replied that she could come, too. In fact, his friend's wife would be very pleased not to be the only woman in a party of men.

I'd have liked to hang up at once, as my employer doesn't approve of one's using the office phone for private calls. But Raymond asked me to hold on; he had something else to tell me, and that was why he'd rung me up, though he could have waited till the evening to pass on the invitation.

'It's like this,' he said. 'I've been shadowed all the morning by some Arabs. One of them's the brother of that girl I had the row with. If you see him hanging round the house when you come back, pass me the word.'

I promised to do so.

Just then my employer sent for me. For a moment I felt uneasy as I expected he was going to tell me to stick to my work and not waste time chattering with friends over the phone. However, it was nothing of the kind. He wanted to discuss a project he had in view, though so far he'd come to no decision. It was to open a branch at Paris, so as to be able to deal with the big companies on the spot, without postal delays, and he wanted to know if I'd like a post there.

'You're a young man,' he said, 'and I'm pretty sure you'd enjoy living in Paris. And, of course, you could travel about France for some months in the year.'

I told him I was quite prepared to go; but really I didn't care much one way or the other.

He then asked if a 'change of life', as he called it, didn't appeal to me, and I answered that one never changed one's real life; anyhow, one life was as good as another and my present one suited me quite well.

At this he looked rather hurt, and told me that I always shilly-shallied, and that I lacked ambition—a grave defect, to his mind, when one was in business.

I returned to my work. I'd have preferred not to vex him, but I saw no reason for 'changing my life'. By and large it wasn't an unpleasant one. As a student I'd had plenty of ambition of the kind he meant. But, when I had to drop my studies, I very soon realized all that was pretty futile.

Marie came that evening and asked me if I'd marry her. I said I didn't mind; if she was keen on it, we'd get married.

Then she asked me again if I loved her. I replied, much as before, that her question meant nothing or next to nothing—but I supposed I didn't.

'If that's how you feel,' she said, 'why marry me?'

I explained that it had no importance really but, if it would give her pleasure, we could get married right away. I pointed out that anyhow the suggestion came from her; as for me, I'd merely said 'Yes'.

Then she remarked that marriage was a serious matter.

To which I answered: 'No.'

She kept silent after that, staring at me in a curious way. Then she asked:

'Suppose another girl had asked you to marry her—I mean, a girl you liked in the same way as you like me—would you have said "Yes" to her, too?'

'Naturally.'

Then she said she wondered if she really loved me or not. I, of course, couldn't enlighten her as to that. And, after another silence, she murmured something about my being 'a queer fellow'. 'And I dare say that's why I love you,' she added. 'But maybe that's why one day I'll come to hate you.'

To which I had nothing to say, so I said nothing.

She thought for a bit, then started smiling, and, taking my arm, repeated that she was in earnest; she really wanted to marry me.

'All right,' I answered. 'We'll get married whenever you like.' I then mentioned the proposal made by my employer and Marie said she'd love to go to Paris.

When I told her I'd lived in Paris for a while, she asked me what it was like.

'A dingy sort of town, to my mind. Masses of pigeons and dark court-yards. And the people have washed-out, white faces.'

Then we went for a walk all the way across the town by the main streets. The women were good-lookers, and I asked Marie if she, too, noticed this. She said 'Yes' and that she saw what I meant. After that we said nothing for some minutes. However, as I didn't want her to leave me, I suggested we should dine together at Céleste's. She'd have loved to dine with me, she said, only she was booked up for the evening. We were near my place, and I said, 'Au revoir, then'.

She looked me in the eyes.

'Don't you want to know what I'm doing this evening?'

I did want to know, but I hadn't thought of asking her, and I guessed she was making a grievance of it. I must have looked embarrassed, for suddenly she started laughing and bent towards me, pouting her lips for a kiss.

I went by myself to Céleste's. When I had just started my dinner an odd-looking little woman came in and asked if she might sit at my table. Of course she might. She had a chubby face like a ripe apple, bright eyes, and moved in a curiously jerky way as if she were on wires. After taking off her close-fitting jacket she sat down and started studying the bill of fare with a sort of rapt attention. Then she called Céleste and gave her order, very fast but quite distinctly; one didn't lose a word. While waiting for the *hors d'œuvre* she opened her bag, took out a slip of paper and a pencil, and added up the bill in advance. Diving into her bag again, she produced a purse and took from it the exact sum, plus a small tip, and placed it on the cloth in front of her.

Just then the waiter brought the *hors d'œuvre*, which she proceeded to wolf down voraciously. While waiting for the next course, she produced another pencil, this time a blue one, from her bag, and the radio magazine for the coming week, and started making ticks against almost all the items of the daily programmes. There were a dozen pages in the magazine and she con-tinued studying them closely throughout the meal. When I'd finished mine she was still ticking off items with the same meticulous attention. Then she rose, put on her jacket again with the same abrupt, robot-like gestures, and walked briskly out of the restaurant.

Having nothing better to do, I followed her for a short distance. Keeping on the kerb of the pavement, she walked straight ahead, never swerving or looking back, and it was extraordinary how fast she covered the ground, considering her smallness. In fact, the pace was too much for me, and I soon lost sight of her and turned back homewards. For a moment the 'little robot' (as I thought of her) had much impressed me, but I soon forgot about her.

As I was turning in at my door I ran into old Salamano. I asked him into my room, and he informed me that his dog was definitely lost. He'd been to the Pound to inquire, but it wasn't there, and the staff told him it had probably been run over. When he asked them whether it was any use inquiring about it at the police station, they said the police had more important things to attend to than keeping records of stray dogs run over in the streets. I suggested he should get another dog, but, reasonably enough, he pointed out that he'd become used to this one, and it wouldn't be the same thing.

I was seated on my bed, with my legs up, and Salamano on a chair beside the table, facing me, his hands spread on his knees. He had kept on his battered felt hat and was mumbling away behind his draggled yellowish moustache. I found him rather boring, but I had nothing to do and didn't feel sleepy. So, to keep the conversation going, I asked some questions about his dog—how long he had had it and so forth. He told me he had got it soon after his wife's death. He'd married rather late in life. When a young man, he'd wanted to go on the stage; during his military service he'd often played in the regimental theatricals and acted rather well, so everybody said. However, finally, he had taken a job in the railway, and he didn't regret it, as now he had a small pension. He and his wife had never hit it off very well, but they'd got used to each other, and when she died he felt lonely. One of his mates on the railway whose bitch had just had pups, had offered him one, and he had taken it, as a companion. He'd had to feed it from the bottle at first. But, as a dog's life is shorter than a man's, they'd so to speak grown old together.

'He was a cantankerous brute,' Salamano said. 'Now and then we had some proper set-tos, he and I. But he was a good tyke all the same.'

I said he looked well bred, and that evidently pleased the old man.

'Ah, but you should have seen him before his illness!' he said. 'He had a wonderful coat; in fact, that was his best point really. I tried hard to cure him; every mortal night after he got that skin disease I rubbed an ointment in. But his real trouble was old age, and there's no curing that.'

Just then I yawned, and the old chap said he'd better make a move. I told him he could stay, and that I was sorry about what had happened to his dog. He thanked me, and mentioned that my mother had been very fond of his dog. He referred to her as 'your poor mother', and was afraid I must be feeling her death terribly. When I said nothing he added hastily and with a rather embarrassed air that some of the people in the street said nasty things about me because I'd sent my mother to the Home. But he, of course, knew better; he knew how devoted to my mother I had always been.

I answered—why, I still don't know—that it surprised me to learn I'd produced such a bad impression. As I couldn't afford to keep her here, it seemed the obvious thing to do, to send her to a Home. 'In any case,' I added, 'for years she'd never had a word to say to me, and I could see she was moping, with no one to talk to.'

'Yes,' he said, 'and at a Home one makes friends, anyhow.'

He got up, saying it was high time for him to be in bed, and added that life was going to be a bit of a problem for him, under the new conditions. For the first time since I'd known him he held out his hand to me—rather shyly, I thought—and I could feel the scales on his skin. Just as he was going out of the door, he turned and, smiling a little, said:

'Let's hope the dogs won't bark again to-night. I always think it's mine I hear. . . .'

6

IT was an effort waking up that Sunday morning; Marie had to jog my shoulders and shout my name. As we wanted to get into the water early, we didn't trouble about breakfast. My head was aching slightly and my first cigarette had a bitter taste. Marie told me I looked like a mourner at a funeral, and I certainly did feel very limp. She was wearing a white dress and had her hair loose. I told her she looked quite ravishing like that, and she laughed happily.

On our way out we banged on Raymond's door, and he shouted that he'd be with us in a jiffy. We went down to the street and, because of my being rather under the weather and our having kept the blind down in my room, the glare of the morning sun hit me in the eyes like a clenched fist.

Marie, however, was almost dancing with delight, and kept repeating, 'What a heavenly day!' After a few minutes I was feeling better, and noticed that I was hungry. I mentioned this to Marie but she paid no attention. She was carrying an oilcloth bag in which she had stowed our bathing kit and a towel. Presently we heard Raymond shutting his door. He was wearing blue trousers, a short-sleeved white shirt, and a straw hat. I noticed that his forearms were rather hairy, but the skin was very white beneath. The straw hat made Marie giggle. Personally, I was rather put off by his get-up. He seemed in high spirits and was whistling as he came down the stairs. He greeted me with, 'Hullo, old boy!' and addressed Marie as 'Mademoiselle'.

On the previous evening we had visited the police station, where I gave evidence for Raymond—about the girl's having been false to him. So they let him off with a warning. They didn't check my statement.

After some talk on the doorstep we decided to take the bus. The beach was within easy walking distance, but the sooner we got there the better. Just as we were starting for the bus stop, Raymond plucked my sleeve and told me to look across the street. I saw some Arabs lounging against the tobacconist's window. They were staring at us silently, in the special way these people have—as if we were blocks of stone or dead trees. Raymond whispered that the second Arab from the left was 'his man', and I thought he looked rather worried. However, he assured me that all that was ancient history. Marie, who hadn't followed his remarks, asked, 'What is it?'

I explained that those Arabs across the way had a grudge against Raymond. She insisted on our going at once. Then Raymond laughed, and squared his shoulders. The young lady was quite right, he said. There was no point in hanging about here. Half-way to the bus stop he glanced back over his shoulder and said the Arabs weren't following. I, too, looked back. They were exactly as before, gazing in the same vague way at the spot where we had been.

When we were in the bus, Raymond, who now seemed quite at ease, kept making jokes to amuse Marie. I could see he was attracted by her, but she had hardly a word for him. Now and again she would catch my eye and smile.

We alighted just outside Algiers. The beach is not far from the bus stop; one has only to cross a patch of high land, a sort of plateau, which overlooks the sea and shelves down steeply to the sands. The ground here was covered with yellowish pebbles and wild lilies that showed snow-white against the blue of the sky, which had already the hard metallic glint it gets on very hot days. Marie amused herself swishing her bag against the flowers and sending the petals showering in all directions. Then we walked between two rows of little houses with wooden balconies and green or white palings. Some of them were half-hidden in clumps of tamarisks; others rose naked from the stony plateau. Before we came to the end of it, the sea was in full view; it lay smooth as a mirror, and in the distance a big headland jutted out over its black reflection. Through the still air came the faint buzz of a motor-engine and we saw a fishing-boat very far out, gliding almost imperceptibly across the dazzling smoothness.

Marie picked some rock-irises. Going down the steep path leading to the sea, we some saw bathers already on the sands.

Raymond's friend owned a small wooden bungalow at the near end of the beach. Its back rested against the cliff-side, while the front stood on piles, which the water was already lapping. Raymond introduced us to his friend, whose name was Masson. He was tall, broad-shouldered and thick-set; his wife was a plump, cheerful little woman, who spoke with a Paris accent.

Masson promptly told us to make ourselves at home. He had gone out fishing, he said, first thing in the morning, and there would be fried fish for lunch. I congratulated him on his little bungalow, and he said he always spent his week-ends and holidays here. 'With the missus, needless to say,' he added. I glanced at her, and noticed that she and Marie seemed to be getting on well together; laughing and chattering away. For the first time, perhaps, I seriously considered the possibility of my marrying her.

Masson wanted to have a swim at once, but his wife and Raymond were disinclined to move. So only the three of us, Marie, Masson and myself, went down to the beach. Marie promptly plunged in, but Masson and I waited for a bit. He was rather slow of speech and had, I noticed, a habit of saying 'and what's more' between his phrases—even when the second added nothing really to the first. Talking of Marie, he said: 'She's an awfully pretty girl, and what's more, charming.'

But I soon ceased paying attention to this trick of his; I was basking in the sunlight which, I noticed, was making me feel much better. The sand was beginning to stoke up under-foot and, though I was eager for a dip, I postponed it for a minute or two more. At last I said to Masson: 'Shall we go in now?' and plunged. Masson walked in gingerly and only began to swim when he was out of his depth. He swam hand over hand and made slow headway, so I left him behind and caught up Marie. The water was cold and I felt all the better for it. We swam a long way out, Marie and I side by side, and it was pleasant feeling how our movements matched, hers and mine, and how we were both in the same mood, enjoying every moment.

Once we were out in the open, we lay on our backs and, as I gazed up at the sky, I could feel the sun drawing up the film of salt water on my lips and cheeks. We saw Masson swim back to the beach and slump down on the sand under the sun. In the distance he looked enormous, like a stranded whale. Then Marie proposed that we should swim tandem. She went ahead and I put my arms round her waist, from behind, and while she drew me forward with her arm-strokes, I kicked out behind to help us on.

That sound of little splashes had been in my ears for so long that I began to feel I'd had enough of it. So I let go of Marie and swam back at an easy pace, taking long, deep breaths. When I made the beach I stretched myself belly-downwards beside Masson, resting my face on the sand. I told him 'it was fine' here and he agreed. Presently Marie came back. I raised my head to watch her approach. She was glistening with brine and holding her hair back. Then she lay down beside me and what with the combined warmth of our bodies and the sun, I felt myself dropping off to sleep.

After a while Marie tugged my arm and said Masson had gone to his place; it must be nearly lunch-time. I rose at once, as I was feeling hungry, but Marie told me I hadn't kissed her once since the early morning. That was so—though I'd wanted to, several times. 'Let's go into the water again,' she said, and we ran into the sea and lay flat amongst the ripples for a moment. Then we swam a few strokes and when we were almost out of our depth she flung her arms round me and hugged me. I felt her legs twining round mine, and my senses tingled.

When we got back, Masson was on the steps of his bungalow, shouting to us to come. I told him I was ravenously hungry, and he promptly turned to his wife and said he'd taken quite a fancy to me. The bread was excellent, and I had my full share of the fish. Then came some steak and chips. None of us spoke while eating. Masson drank a lot of wine and kept refilling my glass the moment it was empty. By the time coffee was handed round I was feeling slightly muzzy, and I started smoking one cigarette after another. Masson, Raymond and I discussed a plan of spending the whole of August on the beach together, sharing expenses.

Suddenly Marie exclaimed: 'I say! Do you know the time? It's only half-past eleven!'

We were all surprised at that, and Masson remarked that we'd had a very early lunch, but really lunch was a movable feast, one had it when one felt like it.

This set Marie laughing, I don't know why. I suspect she'd drunk a bit too much.

Then Masson asked if I'd like to come with him for a stroll on the beach. 'My wife always has a nap after lunch,' he said. 'Personally I find it doesn't agree with me; what I need is a short walk. I'm always telling her it's much better for the health. But of course she's entitled to her own opinion.'

Marie proposed to stay and help with the washing-up. Mme Masson smiled and said that, in that case, the first thing was to get the men out of the way. So we went out together, the three of us.

The light was almost vertical and the glare from the water seared one's eyes. The beach was quite deserted now. One could hear a faint tinkle of knives and forks and crockery in the shacks and bungalows lining the fore-shore. Heat was welling up from the rocks and one could hardly breathe.

At first Raymond and Masson talked of things and people I didn't know. I gathered that they'd been acquainted for some time and had even lived together for a while. We went down to the water's edge and walked along it; now and then a longer wave wetted our canvas shoes. I wasn't thinking of anything, as all that sunlight beating down on my bare head made me feel half asleep.

Just then Raymond said something to Masson that I didn't quite catch. But at the same moment I noticed two Arabs in blue dungarees a long way down the beach, coming in our direction. I gave Raymond a look and he nodded, saying, 'That's him'. We walked steadily on. Masson wondered how they'd managed to track us here. My impression was that they had seen us taking the bus and noticed Marie's oilcloth bathing-bag; but I didn't say anything.

Though the Arabs walked quite slowly they were much nearer already. We didn't change our pace, but Raymond said:

'Listen! If there's a rough house, you, Masson, take on the second one.

I'll tackle the fellow who's after me. And you, Meursault, stand by to help if another one comes up, and lay him out.'

I said, 'Right', and Masson put his hands in his pockets.

The sand was hot as fire and I could have sworn it was glowing red. The distance between us and the Arabs was steadily decreasing. When we were only a few steps away the Arabs halted. Masson and I slowed down, while Raymond went straight up to his man. I couldn't hear what he said, but I saw the native lowering his head, as if to butt him in the chest. Raymond lashed out promptly and shouted to Masson to come. Masson went up to the man he had been marking and struck him twice with all his might. The fellow fell flat into the water and stayed there some seconds with bubbles coming up to the surface round his head. Meanwhile Raymond had been slogging the other man, whose face was streaming with blood. He glanced at me over his shoulder and shouted:

'Just you watch! I ain't finished with him yet!'

'Look out!' I cried. 'He's got a knife.'

I spoke too late. The man had gashed Raymond's arm and his mouth as well.

Masson sprang forward. The other Arab got up from the water and placed himself behind the fellow with the knife. We didn't dare to move. The two natives backed away slowly, keeping us at bay with the knife and never taking their eyes off us. When they were at a safe distance they swung round and took to their heels. We stood stock still, with the sunlight beating down on us. Blood was dripping from Raymond's wounded arm, which he was squeezing hard above the elbow.

Masson remarked that there was a doctor who always spent his Sundays here, and Raymond said: 'Good. Let's go to him at once.' He could hardly get the words out as the blood from his other wound made bubbles in his mouth.

We each gave him an arm and helped him back to the bungalow. Once we were there he told us the wounds weren't so very deep and he could walk to where the doctor was. Marie had gone quite pale, and Mme Masson was in tears.

Masson and Raymond went off to the doctor's while I was left behind at the bungalow to explain matters to the women. I didn't much relish the task and soon dried up and started smoking, staring at the sea.

Raymond came back at about half-past one, accompanied by Masson. He had his arm bandaged and a strip of sticking-plaster on the corner of his mouth. The doctor assured him it was nothing serious, but he was looking very glum. Masson tried to make him laugh, but without success.

Presently Raymond said he was going for a stroll on the beach. I asked him where he proposed to go and he mumbled something about 'wanting to take the air'. We—Masson and I—then said we'd go with him, but he flew into a rage and told us to mind our own business. Masson said we mustn't insist, seeing the state he was in. However, when he went out, I followed him.

It was like a furnace outside, with the sunlight splintering into flakes of fire on the sand and sea. We walked for quite a while, and I had an idea that Raymond had a definite idea where he was going; but probably I was mistaken about this.

At the end of the beach we came to a small stream that had cut a channel in the sand, after coming out from behind a biggish rock. There we found our two Arabs again, lying on the sand in their blue dungarees. They looked harmless enough, as if they didn't bear any malice, and neither made any move when we approached. The man who had slashed Raymond stared at him without speaking. The other man was blowing down a little reed and extracting from it three notes of the scale, which he played over and over again, while he watched us from the corner of an eye.

For a while nobody moved; it was all sunlight and silence except for the tinkle of the stream and those three little lonely sounds. Then Raymond put his hand to his revolver-pocket, but the Arabs still didn't move. I noticed that the man playing on the reed had his big toes splayed out almost at right angles to his feet.

Still keeping his eyes on his man, Raymond said to me: 'Shall I plug him one?'

I thought quickly. If I told him not to, considering the mood he was in, he might very well fly into a temper and use his gun. So I said the first thing that came into my head.

'He hasn't spoken to you yet. It would be a low-down trick to shoot him like that, in cold blood.'

Again, for some moments one heard nothing but the tinkle of the stream and the flute-notes weaving through the hot, still air.

'Well,' Raymond said at last, 'if that's how you feel, I'd better say something insulting, and if he answers back I'll loose off.'

'Right,' I said. 'Only, if he doesn't get out his knife you've no business to fire.'

Raymond was beginning to fidget. The Arab with the reed went on playing, and both of them watched all our movements.

'Listen,' I said to Raymond. 'You take on the fellow on the right, and give me your revolver. If the other one starts making trouble or gets out his knife, I'll shoot.'

The sun glinted on Raymond's revolver as he handed it to me. But nobody made a move yet; it was just as if everything had closed in on us so that we couldn't stir. We could only watch each other, never lowering our eyes; the whole world seemed to have come to a standstill on this little strip of sand between the sunlight and the sea, the twofold silence of the reed and stream. And just then it crossed my mind that one might fire, or not fire—and it would come to absolutely the same thing.

Then, all of a sudden, the Arabs vanished; they'd slipped like lizards under cover of the rock. So Raymond and I turned and walked back. He seemed happier, and began talking about the bus to catch for our return.

When we reached the bungalow Raymond promptly went up the wooden steps, but I halted on the bottom one. The light seemed thudding in my head and I couldn't face the effort needed to go up the steps and make myself amiable to the women. But the heat was so great that it was just as bad staying where I was, under that flood of blinding light falling from the sky. To stay, or to make a move—it came to much the same. After a moment I returned to the beach, and started walking.

There was the same red glare as far as the eye could reach, and small waves were lapping the hot sand in little, flurried gasps. As I slowly walked towards the boulders at the end of the beach I could feel my temples swelling under the impact of the light. It pressed itself upon me, trying to check my progress. And each time I felt a hot blast strike my forehead, I gritted my teeth, I clenched my fists in my trouser-pockets and keyed up every nerve to fend off the sun and the dark befuddlement it was pouring into me. Whenever a blade of vivid light shot upwards from a bit of shell or broken glass lying on the sand, my jaws set hard. I wasn't going to be beaten, and I walked steadily on.

The small black hump of rock came into view far down the beach. It was rimmed by a dazzling sheen of light and feathery spray, but I was thinking of the cold, clear stream behind it, and longing to hear again the tinkle of running water. Anything to be rid of the glare, the sight of women in tears, the strain and effort—and to retrieve the pool of shadow by the rock and its cool silence!

But when I came nearer I saw that Raymond's Arab had returned. He was by himself this time, lying on his back, his hands behind his head, his face shaded by the rock while the sun beat on the rest of his body. One could see his dungarees steaming in the heat. I was rather taken aback; my impression had been that the incident was closed, and I hadn't given a thought to it on my way here.

On seeing me the Arab raised himself a little, and his hand went to his pocket. Naturally, I gripped Raymond's revolver in the pocket of my coat. Then the Arab let himself sink back again, but without taking his hand from his pocket. I was some distance off, at least ten yards, and most of the time I saw him as a blurred dark form wobbling in the heat-haze. Sometimes, however, I had glimpses of his eyes glowing between the half-closed lids. The sound of the waves was even lazier, feebler, than at noon. But the light hadn't changed; it was pounding fiercely as ever on the long stretch of sand that ended at the rock. For two hours the sun seemed to have made no progress; becalmed in a sea of molten steel. Far out on the horizon a steamer was passing; I could just make out from the corner of an eye the small black moving patch, while I kept my gaze fixed on the Arab.

It struck me that all I had to do was to turn, walk away, and think no more about it. But the whole beach, pulsing with heat, was pressing on my back. I took some steps towards the stream. The Arab didn't move. After all, there was still some distance between us. Perhaps because of the shadow on his face, he seemed to be grinning at me.

I waited. The heat was beginning to scorch my cheeks, beads of sweat were gathering in my eyebrows. It was just the same sort of heat as at my mother's funeral, and I had the same disagreeable sensations—especially in my forehead, where all the veins seemed to be bursting through the skin. I couldn't stand it any longer, and took another step forward. I knew it was a fool thing to do; I shouldn't get out of the sun by moving on a yard or so. But I took that step, just one step, forward. And then the Arab drew his knife and held it up towards me, athwart the sunlight.

A shaft of light shot upwards from the steel, and I felt as if a long, thin blade transfixed my forehead. At the same moment all the sweat that had accumulated in my eyebrows splashed down on my eyelids, covering them with a warm film of moisture. Beneath a veil of brine and tears my eyes were blinded; I was conscious only of the cymbals of the sun clashing on my skull, and, less distinctly, of the keen blade of light flashing up from the knife, scarring my eyelashes, and gouging into my eyeballs.

Then everything began to reel before my eyes, a fiery gust came from the sea, while the sky cracked in two, from end to end, and a great sheet of flame poured down through the rift. Every nerve in my body was a steel spring, and my grip closed on the revolver. The trigger gave, and the smooth underbelly of the butt jogged my palm. And so, with that crisp, whipcrack sound, it all began. I shook off my sweat and the clinging veil of light. I knew I'd shattered the balance of the day, the spacious calm of this beach on which I had been happy. But I fired four shots more into the inert body, on which they left no visible trace. And each successive shot was another loud, fateful rap on the door of my undoing.

I WAS questioned several times immediately after my arrest. But they were all formal examinations, as to my identity and so forth. At the first of these, which took place at the police station, nobody seemed to take much interest in the case. However, when I was brought before the examining magistrate a week later, I noticed that he eyed me with distinct curiosity. Like the others, he began by asking my name, address and occupation, the date and place of my birth. Then he inquired if I had chosen a lawyer to defend me. I answered 'No', I hadn't thought about it, and asked him if it was really necessary for me to have one. 'Why do you ask that?' he replied. I replied that I regarded my case as very simple. He smiled. 'Well, it may seem so to you. But we've got to abide by the law, and, if you don't engage a lawyer, the Court will have to appoint one for you.'

It struck me as an excellent arrangement that the authorities should see to details of this kind, and I told him so. He nodded, and agreed that the Code was all that could be desired.

At first I didn't take him quite seriously. The room in which he interviewed me was much like an ordinary sitting-room, with curtained windows and a single lamp standing on the desk. Its light fell on the armchair in which he'd had me sit, while his own face stayed in shadow.

I had read descriptions of such scenes in books, and at first it all seemed like a game. After our conversation, however, I had a good look at him. He was a tall man with clean-cut features, deep-set blue eyes, a big grey moustache and abundant, almost snow-white hair, and he gave me the impression of being highly intelligent and, on the whole, likeable enough. There was only one thing that put one off: his mouth had now and then a rather ugly twist; but it seemed to be only a sort of nervous *tic*. When leaving, I very nearly held out my hand and said 'Good-bye'; just in time I remembered that I'd killed a man.

Next day a lawyer came to my cell; a small, plump, youngish man with sleek black hair. In spite of the heat—I was in my shirt-sleeves—he was wearing a dark suit, stiff collar, and a rather showy tie, with broad black and white stripes. After depositing his brief-case on my bed, he introduced himself, and added that he'd perused the record of my case with the utmost care. His opinion was that it would need cautious handling, but there was every prospect of my getting off, provided I followed his advice. I thanked him, and he said: 'Good. Now let's get down to it.'

Sitting on the bed, he said that they'd been making investigations into my private life. They had learnt that my mother died recently in a Home. Inquiries had been conducted at Marengo and the police informed that I'd shown 'great callousness' at my mother's funeral.

'You must understand,' the lawyer said, 'that I don't relish having to question you about such a matter. But it has much importance and, unless I find some way of answering the charge of "callousness", I shall be handicapped in conducting your defence. And that is where you, and only you, can help me.'

He went on to ask me if I had felt grief on that 'sad occasion'. The question struck me as an odd one; personally I'd have been much embarrassed by having to ask anyone a thing like that.

I answered that in recent years I'd rather lost the habit of noting my feelings, and hardly knew what to answer. I could truthfully say I'd been quite fond of Mother—but really that didn't mean much. All normal people, I added, as an afterthought, had more or less desired the death of those they loved, at some time or another.

Here the lawyer interrupted me, looking greatly perturbed.

'You must promise me not to say anything of that sort at the trial, or to the examining magistrate.'

I promised, to satisfy him; but I explained that my physical condition at any given moment often influenced my feelings. For instance, on the day I attended Mother's funeral, I was fagged out and only half awake. So really I hardly took stock of what was happening. Anyhow I could assure him of one thing: that I'd rather Mother hadn't died.

The lawyer, however, looked displeased. 'That's not enough,' he said curtly.

After considering for a bit he asked me if he could say that on that day I had kept my feelings under control.

'No,' I said. 'That wouldn't be true.'

He gave me a queer look, as if I slightly revolted him; then informed me, in an almost hostile tone, that in any case the Head of the Home and some of the staff would be cited as witnesses.

'And that might do you a very nasty turn,' he concluded.

When I suggested that Mother's death had no connection with the charge against me he merely replied that this remark showed I'd never had any dealings with the Law.

Soon after this he left, looking quite vexed. I wished he had stayed longer and I could have explained that I desired his sympathy, not for him to make a better job of my defence but, if I might put it so, spontaneously. I could see that I got on his nerves; he couldn't make me out and, naturally enough, this irritated him. Once or twice I had a mind to assure him that I was just like everybody else; quite an ordinary person. But really that would have served no great purpose, and I let it go—out of laziness as much as anything else.

Later in the day I was taken again to the examining magistrate's office. It was two in the afternoon and, this time, the room was flooded with light—there was only a thin curtain on the window—and extremely hot.

After inviting me to sit down, the magistrate informed me in a very polite tone that, 'owing to unforeseen circumstances', my lawyer was unable to be present. I should be quite entitled, he added, to reserve my answers to his questions until my lawyer could attend.

To this I replied that I could answer for myself. He pressed a bell-push on his desk and a young clerk came in and seated himself just behind me. Then we—I and the magistrate—settled back in our chairs and the examination began. He led off by remarking that I had the reputation of being a taciturn, rather self-centred person, and he'd like to know what I had to say to that. I answered:

'Well, I rarely have anything much to say. So naturally I keep my mouth shut.'

He smiled as on the previous occasion, and agreed that that was the best of reasons. 'In any case,' he added, 'it has little or no importance.'

After a short silence he suddenly leant forward, looked me in the eyes and said, raising his voice a little:

'What really interests me is—you!'

I wasn't quite clear what he meant, so I made no comment.

'There are several things,' he continued, 'that puzzle me, about your crime. I feel sure that you will help me to understand them.'

When I replied that really it was quite simple, he asked me to give him an account of what I'd done that day. As a matter of fact I had already told him at our first interview—in a summary sort of way, of course—about Raymond, the beach, our swim, the fight, then the beach again, and the five shots I'd fired. But I went over it all again, and after each phrase he nodded. 'Quite so, quite so.' When I described the body lying on the sand, he nodded more emphatically, and said 'Good!' Personally I was tired of repeating the same story; I felt as if I'd never talked so much in all my life before.

After another silence he stood up and said he'd like to help me; I interested him and, with God's help, he would do something for me in my trouble. But, first, he must put a few more questions.

He began by asking bluntly if I'd loved my mother.

'Yes,' I replied, 'like everybody else.' The clerk behind me, who had been typing away at a steady pace, must just then have hit the wrong keys, as I heard him pushing the carrier back and crossing something out.

Next, without any apparent logical connection, the magistrate sprang another question.

'Why did you fire five consecutive shots?'

I thought for a bit; then explained that they weren't quite consecutive. I fired one at first, and the other four after a short interval.

'Why did you pause between the first and second shot?'

I seemed to see it hovering again before my eyes, the red glow of the beach, and to feel that fiery breath on my cheeks—and, this time, I made no answer.

During the silence which followed, the magistrate kept fidgeting, running his fingers through his hair, half rising, then sitting down again. Finally, planting his elbows on the desk, he bent towards me with a queer expression.

'But why, *why* did you go on firing at a prostrate man?'

Again I found nothing to reply.

The magistrate drew his hand across his forehead and repeated in a slightly different tone:

'I ask you "*Why?*" I insist on your telling me.'

I still kept silent.

Suddenly he rose, walked to a file cabinet standing against the opposite wall, pulled a drawer open, and took from it a silver crucifix, which he was waving as he came back to the desk.

'Do you know who this is?' His voice had changed completely; it was vibrant with emotion.

'Of course I do,' I answered.

That seemed to start him off; he began speaking at a great pace. He told me he believed in God, and that even the worst of sinners could obtain forgiveness of Him. But first he must repent, and become like a little child, with a simple, trustful heart, open to conviction. He was leaning right across the table brandishing his crucifix before my eyes.

As a matter of fact I had great difficulty in following his remarks as, for one thing, the office was so stiflingly hot and big flies were buzzing round and settling on my cheeks; also because he rather alarmed me. Of course I realized it was absurd to feel like this, considering that, after all, it was I who was the criminal. However, as he continued talking, I did my best to understand, and I gathered that there was only one point in my confession that badly needed clearing up—the fact that I'd waited before firing a second time. All the rest was, so to speak, quite in order; but this completely baffled him.

I started to tell him that he was wrong in insisting on this; the point was of quite minor importance. But, before I could get the words out, he had drawn himself up to his full height and was asking me very earnestly if I believed in God. When I said 'No', he plumped down into his chair indignantly.

That was unthinkable, he said; all men believe in God, even those who reject Him. Of this he was absolutely sure; if ever he came to doubt it, his life would lose all meaning. 'Do you wish,' he asked indignantly, 'my life to have no meaning?' Really I couldn't see how my wishes came into it, and I told him as much.

While I was talking, he thrust the crucifix again just under my nose and shouted: 'I, anyhow, am a Christian. And I pray Him to forgive you for your sins. My poor young man, how can you not believe that He suffered for your sake?'

I noticed that his manner seemed genuinely solicitous when he said 'My poor young man'—but I was beginning to have enough of it. The room was growing steadily hotter.

As I usually do when I want to get rid of someone whose conversation bores me, I pretended to agree. At which, rather to my surprise, his face lit up.

'You see! You see! Now won't you own that you believe and put your trust in Him?'

I must have shaken my head again, for he sank back in his chair looking limp and dejected.

For some moments there was a silence during which the typewriter, which had been clicking away all the time we talked, caught up with the last remark. Then he gazed at me intently and rather sadly.

'Never in all my experience have I known a soul so case-hardened as yours,' he said in a low tone. 'All the criminals who have come before me until now wept when they saw this symbol of our Lord's sufferings.'

I was on the point of replying that was precisely because they *were* criminals. But then I realized that I, too, came under that description. Somehow it was an idea to which I never could get reconciled.

To indicate, presumably, that the interview was over, the magistrate stood up. In the same weary tone he asked me a last question: Did I regret what I had done?

After thinking a bit, I said that what I felt was less regret than a kind of vexation—I couldn't find a better word for it. But he didn't seem to understand. This was as far as things went at that day's interview.

I came before the magistrate many times more, but on these occasions my lawyer always accompanied me. The examinations were confined to asking me to amplify my previous statements. Or else the magistrate and my lawyer discussed technicalities. At such times they took very little notice of me and, in any case, the tone of the examinations changed as time went on. The magistrate seemed to have lost interest in me, and to have come to some sort of decision about my case. He never mentioned God again or displayed any of the religious fervour I had found so embarrassing at our first interview. The result was that our relations became more cordial. After a few questions, followed by an exchange of remarks with my lawyer, the magistrate closed the interview. My case was 'taking its course', as he put it. Sometimes, too, the conversation was of a general order and the magistrate and lawyer en-

couraged me to join in it. I began to breathe more freely. Neither of the two
men, at these times, showed the least hostility towards me, and everything
went so smoothly, so amiably, that I had an absurd impression of being 'one
of the family'. I can honestly say that during the eleven months these
examinations lasted I got so used to them that I was almost surprised at having
ever enjoyed anything better than those rare moments when the magistrate,
after escorting me to the door of the office, would pat my shoulder and say
in a friendly tone: 'Well, Mr. Antichrist, that's all for the present!' After
which I was made over to my warders.

2

THERE are some things of which I've never cared to talk. And, a few days
after I'd been sent to prison, I decided that this phase of my life was one of
them. However, as time went by, I came to feel that this aversion had no
real substance. In point of fact, during those first few days, I was hardly
conscious of being in prison; I had always a vague hope that something
would turn up, some agreeable surprise.

The change came soon after Marie's first and only visit. From the day
when I got her letter telling me they wouldn't let her come to see me any
more, because she wasn't my wife—it was from that day I realized that this
cell was my last home, a dead end, as one says.

On the day of my arrest they put me in a biggish room with several other
prisoners, mostly Arabs. They grinned when they saw me enter, and asked
me what I'd done. I told them I'd killed an Arab, and they kept mum for a
while. But presently night began to fall, and one of them explained to me
how to lay out my sleeping-mat. By rolling up one end one makes a sort
of bolster. All night I felt bugs crawling over my face.

Some days later I was put by myself in a cell, where I slept on a plank bed
hinged to the wall. The only other furniture was a latrine bucket and a tin
basin. The prison stands on rising ground, and through my little window I
had glimpses of the sea. One day when I was hanging on the bars, straining
my eyes towards the sunlight playing on the waves, a warder entered and
said I had a visitor. I thought it must be Marie, and so it was.

To go the the Visitors' Room, I was taken along a corridor, then up a
flight of steps, then along another corridor. It was a very large room, lit by
a big bow-window, and divided into three compartments by high iron
grilles running transversally. Between the two grilles there was a gap of
some thirty feet, a sort of no-man's-land between the prisoners and their
friends. I was led to a point exactly opposite Marie, who was wearing her
striped dress. On my side of the rails were about a dozen other prisoners,
Arabs for the most part. On Marie's side were mostly Moorish women. She

was wedged between a small old woman with tight-set lips, and a fat matron, without a hat, who was talking shrilly and gesticulated all the time. Because of the distance between the visitors and prisoners I found I, too, had to raise my voice.

When I came into the room the babel of voices echoing on the bare walls, and the sunlight streaming in, flooding everything in a harsh white glare, made me feel quite dizzy. After the relative darkness and the silence of my cell it took me some moments to get used to these conditions. After a bit, however, I came to see each face quite clearly, lit up as if a spotlight played on it.

I noticed a prison official seated at each end of the no-man's-land between the grilles. The native prisoners and their relations on the other side were squatting opposite each other. They didn't raise their voices and, in spite of the din, managed to converse almost in whispers. This murmur of voices coming from below made a sort of accompaniment to the conversations going on above their heads. I took stock of all this very quickly, and moved a step forward towards Marie. She was pressing her brown, sun-tanned face to the bars and smiling as hard as she could. I thought she was looking very pretty, but somehow couldn't bring myself to tell her so.

'Well?' she asked, pitching her voice very high. 'What about it? Are you all right, have you everything you want?'

'Oh, yes. I've everything I want.'

We were silent for some moments; Marie went on smiling. The fat woman was bawling at the prisoner beside me, her husband presumably, a tall, fair, pleasant-looking man.

'Jeanne refused to have him,' she yelled.—'That's just too bad,' the man replied.—'Yes, and I told her you'd take him back the moment you get out; but she wouldn't hear of it.'

Marie shouted across the gap that Raymond sent me his best wishes, and I said, 'Thanks'. But my voice was drowned by my neighbour's, asking, 'if he was quite fit'. The fat woman gave a laugh. 'Fit? I should say he is! The picture of health.'

Meanwhile the prisoner on my left, a youngster with thin, girlish hands, never said a word. His eyes, I noticed, were fixed on the little old woman opposite him, and she returned his gaze with a sort of hungry passion. But I had to stop looking at them as Marie was shouting to me that we mustn't lose hope.

'Certainly not,' I answered. My gaze fell on her shoulders and I had a sudden longing to squeeze them, through the thin dress. Its silky texture fascinated me, and I had a feeling that the hope she spoke of centred on it somehow. I imagine something of the same sort was in Marie's mind, for she went on smiling, looking straight at me.

'It'll all come right, you'll see, and then we shall get married.'

All I could see of her now was the white flash of her teeth, and the little puckers round her eyes. I answered: 'Do you really think so?' but chiefly because I felt it up to me to answer something.

She started talking very fast in the same high-pitched voice.

'Yes, you'll be acquitted, and we'll go bathing again, Sundays.'

The woman beside Marie was still yelling away, telling her husband that she'd left a basket for him in the prison office. She gave a list of the things she'd brought and told him to mind and check them carefully, as some had cost quite a lot. The youngster on my other side and his mother were still gazing mournfully at each other, and the murmur of the Arabs droned on below us. The light outside seemed to be surging up against the window, seeping through, and smearing the faces of the people facing it with a coat of yellow oil.

I began to feel slightly squeamish, and wished I could leave. The strident voice beside me was jarring on my ears. But, on the other hand, I wanted to have the most I could of Marie's company. I've no idea how much time passed. I remember Marie's describing to me her work, with that set smile always on her face. There wasn't a moment's let-up in the noise—shouts, conversations, and always that muttering undertone. The only oasis of silence was made by the young fellow and the old dame gazing into each other's eyes.

Then, one by one, the Arabs were led away; almost everyone fell silent when the first one left. The little old woman pressed herself against the bars and at the same moment a warder tapped her son's shoulder. He called '*Au revoir*, Mother', and, slipping her hand between the bars, she gave him a small, slow wave with it.

No sooner was she gone than a man, hat in hand, took her place. A prisoner was led up to the empty place beside me, and the two started a brisk exchange of remarks—not loud, however, as the room had become relatively quiet. Someone came and called away the man on my right and his wife shouted at him—she didn't seem to realize it was no longer necessary to shout—'Now, mind you look after yourself, dear, and don't do anything rash!'

My turn came next. Marie threw me a kiss. I looked back as I walked away. She hadn't moved; her face was still pressed to the rails, her lips still parted in that tense, twisted smile.

Soon after this I had a letter from her. And it was then that the things I've never liked to talk about began. Not that they were particularly terrible; I've no wish to exaggerate and I suffered less than others. Still, there was one thing in those early days that was really irksome: my habit of thinking like a free man. For instance, I would suddenly be seized with a desire to go down to the beach for a swim. And merely to have imagined the sound of ripples at my feet, and then the smooth feel of the water on my body as I struck out, and the wonderful sensation of relief it gave, brought home still more cruelly the narrowness of my cell.

Still, that phase lasted a few months only. Afterwards, I had prisoner's thoughts. I waited for the daily walk in the courtyard, or a visit from my lawyer. As for the rest of the time, I managed quite well, really. I've often thought that had I been compelled to live in the trunk of a dead tree, with nothing to do but gaze up at the patch of sky just overhead, I'd have got used to it by degrees. I'd have learnt to watch for the passing of birds or drifting clouds, as I had come to watch for my lawyer's odd neckties, or, in another world, to wait patiently till Sunday for a spell of love-making with Marie. Well, here anyhow, I wasn't penned in a hollow tree-trunk. There were others in the world worse off than I was. I remembered it had been one of Mother's pet ideas—she was always voicing it—that in the long run one gets used to anything.

Usually, however, I didn't think things out so far. Those first months were trying, of course; but the very effort I had to make helped me through them. For instance, I was plagued by the desire for a woman—which was natural enough, considering my age. I never thought of Marie especially. I was obsessed by thoughts of this woman or that, of all the ones I'd had, all the circumstances under which I'd loved them; so much so that the cell grew crowded with their faces, ghosts of my old passions. That unsettled me, no doubt; but, at least, it served to kill time.

I gradually became quite friendly with the chief jailer, who went the rounds with the kitchen-hands at meal-times. It was he who brought up the subject of women. 'That's what the men here grumble about most,' he told me. I said I felt like that myself. 'There's something unfair about it,' I added, 'like hitting a man when he's down.'—'But that's the whole point of it,' he said; 'that's why you fellows are kept in prison.'—'I don't follow.'— 'Liberty,' he said, 'means that. You're being deprived of your liberty.' It had never before struck me in that light, but I saw his point. 'That's true,' I said. 'Otherwise it wouldn't be a punishment.' The jailer nodded. 'Yes, you're different, you can use your brains. The others can't. Still, those fellows find a way out; they do it by themselves.' With which remark the jailer left my cell. Next day I did like the others.

The lack of cigarettes, too, was a trial. When I was brought to the prison, they took away my belt, my shoe-laces, and the contents of my pockets, including my cigarettes. Once I had been given a cell to myself I asked to be given back anyhow the cigarettes. Smoking was forbidden, they informed me. That, perhaps, was what got me down the most; in fact, I suffered really badly during the first few days. I even tore off splinters from my plank bed and sucked them. All day long I felt faint and bilious. It passed my understanding why I shouldn't be allowed even to smoke; it could have done no one any harm. Later on, I understood the idea behind it; this privation, too, was part of my punishment. But, by the time I understood, I'd lost the craving, so it had ceased to be a punishment.

Except for these privations, I wasn't too unhappy. Yet again, the whole problem was: how to kill time. After a while, however, once I'd learnt the trick of remembering things, I never had a moment's boredom. Sometimes I would exercise my memory on my bedroom, and, starting from a corner, make the round, noting every object I saw on the way. At first it was over in a minute or two. But each time I repeated the experience, it took a little longer. I made a point of visualizing every piece of furniture, and each article upon or in it, and then every detail of each article, and finally the details of the details, so to speak: a tiny dent or incrustation, or a chipped edge, and the exact grain and colour of the woodwork. At the same time I forced myself to keep my inventory in mind from start to finish, in the right order and omitting no item. With the result that, after a few weeks, I could spend hours merely in listing the objects in my bedroom. I found that the more I thought, the more details, half-forgotten or malobserved, floated up from my memory. There seemed no end to them.

So I learned that even after a single day's experience of the outside world a man could easily live a hundred years in prison. He'd have laid up enough memories never to be bored. Obviously, in one way, this was a compensation.

Then there was sleep. To begin with, I slept badly at night and never in the day. But gradually my nights became better and I managed to doze off in the daytime as well. In fact, during the last months, I must have slept sixteen or eighteen hours out of the twenty-four. So there remained only six hours to fill—with meals, relieving nature, my memories . . . and the story of the Czech.

One day, when inspecting my straw mattress, I found a bit of newspaper stuck to its underside. The paper was yellow with age, almost transparent, but one could still make out the letter-print. It was the story of a crime. The first part was missing, but one gathered that its scene was some village in Czechoslovakia. One of the villagers had left his home to try his luck abroad. After twenty-five years, having made a fortune, he returned to his country with his wife and child. Meanwhile his mother and sister had been running a small hotel in the village where he was born. He decided to give them a surprise and, leaving his wife and child in another inn, he went to stay at his mother's place, booking a room under an assumed name. His mother and sister completely failed to recognize him. At dinner that evening he showed them a large sum of money he had on him, and in the course of the night they slaughtered him with a hammer. After taking the money they flung the body into the river. Next morning his wife came and, without thinking, betrayed the guest's identity. His mother hanged herself. His sister threw herself into a well. I must have read that story thousands of times. In one way it sounded most unlikely; in another, it was plausible enough. Anyhow, to my mind, the man was asking for trouble; one shouldn't play fool tricks of that sort.

So, what with long bouts of sleep, my memories, readings of that scrap of newspaper, the tides of light and darkness, the days slipped by. I'd read, of course, that in jail one ends up by losing track of time. But this had never meant anything definite to me. I hadn't grasped how days could be at once long and short. Long, no doubt, as periods to live through, but so distended that they ended up by overlapping on each other. In fact I never thought of days as such; only the words 'yesterday' and 'to-morrow' still kept some meaning.

When, one morning, the warder informed me I'd now been six months in jail, I believed him—but the words conveyed nothing to my mind. To me it seemed like one and the same day that had been going on since I'd been in my cell, and that I'd been doing the same thing all the time.

After the jailer left me I shined up my tin pannikin and studied my face in it. My expression was terribly serious, I thought, even when I tried to smile. I held the pannikin at different angles, but always my face had the same mournful, tense expression.

The sun was setting and it was the hour of which I'd rather not speak—'the nameless hour', I called it—when evening sounds were creeping up from all the floors of the prison in a sort of stealthy procession. I went to the barred window and in the last rays looked once again at my reflected face. It was as serious as before; and that wasn't surprising, as just then I was feeling serious. But, at the same time, I heard something that I hadn't heard for months. It was the sound of a voice; my own voice, there was no mistaking it. And I recognized it as the voice that for many a day of late had been buzzing in my ears. So I knew that all this time I'd been talking to myself.

And something I'd been told came back to me; a remark made by the nurse at Mother's funeral. No, there was no way out, and no one can imagine what the evenings are like in prison.

3

On the whole I can't say that those months passed slowly; another summer was on its way almost before I realized the first was over. And I knew that with the first really hot days something new was in store for me. My case was down for the last Sessions of the Assize Court, and that Sessions was due to end some time in June.

The day on which my trial started was one of brilliant sunshine. My lawyer assured me the case would take only two or three days. 'From what I hear,' he added, 'the Court will despatch your case as quickly as possible, as it isn't the most important one on the Cause List. There's a case of parricide immediately after, which will take them some time.'

They came for me at half-past seven in the morning and I was conveyed to the Law Courts in the prison van. The two policemen led me into a small room that smelt of darkness. We sat near a door through which came sounds of voices, shouts, chairs scraping on the floor; a vague hubbub which reminded me of one of those small town 'socials' when, after the concert's over, the hall is cleared for dancing.

One of my policemen told me the judges hadn't arrived yet, and offered me a cigarette, which I declined. After a bit he asked me if I was feeling nervous. I said 'No', and that the prospect of witnessing a trial rather interested me; I'd never had occasion to attend one before.

'Maybe,' the other policeman said. 'But after an hour or two one's had enough of it.'

After a while a small electric bell purred in the room. They unfastened my handcuffs, opened the door, and led me to the prisoner's dock.

There was a great crowd in the courtroom. Though the venetian blinds were down, light was filtering through the chinks, and the air was stiflingly hot already. The windows had been kept shut. I sat down, and the police officers took their stand on each side of my chair.

It was then that I noticed a row of faces opposite me. These people were staring hard at me, and I guessed they were the jury. But somehow I didn't see them as individuals. I felt as one does just after boarding a tram and one's conscious of all the people on the opposite seat staring at one in the hope of finding something in one's appearance to amuse them. Of course I knew this was an absurd comparison; what these people were looking for in me wasn't anything to laugh at, but signs of criminality. Still, the difference wasn't so very great, and, anyhow, that's the idea I got.

What with the crowd and the stuffiness of the air I was feeling a bit dizzy. I ran my eyes round the courtroom but couldn't recognize any of the faces. At first I could hardly believe that all these people had come on my account. It was such a new experience, being a focus of interest; in the ordinary way no one ever paid much attention to me. 'What a crush!' I remarked to the policeman on my left, and he explained that the newspapers were responsible for it. He pointed to a group of men at a table just below the jury-box. 'There they are!'—Who?' I asked, and he replied, 'The Press'. One of them, he added, was an old friend of his.

A moment later the man he'd mentioned looked our way and, coming to the dock, shook hands warmly with the policeman. The journalist was an elderly man with a rather grim expression, but his manner was quite pleasant. Just then, I noticed that almost all the people in the courtroom were greeting each other, exchanging remarks and forming groups—behaving, in fact, as in a club where the company of others of one's own tastes and standing makes one feel at ease. That, no doubt, explained the odd impression I had of being *de trop* here, a sort of gate-crasher.

However, the journalist addressed me quite amiably, and said he hoped all would go well for me. I thanked him, and he added with a smile:

'You know, we've been featuring you a bit. We're always rather short of copy in the summer, and there's been precious little to write about except your case and the one that's coming on after it. I expect you've heard about it; it's a case of parricide.'

He drew my attention to one of the group at the Press table, a plump, small man with huge black-rimmed glasses, who made one think of an over-fed weasel.

'That chap's the special correspondent of one of the Paris dailies. As a matter of fact he didn't come on your account. He was sent for the parricide case, but they've asked him to cover yours as well.'

It was on the tip of my tongue to say, 'That was very kind of them', but then I thought it would sound silly. With a friendly wave of his hand he left us, and for some minutes nothing happened.

Then, accompanied by some colleagues, my lawyer bustled in, in his gown. He went up to the Press table and shook hands with the journalists. They remained laughing and chatting together, all seemingly very much at home here, until a bell rang shrilly and everyone went to his place. My lawyer came up to me, shook hands, and advised me to answer all the questions as briefly as possible, not to volunteer information, and to rely on him to see me through.

I heard a chair scrape on my left, and a tall, thin man wearing pince-nez settled the folds of his red gown as he took his seat. The Public Prosecutor, I gathered. A clerk of the Court announced that Their Honours were enter-ing and at the same moment two big electric fans started buzzing overhead. Three judges, two in black and the third in scarlet, with brief-cases under their arms, entered and walked briskly to the bench, which was several feet above the level of the courtroom floor. The man in scarlet took the central, high-backed chair, placed his cap of office of the table, ran a handkerchief over his small bald crown, and announced that the hearing would now begin.

The journalists had their fountain-pens ready; they all wore the same expression of slightly ironical indifference, with the exception of one, a much younger man than his colleagues, in grey flannels with a blue tie, who, leaving his pen on the table, was gazing hard at me. He had a plain, rather chunky face; what held my attention was his eyes, very pale, clear eyes, riveted on me, though not betraying any definite emotion. For a moment I had an odd impression, as if I were being scrutinized by myself. That—and the fact that I was unfamiliar with court procedure—may explain why I didn't follow very well the opening phases: the drawing of lots for the jury, the various questions put by the presiding judge to the Prosecutor, the foreman of the jury and my counsel (each time he spoke all the jurymen's heads swung round together towards the bench), the hurried reading of the charge-sheet, in the course of which I recognized some familiar names of people and places, then some supplementary questions put to my lawyer.

Next, the Judge announced that the Court would call over the witness-list. Some of the names read out by the clerk rather surprised me. From amongst the crowd, which until now I had seen as a mere blur of faces, rose, one after the other, Raymond, Masson, Salamano, the door-keeper from the Home, old Pérez, and Marie, who gave me a little nervous wave of her hand before following the others out by a side door. I was thinking how strange it was I hadn't noticed any of them before when I heard the last name called, that of Céleste. As he rose, I noticed beside him the quaint little woman with a mannish coat and brisk, decided air, who had shared my table at the restaurant. She had her eyes fixed on me, I noticed. But I hadn't time to wonder about her; the Judge had started speaking again.

He said that the trial proper was about to begin, and he need hardly say that he expected the public to refrain from any demonstration whatsoever. He explained that he was there to supervise the proceedings, as a sort of umpire, and he would take a scrupulously impartial view of the case. The verdict of the jury would be interpreted by him in a spirit of justice. Finally, at the least sign of a disturbance he would have the Court cleared.

The day was stoking up. Some of the public were fanning themselves with newspapers, and there was a constant rustle of crumpled paper. On a sign from the presiding judge the clerk of the Court brought three fans of plaited straw, which the three judges promptly put in action.

My examination began at once. The Judge questioned me quite calmly and even, I thought, with a hint of cordiality. For the nth time I was asked to give particulars of my identity and, though heartily sick of this formality, I realized that it was natural enough; after all, it would be a shocking thing for the Court to be trying the wrong man.

The Judge then launched into an account of what I'd done, stopping every two or three sentences to ask me, 'Is that correct?' To which I always replied, 'Yes, sir', as my lawyer had advised me. It was a long business, as the Judge lingered on each detail. Meanwhile the journalists scribbled busily away. But I was sometimes conscious of the eyes of the youngest fixed on me; also those of the queer little robot woman. The jurymen, however, were all gazing at the red-robed judge, and I was again reminded of the row of passengers on one side of a tram. Presently he gave a slight cough, turned some pages of his file, and, still fanning his face, addressed me gravely.

He now proposed, he said, to touch on certain matters which, on a super-ficial view, might seem foreign to the case, but actually were highly relevant. I guessed that he was going to talk about Mother, and at the same moment realized how odious I would find this. His first question was: Why had I sent my mother to an Institution? I replied that the reason was simple; I hadn't enough money to see that she was properly looked after at home. Then he asked if the parting hadn't caused me distress. I explained that neither Mother nor I expected much of one another—or, for that matter, of anybody else; so both of us had got used to the new conditions easily enough. The Judge then said that he had no wish to press the point, and asked the Prosecutor if he could think of any more questions that should be put to me at this stage.

The Prosecutor, who had his back half turned to me, said, without looking in my direction, that, subject to His Honour's approval, he would like to know if I'd gone back to the stream with the intention of killing the Arab. I said 'No'. In that case, why had I taken a revolver with me, and why go back precisely to that spot? I said it was a matter of pure chance. The Prosecutor then observed in a nasty tone: 'Very good. That will be all for the present.'

I couldn't quite follow what came next. Anyhow, after some palavering between the Bench, the Prosecutor and my counsel, the presiding judge announced that the court would now rise; there was an adjournment till the afternoon, when evidence would be taken.

Almost before I knew what was happening, I was rushed out to the prison van, which drove me back, and I was given my midday meal. After a short time, just enough for me to realize how tired I was feeling, they came for me. I was back in the same room, confronting the same faces, and the whole thing started again. But the heat had meanwhile much increased, and by some miracle fans had been procured for everyone: the jury, my lawyer, the Prosecutor, and some of the pressmen, too. The young man and the robot woman were still at their places. But they were not fanning themselves and, as before, they never took their eyes off me.

I wiped the sweat from my face, but I was barely conscious of where or who I was until I heard the Warden of the Home called to the witness-box. When asked if my mother had complained about my conduct, he said 'Yes', but that didn't mean much; almost all the inmates of the Home had grievances against their relatives. The Judge asked him to be more explicit; did she reproach me with having sent her to the Home, and he said 'Yes', again. But this time he didn't qualify his answer.

To another question he replied that on the day of the funeral he was somewhat surprised by my calmness. Asked to explain what he meant by 'my calmness', the Warden lowered his eyes and stared at his shoes for a moment. Then he explained that I hadn't wanted to see Mother's body, or shed a single tear, and that I'd left immediately the funeral ended, without lingering at her grave. Another thing had surprised him. One of the undertaker's men told him that I didn't know my mother's age. There was a short silence; then the Judge asked him if he might take it that he was referring to the prisoner in the dock. The Warden seemed puzzled by this, and the Judge explained: 'It's a formal question. I am bound to put it.'

The Prosecutor was then asked if he had any questions to put, and he answered loudly: 'Certainly not! I have all I want.' His tone and the look of triumph on his face, as he glanced at me, were so marked that I felt as I hadn't felt for ages. I had a foolish desire to burst into tears. For the first time I'd realized how all these people loathed me.

After asking the jury and my lawyer if they had any questions, the Judge heard the door-keeper's evidence. On stepping into the box the man threw a glance at me, then looked away. Replying to questions, he said that I'd declined to see Mother's body, I'd smoked cigarettes and slept, and drunk *café au lait*. It was then I felt a sort of wave of indignation spreading through the courtroom, and for the first time I understood that I was guilty. They got the door-keeper to repeat what he had said about the coffee and my smoking. The Prosecutor turned to me again, with a gloating look in his eyes. My counsel asked the door-keeper if he, too, hadn't smoked. But the Prosecutor took strong exception to this. 'I'd like to know,' he cried indignantly, 'who is on trial in this court. Or does my friend think that by aspersing a witness for the prosecution he will shake the evidence, the abundant and cogent evidence, against his client?' None the less, the Judge told the door-keeper to answer the question.

The old fellow fidgeted a bit. Then, 'Well, I know I didn't ought to have done it,' he mumbled, 'but I did take a fag from the young gentleman when he offered it—just out of politeness.'

The Judge asked me if I had any comment to make. 'None,' I said, 'except that the witness is quite right. It's true I offered him a cigarette.'

The door-keeper looked at me with surprise and a sort of gratitude. Then, after humming and hawing for a bit, he volunteered the statement that it was he who'd suggested I should have some coffee.

My lawyer was exultant. 'The jury will appreciate,' he said, 'the importance of this admission.'

The Prosecutor, however, was promptly on his feet again. 'Quite so,' he boomed above our heads. 'The jury will appreciate it. And they will draw the conclusion that, though a third party might inadvertently offer him a cup of coffee, the prisoner, in common decency, should have refused it, if only out of respect for the dead body of the poor woman who had brought him into the world.'

After which the door-keeper went back to his seat.

When Thomas Pérez was called, a court officer had to help him to the box. Pérez stated that, though he had been a great friend of my mother, he had met me once only, on the day of the funeral. Asked how I had behaved that day, he said:

'Well, I was most upset, you know. Far too much upset to notice things.

My grief sort of blinded me, I think. It had been a great shock, my dear friend's death; in fact I fainted during the funeral. So I didn't hardly notice the young gentleman at all.'

The Prosecutor asked him to tell the court if he'd seen me weep. And when Pérez answered 'No', added emphatically: 'I trust the jury will take note of this reply.'

My lawyer rose at once, and asked Pérez in a tone that seemed to me needlessly aggressive:

'Now think well, my man! Can you swear you saw he didn't shed a tear?'

Pérez answered, 'No'.

At this some people tittered and my lawyer, pushing back one sleeve of his gown, said sternly:

'That is typical of the way this case is being conducted. No attempt is being made to elicit the true facts.'

The Prosecutor ignored this remark; he was making dabs with his pencil on the cover of his brief, seemingly quite indifferent.

There was a break of five minutes, during which my lawyer told me the case was going very well indeed. Then Céleste was called. He was announced as a witness for the defence. The defence meant me.

Now and again Céleste threw me a glance; he kept squeezing his panama hat between his hands as he gave evidence. He was in his best suit, the one he wore when sometimes of a Sunday he went with me to the races. But evidently he hadn't been able to get his collar on; the top of his shirt, I noticed, was secured only by a brass stud. Asked if I was one of his customers, he said, 'Yes, and a friend as well'. Asked to state his opinion of me, he said that I was 'all right' and, when told to explain what he meant by that, he replied that everyone knew what that meant. 'Was I a secretive sort of man?' —'No,' he answered, 'I shouldn't call him that. But he isn't one to waste his breath, like a lot of folks.'

The Prosecutor asked him if I always settled my monthly bill at his restaurant when he presented it. Céleste laughed. 'Oh, he paid on the nail all right. But the bills were just details, like, between him and me.' Then he was asked to say what he thought about the crime. He placed his hands on the rail of the box and one could see he had a speech all ready.

'To my mind it was just an accident, or a stroke of bad luck, if you prefer. And a thing like that takes you off your guard.'

He wanted to continue, but the Judge cut him short. 'Quite so. That's all, thank you.'

For a bit Céleste seemed flabbergasted; then he explained that he hadn't finished what he wanted to say. They told him to continue, but to make it brief.

He only repeated that it was 'just an accident'.

'That's as it may be,' the Judge observed. 'But what we are here for is to try such accidents, according to law. You can stand down.'

Céleste turned and gazed at me. His eyes were moist and his lips trembling. It was exactly as if he'd said: 'Well, I've done my best for you, old chap. I'm afraid it hasn't helped much. I'm sorry.'

I didn't say anything, or make any movement, but for the first time in my life I wanted to kiss a man.

The Judge repeated his order to stand down and Céleste returned to his place amongst the crowd. During the rest of the hearing he remained there, leaning forward, elbows on knees and his panama between his hands, not missing a word of the proceedings.

It was Marie's turn next. She had a hat on and still looked quite pretty, though I much preferred her with her hair free. From where I was I had glimpses of the soft curves of her breasts, and her underlip had the little pout that always fascinated me. She appeared very nervous.

The first question was: How long had she known me? Since the time when she was in our office, she replied. Then the Judge asked her what were the relations between us, and she said she was my girl friend. Answering another question, she admitted promising to marry me. The Prosecutor, who had been studying a document in front of him, asked her rather sharply when our 'liaison' had begun. She gave the date. He then observed with a would-be casual air that apparently she meant the day following my mother's funeral. After letting this sink in he remarked in a slightly ironic tone that obviously this was a 'delicate topic' and he could enter into the young lady's feelings, but—and here his voice grew sterner—his duty obliged him to waive considerations of delicacy.

After making this announcement he asked Marie to give a full account of our doings on the day when I had 'intercourse' with her for the first time. Marie wouldn't answer at first, but the Prosecutor insisted, and then she told him that we had met at the baths, gone together to the pictures, and then to my place. He then informed the court that, as a result of certain statements made by Marie at the proceedings before the magistrate, he had studied the cinema programmes of that date, and turning to Marie asked her to name the film that we had gone to see. In a very low voice she said it was a picture with Fernandel in it. By the time she had finished, the courtroom was so still you could have heard a pin drop.

Looking very grave, the Prosecutor drew himself up to his full height and, pointing at me, said in such a tone that I could have sworn he was genuinely moved:

'Gentlemen of the jury, I would have you note that on the next day after his mother's funeral that man was visiting the swimming-pool, starting a liaison with a girl, and going to see a comic film. That is all I wish to say.'

When he sat down there was the same dead silence. Then all of a sudden

Marie burst into tears. He'd got it all wrong, she said; it wasn't a bit like that really, he'd bullied her into saying the opposite of what she meant. She knew me very well, and she was sure I hadn't done anything really wrong—and so on. At a sign from the presiding judge, one of the court officers led her away, and the hearing continued.

Hardly anyone seemed to listen to Masson, the next witness. He stated that I was a respectable young fellow; 'and, what's more, a very decent chap'. Nor did they pay any more attention to Salamano, when he told them how kind I'd always been to his dog, or when, in answer to a question about my mother and myself, he said that really Mother and I had very little in common and that explained why I'd fixed up for her to enter the Home. 'You've got to understand,' he added. 'You've got to understand.' But no one seemed to understand. He was told to stand down.

Raymond was the next, and last, witness. He gave me a little wave of his hand and led off by saying I was innocent. The Judge rebuked him.

'You are here to give evidence, not your views on the case, and you must confine yourself to answering the questions put you.'

He was then asked to make clear his relations with the deceased, and Raymond took this opportunity of explaining that it was he, not I, against whom the dead man had a grudge, because he, Raymond, had beaten up his sister. The Judge asked him if the deceased had no reason to dislike me, too. Raymond told him that my presence on the beach that morning was a pure coincidence.

'How comes it then,' the Prosecutor inquired, 'that the letter which led up to this tragedy was the prisoner's work?'

Raymond replied that this, too, was due to mere chance.

To which the Prosecutor retorted that in this case 'chance' or 'mere coincidence' seemed to play a remarkably large part. Was it by chance that I hadn't intervened when Raymond assaulted his mistress? Did this convenient term 'chance' account for my having vouched for Raymond at the police station and having made, on that occasion, statements extravagantly favourable to him? In conclusion, he asked Raymond to state what were his means of livelihood.

On his describing himself as a warehouseman, the Prosecutor informed the jury it was common knowledge that the witness lived on the immoral earnings of women. I, he said, was this man's intimate friend and associate; in fact, the whole background of the crime was of the most squalid description. And what made it even more odious was the personality of the prisoner, an inhuman monster wholly without a moral sense.

Raymond began to expostulate, and my lawyer, too, protested. They were told that the Prosecutor must be allowed to finish his remarks.

'I have nearly done,' he said; then turned to Raymond. 'Was the prisoner your friend?'

'Certainly. We were the best of pals, as they say.'

The Prosecutor then put me the same question. I looked hard at Raymond, and he did not turn away.

Then, 'Yes', I answered.

The Prosecutor turned towards the jury.

'Not only did the man before you in the dock indulge in the most shameful orgies on the day following his mother's funeral. He killed a man cold-bloodedly, in pursuance of some sordid vendetta in the underworld of prostitutes and pimps. That, gentlemen of the jury, is the type of man the prisoner is.'

No sooner had he sat down than my lawyer, out of all patience, raised his arms so high that his sleeves fell back, showing the full length of his starched shirt-cuffs.

'Is my client on trial for having buried his mother, or for killing a man?' he asked.

There were some titters in court. But then the Prosecutor sprang to his feet and, draping his gown round him, said he was amazed at his friend's ingenuousness in failing to see that between these two elements of the case there was a vital link. They hung together psychologically, if he might put it so. 'In short,' he concluded, speaking with great vehemence, 'I accuse the prisoner of behaving at his mother's funeral in a way that showed he was already a criminal at heart.'

These words seemed to take much effect on the jury and public. My lawyer merely shrugged his shoulders and wiped the sweat from his forehead. But obviously he was rattled, and I had a feeling things weren't going well for me.

Soon after this incident the court rose. As I was being taken from the courthouse to the prison van, I was conscious for a few brief moments of the once familiar feel of a summer evening out of doors. And, sitting in the darkness of my moving cell, I recognized, echoing in my tired brain, all the characteristic sounds of a town I'd loved, and of a certain hour of the day which I had always particularly enjoyed. The shouts of newspaper-boys in the already languid air, the last calls of birds in the public garden, the cries of sandwich-vendors, the screech of trams at the steep corners of the upper town, and that faint rustling over head as darkness sifted down upon the harbour—all these sounds made my return to prison like a blind man's journey along a route whose every inch he knows by heart.

Yes, this was the evening hour when—how long ago it seemed!—I always felt so well content with life. Then, what awaited me was a night of easy, dreamless sleep. This was the same hour, but with a difference; I was returning to a cell and what awaited me was a night haunted by forebodings of the coming day. And so I learnt that familiar paths traced in the dusk of summer evenings may lead as well to prison as to innocent, carefree sleep.

4

It is always interesting, even in the prisoner's dock, to hear oneself being talked about. And certainly in the speeches of my lawyer and the prosecuting counsel a great deal was said about me; more, in fact, about me personally than about my crime.

Really there wasn't any very great difference between the two speeches. Counsel for the defence raised his arms to heaven and pleaded Guilty, but with extenuating circumstances. The Prosecutor made similar gestures; he agreed that I was guilty, but denied extenuating circumstances.

One thing about this phase of the trial was rather irksome. Quite often, interested as I was in what they had to say, I was tempted to put in a word, myself. But my lawyer had advised me not to. 'You won't do your case any good by talking,' he had warned me. In fact there seemed to be a con-spiracy to exclude me from the proceedings; I wasn't to have any say and my fate was to be decided out of hand.

It was quite an effort at times for me to refrain from cutting them all short, and saying: 'But, damn it all, who's on trial in this court, I'd like to know? It's a serious matter for a man, being accused of murder. And I've something really important to tell you.'

However, on second thoughts, I found I had nothing to say. In any case, I must admit that hearing oneself talked about loses its interest very soon. The Prosecutor's speech, especially, began to bore me before he was half-way through it. The only things that really caught my attention were occasional phrases, his gestures, and some elaborate tirades—but these were isolated patches.

What he was aiming at, I gathered, was to show that my crime was pre-meditated. I remember his saying at one moment, 'I can prove this, gentle-men of the jury, to the hilt. First, you have the facts of the crime; which are as clear as daylight. And then you have what I may call the night side of this case, the dark workings of a criminal mentality.'

He began by summing up the facts, from my mother's death onwards. He stressed my heartlessness, my inability to state Mother's age, my visit to the bathing-pool where I met Marie, our matinée at the pictures where a Fernandel film was showing, and finally my return with Marie to my rooms. I didn't quite follow his remarks at first as he kept on mentioning 'the prisoner's mistress', whereas for me she was just 'Marie'. Then he came to the subject of Raymond. It seemed to me that his way of treating the facts showed a certain shrewdness. All he said sounded quite plausible. I'd written the letter in collusion with Raymond so as to entice his mistress to his room and subject her to ill-treatment by a man 'of more than dubious reputation'.

Then, on the beach, I'd provoked a brawl with Raymond's enemies, in the course of which Raymond was wounded. I'd asked him for his revolver and gone back by myself with the intention of using it. Then I'd shot the Arab. After the first shot I waited. Then, 'to be certain of making a good job of it', I fired four more shots deliberately, point blank and in cold blood, at my victim.

'That is my case,' he said. 'I have described to you the series of events which led this man to kill the deceased, fully aware of what he was doing. I emphasize this point. We are not concerned with an act of homicide committed on a sudden impulse which might serve as extenuation. I ask you to note, gentlemen of the jury, that the prisoner is an educated man. You will have observed the way in which he answered my questions; he is intelligent and he knows the value of words. And I repeat that it is quite impossible to assume that, when he committed the crime, he was unaware what he was doing.'

I noticed that he laid stress on my 'intelligence'. It puzzled me rather why what would count as a good point in an ordinary person should be used against an accused man as an overwhelming proof of his guilt. While thinking this over, I missed what he said next, until I heard him exclaim indignantly: 'And has he uttered a word of regret for his most odious crime? Not one word, gentlemen. Not once in the course of these proceedings did this man show the least contrition.'

Turning towards the dock, he pointed a finger at me, and went on in the same strain. I really couldn't understand why he harped on this point so much. Of course I had to own that he was right; I didn't feel much regret for what I'd done. Still, to my mind he overdid it, and I'd have liked to have a chance of explaining to him, in a quite friendly, almost affectionate way, that I have never been able really to regret anything in all my life. I've always been far too much absorbed in the present moment, or the immediate future, to think back. Of course, in the position into which I had been forced, there was no question of my speaking to anyone in that tone. I hadn't the right to show any friendly feeling or possess good intentions. And I tried to follow what came next, as the Prosecutor was now considering what he called my 'soul'.

He said he'd studied it closely—and had found a blank, 'literally nothing, gentlemen of the jury'. Really, he said, I had no soul, there was nothing human about me, not one of those moral qualities which normal men possess had any place in my mentality. 'No doubt,' he added, 'we should not reproach him with this. We cannot blame a man for lacking what it was never in his power to acquire. But in a criminal court the wholly passive ideal of tolerance must give place to a sterner, loftier ideal, that of Justice. Especially when this lack of every decent instinct is such as that of the man before you, a menace to society.' He proceeded to discuss my conduct towards my mother, repeating what he had said in the course of the hearing. But he spoke at much greater length of my crime; at such length, indeed, that I lost the thread and was conscious only of the steadily increasing heat.

A moment came when the Prosecutor paused and, after a short silence, said in a low, vibrant voice: 'This same court, gentlemen, will be called on to try to-morrow that most odious of crimes, the murder of a father by his son.' To his mind, such a crime was almost unimaginable. But, he ventured to hope, Justice would be meted out without faltering. And yet, he made bold to say, the horror that even the crime of parricide inspired in him paled beside the loathing inspired by my callousness.

'This man, who is morally guilty of his mother's death, is no less unfit to have a place in the community than that other man who did to death the father that begat him. And, indeed, the one crime led on to the other; the first of these two criminals, the man in the dock, set a precedent, if I may put it so, and authorized the second crime. Yes, gentlemen, I am convinced' —here he raised his voice a tone—'that you will not find I am exaggerating the case against the prisoner when I say that he is also guilty of the murder to be tried to-morrow in this court. And I look to you for a verdict accordingly.'

The Prosecutor paused again, to wipe the sweat off his face. He then explained that his duty was a painful one, but he would do it without flinching. 'This man has, I repeat, no place in a community whose basic principles he flouts without compunction. Nor, heartless as he is, has he any claim to mercy. I ask you to impose the extreme penalty of the law; and I ask it without a qualm. In the course of a long career, in which it has often been my duty to ask for a capital sentence, never have I felt that painful duty weigh so little on my mind as in the present case. In demanding a verdict of murder without extenuating circumstances, I am following not only the dictates of my conscience and a sacred obligation, but also those of the natural and righteous indignation I feel at the sight of a criminal devoid of the least spark of human feeling.'

When the Prosecutor sat down there was a longish silence. Personally I was quite overcome by the heat and my amazement at what I had been hearing. The presiding judge gave a short cough, and asked me in a very low tone if I had anything to say. I rose, and as I felt in the mood to speak, I said the first thing that crossed my mind: that I'd had no intention of killing the Arab. The Judge replied that this statement would be taken into consideration by the court. Meanwhile he would be glad to hear, before my counsel addressed the court, what were the motives of my crime. So far, he must admit, he hadn't fully understood the grounds of my defence.

I tried to explain that it was because of the sun, but I spoke too quickly and ran my words into each other. I was only too conscious that it sounded nonsensical, and, in fact, I heard people tittering.

My lawyer shrugged his shoulders. Then he was directed to address the court, in his turn. But all he did was to point out the lateness of the hour and to ask for an adjournment till the following afternoon. To this the Judge agreed.

When I was brought back next day, the electric fans were still churning up the heavy air and the jurymen plying their gaudy little fans in a sort of steady rhythm. The speech for the defence seemed to me interminable. At one moment, however, I pricked up my ears; it was when I heard him saying: 'It is true I killed a man.' He went on in the same strain, saying 'I' when he referred to me. It seemed so queer that I bent towards the policeman on my right and asked him to explain. He told me to shut up; then, after a moment, whispered: 'They all do that.' It seemed to me that the idea behind it was still further to exclude me from the case, to put me off the map, so to speak, by substituting the lawyer for myself. Anyway, it hardly mattered; I already felt worlds away from this courtroom and its tedious 'proceedings'.

My lawyer, in any case, struck me as feeble to the point of being ridiculous. He hurried through his plea of provocation, and then he, too, started in about my 'soul'. But I had an impression that he had much less talent than the Prosecutor.

'I, too,' he said, 'have closely studied this man's soul; but, unlike my learned friend for the prosecution, I have found something there. Indeed I may say that I have read the prisoner's mind like an open book.' What he had read there was that I was an excellent young fellow, a steady, conscientious worker who did his best by his employer; that I was popular with everyone and sympathetic in others' troubles. According to him I was a dutiful son, who had supported his mother as long as he was able. After anxious consideration I had reached the conclusion that, by entering a Home, the old lady would have comforts that my means didn't permit me to provide for her. 'I am astounded, gentlemen,' he added, 'by the attitude taken up by my learned friend in referring to this Home. Surely, if proof be needed of the excellence of such institutions, we need only remember that they are promoted and financed by a Government department.' I noticed that he made no reference to the funeral, and this seemed to me a serious omission. But, what with his long-windedness, the endless days and hours they had been discussing my 'soul', and the rest of it, I found that my mind had gone blurred; everything was dissolving into a greyish, watery haze.

Only one incident stands out; towards the end, while my counsel rambled on, I heard the tin trumpet of an ice-cream vendor in the street, a small, shrill sound cutting across the flow of words. And then a rush of memories went through my mind—memories of a life which was mine no longer and had once provided me with the surest, humblest pleasures: warm smells of summer, my favourite streets, the sky at evening, Marie's dresses and her laugh. The futility of what was happening here seemed to take me by the throat, I felt like vomiting, and I had only one idea: to get it over, to go back to my cell, and sleep . . . and sleep.

Dimly I heard my counsel making his last appeal.

'Gentlemen of the jury, surely you will not send to his death a decent, hard-working young man, because for one tragic moment he lost his self-control? Is he not sufficiently punished by the lifelong remorse that is to be his lot? I confidently await your verdict, the only verdict possible—that of homicide with extenuating circumstances.'

The court rose and the lawyer sat down, looking thoroughly exhausted. Some of his colleagues came to him and shook his hand. 'You put up a magnificent show, old chap,' I heard one of them say. Another lawyer even called me to witness: 'Fine, wasn't it?' I agreed, but insincerely; I was far too tired to judge if it had been 'fine' or otherwise.

Meanwhile the day was ending and the heat becoming less intense. By some vague sounds that reached me from the street I knew that the cool of the evening had set in. We all sat on, waiting. And what we all were waiting for really concerned nobody but me. I looked round the courtroom. It was exactly as it had been on the first day. I met the eyes of the journalist in grey and the robot woman. This reminded me that not once during the whole hearing had I tried to catch Marie's eye. It wasn't that I'd forgotten her; only I was too preoccupied. I saw her now, seated between Céleste and Raymond. She gave me a little wave of her hand, as if to say, 'At last!' She was smiling, but I could tell that she was rather anxious. But my heart seemed turned to stone, and I couldn't even return her smile.

The judges came back to their seats. Someone read out to the jury, very rapidly, a string of questions. I caught a word here and there. 'Murder of malice aforethought . . . Provocation . . . Extenuating circumstances.' The jury went out, and I was taken to the little room where I had already waited. My lawyer came to see me; he was very talkative and showed more cordiality and confidence than ever before. He assured me that all would go well and I'd get off with a few years' imprisonment or transportation. I asked him what were the chances of getting the sentence quashed. He said there was no chance of that. He had not raised any point of law, as this was apt to prejudice the jury. And it was difficult to get a judgment quashed except on technical grounds. I saw his point, and agreed. Looking at the matter dis-passionately, I shared his view. Otherwise there would be no end to litiga-tion. 'In any case,' the lawyer said, 'you can appeal in the ordinary way. But I'm convinced the verdict will be favourable.'

We waited for quite a while, a good three-quarters of an hour, I should say. Then a bell rang. My lawyer left me, saying:

'The foreman of the jury will read out the answers. You will be called on after that to hear the judgment.'

Some doors banged. I heard people hurrying down flights of steps, but couldn't tell whether they were near by or distant. Then I heard a voice droning away in the courtroom.

When the bell rang again and I stepped back into the dock, the silence of the courtroom closed in round me and, with the silence, came a queer sensation when I noticed that, for the first time, the young journalist kept his eyes averted. I didn't look in Marie's direction. In fact, I had no time to look as the presiding judge had already started pronouncing a rigmarole to the effect that 'in the name of the French People' I was to be decapitated in some public place.

It seemed to me then that I could interpret the look on the faces of those present; it was one of almost respectful sympathy. The policemen, too, handled me very gently. The lawyer placed his hand on my wrist. I had stopped thinking altogether. I heard the Judge's voice asking if I had anything more to say. After thinking for a moment, I answered, 'No'. Then the policemen led me out.

5

I HAVE just refused, for the third time, to see the prison chaplain. I have nothing to say to him, don't feel like talking—and shall be seeing him quite soon enough, anyway. The only thing that interests me now is the problem of circumventing the machine, learning if the inevitable admits a loophole.

They have moved me to another cell. In this one, lying on my back, I can see the sky, and there is nothing else to see. All my time is spent in watching the slowly changing colours of the sky, as day moves on to night. I put my hands behind my head, gaze up, and wait.

This problem of a loophole obsesses me; I am always wondering if there have been cases of condemned prisoners escaping from the implacable machinery of justice at the last moment, breaking through the police cordon, vanishing in the nick of time before the guillotine falls. Often and often I blame myself for not having given more attention to accounts of public executions. One should always take an interest in such matters. There's never any knowing what one may come to. Like everyone else I'd read descriptions of executions in the papers. But technical books dealing with this subject must certainly exist; only I'd never felt sufficiently interested to look them up. And in these books I might have found escape stories. Surely they'd have told me that in one case anyhow the wheels had stopped; that once, if only once, in that inexorable march of events, chance or luck had played a happy part. Just once! In a way I think that single instance would have satisfied me. My emotion would have done the rest. The papers often talk of 'a debt owed to society'—a debt which, according to them, must be paid by the offender. But talk of that sort doesn't touch the imagination. No, the one thing that counted for me was the possibility of making a dash for it and defeating their bloodthirsty rite; of a mad stampede to freedom that would anyhow give me a moment's hope, the gambler's last throw. Naturally all that 'hope' could come to was to be knocked down at the corner of a street or picked off by a bullet in my back. But, all things considered, even this luxury was forbidden me; I was caught in the rat-trap irrevocably.

Try as I might, I couldn't stomach this brutal certitude. For really, when one came to think of it, there was a disproportion between the judgment on which it was based and the unalterable sequence of events starting from the moment when that judgment was delivered. The fact that the verdict was read out at 8 p.m. rather than at 5, the fact that it might have been quite different, that it was given by men who change their underclothes, and was credited to so vague an entity as the 'French People'—for that matter, why not to the Chinese or the German People?—all these facts seemed to deprive the court's decision of much of its gravity. Yet I could but recognize that, from the moment the verdict was given, its effects became as cogent, as tangible, as, for example, this wall against which I was lying, pressing my back to it.

When such thoughts crossed my mind, I remembered a story Mother used to tell me about my father. I never set eyes on him. Perhaps the only things I really knew about him were what Mother had told me. One of these was that he'd gone to see a murderer executed. The mere thought of it turned his stomach. But he'd seen it through and, on coming home, was violently sick. At the time I found my father's conduct rather disgusting. But now I understood; it was so natural. How had I failed to recognize that nothing was more important than an execution; that, viewed from one angle, it's the only thing that can genuinely interest a man? And I decided that, if ever I got out of jail, I'd attend every execution that took place. I was unwise, no doubt, even to consider this possibility. For, the moment I'd pictured myself in freedom, standing behind a double rank of policemen—on the right side of the line, so to speak—the mere thought of being an on-looker who comes to see the show, and can go home and vomit afterwards, flooded my mind with a wild, absurd exultation. It was a stupid thing to let my imagination run away with me like that; a moment later I had a shivering fit and had to wrap myself closely in my blanket. But my teeth went on chattering; nothing would stop them.

Still, obviously, one can't be sensible all the time. Another equally ridiculous fancy of mine was to frame new laws, altering the penalties. What was wanted, to my mind, was to give the criminal a chance, if only a dog's chance; say, one chance in a thousand. There might be some drug, or combination of drugs, which would kill the patient (I thought of him as 'the patient') nine hundred and ninety times in a thousand. That he should know this was, of course, essential. For after taking much thought, calmly, I came to the conclusion that what was wrong about the guillotine was that the condemned man had no chance at all, absolutely none. In fact, the patient's death had been ordained irrevocably. It was a foregone conclusion. If by some fluke the knife didn't do its job, they started again. So it came to this, that—against the grain, no doubt—the condemned man had to hope the apparatus was in good working order! This, I thought, was a flaw in the system; and, on the face of it, my view was sound enough. On the other hand, I had to admit it proved the efficiency of the system. It came to this: the man under sentence was obliged to collaborate mentally, it was in his interest that all should go off without a hitch.

Another thing I had to recognize was that, until now, I'd had wrong ideas on the subject. For some reason I'd always supposed that one had to go up steps and climb on to a scaffold to be guillotined. Probably that was because of the 1789 Revolution; I mean, what I'd learnt about it at school, and the pictures I had seen. Then one morning I remembered a photograph the newspapers had featured on the occasion of the execution of a famous criminal. Actually the apparatus stood on the ground; there was nothing very impressive about it, and it was much narrower than I'd imagined. It struck me as rather odd that picture had escaped my memory until now. What had struck me at the time was the neat appearance of the guillotine; its shining surfaces and finish reminded one of some laboratory instrument. One always has exaggerated ideas about what one doesn't know. Now I had to admit it seemed a very simple process, getting guillotined; the machine is on the same level as the man, and he walks towards it as one steps forward to meet somebody one knows. In a sense, that, too, was disappointing. The business of climbing a scaffold, leaving the world below one, so to speak, gave something for a man's imagination to get hold of. But, as it was, the machine dominated everything; they killed you discreetly, with a hint of shame and much efficiency.

There were two other things about which I was always thinking: the dawn, and my appeal. However, I did my best to keep my mind off these thoughts. I lay down, looked up at the sky, and forced myself to study it. When the light began to turn green I knew that night was coming. Another thing I did to deflect the course of my thoughts was to listen to my heart. I couldn't imagine that this faint throbbing, which had been with me for so long, would ever cease. Imagination has never been one of my strong points. Still, I tried to picture a moment when the beating of my heart no longer echoed in my head. But in vain. The dawn and my appeal were still there. And I ended by believing it was a silly thing to try to force one's thoughts out of their natural groove.

They always came for one at dawn; that much I knew. So really all my nights were spent in waiting for that dawn. I have never liked being taken by surprise. When something happens to me I want to be ready for it. That's

why I got into the habit of sleeping off and on in the daytime and watching
through the night for the first hint of daybreak in the dark dome above. The
worst period of the night was that vague hour when, I knew, they usually
come; once it was after midnight I waited, listening intently. Never before
had my ears perceived so many noises, such tiny sounds. Still, I must say I
was lucky in one respect; never during any of those periods did I hear footsteps. Mother used to say that however miserable one is, there's always something to be thankful for. And each morning, when the sky brightened and
light began to flood my cell, I agreed with her. Because I might just as well
have heard footsteps, and felt my heart shattered into bits. Even though the
faintest rustle sent me hurrying to the door and, pressing an ear to the rough,
cold wood, I listened so intently that I could hear my breathing, quick and
hoarse like a dog's panting—even so there was an end; my heart hadn't split,
and I knew I had another twenty-four hours' respite.

Then all day there was my appeal to think about. I made the most of this
idea, studying my effects so as to squeeze out the maximum of consolation.
Thus I always began by assuming the worst; my appeal was dismissed. That
meant, of course, I was to die. Sooner than others, obviously. 'But,' I reminded myself, 'it's common knowledge that life isn't worth living anyhow.' And, on a wide view, I could see that it makes little difference whether
one dies at the age of thirty or three-score and ten—since, in either case, other
men and women will continue living, the world will go on as before. Also,
whether I died now or forty years hence, this business of dying had to be
got through, inevitably. Still, somehow this line of thought wasn't as con-
soling as it should have been; the idea of all those years of life in hand was a
galling reminder! However, I could argue myself out of it, by picturing what
would have been my feelings when my term was up, and death had cornered
me. Once one's up against it, the precise manner of one's death has obviously
small importance. Therefore—but it was hard not to lose the thread of the
argument leading up to that 'therefore'—I should be prepared to face the
dismissal of my appeal.

At this stage, but only at this stage, I had, so to speak, the *right*, and
accordingly I gave myself leave, to consider the other alternative; that my
appeal was successful. And then the trouble was to calm down that sudden
rush of joy racing through my body and even bringing tears to my eyes. But
it was up to me to bring my nerves to heel and steady my mind; for, even
in considering this possibility, I had to keep some order in my thoughts, so
as to make my consolations, as regards the first alternative, more plausible.
When I'd succeeded, I had earned a good hour's peace of mind; and that,
anyhow, was something.

It was at one of these moments that I refused once again to see the chaplain. I was lying down and could mark the summer evening coming on by
a soft golden glow spreading across the sky. I had just turned down my

appeal, and felt my blood circulating with slow, steady throbs. No, I didn't want to see the chaplain. . . . Then I did something I hadn't done for quite a while; I fell to thinking about Marie. She hadn't written for ages; probably, I surmised, she had grown tired of being the mistress of a man sentenced to death. Or she might be ill, or dead. After all, such things happen. How could I have known about it, since, apart from our two bodies, separated now, there was no link between us, nothing to remind us of each other? Supposing she were dead, her memory would mean nothing; I couldn't feel an interest in a dead girl. This seemed to me quite normal; just as I realized people would soon forget me once I was dead. I couldn't even say that this was hard to stomach; really, there's no idea to which one doesn't get acclimatized in time.

My thoughts had reached this point when the chaplain walked in, unannounced. I couldn't help giving a start on seeing him. He noticed this evidently, as he promptly told me not to be alarmed. I reminded him that usually his visits were at another hour, and for a pretty grim occasion. This, he replied, was just a friendly visit; it had no concern with my appeal, about which he knew nothing. Then he sat down on my bed, asking me to sit beside him. I refused—not because I had anything against him; he seemed a mild, amiable man.

He remained quite still at first, his arms resting on his knees, his eyes fixed on his hands. They were slender but sinewy hands, which made me think of two nimble little animals. Then he gently rubbed them together. He stayed so long in the same position that for a while I almost forgot he was there.

All of a sudden he jerked his head up and looked me in the eyes. 'Why,' he asked, 'don't you let me come to see you?'

I explained that I didn't believe in God.

'Are you really so sure of that?'

I said I saw no point in troubling my head about the matter; whether I believed or didn't was, to my mind, a question of so little importance.

He then leant back against the wall, laying his hands flat on his thighs. Almost without seeming to address me, he remarked that he'd often noticed one fancies one is quite sure about something, when in point of fact one isn't. When I said nothing he looked at me again, and asked:

'Don't you agree?'

I said that seemed quite possible. But, though I mightn't be so sure about what interested me, I was absolutely sure about what didn't interest me. And the question he had raised didn't interest me at all.

He looked away and, without altering his posture, asked if it was because I felt utterly desperate that I spoke like this. I explained that it wasn't despair I felt, but fear—which was natural enough.

'In that case,' he said firmly, 'God can help you. All the men I've seen in your position turned to Him in their time of trouble.'

Obviously, I replied, they were at liberty to do so, if they felt like it. I however, didn't want to be helped, and I hadn't time to work up interest for something that didn't interest me.

He fluttered his hands fretfully; then, sitting up, smoothed out his cassock. When this was done he began talking again, addressing me as 'my friend'. It wasn't because I'd been condemned to death, he said, that he spoke to me in this way. In his opinion every man on the earth was under sentence of death.

There, I interrupted him; that wasn't the same thing, I pointed out, and, what's more, could be no consolation.

He nodded. 'Maybe. Still, if you don't die soon, you'll die one day. And then the same question will arise. How will you face that terrible, final hour?'

I replied that I'd face it exactly as I was facing it now.

Thereat he stood up, and looked me straight in the eyes. It was a trick I knew well. I used to amuse myself trying it on Emmanuel and Céleste, and nine times out of ten they'd look away uncomfortably. I could see the chaplain was an old hand at it, as his gaze never faltered. And his voice was quite steady when he said: 'Have you no hope at all? Do you really think that when you die you die outright, and nothing remains?'

I said: 'Yes.'

He dropped his eyes and sat down again. He was truly sorry for me, he said. It must make life unbearable for a man, to think as I did.

The priest was beginning to bore me, and, resting a shoulder on the wall, just beneath the little skylight, I looked away. Though I didn't trouble much to follow what he said, I gathered he was questioning me again. Presently his tone became agitated, urgent, and, as I realized that he was genuinely distressed, I began to pay more attention.

He said he felt convinced my appeal would succeed, but I was saddled with a load of guilt, of which I must get rid. In his view man's justice was a vain thing; only God's justice mattered. I pointed out that the former had condemned me. Yes, he agreed, but it hadn't absolved me from my sin. I told him that I wasn't conscious of any 'sin'; all I knew was that I'd been guilty of a criminal offence. Well, I was paying the penalty of that offence, and no one had the right to expect anything more of me.

Just then he got up again, and it struck me that if he wanted to move in this tiny cell, almost the only choice lay between standing up and sitting down. I was staring at the floor. He took a single step towards me, and halted, as if he didn't dare to come nearer. Then he looked up through the bars at the sky.

'You're mistaken, my son,' he said gravely. 'There's more that might be required of you. And perhaps it *will* be required of you.'

'What do you mean?'

'You might be asked to see . . .'

'To see what?'

Slowly the priest gazed round my cell, and I was struck by the sadness of his voice when he spoke again.

'These stone walls, I know it only too well, are steeped in human suffering. I've never been able to look at them without a shudder. And yet—believe me, I am speaking from the depths of my heart—I *know* that even the wretchedest among you have sometimes seen, taking form upon that greyness, a divine face. It's that face you are asked to see.'

This roused me a little. I informed him that I'd been staring at those walls for months; there was nobody, nothing in the world, I knew better than I knew them. And once upon a time, perhaps, I used to try to see a face. But it was a sun-gold face, glowing with desire—Marie's face. I had no luck; I'd never seen it, and now I'd given up trying. Indeed I'd never seen anything 'taking form', as he called it, against those grey walls.

The chaplain gazed at me mournfully. I now had my back to the wall and light was flowing over my forehead. He muttered some words I didn't catch; then abruptly asked if he might kiss me. I said, 'No'. Then he turned, came up to the wall, and slowly drew his hand along it.

'Do you really love these earthly things so very much?' he asked in a low voice.

I made no reply.

For quite a while he kept his eyes averted. His presence was getting more and more irksome, and I was on the point of telling him to go, and leave me in peace, when all of a sudden he swung round on me, and burst out passionately:

'No! No! I refuse to believe it. I'm sure you've often wished there was an after-life.'

Of course I had, I told him. Everybody has that wish at times. But that had no more importance than wishing to be rich, or to swim very fast, or to have a better-shaped mouth. It was in the same order of things. I was going on in the same vein, when he cut in with a question. How did I picture my life after the grave?

I fairly bawled out at him: 'A life in which I can remember this life on earth. That's all I want of it.' And in the same breath I told him I'd had enough of his company.

But, apparently, he had more to say on the subject of God. I went close up to him and made a last attempt to explain that I'd very little time left, and I wasn't going to waste it on God.

Then he tried to change the subject by asking me why I hadn't once addressed him as 'Father', seeing that he was a priest. That irritated me still more, and I told him he wasn't my father; quite the contrary, he was on the others' side.

'No, no, my son,' he said, laying his hand on my shoulder. 'I'm on *your* side, though you don't realize it—because your heart is hardened. But I shall pray for you.'

Then, I don't know how it was, but something seemed to break inside me, and I started yelling at the top of my voice. I hurled insults at him, I told him not to waste his rotten prayers on me; it was better to burn than to disappear. I'd taken him by the neckband of his cassock, and, in a sort of ecstasy of joy and rage, I poured out on him all the thoughts that had been simmering in my brain. He seemed so cocksure, you see. And yet none of his certainties was worth one strand of a woman's hair. Living as he did, like a corpse, he couldn't even be sure of being alive. It might look as if my hands were empty. Actually, I was sure of myself, sure about everything, far surer than he; sure of my present life and of the death that was coming. That, no doubt, was all I had; but at least that certainty was something I could get my teeth into— just as it had got its teeth into me. I'd been right, I was still right, I was always right. I'd passed my life in a certain way, and I might have passed it in a different way, if I'd felt like it. I'd acted thus, and I hadn't acted otherwise; I hadn't done *x*, whereas I had done *y* or *z*. And what did that mean? That, all the time, I'd been waiting for this present moment, for that dawn, to-morrow's or another day's, which was to justify me. Nothing, nothing had the least importance, and I knew quite well why. He, too, knew why. From the dark horizon of my future a sort of slow, persistent breeze had been blowing towards me, all my life long, from the years that were to come. And on its way that breeze had levelled out all the ideas that people tried to foist on me in the equally unreal years I then was living through. What difference could they make to me, the death of others, or a mother's love, or his God; or the way one decides to live, the fate one thinks one chooses, since one and the same fate was bound to 'choose' not only me but thousands of millions of privileged people who, like him, called themselves my brothers. Surely, surely he must see that? Every man alive was privileged; there was only one class of men, the privileged class. All alike would be condemned to die one day; his turn, too, would come like the others'. And what difference could it make if, after being charged with murder, he were executed because he didn't weep at his mother's funeral, since it all came to the same thing in the end? The same thing for Salamano's wife and for Salamano's dog. That little robot woman was as 'guilty' as the girl from Paris who had married Masson, or as Marie, who wanted me to marry her. What did it matter if Raymond was as much my pal as Céleste, who was a far worthier man? What did it matter if at this very moment Marie was kissing a new boy friend? As a condemned man himself, couldn't he grasp what I meant by that dark wind blowing from my future? . . .

I had been shouting so much that I'd lost my breath, and just then the warders rushed in and started trying to release the chaplain from my grip.

One of them made as if to strike me. The chaplain quietened them down, and gazed at me for a moment without speaking. I could see tears in his eyes. Then he turned and left the cell.

Once he'd gone, I felt calm again. But all this excitement had exhausted me and I dropped heavily on to my sleeping-plank. I must have had a longish sleep, for, when I woke, the stars were shining down on my face. Sounds of the countryside came faintly in, and the cool night air, veined with smells of earth and salt, fanned my cheeks. The marvellous peace of the sleepbound summer night flooded through me like a tide. Then, just on the edge of daybreak, I heard a steamer's siren. People were starting on a voyage to a world which had ceased to concern me, for ever. Almost for the first time in many months I thought of my mother. And now, it seemed to me, I understood why at her life's end she had taken on a 'fiancé'; why she'd played at making a fresh start. There, too, in that Home where lives were flickering out, the dusk came as a mournful solace. With death so near, Mother must have felt like someone on the brink of freedom, ready to start life all over again. No one, no one in the world had any right to weep for her. And I, too, felt ready to start life over again. It was as if that great rush of anger had washed me clean, emptied me of hope, and, gazing up at the dark sky spangled with its signs and stars, for the first time, the first, I laid my heart open to the benign indifference of the universe. To feel it so like myself, indeed so brotherly, made me realize that I'd been happy, and that I was happy still. For all to be accomplished, for me to feel less lonely, all that remained was to hope that on the day of my execution there should be a huge crowd of spectators and that they should greet me with howls of execration.

THE ANIMAL WAITER
ART AT THE HOTEL SPLENDIDE

BY LUDWIG BEMELMANS

from *Hotel Splendide* (1942)

THE ANIMAL WAITER

THE day was one of the rare ones when Mespoulets and I had a guest at our tables. Most of the time I mugged into a large mirror in back of me. Mespoulets stood next to me and shook his head. Mespoulets was a waiter and I was his bus boy. Our station was on the low rear balcony of the main dining-room of a hotel I shall call the Splendide, a vast and luxurious structure with many mirrors which gave up its unequal struggle with economics not long after the boom days and has since most probably been converted into an office building or torn down.

Before coming to America I had worked a short while in a hotel in Tirol that belonged to my uncle. German was my native language and I knew enough English to get along in New York City, but my French was extremely bad. The French language in all its aspects was a passion with Mespoulets, and he had plenty of time to teach it to me.

'When I say "*Le chien est utile*" there is one proposition. When I say "*Je crois que le chien est utile*," there are two. When I say "*Je crois que le chien est utile quand il garde la maison*," how many propositions are there?'

'Three.'

'Very good.'

Mespoulets nodded gravely in approval. At that moment Monsieur Victor, the maître d'hôtel, walked through our section of tables, and the other waiters near by stopped talking to each other, straightened a tablecloth here, moved a chair there, arranged their side towels smoothly over their arms, tugged at their jackets, and pulled their bow ties. Only Mespoulets was indifferent. He walked slowly toward the pantry, past Monsieur Victor, holding my arm. I walked with him and he continued the instruction.

' "*L'abeille fait du miel.*" The verb "*fait*" in this sentence in itself is insufficient. It does not say what the bee does, therefore we round out the idea by adding the words "*du miel*". These words are called "*un complément*". The sentence "*L'abeille fait du miel*" contains then what?'

'It contains one verb, one subject, and one complement.'

'Very good, excellent. Now run down and get the Camembert, the *salade escarole*, the hard water crackers, and the demitasse for Mr. Frank Munsey on Table Eighty-six.'

Our tables—Nos. 81, 82, and 86—were in a noisy, draughty corner of the balcony. They stood facing the stairs from the dining-room and were between two doors. One door led to the pantry and was hung on whining hinges. On wet days it sounded like an angry cat and it was continually kicked by the boots of waiters rushing in and out with trays in their hands. The other door led to a linen closet.

The waiters and bus boys squeezed by our tables, carrying trays. The ones with trays full of food carried them high over their heads; the ones with dirty dishes carried them low, extended in front. They frequently bumped into each other and there would be a crash of silver, glasses, and china, and cream trickling over the edges of the trays in thin streams. Whenever this happened, Monsieur Victor raced to our section, followed by his captains, to direct the cleaning up of the mess and pacify the guests. It was a common sight to see people standing in our section, napkins in hand, complaining and brushing themselves off and waving their arms angrily in the air.

Monsieur Victor used our tables as a kind of penal colony to which he sent guests who were notorious cranks, people who had forgotten to tip him over a long period of time and needed a reminder, undesirables who looked out of place in better sections of the dining-room, and guests who were known to linger for hours over an order of hors d'œuvres and a glass of milk while well-paying guests had to stand at the door waiting for a table.

Mespoulets was the ideal man for Monsieur Victor's purposes. He complemented Monsieur Victor's plan of punishment. He was probably the worst waiter in the world and I had become his bus boy after I fell down the stairs into the main part of the dining-room with eight pheasants à la Souvaroff. When I was sent to him to take up my duties as his assistant, he introduced himself by saying, 'My name is easy to remember. Just think of "my chickens"—"mes poulets"—Mespoulets.'

Rarely did any guest who was seated at one of our tables leave the hotel with a desire to come back again. If there was any broken glass around the dining-room, it was always in our spinach. The occupants of Tables Nos. 81, 82, and 86 shifted in their chairs, stared at the pantry door, looked around and made signs of distress at other waiters and captains while they waited for their food. When the food finally came, it was cold and was often not what had been ordered. While Mespoulets explained what the unordered food was, telling in detail how it was made and what the ingredients were, and offered hollow excuses, he dribbled mayonnaise, soup, or mint sauce over the guests, upset the coffee, and sometimes even managed to break a plate or two. I helped him as best I could.

At the end of a meal, Mespoulets usually presented the guest with somebody else's check, or it turned out that he had neglected to adjust the difference in price between what the guest had ordered and what he had got. By then the guest just held out his hand and cried, 'Never mind, never mind, give it to me, just give it to me! I'll pay just to get out of here! Give it to me, for God's sake!' Then the guest would pay and go. He would stop on the way out at the maître d'hôtel's desk and show Monsieur Victor and his captains the spots on his clothes, bang on the desk, and swear he would never come back again. Monsieur Victor and his captains would listen, make faces of compassion, say 'Oh!' and 'Ah!' and look darkly towards us across the room and promise that we would be fired the same day. But the next day we would still be there.

In the hours between meals, while the other waiters were occupied filling salt and pepper shakers, oil and vinegar bottles, and mustard pots, and counting the dirty linen and dusting the chairs, Mespoulets would walk to a table near the entrance, right next to Monsieur Victor's own desk, overlooking the lounge of the hotel. There he adjusted a special reading lamp which he had demanded and obtained from the management, spread a piece of billiard cloth over the table, and arranged on top of this a large blotter and a small one, an inkstand, and half a dozen penholders. Then he drew up a chair and seated himself. He had a large assortment of fine copper pen points of various sizes, and he sharpened them on a piece of sandpaper. He would select the pen point and the holder he wanted and begin to make circles in the air. Then, drawing towards him a gilt-edged place card or a crested one, on which menus were written, he would go to work. When he had finished, he arranged the cards all over the table to let them dry, and sat there at ease, only a step or two from Monsieur Victor's desk, in a sector invaded by other waiters only when they were to be called down or to be discharged, waiters who came with nervous hands and frightened eyes to face Monsieur Victor. Mespoulets's special talent guaranteed him his job and set him apart from the ordinary waiters. He was further distinguished by the fact that he was permitted to wear glasses, a privilege denied all other waiters no matter how nearsighted or astigmatic.

It was said of Mespoulets variously that he was the father, the uncle, or the brother of Monsieur Victor. It was also said of him that he had once been the director of a lycée in Paris. The truth was that he had never known Monsieur Victor on the other side, and I do not think there was any secret between them, only an understanding, a subtle sympathy of some kind. I learned that he had once been a tutor to a family in which there was a very beautiful daughter and that this was something he did not like to talk about. He loved animals almost as dearly as he loved the French language. He had taken it upon himself to watch over the fish which were in an aquarium in the outer lobby of the hotel, he fed the pigeons in the courtyard, and he extended his interest to the birds and beasts and crustaceans that came alive to the kitchen. He begged the cooks to deal quickly, as painlessly as could be, with lobsters and terrapins. If a guest brought a dog to our section, Mespoulets was mostly under the table with the dog.

At mealtime, while we waited for the few guests who came our way, Mespoulets sat out in the linen closet on a small box where he could keep an eye on our tables through the partly open door. He leaned comfortably against a pile of tablecloths and napkins. At his side was an ancient *Grammaire Française*, and while his hands were folded in his lap, the palms up, the thumbs cruising over them in small, silent circles, he made me repeat exercises, simple, compact, and easy to remember. He knew them all by heart and soon I did, too. He made me go over and over them until my pronunciation was right. All of them were about animals. There were: 'The Sage Salmon,' 'The Cat and the Old Woman,' 'The Society of Beavers,' 'The Bear in the Swiss Mountains,' 'The Intelligence of the Partridge,' 'The Lion of Florence,' and 'The Bird in the Cage.'

We started with 'The Sage Salmon' in January that year and were at the end of 'The Bear in the Swiss Mountains' when the summer garden opened in May. At that season business fell off for dinner, and all during the summer we were busy only at luncheon. Mespoulets had time to go home in the afternoons and he suggested that I continue studying there.

He lived in the house of a relative on West Twenty-fourth Street. On the sidewalk in front of the house next door stood a large wooden horse, painted red, the sign of a saddlemaker. Across the street was a place where horses were auctioned off, and up the block was an Italian poultry market with a picture of a chicken painted on its front. Hens and roosters crowded the market every morning.

Mespoulets occupied a room and bath on the second floor rear. The room was papered green and over an old couch hung a print of van Gogh's *Bridge at Arles*, which was not a common picture then. There were bookshelves, a desk covered with papers, and over the desk a large bird cage hanging from the ceiling.

In this cage, shaded with a piece of the hotel's billiard cloth, lived a miserable old canary. It was bald-headed, its eyes were like peppercorns, its feet were no longer able to cling to the roost, and it sat in the sand, in a corner, looking like a withered chrysanthemum that had been thrown away. On summer afternoons, near the bird, we studied 'The Intelligence of the Partridge' and 'The Lion of Florence'.

Late in August, on a chilly day that seemed like fall, Mespoulets and I began 'The Bird in the Cage'. The lesson was:

L'Oiseau en Cage

Voilà sur ma fenêtre un oiseau qui vient visiter le mien. Il a peur, il s'en va, et le pauvre prisonnier s'attriste, s'agite comme pour s'échapper. Je ferais comme lui, si j'étais à sa place, et cependant je le retiens. Vais-je lui ouvrir? il irait voler, chanter, faire son nid; il serait heureux; mais je ne l'aurais plus, et je l'aime, et je veux l'avoir. Je le garde. Pauvre petit, tu seras toujours prisonnier; je jouis de toi aux dépens de ta liberté, je te plains, et je te garde. Voilà comme le plaisir l'emporte sur la justice.

I translated for him: 'There's a bird at my window, come to visit mine. . . . The poor prisoner is sad. . . . I would feel as he does, if I were in his place, yet I keep him. . . . Poor prisoner, I enjoy you at the cost of your liberty. . . . pleasure before justice.'

Mespoulets looked up at the bird and said to me, 'Find some adjective to use with *"fenêtre"*, *"oiseau"*, *"liberté"*, *"plaisir"*, and *"justice"*,' and while I searched for them in our dictionary, he went to a shelf and took from it a cigar box. There was one cigar in it. He took this out, wiped off the box with his handkerchief, and then went to a drawer and got a large penknife, which he opened. He felt the blade. Then he went to the cage, took the bird out, laid it on the closed cigarbox, and quickly cut off its head. One claw opened slowly and the bird and its head lay still.

Mespoulets washed his hands, rolled the box, the bird, and the knife into a newspaper, put it under his arm, and took his hat from a stand. We went out and walked up Eighth Avenue. At Thirty-fourth Street he stopped at a trash can and put his bundle into it. 'I don't think he wanted to live any more,' he said.

'FROM now on,' lisped Monsieur Victor, as if he were pinning on me the Grand Cross of the Legion of Honour, 'you will be a waiter.'

It was about a year after I had gone to work at the Splendide as Mespoulets's bus boy, and only a month or two after I had been promoted to *commis*. A *commis* feels more self-satisfied than a bus boy and has a better life all round, but to become a waiter is to make a really worthwhile progress.

The cause of my promotion was a waiters' mutiny. On a rainy afternoon several of the waiters had suddenly thrown down their napkins and aprons and walked out. One had punched the chief bus boy in the nose and another had upset a tray filled with Spode demitasse cups. They wanted ten dollars a week instead of six; they wanted to do away with certain penalties that were imposed on them, such as a fine of fifty cents for using a serving napkin to clean an ashtray; and they wanted a full day off instead of having to come back on their free day to serve dinner, which was the custom at the Splendide, as at most other New York hotels. The good waiters did not go on strike. A few idealists spoke too loudly and got fired, and a lot of bad waiters, who had mediocre stations, left.

After my promotion I was stationed at the far end of the room, on the 'undesirables'' balcony, and my two tables were next to Mespoulets's.

It rained all that first day and all the next, and there were no guests on the bad balcony. With nothing to do, Mespoulets and I stood and looked at the ceiling, talked, or sat on overturned linen baskets out in the pantry and yawned. I drew some pictures on my order pad—small sketches of a pantry-man, a row of glasses, a stack of silver trays, a bus boy counting napkins. Mespoulets had a rubber band which, with two fingers of each hand, he stretched into various geometric shapes. He was impressed by my drawings.

The second night the dining-room was half full, but not a single guest sat at our tables. Mespoulets pulled at my serving napkin and whispered, 'If I were you, if I had your talent, that is what I would do', and then he waved his napkin towards the centre of the room.

There a small group of the best guests of the Splendide sat at dinner. He waved his napkin at Table No. 18, where a man was sitting with a very beautiful woman. Mespoulets explained to me that this gentleman was a famous cartoonist, that he drew pictures of a big and a little man. The big man always hit the little man on the head. In this simple fashion the creator of those two figures made a lot of money.

We left our tables to go down and look at him. While I stood off to one side, Mespoulets circled around the table and cleaned the cartoonist's ashtray so that he could see whether or not the lady's jewellery was genuine. 'Yes, that's what I would do if I had your talent. Why do you want to be an actor? It's almost as bad as being a waiter,' he said when we returned to our station. We walked down again later on. This time Mespoulets spoke to the waiter who served Table No. 18, a Frenchman named Herriot, and asked what kind of guest the cartoonist was. Was he liberal?

'Ah,' said Herriot, 'c'ui là? Ah, oui alors! C'est un très bon client, extrêmement généreux. C'est un gentleman par excellence.' And in English he added, 'He's A-1, that one. If only they were all like him! Never looks at the bill, never complains—and so full of jokes! It is a pleasure to serve him. C'est un chic type.'

After the famous cartoonist got his change, Herriot stood by waiting for the tip, and Mespoulets cruised around the table. Herriot quickly snatched up the tip; both waiters examined it, and then Mespoulets climbed back to the balcony. 'Magnifique,' he said to me. 'You are an idiot if you do not become a cartoonist. I am an old man—I have sixty years. All my children are dead, all except my daughter Mélanie, and for me it is too late for anything. I will always be a waiter. But you—you are young, you are a boy, you have talent. We shall see what can be done with it.'

Mespoulets investigated the famous cartoonist as if he were going to make him a loan or marry his daughter off to him. He interviewed chambermaids, telephone operators, and room waiters. 'I hear the same thing from the rest of the hotel,' he reported on the third rainy day. 'He lives here at the hotel, he has a suite, he is married to a countess, he owns a Rolls-Royce. He gives wonderful parties, eats grouse out of season, drinks vintage champagne at ten in the morning. He spends half the year in Paris and has a place in the south of France. When the accounting department is stuck with a charge they've forgotten to put on somebody's bill they just put it on his. He never looks at them.'

'Break it up, break it up. Sh-h-h. Quiet,' said Monsieur Maxim, the maître d'hôtel on our station. Mespoulets and I retired into the pantry, where we could talk more freely.

'It's a very agreeable life, this cartoonist life,' Mespoulets continued, stretching his rubber band. 'I would never counsel you to be an actor or an artist-painter. But a cartoonist, that is different. Think what fun you can have. All you do is think of amusing things, make pictures with pen and ink, have a big man hit a little man on the head, and write a few words over it. And I know you can do this easily. You are made for it.'

That afternoon, between luncheon and dinner, we went out to find a place where cartooning was taught. As we marched along Madison Avenue, Mespoulets noticed a man walking in front of us. He had flat feet and he walked painfully, like a skier going uphill.

Mespoulets said 'Pst', and the man turned round. They recognized each other and promptly said, 'Ah, bonjour'.

'You see?' Mespoulets said to me when we had turned into a side street. 'A waiter. A dog. Call "Pst", click your tongue, snap your fingers, and they turn around even when they are out for a walk and say, "Yes, sir, no sir, bonjour Monsieurdame." Trained poodles! For God's sakes, don't stay a waiter! If you can't be a cartoonist, be a streetcleaner, a dishwasher, anything. But don't be an actor or a waiter. It's the most awful occupation in the world. The abuse I have taken, the long hours, the smoke and dust in my lungs and eyes, and the complaints—ah, c'est la barbe, ce métier. My boy, profit by my experience. Take it very seriously, this cartooning.'

For months one does not meet anybody on the street with his neck in an aluminium-and-leather collar such as is worn in cases of ambulatory cervical fractures, and then in a single day one sees three of them. On one hears Mount Chimborazo mentioned five times. This day was a flat-foot day. Mespoulets, like the waiter we met on Madison Avenue, had flat feet. And so did the teacher in the Andrea del Sarto Art Academy. Before this man had finished interviewing me, Mespoulets whispered in my ear, 'Looks and talks like a waiter. Let's get out of here'.

On our way back to the hotel we bought a book on cartooning, a drawing board, pens and a penholder, and several soft pencils. On the first page of the book we read that before one could cartoon or make caricatures, one must be able to draw a face—a man, a woman—from nature. That was very simple, said Mespoulets. We had lots of time and the Splendide was filled with models. Two days later he bought another book on art and we visited the Metropolitan Museum. We bought all the newspapers that had comic strips. And the next week Mespoulets looked round and everywhere among the guests he saw funny people. He continued to read to me from the book on how to become a cartoonist.

The book said keep a number of sharpened, very soft pencils handy for your work. I did, and for a while I was almost the only waiter who had a pencil when a guest asked for one. 'And remember,' said the book, 'you can never be expert in caricaturing people unless you shake off the fear of drawing people.' I tried to shake off the fear. 'Most people like to have their own pictures drawn,' Mespoulets read solemnly. 'Regular-featured people should be avoided, as they are too simple to draw. Your attention should be concentrated on the faces with unique features.'

The most 'unique' faces at the Splendide belonged to Monsieur and Madame Lawrance Potter Dreyspool. Madame Dreyspool was very rich; her husband was not. He travelled with her as a sort of companion-butler, pulling her chair, helping her to get up, carrying books, flasks, dog leashes, small purchases, and opera glasses. He was also like the attendant at a side-show, for Madame was a monstrosity and everyone stared at her. They were both very fat, but she was enormous. It was said that she got her clothes from a couturier specializing in costumes for women who were *enceinte*, and that to pull everything in shape and get into her dresses she had to lie down on the floor. She was fond of light pastel-coloured fabrics and her ensembles had the colours of pigeons, hyacinths, and boudoir upholstery. Her coat covered her shoes and a wide fur piece her neck, and even in the middle of winter she wore immense garden hats that were as elaborate as wedding cakes.

Monsieur and Madame Dreyspool were the terror of maîtres d'hôtel all over the world. Wherever they stayed, they had the table nearest the entrance to the dining-room. This table was reserved for them at the Splendide in New York, at Claridge's in London, at the Ritz in Paris, and in various restaurants on the luxurious boats on which they crossed. Like the first snow-flakes, Monsieur and Madame Dreyspool always appeared in the Splendide at the beginning of the season. They left for Palm Beach at the first sign of its end.

Their entrance into the dining-room was spectacular. First Madame waddled in, then Monsieur with a Pekinese, one of the few dogs allowed in the main dining-room. Madame answered with one painful nod Monsieur Victor's deep bow, climbed up the two steps to the balcony on the right, where their table was, and elaborately sat down. Everyone in society knew them and nodded, coming in and going out. Monsieur and Madame thanked them briefly from the throne. They never spoke to each other and they never smiled.

Monsieur Dreyspool had consoled himself with whisky so many years that his face was purple. The gossip in the couriers' dining-room, where the valets and maids and chauffeurs ate, was that he also consoled himself with Susanne, Madame's personal maid. He did not seem so fat when he was alone, but when he and Madame were sitting together at their table on the good bal-cony, they looked like two old toads on a lily leaf.

The maître d'hôtel who took care of them was a Belgian and had come from the Hôtel de Londres in Antwerp. He never took his eyes off their table and raced to it whenever Monsieur Dreyspool turned his head. Monsieur and Madame were waited upon by a patient old Italian waiter named Giuseppe. Because he never lost his temper and never made mistakes, he got all the terrible guests, most of whom paid him badly. Madame Dreyspool was not allowed any sugar. Her vegetables had to be cooked in a special fashion. A long letter of instruction about her various peculiarities hung in the offices of the chefs and maîtres d'hôtel of all the hotels she went to. It was mailed ahead to the various managers by Monsieur.

The exit of Monsieur and Madame Dreyspool was as festive as the entrance. When they were ready to leave, the maître d'hôtel pulled Monsieur's chair out. Monsieur pulled out Madame's chair. Madame produced the dog from her generous lap—it had slept there under a fold of the tablecloth while she ate—and gave the dog to Monsieur, who placed it on the carpet. Then the maître d'hôtel, taking steps as small as Madame's, escorted her out, walking on her left side and talking to her solicitously, his face close to hers. Monsieur followed about six feet behind, with a big Belinda Fancy Tales cigar between his teeth, his hands in his pockets, and the leash of the dog slipped over one wrist. From where Mespoulets and I stood on the bad balcony, she looked like several pieces of comfortable furniture piled together under a velvet cover and being slowly pushed along on little wheels.

Mespoulets was convinced that Madame Dreyspool was the very best possible model for me to begin drawing. The book said not to be afraid. 'Take a piece of paper,' it said, 'draw a line down the centre, divide this line, and draw another from left to right so that the paper is divided into four equal parts.' I took an old menu and stood on the good balcony between a screen and a marble column. It was possible there to observe and sketch Madame Dreyspool unnoticed. I divided the back of the menu into four equal parts. Once I started to draw, I saw that Madame's left half-face extended farther out from the nose than her right and that one eye was always half closed. When someone she knew came in, the eyelid went up over the rim of the pupil in greeting and the corners of the lips gave a short upward jump and then sank down again into a steady mask of disgust.

Monsieur and Madame were easy to draw, they hardly moved. They sat and stared—stared, ate, stared, stirred their coffee. Only their eyes moved, when Giuseppe brought the cheese or the pastry tray. Quickly, shiftily, they glanced over it, as one looks at something distasteful or dubious. Always the same sideways glance at the check, at Giuseppe when he took the tip, at the Belgian maître d'hôtel, and at Monsieur Victor as they left.

I took my sketches back to Mespoulets, who had been studying the book on art in the linen closet. 'It shows effort and talent,' he said. 'It is not very good, but it is not bad. It is too stiff—looks too much like pigs, and while there is much pig at that table it is marvellously complicated pig.' He considered the book a moment and then slapped it shut. 'I think,' he said, 'I understand the gist of art without reading any more of this. Try and be free of the helping lines. To-morrow, when they come again, think of the kidney trouble, of the thousand pâtés and sauces they have eaten. Imagine those knees, the knees of Madame under the table—they must be so fat that faces are on each knee—two faces, one on each knee, laughing and frowning as she walks along. All that must be in the portrait. And the ankles that spill over her shoes—this must be evident in your drawing of her face.'

Monsieur and Madame came again the next day, and I stood under a palm and drew them on the back of another menu. Mespoulets came and watched me, broke a roll in half, and kneaded the soft part of the bread into an eraser. 'Much better,' he said. 'Try and try again. Don't give up. Remember the thousand fat sauces, the ankles. The eyes already are wonderful. Go ahead.'

He went back to his station and soon after I heard 'Tsk, tsk, tsk, tsk!' over my shoulder. It was the Belgian maître d'hôtel and he was terror-stricken. He took the menu out of my hand and disappeared with it.

When I came to work the next noon I was told to report to the office of Monsieur Victor. I went to Monsieur Victor's desk. Slowly, precisely, without looking up from his list of reservations, he said, 'Ah, the *Wunderkind*'. Then, in the manner in which he discharged people, he continued. 'You are a talented young man. If I were you, I would most certainly become an artist. I think you should give all your time to it.' He looked up, lifted the top of his desk, and took out the portrait of Monsieur and Madame Lawrance Potter Dreyspool. 'As your first client, I would like to order four of these from you,' he said. 'Nicely done, like this one, but on good paper. If possible with some colour—green and blue and purple. And don't forget Monsieur's nose—the strawberry effect, the little blue veins—or the bags under the eyes. That will be very nice. A souvenir for my colleagues in London, Paris, Nice, and one for the maître d'hôtel on the *Mauretania*. You can have the rest of the day off to start on them.'

THE GENTLEMAN FROM PARIS

BY JOHN DICKSON CARR

Hitherto unpublished

THE GENTLEMAN FROM PARIS

Carlton House Hotel,
Broadway, New York,
14 April 1849

My dear brother:

Were my hand more steady, Maurice, or my soul less agitated, I should have written to you before this. *All is safe*: so much I tell you at once. For the rest, I seek sleep in vain; and this is not merely because I find myself a stranger and a foreigner in New York. Listen and judge.

We discussed, I think, the humiliation that a Frenchman must go to England ere he could take passage in a reliable ship for America. The *Britannia* steam-packet departed from Liverpool on the second of the month, and arrived here on the seventeenth. Do not smile, I implore you, when I tell you that my first visit on American soil was to Platt's Saloon, under Wallack's Theatre.

Great God, that voyage!

On my stomach I could hold not even champagne. For one of my height and breadth I was as weak as a child.

'Be good enough,' I said to a fur-capped coachman, when I had struggled through the horde of Irish immigrants, 'to drive me to some fashionable place of refreshment.'

The coachman had no difficulty in understanding my English, which pleased me. And how extraordinary are these 'saloons'!

The saloon of M. Platt was loud with the thump of hammers cracking ice, which is delivered in large blocks. Though the hand-coloured gas-globes, and the rose-paintings on the front of the bar-counter, were as fine as we could see at the Three Provincial Brothers in Paris, yet I confess that the place did not smell so agreeably. A number of gentlemen, wearing hats perhaps a trifle taller than is fashionable at home, lounged at the bar-counter and shouted. I attracted no attention until I called for a sherry cobbler.

One of the 'bartenders', as they are called in New York, gave me a sharp glance as he prepared the glass.

'Just arrived from the Old Country, I bet?' he said in no unfriendly tone.

Though it seemed strange to hear France mentioned in this way, I smiled and bowed assent.

'Italian, maybe?' said he.

This bartender, of course, could not know how deadly was the insult.

'Sir,' I replied, 'I am a Frenchman.'

And now in truth he was pleased! His fat face opened and smiled like a distorted, gold-toothed flower.

'Is that so, now!' he exclaimed. 'And what might your name be? Unless' —and here his face darkened with that sudden defensiveness and suspicion which, for no reason I can discern, will often strike into American hearts— 'unless,' said he, 'you don't want to give it?'

'Not at all,' I assured him earnestly. 'I am Armand de Lafayette, at your service.'

My dear brother, what an extraordinary effect!

It was silence. All sounds, even the faint whistling of the gas-jets, seemed to die away in that stone-flagged room. Every man along the line of the bar was looking at me. I was conscious only of faces, mostly with whiskers under the chin instead of down the cheek-bones, turned on me in basilisk stare.

'Well, well, well!' almost sneered the bartender. 'You wouldn't be no relation of the *Marquis* de Lafayette, would you?'

It was my turn to be astonished. Though our father has always forbidden us to mention the name of our late uncle, due to his republican sympathies, yet I knew he occupied small place in the history of France and it puzzled me to comprehend how these people had heard of him.

'The late Marquis de Lafayette,' I was obliged to admit, 'was my uncle.'

'You better be careful, young feller,' suddenly yelled a grimy little man with a pistol buckled under his long coat. 'We don't like being diddled, we don't.'

'Sir,' I replied, taking my bundle of papers from my pocket and whacking them down on the bar-counter, 'have the goodness to examine my credentials. Should you still doubt my identity, we can then debate the matter in any way which pleases you.'

'This is furrin writing,' shouted the bartender. '*I* can't read it!'

And then—how sweet was the musical sound on my ear!—I heard a voice addressing me in my own language.

'Perhaps, sir,' said the voice, in excellent French and with great stateliness, 'I may be able to render you some small service.'

The newcomer, a slight man of dark complexion, drawn up under an old shabby cloak of military cut, stood a little way behind me. If I had met him on the boulevards, I might not have found him very prepossessing. He had a wild and wandering eye, with an even wilder shimmer of brandy. He was not very steady on his feet. And yet, Maurice, his manner! It was such that I instinctively raised my hat, and the stranger very gravely did the same.

'And to whom,' said I, 'have I the honour . . . ?'

'I am Thaddeus Perley, sir, at your service.'

'Another furriner!' said the grimy little man, in disgust.

'I am indeed a foreigner,' said M. Perley in English, with an accent like a knife. 'A foreigner to this dram-shop. A foreigner to this neighbourhood. A foreigner to——' Here he paused, and his eyes acquired an almost frightening blaze of loathing. 'Yet I never heard that the reading of French was so *very* singular an accomplishment.'

Imperiously—and yet, it seemed to me, with a certain shrinking nervousness—M. Perley came closer and lifted the bundle of papers.

'Doubtless,' he said loftily, 'I should not be credited were I to translate these. But here,' and he scanned several of the papers, 'is a letter of introduction in English. It is addressed to President Zachary Taylor from the American minister at Paris.'

Again, my brother, what an enormous silence! It was interrupted by a cry from the bartender, who had snatched the documents from M. Perley.

'Boys, this is no diddle,' said he. 'This gent is the real thing!'

'He ain't!' thundered the little grimy man, with incredulity.

'He is!' said the bartender. 'I'll be a son of a roe (*i.e.*, *biche*) if he ain't!'

Well, Maurice, you and I have seen how Paris mobs can change. Americans are even more emotional. In the wink of an eye hostility became frantic affection. My back was slapped, my hand wrung, my person jammed against the bar by a crowd fighting to order me more refreshment.

The name of Lafayette, again and again, rose like a holy diapason. In vain I asked why this should be so. They appeared to think I was joking, and roared with laughter. I thought of M. Thaddeus Perley, as one who could supply an explanation.

But in the first rush towards me M. Perley had been flung backwards. He fell sprawling in some wet stains of tobacco-juice on the floor, and now I could not see him at all. For myself, I was weak from lack of food. A full beaker of whisky, which I was obliged to drink because all eyes were on me, made my head reel. Yet I felt compelled to raise my voice above the clamour.

'Gentlemen,' I implored them, 'will you hear me?'

'Silence for Lafayette!' said a big but very old man, with faded red whiskers. He had tears in his eyes, and he had been humming a catch called *Yankee Doodle*. 'Silence for Lafayette!'

'Believe me,' said I, 'I am full of gratitude for your hospitality. But I have business in New York, business of immediate and desperate urgency. If you will allow me to pay my reckoning . . .'

'Your money's no good here, monseer,' said the bartender. 'You're going to get liquored-up good and proper.'

'But I have no wish, believe me, to become liquored up! It might well endanger my mission! In effect, I wish to go!'

'Wait a minute,' said the little grimy man, with a cunning look. 'What *is* this here business?'

You, Maurice, have called me quixotic. I deny this. You have also called me imprudent. Perhaps you are right; but what choice was left to me?

'Has any gentleman here,' I asked, 'heard of Madame Thevenet? Madame Thevenet, who lives at number 23 Thomas Street, near Hudson Street?'

I had not, of course, expected an affirmative reply. Yet, in addition to one or two sniggers at mention of the street, several nodded their heads.

'Old miser woman?' asked a sportif character, who wore chequered trousers.

'I regret, sir, that you correctly describe her. Madame Thevenet is very rich. And I have come here,' cried I, 'to put right a damnable injustice!'

Struggle as I might, I could not free myself.

'How's that?' asked half a dozen.

'Madame Thevenet's daughter, Mademoiselle Claudine, lives in the worst of poverty at Paris. Madame herself has been brought here, under some spell, by a devil of a woman calling herself . . . Gentlemen, I implore you!'

'And I bet you,' cried the little grimy man with the pistol, 'you're sweet on this daughter what's-her-name?' He seemed delighted. 'Ain't you, now?'

How, I ask of all Providence, could these people have surprised my secret? Yet I felt obliged to tell the truth.

'I will not conceal from you,' I said, 'that I have in truth a high regard for Mlle. Claudine. But this lady, believe me, is engaged to a friend of mine, an officer of artillery.'

'Then what do you *get* out of it? Eh?' asked the grimy little man, with another cunning look.

The question puzzled me. I could not reply. But the bartender with the gold teeth leaned over.

'If you want to see the old Frenchie alive, monseer,' said he, 'you'd better git.' (*Sic*, Maurice.) 'I hearn tell she had a stroke this morning.'

But a dozen voices clamoured to keep me there, though this last intelligence sent me into despair. Then up rose the big and very old man with the faded whiskers: indeed, I had never realized how old, because he seemed so hale.

'Which of you was with Washington?' said he, suddenly taking hold of the fierce little man's neckcloth, and speaking with contempt. 'Make way for the nephew of Lafayette!'

They cheered me then, Maurice. They hurried me to the door, they begged me to return, they promised they would await me. One glance I sought— nor can I say why—for M. Thaddeus Perley. He was sitting at a table by a pillar, under an open gas-jet; his face whiter than ever, still wiping stains of tobacco-juice from his cloak.

Never have I seen a more mournful prospect than Thomas Street, when my cab set me down there. Perhaps it was my state of mind; for if Mme. Thevenet had died without a sou left to her daughter: you conceive it?

The houses of Thomas Street were faced with dingy yellow brick, and a muddy sky hung over the chimney-pots. It had been warm all day, yet I found my spirit intolerably oppressed. Though heaven knows our Parisian streets are dirty enough, we do not allow pigs in them. Except for these, nothing moved in the forsaken street save a blind street-musician, with his dog and an instrument called a banjo; but even he was silent too.

For some minutes, it seemed to me, I plied the knocker at number 23, with hideous noise. Nothing stirred. Finally, one part of the door swung open a little, as for an eye. Whereupon I heard the shifting of a floor-bolt, and both doors were swung open.

Need I say that facing me stood the woman whom we have agreed to call Mademoiselle Jezebel?

She said to me: 'And then, M. Armand?'

'Madame Thevenet!' cried I. 'She is still alive?'

'She is alive,' replied my companion, looking up at me from under the lids of her greenish eyes. 'But she is completely paralysed.'

I have never denied, Maurice, that Mlle. Jezebel has a certain attractiveness. She is not old or even middle-aged. Were it not that her complexion is as muddy as was the sky above us then, she would have been pretty.

'And as for Claudine,' I said to her, 'the daughter of madame——'

'You have come too late, M. Armand.'

And well I remember that at this moment there rose up, in the mournful street outside, the tinkle of the banjo played by the street-musician. It moved closer, playing a popular catch whose words run something thus:

> 'Oh, I come from Alabama
>   With my banjo on my knee;
> I depart for Louisiana
>   My Susannah for to see.'

Across the lips of mademoiselle flashed a smile of peculiar quality, like a razor-cut before the blood comes.

'Gold,' she whispered. 'Ninety thousand persons, one hears, have gone to seek it. Go to California, M. Armand. It is the only place you will find gold.'

This tune, they say, is a merry tune. It did not seem so, as the dreary twanging faded away. Mlle. Jezebel, with her muddy blonde hair parted in the middle and drawn over her ears after the best fashion, faced me implacably. Her greenish eyes were wide open. Her old brown taffeta dress, full at the bust, narrow at the waist, rustled its wide skirts as she glided a step forward.

'Have the kindness,' I said, 'to stand aside. I wish to enter.'

Hitherto in my life I had seen her docile and meek.

'You are no relative,' she said. 'I will not allow you to enter.'

'In that case, I regret, I must.'

'If you had ever spoken one kind word to *me*,' whispered mademoiselle, looking up from under her eyelids, and with her breast heaving, 'one gesture of love—that is to say, of affection—you might have shared five million francs.'

'Stand aside, I say!'

'As it is, you prefer a doll-faced consumptive at Paris. So be it!'

I was raging, Maurice; I confess it; yet I drew myself up with coldness.

'You refer, perhaps to Claudine Thevenet?'

'And to whom else?'

'I might remind you, mademoiselle, that the lady is pledged to my good friend Lieutenant Delage. I have forgotten her.'

'Have you?' asked our Jezebel, with her eyes on my face and a strange hungry look in them. Mlle Jezebel added, with more pleasure: 'Well, she will die. Unless you can solve a mystery.'

'A mystery?'

'I should not have said mystery, M. Armand. Because it is impossible of all solution. It is an Act of God!'

Up to this time the glass-fronted doors of the vestibule had stood open behind her, against a darkness of closed shutters in the house. There breathed out of it an odour of unswept carpets, a sourness of stale living. Someone was approaching, carrying a lighted candle.

'Who speaks?' called a man's voice; shaky, but as French as Mlle. Jezebel's. 'Who speaks concerning an Act of God?'

I stepped across the threshold. Mademoiselle, who never left my side, immediately closed and locked the front doors. As the candle-glimmer moved still closer in gloom, I could have shouted for joy to see the man who (as I correctly guessed) I had come to meet.

'You are M. Duroc, the lawyer!' I said. 'You are my brother's friend!'

M. Duroc held the candle higher, to inspect me.

He was a big, heavy man who seemed to sag in all his flesh. In compensation for his bald head, the greyish-brown moustache flowed down and parted into two hairy fans of beard on either side of his chin. He looked at me through oval gold-rimmed spectacles; in a friendly way, but yet frightened. His voice was deep and gruff, clipping the syllables, despite his fright.

'And you'—*clip-clip*; the candle-holder trembled—'you are Armand de Lafayette. I had expected you by the steam-packet to-day. Well! You are here. On a fool's errand, I regret.'

'But why?' (And I shouted at him, Maurice.)

I looked at mademoiselle, who was faintly smiling.

'M. Duroc!' I protested. 'You wrote to my brother. You said you had persuaded madame to repent of her harshness towards her daughter!'

'Was that your duty?' asked the Jezebel, looking full at M. Duroc with her greenish eyes. 'Was that your right?'

'I am a man of law,' said M. Duroc. The deep monosyllables rapped, in ghostly bursts, through his parted beard. He was perspiring. 'I am correct. Very correct! And yet——'

'Who nursed her?' asked the Jezebel. 'Who soothed her, fed her, wore her filthy clothes, calmed her tempers and endured her interminable abuse? I did!'

And yet, all the time she was speaking, this woman kept sidling and sliding against me, brushing my side, as though she would make sure of my presence there.

'Well!' said the lawyer. 'It matters little now! This mystery . . .'

You may well believe that all these cryptic remarks, as well as reference to a mystery or an Act of God, had driven me almost frantic. I demanded to know what he meant.

'Last night,' said M. Duroc, 'a certain article disappeared.'

'Well, well?'

'It disappeared,' said M. Duroc, drawn up like a grenadier. 'But it could not conceivably have disappeared. I myself swear this! Our only suggestions as to how it might have disappeared are a toy rabbit and a barometer.'

'Sir,' I said, 'I do not wish to be discourteous. But——'

'Am I mad, you ask?'

I bowed. If any man can manage at once to look sagging and uncertain, yet stately and dignified, M. Duroc managed it then. And dignity won, I think.

'Sir,' he replied, gesturing the candle towards the rear of the house, 'Madame Thevenet lies there in her bed. She is paralysed. She can move only her eyes or partially the lips, without speech. Do you wish to see her?'

'If I am permitted.'

'Yes. That would be correct. Accompany me.'

And I saw the poor old woman, Maurice. Call her harridan if you like.

It was a square room of good size, whose shutters had remained closed and locked for years. Can one smell rust? In that room, with faded green wallpaper, I felt I could.

One solitary candle did little more than dispel shadow. It burned atop the mantelpiece well opposite the foot of the bed; and a shaggy man, whom I afterwards learned to be a police-officer, sat in a green-upholstered armchair by an unlighted coal fire in the fireplace grate, picking his teeth with a knife.

'If you please, Dr. Harding!' M. Duroc called softly in English.

The long and lean American doctor, who had been bending over the bed so as to conceal from our sight the head and shoulders of Madame Thevenet, turned round. But this cadaverous body—in such fashion were madame's head and shoulders propped up against pillows—his cadaverous body, I say, still concealed her face.

'Has there been any change?' persisted M. Duroc in English.

'There has been no change,' replied the dark-complexioned Dr. Harding, 'except for the worse.'

'Do you want her to be moved?'

'There has never been any necessity,' said the physician, picking up his beaver hat from the bed. He spoke dryly. 'However, if you want to learn anything more about the toy rabbit or the barometer, I should hurry. The lady will die in a matter of hours, probably less.'

And he stood to one side.

It was a heavy bed with four posts and a canopy. The bed-curtains, of some dullish-green material, were closely drawn on every side except the long side by which we saw Madame Thevenet in profile. Lean as a post, rigid, the strings of her cotton nightcap tightly tied under her chin, Madame Thevenet lay propped up there. But one eye rolled towards us, and it rolled horribly.

Up to this time the woman we call the Jezebel had said little. She chose this moment again to come brushing against my side. Her greenish eyes, lids half-closed, shone in the light of M. Duroc's candle. What she whispered was: 'You don't really hate me, do you?'

Maurice, I make a pause here.

Since I wrote the sentence, I put down my pen, and pressed my hands over my eyes, and once more I thought. But let me try again.

I spent just two hours in the bedroom of Madame Thevenet. At the end of the time—oh, you shall hear why!—I rushed out of that bedroom, and out of number 23 Thomas Street, like the maniac I was.

The streets were full of people, of carriages, of omnibuses, at early evening. Knowing no place of refuge save the saloon from which I had come, I gave its address to a cab-driver. Since still I had swallowed no food, I may have been light-headed. Yet I wished to pour out my heart to the friends who had bidden me return there. And where were they now?

A new group, all new, lounged against the bar-counter under brighter gaslight and brighter paint. Of all those who smote me on the back and cheered, none remained save the ancient giant who had implied friendship with General Washington. *He*, alas, lay helplessly drunk with his head near a sawdust spitting-box. Nevertheless I was so moved that I took the liberty of thrusting a handful of bank-notes into his pocket. He alone remained.

Wait, there was another!

I do not believe he had remained there because of me. Yet M. Thaddeus Perley, still sitting alone at the little table by the pillar, with the open gas-jet above, stared vacantly at the empty glass in his hand.

He had named himself a foreigner; he was probably French. That was as well. For, as I lurched against the table, I was befuddled and all English had fled my wits.

'Sir,' said I, 'will you permit a madman to share your table?'

M. Perley gave a great start, as though roused out of thought. He was now sober: this I saw. Indeed, his shiver and haggard face were due to lack of stimulant rather than too much of it.

'Sir,' he stammered, getting to his feet, 'I shall be—I shall be honoured by your company.' Automatically he opened his mouth to call for a waiter; his hand went to his pocket; he stopped.

'No, no, no!' said I. 'If you insist, M. Perley, you may pay for the second bottle. The first is mine. I am sick at heart, and I would speak with a gentleman.'

At these last words M. Perley's whole expression changed. He sat down, and gave me a grave courtly nod. His eyes, which were his most expressive feature, studied my face and my disarray.

'You are ill, M. de Lafayette,' he said. 'Have you so soon come to grief in this—this *civilized* country?'

'I have come to grief, yes. But not through civilization or the lack of it.' And I banged my fist on the table. 'I have come to grief, M. Perley, through miracles or magic. I have come to grief with a problem which no man's ingenuity can solve!'

M. Perley looked at me in a strange way. But someone had brought a bottle of brandy, with its accessories. M. Perley's trembling hand slopped a generous allowance into my glass, and an even more generous one into his own.

'That is very curious,' he remarked, eyeing the glass. 'A murder, was it?'

'No. But a valuable document has disappeared. The most thorough search by the police cannot find it.'

Touch him anywhere, and he flinched. M. Perley, for some extraordinary reason, appeared to think I was mocking him.

'A document, you say?' His laugh was a trifle unearthly. 'Come, now. Was it by any chance—a letter?'

'No, no! It was a will. Three large sheets of parchment, of the size you call foolscap. Listen!'

And as M. Perley added water to his brandy and gulped down about a third of it, I leaned across the table.

'Madame Thevenet, of whom you may have heard me speak in this café, was an invalid. But (until the early hours of this morning) she was not bed-ridden. She could move, and walk about her room, and so on. She had been lured away from Paris and her family by a green-eyed woman named the Jezebel.

'But a kindly lawyer of this city, M. Duroc, believed that madame suffered and had a bad conscience about her own daughter. Last night, despite the Jezebel, he persuaded madame at last to sign a will leaving all her money to this daughter.

'And the daughter, Claudine, is in mortal need of it! From my brother and myself, who have more than enough, she will not accept a sou. Her affianced, Lieutenant Delage, is as poor as she. But, unless she leaves France for Switzerland, she will die. I will not conceal from you that Claudine suffers from that dread disease we politely call consumption.'

M. Perley stopped with his glass again half-way to his mouth.

He believed me now; I sensed it. Yet under the dark hair, tumbled on his forehead, his face had gone as white as his neat, mended shirt-frill.

'So very little a thing is money!' he whispered. 'So very little a thing!' And he lifted the glass and drained it.

'You do not think I am mocking you, sir?'

'No, no!' says M. Perley, shading his eyes with one hand. 'I knew myself of one such case. She is dead. Pray continue.'

'Last night, I repeat, Madame Thevenet changed her mind. When M. Duroc paid his weekly evening visit with the news that I should arrive to-day, madame fairly chattered with eagerness and a kind of terror. Death was approaching, she said; she had a presentiment.'

As I spoke, Maurice, there returned to me the image of that shadowy, arsenic-green bedroom in the shuttered house; and what M. Duroc had told me.

'Madame,' I continued, 'cried out to M. Duroc that he must bolt the bedroom door. She feared the Jezebel, who lurked but said nothing. M. Duroc drew up to her bedside a portable writing-desk, with two good candles. For a long time madame spoke, pouring out contrition, self-abasement, the story of an unhappy marriage, all of which M. Duroc (sweating with embarrassment) was obliged to write down until it covered three large parchment sheets.

'But it was done, Mr. Perley!

'The will, in effect, left everything to her daughter, Claudine. It revoked a previous will by which all had been left (and this can be done in French law, as we both know) to Jezebel of the muddy complexion and the muddy yellow hair.

'Well, then! . . .

'M. Duroc sallies out into the street, where he finds two sober fellows who come in. Madame signs the will, M. Duroc sands it, and the two men from the street affix their signatures as witnesses. Then *they* are gone. M. Duroc folds the will lengthways, and prepares to put it into his carpet-bag. Now, M. Perley, mark what follows!

' "No, no no!' cries madame, with the shadow of her peaked nightcap wagging on the locked shutters beyond. "I wish to keep it—for this one night!"

' "For this one night, madame?" asks M. Duroc.

' "I wish to press it against my heart," says Madame Thevenet. "I wish to read it once, twice, a thousand times! M. Duroc, what time is it?'

'Whereupon he takes out his gold repeater, and opens it. To his astonishment it is one o'clock in the morning. Yet he touches the spring of the repeater, and its pulse-beat rings one.

' "M. Duroc," pleads Madame Thevenet, "remain here with me for the rest of the night!"

' "Madame!" cried M. Duroc, shocked to the very fans of his beard. "That would not be correct."

' "Yes, you are right," says madame. And never, swears the lawyer, has he seen her less bleary of eye, more alive with wit and cunning, more the great lady of ruin, than there in that green and shadowy and foul-smelling room.

'Yet this very fact puts her in more and more terror of the Jezebel, who is never seen. She points to M. Duroc's carpet-bag.

' "I think you have much work to do, dear sir?"

'M. Duroc groaned. "The Good Lord knows that I have!"

' "Outside the only door of this room," says Madame, "there is a small dressing-room. Set up your writing-desk beside the door there, so that no one may enter without your knowledge. Do your work there; you shall have a lamp or many candles. Do it," shrieks madame, "for the sake of Claudine and for the sake of an old friendship!"

'Very naturally, M. Duroc hesitated.

' "*She* will be hovering," pleads Madame Thevenet, pressing the will against her breast. "*This* I shall read and read and read, and sanctify with my tears. If I find I am falling asleep," and here the old lady looked cunning, "I shall hide it. But no matter! Even *she* cannot penetrate through locked shutters and a guarded door."

'Well, in fine, the lawyer at length yielded.

'He set up his writing-desk against the very doorpost outside that door. When he last saw madame, before closing the door, he saw her in profile with the green bed-curtains drawn except on that side, propped up with a tall candle burning on a table at her right hand.

'Ah, that night! I think I see M. Duroc at his writing-desk, as he has told me, in an airless dressing-room where no clock ticked. I see him, at times, removing his oval spectacles to press his smarting eyes. I see him returning to his legal papers, while his pen scratched through the wicked hours of the night.

'He heard nothing, or virtually nothing, until five o'clock in the morning. Then, which turned him cold and flabby, he heard a cry which he describes as being like that of a deaf-mute.

'The communicating door had not been bolted on Madame Thevenet's side, in case she needed help. M. Duroc rushed into the other room.

'On the table, at madame's right hand, the tall candle had burnt down to a flattish mass of wax over which still hovered a faint bluish flame. Madame herself lay rigid in her peaked nightcap. That revival of spirit last night, or remorse in her bitter heart, had brought on the last paralysis. Though M. Duroc tried to question her, she could move only her eyes.

'Then M. Duroc noticed that the will, which she had clutched as a doomed religious might clutch a crucifix, was not in her hand or on the bed.

' "Where is the will?" he shouted at her, as though she were deaf too. "Where is the will?"

'Madame Thevenet's eyes fixed on him. Then they moved down, and looked steadily at a trumpery toy—a rabbit, perhaps four inches high, made of pink velours or the like—which lay on the bed. Again she looked at M. Duroc, as though to emphasize this. Then her eyes rolled, this time with dreadful effort, towards a large barometer, shaped like a warming-pan, which hung on the wall beside the door. Three times she did this before the bluish candle-flame flickered and went out.'

And I, Armand de Lafayette, paused here in my recital to M. Perley.

Again I became aware that I was seated in a garish saloon, swilling brandy, amid loud talk that beat the air. There was a thumping noise from the theatre above our heads, and faint strains of music.

'The will,' I said, 'was not stolen. Not even the Jezebel could have melted through locked shutters or a guarded door. The will was not hidden, because no inch of the room remains unsearched. *Yet the will is gone!*'

I threw a glance across the table at M. Perley.

To me, I am sure, the brandy had given strength and steadied my nerves. With M. Perley I was not so sure. He was a little flushed. That slightly wild look, which I had observed before, had crept up especially into one eye, giving his whole face a somewhat lop-sided appearance. Yet all his self-confidence had returned. He gave me a little crooked smile.

I struck the table.

'Do you honour me with your attention, M. Perley?'

'What song the Syrens sang,' he said to me, 'or what name Achilles assumed when he hid himself among women, although puzzling questions, are not beyond *all* conjecture.'

'They are beyond *my* conjecture!' I cried. 'And so is this!'

M. Perley extended his hand, spread the fingers, and examined them as one who owns the universe.

'It is some little time,' he remarked, 'since I have concerned myself with these trifles.' His eyes retreated into a dream. 'Yet I have given some trifling aid, in the past, to the Prefect of the Parisian police.'

'You are a Frenchman! I knew it! And the police!' Seeing his lofty look, I added: 'As an amateur, understood?'

'Understood!' Then his delicate hand—it would be unjust to call it claw-like—shot across the table and fastened on my arm. The strange eyes burned towards my face. 'A little more detail!' he pleaded humbly. 'A little more, I beg of you! This woman, for instance, you call the Jezebel?'

'It was she who met me at the house.'

'And then?'

I described for him my meeting with the Jezebel, with M. Duroc, and our entrance to the sick-room, where the shaggy police-officer sat in the armchair and the saturnine doctor faced us from beside the bed.

'This woman,' I exclaimed, with the room vividly before my eyes as I described it, 'seems to have conceived for me (forgive me) a kind of passion. No doubt it was due to some idle compliments I once paid her at Paris.

'As I have explained, the Jezebel is *not* unattractive, even if she would only (again forgive me) wash her hair. Nevertheless, when once more she brushed my side and whispered, "You don't really hate me, do you?" I felt little less than horror. It seemed to me that in some fashion I was responsible for the whole tragedy.

'While we stood beside the bed, M. Duroc the lawyer poured out the story I have recounted. There lay the poor paralytic, and confirmed it with her eyes. The toy rabbit, a detestable pink colour, lay in its same position on the bed. Behind me, hung against the wall by the door, was the large barometer.

'Apparently for my benefit, Madame Thevenet again went through her dumb-show with imploring eyes. She would look at the rabbit; next (as M. Duroc had not mentioned), she would roll her eyes all round her, for some desperate yet impenetrable reason, before fixing her gaze on the barometer.

'It meant . . . what?

'The lawyer spoke then. "More light!" gulped out M. Duroc. "If you must have closed shutters and windows, then let us at least have more light!"

'The Jezebel glided out to fetch candles. During M. Duroc's explanation he had several times mentioned my name. At first mention of it the shaggy police-officer jumped and put away his clasp-knife. He beckoned to the physician, Dr. Harding, who went over for a whispered conference.

'Whereupon the police-officer sprang up.

' "Mr. Lafayette!" And he swung my hand pompously. "If I'd known it was you, Mr. Lafayette, I wouldn't 'a' sat there like a bump on a log."

' "You are an officer of police, sir," said I. "Can *you* think of no explanation?"

'He shook his head.

' "These people are Frenchies, Mr. Lafayette, and you're an American," he said, with somewhat conspicuous lack of logic. "*If* they're telling the truth——"

' "Let us assume that!"

' "I can't tell you where the old lady's will is," he stated positively. "But I can tell you where it ain't. It ain't hidden in this room!"

' "But surely . . . !" I began in despair.

'At this moment the Jezebel, her brown taffeta dress rustling, glided back into the room with a handful of candles and a tin box of the new-style Lucifer matches. She lighted several candles, sticking them on any surface in their own grease.

'There were one or two fine pieces of furniture; but the mottled-marble tops were chipped and stained, the gilt sides cracked. There were a few mirrors, creating mimic spectral life. I saw a little more clearly the faded green paper of the walls, and what I perceived to be the partly open door of a cupboard. The floor was of bare boards.

'All this while I was conscious of two pairs of eyes: the imploring gaze of Madame Thevenet, and the amorous gaze of the Jezebel. One or the other I could have endured, but both together seemed to suffocate me.

' "Mr. Duroc here," said the shaggy police-officer, clapping the distressed advocate on the shoulder, "sent a messenger in a cab at half-past five this morning. And what time did we get here? I ask you and I tell you! Six o'clock!"

'Then he shook his finger at me, in a kind of pride and fury of efficiency.

' "Why, Mr. Lafayette, there's been fourteen men at this room from six this morning until just before you got here!"

' "To search for Madame Thevenet's will, you mean?"

'The shaggy man nodded portentously, and folded his arms.

' "Floor's solid." He stamped on the bare boards. "Walls and ceiling? Nary a inch missed. We reckon we're remarkable smart; and we are."

' "But Madame Thevenet," I persisted, "was not a complete invalid until this morning. She could move about. If she became afraid of"—the name of the Jezebel choked me—"if she became afraid, and *did* hide the will . . ."

' "Where'd she hide it? Tell me!"

' "In the furniture, then?"

' "Cabinet-makers in, Mr. Lafayette. No secret compartments."

' "In one of the mirrors?"

' "Took the backs of 'em off. No will hid there."

' "Up the chimney!' I cried.

' "Sent a chimney-sweep up there," replied my companion in a ruminating way. Each time I guessed, he would leer at me in friendly and complacent challenge. "Ye-es, I reckon we're pretty smart. But we didn't find no will."

'The pink rabbit also seemed to leer from the bed. I saw madame's eyes. Once again, as a desperate mind will fasten on trifles, I observed the strings of the nightcap beneath her scrawny chin. But I looked again at the toy rabbit.

' "Has it occurred to you," I said triumphantly, "to examine the bed and bedstead of Madame Thevenet herself?"

'My shaggy friend went to her bedside.

' "Poor old woman," he said. He spoke as though she were already a corpse. Then he turned round. "We lifted her out, just as gentle as a new-born babe (didn't we, ma'am?). No hollow bedposts! Nothing in the canopy! Nothing in the frame or the feather-beds or the curtains or the bed-clothes!"

'Suddenly the shaggy police-officer became angry, as though he wished to be rid of the whole matter.

' "And it ain't in the toy rabbit," he said, "because you can see we slit it up, if you look close. And it ain't in that barometer there. It just—ain't here."

'There was a silence as heavy as the dusty, hot air of this room.

' "It is here," murmured M. Duroc in his gruff voice. "It must be here!"

'The Jezebel stood there meekly, with downcast eyes.

'And I, in my turn, confess that I lost my head. I stalked over to the barometer, and tapped it. Its needle, which already indicated, "Rain; cold", moved still further towards that point.

'I was not insane enough to hit it with my fist. But I crawled on the floor, in search of a secret hiding-place. I felt along the wall. The police-officer—who kept repeating that nobody must touch anything and he would take no responsibility until he went off duty at something o'clock—the police-officer I ignored.

'What at length gave me pause was the cupboard, already thoroughly searched. In the cupboard hung a few withered dresses and gowns, as though they had shrivelled with Madame Thevenet's body. But on the shelf of the cupboard . . .

'On the shelf stood a great number of perfume-bottles: even to-day, I fear, many of our countrymen think perfume a substitute for water and soap; and the state of madame's hands would have confirmed this. But, on the shelf, were a few dusty novels. There was a crumpled and begrimed copy of yesterday's New York Sun. This newspaper did not contain a will; but it did contain a black beetle, which ran out across my hand.

'In a disgust past describing, I flung down the beetle and stamped on it. I closed the cupboard door, acknowledging defeat. Madame Thevenet's will was gone. And at the same second, in that dim green room—still badly lighted, with only a few more candles—two voices cried out.

'One was my own voice:

' "*In God's name, where is it?*"

'The other was the deep voice of M. Duroc:

' "*Look at that woman! She knows!*"

'And he meant the Jezebel.

'M. Duroc, with his beard-fans a-tremble, was pointing to a mirror; a little blurred, as these mirrors were. Our Jezebel had been looking into the mirror, her back turned to us. Now she dodged, as at a stone thrown.

'With good poise our Jezebel writhed this movement into a curtsy, turning to face us. But not before I also had seen that smile—like a razor-cut before the blood comes—as well as full knowledge, mocking knowledge, shining out of wide-open eyes in the mirror.

' "You spoke to me, M. Duroc?" She murmured the reply, also in French.

' "Listen to me!" the lawyer said formally. "This will is *not* missing. It is in this room. You were not here last night. Something has made you guess. You know where it is."

' "Are you unable to find it?" asked the Jezebel in surprise.

' "Stand back, young man!" M. Duroc said to me. "I ask you something, mademoiselle, in the name of justice."

' "Ask!" said the Jezebel.

' "If Claudine Thevenet inherits the money to which she is entitled, you will be well paid; yes, overpaid! You know Claudine. You know that!"

' "I know it."

' "But if the new will be *not* found," said M. Duroc, again waving me back, "then you inherit everything. And Claudine will die. For it will be assumed——"

' "Yes!" said the Jezebel, with one hand pressed against her breast. "You yourself, M. Duroc, testify that all night a candle was burning at madame's bedside. Well! The poor woman, whom *I* loved and cherished, repented of her ingratitude towards me. She burnt this new will at the candle-flame; she crushed its ashes to powder and blew them away!"

' "Is that true?" cried M. Duroc.

' "They will assume it," smiled the Jezebel, "as you say." She looked at me. "And for you, M. Armand!"

'She glided closer. I can only say that I saw her eyes uncovered; or, if you wish to put it so, her soul and flesh together.

' "I would give you everything on earth," she said. "I will not give you the doll-face in Paris."

' "Listen to me!" I said to her, so agitated that I seized her shoulders. "You are out of your senses! You cannot give Claudine to me! She will marry another man!"

' "And do you think that matters to me," asked the Jezebel, with her green eyes full on mine, "as long as you still love her?"

'There was a small crash as someone dropped a knife on the floor.

'We three, I think, had completely forgotten that we were not alone. There were two spectators, although they did not comprehend our speech.

'The saturnine Dr. Harding now occupied the green armchair. His long thin legs, in tight black trousers with strap under the boot-instep, were crossed and looked spidery; his high beaver hat glimmered on his head. The police-officer, who was picking his teeth with a knife when I first saw him, had now dropped the knife when he tried to trim his nails.

'But both men sensed the atmosphere. Both were alert, feeling out with the tentacles of their nerves. The police-officer shouted at me.

' "What's this gabble?' he said. "What's a-gitting into your head?"

'Grotesquely, it was that word "head" which gave me my inspiration.

' "The nightcap!" I exclaimed in English.

' "What nightcap?"

'For the nightcap of Madame Thevenet had a peak; it was large; it was tightly tied under the chin; it might well conceal a flat-pressed document which—but you understand. The police-officer, dull-witted as he appeared, grasped the meaning in a flash. And how I wished I had never spoken! For the fellow meant well, but he was not gentle.

'As I raced round the curtained sides of the bed, the police-officer was holding a candle in one hand and tearing off Madame's nightcap with the other. He found no will there, no document at all; only straggly wisps of hair on a skull grown old before its time.

'Madame Thevenet had been a great lady, once. It must have been the last humiliation. Two tears overflowed her eyes and ran down her cheeks. She lay propped up there in a nearly sitting position; but something seemed to wrench inside her.

'And she closed her eyes forever. And the Jezebel laughed.

'That is the end of my story. That is why I rushed out of the house like a madman. The will has vanished as though by magic; or is it still there by magic? In any case, you find me at this table: grubby and dishevelled and much ashamed.'

For a little time after I had finished my narrative to M. Perley in the saloon it seemed to me that the bar-counter was a trifle quieter. But a faint stamping continued from the theatre above our heads. Then all was hushed, until a chorus rose to a tinkle of many banjos.

'Oh, I come from Alabama
With my banjo on my knee;
I depart for Louisiana . . .'

Enough! The song soon died away, and M. Thaddeus Perley did not even hear it.

M. Perley sat looking downwards into an empty glass, so that I could not see his face.

'Sir,' he remarked almost bitterly, 'you are a man of good heart. I am glad to be of service in a problem so trifling as this.'

'*Trifling!*'

His voice was a little husky, but not slurred. His hand slowly turned the glass round and round.

'Will you permit two questions?' asked M. Perley.

'Two questions? Ten thousand!'

'More than two will be unnecessary.' Still M. Perley did not look up. 'This toy rabbit, of which so much was made: I would know its exact position on the bed?'

'It was almost at the foot of the bed, and about the middle in a crossways direction.'

'Ah, so I had imagined. Were the three sheets of parchment, forming the will, written upon two sides or upon only one?'

'I had not told you, M. Perley. But M. Duroc said: upon one side only.' M. Perley raised his head.

His face was now flushed and distorted with drink, his eye grown wild. In his cups he was as proud as Satan, and as disdainful of others' intelligence; yet he spoke with dignity, and with careful clearness.

'It is ironic, M. de Lafayette, that I should tell you how to lay your hand on the missing will and the elusive money; since, upon my word, I have never been able to perform a like service for myself.' And he smiled, as at some secret joke. 'Perhaps,' he added, 'it is the very simplicity of the thing which puts you at fault.'

I could only look at him in bewilderment.

'Perhaps the mystery is a little *too* plain! A little *too* self-evident!'

'You mock me, sir! I will not . . .'

'Take me as I am,' said M. Perley, whacking the foot of the glass on the table, 'or leave me. Besides,' here his wandering eye encountered a list of steam-sailings pasted against the wall, 'I—I leave to-morrow by the *Parnassus* for England, and then for France.'

'I meant no offence, M. Perley! If you have knowledge, speak!'

'Madame Thevenet,' he said, carefully pouring himself some more brandy, 'hid the will in the middle of the night. Does it puzzle you that she took such precautions to hide the will? But the element of the outré must always betray itself. The Jezebel *must not* find that will! Yet Madame Thevenet trusted nobody—not even the worthy physician who attended her. If Madame were to die of a stroke, the police would be there and must soon, she was sure, discover her simple device. Even if she were paralysed, it would ensure the presence of other persons in the room to act as unwitting guards.

'Your cardinal error,' M. Perley continued dispassionately, 'was one of ratiocination. You tell me that Madame Thevenet, to give you a hint, looked fixedly at some point near the foot of the bed. Why do you assume that she was looking at the toy rabbit?'

'Because,' I replied hotly, 'the toy rabbit was the only object she could have looked at!'

'Pardon me; but it was *not*. You several times informed me that the bed-curtains were closely drawn together on three sides. They were drawn on all but the "long" side towards the door. Therefore the ideal reasoner, without having seen the room, may safely say that the curtains were drawn together at the foot of the bed?'

'Yes, true!'

'After looking fixedly at this point represented by the toy, Madame Thevenet then "rolls her eyes all round her"—in your phrase. May we assume that she wishes the curtains to be drawn back, so that she may see something *beyond* the bed?'

'It is—possible, yes!'

'It is more than possible, as I shall demonstrate. Let us direct our attention, briefly, to the incongruous phenomenon of the barometer on another wall. The barometer indicates, "Rain; cold".'

Here M. Perley's thin shoulders drew together under the old military cloak.

'Well,' he said, 'the cold is on its way. Yet this day, for April, has been warm outside and indoors, oppressively hot?'

'Yes! Of course!'

'You yourself,' continued M. Perley, inspecting his finger-nails, 'told me what was directly opposite the foot of the bed. Let us suppose that the bed-curtains are drawn open. Madame Thevenet, in her nearly seated position, is looking *downwards*. What would she have seen?'

'The fireplace!' I cried. 'The grate of the fireplace!'

'Already we have a link with the weather. And what, as you have specifically informed me, was in the grate of the fireplace?'

'An unlighted coal fire!'

'Exactly. And what is essential for the composition of such a fire? We need coal; we need wood; but primarily and above all, we need . . .'

'*Paper!*' I cried.

'In the cupboard of that room,' said M. Perley, with his disdainful little smile, 'was a very crumpled and begrimed (mark that; not dusty) copy of *yesterday's* New York *Sun*. To light fires is the most common, and indeed the best, use for our daily press. That copy had been used to build yesterday's fire. But something else, during the night, was substituted for it. You yourself remarked the extraordinarily dirty state of Madame Thevenet's hands.'

M. Perley swallowed the brandy, and his flush deepened.

'Sir,' he said loudly, 'you will find the will crumpled up, with ends most

30

obviously protruding, under the coal and wood in the fireplace grate. Even had anyone taken the fire to pieces, he would have found only what appeared to be dirty blank paper, written side undermost, which could never be a valuable will. It was too self-evident to be seen.—Now go!'

'Go?' I echoed stupidly.

M. Perley rose from his chair.

'Go, I say!' he shouted, with an even wilder eye. 'The Jezebel could not light that fire. It was too warm, for one thing; and all day there were police-officers with instructions that an outsider must touch nothing. But now? *Madame Thevenet kept warning you that the fire must not be lighted, or the will would be destroyed!*'

'Will you await me here?' I called over my shoulder.

'Yes, yes! And perhaps there will be peace for the wretched girl with—with the lung-trouble.'

Even as I ran out of the door I saw him, grotesque and pitiful, slump across the table. Hope, rising and surging, seemed to sweep me along like the crack of the cabman's whip. But when I reached my destination, hope receded.

The shaggy police-officer was just descending the front steps.

'None of us coming back here, Mr. Lafayette!' he called cheerily. 'Old Mrs. What's-her-name went and burnt that will at a candle last night.—Here, what's o'clock?'

The front door was unlocked. I raced through that dark house, and burst into the rear bedroom.

The corpse still lay in the big, gloomy bed. Every candle had flickered almost down to its socket. The police-officer's clasp-knife, forgotten since he had dropped it, still lay on bare boards. But the Jezebel was there.

She knelt on the hearth, with the tin box of Lucifer matches she had brought there earlier. The match spurted, a bluish fire; I saw her eagerness; she held the match to the grate.

'A Lucifer,' I said, 'in the hand of a Jezebel!'

And I struck her away from the grate, so that she reeled against a chair and fell. Large coals, small coals rattled down in puffs of dust as I plunged my hands into the unlighted fire. Little sticks, sawed sticks; and I found it there: crumpled parchment-sheets, but incontestably madame's will.

'M. Duroc!' I called. 'M. Duroc!'

You and I, my brother Maurice, have fought the Citizen-King with bayonets as we now fight the upstart Bonapartist; we need not be ashamed of tears. I confess, then, that the tears overran my eyes and blinded me. I scarcely saw M. Duroc as he hurried into the room.

Certainly I did not see the Jezebel stealthily pick up the police-officer's knife. I noticed nothing at all until she flew at me, and stabbed me in the back.

Peace, my brother: I have assured you all is well. At that time, faith, I was not much conscious of any hurt. I bade M. Duroc, who was trembling, to wrench out the knife; I borrowed his roomy greatcoat to hide the blood; I must hurry, hurry, hurry back to that little table under the gas-jet.

I planned it all on my way back. M. Perley, apparently a stranger in this country, disliked it and was evidently very poor even in France. But *we* are not precisely paupers. Even with his intense pride, he could not refuse (for such a service) a sum which would comfort him for the rest of his life.

Back I plunged into the saloon, and hurried down it. Then I stopped. The little round table by the pillar, under the flaring gas-jet, was empty.

How long I stood there I cannot tell. The back of my shirt, which at first had seemed full of blood, now stuck to the borrowed greatcoat. All of a sudden I caught sight of the fat-faced bartender with the gold teeth, who had been on service that afternoon and had returned now. As a mark of respect, he came out from behind the bar-counter to greet me.

'Where is the gentleman who was sitting at that table?'

I pointed to it. My voice, in truth, must have sounded so hoarse and strange that he mistook it for anger.

'Don't you worry about that, monseer!' said he reassuringly. '*That's* been tended to! We threw the drunken tramp out of here!'

'You threw . . .'

'Right bang in the gutter. Had to crawl along in it before he could stand up.' My bartender's face was pleased and vicious. 'Ordered a bottle of best brandy, and couldn't pay for it.' The face changed again. 'Goddelmighty, monseer, what's wrong?'

'*I* ordered that brandy.'

'*He* didn't say so, when the waiter brought me over. Just looked me up and down, crazy-like, and said a gentleman would give his I.O.U. Gentleman!'

'M. Perley,' I said, restraining an impulse to kill that bartender, 'is a friend of mine. He departs for France early to-morrow morning. Where is his hotel? Where can I find him?'

'Perley!' sneered my companion. 'That ain't even his real name, I hearn tell. Gits high-and-mighty ideas from upper Broadway. But his real name's on the I.O.U.'

A surge of hope, once more, almost blinded me. 'Did you keep that I.O.U.?'

'Yes, I kepp it,' growled the bartender, fishing in his pocket. 'God knows why, but I kepp it.'

And at last, Maurice, I triumphed!

True, I collapsed from my wound; and the fever would not let me remember that I must be at the dock when the *Parnassus* steam-packet departed from New York next morning. I must remain here, shut up in a hotel-room and unable to sleep at night, until I can take ship for home. But where I failed, you can succeed. He was to leave on the morrow by the *Parnassus* for England, and then for France—so he told me. You can find him—in six months at the most. In six months, I give you my word, he will be out of misery for ever!

'*I.O.U.*,' reads the little slip, '*for one bottle of your best brandy, forty-five cents. Signed: Edgar A. Poe.*'

I remain, Maurice,
Your affectionate brother,
Armand

PEARLS ARE A NUISANCE

BY RAYMOND CHANDLER

from *The Simple Art of Murder* (1950)

PEARLS ARE A NUISANCE

IT is quite true that I wasn't doing anything that morning except looking at a blank sheet of paper in my typewriter and thinking about writing a letter. It is also quite true that I don't have a great deal to do any morning. But that is no reason why I should have to go out hunting for old Mrs. Penruddock's pearl necklace. I don't happen to be a policeman.

It was Ellen Macintosh who called me up, which made a difference, of course. 'How are you, darling?' she asked. 'Busy?'

'Yes and no,' I said. 'Mostly no. I am very well. What is it now?'

'I don't think you love me, Walter. And anyway you ought to get some work to do. You have too much money. Somebody has stolen Mrs. Penruddock's pearls and I want you to find them.'

'Possibly you think you have the police department on the line,' I said coldly. 'This is the residence of Walter Gage. Mr. Gage talking.'

'Well, you can tell Mr. Gage from Miss Ellen Macintosh,' she said, 'that if he is not out here in half an hour, he will receive a small parcel by registered mail containing one diamond engagement ring.'

'And a lot of good it did me,' I said. 'That old crow will live for another fifty years.'

But she had already hung up so I put my hat on and went down and drove off in the Packard. It was a nice late April morning, if you care for that sort of thing. Mrs. Penruddock lived on a wide quiet street in Carondelet Park. The house had probably looked exactly the same for the last fifty years, but that didn't make me any better pleased that Ellen Macintosh might live in it another fifty years, unless old Mrs. Penruddock died and didn't need a nurse any more. Mr. Penruddock had died a few years before, leaving no will, a thoroughly tangled-up estate, and a list of pensioners as long as a star boarder's arm.

I rang the front doorbell and the door was opened, not very soon, by a little old woman with a maid's apron and a strangled knot of grey hair on the top of her head. She looked at me as if she had never seen me before and didn't want to see me now.

'Miss Ellen Macintosh, please,' I said. 'Mr. Walter Gage calling.'

She sniffed, turned without a word and we went back into the musty recesses of the house and came to a glassed-in porch full of wicker furniture and the smell of Egyptian tombs. She went away, with another sniff.

In a moment the door opened again and Ellen Macintosh came in. Maybe you don't like tall girls with honey-coloured hair and skin like the first strawberry peach the grocer sneaks out of the box for himself. If you don't, I'm sorry for you.

'Darling, so you did come,' she cried. 'That was nice of you, Walter. Now sit down and I'll tell you all about it.'

We sat down.

'Mrs. Penruddock's pearl necklace has been stolen, Walter.'

'You told me that over the telephone. My temperature is still normal.'

'If you will excuse a professional guess,' she said, 'it is probably subnormal —permanently. The pearls are a string of forty-nine matched pink ones which Mr. Penruddock gave to Mrs. Penruddock for her golden wedding present. She hardly ever wore them lately, except perhaps on Christmas or when she had a couple of very old friends in to dinner and was well enough to sit up. And every Thanksgiving she gives a dinner to all the pensioners and friends and old employees Mr. Penruddock left on her hands, and she wore them then.'

'You are getting your verb tenses a little mixed,' I said, 'but the general idea is clear. Go on.'

'Well, Walter,' Ellen said, with what some people call an arch look, 'the pearls have been stolen. Yes, I know that is the third time I told you that, but there's a strange mystery about it. They were kept in a leather case in an old safe which was open half the time and which I should judge a strong man could open with his fingers even when it was locked. I had to go there for a paper this morning and I looked in at the pearls just to say hello——'

'I hope your idea in hanging on to Mrs. Penruddock has not been that she might leave you that necklace,' I said stiffly. 'Pearls are all very well for old people and fat blondes, but for tall willowy——'

'Oh shut up, darling,' Ellen broke in, 'I should certainly not have been waiting for these pearls—because they were false.'

I swallowed hard and stared at her. 'Well,' I said, with a leer, 'I have heard that old Penruddock pulled some cross-eyed rabbits out of the hat occasionally, but giving his own wife a string of phoney pearls on her golden wedding gets my money.'

'Oh, don't be such a fool, Walter! They were real enough then. The fact is Mrs. Penruddock sold them and had imitations made. One of her old friends, Mr. Lansing Gallemore of the Gallemore Jewellery Company, handled it all for her very quietly, because of course she didn't want anyone to know. And that is why the police have not been called in. You will find them for her, won't you, Walter?'

'How? And what did she sell them for?'

'Because Mr. Penruddock died suddenly without making any provision for all these people he had been supporting. Then the depression came, and there was hardly any money at all. Only just enough to carry on the household and pay the servants, all of whom have been with Mrs. Penruddock so long that she would rather starve than let any of them go.'

'That's different,' I said. 'I take my hat off to her. But how the dickens am I going to find them, and what does it matter anyway—if they were false?'

'Well, the pearls—imitations, I mean—cost two hundred dollars and were specially made in Bohemia and it took several months and the way things are over there now she might never be able to get another set of really good imitations. And she is terrified somebody will find out they were false, or that the thief will blackmail her, when he finds out they were false. You see, darling, I know who stole them.'

I said, 'Huh?' a word I very seldom use as I do not think it part of the vocabulary of a gentleman.

'The chauffeur we had here a few months, Walter—a horrid big brute named Henry Eichelberger. He left suddenly the day before yesterday, for no reason at all. Nobody ever leaves Mrs. Penruddock. Her last chauffeur was a very old man and he died. But Henry Eichelberger left without a word and I'm sure he had stolen the pearls. He tried to kiss me once, Walter.'

'Oh, he did,' I said in a different voice. 'Tried to kiss you, eh? Where is this big slab of meat, darling? Have you any idea at all? It seems hardly likely he would be hanging around on the street corner for me to punch his nose for him.'

Ellen lowered her long silky eyelashes at me—and when she does that I go limp as a scrubwoman's back hair.

'He didn't run away. He must have known the pearls were false and that he was safe enough to blackmail Mrs. Penruddock. I called up the agency he came from and he has been back there and registered again for employment. But they said it was against their rules to give his address.'

'Why couldn't somebody else have taken the pearls? A burglar, for instance?'

'There is no one else. The servants are beyond suspicion and the house is locked up as tight as an icebox every night and there were no signs of anybody having broken in. Besides, Henry Eichelberger knew where the pearls were kept, because he saw me putting them away after the last time she wore them—which was when she had two very dear friends in to dinner on the occasion of the anniversary of Mr. Penruddock's death.'

'That must have been a pretty wild party,' I said, 'All right, I'll go down to the agency and make them give me his address. Where is it?'

'It is called the Ada Twomey Domestic Employment Agency, and it is in the two-hundred block on East Second, a very unpleasant neighbourhood.'

'Not half as unpleasant as my neighbourhood will be to Henry Eichelberger,' I said. 'So he tried to kiss you, eh?'

'The pearls, Walter,' Ellen said gently, 'are the important thing. I do hope
he hasn't already found out they are false and thrown them in the ocean.'

'If he has, I'll make him dive for them.'

'He is six feet three and very big and strong, Walter,' Ellen said coyly.
'But not handsome like you, of course.'

'Just my size,' I said. 'It will be a pleasure. Good-bye, darling.'

She took hold of my sleeve. 'There is just one thing, Walter I don't mind
a little fighting because it is manly. But you mustn't cause a disturbance that
would bring the police in, you know. And although you are very big and
strong and played right tackle at college, you are a little weak about one
thing. Will you promise me not to drink any whisky?'

'This Eichelberger,' I said, 'is all the drink I want.'

2

The Ada Twomey Domestic Employment Agency on East Second Street
proved to be all that the name and location implied. The odour of the ante-
room, in which I was compelled to wait for a short time, was not at all
pleasant. The agency was presided over by a hard-faced middle-aged woman
who said that Henry Eichelberger was registered with them for employment as a chauffeur, and that she could arrange to have him call upon me, or
could bring him there to the office for an interview. But when I placed a ten-
dollar bill on her desk and indicated that it was merely an earnest of good
faith, without prejudice to any commission which might become due to her
agency, she relented and gave me his address, which was out west on Santa
Monica Boulevard, near the part of the city which used to be called Sherman.

I drove out there without delay, for fear that Henry Eichelberger might
telephone in and be informed that I was coming. The address proved to be a
seedy hotel, conveniently close to the inter-urban car tracks and having its
entrance adjoining a Chinese laundry. The hotel was upstairs, the steps being
covered—in places—with strips of decayed rubber matting to which were
screwed irregular fragments of unpolished brass. The smell of the Chinese
laundry ceased about halfway up the stairs and was replaced by a smell of
kerosene, cigar butts, slept-in air and greasy paper bags. There was a register
at the head of the stairs on a wooden shelf. The last entry was in pencil, three
weeks previous as to date, and had been written by someone with a very
unsteady hand. I deduced from this that the management was not over-
particular.

There was a bell beside the book and a sign reading: MANAGER. I rang the
bell and waited. Presently a door opened down the hall and feet shuffled

towards me without haste. A man appeared wearing frayed leather slippers and trousers of a nameless colour, which had the two top buttons unlatched to permit more freedom to the suburbs of his extensive stomach. He also wore red suspenders, his shirt was darkened under the arms, and elsewhere, and his face badly needed a thorough laundering and trimming.

He said: 'Full up, bud', and sneered.

I said: 'I am not looking for a room, I am looking for one Eichelberger, who, I am informed, lives here, but who, I observe, has not registered in your book. And this, as of course you know, is contrary to the law.'

'A wise guy,' the fat man sneered again. 'Down the hall, bud. Two-eighteen.' He waved a thumb the colour and almost the size of a burnt baked potato.

'Have the kindness to show me the way,' I said.

'Geez, the lootenant-governor,' he said, and began to shake his stomach. His small eyes disappeared in folds of yellow fat. 'Okay, bud. Follow on.'

We went into the gloomy depths of the back hall and came to a wooden door at the end with a closed wooden transome above it. The fat man smote the door with a fat hand. Nothing happened.

'Out,' he said.

'Have the kindness to unlock the door,' I said. 'I wish to go in and wait for Eichelberger.'

'In a pig's valise,' the fat man said nastily. 'Who the hell you think you are, bum?'

This angered me. He was a fair-sized man, about six feet tall, but too full of the memories of beer. I looked up and down the dark hall. The place seemed utterly deserted.

I hit the fat man in the stomach.

He sat down on the floor and belched and his right kneecap came into sharp contact with his jaw. He coughed and tears welled up in his eyes.

'Cripes, bud,' he whined. 'You got twenty years on me. That ain't fair.'

'Open the door,' I said. 'I have no time to argue with you.'

'A buck,' he said, wiping his eyes on his shirt. 'Two bucks and no tip-off.'

I took two dollars out of my pocket and helped the man to his feet. He folded the two dollars and produced an ordinary pass-key which I could have purchased for five cents.

'Brother, you sock,' he said. 'Where you learn it? Most big guys are muscle-bound.' He unlocked the door.

'If you hear any noises later on,' I said, 'ignore them. If there is any damage, it will be paid for generously.'

He nodded and I went into the room. He locked the door behind me and his steps receded. There was silence.

The room was small, mean and tawdry. It contained a brown chest of drawers with a small mirror hanging over it, a straight wooden chair, a wooden rocking chair, a single bed of chipped enamel, with a much mended cotton counterpane. The curtains at the single window had fly marks on them and the green shade was without a slat at the bottom. There was a washbowl in the corner with two paper-thin towels hanging beside it. There was, of course, no bathroom, and there was no closet. A piece of dark figured material hanging from a shelf made a substitute for the latter. Behind this I found a grey business suit of the largest size made, which would be my size, if I wore ready-made clothes, which I do not. There was a pair of black brogues on the floor, size number twelve at least. There was also a cheap fibre suitcase, which of course I searched, as it was not locked.

I also searched the bureau and was surprised to find that everything in it was neat and clean and decent. But there was not much in it. Particularly there were no pearls in it. I searched in all other likely and unlikely places in the room but I found nothing of interest.

I sat on the side of the bed and lit a cigarette and waited. It was now apparent to me that Henry Eichelberger was either a very great fool or entirely innocent. The room and the open trail he had left behind him did not suggest a man dealing in operations like stealing pearl necklaces.

I had smoked four cigarettes, more than I usually smoke in an entire day, when approaching steps sounded. They were light quick steps but not at all clandestine. A key was thrust into the door and turned and the door swung carelessly open. A man stepped through it and looked at me.

I am six feet three inches in height and weigh over two hundred pounds. This man was tall, but he seemed lighter. He wore a blue serge suit of the kind which is called neat for lack of anything better to say about it. He had thick wiry blond hair, a neck like a Prussian corporal in a cartoon, very wide shoulders and large hard hands, and he had a face that had taken much battering in its time. His small greenish eyes glinted at me with what I then took to be evil humour. I saw at once that he was not a man to trifle with, but I was not afraid of him. I was his equal in size and strength, and, I had small doubt, his superior in intelligence.

I stood up off the bed calmly and said: 'I am looking for one Eichelberger.'

'How you get in here, bud?' It was a cheerful voice, rather heavy, but not unpleasant to the ear.

'The explanation of that can wait,' I said stiffly. 'I am looking for one Eichelberger. Are you he?'

'Haw,' the man said. 'A gut-buster. A comedian. Wait'll I loosen my belt.' He took a couple of steps farther into the room and I took the same number towards him.

'My name is Walter Gage,' I said. 'Are you Eichelberger?'

'Gimme a nickel,' he said, 'and I'll tell you.'

I ignored that. 'I am the fiancé of Miss Ellen Macintosh,' I told him coldly. 'I am informed that you tried to kiss her.'

He took another step towards me and I another towards him. 'Whaddaya mean—tried?' he sneered.

I led sharply with my right and it landed flush on his chin. It seemed to me a good solid punch, but it scarcely moved him. I then put two hard left jabs into his neck and landed a second hard right at the side of his rather wide nose. He snorted and hit me in the solar plexus.

I bent over and took hold of the room with both hands and spun it. When I had it nicely spinning I gave it a full swing and hit myself on the back of the head with the floor. This made me lose my balance temporarily and while I was thinking about how to regain it a wet towel began to slap at my face and I opened my eyes. The face of Henry Eichelberger was close to mine and bore a certain appearance of solicitude.

'Bud,' his voice said, 'your stomach is as weak as a Chinaman's tea.'

'Brandy!' I croaked. 'What happened?'

'You tripped on a little bitty tear in the carpet, bud. You really got to have liquor?'

'Brandy,' I croaked again, and closed my eyes.

'I hope it don't get me started,' his voice said.

A door opened and closed. I lay motionless and tried to avoid being sick at my stomach. The time passed slowly, in a long grey veil. Then the door of the room opened and closed once more and a moment later something hard was being pressed against my lips. I opened my mouth and liquor poured down my throat. I coughed, but the fiery liquid coursed through my veins and strengthened me at once. I sat up.

'Thank you, Henry,' I said. 'May I call you Henry?'

'No tax on it, bud.'

I got to my feet and stood before him. He stared at me curiously. 'You look okay,' he said. 'Why'n't you told me you was sick?'

'Damn you, Eichelberger!' I said and hit with all my strength on the side of his jaw. He shook his head and his eyes seemed annoyed. I delivered three more punches to his face and jaw while he was still shaking his head.

'So you wanta play for keeps!' he yelled and took hold of the bed and threw it at me.

I dodged the corner of the bed, but in doing so I moved a little too quickly and lost my balance and pushed my head about four inches in the baseboard under the window.

A wet towel began to slap at my face. I opened my eyes.

'Listen, kid. You got two strikes and no balls on you. Maybe you oughta try a lighter bat.'

'Brandy,' I croaked.

'You'll take rye,' He pressed a glass against my lips and I drank thirstily. Then I climbed to my feet again.

The bed, to my astonishment, had not moved. I sat down on it and Henry
Eichelberger sat down beside me and patted my shoulder.

'You and me could get along,' he said. 'I never kissed your girl, although I
ain't saying I wouldn't like to. Is that all is worrying at you?'

He poured himself half a waterglassful of the whisky out of the pint bottle
which he had gone out to buy. He swallowed the liquor thoughtfully.

'No, there is another matter,' I said.

'Shoot. But no more haymakers. Promise?'

I promised him rather reluctantly. 'Why did you leave the employ of Mrs.
Penruddock?' I asked him.

He looked at me from under his shaggy blond eyebrows. Then he looked
at the bottle he was holding in his hand. 'Would you call me a looker?' he
asked.

'Well, Henry——'

'Don't pansy up on me,' he snarled.

'No, Henry, I should not call you very handsome. But unquestionably you
are virile.'

He poured another half-waterglassful of whisky and handed it to me.
'Your turn,' he said. I drank it down without fully realizing what I was doing.
When I had stopped coughing Henry took the glass out of my hand and
refilled it. He took his own drink moodily. The bottle was now nearly
empty.

'Suppose you fell for a dame with all the looks this side of heaven. With
a map like mine. A guy like me, a guy from the stockyards that played himself a lot of very tough left end at a cow college and left his looks and education on the scoreboard. A guy that has fought everything but whales and
freight hogs—engines to you—and licked em' all, but naturally had to take a
sock now and then. Then I get a job where I see this lovely all the time and
every day and know it's no dice. What would do you, pal? Me, I just quit
the job.'

'Henry, I'd like to shake your hand,' I said.

He shook hands with me listlessly. 'So I ask for my time,' he said. 'What
else would I do?' He held the bottle up and looked at it against the light. 'Bo,
you made an error when you had me get this. When I start drinking it's a
world cruise. You got plenty dough?'

'Certainly,' I said. 'If whisky is what you want, Henry, whisky is what you
shall have. I have a very nice apartment on Franklin Avenue in Hollywood
and while I cast no aspersions on your own humble and of course quite
temporary abode, I now suggest we repair to my apartment, which is a good
deal larger and gives one more room to extend one's elbow.' I waved my
hand airily.

'Say, you're drunk,' Henry said, with admiration in his small green eyes.

'I am not yet drunk, Henry, although I do in fact feel the effect of that whisky and very pleasantly. You must not mind my way of talking which is a personal matter, like your own clipped and concise method of speech. But before we depart there is one other rather insignificant detail I wish to discuss with you. I am empowered to arrange for the return of Mrs. Penruddock's pearls. I understand there is some possibility that you may have stolen them.'

'Son, you take some awful chances,' Henry said softly.

'This is a business matter, Henry, and plain talk is the best way to settle it. The pearls are only false pearls, so we should very easily be able to come to an agreement. I mean you no ill will, Henry, and I am obliged to you for procuring the whisky, but business is business. Will you take fifty dollars and return the pearls and no questions asked?'

Henry laughed shortly and mirthlessly, but he seemed to have no animosity in his voice when he said: 'So you think I stole some marbles and am sitting around here waiting for a flock of dicks to swarm me?'

'No police have been told, Henry, and you may not have known the pearls were false. Pass the liquor, Henry.'

He poured me most of what was left in the bottle, and I drank it down with the greatest good humour. I threw the glass at the mirror, but unfortunately missed. The glass, which was of heavy and cheap construction, fell on the floor and did not break. Henry Eichelberger laughed heartily.

'What are you laughing at, Henry?'

'Nothing,' he said. 'I was just thinking what a sucker some guy is finding out he is—about them marbles.'

'You mean you did not steal the pearls, Henry?'

He laughed again, a little gloomily. 'Yeah,' he said, 'meaning no. I oughta sock you, but what the hell? Any guy can get a bum idea. No, I didn't steal no pearls, bud. If they was ringers, I wouldn't be bothered, and if they was what they looked like the one time I saw them on the old lady's neck, I wouldn't decidedly be holed up in no cheap flop in L.A. waiting for a couple carloads of johns to put the sneeze on me.'

I reached for his hand again and shook it.

'That is all I required to know,' I said happily. 'Now, I am at peace. We shall now go to my apartment and consider ways and means to recover these pearls. You and I together should make a team that can conquer any opposition, Henry.'

'You ain't kidding me, huh?'

I stood up and put my hat on—upside down. 'No, Henry, I am making you an offer of employment which I understand you need, and all the whisky you can drink. Let us go. Can you drive a car in your condition?'

'Hell, I ain't drunk,' Henry said, looking surprised.

We left the room and walked down the dark hallway. The fat manager very suddenly appeared from some nebulous shade and stood in front of us rubbing his stomach and looking at me with small greedy expectant eyes. 'Everything oke?' he inquired, chewing on a time-darkened toothpick.

'Give him a buck,' Henry said.

'What for, Henry?'

'Oh, I dunno. Just give him a buck.'

I withdrew a dollar bill from my pocket and gave it to the fat man.

'Thanks, pal,' Henry said. He chucked the fat man under the Adam's apple, and removed the dollar bill deftly from between his fingers. 'That pays for the hooch,' he added. 'I hate to have to bum dough.'

We went down the stairs arm in arm, leaving the manager trying to cough the toothpick up from his œsophagus.

3

At five o'clock that afternoon I awoke from slumber and found that I was lying on my bed in my apartment in the Chateau Moraine, on Franklin Avenue near Ivar Street, in Hollywood. I turned my head, which ached, and saw that Henry Eichelberger was lying beside me in his undershirt and trousers. I then perceived that I also was as lightly attired. On the table near by there stood an almost full bottle of Old Plantation rye whisky, the full quart size, and on the floor lay an entirely empty bottle of the same excellent brand. There were garments lying here and there on the floor, and a cigarette had burned a hole in the brocaded arm of one of my easy chairs.

I felt myself over carefully. My stomach was stiff and sore and my jaw seemed a little swollen on one side. Otherwise I was none the worse for wear. A sharp pain darted through my temples as I stood up off the bed, but I ignored it and walked steadily to the bottle on the table and raised it to my lips. After a steady draught of the fiery liquid I suddenly felt much better. A hearty and cheerful mood came over me and I was ready for any adventure. I went back to the bed and shook Henry firmly by the shoulder.

'Wake up, Henry,' I said. 'The sunset hour is nigh. The robins are calling and the squirrels are scolding and the morning glories furl themselves in sleep.'

Like all men of action Henry Eichelberger came awake with his fist doubled. 'What was that crack?' he snarled. 'Oh, yeah. Hi, Walter. How you feel?'

'I feel splendid. Are you rested?'

'Sure.' He swung his shoeless feet to the floor and rumpled his thick blond hair with his fingers. 'We was going swell until you passed out,' he said. 'So I had me a nap. I never drink solo. You okay?'

'Yes, Henry, I feel very well indeed. And we have work to do.'

'Swell.' He went to the whisky bottle and quaffed from it freely. He rubbed his stomach with the flat of his hand. His green eyes shone peacefully. 'I'm a sick man,' he said, 'and I got to take my medicine.' He put the bottle down on the table and surveyed the apartment. 'Geez,' he said, 'we thrown it into us so fast I ain't hardly looked at the dump. You got a nice little place here, Walter. Geez, a white typewriter and a white telephone. What's the matter, kid—you just been confirmed?'

'Just a foolish fancy, Henry,' I said, waving an airy hand.

Henry went over and looked at the typewriter and the telephone side by side on my writing desk, and the silver-mounted desk set, each piece chased with my initials.

'Well fixed, huh?' Henry said, turning his green gaze on me.

'Tolerably so, Henry,' I said modestly.

'Well, what next, pal? You got any idea or do we just drink some?'

'Yes, Henry, I do have an idea. With a man like you to help me I think it can be put into practice. I feel that we must, as they say, tap the grapevine. When a string of pearls is stolen, all the underworld knows it at once. Pearls are hard to sell, Henry, inasmuch as they cannot be cut and can be identified by experts, I have read. The underworld will be seething with activity. It should not be too difficult for us to find someone who would send a message to the proper quarter that we are willing to pay a reasonable sum for their return.'

'You talk nice—for a drunk guy,' Henry said, reaching for the bottle. 'But ain't you forgot these marbles are phonies?'

'For sentimental reasons I am quite willing to pay for their return, just the same.'

Henry drank some whisky, appeared to enjoy the flavour of it and drank some more. He waved the bottle at me politely.

'That's okay—as far as it goes,' he said. 'But this underworld that's doing all this here seething you spoke of ain't going to seethe a hell of a lot over a string of glass beads. Or am I screwy?'

'I was thinking, Henry, that the underworld probably has a sense of humour, and the laugh that would go around would be quite emphatic.'

'There's an idea in that,' Henry said. 'Here's some mug finds out lady Penruddock has a string of oyster fruit worth oodles of kale, and he does hisself a neat box little job and trots down to the fence. And the fence gives him the belly laugh. I would say something like that could get around the poolrooms and start a little idle chatter. So far, so nutty. But this box man is going to dump them beads in a hurry, because he has a three-to-ten on him even if they are only worth a nickel plus sales tax. Breaking and entering is the rap, Walter.'

'However, Henry,' I said, 'there is another element in the situation. If this thief is very stupid, it will not, of course, have much weight. But if he is even moderately intelligent, it will. Mrs. Penruddock is a very proud woman and lives in a very exclusive section of the city. If it should become known that she wore imitation pearls, and above all, if it should be even hinted in the public Press that these were the very pearls her own husband had given her for her golden wedding present—well, I am sure you see the point, Henry.'

'Box guys ain't too bright,' he said, and rubbed his stony chin. Then he lifted his right thumb and bit it thoughtfully. He looked at the windows, at the corner of the room, at the floor. He looked at me from the corners of his eyes.

'Blackmail, huh?' he said. 'Maybe. But crooks don't mix their rackets much. Still, the guy might pass the word along. There's a chance, Walter. I wouldn't care to hock my gold fillings to buy me a piece of it, but there's a chance. How much you figure to put out?'

'A hundred dollars should be ample, but I am willing to go as high as two hundred, which is the actual cost of the imitations.'

Henry shook his head and patronized the bottle. 'Nope. The guy wouldn't uncover hisself for that kind of money. Wouldn't be worth the chance he takes. He'd dump the marbles and keep his nose clean.'

'We can at least try, Henry.'

'Yeah, but where? And we're getting low on liquor. Maybe I better put my shoes on and run out, huh?'

At that very moment, as if in answer to my unspoken prayer, a soft dull thump sounded on the door of my apartment. I opened it and picked up the final edition of the evening paper. I closed the door again and carried the paper back across the room, opening it up as I went. I touched it with my right forefinger and smiled confidently at Henry Eichelberger.

'Here. I will wager you a full quart of Old Plantation that the answer will be on the crime page of this paper.'

'There ain't any crime page,' Henry chortled. 'This is Los Angeles. I'll fade you.'

I opened the paper to page three with some trepidation, for, although I had already seen the item I was looking for in an early edition of the paper while waiting in Ada Twomey's Domestic Employment Agency, I was not certain it would appear intact in the later editions. But my faith was rewarded. It had not been removed, but appeared midway of column three exactly as before. The paragraph, which was quite short, was headed: LOU GANDESI QUESTIONED IN GEM THEFTS. 'Listen to this, Henry,' I said, and began to read. 'Acting on an anonymous tip police late last night picked up Louis G. (Lou) Gandesi, proprietor of a well-known Spring Street tavern, and quizzed him intensively concerning the recent wave of dinner-party hold-ups in an exclusive western section of this city, hold-ups during which, it is alleged, more than two hundred thousand dollars' worth of valuable jewels have been torn at gun's point from women guests in fashionable homes. Gandesi was released at a late hour and refused to make any statement to reporters. "I never kibitz the cops," he said modestly. Captain William Norgaard, of the

General Robbery Detail, announced himself as satisfied that Gandesi had no connection with the robberies, and that the tip was merely an act of personal spite.'

I folded the paper and threw it on the bed.

'You win, bo,' Henry said, and handed me the bottle. I took a long drink and returned it to him. 'Now what? Brace this Gandesi and take him through the hoops?'

'He may be a dangerous man, Henry. Do you think we are equal to it?'

Henry snorted contemptuously. 'Yah, a Spring Street punk. Some fat slob with a phoney ruby on his mitt. Lead me to him. We'll turn the slub inside out and drain his liver. But we're just about fresh out of liquor. All we got is maybe a pint.' He examined the bottle against the light.

'We have had enough for the moment, Henry.'

'We ain't drunk, are we? I only had seven drinks since I got here, maybe nine.'

'Certainly we are not drunk, Henry, but you take very large drinks, and we have a difficult evening before us. I think we should now get shaved and dressed, and I further think that we should wear dinner clothes. I have an extra suit which will fit you admirably, as we are almost exactly the same size. It is certainly a remarkable omen that two such large men should be associated in the same enterprise. Evening clothes impress these low characters, Henry.'

'Swell,' Henry said. 'They'll think we're mugs workin' for some big shot. This Gandesi will be scared enough to swallow his necktie.'

We decided to do as I had suggested and I laid out clothes for Henry, and while he was bathing and shaving I telephoned to Ellen Macintosh.

'Oh, Walter, I am so glad you called up,' she cried. 'Have you found anything?'

'Not yet, darling,' I said. 'But we have an idea. Henry and I are just about to put it into execution.'

'Henry, Walter? Henry who?'

'Why, Henry Eichelberger, of course, darling. Have you forgotten him so soon? Henry and I are warm friends and we——'

She interrupted me coldly. 'Are you drinking, Walter?' she demanded in a very distant voice.

'Certainly not, darling. Henry is a teetotaler.'

She sniffed sharply. I could hear the sound distinctly over the telephone. 'But didn't Henry take the pearls?' she asked, after quite a long pause.

'Henry, angel? Of course not. Henry left because he was in love with you.'

'Oh, Walter. That ape? I'm sure you're drinking terribly. I don't ever want to speak to you again. Good-bye.' And she hung the phone up very sharply so that a painful sensation made itself felt in my ear.

I sat down in a chair with a bottle of Old Plantation in my hand wondering what I had said that could be construed as offensive or indiscreet. As I was unable to think of anything, I consoled myself with the bottle until Henry came out of the bathroom looking extremely personable in one of my pleated shirts and a wing collar and black bow tie.

It was dark when we left the apartment and I, at least, was full of hope and confidence, although a little depressed by the way Ellen Macintosh had spoken to me over the telephone.

4

Mr. Gandesi's establishment was not difficult to find, inasmuch as the first taxicab driver Henry yelled at on Spring Street directed us to it. It was called the Blue Lagoon and its interior was bathed in an unpleasant blue light. Henry and I entered it steadily, since we had consumed a partly solid meal at Mandy's Caribbean Grotto before starting out to find Mr. Gandesi. Henry looked almost handsome in my second-best dinner suit, with a fringed white scarf hanging over his shoulder, a lightweight black felt hat on the back of his head (which was only a little larger than mine), and a bottle of whisky in each of the side pockets of the summer overcoat he was wearing.

The bar of the Blue Lagoon was crowded, but Henry and I went on back to the small dim dining-room behind it. A man in a dirty dinner suit came up to us and Henry asked for Gandesi, and he pointed out a fat man who sat alone at a small table in the far corner of the room. We went that way.

The man sat with a small glass of red wine in front of him and slowly twisted a large green stone on his finger. He did not look up. There were no other chairs at the table, so Henry leaned on it with both elbows.

'You Gandesi?' he said.

The man did not look up even then. He moved his thick black eyebrows together and said in an absent voice: 'Si. Yes.'

'We got to talk to you in private,' Henry told him. 'Where we won't be disturbed.'

Gandesi looked up now and there was extreme boredom in his flat black almond-shaped eyes. 'So?' he asked and shrugged. 'Eet ees about what?'

'About some pearls,' Henry said. 'Forty-nine on the string, matched and pink.'

'You sell—or you buy?' Gandesi inquired and his chin began to shake up and down as if with amusement.

'Buy,' Henry said.

The man at the table crooked his finger quietly and a very large waiter appeared at his side. 'Ees dronk,' he said lifelessly. 'Put dees men out.'

The waiter took hold of Henry's shoulder. Henry reached up carelessly, and took hold of the waiter's hand and twisted it. The waiter's face in that bluish light turned some colour I could not describe, but which was not at all healthy. He put out a low moan. Henry dropped the hand and said to me: 'Put a C-note on the table.'

I took my wallet out and extracted from it one of the two hundred-dollar bills I had taken the precaution to obtain from the cashier at the Chateau Moraine. Gandesi stared at the bill and made a gesture to the large waiter, who went away rubbing his hand and holding it tight against his chest.

'What for?' Gandesi asked.

'Five minutes of your time alone.'

'Ees very fonny. Okay, I bite.' Gandesi took the bill and folded it neatly and put it in his vest pocket. Then he put both hands on the table and pushed himself heavily to his feet. He started to waddle away without looking at us.

Henry and I followed him among the crowded tables to the far side of the dining-room and through a door in the wainscoting and then down a narrow dim hallway. At the end of this Gandesi opened a door into a lighted room and stood holding it for us, with a grave smile on his olive face. I went in first.

As Henry passed in front of Gandesi into the room the latter, with surprising agility, took a small shiny black leather club from his clothes and hit Henry on the head with it very hard. Henry sprawled forward on his hands and knees. Gandesi shut the door of the room very quickly for a man of his build and leaned against it with the small club in his left hand. Now, very suddenly, in his right appeared a short but heavy black revolver.

'Ees very fonny,' he said politely, and chuckled to himself.

Exactly what happened then I did not see clearly. Henry was at one instant on his hands and knees with his back to Gandesi. In the next, or possibly even in the same instant, something swirled like a big fish in water and Gandesi grunted. I then saw that Henry's hard blond head was buried in Gandesi's stomach and that Henry's large hands held both of Gandesi's hairy wrists. Then Henry straightened his body to its full height and Gandesi was high up in the air balanced on top of Henry's head, his mouth strained wide open and his face a dark purple colour. Then Henry shook himself, as it seemed, quite lightly, and Gandesi landed on his back on the floor with a terrible thud and lay gasping. Then a key turned in the door and Henry stood with his back to it, holding both the club and the revolver in his left hand, and solicitously feeling the pockets which contained our supply of whisky. All this happened with such rapidity that I leaned against the side wall and felt a little sick at my stomach.

'A gut-buster,' Henry drawled. 'A comedian. Wait'll I loosen my belt.'

Gandesi rolled over and got to his feet very slowly and painfully and stood swaying and passing his hand up and down his face. His clothes were covered with dust.

'Ths here's a cosh,' Henry said, showing me the small black club. 'He hit me with it, didn't he?'

'Why, Henry, don't you know?' I inquired.

'I just wanted to be sure,' Henry said. 'You don't do that to the Eichelbergers.'

'Okay, what you boys want?' Gandesi asked abruptly, with no trace whatever of his Italian accent.

'I told you what we wanted, dough-face.'

'I don't think I know you boys,' Gandesi said and lowered his body with care into a wooden chair beside a shabby office desk. He mopped his face and neck and felt himself in various places.

'You got the wrong idea, Gandesi. A lady living in Carondelet Park lost a forty-nine bead pearl necklace a couple of days back. A box job, but a pushover. Our outfit's carrying a little insurance on those marbles. And I'll take that C note.'

He walked over to Gandesi and Gandesi quickly reached the folded bill from his pocket and handed it to him. Henry gave me the bill and I put it back in my wallet.

'I don't think I hear about it,' Gandesi said carefully.

'You hit me with a cosh,' Henry said. 'Listen kind of hard.'

Gandesi shook his head and then winced. 'I don't back no petermen,' he said, 'nor no heist guys. You got me wrong.'

'Listen hard,' Henry said in a low voice. 'You might hear something.' He swung the small black club lightly in front of his body with two fingers of his right hand. The slightly too-small hat was still on the back of his head, although a little crumpled.

'Henry,' I said, 'you seem to be doing all the work this evening. Do you think that is quite fair?'

'Okay, work him over,' Henry said. 'These fat guys bruise something lovely.'

By this time Gandesi had become a more natural colour and was gazing at us steadily. 'Insurance guys, huh?' he inquired dubiously.

'You said it, dough-face.'

'You try Melachrino?' Gandesi asked.

'Haw,' Henry began raucously, 'a gut-buster. A——' but I interrupted him sharply.

'One moment, Henry,' I said. Then turning to Gandesi, 'Is this Melachrino a person?' I asked him.

Gandesi's eyes rounded in surprise. 'Sure—a guy. You don't know him, huh?' A look of dark suspicion was born in his sloe-black eyes, but vanished almost as soon as it appeared.

'Phone him,' Henry said, pointing to the instrument which stood on the shabby office desk.

'Phone is bad,' Gandesi objected thoughtfully.

'So is cosh poison,' Henry said.

Gandesi sighed and turned his thick body in the chair and drew the telephone towards him. He dialled a number with an inky nail and listened. After an interval he said: 'Jo? . . . Lou. Couple insurance guys tryin' to deal on a Carondelet Park job. . . . Yeah. . . . No, marbles. . . . You ain't heard a whisper, huh?. . . . Okay, Joe.'

Gandesi replaced the phone and swung round in the chair again. He studied us with sleepy eyes. 'No soap. What insurance outfit you boys work for?'

'Give him a card,' Henry said to me.

I took my wallet out once more and withdrew one of my cards from it. It was an engraved calling card and contained nothing but my name. So I used my pocket pencil to write, Chateau Moraine Apartments, Franklin near Ivar, below the name. I showed the card to Henry and then gave it to Gandesi.

Gandesi read the card and quietly bit his finger. His face brightened suddenly. 'You boys better see Jack Lawler,' he said.

Henry stared at him closely. Gandesi's eyes were now bright and unblinking and guileless.

'Who's he?' Henry asked.

'Runs the Penguin Club. Out on the Strip—Eighty-six Forty-four Sunset or some number like that. He can find out, if any guy can.'

'Thanks,' Henry said quietly. He glanced at me. 'You believe him?'

'Well, Henry,' I said, 'I don't really think he would be above telling us an untruth.'

'Haw!' Gandesi began suddenly. 'A gut-buster! A——'

'Can it!' Henry snarled. 'That's my line. Straight goods, is it, Gandesi? About this Jack Lawler?'

Gandesi nodded vigorously. 'Straight goods, absolute. Jack Lawler got a finger in everything high-class that's touched. But he ain't easy to see.'

'Don't worry none about that. Thanks, Gandesi.'

Henry tossed the black club into the corner of the room and broke open the breech of the revolver he had been holding all this time in his left hand. He ejected the shells and then bent down and slid the gun along the floor until it disappeared under the desk. He tossed the cartridges idly in his hand for a moment and then let them spill on the floor.

'So long, Gandesi,' he said coldly. 'And keep that schnozzle of yours clean, if you don't want to be looking for it under the bed.'

He opened the door then and we both went out quickly and left the Blue Lagoon without interference from any of the employees.

5

My car was parked a short distance away down the block. We entered it and Henry leaned his arms on the wheel and stared moodily through the windshield.

'Well, what you think, Walter?' he inquired at length.

'If you ask my opinion, Henry, I think Mr. Gandesi told us a cock-and-bull story merely to get rid of us. Furthermore I do not believe he thought we were insurance agents.'

'Me too, and an extra helping,' Henry said. 'I don't figure there's any such guy as this Melachrino or this Jack Lawler and this Gandesi called up some dead number and had himself a phoney chin with it. I oughta go back there and pull his arms and legs off. The hell with the fat slub.'

'We had the best idea we could think of, Henry, and we executed it to the best of our ability. I now suggest that we return to my apartment and try to think of something else.'

'And get drunk,' Henry said, starting the car and guiding it away from the kerb.

'We could perhaps have a small allowance of liquor, Henry.'

'Yah!' Henry snorted. 'A stall. I oughta go back there and wreck the joint.'

He stopped at the intersection, although no traffic signal was in operation at the time; and raised a bottle of whisky to his lips. He was in the act of drinking when a car came up behind us and collided with our car, but not very severely. Henry choked and lowered his bottle, spilling some of the liquor on his garments.

'This town's getting too crowded,' he snarled. 'A guy can't take hisself a drink without some smart monkey bumps his elbow.'

Whoever it was in the car behind us blew a horn with some insistence, inasmuch as our car had not yet moved forward. Henry wrenched the door open and got out and went back. I heard voices of considerable loudness, the louder being Henry's voice. He came back after a moment and got into the car and drove on.

'I oughta have pulled his mush off,' he said, 'but I went soft.' He drove rapidly the rest of the way to Hollywood and the Chateau Moraine and we went up to my apartment and sat down with large glasses in our hands.

'We got better than a quart and a half of hooch,' Henry said, looking at the two bottles which he had placed on the table beside others which had long since been emptied. 'That oughta be good for an idea.'

'If it isn't enough, Henry, there is an abundant further supply where it came from,' I drained my glass cheerfully.

'You seem a right guy,' Henry said. 'What makes you always talk so funny?'

'I cannot seem to change my speech, Henry. My father and mother were both severe purists in the New England tradition, and the vernacular has never come naturally to my lips, even while I was in college.'

Henry made an attempt to digest this remark, but I could see that it lay somewhere heavily on his stomach.

We talked for a time concerning Gandesi and the doubtful quality of his advice, and thus passed perhaps half an hour. Then rather suddenly the white telephone on my desk began to ring. I hurried over to it, hoping that it was Ellen Macintosh, and that she had recovered from her ill humour. But it proved to be a male voice and a strange one to me. It spoke crisply, with an unpleasant metallic quality of tone.

'You Walter Gage?'

'This is Mister Gage speaking.'

'Well, *Mister* Gage, I understand you're in the market for some jewellery.'

I held the phone very tightly and turned my body and made grimaces to Henry over the top of the instrument. But he was moodily pouring himself another large portion of Old Plantation.

'That is so,' I said into the telephone, trying to keep my voice steady, although my excitement was almost too much for me. 'If by jewellery you mean pearls.'

'Forty-nine in a rope, brother. And five grand is the price.'

'Why that is entirely absurd,' I gasped. 'Five thousand dollars for those——'

The voice broke in on me rudely. 'You heard me, brother. Five grand. Just hold up the hand and count the fingers. No more, no less. Think it over. I'll call you later.'

The phone clicked dryly and I replaced the instrument shakily in its cradle. I was trembling. I walked back to my chair and sat down and wiped my face with my handkerchief.

'Henry,' I said in a low tense voice, 'it worked. But how strangely.'

Henry put his empty glass down on the floor. It was the first time that I had ever seen him put an empty glass down and leave it empty. He stared at me closely with his tight unblinking green eyes.

'Yeah?' he said gently. 'What worked, kid?' He licked his lips slowly with the tip of his tongue.

'What we accomplished down at Gandesi's place, Henry. A man just called me on the telephone and asked me if I was in the market for pearls.'

'Geez.' Henry pursed his lips and whistled gently. 'That damn dago had something after all.'

'But the price is five thousand dollars, Henry. That seems beyond reasonable explanation.'

'Huh?' Henry's eyes seemed to bulge as if they were about to depart from their orbits. 'Five grand for them ringers? The guy's nuts. They cost two C's, you said. Bugs completely is what the guy is. Five grand? Why, for five grand I could buy me enough phoney beads to cover an elephant's caboose.'

I could see that Henry seemed puzzled. He refilled our glasses silently and we stared at each other over them. 'Well, what the heck can you do with that, Walter?' he asked after a long silence.

'Henry,' I said firmly, 'there is only one thing to do. It is true that Ellen Macintosh spoke to me in confidence, and as she did not have Mrs. Penruddock's express permission to tell me about the pearls, I suppose I should respect that confidence. But Ellen is now angry with me and does not wish to speak to me, for the reason that I am drinking whisky in considerable quantities, although my speech and brain are still reasonably clear. This last is a very strange development, and I think, in spite of everything, some close friend of the family should be consulted. Preferably of course, a man, some-one of large business experience, and in addition to that a man who under-stands about jewels. There *is* such a man, Henry, and to-morrow morning I shall call upon him.'

'Geez,' Henry said. 'You coulda said all that in nine words, bo. Who is this guy?'

'His name is Mr. Lansing Gallemore, and he is president of the Gallemore Jewellery Company on Seventh Street. He is a very old friend of Mrs. Penruddock—Ellen has often mentioned him—and is, in fact, the very man who procured for her the imitation pearls.'

'But this guy will tip the bulls,' Henry objected.

'I do not think so, Henry. I do not think he will do anything to embarrass Mrs. Penruddock in any way.'

Henry shrugged. 'Phonies are phonies,' he said. 'You can't make nothing else outa them. Not even no president of no jewellery store can't.'

'Nevertheless, there must be a reason why so large a sum is demanded, Henry. The only reason that occurs to me is blackmail and, frankly, that is a little too much for me to handle alone, because I do not know enough about the background of the Penruddock family.'

'Oke,' Henry said, sighing. 'If that's your hunch, you better follow it, Walter. And I better breeze on home and flop so as to be in good shape for the rough work, if any.'

'You would not care to pass the night here, Henry?'

'Thanks, pal, but I'm okay back at the hotel. I'll just take this spare bottle of the tiger sweat to put me to sleep. I might happen to get a call from the agency in the a.m. and would have to brush my teeth and go after it. And I guess I better change my duds back to where I can mix with the common people.'

So saying he went into the bathroom and in a short time emerged wearing his own blue serge suit. I urged him to take my car, but he said it would not be safe in his neighbourhood. He did, however, consent to use the topcoat he had been wearing, and, placing in it carefully the unopened quart of whisky, he shook me warmly by the hand.

'One moment, Henry,' I said and took out my wallet. I extended a twenty-dollar bill to him.

'What's that in favour of?' he growled.

'You are temporarily out of employment, Henry, and you have done a noble piece of work this evening, puzzling as are the results. You should be rewarded and I can well afford this small token.'

'Well, thanks, pal,' Henry said. 'But it's just a loan.' His voice was gruff with emotion. 'Should I give you a buzz in the a.m.?'

'By all means. And there is one thing more that has occurred to me. Would it not be advisable for you to change your hotel? Suppose, through no fault of mine, the police learn of this theft. Would they not at least suspect you?'

'Hell, they'd bounce me up and down for hours,' Henry said. 'But what'll it get them? I ain't no ripe peach.'

'It is for you to decide, of course, Henry.'

'Yeah. Good night, pal, and don't have no nightmares.'

He left me then and I felt suddenly very depressed and lonely. Henry's company had been very stimulating to me, in spite of his rough way of talking. He was very much of a man. I poured myself a rather large drink of whisky from the remaining bottle and drank it quickly but gloomily.

The effect was such that I had an overmastering desire to speak to Ellen Macintosh at all costs. I went to the telephone and called her number. After a long wait a sleepy maid answered. But Ellen, upon hearing my name, refused to come to the telephone. That depressed me still further, and I finished the rest of the whisky almost without noticing what I was doing. I then lay down on the bed and fell into fitful slumber.

6

The busy ringing of the telephone awoke me and I saw that the morning sunlight was streaming into the room. It was nine o'clock and all the lamps were still burning. I arose feeling a little stiff and dissipated, for I was still wearing my dinner suit. But I am a healthy man with very steady nerves and I did not feel as bad as I expected. I went to the telephone and answered it.

Henry's voice said: 'How you feel, pal? I got a hangover like twelve Swedes.'

'Not too bad, Henry.'

'I got a call from the agency about a job. I better go down and take a gander at it. Should I drop around later?'

'Yes, Henry, by all means do that. By eleven o'clock I should be back from the errand about which I spoke to you last night.'

'Any more calls from you know?'

'Not yet, Henry.'

'Check. Abyssinia.' He hung up and I took a cold shower and shaved and dressed. I donned a quiet brown business suit and had some coffee sent up from the coffee shop downstairs. I also had the waiter remove the empty bottles from my apartment and gave him a dollar for his trouble. After drinking two cups of black coffee I felt my own man once more and drove downtown to the Gallemore Jewellery Company's large and brilliant store on West Seventh Street.

It was another bright, golden morning and it seemed that somehow things should adjust themselves on so pleasant a day.

Mr. Lansing Gallemore proved to be a little difficult to see, so that I was compelled to tell his secretary that it was a matter concerning Mrs. Penruddock and of a confidential nature. Upon this message being carried in to him I was at once ushered into a long panelled office, at the far end of which Mr. Gallemore stood behind a massive desk. He extended a thin, pink hand to me.

'Mr. Gage? I don't believe we have met, have we?'

'No, Mr. Gallemore, I do not believe we have. I am the fiancé—or was until last night—of Miss Ellen Macintosh, who, as you probably know, is Mrs. Penruddock's nurse. I am come to you upon a very delicate matter and it is necessary that I ask for your confidence before I speak.'

He was a man of perhaps seventy-five years of age, and very thin and tall and correct and well preserved. He had cold blue eyes but a warming smile. He was attired youthfully enough in a grey flannel suit with a red carnation at his lapel.

'That is something I make it a rule never to promise. Mr. Gage,' he said. 'I think it is almost always a very unfair request. But if you assure me the matter concerns Mrs. Penruddock, and is really of a delicate and confidential nature, I will make an exception.'

'It is indeed, Mr. Gallemore,' I said, and thereupon told him the entire story, concealing nothing, not even the fact that I had consumed far too much whisky the day before.

He stared at me curiously at the end of my story. His finely shaped hand picked up an old-fashioned white quill pen and he slowly tickled his right ear with the feather of it.

'Mr. Gage,' he said, 'can't you guess why they ask five thousand dollars for that string of pearls?'

'If you permit me to guess, in a matter of so personal a nature, I could perhaps hazard an explanation, Mr. Gallemore.'

He moved the white feather around to his left ear and nodded. 'Go ahead, son.'

'The pearls are in fact real, Mr. Gallemore. You are a very old friend of Mrs. Penruddock—perhaps even a childhood sweetheart. When she gave you her pearls, her golden wedding present, to sell because she was in sore need of money for a generous purpose, you did not sell them, Mr. Gallemore. You only pretended to sell them. You gave her twenty thousand dollars of your own money, and you returned the real pearls to her, pretending that they were an imitation made in Czechoslovakia.'

'Son, you think a lot smarter than you talk,' Mr. Gallemore said. He rose and walked to a window, pulled aside a fine net curtain and looked down on the bustle of Seventh Street. He came back to his desk and seated himself and smiled a little wistfully.

'You are almost embarrassingly correct, Mr. Gage,' he said, and sighed. 'Mrs. Penruddock is a very proud woman, or I should simply have offered her the twenty thousand dollars as an unsecured loan. I happened to be the co-administrator of Mr. Penruddock's estate and I knew that in the condition of the financial market at that time it would be out of the question to raise enough cash, without damaging the corpus of the estate beyond reason, to care for all those relatives and pensioners. So Mrs. Penruddock sold her pearls—as she thought—but she insisted that no one should know about it. And I did what you have guessed. It was unimportant. I could afford the gesture. I have never married, Gage, and I am rated a wealthy man. As a matter of fact, at that time, the pearls would not have fetched more than half of what I gave her, or of what they should bring to-day.'

I lowered my eyes for fear this kindly old gentleman might be troubled by my direct gaze.

'So I think we had better raise that five thousand, son,' Mr. Gallemore at once added in a brisk voice. 'The price is pretty low, although stolen pearls are a great deal more difficult to deal in than cut stones. If I should care to trust you that far on your face, do you think you could handle the assignment?'

'Mr. Gallemore,' I said firmly but quietly, 'I am a total stranger to you and I am only flesh and blood. But I promise you by the memories of my dead and revered parents that there will be no cowardice.'

'Well, there is a good deal of the flesh and blood, son,' Mr. Gallemore said kindly. 'And I am not afraid of your stealing the money, because possibly I know a little more about Miss Ellen Macintosh and her boy friend than you might suspect. Furthermore, the pearls are insured, in my name, of course, and the insurance company should really handle this affair. But you and your funny friend seem to have got along very nicely so far, and I believe in playing out a hand. This Henry must be quite a man.'

'I have grown very attached to him, in spite of his uncouth ways,' I said.

Mr. Gallemore played with his white quill pen a little longer and then he brought out a large cheque-book and wrote a cheque, which he carefully blotted and passed across the desk.

'If you get the pearls, I'll see that the insurance people refund this to me,' he said. 'If they like my business, there will be no difficulty about that. The bank is down at the corner and I will be waiting for their call. They won't cash the cheque without telephoning me, probably. Be careful, son, and don't get hurt.'

He shook hands with me once more and I hesitated. 'Mr. Gallemore, you are placing a greater trust in me than any man ever has,' I said. 'With the exception, of course, of my own father.'

'I am acting like a damn fool,' he said with a peculiar smile. 'It is so long since I heard anyone talk the way Jane Austen writes that it is making a sucker out of me.'

'Thank you, sir. I know my language is a bit stilted. Dare I ask you to do me a small favour, sir?'

'What is it, Gage?'

'To telephone Miss Ellen Macintosh, from whom I am now a little estranged, and tell her that I am not drinking to-day, and that you have entrusted me with a very delicate mission.'

He laughed aloud. 'I'll be glad to, Walter. And as I know she can be trusted, I'll give her an idea of what's going on.'

I left him then and went down to the bank with the cheque, and the teller, after looking at me suspiciously, then absenting himself from his cage for a long time, finally counted out the money in hundred-dollar bills with the reluctance one might have expected, if it had been his own money.

I placed the flat packet of bills in my pocket and said: 'Now give me a roll of quarters, please.'

'A roll of quarters, sir?' His eyebrows lifted.

'Exactly. I use them for tips. And naturally I should prefer to carry them home in the wrappings.'

'Oh, I see. Ten dollars, please.'

I took the fat hard roll of coins and dropped it into my pocket and drove back to Hollywood.

Henry was waiting for me in the lobby of the Chateau Moraine, twirling his hat between his rough hard hands. His face looked a little more deeply lined than it had the day before and I noticed that his breath smelled of whisky. We went up to my apartment and he turned to me eagerly.

'Any luck, pal?'

'Henry,' I said, 'before we proceed further into this day I wish it clearly understood that I am not drinking. I see that already you have been at the bottle.'

'Just a pick-up, Walter,' he said a little contritely. 'That job I went out for was gone before I got there. What's the good word?'

I sat down and lit a cigarette and stared at him evenly. 'Well, Henry, I don't really know whether I should tell you or not. But it seems a little petty not to do so after all you did last night to Gandesi.' I hesitated a moment longer while Henry stared at me and pinched the muscles of his left arm. 'The pearls are real, Henry. And I have instructions to proceed with the business and I have five thousand dollars in cash in my pocket at this moment.'

I told him briefly what had happened.

He was more amazed than words could tell. 'Cripes!' he exclaimed, his mouth hanging wide open. 'You mean you got the five grand from this Gallemore—just like that?'

'Precisely that, Henry.'

'Kid,' he said earnestly, 'you got something with that daisy pan and that fluff talk that a lot of guys would give important dough to cop. Five grand—out of a business guy—just like that. Why, I'll be a monkey's uncle, I'll be a snake's daddy. I'll be a mickey finn at a woman's-club lunch.'

At that exact moment, as if my entrance to the building had been observed, the telephone rang again and I sprang to answer it.

It was one of the voices I was awaiting, but not the one I wanted to hear with the greater longing. 'How's it looking to you this morning, Gage?'

'It is looking better,' I said. 'If I can have any assurance of honourable treatment, I am prepared to go through with it.'

'You mean you got the dough?'

'In my pocket at this exact moment.'

The voice seemed to exhale a slow breath. 'You'll get your marbles okay—if we get the price, Gage. We're in this business for a long time and we don't welsh. If we did, it would soon get around and nobody would play with us any more.'

'Yes, I can readily understand that,' I said. 'Proceed with your instructions,' I added coldly.

'Listen close, Gage. To-night at eight sharp you be in Pacific Palisades. Know where that is?'

'Certainly. It is a small residential section west of the polo fields on Sunset Boulevard.'

'Right. Sunset goes slap through it. There's one drugstore there—open till nine. Be there waiting a call at eight sharp to-night. Alone. And I mean alone, Gage. No cops and no strong-arm guys. It's rough country down there and we got a way to get you to where we want you and know if you're alone. Get all this?'

'I am not entirely an idiot,' I retorted.

'No dummy packages, Gage. The dough will be checked. No guns. You'll be searched and there's enough of us to cover you from all angles. We know your car. No funny business, no smart work, no slip-up and nobody hurt. That's the way we do business. How's the dough fixed?'

'One-hundred-dollar bills,' I said. 'And only a few of them are new.'

'Attaboy. Eight o'clock then. Be smart, Gage.'

The phone clicked in my ear and I hung up. It rang again almost instantly. This time it was the *one* voice.

'Oh, Walter,' Ellen cried. 'I was so mean to you! Please forgive me, Walter. Mr. Gallemore has told me everything and I'm so frightened.'

'There is nothing of which to be frightened,' I told her warmly. 'Does Mrs. Penruddock know, darling?'

'No, darling. Mr. Gallemore told me not to tell her. I am phoning from a store down on Sixth Street. Oh, Walter, I really am frightened. Will Henry go with you?'

'I am afraid not, darling. The arrangements are all made and they will not permit it. I must go alone.'

'Oh, Walter! I'm terrified. I can't bear the suspense.'

'There is nothing to fear,' I assured her. 'It is a simple business transaction. And I am not exactly a midget.'

'But, Walter—oh, I *will* try to be brave, Walter. Will you promise me just one teensy-weensy little thing?'

'Not a drop, darling,' I said firmly. 'Not a single solitary drop.'

'Oh, Walter!'

There was a little more of that sort of thing, very pleasant to me in the circumstances, although possibly not of great interest to others. We finally parted with my promise to telephone as soon as the meeting between the crooks and myself had been consummated.

I turned from the telephone to find Henry drinking deeply from a bottle he had taken from his hip pocket.

'Henry!' I cried sharply.

He looked at me over the bottle with a shaggy determined look. 'Listen, pal,' he said in a low hard voice. 'I got enough of your end of the talk to figure the set-up. Some place out in the tall weeds and you go alone and they feed you the old cosh poison and take your dough and leave you lying—with the marbles still in their kitty. Nothing doing, pal, I said—nothing doing!' He almost shouted the last words.

'Henry, it is my duty and I must do it,' I said quietly.

'Haw!' Henry snorted. 'I say no. You're a nut, but you're a sweet guy on the side. I say no. Henry Eichelberger of the Wisconsin Eichelbergers—in fact, I might just as leave say of the Milwaukee Eichelbergers—says no. And he says it with both hands working.' He drank again from the bottle.

'You certainly will not help matters by becoming intoxicated,' I told him rather bitterly.

He lowered the bottle and looked at me with amazement written all over his rugged features. 'Drunk, Walter?' he boomed. 'Did I hear you say drunk? An Eichelberger drunk? Listen, son. We ain't got a lot of time now. It would take maybe three months. Some day when you got three months and maybe five thousand gallons of whisky and a funnel, I would be glad to take my own time and show you what an Eichelberger looks like when drunk. You wouldn't believe it. Son, there wouldn't be nothing left of this town but a few sprung girders and a lot of busted bricks, in the middle of which— Geez, I'll get talking English myself if I hang around you much longer—in the middle of which, peaceful, with no human life nearer than maybe fifty miles, Henry Eichelberger will be on his back smiling at the sun. Drunk, Walter. Not stinking drunk, not even country-club drunk. But you could use the word drunk and I wouldn't take no offence.'

He sat down and drank again. I stared moodily at the floor. There was nothing for me to say.

'But that,' Henry said, 'is some other time. Right now I am just taking my medicine. I ain't myself without a slight touch of delirium tremens, as the guy says. I was brought up on it. And I'm going with you, Walter. Where is this place at?'

'It's down near the beach, Henry, and you are not going with me. If you must get drunk—get drunk, but you are not going with me.'

'You got a big car, Walter. I'll hide in back on the floor under a rug. It's a cinch.'

'No, Henry.'

'Walter, you are a sweet guy,' Henry said, 'and I am going with you into this frame. Have a smell from the barrel, Walter. You look to me kind of frail.'

We argued for an hour and my head ached and I began to feel very nervous and tired. It was then that I made what might have been a fatal mistake. I succumbed to Henry's blandishments and took a small portion of whisky purely for medicinal purposes. This made me feel so much more relaxed that I took another and larger portion. I had had no food except coffee that morning and only a very light dinner the evening before. At the end of another hour Henry had been out for two more bottles of whisky and I was as bright as a bird. All difficulties had now disappeared and I had agreed heartily that Henry should lie in the back of my car hidden by a rug and accompany me to the rendezvous.

We had passed the time very pleasantly until two o'clock, at which hour I began to feel sleepy and lay down on the bed, and fell into a deep slumber.

7

When I awoke again it was almost dark. I rose from the bed with panic in my heart, and also a sharp shoot of pain through my temples. It was only six-thirty, however, I was alone in the apartment and lengthening shadows were stealing across the floor. The display of empty whisky bottles on the table was very disgusting. Henry Eichelberger was nowhere to be seen. With an instinctive pang, of which I was almost immediately ashamed, I hurried to my jacket hanging on the back of a chair and plunged my hand into the inner breast pocket. The packet of bills was there intact. After a brief hesitation, and with a feeling of secret guilt, I drew them out and slowly counted them over. Not a bill was missing. I replaced the money and tried to smile at myself for this lack of trust, and then switched on a light and went into the bathroom to take alternate hot and cold showers until my brain was once more comparatively clear.

I had done this and was dressing in fresh linen when a key turned in the lock and Henry Eichelberger entered with two wrapped bottles under his arm. He looked at me with what I thought was genuine affection.

'A guy that can sleep it off like you is a real champ, Walter,' he said admiringly. 'I snuck your keys so as not to wake you. I had to get some eats and some more hooch. I done a little solo drinking, which as I told you is against my principles, but this is a big day. However, we take it easy from now on as to the hooch. We can't afford no jitters till it's all over.'

He had unwrapped a bottle while he was speaking and poured me a small drink. I drank it gratefully and immediately felt a warm glow in my veins.

'I bet you looked in your poke for that deck of mazuma,' Henry said, grinning at me.

I felt myself reddening, but I said nothing. 'Okay, pal, you done right. What the heck do you know about Henry Eichelberger anyways? I done something else.' He reached behind him and drew a short automatic from his hip pocket. 'If these boys wanta play rough,' he said, 'I got me five bucks worth of iron that don't mind playin' rough a little itself. And the Eichelbergers ain't missed a whole of the guys they shot at.'

'I don't like that, Henry,' I said severely. 'That is contrary to the agreement.'

'Nuts to the agreement,' Henry said. 'The boys get their dough and no cops. I'm out to see that they hand over them marbles and don't pull any fast footwork.'

I saw there was no use arguing with him, so I completed my dressing and prepared to leave the apartment. We each took one more drink and then Henry put a full bottle in his pocket and we left.

On the way down the hall to the elevator he explained in a low voice: 'I got a hack out front to tail you, just in case these boys got the same idea. You might circle a few quiet blocks so as I can find out. More like they don't pick you up till down close to the beach.'

'All this must be costing you a great deal of money, Henry,' I told him, and while we were waiting for the elevator to come up I took another twenty-dollar bill from my wallet and offered it to him. He took the money reluctantly, but finally folded it and placed it in his pocket.

I did as Henry had suggested, driving up and down a number of the hilly streets north of Hollywood Boulevard, and presently I heard the unmistakable hoot of a taxicab horn behind me. I pulled over to the side of the road. Henry got out of the cab and paid off the driver and got into my car beside me.

'All clear,' he said. 'No tail. I'll just keep kind of slumped down and you better stop somewhere for some groceries on account of if we have to get rough with these mugs, a full head of steam will help.'

So I drove westward and dropped down to Sunset Boulevard and presently stopped at a crowded drive-in restaurant where we sat at the counter and ate a light meal of omelette and black coffee. We then proceeded on our way. When we reached Beverly Hills, Henry again made me wind in and out through a number of residential streets where he observed very carefully through the rear window of the car.

Fully satisfied at last we drove back to Sunset, and without incident onwards through Bel-Air and the fringes of Westwood, almost as far as the Riviera polo field. At this point, down in the hollow, there is a canyon called Mandeville Canyon, a very quiet place. Henry had me drive up this for a short distance. We then stopped and had a little whisky from his bottle and he climbed into the back of the car and curled his big body up on the floor, with the rug over him and his automatic pistol and his bottle down on the floor conveniently to his hand. That done I once more resumed my journey.

Pacific Palisades is a district whose inhabitants seem to retire rather early. When I reached what might be called the business centre nothing was open but the drugstore beside the bank. I parked the car, with Henry remaining silent under the rug in the back, except for a slight gurgling noise I noticed as I stood on the dark sidewalk. Then I went into the drugstore and saw by its clock that it was now fifteen minutes to eight. I bought a package of cigarettes and lit one and took up my position near the open telephone booth.

The druggist, a heavy set red-faced man of uncertain age, had a small radio up very loud and was listening to some foolish serial. I asked him to turn it down, as I was expecting an important telephone call. This he did, but not with any good grace, and immediately retired to the back part of his store whence I saw him looking out at me malignantly through a small glass window.

At precisely one minute to eight by the drugstore clock the phone rang sharply in the booth. I hastened into it and pulled the door tight shut. I lifted the receiver, trembling a little in spite of myself.

It was the same cool metallic voice, 'Gage?'

'This is Mr. Gage.'

'You done just what I told you?'

'Yes,' I said. 'I have the money in my pocket and I am entirely alone.' I did not like the feeling of lying so brazenly, even to a thief, but I steeled myself to it.

'Listen, then. Go back about three hundred feet the way you come. Beside the firehouse there's a service station, closed up, painted green and red and white. Beside that, going south, is a dirt road. Follow it three-quarters of a mile and you come to a white fence of four-by-four built almost across the road. You can just squeeze your car by at the left side. Dim your lights and get through there and keep going down the little hill into a hollow with sage all around. Park there, cut your lights, and wait. Get it?'

'Perfectly,' I said coldly, 'and it shall be done exactly that way.'

'And listen, pal. There ain't a house in half a mile, and there ain't any folks around at all. You got ten minutes to get there. You're watched right this minute. You get there fast and you get there alone—or you got a trip for biscuits. And don't light no matches or pills nor use no flashlights. On your way.'

The phone went dead and I left the booth. I was scarcely outside the drug-store before the druggist rushed at his radio and turned it up to a booming blare. I got into my car and turned it and drove back along Sunset Boulevard, as directed. Henry was as still as the grave on the floor behind me.

I was now very nervous and Henry had all the liquor which we had brought with us. I reached the firehouse in no time at all and through its front window I could see four firemen playing cards. I turned to the right down the dirt road past the red-and-green-and-white service station and almost at once the night was so still, in spite of the quiet sound of my car, that I could hear the cricket and treefrogs chirping and trilling in all direc-tions, and from some nearby watery spot came the hoarse croak of a solitary bull-frog.

The road dipped and rose again and far off there was a yellow window. Then ahead of me, ghostly in the blackness of the moonless night, appeared the dim white barrier across the road. I noted the gap at the side and then dimmed my headlamps and steered carefully through it and so on down a rough short hill into an oval-shaped hollow space surrounded by low brush and plentifully littered with empty bottles and cans and pieces of paper. It was entirely deserted, however, at this dark hour. I stopped my car and shut off the ignition, and the lights, and sat there motionless, hands on the wheel.

Behind me I heard no murmur of sound from Henry. I waited possibly five minutes, although it seemed much longer, but nothing happened. It was very still, very lonely, and I did not feel happy.

Finally there was a faint sound of movement behind me and I looked back to see the pale blur of Henry's face peering at me from under the rug.

His voice whispered huskily: 'Anything stirring, Walter?'

I shook my head at him vigorously and he once more pulled the rug over his face. I heard a faint sound of gurgling.

Fully fifteen minutes passed before I dared to move again. By this time the tensity of waiting had made me stiff. I therefore boldly unlatched the door of the car and stepped out upon the rough ground. Nothing happened. I walked slowly back and forth with my hands in my pockets. More and more time dragged by. More than half an hour had now elapsed and I became impatient. I went to the rear window of the car and spoke softly into the interior.

'Henry, I fear we have been victimized in a very cheap way. I fear very much that this is nothing but a low practical joke on the part of Mr. Gandesi in retaliation for the way you handled him last night. There is no one here and only one possible way of arriving. It looks to me like a very unlikely place for the sort of meeting we have been expecting.'

'The son of a bitch!' Henry whispered back, and the gurgling sound was repeated in the darkness of the car. Then there was movement and he appeared free of the rug. The door opened against my body. Henry's head emerged. He looked in all directions his eyes could command. 'Sit down on the running board,' he whispered. 'I'm getting out. If they got a bead on us from them bushes, they'll only see one head.'

I did what Henry suggested and turned my collar up high and pulled my hat down over my eyes. As noiselessly as a shadow Henry stepped out of the car and shut the door without sound and stood before me ranging the limited horizon with his eyes. I could see the dim reflection of light on the gun in his hand. We remained thus for ten more minutes.

Henry then got angry and threw discretion to the winds. 'Suckered!' he snarled. 'You know what happened, Walter?'

'No, Henry. I do not.'

'It was just a tryout, that's what it was. Somewhere along the line these dirty so-and-so's checked on you to see did you play ball, and then again they checked on you at that drugstore back there. I bet you a pair of solid platinum bicycle wheels that was a long-distance call you caught back there.'

'Yes, Henry, now that you mention it, I am sure it was,' I said sadly.

'There you are, kid. The bums ain't even left town. They are sitting back there beside their plush-lined spittoons giving you the big razzo. And to-morrow this guy calls you again on the phone and says Okay so far, but they had to be careful, and they will try again to-night maybe out in San Fernando Valley and the price will be upped to ten grand, on account of their extra trouble. I oughta go back there and twist that Gandesi as he would be lookin' up his left pants leg.'

'Well, Henry,' I said, 'after all, I did not do exactly what they told me to, because you insisted on coming with me. And perhaps they are more clever than you think. So I think the best thing now is to go back to town and hope there will be a chance to-morrow to try again. And you must promise me faithfully not to interfere.'

'Nuts!' Henry said angrily. 'Without me along they would take you the way the cat took the canary. You are a sweet guy, Walter, but you don't know as many answers as Baby Leroy. These guys are thieves and they have a string of marbles that might probably bring them twenty grand with careful handling. They are out for a quick touch, but they will squeeze all they can just the same. I oughta go back to that fat wop Gandesi right now. I could do things to the slob that ain't been invented yet.'

'Now, Henry, don't get violent,' I said.

'Haw,' Henry snarled. 'Them guys give me an ache in the back of my lap.' He raised his bottle to his lips with his left hand and drank thirstily. His voice came down a few tones and sounded more peaceful. 'Better dip the bill, Walter. The party's a flop.'

'Perhaps you are right, Henry,' I sighed. 'I will admit that my stomach has been trembling like an autumn leaf for all of half an hour.'

So I stood up boldly beside him and poured a liberal portion of the fiery liquid down my throat. At once my courage revived. I handed the bottle back to Henry and he placed it carefully down on the running board. He stood beside me dancing the short automatic pistol up and down on the broad palm of his hand.

'I don't need no tools to handle that bunch. The hell with it.' And with a sweep of his arm he hurled the pistol off among the bushes, where it fell to the ground with a muffled thud. He walked away from the car and stood with his arms akimbo, looking up at the sky.

I moved over beside him and watched his averted face, in so far as I was able to see it in that dim light. A strange melancholy came over me. In the brief time I had known Henry I had grown very fond of him.

'Well, Henry,' I said at last, 'what is the next move?'

'Beat it on home, I guess,' he said slowly and mournfully. 'And get good and drunk.' He doubled his hands into fists and shook them slowly. Then he turned to face me. 'Yeah,' he said. 'Nothing else to do. Beat it on home, kid, is all that is left to us.'

'Not quite yet, Henry,' I said softly.

I took my right hand out of my pocket. I have large hands. In my right hand nestled the roll of wrapped quarters which I had obtained at the bank that morning. My hand made a large fist around them.

'Good night, Henry,' I said quietly, and swung my fist with all the weight

of my arm and body. 'You had two strikes on me, Henry,' I said. 'The big
one is still left.'

But Henry was not listening to me. My fist with the wrapped weight of
metal inside it had caught him fairly and squarely on the point of his jaw.
His legs became boneless and he pitched straight forward, brushing my sleeve
as he fell. I stepped quickly out of his way.

Henry Eichelberger lay motionless on the ground, as limp as a rubber
glove.

I looked down at him a little sadly, waiting for him to stir, but he did not
move a muscle. He lay inert, completely unconscious. I dropped the roll of
quarters back into my pocket, bent over him, searched him thoroughly,
moving him around like a sack of meal, but it was a long time before I found
the pearls. They were twined around his ankle inside his left sock.

'Well, Henry,' I said, speaking to him for the last time, although he could
not hear me, 'you are a gentleman, even if you are a thief. You could have
taken the money a dozen times this afternoon and given me nothing. You
could have taken it a little while ago when you had the gun in your hand,
but even that repelled you. You threw the gun away and we were man to
man, far from help, far from interference. And even then you hesitated,
Henry. In fact, Henry, I think for a successful thief you hesitated just a little
too long. But as a man of sporting feelings I can only think the more highly
of you. Good-bye, Henry, and good luck.'

I took my wallet out and withdrew a one-hundred-dollar bill and placed it
carefully in the pocket where I had seen Henry put his money. Then I went
back to the car and took a drink out of the whisky bottle and corked it
firmly and laid it beside him, convenient to his right hand.

I felt sure that when he awakened he would need it.

8

It was past ten o'clock when I returned home to my apartment, but I at
once went to the telephone and called Ellen Macintosh. 'Darling!' I cried.
'I have the pearls.'

I caught the sound of her indrawn breath over the wire. 'Oh darling,' she
said tensely and excitedly, 'and you are not hurt? They did not hurt you,
darling? They just took the money and let you go?'

'There were no "they" darling,' I said proudly. 'I still have Mr. Gallemore's money intact. There was only Henry.'

'Henry!' she cried in a very strange voice. 'But I thought—Come over
here at once, Walter Gage, and tell me——'

'I have whisky on my breath, Ellen.'

'Darling! I'm sure you needed it. Come at once.'

So once more I went down to the street and hurried to Carondelet Park and in no time at all was at the Penruddock residence. Ellen came out on the porch to meet me and we talked there quietly in the dark, holding hands, for the household had gone to bed. As simply as I could I told her my story.

'But, darling,' she said at last, 'how did you know it was Henry? I thought Henry was your friend. And this other voice on the telephone——'

'Henry *was* my friend,' I said a little sadly, 'and that is what destroyed him. As to the voice on the telephone, that was a small matter and easily arranged. Henry was away from me a number of times to arrange it. There was just one small point that gave me thought. After I gave Gandesi my private card with the name of my apartment house scribbled upon it, it was necessary for Henry to communicate to his confederate that we had seen Gandesi and given him my name and address. For of course when I had this foolish, or perhaps not so very foolish idea of visiting some well-known underworld character in order to send a message that we would buy back the pearls, this was Henry's opportunity to make me think the telephone message came as a result of our talking to Gandesi, and telling him our difficulty. But since the first call came to me at my apartment before Henry had had a chance to inform his confederate of our meeting with Gandesi, it was obvious that a trick had been employed.

'Then I recalled that a car had bumped into us from behind and Henry had gone back to abuse the driver. And of course the bumping was deliberate, and Henry had made the opportunity for it on purpose, and his confederate was in the car. So Henry, while pretending to shout at him, was able to convey the necessary information.'

'But, Walter,' Ellen said, having listened to this explanation a little impatiently, 'that is a very small matter. What I really want to know is how you decided that Henry had the pearls at all.'

'But you told me he had them,' I said. 'You were quite sure of it. Henry is a very durable character. It would be just like him to hide the pearls somewhere, having no fear of what the police might do to him, and get another position and then after perhaps quite a long time, retrieve the pearls and quietly leave this part of the country.'

Ellen shook her head impatiently in the darkness of the porch. 'Walter,' she said sharply, 'you are hiding something. You could not have been sure and you would not have hit Henry in that brutal way, unless you had been sure. I know you well enough to know that.'

'Well, darling,' I said modestly, 'there was indeed another small indication, one of those foolish trifles which the cleverest men overlook. As you know, I do not use the regular apartment-house telephone, not wishing to be annoyed by canvassers and such people. The phone which I use is a private line and its number is unlisted. But the calls I received from Henry's confederate came over that phone, and Henry had been in my apartment a great deal, and I had been careful not to give Mr. Gandesi that number, as I was perfectly sure from the beginning that Henry had the pearls, if only I could get him to bring them out of hiding.'

'Oh, darling,' Ellen cried, and threw her arms around me. 'How brave you are, and I really think that you are actually clever in your own peculiar way. Do you believe that Henry was in love with me?'

But that was a subject in which I had no interest whatever. I left the pearls in Ellen's keeping and late as the hour now was I drove at once to the residence of Mr. Lansing Gallemore and told him my story and gave him back his money.

A few months later I was happy to receive a letter postmarked in Honolulu and written on a very inferior brand of paper.

Well, pal, that Sunday punch of yours was the money and I did not think you had it in you, altho of course I was not set for it. But it was a pip and made me think of you for a week every time I brushed my teeth. It was too bad I had to scram because you are a sweet guy altho a little on the goofy side and I'd like to be getting plastered with you right now instead of wiping oil valves where I am at which is not where this letter is mailed by several thousand miles. There is just two things I would like you to know and they are both kosher. I did fall hard for that tall blonde and this was the main reason I took my time from the old lady. Glomming the pearls was just one of those screwy ideas a guy can get when he is dizzy with a dame. It was a crime the way they left them marbles lying around in that bread box and I worked for a Frenchy once in Djibouty and got to know pearls enough to tell them from snowballs. But when it came to the clinch down there in that brush with us two alone and no holds barred I just was too soft to go through with the deal. Tell that blonde you got a loop on I was asking for her.

Yrs. as ever,

HENRY EICHELBERGER (*Alias*)

P.S. What do you know, that punk that did the phone work on you tried to take me for a fifty cut on that C note you tucked in my vest. I had to twist the sucker plenty.

Yrs. H.E. (*Alias*)

DE MORTUIS...

BY JOHN COLLIER

from *Fancies and Goodnights*

(1952)

DE MORTUIS . . .

DR. RANKIN was a large and rawboned man on whom the newest suit at once appeared outdated, like a suit in a photograph of twenty years ago. This was due to the squareness and flatness of his torso, which might have been put together by a manufacturer of packing cases. His face also had a wooden and a roughly constructed look; his hair was wiglike and resentful of the comb. He had those huge and clumsy hands which can be an asset to a doctor in a small upstate town where people still retain a rural relish for paradox, thinking that the more apelike the paw, the more precise it can be in the delicate business of a tonsillectomy.

This conclusion was perfectly justified in the case of Dr. Rankin. For example, on this particular fine morning, though his task was nothing more ticklish than the cementing over of a large patch on his cellar floor, he managed those large and clumsy hands with all the unflurried certainty of one who would never leave a sponge within or create an unsightly scar without.

The Doctor surveyed his handiwork from all angles. He added a touch here and a touch there till he had achieved a smoothness altogether professional. He swept up a few last crumbs of soil and dropped them into the furnace. He paused before putting away the pick and shovel he had been using, and found occasion for yet another artistic sweep of his trowel, which made the new surface precisely flush with the surrounding floor. At this moment of supreme concentration the porch door upstairs slammed with the report of a minor piece of artillery, which, appropriately enough, caused Dr. Rankin to jump as if he had been shot.

The Doctor lifted a frowning face and an attentive ear. He heard two pairs of heavy feet clump across the resonant floor of the porch. He heard the house door opened and the visitors enter the hall, with which his cellar communicated by a short flight of steps. He heard whistling and then the voices of Buck and Bud crying, 'Doc! Hi, Doc! They're biting!'

Whether the Doctor was not inclined for fishing that day, or whether, like others of his large and heavy type, he experienced an especially sharp, unsociable reaction on being suddenly startled, or whether he was merely anxious to finish undisturbed the job in hand and proceed to more important duties, he did not respond immediately to the inviting outcry of his friends.

959

Instead, he listened while it ran its natural course, dying down at last into a puzzled and fretful dialogue.

'I guess he's out.'

'I'll write a note—say we're at the creek, to come on down.'

'We could tell Irene.'

'But she's not here, either. You'd think *she'd* be around.'

'Ought to be, by the look of the place.'

'You said it, Bud. Just look at this table. You could write your name——'

'Sh-h-h! Look!'

Evidently the last speaker had noticed that the cellar door was ajar and that a light was shining below. Next moment the door was pushed wide open and Bud and Buck looked down.

'Why, Doc! There you are!'

'Didn't you hear us yelling?'

The Doctor, not too pleased at what he had overheard, nevertheless smiled his rather wooden smile as his two friends made their way down the steps. 'I thought I heard someone,' he said.

'We was bawling our heads off,' Buck said. 'Thought nobody was home. Where's Irene?'

'Visiting,' said the Doctor. 'She's gone visiting.'

'Hey, what goes on?' said Bud. 'What are you doing? Burying one of your patients, or what?'

'Oh, there's been water seeping up through the floor,' said the Doctor. 'I figured it might be some spring opened up or something.'

'You don't say!' said Bud, assuming instantly the high ethical standpoint of the realtor. 'Gee, Doc, I sold you this property. Don't say I fixed you up with a dump where there's an underground spring.'

'There was water,' said the Doctor.

'Yes, but, Doc, you can look on that geological map the Kiwanis Club got up. There's not a better section of subsoil in the town.'

'Looks like he sold you a pup,' said Buck, grinning.

'No,' said Bud. 'Look. When the Doc came here he was green. You'll admit he was green. The things he didn't know!'

'He bought Ted Webber's jalopy,' said Buck.

'He'd have bought the Jessop place if I'd let him,' said Bud. 'But I wouldn't give him a bum steer.'

'Not the poor, simple city slicker from Poughkeepsie,' said Buck.

'Some people would have taken him,' said Bud. 'Maybe some people did. Not me. I recommended this property. He and Irene moved straight in as soon as they were married. I wouldn't have put the Doc on to a dump where there'd be a spring under the foundations.'

'Oh, forget it,' said the Doctor, embarrassed by this conscientiousness. 'I guess it was just the heavy rains.'

'By gosh!' Buck said, glancing at the besmeared point of the pickaxe. 'You certainly went deep enough. Right down into the clay, huh?'

'That's four feet down, the clay,' Bud said.

'Eighteen inches,' said the Doctor.

'Four feet,' said Bud. 'I can show you on the map.'

'Come on. No arguments,' said Buck. 'How's about it, Doc? An hour or two at the creek, eh? They're biting.'

'Can't do it, boys,' said the Doctor. 'I've got to see a patient or two.'

'Aw, live and let live, Doc,' Bud said. 'Give 'em a chance to get better. Are you going to depopulate the whole darn town?'

The Doctor looked down, smiled, and muttered, as he always did when this particular jest was trotted out. 'Sorry, boys,' he said. 'I can't make it.'

'Well,' said Bud, disappointed. 'I suppose we'd better get along. How's Irene?'

'Irene?' said the Doctor. 'Never better. She's gone visiting. Albany. Got the eleven-o'clock train.'

'Eleven o'clock?' said Buck. 'For Albany?'

'Did I say Albany?' said the Doctor. 'Watertown, I meant.'

'Friends in Watertown?' Buck asked.

'Mrs. Slater,' said the Doctor. 'Mr. and Mrs. Slater. Lived next door to 'em when she was a kid, Irene said, over on Sycamore Street.'

'Slater?' said Bud. 'Next door to Irene. No.'

'Oh, yes,' said the Doctor. 'She was telling me all about them last night. She got a letter. Seems this Mrs. Slater looked after her when her mother was in hospital one time.'

'No,' said Bud.

'That's what she told me,' said the Doctor. 'Of course, it was a good many years ago.'

'Look, Doc,' said Buck. 'Bud and I were raised in this town. We've known Irene's folks all our lives. We were in and out of their house all the time. There was never anybody next door called Slater.'

'Perhaps,' said the Doctor, 'she married again, this woman. Perhaps it was a different name.'

Bud shook his head.

'What time did Irene go to the station?' Buck asked.

'Oh, about a quarter of an hour ago,' said the Doctor.

'You didn't drive her?' said Buck.

'She walked,' said the Doctor.

'We came down Main Street,' Buck said. 'We didn't meet her.'

'Maybe she walked across the pasture,' said the Doctor.

'That's a tough walk with a suitcase,' said Buck.

'She just had a couple of things in a little bag,' said the Doctor.

Bud was still shaking his head.

Buck looked at Bud, and then at the pick, at the new, damp cement on the floor. 'Jesus Christ!' he said.

'Oh, God, Doc!' Bud said. 'A guy like you!'

'What in the name of heaven are you two bloody fools thinking?' asked the Doctor. 'What are you trying to say?'

'A spring!' said Bud. 'I ought to have known right away it wasn't any spring.'

The Doctor looked at his cement-work, at the pick, at the large worried faces of his two friends. His own face turned livid. 'Am I crazy?' he said. 'Or are you? You suggest that I've—that Irene—my wife—oh, go on! Get out! Yes, go and get the sheriff. Tell him to come here and start digging. You—get out!'

Bud and Buck looked at each other, shifted their feet, and stood still again.

'Go on,' said the Doctor.

'I don't know,' said Bud.

'It's not as if he didn't have the provocation,' Buck said.

'God knows,' Bud said.

'God knows,' Buck said. 'You know. I know. The whole town knows. But try telling it to a jury.'

The Doctor put his hand to his head. 'What's that?' he said. 'What is it? Now what are you saying? What do you mean?'

'If this ain't being on the spot!' said Buck. 'Doc, you can see how it is. It takes some thinking. We've been friends right from the start. Damn good friends.'

'But we've got to think,' said Bud. 'It's serious. Provocation or not, there's a law in the land. There's such a thing as being an accomplice.'

'You were talking about provocation,' said the Doctor.

'You're right,' said Buck. 'And you're our friend. And if ever it could be called justified——'

'We've got to fix this somehow,' said Bud.

'Justified?' said the Doctor.

'You were bound to get wised up sooner or later,' said Buck.

'We could have told you,' said Bud. 'Only—what the hell?'

'We could,' said Buck. 'And we nearly did. Five years ago. Before ever you married her. You hadn't been here six months, but we sort of cottoned to you. Thought of giving you a hint. Spoke about it. Remember, Bud?'

Bud nodded. 'Funny,' he said. 'I came right out in the open about that Jessop property. I wouldn't let you buy that, Doc. But getting married, that's something else again. We could have told you.'

'We're that much responsible,' Buck said.

'I'm fifty,' said the Doctor. 'I suppose it's pretty old for Irene.'

'If you was Johnny Weissmuller at the age of twenty-one, it wouldn't make any difference,' said Buck.

'I know a lot of people think she's not exactly a perfect wife,' said the Doctor. 'Maybe she's not. She's young. She's full of life.'

'Oh, skip it!' said Buck sharply, looking at the raw cement. 'Skip it, Doc, for God's sake.'

The Doctor brushed his hand across his face. 'Not everybody wants the same thing,' he said. 'I'm a sort of dry fellow. I don't open up very easily. Irene—you'd call her gay.'

'You said it,' said Buck.

'She's no housekeeper,' said the Doctor. 'I know it. But that's not the only thing a man wants. She's enjoyed herself.'

'Yeah,' said Buck. 'She did.'

'That's what I love,' said the Doctor. 'Because I'm not that way myself. She's not very deep, mentally. All right. Say she's stupid. I don't care. Lazy. No system. Well, I've got plenty of system. She's enjoyed herself. It's beautiful. It's innocent. Like a child.'

'Yes. If that was all,' Buck said.

'But,' said the Doctor, turning his eyes full on him, 'you seem to know there was more.'

'Everybody knows it,' said Buck.

'A decent, straightforward guy comes to a place like this and marries the town floozy,' Bud said bitterly. 'And nobody'll tell him. Everybody just watches.'

'And laughs,' said Buck. 'You and me, Bud, as well as the rest.'

'We told her to watch her step,' said Bud. 'We warned her.'

'Everybody warned her,' said Buck. 'But people get fed up. When it got to truck-drivers——'

'It was never us, Doc,' said Bud, earnestly. 'Not after you came along, anyway.'

'The town'll be on your side,' said Buck.

'That won't mean much when the case comes to trial in the county seat,' said Bud.

'Oh!' cried the Doctor, suddenly. 'What shall I do? What shall I do?'

'It's up to you, Bud,' said Buck. 'I can't turn him in.'

'Take it easy, Doc,' said Bud. 'Calm down. Look, Buck. When we came in here the street was empty, wasn't it?'

'I guess so,' said Buck. 'Anyway, nobody saw us come down cellar.'

'And we haven't been down,' Bud said, addressing himself forcefully to the Doctor. 'Get that, Doc? We shouted upstairs, hung around a minute or two, and cleared out. But we never came down into this cellar.'

'I wish you hadn't,' the Doctor said heavily.

'All you have to do is say Irene went out for a walk and never came back,' said Buck. 'Bud and I can swear we saw her headed out of town with a fellow in a tan roadster. Everybody'll believe that, all right. We'll fix it. But later. Now we'd better scram.'

'And remember, now. Stick to it. We never came down here and we haven't seen you to-day,' said Bud. 'So long!'

Buck and Bud ascended the steps, moving with a rather absurd degree of caution. 'You'd better get that . . . that thing covered up,' Buck said over his shoulder.

Left alone, the Doctor sat down on an empty box, holding his head with both hands. He was still sitting like this when the porch door slammed again. This time he did not start. He listened. The house door opened and closed. A voice cried, 'Yoo-hoo! Yoo-hoo! I'm back.'

The Doctor rose slowly to his feet. 'I'm down here, Irene!' he called.

The cellar door opened. A young woman stood at the head of the steps. 'Can you beat it?' she said. 'I missed the damn train.'

'Oh!' said the Doctor. 'Did you come back across the field?'

'Yes, like a fool,' she said. 'I could have hitched a ride and caught the train up the line. Only I didn't think. If you'd run me over to the junction, I could still make it.'

'Maybe,' said the Doctor. 'Did you meet anyone coming back?'

'Not a soul,' she said. 'Aren't you finished with that old job yet?'

'I'm afraid I'll have to take it all up again,' said the Doctor. 'Come down here, my dear, and I'll show you.'

FOR ESMÉ—
WITH LOVE AND SQUALOR

BY J. D. SALINGER

Author of *The Catcher in the Rye* (1951)

FOR ESMÉ—WITH LOVE AND SQUALOR

=====

JUST recently by air mail, I received an invitation to a wedding that will take place in England on 18 April. It happens to be a wedding I'd give a lot to be able to get to, and when the invitation first arrived, I thought it might just be possible for me to make the trip abroad, by plane, expenses be hanged. However, I've since discussed the matter rather extensively with my wife, a breathtakingly levelheaded girl, and we've decided against it— for one thing, I'd completely forgotten that my mother-in-law is looking forward to spending the last two weeks in April with us. I really don't get to see Mother Grencher terribly often, and she's not getting any younger. She's fifty-eight. (As she'd be the first to admit.)

All the same, though, where*ever* I happen to be, I don't think I'm the type that doesn't even lift a finger to prevent a wedding from flatting. Accordingly, I've gone ahead and jotted down a few revealing notes on the bride as I knew her almost six years ago. If my notes should cause the groom, whom I haven't met, an uneasy moment or two, so much the better. Nobody's aiming to please, here. More, really, to edify, to instruct.

In April of 1944, I was among some sixty American enlisted men who took a rather specialized pre-Invasion training course, directed by British Intelligence, in Devon, England. And as I look back, it seems to me that we were fairly unique, the sixty of us, in that there wasn't one good mixer in the bunch. We were all essentially letter-writing types, and when we spoke to each other out of the line of duty, it was usually to ask somebody if he had any ink he wasn't using. When we weren't writing letters or attending classes, each of us went pretty much his own way. Mine usually led me, on clear days, in scenic circles around the countryside. Rainy days, I generally sat in a dry place and read a book, often just an axe length away from a ping-pong table.

The training course lasted three weeks, ending on a Saturday, a very rainy one. At seven that last night, our whole group was scheduled to entrain for London, where, as rumour had it, we were to be assigned to infantry and airborne divisions mustered for the D-Day landings. By three in the afternoon, I'd packed all my belongings into my barrack bag, including a canvas gas mask container full of books I'd brought over from the Other Side. (The gas mask itself I'd slipped through a porthole of the *Mauretania* some weeks earlier, fully aware that if the enemy ever *did* use gas I'd never get the damn thing on in time.) I remember standing at an end window of our Quonset hut for a very long time, looking out at the slanting, dreary rain, my trigger finger itching imperceptibly, if at all. I could hear behind my back the uncomradely scratching of many fountain pens on many sheets of V-mail paper. Abruptly, with nothing special in mind, I came away from the window and put on my raincoat, cashmere muffler, galoshes, woollen gloves, and overseas cap (the last of which, I'm still told, I wore at an angle all my own—slightly down over both ears). Then, after synchronizing my wristwatch with the clock in the latrine, I walked down the long, wet cobblestone hill into town. I ignored the flashes of lightning all around me. They either had your number on them or they didn't.

In the centre of town, which was probably the wettest part of town, I stopped in front of a church to read the bulletin board, mostly because the featured numerals, white on black, had caught my attention but partly because, after three years in the Army, I'd become addicted to reading bulletin boards. At three-fifteen, the board stated, there would be children's-choir practice. I looked at my wristwatch, then back at the board. A sheet of paper was tacked up, listing the names of the children expected to attend practice. I stood in the rain and read all the names, then entered the church.

A dozen or so adults were among the pews, several of them bearing pairs of small-size rubbers, soles up, in their laps. I passed along and sat down in the front row. On the rostrum, seated in three compact rows of auditorium chairs, were about twenty children, mostly girls, ranging in age from about seven to thirteen. At the moment, their choir coach, an enormous woman in tweeds, was advising them to open their mouths wider when they sang. Had anyone, she asked, ever heard of a little dickey-bird that *dared* to sing his charming song without first opening his little beak wide, wide, wide? Apparently nobody ever had. She was given a steady, opaque look. She went on to say that she wanted *all* her children to absorb the *meaning* of the words they sang, not just *mouth* them, like silly-billy parrots. She then blew a note on her pitch pipe, and the children, like so many under-age weight-lifters, raised their hymn books.

They sang without instrumental accompaniment—or, more accurately in their case, without any interference. Their voices were melodious and un-sentimental, almost to the point where a somewhat more denominational man than myself might, without straining, have experienced levitation. A couple of the very youngest children dragged the tempo a trifle, but in a way that only the composer's mother could have found fault with. I had never heard the hymn, but I kept hoping it was one with a dozen or more verses. Listening, I scanned all the children's faces but watched one in par-ticular, that of the child nearest me, on the end seat in the first row. She was about thirteen, with straight ash-blond hair of ear-lobe length, an exquisite forehead, and blasé eyes that, I thought, might very possibly have counted the house. Her voice was distinctly separate from the other children's voices, and not just because she was seated nearest me. It had the best upper register, the sweetest-sounding, the surest, and it automatically led the way. The young lady, however, seemed slightly bored with her own singing ability, or perhaps just with the time and place; twice, between verses, I saw her yawn. It was a ladylike yawn, a closed-mouth yawn, but you couldn't miss it; her nostril wings gave her away.

The instant the hymn ended, the choir coach began to give her lengthy opinion of people who can't keep their feet still and their lips sealed tight during the minister's sermon. I gathered that the singing part of the rehearsal was over, and before the coach's dissonant speaking voice could entirely break the spell the children's singing had cast, I got up and left the church.

It was raining even harder. I walked down the street and looked through the window of the Red Cross recreation room, but soldiers were standing two and three deep at the coffee counter, and, even through the glass, I could hear ping-pong balls bouncing in another room. I crossed the street and entered a civilian tearoom, which was empty except for a middle-aged waitress, who looked as if she would have preferred a customer with a dry raincoat. I used a coat tree as delicately as possible, and then sat down at a table and ordered tea and cinnamon toast. It was the first time all day that I'd spoken to anyone. I then looked through all my pockets, including my raincoat, and finally found a couple of stale letters to re-read, one from my wife, telling me how the service at Schrafft's Eighty-eighth Street had fallen off, and one from my mother-in-law, asking me to please send her some cashmere yarn first chance I got away from 'camp'.

While I was still on my first cup of tea, the young lady I had been watching and listening to in the choir came into the tearoom. Her hair was soaking wet, and the rims of both ears were showing. She was with a very small boy, unmistakably her brother, whose cap she removed by lifting it off his head with two fingers, as if it were a laboratory specimen. Bringing up the rear was an efficient-looking woman in a limp felt hat—presumably their governess. The choir member, taking off her coat as she walked across the floor, made the table selection—a good one, from my point of view, as it was just eight or ten feet directly in front of me. She and the governess sat down. The small boy, who was about five, wasn't ready to sit down yet. He slid out of and discarded his reefer; then, with the deadpan expression of a born heller, he methodically went about annoying his governess by pushing in and pulling out his chair several times, watching her face. The governess, keeping her voice down, gave him two or three orders to sit down and, in effect, stop the monkey business, but it was only when his sister spoke to him that he came around and applied the small of his back to his chair seat.

He immediately picked up his napkin and put it on his head. His sister removed it, opened it, and spread it out on his lap.

About the time their tea was brought, the choir member caught me staring over at her party. She stared back at me, with those house-counting eyes of hers, then, abruptly, gave me a small, qualified smile. It was oddly radiant, as certain, small, qualified smiles sometimes are. I smiled back much less radiantly, keeping my upper lip down over a coal-black G.I. temporary filling showing between two of my front teeth. The next thing I knew, the young lady was standing, with enviable poise, beside my table. She was wearing a tartan dress—a Campbell tartan, I believe. It seemed to me to be a wonderful dress for a very young girl to be wearing on a rainy, rainy day. 'I thought Americans despised tea,' she said.

It wasn't the observation of a smart aleck but that of a truth-lover or a statistics-lover. I replied that some of us never drank anything *but* tea. I asked her if she'd care to join me.

'Thank you,' she said. 'Perhaps for just a fraction of a moment.'

I got up and drew a chair for her, the one opposite me, and she sat down on the forward quarter of it, keeping her spine easily and beautifully straight. I went back—almost hurried back—to my own chair, more than willing to hold up my end of a conversation. When I was seated, I couldn't think of anything to say, though. I smiled again, still keeping my coal-black filling under concealment. I remarked that it was certainly a terrible day out.

'Yes; quite,' said my guest, in the clear, unmistakable voice of a small-talk detester. She placed her fingers flat on the table edge, like someone at a séance, then, almost instantly, closed her hands—her nails were bitten down to the quick. She was wearing a wristwatch, a military-looking one that looked rather like a navigator's chronograph. Its face was much too large for her slender wrist. 'You were at choir practice,' she said matter-of-factly. 'I saw you.'

I said I certainly had been, and that I had heard her voice singing separately from the others. I said I thought she had a very fine voice.

She nodded. 'I know. I'm going to be a professional singer.'

'Really? Opera?'

'Heavens, no. I'm going to sing jazz on the radio and make heaps of money. Then, when I'm thirty, I shall retire and live on a ranch in Ohio.' She touched the top of her soaking-wet head with the flat of her hand. 'Do you know Ohio?' she asked.

I said I'd been through it on the train a few times but that I didn't really know it. I offered her a piece of cinnamon toast.

'No, thank you,' she said. 'I eat like a bird, actually.'

I bit into a piece of toast myself, and commented that there's some mighty rough country around Ohio.

'I know. An American I met told me. You're the eleventh American I've met.'

Her governess was now urgently signalling her to return to her own table —in effect, to stop bothering the man. My guest, however, calmly moved her chair an inch or two so that her back broke all possible further communication with the home table. 'You go to that secret Intelligence school on the hill, don't you?' she inquired coolly.

As security-minded as the next one, I replied that I was visiting Devonshire for my health.

'*Really*,' she said, 'I wasn't quite born yesterday, you know.'

I said I'd bet she hadn't been, at that. I drank my tea for a moment. I was getting a trifle posture-conscious, and I sat up somewhat straighter in my seat.

'You seem quite intelligent for an American,' my guest mused.

I told her that was a pretty snobbish thing to say, if you thought about it at all, and that I hoped it was unworthy of her.

She blushed—automatically conferring on me the social poise I'd been missing. 'Well. Most of the Americans *I've* seen act like animals. They're forever punching one another about, and insulting everyone, and—— You know what one of them did?'

I shook my head.

'One of them threw an empty whisky bottle through my aunt's window. *Fortunately*, the window was open. But does that sound very intelligent to you?'

It didn't especially, but I didn't say so. I said that many soldiers, all over the world, were a long way from home, and that few of them had had many real advantages in life. I said I'd thought that most people could figure that out for themselves.

'Possibly,' said my guest, without conviction. She raised her hand to her wet head again, picked at a few limp filaments of blond hair, trying to cover her exposed ear rims. 'My hair is soaking wet,' she said. 'I look a fright.' She looked over at me. 'I have quite wavy hair when it's dry.'

'I can see that, I can see you have.'

'Not actually curly, but quite wavy,' she said. 'Are you married?'

I said I was.

She nodded. 'Are you very deeply in love with your wife? Or am I being too personal?'

I said that when she was, I'd speak up.

She put her hands and wrists farther forward on the table, and I remember wanting to do something about that enormous-faced wristwatch she was wearing—perhaps suggest that she try wearing it round her waist.

'Usually, I'm not terribly gregarious,' she said, and looked over at me to see if I knew the meaning of the word. I didn't give her a sign, though, one way or the other. 'I purely came over because I thought you looked extremely lonely. You have an extremely sensitive face.'

I said she was right, that I *had* been feeling lonely, and that I was very glad she'd come over.

'I'm training myself to be more compassionate. My aunt says I'm a terribly cold person,' she said, and felt the top of her head again. 'I live with my aunt. She's an extremely kind person. Since the death of my mother, she's done everything within her power to make Charles and me feel adjusted.'

'I'm glad.'

'Mother was an extremely intelligent person. Quite sensuous, in many ways.' She looked at me with a kind of fresh acuteness. 'Do you find me terribly cold?'

I told her absolutely not—very much to the contrary, in fact. I told her my name and asked for hers.

She hesitated. 'My first name is Esmé. I don't think I shall tell you my full name, for the moment. I have a title and you may just be impressed by titles. Americans are, you know.'

I said I didn't think I would be, but that it might be a good idea, at that, to hold on to the title for a while.

Just then, I felt someone's warm breath on the back of my neck. I turned round and just missed brushing noses with Esmé's small brother. Ignoring me, he addressed his sister in a piercing treble: 'Miss Megley said you must come and finish your tea!' His message delivered, he retired to the chair between his sister and me, on my right. I regarded him with high interest. He was looking very splendid in brown Shetland shorts, a navy-blue jersey, white shirt, and striped necktie. He gazed back at me with immense green eyes. 'Why do people in films kiss sideways?' he demanded.

'Sideways?' I said. It was a problem that had baffled me in my own childhood. I said I guessed it was because actors' noses are too big for kissing anyone head on.

'His name is Charles,' Esmé said. 'He's extremely brilliant for his age.'

'He certainly has green eyes. Haven't you, Charles?'

Charles gave me the fishy look my question deserved, then wriggled downward and forward in his chair till all of his body was under the table except his head, which he left, wrestler's-bridge style, on the chair seat. 'They're orange,' he said in a strained voice, addressing the ceiling. He picked up a corner of the tablecloth and put it over his handsome, deadpan little face.

'Sometimes he's brilliant and sometimes he's not,' Esmé said. 'Charles, do sit up!'

Charles stayed right where he was. He seemed to be busy holding his breath.

'He misses our father very much. He was s-l-a-i-n in North Africa.'

I expressed regret to hear it.

Esmé nodded. 'Father adored him.' She bit reflectively at the cuticle of her thumb. 'He looks very much like my mother—Charles, I mean. I look exactly like my father.' She went on biting at her cuticle. 'My mother was quite a passionate woman. She was an extrovert. Father was an introvert. They were quite well mated, though, in a superficial way. To be quite candid, Father really needed more of an intellectual companion than Mother was. He was an extremely gifted genius.'

I waited, receptively, for further information, but none came. I looked down at Charles, who was now resting the side of his face on his chair seat. When he saw that I was looking at him, he closed his eyes, sleepily, angelically, then stuck out his tongue—an appendage of startling length—and gave out what in *my* country would have been a glorious tribute to a myopic baseball umpire. It fairly shook the tearoom.

'Stop that,' Esmé said, clearly unshaken. 'He saw an American do it in a fish-and-chips queue, and now he does it whenever he's bored. Just stop it, now, or I shall send you directly to Miss Megley.'

Charles opened his enormous eyes as sign that he'd heard his sister's threat, but otherwise didn't look especially alerted. He closed his eyes again, and continued to rest the side of his face on the chair seat.

I mentioned that maybe he ought to save it—meaning the Bronx cheer—till he started using his title regularly. That is, if he had a title, too.

Esmé gave me a long, faintly clinical look. 'You have a dry sense of humour, haven't you?' she said—wistfully. 'Father said I have no sense of humour at all. He said I was unequipped to meet life because I have no sense of humour.'

Watching her, I lit a cigarette and said I didn't think a sense of humour was of any use in a real pinch.

'Father said it was.'

This was a statement of faith, not a contradiction, and I quickly switched horses. I nodded and said her father had probably taken the long view, while I was taking the short (whatever *that* meant).

'Charles misses him exceedingly,' Esmé said, after a moment. 'He was an exceedingly lovable man. He was extremely handsome, too. Not that one's appearance matters greatly, but he was. He had terribly penetrating eyes, for a man who was intrinsically kind.'

I nodded. I said I imagined her father had had quite an extraordinary vocabulary.

'Oh yes; quite,' said Esmé. 'He was an archivist—amateur, of course.'

At that point, I felt an importunate tap, almost a punch, on my upper arm, from Charles's direction. I turned to him. He was sitting in a fairly normal position in his chair now, except that he had one knee tucked under him. 'What did one wall say to the other wall?' he asked shrilly. 'It's a riddle!'

I rolled my eyes reflectively ceilingward and repeated the question aloud. Then I looked at Charles with a stumped expression and said I gave up.

'Meet you at the corner!' came the punch line, at top volume.

It went over biggest with Charles himself. It struck him as unbearably funny. In fact, Esmé had to come round and pound him on the back, as if treating him for a coughing spell. 'Now, stop that,' she said. She went back to her own seat. 'He tells that same riddle to everyone he meets and has a fit every single time. Usually he drools when he laughs. Now, just stop, please.'

'It's one of the best riddles I've heard, though,' I said, watching Charles, who was very gradually coming out of it. In response to this compliment, he sank considerably lower in his chair and again masked his face up to the eyes with a corner of the tablecloth. He then looked at me with his exposed eyes, which were full of slowly subsiding mirth and the pride of someone who knows a really good riddle or two.

'May I inquire how you were employed before entering the Army?' Esmé asked me.

I said I hadn't been employed at all, that I'd only been out of college a year but that I liked to think of myself as a professional short-story writer.

She nodded politely. 'Published?' she asked.

It was a familiar but always touchy question, and one that I didn't answer just one, two, three. I explained how most editors in America were a bunch——

'My father wrote beautifully,' Esmé interrupted. 'I'm saving a number of his letters for posterity.'

I said that sounded like a very good idea. I happened to be looking at her enormous-faced, chronographic-looking wristwatch again. I asked if it had belonged to her father.

She looked down at her wrist solemnly. 'Yes, it did,' she said. 'He gave it to me just before Charles and I were evacuated.' Self-consciously, she took her hands off the table, saying, 'Purely as a memento, of course'. She guided the conversation in a different direction. 'I'd be extremely flattered if you'd write a story exclusively for me sometime. I'm an avid reader.'

I told her I certainly would, if I could. I said that I wasn't terribly prolific.

'It doesn't have to be terribly prolific! Just so that it isn't childish and silly.' She reflected. 'I prefer stories about squalor.'

'About what?' I said, leaning forward.

'Squalor. I'm extremely interested in squalor.'

I was about to press her for more details, but I felt Charles pinching me, hard, on my arm. I turned to him, wincing slightly. He was standing right next to me. 'What did one wall say to the other wall?' he asked, not unfamiliarly.

'You asked him that,' Esmé said. 'Now, stop it.'

Ignoring his sister, and stepping up on one of my feet, Charles repeated the key question. I noticed that his necktie knot wasn't adjusted properly. I slid it up into place, then, looking him straight in the eye, suggested, 'Meetcha at the corner?'

The instant I'd said it, I wished I hadn't. Charles's mouth fell open. I felt as if I'd struck it open. He stepped down off my foot and, with white-hot dignity, walked over to his own table, without looking back.

'He's furious,' Esmé said. 'He has a violent temper. My mother had a propensity to spoil him. My father was the only one who didn't spoil him.'

I kept looking over at Charles, who had sat down and started to drink his tea, using both hands on the cup. I hoped he'd turn round, but he didn't.

Esmé stood up. '*Il faut que je parte aussi,*' she said, with a sigh. 'Do you know French?'

I got up from my own chair with mixed feelings of regret and confusion. Esmé and I shook hands; her hand, as I'd suspected, was a nervous hand, damp at the palm. I told her, in English, how very much I'd enjoyed her company.

She nodded. 'I thought you might,' she said. 'I'm quite communicative for my age.' She gave her hair another experimental touch. 'I'm dreadfully sorry about my hair,' she said. 'I've probably been hideous to look at.'

'Not at all! As a matter of fact, I think a lot of the wave is coming back already.'

She quickly touched her hair again. 'Do you think you'll be coming here again in the immediate future?' she asked. 'We come here every Saturday, after choir practice.'

I answered that I'd like nothing better but that, unfortunately, I was pretty sure I wouldn't be able to make it again.

'In other words, you can't discuss troop movements,' said Esmé. She made no move to leave the vicinity of the table. In fact, she crossed one foot over the other and, looking down, aligned the toes of her shoes. It was a pretty little execution, for she was wearing white socks and her ankles and feet were lovely. She looked up at me abruptly. 'Would you like me to write to you?' she asked, with a certain amount of colour in her face. 'I write extremely articulate letters for a person my——'

'I'd love it.' I took out pencil and paper and wrote down my name, rank, serial number, and A.P.O. number.

Esmé was standing with crossed ankles again. 'You're quite sure you won't forget to write that story for me?' she asked. 'It doesn't have to be *exclu*sively for me. It can——'

I said there was absolutely no chance that I'd forget. I told her that I'd never written a story *for* anybody, but that it seemed like exactly the right time to get down to it.

She nodded. 'Make it extremely squalid and moving,' she suggested. 'Are you at all acquainted with squalor?'

I said not exactly but that I was getting better acquainted with it, in one form or another, all the time, and that I'd do my best to come up to her specifications. We shook hands.

'Isn't it a pity that we didn't meet under less extenuating circumstances?' I said it was. I said it certainly was.

'Good-bye,' Esmé said. 'I hope you return from the war with all your faculties intact.'

I thanked her, and said a few other words, and then watched her leave the tearoom. She left it slowly, reflectively, testing the ends of her hair for dryness.

THIS is the squalid, or moving, part of the story, and the scene changes. The people change, too. I'm still around, but from here on in, for reasons I'm not at liberty to disclose, I've disguised myself so cunningly that even the cleverest reader will fail to recognize me.

It was about ten-thirty at night in Gaufurt, Bavaria, several weeks after V-E Day. Staff Sergeant X was in his room on the second floor of the civilian home in which he and nine other American soldiers had been quartered, even before the armistice. He was seated on a folding wooden chair at a small, messy-looking writing table, with a paperback overseas novel open before him, which he was having great trouble reading. The trouble lay with him, not the novel. Although the men who lived on the first floor usually had first grab at the books sent each month by Special Services, X usually seemed to be left with the book he might have selected himself. But he was a young man who had not come through the war with all his faculties intact, and for more than an hour he had been triple-reading paragraphs, and now he was doing it to the sentences. He suddenly closed the book, without marking his place. With his hand, he shielded his eyes for a moment against the harsh, watty glare from the naked bulb over the table.

He took a cigarette from a pack on the table and lit it with fingers that bumped gently and incessantly against one another. He sat back a trifle in his chair and smoked without any sense of taste. He had been chain-smoking for weeks. His gums bled at the slightest pressure of the tip of his tongue, and he seldom stopped experimenting; it was a little game he played, sometimes by the hour. He sat for a moment smoking and experimenting. Then, abruptly, familiarly, and, as usual, with no warning, he thought he felt his mind dislodge itself and teeter, like insecure luggage on an overhead rack. He quickly did what he had been doing for weeks to set things right: he pressed his hands hard against his temples. He held on tight for a moment. His hair needed cutting, and it was dirty. He had washed it three or four times during his two weeks' stay at the hospital in Frankfurt on the Main, but it had got dirty again on the long dusty jeep ride back to Gaufurt. Corporal Z, who had called for him at the hospital, still drove a jeep combat-style, with the windshield down on the hood, armistice or no armistice. There were thousands of new troops in Germany. By driving with his windshield down, combat-style, Corporal Z hoped to show that he was not one of them, that not by a long shot was he some new son of a bitch in the E.T.O.

When he let go of his head, X began to stare at the surface of the writing table, which was a catchall for at least two dozen unopened letters and at least five or six unopened packages, all addressed to him. He reached behind the debris and picked out a book that stood against the wall. It was a book by Goebbels, entitled *Zeit Ohne Beispiel*. It belonged to the thirty-eight-year-old, unmarried daughter of the family that, up to a few weeks earlier, had been living in the house. She had been a low official in the Nazi Party, but high enough, by Army Regulations standards, to fall into an automatic-arrest category. X himself had arrested her. Now, for the third time since he had returned from the hospital that day, he opened the woman's book and read the brief inscription on the flyleaf. Written in ink, in German, in a small, hopelessly sincere handwriting, were the words 'Dear God, life is hell'. Nothing led up to or away from it. Alone on the page and in the sickly stillness of the room, the words appeared to have the stature of an incontestable, even classic indictment. X stared at the page for several minutes, trying, against heavy odds, not to be taken in. Then, with far more zeal than he had done anything in weeks, he picked up a pencil stub and wrote down under the inscription, in English, 'Fathers and teachers, I ponder "What is hell?" I maintain that it is the suffering of being unable to love'. He started to write Dostoievski's name under the inscription, but saw—with fright that ran through his whole body—that what he had written was almost entirely illegible. He shut the book.

He quickly picked up something else from the table, a letter from his older brother in Albany. It had been on his table even before he had checked into the hospital. He opened the envelope, loosely resolved to read the letter straight through, but read only the top half of the first page. He stopped after the words 'Now that the g.d. war is over and you probably have a lot of time over there, how about sending the kids a couple of bayonets or swastikas . . .' After he'd torn it up, he looked down at the pieces as they lay in the waste-basket. He saw that he had overlooked an enclosed snapshot. He could make out somebody's feet standing on a lawn somewhere.

He put his arms on the table and rested his head on them. He ached from head to foot, all zones of pain seemingly interdependent. He was rather like a Christmas tree whose lights, wired in series, must all go out if even one bulb is defective.

The door banged open, without having been rapped on. X raised his head, turned it, and saw Corporal Z standing in the door. Corporal Z had been X's jeep partner and constant companion from D-Day straight through five campaigns of the war. He lived on the first floor and he usually came up to see X when he had a few rumours or gripes to unload. He was a huge, photogenic young man of twenty-four. During the war, a national magazine had photographed him in Hürtgen Forest; he had posed with a Thanksgiving turkey in each hand. 'Ya writin' letters?' he asked X. 'It's spooky in here, for Chrissake.' He preferred always to enter a room that had the overhead light on.

X turned around in his chair and asked him to come in, and to be careful not to step on the dog.

'The what?'

'Alvin. He's right under your feet, Clay. How 'bout turning on the goddam light?'

Clay found the overhead light switch, flicked it on, then stepped across the puny, servant's-size room and sat down on the edge of the bed, facing his host. His brick-red hair, just combed, was dripping with the amount of water he required for satisfactory grooming. A comb with a fountain-pen clip protruded, familiarly, from a right-hand pocket of his olive-drab shirt. Over the left-hand pocket he was wearing the Combat Infantryman's Badge (which technically, he wasn't authorized to wear), the European Theatre ribbon, with five bronze battle stars in it (instead of a lone silver one, which was the equivalent of five bronze ones), and the pre-Pearl Harbour service ribbon. He sighed heavily and said, 'Christ Almighty'. It meant nothing; it was Army. He took a pack of cigarettes from his shirt pocket, tapped one out, then put away the pack and rebuttoned the pocket flap. Smoking, he looked vacuously around the room. His look finally settled on the radio. 'Hey,' he said. 'They got this terrific show comin' on the radio in a coupla minutes. Bob Hope, and everybody.'

X, opening a fresh pack of cigarettes, said he had just turned the radio off.

Undarkened, Clay watched X trying to get a cigarette lit. 'Jesus,' he said, with spectator's enthusiasm, 'you oughta see your goddam hands. Boy, have you got the shakes. Ya know that?'

X got his cigarette lit, nodded, and said Clay had a real eye for detail.

'No kidding, hey. I goddam near fainted when I saw you at the hospital. You looked like a goddam *corpse*. How much weight ya lose? How many pounds? Ya know?'

'I don't know. How was your mail when I was gone? You heard from Loretta?'

Loretta was Clay's girl. They intended to get married at their earliest convenience. She wrote to him fairly regularly, from a paradise of triple exclamation points and inaccurate observations. All through the war, Clay had read all Loretta's letters aloud to X, however intimate they were—in fact, the more intimate, the better. It was his custom after each reading, to ask X to plot out or pad out the letter of reply, or to insert a few impressive words in French or German.

'Yeah, I had a letter from her yesterday. Down in my room. Show it to ya later,' Clay said, listlessly. He sat up straight on the edge of the bed, held his breath, and issued a long, resonant belch. Looking just semi-pleased with the achievement, he relaxed again. 'Her goddam brother's getting outa the Navy on account of his hip,' he said. 'He's got this hip, the bastard.' He sat up again and tried for another belch, but with below-par results. A jot of alertness came into his face. 'Hey. Before I forget. We gotta get up at five to-morrow and drive to Hamburg or someplace. Pick up Eisenhower jackets for the whole detachment.'

X, regarding him hostilely, stated that he didn't want an Eisenhower jacket.

Clay looked surprised, almost a trifle hurt. 'Oh, they're good! They look good. How come?'

'No reason. Why do we have to get up at five? The war's over, for God's sake.'

'I don't know—we gotta get back before lunch. They got some new forms in we gotta fill out before lunch. . . . I asked Bulling how come we couldn't fill 'em out to-night—he's *got* the goddam forms right on his desk. He don't want to open the envelopes yet, the son of a bitch.'

The two sat quiet for a moment, hating Bulling.

Clay suddenly looked at X with new—higher—interest than before. 'Hey,' he said. 'Did you know the goddam side of your face is jumping all over the place?'

X said he knew all about it, and covered his tic with his hand.

Clay stared at him for a moment, then said, rather vividly, as if he were the bearer of exceptionally good news, 'I wrote Loretta you had a nervous breakdown.'

'Oh?'

'Yeah. She's interested as hell in all that stuff. She's majoring in psychology.' Clay stretched himself out on the bed, shoes included. 'You know what she said? She says nobody gets a nervous breakdown just from the war and all. She says you probably were unstable like, your whole goddam life.'

X bridged his hand over his eyes—the light over the bed seemed to be blinding him—and said that Loretta's insight into things was always a joy.

Clay glanced over at him. 'Listen, ya bastard,' he said. 'She knows a goddam sight more psychology than *you* do.'

'Do you think you can bring yourself to take your stinking feet off my bed?' X asked.

Clay left his feet where they were for a few don't-tell-me-where-to-put-my-feet seconds, then swung them around to the floor and sat up. 'I'm goin' downstairs anyway. They got the radio on in Walker's room.' He didn't get up from the bed, though. 'Hey. I was just tellin' that new son of a bitch, Bernstein, downstairs. Remember that time I and you drove into Valognes, and we got shelled for about two goddam hours, and that goddam cat I shot that jumped up on the hood of the jeep when we were layin' in that hole? Remember?'

'Yes—don't start that business with that cat again, Clay, God damn it. I don't want to hear about it.'

'No, all I mean is I wrote Loretta about it. She and the whole psychology class discussed it. In class and all. The goddam professor and everybody.'

'That's fine. I don't want to hear about it, Clay.'

'No, you know the reason I took a pot shot at it, Loretta says? She says I was temporarily insane. No kidding. From the shelling and all.'

X threaded his fingers once, through his dirty hair, then shielded his eyes against the light again. 'You weren't insane. You were simply doing your duty. You killed that pussycat in as manly a way as anybody could've, under the circumstances.'

Clay looked at him suspiciously. 'What the hell are you talkin' about?'

'That cat was a spy. You *had* to take a pot shot at it. It was a very clever German midget dressed up in a cheap fur coat. So there was absolutely nothing brutal, or cruel, or dirty, or even——'

'God damn it!' Clay said, his lips thinned. 'Can't you ever be *sincere*?'

X suddenly felt sick, and he swung around in his chair and grabbed the wastebasket—just in time.

When he had straightened up and turned towards his guest again, he found him standing, embarrassed, half-way between the bed and the door. X started to apologize, but changed his mind and reached for his cigarettes.

'C'mon down and listen to Hope on the radio, hey,' Clay said, keeping his distance but trying to be friendly over it. 'It'll do ya good. I mean it.'

'You go ahead, Clay. . . . I'll look at my stamp collection.'

'Yeah? You got a stamp collection? I didn't know you——'

'I'm only kidding.'

Clay took a couple of slow steps towards the door. 'I may drive over to Ehstadt later,' he said. 'They got a dance. It'll probably last till around two. Wanna go?'

'No thanks. . . . I may practise a few steps in the room.'

'O.K. G'night! Take it easy, now, for Chrissake.' The door slammed shut, then instantly opened again. 'Hey. O.K. if I leave a letter to Loretta under your door? I got some German stuff in it. Willya fix it up for me?'

'Yes. Leave me alone now, God damn it.'

'Sure,' said Clay. 'You know what my mother wrote me? She wrote me she's glad you and I were together and all the whole war. In the same jeep and all. She says my letters are a helluva lot more intelligent since we been goin' around together.'

X looked up and over at him, and said, with great effort, 'Thanks. Tell her thanks for me.'

'I will. G'night!' The door slammed shut, this time for good.

X sat looking at the door for a long while, then turned his chair around towards the writing table and picked up his portable typewriter from the floor. He made space for it on the messy table surface, pushing aside the collapsed pile of unopened letters and packages. He thought if he wrote a letter to an old friend of his in New York there might be some quick, however slight, therapy in it for him. But he couldn't insert his notepaper into the roller properly, his fingers were shaking so violently now. He put his hands down at his sides for a minute, then tried again, but finally crumpled the notepaper in his hand.

He was aware that he ought to get the wastebasket out of the room, but instead of doing anything about it, he put his arms on the typewriter and rested his head again, closing his eyes.

A few throbbing minutes later, when he opened his eyes, he found himself squinting at a small, unopened package wrapped in green paper. It had probably slipped off the pile when he had made space for the typewriter. He saw that it had been readdressed several times. He could make out, on just one side of the package, at least three of his old A.P.O. numbers.

He opened the package without any interest, without even looking at the return address. He opened it by burning the string with a lighted match. He was more interested in watching the string burn all the way down than in opening the package, but he opened it, finally.

Inside the box, a note written in ink, lay on top of a small object wrapped in tissue paper. He picked out the note and read it.

17, ———— Road,

————, Devon,

7 June 1944

Dear Sergeant X,

I hope you will forgive me for having taken 38 days to begin our correspondence, but I have been extremely busy as my aunt has undergone streptococcus of the throat and nearly perished and I have been justifiably saddled with one responsibility after another. However I have thought of you frequently and of the extremely pleasant afternoon we spent in each other's company on 30 April 1944, between 3.45 and 4.15 p.m. in case it slipped your mind.

We are all tremendously excited and overawed about D-Day and only hope that it will bring about the swift termination of the war and a method of existence that is ridiculous to say the least. Charles and I are both quite concerned about you; we hope you were not among those who made the first initial assault upon the Cotentin Peninsula. Were you? Please reply as speedily as possible. My warmest regards to your wife.

Sincerely yours,

ESMÉ

P.S. I am taking the liberty of enclosing my wristwatch which you may keep in your possession for the duration of the conflict. I did not observe whether you were wearing one during our brief association, but this one is extremely waterproof and shock-proof as well as having many other virtues among which one can tell at what velocity one is walking if one wishes. I am quite certain that you will use it to greater advantage in these difficult days than I ever can and that you will accept it as a lucky talisman.

Charles, whom I am teaching to read and write and whom I am finding an extremely intelligent novice, wishes to add a few words. Please write as soon as you have the time and inclination.

HELLO HELLO HELLO HELLO HELLO
HELLO HELLO HELLO HELLO HELLO
LOVE AND KISSES CHARLES

IT was a long time before X could set the note aside, let alone lift Esmé's father's wristwatch out of the box. When he did finally lift it out, he saw that its crystal had been broken in transit. He wondered if the watch was otherwise undamaged, but he hadn't the courage to wind it and find out. He just sat with it in his hand for another long period. Then, suddenly, almost ecstatically, he felt sleepy.

You take a really sleepy man, Esmé, and he *always* stands a chance of again becoming a man with all his fac—with all his f-a-c-u-l-t-i-e-s intact.

THE SECRET LIFE OF
WALTER MITTY
from *My World and Welcome To It* (1942)

THE CATBIRD SEAT
from *The Thurber Carnival* (1945)

THE LILIES-AND-BLUEBIRD DELUSION
from *Is Sex Necessary?* (1947)

A CALL ON MRS. FORRESTER

THE LADY ON THE BOOKCASE
from *The Beast in Me* (1950)

BY JAMES THURBER

cop as the light changed, and Mitty hastily pulled on his gloves and lurched
ahead. He drove around the streets aimlessly for a time, and then he drove
ahead. It's the millionaire banker, Wellington McMillan, said the pretty
nurse. 'Yes?' said Walter Mitty removing his gloves slowly. 'Who has the
case?' Dr. Renshaw and Dr. ——————— here are two specialists here,
Dr. Remington from New York and Mr. Pritchard-Mitford from London.
He flew over. A door opened down a long, cool corridor and Dr. Renshaw
came out. He looked distraught and haggard. 'Hello Mitty,' he said. 'We're

THE SECRET LIFE OF WALTER MITTY

'WE'RE going through!' The Commander's voice was like thin ice breaking.
He wore his full-dress uniform, with the heavily braided white cap pulled
down rakishly over one cold grey eye. 'We can't make it, sir. It's spoiling
for a hurricane, if you ask me.' 'I'm not asking you, Lieutenant Berg,' said
the Commander. 'Throw on the power lights! Rev her up to 8,500! We're
going through!' The pounding of the cylinders increased: ta-pocketa-
pocketa-pocketa-*pocketa-pocketa*. The Commander stared at the ice forming
on the pilot window. He walked over and twisted a row of complicated
dials. 'Switch on No. 8 auxiliary!' he shouted. 'Switch on No. 8 auxiliary!'
repeated Lieutenant Berg. 'Full strength in No. 3 turret!' shouted the Commander. 'Full strength in No. 3 turret!' The crew, bending to their various
tasks in the huge, hurtling eight-engined Navy hydroplane, looked at each
other and grinned. 'The Old Man'll get us through,' they said to one
another. 'The Old Man ain't afraid of Hell!' . . .

'Not so fast! You're driving too fast!' said Mrs. Mitty. 'What are you
driving so fast for?'

'Hmm?' said Walter Mitty. He looked at his wife, in the seat beside him,
with shocked astonishment. She seemed grossly unfamiliar, like a strange
woman who had yelled at him in a crowd. 'You were up to fifty-five,' she
said. 'You know I don't like to go more than forty. You were up to fifty-
five.' Walter Mitty drove on towards Waterbury in silence, the roaring of
the SN202 through the worst storm in twenty years of Navy flying fading
in the remote, intimate airways of his mind. 'You're tensed up again,' said
Mrs. Mitty. 'It's one of your days. I wish you'd let Dr. Renshaw look you
over.'

Walter Mitty stopped the car in front of the building where his wife went
to have her hair done. 'Remember to get those overshoes while I'm having
my hair done,' she said. 'I don't need overshoes,' said Mitty. She put her
mirror back into her bag. 'We've been all through that,' she said, getting
out of the car. 'You're not a young man any longer.' He raced the engine a
little. 'Why don't you wear your gloves? Have you lost your gloves?'
Walter Mitty reached in a pocket and brought out the gloves. He put them
on, but after she had turned and gone into the building and he had driven
on to a red light, he took them off again. 'Pick it up, brother!' snapped a

cop as the light changed, and Mitty hastily pulled on his gloves and lurched
ahead. He drove around the streets aimlessly for a time, and then he drove
past the hospital on his way to the parking lot.

. . . 'It's the millionaire banker, Wellington McMillan,' said the pretty
nurse. 'Yes?' said Walter Mitty, removing his gloves slowly. 'Who has the
case?' 'Dr. Renshaw and Dr. Benbow, but there are two specialists here,
Dr. Remington from New York and Mr. Pritchard-Mitford from London.
He flew over.' A door opened down a long, cool corridor and Dr. Renshaw
came out. He looked distraught and haggard. 'Hello, Mitty,' he said. 'We're
having the devil's own time with McMillan, the millionaire banker and
close personal friend of Roosevelt. Obstreosis of the ductal tract. Tertiary.
Wish you'd take a look at him.' 'Glad to,' said Mitty.

In the operating room there were whispered introductions: 'Dr. Remington, Dr. Mitty. Mr. Pritchard-Mitford, Dr. Mitty.' 'I've read your book on
streptothricosis,' said Pritchard-Mitford, shaking hands. 'A brilliant performance, sir.' 'Thank you,' said Walter Mitty. 'Didn't know you were in
the States, Mitty,' grumbled Remington. 'Coals to Newcastle, bringing
Mitford and me up here for a tertiary.' 'You are very kind,' said Mitty. A
huge, complicated machine, connected to the operating table, with many
tubes and wires, began at this moment to go pocketa-pocketa-pocketa. 'The
new anæsthetizer is giving way!' shouted an interne. 'There is no one in the
East who knows how to fix it!' 'Quiet, man!' said Mitty, in a low, cool voice.
He sprang to the machine, which was now going pocketa-pocketa-queep-
pocketa-queep. He began fingering delicately a row of glistening dials. 'Give
me a fountain pen!' he snapped. Someone handed him a fountain pen. He
pulled a faulty piston out of the machine and inserted the pen in its place.
'That will hold for ten minutes,' he said. 'Get on with the operation.' A
nurse hurried over and whispered to Renshaw, and Mitty saw the man turn
pale. 'Coreopsis has set in,' said Renshaw nervously. 'If you would take
over, Mitty?' Mitty looked at him and at the craven figure of Benbow, who
drank, and at the grave, uncertain faces of the two great specialists. 'If you
wish,' he said. They slipped a white gown on him; he adjusted a mask and
drew on thin gloves; nurses handed him shining . . .

'Back it up, Mac! Look out for that Buick!' Walter Mitty jammed on the
brakes. 'Wrong lane, Mac,' said the parking-lot attendant, looking at Mitty
closely. 'Gee. Yeh,' muttered Mitty. He began cautiously to back out of the
lane marked 'Exit Only'. 'Leave her sit there,' said the attendant. 'I'll put her
away.' Mitty got out of the car. 'Hey, better leave the key.' 'Oh,' said Mitty,
handing the man the ignition key. The attendant vaulted into the car, backed
it up with insolent skill, and put it where it belonged.

They're so damn cocky, thought Walter Mitty, walking along Main
Street; they think they know everything. Once he had tried to take his
chains off, outside New Milford, and he had got them wound round the

axles. A man had had to come out in a wrecking car and unwind them, a young, grinning garageman. Since then Mrs. Mitty always made him drive to a garage to have the chains taken off. The next time, he thought, I'll wear my right arm in a sling; they won't grin at me then. I'll have my right arm in a sling and they'll see I couldn't possibly take the chains off myself. He kicked at the slush on the sidewalk. 'Overshoes,' he said to himself, and he began looking for a shoe store.

When he came out into the street again, with the overshoes in a box under his arm, Walter Mitty began to wonder what the other thing was his wife had told him to get. She had told him, twice, before they set out from their house for Waterbury. In a way he hated these weekly trips to town—he was always getting something wrong. Kleenex, he thought, Squibb's, razor blades? No. Toothpaste, toothbrush, bicarbonate, carborundum, initiative and referendum? He gave it up. But she would remember it. 'Where's the what's-its-name?' she would ask. 'Don't tell me you forgot the what's-its-name.' A newsboy went by shouting something about the Waterbury trial. . . . 'Perhaps this will refresh your memory.' The District Attorney suddenly thrust a heavy automatic at the quiet figure on the witness stand. 'Have you ever seen this before?' Walter Mitty took the gun and examined it expertly. 'This is my Webley-Vickers 50.80,' he said calmly. An excited buzz ran round the courtroom. The Judge rapped for order. 'You are a crack shot with any sort of firearms, I believe?' said the District Attorney, insinuatingly. 'Objection!' shouted Mitty's attorney. 'We have shown that the defendant could not have fired the shot. We have shown that he wore his right arm in a sling on the night of the fourteenth of July.' Walter Mitty raised his hand briefly and the bickering attorneys were stilled. 'With any known make of gun,' he said evenly, 'I could have killed Gregory Fitzhurst at three hundred feet *with my left hand*.' Pandemonium broke loose in the courtroom. A woman's scream rose above the bedlam and suddenly a lovely, dark-haired girl was in Walter Mitty's arms. The District Attorney struck at her savagely. Without rising from his chair, Mitty let the man have it on the point of the chin. 'You miserable cur!' . . .

'Puppy biscuit,' said Walter Mitty. He stopped walking and the buildings of Waterbury rose up out of the misty courtroom and surrounded him again. A woman who was passing laughed. 'He said "Puppy biscuit",' she said to her companion. 'That man said "Puppy biscuit" to himself.' Walter Mitty hurried on. He went into an A. & P., not the first one he came to but a smaller one farther up the street. 'I want some biscuit for small, young dogs,' he said to the clerk. 'Any special brand, sir?' The greatest pistol shot in the world thought a moment. 'It says "Puppies Bark for It" on the box,' said Walter Mitty.

His wife would be through at the hairdresser's in fifteen minutes, Mitty saw in looking at his watch, unless they had trouble drying it; sometimes they had trouble drying it. She didn't like to get to the hotel first; she would want him to be there waiting for her as usual. He found a big leather chair in the lobby, facing a window, and he put the overshoes and the puppy biscuit on the floor beside it. He picked up an old copy of *Liberty* and sank down into the chair. 'Can Germany Conquer the World Through the Air?' Walter Mitty looked at the pictures of bombing planes and of ruined streets.

. . . 'The cannonading has got the wind up in young Raleigh, sir,' said the sergeant. Captain Mitty looked up at him through tousled hair. 'Get him to bed,' he said wearily. 'With the others. I'll fly alone.' 'But you can't, sir,' said the sergeant anxiously. 'It takes two men to handle that bomber and the Archies are pounding hell out of the air. Von Richtman's circus is between here and Saulier.' 'Somebody's got to get that ammunition dump,' said Mitty. 'I'm going over. Spot of brandy?' He poured a drink for the sergeant and one for himself. War thundered and whined around the dugout and battered at the door. There was a rending of wood and splinters flew through the room. 'A bit of a near thing,' said Captain Mitty carelessly. 'The box barrage is closing in,' said the sergeant. 'We only live once, Sergeant,' said Mitty, with his faint, fleeting smile. 'Or do we?' He poured another brandy and tossed it off. 'I never see a man could hold his brandy like you, sir,' said the sergeant. 'Begging your pardon, sir.' Captain Mitty stood up and strapped on his huge Webley-Vickers automatic. 'It's forty kilometres through hell, sir,' said the sergeant. Mitty finished one last brandy. 'After all,' he said softly, 'what isn't?' The pounding of the cannon increased; there was the rat-tat-tatting of machine-guns, and from somewhere came the menacing pocketa-pocketa-pocketa of the new flame-throwers. Walter Mitty walked to the door of the dugout humming 'Auprès de Ma Blonde'. He turned and waved to the sergeant. 'Cheerio!' he said. . . .

Something struck his shoulder. 'I've been looking all over this hotel for you,' said Mrs. Mitty. 'Why do you have to hide in this old chair? How did you expect me to find you?' 'Things close in,' said Walter Mitty vaguely. 'What?' Mrs. Mitty said. 'Did you get the what's-its-name? The puppy biscuit? What's in that box?' 'Overshoes,' said Mitty. 'Couldn't you have put them on in the store?' 'I was thinking,' said Walter Mitty. 'Does it ever occur to you that I am sometimes thinking?' She looked at him. 'I'm going to take your temperature when I get you home,' she said.

They went out through the revolving doors that made a faintly derisive whistling sound when you pushed them. It was two blocks to the parking lot. At the drugstore on the corner she said, 'Wait here for me. I forgot something. I won't be a minute'. She was more than a minute. Walter Mitty lighted a cigarette. It began to rain, rain with sleet in it. He stood up against the wall of the drugstore, smoking. . . . . He put his shoulders back and his

heels together. 'To hell with the handkerchief,' said Walter Mitty scornfully.
He took one last drag on his cigarette and snapped it away. Then, with that
faint, fleeting smile playing about his lips, he faced the firing squad; erect
and motionless, proud and disdainful, Walter Mitty the Undefeated, inscrutable to the last.

THE CATBIRD SEAT

MR. MARTIN bought the pack of Camels on Monday night in the most crowded cigar store on Broadway. It was theatre time and seven or eight men were buying cigarettes. The clerk didn't even glance at Mr. Martin, who put the pack in his overcoat pocket and went out. If any of the staff at F & S had seen him buy the cigarettes, they would have been astonished, for it was generally known that Mr. Martin did not smoke, and never had. No one saw him.

It was just a week to the day since Mr. Martin had decided to rub out Mrs. Ulgine Barrows. The term 'rub out' pleased him because it suggested nothing more than the correction of an error—in this case an error of Mr. Fitweiler. Mr. Martin had spent each night of the past week working out his plan and examining it. As he walked home now he went over it again. For the hundredth time he resented the element of imprecision, the margin of guesswork that entered into the business. The project as he had worked it out was casual and bold, the risks were considerable. Something might go wrong anywhere along the line. And therein lay the cunning of his scheme. No one would ever see in it the cautious, painstaking hand of Erwin Martin, head of the filing department at F & S, of whom Mr. Fitweiler had once said, 'Man is fallible but Martin isn't'. No one would see his hand, that is, unless it were caught in the act.

Sitting in his apartment, drinking a glass of milk, Mr. Martin reviewed his case against Mrs. Ulgine Barrows, as he had every night for seven nights. He began at the beginning. Her quacking voice and braying laugh had first profaned the halls of F & S on 7 March 1941 (Mr. Martin had a head for dates). Old Roberts, the personnel chief, had introduced her as the newly appointed special adviser to the president of the firm, Mr. Fitweiler. The woman had appalled Mr. Martin instantly, but he hadn't shown it. He had given her his dry hand, a look of studious concentration, and a faint smile. 'Well,' she had said, looking at the papers on his desk, 'are you lifting the oxcart out of the ditch?' As Mr. Martin recalled that moment, over his milk, he squirmed slightly. He must keep his mind on her crimes as a special adviser, not on her peccadillos as a personality. This he found difficult to do, in spite of entering an objection and sustaining it. The faults of the woman as a woman kept chattering on in his mind like an unruly witness. She had, for almost two years now, baited him. In the halls, in the elevator, even in his own office, into which she romped now and then like a circus horse, she was constantly shouting these silly questions at him. 'Are you lifting the oxcart out of the ditch? Are you tearing up the pea patch? Are you hollering down the rain barrel? Are you scraping around the bottom of the pickle barrel? Are you sitting in the catbird seat?'

It was Joey Hart, one of Mr. Martin's two assistants, who had explained what the gibberish meant. 'She must be a Dodger fan,' he had said. 'Red Barber announces the Dodger games over the radio and he uses those expressions—picked 'em up down South.' Joey had gone on to explain one or two. 'Tearing up the pea patch' meant going on a rampage; 'sitting in the catbird seat' meant sitting pretty, like a batter with three balls and no strikes on him. Mr. Martin dismissed all this with an effort. It had been annoying, it had driven him near to distraction, but he was too solid a man to be moved to murder by anything so childish. It was fortunate, he reflected as he passed on to the important charges against Mrs. Barrows, that he had stood up under it so well. He had maintained always an outward appearance of polite tolerance. 'Why, I even believe you like the woman,' Miss Paird, his other assistant, had once said to him. He had simply smiled.

A gavel rapped in Mr. Martin's mind and the case proper was resumed. Mrs. Ulgine Barrows stood charged with wilful, blatant, and persistent attempts to destroy the efficiency and system of F & S. It was competent, material, and relevant to review her advent and rise to power. Mr. Martin had got the story from Miss Paird, who seemed always able to find things out. According to her, Mrs. Barrows had met Mr. Fitweiler at a party, where she had rescued him from the embraces of a powerfully built drunken man who had mistaken the president of F & S for a famous retired Middle Western football coach. She had led him to a sofa and somehow worked upon him a monstrous magic. The ageing gentleman had jumped to the conclusion there and then that this was a woman of singular attainments, equipped to bring out the best in him and in the firm. A week later he had introduced her into F & S as his special adviser. On that day confusion got its foot in the door. After Miss Tyson, Mr. Brundage, and Mr. Bartlett had been fired and Mr. Munson had taken his hat and stalked out, mailing in his resignation later, old Roberts had been emboldened to speak to Mr. Fitweiler. He mentioned that Mr. Munson's department had been 'a little disrupted' and hadn't they perhaps better resume the old system there? Mr. Fitweiler had said certainly not. He had the greatest faith in Mrs. Barrows's ideas. 'They require a little seasoning, a little seasoning, is all,' he had added. Mr. Roberts had given it up. Mr. Martin reviewed in detail all the changes wrought by Mrs. Barrows. She had begun chipping at the cornices of the firm's edifice and now she was swinging at the foundation stones with a pickaxe.

Mr. Martin came now, in his summing up, to the afternoon of Monday, 2 November 1942—just one week ago. On that day, at 3 p.m., Mrs. Barrows had bounced into his office. 'Boo!' she had yelled. 'Are you scraping around the bottom of the pickle barrel?' Mr. Martin had looked at her from under his green eyeshade, saying nothing. She had begun to wander about the office, taking it in with her great, popping eyes. 'Do you really need *all* these filing cabinets?' she had demanded suddenly. Mr. Martin's heart had jumped. 'Each of these files,' he had said, keeping his voice even, 'plays an indispensable part in the system of F & S.' She had brayed at him, 'Well, don't tear up the pea patch!' and gone to the door. From there she had bawled, 'But you sure have got a lot of fine scrap in here!' Mr. Martin could no longer doubt that the finger was on his beloved department. Her pickaxe was on the upswing, poised for the first blow. It had not come yet; he had received no blue memo from the enchanted Mr. Fitweiler bearing nonsensical instructions deriving from the obscene woman. But there was no doubt in Mr. Martin's mind that one would be forthcoming. He must act quickly. Already a precious week had gone by. Mr. Martin stood up in his living-room, still holding his milk glass. 'Gentlemen of the jury,' he said to himself, 'I demand the death penalty for this horrible person.'

The next day Mr. Martin followed his routine, as usual. He polished his glasses more often and once sharpened an already sharp pencil, but not even Miss Paird noticed. Only once did he catch sight of his victim; she swept past him in the hall with a patronizing 'Hi!' At five-thirty he walked home, as usual, and had a glass of milk, as usual. He had never drunk anything stronger in his life—unless you could count ginger ale. The late Sam Schlosser, the S of F & S, had praised Mr. Martin at a staff meeting several years before for his temperate habits. 'Our most efficient worker neither drinks nor smokes,' he had said. 'The results speak for themselves.' Mr. Fitweiler had sat by, nodding approval.

Mr. Martin was still thinking about that red-letter day as he walked over to the Schrafft's on Fifth Avenue near Forty-sixth Street. He got there, as he always did, at eight o'clock. He finished his dinner and the financial page of the *Sun* at a quarter to nine, as he always did. It was his custom after dinner to take a walk. This time he walked down Fifth Avenue at a casual pace. His gloved hands felt moist and warm, his forehead cold. He transferred the Camels from his overcoat to a jacket pocket. He wondered, as he did so, if they did not represent an unnecessary note of strain. Mrs. Barrows smoked only Luckies. It was his idea to puff a few puffs on a Camel (after the rubbing-out), stub it out in the ashtray holding her lipstick-stained Luckies, and thus drag a small red herring across the trail. Perhaps it was not a good idea. It would take time. He might even choke, too loudly.

Mr. Martin had never seen the house on West Twelfth Street where Mrs. Barrows lived, but he had a clear enough picture of it. Fortunately, she had bragged to everybody about her ducky first-floor apartment in the perfectly darling three-storey red-brick. There would be no doorman or other attendants; just the tenants of the second and third floors. As he walked along, Mr. Martin realized that he would get there before nine-thirty. He had considered walking north on Fifth Avenue from Schrafft's to a point from which it would take him until ten o'clock to reach the house. At that hour people were less likely to be coming in or going out. But the procedure would have made an awkward loop in the straight thread of his casualness, and he had abandoned it. It was impossible to figure when people would be entering or leaving the house, anyway. There was a great risk at any hour. If he ran into anybody, he would simply have to place the rubbing-out of Ulgine Barrows in the inactive file forever. The same thing would hold true if there were someone in her apartment. In that case he would just say that he had been passing by, recognized her charming house and thought to drop in.

It was eighteen minutes after nine when Mr. Martin turned into Twelfth Street. A man passed him, and a man and a woman talking. There was no one within fifty paces when he came to the house, half-way down the block. He was up the steps and in the small vestibule in no time, pressing the bell under the card that said 'Mrs. Ulgine Barrows'. When the clicking in the lock started, he jumped forward against the door. He got inside fast, closing the door behind him. A bulb in a lantern hung from the hall ceiling on a chain seemed to give a monstrously bright light. There was nobody on the stair, which went up ahead of him along the left wall. A door opened down the hall in the wall on the right. He went towards it swiftly, on tiptoe.

'Well, for God's sake, look who's here!' bawled Mrs. Barrows, and her braying laugh rang out like the report of a shotgun. He rushed past her like a football tackle, bumping her. 'Hey, quit shoving!' she said, closing the door behind them. They were in her living-room, which seemed to Mr. Martin to be lighted by a hundred lamps. 'What's after you?' she said. 'You're as jumpy as a goat.' He found he was unable to speak. His heart was wheezing in his throat. 'I—yes,' he finally brought out. She was jabbering and laughing as she started to help him off with his coat. 'No, no,' he said. 'I'll put it here.' He took it off and put it on a chair near the door. 'Your hat and gloves, too,' she said. 'You're in a lady's house.' He put his hat on top of the coat. Mrs. Barrows seemed larger than he had thought. He kept his gloves on. 'I was passing by,' he said. 'I recognized—is there anyone here?' She laughed louder than ever. 'No,' she said, 'we're all alone. You're as white as a sheet, you funny man. Whatever *has* come over you? I'll mix you a toddy.' She started towards a door across the room. 'Scotch-and-soda be all right? But say, you don't drink, do you?' She turned and gave him her amused look. Mr. Martin pulled himself together. 'Scotch-and-soda will be

all right,' he heard himself say. He could hear her laughing in the kitchen.
Mr. Martin looked quickly round the living-room for the weapon. He
had counted on finding one there. There were andirons and a poker and
something in a corner that looked like an Indian club. None of them would
do. It couldn't be that way. He began to pace around. He came to a desk.
On it lay a metal paper knife with an ornate handle. Would it be sharp
enough? He reached for it and knocked over a small brass jar. Stamps spilled
out of it and it fell to the floor with a clatter. 'Hey,' Mrs. Barrows yelled
from the kitchen, 'are you tearing up the pea patch?' Mr. Martin gave a
strange laugh. Picking up the knife, he tried its point against his left wrist.
It was blunt. It wouldn't do.

When Mrs. Barrows reappeared, carrying two highballs, Mr. Martin,
standing there with his gloves on, became acutely conscious of the fantasy
he had wrought. Cigarettes in his pocket, a drink prepared for him—it was
all too grossly improbable. It was more than that; it was impossible. Somewhere in the back of his mind a vague idea sprouted. 'For heaven's sake, take
off those gloves,' said Mrs. Barrows. 'I always wear them in the house,' said
Mr. Martin. The idea began to bloom, strange and wonderful. She put the
glasses on a coffee table in front of a sofa and sat on the sofa. 'Come over
here, you odd little man,' she said. Mr. Martin went over and sat beside her.
It was difficult getting a cigarette out of the pack of Camels, but he managed
it. She held a match for him, laughing. 'Well,' she said, handing him his
drink, 'this is perfectly marvellous. You with a drink and a cigarette.'

Mr. Martin puffed, not too awkwardly, and took a gulp of the highball.
'I drink and smoke all the time,' he said. He clinked his glass against hers.
'Here's nuts to that old windbag, Fitweiler,' he said, and gulped again. The
stuff tasted awful, but he made no grimace. 'Really, Mr. Martin,' she said,
her voice and posture changing, 'you are insulting your employer.' Mrs.
Barrows was now all special adviser to the president. 'I am preparing a
bomb,' said Mr. Martin, 'which will blow the old goat higher than hell.'
He had only had a little of the drink, which was not strong. It couldn't be
that. 'Do you take dope or something?' Mrs. Barrows asked coldly. 'Heroin,'
said Mr. Martin. 'I'll be coked to the gills when I bump that old buzzard off.'
'Mr. Martin!' she shouted, getting to her feet. 'That will be all of that. You
must go at once.' Mr. Martin took another swallow of his drink. He tapped
his cigarette out in the ashtray and put the pack of Camels on the coffee
table. Then he got up. She stood glaring at him. He walked over and put
on his hat and coat. 'Not a word about this,' he said, and laid an index finger
against his lips. All Mrs. Barrows could bring out was 'Really!' Mr. Martin
put his hand on the doorknob. 'I'm sitting in the catbird seat,' he said. He
stuck his tongue out at her and left. Nobody saw him go.

Mr. Martin got to his apartment, walking, well before eleven. No one saw him go in. He had two glasses of milk after brushing his teeth, and he felt elated. It wasn't tipsiness, because he hadn't been tipsy. Anyway, the walk had worn off all effects of the whisky. He got in bed and read a magazine for a while. He was asleep before midnight.

Mr. Martin got to the office at eight-thirty the next morning, as usual. At a quarter to nine, Ulgine Barrows, who had never before arrived at work before ten, swept into his office. 'I'm reporting to Mr. Fitweiler now!' she shouted. 'If he turns you over to the police, it's no more than you deserve!' Mr. Martin gave her a look of shocked surprise. 'I beg your pardon?' he said. Mrs. Barrows snorted and bounced out of the room, leaving Miss Paird and Joey Hart staring after her. 'What's the matter with that old devil now?' asked Miss Paird. 'I have no idea,' said Mr. Martin, resuming his work. The other two looked at him and then at each other. Miss Paird got up and went out. She walked slowly past the closed door of Mr. Fitweiler's office. Mrs. Barrows was yelling inside, but she was not braying. Miss Paird could not hear what the woman was saying. She went back to her desk.

Forty-five minutes later, Mrs. Barrows left the president's office and went into her own, shutting the door. It wasn't until half an hour later that Mr. Fitweiler sent for Mr. Martin. The head of the filing department, neat, quiet, attentive, stood in front of the old man's desk. Mr. Fitweiler was pale and nervous. He took his glasses off and twiddled them. He made a small, bruffing sound in his throat. 'Martin,' he said, 'you have been with us more than twenty years.' 'Twenty-two, sir,' said Mr. Martin. 'In that time,' pursued the president, 'your work and your—uh—manner have been exemplary.' 'I trust so, sir,' said Mr. Martin. 'I have understood, Martin,' said Mr. Fitweiler, 'that you have never taken a drink or smoked.' 'That is correct, sir,' said Mr. Martin. 'Ah, yes.' Mr. Fitweiler polished his glasses. 'You may describe what you did after leaving the office yesterday, Martin,' he said. Mr. Martin allowed less than a second for his bewildered pause. 'Certainly, sir,' he said. 'I walked home. Then I went to Schrafft's for dinner. Afterwards I walked home again. I went to bed early, sir, and read a magazine for a while. I was asleep before eleven.' 'Ah, yes,' said Mr. Fitweiler again. He was silent for a moment, searching for the proper words to say to the head of the filing department. 'Mrs. Barrows,' he said finally. 'Mrs. Barrows has worked hard, Martin, very hard. It grieves me to report that she has suffered a severe breakdown. It has taken the form of a persecution complex accompanied by distressing hallucinations.' 'I am very sorry, sir,' said Mr. Martin. 'Mrs. Barrows is under the delusion,' continued Mr. Fitweiler, 'that you visited her last evening and behaved yourself in an—uh—unseemly manner.' He raised his hand to silence Mr. Martin's little pained outcry. 'It is the nature of these psychological diseases,' Mr. Fitweiler said, 'to fix upon the least likely and most innocent party as the—uh—source of persecution. These matters are not for the lay mind to grasp, Martin. I've just had my psychiatrist, Dr. Fitch, on the phone. He would not, of course, commit himself, but he made enough generalizations to substantiate my suspicions. I suggested to Mrs. Barrows when she had completed her—uh—story to me this morning, that she visit Dr. Fitch, for I suspected a condition at once. She flew, I regret to say, into a rage, and demanded—uh—requested that I call you on the carpet. You may not know, Martin, but Mrs. Barrows had planned a reorganization of your department—subject to my approval, of course, subject to my approval. This brought you, rather than anyone else, to her mind—but again that is a phenomenon for Dr. Fitch and not for us. So, Martin, I am afraid Mrs. Barrows's usefulness here is at an end.' 'I am dreadfully sorry, sir,' said Mr. Martin.

It was at this point that the door to the office blew open with the suddenness of a gas-main explosion and Mrs. Barrows catapulted through it. 'Is the little rat denying it?' she screamed. 'He can't get away with that!' Mr. Martin got up and moved discreetly to a point beside Mr. Fitweiler's chair. 'You drank and smoked at my apartment,' she bawled at Mr. Martin, 'and you know it! You called Mr. Fitweiler an old windbag and said you were going to blow him up when you got coked to the gills on your heroin!' She stopped yelling to catch her breath and a new glint came into her popping eyes. 'If you weren't such a drab, ordinary little man,' she said, 'I'd think you'd planned it all. Sticking your tongue out, saying you were sitting in the catbird seat, because you thought no one would believe me when I told it! My God, it's really too perfect!' She brayed loudly and hysterically, and the fury was on her again. She glared at Mr. Fitweiler. 'Can't you see how he has tricked us, you old fool? Can't you see his little game?' But Mr. Fitweiler had been surreptitiously pressing all the buttons under the top of his desk and employees of F & S began pouring into the room. 'Stockton,' said Mr. Fitweiler, 'you and Fishbein will take Mrs. Barrows to her home. Mrs. Powell, you will go with them.' Stockton, who had played a little football in high school, blocked Mrs. Barrows as she made for Mr. Martin. It took him and Fishbein together to force her out of the door into the hall, crowded with stenographers and office boys. She was still screaming imprecations at Mr. Martin, tangled and contradictory imprecations. The hubbub finally died out down the corridor.

'I regret that this has happened,' said Mr. Fitweiler. 'I shall ask you to dismiss it from your mind, Martin.' 'Yes, sir,' said Mr. Martin, anticipating his chief's 'That will be all' by moving to the door. 'I will dismiss it.' He went out and shut the door, and his step was light and quick in the hall. When he entered his department he had slowed down to his customary gait, and he walked quietly across the room to the W20 file, wearing a look of studious concentration.

THE LILIES-AND-BLUEBIRD DELUSION

THE young bridegroom who unexpectedly discovers that his wife has been brought up in extreme unawareness of the true facts of life and believes in some variant of the Birds and Flowers Delusion (that is, that birds and flowers have something to do with the emotional life of persons), is faced with a situation calling for the greatest tact and tenderness. It won't do any good for him to get mad, or to indulge in self-pity, crying, 'Oh, how sorry I am for me!' and only a coward would go directly into a psycho-neurosis without first trying to win his wife over to acceptance of things as they are.

I have in mind the case of a young lady whose silly mother had taught her to believe that she would have a little son, three years old, named Ronald, as soon as her husband brought a pair of bluebirds into a room filled with lilies-of-the-valley. The young woman (to say nothing of the young man) was thus made the victim of one of the extremest cases of Birds and Flowers Fixation which has ever come to my attention. I shall transcribe, from Dr. Tithridge's notes, the first dialogue on the subject that took place between the young couple. This dialogue was carefully reconstructed by Tithridge from the account of the incident as given by the young husband, who sought his advice and counsel.

On the evening of 25 June, when the couple were married, the young husband entered their hotel suite to find it literally a garden of lilies-of-the-valley. He was profoundly touched, but baffled, and asked his wife who was dead.

'Where are the bluebirds?' she replied, coyly.

'What bluebirds?' he demanded.

'*The* bluebirds,' she said, blushing.

Unfortunately, but not unnaturally, the bridegroom did not know what the bride was talking about. What was of the extremest importance to her, was to her husband merely an idle whim, a shadowy fancy. Obviously, the young couple should have talked such matters over long before, but they hadn't, and there they were. He strove to change the subject, whistled, lighted cigarettes, for he was nervous enough the way it was, but she kept recurring to the bluebirds. His bewilderment became tinged with some alarm, for during their courtship he had put forth no great effort to examine into her mental capacity, and he was now assailed by the excusable suspicion

MALE TYPE (EASTERN SEABOARD)

Definitely interested in, but uncertain what to do about, the Female.
To men of this type many aspects of the Sexual Revolution never
became clear at all

that she was perhaps not exactly bright. He talked rapidly, apprehensively, of many things. Among the things he talked about were the St. Louis Cardinals (a baseball club). From there it was but an easy associative step for his wife to go back to the bluebirds again.

'Aren't you going to *get* any bluebirds?' she persisted.

'I don't know where the hell I'd get any bluebirds to-night,' he said, rather irritably, 'me not being Bo-Peep.'

The nuclear complex was made right then and there. There was a long tense silence, after which the bride burst into bitter tears.

'Now, dear,' said her husband, more reasonably, 'let's try to get this thing straightened out. What are you talking about, anyway?'

'Sex—if you want to know!' she blurted out, and swooned.

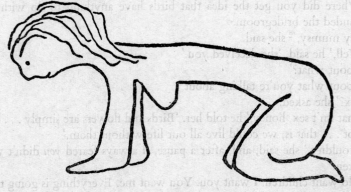

EARLY WOMAN

Instead of getting her a glass of water, he excitedly phoned the room clerk, but became embarrassed once he had got him, and merely asked that a couple of blankets be sent up. It was, unfortunately, as I have said, June—and warmish. Thus when the wife revived sufficiently to become aware of her surroundings, the husband was standing above her holding a pair of blankets, and looking pale and warm.

'What are those for?' she demanded, suspiciously, for the notion had now formed in her own mind (Dr. Tithridge feels, and I agree) that she very likely had married a dementia præcox case. These mutual suspicions of mental inadequacy are common during the first year of any marriage, but rarely are they aggravated by factors so clearly calculated to upset the mental equilibrium as bluebirds at midnight and blankets in June. This husband and wife were drifting farther and farther apart. The solution to their problem was becoming more and more remote, what with this setting up of involved artificial barriers, this almost fantastical beclouding of the issue. Dr. Tithridge tells me that he believes the young man's reason would have been permanently dethroned had he (Dr. Tithridge) tweeted or chirped like a bird[1] on the occasion of the husband's first visit to him.

When the wife beheld her husband standing there with the blankets, she demanded, again, 'What are you doing with those blankets?'

'I get cold,' he mumbled, and he proceeded to put the blankets on the shelf of a closet which already held several extra pair. He was, furthermore, decidedly warm, and kept patting his brow with a handkerchief.

'Let's go out and take a walk,' suggested his wife, apprehensively. To this her husband very readily agreed. They were getting afraid to stay in the same room with each other, than which there is no other condition in the world more certain to break up a marriage. Out in the street, among people, they both felt safer, and they wandered to a bench in a fairly crowded park, and sat down.

'Where did you get the idea that birds have anything to do with us?' demanded the bridegroom.

'My mumsy,'[2] she said.

'Well,' he said, 'she deceived you.'

'About what?'

'About what you're talking about.'

'Sex?' she asked.

'That isn't sex, honey,' he told her. 'Birds and flowers are simply . . . they do not . . . that is, we could live all our life without them.'

'I couldn't,' she said, and, after a pause, 'I always feared *you* didn't want children.'

'I do want children. I want you. You want me. Everything is going to be all right.'

'How is it?' she demanded.

'In the first place,' he began, pulling at his collar, 'it's this way. Now here's the way it is. Now you take me . . . or take you, say. In the first place the girl, that is Woman . . . why, Woman[3] . . .' He lapsed into a profound silence.

'Well, go on,' she prompted.

'Well,' he said, 'you know how women are, don't you?'

'Yes,' she said, doubtfully.

---

[1] Experiments of this sort, calculated to determine the possible effects of tweeting, or chirping, in the case of a Birds Fixation, fall, of course, outside the province of the psycho-analyst, and not only is the legality of their practice questionable, but the value of the results obtained is highly doubtful.

[2] Young women who allude to their mothers as 'mumsy' almost invariably present difficult problems in adjustment. The word is a sentimentalization of the more common 'mamma' and indicates a greater dependence upon maternal direction and supervision than may be expected in the case of young women who use the more familiar term.

[3] Explanations of natural phenomena in terms of the collective noun, particularly where the noun becomes capitalized in the mind of the person striving to explain, are almost never successful.

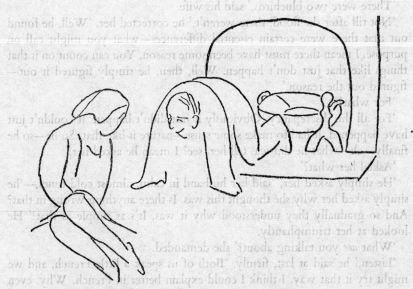

EMOTIONAL CHARADES

*One young man every night tenderly placed, with much strange
clucking, a basket near the hearth into which he had some expectation
that a baby would be deposited by a stork*

'That's fine,' he said, brightening. 'Now women are that way, then——'

'What way?' she asked.

'Why, the way you are . . . from me . . . than I am, I mean.' He made a vague gesture.

'I don't see what you mean,' she said. Her husband gave a light laugh.

'Hell's bells, it's simple enough,' he cried, suddenly, giving the light laugh again; 'it's certainly simple enough. Now, here. We'll take Adam and Eve. There they were, all alone, see?'

'There were two bluebirds,' said his wife.

'Not till after the flood, there weren't,' he corrected her. 'Well, he found out that there were certain essential differences—what you might call on purpose. I mean there must have been some reason. You can count on it that things like that just don't happen. Well, then, he simply figured it out—figured out the reason.'

'For what?'

'For all this discrepancy. Obviously it just didn't happen. It couldn't just have happened. It had to make some sense—nature is like that. So he—so he finally—ah—what he did was tell her, see? I mean he asked her.'

'Asked her what?'

'He simply asked her,' said her husband in calm, almost cold tones,—'he simply asked her why she thought this was. Is there anything wrong in that? And so gradually they understood why it was. It's as simple as that!' He looked at her triumphantly.

'What *are* you talking about?' she demanded.

'Listen,' he said at last, firmly. 'Both of us speak a little French, and we might try it that way. I think I could explain better in French. Why, even little children, tiny girls, sing *Auprès de ma blonde* in France, and think nothing of it. It's just a nice, wholesome idea—*auprès de ma blonde*—and it sounds like poetry—but take it in English and what do you get?'

' "Quite close to my blonde" . . .' answered his wife.

'. . . "Qu'il fait bon dormir,"' her husband hurried on.

' "How good it is to sleep," ' she translated.

'Fine! Now you're talking.'

'Go on,' she said, '*you're* talking.'

'Well, all right, but first I wanted you to see that there is no reason to get embarrassed, because everything is lovely in French. So don't mind my frankness.'

'I don't,' said the bride.

'All right,' he began again, '*Alors*, now, *il y a quelque chose que vous avez que je n'en ai pas: n'est-ce pas?*'

'*Oui*,' she said.

'*Bon*,' he said. '*Alors, ça c'est naturel—ah—ça c'est bien naturel . . .*'

'*Par exemple*,' put in his wife, a little illogically.

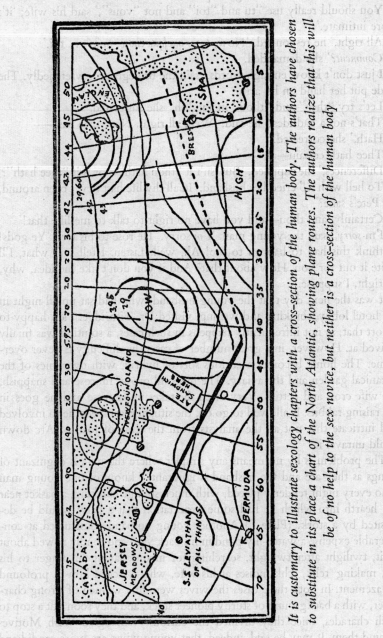

It is customary to illustrate sexology chapters with a cross-section of the human body. The authors have chosen to substitute in its place a chart of the North Atlantic, showing plane routes. The authors realize that this will be of no help to the sex novice, but neither is a cross-section of the human body

'*Dites*,' he said, and after a great pause, '*Dites donc—dites vous——*'

'You should really use "tu and "toi" and not "vous",' said his wife; 'it's more intimate.'

'All right,' he responded. 'Now, *tu as quelque chose, tu as . . . toi.*'

'*Comment?*' she demanded.

'I just don't know enough words,' said the bridegroom, wretchedly. The bride put her hand on his arm.

'Let's try "thee" and "thou" in English,' she suggested.

'That's not a bad idea,' he said. 'Well, all right. Now thee has——'

'Hath,' she corrected.

'Thee hath certain—ah——'

'Differences,' she supplied. 'But isn't it "thou hath"—or is it "thee hath"?'

'To hell with it!' cried her husband. 'In all thy life hast never been around, for Pete's sake?'

'Certainly, and thou—and you have no right to talk to me like that!'

'I'm *sorry*,' said the young man. '*I'm* sorry.' He rose to his feet. 'Ye gods! to think this had to happen to me! Ah, well. Listen. I tell you what, I'll write it out for you. How about that? And if you don't like the idea, why, all right, I suppose.'

It was the next day that the young husband, who had sat up all night in the hotel lobby, thinking and writing, visited Dr. Tithridge. I am happy to report that, as not infrequently happens in such cases, a solution was finally arrived at. However, in a great number of cases the difficulty is never overcome. The home becomes a curious sort of hybrid, with overtones of the botanical garden and the aviary. The husband grows morose and snappish, the wife cross and pettish. Very often she takes up lacrosse and he goes in for raising rabbits. If allowed to go on, the situation can become so involved and intricate that not all the analysts from the time of Joan of Arc down could unravel it.

The problem is by no means any simpler where the wife is cognizant of things as they are and the husband is ignorant. I know of one young man who every night tenderly placed, with much strange clucking, a basket near the hearth into which he had some expectation that a baby would be deposited by a stork. (Plate I.) Another young husband constructed at considerable expense a water-lily pond in his back yard and fondly rowed about in it, twilight after twilight, searching for infants, laying his finger to his lip, making 'tchk, tchk' noises at his wife, who watched him in profound amazement. In both these cases the wives were fine women of strong character, with a background of sturdy pioneer stock, and they soon put a stop to such charades, once they divined the curiously entangled Wish Motives behind them. It may be said, indeed, that young wives are more candid and direct in their explanations of natural phenomena than young husbands, when they have to be.

The existence of such deplorable ignorance is a sad commentary on the sentimentality of a nation which sets itself up to be frankly sexual. There is much reason to be hopeful, however. The future parents of the land will doubtless come straight to the point in matters of this sort, when talking with their children. The children of to-day will be the parents of to-morrow, and you know how the children of to-day are.

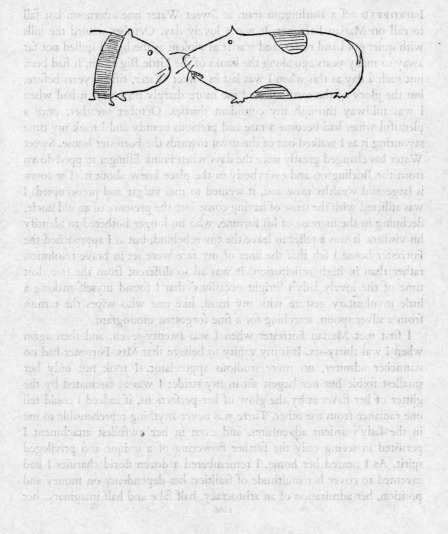

A CALL ON MRS FORRESTER

(AFTER RE-READING, IN MY MIDDLE YEARS, WILLA CATHER'S 'A LOST LADY' AND HENRY JAMES'S 'THE AMBASSADORS')

=====

I DROPPED off a Burlington train at Sweet Water one afternoon last fall to call on Marian Forrester. It was a lovely day. October stained the hills with quiet gold and russet, and scarlet as violent as the blood spilled not far away so many years ago along the banks of the Little Big Horn. It had been just such a day as this when I was last in Sweet Water, fifteen years before, but the glory of the earth affected me more sharply now than it had when I was midway through my confident thirties. October weather, once a plentiful wine, had become a rare and precious brandy and I took my time savouring it as I walked out of the town towards the Forrester house. Sweet Water has changed greatly since the days when Frank Ellinger stepped down from the Burlington and everybody in the place knew about it. The town is large and wealthy now and, it seemed to me, vulgar and preoccupied. I was afflicted with the sense of having come into the presence of an old uncle, declining in the increase of his fortune, who no longer bothered to identify his visitors. It was a relief to leave the town behind, but as I approached the Forrester house I felt that the lines of my face were set in brave resolution rather than in high anticipation. It was all so different from the free, lost time of the lovely lady's 'bright occasions' that I found myself making a little involuntary gesture with my hand, like one who wipes the tarnish from a silver spoon, searching for a fine forgotten monogram.

I first met Marian Forrester when I was twenty-seven, and then again when I was thirty-six. It is my vanity to believe that Mrs. Forrester had no stauncher admirer, no more studious appreciator. I took not only her smallest foible but her largest sin in my stride; I was as fascinated by the glitter of her flaws as by the glow of her perfections, if indeed I could tell one radiance from the other. There was never anything reprehensible to me in the lady's ardent adventures, and even in her awfullest attachment I persisted in seeing only the further flowering of a unique and privileged spirit. As I neared her home, I remembered a dozen florid charities I had invented to cover her multitude of frailties: her dependence on money and position, her admiration of an aristocracy, half false and half imaginary, her

1006

lack of any security inside herself, her easy loneliness. It was no use, I was fond of telling myself, to look for the qualities of the common and whole-some morning glory in the rare and wanton Nicotiana. From the darkest earth, I would add, springs ever the sweetest rose. A green isle in the sea, if it has the sparkling fountain, needs not the solemn shrine, and so forth and so on.

I had built the lady up very high, as you see. I had commanded myself to believe that emotional literacy, a lively spirit, and personal grace, so rarely joined in American females, particularly those who live between Omaha and Denver, were all the raiment a lady needed. As I crossed the bridge, with the Forrester house now in full view, I had, all of a sudden, a disturbing fancy. There flashed into my consciousness a vivid vision of the pretty lady, seated at her dressing table, practising in secrecy her little arts, making her famous earrings gleam with small studied turnings of her head, revealing her teeth for a moment in a brief mocking smile, and, unhappiest picture of all, rehearsing her wonderful laughter.

I stopped on the bridge and leaned against the rail and felt old and tired. Black clouds had come up, obscuring the sun, and they seemed to take the mushroom shape of atomic dust, threatening all frail and ancient satisfac-tions. It began to rain.

I wondered what I would say to Marian Forrester if she appeared at the door in one of her famous, familiar postures, *en déshabillé*, her hair down her back, a brush in her hand, her face raised in warm, anachronistic gaiety. I tried to remember what we had ever talked about, and could think only of the dreadful topic of grasping women and eligible men. We had never discussed any book that I could recall, and she had never mentioned music. I had another of my ungallant fancies, a vision of the lovely lady at a concert in the town, sitting with bright eye and deaf ear, displaying a new bonnet and gown, striving, less subtly than of old, to capture the attention of worried and oblivious gentlemen. I recalled with sharp clarity a gown and bonnet she had once worn, but for the life of me I could not put a face be-tween them. I caught the twinkle of earrings, and that was all.

The latest newspaper lying open on a chair, a note stuck in a milk bottle on the back porch, are enough to indicate the pulse of a living house, but there would not even be these faint signs of to-day and to-morrow in Marian Forrester's house, only the fibrillation of a yesterday that had died but would not stay dead. There would be an old copy of *Ainslee's* on the floor somewhere, a glitter of glass under a broken windowpane, springs leaking from a ruptured sofa, a cobweb in a chandelier, a dusty etching of Notre Dame unevenly hung on the wall, and a stopped clock on the marble mantel above a cold fireplace. I could see the brandy bottle, too, on a stained table, wearing its cork drunkenly.

Just to the left of the front door, the big hall closet would be filled with relics of the turn of the century, the canes and guns of Captain Forrester, a crokinole board, a diavolo, a frivolous parasol, a collection of McKinley campaign buttons, a broken stereopticon, a table tennis net, a toppled stack of blue poker chips and a scatter of playing cards, a woodburning set, and one of those large white artificial Easter eggs you put to your eye and, squinting into it, behold the light that never was, in a frosty fairyland. There would be a crack in the crusty shell, and common daylight would violate the sanctuary of the yellowed and tottery angels. You could find, in all the litter, as measuring sticks of calamity, nothing longer than an envelope firmly addressed in a gentleman's hand, a cancelled cheque, a stern notice from the bank.

The shade of one upstairs window was pulled all the way down, and it suddenly had the effect of making the house appear to wink, as if it were about to whisper, out of the corner of its door, some piece of scandal. If I went in, I might be embarrassed by the ungainly sounds of someone moving about upstairs, after the lady had descended, sounds which she would cover by riffling nervously through a dozen frilly seasons of her faded past, trying a little shrilly to place me among the beaux in some half-remembered ball-room. I was afraid, too, that I might encounter in some dim and dusty mirror a young man frowning disapproval of an older self come to make judgment on a poor lady not for her sake and salvation but, in some strange way, for his own. And what if she brought out, in the ruins of her famous laughter, what was left of the old disdain, and fixed me shrewdly for what I was, a frightened penitent, come to claim and take away and burn the old praises he had given her? I wouldn't succeed, of course, standing there in my unbecoming middle years, foolishly clutching reasons and arguments like a shopper's husband loaded down with bundles. She would gaily accuse me of being in love with another and, with the ghost of one of her poses of charming bewilderment, would claim a forfeit for my cruelty and insist that I sit down and have a brandy. I would have one—oh, several—and in the face of my suspicions of the presence of a man upstairs, my surrender would compromise the delicacy of my original cool intentions, and the lost individual would be, once again as always in this house, myself. I wondered, standing there in the rain, how it would all come out.

She would get the other lady's name out of me easily enough, when the brandy began to ebb in the bottle, and being Marian Forrester, for whom jealousy was as simple as a reflex, she would be jealous of the imaginary relations of a man she could not place, with a woman she had never heard of. I would then confess my love for Madame de Vionnet, the lady of the lilacs, of Gloriani's bright Sunday garden, of the stately house in the Boulevard Malsherbes, with its cool parlour and dark medallions. I would rise no doubt to the seedy grandiloquence of which I am capable when the cognac is flowing, and I could hear her pitiless comment. 'One of those women who have something to *give*, for heaven's sake!' she would say. 'One of those women who save men, a female whose abandon might possibly tiptoe to the point of tousling her lover's hair, a woman who at the first alarm of a true embrace would telephone the gendarmes.' 'Stop it!' I heard myself shout there in the rain. 'I beg you to remember it was once said of Madame de Vionnet that when she touched a thing the ugliness, God knows how, went out of it.' 'How sweet!' I could hear Mrs. Forrester go on. 'And yet, according to you, she lost her lover, for all her charm, and to a snippet of an apple-cheek from New England. Did the ugliness go out of *that*? And if it did, what did the poor lady do with all the prettiness?'

As I stood there in the darkening afternoon, getting soaked, I realized sharply that in my fantasy I had actually been handing Marian Forrester stones to throw at the house in Paris, and the confusion in my viewpoint of the two ladies, if up to that moment I had had a viewpoint, overwhelmed me. I figured what would happen as the shadows deepened in the Forrester house, and we drank what was left of the brandy out of ordinary tumblers —the ballons of the great days would long since have been shattered. Banter would take on the sharp edge of wrangling, and in the end she would stand above me, maintaining a reedy balance, and denounce the lady of the lilacs in the flat terms she had overheard gentlemen use so long ago over their cigars and coffee in the library. I would set my glass down on the sticky arm of the chair and get up and stalk out into the hall. But though she had the last word, she would not let me have the last silence, the gesture in conclusion. She would follow me to the door. In her house, by an ancient rule, Marian Forrester always had the final moment—standing on the threshold, her face lifted, her eyes shining, her hand raised to wave good-bye. Yes, she would follow me to the door, and in the hall—I could see it so clearly I shivered there on the bridge—something wonderful would happen. With the faintest of smiles and the slightest of murmurs I would bow to my hostess, open the door and walk, not out into the rain, but into that damn closet, with its junk and clutter, smashing the Easter egg with my shoe, becoming entangled in the table tennis net, and holding in my hand, when I regained my balance, that comic parasol. Madame de Vionnet would ignore such a calamity, she would pretend not to see it, on the ground that a hostess is blind—a convention that can leave a man sitting at table with an omelette in his lap, unable to mention it, forced to go on with the conversation. But Marian would laugh, the lost laugh of the bright occasions, of the day of her shameless passion in the snow, and it would light the house like candles, reducing the sounds upstairs, in some miraculous way, to what they really were, the innocent creaking of the old floor boards. 'What's all this about saving men?' I would cry. 'Look who's talking!' And, still holding the parasol, I would kiss her on the cheek, mumble something about coming back some day, and leave, this time by the right door, finding, as I went to rejoin myself at the bridge, a poker chip in the cuff of my trousers.

It seems a long time ago, my call on Mrs. Forrester. I have never been back. I didn't even send her a Valentine last February. But I did send a pretty book of impeccable verses to Madame de Vionnet, writing in the inscription something polite and nostalgic about 'ta voix dans le Bois de Boulogne'. I did this, I suppose, out of some obscure guilt sense—these things are never very clear to any man, if the truth were told. I think the mental process goes like this, though. Drinking brandy out of a water glass in the amiable company of a lady who uses spirits for anodyne and not amenity, a timid gentleman promises his subconscious to make up for it later on by taking a single malaga before *déjeuner à midi* with a fastidious lady, toying with aspic, discussing Thornton Wilder, praising the silver point in the hall on the way out, and going home to lie down, exhausted but somehow purified.

I will carry lilacs, one of these summers, to the house in the Boulevard Malesherbes, and take Madame de Vionnet to a matinée of *Louise*, have a white port with her at one of the little terraces at the quietest corner of the Parc Monceau, and drop her at the door well before the bold moon has begun to wink at the modest twilight. Since, in the best Henry James tradition, I will get nothing out of this for myself, it ought to make up for something. I could do worse than spend my last summers serenely, sipping wine, clopping around town, listening to good music, kissing a lady's hand at the door, going to bed early and getting a good night's sleep. A man's a fool who walks in the rain, drinks too much brandy, risks his neck floundering around in an untidy closet. Besides, if you miss the six-fifteen, the east-bound Burlington that has a rendezvous with dusk in Sweet Water every day except Sundays and holidays, you have to wait till midnight for the next train east. A man could catch his death, dozing there in that cold and lonesome station.

O NE day twelve years ago an outraged cartoonist, four of whose drawings had been rejected in a clump by *The New Yorker*, stormed into the office of Harold Ross, editor of the magazine. 'Why is it,' demanded the cartoonist, 'that you reject my work and publish the drawings by a fifth-rate artist like

'With you I have known peace, Lida, and now you say you're going crazy.'

Thurber?' Ross came quickly to my defence like the true friend and devoted employer he is. 'You mean third-rate,' he said quietly, but there was a warning glint in his steady grey eyes that caused the discomfited cartoonist to beat a hasty retreat.

Home

With the exception of Ross, the interest of editors in what I draw has been rather more journalistic than critical. They want to know if it is true that I draw by moonlight, or under water, and when I say no, they lose interest until they hear the rumour that I found the drawings in an old trunk or that I

'All right, have it your way—you heard a seal bark.'

do the captions while my nephew makes the sketches.

The other day I was shoving some of my originals around on the floor (I do not draw on the floor; I was just shoving the originals around) and they fell, or perhaps I pushed them, into five separate and indistinct categories. I have never wanted to write about my drawings, and I still don't want to, but

With the exception of Ross, the interest of editors in what I drew has been rather more journalistic than critical. They want to know if it is true that I draw by _____ until they hear the rumour that I found the drawings in an old trunk _____

'That's my first wife up there, and this is the present Mrs. Harris.'

do the captions while my nephew makes the sketch.

The other day I was showing some of my originals around on the floor (I do not draw on the floor; I was just showing the originals around) and they fell, or perhaps I pushed them, into five separate and indistinct categories. I have never wanted to write about my drawings, and I still don't want to becit occurred to me that it might be a good idea to do it now, when everybody is busy with something else, and get it over quietly.

Category No. 1, then, which may be called the Unconscious or Stream of Nervousness category, is represented by 'With you I have known peace, Lida, and now you say you're going crazy' and the drawing entitled with simple dignity, 'Home'. These drawings were done while the artist was thinking of something else (or so he has been assured by experts) and hence

'For the last time, you and your horsie get away from me and stay away!'

his hand was guided by the Unconscious which, in turn, was more or less influenced by the Subconscious.

Students of Jung have instructed me that Lida and the House-Woman are representations of the *anima*, the female essence or directive which floats around in the ageless universal Subconscious of Man like a tadpole in a cistern. Less intellectual critics insist that the two ladies are actual persons I have consciously known. Between these two schools of thought lies a discouragingly large space of time extending roughly from 1,000,000 B.C. to the middle Nineteen Thirties.

Whenever I try to trace the true identity of the House-Woman, I get to thinking of Mr. Jones. He appeared in my office one day twelve years ago, said he was Mr. Jones, and asked me to lend him 'Home' for reproduction in an art magazine. I never saw the drawing again. Tall, well-dressed, kind of sad-looking chap, and as well spoken a gentleman as you would want to meet.

Category No. 2 brings us to Freud and another one of those discouragingly

'The father belonged to some people who were driving through in a Packard.'

large spaces—namely, the space between the Concept of the Purely Accidental and the Theory of Haphazard Determination. Whether chance is capricious or we are all prisoners of pattern is too long and cloudy a subject to go into here. I shall consider each of the drawings in Category No. 2, explaining what happened and leaving the definition of the forces involved up to you. The seal on top of the bed, then ('All right, have it your way—you heard a seal bark'), started out to be a seal on a rock. The rock, in the process of being drawn, began to look like the head of a bed, so I made a bed out of it, put a man and wife in the bed, and stumbled on to the caption as easily and unexpectedly as the seal had stumbled into the bedroom.

The woman on top of the bookcase ('That's my first wife up there, and this is the *present* Mrs. Harris') was originally designed to be a woman crouched on the top step of a staircase, but since the tricks and conventions of perspective and planes sometimes fail me, the staircase assumed the shape of a bookcase and was finished as such, to the surprise and embarrassment of the first Mrs. Harris, the present Mrs. Harris, the lady visitor, Mr. Harris and me. Before *The New Yorker* would print the drawing, they phoned me long distance to inquire whether the first Mrs. Harris was alive or dead or stuffed. I replied that my taxidermist had advised me that you cannot stuff a woman,

'*What have you done with Dr. Millmoss?*'

and that my physician had informed me that a dead lady cannot support herself on all fours. This meant, I said, that the first Mrs. Harris was unquestionably alive.

The man riding on the other man's shoulders in the bar ('For the last time, you and your horsie get away from me and stay away!') was intended to be standing alongside the irate speaker, but I started his head up too high and made it too small, so that he would have been nine feet tall if I had completed his body that way. It was but the work of thirty-two seconds to put him on another man's shoulders. As simple or, if you like, as complicated as that.

The psychological factors which may be present here are, as I have indicated, elaborate and confused. Personally, I like Dr. Claude Thornway's theory of the Deliberate Accident or Conditioned Mistake.

Category No. 3 is perhaps a variant of Category No. 2; indeed, they may even be identical. The dogs in 'The father belonged to some people who were driving through in a Packard' were drawn as a captionless spot, and the interior with figures just sort of grew up around them. The hippopotamus in 'What have you done with Dr. Millmoss?' was drawn to amuse my small

'Touché!'

daughter. Something about the creature's expression when he was completed convinced me that he had recently eaten a man. I added the hat and pipe and Mrs. Millmoss, and the caption followed easily enough. Incidentally, my daughter, who was 2 years old at the time, identified the beast immediately. 'That's a hippotomanus,' she said. *The New Yorker* was not so smart. They described the drawing for their files as follows: 'Woman with strange animal.' *The New Yorker* was nine years old at the time.

Category No. 4 is represented by perhaps the best known of some fifteen drawings belonging to this special grouping, which may be called the Contributed Idea Category. This drawing ('Touché!') was originally done for *The New Yorker* by Carl Rose, caption and all. Mr. Rose is a realistic artist, and his gory scene distressed the editors, who hate violence. They asked Rose if he would let me have the idea, since there is obviously no blood to speak of in the people I draw. Rose graciously consented. No one who looks at 'Touché!' believes that the man whose head is in the air is really dead. His opponent will hand it back to him with profuse apologies, and the discommoded fencer will replace it on his shoulders and say, 'No harm done, forget

'Well, I'm disenchanted, too. We're all disenchanted.'

it'. Thus the old controversy as to whether death can be made funny is left just where it was before Carl Rose came along with his wonderful idea.

Category No. 5, our final one, can be called, believe it or not, the Intentional or Thought-Up Category. The idea for each of these two drawings just came to me and I sat down and made a sketch to fit the prepared caption. Perhaps, in the case of 'Well, I'm disenchanted, too. We're all disenchanted', another one of those Outside Forces played a part. That is, I may have overheard a husband say to his wife, on the street or at a party, 'I'm disenchanted'. I do not think this is true, however, in the case of the rabbit-headed doctor and his woman patient. I believe that scene and its caption came to me one night in bed. I *may* have got the idea in a doctor's office or a rabbit hutch, but I don't think so.

If you want to, you can cut these drawings out and push them around on the floor, making your own categories or applying your own psychological theories; or you can even invent some fresh rumours. I should think it would be more fun, though, to take a nap, or baste a roast, or run around the reservoir in Central Park.

'You said a moment ago that everybody you look at seems to be a rabbit.
Now just what do you mean by that, Mrs. Sprague?'

WHEN I WAS THIRTEEN

BY DENTON WELCH

from *Brave and Cruel* (1949)

WHEN I WAS THIRTEEN

When I was thirteen, I went to Switzerland for the Christmas holidays in the charge of an elder brother, who was at that time still up at Oxford.

In the hotel we found another undergraduate whom my brother knew. His name was Archer. They were not at the same college, but they had met and evidently had not agreed with each other. At first my brother would say nothing about Archer, then one day, in answer to a question of mine, he said: 'He's not very much liked; although he's a very good swimmer.' As he spoke, my brother held his lips in a very firm, almost pursed, line which was most damaging to Archer.

After this I began to look at Archer with more interest. He had broad shoulders but was not tall. He had a look of strength and solidity which I admired and envied. He had rather a nice pug face with insignificant nose and broad cheeks. Sometimes, when he was animated, a tassel of fair, almost colourless, hair would fall across his forehead, half-covering one eye. He had a thick beautiful neck, rather meaty barbarian hands, and a skin as smooth and evenly coloured as a pink fondant.

His whole body appeared to be suffused with this gentle pink colour. He never wore proper skiing clothes of water-proof material like the rest of us. Usually he came out in nothing but a pair of grey flannels and a white cotton shirt with all the buttons left undone. When the sun grew very hot, he would even discard this thin shirt, and ski up and down the slopes behind the hotel in nothing but his trousers. I had often seen him fall down in this half-naked state and get buried in snow. The next moment he would jerk himself to his feet again, laughing and swearing.

After my brother's curt nod to him on our first evening at the hotel, we had hardly exchanged any remarks. We sometimes passed on the way to the basement to get our skis in the morning, and often we found ourselves sitting near one another on the glassed-in terrace; but some Oxford snobbery I knew nothing of, or some more profound reason, always made my brother throw off waves of hostility. Archer never showed any signs of wishing to approach. He was content to look at me sometimes with a mild inoffensive curiosity, but he seemed to ignore my brother completely. This pleased me more than I would have admitted at that time. I was so used to being passed over myself by all my brother's friends that it was pleasant when someone who knew him seemed to take a sort of interest, however slight and amused, in me.

My brother was often away from the hotel for days and nights together, going for expeditions with guides and other friends. He would never take me because he said I was too young and had not enough stamina. He said that I would fall down a crevasse or get my nose frost-bitten, or hang up the party by lagging behind.

In consequence I was often alone at the hotel; but I did not mind this; I enjoyed it. I was slightly afraid of my brother and found life very much easier and less exacting when he was not there. I think other people in the hotel thought that I looked lonely. Strangers would often come up and talk to me and smile, and once a nice absurd Belgian woman, dressed from head to foot in a babyish suit of fluffy orange knitted wool, held out a bright five-franc piece to me and told me to go and buy chocolate caramels with it. I think she must have taken me for a much younger child.

On one of these afternoons when I had come in from the Nursery Slopes and was sitting alone over my tea on the sun-terrace, I noticed that Archer was sitting in the corner huddled over a book, munching greedily and absent-mindedly.

I, too, was reading a book, while I ate delicious rhumbabas and little tarts filled with worm-castles of chestnut purée topped with caps of whipped cream. I have called the meal tea, but what I was drinking was not tea but chocolate. When I poured out, I held the pot high in the air, so that my cup, when filled, should be covered in a rich froth of bubbles.

The book I was reading was Tolstoy's *Resurrection*. Although I did not quite understand some parts of it, it gave me intense pleasure to read it while I ate the rich cakes and drank the frothy chocolate. I thought it a noble and terrible story but, I was worried and mystified by the words 'illegitimate child' which had occurred several times lately. What sort of child could this be? Clearly a child that brought trouble and difficulty. Could it have some terrible disease, or was it a special sort of imbecile? I looked up from my book, still wondering about this phrase 'illegitimate child', and saw that Archer had turned in his creaking wicker chair and was gazing blankly in my direction. The orchestra was playing 'The Birth of the Blues' in a rather remarkable Swiss arrangement, and it was clear that Archer had been distracted from this book by the music, only to be lulled into a day-dream, as he gazed into space.

Suddenly his eyes lost their blank look and focused on my face. 'Your brother off up to the Jungfrau Joch again, or somewhere?' he called out.

I nodded my head, saying nothing, becoming slightly confused.

Archer grinned. He seemed to find me amusing.

'What are you reading?' he asked.

'This,' I said, taking my book over to him. I did not want to call out either the word 'Resurrection' or 'Tolstoy'. But Archer did not make fun of me for reading a 'classic', as most of my brother's friends would have done. He only said: 'I should think it's rather good. Mine's frightful; it's called *The Story of my Life*, by Queen Marie of Roumania.' He held the book up and I saw an extraordinary photograph of a lady who looked like a snake-charmer in full regalia. The head-dress seemed to be made of white satin, embroidered with beads, stretched over cardboard. There were tassels and trailing things hanging down everywhere.

I laughed at the amusing picture and Archer went on: 'I always read books like this when I can get them. Last week I had Lady Oxford's autobiography, and before that I found a perfectly wonderful book called *Flaming Sex*. It was by a French woman who married an English knight and then went back to France to shoot a French doctor. She didn't kill him, of course, but she was sent to prison, where she had a very interesting time with the nuns who looked after her in the hospital. I also lately found an old book by a Crown Princess of Saxony who ended up picnicking on a haystack with a simple Italian gentleman in a straw hat. I love these "real life" stories, don't you?'

I again nodded my head, not altogether daring to venture on a spoken answer. I wondered whether to go back to my own table or whether to pluck up courage and ask Archer what an 'illegitimate child' was. He solved the problem by saying 'Sit down' rather abruptly.

I subsided next to him with 'Tolstoy' on my knee. I waited for a moment and then plunged.

'What exactly does "illegitimate child" mean?' I asked rather breathlessly.

'Outside the law—when two people have a child although they're not married.'

'Oh.' I went bright pink. I thought Archer must be wrong. I still believed that it was quite impossible to have a child unless one was married. The very fact of being married produced the child. I had a vague idea that some particularly reckless people attempted, without being married, to have children in places called 'night clubs', but they were always unsuccessful, and this made them drink, and plunge into the most hectic gaiety.

I did not tell Archer that I thought he had made a mistake, for I did not want to hurt his feelings. I went on sitting at his table and, although he turned his eyes back to his book and went on reading, I knew that he was friendly.

After some time he looked up again and said: 'Would you like to come out with me to-morrow? We could take our lunch, go up the mountain and then ski down in the afternoon.'

I was delighted at the suggestion, but also a little alarmed at my own shortcomings. I thought it my duty to explain that I was not a very good skier, only a moderate one, and that I could only do stem turns. I hated the thought of being a drag on Archer.

'I expect you're much better than I am. I'm always falling down or crashing into something,' he answered.

It was all arranged. We were to meet early, soon after six, as Archer wanted to go to the highest station on the mountain railway and then climb on skis to a nearby peak which had a small rest-house of logs.

I went to bed very excited, thankful that my brother was away on a long expedition. I lay under my enormous feather-bed eiderdown, felt the freezing mountain air on my face, and saw the stars sparkling through the open window.

I got up very early in the morning and put on my most sober ski socks and woollen shirt, for I felt that Archer disliked any suspicion of bright colours or dressing-up. I made my appearance as workmanlike as possible, and then went down to breakfast.

I ate several crackly rolls, which I spread thickly with dewy slivers of butter and gobbets of rich black cherry jam; then I drank my last cup of coffee and went to wax my skis. As I passed through the hall I picked up my picnic lunch in its neat grease-proof paper packet.

The nails in my boots slid and then caught on the snow, trodden hard down to the basement door. I found my skies in their rack, took them down and then heated the iron and the wax. I loved spreading the hot black wax smoothly on the white wood. Soon they were both done beautifully.

I will go like a bird, I thought.

I looked up and saw Archer standing in the doorway.

'I hope you haven't put too much on, else you'll be sitting on your arse all day,' he said gaily.

How fresh and pink he looked! I was excited.

He started to wax his own skis. When they were finished, we went outside and strapped them on. Archer carried a rucksack and he told me to put my lunch and my spare sweater into it.

We started off down the gentle slopes to the station. The sun was shining prickingly. The lovely snow had rainbow colours in it. I was so happy I swung my sticks with their steel points and basket ends. I even tried to show off, and jumped a little terrace which I knew well. Nevertheless it nearly brought me down. I just regained my balance in time. I would have hated at that moment to have fallen down in front of Archer.

When we got to the station we found a compartment to ourselves. It was still early. Gently we were pulled up the mountain, past the water station stop and the other three halts.

We got out at the very top where the railway ended. A huge unused snow-plough stood by the side of the track, with its vicious shark's nose pointed at me. We ran to the van to get out our skis. Archer found mine as well as his own and slung both pairs across his shoulders. He looked like a very tough Jesus carrying two crosses, I thought.

We stood by the old snow-plough and clipped on our skis; then we began to climb laboriously up the ridge to the wooden rest-house. We hardly talked at all, for we needed all our breath, and also I was still shy of Archer. Sometimes he helped me, telling me where to place my skis, and, if I slipped backwards, hauling on the rope which he had half-playfully tied round my waist.

In spite of growing tired, I enjoyed the grim plodding. It gave me a sense of work and purpose. When Archer looked round to smile at me, his pink face was slippery with sweat. His white shirt above the small rucksack was plastered to his shoulder-blades. On my own face I could feel the drops of sweat just being held back by my eyebrows. I would wipe my hand across my upper lip and break all the tiny beads that had formed there.

Every now and then Archer would stop. We would put our skis sideways on the track and rest, leaning forward on our sticks. The sun struck down on our necks with a steady seeping heat and the light striking up from the snow was as bright as the fiery dazzle of a mirror. From the ridge we could see down into two valleys; and standing all round us were the other peaks, black rock and white snow, tangling and mixing until the mountains looked like vast teeth which had begun to decay.

I was so tired when we reached the long gentle incline to the rest-house that I was afraid of falling down. The rope was still round my waist, and so the slightest lagging would have been perceptible to Archer. I think he must have slackened his pace for my benefit, for I somehow managed to reach the iron seats in front of the hut. I sank down, still with my skis on. I half-shut my eyes. From walking so long with my feet turned out, my ankles felt almost broken.

The next thing I knew was that Archer had disappeared into the rest-house. He came out, carrying a steaming cup.

'You must drink this,' he said, holding out black coffee which I hated. He unwrapped four lumps of sugar and dropped them in the cup.

'I don't like it black,' I said.

'Never mind,' he answered sharply, 'drink it.'

Rather surprised, I began to drink the syrupy coffee. 'The sugar and the strong coffee will be good for you,' said Archer. He went back into the rest-house and brought out a glass of what looked like hot water with a piece of lemon floating in it. The mountain of sugar at the bottom was melting into thin Arabian Nights wreaths and spirals, smoke-rings of syrup.

'What else has it got in it?' I asked, with an attempt at worldliness.

'Rum!' said Arthur.

We sat there on the terrace and unwrapped our picnic lunches. We both had two rolls, one with tongue in it, and one with ham, a hard-boiled egg, sweet biscuits, and a bar of delicious bitter chocolate; tangerine oranges were our dessert.

We began to take huge bites out of our rolls. We could not talk for some time. The food brought out a thousand times more clearly the beauty of the mountain peaks and sun. My tiredness made me thrillingly conscious of delight and satisfaction. I wanted to sit there with Archer for a long time.

At the end of the meal Archer gave me a piece of his own bar of chocolate, and then began to skin pigs of tangerine very skilfully and hand them to me on his outstretched palm, as one offers a lump of sugar to a horse. I thought for one moment of bending down my head and licking the pigs up in imitation of a horse; then I saw how mad it would look.

We threw the brilliant tangerine peel into the snow, which immediately seemed to dim and darken its colour.

Archer felt in his hip pocket and brought out black, cheap Swiss cigarettes, wrapped in leaf. They were out of a slot machine. He put one between my lips and lighted it. I felt extremely conscious of the thing jutting out from my lips. I wondered if I would betray my ignorance by not breathing the smoke in and out correctly. I turned my head a little away from Archer and experimented. It seemed easy if one did not breathe too deeply. It was wonderful to be really smoking with Archer. He treated me just like a man.

'Come on, let's get cracking,' he said, 'or, if anything happens, we'll be out all night.'

I scrambled to my feet at once and snapped the clips of the skis around my boot heels. Archer was in high spirits from the rum. He ran on his skis along the flat ridge in front of the rest-house and then fell down.

'Serves me right,' he said. He shook the snow off and we started properly. In five minutes we had swooped down the ridge we had climbed so painfully all morning. The snow was perfect, new and dry with no crust. We followed a new way which Archer had discovered. The ground was uneven with dips and curves. Often we were out of sight of each other. When we came to the icy path through a wood, my courage failed me.

'Stem like hell and don't get out of control,' Archer yelled back at me. I pointed my skis together, praying that they would not cross. I leant on my sticks, digging their metal points into the compressed snow. Twice I fell, though not badly.

'Well done, well done!' shouted Archer, as I shot past him and out of the wood into a thick snowdrift. He hauled me out of the snow and stood me on my feet, beating me all over to get off the snow, then we began the descent of a field called the 'Bumps'. Little hillocks, if manœuvred successfully, gave one that thrilling sinking and rising feeling experienced on a scenic railway at a fun fair.

Archer went before me, dipping and rising, shouting and yelling in his exuberance. I followed more sedately. We both fell several times, but in that not unpleasant, bouncing way which brings you to your feet again almost at once.

Archer was roaring now and trying to yodel in an absurd, rich contralto.

I had never enjoyed myself quite so much before. I thought him the most wonderful companion, not a bit intimidating, in spite of being rather a hero.

When at last we swooped down into the village street, it was nearly evening. Early orange lights were shining in the shop windows. We planked our skis down on the hard, iced road, trying not to slip.

I looked in at the *patisserie, confiserie* window, where all the electric bulbs had fluffy pink shades like powder-puffs. Archer saw my look.

'Let's go in,' he said. He ordered me hot chocolate with whipped cream, and *croissant* rolls. Afterwards we both went up to the little counter and chose cakes. I had one shaped like a little log. It was made of soft chocolate, and had green moss trimmings made in pistachio nut. When Archer went to pay the bill he bought me some chocolate caramels, in a little bird's-eye maple box, and a bar labelled '*Chocolat Polychrome*'. Each finger was a different-coloured cream: mauve, pink, green, yellow, orange, brown, white, even blue.

We went out into the village street and began to climb up the path to the hotel. About half-way up Archer stopped outside a little wooden chalet and said: 'This is where I hang out.'

'But you're staying at the hotel,' I said incredulously.

'Oh yes, I have all my meals there, but I sleep here. It's a sort of little annex when there aren't any rooms left in the hotel. It's only got two rooms; I've paid just a bit more and got it to all to myself. Someone comes every morning and makes the bed and stokes the boiler and the stove. Come in and see it.'

I followed Archer up the outside wooden staircase and stood with him on the little landing outside the two rooms. The place seemed wonderfully warm and dry. The walls were unpainted wood; there were double windows. There was a gentle creaking in all the joints of the wood when one moved. Archer pushed open one of the doors and ushered me in. I saw in one corner a huge white porcelain stove, the sort I had only before seen in pictures. Some of Archer's skiing gloves and socks were drying round it on a ledge. Against another wall were two beds, like wooden troughs built into the wall. The balloon-like quilts bulged up above the wood.

'I hardly use the other room,' said Archer. 'I just throw my muck into it and leave my trunks there.' He opened the connecting door and I saw a smaller room with dirty clothes strewn on the floor; white shirts, hard evening collars, some very short pants, and many pairs of thick grey socks. The room smelt mildly of Archer's old sweat. I didn't mind at all.

Archer shut the door and said: 'I'm going to run the bath.'

'Have you a bathroom too—all your own?' I exclaimed enviously. 'Every time anyone has a bath at the hotel, he has to pay two francs fifty to the fräulein before she unlocks the door. I've only had two proper baths since I've been here. I don't think it matters though. It seems almost impossible to

get really dirty in Switzerland, and you can always wash all over in your
bedroom basin.'

'Why don't you have a bath here after me? The water's lovely and hot,
although there's not much of it. If you went back first and got your evening
clothes, you could change straight into them.'

I looked at Archer a little uncertainly. I longed to soak in hot water after
my wonderful but gruelling day.

'Could I really bath here?' I asked.

'If you don't mind using my water. I'll promise not to pee in it. I'm not
really filthy, you know.'

Archer laughed and chuckled, because he saw me turning red at his coarse-
ness. He lit another of his peasant cigarettes and began to unlace his boots.
He got me to pull them off. I knelt down, bowed my head and pulled. When
the ski boot suddenly flew off, my nose dipped forward and I smelt Archer's
foot in its woolly, hairy, humid casing of sock.

'Would you just rub my foot and leg?' Archer said urgently, a look of
pain suddenly shooting across his face. 'I've got cramp. It often comes on at
the end of the day.'

He shot his leg out rigidly and told me where to rub and massage. I felt
each of his curled toes separately and the hard tendons in his leg. His calf was
like a firm sponge ball. His thigh, swelling out, amazed me. I likened it in
my mind to the trumpet of some musical instrument. I went on rubbing
methodically. I was able to feel his pain melting away.

When the tense look had quite left his face, he said, 'Thanks', and stood up.
He unbuttoned his trousers, let them fall to the ground, and pulled his shirt
up. Speaking to me with his head imprisoned in it, he said: 'You go and get
your clothes and I'll begin bathing.'

I left him and hurried up to the hotel, carrying my skis on my shoulder. I
ran up to my room and pulled my evening clothes out of the wardrobe. The
dinner jacket and trousers had belonged to my brother six years before, when
he was my age. I was secretly ashamed of this fact, and had taken my brother's
name from the inside of the breast pocket and had written my own in
elaborate lettering.

I took my comb, face flannel and soap, and getting out my toboggan slid
back to Archer's chalet in a few minutes. I let myself in and heard Archer
splashing. The little hall was full of steam and I saw Archer's shoulders and
arms like a pink smudge through the open bathroom door.

'Come and scrub my back,' he yelled, 'it gives me a lovely feeling.' He
thrust a large stiff nailbrush into my hands and told me to scrub as hard as I
could.

I ran it up and down his back until I'd made harsh red tramlines.
Delicious tremors seemed to be passing through Archer.

'Ah! go on!' said Archer in a dream, like a purring cat. 'When I'm rich

I'll have a special back-scratcher slave.' I went on industriously scrubbing his back till I was afraid that I would rub the skin off. I liked to give him pleasure.

At last he stood up all dripping and said: 'Now it's your turn.'

I undressed and got into Archer's opaque, soapy water. I lay back and wallowed. Archer poured some very smelly salts on to my stomach. One crystal stuck in my navel and tickled and grated against me.

'This whiff ought to cover up all remaining traces of me!' Archer laughed.

'What's the smell supposed to be?' I asked, brushing the crystals off my stomach into the water, and playing with the one that lodged so snugly in my navel.

'Russian pine,' said Archer, shutting his eyes ecstatically and making inbreathing dreamy noises. He rubbed himself roughly with the towel and made his hair stand up on end.

I wanted to soak in the bath for hours, but it was already getting late, and so I had to hurry.

Archer saw what difficulty I had in tying my tie. He came up to me and said 'Let me do it'. I turned round relieved, but slightly ashamed of being incompetent.

I kept very still, and he tied it tightly and rapidly with his ham-like hands. He gave the bows a little expert jerk and pat. His eyes had a very concentrated, almost crossed look and I felt him breathing down on my face. All down the front our bodies touched featherily; little points of warmth came together. The hard-boiled shirts were like slightly warmed dinner-plates.

When I had brushed my hair, we left the chalet and began to walk up the path to the hotel. The beaten snow was so slippery, now that we were shod only in patent-leather slippers, that we kept sliding backwards. I threw out my arms, laughing, and shouting to Archer to rescue me; then, when he grabbed me and started to haul me to him, he too would begin to slip. It was a still, Prussian-blue night with rather weak stars. Our laughter seemed to ring across the valley, to hit the mountains and then to travel on and on and on.

We reached the hotel a little the worse for wear. The soles of my patent-leather shoes had become soaked, and there was snow on my trousers. Through bending forward, the studs in Archer's shirt had burst undone, and the slab of hair hung over one of his eyes. We went into the cloakroom to readjust ourselves before entering the dining-room.

'Come and sit at my table,' Archer said; then he added: 'No, we'll sit at yours; there are two places there already.'

We sat down and began to eat Roman *gnocchi*. (The proprietor of the hotel was Italian-Swiss.) I did not like mine very much and was glad when I could go on to *œufs au beurre noir*. Now that my brother was away I could pick and choose in this way, leaving out the meat course, if I chose to, without causing any comment.

Archer drank Pilsner and suggested that I should too. Not wanting to disagree with him, I nodded my head, although I hated the pale, yellow, bitter water.

After the meal Archer ordered me *crême de menthe* with my coffee; I had seen a nearby lady drinking this pretty liquid and asked him about it. To be ordered a liqueur in all seriousness was a thrilling moment for me. I sipped the fumy peppermint, which left such an artificial heat in my throat and chest, and thought that apart from my mother who was dead, I had never liked anyone so much as I liked Archer. He didn't try to interfere with me at all. He just took me as I was and yet seemed to like me.

Archer was now smoking a proper cigar, not the leaf-rolled cigarettes we had had at lunch-time. He offered me one too, but I had the sense to realize that he did not mean me to take one and smoke it there before the eyes of all the hotel. I knew also that it would have made me sick, for my father had given me a cigar when I was eleven, in an attempt to put me off smoking for ever.

I always associated cigars with middle-aged men, and I watched Archer interestedly, thinking how funny the stiff fat thing looked sticking out of his young mouth.

We were sitting on the uncurtained sun-terrace, looking out on to the snow in the night; the moon was just beginning to rise. It made the snow glitter suddenly, like fish-scales. Behind us people were dancing in the salon and adjoining rooms. The music came to us in angry snatches, some notes distorted, others quite obliterated. Archer did not seem to want to dance. He seemed content to sit with me in silence.

Near me on a what-not stand stood a high-heeled slipper made of china. I took it down and slipped my hand into it. How hideously ugly the china pom–poms were down the front. The painted centipede climbing up the red heel wore a knowing, human expression. I moved my fingers in the china shoe, pretending they were toes.

'I love monstrosities, too,' said Archer, as I put the shoe back beside the fern in its crinkly paper-covered pot.

Later we wandered to the buffet bar and stood there drinking many glasses of the *limonade* which was made with white wine. I took the tinkly pieces of ice into my mouth and sucked them, trying to cool myself a little. Blood seemed to rise in my face; my head buzzed.

Suddenly I felt full of *limonade* and lager. I left Archer to go to the cloak-room, but he followed and stood beside me in the next china niche, while the water flushed and gushed importantly in the polished copper tubes, and an interesting, curious smell came from the wire basket which held some strange disinfectant crystals. Archer stood so quietly and guardingly beside me there that I had to say: 'Do I look queer?'

'No, you don't look queer; you look nice,' he said simply.

A rush of surprise and pleasure made me hotter still. We clanked over the tiles and left the cloak-room.

In the hall, I remembered that I had left all my skiing clothes at the chalet.

'I shall need them in the morning,' I said to Archer.

'Let's go down there now, then I can make cocoa on my spirit-lamp, and you can bring the clothes back with you.'

We set out in the moonlight; Archer soon took my arm, for he saw that I was drunk, and the path was more slippery than ever. Archer sang 'Silent Night' in German, and I began to cry. I could not stop myself. It was such a delight to cry in the moonlight with Archer singing my favourite song; and my brother far away up the mountain.

Suddenly we both sat down on our behinds with a thump. There was a jarring pain at the bottom of my spine but I began to laugh wildly; so did Archer. We lay there laughing, the snow melting under us and soaking through the seats of our trousers and the shoulders of our jackets.

Archer pulled me to my feet and dusted me down with hard slaps. My teeth grated together each time he slapped me. He saw that I was becoming more and more drunk in the freezing air. He propelled me along to the chalet, more or less frog-marching me in an expert fashion. I was quite content to leave myself in his hands.

When he got me upstairs, he put me into one of the bunks and told me to rest. The feathers ballooned out round me. I sank down deliciously. I felt as if I were floating down some magic staircase for ever.

Archer got his little meta-stove out and made coffee—not cocoa as he had said. He brought me over a strong cup and held it to my lips. I drank it unthinkingly and not tasting it, doing it only because he told me to.

When he took the cup away, my head fell back on the pillow, and I felt myself sinking and floating away again. I was on skis this time, but they were liquid skis, made of melted glass, and the snow was glass too, but a sort of glass that was springy, like gelatine, and flowing like water.

I felt a change in the light, and knew that Archer was bending over me. Very quietly he took off my shoes, undid my tie, loosened the collar and unbuttoned my braces in front. I remember thinking, before I finally fell asleep, how clever he was to know about undoing the braces; they had begun to feel so tight pulling down on my shoulders and dragging the trousers up between my legs. Archer covered me with several blankets and another quilt.

When I woke in the morning, Archer was already up. He had made me some tea and had put it on the stove to keep warm. He brought it over to me and I sat up. I felt ill, rather sick. I remembered what a glorious day yesterday had been, and thought how extraordinary it was that I had not slept in my own bed at the hotel, but in Archer's room, in my clothes.

I looked at him shamefacedly. 'What happened last night? I felt peculiar,' I said.

'The lager and the lemonade, and the *crème de menthe* made you a bit tight, I'm afraid,' Archer said, laughing. 'Do you feel better now? We'll go up to the hotel and and have breakfast soon.'

I got up and washed and changed into my skiing clothes. I still felt rather sick. I made my evening clothes into a neat bundle and tied them on to my toboggan. I had the sweets Archer had given me in my pocket.

We went up to the hotel, dragging the toboggan behind us.

And there on the doorstep we met my brother with one of the guides. They had had to return early, becuse someone in the party had broken a ski.

He was in a temper. He looked at us and then said to me: 'What have you been doing?'

I was at a loss to know what to answer. The very sight of him had so troubled me that this added difficulty of explaining my actions was too much for me.

I looked at him miserably and mouthed something about going in to have breakfast.

My brother turned to Archer fiercely, but said nothing.

Archer explained: 'Your brother's just been down to my place. We went skiing together yesterday and he left some clothes at the chalet.'

'It's very early,' was all my brother said; then he swept me on into the hotel before him, without another word to the guide or to Archer.

He went with me up to my room and saw that the bed had not been slept in.

I said clumsily: 'The maid must have been in and done my room early.' I could not bear to explain to him about my wonderful day, or why I had slept at the chalet.

My brother was so furious that he took no more notice of my weak explanations and lies.

When I suddenly said in desperation, 'I feel sick,' he seized me, took me to the basin, forced his fingers down my throat and struck me on the back till a yellow cascade of vomit gushed out of my mouth. My eyes were filled with stinging water; I was trembling. I ran the water in the basin madly, to wash away this sign of shame.

Gradually I grew a little more composed. I felt better, after being sick, and my brother had stopped swearing at me. I filled the basin with freezing water, and dipped my face into it. The icy feel seemed to bite round my eye-sockets and make the flesh round my nose firm again. I waited, holding my breath for as long as possible.

Suddenly my head was pushed down and held, I felt my brother's hard fingers digging into my neck. He was hitting me now with a slipper, beating my buttocks and my back with slashing strokes, hitting a different place each time, as he had been taught when a prefect at school, so that the flesh should not be numbed from a previous blow.

I felt that I was going to choke. I could not breathe under the water, and realized that I would die. I was seized with such a panic that I wrenched myself free and darted round the room, with him after me. Water dripped on the bed, the carpet, the chest of drawers. Splashes of it spat against the mirror in the wardrobe door. My brother aimed vicious blows at me until he had driven me into a corner. There he beat against my uplifted arms, yelling in a hoarse, mad, religious voice, 'Bastard, Devil, Harlot, Sod!'

As I cowered under his blows, I remember thinking that my brother had suddenly become a lunatic and was talking gibberish in his madness, for, of the words he was using, I had not heard any before, except 'Devil'.